Lecture Notes in Computer Science 3220

Commenced Publication in 1973
Founding and Former Series Editors:
Gerhard Goos, Juris Hartmanis, and Jan van Leeuwen

James C. Lester Rosa Maria Vicari
Fábio Paraguaçu (Eds.)

Intelligent Tutoring Systems

7th International Conference, ITS 2004
Maceió, Alagoas, Brazil, August 30 – September 3, 2004
Proceedings

Springer

Volume Editors

James C. Lester
North Carolina State University, Department of Computer Science
Box 7535, Raleigh, NC 27695-7535, USA
E-mail: lester@csc.ncsu.edu

Rosa Maria Vicari
Federal University of Rio Grande do Sul, Instituto de Informática
Av. Bento Goncalves, 1500, Campus do Vale, Bloco IV, Bairro Agronomia
9500, Porto Alegre, RS, Brazil
E-mail: rosa@inf.ufrgs.br

Fábio Paraguaçu
Federal University of Alagoas, Department of Information Technologies
Campus A.C. Simões, Tabuleiro dos Martins, Maceió, AL 57072-970, Brazil
E-mail: paragua@tci.ufal.br

Library of Congress Control Number: 2004110895

CR Subject Classification (1998): K.3, I.2.6, H.5, J.1

ISSN 0302-9743
ISBN 3-540-22948-5 Springer Berlin Heidelberg New York

Springer is a part of Springer Science+Business Media

springeronline.com

Printed in Germany

Typesetting: Camera-ready by author, data conversion by PTP-Berlin, Protago-TeX-Production GmbH
Printed on acid-free paper SPIN: 11316176 06/3142 5 4 3 2 1 0

Preface

Welcome to the proceedings of the 7th International Conference on Intelligent Tutoring Systems! In keeping with the rich tradition of the ITS conferences, ITS 2004 brought together an exciting mix of researchers from all areas of intelligent tutoring systems. A leading international forum for the dissemination of original results in the design, implementation, and evaluation of ITSs, the conference drew researchers from a broad spectrum of disciplines ranging from artificial intelligence and cognitive science to pedagogy and educational psychology.

Beginning with the first ITS conference in 1988, the gathering has developed a reputation as an outstanding venue for AI-based learning environments. Following on the great success of the first meeting, subsequent conferences have been held in 1992, 1996, 1998, 2000, and 2002. The conference has consistently created a vibrant convocation of scientists, developers, and practitioners from all areas of the field.

Reflecting the growing international involvement in the field, ITS 2004 was hosted in Brazil. The previous conferences were convened in Canada, the USA, and Europe. We are grateful to the Brazilian ITS community for organizing the first ITS conference in Latin America—in Maceió, Alagoas. With its coconut palm-lined beaches and warm, crystal-clear waters, Maceió, the capital city of the state of Alagoas, is fittingly known as "The Water Paradise." The conference was held at the Ritz Lagoa da Anta Hotel, which is by Lagoa da Anta Beach and close to many of the city's beautiful sights.

The papers in this volume represent the best of the more than 180 submissions from authors hailing from 29 countries. Using stringent selection criteria, submissions were rigorously reviewed by an international program committee consisting of more than 50 researchers from Australia, Austria, Brazil, Canada, Colombia, France, Germany, Hong Kong, Japan, Mexico, the Netherlands, Portugal, Singapore, Spain, Taiwan, Tunisia, the UK, and the USA. Of the submissions, only 39% were accepted for publication as full technical papers. In addition to the 73 full papers, 39 poster papers are also included in the proceedings. We are pleased to announce that in cooperation with the AI in Education Society, a select group of extended full papers will be invited to appear in a forthcoming special issue of the *International Journal of Artificial Intelligence in Education.*

Participants of ITS 2004 encountered an exciting program showcasing the latest innovations in intelligent learning environment technologies. The diversity of topics discussed in this volume's papers is a testament to the breadth of ITS research activity today. The papers address a broad range of topics: classic ITS issues in student modeling and knowledge representation; cognitive modeling, pedagogical agents, and authoring systems; and collaborative learning environments, novel applications of machine learning to ITS problems, and new natural language techniques for tutorial dialogue and discourse analysis.

The papers also reflect an increased interest in affect and a growing emphasis on evaluation. In addition to paper and poster presentations, ITS 2004 featured a full two-day workshop program with eight workshops, an exciting collection of panels, an exhibition program, and a student track. We were honored to have an especially strong group of keynote speakers: Stefano A. Cerri (University of Montpellier II, France), Bill Clancey (NASA, USA), Cristina Conati (University of British Columbia, Canada), Riichiro Mizoguchi (Osaka University, Japan), Cathleen Norris (University of North Texas, USA), Elliot Soloway (University of Michigan, USA), and Liane Tarouco (Federal University of Rio Grande do Sul, Brazil).

We are very grateful to the many individuals and organizations that made ITS 2004 possible. Thanks to the members of the Program Committee, the external reviewers, and the Poster Chairs for their thorough reviewing. We thank the Brazilian organizing committee for their considerable effort in planning the conference and making it a reality. We appreciate the sagacious advice of the ITS Steering Committee. We extend our thanks to the Workshop, Panel, Poster, Student Track, and Exhibition Chairs for assembling such a strong program. We thank the General Information & Registration Chairs for making the conference run smoothly, and the Press & Web Site Art Development Chair and the Press Art Development Chair for their work with publicity. Special thanks to Thomas Preuß of ConfMaster for his assistance with the paper review management system, to Bradford Mott for his invaluable assistance in the monumental task of collating the proceedings, and the editorial staff of Springer-Verlag for their assistance in getting the manuscript to press. We gratefully acknowledge the sponsoring institutions and corporate sponsors (CNPq, CAPES, FAPEAL, FINEP, FAL, and PETROBRAS) for their generous support of the conference, and AAAI and the AI in Education Society for their "in cooperation" sponsorship.

Finally, we extend a heartfelt thanks to Claude Frasson, the conference's founder. Claude continues to be the guiding force of the conference after all of these years. Even with his extraordinarily busy schedule, he made himself available for consultation on matters ranging from the mundane to the critical and everything in between. He has been a constant source of encouragement. The conference is a tribute to his generous spirit.

July 2004

James C. Lester
Rosa Maria Viccari
Fábio Paraguaçu

Conference Chairs

Rosa Maria Viccari (Federal University of Rio Grande do Sul, Brazil)
Fábio Paraguaçu (Federal University of Alagoas, Brazil)

Program Committee Chair

James Lester (North Carolina State University, USA)

Program Committee

Esma Aïmeur (University of Montréal, Canada)
Vincent Aleven (Carnegie Mellon University, USA)
Elisabeth André (University of Augsburg, Germany)
Guy Boy (Eurisco, France)
Karl Branting (North Carolina State University, USA)
Joost Breuker (University of Amsterdam, Netherlands)
Paul Brna (Northumbria University, Netherlands)
Peter Brusilovsky (University of Pittsburgh, USA)
Stefano Cerri (University of Montpellier II, France)
Tak-Wai Chan (National Central University, Taiwan)
Cristina Conati (University of Vancouver, Canada)
Ricardo Conejo (University of Malaga, Spain)
Evandro Barros Costa (Federal University of Alagoas, Brazil)
Ben du Boulay (University of Sussex, UK)
Isabel Fernandez de Castro (University of the Basque Country, Spain)
Claude Frasson (University of Montréal, Canada)
Gilles Gauthier (University of Québec at Montréal, Canada)
Khaled Ghedira (ISG, Tunisia)
Guy Gouardères (University of Pau, France)
Art Graesser (University of Memphis, USA)
Jim Greer (University of Saskatchewan, Canada)
Mitsuru Ikeda (Japan Advanced Institute of Science and Technology)
Lewis Johnson (USC/ISI, USA)
Judith Kay (University of Sydney, Australia)
Ken Koedinger (Carnegie Mellon University, USA)
Fong Lok Lee (Chinese University of Hong Kong)
Chee-Kit Looi (Nanyang Technological University, Singapore)
Rose Luckin (University of Sussex, UK)
Stacy Marsella (USC/ICT, USA)
Gordon McCalla (University of Saskatchewan, Canada)
Riichiro Mizoguchi (University of Osaka, Japan)
Jack Mostow (Carnegie Mellon University, USA)
Tom Murray (Hampshire College, USA)
Germana Nobrega (Catholic University of Brasília, Brazil)
Toshio Okamoto (Electro-Communications University, Japan)

Demetrio Arturo Ovalle Carranza (National University of Colombia)
Helen Pain (University of Edinburgh, UK)
Ana Paiva (Higher Technical Institute, Portugal)
Fábio Paraguaçu (Federal University of Alagoas, Brazil)
Jean-Pierre Pecuchet (INSA of Rouen, France)
Paolo Petta (Research Institute for AI, Austria)
Sowmya Ramachandran (Stottler Henke, USA)
David Reyes (University of Tijuana, Mexico)
Thomas Rist (DFKI, Germany)
Elliot Soloway (University of Michigan, USA)
Dan Suthers (University of Hawaii, USA)
João Carlos Teatini (Ministry of Education, Brazil)
Gheorge Tecuci (George Mason University, USA)
Patricia Tedesco (Federal University of Pernambuco, Brazil)
Kurt VanLehn (University of Pittsburgh, USA)
Julita Vassileva (University of Saskatchewan, Canada)
Rosa Maria Viccari (Federal University of Rio Grande do Sul, Brazil)
Beverly Woolf (University of Massachusetts, USA)

ITS Steering Committee

Stefano Cerri (University of Montpellier II, France)
Isabel Fernandez-Castro (University of the Basque Country, Spain)
Claude Frasson (University of Montréal, Canada)
Gilles Gauthier (University of Québec at Montréal, Canada)
Guy Gouardères (University of Pau, France)
Mitsuru Ikeda (Japan Advanced Institute of Science and Technology)
Marc Kaltenbach (Bishop's University, Canada)
Judith Kay (University of Sydney, Australia)
Alan Lesgold (University of Pittsburgh, USA)
Elliot Soloway (University of Michigan, USA)
Daniel Suthers (University of Hawaii, USA)
Beverly Woolf (University of Massachussets, USA)

Organizing Committee

Evandro de Barros Costa (Federal University of Alagoas, Brazil)
Cleide Jane Costa (Seune University of Alagoas, Maceió, Brazil)
Clovis Torres Fernandes (Technological Institute of Aeronautics, Brazil)
Lucia Giraffa (Pontifical Catholic University of Rio Grande do Sul, Brazil)
Leide Jane Meneses (Federal University of Rondônia, Brazil)
Germana da Nobrega (Catholic University of Brasília, Brazil)
David Nadler Prata (FAL University of Alagoas, Maceió, Brazil)
Patricia Tedesco (Federal University of Pernambuco, Brazil)

Panels Chairs

Vincent Aleven (Carnegie Mellon University, USA)
Lucia Giraffa (Pontifical Catholic University of Rio Grande do Sul, Brazil)

Workshops & Tutorials Chairs

Jack Mostow (Carnegie Mellon University, USA)
Patricia Tedesco (Federal University of Pernambuco, Brazil)

Poster Chairs

Mitsuru Ikeda (JAIST, Japan)
Marco Aurélio Carvalho (Federal University of Brasília, Brazil)

Student Track Chairs

Roger Nkambou (University of Québec at Montréal, Canada)
Maria Fernanda Rodrigues Vaz (University of São Paulo, Brazil)

General Information & Registration Chairs

Breno Jacinto (FAL University of Alagoas, Maceió, Brazil)
Carolina Mendonça de Moraes (Federal University of Alagoas, Brazil)

Exhibition Chair

Clovis Torres Fernandes (Technological Institute of Aeronautics, Brazil)

Press & Web Site Art Development Chair

Elder Lima (Federal University of Alagoas, Brazil)
Demian Borba (Federal University of Alagoas, Brazil)

Press Art Development Chair

Elder Lima (Federal University of Alagoas, Brazil)

External Reviewers

C. Brooks
A. Bunt
B. Daniel
C. Eliot
H. McLaren
K. Muldner
T. Tang
M. Winter

Table of Contents

Adaptive Testing

Affect

Architectures for ITS

Authoring Systems

Cognitive Modeling

Evaluation

Machine Learning in ITS

Pedagogical Agents

Student Modeling

Teaching and Learning Strategies

Poster Papers

Invited Presentations

Panels

Workshops

A Learning Environment for English for Academic Purposes Based on Adaptive Tests and Task-Based Systems*

Jean P. Gonçalves[1], Sandra M. Aluisio[1], Leandro H.M. de Oliveira[1], and Osvaldo N. Oliveira Jr. [1,2]

[1]Núcleo Interinstitucional de Lingüística Computacional (NILC), ICMC-University of São Paulo (USP), CP 668, 13560-970 São Carlos, SP, Brazil
jpiton@yahoo.com, sandra@icmc.usp.br, leandroh@nilc.icmc.usp.br

[2]Instituto de Física de São Carlos, USP, CP 369, 13560-970 São Carlos, SP, Brazil
chu@if.sc.usp.br

Abstract. This paper introduces the environment CALEAP-Web that integrates adaptive testing into a task-based environment in the domain of English for Academic Purposes. It is aimed at assisting graduate students for the proficiency English test, which requires them to be knowledgeable of the conventions of scientific texts. Both testing and learning systems comprise four modules dealing with different aspects of Instrumental English. These modules were based on writing tools for scientific writing. In CALEAP-Web, the students are assessed on an individual basis and are guided through appropriate learning tasks to minimize their deficiencies, in an iterative process until the students perform satisfactorily in the tests. An analysis was made of the item exposure in the adaptive testing, which is crucial to ensure high-quality assessment. Though conceived for a particular domain, the rationale and the tools may be extended to other domains.

1 Introduction

There is a growing need for students from non-English speaking countries to learn and employ English in their research and even in school tasks. Only then can these students take full advantage of the enormous amount of teaching material and scientific information in the WWW, which is mostly in English. For graduate students, in particular, a minimum level of instrumental English is required, and indeed universities tend to require the students to undertake proficiency exams. There are various paradigms for both the teaching and the exams which may be adopted. In the Institute for Mathematics and Computer Science (ICMC) of University of São Paulo, USP, we have decided to emphasize the mastering of English for Academic Purposes. Building upon previous experience in developing writing tools for academic works [1, 2, 3],

* This work was financially supported by FAPESP and CNPq.

J.C. Lester et al. (Eds.): ITS 2004, LNCS 3220, pp. 1–11, 2004.

we conceived a test that checks whether the students are prepared to understand and make use of the most important conventions of scientific texts in English [4]. This fully-automated test, called CAPTEAP[1], consists of objective questions in which the user is asked to choose or provide a response to a question whose correct answer is predetermined. CAPTEAP comprises four modules, explained in Section 2. In order to get ready for the test – which is considered as an official proficiency test required for the MSc. at ICMC, students may undertake training tests that are offered in the CAPTEAP system. However, until recently there was no module that assisted students in the learning process or that could assess their performance in their early stage of learning. This paper describes the Computer-Aided Learning of English for Academic Purposes (CALEAP-Web) system that fills in this gap, by providing students with adaptive tests integrated into a computational environment with a variety of learning tasks.

CALEAP-Web employs a computer-based adaptive test (CAT) named Adaptive English Proficiency Test for Web (ADEPT), with questions selected on the basis of the estimated knowledge of a given student, being therefore a fully customized system. This is integrated into the Computer-Aided Task Environment for Scientific English (CATESE) [5] to train the students about conventions of the scientific texts, in the approach known as learning by doing [6].

2 Computer-Based Adaptive Tests

The main idea behind adaptive tests is to select the items of a test according to the ability of the examinee. That is to say, the questions proposed should be appropriate for each person. An examinee is given a test that adjusts to the responses given previously. If the examinee provides the correct answer for a given item, then the next one is harder. If the examinee does not answer correctly, the next question can be easier. This allows a more precise assessment of the competences of the examinees than traditional multiple-choice tests because it reduces fatigue, a factor that can significantly affect an examinee's test results [7]. Other advantages are an immediate feedback, the challenge posed as the examinees are not discouraged or annoyed by items that are far above or below their ability level, and reduction in the time required to take the tests.

2.1 Basic Components of a CAT

According to Conejo et al. [8], Adaptive Testing based on Item Response Theory (IRT) comprises the following basic components: a) an IRT model describing how the examinee answers a given question, according to his/her level of knowledge. When the level of knowledge is assessed, one expects that the result should not be affected by the instrument used to assess, i.e. computer or pen and paper; b) a bank of

[1] http://www.nilc.icmc.usp.br/capteap/

items containing questions that may cover part or the whole knowledge of the domain. c) the level of initial knowledge of the examinee, which should be chosen appropriately to reduce the time of testing. d) a method to select the items, which is based on the estimated knowledge of the examinee, depending obviously on the performance in previous questions. e) stopping criteria that are adopted to discontinue the test once the pre-determined level of capability is achieved or when the maximum number of items have been applied, or if the maximum time for the test is exceeded.

2.2 ADEPT

ADEPT provides a customized test capable of assessing the students with only a few questions. It differs from the traditional tests that employ a fixed number of questions for all examiees and do not take into account the previous knowledge of each examinee.

2.2.1 Item Response Theory. This theory assumes some relationship between the level of the examinee and his/her ability to get the answers right for the questions, based on statistical models. ADEPT employs the 3-parameter logistic model [9] given by the expression:

$$P(\theta) = c + (1-c)\frac{1}{1+e^{-1.7a(\theta-b)}}$$

where a (discrimination) denotes how well one item is able to discriminate between examinees of slightly different ability, b (difficulty) is the level of difficulty of one item and c (guessing) is the probability that an examinee will get the answer right simply by guessing.

2.2.2 Item calibration. It consists in assigning numerical parameters to each item, which depends on the ITR adopted. In our case, we adopted the 3-parameter logistic model proposed by Huang [10], as follows. The bank of items employed by ADEPT contains questions used in the proficiency tests of the ICMC in the years 2001 through 2003, for Computer Science, Applied Mathematics and Statistics. There are 30 tests, with about 20 questions each. The insertion in the bank and checking of the questions were carried out by the first author of this paper. Without considering reuse of an item, there are 140 questions with no repetition of texts in the bank.

The proficiency test contains four modules: **Module 1** - conventions of the English language in scientific writing. It deals with knowledge about morphology, vocabulay, syntax, the verb tenses and discourse markers employed in scientific writing. Today, this module covers two components of Introductions[2], namely Gap and Purpose; **Module 2** - structures of scientific texts. It deals with the function of each section of a paper, covering particularly the Introduction and Abstract; **Module 3** - text compre-

2 According to Weissberg and Buker [12], the main components of an Introduction are Setting, Review of the Literature, Gap, Purpose, Methodology, Main Results, Value of the Work and Layout of the Article.

hension, aimed to check whether the student recognizes the relationships between the ideas conveyed in a given section of the paper. **Module 4** - strategies of scientific writing. It checks whether the student can distinguish between rhetorical strategies such as definitions, descriptions, classifications and argumentations. Today this module covers two components of Introductions, namely Setting and Review of the Li-t-erature.

The questions for Modules 1 and 4 are simple, independent from each other. However, the questions for Modules 2 and 3 are testlets, which are a group of items related to a given topic to be assessed. Testlets are thus considered as "units of test"; for instance, in a test there may be four questions about a particular item [12]. Calibration of the items is carried out with the algorithm of Huang [10], viz. the Content Balanced Adaptive Testing (CBAT-2), a self-adaptive testing which calibrates the parameters of the items during the test, according to the performance of the students. In the ADEPT, there are three options for the answers (choices a, b, or c). Depending on the answer (correct or incorrect), the parameter b is calibrated and there is the updating of the parameters *R* (number of times that the question was answered correctly in the past), *W* (number of times the question was answered incorrectly in the past) and Φ (difficulty accumulator) [10]. Even though the bank of items in ADEPT covers only Instrumental English, several subjects may be present. Therefore, the contents of the items had to be balanced [13], with the items being classified according to several components grouped in modules. In ADEPT, the contents are split into the Modules 1 through 4 with 15%, 30%, 30% and 25%, respectively. As for the weight of each component and Module in the curriculum hierarchy [14], 1 was adopted for all levels. In ADEPT, the student is the agent of calibration in real time of the test, with his/her success (failure) in the questions governing the calibration of the items in the bank.

2.2.3 Estimate of the Student Ability. In order to estimate the ability θ of a given student, ADEPT uses the modified iterative Newton-Raphson method [9], using the following formulas:

$$\theta_{n+1} = \theta_n + \frac{\sum_{i=1}^{n} S_i(\theta_n)}{\sum_{i=1}^{n} I_i(\theta_n)}$$

$$S_i(\theta) = [r_i - P_i(\theta)] \frac{P_i'(\theta)}{P_i(\theta)[1 - P_i(\theta)]}$$

where θ_n is the estimated ability after the nth question. r_i = 1 if the ith-answer was correct and r_i = 0 if the anwer was wrong. For the initial ability θ_0= 0.0 was adopted. The Newton-Raphson model was chosen due to the ease with which it is implemented.

2.2.4 Stopping Criteria. The criteria for stopping an automated test are crucial. In ADEPT two criteria were adopted: i) The number of questions per module of the test is between 3 (minimum) and 6 (maximum), because we did not the test to be too long. In case deficiencies were detected, the student would be recommended to perform tasks in the corresponding learning module. ii) θ should lie between -3.0 and 3.0 [15].

3 Task-Based Environments

A task-based environment provides the student with tasks for a specific domain. The rationale of this type of learning environment is that the student will learn by doing, in a real-world task related to the domain being taught. There is no assessment of the performance from the students while carrying out the tasks, but in some cases explanations on the tasks are provided.

3.1 CATESE

The Computer-Aided Task Environment for Scientifc English (CATESE) comprises tasks associated with the 4 modules of the Proficiency tests described in Section 2. The tasks are suggested to each student after performing the test of a specific module. This is done first for the Modules 1 and 2 and then for the Modules 4 and 3, seeking a balance for the reading of long (Modules 2 and 3) and short chunks of text (Modules 1 and 4).

The four tasks are as follows: **Task 1** (T1): identification and classification of discourse markers in sentences of the component Gap of an Introduction. Identification of verb tenses of the component Purpose; **Task 2** (T2): selection of the components for an Introduction and retrieval of well-written related texts from a text base for subsequent reading; **Task 3** (T3): reading of sentences with discourse markers for the student to establish relationships between the functions of the discourse and the markers, and **Task 4** (T4): identification and classification of writing strategies for the components Background and Review of the Literature.

The text base for Tasks 1, 3 and 4 of CATESE was extracted from the Support tool of AMADEUS [1], with the sample texts being displayed in XML. Task 2 is an adaptation of CALESE (http://www.nilc.icmc.usp.br/calese/) with filters for displaying the cases. Task 1 has 13 excerpts of papers with the components Gap and 40 for the Purpose, Task 2 has 51 Introductions of papers, Task 3 contains 46 excerpts from scientific texts and Task 4 has 34 excerpts from the component Setting and 38 for the component Purpose.

4 Integration of ADEPT and CATESE

The CALEAP-Web integrates two systems associated with assessing and learning tasks, as follows [5]: **Module 1** (Mod1) – assessment of the student with ADEPT to determine his/her level of knowledge of Instrumental English and **Module 2** (Mod2)

– tasks are suggested to the student using CATESE, according to his/her estimated knowledge, particularly to address difficulties detected in the assessment stage. Mod1 and Mod2 are integrated as illustrated in Fig. 1.

The sequence suggested by CALEAP-Web involves activities for Modules 1, 2, 4 and 3 of the EPI, presented below. In all tasks, chunks of text from well-written scientific papers are retrieved. The cases may be retrieved as many times as the student needs, and the selection is random.

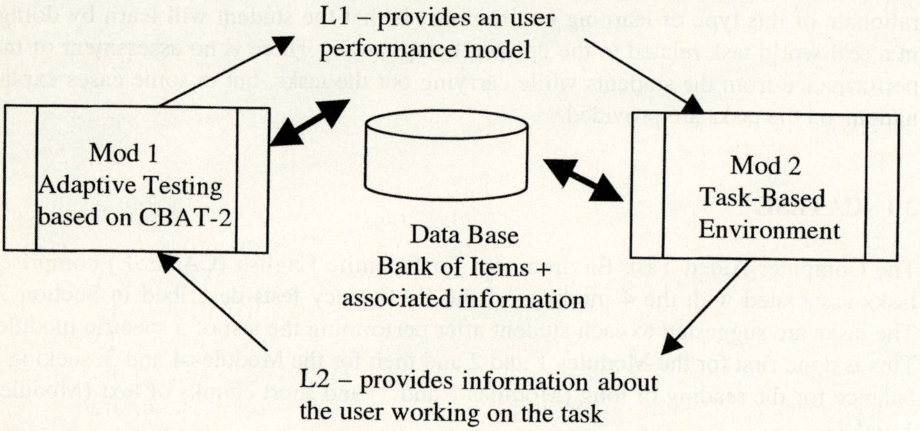

Fig. 1. Integration Scheme in CALEAP-Web. Information for modeling the user performance (L1) comes from the EPI Module in which the student is deficient, θ and $P(\theta)$, normalized score of the student in the test, number of correct and incorrect answers and time taken for the test in the EPI module being assessed. At the end of the test of each module of the EPI, the student will be directed to CATESE if his/her performance was below a certain level (if 2 or more answers are wrong in a given module). This criterion is being used in an experimental basis. In the future, other criteria will be employed to improve the assessment of the users' abilities, which may include: final abilities, number of questions answered, time of testing, etc. As an example of the interaction between ADEPT and CATESE is the following: if the student does not do well in Module 1 (involving Gap and Purpose) for questions associated with the component Gap, he/she will be asked to perform a task related to Gap (see Task 1 in Section 3.1), but not Purpose. If the two wrong answers refer to Gap and Purpose, then two tasks will be offered, one for each component. The information about the student (L2) includes the tasks recommended to the student and monitoring of how these tasks were performed. It is provided by CATESE to ADEPT, so that the student can take another EPI test in the module where deficiencies were noted. If the performance is now satisfactory, the student will be taken to the next test module.

Task 1 deals with the components Gap and Purpose of Module 1 from EPI, with the texts retrieved belonging to two classes for the Gap component: **Class A**: special words are commonly used to indicate the beginning of the Gap. Connectors such as "however" and "but" are used for this purpose. The connector is followed immediately by a gap statement in the present or present perfect tense, which often contains modifiers such as "few", "little", or "no": Signal word + Gap (present or present perfect) + Research topic; **Class B**: subordinating conjunctions like "while", "although" and "though" can also be used to signal the gap. When such signals are used, the sentence will typically include modifiers such as "some", "many", or "much" in the first clause, with modifiers such as "little", "few", or "no" in the second clause: Signal word + Previous work (present or present perfect) + Gap + topic.

In this classification two chunks of text are retrieved, where the task consists in the identification and classification of markers in the examples, two of which are shown below.

> Class A: However, in spite of this rapid progress, many of the basic physics issues of x-ray lasers remain poorly understood.
> Class B: Although the origin of the solitons has been established, some of their physical properties remained unexplained.

The texts retrieved for the Purpose component are classified as: **Class A**: the orientation of the statement of purpose may be towards the report itself. If you choose the report orientation you should use the present or future tense: Report orientation + Main Verb (present or future) + Research question; **Class B**: the orientation of the statement of purpose may be towards the research activity. If you choose the research orientation you should use the past tense, because the research activity has already been completed: Research orientation + Main Verb (past) + Research question.

The Tasks consists in identifying and classifying the markers in the examples for each class, illustrated below.

> Class A: In this paper we report a novel resonant-like behavior in the latter case of diffusion over a fluctuating barrier.
> Class B: The present study used both methods to produce monolayers of C16MV on silver electrode surfaces.

Task 2 is related to the Introduction of Module 2 of EPI, which provides information about the components of an Introduction of a scientific paper. The student selects the components and strategies so that the system retrieves the cases (well-written papers) that are consistent with the requisition and reads them. With this process, the student may learn by examples where and how the components and strategies should be used. This task was created from the Support Tool of AMADEUS [4], which employs case-based reasoning (CBR) to model the three stages of the writing process: the user selects the intended characteristics of the Introduction of a scientific paper, the best cases are retrieved from the case base, and the case chosen is modified to cater for the user intentions. The student may repeat this task and select new strategies (with the corresponding components).

Task 4 deals with the Setting and Review of the Literature from Module 4 or EPI. For the Setting, the cases retrieved are classified into three classes: **Class A**: Arguing about the topic prominence: uses arguments; **Class B**: Familiarizing terms or objects or processes: follows one of the three patterns: description, definition or classification; **Class C**: Introducing the research topic from the research area: follows the general to particular ordering of details.

For the Review of the Literature, there are also three classes: **Class A**: Citations grouped by approaches: better suited for reviews of the literature which encompass different approaches; **Class B**: Citations ordered from general to specific: citations are organized in order from those most distantly related to the study to those most closely related; **Class C**: Citations ordered chronologically: used, for example, when describing the history of research in an area.

The last Task is related to Comprehension of Module 3 of EPI. Here a sequence of discourse markers are presented to the student, organized according to their function in the clause (or sentence). Also shown is an example of well-written text in English with annotated discourse markers. Task 3 therefore consists in reading and verifying examples of markers for each discourse function. The nine functions considered are: contrast/opposition, signaling of further information/addition, similarity, exemplification, reformulation, consequence/result, conclusion, explanation, deduction/inference. The student may navigate through the cases and after finishing, he/she will be assessed by the CAT. It is believed that after being successful in the four stages described above in the CALEAP-Web system, the student is prepared to undertake the official test at ICMC-USP.

5 Evaluating CALEAP-Web

CALEAP-Web has been assessed according to two main criteria: item exposure of the CAT module and robustness of the whole computational environment. With regard to robustness, we ensured that the environment works as specified in all stages, with no crash or error, by simulating students using the 4 tasks presented in Section 4. The data from four students that evaluated ADEPT, graded as having intermediate level of proficiency (θ in the range $-1.0 <= \theta <= 1.0$), were selected as a starting point of the simulation. All the four tasks were performed and the environment was proven to be robust to be used by prospective students in preparation for the official exam in 2004 at ICMC-USP. The analysis of item exposure is crucial to ensure a quality assessment. Indeed, item exposure is critical because adaptive algorithms are designed to select optimal items, thus tending to choose those with high discriminating power (parameter a). As a result, these items are selected far more often than other ones, leading to both over-exposure of some parts of the item pool and under-utilization of others. The risk is that over-used items are often compromised as they create a security problem that could jeopardize a test, especially if it's a summative one. In our CAT parameters a and c were constant for all the items, and therefore item exposure depends solely on parameter b. To measure item exposure rate of the two types of item from our EPI (simple and testlet) we performed two experiments, the first with 12 students who failed the 2003 EPI and another with 9 students that passed it. From the 140 items only 66 were accessed and re-calibrated[3] after both experiments, where

[3] The second author has realized a pre-calibration of the parameter b of all the 140 items from the bank, using a 4-value table including difficult, medium, easy and very easy item category with respectively 2.5, 1.0, -1.0 and -2.5 value.

30 of them were from testlets. Testlets are problematic because they impose application of questions as soon as selected. The 21 testlets of CAT involve 78 questions, with 48 remaining non re-calibrated. As for the EPI modules, most calibrated questions were from modules 1 and 4 because they include simple questions, allowing more variability in items choice. In experiment 1 questions 147 and 148 were accessed 9 times, with 16 questions being accessed only once and 89 were not accessed at all. In experiment 2, the most accessed questions were 138, 139 and 51 with 9 accesses each. On the other hand, 16 questions had only one access and 83 were not accessed at all. Taken together these results show the need to extend the studies with a larger number of students in order to achieve a more precise item calibration.

6 Related Work

Particularly with the rapid expansion of open and distance-learning programs, fully-automated tests are being increasingly used to measure student performance as an important component in educational or training processes. This is illustrated by a computer-based large-scale evaluation using specifically adaptive testing to assess several knowledge types, viz. the Test of English as a Foreign Language (http://www.toefl.org/). Other examples of learning environments with an assessment module are the Project entitled Training of European Environmental trainers and technicians in order to disseminate multinational skills between European countries (TREE) [16, 17, 8] and the Intelligent System for Personalized Instruction in a Remote Environment (INSPIRE) [18]. TREE is aimed at developing an Intelligent Tutoring System (ITS) for classification and identification of European vegetations. It comprises three main subsystems, namely, an Expert System, a Tutoring System and a Test Generation System. The latter, referred to as Intelligent Evaluation System using Tests for Teleducation (SIETTE), assesses the student with a CAT implemented with the CBAT-2 algorithm, the same we have used in this work. The task module is the ITS. INSPIRE monitors the students' activities, adapting itself in real time to select lessons that are adequate to the level of knowledge of the student. It differs from CALEAP-Web, which is based in the learn by doing paradigm. In INSPIRE there is a module to assess the student with adaptive testing [19], also using the CBAT-2 algorithm.

7 Conclusions and Further Work

The environment presented here and its preliminary evaluation, referred to as CALEAP-Web, is a first, important step in implementing adaptive assessment in relatively small institutions, as it offers a mechanism to escape from a pre-calibration of test items [10]. It integrates a CAT system and a task-based system, which serve to assess the performance of users (i.e. to detect their level of knowledge on scientific texts genre) and assist them with a handful of learning strategies, respectively. The ones implemented in CALEAP-Web were all associated with English for academic purposes, but the rationale and the tools developed can be extended to other domains. ADEPT is readily amenable to be portable because it only requires a change in the bank of items. CATESE, on the other hand, needs to be rebuilt because the tasks are domain specific. One major present limitation of CALEAP-Web is the small size of the bank of items; furthermore, increasing this size is costly in terms of man power due to the time-consuming corpus analysis to annotate the scientific papers used in both the adaptive testing and the task-based environment. With a reduced bank of items, at the moment we recommend the use of the adaptive test of CALEAP-Web only in formative tests and not in summative tests as we still have items with over-exposure and a number of them under-utilized.

References

1. Aluisio, S.M., Oliveira Jr. O.N.: A case-based approach for developing writing tools aimed at non-native English users. Lectures Notes in Artificial Intelligence, Vol. 1010. Springer-Verlag, Berlin Heidelberg New York (1995) 121-132
2. Aluísio, S.M., Gantenbein, R.E.: Towards the application of systemic functional linguistics in writing tools. Proceedings of International Conference on Computers and their Applications (1997) 181-185
3. Aluísio, S.M., Barcelos, I. Sampaio, J., Oliveira Jr., O N.: How to learn the many unwritten "Rules of the Game" of the Academic Discourse: A hybrid Approach based on Critiques and Cases. Proceedings of the IEEE International Conference on Advanced Learning Technologies, Madison/Wisconsin (2001) 257-260
4. Aluísio, S. M., Aquino, V. T., Pizzirani, R., Oliveira JR, O. N.: High Order Skills with Partial Knowledge Evaluation: Lessons learned from using a Computer-based Proficiency Test of English for Academic Purposes. Journal of Information Technology Education, Califórnia, USA, Vol. 2, N. 1 (2003)185-201
5. Gonçalves, J. P.: A integração de Testes Adaptativos Informatizados e Ambientes Computacionais de Tarefas para o aprendizado do inglês instrumental. (Portuguese). Dissertação de mestrado, ICMC-USP, São Carlos, Brasil (2004)
6. Schank, R.: Engines for Education (Hyperbook ed.). Chicago, USA: ILS, Northwestern University (2002). URL http://www.engines4ed.org/hyperbook/index.html
7. Olea, J., Ponsoda V., Prieto, G.: Tests Informatizados Fundamentos y Aplicaciones. Ediciones Pirámede (1999)
8. Conejo, R., Millán, E., Cruz, J.L.P., Trella, M.: Modelado del alumno: um enfoque bayesiano. Inteligencia Artificial, Revista Iberoamericana de Inteligencia Artificial N. 12 (2001) 50–58. URL http://tornado.dia.fi.upm.es/caepia/numeros/12/Conejo.pdf
9. Lord, F. M.: Application of Item Response Theory to Practical Testing Problems. Hilsdale, New Jersey, EUA: Lawrence Erlbaum Associates (1980)
10. Huang, S.X.: A Content-Balanced Adaptive Testing Algorithm for Computer-Based Training Systems. Intelligent Tutoring Systems (1996) 306-314
11. Weissberg, R., Buker, S.: Writing Up Research - Experimental Research Report Writing for Students of English. Prentice Hall Regents (1990)

12. Oliveira, L. H. M.: Testes adaptativos sensíveis ao conteúdo do banco de itens: uma aplicação em exames de proficiência em inglês para programas de pós-graduação. (Portuguese). Dissertação de mestrado, ICMC-USP, São Carlos, Brasil (2002)
13. Huang, S.X.: On Content-Balanced Adaptive Testing. CALISCE (1996) 60-68
14. Collins, J.A., Geer, J.E., Huang, S.X.: Adaptive Assessment Using Granularity Hierarchies and Bayesian Nets. Intelligent Tutoring Systems (1996) 569-577
15. Baker, F.: The Basics of Item Response. College Park, MD: ERIC Clearinghouse, University of Maryland (2001)
16. Conejo, R.; Rios, A., Millán, M.T.E., Cruz, J.L.P.: Internet based evaluation system. AIED-International Conference Artificial Intelligence in Education, IOS Press (1999). URL http://www.lcc.uma.es/~eva/investigacion/papers/aied99a.ps.
17. Conejo, R., Millán, M.T.E., Cruz, J.L.P., Trella,M.: An empirical approach to online learning in Siette. Intelligent Tutorial Systems (2000) 604–615
18. Papanikolaou, K., Grigoriadou, M., Kornilakis, H., Magoulas, G.D.: Inspire: An intelligent system for personalized instruction in a remote environment. Third Workshop on Adaptive Hypertext and Hypermedia (2001) URL http://wwwis.win.tue.nl/ah2001/papers/papanikolaou.pdf.
19. Gouli, E, Kornilakis, H.; Papanikolaou, K.; Grigoriadou. M.: Adaptive assessment improving interaction in an educational hypermedia system. PC-HCI Conference (2001). URL http://hermes.di.uoa.gr/lab/CVs/papers/gouli/F51.pdf

A Model for Student Knowledge Diagnosis Through Adaptive Testing*

Eduardo Guzmán and Ricardo Conejo

Departamento de Lenguajes y Ciencias de la Computación
E.T.S.I. Informática. Universidad de Málaga. Apdo. 4114. Málaga 29080. SPAIN
{guzman,conejo}@lcc.uma.es

Abstract. This work presents a model for student knowledge diagnosis that can be used in ITSs for student model update. The diagnosis is accomplished through *Computerized Adaptive Testing* (CAT). CATs are assessment tools with theoretical background. They use an underlying psychometric theory, the *Item Response Theory* (IRT), for question selection, student knowledge estimation and test finalization. In principle, CATs are only able to assess one topic for each test. IRT models used in CATs are dichotomous, that is, questions are only scored as correct or incorrect. However, our model can be used to simultaneously assess multiple topics through content-balanced tests. In addition, we have included a polytomous IRT model, where answers can be given partial credit. Therefore, this polytomous model is able to obtain more information from student answers than the dichotomous ones. Our model has been evaluated through a study carried out with simulated students, showing that it provides accurate estimations with a reduced number of questions.

1 Introduction

One of the most important features of Intelligent Tutoring Systems (ITSs) is the capability of adapting instruction to student needs. To accomplish this task, the ITS must know the student's knowledge state accurately. One of the most common solutions for student diagnosis is testing. The main advantages of testing are that it can be used in quite a few domains and it is easy to implement. Generally, test-based diagnosis systems use heuristic solutions to infer student knowledge. In contrast, *Computerized Adaptive Testing* (CAT) is a well-founded technique, which uses a psychometric theory called *Item Response Theory* (IRT). The CAT theory is not used only with conventional paper-and-pencil test questions, that is, questions comprising a stem and a set of possible answers. CAT can also include a wide range of exercises [5]. On the contrary, CATs are only able to assess a single atomic topic [6]. This restricts its applicability to structured domain models, since when in a test more than one content area is being assessed, the test is only able to provide one student

---

* This work has been partially financed by LEActiveMath project, funded under FP6 (Contr. Nº 507826). The author is solely responsible for its content, it does not represent the opinion of the EC, and the EC is not responsible for any use that might be made of data appearing therein.

J.C. Lester et al. (Eds.): ITS 2004, LNCS 3220, pp. 12–21, 2004.

knowledge estimation for all content areas. In addition, in these multiple topic tests, the content balance cannot be guaranteed.

In general, systems that implement CATs use dichotomous IRT based models. This means that student answers to a question can only be evaluated as correct or incorrect, i.e. no partial credit can be given. IRT has defined other kinds of response models called polytomous. These models allow giving partial credit to item answers. They are more powerful, since they make better use of the responses provided by students, and as a result, student knowledge estimations can be obtained faster and more accurately. Although in literature there are a lot of polytomous models, they are not usually applied to CATs [3], because they are difficult to implement.

In this paper, a student diagnosis model is presented. This model is based on a technique [4] of assessing multiple topics using content-balanced CATs. It can be applied to declarative domain models structured in granularity hierarchies [8], and it uses a discrete polytomous IRT inference engine. It could be applied in ITS as a student knowledge diagnosis engine. For instance, at the beginning of instruction, to initialize the student model by pretesting; during instruction, to update the student model; and/or at the end of instruction, providing a global snapshot of the state of knowledge.

The next section is devoted to showing the modus operandi of adaptive testing. Section 3 supplies the basis of IRT. Section 4 is an extension of Section 3, introducing polytomous IRT. In Section 5 our student knowledge diagnosis model is explained. Here, the diagnosis procedure of this model is described in detail. Section 6 checks the reliability and accuracy of the assessment procedure through a study with simulated students. Finally, Section 7 discusses the results obtained.

2 Adaptive Testing

A CAT [11] is a test-based measurement tool administered to students by means of a computer instead of the conventional paper-and-pencil format. Generally, in CATs questions (called "items") are posed one at a time. The presentation of each item and the decision to finish the test are dynamically adopted, based on students' answers. The final goal of a CAT is to estimate quantitatively student knowledge level expressed by means of a numerical value. A CAT applies an iterative algorithm that starts with an initial estimation of the student's knowledge level and has the following steps: 1) all the items (that have not been administered yet) are examined to determine which is the best item to ask next, according to the current estimation of the student's knowledge level; 2) the item is asked, and the student responds; 3) in terms of the answer, a new estimation of his knowledge level is computed; 4) steps 1 to 3 are repeated until the defined test finalization criterion is met. The selection and finalization criteria are based on theoretically based procedures that can be controlled with parameters. These parameters define the required assessment accuracy. The number of items is not fixed, and each student usually takes different sequences of items, and even different items. The basic elements in the development of a CAT are: 1) The *response model associated to each item*: This model describes how students answer the item depending on their knowledge level. 2) The *item pool*: It may contain a large number of correctly calibrated items at each knowledge level. The better the quality of the item pool, the better the job that the CAT can perform . 3) *Item selection method*: Adaptive tests select the next item to be posed depending on the student's estimated knowledge level (obtained from the answers to items previously administered). 4) *The termination criterion*: Different criteria can be used to decide when the test should finish, in terms of the purpose of the test.

The set of advantages provided by CATs is often addressed in the literature [11]. The main advantage is that it reduces the number of questions needed to estimate student knowledge level, and as a result, the time devoted to that task. . This entails an improvement in student motivation. However, CATs contain some drawbacks. They require the availability of huge item pools, techniques to control item exposure and to detect compromised items. In addition, item parameters must be calibrated. To accomplish this task, a large number of student performances are required, and this is not always available.

3 Item Response Theory

IRT [7] has been successfully applied to CATs as a response model, item selection and finalization criteria. It is based on two principles: a) Student performance in a test can be explained by means of the knowledge level, which can be measured as an unknown numeric value. b) The performance of a student with an estimated knowledge level answering an item *i* can be probabilistically predicted and modeled by means of a function called *Item Characteristic Curve* (ICC). It expresses the probability that a student with certain knowledge level θ has to answer the item correctly. Each item must define an ICC, which must be previously calibrated. There are several functions to characterize ICCs. One of the most extended is the logistic function of three parameters (3PL) [1] defined as follows:

$$P(u_i = 1 | \theta) = c_i + (1 - c_i) \frac{1}{1 + e^{-1.7 a_i (\theta - b_i)}} \quad (1)$$

where $u_i=1$ represents that the student has successfully answered item *i*. If the student answers incorrectly, $P(u_i=0|\theta)=1-P(u_i=1|\theta)$. The three parameters that determine the shape of this curve are:

- *Discrimination factor* (a_i): It is proportional to the slope of the curve. High values indicate that the probability of success from students with a knowledge level higher than the item difficulty is high.
- *Difficulty* (b_i): It corresponds to the knowledge level at which the probability of answering correctly is the same as answering incorrectly . The range of values allowed for this parameter is the same as the ones allowed for the knowledge levels.
- *Guessing factor* (c_i): It is the probability of that a student with no knowledge at all will answer the item correctly by randomly selecting a response.

In our proposal, and therefore throughout this paper, the knowledge level is measured using a discrete IRT model. Instead of taking real values, the knowledge level takes K values (or latent classes) from 0 to K-1. Teachers decide the value of *K* in terms of the assessment granularity desired. Likewise, each ICC is turned into a probability vector $p(u_i=1|\theta=0), p(u_i=1|\theta=1), p(u_i=1|\theta=2), \ldots, p(u_i=1|\theta=K-1)$.

3.1 Student Knowledge Estimation

IRT supplies several methods to estimate student knowledge. All of them calculate a probability distribution curve $P(\theta|\mathbf{u})$, where $\mathbf{u}=u_1, .., u_n$ is the vector of items administered to students. When applied to adaptive testing, knowledge estimation is accomplished every time the student answers each item posed, obtaining a temporal estimation. The distribution obtained after posing the last item of the test becomes the final student knowledge estimation. One of the most popular estimation methods is the Bayesian method [9]. It applies the Bayes theorem to calculate student knowledge distribution after posing an item i:

$$\mathrm{P}(\theta|\mathrm{u}_1,..,\mathrm{u}_i) \propto P(\mathrm{u}_i=1|\theta)^{u_i}(1-P(\mathrm{u}_i=1|\theta))^{(1-u_i)}P(\theta|u_1,..u_{i-1}) \quad (2)$$

where $P(\theta|u_1, .., u_{i-1})$ represents temporary student knowledge distribution before posing i.

3.2 Item Selection Procedure

One of the most popular methods for selecting items is the Bayesian method [9]. It selects the item that minimizes the expectation of a posteriori student knowledge distribution variance. That is, taking the current estimation, it calculates the posterior expectation for every non-administered item, and selects the one with the smallest expectation value. Expectation is calculated as follows:

$$\begin{aligned}&\mathrm{P}'(\theta|u_1,...,\mathrm{u}_i=\mathrm{r})=\mathrm{P}(\mathrm{u}_i=\mathrm{r}|\theta)\cdot P(\theta|u_1,...,u_{i-1})\\&\mathrm{E}[\sigma^2(\mathrm{P}(\theta|\mathrm{u}_1,...,\mathrm{u}_i))]=\sum_r \mathrm{P}'(\theta|u_1,...,\mathrm{u}_i=\mathrm{r})\,\sigma^2(\mathrm{P}(\theta|u_1,...,\mathrm{u}_i=\mathrm{r}))\end{aligned} \quad (3)$$

where r can take value 0 or 1. It is $r=1$-, if the response is correct, or $r=0$ otherwise. $P'(\theta|u_1,...,u_i=r)$ is the scalar product between ICC (or its inverse) of item i and the current estimated knowledge distribution.

4 Polytomous IRT

In dichotomous IRT models, items are only scored as correct or incorrect. In contrast, polytomous models try to obtain as much information as possible from the student's response. They take into account the answer selected by students in the estimation of knowledge level and in the item selection. For this purpose, these models add a new type of characteristic curve associated to each answer, in the style of ICC. In the literature these curves are called *trace lines* (TC) [3], and they represent the probability that certain student will select an answer given his knowledge level.

To understand the advantages of this kind of model, let us look at the item represented in Fig. 1 (a). A similar item was used in a study carried out in 1992 [10]. Student performances in this test were used to calibrate the test items. The calibrated TCs for the item of Fig. 1 (a) are represented in Fig. 1 (b). Analyzing these curves, we see that the correct answer is B, since students with the highest knowledge levels have high probabilities of selecting this answer. Options *A* and *D* are clearly wrong, because students with the lowest knowledge levels are more likely to select these answers. However, option *C* shows that a considerable number of students with medium knowledge levels tends to select this option. If the item is analyzed, it is evident that for option *C*, although incorrect , the knowledge of students selecting *it* is higher than the knowledge of students selecting *A* or *D*. Selecting *A* or *D* may be assessed more negatively than selecting *B*. Answers like *C* are called *distractors*, since, even though these answers are not correct, they are very similar to the correct answers. In addition, polytomous models make a difference between selecting an option or leave the item blank. Those students who do not select any option are modeled with the DK option TC. This answer is considered as an additional possible option and is known as *don't know* option.

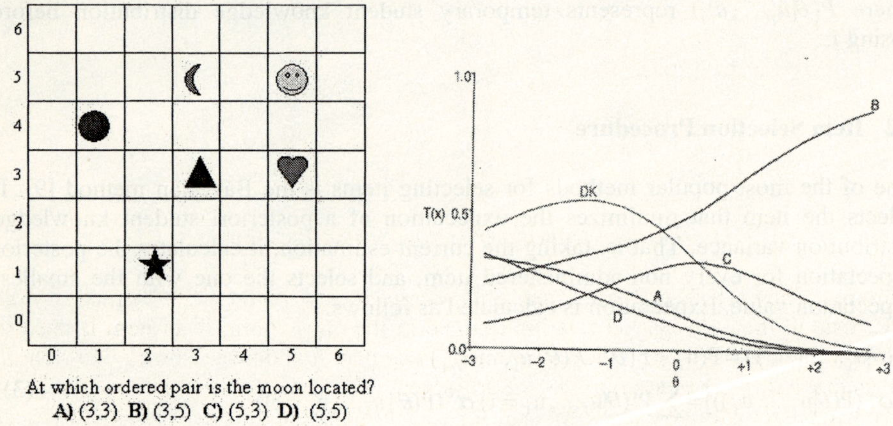

Fig. 1. (a) A multiple-choice item, and (b) its trace lines (adapted from [10])

5 Student Knowledge Diagnosis Through Adaptive Testing

Domain models can be structured on the basis of subjects. Subjects may be divided into different topics. A topic can be defined as a concept regarding which student knowledge can be assessed. They can also be decomposed into other topics and so on, forming a hierarchy with a degree of granularity decided by the teacher. In this hierarchy, leaf nodes represent a unique concept or a set of concepts that are indivisible from the assessment point of view. Topics and their subtopics are related by means of aggregation relations, and no precedence relations are considered. For diagnosis purposes, this domain model could be extended by adding a new layer to include two kinds of components: items and test specifications. This extended model has been represented in Fig. 2. The main features of these new components are the following:

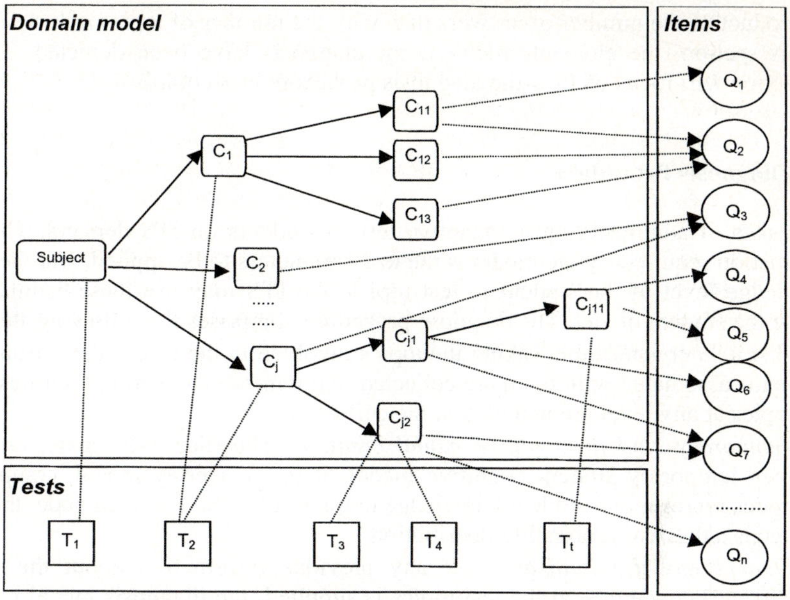

Fig. 2. A domain model extended for diagnosis

Items. They are related to a topic. This relationship is materialized by means of an ICC. Due to the aggregation relation defined in the curriculum, if an item is used to assess a topic *j*, it also provides assessment information about the knowledge state in topics preceding *j*, and even in the whole subject. To model this feature, several ICCs have been associated to each item , one for each topic the item is used to assess. These curves collect the probability of answering the item correctly given the student knowledge level in the corresponding topic. Accordingly, the number of ICCs of an item is equal to the number of topics, in different levels of the hierarchy, which are related to the item including the subject. This means that for item Q_5 (Fig. 2), the ICCs defined are: $P(u_5=1|\theta_{j11})$, $P(u_5=1|\theta_{j1})$, $P(u_5=1|\theta_j)$ and $P(u_5=1|\theta_{subject})$.

Tests. They are specifications of adaptive assessment sessions defined on topics. Therefore, after a student takes a test, it will diagnose his knowledge levels in the test topics, and in all their descendant topics. For instance, let us consider test T_2 (Fig. 2). Topics of this test are C_1 and C_j. After a testing session, the knowledge of students in these topics will be inferred. Additionally, the knowledge in topics C_{11}, C_{12}, C_{13}, C_{j1}, C_{j2} and C_{j11} can also be inferred That is, if $\boldsymbol{u}= u_1, ..., u_n$ is the set of items administered, the following knowledge distributions could be inferred: $P(\theta_1|\boldsymbol{u})$, $P(\theta_j|\boldsymbol{u})$, $P(\theta_{11}|\boldsymbol{u})$, $P(\theta_{12}|\boldsymbol{u})$, $P(\theta_{13}|\boldsymbol{u})$, $P(\theta_{j1}|\boldsymbol{u})$, $P(\theta_{j2}|\boldsymbol{u})$ and $P(\theta_{j11}|\boldsymbol{u})$.

As mentioned earlier, even though CATs are used to assess one single topic, in [4] we introduce a technique to simultaneously assess multiple topics in the same test, which is content-balanced. This technique has been included in a student knowledge diagnosis model that uses the extended domain model of Fig. 2. The model assesses through adaptive testing, and uses a discrete response model where the common dichotomous approach has been replaced by a polytomous one. Accordingly, the relationship between topics and items is modified. Now, each ICC is replaced by a set of TCs (one for each item answer), that is, the number of TCs of an item *i* is equal to the product of the number of answers of *i*, with the number of topics assessed using *i*. In this section, the elements required for diagnosis have been depicted. The next subsection will focus on how the diagnosis procedure is accomplished.

5.1 Diagnosis Procedure

It consists of administering an adaptive test to students on ITS demand. The initial information required by the model is the test parameters to be applied, and the current knowledge level of the student in test topics. An ITS may use these estimations to update the student model. The diagnose procedure comprises the following steps:

- *Test item compilation*: Taking the topics involved in the test as the starting point, items associated with them are collected. All items associated to their descendant topics at any level are included in the collection.
- *Temporary student cognitive model creation*: The diagnosis model creates its own temporary student cognitive model. It is an overlay model, composed of nodes representing student knowledge in the test topics. For each node, the model keeps a discrete probability distribution.
- *Student model initialization*: If any previous information about the state of student knowledge in the test topics is supplied, the diagnosis model could use this information as a priori estimation of student knowledge. In other cases, this model offers the possibility of selecting several values by default
- *Adaptive testing stage*: The student is administered the test adaptively.

5.2 Adaptive Testing Stage

This testing algorithm follows the steps described in Section 2, although item selection and knowledge estimation procedures differ because of the addition of a discrete polytomous response model. Student knowledge estimation uses a variation of the Bayesian method described in Equation 2. After administering item *i*, the new estimated knowledge level in topic *j* is calculated using Equation 4.

$$\mathrm{P}(\theta_j | u_1,...,u_{i-1},\mathrm{u_i}) \propto P(\mathrm{u_i} = \mathrm{r} \mid \theta_j) P(\theta_j \mid u_1,...,u_{i-1}) \quad (4)$$

Note that the TC corresponding to the student answer, $P(u_i=r|\theta_j)$, has replaced the ICC term. Being *r* the answer selected by the student, it can take values between 1 to the number of answers *R*. When *r* is zero, it represents the *don't know* answer.

Once the student has answered an item, this response is used to update student knowledge in all topics that are descendents of topic *j*. Let us suppose test T_2 (Fig. 1(b)) is being administered. If item Q_5 has just been administered, student knowledge estimation in topic C_j is updated according to Equation 4. In addition, item Q_5 provides information about student knowledge in topics C_{j1} and C_{j11}. Consequently, the student knowledge estimation in these topics is also updated using the same equation.

The item selection mechanism modifies the dichotomous Bayesian one (Equation 3). In this modification, expectation is calculated from the TCs, instead of the ICC (or its inverse), in the following way:

$$E\left[\sigma^2(P(\theta_j|u_1,..,u_i))\right]=\sum_{r=0}^{n}\left[P(u_i=r\,|\,\theta_j)\cdot P(\theta_j\,|\,u_1,..,u_{i-1})\right]\sigma^2(P(\theta_j\,|\,u_1,..,u_i=r)) \quad (5)$$

θ_j represents student knowledge in topic *j*. Topic *j* is one of the test topics. Let us take test T_2 again. Expectation is calculated for all (non-administered) items that assess topics C_1, C_j or any descendent. Note that Equation 5 must always be applied to knowledge distributions in test topics (i.e. C_1 and C_j), since the main goal of the test is to estimate student knowledge in these topics. The remaining estimations can be considered as a collateral effect. Additionally, this model guarantees content-balanced tests. The adaptive selection engine itself tends to select the item that makes the estimation more accurate [4]. If several topics are assessed, the selection mechanism is separated in two phases. In the first one, it will select the topic whose student knowledge distribution is the least accurate. The second one selects, from items of this topic, the one that contributes the most to increase accuracy.

6 Evaluation

Some authors have pointed out the advantages of using simulated students for evaluation purposes [12], since this kind of student allows having a controlled environment, and contributes to ensuring that the results obtained in the evaluation are correct. This study consists of a comparison of two CAT-based assessment methods: the polytomous versus the dichotomous one. It uses a test of a single topic, which contains an item pool of 500 items. These items are multiple-choice items with four answers, where the *don't know* answer is included. The test stops when the knowledge estimation distribution has a variance that is less than 10^{-5}. The test has been administered to a population of 150 simulated students. These students have been generated with a real knowledge level that is used to determine their behavior during the test. Let us assume that the knowledge level of the student John is θ_j. When an item *i* is posed, John's response is calculated by generating a random probability value v. The answer *r* selected by John ($r \in \{0, 1, 2, 3, 4\}$) is the one that fulfils,

$$\sum_{m=0}^{r} P\,(u_i = r\,|\,\theta_j) >= v$$

Using the same population and the same item pool, two adaptive tests have been administered for each simulation. The former uses polytomous item selection and knowledge estimation, and the latter dichotomous item selection and knowledge estimation. Different simulations of test execution have been accomplished changing the parameters of the item curves. ICCs have been generated (and are assumed to be well calibrated), before each simulation, according to these conditions. The correct answer TC corresponds to the ICC, and the incorrect response TCs are calculated in such a way that their sum is equal to *1-ICC*. Simulation results are shown in Table 1.

In Table 1 each row represents a simulation of the students taking a test with the features specified in the columns. Discrimination factor and difficulty of all items of the pool are assigned the value indicated in the corresponding column, and the guessing factor is always zero. When the value is "uniform", item parameter values

Table 1. Simulation results of polytomous testing versus dichotomous testing

Assessment & item selection	Item discrim.	Item difficult.	Item number average	Estimation variance average	Success rate
polytomous	0,4	uniform	67,77	0,000577216	100%
dichotomous	0,4	uniform	146,51	0,000366659	98%
polytomous	0,7	uniform	40,35	0,000007113	100%
dichotomous	0,7	uniform	50,56	0,000186682	100%
polytomous	1,2	uniform	20,30	0,000006597	100%
dichotomous	1,2	uniform	18,57	0,000007863	100%
polytomous	uniform	uniform	20,60	0,000007476	100%
dichotomous	uniform	uniform	28,97	0,000028836	100%

have been generated uniformly along the allowed range. The last three columns represent the results of simulations. "Item number average" is the average of items posed to students in the test; "estimation variance average" is the average of the final knowledge estimation variances. Finally , "success rate" is the percentage of students assessed correctly. This last value has been obtained by comparing real student knowledge with the student knowledge inferred by the test. As can be seen, the best improvements have been obtained for a pool of items with a low discrimination factor. In this case, the number of items has been reduced drastically. The polytomous version requires less than half of the dichotomous one, and the estimation accuracy is only a bit lower . The worst performance of the polytomous version takes place when items have a high discrimination factor. This can be explained because high discrimination ICCs get the best performance in dichotomous assessment. In contrast, for the polytomous test, TCs have been generated with random discriminations, and as a result, TCs are not able to discriminate as much as dichotomous ICCs. In the most realistic case, i.e. the last two simulations, item parameters have been calculated uniformly. In this case, test results for the polytomous version is better than the dichotomous one, since the higher the accuracy, the lower the number of items required. In addition, the evaluation results obtained in [4] showed that the assessment of multiple topics is simultaneously able to make a content-balanced item selection. Teachers do not have to specify, for instance, the percentage of items that must be administered for each topic involved in the test.

7 Discussion

This work proposes a well-founded student diagnosis model, based on adaptive testing. It introduces some improvements in traditional CATs. It allows simultaneous assessment of multiple topics through content-balanced tests. Other approaches have presented content-balanced adaptive testing, like the CBAT-2 algorithm [6]. It is able to generate content-balanced tests, but in order to do so, teachers must manually introduce the weight of topics in the global test for the item selection. However, in our model, item selection is carried out adaptively by the model itself. It selects the next item to be posed from the topic whose knowledge estimation is the least accurate. Additionally, we have defined a discrete , IRT-based polytomous response model. The evaluation results (where accuracy has been overstated to demonstrate the

strength of the model) have shown that, in general, our polytomous model makes more accurate estimations and requires fewer items.
The model presented has been implemented and is currently used in the SIETTE system [2]. SIETTE is a web-based CAT delivery and elicitation tool (http://www.lcc.uma.es/siette) that can be used as a diagnosis tool in ITSs. Currently, we are working on TC calibration techniques. The goal is to obtain a calibration mechanism that minimizes the number of prior student performances required to calibrate the TCs.

References

1. Birnbaum, A. Some Latent Trait Models and Their Use in Inferring an Examinee's Mental Ability. In : Lord, F. M. and Novick, M. R, eds. *Statistical Theories of Mental Test Scores*. Reading, MA: Addison-Wesley; 1968.
2. Conejo, R.; Guzmán, E.; Millán, E.; Pérez-de-la-Cruz, J. L., and Trella, M. SIETTE: A web-based tool for adaptive testing. *International Journal of Artificial Intelligence in Education* (forthcoming).
3. Dodd, B. G.; DeAyala, R. J., and Koch, W. R. Computerized Adaptive Testing with Polytomous Items. *Applied Psychological Measurement*. 1995; 19(1):pp. 5-22.
4. Guzmán, E. and Conejo, R. Simultaneous evaluation of multiple topics in SIETTE. *LNCS, 2363. ITS 2002*. Springer Verlag; 2002: 739-748.
5. Guzmán, E. and Conejo, R. A library of templates for exercise construction in an adaptive assessment system. *Technology, Instruction, Cognition and Learning (TICL)* (forthcoming).
6. Huang, S. X. A Content-Balanced Adaptive Testing Algorithm for Computer-Based Training Systems. *LNCS, 1086. ITS 1996*. Springer Verlag; 1996: pp. 306-314.
7. Lord, F. M. *Applications of item response theory to practical testing problems*. Hillsdale, NJ: Lawrence Erlbaum Associates; 1980.
8. McCalla, G. I. and Greer, J. E. Granularity-Based Reasoning and Belief Revision in Student Models. In: Greer, J. E. and McCalla, G., eds. *Student Modeling: The Key to Individualized Knowledge-Based Instruction*. Springer Verlag; 1994; 125 pp. 39-62.
9. Owen, R. J. A Bayesian Sequential Procedure for Quantal Response in the Context of Adaptive Mental Testing. *Journal of the American Statistical Association*. 1975 Jun; 70(350):351-371.
10. Thissen, D. and Steinberg, L. A Response Model for Multiple Choice Items. In: Van der Linden, W. J. and Hambleton, R. K., (eds.). *Handbook of Modern Item Response Theory*. New York: Springer-Verlag; 1997; pp. 51-65.
11. van der Linden, W. J. and Glas, C. A. W. *Computerized Adaptive Testing: Theory and Practice*. Netherlands: Kluwer Academic Publishers; 2000.
12. VanLehn, K.; Ohlsson, S., and Nason, R. Applications of Simulated Students: An Exploration. *Journal of Artificial Intelligence and Education*. 1995; 5(2):135-175.

A Computer-Adaptive Test That Facilitates the Modification of Previously Entered Responses: An Empirical Study

Mariana Lilley[1] and Trevor Barker[2]

[1] University of Hertfordshire, School of Computer Science
College Lane, Hatfield, Hertfordshire AL10 9AB, United Kingdom
M.Lilley@herts.ac.uk

[2] University of Hertfordshire, School of Computer Science
College Lane, Hatfield, Hertfordshire AL10 9AB, United Kingdom
T.1.Barker@herts.ac.uk

Abstract. In a computer-adaptive test (CAT), learners are not usually allowed to revise previously entered responses. In this paper, we present findings from our most recent empirical study, which involved two groups of learners and a modified version of a CAT application that provided the facility to revise previously entered responses. Findings from this study showed that the ability to modify previously entered responses did not lead to significant differences in performance for one group of learners ($p>0.05$), and only relatively small yet significant differences for the other ($p<0.01$). The implications and the reasons for the difference between the groups are explored in this paper. Despite the small effect of the modification, it is argued that this option is likely to lead to a reduction in student anxiety and an increase in student confidence in this assessment method.

1 Introduction

The use of computer-adaptive tests (CAT) has been increasing, and indeed replacing traditional computer-based tests (CBTs) in various areas of education and training. Projects such as SIETTE [4] and the replacement of CBTs with CATs in large scale examinations such as the Graduate Management Admission Test (GMAT) [6], Test of English as a Foreign Language (TOEFL) [20], Graduate Records Examination (GRE) [20], Armed Sciences Vocational Aptitude Battery (ASVAB) [20] and Microsoft Certified Professional [13] are evidence of this trend.

CATs differ from the conventional CBTs primarily in the approach used to select the set of questions to be administered during a given assessment session. In a CBT, the same set of questions is administered to all students. Because of individual differences in knowledge levels within the subject domain being tested, this static approach often poses problems for certain students. For instance, what might seem a difficult

J.C. Lester et al. (Eds.): ITS 2004, LNCS 3220, pp. 22–33, 2004.

and therefore bewildering question to one student could seem too easy and thus uninteresting to another.

By dynamically selecting questions to match the estimated ability level of each individual student, the CAT approach offers higher levels of individualisation and interaction than those offered by traditional CBTs. By tailoring the level of difficulty of the questions presented to each individual student according to his or her previous responses, it is intended that a CAT would mimic aspects of an oral examination [5, 19]. Similar to a real oral exam, the first question to be administered within a CAT is typically one of medium difficulty. In the event of the student providing a correct response, a more difficult question will be administered next. Conversely, an incorrect response will cause an easier question to follow.

The underlying concept within CATs is that questions that are too difficult or too easy provide little or no information regarding a student's knowledge within the subject domain. Only those few questions exactly at the boundary of the student's knowledge provide tutors with valuable information about the level of a student's ability. The questions administered during a given session of CAT are intended to be at this level of difficulty and therefore continually re-evaluated in order to establish the boundary of the learner's knowledge.

Adaptive algorithms within CATs are usually based on Item Response Theory (IRT), which is a family of mathematical functions used to predict the probability of a student answering a given question correctly [12]. The CAT prototype used in this study is based on the Three-Parameter Logistic Model and the mathematical function shown in Equation 1 [12] is used to evaluate the probability P of a student with an unknown ability θ correctly answering a question of difficulty b, discrimination a and pseudo-chance c.

In order to evaluate the probability Q of a student with an unknown ability θ incorrectly answering a question of difficulty b, the function $Q(\theta) = 1 - P(\theta)$ is used [12]. Within a CAT, the question to be administered next as well as the final score obtained by any given student is computed based on the set of previous responses, which is obtained using the mathematical function shown in Equation 2 [12].

$$P(\theta) = c + \frac{1-c}{1+e^{-1.7a(\theta-b)}} \tag{1}$$

$$L(u_1, u_2, \ldots, u_n \mid \theta) = \prod_{j=1}^{n} P_j^{u_j} Q_j^{1-u_j} \tag{2}$$

Questions within the Three-Parameter Logistic Model are dichotomously scored. As an example, consider a student who answered a set of three questions, in which the first and second responses were incorrect and the third response was correct, such as $u1 = 0$, $u2 = 0$ and $u3 = 1$. The likelihood function for this example is $L(u1, u2, u3 \mid \theta) = (P_1^0 Q_1^1)(P_2^0 Q_2^1)(P_3^1 Q_3^0)$, or more concisely $L(u1, u2, u3 \mid \theta) = Q_1 Q_2 P_3$.

In the event of a student entering at least one correct and one incorrect response, the response likelihood curve (see Equation 2), assumes a bell-shape. IRT suggests that the peak of this curve is the most likely value for this student's ability θ estimate. The discussion on IRT here is necessarily brief, but the interested reader is referred to the work of Lord [12] and Wainer [20].

This paper marks further progress in research previously done at the University of Hertfordshire on the use of computerised adaptive testing in Higher Education. In the next section of this paper, we present a summary of two empirical studies concerning the use of CATs in Higher Education, followed by the main findings of our most recent study.

2 The Use of Computer-Adaptive Tests in a Real Educational Context: Findings from Two Empirical Studies

In our first study, a high-fidelity prototype of a CAT based on the Three-Parameter Logistic Model from IRT [12] was designed, developed and evaluated in a UK University. The prototype, which aimed to assess student ability in the domain of English as a second language, comprised a Graphical User Interface and a 250-question database in the subject domain. Twenty-seven international students and a panel of 11 experts, namely lecturers of Computer Science and English for Academic Purposes, participated in this first empirical study. The evaluation of the CAT prototype was performed in a real educational context, and entailed a series of techniques, which ranged from statistical analysis of student performance, heuristic evaluation by a panel of experts [14] and evaluation using potential real users as subjects. Findings from this first empirical study were taken to indicate that the prototype's interface was unlikely to negatively affect student performance. Moreover, findings from the statistical analysis of student performance were taken to suggest that the CAT approach was a fair method of assessment. The findings from this evaluation are briefly outlined here, and the interested reader is referred to Lilley & Barker [9, 10] and Lilley, Barker & Britton [11] for a more comprehensive account.

The prototype's user interface was then enhanced to support images within the question stem, rather than text-only. In addition, a new database consisting of 119 objective questions in the domain of Computer Science was created and independently moderated and calibrated by subject experts. This enhanced version of the application was then used to support two sessions of summative assessment of a second year Visual Basic programming module of the Higher National Diploma programme in Computer Science at the University of Hertfordshire. One hundred and thirty three students were enrolled for this module, and this group of students was invited to take a computerised Cognitive Style Analysis (CSA) test. The CSA test is a simple computer-based test developed by Riding [18], which aims to classify learners according to their position along two bipolar dimensions of cognitive style, namely the Wholist/Analytic (WA) and Verbaliser/Imager (VI) dimensions.

In addition to the CSA test, all 133 students took part in four different types of summative assessment, namely computer-adaptive test, computer-based test, practical project and practical exam. The results obtained by this student group in all assessments were subjected to a Pearson's Product Moment correlation, and the findings from this statistical analysis corroborate the findings from the first empirical study in that the CAT approach was a fair method of assessment and also potentially capable of offering a more consistent and accurate measurement of student ability than that offered by conventional CBTs. The latter student performance analysis also indicated that a score obtained by a student in one of the four assessments was a fair and satisfactory predictor of performance in any other. A further finding from this second empirical study was that learners with different cognitive styles were not disadvantaged by the CAT approach. This is a brief account of the findings from our second empirical study, which are described in full by Barker & Lilley [2] and Lilley & Barker [8].

In both studies, student feedback regarding the CAT approach was mainly positive. Although students were receptive to the idea of computerised adaptive testing, some students expressed their concern about not being able to review and modify previously entered responses. This aspect of computerised adaptive testing is discussed in the next section of this paper.

3 Reviewing and Modifying Previously Entered Responses

The underlying idea within a CAT is that the ability of a test-taker can be estimated based on his or her responses to a set of items by using the mathematical functions provided by Item Response Theory. There is a common assumption that, within a CAT, test-takers should not be allowed to review and modify previously entered responses [17, 20], as this might compromise the legitimacy of the test and the appropriateness of the set of questions selected for each individual participant. For instance, it is often assumed that returning to previously answered questions might provide students with an opportunity to obtain correct responses by intelligent guessing. Based on the premise that a student has an understanding of how the adaptive algorithm works, if this student answers a question and the following question is an easier one, he or she can deduce that the previous response was incorrect. This would, in turn, allow the student to keep modifying his/her responses until the following question was a more difficult one.

Nevertheless, previous work by the authors [8, 10] suggest that the inability to review and modify previously entered responses could lead to an increase of student anxiety levels and perceived loss of control over the application. Test-takers from a study by Rafacz & Hetter [17] expressed a similar concern. Olea et al. have also reported student preference towards CATs in which the review and modification of previously entered responses is permitted [15]. In summary, students seem to favour a computer-assisted assessment in which they have more control over the application and the review and modification of previously entered responses is permitted. Furthermore, the inability to return to and modify responses seemed to be contrary to previous experiences of most students who have taken tests either in the traditional CBT or paper-and-pencil formats.

In order to provide students with more control over the application, we first considered allowing students to review and modify previously entered responses at any given point. This alternative presented complications in terms of question administration algorithm. Our current algorithm requires that the next question administered is based on previous answers. For instance, assume a given student whose current set of responses is equal to $u1$=0, $u2$=0, $u3$=1 and $u4$ =1 and he or she decides to modify his/her response to question 2 (from $u2$=0 to $u2$=1). How should that response reflect on the question to be administered next? Should question 5 be selected using the likelihood function $L(u1,u2,u3,u4\,|\,\theta) = (P_1^0 Q_1^1)(P_2^1 Q_2^0)(P_3^1 Q_3^0)(P_4^1 Q_4^0)$ or the likelihood function $L(u1,u2\,|\,\theta) = (P_1^0 Q_1^1)(P_2^1 Q_2^0)$? More importantly, it did not seem clear how illegitimately inflated scores could be prevented and/or identified. Thus, this alternative was discarded.

Given that both iterations of the CAT prototype introduced here were of fixed-length, it seemed feasible to allow students to revise previous responses immediately after all questions had been answered. A further benefit would be reduced risk of students using response strategies that yield inflated ability estimates. As soon as the test is finished and the reviewing process completed, the student ability θ would be recalculated using the final values for each individual response. As an example, consider a student whose initial set of responses was equal to $u1$=0, $u2$=0, $u3$=1 and $u4$ =1 and he or she modified his/her response to question 2, such as the new set of responses is equal to u1=0, $u2$=1, $u3$=1 and $u4$ =1. The ability θ for this student would be evaluated using the latter set of responses, such as $L(u1,u2,u3,u4\,|\,\theta) = (P_1^0 Q_1^1)(P_2^1 Q_2^0)(P_3^1 Q_3^0)(P_4^1 Q_4^0)$.

Our CAT prototype was modified to allow students to revise previously entered responses immediately after all questions have been administered and answered. In order to investigate the feasibility of the approach, we performed an empirical study using the modified version of the prototype. This empirical study is described in the next section of this paper.

4 The Study

Within this most recent version of the prototype, students were expected to answer 30 multiple-choice questions within a 40-minute time limit. The 30 questions were divided into 2 groups. First, a set of 10 non-adaptive questions (i.e. CBT) followed by 20 adaptive questions (i.e. CAT). The set of CBT questions was identical for all participanting students. Not only would this be a useful addition for comparative purposes, but it would also help ensure that the test was fair and that no student would be disadvantaged by taking part in the study. Students were allowed to review and modify CBT and/or CAT responses only after all 30 questions had been answered.

The empirical study described here had two groups of participants. The first group (CD2) comprised second year students from a Higher National Diploma (HND) programme in Computer Science. The second group (CS2) consisted of second year students from a Bachelor of Science (BSc) programme in Computer Science. Both groups of participants took the same tests as part of their normal assessment for a programming module. The first assessment took place after 6 weeks of the course and the second after 9 weeks.

The CAT was based on a database of 215 questions that were independently ranked according to their difficulty by experts and assigned a value for the *b* parameter. Values to the *b* parameter were assigned according to Bloom's taxonomy of cognitive skills [1, 16], as shown in Table 1.

Table 1. Values assigned to the *difficulty* parameter

Difficulty *b*	Cognitive skill	Skill involved
-2 *b* -0.6	Knowledge	Ability to recall taught material
-0.6 *b* 0.8	Comprehension	Ability to interpret and/or translate knowledge
0.8 *b* 2	Application	Ability to apply knowledge to novel situations

Questions for the CBT component of the tests were also drawn from this database across the range of difficulty levels. Participants were given a brief introduction to the use of the software, but were unaware of the full purpose of the study and to the CAT component of the tests until after both assessments had been completed. Each assessment was conducted under supervision in computer laboratories. We present the main findings from this study in the next section of this paper.

5 Results

The mean scores obtained by both groups of students are shown in Table 2. In Table 2, the mean value of the estimated ability θ for the adaptive component of the assessment session is presented in the column named "CAT Level". The estimated ability θ ranged from +2 to –2, with 0.01 intervals.

Table 2. Mean scores obtained by CS2 and CD2 groups in both tests

Test	N	CBT score (% Correct responses)	CAT score (% Correct responses)	CAT Level
CS2				
Test 1	96	52.72	50.52	-0.89
Test 2	118	28.0	49.33	-0.84
CD2				
Test 1	81	50.0	51.60	-0.81
Test 2	81	24.32	42.35	-1.45

Table 3 shows the results obtained by those students who made use of the option to modify their previous answers. It can be seen from Table 3 that, for both groups, most students who used the review facility increased rather than lowered their final scores. Further analysis was performed on the data from only one test (Test 2), as the data from this test was the most complete.

Table 4 shows the number of students who made use of the review option on Test 2. Olea et al. [15] have reported that 60% of the participants in their study changed at least one answer. Similarly, approximately 92% of CD2 participants in this study used the review function on Test 2 and 60% of the participants changed at least one answer. As for the CS2 group, it can be seen from Tables 3 and 4 that 92% of this group used the review functions, but only 46% of the students changed at least one answer.

Table 3. Summary of results obtained by those students who made use of review option

Test	Score *raised*	Score *lowered*	CAT Level *raised*	CAT Level *lowered*
CS2				
Test 1	39	13	27	11
Test 2	45	9	33	9
CD2				
Test 1	30	13	19	10
Test 2	37	11	9	8

Table 4. Number of students who made use of the review option on Test 2

Group	Number of students who used review option	Number of students who did *not* use the option	Total
CS2			
Test 2	98	20	118
CD2			
Test 2	74	7	81

Table 5. Analysis of Variance (ANOVA) on the mean scores before and after use of review option

Test	Mean score before review	Mean score after review	Mean Change	Significance (P)
CS2 Test 2				
CAT Level	-0.97	-0.86	0.11	<0.001
CBT %	26.18	29.14	2.96	<0.01
CAT %	48.16	49.80	1.63	<0.001
CD2 Test 2				
CAT Level	-1.38	-1.42	-0.04	0.38
CBT %	23.78	24.05	0.27	0.75
CAT %	40.47	42.36	1.89	<0.001

Table 5 shows the mean changes in scores obtained on Test 2 for students from CS2 and CD2 groups. In addition, it shows the results of an Analysis of Variance (ANOVA) on the data summarised in the columns "Mean score before review", "Mean score after review" and "Mean change".

Table 6 shows the mean scores obtained by CS2 students who took Test 2, according to their usage of the review option. An Analysis of Variance (ANOVA) was performed on the data summarised in Table 6 to examine any significance of differences in the mean scores obtained for the two groups.

Table 6. Mean scores obtained by CS2 students

Students who	N	**Mean CBT** % Correct responses	**Mean CAT** % Correct responses	**Mean** CAT Level
Used review option	98	29.14	49.80	-0.86
Did *not* use review option	20	18.50	40.0	-1.47

Table 7. Analysis of Variance (ANOVA) on the data summarised in Table 6

Condition	**Df**	**F**	**Significance**
CBT Score			
Between groups	1	5.270	0.023
Within groups	116		
CAT Score			
Between groups	1	5.701	0.019
Within groups	116		
CAT Level			
Between groups	1	8.26	0.005
Within groups	116		

Mean standard error is presented in Figure 1 for a random sample of 45 CS2 students who took Test 2. The subject sample was subdivided into three groups: 15 students who performed well, 15 students who performed in the middle range and 15 students who performed poorly. Figure 2 shows the standard error for a random sample of 45 CD2 students who took Test 2. Similarly to Figure 1, the CD2 subject sample is subdivided into three groups: 15 students who performed well (i.e. "high performing participants"), 15 students who performed in the middle range (i.e. "mid-range performing participants") and 15 students who performed poorly (i.e. "low performing participants").

It can be seen from Figures 1 and 2 that, irrespective of group or performance, the standard error tends to a constant value of approximately 0.1.

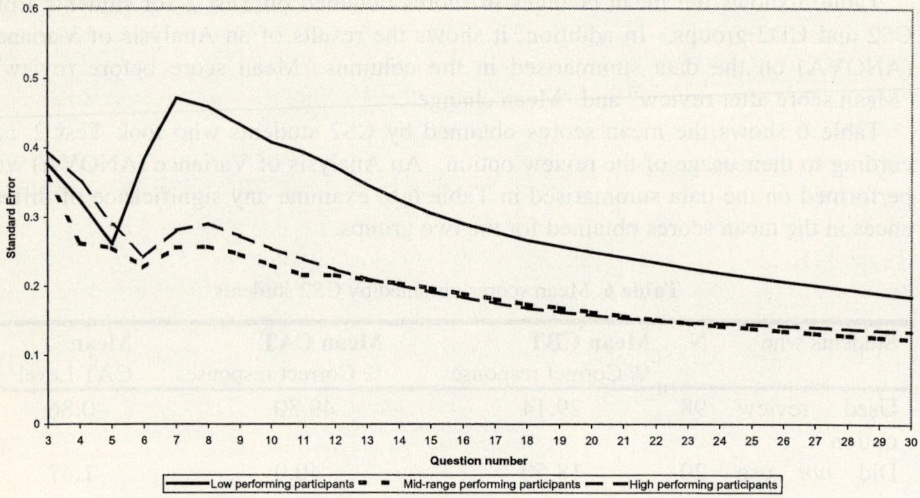

Fig. 1. Standard error curves for a sample of 45 CS2 students on Test 2

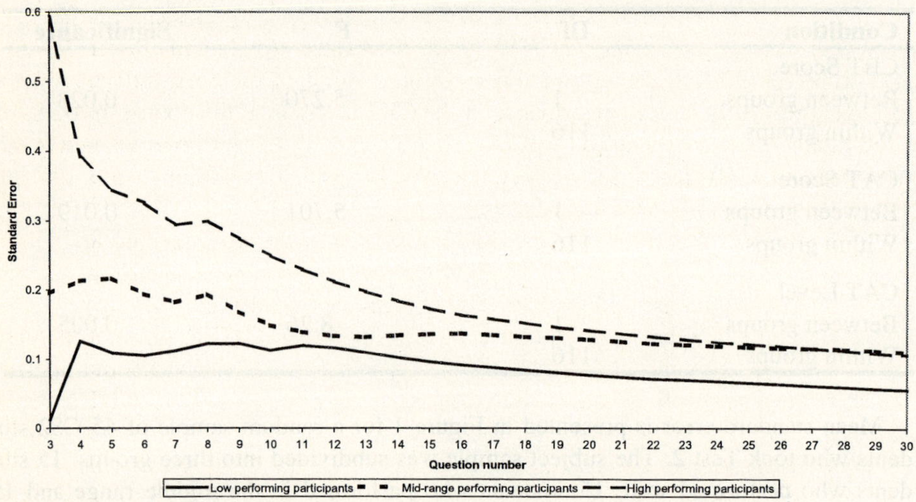

Fig. 2. Standard error curves for a sample of 45 CS2 students on Test 2

6 Discussion and Future Work

An important finding from our earlier work [8, 9, 10, 11] was that students valued the ability to review and change answers in paper-based and traditional CBT assessments. Similarly, in focus group studies, participants reported that they would like the ability to review and change response to CAT test questions before they were submitted. A basic assumption of the CAT method is that the next question to be administered to a test-taker is determined by his or her set of previous answers. In this study, the CAT software was modified to allow review and change of selection at the end of the test. This method presented itself as the simplest from a limited range of options. The solution implemented allowed students the flexibility to modify their responses to questions prior to submission, without the need for the programmers to change the adaptive algorithm upon which the CAT was based. At the end of the test, the ability of each individual student was recalculated using his/her latest set of responses. It was important to test the effect of this modification to the CAT on the performance of students. Overall, the data presented in Table 3 suggested that most learners were able to improve their scores on the CAT and CBT components of the tests by reviewing their answers prior to submission.

Differences in the performance of the two different groups of learners were interesting. Table 5 showed that for the CS2 (BSc Computer Science) group the option to review scores led to significant increase in performance in terms of the percentage of correct responses in the CBT ($p<0.01$), the percentage of correct responses in the CAT ($p<0.001$) and the CAT level obtained ($p<0.001$). This was not the case for the CD2 group. The CD2 (HND Computer Science) group had performed less well than the CS2 group on both tests. Analysis of Variance of the data presented in Table 2 showed that for Tests 1 and 2, the CS2 group performed significantly better than the CD2 group ($p<0.001$). The option to review, although used by most students, did not lead to significantly better performance in the CBT sections of the course ($p=0.38$) or in the final CAT level achieved ($p=0.75$). There was a significant improvement in the percentage of CAT responses answered correctly ($p<0.001$), although this did not lead to a significant increase in CAT level.

The reasons for this difference are possibly related to the CAT method and to the ability of the students in each group. Only by getting the difficult questions correct during the review process will the CAT level be affected significantly.

This seemed to be harder to do for the CD2 students. The CS2 learners perform significantly better on the CAT test than the CD2 group. CS2 learners are more likely to correct the more difficult questions they got wrong prior to review. CD2 learners are more likely to correct the simpler questions they got wrong the first time, which has little effect on the CAT level, but has an effect on the CAT % score. It is as if there is a barrier above which the CD2 learners were not able to go. This is supported by the fact that there was no significant change in the CBT % after review for the CD2 group, showing that when the questions are set above their CAT level (as many of the CBT questions were) then they did not improve their score by changing their answers to them. When the answers to the more difficult questions were reviewed and modified, they were less likely to get them right. Changing only the easier questions has little effect up or down on the CAT level. CS2 students are able to perform at a higher level and the barrier was not evident for them. It is interesting to note that they were able to change significantly their performance on CBT and CBT sections of the test after review.

Of further interest is a comparison of the standard error curves for CS2 and CD2 groups of students. The standard error for both groups and for all levels of performance was very similar and relatively constant. The adaptive nature of the CAT test will ensure that the final CAT level achieved by learners on the test is fairly constant after relatively few questions. The approach of allowing students to modify their responses at the end of the CAT is not likely to change the final level of the test-taker significantly, unless they have performed slightly below their optimum level first time round. It is possible that CS2 students adopt a different strategy when answering the CAT from CD2 students. Perhaps CS2 students enter their answers more quickly and rely on the review process to modify them, whereas CD2 students enter them at their best level first time. This would explain the difference in performance after the review for both groups. It would be of interest to investigate the individual strategies adopted by learners on CATs in future work.

In summary, all students valued the option to review, even though in many cases this had little effect on the final levels achieved. Certainly less able learners did not significantly improve performance by reviewing their answers, though most were able to improve their scores slightly. Some learners performed less well after review, though slightly more gained than lost by reviewing.

It is likely that the attitude of learners to the review process was an important feature. The effect on motivation was reported in earlier studies and for this reason alone it is probably worth allowing review in CATs. Reflection is an important study skill that should be fostered. A mature approach to examination requires reflection and it is still the best advice to students to read over their answers before finishing a test.

Standard error (SE) was shown to be a reliable stopping condition for a CAT, since for both groups of students at three levels of performance the SE was approximately the same.

References

1. Anderson, L.W. & Krathwohl, D.R. (Eds.) (2001). A Taxonomy for Learning, Teaching, and Assessing: A Revision of Bloom's Taxonomy of Educational Objectives. New York: Longman.
2. Barker, T. & Lilley, M. (2003). Are Individual Learners Disadvantaged by the Use of Computer-Adaptive Testing? In Proceedings of the 8th Learning Styles Conference. University of Hull, United Kingdom, European Learning Styles Information Network (ELSIN), pp. 30-39.
3. Carlson, R. D. (1994). Computer-Adaptive Testing: a Shift in the Evaluation Paradigm. Journal of Educational Technology Systems, 22(3), pp 213-224.
4. Conejo, R., Millán, E., Pérez-de-la-Cruz, J. L. & Trella, M. (2000). An Empirical Approach to On-Line Learning in SIETTE. Lecture Notes in Computer Science (2000) 1839, pp. 605-614.
5. Freedle, R. O. & Duran, R. P. (1987). Cognitive and Linguistic Analyses of test performance. New Jersey: Ablex.

6. Graduate Management Admission Council (2002). Computer-Adaptive Format [online]. Available from http://www.mba.com/mba/TaketheGMAT/TheEssentials/WhatIstheGMAT/ComputerAdaptiveFormat.html [Accessed 21 Mar 2004].
7. Jacobson, R. L. (1993). New Computer Technique Seen Producing a Revolution in Educational Testing. The Chronicle of Higher Education, 40(4), 15 September 1993, pp. 22-23, 26.
8. Lilley, M. & Barker, T. (2003). Comparison between computer-adaptive testing and other assessment methods: An empirical study In Research Proceedings of the 10th Association for Learning and Teaching Conference. The University of Sheffield and Sheffield Hallam University, United Kingdom, pp. 249-258.
9. Lilley, M. & Barker, T. (2002). The Development and Evaluation of a Computer-Adaptive Testing Application for English Language In Proceedings of the 6th Computer-Assisted Assessment Conference. Loughborough University, United Kingdom, pp. 169-184.
10. Lilley, M. & Barker, T. (2003). An Evaluation of a Computer-Adaptive Test in a UK University context In Proceedings of the 7th Computer-Assisted Assessment Conference. Loughborough University, United Kingdom, pp. 171-182.
11. Lilley, M., Barker, T. & Briton, C. (2004). The development and evaluation of a software prototype for computer adaptive testing. Computers & Education Journal 43(1-2), pp. 109-123.
12. Lord, F. M. (1980). Applications of Item Response Theory to practical testing problems. New Jersey: Lawrence Erlbaum Associates.
13. Microsoft Corporation (2002). Exam and Testing Procedures [online]. Available from http://www.microsoft.com/traincert/mcpexams/faq/procedures.asp [Accessed 21 Mar 2004].
14. Molich, R. & Nielsen, J. (1990). Improving a human-computer dialogue. Communications of the ACM, 33(3), pp. 338-348.
15. Olea, J., Revuelta, J., Ximénez, M. C. & Abad, F. J. (2000). Psychometric and psychological effects of review on computerized fixed and adaptive tests. Psicológica (2000) 21, pp. 157-173.
16. Pritchett, N. (1999). Effective Question Design In S. Brown, P. Race & J. Bull. Computer-Assisted Assessment in Higher Education. London: Kogan Page.
17. Rafacz, B. & Hetter, R. D (2001). ACAP Hardware Selection, Software Development, and Acceptance Testing In W. A. Sands, B. K. Waters & J. R. McBride. Computerized Adaptive Testing: from Inquiry to Operation. Washington, DC: American Psychological Association.
18. Riding, R. J. (1991). Cognitive Style Analysis, Users Manual. Birmingham Learning and Training Technology, United Kingdom.
19. Syang, A. & Dale, N. B. Computerized adaptive testing in computer science: assessing student programming abilities. ACM SIGCSE Bulletin, 25 (1), March 1993, pp. 53-57.
20. Wainer, H. (2000). Computerized Adaptive Testing (A Primer). 2nd Edition. New Jersey: Lawrence Erlbaum Associates.

An Autonomy-Oriented System Design for Enhancement of Learner's Motivation in E-learning

Emmanuel Blanchard and Claude Frasson

Computer Science Department, University of Montréal,
CP 6128 succ. Centre Ville, Montréal, QC Canada, H3C 3J7.
{blanchae, frasson}@iro.umontreal.ca

Abstract. Many e-Learning practices don't care about learner's motivation. There are elements showing that this is an important factor in learner's success and that a lack of motivation produces a negative emotional impact. This work is aimed at establishing a survey of motivation literature and proposing a Motivation-Oriented System Design for e-Learning. Psychological theories underline the importance of giving control of his activities (i.e. providing autonomy) to a learner in order to enhance learner's self-beliefs, hence motivation. Coaching is also important to keep learners focused on an activity. ITS and Pedagogical Agents provide coaching whereas Open Environments offer autonomy to learners. The presented system is a hybrid solution taking motivational positive aspects of Open-Environments and Pedagogical Agents. It also uses role-playing practices in order to enhance constructivist learning.

Keywords: Achievement Motivation, Emotions, e-Learning, Intelligent Tutoring Systems, Pedagogical Agents, Agents Collaboration, Open-Environment, Role-Playing, Constructivist Learning.

1 Introduction

How to keep students interested in a learning activity? This question is one of teacher's major challenges. Eccles et al [6] cited Dewey to argue that "people will identify with, and be totally absorbed by, the materiel to be learned only if they are sufficiently interested in it". What is true in a classroom become tremendously important in e-Learning activities.

According to O'Regan's study [12], some actual e-Learning practices produce negative emotions on learners (frustration, fear, shame, anxiety and embarrassment) more frequently than positive ones (excitation, pride). It has been demonstrated that negative emotions, such as anxiety, are strongly linked to learner's motivation [9, 17]. Given O'Regan's outcomes, where is the problem in those e-Learning practices? What is missing in some e-Learning activities in order to procure interest to learners? What could be done to maintain and enhance learner's motivation for an e-Learning activity?

Achievement Motivation (AM) is the part of psychology dedicated to the study of motivation to succeed that a learner has and how this motivation can affect learner's results and behaviors. Many researches in AM demonstrated the importance of giving the belief to a learner that he has control on his activities and results (i.e. he has some

J.C. Lester et al. (Eds.): ITS 2004, LNCS 3220, pp. 34–44, 2004.

autonomy). But other researches also underlined the necessity of monitoring and sometime guiding and helping (i.e. coaching) students in order to keep them focused on learning activities [5, 6, 11]. In this paper, we will propose a system design in order to give autonomy and, at the same time, monitor/coach learners in an e-Learning system.

Contrary to O'Regan's outcomes, *non-controlling virtual environments* (for example Virtual Harlem [13]) have positive feedbacks from learners and appear to be very motivating. But those systems don't adapt to learners specificities. On their side, ITS provide organized knowledge and personalized help to learners but are very controlling systems. Thus, we propose a hybrid e-Learning system design using non-controlling virtual environment and agents inspired by pedagogical agents [8]. We demonstrate how this system can enhance learner's motivation.

In section two, we give an overview of some of the main AM theories and also present some of the motivation factors that have been defined in the AM field. In section three, we emphasize the importance of learner's autonomy in order to maintain a high level of motivation. We also focus on the necessity of finding balance between coaching and autonomy. In section four, we propose a virtual learning environment system for maintaining and enhancing motivation in an e-Learning activity. This environment will enhance learner's motivation by giving him more control on his learning activity, allowing him to explore solutions, to make hypothesis, to interact and play different roles.

2 Overview of Achievement Motivation

Petri [14] defines motivation as "the concept we use when we describe the forces acting on or within an organism to initiate and direct behavior". He also notices that motivation is used "to explain differences in the intensity of behavior" and "to indicate the direction of behavior. When we are hungry, we direct our behavior in ways to get food".

Study of motivation is a huge domain in psychology. AM is a sub-part of this domain where "theorists attempt to explain people's choice of achievement tasks, persistence on those tasks, vigor in carrying them out, and quality of task engagement" [5]. There are many different theories dealing with AM. Actual ones are mostly referring to a social-cognitive model of motivation proposed by Bandura [1], described by Eccles and her colleagues [5] as a postulate that "human achievement depends on interactions between one's behavior, personal factors (e.g. thoughts, beliefs) and environmental conditions". In the next part, we give a review of some of the main actual AM theories.

2.1 Theories of Achievement Motivation

The Attribution Theory is concerned with interpretations people have of their achievement outcomes and how it can determine future achievement strivings. Weiner [17] classified attribution using three dimensions: locus of control, stability and controllability. The locus of control (also called locus of causality: "attribution term" for sense of autonomy [15]) dimension can be internal or external depending if success is attributed to internal (depending of the learner) causes or not. The stability dimension determines if causes changes over time or not. The controllability dimension makes a distinction between controllable attribution causes like skill/efficacy and uncontrollable ones like aptitude, mood.

Controls Theories [3, 16] are focused on beliefs people have on how they (and/or their environment) control their achievement.

Intrinsic Motivation Theories are focused on the distinction between intrinsic motivation (where people will do an activity "for their own sake") and extrinsic motivation (people have an external interest in doing the activity, like receiving an award). As Eccles and al [6] noticed, the distinction between intrinsic and extrinsic motivation "is assumed to be fundamental throughout the motivation literature". Deci and Ryan's *self-determination theory* [15] is one of the major intrinsic motivation theories.

Theories of Self-Regulation study how people regulate their behaviors in order to succeed in a task or activity. Zimmerman [19] enumerated three processes in which self-regulated learners are engaged: self-observation (monitoring one's activities), self-judgment (making an evaluation of one's performances) and self-reaction (dealing with one's reaction to its performance outcomes). Self-determination theory, seen in the precedent paragraph, also deals with self-regulation.

*Theories Concerning Volition***.** According to Corno [2], Eccles et al [6] say that "the term volition refers to both the strength of will needed to complete a task and diligence of pursuit". Kulh [9] enounces different volitional strategies (cognitive, emotional and motivational control strategies) to explain persistence when there are distractive elements.

Academic Help Seeking is focused on finding appropriate moments for help and is closely-linked to self-regulation and volition concepts. Providing help whereas the student never tried may result in a work-avoidant strategy. But, according to Newman [11], Eccles and her colleagues [6] pointed that "instrumental help seeking can foster motivation by keeping children engaged in an activity when they experience difficulties".

In all those theories, many factors have been said to affect motivation. In the next part, we will go deeper in the explanation of those factors.

2.2 Factors of Achievement Motivation

Elements that can affect AM are numerous. In AM literature, those which appear most frequently are individual goals, social environment, emotions, intrinsic interest for an activity and self beliefs. It exist relations between all those factors so they must not be seen as being independent of the others.

Individual Goals. As explained by Eccles et al [6], researches show that a learner can develop ego-involved goals (if he wants to maximize the probability of a good evaluation of his competences and create a positive image of himself), task-involved goals (if he wants to master tasks and improve his competences) or also work-avoidant goals (if he wants to minimize the effort). In fact, goals are generally said to be oriented to performance (ego-involved) or mastery (task-involved).

The Social Environment. Because it affect self-belief, social environment is an important factor of individual's motivation. Parents, peers, school, personal specificities (such as gender or ethnic group) and instructional contexts have a strong impact on learner's motivation to succeed [5, 6]. Ego-involved goals are particularly linked with the social environment. If a learner has such goals, the importance of the evaluation that his environment do on him will be increased. The objective of that kind of learner is to maintain a positive self-image and also to outperform other learners. For example, if in some case, failure seems likely, a learner may decide not to try in order to avoid to be judged by his peers. Those learners think that it is better their peers attribute the failure to a lack of effort instead of low ability. It is commonly called a "face saving tactic".

Emotions. Inserting emotions in e-Learning is a growing practice that needs to be enhanced. O'Regan [12] emphasizes the fact that some actual e-Learning practices produce negative emotions on learners more frequently than positive ones. That means emotional control has to be enhanced in e-Learning. Many researches explain that emotions can act as motivators [14]. But motivation can also influence emotions [5, 6]. Eccles et al [6] say that, in Weiner's attribution theory [17], "the locus of control dimension was linked most strongly to affective reactions" and "attributing success to internal causes should enhance pride or self-esteem; attributing it to external causes should enhance gratitude; attributing failure to internal causes should produce shame; attributing it to external causes should induce anger". In his volition theory, Kulh [9] proposed volitional strategies to explain persistence when a learner is confronted to distraction or others possibilities. One of these strategies refers to emotional control and its goal is "to keep inhibiting emotional states such as anxiety or depression in check" [6]. What is interesting to notice is that, in O'Regan [12] experimentation, learners reported emotions discussed by Weiner [17] and Kuhl [9] as being linked to a lack of motivation.

The Intrinsic Interest for an Activity. An individual is intrinsically motivated by a learning activity when he decides to perform this activity without external needs, without trying to be rewarded. According to different researches, there are individual differences and orientations in intrinsic interest. Some learners will be attracted by hard and challenging tasks. For others, curiosity will be a major element of intrinsic interest. A third category of learners will look for activities that will enhance their competence and mastery. Furthermore, Eccles et al [6] cited Matsumoto and Sanders [10] to tell that "evidence suggests that high levels of traitlike intrinsic motivation facilitate positive emotional experience". As we have seen before, learners using e-Learning often have a lack of positive emotions [12]. We suppose that is partly due to a lack of motivation.

Self-Beliefs. Many different self-beliefs can affect the AM of a learner. A learner can have outcome expectations before performing an activity. If the expected outcomes are low, the learner may decide not to try (see also part 2.2.1). A learner can also have efficacy expectations, which means he believes he can perform needed behaviors in order to succeed in the activity. Self-beliefs are also proposed in control [3, 16] and intrinsic motivation theories ([15], see also part 3.1) concerning the control a learner believes to have on a task and on his achievement. According to Eccles et al [6], many researches "confirmed the positive association between internal locus of control and academic achievement". Connell and Wellborn [3] proposed that children who believe they control their achievement outcomes should feel more competent. They also made a link between control beliefs and competence needs and hypothesized that the fulfillment of needs was influenced by social environment characteristics (such as autonomy provided to the learner). In her AM model, Skinner [16] described a control belief as an expectation a person has to be able to produce desired events.

In the next part, we show the interest for e-Learning of giving to the learner the belief that he has control (i.e. autonomy) on his activities and achievements.

3 Coaching Versus Autonomy in E-learning: Finding Balance

3.1 Importance of Autonomy

Eccles et al [6] reported that many psychologists "have argued that intrinsic motivation is good for learning" and that "classroom environments that are overly controlling and do not provide adequate autonomy, undermine intrinsic motivation, mastery orientation, ability self-concepts and expectation and self-direction, and induce a learner helplessness response to difficult tasks". Flink et al [7] made experimentation in this way. They created homogeneous groups of learners and asked different teachers to teach with either controlling methodology or by giving autonomy to the learner. All the sessions were videotaped. After that, they showed the tapes to a group of observers and asked them who the best teachers were. Observers answered that teachers having the controlling style were better (maybe because they seemed more active, directive and better organized [6]). In fact learners having more autonomy obtained results significantly better. Others researchers found similar results.

In Deci and Ryan's Self-Determination Theory [15], a process called internalization is presented. As Eccles et al mentioned [6], "Internalization is the process of transferring the regulation of behavior from outside to inside the individual". Ryan and Deci also proposed different regulatory styles which correspond to different level of autonomy. Figure 1 represents these different levels, their corresponding locus of control (i.e. "perceived locus of control") and the relevant regulatory processes.

In this figure, we can see that the more internal the locus of control is, the better the regulatory processes. That means that, if a learner has intrinsic motivation for an activity, his regulation style will be intrinsic, his locus of control will be intern and he will resent inherent satisfaction, enjoyment, and interest. Intrinsic motivation will only occur if the learner is highly interested in the activity. In many e-Learning activities, interest for the activity will be lower. And motivation will be somewhat extrinsic. So, in e-Learning, we have to focus on enhancing an learner‘s internal perception of locus of control.

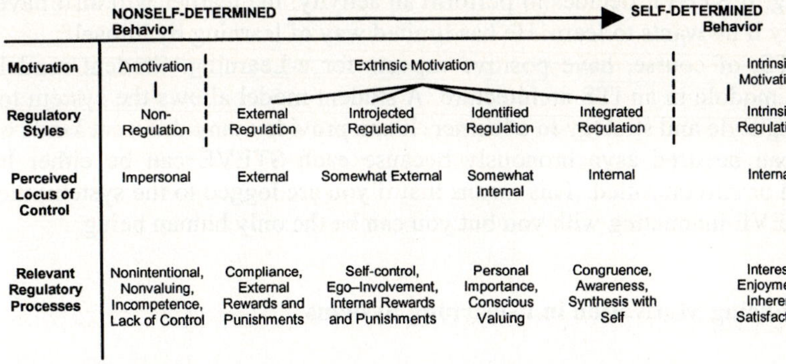

Fig. 1. A taxonomy of Human Motivation (as proposed by Ryan and Deci [15])

3.2 Virtual Harlem: An Example of "Open Environment" for Autonomy in E-learning

Some e-Learning systems already provide autonomy without being focused on it. Virtual Harlem [13] for example is a reconstruction of Harlem during the 1920s. The aim of this system is to provide a Distance Learning Classroom concerning African-American Literature of that period. Some didactic elements like sound or text can be inserted in the virtual world and the learner is able to retrieve those didactic elements.

Virtual Harlem is also a collaborative environment and learners can interact with other learners or teachers in order to share the experience they acquired in the virtual world. An interesting element in Virtual Harlem is that learners can add content to the world, expressing what they felt and making the virtual world richer (this is some kind of asynchronous help for future students). Virtual Harlem provides autonomy not because it is Virtual Reality but because this is an "open world". By "open environment", we mean that constraints in term of movements and actions are limited. Contrary to O'Regan's study, Virtual Harlem received positive feedbacks from learners who said there should be more exposure to technologies in classrooms.

But Virtual Harlem has also problems. The system itself has few pedagogical capabilities. There is no adaptation to learner specificities, which limits learning strategies. Asynchronous learning remains difficult because a huge part of the learning depends on the interaction with other human beings connected to the system.

3.3 Interest of Coaching

We have seen that autonomy is positive for learning. Many ITS systems are used to support e-Learning activities. They can be described as extremely controlling because they adopt a state-transition scheme (i.e. the learner does an activity, the ITS assesses the learner and, given the results ask the learner to do another activity). Locus of control is mainly external. Virtual reality pedagogical agents like STEVE [8] are also controlling. If STEVE decides to perform an activity, the learner will also have to do the activity if he wants to learn. He has limited way of learning by himself.

But ITS, of course, have positive aspects for e-Learning. Student model is an important module in an ITS architecture. A student model allows the system to adapt its teaching style and strategy to a learner. It can provide many different kinds of help. STEVE can be used asynchronously because each STEVE can be either human-controlled or AI-controlled. This means that if you are logged to the system, there can be ten STEVE interacting with you but you can be the only human being.

3.4 Enhancing Motivation in E-learning Systems

We have seen that actual e-Learning Systems, which don't provide autonomy, provoke more negatives than positive emotions on learners and lower the interest for the learning activity [12]. We have shown that "open world" can deal with learners autonomy needs. But actual systems like Virtual Harlem lack of pedagogical capabilities and adaptation to the learner. ITS provide that adaptation but are very controlling systems.

In the next part, we propose to define a motivation-oriented hybrid system. The aim of this system is to provide an environment where learning initiatives (i.e. autonomy) are encouraged in order to increase learner's intrinsic interest for the learning activity. This system is a multi-learner online system using role-playing practices. Thus, it has a constructivist learning approach [18]. As we pointed before, if they are used with parsimony, help and guidance are useful for learner's motivation and success. Our system monitors learner's behaviors and takes the initiative to propose help to the learner only when a problem is detected.

To go further Virtual Harlem and other systems, we propose to define motivational e-Learning systems.

4 A Description of MeLS: Motivational E-learning System

4.1 Role-Playing in MeLS: Using Scenarios for Constructivist Learning

How do people learn with MeLS? As in Virtual Harlem, the objective of MeLS is to immerse learners in the domain to learn in order to enhance constructivist learning [18]. For example, in a MeLS activity concerning medicine we can imagine to model a 3D Hospital with rooms containing some surgery tools, radiographic devices… By clicking on an object, a learner can have information on its use, exercises, simulation. If the learner decides to visit the hospital, he can also meet and communicate with avatars representing doctors, nurses, patients. Patients can have different problems: fractures, burns, diseases… And the learner can try to determine the pathology of the patient with whom he communicates.

If it appears to MeLS that the learner is not actively learning by himself, the system can generate a scenario. For example, a doctor will come to tell the learner that there is a fire next to the hospital and that many injured persons (new patients) are coming. The doctor will then ask the learner to make diagnostic on those new patients and determine whose patients have to be cured first.

4.2 MeLS Elements

There are three types of entities that can communicate together in the system: the learner application, Motivational Pedagogical Agents (MPAs) and the Motivational Strategy Controller (MSC). Two other elements complete MeLS design: the Open Environment and the Curriculum Module. Figure 2 represents the global architecture of MeLS.

The Open Environment is a 3D environment. Some interactive objects can be added to the environment in order to ameliorate constructivist learning.

The Learner Application contains the student model of the learner and sensors to analyze the activity of the learner. If the learner is passive, MeLS will deduce that he needs to be motivated. Those sensors also help to maintain the student model of the learner. In the open environment, each learner is represented by an avatar.

An MPA is an extension of the pedagogical agent concept proposed by Johnson and his colleagues [8]. Each MPA is represented by an avatar and has particular behavior, personality and knowledge given their assigned role (doctors and nurses don't know the same things about medicine) in the virtual environment. Given the behavior of the learner, an MPA can also decide to contact a learner (when he is passive) in order to propose him an activity. To compare with ITS and depending of the learning strategy used, MPAs can be seen as companion or tutor.

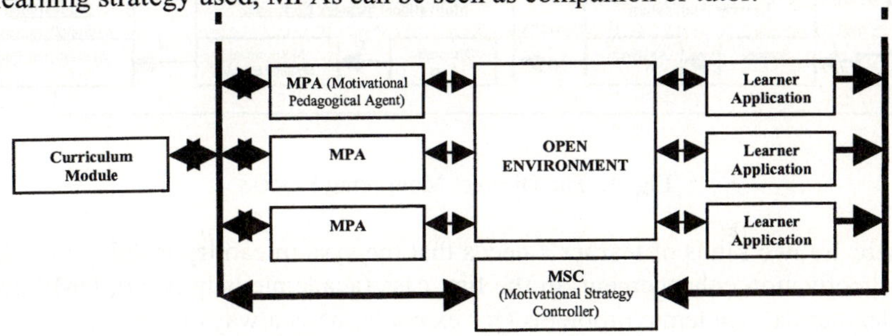

Fig. 2. Architecture of MeLS

The MSC has no physical representation in the open environment. Its meaning is to define a more global strategy for enhancing learners' motivation. The MSC is also in charge of proposing scenario (adapted from a bank of scenario template) and, for this purpose, he can generate new MSC. As we said before, there can be many learners on the system. The MSC can organize collaborative activities (collaboration enhances motivation [6]) within a scenario. MSC is in someway the equivalent of the planner in ITS.

The Curriculum Module has the same meaning than in an ITS. When we say that an MPA has certain knowledge, we mean they have the right to access to corresponding knowledge resources in the curriculum module. We decide to exteriorize knowledge of MPAs in order to facilitate the process of knowledge update (there will be only one module to update).

4.3 Discreet Monitoring Process

Discreet Monitoring Process (DMP) is a process of interaction between three modules of MeLS: the Learner Application, the MSC and MPAs. The aim of DMP is to produce an adapted reaction only when students really need it. In this case, as shown by Newman [11], providing help can stimulate motivation by keeping children focused on a difficult activity. Thus, the negative impact of controlling the learner is avoided. Figure 3 presents the DMP.

The process is the following:

(a) Sensors of the learner application monitor the learner.

(b) Data concerning the learner are transmitted to the analyzer of the learner application.

(c) The analyzer detects that there is a problem and send information to the MSC.

(d) MSC identifies the problem type with its diagnostic tool and refers it to a strategy engine

(e) Given the diagnostic, MSC elaborates a strategy to resolve the problem (ex: fire scenario proposed in 4.1). Once a strategy is defined, one (or more in case of a collaborative strategy) MPA is initialized in order to carry out the strategy.

(f) One of the initialized MPA contacts the learner and, if the learner accepts, integrates the learner in the strategy in order to correct the problem.

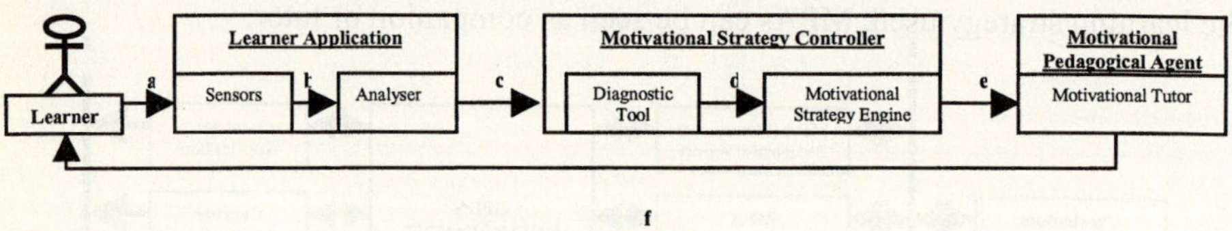

Fig. 3. The Discreet Monitoring Process

There are two kinds of learner's needs that the system can try to fulfill: academic help or motivation enhancement. In the first case (academic help need), DMP detects that a learner has academic problems (for example, he is always failing to achieve an activity). In the second case (motivation enhancement need) DMP detects that a learner is passive (some work on motivation diagnosis in ITS was done by De Vicente and Pain [4]). DMP deduce that this learner needs to be motivated. Once a problem is detected, a strategy (ex: a scenario) to resolve it will be elaborate by the MSC.

5 Conclusions and Future Works

In this paper, we made a survey of the "Achievement Motivation" field and underlined the importance of learner's motivation to succeed. From this work and from O'Regan's study [12] about emotions produced on learners by e-Learning, we deduced that enhancing autonomy in e-Learning will increase learners' intrinsic interest for e-Learning and, by the way, learners' success. But coaching can also be positive for learner's success.

In order to mix coaching and learner's autonomy in e-Learning systems, we defined an hybrid system design between open environments and ITS, called Motivational e-Learning System (MeLS). This system resolves problems of learner's autonomy that we described in ITS: it gives possibilities of self-learning to learners by interacting with the environment, which can be seen as a constructivist learning approach. The Discreet Monitoring Process (DMP) was proposed to foster learner's motivation. DMP can deal with academic or learner's passive behavior problems. DMP is able to generate strategies (such as scenarios) to correct learner's problems. Motivational Pedagogical Agents (MPAs), inspired by pedagogical agents like STEVE [8] and represented in the virtual world by avatars, are in charge of executing those strategies.

Next step will be to create a whole course using MeLS design. Motivational student model, strategies (local or global) have to be clarified. In this purpose, further readings on volition and intrinsic motivation concepts and on academic help seeking are planned.

Acknowledgements. We acknowledge the support for this work from Valorisation Recherche Québec (VRQ). This research is part of the DIVA project: 2200-106.

References

[1] Bandura, A. (1986). Social foundations of thought and action: a social-cognitive theory. Englewood Cliffs, NJ: Prentice Hall.

[2] Corno, L. (1993). The best-laid plans: modern conceptions of volition and educational research. Educational Researcher, 22. pp 14-22.

[3] Connell, J. P. & Wellborn J. G. (1991). Competence, autonomy and relatedness: a motivational analysis of self-system processes. R Gunnar & L. A. Sroufe (Eds), Minnesota Symposia on child psychology, 23. Hillsdale, NJ: Erlbaum. pp 43-77.

[4] De Vicente, A. and Pain, H. (2002). Informing the detection of the students' motivational state: An empirical study. In S.A. Cerri, G. Gouardères, & F. Paraguaçu (Eds.), Proceedings of the 6th International Conference on Intelligent Tutoring Systems. Berlin: Springer-Verlag. pp 933-943.

[5] Eccles, J. S. & Wigfield A. (2002). Development of achievement motivation. San Diego, CA: Academic Press.

[6] Eccles, J. S., Wigfield A. & Schiefele U. (1998). Motivation to succeed. N. Eisenberg (Eds), Handbook of child psychology, 3. Social, emotional, and personality development (5th ed.), New York: Wiley. pp 1017-1095.

[7] Flink, C., Boggiano A. K., Barrett M. (1990). Controlling teaching strategies: undermining children's self-determination and performance. Journal of Personality and Social Psychology, 59. pp 916-924.

[8] Johnson, W.L., Rickel J.W. & Lester J.C. (2000) Animated pedagogical agents: face-to-face interaction in interactive learning environments. International Journal of Artificial Intelligence in Education, 1. pp 47-78.

[9] Kuhl, J. (1987). Action control: The maintenance of Motivational states. F. Halisch & J. Kuhl (Eds), Motivation, Intention and Volition. Berlin: Springer-Verlag. pp 279-307.

[10] Matsumoto, D., Sanders, M. (1988). Emotional experiences during engagement in intrinsically and extrinsically motivated tasks. Motivation and Emotion, 12. pp 353-369.
[11] Newman, R. S. (1994). Adaptive help-seeking: a strategy of self-regulated learning. In D.H Schunk & B.J. Zimmerman (Eds), Self-Regulation of Learning and Performance: Issues and Educational Applications. Hillsdale, NJ: Erlbaum. pp 283-301.
[12] O'Regan, K. (2003). Emotion and e-Learning. Journal of Asynchronous Learning Network, 7(3). pp 78-92.
[13] Park, K., Leigh, J., Johnson, A. E. Carter B., Brody J. & Sosnoski J. (2001). Distance learning classroom using Virtual Harlem, Proceedings of 7th International Conference on Virtual Systems and Multimedia. pp 489-498.
[14] Petri, H. L. (1996). Motivation: theory, research and applications (4th ed). Pacific Grove, CA: Brooks/Cole.
[15] Ryan, R. M., & Deci, E. L. (2000). Self-determination theory and the facilitation of intrinsic motivation, social development, and well-being. American Psychologist, 55, pp 68-78.
[16] Skinner, E. A. (1995). Perceived control, motivation, and coping. Thousand Oaks, CA: Sage.
[17] Weiner, B. (1985). An Attributional Theory of Achievement Motivation and Emotion. Psychological Review, 92. pp 548-573.
[18] Wilson, B. (Ed.) (1996). Constructivist learning environments: Case studies in instructional design. New Jersey: Educational Technology Publications.
[19] Zimmerman, B. J. (1989). A Social Cognitive View of Self Regulated Learning. Journal of Educational Psychology, 81. pp 329-339.

Inducing Optimal Emotional State for Learning in Intelligent Tutoring Systems

Soumaya Chaffar and Claude Frasson

Département d'informatique et de recherche opérationnelle
Université de Montréal C.P. 6128, Succ. Centre-ville
Montréal, Québec Canada H3C 3J7
{chaffars, frasson}@iro.umontreal.ca

Abstract. Emotions play an important role in cognitive processes and specially in learning tasks. Moreover, there are some evidences that the emotional state of the learner correlated with his performance. Furthermore, it's important that new Intelligent Tutoring Systems involve this emotional aspect; they may be able to recognize the emotional state of the learner, and to change it so as to be in the best conditions for learning. In this paper we describe such an architecture developed in order to determine the optimal emotional state for learning and to induce it. Based on experimentation, we have used the Naïve Bayes classifier to predict the optimal emotional state according to the personality and then we induce it using a hybrid technique which combines the guided imagery technique, music and images.

1 Introduction

Researches in neurosciences and psychology have shown that emotions exert influences in various behavioral and cognitive processes, such as attention, long-term memorizing, decision-making, etc. [5, 18]. Moreover, positive affects are fundamental in cognitive organization and thought processes; they also play an important role to improve creativity and flexibility in problem solving [11]. However, negative affects can block thought processes; people who are anxious have deficit in inductive reasoning [15], slow decision latency [20] and reduced memory capacity [10]. This is not new to teachers involved in traditional learning; students who are bored or anxious could not retain knowledge and think efficiently.

Intelligent Tutoring Systems (ITS) are used to support and improve the process of learning for any field of knowledge [17].Thus, new ITS should deal with student's emotional states such as sadness or joy, by identifying his current emotional state and attempting to address it. Some ITS architectures integrate learner emotion in the student model. For instance, Conati [4] used a probabilistic model based on Dynamic Decision Networks to assess the emotional state of the user with educational games. In the best of our knowledge; there is no ITS systems dealt with the optimal emotional state.

J.C. Lester et al. (Eds.): ITS 2004, LNCS 3220, pp. 45–54, 2004.

So, we define the optimal emotional state as the affective state which maximizes learner's performance such as memorization, comprehension, etc. To achieve this goal, we address here the following fundamental questions: how can we detect the current emotional state of the learner? How can we recognize his optimal emotional state for learning? How can we induce this optimal emotional state in the learner?

In the present work we have developed and implemented a system called ESTEL (Emotional State Towards Efficient Learning system) which is able to predict the optimal emotional state of the learner and to induce it, that means to trigger actions so that the learner be in his optimal emotional state.

After reviewing some previous work realized we present ESTEL, architecture of a system intended to generate emotions able to improve learning. We detail all its components and show how we obtained from experiment various elements of theses modules. We present in particular this experiment.

2 Previous Work

This section will survey some of previous work in inducing emotion in psychology and in computer science domains.

Researchers in psychology have developed a variety of experimental techniques for inducing emotional state aiming to find a relationship between emotions and thought tasks; one of them is the Velten procedure which consists of randomly assigning participants to read a graded set of self-referential statements for example, "I am physically feeling very good today" [19]. A variety of other techniques exists including guided imagery [2] which consists of asking participants to imagine themselves in a series of described situations, for example: "You are sitting in a restaurant with a friend and the conversation becomes hilariously funny and you can't stop from laughing". Some other existing techniques are based upon exposing to participants films, music or odors. Gross and Levenson (1995) found that 16 film clips could induce really one of the following emotions (amusement, anger, contentment, disgust, fear, neutrality, sadness, and surprise) from the 78 films shown to 494 subjects [9]. Researchers in psychology have also developed hybrid techniques which combine two or more procedures; Mayer et al. (1995) used the guided imagery procedure with music procedure to induce four types of emotions, joy, anger, fear, sadness. They used the guided imagery to occupy the foreground attention and the music to emphasize the background.

However, few works in computer science attempted to induce emotions. For instance, at MIT Media Lab, Picard et al. (2001) used pictures to induce a set of emotions which include happiness, sadness, anger, fear, disgust, surprise, neutrality, platonic love and romantic love [14]. Moreover at affective Social Computing Laboratory, Nasoz et al. used results of Gross and Levenson (1995) to induce sadness, anger, surprise, fear, frustration, and amusement [13].

As mentioned previously, emotions play a fundamental role in thought processes; Estrada et al. have found that positive emotions may increase intrinsic motivation [6]. In addition, two recent studies, trying to check the influence of positive emotions on motivation, have also found that positive affects can enhance performance on the task at hand [11]. For these reasons, our present work aims to induce optimal emotional state which is a positive emotion that maximizes learner's performance.

In the next section, we present the architecture of the ESTEL.

3 ESTEL Architecture

In order to answer to the questions mentioned in the introduction, we need to develop a system able to: (1) detect the current emotional state; (2) recognize the optimal emotional state according to the personality of the learner; (3) induce this optimal emotional state; (4) evaluate the knowledge acquisition of the learner in each state of emotions. Furthermore, the corresponding modules able to achieve the previous functionalities are indicated in the architecture shown in Fig. 1.

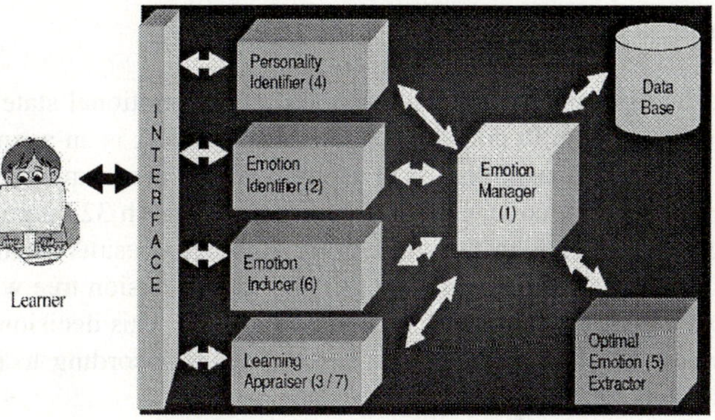

Fig. 1. ESTEL architecture

The different modules of this architecture intervene according to the following sequence; we detail further the functionalities of each module:

- the learner has first to accede to the system through a user interface and his actions are intercepted by the Emotion Manager,
- the Emotion Manager module launches the Emotion Identifier module which identifies the current emotion of the learner (2),
- the Learning Appraiser module receives instruction (3) from the Emotion Manager to submit the learner to a pre-test in order to evaluate his performance in the current emotional state,
- the Emotion Manager module triggers the Personality Identifier module (4) which identifies the personality of the learner,
- in the same way, the Optimal Emotion Extractor (5) is started to predict the optimal emotional state of the learner according to his personality,

- then next module launched is the Emotion Inducer (6),which will induce the optimal emotional state for the learner,
- finally, the Learning Appraiser (7) module will submit the learner to a post-test to evaluate his performance under the optimal emotional state.

The different modules mentioned previously are described bellow:

3.1 Emotion Manager

The role of this module is to monitor the entire emotional process of ESTEL, to distribute and synchronize tasks, and to coordinate between the other modules. In fact the emotion manager is a part of the student model in an ITS. It receives various parameters from the other modules. As we can see in Fig. 1, ESTEL architecture is centralized, all the information passes by the Emotion Manager module which will successively trigger the other modules.

3.2 Emotion Identifier

The Emotion Identifier module recognizes the current emotional state of the learner; it is based on the Emotion Recognition Agent (ERA). ERA is an agent that has been developed in our lab to identify a user's emotion given a sequence of colors. To achieve this goal, we have conducted an experiment in which 322 participants have to associate color sequences with their emotions. Based on results obtained in the experiment, the agent uses an ID3 algorithm to provide a decision tree which represents the sequence of colors with the corresponding emotions. This decision tree allows us to predict the current emotional state of a new learner according to his choice of a color sequence with 57, 6 % accuracy.

3.3 Personality Identifier

Personality traits were identified by applying Abbreviated form of the Revised Eysenck Personality Questionnaire (EPQR-A) [8] which contains 24 items to identify personality from a set of personality traits (Psychoticism, Extraversion, Neuroticism, And Lie Scale). Extravert people are characterized by active and talkative behaviour, high on positive affects. However, Neuroticism is characterized by high levels of negative affects. People with high neuroticism are easily affected by the surrounding atmosphere, get worried easily, quick to anger, and easily discouraged. Psychoticism is characterized by non-conformity, tough-mindedness, hostility, anger, and impulsivity. People with high Lie scale are sociably desirable, agreeable and generally respect the laws in the society [7]. After identifying the personality of the learner, the Personality Identifier module communicates this information to the Emotion Manager which triggers the Optimal Emotion Extractor for determining the optimal emotional state of the learner according to his personality.

3.4 Optimal Emotion Extractor

The Optimal Emotion Extractor module uses a set of rules that we have obtained from the experiment which will be described later. Those rules allow us to determine the learner's optimal emotional state according to his personality. Let us take an example to show how the Optimal Emotion Extractor works; we suppose that the learner's personality is extraversion. To predict his optimal emotional state, the Optimal Emotion Extractor browses the rules to find a case corresponding to the personality of the learner; the rules are represented as:
If (personality = Extraversion) then optimal-emotional-state = joy.

By applying the rule above, the Optimal Emotion Extractor module will identify the learner's optimal emotional state as joy.

After identifying the optimal emotional state of the learner, ESTEL will induce it via the Emotion Inducer module.

3.5 Emotion Inducer

The Emotion Inducer module attempts to induce the optimal emotional state, which represents a positive state of mind that maximizes learner's performance, found by the Optimal Emotion Extractor. For example, when a new learner accedes to ESTEL; the Personality Identifier determines his personality as extraversion, and then the Optimal Emotion Extractor retrieves joy as the optimal emotional state for this personality. Emotion Inducer will elicit joy in this learner by using the hybrid technique which consists of displaying different interfaces. These interfaces include guided imagery vignettes, music and images. The Emotion Inducer is inspired by the study of Mayer et al. [12] that has been done to induce four specific emotions (joy, anger, fear, and sadness). After inducing emotion, the Emotion Manager module will restart the Learning Appraiser module for evaluating learning efficiency.

3.6 Learning Appraiser

This module allows us to assess the performance of the learner in his current emotional state and then in his optimal one. The Learning Appraiser module uses, firstly, a pre-test for measuring the knowledge retention of the learner in the current emotional state. Secondly, it uses a post-test to evaluate the learner in the optimal emotional state. The results obtained will be transferred to the Emotion Manager to find out which of the two emotional states really enhances learning. If the results of the learner obtained in the pre-test (current emotional state) are better than those obtained in the post-test (optimal emotional state), ESTEL will take into consideration the current emotional state of this learner to eventually update the set of possible optimal emotional state for new learners.

As follows, we present the results of the experiment conducted to predict learner's optimal emotional state and to induce it.

4 Experiment and Results

Since different people have different optimal emotional states for learning, we have conducted an experiment to predict optimal emotional state according to the learner's personality. The sample included 137 participants from different genders and ages. First, participants choose the optimal emotional state that maximizes their learning from a set of sixteen emotions (as shown in Fig. 2).

Fig. 2. Emotions Set

After selecting their optimal emotional state, subjects answer to the 24-items of the EPQR-A [8]. The data collected was used to establish a relationship between optimal emotional state and personality.

Table 1. Experiment Results

	Extraversion	Lie	Neuroticism	Psychoticism
Anger	2	0	0	0
Anxious	8	3	3	2
Bored	2	0	2	0
Confident	12	14	8	0
Disgusted	0	1	0	1
Distressed	0	0	3	0
Fear	1	0	0	0
Joy	15	10	7	3
Pride	5	4	11	0
Resentment	0	0	1	0
Self-Gratification	4	7	3	0
Surprised	3	0	1	0
Remorseful	1	0	0	0

As shown in the table above, from the initial set of sixteen emotions given to the 137 participants, just thirteen have been selected. As you notice more than 28% of the participants, who their personality is extraversion, select joy as the optimal emotional state. There are also about 36% of the participants who have the most score in the lie scale, choose confident for representing their optimal emotional state. Nearly, 29% of the neurotic participants find that their optimal emotional state is pride. Moreover, from the 137, we have found just six psychotic participants, 50% of them have selected joy as the optimal emotional state.

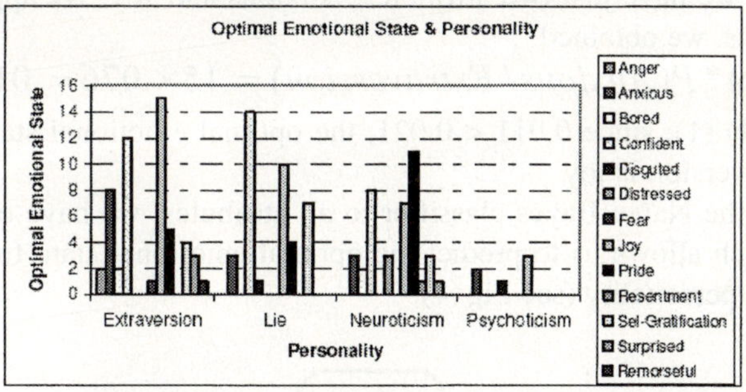

Fig. 3. Optimal emotional state & personality

As shown in Fig. 3, we have learner's personalities and their corresponding optimal emotional states. However, we need to select the most chosen by participants; we have applied the Naïve Bayes classifier to do that. Suppose that personality traits are noted by p_i, and those optimal emotional states variables are noted by o_i, the Naïve Bayes Classifier helps us to find the best class o_i given to p_i in the case of two independents variables [16]. By a direct application of Bayes' theorem, we get:

$$\mathrm{O}^* = agr\max_{o_j \in O} P(o_j) * P(p_i / o_j) \; . \tag{1}$$

We generally estimate $P(p_i / o_j)$ using m-estimates:

$$P(p_i / o_j) = \frac{n_c + mp}{n + m} \; . \tag{2}$$

Where:

n = the number of the users who their optimal emotional state is o_j

n_c = the number of the users who their optimal emotional state is o_j and their personality is p_i.

p = a priori estimate for $P\,(p_i/o_j)$.

m = the size of the sample.

Looking at P (Joy/Extraversion), we have 53 cases where p_i = Extraversion, and in 15 of those cases o_j = Joy. Thus, n = 53 and n_c = 15, since we have just one attribute value and p = 1/ (number-of attribute values), so p = 1 for all attributes. The size of the sample is m = 137, therefore, from formula (2), we get:

$$P(Joy / Extraversion) = \frac{15+137}{53+137} = {}^{15}\!/_{53} = .28$$

$$P(Joy) = \frac{1}{13} = .076$$

and, therefore,

$$P(Joy) * P(Joy / Extraversion) = .28 \times .076 = .021$$

Suppose that we have just two attributes: Anxious and Joy. By applying the same steps for Anxious, we obtained:

$$P(Anxious) * P(Anxious / Extraversion) = .15 \times .076 = .011$$

Using formula (1): since 0.011 < 0.021, the optimal emotional state predicted according to extraversion is joy.

By applying the Naïve Bayes classifier to all attributes, we have obtained the following tree which allows us to predict the optimal emotional state for a new learner according to his personality (see Fig. 4).

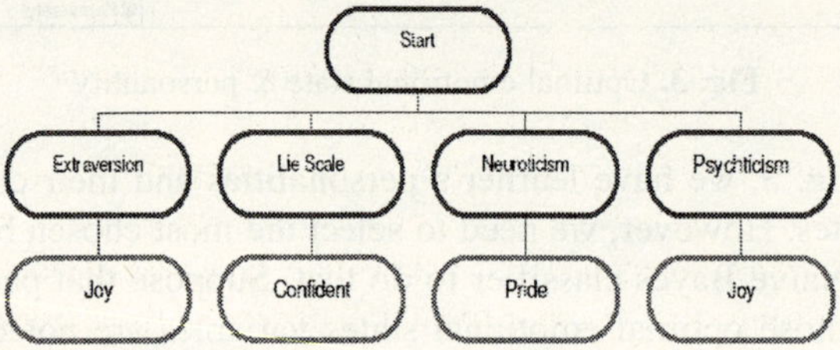

Fig. 4. The predicted optimal emotional state

Fig. 5. Example of interface inducing joy

Furthermore, for each personality we try to induce the corresponding optimal emotional state. The figure bellow (Fig. 5) shows how the hybrid technique allows us to induce joy for the extravert learner, so, we integrate in the interface a guided imagery vignette to engage the foreground attention and in the background we set an image that expresses what was said by the vignette in order to help in the guided imagery, we also put music to improve the background. For example, we say to the learner imagine that "It's your birthday and friends throw you a terrific surprise party" [12], we show him an image that reflects this situation to help him in his imagination, in the background we put to him a music expressing joy such as Brandenburg Concerto #2 composed by Bach [3]. We use the same principle to induce the two other optimal emotional states.

5 Conclusion and Future Research

In this paper, we have presented the architecture of our system ESTEL. By which, we proposed a way to predict optimal emotional state for learning and to induce it. We know that it is hard to detect the optimal emotional state for learning. For this reason, we have used the Naïve Bayes classifier which helps us to find the optimal emotional state for each personality. Moreover, we are also aware of the fact that inducing emotions in humans is not easy. That is why we have used the hybrid technique including; guided imagery, music and images attempting to change learner's emotion.

It remains for future research to study the effect of the emotion intensity in thought processes. On one hand, as mentioned previously, positive affects play an important role to enhance learning; on the other hand, the excess of the emotion sensed could go in the opposite direction. So, the learner will be submerged by this emotion and could not achieve the learning tasks in a good way. For this reason, future studies will concentrate on emotion intensities to regulate the emotion induced by ESTEL. So, we are thinking to add a new module called the Emotion Regulator which will be able to control and to regulate the optimal emotional state intensity in order to improve even more the learner's performance.

Acknowledgements. We address our thanks to the Ministry of Research, Sciences and the Technology of Quebec which supports this project within the framework of Valorisation-Recherche Québec (VRQ).

References

1. Abou-Jaoude, S., Frasson, C. Charra, O., Troncy, R.: On the Application of a Believable Layer in ITS. Workshop on Synthetic Agents, 9th International Conference on Artificial Intelligence in Education, Le Mans (1999)
2. Ahsen, A.: Guided imagery: the quest for a science. Part I: Imagery origins. Education, Vol. 110, (1997) 2-16
3. Bach, J. S.: Brandenburg Concerto No.2. In Music from Ravinia series, New York, RCA Victor Gold Seal, (1721) 60378-2-RG
4. Conati C.: Probabilistic Assessment of User's Emotions in Educational Games. Journal of Applied Artificial Intelligence, Vol. 16, (2002) 555-575

5. Damasio, A.: Descartes Error. Emotion, Reason and the Human Brain, Putnam Press, New York (1994)
6. Estrada, C.A., Isen, A.M., Young, M. J.: Positive affect influences creative problem solving and reported source of practice satisfaction in physicians. Motivation and Emotion, Vol. 18, (1994) 285-299
7. Eysenck, H. J., Eysenck, M. W.: Personality and individual differences. A natural science approach, New York: Plenum press (1985)
8. Francis, L., Brown, L., Philipchalk, R.: The development of an Abbreviated form of the Revised Eysenck Personality Questionnaire (EPQR-A). Personality and Individual Differences, Vol. 13, (1992) 443-449
9. Gross, J.J., Levenson, R.W.: Emotion elicitation using films. Cognition and Emotion, Vol. 9, (1995) 87-108
10. Idzihowski, C., Baddeley, A.: Fear and performance in novice parachutists. Ergonomics, Vol. 30, (1987) 1463-1474
11. Isen, A. M.: Positive Affect and Decision Making. Handbook of Emotions, New York: Guilford (1993) 261-277
12. Mayer, J., Allen, J., Beauregard, K.: Mood Inductions for Four Specific Moods. Journal of Mental imagery, Vol. 19, (1995) 133-150
13. Nasoz, F., Lisetti, C.L., Avarez, K., Finkelstein, N.: Emotion Recognition from Physiological Signals for User Modeling of Affect. The 3rd Workshop on Affective and Attitude User Modeling, USA (2003)
14. Picard, R. W., Healey, J., Vyzas, E.: Toward Machine Emotional Intelligence Analysis of Affective Physiological State. IEEE Transactions onPattern Analysis and Machine Intelligence, Vol. 23 (2001) 1175-1191
15. Reed, G. F.: Obsessional cognition: performance on two numerical tasks. British Journal of Psychiatry, Vol. 130 (1977) 184-185
16. Rish, I.: An empirical study of the naive Bayes classifier. Workshop on Empirical Methods in AI (2001)
17. Rosic, M., Stankov, S. Glavinic, V.: Intelligent tutoring systems for asynchronous distance education. 10th Mediterranean Electrotechnical Conference (2000) 111-114

Evaluating a Probabilistic Model of Student Affect

Cristina Conati and Heather Maclare

Dept. of Computer Science, University of British Columbia
2366 Main Mall, Vancouver, BC, V6T 1Z4, Canada
{conati, maclaren}@cs.ubc.ca

Abstract. We present the empirical evaluation of a probabilistic model of student affect based on Dynamic Bayesian Networks and designed to detect multiple emotions. Most existing affective user models focus on recognizing a specific emotion or lower level measures of emotional arousal, and none of these models have been evaluated with real users. We discuss our study in terms of the accuracy of various model components that contribute to the assessment of student emotions. The results provide encouraging evidence on the effectiveness of our approach, as well as invaluable insights on how to improve the model's performance.

1 Introduction

Electronic games for education are learning environments that try to increase student motivation by embedding pedagogical activities in highly engaging, game-like interactions. Several studies have shown that these games are usually successful at increasing the level of student engagement, but they often fail to trigger learning [10] because students play the game without actively reasoning about the underlying instructional domain. To overcome this limitation, we are designing pedagogical agents that generate tailored interactions to improve student learning during game playing. In order not to interfere with the student's level of engagement, these agents should take into account the student's affective state (as well as their cognitive state) when determining when and how to intervene. However, understanding someone's emotions is hard, even for human beings. The difficulty is largely due to the high level of ambiguity in the mapping between emotional states, their *causes* and their *effects* [12].

One possible approach to tackling the challenge of recognizing user affect is to reduce the ambiguity in the modeling task, either by focusing on a specific emotion in a fairly constraining interaction (e.g. [9]) or by only recognizing emotion intensity and valence (e.g. [1]). In contrast, our goal is to devise a framework for affective modeling that pedagogical agents can use to detect multiple specific emotions in interactions in which this information can improve the effectiveness of the adaptive support provided. To handle the high level of uncertainty in this modeling task, the framework integrates in a Dynamic Bayesian Network (DBN [8]) information on both the

J.C. Lester et al. (Eds.): ITS 2004, LNCS 3220, pp. 55–66, 2004.

causes of a student's emotional reactions and their *effects* on the student's bodily expressions. Model construction is done as much as possible from data, integrated with relevant psychological theories of emotion and personality.

While the model structure and construction is described in previous publications [3,13], in this paper we focus on model evaluation. In particular, we focus on evaluating the *causal part* of the model. To our knowledge, whilst there have been user studies to evaluate sources of affective data (e.g., [2]), this is the first empirical evaluation of an affective user model, embedded in a real system and tested with real users.

We start by describing our general framework for affective modeling. We then summarize how we built the causal part of the model for Prime Climb, an educational game for number factorization. Finally we describe the user study, its results and the insights that it generated on how to improve the model's accuracy.

2 A DBN for Emotion Recognition

Fig. 1 shows two time slices of our DBN for affective modeling. The nodes represent classes of variables in the actual DBN, which combines evidence on both causes and effects of emotional reactions, to compensate for the fact that often evidence on causes or effects alone is insufficient to accurately assess the student's emotional state.

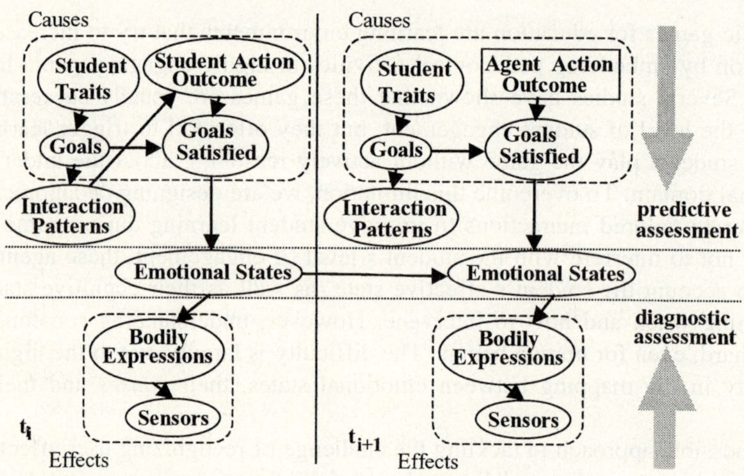

Fig. 1. Two time slices of our general affective model

The part of the network above the nodes *Emotional States* represents the relations between possible causes and emotional states, as they are described in the OCC theory of emotions [11]. In this theory, emotions arise as a result of one's *appraisal* of the current situation in relation to one's goals. Thus, our DBN includes variables for

Goals that a student may have during interaction with the game. Situations consist of the outcome of any event caused by either a student's or an agent's action (nodes *Student Action Outcome* and *Agent Action Outcome* in Fig. 1). Agent actions are represented as decision variables, indicating points where the agent must decide how to intervene in the interaction. The desirability of an event in relation to the student's goals is represented by the node class *Goals Satisfied,* which in turn influences the student's *Emotional States*.

Assessing student goals is non-trivial, especially when asking the student directly is not an option (as is the case in educational games). Thus, our DBN includes nodes to infer student goals from both *User Traits* that are known to influence goals (such as personality [7]) and *Interaction Patterns*.

The part of the network below *Emotional States* represents the interaction between emotional states, their observable effects on student behavior (*Bodily Expressions*) and sensors that can detect them. It is designed to modularly combine any available sensor information, to compensate for the fact that a single sensor can seldom reliably identify a specific emotional state.

In the next section, we show how we instantiated the causal part of the model to assess students' emotions during the interaction with the Prime Climb educational game. For details on the diagnostic part see [5].

3 Causal Model Construction for Prime Climb

Fig. 2 shows a screenshot of Prime Climb, a game designed to teach number factorization to 6th and 7th grade students. Two players must cooperate to climb a series of mountains that are divided in numbered sectors. Each player should move to a number that does not share any factors with her partner's number, otherwise she falls. Prime Climb provides two tools to help students: a *magnifying glass* to see a number's factorization, and a *help box* to communicate with the pedagogical agent we are building for the game. In addition to providing help when a student is playing with a partner, the agent engages its player in a "Practice Climb" during which it climbs with the student as a climbing instructor. The affective user model described here assesses the player's emotions during these practice climbs, and will eventually be integrated with a model of student learning [6] to inform the agent's pedagogical decisions.

We start by summarizing how we defined the sub-network that assesses students' goals. For more details on the process see [13]. Because all the variables in this sub-network are observable, we identified the variables and built the corresponding conditional probability tables (CPTs) using data collected through a Wizard of Oz study where students interacted with the game whilst an experimenter guided the pedagogical agent. The students took a pretest on factorization knowledge, a personality test based on the Five Factor personality theory [7], and a post-game questionnaire to express what goals they had during the interaction. The probabilistic dependencies

Fig. 2. Prime Climb interface

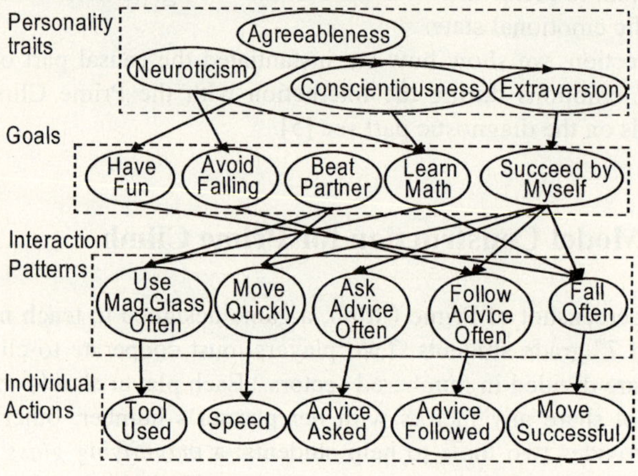

Fig. 3. Sub-network for goal assessment

among goals, personalities, interaction patterns and student actions were established through correlation analysis between the test results, the questionnaire results and student actions logged during the interactions.

Fig. 3 shows the resulting sub-network, incorporating both positive and negative correlations. The bottom level specifies how interaction patterns are recognized from the relative frequency of individual actions [13]. We intended to represent different degrees of personality type and goal priority by using multiple values in the corresponding nodes. However, we did not have enough data to populate the larger CPTs and resorted to binary nodes. Let's consider now the part of the network that represents the *appraisal mechanism* (i.e. how the mapping between student goals and game states influences student emotions). We currently represent in our DBN only 6 of the 22 emotions defined in the OCC model. They are *joy /distress* for the current state of the game, *pride/shame* of the student toward herself, and *admiration/reproach* toward the agent, modeled in the network by three two-valued nodes: *emotion for event*, *emotion for self* and *emotion for agent* (see Fig. 4).

The links and CPTs between *Goal* nodes, the outcome of student or agent actions and *Goal Satisfied* nodes, are currently based on subjective judgment. For some of these links, the connections are quite obvious. For instance, if the student has the goal *Avoid Falling*, a move resulting in a fall will lower the probability that the goal is achieved. Other links (e.g., those modeling which student actions cause a student to have fun or learn math) are less obvious, and could be built only through explicit student interviews that we had no way to conduct during our studies. When we did not have good heuristics to create these links, we did not include them in the model. The links between *Goal Satisfied* nodes and the emotion nodes are defined as follows. We assume that the outcome of every agent or student action is subject to student appraisal. Thus, each *Goal Satisfied* node influences *emotion-for-event* in every slice. Whether a *Goal Satisfied* node influences *emotion-for-self* or *emotion-for-agent* in a given slice depends upon whether the slice was generated, respectively, by a student action (slice t_i in Fig. 4) or agent's action (not shown due to lack of space). The CPTs for emotion nodes are defined so that the probability of each positive emotion is proportional to the number of true *Goal Satisfied* nodes.

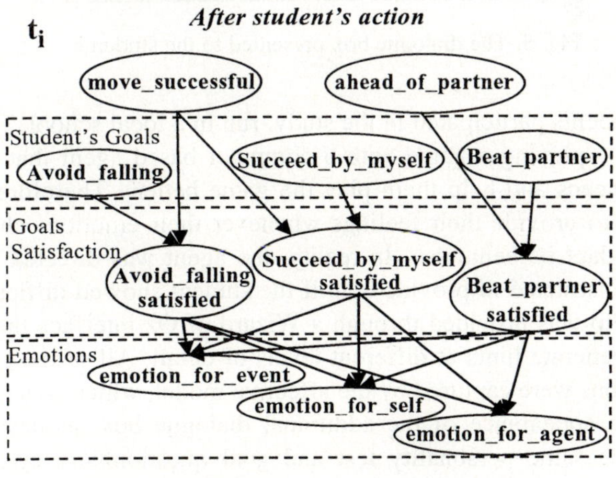

Fig. 4. Sample sub-network for appraisal

4 Evaluation

In order to gain an idea of how approximation due to lack of data affected the causal affective model we ran a study to produce an empirical evaluation of its accuracy. However, evaluating an affective user model directly is difficult. It requires assessing the students' actual emotions, which are ephemeral and can change multiple times during the interaction. Therefore it is not feasible to ask the students to describe them after game playing. Asking the students to describe them *during* the interaction, if not done properly, can significantly interfere with the very emotional states that we want to assess. Pilot testing various ways to try this second option showed that the least intrusive solution consisted of using two identical dialogue boxes [4]. One dialogue box (Fig. 5) is always available next to the game window for students to input their emotional states spontaneously. A similar dialogue box pops up if a student does not do this frequently enough, or if the model assesses that the student's emotional state has likely changed. Students were asked to report feelings toward the game and the agent only, as it was felt that our 11-year-old subjects would be too confused if asked to describe three separate feelings.

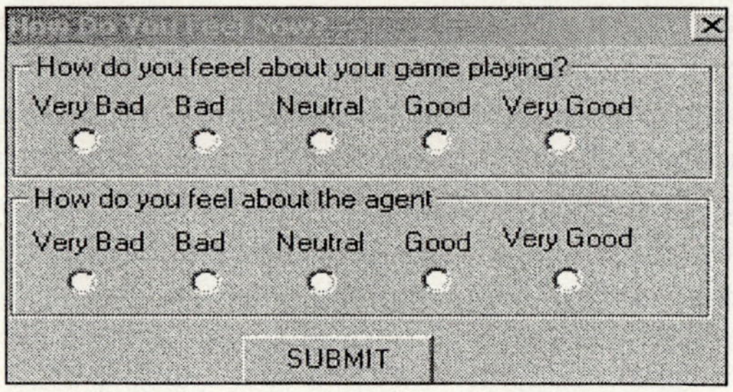

Fig. 5. The dialogue box presented to the students

20 7th grade students participated in the study, run in a local school. They were told that they would be playing a game with a computer-based agent that was trying to understand their needs and help them play the game better. Therefore, the students were encouraged to provide their feelings whenever their emotions changed so that the agent could adapt its behavior. In reality, the agent was directed by an experimenter who was instructed to provide help if the student showed difficulties with the climbing task. Help was provided through a Wizard of Oz interface that allowed the experimenter to generate hints at different levels of detail. All of the experimenter's and student's actions were captured by the affective model, which was updated in real time to direct the appearance of the additional dialogue box, as described earlier. Students filled the same personality test and goal questionnaire used in previous studies. Log files of the interaction included the student's reported emotions and corresponding model assessment.

4.1 Results: Accuracy of Emotion Assessment

We start our data analysis by measuring how often the model's assessment agreed with the student's reported emotion. We translated the students' reports for each emotion pair (e.g. joy/distress) and the model's corresponding probabilistic assessment into 3 values; 'positive' (any report higher than 'neutral' in the dialogue box), 'negative' (any report lower than 'neutral') and 'neutral' itself. If the model's assessment was above a simple threshold then it was predicting a positive emotion, if not then it was predicting a negative emotion. We did not include a 'neutral' value in the model's emotion nodes because we did not have sufficient knowledge from previous studies to populate the corresponding CPTs.

Making a binary prediction from the model's assessment is guaranteed to disagree with any neutral reports given. However, we found that 25 student reports (53% and 35% of the neutral joy and admiration reports respectively) were neutral for both joy and admiration. If, as these reports indicate, the student had a low level of emotional arousal, then this state that can be easily picked up by biometric sensors in the diagnostic part of the model [5]. This is a clear example of a situation where the observed evidence of a student's emotional state can inform the causal assessment of the model.

Table 1. Emotional belief accuracy using data from all 20 students

	Accuracy (%)		
Emotion	Mean	Std. Dev.	Data points
Joy	68.63	2.49	121
Distress	91.67	14.43	9
Combined J/D	80.15		
Admiration	20.61	3.39	97
Reproach	81.67	22.91	6
Combined A/R	51.14		

Table 2. Affective belief accuracy using data from 17 students with declared goals

	Accuracy (%)	
Emotion	Without Goals	With Goals
Joy	66.39	50.45
Distress	85.71	57.14
Combined J/D	76.05	53.78
Admiration	20.52	62.87
Reproach	75	75
Combined A/R	47.76	68.94

Using a threshold to classify the model's belief as positive or negative involves a trade-off between correctly classifying positive and negative emotions. We could argue that it will be more crucial for the pedagogical agent to accurately detect negative emotional states, but for the purpose of this evaluation we gave equal weight to positive and negative accuracy. Using this approach, threshold analysis showed that values between 0.6 and 0.7 produced the best overall results. We used the results at value 0.65, shown in Table 1, as the starting point for our data analysis.

The results were obtained from the model without using prior knowledge on individual students (i.e. the root personality nodes were initialized to 0.5 for every subject). For each emotion, we calculated the percentage of reports where the model

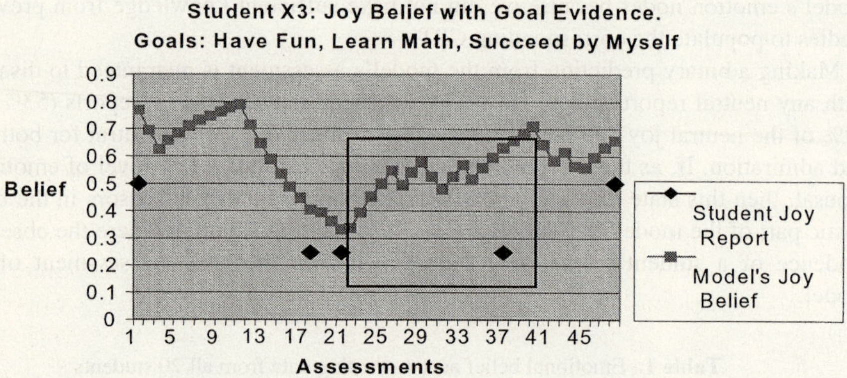

Fig. 6. A game session in which the student experienced frustration

agreed with the student. To determine whether any students had significantly different accuracy, we performed cross-validation to produce a measure of standard deviation. This measure is quite high for reproach and distress because far fewer data points were recorded for these negative emotions, but it is low for the other emotions, showing that the model produced similar performances for each student.

Table 1 shows that the combined accuracy for admiration/reproach is much lower than the combined accuracy for joy/distress. To determine to what extent these results are due to problems with the sub-network assessing student goals or with the sub-network modeling the appraisal process, we analyzed how the accuracy changed if we added evidence on student goals into the model, simulating a situation in which the model assesses goals correctly.

Table 2 shows that, when we add evidence on student goals, the accuracy for admiration improves, but the accuracy for joy is reduced. To understand why, we took a closer look at the data for individual students. While the increase in accuracy for admiration was a general improvement for all students who reported this emotion, the decreases in accuracy for joy and distress were due to a small number of students for whom the model no longer gave a good performance. We have identified 2 reasons for this result:

Reason 1. As we mentioned in a previous section, we currently have no links connecting student actions to the satisfaction of the goals Have Fun and Learn Math because we did not have sufficient knowledge to build these links. However, in this study, 4 students reported that they only had goals of Have Fun or Learn Math (or both). For these students, the model's belief for joy only changed after agent actions. Since the agent acted infrequently, the model's joy belief changed very little from its initial value of 0.5. Thus, because of the 0.65 threshold, all student reports for joy/distress were classified as distress, and the model's accuracy for this emotion pair was reduced. Removing these 4 students from the data set improved the accuracy for detecting joy when goal evidence was used from 50% to 74%. An obvious fix for this problem is to add to the model the links that relate the goals Have Fun and Learn

Math to student actions. We plan to run a study explicitly designed to gather the relevant information from student interviews after game playing.

Reason 2. Of the 7 distress reports collected, 4 were not classified correctly because they occurred in a particular game situation. The section of the graph within the rectangle in Fig. 6 shows the comparison between the model's assessment and the student's reported emotions (normalized between 0 and 1 for the sake of comparison) during one such occurrence. In this segment of the interaction, the student falls and then makes a rapid series of successful climbs to get back to the position that she fell from. She then falls again and repeats the process until eventually she solves the problem. This student has declared the goals Have Fun, Learn Math, and Succeed by Myself but, for reason 1 above, only the latter goal influences the student's emotional state after a student action. Thus, each fall reduces the model's belief for joy because the student is not succeeding. Each successful move without the agent's help (i.e. in most of her moves) increases the model's belief for joy. However, apparently the model overestimated how quickly the student's level of joy recovered because of the successful moves. This was the case for all students whose reports of distress were misclassified. In order to fix this problem the model needs a long-term assessment of the student's overall mood that will influence the priorities of student goals. It also needs an indication of whether moves represent actual progress in the game, adding links that relate this to the satisfaction of the goal Have Fun. Finally, we can use personality information to distinguish between students who experience frustration in such a situation and those who are merely 'playing' (some students enjoy falling and do not care about succeeding).

The improvement in the accuracy of emotional assessment (after taking into account the problems just discussed) when goal evidence is included shows that the model was not always accurate in predicting student goals. Why then was the accuracy for joy and distress so high when goal evidence was not included? Without this information, the model's belief for each goal tended to stay close to its initial value of 0.5, indicating that it did not know whether the student had the goal or not. Because successful moves can satisfy three out of the five goals in the model (Succeed by Myself, Avoid Falling and Beat Partner) and all students moved successfully more often than they fell, the model's assessment for joy tended to stay above the threshold value of 0.65, leading to a high number of reports being classified as joy. Most of the 5 distress reports related to the frustrating situations described earlier were also classified correctly. This is because the model did not correctly assess the fact that all the students involved in these situations had the goal Succeed by Myself and therefore did not overestimate the rising of joy as it did in the presence of goal evidence. This behavior may suggest that we don't always need an accurate assessment of goals to have an acceptable model of student affect. However, we argue that knowing the exact causes of the student's affective states can help an intelligent agent to react to these states more effectively. Thus, the next stage of our analysis relates to understanding the model's performance in assessing goals and how to improve it. In particular we explore whether having information on personality and interaction patterns is enough to accurately determine a person's goals.

4.2 Results: Accuracy of Goal Assessment

Only 10 students completed the personality test in our study. Table 3 shows, for each goal, the percentage of these students for whom the declaration of that goal was correctly identified, and how these percentages change when personality information is used. A threshold of 0.6 was used to determine whether the model thought that a student had a particular goal, because goals will begin to substantially affect the assessment of student emotions at this level of belief. The results show that personality information improves the accuracy for only two of the five goals, Have Fun and Beat Partner. For the other goals, the results appear to indicate that the model's belief about these goals did not change. However, what actually happened is that in these cases the belief simply did not change enough to alter the models predictions using the threshold.

Table 3. The model's goal assessment accuracy when personality information is included.

	Accuracy (%)	
Goals	Without Personality	With Personality
Have Fun	30	100
Avoid Falling	70	70
Beat Partner	60	80
Learn Math	50	50
Succeed by Myself	40	40

The model's belief about a student's goals is constructed from causal knowledge (personality traits) and evidence (student actions). Fig. 3 showed the actions identified as evidence for particular goals . When personality traits are used, they produce an initial bias towards a particular set of goals. Evidence collected during the game should then refine this bias, because personality traits alone cannot always accurately assess which goals a student has. However, currently the bias produced by personality information is stronger than the evidence coming from game actions. There are two reasons for this strong bias:

Reason 1. Unfortunately, some of the actions collected as evidence (e.g. asking the agent for advice) did not occur very frequently, even when the student declared the particular goal that the action was evidence for. One possible solution is to add to the model a goal prior for each of the covered goals. The priors would be produced by a short test before the game and only act as an initial influence since the model's goal assessments will be dynamically refined by evidence. Integration of the prior information with the information on personality and interaction patterns will require fictitious root goal nodes to be added the model.

Reason 2. Two of the personality traits that affect the three goals Learn Math, Avoid Falling, and Succeed by Myself (see Fig. 3) are Neuroticism and Extraversion. However, the significant correlations that are represented by the links connecting these goals and personality traits were based on very few data points. This has probably led to stronger correlations than would be found in the general population. Because evidence coming from interaction patterns is often not strong enough (see Reason 1 above), then the model is not able to recover from the bias that evidence on these two personality traits brings to the model assessment. An obvious fix to these problems is to collect more data to refine the links between personality and goals.

5 Discussion and Future Work

In this paper, we have discussed the evaluation of a probabilistic model of student affect that relies on DBNs to assess multiple student emotions during interaction with educational games. Although other researchers have started using this probabilistic approach to deal with the high level of uncertainty involved in recognizing multiple user emotions (e.g. [3,12]), so far there has been no empirical evaluation of the proposed models, or of any other existing affective user model for that matter.

The results presented show that if a student's goals can be correctly determined, then the affective model described can maintain a fairly accurate assessment of the student's current emotional state. Furthermore, we can increase this accuracy by implementing the solutions that we described to overcome the sources of error detected in the model structure and parameters. Accurate assessment of student goals, however, has been shown to be more problematic, which is not surprising given that what we are trying to do is basically *plan recognition*, which is one of AI's notoriously difficult problems. We reported two main sources of inaccuracy in goal assessment in our model, and presented suggestions on how to tackle them. However, it is unlikely that we will ever achieve consistently high accuracy in goal assessment for all students in all situations. This is where having a model that combines information on both causes and effects of emotional reaction can compensate for the fact that often evidence on causes or effects alone is insufficient to accurately assess the student's emotional state. Thus, we believe that our results provide encouraging evidence that confirms the potential of using DBNs to successfully model user affect in general.

In addition to collecting more data to refine the model as suggested by our data analysis, other improvements that we are planning include (1) investigating adding to the model varying degrees of goal priority and personality traits (2) combining the causal part of the model with a diagnostic model [5], that makes use of evidence from biometric sensors, to produce a model that integrates both causes and effects into a single emotional assessment.

References

1. Ball, G. and Breese, J. 1999. Modeling the Emotional State of Computer Users. *Workshop on 'Attitude, Personality and Emotions in User-Adapted Interaction', UM'99*, Canada.
2. Bosma, W. and André, E. 2004. Recognizing Emotions to Disambiguate Dialogue Acts. *International Conference on Intelligent User Interfaces 2004*. Madeira, Portugal.

3. Conati, C. 2002. Probabilistic Assessment of User's Emotions in Educational Games. *Journal of Applied Artificial Intelligence, special issue on "Merging Cognition and Affect in HCI"*, **16**(7-8):555-575.
4. Conati, C. 2004. How to Evaluate models of User Affect? *Tutorial and Research Workshop on Affective Dialogue Systems*. Kloster Irsee, Germany.
5. Conati, C., Chabbal, R., and Maclaren, H. 2003. A Study on Using Biometric Sensors for Monitoring User Emotions in Educational Games. *Workshop on Modeling User Affect and Actions: Why, When and How. *UM'03, Int. conf. On User Modeling*. Johnstown, PA.
6. Conati C. and Zhao X. 2004. Building and Evaluating an Intelligent Pedagogical Agent to Improve the Effectiveness of an Educational Game. *International Conference on Intelligent User Interfaces 2004*. Madeira, Portugal.
7. Costa, P.T. and McCrae, R.R. 1992. Four Ways Five Factors are Basic. *Personality and Individual Differences* 1. **13**:653-665.
8. Dean, T. and Kanazawa, K. 1989. A Model for Reasoning about Persistence and Causation. *Computational Intelligence* **5**(3):142-150.
9. Healy, J. and Picard, R. 2000. SmartCar: Detecting Driver Stress. *15th Int. Conf. on Pattern Recognition*. Barcelona, Spain.
10. Klawe, M. 1998. When Does The User Of Computer Games And Other Interactive Multimedia Software Help Students Learn Mathematics? *NCTM Standards 2000 Technology Conference*, 1998. Arlington, VA.
11. Ortony, A., Clore, G.L., and Collins, A. 1988. *The Cognitive Structure of Emotions*. Cambridge University Press.
12. Picard, R. 1995. *Affective computing*. Cambridge: MIT Press.
13. Zhou, X. and Conati, C. 2003. Inferring User Goals from Personality and Behavior in a Causal Model of User Affect. *International Conference on Intelligent User Interfaces 2003*. Miami, FL.

Politeness in Tutoring Dialogs: "Run the Factory, That's What I'd Do"

W. Lewis Johnson[1] and Paola Rizzo[2]

[1] Center for Advanced Research in Technology for Education
Information Sciences Institute, University of Southern California
4676 Admiralty Way, Marina del Rey, CA 90292-6695 USA
johnson@isi.edu, http://www.isi.edu/isd/carte/

[2] Department of Historical-Philosophical and Pedagogical Research
University of Rome "La Sapienza"
Via Carlo Fea 2, 00161, Rome, Italy
paola.rizzo@uniroma1.it

Abstract. Intelligent Tutoring Systems usually take into account only the cognitive aspects of the student: they may suggest the right actions to perform, correct mistakes, and provide explanations. However, besides cognition, educational researchers increasingly recognize the importance of factors such as self-confidence and interest that contribute to learner intrinsic motivation. We believe that the student affective goals can be taken into account by implementing a model of politeness into the tutoring system. This paper aims at providing an overall account of politeness in tutoring interactions (in particular, natural language dialogs), and describes the way in which politeness has been implemented in an intelligent tutoring system based on an animated pedagogical agent. The work is part of a larger project building a socially intelligent pedagogical agent able to monitor learner performance and provide socially sensitive coaching and feedback at appropriate times. The project builds on the experience gained in realizing several other pedagogical agents.

1 Introduction

Intelligent Tutoring Systems usually take into account only the cognitive aspects of the student: they may suggest the right actions to perform, correct mistakes, and provide explanations. However, besides cognition, educational researchers increasingly recognize the importance of factors such as self-confidence and interest that contribute to learner intrinsic motivation [21]. ITSs not only usually ignore the motivational states of the student, but might even undermine them, for instance when the system says "Your answer is wrong" (affecting learner self-confidence), or "Now execute this action" (affecting learner initiative).

We believe that the student affective goals can be taken into account by implementing a model of politeness into a tutoring system. A polite tutor would respect the student need to be in control, by suggesting rather than imposing actions; it would reinforce the student self-confidence, by emphasizing his successful performances, or by leveraging on the assumption that he and the tutor are solving the problems to-

J.C. Lester et al. (Eds.): ITS 2004, LNCS 3220, pp. 67–76, 2004.

gether; it would make the student more comfortable and motivated towards the learning task, by trying to build up a positive relationship, or "rapport", with him; and it would stimulate the student interest, by unobtrusively highlightling open and unresolved issues.

This paper aims at providing an overall account of politeness in tutoring interactions (in particular, natural language dialogs), and describes the way in which politeness has been implemented in an intelligent tutoring system incorporating an animated pedagogical agent. The work is part of a larger project building a socially intelligent pedagogical agent able to monitor learner performance and provide socially sensitive coaching and feedback and appropriate times [11]. Animated pedagogical agents can produce a positive affective response on the part of the learner, sometimes referred to as the persona effect [16]. This is attributed to the natural tendency for people to relate to computers as social actors [20], a tendency that animate agents exploit. Regarding politeness, the social actor hypothesis lead us to expect that humans not only respond to social cues, but also that they behave politely toward the agents.

2 The Politeness Theory of Brown and Levinson

Brown and Levinson [4] have devised a cross-cultural theory of politeness, according to which everybody has a positive and negative "face". Negative face is the want to be unimpeded by others, while positive face is the want to be desirable to others. Some communicative acts, such as requests and offers, can threaten the hearer's negative face, positive face, or both, and therefore are referred to as Face Threatening Acts (FTAs). Two examples of FTAs in the context of tutoring interactions are the following: (a) "Your answer is wrong": this threatens the student positive face; (b) "You have to do this": this threaten the student negative face.

Speakers use various types of politeness strategies to mitigate face threats, according to the severity, or "weightiness", of the FTA. The assessment is based on three sociological factors: the "social distance" between speaker and hearer (the level of their reciprocal acquaintance), the "relative power" of hearer and speaker (e.g., the employer has more power than the employee), and the "absolute ranking of impositions" (the severity that each face threat is considered to impose, according to cultural norms). The values of these factors dynamically change according to the context; for instance, social distance tends to diminish over time as speaker and hearer interact with each other.

Brown and Levinson group politeness strategies into 5 categories, ranked from least to most polite. These are listed below, together with examples of utterances that might be spoken by a tutor in an industrial engineering learning environment.

1. Bald on record: the speaker communicates directly, without trying to redress the hearer's face, e.g.: "Now set the planning methodology of the factory."
2. Positive politeness: the speaker tries to redress the hearer's positive face by attending to his interests and wants, e.g.: "You did very well on setting the parameters of your factory! Now set the planning methodology."

3. Negative politeness: the speaker redresses the hearer's negative face by suggesting that the hearer is free to decide whether to comply with the FTA, e.g.: "Now you might want to set the planning methodology of the factory."
4. Off record: the speaker provides some sort of hint to what he means, without committing to a specific attributable intention, for example: "What about the planning methodology of the factory?"
5. Don't do the FTA: when the weightiness of the FTA is considered too high, the speaker might simply avoid performing the FTA.

3 Analyzing Politeness in Real Tutoring Interactions

To investigate the role that politeness plays in learner-tutor interaction, we videotaped interactions between learners and a human tutor while the students were working with a particular on-line learning environment, the Virtual Factory Teaching System (VFTS) [9]. Students read through an on-line tutorial in a Web browser, and carried out actions on the VFTS as indicated by the tutorial. Learners were supposed to analyse the history of previous factory orders in order to forecast future demand, develop a production plan, and then schedule the processing of jobs within the factory in order to meet the demand. The tutor sat next to the students as they worked, and could interact with them as the student or the tutor felt appropriate. Completing the entire scenario required approximately two hours of work, divided into two sessions of around one hour. To analyse the interactions, and use them in designing learner-agent dialog, we transcribed them and annotated them using the DISCOUNT scheme [18].

The analysis showed that the tutor often applied politeness strategies to mitigate face threats. The following patterns of politeness strategies were associated with each type of tutor support (listed from most to least frequent):

- Suggesting actions:
  - this might threaten the student negative face, so the tutor mostly applied negative politeness strategies, e.g.: "You will probably want to look at the work centers", or "Want to look at your capacity?". A negative politeness strategy used quite often by the tutor is "conventional indirectness": a compromise between the desires to be direct and to be indirect, resulting in a communicative act that has a non-literal meaning based on conventions. Examples from our transcripts are: "They're asking you to go back and maybe change it", or "What they're telling you is go and try to get the error terms". This strategy enables the tutor to deflect to the system or interface the responsibility of requesting the student to perform an action.
  - in other cases the tutor chose a positive politeness strategy, by phrasing suggestions as activities to be performed jointly by the tutor and the learner, e.g.: "So why don't we go back to the tutorial factory…", or by showing concern for the student's goals, e.g. "Run your factory, that's what I'd do."
- Providing feedback:

- o negative feedback might threaten the student's positive face, so the tutor mostly used off-record politeness strategies, e.g.: "So the methodology you used for product 1 probably wasn't that good." In some cases, the tutor provides feedback by promoting interest and reflection, as well as affecting face, using "socratic" communicative acts such as: "Well, think about what you did…".
- Explaining concepts: this does not seems to be face threatening, because the tutor is usually bald on record, e.g.: "stochastic […] means the parameters in your factory are going to be random."

4 Politeness and Student Motivation

As already noticed, a striking feature of the tutoring dialogs was that although they involved many episodes where the tutor was offering advice, in very few cases did the tutor give explicit instructions of what to do. Rather, the tutor would phrase his comments so as to subtly engage the learner's interest and motivation, while leaving the learner the choice of what to do and how.

Following the work of Sansone, Harackiewicz, and Lepper and others [21, 15], we analyze these comments as intended to influence learner intrinsic motivation. Learners tend to learn better and more deeply if they are motivated by an internal interest and desire to master the material, as opposed to extrinsic rewards and punishments such as grades. Researchers in motivation have identified the following factors as conducive to intrinsic motivation:

- o Curiosity in the subject matter,
- o An optimal level of challenge – neither too little nor too much,
- o Confidence, i.e., a sense of self-efficacy, and
- o A sense of control – being free to choose what problems to solve and how, as opposed to being told what to do.

The tutorial comments observed in the dialogs tend to be phrased in such a way as to have an indirect effect on these motivational factors, e.g., phrasing a hinted action as a question reinforces the learner's sense of control, since the learner can choose whether or not to answer the question affirmatively. Also, the tutor's comments often would reinforce the learner's sense of being an active participant in the problem solving process, e.g., by phrasing suggestions as activities to be performed jointly by the tutor and the learner.

A particularly interesting communicative strategy we have frequently observed in the transcripts is what can be considered a "socratic hint", i.e., an indirect comment or question that raises unresolved issues or wrong student actions. Examples are: "Did you take a look at number 2's results?", "Take a look at the data, and see what you think", or "You like this one?". The socratic hint is a cognitive and motivational strategy aimed at evoking the student curiosity and requiring further thought from him [15]. From our perspective, it is also an off-record politeness strategy, in that it is indirect and provides hints to what the tutor actually means. This strategy minimizes both the threat to the student positive face, because criticisms are veiled, and the threat to his negative face, since the student is not pushed towards any specific action.

In other words, the socratic hint is a case in which politeness is used not only for mitigating face threats, but also for indirectly influencing the student motivation.

Although politeness theory and motivation theory come out of distinct literatures, their predictions regarding the choice to tutorial interaction tactics are broadly consistent. This is not surprising, since the wants described by politeness theory have a clear motivational aspect; negative face corresponds to control, and positive face corresponds somewhat to confidence in educational settings. Therefore, we are led to think that tutors may use politeness strategies not only for minimizing the weightiness of face threatening acts, but also for indirectly supporting the student's motivation. For instance, the tutor may use positive politeness for promoting the student positive face (e.g. his desire for successful learning), and negative politeness for supporting the student negative face (e.g. his desire for autonomous learning).

5 A Model of Politeness for Tutoring Dialogs

In order to apply the theory by Brown and Levinson to the context of interactions in ITSs, we have realized a computational model that has the following features. First, positive and negative politeness values are assigned beforehand to each possible natural language template that may be used by the tutor; for instance, a bald on record template has a lower politeness value than an off-record template. The politeness value measures the degree to which a template redresses the student's face, and can be considered the inverse of the weightiness of an FTA. During the interaction between tutor and student, we compute the politeness value of the tutor, i.e. the degree to which we want the tutor to be polite with the student. The value is computed according to the values of D(T,S) (the social distance between the tutor and the student) and P(T,S) (the amount of social power that the tutor has over the student) , and if D and P vary, the tutor politeness will change accordingly. When the tutor has to perform a communicative act, the template having a politeness value which minimizes the difference from the tutor politeness value will be selected and used for producing an utterance.

Secondly, to bring the politeness and motivation together, we extend the Brown & Levinson model as follows. First, whereas Brown & Levinson's model assigns a single numeric value to each face threat, we extend their model to consider positive face threat and negative face threat separately. This enables us to select a redressive strategy that is appropriate to the type of face threat. For example, if an FTA threatens negative face but not positive face, then the politeness model should choose a redressive strategy that mitigates negative face threat; in contrast the basic Brown & Levinson model would consider a redressive strategy aimed at positive face to be equally appropriate. Second, we allow for the possibility that the tutor might wish to explicitly enhance the learner's face, beyond what is required to mitigate immediate face threats. For example, if the tutor judges that the learner needs to feel more in control, he or she will make greater use of redressive strategies that augment negative face.

Altogether, the amount of face threat redress is determined by the following formulas, which extend the weightiness formulas proposed by Brown & Levinson [4]:

$$Wx+ = D(T,S) - P(T,S) + Rx+ + D+$$
$$Wx- = D(T,S) - P(T,S) + Rx- + D -.$$

Here Wx+ and Wx- are the amounts of positive and negative face threat redress, respectively, T represents the tutor and S represents the student. Rx+ is the inherent positive face threat of the communicative act (e.g., advising, critiquing, etc.,), Rx- is the inherent negative face threat of the act, D+ is the amount of augmentation of positive face desired by the tutor, and D - is the augmentation of learner negative face.

As a final modification of Brown and Levinson's theory, we have grouped politeness strategies in a more fine-grained categorization (see Table 1), that takes into account the types of speech acts observed in the transcripts of real tutoring dialogs.

Table 1. Categorization of politeness strategies in tutoring interactions

Politeness strategies	Example sentences
Joint goal	We should set the planning methodology
Question	Did you set the planning methodology?
Bald on record	Now set the planning methodology
Tutor Goal	I would set the planning methodology
Conventional indirectness	The machine wants you to set the planning methodology
Request	I suggest that you set the planning methodology
Student goal	You could set the planning methodology
Socratic hint	What about the planning methodology?

6 Implementing the Politeness Model

The implementation of our politeness model is based on a natural language generator for producing appropriate interaction tactics [12]. The generator takes as input a set of language elements – short noun phrases and short verb phrases in the target domain – and DISCOUNT predicates describing the desired dialog move. It chooses an utterance pattern that matches the dialog move predicates most closely, instantiates it with the language elements, and synthesizes an utterance, which is then passed to the animated tutor for uttering using text-to-speech synthesis.

The move templates and language elements are specified using an XML syntax and all defined in one language definition file. Figure 1 shows an example move from the language definition file. The moves are based upon utterances found in the dialog transcripts; the comments at the top of the move template show the original utterance and the transcript and time code where it was found. The move template may classify the move in multiple ways, since the same utterance may have multiple communicative roles, and different coders may code the same utterance differently.

A politeness module [12] implements the politeness / motivation model described above. It selects an appropriate face threat mitigation strategy to apply to each utter-

```
<move> <!-- 7S P1 47:11 T -->
<!-- So number 2, the number of seasons may not be 2 then.-->
    <predicate role="initiating" move="all" name="action1"/>
    <predicate role="initiating" move="all" name="noun1"/>
    <predicate role="initiating" move="hint" name="suggest"/>
    <predicate role="initiating" move="inform" name="identify"/>
    <predicate role="initiating" move="reason" name="explain"/>
    <template>
      So <nounphrase case="object" type="parameter"
                    name="noun1.nounphrase1"/>
        may not
        <verbphrase type="parameter" name="action1.action1" form="infinite"/>
    </template>
</move>
```

Fig. 1. An example dialog move template

ance. For each utterance type a set of politeness strategies are available, ordered by the amount of face threat mitigation they offer. Each strategy is in turn described as a set of dialog moves, similar to those shown in Figure 1. These are passed to the natural language generator, which selects a dialog move. The combined dialog generator takes as input the desired utterance type, language elements, and a set of parameters governing face threat mitigation (social distance, social power, and motivational support) and generates an utterance with the appropriate degree of face threat redress. Using this generation framework, it is possible to present the same tutorial comment with different degrees of politeness. For example, a suggestion to save the current factory description, can be stated either bald on record (e.g., "Save the factory now"), as a hint, ("Do you want to save the factory now?"), as a suggestion of what the tutor would do ("I would save the factory now"), as a suggestion of a joint action ("Why don't we save our factory now?"), etc.

7 Evaluating the Politeness of Natural Language Templates

To set the positive and negative politeness values of NL templates, we submitted to 9 subjects a questionnaire where they were asked to assign positive and negative politeness values to example sentences. Each sentence was representative of a given politeness category, and was put into the context of a possible interaction between student and tutor. The politeness values could range from 1 (very impolite) to 7 (very polite).

The data collected from the questionnaire, as we expected, showed that the politeness categories have different average negative and politeness values, and can therefore be ordered differently according to those values. However, the standard deviations were high, which meant that there was strong variability among the subjects' evaluations of politeness. Furthermore, there was a correlation between the rankings of positive and negative politeness, which might mean that it is difficult to clearly separate positive from negative politeness strategies, or that our instructions about how to evaluate positive and negative politeness were not clear enough to the subjects. We revised the wording of the questionnaire, based on feedback from this set of subjects, and collected data from 47 subjects from University of California Santa Barbara, with much more consistent results.

8 Planning an Evaluation of the Effect of Politeness

In order to test the impact of different politeness strategies on learner performance, we have developed a Wizard of Oz experimental setting, where a human plays the role of the automated tutor, assisted by the politeness model. The experimenter uses a graphical interface that enables him to: (a) choose a pedagogical goal, such as "Suggest action", or "Explain concept", (b) select the object of the communicative act (e.g. the action "create the factory"), and (c) select the type of communicative act from the radio buttons (for instance, a simple indication of the action to execute, or also a description of the reasons for executing it). The communicative act is sent to the Politeness Module, which applies a politeness strategy and then sends it to the NLG, which in its turn selects a template corresponding to the desired type of utterance.

The experiment will be based on a between-subjects design with two conditions: "polite tutor" vs "impolite tutor". In the "polite" condition, the communicative acts chosen by the experimenter undergo politeness strategies before being sent to the student, while in the "impolite" condition the experimenter utterances are produced in a direct, bald on record way, without applying any politeness strategy. We expect that in the "polite tutor" condition the students will be more intrinsically motivated to learn and have a better rapport with the tutor, and this should result in a better learning score with respect to the students who have learned with the "impolite tutor".

9 Related Work

Affect and motivation in learning environments are attracting increasing interest, e.g., the work of del Soldato et al [8] and de Vicente [7]. Heylen et al. [10] highlight the importance of these factors in tutors, and examine the interpersonal factors that should be taken into account when creating sociallly intelligent computer tutors. Cooper [6] has shown that profound empathy in teaching relationships is important because it stimulates positive emotions and interactions that favor learning. Baylor [3] has conducted experiments in which learners interact with multiple pedagogical agents, one of which seeks to motivate the learner. User interface and agent researchers are also beginning to apply the Brown & Levinson model to human-computer interaction in other contexts [5; 17]; see also André's work in this area [2].

Porayska-Pomsta [19] has also been using the Brown & Levinson model to analyze teacher communications in classroom settings. Although there are similarities between her approach and the approach described here, her model makes relatively less use of face threat mitigating strategies. This may be due to the differences in the social contexts being modeled: one-on-one coaching and advice giving is likely to result in a greater degree of attention to face work.

Other researchers such as Kort et al. [1, 13], and Zhou and Conati [22] have been addressing the problem of detecting learner affect and motivation, and influencing it. Comparisons with this work are complicated by differences in terminology regarding affect and emotion. We adhere to the terminological usage of Lazarus [14], who consider all emotions to be appraisal-based, and distinguish emotions from other states and attitudes that may engender emotions in specific context. In this sense our focus is not on emotions per se, but on states (i.e., motivation, face wants) that can engender emotions in particular contexts (e.g., frustration, embarassment). Although nonverbal emotional displays were not prominent in the tutorial dialogs described in this paper, they do arise in tutorial dialogs that we have studied in other domains, and we plan in our future work to incorporate them into our model.

10 Conclusion

This paper has presented a model of politeness in tutorial dialog, based on transcripts of student-tutor interaction. We have shown how politeness theory, extended to address the specifics of tutorial dialog, can provide a common account for tutorial advice giving, motivational tactics, and Socratic dialog. We believe that this model could be applied broadly to intelligent tutoring systems to engender a more positive learner attitude, both toward the subject matter and toward the tutoring system.

Once we complete our experimental evaluations of the model, we plan to extend it to other domains, such as foreign language learning. Future work will then investigate how to integrate nonverbal gesture and affective displays into the model, in order to control the behavior of an animated pedagogical agent.

Acknowledgements. Various people who have contributed to the Social Intelligence Project, including Wauter Bosma, Maged Dessouky, Mattijs Ghijsen, Sander Kole, Kate LaBore, Hyokeong Lee, Richard Mayer, Helen Pain, Lei Qu, Sahiba Sandhu, Erin Shaw, Ning Wang, and Herwin van Welbergen. This work was supported by the National Science Foundation under Grant No. 0121330, and by Microsoft Research. Paola Rizzo was partially supported by a scholarship from the Italian National Research Council. Any opinions, findings, and conclusions or recommendations expressed in this material are those of the authors and do not necessarily reflect the views of the funders.

References

1. Aist G., Kort B., Reilly R., Mostow J., Picard R.W: Adding Human-Provided Emotional Scaffolding to an Automated Reading Tutor that Listens Increases Student Persistence. In S. A. Cerri, G. Gouardères, F. Paraguaçu (Eds.): ITS 2002. Springer, Berlin (2002)
2. André, E. Rehm, M., Minker, W., Bühner, D.: Endowing spoken language dialogue systems with emotional intelligence. In: Proceedings ADS04. Springer, Berlin (2004)

3. Baylor, A.L., Ebbers, S.: Evidence that Multiple Agents Facilitate Greater Learning. International Artificial Intelligence in Education (AI-ED) Conference. Sydney (2003)
4. Brown, P., Levinson, S.C.: Politeness: Some universals in language use. Cambridge University Press, New York (1987)
5. Cassell, J., Bickmore, T.: Negotiated Collusion: Modeling Social Language and its Relationship Effects in Intelligent Agents. User Modeling and User-Adapted Interaction, 13, 1-2 (2003) 89 – 132
6. Cooper B.: Care – Making the affective leap: More than a concerned interest in a learner's cognitive abilities. International Journal of Artificial Intelligence in Education, 13, 1 (2003)
7. De Vicente, A., Pain, H.: Informing the detection of the students' motivatonal state: An empirical study. In: S.A. Cerri, G. Gouardères, F. Paraguaçu (Eds.): Intelligent Tutoring Systems. Springer, Berlin (2002) 933-943
8. Del Soldato, T., du Boulay, B.: Implementation of motivational tactics in tutoring systems. Journal of Artificial Intelligence in Education, 6, 4 (1995) 337-378
9. Dessouky, M.M., Verma, S., Bailey, D., Rickel, J.: A methodology for developing a Web-based factory simulator for manufacturing education. IEE Transactions 33 (2001) 167-180
10. Heylen, D., Nijholt, A., op den Akker, R., Vissers, M.: Socially intelligent tutor agents. Social Intelligence Design Workshop (2003)
11. Johnson, W.L.: Interaction tactics for socially intelligent pedagogical agents. Int'l Conf. on Intelligent User Interfaces. ACM Press, New York (2003) 251-253
12. Johnson, W.L., Rizzo, P., Bosma W., Kole S., Ghijsen M., Welbergen H.: Generating Socially Appropriate Tutorial Dialog. In: Proceedings of the Workshop on Affective Dialogue Systems (ADS04). Springer, Berlin (2004)
13. Kort B., Reilly R., Picard R.W.: An Affective Model of Interplay between Emotions and Learning: Reengineering Educational Pedagogy – Building a Learning Companion. In: ICALT (2001)
14. Lazarus, R.S.: Emotion and adaptation. Oxford University Press, New York (1991)
15. Lepper, M.R., Woolverton, M., Mumme, D., Gurtner, J.: Motivational techniques of expert human tutors: Lessons for the design of computer-based tutors. In: S.P. Lajoie, S.J. Derry (Eds.): Computers as cognitive tools. LEA, Hillsdale, NJ (1993) 75-105
16. Lester, J. C., Converse, S. A., Kahler, S. E., Barlow, S. T., Stone, B. A., Bhogal, R. S.: The persona effect: Affective impact of animated pedagogical agents. In: CHI '97. (1997) 359-366
17. Miller C. (ed.): Etiquette for Human-Computer Work. Papers from the AAAI Fall Symposium. AAAI Technical Report FS-02-02 (2002)
18. Pilkington, R.M.: Analysing educational discourse: The DISCOUNT scheme. Technical report 99/2, Computer-Based Learning Unit, University of Leeds (1999)
19. Porayska-Pomsta, K.: Influence of Situational Context on Language Production. Ph.D. thesis. University of Edinburgh (2004)
20. Reeves, B. ,Nass, C.: The media equation. Cambridge University Press, New York (1996)
21. Sansone, C., Harackiewicz, J.M.: Intrinsic and extrinsic motivation: The search for optimal motivation and performance. Academic Press, San Diego (2000)
22. Zhou X., Conati C.: Inferring User Goals from Personality and Behavior in a Causal Model of User Affect. In: Proceedings of IUI 2003 (2003).

Providing Cognitive and Affective Scaffolding Through Teaching Strategies: Applying Linguistic Politeness to the Educational Context

Kaśka Porayska-Pomsta and Helen Pain

Edinburgh University
ICCS/HCRC
2, Buccleuch Place, Edinburgh EH8 9LW, United Kingdom
{kaska, helen} @inf.ed.ac.uk

Abstract. Providing students with cognitive and affective support is generally recognised as important to their successful learning. There is an intuitive recognition of the two types of support being related, but little research explains how such a relationship may be manifested in teaching strategies, or what conditions tutors' strategic choices in relation to those two types of support. Research on politeness provides plausible answers to those questions. In this paper we present a model of teachers selecting corrective feedback based on the politeness notion of face. We adapt the existing definition of face to the educational genre and we demonstrate how it can be used to relate cognitive and affective scaffolding and to model the selection of teaching strategies given specific contexts.

1 Introduction

Teaching strategies are teachers' primary tool for controlling the flow of a lesson and the flow of the student's progress. Traditionally a teaching strategy is associated with a method for teaching a particular topic, with its nature being dictated either by the content taught, the student's cognitive needs and abilities, or both. For example, the content may dictate that the strategy of presenting a particular problem by analogy is better than a strategy, which simply describes it. On the other hand, a student's current cognitive demands may indicate that a problem decomposition strategy may be more advantageous to him than prompting. The relevant literature (e.g., [2]; [7]) reveals that depending on the task and the student, on average, a teacher may have to choose between at least eight different high level strategies, each of which may provide her with as many more sub-strategies. A teacher needs to discriminate between the available strategies and, for each feedback move, to choose the one that brings the most significant educational benefits. Unfortunately, as McArthur *et al.* [7] point out, teaching strategies constitute the aspect of teaching, which is the least developed and understood to date. This may be due to the general lack of understanding of the con

J.C. Lester et al. (Eds.): ITS 2004, LNCS 3220, pp. 77–86, 2004.

ditions under which particular strategies may be used, and of the effects that their use has on student's learning.

Most of the catalogued strategies are aimed at remedying students' misconceptions through corrective feedback of a sort, which structures the content appropriately or gives at least part of the answer away (*cognitive scaffolding*). However, it is recognised in education that the success of cognitive development of students also depends on the support that the teacher provides with respect to their emotional needs (e.g. [4]). Several attempts to define a list of *affective scaffolding* strategies have been made to date. Malone and Lepper [5] propose that as well as having purely content-oriented pedagogical goals, teachers also have motivational goals such as to challenge the student, to arouse his curiosity, and to support his sense of self-control or self-confidence. Clearly, certain of these motivational goals (challenge/curiosity support) are strongly related to both providing the student with cognitive scaffolding (e.g., appropriate level of difficulty, suitable representation of a problem to be solved by the student, goals of the task, etc.), and with affective scaffolding (e.g., suitable level of challenge should allow the student to solve the problem independently of the teacher, resulting in the student's sense of accomplishment and a raised level of self-esteem).

Despite useful progress being made with respect to defining what constitutes a good teaching strategy and despite there being a number of catalogues of teaching strategies, there are still no systematic accounts of: (1) the relationship between cognitive and affective type of support, (2) the conditions under which given strategies may be used in terms of providing the student with both cognitive and affective scaffolding most effectively, or (3) the way in which the two types of support are manifested in teachers' concrete actions. Natural language is widely recognised as a powerful means for delivering the appropriate guidance and affective support to the student: in this paper we take it as the basis for explaining the nature of and the relationship between the cognitive and the affective scaffolding. Based on dialogue analysis, we relate these two types of support to concrete strategies that tutors tend to use in student corrective situations, and we specify the contextual conditions under which these strategies may be used successfully. We present a model of teachers' selecting corrective feedback and show how the cognitive and the affective nature of instruction can be consolidated in terms of language general communicative strategies as accounted for in research on linguistic politeness.

2 Language Theoretical Basis for Defining and Choosing Strategies

In human-human educational interactions appropriate use of natural language seems to be the most common means used for guiding the student cognitively and for providing him with affective support (e.g., [3]). With respect to affective support, the usefulness of natural language is especially apparent in student corrective situations in which the tutor needs to reject or partly reject the student's erroneous action. In such situations the tutor is often unable to provide fully positive feedback such as *"Well done!"* or *"Good!"* without being untrue to her assessment of the student's action; such positive feedback is typically reserved for praising the student for what he did correctly. Instead, as Fox [3] observes, tutors use indirect language (e.g., *"Why don't you try again?"* or *"Okay"* said in a hesitating manner) to convey to the student in as motivating a way as possible that his answer was problematic, while leading him to the desired cognitive goals. Through appropriate use of indirect language experienced tutors maintain a necessary balance between allowing students as much learning initiative as possible while giving them enough guidance and encouragement to prevent their frustration. Tutors adjust their language according to what they think are the current cognitive and psychological needs of their students, in order to achieve specific communicative and pedagogical goals, i.e. they choose language in a highly strategic way based on the current socio-situational settings.

Strategic language use based on social interactions is a primary notion in research on linguistic politeness. In particular, Brown and Levinson's theory [1], henceforth B&L, provides many valuable insights as to the way in which the social and the emotional aspects of participants in an interaction affect communication in general. In this theory the cognitive and the affective states of the participants, and their ability to recognise those states accurately, are inherently linked to the success of communication. According to B&L every social interaction involves face – a psychological dimension that applies to all members of society. Face is a person's self-image, which can be characterised by two dimensions:

1. Negative Face: a need for freedom of action and freedom from imposition, i.e., a desire for *autonomy*
2. Positive Face: a need to be approved of by others, i.e., the need for *approval.*

In addition to face, all members of society are equipped with an ability to behave in a rational way. The public self-image regulates all speakers' linguistic actions at all times. Speakers choose their language to minimise the threat to their own and to others' face, i.e., they engage in *facework.* The ability of speakers to behave rationally enables them to assess the extent of the potential threat of their intended actions and to accommodate (in various degrees) for others' face while achieving their own goals and face needs. Every community provides its members with a set of rules (conventions) which define means for achieving their goals in a socially and culturally acceptable, i.e., polite, manner. In terms of language, these conventions are manifested in concrete *communicative strategies* that are available to speakers.

B&L propose four main strategies (Fig. 1) which represent the social conventions that speakers use to make appropriate linguistic choices: the *On-record, bald* (e.g. to a perfect stranger: *"Give me your money!"*), the *On-record, redressive* (e.g. To a friend: *"Look, I know you're broke right now, but could you lend me some money, please?"*) the *Off-record* (e.g. To a friend: *"I can't believe it! I forgot my wallet at home"*) and the *Don't do face threatening action* (FTA) strategies. Each strategy leads to a number of different sub-strategies and their prototypical surface form realisations.

The appropriateness of a communicative strategy for achieving a particular speaker goal is determined along the two dimensions of face. According to B&L, speakers tend to choose the strategies and consequently their language based on three variables: (1) the social distance between them and the hearer, (2) the power that the hearer has over them, and (3) a ranking of imposition for the act that they want to commit. Speakers establish the values of those variables based on the current situation and the cultural conventions under which a given social interaction takes place. For example, power may depend on the interlocutors' status or their access to goods or information; distance depends on the degree of familiarity between the parties involved, while rank of imposition typically reflects social and cultural conventions of a given speech community, which ranks different acts with respect to how much they interfere with people's need for autonomy and approval. A speaker's ability to assess the situation with respect to a hearer's social, cultural and emotional needs constitutes a crucial facet of his social and linguistic competence.

3 Teaching Strategies Viewed as Communicative Strategies

Intuitively, in education, the two dimensions of face seem to play an important role in guiding teachers in their selection of strategies. In particular, in situations which require the teacher to correct her student, i.e., to perform a potentially face threatening action, the teacher's awareness and her will to find the means to accommodate for the student's desire for autonomy and approval seem essential to the pedagogical success of her actions. A teacher's obligation vis à vis the student is to promote his cognitive progress. As many researchers currently accept, such progress is achieved best by having the student recognise that he made an error and by allowing him the initiative to find the correct solution. (e.g., [2]). This means that teachers should avoid giving the answers to students. Thus, the need to provide the student with autonomy of action seems to be a well recognised aspect of good teaching. However, cognitive progress is said to be facilitated also by avoiding any form of demotivation (e.g., [4]). This means that teachers should avoid criticising (or disapproving of) students' actions in a *point blank* manner, i.e. in B&L's terms they ought to use Off-record strategies. As with autonomy, the notion of approval seems to constitute an integral part of good teaching. This suggests that, in line with the communicative strategies referred by B&L in the language-general context, teaching strategies can be defined along the two dimensions of face: teaching strategies may be viewed as a specialised form of communicative strategies.

To date, there has been relatively little effort made towards relating the theory of linguistic politeness to teachers' strategic language use. The most prominent attempt is that by Person *et al.* [7] in which they analyse tutorial dialogues to assess whether or not facework impacts the effectiveness of student's learning. They confirm that, just as speakers in normal conversations, tutors also engage in facework during tutoring. The resulting language varies in terms of the degree of indirectness of the communicated messages, with a given degree of indirectness being dependent on the level of politeness that the tutor deems necessary in a particular situation and with respect to a particular student. For example, students who are not very confident may need to be informed about the problems in their answers more indirectly than students who are fairly self-satisfied. However, the overall conclusions of Person's analysis do not bode well for the role of politeness in tutoring which, they claim, may inhibit a tutor's ability to give adequately informative feedback to students as a way of avoiding face threat. In turn, vagueness of the tutor's feedback may lead to the student's confusion and lack of progress.

Although valuable in many respects, Person *et al.*'s analysis is problematic in that it assumes that tutorial interactions belong to the genre of normal conversation for which B&L's model was developed. However, B&L's theory is not entirely applicable to teaching in that language produced in tutoring circumstances is governed by different conventions than that of normal conversations [8]. These differences impact both the type of contextual information that is relevant to making linguistic choices and the nature of the strategies. With respect to the strategies, teachers do not tend to offer gifts or information as a way of fulfilling their students' face needs, nor do they tend to apologise for requesting information from them; their questions are typically asked not to gain information in the conventional sense, but to test the students' knowledge, to highlight problematic aspects of his reasoning, to prompt or to hint. Similarly, instructions and commands are not typically perceived by teachers as out of the ordinary in the teaching circumstances. While some of B&L's strategies simply do not apply to educational contexts, others require a more detailed specification or complete redefinition. With respect to the contextual information used to guide the selection of the strategies, power and distance seem relatively constant in the educational, student-corrective genre, rendering the rank of imposition the only immediately contextual variable relevant to teachers' corrective actions [13].

4 The Cognitive and the Affective as the Two Dimensions of Face

In order to explore the relationship between the Positive and the Negative face dimensions, and the cognitive and the affective aspects of instruction, in terms of a formal model, and given the observation that the language of education is governed by different conventions than that of normal conversation, it is necessary to (1) define face and facework for an educational context; (2) determine a system of strategies representative of the linguistic domain under investigation; (3) define the strategies included in our model in terms of face. Furthermore it is necessary to identify the contextual variables which affect teachers' linguistic choices and to relate them to the notion of face.

4.1 Defining Face for Tutorial Interactions

We analysed two sets of human-human tutorial and classroom dialogues: one in the domain of basic electricity and electronics (BEE) and one in the domain of literary analysis. In line with Person *et al.*'s analysis, we observed that facework plays a crucial role in education: teachers tend to employ linguistic indirectness so as not to threaten the student's face. However, we found B&L's definitions of the face dimensions not to be precise enough to explain the nature of face and facework in educational circumstances. Our dialogue analysis confirms other researchers' suggestions that indirect use of language by teachers results from their attempt to allow their students as much freedom of initiative as possible (pedagogical/cognitive considerations) while making sure that they do not flounder and become demotivated (motivational concerns) [4]. Specifically, we found that all of teachers' corrective feedback can be interpreted in terms of both differing amount of *content specificity*, that is, how specific and how structured the tutor's feedback is with respect to the answer sought from the student (compare: *"No, that's incorrect"* with *"Well, if you put the light bulb in the oven then it will get a lot of heat, but will it light up?"*), and *illocutionary specificity,* that is, how explicitly accepting or rejecting the tutor's feedback is (compare: *"No that's incorrect"* with *"Well, why don't you try again?"*).

Based on these observations we define the Negative and the Positive face directly in terms of:

- <u>Autonomy</u>: letting the student do as much of the work as possible (determination of the appropriate level of content specificity and accommodation for the student's cognitive needs)
- <u>Approval</u>: providing the student with as positive feedback as possible (determination of the appropriate level of illocutionary specificity and accommodation for the student's affective needs).

The less information the teacher gives to the student, the more autonomy she gives him and vice versa. The more explicit the references to the student's good traits, his prior or current achievements or the correctness of his answer, the more approval the teacher gives to the student. However, if the teacher supports the student's reasoning without giving away too much of the answer, she can be said also to approve of the student to an extent. Thus the level of approval given by the tutor can be affected by the amount of autonomy given and vice versa, which suggests that the two dimensions are not fully independent from each other. It can be further inferred from this that cognitive and affective support, as provided through teachers' language, are also dependent of each other.

4.2 Determining the System of Strategies and Relating Them to Face

The tightened definitions of the face dimensions allowed us to identify the student corrective strategies used by tutors and teachers in our dialogues, and to characterise them in terms of the *degree* to which each accommodates for the student's need for autonomy and approval (henceforth <Aut, App>). In defining the system of strategies representative of our data, first we identified those of B&L strategies which seem to apply to the educational settings. We then identified other strategies used in the dialogues, whenever possible we related them to the teaching strategies proposed by other researchers, and combined them with those proposed by B&L. The resulting strategic system differs in a number of respects from that of B&L. Whilst B&L's system proposes a clear separation between those strategies which address Negative and Positive face, in our model all strategies are characterised in terms of the two face dimensions. In B&L's model the selection of a strategy was based only on one numeric value – the result of summing the three social variables. In our model two values are used in such a selection: one referring to the way in which a given strategy addresses a student's need for autonomy and another to the way in which the strategy addresses a student's need for approval.

Although we retain B&L's high-level distinction between On-record, Off-record and Don't do FTA strategies, the lower level strategies refer explicitly to both the pedagogical goals of tutors' corrective actions as encapsulated in our definition of autonomy, and to the affective goals as expressed in our definition of approval. We split the strategies into two types: the main strategies which are used to express the main message of the corrective act, i.e., the teacher's rejection of the student's previous answer, and the auxiliary strategies which are used primarily to express redress. Although both types of strategies affect both face dimensions, the auxiliary strategies tend to increase the overall level of approval given to the student. For example one of the main on-record strategies, `give complete answer away` (e.g. *"The answer is..."*), which is characterised by no autonomy and lack of explicit approval, and thus as being quite threatening to the student's face, can combine with the auxiliary strategy `state FTA as a general rule` (e.g. *"We are running out of time, so I will tell you the answer"*) to reduce the overall face threat. Unlike in B&L's model in which the strategies are rigidly assigned to a particular type of facework, in our approach the split between the strategies provides for a more flexible generative model which reflects the way in which teachers tend to provide corrective feedback: in a single act a teacher often makes use of several different strategies simultaneously.

The assignment of the <Aut, App> values, each being anything between 0 and 1, to the individual strategies is done relative to other strategies in our system. For example when contrasting a strategy such as `give complete answer away` (e.g. *"The answer is..."*) with a strategy such as `use direct hinting` (e.g. *"That's one way, but there is a better way to do this"*) we assessed the first strategy as giving less autonomy and less approval to the student than the second strategy. On the other hand, when compared with a third strategy such as `request self-explanation` (e.g., *"Why?"*), the hinting strategy seems to give less autonomy, but more approval. For each strategy we compiled a list of its possible surface realisations and we also ordered them according to the degrees of <Aut, App> that they seem to express.

5 The Conditions for Selecting Strategies

To determine the contextual variables affecting teachers' feedback we compiled the following list of situational factors based on the relevant educational literature, our dialogue analysis and informal interviews with a number of teachers:

Student-oriented factors
- student confidence
- student interest (bored/motivated)

Lesson-oriented factors
- time left for lesson

- amount of material left to be covered
- difficulty of material
- importance of material

Performance-oriented factors

- correctness of student's previous answer(s)
- ability of student

In order to (1) validate the situational factors, (2) relate the individual factors to the <Aut, App> dimensions and (3) to enable us to calculate the degree of <Aut, App> based on specific situations, we ran a study in which teachers were given situations as characterised by combinations of the factors and their values. The factor-values in our current model are binary, e.g., the possible values of the factor student's confidence are confident or not confident. For each combination, the teachers were asked to rate each factor-value according to how important they thought it to be in affecting the form of their feedback. The results of the study were used to inform the design and the implementation of the situational component. Specifically, the Principle Component Analysis enabled the grouping of factors, while teachers' written comments and post-hoc interviews allowed us to determine their possible relation to the <Aut, App> dimensions. We also derived the means from teachers' ratings for each situation given in the study. We used these means to represent the relative importance (salience) of each factor-value in a given combination. Based on the groupings of factors along with their salience we derived rules, which (1) combine situational factor-values, (2) relate them to either guidance or approval goals in terms of which the two face dimensions are defined, (3) calculate <Aut, App>. For example, the effect of the rule with preconditions *little time left* and *high student's ability* is a numerically expressed degree of guidance, calculated using a weighted means function from the salience of the two contributing factors.

6 Implementation of the Model

We implemented the model in a system, shown in figure 1. The surface forms coded for <Aut, App> values are stored in a case base (CB2) which provides different feedback alternatives using a standard Case Based Reasoning technique. A Bayesian network (BN) combines evidence from the factors to compute values for <Aut, App> for every situational input. The structure of the network reflects the relationship of factors as determined by the study with teachers. The individual nodes in the network are populated with the conditional probabilities calculated using the types of rules described above. To generate feedback recommendations, the system expects an input in the form of factor-values. The factor-values are interpreted by the Pre-processing unit (PPU) as evidence required by the BN. The evidence consists of salience of each factor-value in the input. It is either retrieved directly from the Case Base 1 (CB1) which stores all the situations seen and ranked by the teachers in the study or, if there is no situation in the CB1 that matches the input, it is calculated for each factor-value from the mean salience of three existing nearest matching situations using the K-nearest neighbour algorithm (KNN1). When evidence is set, the BN calculates <Aut, App>. These are passed to the linguistic component. KNN2 finds N closest matching pairs of <Aut, App> (N being specified by the user) which are associated with specific linguistic alternatives stored in CB2, and which constitute the output of the system.

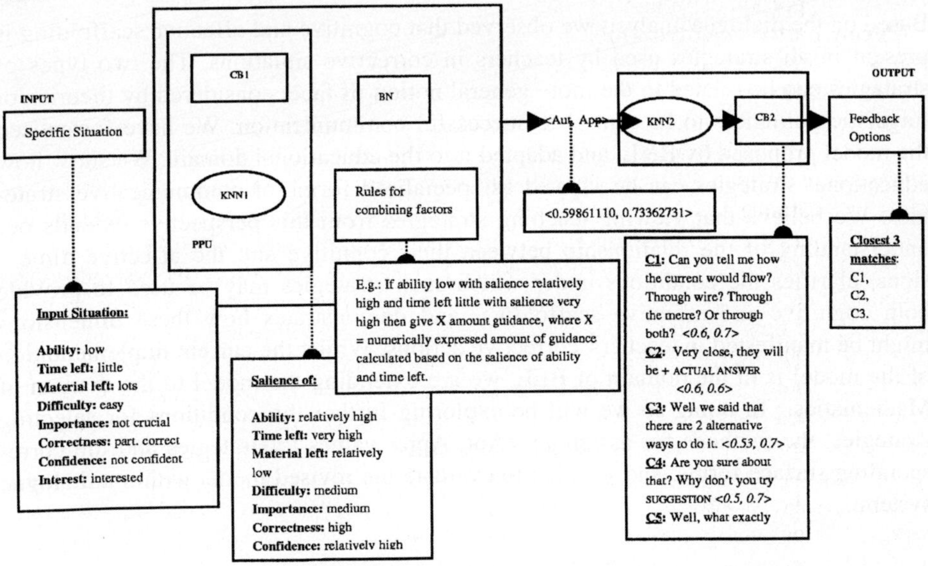

Fig. 1. The structure of the system with an example.

7 Evaluation of the Model

The model was evaluated by four experienced BEE tutors. Each tutor was presented with twenty different situations in the form of short dialogues between a student and a tutor. Each interaction ended with either incorrect or partially correct student answer. For each situation, the participants were provided with three possible tutor responses to the student's answer and were asked to rate each of them on a scale from 1 to 5 according to how appropriate they thought the response was in a given situation. They were asked to pay special attention to the manner in which each response attempted to correct the student. The three types of responses rated included: a response that a human gave, the system's preferred response, and a response that the system was less likely to recommend for the same situation (the less preferred response).

A t-test was performed to determine any significant differences between the three types of responses. The analysis revealed a significant difference between human responses and the system's less preferred responses ($t(19) = 4.40$, $p < 0.001$), as well as a significant difference between the system's preferred and the system's less preferred responses ($t(19) = 2.72$, $p = 0.013$). However, there was no significant difference between the ratings of the human responses and the system's preferred responses, ($t(19)=1.99$, $p=0.61$). This preliminary evaluation suggests that the model's choices are in line with those made by a human tutor in identical situations.

8 Conclusions and Further Work

Based on the dialogue analysis we observed that cognitive and affective scaffolding is present in all strategies used by teachers in corrective situations. The two types of strategies can be related to the more general notion of face, considered by theories of linguistic politeness to be central to successful communication. We have formalised the model proposed by B&L, and adapted it to the educational domain. We show how educational strategies can be viewed as specialised forms of communicative strategies. We believe that viewing teaching strategies from this perspective extends our understanding of the relationship between their cognitive and the affective dimensions, clarifies the conditions under which such strategies may be used to provide both cognitive and affective scaffolding, and demonstrates how these dimensions might be manifested in teachers' corrective actions. Whilst the current implementation of the model is in the domain of BEE, we are extending the model to the domain of Mathematics. In doing so we will be exploring further the conditions for selecting strategies, the methods for assigning <Aut, App> values to strategies and the corresponding surface forms, and we plan to evaluate the revised model within a dialogue system.

References

1. Brown, P., and Levinson, S. (1987). *Politeness: Some Universals in Language Use*, CUP.
2. Chi, M.T. H., Siler, S. A., Jeong, H., Yamauchi, T., and Hausmann, R.G. (2001). Learning from human tutoring. *Cognitive Science Society*, **(25)**, 471-533.
3. Fox, B. (1991). Cognitive Interactional aspects of correction in tutoring. P Goodyear (eds.), *Teaching knowledge and intelligent tutoring., pp.* 149-172, Ablex, Norwood, N.J.
4. Lepper, M.R., Woolverton, M., Mumme, D. L., and Gurtner, J. (1993). *Motivational Techniques of Expert Tutors: Lessons for the Design of Computer-Based Tutors*, chapter 3, pages 75-107, LEA, NJ.
5. Malone, T. W. and Lepper, M. R. (1987). Making learning fun: a taxonomy of intrinsic motivations for learning. In R.E. Snow and M.J. Farr eds, *Aptitude, Learning and Instruction: Conative and Affective Process Analyses.*, pages 261-265, AAAI.
6. McArthur, D., Stasz, C., and Zmuidzinas, M. (1990). Tutoring techniques in algebra. *Cognition and Instruction*, **(7)**, 197-244.
7. Person, N. K., Kreuz, R. J., Zwaan, R. A., Graesser, A. C. (1995). Pragmatics and pedagogy: Conversational rules of politeness strategies may inhibit effective tutoring. *Cognition and Instruction,* **2**(13), 161-188. Lawrence Erlbaum Associates, Inc.
8. Porayska-Pomsta, K. (2003). Influence of situational context on language prduction: Modelling teachers' corrective responses. PhD thesis, Edinburgh University.

Knowledge Representation Requirements for Intelligent Tutoring Systems

Ioannis Hatzilygeroudis[1,2] and Jim Prentzas[1]

University of Patras, School of Engineering
Department of Computer Engineering & Informatics, 26500 Patras, Greece
{prentzas, ihatz}@ceid.upatras.gr
Research Academic Computer Technology Institute, P.O. Box 1122, 26110 Patras, Greece
ihatz@cti.gr

Abstract. In this paper, we make a first effort to define requirements for knowledge representation (KR) in an ITS. The requirements concern all stages of an ITS's life cycle (construction, operation and maintenance), all types of users (experts, engineers, learners) and all its modules (domain knowledge, user model, pedagogical model). We also briefly present and compare various KR formalisms used (or that could be used) in ITSs as far as the specified KR requirements are concerned. It appears that various hybrid approaches to knowledge representation can satisfy the requirements in a greater degree than that of single representations. Another finding is that there is not a hybrid formalism that can satisfy the requirements of all of the modules of an ITS, but each one individually. So, a multi-paradigm representation environment could provide a solution to requirements satisfaction.

1 Introduction

Intelligent Tutoring Systems (ITSs), either Web-based or not, form an advanced generation of Computer Aided Instruction (CAI) systems. The key feature of ITSs is their ability to provide a user-adapted presentation of the teaching material. This is mainly accomplished by using Artificial Intelligence (AI) techniques.

A crucial aspect in the development of an ITS is how related knowledge is represented and how reasoning for problem solving is accomplished. Various single knowledge representation (KR) schemes have been used in ITSs such as, symbolic rules [10], fuzzy logic [7], Bayesian networks [9], case-based reasoning [3]. Also, hybrid representations such as, neuro-symbolic [5], [8] and neuro-fuzzy [6], have been recently used. Hybrid approaches integrate two or more single formalisms and are an emerging type of knowledge representation in ITSs in an effort to enhance the representational and reasoning capabilities of them.

An aspect that has not received much attention yet is defining requirements for knowledge representation in ITSs. The definition of such requirements is important, since it can assist in the selection of the KR formalism(s) to be employed by an ITS.

J.C. Lester et al. (Eds.): ITS 2004, LNCS 3220, pp. 87–97, 2004.

It is desirable that a knowledge representation formalism satisfy most, if not all, of them.

In this paper, we present a first effort to specify a number of requirements that a KR&R formalism, which is going to be used in an ITS, should meet in order to be adequate. The requirements refer to all stages of an ITS's life cycle (construction, operation and maintenance). They are also based on all types of users involved in those phases (experts, knowledge engineers, learners) as well as on the three basic modules of an ITS (domain knowledge, user model and pedagogical model). Based on them and a comparison of various KR formalisms, we argue that hybrid formalisms satisfy those requirements in a larger degree than single formalisms, because hybrid formalisms exhibit significant improvements compared to their component formalisms. Our final argument is that only a multi-paradigm environment would be adequate for the development of an ITS.

The paper is organized as follows. Section 2 specifies the KR requirements. Section 3 presents a number of KR formalisms and how they satisfy the requirements. Section 4 makes a comparison of the KR formalisms and, finally, Section 5 concludes.

2 KR Requirements for ITSs

Like other knowledge-based systems, we distinguish three main phases in the life-cycle of an ITS, the *construction phase*, the *operation phase* and the *maintenance phase*. The main difference is that an ITS requires a great deal of feedback with the users and iteration between phases. Three types of users are involved in those phases: *domain experts*, *knowledge engineers* (both mainly involved in the construction and maintenance phases) and *learners* (mainly involved in the operation phase). Each type of user has different requirements from the KR formalism(s) to be used.

On the other hand, the system itself imposes a number of requirements to the KR formalism. An ITS consists of three main modules: (a) the *domain knowledge*, which contains the teaching content and information about the subject to be taught, (b) the *user model*, which records information concerning the user, and (c) the *pedagogical model*, which encompasses knowledge regarding various pedagogical decisions. Each component imposes different KR requirements.

2.1 Users Requirements

2.1.1 Domain Expert

The domain expert provides knowledge concerning the application domain. He/she is a person that has worked in the application field for an ample time period and knows in-depth the possible problems, the way of dealing with them as well as various practices obtained through his/her experience. In ITSs, the domain experts are mainly the tutors. Tutors are interested in testing teaching theories in practice to demonstrate their usability. They consider that the effectiveness of the theories in assisting students to learn the teaching subject is of extreme importance. Tutors are highly involved in the construction and maintenance stages. However, in most cases, their relation to AI is rather superficial. Sometimes even their experience in computers is low. This may potentially make them restrained in their interaction with the knowledge engineer. Furthermore, the teaching theories they want to incorporate within the system can be rather difficult to express.

So, it is evident that one main requirement that tutors impose on the knowledge representation formalism is *naturalness* of representation. Naturalness facilitates interaction with the knowledge engineer and helps the tutor in overcoming his/her possible restraints with AI and computers in general. In addition, it assists the tutor in proposing updates to the existing knowledge. The more natural the knowledge representation formalism, the better understanding of the existing knowledge and communication with the knowledge engineer.

Also, checking knowledge during the knowledge acquisition process is a tedious task. Capability of *providing explanations* is quite helpful for the expert. So, this is another requirement. On the other hand, if the knowledge base can be easily updated, then existing items of the acquired knowledge can be easily removed or updated and new items can be easily inserted. This demands *ease of update*.

2.1.2 Knowledge Engineer

The knowledge engineer manages the development of the ITS and directs its various phases. The main tasks of the knowledge engineer are to select the implementation tools, to acquire knowledge from the domain expert and/or other knowledge sources and to effectively represent the acquired knowledge. He/she is the one who decides on how expert knowledge is to be represented. He/she chooses or designs the knowledge representation formalism to be employed. Finally, he/she is who maintains the produced knowledge base.

Obviously, naturalness is again a basic requirement. The more natural the KR formalism, the easier it will be for the knowledge engineer to translate expert knowledge. Furthermore, tutors, during construction, may frequently change part (small or big) of the knowledge imparted to the knowledge engineer. Also, even if the system's operation is satisfactory, changes and updates of the incorporated expert knowledge may be required.

Additionally, the KR formalism should facilitate the knowledge acquisition process. This can be achieved if the KR formalism allows acquiring knowledge from alternative (to experts) sources, such as databases of empirical data or past cases, in an automated or semi-automated way. In this way, more existing knowledge sources can be exploited and the knowledge acquisition process will not be hindered by the unavailability of a type of source (e.g. experts). So, *ease of knowledge acquisition* is another requirement.

Usually, in developing knowledge-based systems, a prototype is constructed before the final system. Testing the prototype can call for arduous efforts. As far as the KR formalism is concerned, two important factors are the inference engine performance and the capability of providing explanations. If the inference engine associated with the KR formalism is efficient, the time spent by the knowledge engineer is reduced. Also, the possibility of an explanation mechanism associated with the KR formalism is important, because explanations justifying how conclusions were reached can be produced. This feature can assist in the location of deficiencies in the knowledge base. Hence, two other requirements are *efficient inferences* and *explanation facility*.

2.1.3 End-User

An end-user (learner) is the one who uses the system in its operation stage. He/she imposes constraints regarding the user-interface and the time performance of the system. The basic requirement for KR, from the point of view of end-users, concerns time efficiency. ITSs are highly interactive knowledge-based systems requiring time-efficient responses to the users' actions. The decisions an ITS makes during a training session are based on the conclusions reached by the inference engine associated with the knowledge representation formalism. The faster the conclusions can be reached, the faster will the system interact with the user. Therefore, the time performance of an ITS significantly depends on the time-efficiency of the inference engine. In case of Web-based ITSs, time performance is even more crucial since the Web imposes additional time constraints. The server hosting the ITS may be accessed by a significant number of users. Some of them may even possess a low communication bandwidth. The server must respond as fast as possible. Besides efficiency, the inference engine should also be able to *reach conclusions from partially known inputs*. It is very common that, during a learning session, certain parameters may be unknown. However, the system should be able to make inferences and reach conclusion, no matter whether all or some of the inputs are known.

2.2 System Requirements

2.2.1 Domain Knowledge

The domain knowledge module contains knowledge regarding the subject to be taught as well as the actual teaching content. It usually consists of two parts: (a) knowledge concepts and (b) course units. Knowledge concepts refer to the basic entities/concepts that constitute the subject to be taught. Furthermore, various concepts are related among them, e.g. by the prerequisite relation, specialization relation etc. Finally, they are associated with course units. Course units constitute the teaching content.

Usually, concepts are organized in a type of structure. So, it is evident that a requirement that comes out of domain knowledge is the capability of the KR formalism to be able to naturally represent *structural and relational knowledge*.

2.2.2 User Model

The user model records information about the learner's knowledge state and traits. This information is vital for the system to be able to adapt to the user's needs. The process of inferring a user model from observable behavior is called diagnosis, because it is much like the medical task of inferring a hidden physiological state from observable signs. There are many possible user characteristics that can be recorded in the user model. One of them is the knowledge that he/she has learned. In this case, diagnosis refers to evaluation of learner's knowledge level. Other characteristics may be 'learning ability' and 'concentration'. Diagnosis in those cases means estimation of the learning ability and the concentration of the learner, based on his/her behavior while interacting with the system. Measurement and interpretation of such user behavior is quite uncertain.

There is not a clear process for evaluating learner's characteristics. Also, there is no a clear-cut between various levels (values) of the characteristics (e.g. between 'low' and 'medium' concentration). It is quite clear that a representation and reasoning formalism for the user model should be able to deal with *uncertain and vague knowledge*. Also, *heuristic (rule of thumb) knowledge* is required to make evaluations.

Table 1. Users Requirements

USERS REQUIREMENTS		
Expert	Engineer	Learner
• *naturalness* • *ease of update*	• *naturalness* • *ease of update* • *multi-source knowledge acquisition* • *explanation facility*	• *efficient inferences* • *partial input inferences*

Table 2. System Requirements

SYSTEM REQUIREMENTS		
Domain Knowledge	User Model	Pedagogical Model
• *structural knowledge* • *relational knowledge*	• *uncertain knowledge* • *heuristic knowledge*	• *heuristic knowledge*

2.2.3 Pedagogical Model

The pedagogical model represents the teaching process. It provides the knowledge infrastructure in order to tailor the presentation of teaching the content according to the information recorded in the user model. The pedagogical model of a 'classical' ITS mainly performs the following tasks: (a) course planning (or knowledge sequencing), (b) teaching method selection and (c) learning content selection. The main task in (a) is planning, that is selecting and appropriately ordering the concepts to be taught. The main task involved in (b) and (c) is also selection, e.g. how a teaching method is selected based on the learner's state and the learning goal. This is a reasoning process whose resulting conclusion depends on the logical combinations of the values of the user model characteristics, which reminds of a rule-type of knowledge or generally of heuristic knowledge. The above analysis of the requirements of knowledge representation for an ITS is depicted in Tables 1 and 2.

3 Knowledge Representation Formalisms

In this section, we investigate to what extent various well-known knowledge representation formalisms satisfy the requirements imposed by the developers, the users and the components of an ITS. We distinguish between single and hybrid KR formalisms.

3.1 Single Formalisms

Semantic nets and their descendants (*frames* or *schemata*) represent knowledge in the form of a graph (or a hierarchy). Nodes in the graph represent concepts and edges represent relations between concepts. Nodes in a hierarchy also represent concepts, but they have internal structure describing concepts via sets of attributes. They are very natural and well suited for representing structural and relational knowledge. They can also make efficient inferences for small to medium graphs (hierarchies). However, it is difficult to represent heuristic knowledge, uncertain knowledge and make inferences from partial inputs. Also explanations knowledge updates are difficult.

Symbolic rules (of prepositional type) represent knowledge in the form of if-then rules. They satisfy a number of the requirements. Symbolic rules are natural since one can easily comprehend the encompassed knowledge and follow the inference steps. Due to their modularity, updates such as removing existing rules or inserting new rules are easy to make. Explanations of conclusions are straightforward and of various types. Heuristic knowledge representation is feasible and procedural knowledge can be represented in their conclusions too. The inference process may be not very efficient, when there is a large number of rules and multiple paths are to be followed. Knowledge acquisition is one of their major drawbacks. Also, conclusions cannot be reached if some of the inputs are unknown. Finally, they cannot represent uncertain knowledge and are not suitable for representing structural and relational knowledge.

Fuzzy logic is used to represent imprecise and fuzzy terms. Sets of *fuzzy rules* are used to infer conclusions based on input data. Fuzzy rules outperform symbolic rules and other formalisms in representing uncertainty. However, fuzzy rules are not as natural as symbolic rules, because the concepts contained in them are associated with membership functions. Furthermore, for the same reason, compared to symbolic rules, they have great difficulties in making updates, providing explanations and acquiring knowledge (e.g. for specifying membership functions). Inference is more complicated and less natural than symbolic rule-based reasoning, but its overall performance is not worse due, because a fuzzy rule can replace more than one symbolic rule. Explanations are feasible, but not all reasoning steps can be explained. Finally, fuzzy rules are much like symbolic rules as to structural, heuristic and relational knowledge as well as the ability to perform partial input inferences.

Case-based representations store a large set of previous cases with their solutions and use them whenever a similar new case has to be dealt with. Case-based representation satisfies several requirements. Cases are usually easy to obtain in most domains and unlike other formalisms case acquisition can also take place during the system's operation further enhancing the knowledge base. Cases are natural since their knowledge is quite comprehensible by humans. Explanations cannot be easily provided in most situations, due to the complicated numeric similarity functions. Conclusions can be reached even if some of the inputs are not known, through similarity to stored cases. Updates can be made easier compared to other formalisms, since no changes need to be made in preexisting knowledge. However, inference efficiency is not always the desirable when the case library becomes very large. Finally, cases are not suitable for representing structural, uncertain and heuristic knowledge.

Neural networks represent a totally different approach to AI, known as connectionism. Neural networks can easily obtain knowledge from training examples, which are usually available in abundance for most application domains. Neural networks are very efficient in producing conclusions and can reach conclusions based on partially known inputs due to their generalization ability. On the other hand, neural networks lack naturalness. The encompassed knowledge is in most cases incomprehensible and explanations for the reached conclusions cannot be provided. It is also difficult to make updates to specific parts of the network. The neural network is not decomposable and any changes affect the whole network. Neural networks do not possess inherent mechanisms for representing structural, relational and uncertain knowledge. Heuristic knowledge can be represented to some degree since it can be implicitly incorporated into a trained neural network.

Belief networks (or *probabilistic nets*) are graphs, where nodes represent statistical concepts and links represent mainly causal relations between them. Each link is assigned a probability, which represents how certain is that the concept where the link departs from causes (lead to) the concept where the link arrives at. Belief nets are good at representing causal relations between concepts. Also, they can represent heuristic knowledge to some extend. Furthermore, they can represent uncertain knowledge through the probabilities and make relatively efficient inferences (via computations of probabilities propagation). However, estimation of probabilities is a difficult task, which gives great problems to the knowledge acquisition process. For the same reason, it is difficult to make updates. Also, explanations are difficult to produce, since the inference steps cannot be easily followed by humans. Furthermore, given that belief networks representation and reasoning are based on numerical computation, their naturalness is reduced.

3.2 Hybrid Formalisms

Hybrid formalisms are integrations of two or more single KR formalisms. In this section we focus on approaches belonging to the most popular categories of hybrid formalisms that is, symbolic-symbolic, neuro-symbolic, neuro-fuzzy and integrations of rule-based and case-based formalisms.

Connectionist expert systems [1] are neuro-symbolic integrations combining neural networks with expert systems. The knowledge base is a network whose nodes correspond to domain concepts. They also consist of an inference engine and an explanation mechanism. Compared to neural networks, they offer more natural representation and can provide some type of explanation. Naturalness is enhanced due to the fact that most of the nodes correspond to domain concepts. However, the additional (unknown) nodes inserted to deal with inseparability affect negatively the naturalness of the knowledge base and the provided explanations. In all other aspects, connectionist expert systems behave like neural networks.

There are various ways to integrate neural networks and fuzzy logic. We are interested in integrations that the two component representations are indistinguishable. Such integrations are the *fuzzy neural networks* and the *hybrid neuro-fuzzy representations*. Fuzzy neural networks are fuzzified neural networks, that is they retain the basic properties and architectures of neural networks and "fuzzify" some of their elements (i.e., input values, weights, activations, outputs). In a hybrid neuro-fuzzy system both fuzzy techniques and neural networks play a key role. Each does its own job in serving different functions in the system (usually knowledge is contained and applied by the connectionist part, but is described and presented by the fuzzy model). Hybrid neuro-fuzzy systems seem to satisfy KR requirements in a greater degree than fuzzy neural networks. They combine more and in a more satisfactory way the benefits of their component representations.

Another trend to hybrid knowledge representation are the *integrations of rule-based with case-based reasoning* [2]. We refer here to the approaches where rules dominate. Rules correspond to general knowledge, whereas cases correspond to specific knowledge. These hybrid approaches effectively combine the best features of rules and cases. Naturalness of the underlying components is retained. Compared to 'pure' case-based reasoning, their key advantage is the improvement in the performance of the inference engine and the ability to represent heuristic and relational knowledge. Furthermore, the synergism of rules and cases can cover up deficiencies in the rule base (improved knowledge acquisition) and also enable partial input inferences. The existence of rules in these hybrid formalisms makes updates more difficult than 'pure' case-based representations. Also explanations can be provided but not as easily as in 'pure' rule-based reasoning because inference becomes more complicated, since similarity functions are still present.

Description Logics (DLs) can be also considered as hybrid KR formalisms, since they combine aspects from frames, semantic nets and logic. They consist of two main components, the Tbox and the Abox. Tbox contains definitions of concepts and roles (i.e. their attributes), which are called terminological knowledge, whereas ABox contains logical assertions about concepts and roles, which are called assertional knowledge. DLs offer clear semantics and sound inferences. They are usually used for building and maintaining ontologies as well as for classification tasks related to ontologies. Also, DLs can be built on existing Semantic Web standards (XML, RDF, RDFS). So, they are quite suitable for representing structural and relational knowledge. Also, since they are based on logic, they can represent heuristic knowledge. Furthermore, their Tboxes can be formally updated. Their representation is natural, but not as much as that of symbolic rules. Inferences in DLs may have efficiency problems. Explanations cannot be easily provided.

Neurules are a type of hybrid rules integrating symbolic rules with neurocomputing, introduced by us [4]. The most attractive features of neurules are that they improve the performance of symbolic rules and simultaneously retain their modularity and, in a large degree, their naturalness, in contrast to other hybrid approaches. So, neurules offer a number of benefits for knowledge representation in an ITS. Apart from the above, updating a neurule base (add to or remove neurules from) is easy, due to the modularity of neurules [5]. The explanation mechanism produces natural explanations. Neurule-based inference is more efficient than symbolic rule-based reasoning and inference in other hybrid neuro-symbolic approaches. Neurules can be constructed either from symbolic rules or from empirical data enabling the exploitation of various knowledge sources [5]. In contrast to symbolic rules, neurule-based reasoning can derive conclusions from partially known inputs, due to its connectionist part.

Table 3. Comparison of KR formalisms

	USERS REQUIREMENTS						SYSTEM REQUIREMENTS			
	Naturalness	*Ease of Update*	*Efficient Inference*	*Explanations*	*Knowledge Acquisition*	*Partial input inferences*	*Structural knowledge*	*Relational knowledge*	*Uncertain knowledge*	*Heuristic knowledge*
Semantic nets/frames	√+	√-	√+	-	√	-	√+	√+	-	-
Symbolic rules	√+	√+	√	√+	√-	-	-	√-	-	√+
Fuzzy logic	√-	-	√	-	√-	-	-	√-	√+	√+
Case-based representations	√+	√+	√	√	√+	√	-	√	-	-
Belief networks	√-	-	√+	-	√-	-	√	√+	√+	√-
Neural networks	-	-	√+	-	√+	√+	-	√-	-	√-
Connectionist expert systems	√-	√-	√+	√-	√+	√+	-	√-	-	√-
Neuro-fuzzy representations	√-	-	√	-	√	√-	-	√-	√+	√
Cases and rules	√+	√	√	√	√	√	-	√	-	√
Description logics	√	√-	√-	√-	√	-	√+	√+	-	√
Neurules	√	√	√+	√+	√+	√+	-	√-	-	√+

4 Discussion

Table 3 compares the KR formalisms discussed in Section 3, as far as satisfaction of KR requirements for ITSs are concerned. Symbol '-' means 'unsatisfactory', '√-' average, '√' 'good' and '√+' 'very good'. A conclusion that can be drawn from the table is that none of the single or hybrid formalisms satisfies all the requirements for an ITS. However, some of them satisfy the requirements of the different modules of an ITS. Hybrid formalisms demonstrate improvements compared to most or all of their component formalisms. So, a solution to the representational problem of an ITS could be the use of different representation formalisms (single or hybrid) for the implementation for different ITS modules (i.e. domain knowledge, user model, pedagogical model). Then, the idea of a multi-paradigm development environment seems to be interesting. The next problem, though, is which KR paradigms should be included in such an environment.

5 Conclusions

In this paper, we make a first effort to define requirements for KR in an ITS. The requirements concern all stages of an ITS's life cycle (construction, operation and maintenance), all types of users (experts, engineers, kearners) and all its modules (domain knowledge, user model, pedagogical model). According to our knowledge, such requirements have not been defined yet in the ITS literature. However, we consider them of great importance as they can assist in choosing the KR formalisms for representing knowledge in the components of an ITS.

From our analysis, it appears that various hybrid approaches to knowledge representation can satisfy the requirements in a greater degree than that of single representations. So, we believe that use of hybrid KR approaches in ITSs can become a popular research trend, although, till now, only a few efforts exist. Another finding is that there is not a hybrid formalism that can satisfy the requirements of all of the modules of an ITS. So, a multi-paradigm representation could provide a solution.

We feel that our research needs to be further completed by getting more detailed and more specific to ITSs nature. What is further needed is a more in-depth analysis of the three modules of an ITS. Also, a more fine-grained comparison of the KR formalisms may be required. These are the main concerns of our future work.

Acknowledgements. This work was supported by the Research Committee of the University of Patras, Greece, Program "Karatheodoris", project No 2788.

References

1. Gallant, S.I.: Neural Network Learning and Expert Systems. MIT Press (1993).
2. Golding, A.R., Rosenbloom, P.S.: Improving accuracy by combining rule-based and case-based reasoning. Artificial Intelligence 87 (1996) 215-254.
3. Guin-Duclosson, N., Jean-Danbias, S., Norgy, S.: The AMBRE ILE: How to Use Case-Based Reasoning to Teach Methods. In Cerri, S.A., Gouarderes, G., Paraguacu, F. (eds.): Sixth International Conference on Intelligent Tutoring Systems. Lecture Notes in Computer Science, Vol. 2363. Springer-Verlag, Berlin (2002) 782-791.
4. Hatzilygeroudis, I., Prentzas, J.: Neurules: Improving the Performance of Symbolic Rules. International Journal on Artificial Intelligence Tools 9 (2000) 113-130.

5. Hatzilygeroudis, I., Prentzas, J.: Using a Hybrid Rule-Based Approach in Developing an Intelligent Tutoring System with Knowledge Acquisition and Update Capabilities. Journal of Expert Systems with Applications 26 (2004) 477-492.
6. Magoulas, G.D., Papanikolaou, K.A., Grigoriadou, M.: Neuro-fuzzy Synergism for Planning the Content in a Web-based Course. Informatica 25 (2001) 39-48.
7. Nkambou, R.: Managing Inference Process in Student Modeling for Intelligent Tutoring Systems. In Proceedings of the Eleventh IEEE International Conference on Tools with Artificial Intelligence. IEEE Computer Society Press (1999).
8. Prentzas, J., Hatzilygeroudis, I., Garofalakis J.: A Web-Based Intelligent Tutoring System Using Hybrid Rules as its Representational Basis. In Cerri, S.A., Gouarderes, G., Paraguacu, F. (eds.): Sixth International Conference on Intelligent Tutoring Systems. Lecture Notes in Computer Science, Vol. 2363. Springer-Verlag, Berlin (2002) 119-128.
9. Vanlehn, K., Zhendong, N.: Bayesian student modeling, user interfaces and feedback: a sensitivity analysis. International Journal of AI in Education 12 (2001) 155-184.
10. Vassileva, J.: Dynamic Course Generation on the WWW. British Journal of Educational Technologies 29 (1998) 5-14.

Coherence Compilation: Applying AIED Techniques to the Reuse of Educational TV Resources

Rosemary Luckin, Joshua Underwood, Benedict du Boulay, Joe Holmberg, and Hilary Tunley

IDEAs Laboratory, Human Centred Technology Research group,
School of Science and Technology
University of Sussex
Brighton BN1 9Q UK
rosel@sussex.ac.uk

Abstract. The HomeWork project is building an exemplar system to provide individualised experiences for individual and groups of children aged 6-7 years, their parents, teachers and classmates at school. It employs an existing set of broadcast video media and associated resources that tackle both numeracy and literacy at Key Stage 1. The system employs a learner model and a pedagogical model to identify what resource is best used with an individual child or group of children collaboratively at a particular learning point and at a particular location. The Coherence Compiler is that component of the system which is designed to impose an overall narrative coherence on the materials that any particular child is exposed to. This paper presents a high level vision of the design of the Coherence Compiler and sets its design within the overall framework of the HomeWork project and its learner and pedagogical models.

1 Introduction

The use of TV (and radio) in education has a long history — longer than the use of computers in education. But the traditions within which TV operates, such as the strong focus on narrative and the emphasis on viewer engagement, are rather different from those within which computers in education, and more particularly ITS & AIED systems operate. We can characterise ITS & AIED systems as being fundamentally concerned with individualising the experience of learners and groups of learners and supporting a range of representations and reifications of either the domain being explored or the learning process. The traditional division of the subject into student modelling, domain modelling, modelling teaching and interface issues reflects this concern with producing systems that react intelligently to the learner or group of learners using the system. Even where the system is simply a tool or a vehicle to promote collaboration (say), there will be a concern to monitor and perhaps adjust the parameters within which that collaboration takes place, if the system is to be regarded as of interest to the ITS & AIED community. One novel aspect of the HomeWork system is its concern with modelling and managing the narrative flow of the learners' experience both at the micro level within sessions and at the macro level between sessions and over extended use. This project is building an exemplar system for

J.C. Lester et al. (Eds.): ITS 2004, LNCS 3220, pp. 98–107, 2004.

children aged 6-7 years, their parents, teachers and classmates at school to tackle both numeracy and literacy at Key Stage 1. In the classroom the child will be able to work alone or as part of a group and interact both with a large interactive whiteboard and with a handheld digital slate as directed by the teacher. When the handheld slate is taken home further activities can be completed using a home TV and the slate either working alone, with their family, or with other classmates who may be co-located or at a distance in their own homes.

This paper concentrates on the narrative aspects of the HomeWork project and on the Coherence Compiler that ensures narrative coherence. We start by outlining the HomeWork project. We then give the theoretical background to the narrative work. Finally we discuss how the coherence compiler is being designed to maintain narrative coherence across different technologies in different locations despite the interactive interventions of the learners.

2 The HomeWork Project

Most homes and schools possess a TV, and many schools now also possess interactive whiteboards. TV is a technology that has been used to deliver motivating, gripping and captivating content to millions of learners of all ages. The introduction of digital interactive broadband systems that can carry information both to and from the user opens up the possibility of personalised, adaptive learning experiences. However, learners are not yet used to interacting through their TV screens, which are not appropriate when it comes to text and navigation. What is required is a learning experience designed for delivery across multiple technologies and interfaces in which the educational media are integrated into a coherent, non-linear narrative and experienced by the learner through the technological artefact that best delivers the media being used. In this way the rich television media can be viewed through the TV interface and the text and associated interactive components through the PC (slate). Our previous work has shown that young children can co-ordinate the integration of multiple interfaces and artefacts [1].ADDIN

The design challenge is how to string together bits of content (potentially from different providers) across a variety of devices (TV, tablets, paper) and locations (school and home) in such a way that enables learners to engage with the concepts of the discipline being studied (not the technology being employed or the effort of mentally linking the episodes), and to collaborate within and across locations. This requires the development of an underpinning pedagogical framework. To be effective, this framework needs to be grounded in a pedagogy that recognises that education is interactive with a multiplicity of potential participants both human and artefact. It also needs to be flexible enough to apply to a range of devices (both technological and non-technological), real educational contexts, constantly changing policy, and to the evolving future.

InADDIN [2] we identified potential points of contact between Social Constructivism and broadband learning, and proposed key actions that provide a starting point for a future design framework. In this framework we expanded the definition of Broadband to describe a concept that accommodates a wide 'bandwidth' of participants, senses, devices and contexts. This Broadband Learner Modelling (BLM) approach expands the theoretical framework previously developed for the design of a single user Interactive Learning Environment [3,4]ADDIN and a Multimedia Interactive CD-ROM [5].ADDIN

Within the BLM framework a pivotal role is played by the learner-modelling component that is used to profile each learner or group of learners and teachers. This component allows a dynamic description of the learner/s to be maintained and used to shape their interactions and collaborations. The design of the learner model is also used as a template for the design of the descriptive tags that are used to organise the educational resources at the system's disposal. These resources include multiple media (such as text, audio and video) about particular areas of the curriculum (primary maths and literacy in the instance of this grant application) as well as other learners and teachers who can offer collaborative support.

3 The Learner Model

Within different contexts such as school and home there are models of learners in the minds of teachers, parents, peers and the learners themselves. These are not linked, but in sum they tell a story of a learner's intellectual development. Through the creation and maintenance of the Broadband Learner Model these different perspectives are brought together as different participants are able to access and update their view of the learner. The minimum core components in the Learner Model have been specified through the ieTV pilot system developed by the authors [2].

This system matches learners, both as individuals and as groups, to the best available learning resources described in its database. This database contains information about multiple media including video, audio and text as well as profiles of other learners and teachers who may be able to offer assistance. The HomeWork system expands this learner model for use across multiple contexts and devices: the learners' slates for use in class and at home, teacher workstation, large screen classroom TV or interactive whiteboard and home TV screen and set-top box. Learners will be able to access an up-to-date representation of themselves in the shape of the Learner Model between the home and school learning contexts via their slates.

4 An Example Scenario

The scenario presented in Table 1 below describes the desired learner experience and the proposed system behaviour.

5 Coherence Compilation

The Coherence compiler is an attempt to operationalise guidelines drawn from the Non-linear Interactive Narrative Framework. The original Non-linear Interactive Narrative Framework (NINF) was the product of the MENO research project [6]. This framework was subsequently adapted and used in the design of the IETV pilot system developed at Sussex [2] and is now being further expanded for use in the HomeWork project. In this section of the document we discuss the relevant theoretical grounding

Table 1. Sample Scenario of Use and associated system behaviour

Sample Scenario	System Behaviour
Mary is 6 years old and her school is tuned into the 'Number Crew' from Channel 4. The programme and associated interactive materials are broadcast to the class's set-top box and the children watch Bradley and the crew solve number problems on the good ship Mathematical. Whilst the TV pictures on the large classroom screen engage the class, interactive exercises and activity sheets are transferred from the set-top box to each child's 'digital slate'. These exercises are differentiated and personalised to each child through the Broadband Learner Model maintained by the system for each child. The Coherence Compiler ensures the relationship between these exercises and the opening TV episode are clear	Registration details for Mary and her classmates have already been used by the system in collaboration with the teacher to construct initial learner profiles. At the start of today's session the teacher has entered the lesson parameters (e.g. length) for which she would like TV programmes and associated interactive activities. The BLM coherence compiler matches the details of the class profile and the individual learner profiles to the most appropriate resources in the BLM content database. These are offered to the teacher who makes the final selection for class session and for the individual learners. Once these selections are made, the TV material is displayed on the classroom large screen. The teacher workstation and the children's slates are synchronized and the learner profiles updated to reflect the activities completed.
When Bradley and the crew say goodbye each child's slate comes to life and the children can work as individuals (or in pairs or small groups) with the interactive materials on the Number Crew website in the Channel 4 Collaborative Learning Community. Mary and Jo, her classmate, work together.	After (and possibly during) the TV programme the children complete the interactive activities selected for them. The Learner model for each child is updated on the slate as they progress and subsequently synchronised with the teacher's workstation. At the end of the lesson the teacher can select the material for the child to take home or.
That night at home, Mary switches on her slate and it automatically synchronises with the home set-top box. The Coherence Compiler provides her with a televisual summary of her recent study leading to Mary's teacher's suggestion that some consolidation on addition would be good. When Mary's mum turns on the TV, Bradley engages Mary in some number puzzles that she then completes on her slate with some help from classmate Jo, who lives on the other side of town.	At home the Leaner model on the slate is synchronised with that stored on, or delivered to the TV, set top box so that when the slate is turned on the relevant TV programme material can be played. Mary can contact Jo, who has the same set up at his house and they can once again work together for a while. Both Mary and Jo's Leaner model is updated by the system. When they go to school the next day their slates are synchronised with that of the teacher workstation.

for the NINF, and the influence of previous work, in particular that of the MENO project on the NINF. We then present the current version of the NINF for use in the HomeWork Project.

5.1 Theoretical Grounding

[7] describes narrative as "a mode of thought and an expression of a culture's worldview". He suggests that we make sense of our own thoughts and experiences, and those of others through the active generation of narrative. In this sense, narrative shapes our knowledge and experience and is central to our cognition. A narrative can take the form of a story that entices us through a sequence of events. The narrative process allows us to make sense of the world and to share this with others. Narrative can also be used as a framework within which explorations can occur, a macro-structure with a network of causal links and signposts [6]. Within this overarching structure there are inter-related elements each with their own micro-narrative. In fact, within formal education there may be several layers of this structure with a macro-narrative that is, for example, at the level of a lesson within which there are different elements. This lesson is itself also part of a term's curriculum and therefore in a sense a micro–narrative too. From the point of view of learning and the HomeWork project in particular, we need to offer a means of helping teachers and learners see the links between the layers of macro and micro narratives as well as to keep track of the individual narrative elements themselves. This is what we refer to as Narrative Guidance. This guidance needs to be adaptive to the needs of the learner/s, it needs to offer a strong 'storyline' when a learner is new to a subject and then fade as he becomes more accomplished. The important factor here is that the learner/s must participate in the activity of creating the links between the elements of the narrative.

Social Constructivism [8] has been influential within mainstream education and the design of educational technology alike for the latter part of the twentieth century. It requires that both learners and teachers are active participants in a process of mediated communication. So what does all this have to do with the role of interactive technology? The point about interactive technology is that it allows us to 'play around' with the nature of the narrative guidance we offer to a learner, it allows the learner to be more active in the path they take (or create) through the resources and experiences they are offered. The problem that can arise is that learners have too much freedom to explore and end up being confused and lost. There is a fluctuating tension between the strength of the guidance we need to offer and the amount of control we leave with the learner. We need to provide them with tools to help them construct their own understanding from their experiences. We also need to free learners to explore their own curiosity and to be creative.

It is this need to support learner creativity that provides us with a third theoretical position to explore. Creativity can be considered as a process through which individuals, groups and even entire societies are able to transcend an accepted model of reality. It has been differentiated by [9] into three broad categories: combinatorial, exploratory and transformational all of which require the manipulation of an accepted familiarity, pattern or structure in order to produce a novel outcome. The perceptions of reality that are the backdrop for creativity vary not only from individual to individual, but also from culture to culture. Communities explore and transform these realities in many ways, through art, drama and narrative for example. In developing the coherence compiler we are particularly interested in the relationship between creativity and narrative as applied to education. Narrative offers us a way to play with the constraints of reality: to help learners to be creative. Used appropriately it also allows us to engage learners.

The narrative context of a learning episode has both cognitive and affective consequences. Incoherent or unclear narrative requires extra cognitive effort on the listener's part to disentangle the ambiguities. As a consequence the learner may be distracted from the main message of the learning episode, which may in turn detract from her ability to understand the concepts to be communicated. It may also disengage her altogether. On the other hand engaging narrative may motivate her to expend cognitive effort in understanding concepts to which she would not otherwise be inclined to attend. The Non-linear Interactive Narrative Framework identifies ways in which narrative might be exploited in interactive learning environments. The NINF distinguishes two key aspects of narrative:

Narrative guidance (NG): the design elements that teachers and/or software need to provide in order to help learners interpret the resources and experiences they are offered, and
Narrative construction (NC): the process through which learners discern and impose a structure on their learning experiences, making links and connections in a personally meaningful way.

5.2 What Is the Coherence Compiler?

The Coherence Compiler is responsible for giving learners a coherent learning experience. The need for providing coherence is perhaps not very clear if you are imagining material drawn from a single source (say the 'Number Crew') as this content will already have 'coherence' designed into it; the content goes together, has a built in sequence with a clear structure contained in storylines and lesson plans that link video clips, worksheet and other activities in a coherent narrative (there is implicit narrative guidance). However, when we consider how we may wish to link diverse content, drawn from a variety of sources, into a unified learning experience the need for some means of maintaining coherence or supporting learners and their helpers in constructing this coherence becomes more evident (this may require more explicit narrative guidance). Somehow the Coherence Compiler needs to be able to generate or know about routes through appropriate (where appropriate means relevant to the learner's needs) content that make 'narrative' sense. The Coherence Compiler should also be able to guide learners and/or authors of learning experiences in creating their own coherent routes through potentially diverse and otherwise unrelated but relevant content, perhaps by providing access to suitable tools; e.g. search tools, guides that relate content to learning objectives, ways of relating past learning to current learning, etc. The issues raised here are common for a variety of schemes that wish to amalgamate materials from diverse sources into a coherent whole, see e.g. [10].

5.3 How Does the Coherence Compiler Interact with Other System Components?

In order to provide the kind of services suggested above the Coherence Compiler needs information about: the available content and its relation to other content; the learner's characteristics; the learner's history of activity; the learner's personal goals and curriculum goals; the tools available to help learners relate content, learning objectives and past learning; the tools available to help teachers build routes through content; and existing coherent routes through content (lesson plans, schemes of work, ways of identifying content that is part of a series, and popular associations between content).

Much of this information might be provided by the content management system or other system components: the content metadata, including relationship data; the Learner Model; logs of learner activity; a Curriculum or Pedagogic Model; a collection of suitable user interfaces (teacher / child / helper) for visualising content search results, learner activity and learning / curriculum objectives; a database of coherent trail information (e.g. lesson plans, other authored routes, popular routes, i.e. sequences of content that many similar learners have followed).

So, while the content management system and other components are able to successfully identify and retrieve content that is suited to a learner's needs and to present that content along with information about how it relates to other content elements, the value of the Coherence Compiler is that it enables the teacher and/or learner to create a coherent route through that suitable content. The Coherence Compiler provides user interfaces appropriate to each of its user groups (teacher / learners / learner collaborators, parents etc…) for those of its services, which are visible to users, i.e. tools for narrative construction and explicit narrative guidance.

5.4 Coherence Compiler Interfaces Requirements

Primarily for Teacher. The interface for teachers should: (i) Be able to assist primary teachers to find suitable content and make 'coherent paths' through it (e.g. lesson plans or schemes of work). (ii) Be capable of performing search on available content metadata in order to find content that suits the purpose of the author. (iii) Enable (and possibly encourage) teachers to add guidance and scaffolding elements to the lessons they create e.g. Reminders of the goal of the session, identification of sub-goals and prompts to ask for help. (iv) Allow the teacher to reference content not known to the system but available to the teacher. (v) Allow the teacher to annotate links between content and activities and include instructions; e.g. (instructions and annotation in italic) – *First watch section 1 of the video about elephant being max weight for the roller coaster* {ref clip and start and stop times} *think about the problem. How do you think the crew can work out which combinations of animals weigh less than the elephant? Now watch the solution* {ref clip}. *Now play the game* {ref interactive} *to help find combinations of animals that weigh less than the elephant.* (vi) Allow the teacher to select level of system or learner control applicable to the session. (vii) Allow the teacher to select from amongst options for the nature and strength of the narrative guidance to be offered, see Figure 1.

Primarily for Learners. The interface for learners should: (i) Provide access to the data and information that learners will need to construct their personal narrative understanding: i.e. learning history, available content, learning objectives, content menus and search facilities, etc. (ii) Remind learners of (macro and micro) objectives in a timely manner in order to focus their attention on a purposeful interpretation of the content. (iii) Guide learners towards accessing content that delivers these learning goals. Guidance may be more or less constraining depending on the learner's independence. (iv) Vary the degree of (system-user) narrative control over the sequence of events and activities or route through content, to match the needs of different learners. (v) Guide a child in choosing what to do next (for young children this guidance is likely to be very constraining – a linear progression of 'next' and 'back' buttons or a limited number of choices. For more independent learners guidance (and interface) would become less constraining. (vi) Enable the learner to record and reflect on their activity and progress towards goals. Possibly by annotating suitable representations of her activity log and objectives. Again, this needs to be done in a way that is intelligible and accessible to young children. (vii) Be able to suggest 'coherent paths' through content (to learners, parents, teachers) through analysis of content usage in authored paths and in other learners' activity histories. For example, if I choose to use a certain piece of video, and learners with similar profiles have used this perhaps what they chose to do next will also be suitable for me (something like the way Amazon suggests purchases?). Or if a piece of content I choose to incorporate in a 'lesson plan' has been used on other lesson plans maybe other pieces of content used to follow on from this content in those plans will be appropriate to the new plan. This feature will obviously become more useful over time as the system incorporates larger volumes of content and usage but will have to be careful not to confuse users with divergent recommendations.

Primarily for Learners with Collaborators. The interface for learners with collaborators should allow learners (and their parents/guardian/teachers) to review and annotate the learner's history of interaction with the system. This could facilitate a form of collaborative parent child narrative construction. This interface might be a bit like a browser history, learners would be able to revisit past interactions. Maybe if asked what did you do today at school a child would be able to show as well as tell through the use of this feature. There are many challenging issues to address here including separating out individual and group learner models as well as assignment of credit.

Not Visible to Users. Although not directly visible to users, the system should: (i) Have access to a record of a child's activity with the system. (ii) Have access to authored 'coherent journeys' through available content: coherent journeys are linked sequences of guidance comments, activities and content that make sense (e.g. existing lesson plans and schemes of work authored by material producers and/or users of the system, other sensible sequences of interaction and guidance possibly obtained through analysis of content usage by all learners). (iii) Be able to identify suitable content for a child's next interaction based on the record of her activity and the 'coherent journeys' described above. Decisions about suitable content will also involve consideration of the learner's individual identity and needs described in the

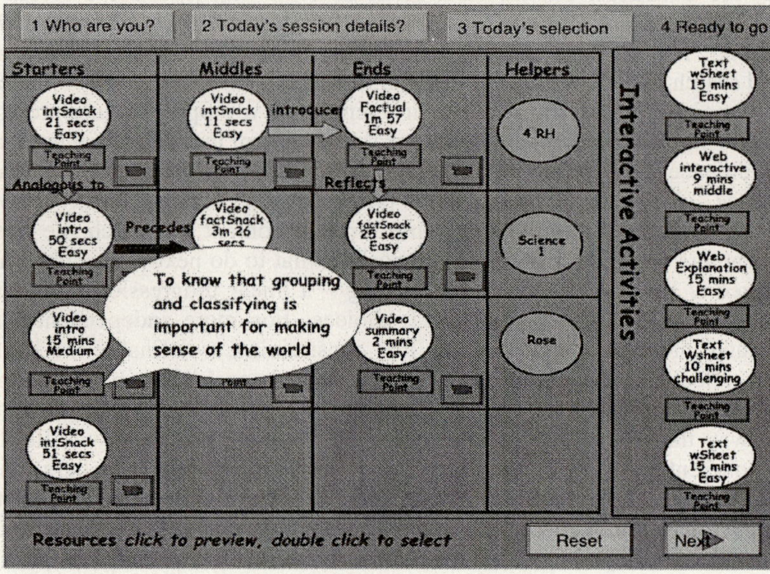

Fig. 1. Mock up of interface for teachers

learner model and pedagogic objectives (possibly described by the curriculum). (iv) Be able to choose/suggest 'paths' through content that are interesting/motivating to individual learners; i.e. if there are several paths through content/plans for learning at an appropriate level for this learner choose the one that is most likely to be interesting/motivating to this learner

6 Conclusions

In this paper we have described the initial design of the Coherence Compiler for the HomeWork project. The HomeWork project is making existing content materials, including TV programs, available to learners. The original programs may not be used in their original entirety, but parts selected, re-ordered or repeated and interspersed with other materials and activities according to the needs of individual or groups of children. The Coherence Compiler is responsible for maintaining narrative coherence across these materials and across devices so that the learner experiences a well-ordered sequence that supports her learning effectively. Such support may be provided both through narrative guidance and tools to support the learner's own personal narrative construction. Narrative guidance should be adaptive to the needs of the learner, it initially offers a strong 'storyline' explicitly linking new and old learning and then fades as the learner becomes more accomplished at making these links for herself. Such support may be provided both through narrative guidance and tools to support the learner's own personal narrative construction.

References

1. Luckin, R., Connolly, D., Plowman, L., and Airey, (2002) The Young Ones: the Implications of Media Convergence for Mobile Learning with Infants, in S. Anastopolou, M. Sharples & G. Vavoula (Eds.) *Proceedings of the European Workshop on Mobile and Contextual Learning*, University of Birmingham, 7-11.
2. Luckin, R. and du Boulay, B. (2001) Imbedding AIED in ie-TV through Broadband User Modelling (BbUM). In Moore, J.D., Redfield, C.L. and Johnson, W.L. (Eds.) *Artificial Intelligence in Education: AI-ED in the Wired and Wireless Future*, Amsterdam: IOS Press, 322--333.
3. Luckin, R. and du Boulay, B. (1999) Capability, potential and collaborative assistance, in J. Kay (Ed) *UM99 User Modelling: 7th International conference on user modeling*, Banff, Alberta, Canada, CISM Courses and Lectures, No. 407, Springer-Verlag, Wien, 139–148.
4. Luckin, T. and Hammerton, L. (2002) Getting to Know me: Helping Learners Understand their Own Learning Needs through Metacognitive Scaffolding, in S.A. Cerri, G. Gouarderes & F. Paranguaca (Eds), *Intelligent Tutoring Systems*, Berlin: Springer-Verlag, 759-771.
5. Luckin, R., Plowman, L. Laurillard, D, Stratfold, M. and Taylor, J. (1998) Scaffolding Learners' Constructions of narrative in A. Bruckerman, M. Guzdial, J. Kolodner and A Ram (Eds) *International Conference of the Learning Sciences,* Atlanta: AACE, 181-187.
6. Plowman, L., Luckin, R., Laurillard, D., Stratfold, M., & Taylor, J. (1999). Designing Multimedia for Learning: Narrative Guidance and Narrative Construction, *in the proceedings of CHI 99* (pp. 310-317). May 15-20, 1999, Pittsburgh, PA USA.: ACM.
7. Bruner, J. (1996). *The Culture of Education.* Harvard University Press, Cambridge MA.
8. Vygotsky, L. S. (1986). *Thought and Language.* Cambridge, Mass: The MIT Press.
9. Boden, M. A. (2003) The Creative Mind: Myths and Mechanisms. London, Weidenfeld and Nicolson.
10. AFAIDL Distance Learning Initiatve: www.cbd-net.com/index.php/search/show/536227

The Knowledge Like the Object of Interaction in an Orthopaedic Surgery-Learning Environment

Vanda Luengo, Dima Mufti-Alchawafa, and Lucile Vadcard

Laboratoire CLIPS/ IMAG, 385 rue de la Bibliothèque,
Domaine Universitaire, BP 53, 38041 Grenoble cedex 9, FRANCE
{vanda.luengo,dima.mufti-alchawafa,lucile.vadcard}@imag.fr

Abstract. In this paper, we present the design of a computer environment for the learning of procedural concepts in orthopedic surgery. We particularly focus on the implementation of a model of knowledge for the definition of feedback. In our system, the feedback is produced according to the user's knowledge during the problem-solving activity. Our aim is to follow the consistency of the user's actions instead of constraining him/her into the expert's model of doing. For this, we are basing the system feedback on local consistency checks of student utterances rather than on an a priori normative solution trace.

1 Introduction

The work we present in this paper is motivated by the conjunction of two categories of problems in surgery. First, there are some well-known instructional difficulties. In the traditional approach, the student interacts with an experienced surgeon to learn operative procedures, learning materials being patient cases and cadavers. This principally presents the following problems: it requires one surgeon for one learner, it is unsafe for patients, cadavers must be available and there is no way to quantify the learning curve. The introduction of computers in medical education is seen by several authors as something to develop to face these issues in medical education [7], but on the condition that real underlying educational principles are integrated [2], [9]. In particular, the importance of individual feedback is stressed [13]; from our point of view, it is the backbone of the relevance of computer based systems for learning.

As pointed by Eraut and du Boulay [7], we can consider Information Technology in medicine as divided into "tools" and "training systems". Tools support surgeons in their practice, while training systems are dedicated to the apprenticeship. Our personal aim is to use the same tools developed in the framework of computer assisted surgical techniques to create also training systems for conceptual notions useful in both computer assisted and classical surgery.

We want to take explicitly into account the issue of provided feedback by embedding a model of knowledge in our system. We want to provide a feedback linked to the user current knowledge that is diagnosed according to the user's actions on the system. This article presents the design of an environment for the learning of screw

J.C. Lester et al. (Eds.): ITS 2004, LNCS 3220, pp. 108–117, 2004.

placement trajectory, based on a computer assisted surgical tool. We describe the methodology adopted to integrate a diagnosis system in a pedagogical and didactical component for user/system interaction.

2 The Surgical Knowledge

Traditionally, knowledge in orthopedic surgery is considered to be divided into two main categories: declarative and gestural. The first category includes intellectual, diagnostic and personal abilities. This kind of knowledge is usually learned in a context of formal schooling, and measured by well-established examinations such as multiple-choice questionnaires, written or oral tests, and ward rounds. The gestural skills, also referred to as technical or motor skills, are dexterity, eye-hand coordination, and spatial skills.

However, this dual classification is neglecting a key aspect of surgical knowledge: surgery takes place in a specific context and is based on actions. Regarding the question of learning, expert practice cannot be solely divided into a formal part and a gestural part. Medical reasoning, reaction in the case of complications, validation and control are some issues that cannot be placed at the same level as declarative knowledge, which is explicit and consensual.

According to De Oliveira & al. [6], declarative knowledge deals with anatomy, findings (concepts used in the physician's investigation process), therapy (kinds of therapy and their features), diagnosis (concepts and characteristics that identify syndrome and aetiology diagnoses), and pathologies (representing different situations whose classification and features are important for the purpose of the domain theory). These elements are theoretical, explicit, made for communication (encyclopedic knowledge). Procedural knowledge allows the surgeon to use the declarative knowledge and apply it to a particular patient case. It involves problem solving, reasoning and prediction. It is an experimental part of knowledge, and it is validated by empirical means. However, it still remains a worded part of knowledge, which enables communication.

This is not the case for the last part of surgical knowledge: operative knowledge, the gestural part of the surgical practice. It deals with dexterity, eye-hand coordination, spatial skills, and it is transmitted by ostentation. It cannot be worded, and remains in some pragmatic representation and validation frameworks.

The declarative part of a surgeon's knowledge is predicative; it can be expressed and transmitted. In contrast, the procedural component of surgical knowledge contains both predicative and operative features. Diagnosis abilities (intellectual skills), attitudes towards patient, cognitive strategies and even motor skills can be partly explicited and transmitted, particularly for continuing education. However, they are also some subjective, personal and context-specific knowledge. Finally, operational knowledge is dealing with the use value: it is the "knowing in action" for the surgeon. In surgery, the operative part of the expert practice is both occurring during the diagnosis and the treatment delivery phases.

Based on this analysis of surgical knowledge, we developed for the last two years, in the framework of VOEU, the Virtual European Orthopedics University project (European Union IST-1999-13079 [4]), different multimedia educational modules related to these different knowledge types. Declarative knowledge is well adapted to multimedia courses, both classical and case-based. Operational knowledge is obviously adapted to simulators, including those with haptic feedback. Our objective is now to create an environment for the learning of procedural knowledge, which is more complex.

3 Tool Presentation

The system we use is an image-guided system for the percutaneous placement of screws. The goals of this computer-assisted approach are to decrease surgical complications, with a mini-invasive technique, and to increase the accuracy and security of screw positioning. The general procedure of this kind of computer assisted screwing surgery is the following. Pre-operative planning is performed. It is the identification of the best possible trajectory on a reconstructed 3D model of the bone from CT-scans – this trajectory will be used to guide the surgeon during the intervention. During surgery, tools are tracked with an optical localizer. An ultrasound acquisition is performed and images are segmented to obtain 3D intra-operative data that are registered with the CT-scan 3D model. The surgeon is assisted during drilling and screwing processes with re-sliced CT-scan images displayed on the computer screen and comparison between pre-operative planning and tools position. In the context of the VOEU project, our university develops a training simulator for the first two aspects of this computer-assisted procedure: the surgical planning and the intra operative ultrasound acquisition. The components of the simulator correspond to the different components of the computer-aided system for screw placement. They are designed to answer the potential difficulties of the clinician when using this computer-aided procedure.

Concerning the ultrasound acquisition, the simulation can be split into a visual and a gestural part. The visual part concerns the generation of realistic images to be displayed on a screen from the position of the probe relatively to the anatomical structures. The gestural part deals with the force feedback to be sent to the user so that he can feel the reaction of the tissues to the pressure exerted by the virtual probe onto the modeled part of the body. Concerning the planning step of the procedure, the simulator provides a reconstructed 3D model of the relevant anatomical structures, and allows the visualization of re-sliced CT images along the screw axis (see Fig. 1). This training solution consists in learning by doing thanks to a virtual environment. Using this system, the learner is able to train the gestual parts of the procedure and to make use of declarative knowledge on the surgical screwing (choice of the number and the position of screws).

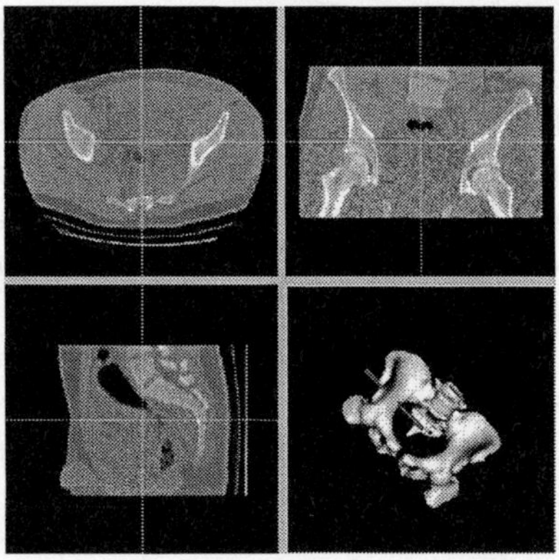

Fig. 1. Re-sliced CT images along the screw axis and sacrum 3D model

In the work we present here, we focus on the planning step of this surgical tool; the principal reason is that in this step we can see to appear the procedural knowledge.

4 Methodology

In our learning environment, we separate the simulation component from the system component dealing with didactical and pedagogical intentions [5], [8]. The simulation is not intended for learning: it is designed to be used by an expert who wants to define a screw placement trajectory.

From the software point of view, we would like to respect the simulation architecture. The system part concerned with didactical and pedagogical intentions is to be plugged only in learning situations; we call this complete configuration the learning level. The learning level must also allow the construction of learning situations.

Concerning interactions, we chose the architecture describe en the next figure (Fig. 2):

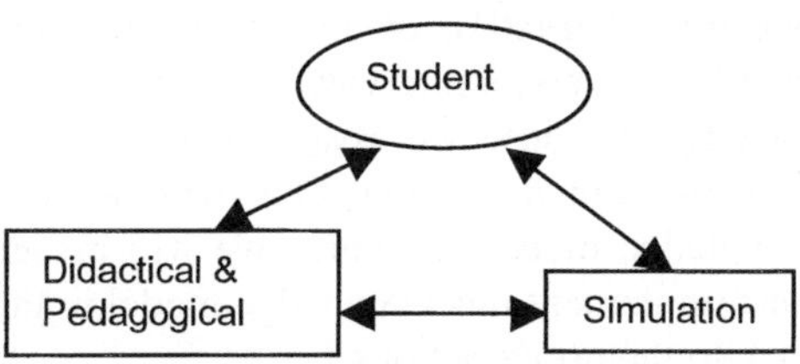

Fig. 2. Architecture.

We chose this architecture because we would like to observe the student's activity while he/she uses the simulation. The feedback produced by the simulation is not necessarily in terms of knowledge: for example, the system can send feedback about the segmentation of the images or about the gestural process. Our system must intervene when it detects a didactical or pedagogical reason, and then generate an interaction. We do not want to constrain "a priori" the student in his/her activity with the simulation. On the other hand, the didactical and pedagogical system has to determine the feedback in relation to the knowledge that the user manipulates.

In this case, the simulation will produce traces about the user's activity. We want these traces to give information about the piece of knowledge that the system has detected [11]. In this work, we try to determine this information from the actions on the interface and to deduce the knowledge that the user manipulates. We determined how the simulation system transmits this information to the learning level. The first version that we produced is based on a DTD specification; the XML file describes all test trajectories that the user proposes in the planning software.

We differentiate two kinds of feedback: feedback related to the validity of the knowledge, and feedback related to the control activity.

We define the first kind of feedback as a function of the knowledge object.

A control feedback is defined according to the knowledge of the expert and to the manner that the expert wants to transmit his/her expertise to the novice. The idea is to reproduce the interaction between expert and novice in a learning situation. In this case, the expert uses his/her own controls to validate or invalidate the novice action and consequently he/she determines the feedback to the novice.

In our methodology, we take into account the didactical and computers considerations for produce the learning level.

4.1 Didactical Considerations

We use the framework of the didactical situations theory [3]. This implies that the system has to allow interactions for actions, formulations and validations. In this case, the system will be a set of properties [10].

In this paper, our objective is to specify a methodology for designing the validation interactions.

The aim of our research in this paper is to allow the acquisition of procedural knowledge in surgery. The adopted methodology is based on two linked phases. In the first phase, we must identify some procedural components of the surgeon's knowledge. This is done by observation of expert and learner interactions during surgical interventions, and by surgeon's interviews. In this part, we focus on the control component of knowledge, because we assume that control is the main role of procedural knowledge during problem solving. This hypothesis is related to the theoretical framework of knowledge modeling, which we will present just after. During the second phase, we must implement this knowledge model in the system, in order to link the provided feedback to the user's actions.

We adopt the point of view described by Balacheff to define the notion of conception, which "has been used for years in educational research, but most often as common sense, rather than being explicitly defined" [1]. To shorten the presentation of the cK¢ model, we will just describe its structure and specificity.

A first aspect of this model is rather classical: it defines a conception as a set of related problems (P), a set of operators to act on these problems (R), and an associated representation system (L). It also takes into account a control structure, called Σ. Schoenfeld [14] has already pointed out the crucial role of control in problem solving. In the problem-solving process, the control elements allow the subject to decide whether an action is relevant or not, or to decide that a problem is solved. In the chosen model, a problem solving process can thus be formally described as a succession of solving steps: $\sigma(r(p))$=right, with $\sigma \in \Sigma$, $r \in R$ and $p \in P$. In an apprenticeship perspective, we will focus on differences between novice's and expert's conceptions. Below is an example of formalization, to illustrate the way we use the cK¢ model.

Let us consider the problem P2: "define a correct trajectory for a second screw in the vertebra". Indeed, the surgeon has often two screws to introduce, each on one side of the vertebra, through the pedicles (see Fig. 3):

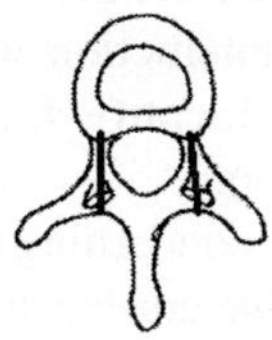

Fig. 3. Vertebra with rough position of the screws

In a general way, the screw trajectory is defined according to anatomical landmarks and to knowledge on the vertebra (and spine) structure. Control of the chosen trajectory is partly made by perceptual and visual elements like the feeling of the bone density during the drilling, and X-rays [15]. When a first screw has been correctly introduced, there is at least two ways to solve P2. First, the second screw trajectory can be defined regardless of the first one. In this case, operators and controls that will act during the problem solving are the same ones as for the former problem P1 ("define a correct trajectory for a first screw in the vertebra"). A second approach is to consider the symmetrical structure of the vertebra. In this case, the involved operators are not the same. They are linked to the construction of a symmetrical point in relation to an axis. Controls are partly the ones involved in the recognition of symmetry. Other controls, like perceptual and visual elements, are also present in this case. The main problem of this second way of P2-solving is that it is neglecting some false symmetrical configurations: a slight scoliosis, a discrepancy between the spinal axis and the table axis due to the patient position, etc. This is the reason why the expert will always solve P2 with the same approach he used to solve P1.

4.2 Computer Considerations

The didactical analysis of the knowledge objects will be the key to the success of our model implementation. The choice that will be suitable in relation to knowledge will determine the main characteristics of the design. For the judgment interaction design, we identified a set of pedagogical constraints: no blocking system response, any true/false feedback and feedback after every step. According to the point of view of the expert model, we should not compare this model to the student activity. Our objective is to follow the student's work. Thus, if there are automatic deduction tools, they should not provide an expected solution because it would constrain the student's work [11], but they should rather be used to facilitate the system-student interaction. We can use this kind of tools to give the system the capacities to argue or to refuse through counter-examples.

For our computer learning level, this implies that we have to link a judgment interaction with declarative knowledge. For example, if the student chooses a trajectory that can touch a nerve, the interaction can be refer to the anatomy knowledge in order to explain (to show) that in these body parts there can be a nerve.

In other words, one kind of judgment interaction is the explanation of an error. For this, we will identify the declarative knowledge in relation to the procedural knowledge in order to produce an explanation related to the error.

For the generation of validation interaction we identify the knowledge that intervenes in the planning activity. We identify four kinds of necessary knowledge to validate the screw trajectory's planning:

- Pathology: declarative knowledge concerning the illness type;
- Morphology: declarative knowledge concerning the patient's state;
- Anatomy: declarative knowledge concerning the anatomy of body part;
- Planning: procedural knowledge concerning the screw and its position in the bone.

We have an example for the vertebra classification knowledge [12]. We can see that procedural knowledge have a relationship with declarative knowledge. The procedural knowledge is based on the declarative one, in consequence in order to validate procedural knowledge the system needs to know declarative knowledge, which intervene to build the other.

In the case of the learning situation about the screw trajectory's planning, we also identified for the validation a hierarchical deduction's relationships between these kinds of knowledge (Fig. 4).

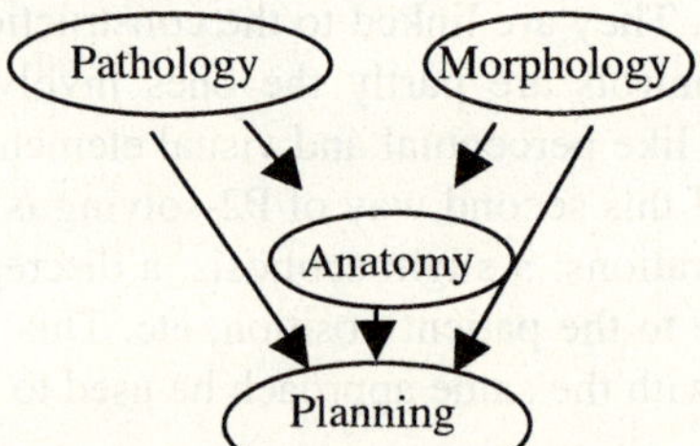

Fig. 4. Relationships between kinds of knowledge.

Firstly the pathology and morphology knowledge deduce which part of the patient's body will be operated (the anatomy part). Secondly, the declarative knowledge determines the learning situation for the validation of the planning knowledge.

For the production of validation interactions, we have a set of surgical conceptions (that we obtain with a didactical analyses). Starting from surgical conceptions, the surgery-learning environment has to identify the conceptions that the student applies in his/her activity.

From the computer point of view, the learning environment contains a learning component. This component has to represent the surgical knowledge and to produce a diagnostic of the student's knowledge. Our approach based on a representation and knowledge diagnosis system "Emergent Diagnosis via coalition formation" [16].

The Webber approach [16] represents knowledge in the form of MAS (Multi-Agents System). This representation uses the cK¢ model [1] (explained above). Conceptions are characterized by sets of agents. The society of agents is composed of four categories: problems, operators, language and control. Each element from the quadruplet C (P, R, L, Σ) is the core of one reactive agent. This approach [16] considers diagnosis as the emergent result of collective actions of reactive agents.

The general role of any agent is to check whether the element it represents is present in the environment. If the element is found, the agent becomes satisfied. Once satisfied, the agent is able to influence the satisfaction of other agents by voting. The diagnosis result is the identification of a set of conceptions, which the system deduces, in the form of a vector of the votes.

This approach has been created for a geometry proof system. We identified a set of differences in the nature of knowledge between the geometry and surgical domain. In particular, for the diagnosis of the geometry students' knowledge, the representation of knowledge is only declarative and the results of the diagnosis are the identification of conceptions related also to the declarative knowledge. However, in the surgical domain, we showed how the declarative and procedural knowledge can intervene in the student's activity. Furthermore, for the validation of the procedural knowledge, is not sufficient to identify the conceptions related to procedural knowledge (planning), it is also necessary to identify the conceptions related to the learning situation; in other words, the declarative knowledge (pathology, morphology, anatomy). For example, if the system deduces that the screw is in the bone and there is no lesion, that is not sufficient to validate the screw trajectory. The system has to deduce if this trajectory is the solution of the clinical case or not.

In our system, we distinguish two diagnosis levels according to the type of knowledge. The first diagnosis level allows the deduction of the student's errors related to declarative knowledge. For example, the system may deduce that the student has applied a false screw trajectory's theory for this type of illness. In this case, we give a link feedback to a semantic web that we are building.

If the system deduces that, there are no errors for this level that means the student knows the declarative surgical knowledge. In the second diagnosis level, the system will evaluate his procedural surgical knowledge. Consequently, we adapt the representation and diagnosis system "Emergent Diagnosis via coalition formation" to our knowledge representation. We choose to use a "computer mask" that the system applies to the vector of votes resulting from the diagnosis. This mask filters a set of conceptions, which are related to the declarative knowledge in the vote vector. It allows to "see" the piece of knowledge that we try to identify at the first diagnosis level.

The system generates the mask by an "a priori" analysis of the expected vector. This analysis is applied to the declarative knowledge (learning situation) before the diagnosis phase. After this phase, the system applies the mask and then starts the first diagnosis level (the declarative knowledge). If the system deduces that there is an error in this level, it generates an interaction with the student in order to explain which knowledge he/she has to revise. If there are no errors in the first level, it starts the second diagnosis level to validate the screw trajectory. Finally, the system generates the validation interaction to the student.

5 Conclusion and Future Work

The research involved in the work presented here come from tow domains, the didactic and computer fields. By its nature, this project consists of two interrelated parts. The first part is the modeling of surgical knowledge and it is related to didactic research, the latter is the design a computer system of this model and the definition of system's feedback.

We searched to design a computer system for surgical learning environment. This environment should provide to student a feedback related to his/her knowledge during the problem-solving activity. In other words, the knowledge, in the learning situation, is the object of feedback. To realize this idea, we based on a didactical methodology for the design of our system.

The design of the computer system for a learning environment depends to the learning domain. In consequence, we analyzed the knowledge of domain (didactic work) before the representation of the computer system. That allows to identify the knowledge domain's constraints for the representation's model.

For validate our work, it will involve some junior surgeons in the task of defining good screw trajectories for a learning situation in the simulator. The provided feedback and the students reactions will be analyzed in terms of apprenticeship (that is, regarding knowledge at stake).

We will also validate the model of knowledge and the chosen representation. By the analyze of the generality of the cK¢ model, we will try to distinguish the differences with other cK¢ representations and their implementations in the computer systems.

In addition, we will analyze our computer system with the objective of evaluating our diagnostic system and the relationships between the diagnostic system and the feedback system. We started to work on the feedback system and we decided to use a Bayesian network for the representation of the didactical decisions. The idea is to represent -whenever a procedural conception is detected by our diagnostic system - what are the possible situations problems that can destabilize this conception.

In this paper, we studied the learning of the planning level of simulator. In this level, there are two types of surgical knowledge: the declarative and procedural. In our future work, we want to complete the research, by including the operational knowledge, the third type of surgical knowledge [15].

Our final objective is the implementation of a complete surgical learning environment with declarative, procedural and operational surgical knowledge. This environment will be contains also a component for the medical diagnosis and another component for the construction of the learning situation by the teacher in surgery.

References

1. Balacheff N. (2000), Les connaissances, pluralité de conceptions (le cas des mathématiques). In: Tchounikine P. (ed.) Actes de la conférence Ingénierie de la connaissance (IC 2000, pp.83-90), Toulouse.
2. Benyon D., Stone D., Woodroffe M. (1997), Experience with developing multimedia courseware for the world wide web: the need for better tools and clear pedagogy, International Journal of Human Computer Studies, n° 47, 197-218.
3. Brousseau G., (1997). Theory of Didactical Situations. Dordrecht : Kluwer Academic Publishers edition and translation by Balacheff N., Cooper M., Sutherland R. and Warfield V.
4. Conole G., Wills G., Carr L., Hall W., Vadcard L., Grange S. (2003), Building a virtual university for orthopaedics, in Ed-Media 2003 World conference on educational multimedia, hypermedia & telecommunications, 23-28 juin 2003, Honolulu, Hawaii, USA.
5. De Jong T. (1991), Learning and instruction with computer simulations, in Education & Computing 6, 217-229.
6. De Oliveira K., Ximenes A., Matwin S., Travassos G., Rocha A.R. (2000), A generic architecture for knowledge acquisition tools in cardiology, proceedings of IDAMAP 2000, Fifth international workshop on Intelligent Data Analysis in Medicine and Pharmacology, at the 14th European conference on Artificial Intelligence, Berlin.
7. Eraut M., du Boulay B. (2000), Developing the attributes of medical professional judgement and competence, IN Cognitive Sciences Research Paper 518, University of Sussex, http://www.cogs.susx.ac.uk/users/bend/doh.
8. Guéraud V., Pernin J.P. et al. (1999), Environnements d'apprentissage basés sur la simulation : outils auteur et expérimentations, in Sciences et Techniques Educatives, special issue "Simulation et formation professionnelle dans l'industrie", vol.6 n°1, 95-141.
9. Lillehaug S.I., Lajoie S. (1998), AI in medical education – another grand challenge for medical informatics, In Artificial intelligence in medecine 12, 197-225.
10. Luengo V. (1997). Cabri-Euclide : un micromonde de preuve intégrant la réfutation. Principes didactiques et informatiques. Réalisation. Thèse. Grenoble : Université Joseph Fourier.
11. Luengo V. (1999), Analyse et prise en compte des contraintes didactiques et informatiques dans la conception et le développement du micromonde de preuve Cabri-Euclide, In Sciences et Techniques Educatives Vol. 6 n°1.
12. Mufti-Alchawafa, D. (2003), Outil pour l'apprentissage de la chirurgie orthopédique à l'aide de simulateur, Mémoire DEA Informatique, Systèmes et Communications, Université Joseph Fourier.
13. Rogers D., Regehr G., Yeh K., Howdieshell T. (1998), Computer-assisted learning versus a lecture and feedback seminar for teaching a basic surgical technical skill, The American Journal of Surgery, 175, 508-510.
14. Schoenfeld A. (1985). Mathematical Problem Solving. New York: Academic Press.
15. Vadcard L., First version of the VOEU pedagogical strategy, Intermediate deliverable (n°34.07), VOEU IST 1999 – 13079. 2002.
16. Webber, C., Pesty, S. Emergent diagnosis via coalition formation. In: IBERAMIA 2002 - Proceedings of the 8th Iberoamerican Conference on Artificial Intelligence. Garijo,F. (ed.), Springer Verlag, 2002.

Towards Qualitative Accreditation with Cognitive Agents

Anton Minko[1] and Guy Gouardères[2]

[1]Interactive STAR, Centre Condorcet Développement 162, av. du Dr.A.Schweitzer
33600 PESSAC, France
anton.minko@star-ima.com
[2]Equipe ISIHM - LIUPPA - IUT de Bayonne, 64100
Bayonne, France
Guy.Gouarderes@iutbay.univ-pau.fr

Abstract. This paper presents the results of application of cognitive models to aeronautic training through the usage of a multi-agent based ITS (Intelligent Tutoring Systems). More particularly, the paper deals with models of human error and application of multi-agent technologies to diagnose human errors and underlying cognitive gaps. The model of reasoning based on qualitative simulation supplies a wide variety of parameters as the base for pedagogical evaluation of the trainee. The experimental framework is simulation-based ITS, which uses a «learning by doing errors» approach. The overall process is intended to be used in the perspective of e-accreditation of training, which seems to become unavoidable in the context of globalisation and development of e-learning in aeronautic companies.

1 Introduction

In the world of aeronautical training, many training tasks are more and more performed in simulators. Aeronautical simulators are very powerful training tools which allow to reach a very high degree of realism (perception of the simulator as a real aircraft by trainee). However, several problems may appear. One of the most critical problems is taking into account the behaviour of the trainee, which remains relatively limited because of the lack of the online feedback on the users' behaviour.

Our research is centred on the description and the qualification of various types of behaviours in critical situations (resolution of a problem under risk constraints) depending on committed errors. We articulated these two issues by describing two major sources of errors that come from the trainee's behaviour, using an adapted version of the ACT-R/PM model [3]. The first, fairly general source of errors in ACT-R models, is the failure of retrieval or mis-retrieval of various pieces of knowledge (in CBT, Computer-Based Training, systems – checked Flow-Charts, or in PFC – Procedures Follow-Up Component – in terms of ASIMIL, see end of paragraph). The second and more systematic error source is the time/accuracy trade-off in decision-making.

There are also other secondary sources of error, such as the trainee failing to see a necessary sign/indicator in the time provided in order to perform the needed operation. These sources of error are mainly due to ergonomics or psychology affects.

J.C. Lester et al. (Eds.): ITS 2004, LNCS 3220, pp. 118–127, 2004.

In this work we try to translate all of the above-mentioned sources/parameters of errors into triggered hallmarks that are in the learner profile [15]. We have considered a number and the possible extensions of the error types after Rasmussen's framework [12] and performed partial in-depth analyses about: level of reflexes (sensor-motor ability), level of rule-based errors (widely revised in aeronautic research [7]), level of trainee's cognitive abilities based on John Self's [15] theory about learner profile.
Our idea consisted in proposing a multi-agent system including open and revisable competencies of a human tutor in the framework of Actors-like agents architecture (autonomous and concurrent), where different agents are specialised in their respective types of errors.
This research was undertaken within the framework of project ASIMIL (Aero user friendly SIMulation based dIstance Learning) financed by the 5th Framework Program of of the European Community. The main objective of ASIMIL project consisted in exploring new approaches in the aeronautical training, including distance training, simulation, technologies of intelligent agents and virtual reality. The final prototype represents a real desktop simulator installed on a workstation over the network.

2 Cognitive Modelling of Learning (Training) Process

The general question raised in this paper: how to ensure a good quality of computer-assisted training equivalent or higher than that obtained in the classical training. We found the answer in the use of ITS and in the modification of the conventional training loop [11] by introducing cognitive models.
By definition, ITS is an adaptive system. Its adaptation is carried out via the modification of the internal representation of learning recorded and used by the ITS (learner profile). The system must build a personalised model of learner, allowing to adapt the course curriculum to the trainee, to help him/her browse the course and to carry out exercises, by providing personalised help.
Cognitive models provide the means of applying psychology to predict time, errors, and other measures of user interaction. [16]
This leads us to restore the role of the instructor in the training, because the main task of computerisation in the training consists in returning to the instructor all the freedom of diagnosis and decision by decreasing his/her logistics' tasks for the profit of teaching. Moreover, the ITS is obliged to interact with all the components present in the conventional loop of training (trainee, trainer, simulator, training procedures).
According to Piaget model, the declarative knowledge is posterior to the procedural knowledge. In the model ACT (Component of Though Activates) of John Anderson, (here we ACT-R/PM of Anderson & Byrnes) [3], the formalised articulation is opposite to the processes of knowledge acquisition. The cognition is analysed on the symbolic level and the basic cognitive unit is the condition-action rule (see Fig.1). The working memory of R/PM engine is only seen as a system, which is independent of the long-term working memory. Cognition is then considered as a succession of cognitive processes which are connected dynamically, posing with a great acuity the

problem of centralised control (Amygdala) or not (sensory effectors). The basic level is the activation of a concept, which characterises the state of a concept at rest. That level is more significant for experts than for non-experts.

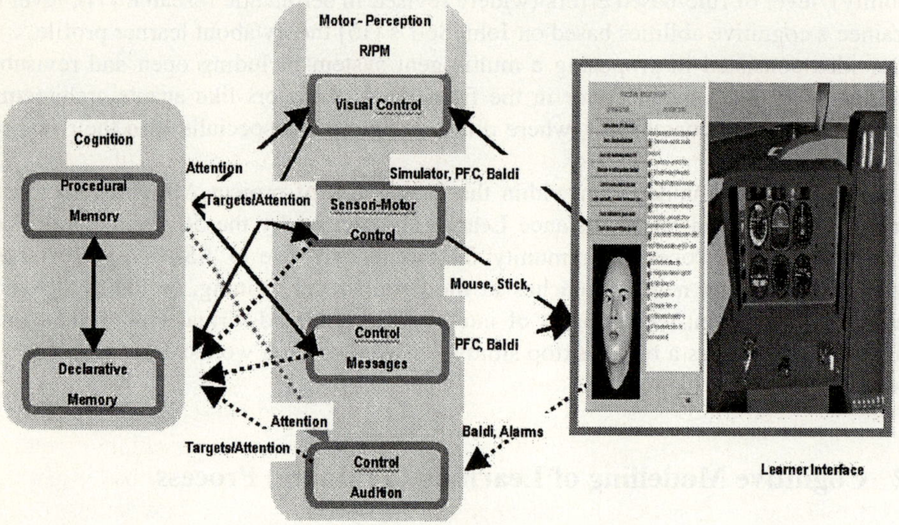

Fig. 1. Cognitive control of dialogue's modalities by ACT-R/PM model in ASIMIL[1]

The expertise of knowledge acquisition can be described like the sequential application of independent rules, which are compiled and reinforced by the exercise of automation, thus allowing the acquisition of procedural knowledge. Moreover, in ASIMIL, we have needed to control several methods of parallel dialogue and exchanges (messages – texts/word, orders – mouse/stick/caps/instructions, alarms – visual/sound...). In this model, one can also specify the role of the cognitive resources in the high level cognitive tasks and adopt proposals exchanged at the time of a conversation.

We have used the interaction in a manner of ACT-R/PM model, which provides an integrated model (module of cognition connected to perception-motor module) and a strong psychology theory on how interaction occurs. Furthermore, ACT-R/PM model allows to produce diagnostics in real-time, what is very important in the context of aeronautic training exercises, which are often time-critical.

[1] ACT-R/PM architecture is presented on the left part of figure. ASIMIL interface – on the right part (System of procedures follow-up on the left, flight simulator on the right and an animated agent (Baldi))

3 Theoretic Modelling of Error

Often, methods of systems' design, applied to the modelling of the human operator, give the results too oriented towards the system, and not oriented towards the individual. Among the models used we can mention the following: scalar, overlay, error-based, genetic [2]. Usually, the activity of a human operator uses cognitive factors (motivation, stress, emotions), and cannot be evaluated efficiently via conventional mathematical equations. It becomes necessary to use other techniques resulting from research in the field of belief-based logic [8] or qualitative modelling [14].

The committed errors are used as reference marks for the detection of changes in behaviour. Three reference frames are defined to cover various solutions which the trainee is able to adopt in the course of the realisation of a given task [6]: (a) frame of the prescribed task: the error is defined like a non-respect or non-application of the procedure, (b) standard frame of the typical user: this frame represents the set of tasks carried out by a standard operator in the same profession, (c) frame of the operator himself/herself (individual activity).

A primary typology of gaps ("tunnel", intervals of motivation) was already established [5]. The analysis of works carried out by Rasmussen [12], Norman [10], Reason [13], brought us to extend this typology, by distinguishing three different types of errors: the errors due to an insufficient knowledge, the errors due to a bad ergonomy of the ITS (they can be detected after the observations of the interactions of the trainee with the ITS), errors in connection with psychophysiologic factors of the human operator (i.e. human factor in order to determine the level of trainee's self-confidence [1]).

The general outline of the evaluation process is presented on the Fig.2, next page.

According to [9], one of the main characteristics of an ITS, as well as for the human teacher, is to be qualified in the subject which ITS teaches. For ITS, the approach consists in equipping the system with capabilities to reason on any problem of the field (within the limits imposed by the syntax of the command language). A major consequence of this projection is reflected by the overall evolution of computer-based instruction systems, which evolved from the principle of codification of pre-set solutions towards the processes of resolution.

In qualitative representation, it is important that trainees become designers because during the process of design, they are brought to articulate the relations between the entities and the various beliefs about these entities. The suggested qualitative models must provide the means for beliefs' externalisation and the support for the reasoning, for the discussion and for the justification of decisions [14].

Another characteristic of our system of trainee's modelling consists in the fact that the evaluation and the integral note include the components of three kinds: knowledge, ergonomy, psychology (see Fig.2).

Inside each criterion, there are elements (for example, knowledge and know-how of the trainee in the criterion "knowledge") which are viewed as quasi-constant during a session of training.

Then, at the time of training session, each criterion performs an analysis of the trainee's actions from its own "point of view" (that of the criterion in question).

The evaluation of each criterion gives a qualitative coefficient (Kc, Ke or Kp according to the name of the criterion – knowledge, ergonomy, psychology), which is used in the calculation of the current performance.

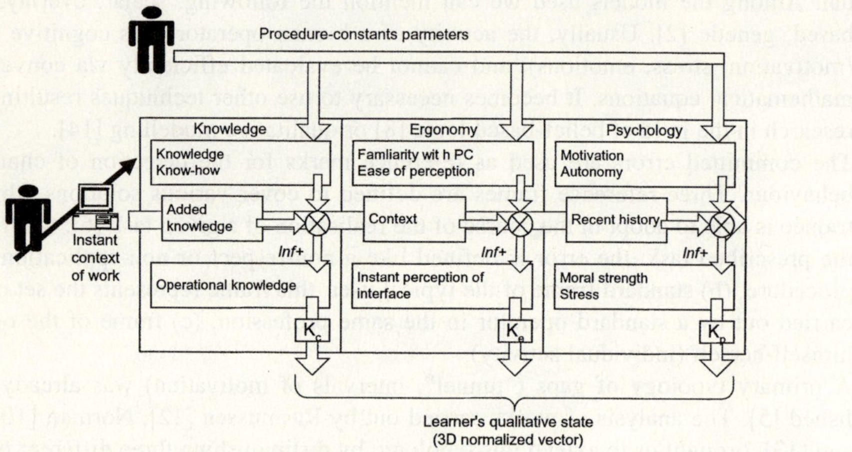

Fig. 2. Process of qualitative evaluation

According to the error's gravity, the graph of total performance is built online. Teacher's intervention is carried out in different cases detected according to score's and its derivatives' changes.

Moreover, the terms of surprised error and awaited error are introduced in order to be able to calculate the rate of error's expectation by the ITS. This coefficient is used in the process of decision-making – is this particular error expected by the ITS or not? More coefficients K are high, more error's expectation is low (error's surprise is high). Thus, K determines the character of teacher's assistance provided to learner.

As learner evolves in three-dimensional space (knowledge, ergonomy, psychology), we have the possibility to follow his/her integral progression (by measuring instantaneous length of the vector of error $\vec{E}$ like its performances on each one of the criteria c, e or p, see also results presented in section 5).

4 Multi-agent System Architecture

As ITS was designed under the form of a Multi-Agent System (MAS), this section briefly presents its main components.

Multi-agent technologies are widely used in the field of ITS [4], [5]. The aeronautical training has five characteristics which make it particularly adapted to agent applications: it is modular, decentralised, variable, ill-structured and complex. Three main components of an ITS (student, knowledge and pedagogical models) were integrated

in the architecture of intelligent agents such as Actors [4]. This architecture is presented on the Fig.2, and the interface of the whole system on Fig.3.
The experimental framework for the ASIMIL training system is simulation-based intelligent peer-to-peer review process which is performed by autonomous agents (as Knowledge, Ergonomic, Psychologic). Each agent scans separately a common stream of messages coming from other actors (Human, intelligent agents, physical disposals). They perform coalitions in order to supply a given community of users (instructors, learners, moderators,...) with diagnoses and advises as well as to allow actors mutually help one another.
A dedicated architecture called ASITS [5] was directly adopted from Actors [4] by including a cognitive architecture based on ACT-R/PM. Within the ASITS agent's framework, ACT ("Adaptive Control of Thought") is preferred to "Atomic Components of Thought", R stands for "rationale accepted as Revision or Reviewing", and PM stands for "perceptual and motor" monitoring of task. [3]

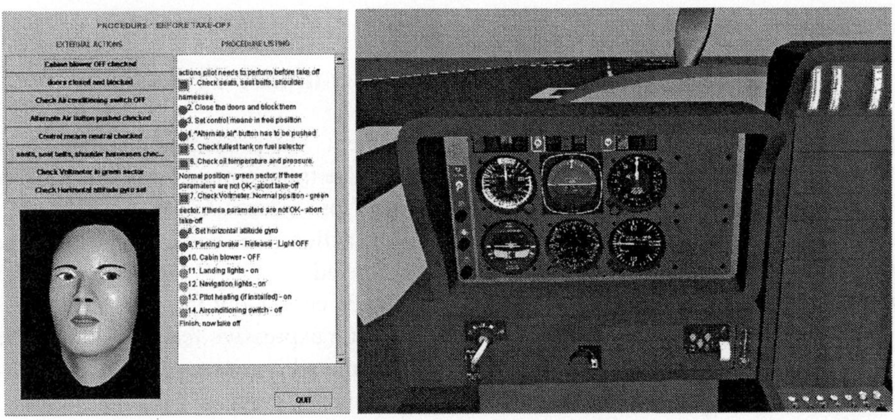

Fig. 3. System of procedures follow-up on the left, flight simulator on the right and an animated agent (Baldi)

The various agents of this architecture are:

- Interface agent ensures the communication between the MAS and the other components of the system (simulator, virtual reality, procedures)
- Curriculum agent traces the evolution of learner in interaction with the system and builds history
- team of agents-Evaluators of errors realises diagnoses of trainee's errors according to three axes: knowledge, ergonomy or psychology
- Pedagogical agent carries out the evaluation and brings a help to learning
- agent-Manager of the didactic resources looks up for pedagogical resources required.

The effectiveness of the follow-up by agents ASITS was already shown in CMOS prototype [5]. Today, the presence of several agents-evaluators allows the diagnosis of several types of errors. The agents-evaluators launch the evaluation, then the

variation is quantified, evaluated and redirected towards the Pedagogical agent in order to be operated (announced and/or stored for the debriefing).
The system ASIMIL was the object of evaluations during 8 months in real conditions. These evaluations have involved trainees and private pilots from France and Italy (since they were conducted in the framework of ASIMIL project). The evaluations allowed to underline the following tendencies:

- trainers perceive the tool positively: according to them, such a software could become of a good support for trainees (Pedagogical agent doesn't miss any error) and for trainers themselves (the agents' debriefing is explicit and can serve as a base for face-to-face debriefing)
- trainees also have approved the software, but they pointed out the disturbing character of Pedagogical Agent who spoke in English only. In reality, the training is often performed in native language (French or Italian, in our case) even if international aeronautic requirements (JAR, FAR)[2] are formal and recognise English as the only official training language.

5 Example of Agents' Functioning in Aeronautic Training

Fig.3 shows three components of training environment. The procedure presented here is the procedure of takeoff ("Takeoff Procedure"). The trainee must carry out a series of actions on the simulator, whereas the system of procedures follow-up PFC validates the actions carried out by learner. If learner's action does not correspond to the action required by the procedure, a red light is displayed.
The Pedagogical agent (animated character on Fig.3) carries out the teaching expertise on trainee (similar to Steve but with more realistic expressive features – [17]). Its diagnoses are based on the trainee's history. The animated agent was developed in cooperation with the university of Santa Cruz, California.
In complement of traditional means of trainee's evaluation, which are proposed in ITS, we concentrated our efforts on the means at the disposal of the human tutor (instructor). Two main functions were identified as essential for an effective follow-up of a trainee by the instructor:

- synchronous or asynchronous follow-up of the trainee: show of the events recorded in the history of each training session (see Fig.4)
- customisation of Pedagogical agent: changing its physical appearance (face aspect, gravity of voice) as well as its reasoning (thresholds of help messages, conditions of stopping procedure).

Two undeniable advantages consist in the fact that the agents do not let pass any deviation/error, and in carrying out, for the instructor, the supervision of several trainees simultaneously.

[2] The Joint Aviation Authorities (JAA) is an associated body of the European Civil Aviation Conference (ECAC) publishes the Joint Aviation Requirements (JARs) whereas the Federal Aviation Administration edits the Federal Aviation Regulations (FAR).

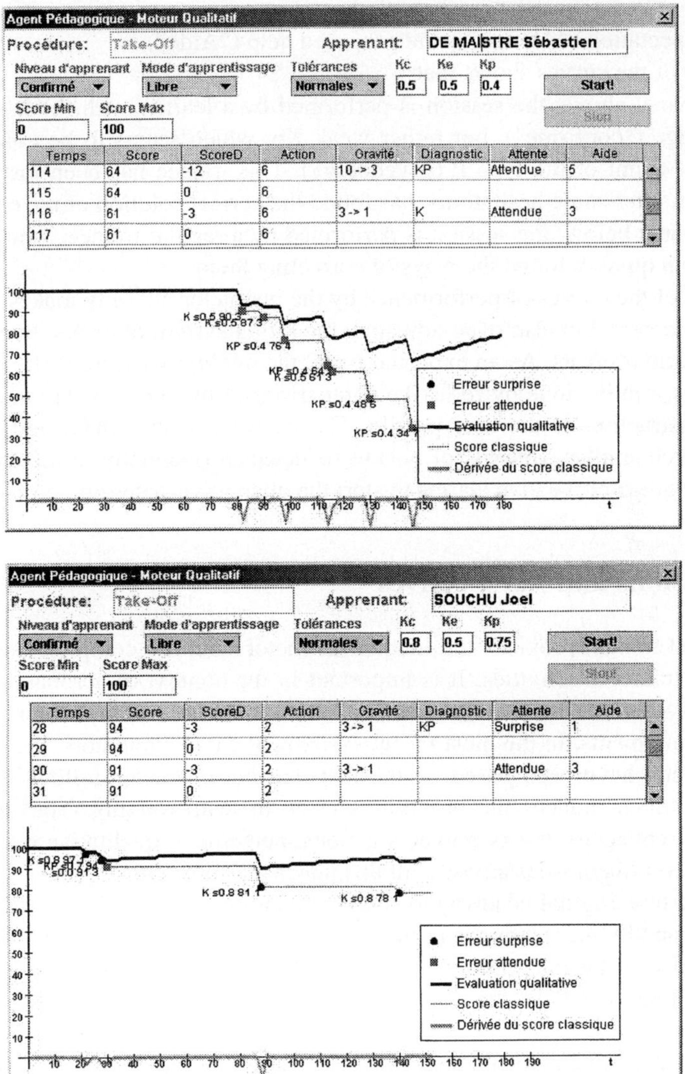

Fig. 4. Instructor's «Dashboard» cases – "disturbed" trainee (above) and "normal" trainee (below)

The following details are presented in the window of instructor (see Fig.4). The axis of abscissa means time starting from the beginning of the exercise. The axis of ordinates means the variation of the objective of the exercise (also called user's "qualitative score"). A certain number of general options enters in account, such as level of learner, mode of training, tolerances, coefficients of performance Kc, Ke, Kp etc. The monitoring table (in the middle of each panel on Fig.4) holds the chronology of the session. One can see the moment when an error has appeared (column "Temps"), the qualification of the error ("Diagnostic"), its gravity ("Gravité", a number of points to

be removed, associated with gravity with the error – slight, serious or critical), degree of error's expectation ("Attente"), and proposed help ("Aide").
The analysis of the curves shows that:

- on the panel above, the session is performed by a learner with the high level of knowledge ("confirmé"), but rather weak Kp, which seems to be confirmed by the error count of the type P (psychology). This trainee has been lost facing an error but, after some hesitations, has found the correct solution of the exercise
- on the panel below, the session is performed by a regular trainee, who made two errors, but quickly found the ways of correcting them.

The analysis of the curves of performance by the instructor not only makes it possible to evaluate learners, but also of re-adjusting the rating system of errors, by modifying weights of various errors. As an expected issue, the qualitative accreditation of differentiated users, can be done by reflexive comparison of the local deviation during the dynamic construction of the user profile. The analysis of the curves red and black allows to match similar patterns (or not) to be detected (manually in the current version) and the green curve give alarms to start the qualitative accreditation process.

6 Conclusions and Perspectives

The presented system provides the human instructor with the complete and detailed report about trainee's activities. It is important in the context of aeronautic training, because the system has been designed in collaboration with real instructors and satisfies their requirements. In the most recent systems of cabin simulators, the evaluation and certification have been based on the fact that the instructor follows the trainee step-by-step which induces the prohibitive costs of team training. The multi-agent ACT-R/PM architecture tracks trainee's actions, performs a qualitative reasoning on them and deliver diagnostics/advises, all this under real-time constraints.
We presented one original headway to supply an additional evaluation which is traditionally obtained by the instructor in the course of training. This innovative step was possible thanks to the integration of techniques resulting from various fields (ITS, MAS, Modelling) but with the concern of keeping the reasoning close to human logic.
Qualitative evaluation allows to reach two objectives: evaluate each learner separately by using instructor's terms (core of qualitative reasoning engine), but also compare learners' performances and tie them with psychological profiles.
Characteristics like the follow-up in real-time by the instructor of the trainee's cognitive discrepancies, by making the distinction between the errors relative to the simulator, to the procedures or to the cognitive tasks, established the base of our study. Nevertheless, we planned and carried out a reasonable but rigorous assessment of the variables and general options of the method of qualitative simulation which led to the establishment of a hierarchy of errors representing a significant progress compared with the previous work. The extension of the evaluation of the errors represents an unavoidable phase in the process of certification and qualification of the prototype for vocational training in aeronautics.

References

1. E. Aïmeur, C. Frasson. Reference Model For Evaluating Intelligent Tutoring Systems. Université de Montréal, TICE 2000 Troyes – Technologie de l'Information et de la Communication dans les Enseignements d'ingénieurs et dans l'industrie.
2. P. Brusilovsky. Intelligent tutor, environment, and manual for introductory programming. Educational and Training Technology International 29: pp.26-34.
3. M.D. Byrnes, J.R. Anderson, Serial modules in parallel: The psychological refractory period and perfect time-sharing, Psychological Review, 108, 847–869. 2001.
4. C. Frasson, T. Mengelle, E. Aïmeur, G. Gouardères. «An actor-based architecture for intelligent tutroing systems», Intl Conference on ITS, Montréal–96.
5. G. Gouardères, A. Minko, L. Richard. «Simulation et Systèmes Multi-Agents pour la formation professionnelle dans le domaine aéronautique», Dans Simulation et formation professionelle dans l'industrie, Coordonnateurs M. Joab et G. Gouardères, Hermès Science, Vol.6, No.1, pp.143-188, 1999.
6. F. Jambon. "Erreurs et interruptions du point de vue de l'ingénierie de l'interaction homme-machine". Thèse de doctorat de l'Université Joseph Fourier (Grenoble 1). Soutenue le 05 décembre 1996.
7. A.A. Krassovski. Bases of simulators' theory in aviation. Moscow, Machinostroenie, 1995, 304p. (in Russian)
8. K. Van Lehn, S. Ohlsson, R. Nason. Application of Simulated Students: an exploration. Journal of Artificial Intelligence in Education, vol.5, n.2, 1994; p.135-175.
9. P. Mendelsohn, P. Dillenbourg. Le développement de l'enseignement intelligemment assisté par ordinateur. Conférence donnée à l'Association de Psychologie Scientifique de Langue Française Symposium Intelligence Naturelle et Intelligence Artificielle, Rome, 23-25 septembre 1991.
10. K.L. Norman. «The psychology of menu selection: designing cognitive control at the human/computer interface», Ables Publishing, Norwood NJ, 1991.
11. O. Popov, R. Lalanne, G. Gouardères, A. Minko, A. Tretyakov. Some Tasks of Intelligent Tutoring Systems Design for Civil Aviation Pilots. Advanced Computer Systems. The Kluwer International Series in Engineering and Computer Science. Kluwer Academic Publishers. Boston/Dordrecht/London, 2002
12. J. Rasmussen. «Information processing and human-machine interaction: an approach to cognitive engineering», North-Holland, 1986.
13. J. Reason. Human error. Cambridge University Press. Cambridge,1990.
14. P. Salles, B. Bredeweg. «A case study of collaborative modelling: building qualitative models in ecology». ITS-2002, Workshop on Model-Based Educational Systems and Qualitative Reasoning, San-Sebastian, Spain, June 2002.
15. J. Self. The Role of Student Models in Learning Environments. AAI/AI-ED Technical Report No.94. In Transactions of the Institute of Electronics, Information and Communication Engineers, E77-D(1), 3-8, 1994.
16. F.E. Ritter, D. Van Rooy, F. St Amant. A user modeling design tool based on a cognitive architecture for comparing interfaces. Proceedings of the Fourth International Conference on Computer-Aided Design of User Interfaces (CADUI), 2002.
17. W. Lewis Johnson: Interaction tactics for socially intelligent pedagogical agents. Intelligent User Interfaces 2003: 251-253.

Integrating Intelligent Agents, User Models, and Automatic Content Categorization in a Virtual Environment

Cássia Trojahn dos Santos and Fernando Santos Osório

Master Program in Applied Computing, Unisinos University
Av. Unisinos, 950 – 93.022-000 – São Leopoldo – RS – Brazil
{cassiats,osorio}@exatas.unisinos.br

Abstract. This paper presents an approach that aims to integrate intelligent agents, user models and automatic content categorization in a virtual environment. In this environment, called AdapTIVE (Adaptive Three-dimensional Intelligent and Virtual Environment), an intelligent virtual agent assists users during navigation and retrieval of relevant information. The users' interests and preferences, represented in a user model, are used in the adaptation of environment structure. An automatic content categorization process, that applies machine-learning techniques, is used in the spatial organization of the contents in the environment. This is a promising approach for new and advanced forms of education, entertainment and e-commerce. In order to validate our approach, a case study of a distance-learning environment, used to make educational content available, is presented.

1 Introduction

Virtual Reality (VR) becomes an attractive alternative for the development of more interesting interfaces for the user. The environments that make use of VR techniques are referred as Virtual Environments (VEs). In VEs, according to [2], the user is part of the system, an autonomous presence in the environment. He is able to navigate, to interact with objects and to examine the environment from different points of view. As indicated in [11], the 3D paradigm is useful mainly because it offers the possibility of representing information in a realistic way, while it organizes content in a spatial manner. In this way, a larger intuition in the visualization of the information is obtained, allowing the user to explore it in an interactive way, more natural to humans. Nowadays, the use of intelligent agents in VEs has been explored. According to [3], these agents when inserted in virtual environments are called Intelligent Virtual Agents (IVAs). They act as users' assistants in order to help to explore the environment and to locate information [8,15,16,18], being able to establish a verbal communication (e.g., using natural language) or non verbal (through body movement, gestures and face expressions) with the user. The use of these agents has many advantages: to enrich the interaction with the virtual environment [25]; to turn the environ

J.C. Lester et al. (Eds.): ITS 2004, LNCS 3220, pp. 128–139, 2004.

ment less intimidating, more natural and attractive to the user [8]; to prevent the users from feeling lost in the environment [24].

At the same time, the systems capable of adapting its structure from a user model have received special attention on research community, especially Intelligent Tutoring Systems and Adaptive Hypermedia. According to [13], a user model is a collection of information and suppositions on individual users or user groups, necessary for the system to adapt several aspects of its functionalities and interface. The adoption of a user model has been showing great impact in the development of filter systems and information retrieval [4,14], electronic commerce [1], learning systems [29] and adaptive interfaces [5,21]. These systems have already proven to be more effective and/or usable that non adaptive ones [10]. However, the research effort in adaptive systems has being focused in the adaptation of traditional 2D/textual environments. Adaptation of 3D VEs is still few explored, but considered promising [6,7].

Moreover, in relation to organizing of content in VEs, the grouping of the contents, according to some semantic criterion, is interesting and sometimes necessary. An approach to organization of content consists in the automatic content categorization process. This process is based on machine learning techniques (see e.g, [28]) and comes being applied in general context, such as web pages classification [9,20]. However, it can be adopted in the organization of content in VE context.

In this paper we present an approach that aims to integrate intelligent agents, user models and automatic content categorization in a virtual environment. In this environment, called AdapTIVE (Adaptive Three-dimensional Intelligent and Virtual Environment), an intelligent virtual agent assists users during navigation and retrieval of relevant information. The users' interests and preferences, represented in a user model, are used in the adaptation of environment structure. An automatic content categorization process is used in the spatial organization of the contents in the environment. In order to validate our approach, a case study of a distance-learning environment, used to make educational contents available, is presented.

The paper is organized as follow. In section 2, the AdapTIVE architecture is presented and its main components are detailed. In section 3, the case study is presented. Finally, section 4 presents the final considerations and future works.

2 AdapTIVE Architecture

The environment consists of the representation of a three-dimensional world, accessible through the Web, used to make content available, which are organized by the area of knowledge that they belong. In the environment (Fig. 1), there is support for two types of users: information *consumer* (e.g., student) and information *provider* (e.g., teacher). The users are represented by avatars, they can explore the environment searching relevant content and can be aided by the *intelligent agent*, in order to navigate and to locate information. The user models are used in the environment adaptation and are managed by the *user model manager* module. The contents are added or removed by the provider through the *content manager module* and stored in a *content database*. Each content contains a *content model*. The *provider*, aided by the automatic content categorization process, acts in the definition of this model. From the *content model*, the spatial position of each content in the environment is defined. The representation of the contents in the environment is made by three-dimensional objects and links to the data (e.g., text document, web page). The *environment generator module* is the responsible for the generation of different three-dimensional structures that form the environment and to arrange the information in the environment, according to the user and content models. The environment adaptation involves its reorganization, in relation to the arrangement of the contents and aspects of its layout (e.g. use of different textures and colors, according to user's preference). In the following sections are detailed the main components of the environment: user model manager, content manager and intelligent agent.

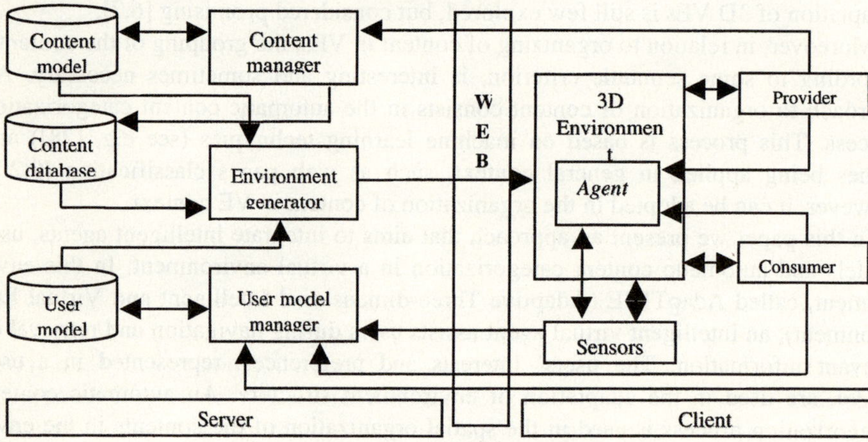

Fig. 1. AdapTIVE architecture.

2.1 User Model Manager

This module is responsible for the initialization and updating of user models. The user model contains information about the user's interests, preferences and behaviors. In order to collect the data used in the composition of the model, the explicit and implicit approaches [19,20] are used. The explicit approach is adopted to acquire the user's preferences compounding an initial user model and the implicit one is applied to update this model. In the explicit approach, a form is used to collect fact data (e.g., name, gender, areas of interest and preferences for colors). In the implicit approach, the monitoring of user navigation in the environment and his interactions with the agent are made. Through this approach, the environment places visited by the user and the requested (through the search mechanism) and accessed (clicked) contents are monitored. These data are used to update the initial user model.

The process of updating the user model is based on rules and certainty factors (CF) [12,17]. The rules allow to infer conclusions (hypothesis) from antecedents (evidences). To each conclusion, it is possible to associate a CF, which represents the degree of belief associated to corresponding hypothesis. Thus, the rules can be described in the following format: **IF** Evidence (s) **THEN** Hypothesis with **CF = x degree**. The CFs associate measures of belief (MB) and disbelief (MD) to a hypothesis (H), given an evidence (E). A CF=1 indicates total belief in a hypothesis, while CF=-1 corresponds a total disbelief. The calculation of the CF is accomplished by the formulas (1), (2) and (3), where P(H) represents the probability of the hypothesis (i.e. the interest in some area), and P(H|E) is the probability of the hypothesis (H), given that some evidence (E) exists. In the environment, the user's initial interest in a given area (initial value of P(H)) is determined by the explicit data collection and it may vary during the process of updating the model (based on threshold of increasing and decreasing belief), where P(H|E) is obtained from the implicit approach.

$$CF = \frac{MB - MD}{1 - MIN(MB, MD)} \tag{1}$$

$$MB = \begin{cases} 1 & \text{if } P(H) = 1 \\ \dfrac{MAX[P(H|E), P(H)] - P(H)}{1 - P(H)} & \text{otherwise} \end{cases} \tag{2}$$

$$MD = \begin{cases} 1 & \text{if } P(H) = 0 \\ \dfrac{MIN[P(H|E), P(H)] - P(H)}{0 - P(H)} & \text{otherwise} \end{cases} \tag{3}$$

The evidences are related to the environment areas visited and to the requested and accessed contents by the user. They are used to infer the hypothesis of the user's interest in each area of knowledge, from the rules and corresponding CFs. To update the model the rules (4), (5), (6) and (7) were defined. The rules (4), (5) and (6) are used when evidences of request, navigation and/or access exist. In this case, the combination of the rules is made and the resultant CF is calculated - formula (8), where two rules with CF1 and CF2 are combined. The rule (7) is used when does not exist any evidence, indicating total lack of user interest in the corresponding area.

IF request **THEN** interest in Y with **CF = x** (4)
IF navigation **THEN** interest in Y with **CF = x** (5)
IF access **THEN** interest in Y with **CF = x** (6)
IF (not request) and (not navigation) and (not access) **THEN** interest in Y with **CF = x** (where x<0) (7)

$$CF = \begin{cases} CF1 + CF2\,(1 - CF1) & \text{if both} > 0 \\ \dfrac{CF1 + CF2}{1 - MIN(|CF1|, |CF2|)} & \text{if one} < 0 \\ CF1 + CF2\,(1 + CF1) & \text{if both} < 0 \end{cases} \tag{8}$$

Each *n* sessions (adjustable time window), for each area, the evidences (navigation, request and access) are verified, the inferences with the rules are made, and the CFs corresponding to the hypothesis of interest are updated. By sorting the resulting CFs, it is possible to establish a ranking of user's areas of interest. Therefore, it is possible to verify the alterations in the initial model (obtained from the explicit data collection) and, thus, to update the user model. From this update, the reorganization of the environment is made - contents that correspond to the areas of major user's interest are placed, in a visualization order, before the contents which are less interesting (easier access). It must be addressed that each modification in the environment is always suggested to the user and accomplished only under user's acceptance.

Our motivation to adopt rules and CFs is based on the following main ideas. First, it is a formalism that allows to infer hypothesis of the user's interests in the areas from a set of evidences (e.g., navigation, request and access), also considering a degree of uncertainty about the hypothesis. Second, it can be an alternative to Bayesian Nets, an other common approach used in user modeling, considering that it doesn't require to know a full priori set of probabilities and conditional tables. Third, it doesn't require the pre-definition of user categories, as in the techniques based on stereotypes. Moreover, it has low computational cost, is intuitive, robust and extensible (considering that it was extended, allowing to create the new type of rule). In this way, this formalism can be considered an alternative technique in user modeling.

2.2 Content Manager

This module is responsible for insertion and removal of contents, and management of its models. The content models contain the following data: category (among a predefined set), title, description, keywords, type of media and corresponding file. From content model, the spatial position that the content will occupy in the environment is defined. The contents are also grouped into virtual rooms by main areas (categories). For textual contents, an automatic categorization process is available, thus the category and the keywords of the content are obtained. For non textual contents (for instance, images and videos), textual descriptions of contents can be used in the automatic categorization process.

The automatic categorization process is formed by a sequence of stages: (a) document base collection; (b) pre-processing; and (c) categorization. The document base collection consists of obtaining the examples to be used for training and test of the learning algorithm. The pre-processing involves, for each example, the elimination of irrelevant words (e.g., articles, prepositions, pronouns), the removal of affix of the words and the selection of the most important words (e.g., considering the word frequency occurrence), used to characterize the document. In the categorization stage, the learning technique is then determined, the examples are coded, and the classifier learning is accomplished. After these stages, the classifier can be used in the categorization of new documents. In a set of preliminary experiments (details in [26]), decision trees [23] showed to be more robust and were selected for use in the categorization process proposed in the environment. In these experiments, the pre-processing stage was supported by an application, extended from a *framelet* (see [22]), whose kernel contemplates the basic flow of data among the activities of the pre-processing stage and generation of scripts submitted to the learning algorithms. After, the "learned model" - rules extracted from the decision tree - is connected to the content manager module, in order to use it in the categorization of new documents. Thus, when a new document is inserted in the environment, it is pre-processed, has its keywords extracted and is automatically categorized and positioned in the environment.

2.3 Intelligent Virtual Agent

The intelligent virtual agent assists users during navigation and retrieval of relevant information. The agent's architecture reflects the following modules: knowledge base, perception, decision and action. The agent's knowledge base stores the information that it holds about the user and the environment. This knowledge is built from two sources of information: external source and perception of the interaction with the user. The external source is the information about the environment and the user, and they are originated from the environment generator module. A perception module observes the interaction with the user, and the information obtained from this observation is used to update the agent's knowledge. It is through the perception module that the agent detects the requests from user and observes the user's actions in the environment. Based on its perception and in the knowledge that it holds, the agent decides how to act in the environment. A decision module is responsible for this activity. The decisions are passed to an action module, responsible to execute the actions (e.g., animation of graphic representation and speech synthesis).

The communication between the agent and the users can be made by three ways: in a verbal way, through a pseudo-natural language and speech synthesis[1], and non verbal way, by the agent's actions in the environment. The dialogue in pseudo-natural language consists of a certain group of questions and answers and short sentences, formed by a verb that corresponds to the type of user request and a complement, regarding the object of user interest. During the request for helping to locate information, for instance, the user can indicate (in textual interface) *Locate <content>*. The agent's answers are suggested by its own movement through the environment, by indications through short sentences, and by text-to-speech synthesis. In the interaction with provider, during the insertion of content, he can indicate *Insert <content>*, and the agent presents the data entry interface for the specification, identification and automatic categorization of the content model.

Moreover, a topological map of the environment is kept in the agent's knowledge base. In this map, a set of routes for key-positions of the environment is stored. In accordance with the information that the agent has about the environment and with the map, it defines a set of routes that must be used in the localization of determined content or used to navigate until determined environment area. Considering that the agent updates its knowledge for each modification in the environment, it is always able to verify the set of routes that leads to a new position of a specific content.

[1] JSAPI (Java Speech API)

3 Case Study Using AdapTIVE

In order to validate our proposal, a prototype of a distance learning environment [27], used to make educational content available, was developed. In the prototype, a division of the virtual environment is adopted according to the areas of the contents. In each area a set of sub-areas can be associated. The sub-areas are represented as subdivisions of the environment. In the prototype the following areas and sub-areas were selected: Artificial Intelligence (AI) – Artificial Neural Networks, Genetic Algorithms and Multi Agents Systems; Computer Graphics (CG) – Modeling, Animation and Visualization; Computer Networks (CN) – Security, Management and Protocols; Software Engineering (SE) – Analysis, Patterns and Software Quality. A room is associated to each area in the environment and the sub-areas are represented as subdivisions of rooms. Fig. 2 (a) and (b) show screen-shots of the prototype that illustrate the division of the environment in rooms and sub-rooms. In screen-shots, a system version in Portuguese is presented, where the description "Inteligência Artificial" corresponds to "Artificial Intelligence".

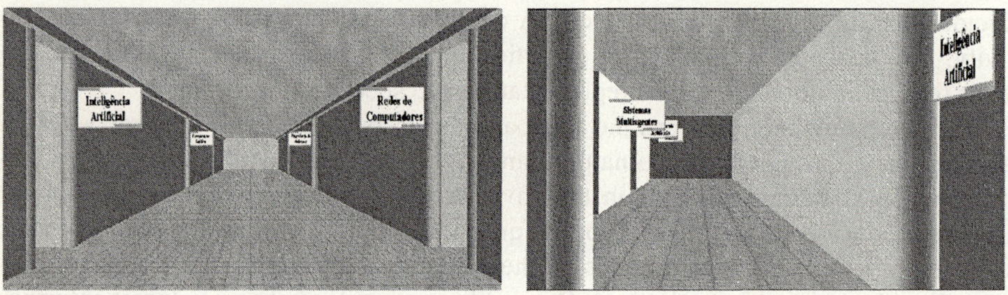

(a) (b)

Fig. 2. (a) Rooms of the environment; (b) Sub-rooms of the environment.

According to the user model, the reorganization of this environment is made: the rooms that correspond to the areas of major user's interest are placed, in a visualization order, before the rooms which contents are less interesting. The initial user model, based on explicit approach, is used to structure the initial organization of the environment. This involves also the use of avatars according to gender of user and the consideration of users' preferences by colors. As the user interacts with the environment, his model is updated and changes in the environment are made. After n sessions (time window), for each area, the evidences of interest (navigation, request and access) are verified, in order to update the user model. For instance, with a user, who is interested about Artificial Intelligence (AI), is indifferent to contents related to the areas of Computer Networks (CN) and Computer Graphics (CG), and does not show initial interest about Software Engineering (SE), the initial values of the CFs, at the beginning of the first session of interaction (without evidences), would be respectively 1, 0, 0 e -1. After doing some navigations (N), requests (R) and access (A), presented in the graph of Fig. 3, the CFs can be reevaluated. According to Fig. 3, it is verified that the CN area was not navigated, requested and accessed, and on the other side, the user started to navigate, to request, and to access contents in SE area. As presented in the graph of Fig. 4, an increasing of the CFs had been identified as related to the SE area. In that way, at end of the seventh session, the resulting CFs would be 1, -1, 0.4 and 0.2 (AI, CN, CG, SE, respectively). By sorting the resulting CFs, it would be possible to detect an alteration in the user model, whose new ranking of the interest areas would be AI, CG, SE, CN.

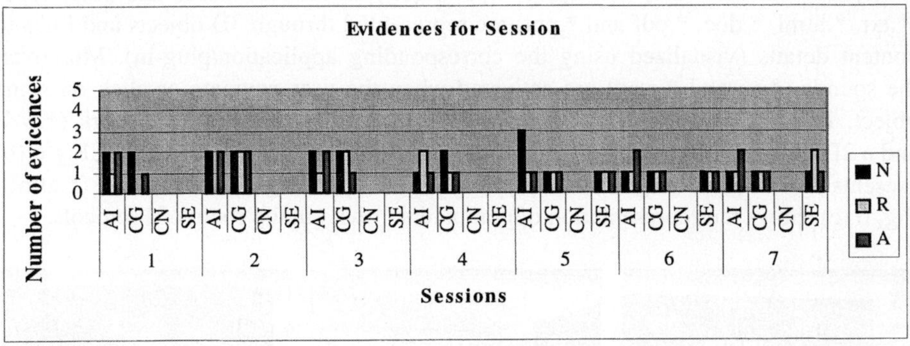

Fig. 3. Number of navigations (N), requests (R) and access (A) of each area, for session.

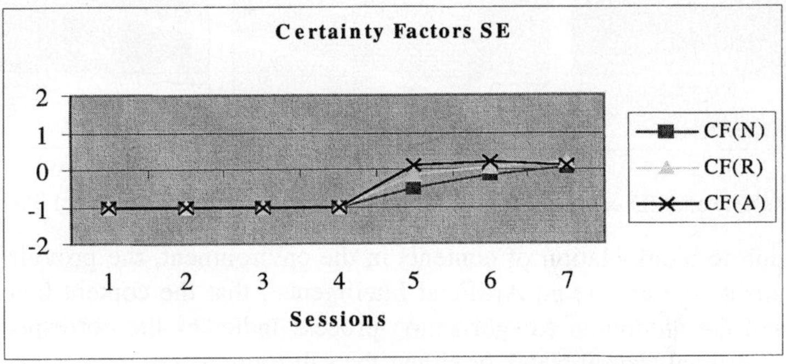

Fig. 4. Certainty factors corresponding to evidences of the SE area.

Fig. 5 (a) and (b) represent an example of the organization of the environment (2D view) before and after a modification in the user model, respectively, as showed in the example above.

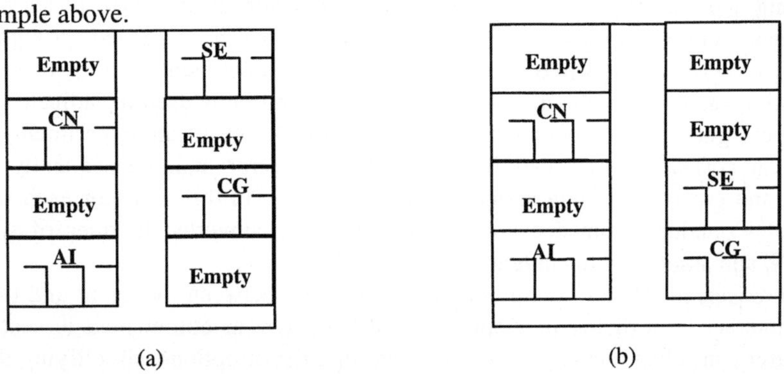

Fig. 5. (a) Organization of the environment according to initial user model; (b) Organization of the environment after the user model changes.

On the other side, in relation to contents in the environment, the following types are supported: *.txt, *.html, *.doc, *.pdf, *.ppt, *.jpg, *.bmp, *.wrl (VRML), *.avi, *.wav e *.au. The types that correspond to 2D and 3D images (*.bmp, *.jpg and *.wrl) and videos (*.avi) are represented directly in the 3D space. The other types (*.txt, *.html, *.doc, *.pdf and *.ppt) are represented through 3D objects and links to content details (visualized using the corresponding application/plug-in). Moreover, the sounds (*.au and *.wav) are activated when the user navigate or click on some object. The Fig. 6 (a) shows a simplified representation of a neural network (*.wrl) and a 2D image (*.jpg) of a type of neural network (Self Organizing Maps); Fig 6 (b) presents a 3D object and the visualization of corresponding content details (*.html); Fig. 6 (c) shows the representation of computers (*.wrl) in the room of Protocols.

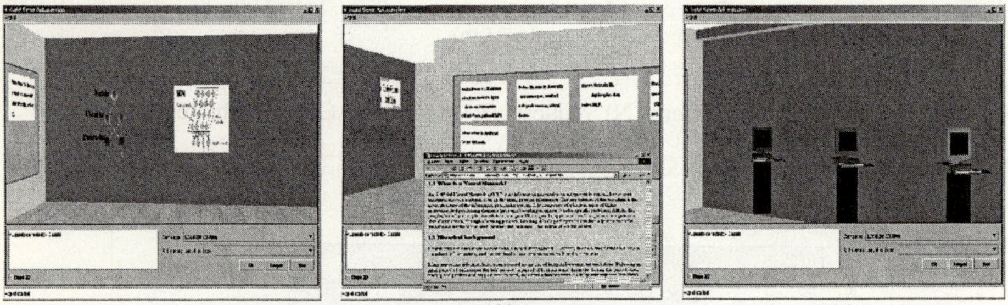

(a) (b) (c)

Fig. 6. (a) 3D and 2D contents; (b) 3D object and link to content details; (c) 3D content.

In relation to manipulation of contents in the environment, the provider model is used to indicate the area (e.g., Artificial Intelligence) that the content being inserted belongs, and the automatic categorization process indicates the corresponding sub-area (e.g., Artificial Neural Nets), or either, the sub-room where the content should be inserted. In this way, the spatial disposal of the content is made automatically by the environment generator, on the basis of its category. In the prototype, thirty examples of scientific papers, for each sub-area, had been collected from the Web, and used for learning and validation of the categorization algorithm. In the stage of learning, experiments with binary and multiple categorizations had been carried through. In the binary categorization, a tree is used to indicate if a document belongs or not to the definitive category. In the multiple categorization, a tree is used to indicate the most likely category of one document, amongst a possible set. In the experiments, the binary categorization presented better results (less error and, consequently, greater recall and precision), being adopted in the prototype. In this way, for each sub-area, the rules obtained from decision tree (C4.5) were converted to rules of type IF - THEN, and associated to content manager module.

Moreover, in relation to communication process between the agent and the users, they interact by a dialog in pseudo-natural language, as commented in section 2.1. The user can select one request to the agent in a list of options, simplifying the communication. The agent's answers are showed in the corresponding text interface window and synthesized to speech. Fig. 7 (a), (b), and (c) illustrate, respectively: a request of the user for the localization of determined area and the movement of the agent, together with a 2D environment map, used as an additional navigation resource; the localization of an sub-area by the agent; the user visualization of a content and the visualization of details of it, after selection and click in a specific content description.

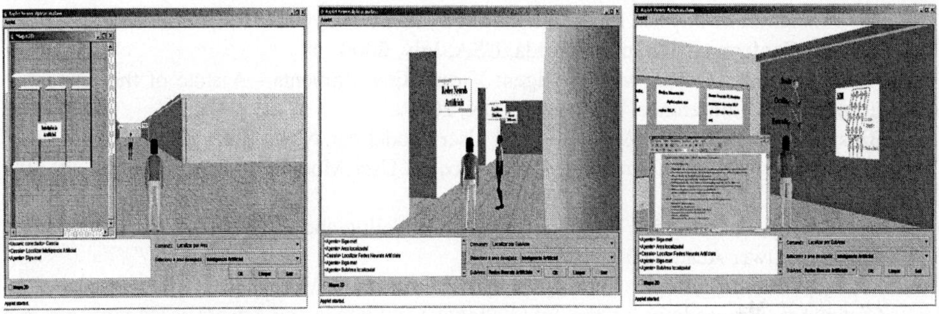

(a) (b) (c)

Fig. 7. (a) Request of the user; (b) Localization of a sub-area; (c) Visualization of contents.

4 Final Remarks

This paper presented an approach that integrates intelligent agents, user models and automatic content categorization in a virtual environment. The main objective was to explore the resources of Virtual Reality, seeking to increase the interactivity degree between the users and the environment. A large number of distance learning environments make content available through 2D environments, usually working with interfaces in HTML, offering poor interaction with the user. The spatial reorganization possibilities and the environment customization, according to the modifications in the available contents and the user models were presented. Besides, an automatic content categorization process that aims to help the specialist of the domain (provider) in the information organization in this environment was also shown. An intelligent agent that knows the environment and the user and acts assisting him in the navigation and location of information in this environment was described. A standout of this work is that it deals with the acquisition of users' characteristics in a three-dimensional environment. Most of the works related to user model acquisition and environment adaptation are accomplished using 2D interfaces. Moreover, a great portion of these efforts in the construction of Intelligent Virtual Environments don't provide the combination of user models, assisted navigation and retrieval of information, and, mainly, don't have the capability to reorganize the environment, and display the contents in a 3D space. Usually, only a sub-group of these problems is considered. This work extends and improves these capabilities 3D environments.

References

1. Abbattista, F.; Degemmis, M; Fanizzi, N.; Licchelli, O. Lops, P.; Semeraro, G.; Zambetta, F.: Learning User Profile for Content-Bases Filtering in e-Commerce. Workshop Apprendimento Automatico: Metodi e Applicazioni, Siena, Settembre, 2002.
2. Avradinis, N.; Vosinakis, S.; Panayiotopoulos, T.: Using Virtual Reality Techniques for the Simulation of Physics Experiments. 4th Systemics, Cybernetics and Informatics International Conference, Orlando, Florida, USA, July, 2000.
3. Aylett, R. and Cavazza, M.: Intelligent Virtual Environments - A state of the art report. Eurographics Conference, Manchester, UK, 2001.
4. Billsus, D. and Pazzani, M.: A Hybrid User Model for News Story Classification. Proceedings of the 7th International Conference on User Modeling, Banff, Canada, 99-108, 1999.
5. Brusilovsky, P.: Adaptive Hypermedia. User Modeling and User-Adapted Interaction, 11, 87-110, Kluwer Academic Publishers, 2001.
6. Chittaro L. and Ranon R.: Adding Adaptive Features to Virtual Reality Interfaces for E-Commerce. Proceedings of the International Conference on Adaptive Hypermedia and Adaptive Web-based Systems, Lecture Notes in Computer Science 1892, Springer-Verlag, Berlin, August, 2000.
7. Chittaro, L. and Ranon, R.: Dynamic Generation of Personalized VRML Content: A General Approach and its Application to 3D E-Commerce. Proceedings of 7th Conference on 3D Web Technology, USA, February, 2002.
8. Chittaro, R.; Ranon, R.; Ieronutti, L.: Guiding Visitors of Web3D Worlds through Automatically Generated Tours. Proceedings of the 8th Conference on 3D Web Technology, ACM Press, New York, March, 2003.
9. Duarte, E.; Braga, A.; Braga, J.: Agente Neural para Coleta e Classificação de Informações Disponíveis na Internet. Proceeding of the 16th Brazilian Symposium on Neural Networks, PE, Brazil, 2002.
10. Fink. J. and Kobsa, A.: A Review and Analysis of Commercial User Modeling Server for Personalization on the World Wide Web. User Modeling and User Adapted Interaction, 10(3-4), 209-249, 2000.
11. Frery, A.; Kelner, J.; Moreira, J., Teichrieb, V.: Satisfaction through Empathy and Orientation in 3D Worlds. CyberPsychology and Behavior, 5(5), 451-459, 2002.
12. Giarratano, J. and Riley, G.: Expert Systems - Principles and Programming. 3 ed., PWS, Boston, 1998.
13. Kobsa, A.: Supporting User Interfaces for All Through User Modeling. Proceedings of HCI International, Japan, 1995.
14. Lieberman, H.: Letizia: An Agent That Assist Web Browsing. International Joint Conference on Artificial Intelligence, Montreal, 924-929, 1995.
15. Milde, J.: The instructable Agent Lokutor. Workshop on Communicative Agents in Intelligent Virtual Environments, Spain, 2000.
16. Nijholt, A. and Hulstijn, J.: Multimodal Interactions with Agents in Virtual Worlds. In: Kasabov, N. (ed.): Future Directions for Intelligent Information Systems and Information Science, Physica-Verlag: Studies in Fuzziness and Soft Computing, 2000.
17. Nikolopoulos, C.: Expert Systems - Introduction to First and Second Generation and Hybrid Knowledge Based Systems. Eds: Marcel Dekker, New York, 1997.
18. Panayiotopoulos, T.; Zacharis, N.; Vosinakis, S.: Intelligent Guidance in a Virtual University. Advances in Intelligent Systems - Concepts, Tools and Applications, 33-42, Kluwer Academic Press, 1999.

19. Papatheodorou, C.: Machine Learning in User Modeling. Machine Learning and Applications. Lecture Notes in Artificial Intelligence. Springer Verlag, 2001.
20. Pazzani, M. and Billsus, D.: Learning and Revising User Profiles: The identification on Interesting Web Sites. Machine Learning, 27(3), 313-331, 1997.
21. Perkowitz, M. and Etzioni, O.: Adaptive Web Sites: Automatically synthesizing Web pages. Fifteen National Conference in Artificial Intelligence, Wisconsin, 1998.
22. Pree, W. and Koskimies, K.: Framelets-Small Is Beautiful, A Chapter in Building Application Frameworks: Object Oriented Foundations of Framework Design. Eds: M.E. Fayad, D.C. Schmidt, R.E. Johnson, Wiley & Sons, 1999.
23. Quinlan, R. C4.5: Programs for Machine Learning. Morgan Kaufmann, Sao Mateo, California, 1993.
24. Rickel, J. and Johnson, W.: Task-Oriented Collaboration with Embodied Agents in Virtual Worlds. In J. Cassell, J. Sullivan, S. Prevost, and E. Churchill (Eds.), Embodied Conversational Agents, 95-122. Boston: MIT Press, 2000.
25. Rickel, J.; Marsella, S.; Gratch, J.; Hill, R.; Traum, D.; Swartout W.: Toward a New Generation of Virtual Humans for Interactive Experiences. IEEE Intelligent Systems, 17(4), 2002.
26. Santos, C. and Osorio, F.: Técnicas de Aprendizado de Máquina no Processo de Categorização de Textos. Internal Research Report (http://www.inf.unisinos.br/~cassiats/mestrado), 2003.
27. Santos, C. and Osório, F.: An Intelligent and Adaptive Virtual Environment and its Application in Distance Learning. Advanced Visual Interfaces, Italy, May, ACM Press, 2004.
28. Sebastiani, F.: Machine learning in automated text categorization. ACM Computing Surveys, 34(1), 1-47, 2002.
29. Self, J.: The defining characteristics of intelligent tutoring systems research: ITSs care, precisely. International Journal of Artificial Intelligence in Education, 10, 350-364, 1999.

EASE: Evolutional Authoring Support Environment

Lora Aroyo[1], Akiko Inaba[2], Larisa Soldatova[2], and Riichiro Mizoguchi[2]

[1]Department of Computer Science and Mathematics
Eindhoven University of Technology
P.O. Box 513, 5600 MB Eindhoven, The Netherlands
l.m.aroyo@tue.nl

[2]ISIR, Osaka University, 8-1 Mihogaoka, Ibaraki, Osaka, 567-0047 Japan
{ina,larisa,miz }@ei.sanken.osaka-u.ac.jp

Abstract. How smart should we be in order to cope with the complex authoring process of smart courseware? Lately this question gains more attention with attempts to simplify the process and efforts to define authoring systems and tools to support it. The goal of this paper is to specify an *evolutional perspective* on the Intelligent Educational Systems (IES) authoring and in this context to define the authoring framework EASE: powerful in its functionality, generic in its support of instructional strategies and user-friendly in its interaction with the author. The *evolutional authoring support* is enabled by an authoring task ontology that at a meta-level defines and controls the configuration and tuning of an authoring tool for a specific authoring process. In this way we achieve more control over the evolution of the intelligence in IES and reach a computational formalization of IES engineering.

1 Introduction and Background

For many years now, various types of Intelligent Educational Systems (IES) have proven to be well accepted and have gained a prominent place in the field of courseware [15]. IES also have proven [8, 14] that they are rather difficult to build and maintain, which became, and still is, a prime obstacle for their wide spread popularization. The dynamic user demands in many aspects of software production are influencing research in the field of intelligent educational software as well [1]. Problems are related to keeping up with the constant requirements for flexibility and adaptability of content and for reusability and sharing of learning objects [10].

Thus, the IES engineering is a complex process, which could benefit from a systematic approach, based on a common models and a specification framework. This will offer a common framework, to identify general design and development phases, to modularize the system components, to separate the modeling of various types of knowledge, to define interoperability points with other applications, to reuse subject domains, tutoring and application independent knowledge structures, and finally to achieve more flexibility and consistency within the entire authoring process. Beyond the point of creation of IES, such a common engineering framework will allow for structured analysis and comparison of IES and their easy maintainability.

Currently, a lot of effort is focused on improving of IES authoring tools to simplify the process and allow time-efficient creation of IES [14, 17, 21]. Despite this massive

J.C. Lester et al. (Eds.): ITS 2004, LNCS 3220, pp. 140–149, 2004.

effort, there is still no complete integrated methodology that allows to distinguish between the various stages of IES design, and also to (semi-)automate the modeling and engineering of IES components, as well as providing structured guidance and feedback to the author. There are efforts to decrease the level of complexity of ITS building by narrowing down the focus to a set of programming tasks and tools to support them [5], and by limiting the view to only correct or incorrect 'solutions to a set of tasks' [18]. As a way to overcome the complexity without decreasing the level of 'intelligence' in IES, [18] proposes an approach for separation of authoring components, and [14] offers a KBT-MM a reference model for authoring system of a knowledge-based tutor, which is storing the domain and tutoring knowledge in "modular components that can be combined, visualized and edited in the process of tutor creation".

A considerable amount of the research on knowledge-based and intelligent systems moves towards concepts and ontologies [13] and focuses on knowledge sharing and reusability [9, 11]. Ontologies allow the definition of an infrastructure for integrating IES at the knowledge level, independent of particular implementations, thus enabling knowledge sharing [7]. Ontologies can be used as a basis for development of libraries of shareable and reusable knowledge modules [2] and help IES authoring tools to move towards semantics-aware environments.

In compliance with the principles given by [14] we present an integrated framework that allows for a structured approach to IES authoring, as well as for automation of authoring activities. Characteristic aspect of our approach is the definition of different ontology-based IES intelligence components and the definition of their interaction. We finally aim in obtaining an *evolutional (self-evolving) authoring system*, which will be able to reason over its own behavior and subsequently change it if is necessary. In Section 2 we illustrate aspects of the authoring support process. In Section 3 we consider IES in terms of a reference model. In Section 4 we describe the EASE framework for IES authoring, and subsequently in Section 5 we describe an EASE-based architecture.

2 Authoring Support Approach

The approach we take follows up on the efforts to elicit requirements for IES authoring, define a reference model and modularize the architecture of IES authoring tools. We describe a model-driven design and specification framework that provides functionality to bridge the gap between the author and the authoring system by managing the *increased intelligence*. It accentuates the separation of concerns between subject domain, user aspects, application and the final presentation of the educational content. It allows to overcome inconsistencies and to automate the authoring tasks. We show how the scheme from [14] can be filled with the 'entire intelligence of IES', split into collaborative knowledge components.

First, we look at the increased intelligence. Authoring of IES is a process with an exponentially growing complexity and it requires many different types of knowledge and considering various constraints, requirements and educational strategies [16]. Aiming at (semi)-automated IES authoring we need to have explicit representations of the strategic knowledge (rules, requirements, constraints) in order to be able to reason within different authoring contexts and situations. Managing of the increased intelligence is therefore a key issue in authoring support.

Second, we consider the conceptual distance between the user and the system. According to [13, 17] the authoring tools are neither intelligent nor user-friendly. Special-purpose systems provide extensive guidance, but the disadvantage is that changing such systems is not easy, and the knowledge and content can hardly be reused for their educational purposes [15]. Thus, structured guidance is needed in this complex authoring process.

Our ultimate aim is to attain seemingly conflicting goals: to define authoring support in a powerful, generic and easy to use way. The *power* comes from the use of ontology-based approach. The *generality* is achieved with the help of a meta-authoring tool, instantiated with the concrete learning context to achieve also the power of a domain specific tool. The *ease of use* comes from the combination of the previous two. A characteristic aspect of our approach is the use of Authoring Task Ontology (ATO) [3] as part of the authoring environment, which enables us to build a meta-authoring tool [4] and to tailor the general architecture to the needs of each individual system.

3 Intelligent Educational Systems

Characteristically, ITS [14], maintain and work with knowledge of the *expert*, *learner*, and *tutoring strategies*, to capture the student's understanding of the domain and to tailor instructional strategies to the concrete student's needs. Adaptive Hypermedia reference architectures [8] define a *domain,* a *user* and an *adaptation (teaching) model* used to achieve the content adaptation.

Analogously, Web-based Educational Systems [2] distinguish a *domain*, a *user* and an *application models*, connecting the domain and user models to give a personalized view of the learning resources. A *task model* specifies the concrete sequence of tasks

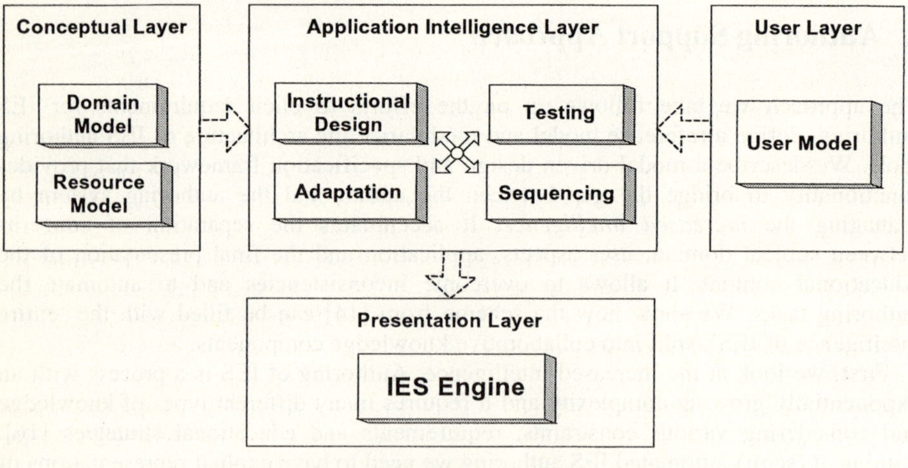

Fig. 1. IES Reference Model

in an adaptive way. As a consequence, [4] distinguish three IES design stages: (1) conceptual modeling of domain and resources, (2) the modeling of application aspects, and (3) simulated use of the user model. Thus, the provision of user-oriented (adapted) instruction and adequate guidance in IES depends on:

- maintaining a model of the *domain*, describing the structure of the information content within IES (based on concepts and their relationships);
- maintaining a personalized portal to a large collection of well organized and structured learning/teaching material *resources*.
- maintaining a model of the *user* to reflect the user's preferences, knowledge, goals, and other relevant instructional aspects;
- maintaining the application intelligence in *instructional design*, *testing*, *adaptation* and *sequencing models*;
- a specific engine to execute the prepared educational structure or sequences.

We organize the common aspects of IES in a model-driven reference approach to allow for a modularization of authoring concerns interoperability of IES components.

4 IES Authoring Context

In line with the IES model defined in the previous section we structure the complexity of the entire authoring process by grouping various authoring activities to:

- model the *domain* as a representation of the domain knowledge;
- annotate, maintain, update and create *learning objects*;
- define the *learning goals*;
- select and apply *instructional strategies* for individual and group learning;
- select and apply *assessment strategies* for individual and group learning;
- specify a *learner model* with learner characteristics;
- specify *learning sequence(s)* out of learning and assessment activities.

To support these authoring tasks we employ knowledge models and capture all the processes related to those tasks in corresponding *authoring modules* as shown in Figure 2. It defines three levels of abstraction for building an IES. At the *product level* we see the final IES. At the *authoring instance level* the actual IES authoring takes place by instantiation of the meta-schema with the actual IES authoring concepts, models and behavior. At the *meta-authoring* we exploit the generic authoring task ontology (ATO) [3, 4] as a main knowledge component in a meta-authoring system and as a conceptual structure of the entire authoring process. A repository of domain-independent authoring components is defined at this level.

At the instance level we exploit ontologies as a way to conceptualize the authoring knowledge in IES. Corresponding ontologies (e.g. for Domain Model, Instructional Strategies, Learning Goal, Test Generation, Resource Management, User Model) are defined to represent the knowledge and important concepts in each of those authoring modules.

Our final goal with this three-layer approach is to realize an evolutional (self-evolving) authoring system, which will be able to reason over its own behavior and based on statistical and other intelligent computations will be able to add new rules or change existing ones in the different parts of the authoring process.

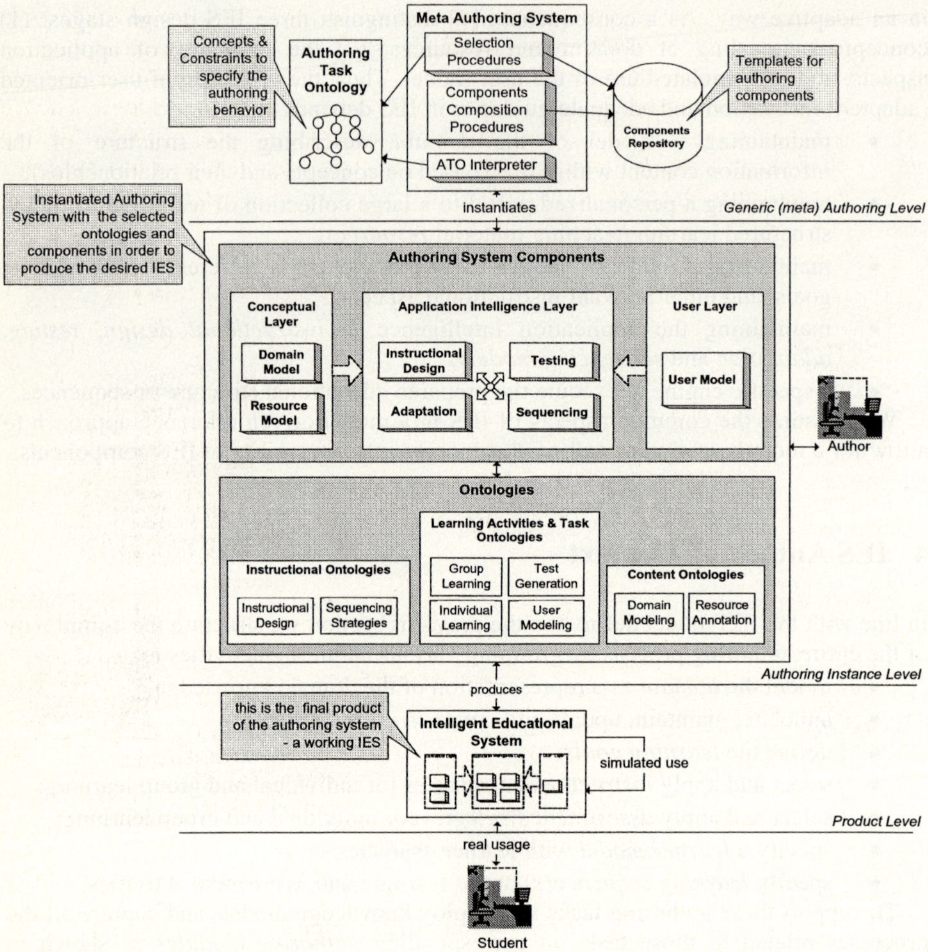

Fig. 2. The IES Authoring Process as captured further in EASE

5 EASE Architectural Issues

To achieve separation of data (content), application (educational strategy), the instructional goals and the assessment activities, we take a goal-centered approach, where a learning goal module is separated from the knowledge on instructional strategies and course sequencing. This allows high reusability of general knowledge on instructional design and strategies. Thus, we have a clear distinction between the content and the computational knowledge, where the learning goal plays a connecting role in order to bring them together within the specific context of each IES.

For example, in Figure 3, the *Collaborative Learning Strategy (CLS)* authoring module provides appropriate group learning strategies for intended users, and requirements for the strategies to the author via the *Sequence Strategies Authoring (SS)* module. To generate explanations and guidance about the recommended strategies *CLS* uses Collaborative Learning Ontology which is a system of concepts to represent collaborative learning sessions and Collaborative Learning Models inspired by learning theories [12, 20].

Another example is given by the *Assessment (A)* module which provides assistance to the author in assessing the learner's (or group of learners) level of understanding and in checking whether a learning goal has been achieved. It uses a test ontology [19] to estimate the effectiveness of the learning process and the preparation/selection of learning objects.

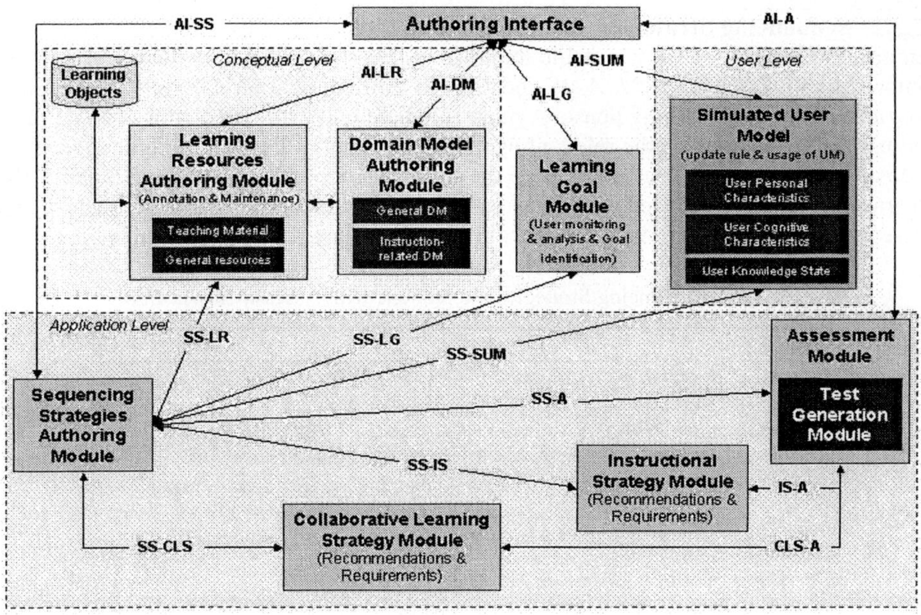

Fig. 3. EASE Reference Architecture

In EASE we follow explicitly the principles supported also by KBT-MM [14] to separate 'what to teach' into modular units independent of 'how to teach' and to present learning goals separately from the instructional content. The rest of the principles we follow implicitly with our use of ontology-based models.

5.1 Communication

The core of the intelligence in the EASE architecture comes from the communication or interactions between the components. There are two "central" components here, the *Sequencing Strategies Authoring (SS)* and the *Authoring Interface (AI)*. The *AI* is the access point for the author to interact with the underlying concepts, models and content. The *SS* interacts with the other components in order to achieve the most appropriate learning sequence for the targeted learner. In this section we illustrate the communication exchange among EASE components, which will further result in the authoring support guidance provided by an EASE-based authoring system.

5.2.1 Authoring Interface (AI) Interactions

At a *conceptual level* the IES author interacts with the *Learning Resources (LR)* and with the *Domain Model (DM)* authoring modules, for example to handle the learning objects. While the author is working with *DM*, an interaction is required between *DM* and *LR* to determine available resources to link to domain concepts. At the *user (learner) level* the author interacts with the *Simulated User Model (SUM)* component in order to determine the use of *UM* (update rules) within the IES application. At the *application level* the author interacts with the *A* and *SS* modules.

5.2.2 Sequencing Strategies (SS) Interactions

In order to realize the most suitable learning task sequence for individual learners, *SS* interacts with *LR, LG, SUM, A, IS* and *CLS* to estimate learner's current knowledge, cognitive state and learning phase. A main role here plays the interaction with *SUM* to adjust the sequencing to the relevant attributes and their values in the user model. *SS* consults *A* for the right evaluation of the user's states and *A* consults SS about the learning history, knowledge values of domain concepts, cognitive states and assessment goals. The *SS* interactions with *A* via *CLS* are presented in Table 1.

Table 1. Sequencing Strategies interactions with Assessment via *CLS*

SS-CLS	CLS-SS
`SendLOCharacteristics`	`RequestAll`
`SendAttrValues`	`SendLearningStyle`
`SendCognitiveAttrValues`	`SendGLstrategy`
`SendLearningHistory`	`ReqsGroupFormation`
`SendLearningGoals`	`ReqsInteractionTypes`
	`ReqsGLsequenceTypes`
	`ReqsGLproblemTypes`
	`ReqsGLtools`
	`SelectLearningGoal`

CLS-A	A-CLS
`SelectFromGoalList`	`ListTestGoals`
`Fill-InTestProperties`	`ListTestPropoerties`

5.3 Example of IES Authoring Interactions

In order to illustrate in practice the intelligence of the IES authoring architecture we will look at the interactions of the *Assessment (A)* authoring module. A typical example is given in Figure 4: an author wants to make a test to assess the learners knowledge after studying a theme. For this, *A* infers an assessment goal, test properties, learner's and domain characteristics from the interaction with *SS* and *IS*. Further, *A* provides an explanation of the most important actions. *A* generates test items and allows the author to edit them, then checks their compatibility with the domain and the test structure. The output of *A* to the author is a generated test, the test documentation, recommendations how to improve the test if necessary, and test characteristics. After the test application *A* interprets the results and checks whether they correspond to the teaching goal.

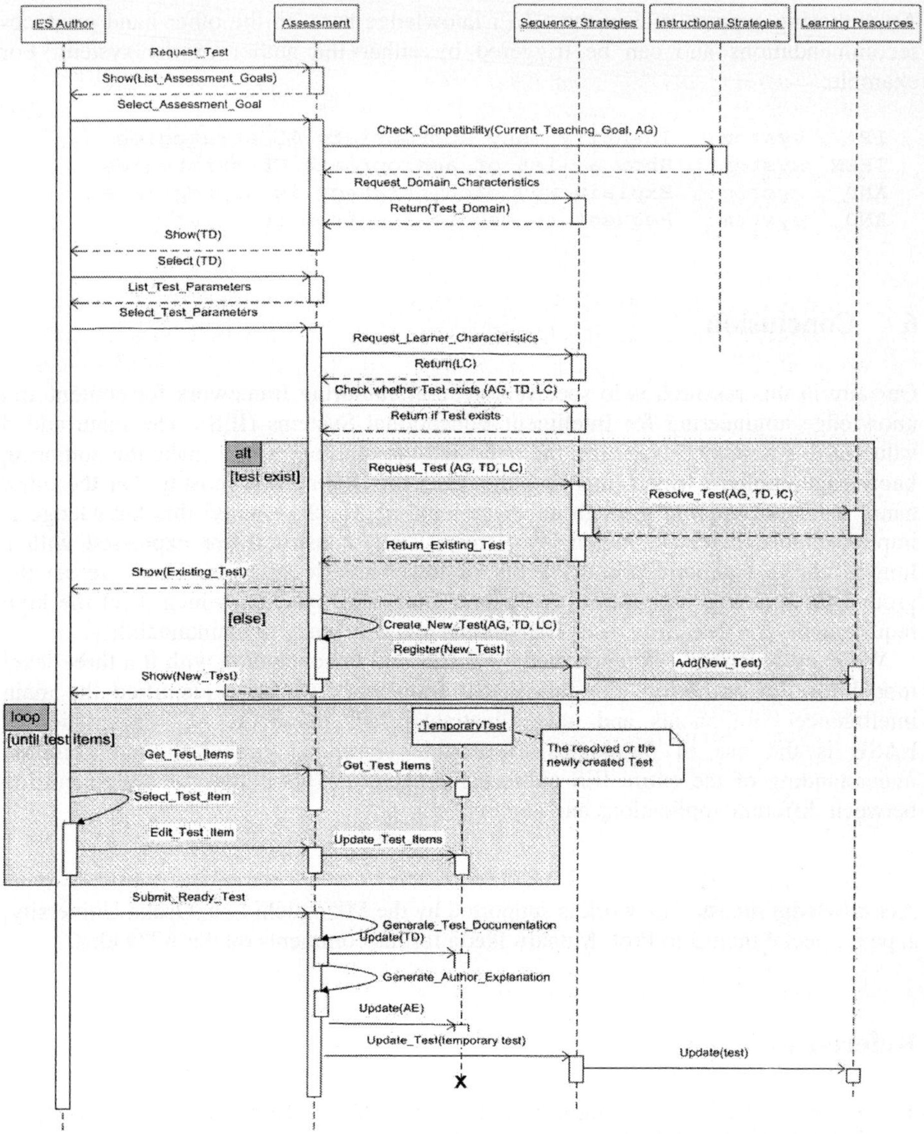

Fig. 4. Assessment Module Interactions

Authoring rules in the *Assessment* knowledge base trigger interaction in order to realize various aspects of the test generation process. For example:

```
IF   author: Edit a test item TI
THEN system: Update the test item
AND  system: Check if TI compatible with the test domain
AND  system: Alert if not compatible with test domain
AND  system: Check if TI compatible with the test structure
AND  system: Alert if not compatible with test structure
```

An authoring support rule in the *CLS's* knowledge base on the other hand produces recommendations and can be triggered by either the author or the system. For example:

```
IF    system:  Identify many appropriate GL strategies
THEN  system:  Show a list of appropriate GL strategies
AND   system:  Explain why each strategy is appropriate
AND   system:  Request to choose one from the list
```

6 Conclusion

Our aim in this research is to specify a general authoring framework for content and knowledge engineering for Intelligent Educational Systems (IES). The main added value of this approach is that on the one hand the ontologies in it make the authoring knowledge explicit, which improves the basis for sharing and reusing. On the other hand, it is configurable through an evolutional approach. Finally, this knowledge is implementable, since all higher-level (meta-level) constructs are expressed with a limited class of generic primitives out of lower-level constructs. Thus, we set the ground for a new generation of evolutional authoring systems, which meet the high requirements for flexibility, user-friendliness and efficiency in maintainability.

We have described reference model for IES and in connection with it a three-level model for IES authoring. For this EASE framework we have identified the main intelligence components and have illustrated their interaction. Characteristic for EASE is the use of ontologies to provide common vocabulary and common understanding of the entire IES authoring processes. This allows for interoperation between different applications and authors.

Acknowledgements. The work is supported by the Mizoguchi Lab, Osaka University, Japan. Special thanks to Prof. Mitsuru Ikeda for his comments on the ATO idea.

References

1. Ainsworth, S., Major, N., Grimshaw, S., Hayes, M., Underwood, J., Williams, B., & Wood, D. (2003). REDEEM: Simple Intelligent Tutoring Systems from Usable Tools, In Murray, Ainsworth, & Blessing (eds.), Authoring Tools for Adv. Tech. Learning Env., 205-232.
2. Aroyo, L., Dicheva, D., & Cristea, A. (2002). Ontological Support for Web Courseware Authoring. In Proceedings of ITS 2002 Conference, 270-280.
3. Aroyo, L, & Mizoguchi, R. (2003). Authoring Support Framework for Intelligent Educational Systems. In Proceedings of AIED 2003 Conference.
4. Aroyo, L. & Mizoguchi, R. (2004). Towards Evolutional Authoring Support. Journal for Interactive Learning Research. (in print)
5. Anderson, J., Corbett, A. Koedinger, K., & Pelletier, R. (1995). Cognitive tutors: Lessons learned. The Journal of the Learning Sciences, 4(2), 167-207.

6. Bourdeau, J., Mizoguchi, R. (2000). Collaborative Ontological Engineering of Instructional Design Knowledge for an ITS Authoring Environment, In Proceedings of ITS 2000 Conference.
7. Breuker, J., Bredeweg, B. (1999). Ontological Modelling for Designing Educational Systems, In Proceedings of the Workshop on Ontologies for Intelligent Educational Systems at AIED'99 Conference.
8. Brusilovsky, P. (2003). Developing Adaptive Educational Hypermedia Systems. In Murray, Ainsworth, & Blessing (eds.), Authoring Tools for Advanced Technology Learning Environments, Kluwer Academic Publishers, 377-409.
9. Chen, W. Hayashi, Y., Kin, L. Ikeda, M. and Mizoguchi, R. (1998) Ontological Issues in an Intelligent Authoring Tool, In Proceedings of ICCE 1998 Conference, (1), 41-50.
10. Devedzic, V., Jerinic, L., Radovic, D. (2000). The GET-BITS Model of Intelligent Tutoring Systems. Journal of Interactive Learning Research, 11(3), 411-434.
11. Ikeda, M., Seta, K., Mizoguchi, R. (1997). Task Ontology Makes It Easier To Use Authoring Tools. In Proceedings of IJCAI 1997 Conference.
12. Inaba, A., Supnithi, T., Ikeda, M., Mizoguchi, R., & Toyoda, J., (2000). How Can We Form Effective Collaborative LearnningGroups - Theoretical justification of Opportunistic Group Formation with ontological engineering. In Proceedings of ITS 2000 Conference, 282-291.
13. Mizoguchi, R., & Bourdeau, J. (2000). Using Ontological Engineering to Overcome Common AI-ED Problems, International Journal of AIED, 11(2), 107-121.
14. Murray, T. (2003a). Principles for pedagogy-oriented Knowledge-based Tutor Authoring Systems. In Murray, Ainsworth, & Blessing (eds.), Authoring Tools for Advanced Technology Learning Environments, Kluwer Academic Publishers, 439–466.
15. Murray, T. (2003b). An Overview of ITS authoring tools. In Murray, Ainsworth, & Blessing (eds.), Authoring Tools for Advanced Technology Learning Environments, Kluwer Publishers, 491–544.
16. Nkambou, R., Gauthier, G., Frasson, C. (1996). CREAM-Tools: An Authoring Environment for Curriculum and Course Building in an ITS. Computer Aided Learning and Instruction in Science and Engineering, 186-194.
17. Redfield, C. L. (1997). An ITS Authoring Tools: Experimental Advanced Instructional Design Advisor, AAAI Fall Symposium, 72-82.
18. Ritter, S., Blessing, S., & Wheeler, L. (2003). Authoring tools for Component-based Learning Environments. In Murray, Ainsworth, & Blessing (eds.), Authoring Tools for Advanced Technology Learning Environments, Kluwer Academic Publishers, 467-489.
19. Soldatova, L., & Mizoguchi, R. (2003). Ontology of tests. Proc. Computers and Advanced Technology in Education, In Proceedings of CATE 2003 Conference, 175-180.
20. Supnithi, T., Inaba, A., Ikeda, M., Toyoda, J., & Mizoguchi, R. (1999) Learning Goal Ontology Supported by LearningTheories for Opportunistic Group Formation, Proc. of AIED'99, Le Mans France, 67-74.
21. Vassileva, J. (1995). Dynamic Courseware Generation: at the Cross Point of CAL, ITS and Authoring. In Proceedings of ICCE 1995 Conference, 290-297.

Selecting Theories in an Ontology-Based ITS Authoring Environment

Jacqueline Bourdeau[1], Riichiro Mizoguchi[2], Valéry Psyché[1, 3], and Roger Nkambou[3]

[1] Centre de recherche LICEF, Télé-université
4750 Henri-Julien, Montréal (Québec) H2T 3E4, Canada ; Tel: 514-840-2747
{bourdeau, vpsyche}@licef.teluq.uquebec.ca,

[2] ISIR, Osaka University, 8-1 Mihogaoka, Ibaraki, Osaka, 567-0047 Japan,
miz@ei.sanken.osaka-u.ac.jp

[3] Département d'informatique, Université du Québec à Montréal
Case postale 8888, succursale Centre-ville, Montréal (Québec) Canada - H3C 3P8
nkambou.roger@uqam.ca

Abstract. This paper introduces the rationale for concrete situations in the authoring process that can exploit a theory-aware Authoring Environment. It illustrates how Ontological Engineering (OE) can be instrumental in representing the declarative knowledge needed, and how an added value in terms of intelligence can be expected for both authoring and for learning environments.

1 Introduction

Ontological Engineering may prove to be instrumental in solving several problems known in the field of Artificial Intelligence and Education (AIED) [1]. Preliminary work shows that significant results can be obtained in terms of knowledge systematization and of instructional planning [2];[3];[4]. Results obtained in other fields [5], [6], [7] indicate significant added value and justify efforts to further explore this direction. In a previous paper [8], we envisioned the power of ontologies to sustain the ITS authoring process in an ITS Authoring Environment, and explored methodologies for engineering declarative knowledge from instructional and learning sciences. This paper introduces the rationale for concrete situations in the authoring process that exploits a theory-aware Authoring Environment. It illustrates how Ontological Engineering can be instrumental in representing the declarative knowledge needed, and how an added value in terms of intelligence can be expected for Intelligent Tutoring Systems (ITS) authoring environments.

J.C. Lester et al. (Eds.): ITS 2004, LNCS 3220, pp. 150–161, 2004.

2 Value of Ontologies for ITS and for the Authoring Process

2.1 Why Should a Theory-Aware Environment Be Beneficial to the Authoring of ITS?

Existing ITS authoring environments aim at combining authoring tools and knowledge representation [9], but so far no ITS authoring environment possesses the desired functionalities of an intelligent authoring system such as Retrieve appropriate theories for selecting instructional strategies or Provide principles for structuring a learning environment. Declarative knowledge is mainly absent in those systems, as is the maintenance of knowledge base's integrity. Ontological Engineering can solve these problems by proposing a declarative knowledge modeling approach. The semantic-based knowledge systematization that would result from this approach could provide a gateway to learning objects and their management. Ontologies are considered a solution to the problems of indexing, assembling and aggregating Learning Objects in a coherent way [10], [11], [12], either automatically, semi-automatically or done by humans.

Viewing the authoring task as part of instructional design (in which design decisions are made) access to theoretical knowledge should improve quality and consistency of the design. From the ontological point of view, it is possible to suggest common concepts and a conceptual structure to explain existing theories in a harmonized way. Our effort to systematize theoretical knowledge and to integrate it into a design methodology for authoring tasks is described in [6]. We have developed a minimal ontology for illustrating how our ideas can help an author or an agent to build a learning scenario by reflecting on possible variations based on instructional theories. A long term perspective for this work is to provide the next generation of authoring systems with a scientific basis for semantic standards of learning objects and their management.

2.2 What Is the Full Power of an Ontology-Based System When Adequately Deployed?

Exploring the power of ontologies for ITS and for the authoring process raises the following question: what is the full power of an ontology-based system when adequately deployed? A successful experiment was conducted by Mizoguchi [6] in deploying ontology-based knowledge systematization of functional knowledge into a production division of a large company. Although the domain is different from educational knowledge, we believe that it is applicable to the knowledge systematization of learning and instructional sciences. One of the key claims of our knowledge systematization is that the concept of function should be defined independently of an object that can possess it and of its realization method. This in effect releases the function for re-use in multiple domains.

Consider: If functions are defined depending on objects and their realization, few functions are reused in different domains. In the systematization reported in

Mizoguchi, a six-layer ontology and knowledge base was built using functional knowledge representation frameworks to capture, store and share functional knowledge among engineers and enable them to reuse that functional knowledge in their daily work life with the help of a functional knowledge server. It was successfully deployed inside the Production Systems Division of Sumitomo Electric Industry, Ltd., with the following results: 1) the same document can be used for redesign, design review, patent writing and troubleshooting; 2) Patent writing process is reduced by one third; 3) design review goes extremely better than before, 4) troubleshooting is much easier than before, 5) it enables collaborative work among several kinds of engineers. It demonstrates that operational knowledge systems based on developed ontologies can work effectively in a real world situation.

What is the similarity of situations in the manufacturing and the educational domains? Both have rich concepts and experiential knowledge. However, neither a common conceptual infrastructure nor shareable knowledge bases are available in those domains. Rather, each is characterized by multiple viewpoints and a variety of concepts. The success reported in [6] leads us to believe that similar results can be obtained in the field of ITS, and that efforts should be made towards achieving this goal of building ITS frameworks capable of sharing educational knowledge.

3 Intelligence in ITS Authoring and Learning Environments

3.1 Value of Ontology for ITS Learning Environments

The power of the intelligent behaviour of an ITS Learning Environment relies on the knowledge stored in it. This knowledge deals with domain expertise, pedagogy, interaction and tutoring strategy. Each of those dimensions is usually implemented as an agent-based system. A simplified view of an ITS is that of a multi-agent system in which domain expert, pedagogical and tutoring agents cooperate to deliver an optimal learning environment with respect to the learning goals. In order to achieve this, ITS agents need to share common interpretations during their interactions. How does ontology engineering contribute to this?

Several views or theories of domain knowledge taxonomy can be found in the literature as well as discussions of how this knowledge can be represented in a knowledge-based system for learning/teaching purposes. For instance, Gagné et al. suggested five categories of knowledge that are responsible for most human activity; some of these categories include several types of knowledge. Merrill suggested a different view of possible learning outcomes or domain knowledge. Even if there are some intersections between existing taxonomies, it is very difficult to implement a system that can integrate these different views without a prior agreement on the semantics of what the student should learn.

We believe that ontological engineering can help the domain expert agent to deal with these different views in two ways: 1) by defining "things" associated with each taxonomy and their semantics, the domain knowledge expert can then inform other agents of the system in the course of their interaction. 2) by creating an ontology for a meta-taxonomy which can include different views. We are experimenting with each of these approaches.

Ontological engineering can also be instrumental for including different instructional theories into the same pedagogical agent: for example Gagné's learning events theory, or Merrill component-based theory. This could lead to the development of multi-instructional theories-based ITS which could exploit principles from one instructional theory or another with respect to the current instructional goal.

Furthermore, ontology engineering is essential for the development of ITSs in which several agents (tutor, instructional planner, expert, profiler) need to agree about the definition and the semantics of the things they share during a learning session. Even if pure multi-agent platforms based on standards such as FIPA offer ontology-free ACL (Agent Communication Language), ontological engineering is still necessary because the ontology defines shared concepts, which are in turn sent to the other party during the communication. It is possible to implement using FIPA-ACL standards in which "performatives" (communication acts between agents) can take a given ontology as a parameter to make it possible for the other party to understand and to interpret concepts or things included in the content of the message.

By adding intelligence to ITS authoring environments in the form of theory-aware environments, we could also provide not only curriculum knowledge, not only instructional strategies, but also the foundations, the rationale upon which the tutoring system relies and acts. As a result of having ontology-based ITS authoring environments, we can ensure that: 1) the ITS generated can be more coherent, well-founded, scrutable, and expandable; 2) the ITS can explain and justify to learners the rationale behind an instructional strategy (based on learning theories), and therefore support metacognition; 3) the ITS can even offer some choice to learners in terms of instructional strategies, with pros and cons for each option, thus supporting the development of autonomy and responsibility.

Having access to multiple theories (instead of one) in an ITS authoring environment such as CREAM-tools [13] would offer added value through: 1) the possible diversity offered to authors and learners, through the integration of multiple theories into a common knowledge base, 2) a curriculum planning module that would then be challenged to select among theories, and would therefore have to be more intelligent, and 3) an opportunity for collaboration between authors (even with different views of instructional or learning theory) in the development of ITS modules.

3.2 What Benefits Would the General Functionalities of a Theory-Aware ITS Authoring Environment Offer?

In an Ontology-based Authoring Environment, authors (human or software) could benefit from accessing theories to: 1) make design decisions (macro, micro) after reflection and reasoning, 2) communicate about or explain their design decisions, 3) check consistency among design decisions, intra-theory and inter-theories, 4) produce scrutable learning environments, 5) use heuristical knowledge grounded in theoretical knowledge.

Useful functionalities could include such queries as: 1) asking the system what theories apply best to this or that learning situation/goal, 2) asking the system to show examples, 3) asking the system for advice on whether this element of a theory can be combined to an element from another theory, the risk in doing so, other preferable solutions, etc.

Among the variations depending on theories in design or authoring decisions, some can be called paradigmatic, since they refer to a fundamental view of learning or of instruction [8]: instructivist, constructivist, or socioconstructivist. Other variations refer to educational strategies, some are specific to the characteristics of learners or to the subject matter. The following section describes a decision to be made by authors among variations from theories, and illustrates how an ontology can support this decision-making process.

Currently such functionalities are not available in existing ITS authoring environments, as stated by Murray in his review of existing ITS authoring environments [13]. When these environments include theoretical knowledge, it is hard-wired and procedurally implemented in the system so that it cannot be flexible enough to satisfy users' goal. Moreover, these environments cannot know if the hard-wired theory is appropriate or not for the user's goal, they merely impose it on the authors. In Murray's classification, pedagogy-oriented systems rely upon instructional or teaching strategies for curriculum planning, but they do not take into account commonalities nor variations among theories. This limitation can be overcome by having theory-aware systems with multi-instructional theories, exploited by authors or agents.

4 Selecting an Instructional Strategy

In the course of designing instruction or authoring a learning environment, decisions are made as to what will be provided to learners in order to support, to foster or to assess their learning. Such decisions may either rely on well-thought-out, explicit reasons, or simply be intuitive, or ad hoc, or based on personal experience. In order to obtain science-based ITS design, these decisions need to be based on theories. Since ontologies are an effective form of declarative knowledge representation, and if ontological engineering is a methodology to develop this knowledge representation, a theory-aware authoring environment could effectively serve the decisions to be made for selecting an instructional strategy. This section will introduce the decision-making process for selecting an instructional strategy, and the variations based on respective theories. An implementation of a theory-aware environment to support these decisions will be described, as it illustrates the design process of a lesson in the field of Optics.

4.1 The Case of Selecting an Instructional Strategy in the Authoring Process

When designing instruction or authoring a learning environment, two types of decisions are to be made: macro-decisions for strategies, and micro-decisions for designing the learning material or the organization of learning activities. Decisions about instructional strategies are the most strategic and govern the decisions about learning material and organization. These decisions are based on: 1) theories that are accepted and respected by authors, 2) results of the analysis conducted before the design, such as analysis of content, context, expectations, etc. Such decisions are made by a person or a team acting as designers if the authoring process is done by humans; Otherwise, the choices are made by a system if the ITS authoring environment has a curriculum planning component; by an instructor or even a learner if provided with this freedom to choose.

The impact of such decisions is the following: selecting an instructional strategy should 'govern' or 'orient' or 'inspire' the development of the learning environment and organization and therefore influence the learning process. A good decision is a strategy that is coherent with the theory, which is the most adequate one as it relates to the goals and the conditions of learning, and respects the philosophy of the persons or organizations. In terms of granularity, this decision applies to the level of the 'learning unit', with objectives, learning activities and assessment. A decision remains good as long as it proves to have coherence and potential effectiveness. In some situations, designers have good reasons to combine elements from various theories into one scenario. If theoretical knowledge is specified and structured in an ontology, it allows for such combinations under constraint checking, thus reducing the risk of errors.

4.2 Variations Around Three Theories to Design a Lesson in Optics

Dependence between instructional theory and strategy is best illustrated in the book edited by Reigeluth: 'Instructional Theories in Action: Lessons Illustrating Selected Theories and Models [14]. Reigeluth asked several authors to design a lesson based on a specific theory, having in common the subject matter, the objectives, and the test items. The objectives included both concept learning and skill development. The lesson is an introduction to the concepts of lens, focus and magnitude in optics. The book offers eight variations of the lesson, each one being an implementation of eight existing and recognized theories. Reigeluth gives as warnings to this exercise that: 1) despite the fact that each theory uses its own terminology, they have much in common, 2) each theory has its limitations, and none of them covers the full complexity of the design problem, none of them takes into account the large number of variables that play a role, 3) the main variation factor is how much the strategy is appropriate to the situation, 4) authors would benefit to know and have access to all existing ones. In the same book, Schnellbecker, in his effort to compare and contrast the different approaches, underlines that there is no such thing as a 'truth character' in the selection of a model. Variations among the lessons are of two kinds: intra-theory and inter-theory. Each implementation of one theory is specific, and could give room to a range of other strategies, all of them referring to the same principles. Inter-theory variations represent fundamental differences in how one views learning and instruction, in terms of paradigm.

Since we are mainly interested in the examination of variations among theories, we concentrated on inter-theories variations. We selected three theories: Gagné-Briggs, Merrill, and Collins, and we selected one objective of concept learning (skill development is to be examined under a different study). The Gagné-Briggs theory of instruction was the first one to directly and explicitly rely on a learning theory. It is comprehensive of cognitive, affective and psycho-motor knowledge; the goal of learning is performance, and the goal of instruction is effectiveness. Merrill's Component Display theory shares the same paradigm as Gagné-Briggs', but suggests a different classification of objectives, and provides more detailed guidelines for learning organization and learning material. The lesson drawn by Collins refers to principles extracted from good practices and to scientific inquiry as a metaphor to learning; its goals are oriented towards critical thinking rather than performance.

4.3 Ontological Engineering Methodology and Results

This section documents the methodology used for building the ontology and the models, and presents the results. The view of an ontology and of ontological engineering is the one developed and applied at Mizlab [15]. From the three steps proposed by Mizoguchi [15], the first one, called Level 1, has been developed, and consists of term extraction and definition, hierarchy building, relation setting, and model building. A Use Case was built to obtain the ontological commitments needed [16], and competency questions were sketched as suggested by Gruninger and Fox [17]. Concept extraction was performed based on the assumptions expressed by Noy and McGuiness [18]. The definition of a 'role' refers to Kozaki [19].

The Ontology environment used for the development of the ontology is Hozo [19], an environment composed of a graphic interface, an ontology editor and an ontology and models server in a client-server architecture.

Use-case. The definition of the domain of instruction has been done based on the ideas developed in [8]. A set of competency questions [17] was also sketched, as well as preliminary queries that our authoring environment prototype should be able to answer, such as: What is the most appropriate instructional theory? Which kind of learning activity or material do we need based on instructional theory chosen? At this stage we made ontological commitments [16] to which domain we wanted to model, how we wanted to do it, under which goals, in which order, and in which environment. The use case was done from the point of view of an author (human or software) having to select an instructional strategy to design a lesson. The lesson selection is usually done based on the learning conditions that have been previously identified. The result generated by the authoring environment is an instructional scenario based on the instructional strategy which best satisfies the learning conditions. Building the Use Cases was done by analyzing the expectations for theory-aware authoring, and by analyzing commonalities and variations among the three lessons. Figure 1 shows the result of this analysis in the form of a synoptic table. This use case illustrates an instructional scenario for teaching a concept in optics to secondary school learners, based on the three theories.

Table 1. Use Case of Instructional Scenario

Use Case of Instructional Scenario Based on Objective : Student will be able to define focal length Learning Content : Focal length	
1 Instructional Theory	**Gagné-Briggs' theory of Instruction**
1.1. Prerequisite	Identify Focal Point
1.2. Teaching Strategy	Expository
1.3. Teaching Material	Workbook with visual representation
1.4. Assessment	Quiz
1.5. Activity type	**1)** Informing the learner of the lesson objective, **2)** Presenting the stimulus material with distinctive features, **3)** Providing learning guidance, **4)** Eliciting performance, **5)** Providing informative feedback, **6)** Assessing Performance
2 Instructional Theory	**Component display theory by M.D. Merrill**
2.1. Prerequisite	Remember – Instance – Fact, Use - Concept
2.2. Learning Content	Focal Length
2.3. Teaching Strategy	Expository and Practice
2.4. Teaching Material	Printed Study Sheet
2.5. Assessment	Fill in the blank test
2.6. Activity type	**1)** Introduction, **2)** Reference Example, **3)** Definition, **4)** Learning Tip, **5)** Practice, **6)** Study Problems, **7)** Feedback
3. Instructional Theory	**Theory of Inquiry Teaching by A. Collins**
3.1. Prerequisite	Terminology about lens
3.2. Learning Content	Focal Length
3.3. Teaching Strategy	Inquiry Dialogue
3.4. Teaching Material	Lenses, magnifying glass, lenses
3.5. Assessment type	Question test
3.6. Activitiy type	**1)** Preliminary, **2)** Forming hypothesis, **3)** Testing hypothesis, **4)** Entrapping Students, **5)** Varying cases systematically, **6)** Questioning authority, **7)** Testing hypothesis

According to these uses cases, the author is informed of: the necessary prerequisites to reach the lesson objective, the learning content, the teaching strategy, the teaching material, the assessment, the activities order and type. The activities proposed are based on Gagné's instructional events, Merrill's performance/content matrix and Collins's instructional techniques.

Term extraction and definition. This operation was conducted based on the assumptions [18] that; 1) there is no one correct way to model a domain, 2) ontology development is necessarily an iterative process, 3) concepts in the ontology should be close to objects (physical or logical) and relationships in your domain of interest. As a result, we obtained a set of concepts as shown in Fig. 1.

Hierarchy Building. Once the concepts were defined, we created a hierarchy by identifying "*is-a*" and "*part-of*" relations. The concepts of higher level selected for the main ontology appear in the primitive concept hierarchy presented in figure 1. We developed middle-out hierarchy approach for the lesson scenario and a top-down approach for the optic domain ontology. As a result, the hierarchy of the main ontology, that we call the Core ontology, has four levels.

Relation setting. Most of the concepts defined need a set of properties and role relations to explicit the context in which they should be understood by agents. In that sense, the "*attribute-of*" relation was used as a property slot and the "*part-of*" relation as a role slot, as suggested by Kozaki [19]. Other relations can be created between concepts. The "*participate-in*" relation (or *p/i* in the editor), is similar to the "*part-of*" relation, but is not included in the relational concept. This step allows us to describe connections between these concepts. For example, one stake of the ontology was to express a dynamic scenario showing a sequence of teaching/learning activities. To model these, we used a "*before-after*" relation which allowed expression of which activities happened before the current activity and which one happened after.

Figure 1 shows the Core Ontology that resulted from this development.

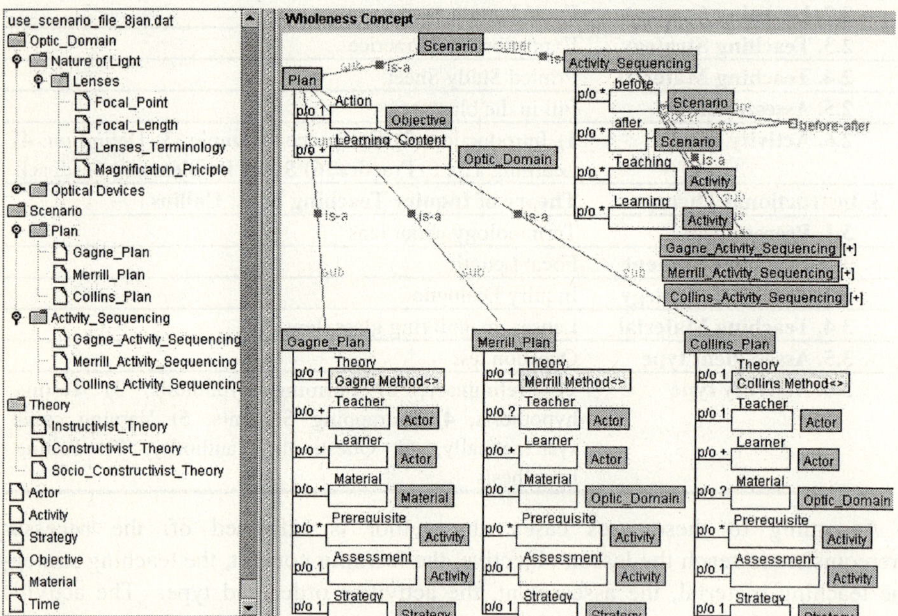

Fig. 1. Core Ontology

Create instances (models). The models were built by instantiating the ontology concepts, then by connecting the instances to each other. The consistency checking

of the model is done using the axioms defined in the ontology. The model is then ready to be used by others agents (human, software or both).
Three models have been built that rely on the main ontology, and relate to the Use Cases. These models of scenarios focus on the teaching/learning interaction based on each respective Instructional Theory. Figure 2 presents the model for the Gagné-Briggs theory.

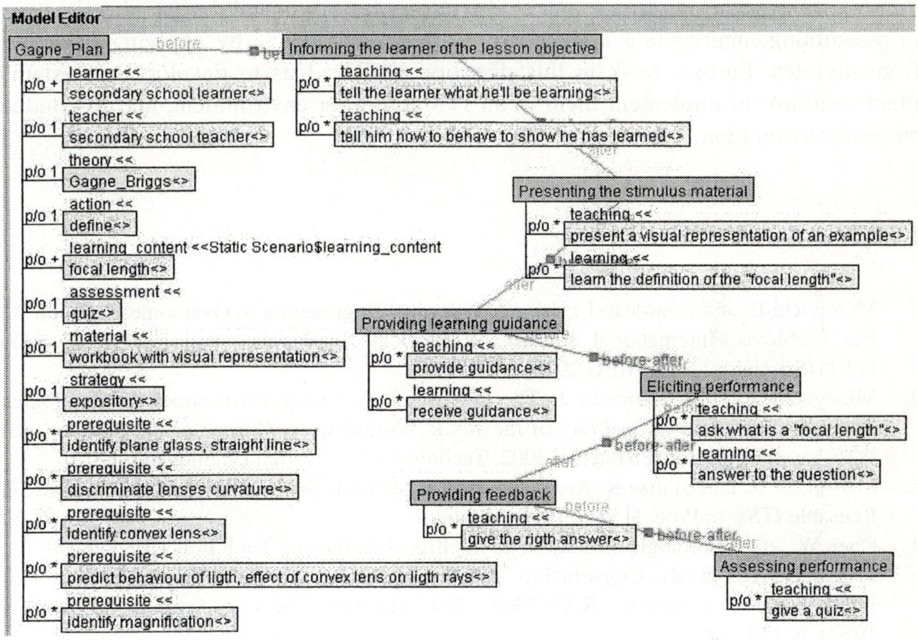

Fig. 2. Model of Gagné-Briggs Theory

Six out of Gagné's nine events of instruction, which are needed to achieve the lesson scenario, are presented in Figure 2. The activities involved in the achievement of the lesson objective, are represented according to "Remember-Generality-Concept" from Merrill's performance/content matrix. In the same way, six of Collins's ten techniques of instruction, which are needed to achieve the lesson scenario according to this Theory, are represented in their event order. The most interesting part of these three models is that they explicitly show the role of each participant during the activities based on each theory.

5 Conclusion

As a conclusion, ontological engineering allowed for unifying the commonalities as well as specifying the variations in linking theories to concrete instructional strategies. Obviously, ontologies cannot go beyond the power of the theories themselves, and one should not expect from ontological engineering of theoretical knowledge more than what can be expected from the theories themselves.

This paper illustrates the idea that an Ontology-based ITS Authoring Environment can enrich the authoring process as well curriculum planning. One example is provided of how a theory-aware authoring environment allows for principled design, provides explicit justification for selection, may stimulate reflection among authors, and may pave the way to an integrated knowledge base of instructional theories. A theory-aware Authoring Environment also allows for principled design when it comes to assembling, aggregating and integrating learning objects by applying principles from theories. Further work in this direction will lead us to develop the system's functionalities, to implement them in an ITS authoring environment, and to conduct empirical evaluation.

References

1. Mizoguchi R. and Bourdeau J., Using Ontological Engineering to Overcome Common AI-ED Problems. International Journal of Artificial Intelligence and Education, 2000. vol.11(Special Issue on AIED 2010): p. 107-121.
2. Mizoguchi R. and Bourdeau J. Theory-Aware Authoring Environment : Ontological Engineering Approach. in Proc. of the ICCE Workshop on Concepts and Ontologies in Web-based Educational Systems. 2002. Technische Universiteit Eindhoven.
3. Mizoguchi R. and Sinitsa K. Architectures and Methods for Designing Cost-Effective and Reusable ITSs. in Proc. ITS'96. 1996. Montreal.
4. Chen W., et al. Ontological Issues in an Intelligent Authoring Tool. in ICCE'98. 1998.
5. Mizoguchi R., et al., Construction and Deployment of a Plant Ontology. The 12th International Conference, EKAW2000,, 2000 (Lecture Notes in Artificial Intelligence 1937): p. 113-128.
6. Mizoguchi R. Ontology-based systematization of functional knowledge. in TMCE2002:Tools and methods of competitive engineering. 2002. China.
7. Rubin D. L., et al., Representing genetic sequence data for pharmacogenomics: an evolutionary approach using ontological and relational models. 2002. 18(1): p. 207-215.
8. Bourdeau J. and Mizoguchi R. Collaborative Ontological Engineering of Instructional Design Knowledge for an ITS Authoring Environment. in ITS 2002. 2002: Springer, Heidelberg.
9. Murray T., Authoring intelligent tutoring systems: an analysis of the state of the art. IJAIED, 1999. 10: p. 98-129.
10. Kay J. and Holden S. Automatic Extraction fo Ontologies from Teaching Document Metadata. in ICCE Workshop on Concepts and Ontologies in Web-based Educational Systems. 2002. Technische Universiteit Eindhoven.
11. Paquette G. and Rosca I., Organic Aggregation of Knowledge Objects in Educational Systems. Canadian Journal of Learning and Technology, 2002. vol. 28(No. 3): p. 11-26.
12. Aroyo L. and Dicheva D. Authoring Framework for Concept-based Web Information Systems. in ICCE Workshop on Concepts and Ontologies in Web-based Educational Systems. 2002. Technische Universiteit Eindhoven.

13. Nkambou R., Frasson C., and Gauthier G., Cream-Tools: an authoring environment for knowledge engineering in intelligent tutoring systems, in Authoring Tools for Advanced Technology Learning Environments : Toward cost-effective adaptative, interactive, and intelligent educational software, B.S.a.A.S. Murray T., Editor. 2002, Kluwer Academic Publishers.
14. Reigeluth C. M., ed. Instructional theories in action: lessons illustrating, selected theories and models. 1993, LEA.
15. Mizoguchi R. A Step Towards Ontological Engineering. in 12th National Conference on AI of JSAI. 1998.
16. Davis R., Shrobe H., and Szolovits P., What Is a Knowledge Representation? AI Magazine, 1993.
17. Gruninger M. and Fox M.S. Methodology for the Design and Evaluation of Ontologies. in Workshop on Basic Ontological Issues in Knowledge Sharing, IJCAI-95. 1995. Montreal.
18. Noy N. F. and McGuinness D. L., Ontology Development 101: A Guide to Creating Your First Ontology. 2000.
19. Kozaki K., et al., Development of an environment for building ontologies which is based on a fundamental consideration of relationship and role. 2001.

Opening the Door to Non-programmers: Authoring Intelligent Tutor Behavior by Demonstration

Kenneth R. Koedinger[1], Vincent Aleven[1], Neil Heffernan[2], Bruce McLaren[1], and Matthew Hockenberry [1]

[1] Human-Computer Interaction Institute, Carnegie Mellon University, Pgh, PA, 15213
{koedinger, aleven, bmclaren}@cs.cmu.edu , mch2@andrew.cmu.edu

[2] Computer Science Dept., Worcester Polytechnic Institute, Worcester, MA 01609-2280
nth@wpi.edu

Abstract. Intelligent tutoring systems are quite difficult and time intensive to develop. In this paper, we describe a method and set of software tools that ease the process of cognitive task analysis and tutor development by allowing the author to demonstrate, instead of programming, the behavior of an intelligent tutor. We focus on the subset of our tools that allow authors to create "Pseudo Tutors" that exhibit the behavior of intelligent tutors without requiring AI programming. Authors build user interfaces by direct manipulation and then use a Behavior Recorder tool to demonstrate alternative correct and incorrect actions. The resulting behavior graph is annotated with instructional messages and knowledge labels. We present some preliminary evidence of the effectiveness of this approach, both in terms of reduced development time and learning outcome. Pseudo Tutors have now been built for economics, analytic logic, mathematics, and language learning. Our data supports an estimate of about 25:1 ratio of development time to instruction time for Pseudo Tutors, which compares favorably to the 200:1 estimate for Intelligent Tutors, though we acknowledge and discuss limitations of such estimates.

1 Introduction

Intelligent Tutoring Systems have been successful in raising student achievement and have been disseminated widely. For instance, Cognitive Tutor Algebra is now in more than 1700 middle and high schools in the US [1] (www.carnegielearning.com). Despite this success, it is recognized that intelligent tutor development is costly and better development environments can help [2, 3]. Furthermore, well-designed development environments should not only ease implementation of tutors, but also improve the kind of cognitive task analysis and exploration of pedagogical content knowledge that has proven valuable in cognitively-based instructional design more generally [cf., 4, 5]. We have started to create a set of Cognitive Tutor Authoring Tools (CTAT) that support both objectives. In a previous paper, we discussed a number of stages of tutor development (e.g., production rule writing and debugging) and presented some preliminary evidence that the tools potentially lead to substantial

J.C. Lester et al. (Eds.): ITS 2004, LNCS 3220, pp. 162–174, 2004.

savings in the time needed to construct executable cognitive models [6]. In the current paper, we focus on the features of CTAT that allow developers to create intelligent tutor behavior without programming. We describe how these features have been used to create "Pseudo Tutors" for a variety of domains, including economics, LSAT preparation, mathematics, and language learning, and present data consistent with the hypothesis that these tools reduce the time to develop educational systems that provide intelligent tutor behavior.

A Pseudo Tutor is an educational system that emulates intelligent tutor behavior, but does so without using AI code to produce that behavior. (It would be more accurate, albeit more cumbersome, to call these "Pseudo Intelligent Tutors" to emphasize that it is the lack of an internal AI engine that makes them "pseudo," not any significant lack of intelligent behavior.) Part of our investigation in exploring the possibilities of Pseudo Tutors is to investigate the cost-benefit trade-offs in intelligent tutor development, that is, in what ways can we achieve the greatest instructional "bang" for the least development "buck." Two key features of Cognitive Tutors, and many intelligent tutoring systems more generally, are 1) helping students in constructing knowledge by getting feedback and instruction in the context of doing and 2) providing students with flexibility to explore alternative solution strategies and paths while learning by doing. Pseudo Tutors can provide these features, but with some limitations and trade-offs in development time. We describe some of these limitations and trade-offs. We also provide preliminary data on authoring of Pseudo Tutors, on student learning outcomes from Pseudo Tutors, and development time estimates as compared with estimates of full Intelligent Tutor development.

2 Pseudo Tutors Mimic Cognitive Tutors

Cognitive Tutors are a kind of "model-tracing" intelligent tutoring systems that are based on cognitive psychology theory [7], particularly the ACT-R theory [8]. Developing a Cognitive Tutor involves creating a cognitive model of student problem solving by writing production rules that characterize the variety of strategies and misconceptions students may acquire. Productions are written in a modular fashion so that they can apply to a goal and context independent of what led to that goal. Consider the following example of three productions from the domain of equation solving:

Strategy 1:	IF the goal is to solve a(bx+c) = d THEN rewrite this as bx + c = d/a
Strategy 2:	IF the goal is to solve a(bx+c) = d THEN rewrite this as abx + ac = d
Misconception:	IF the goal is to solve a(bx+c) = d THEN rewrite this as abx + c = d

The first two productions illustrate alternative correct strategies for the same goal. By representing alternative strategies, the cognitive tutor can follow different students down different problem solving paths. The third "buggy" production represents a common error students make when faced with this same goal. A Cognitive Tutor makes use of the cognitive model to follow students through their individual approaches to a problem. A technique called "model tracing" allows the tutor to provide individualized assistance in the context of problem solving. Such assistance comes in the form of instructional message templates that are attached to the correct and buggy production rules. The cognitive model is also used to estimate students' knowledge growth across problem-solving activities using a technique known as "knowledge tracing" [9]. These estimates are used to adapt instruction to individual student needs.

The key behavioral features of Cognitive Tutors, as implemented by model tracing and knowledge tracing, are what we are trying to capture in Pseudo Tutor authoring. The Pseudo Tutor authoring process does not involve writing production rules, but instead involves demonstration of student behavior.

3 Authoring Pseudo Tutors in CTAT

Authoring a Pseudo Tutor involves several development steps that are summarized below and illustrated in more detail later in this section.

1. Create the graphical user interface (GUI) used by the student
2. Demonstrate alternative correct and incorrect solutions
3. Annotate solutions steps in the resulting "behavior graph" with hint messages, feedback messages, and labels for the associated concepts or skills
4. Inspect skill matrix and revise

The subset of the Cognitive Tutor Authoring Tools that support Pseudo Tutor development and associated cognitive task analysis are:

1. ***Tutor GUI Builder*** — used to create a graphical user interface (GUI) for student problem solving.
2. ***Behavior Recorder*** —records alternate solutions to problems as they are being demonstrated in the interface created with the Tutor GUI Builder. The author can annotate these "behavior graphs" (cf., [10]) with hints, feedback and knowledge labels. When used in "pseudo-tutor mode", the Behavior Recorder uses the annotated behavior graph to trace students' steps through a problem, analogous to the methods of model-tracing tutors.

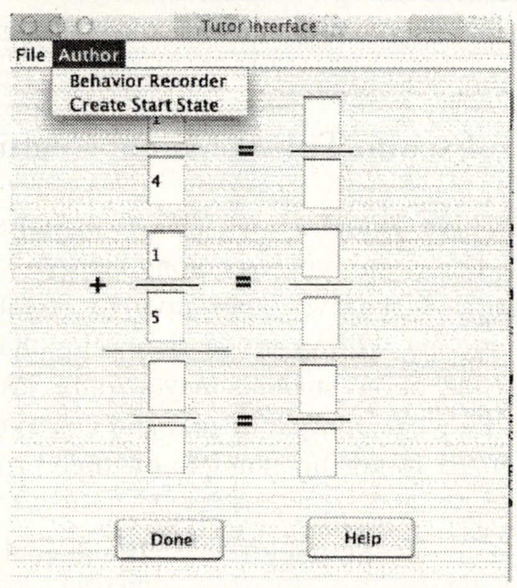

Fig. 1. The author creates the initial state of a problem that the learner will later see. Here, the initial state displays the fraction addition problem 1/4 + 1/5.

Create the Graphical User Interface. Figure 1 shows an interface for fraction addition created using a "recordable widget" palette we added to Java NetBeans, a shareware programming environment. To create this interface, the author clicks on the text field icon in the widget palette and uses the mouse to position text fields.

Typically in the tutor development process new ideas for interface design, particularly "scaffolding" techniques, may emerge (cf., [11]). The interface shown in Figure 1 provides scaffolding for converting the given fractions into equivalent fractions that have a common denominator. The GUI Builder tool can be used to create a number of kinds of scaffolding strategies for the same class of problems. For instance, story problems sometimes facilitate student performance and thus can serve as a potential scaffold. Consider this story problem: "Sue has 1/4 of a candy bar and Joe has 1/5 of a candy bar. How much of candy bar do they have altogether?" Adding such stories to the problem in Figure 1 is a minor interface change (simply add a text area widget). Another possible scaffold early in instruction is to provide students with the common denominator (e.g., 1/4 + 1/5 = __/20 + __/20). An author can create such a subgoal scaffold simply by entering the 20's before saving the problem start state. Both of these scaffolds can be easily implemented and have been shown to reduce student errors in learning fraction addition [12].

The interface widgets CTAT provides can be used to create interfaces that can scaffold a wide variety of reasoning and problem solving processes. A number of non-trivial widgets exist including a "Chooser" and "Composer" widget. The Chooser widget allows students to enter hypotheses (e.g., [13]). The Composer widget allows students to compose sentences by combining phrases from a series of menus (e.g., [14]).

Demonstrate Alternative Correct and Incorrect Solutions. Once an interface is created, the author can use it and the associated "Behavior Recorder" to author problems and demonstrate alternate solutions. Figure 1 shows the interface just after the author has entered 1, 4, 1, and 5 in the appropriate text fields. At this point, the author chooses "Create Start State" from the Author menu and begins interaction with the Behavior Recorder, shown on the left in Figure 2. After creating a problem start state, the author demonstrates alternate solutions as well as

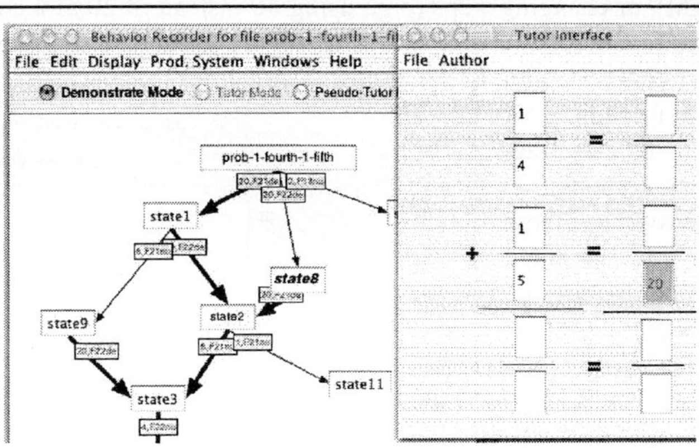

Fig. 2. The Behavior Recorder records authors' actions in any interface created with CTAT's recordable GUI widgets. The author demonstrates alternative correct and incorrect paths. Coming out of the start state (labeled "prob-1-fourth-1-fifth") are two correct paths ("20, F21den" and "20, F22den") and one incorrect path ("2, F13num"). Since *state8* is selected in the Behavior Recorder, the Tutor Interface displays that state, namely with the 20 entered in the second converted fraction.

common errors that students tend to make. Each interaction with the interface (e.g., typing a 20 in the cell to the right of the 4) produces a new action link and interface state node in the behavior graph displayed in the Behavior Recorder.

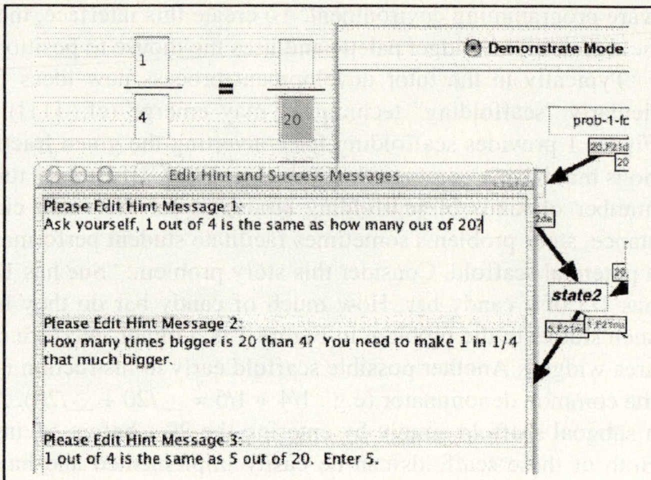

Fig. 3. The author adds a sequence of hint messages for a step by control-clicking on the associated action link (e.g., "5, F21num" just below state2) and then typing messages.

Figure 2 shows the Behavior Recorder after the author has demonstrated a complete solution and some alternatives. The link from the start state (prob-1-fourth-1-fifth) off to the left to state1 represents the action of entering 20. The links to the right from the start state represent either alternative solution strategies or common errors. Alternative solutions may involve reordering steps (e.g., putting the common denominator 20 across from the 5 before putting the 20 across from the 4), skipping steps (e.g., entering the final answer 9/20 without using the equivalent fraction scaffold on the right), or changing steps (e.g., using 40 instead of 20 as a common denominator). The common student errors shown in Figure 2 capture steps involved in adding the numerators and denominators of the given fractions without first converting them to a common denominator (e.g., entering 2/9 for 1/4 + 1/5).

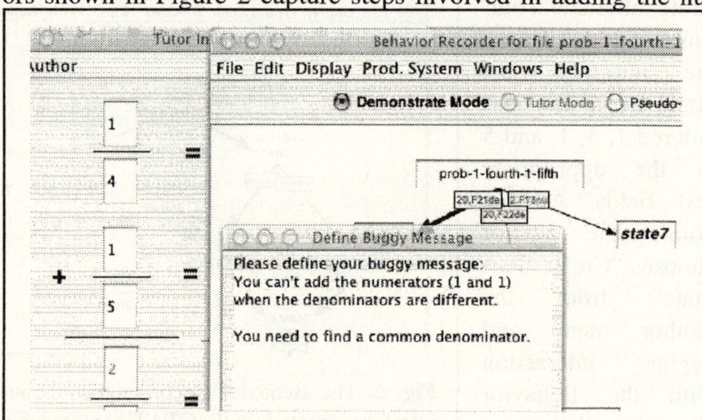

Fig. 4. The author enters an error feedback or "buggy" message by control-clicking on the link corresponding with the incorrect action (e.g.,"2, F13num" going to state7). The error of adding the numerators of fractions with unlike denominators is shown.

Label Behavior Graph with Hints and Feedback Messages. After demonstrating solutions, the author can annotate links on the behavior graph by adding hint messages to the correct links and error feedback messages to the incorrect links. Figure 3 shows an example of an author entering hint messages and Figure 4 shows an example of entering a feedback message. In Figure 3, the author has entered three layers of hint messages for finding the equivalent numerator in the blank cell in 1/4 = __/20. When a student requests a hint at this step in the resulting Pseudo Tutor, message 1 is presented and, only if further requests are made are the subsequent messages given.

When an author encounters a new step, in the same or different problem, in which a similar hint would make sense, this is a cue that that step draws on the same knowledge (concepts or skills) as the prior step. For instance, the hint sequence shown in Figure 3 can be re-used for the later step in this problem where the student needs to find the equivalent numerator to fill in the blank cell in 1/5 = __/20. The author need only substitute 5 for 4 and 4 for 5 in the message. Such similarity in the hint messages across different steps is an indication that learners can learn or use the same underlying knowledge in performing these steps. As described in the next section, the tools allow the author to annotate links in the behavior graph with knowledge labels that indicate commonalities in underlying knowledge requirements.

After demonstrating correct and incorrect solutions and adding hint and buggy messages, authors can have students use the Pseudo Tutor. The Pseudo Tutor provides feedback and context-sensitive error messages in response to students' problem-solving steps and provides context-sensitive hints at the students' request. Figure 5 shows a student receiving a hint message that may have been rewritten moments ago in response to observations of a prior learner using the Pseudo Tutor.

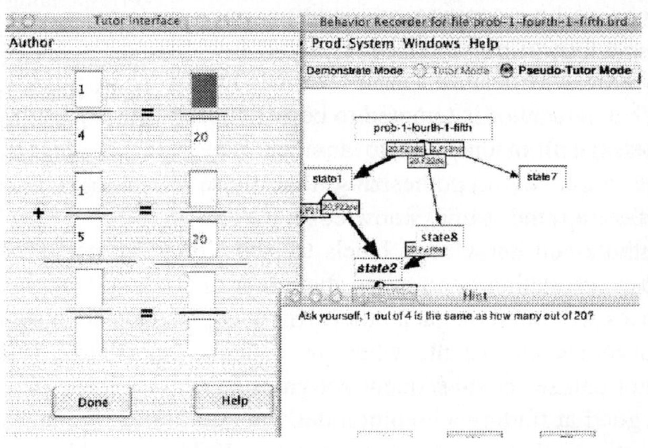

Fig. 5. The author begins testing tutor behavior by putting the Behavior Recorder in Pseudo-Tutor Mode (top right). She "plays student" by entering two correct steps (the 20's), which the Behavior Recorder has traced to follow the student to *state2*. She then clicks the Help button and the tutor highlights the relevant interface element (F21num cell) and displays the preferred hint (thicker line) out of *state2*.

Adding Knowledge Labels. Once the behavior graph has been completed the author can attach knowledge labels to links in the behavior graph to represent the knowledge behind these problem-solving steps, as illustrated in Figure 6. While these labels are referred to as "rules" in the tutor interface (reflecting a connection with the use of production rules in the ACT-R theory), the approach is neutral to the specific nature of the knowledge elements, whether they are concepts, skills, schemas, etc. One consequence of using knowledge labels is that it provides a way for the author to copy hint messages from one step to a similar step.

In Figure 6 the author has labeled the step of entering 5 in 5/20 (i.e., the one between *state2* and *state3*) with *find-equivalent-numerator*. If the author believes the next step of entering the 4 in 4/20 (i.e., between *state3* and *state4*) draws upon the same knowledge, he or she can label it as *find-equivalent-numerator* as well. Doing so has the direct benefit that the hint that was written before will be copied to this link. The author needs to make some modifications to the messages, in this case by changing 4 to 5 and 5 to 4 so that, for instance, message 1 in Figure 3 now becomes "Ask yourself, 1 out of 5 is the same as how many out of 20?" These steps of hint copying and editing push the author to make decisions about how to represent desired learner knowledge. When an author is tempted to copy a hint message from one link to another, they are implicitly hypothesizing that those links tap the same knowledge. When authors add knowledge labels to steps, they are performing cognitive task analysis. They are stating hypotheses about learning transfer and how repeated learning experiences will build on each other. Knowledge labels are also used by the Pseudo Tutor to do *knowledge tracing* whereby students' knowledge gaps can be assessed and the tutor can select subsequent activities to address those gaps. For instance, if a student is good at finding a common denominator, but is having difficulty finding equivalent fractions, the tutor can select a "scaffolded" problem, like "1/4 + 1/5 = __/20 + __/20", where the common denominator is provided and the student is focused on the *find-equivalent-numerator* steps.

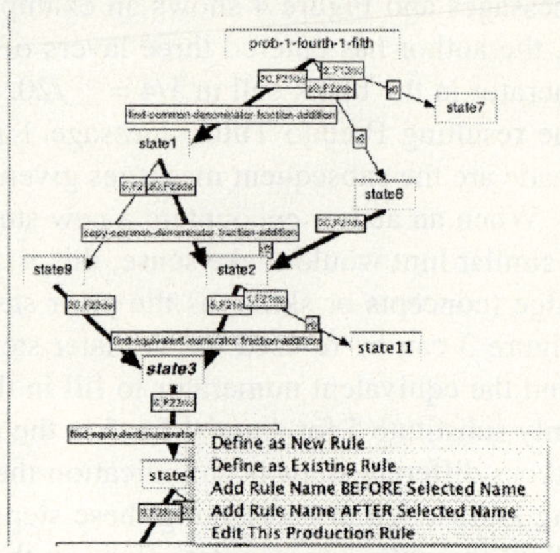

Fig. 6. The author labels links in the behavior graph to represent hypotheses about the knowledge needed to perform the corresponding step. Some steps are labeled the same, for instance, "find-equivalent-numerator" is on both the state2-state3 and state3-state4 link. The "Define as Existing Rule" option shown allows the selection of an existing label and copies associated hint messages.

Inspect Skill Matrix and Revise Tutor Design. Not only can knowledge labels be reused within problems, as illustrated above, they can also be reused across problems. Doing so facilitates the creation of a "skill matrix" as illustrated in Figure 7. The rows of the skill matrix indicate the problems the author has created and the columns are the knowledge elements required to solve each problem. The problems in the skill matrix are 1) prob-1-fourth-1-fifth described above, 2) prob-multiples is "1/3 + 1/6", 3) prob-same-denom is "2/5 + 1/5", and 4) prob-with-scaffold is "1/4 + 1/5 = __/20 + __/20" where the start state includes the common denominator already filled in. Inspecting the skill matrix, one can see how the problems grow in complexity from prob-same-denom, which only requires add-common-denominators and add-numerators, to prob-with-scaffold, which adds find-equivalent-numerators, to prob-1-fourth-1-fifth and prob-multiples which add more skills as shown in the matrix.

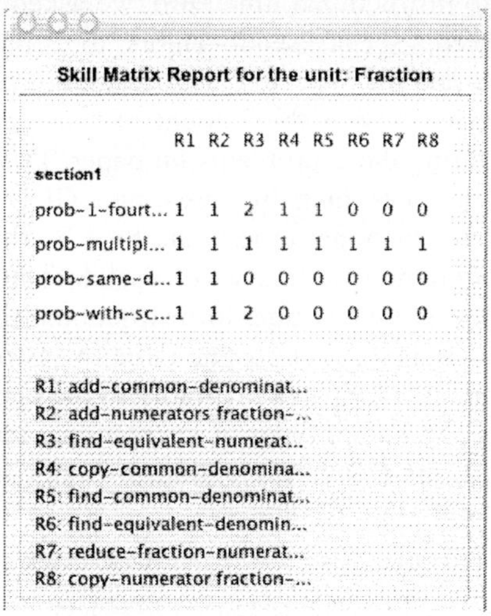

Skill Matrix Report for the unit: Fraction

	R1	R2	R3	R4	R5	R6	R7	R8
section1								
prob-1-fourt...	1	1	2	1	1	0	0	0
prob-multipl...	1	1	1	1	1	1	1	1
prob-same-d...	1	1	0	0	0	0	0	0
prob-with-sc...	1	1	2	0	0	0	0	0

R1: add-common-denominat...
R2: add-numerators fraction-...
R3: find-equivalent-numerat...
R4: copy-common-denomina...
R5: find-common-denominat...
R6: find-equivalent-denomin...
R7: reduce-fraction-numerat...
R8: copy-numerator fraction-...

Fig. 7. The skill matrix shows what knowledge elements (columns) are used in which problems (rows). For example, the 2 in the "prob-1-fourt" row means this problem requires two uses of knowledge element R3.

The skill matrix makes predictions about transfer. For instance, practice on problems like prob-with-scaffold should improve performance of the find-equivalent-numerator steps of problems like prob-1-fourth-1-fifth but should not improve performance of the find-common-denominator step. The author can reflect on the plausibility of these predictions and, better yet, use the Pseudo Tutor to collect student performance data to test these predictions. The cognitive task analysis and tutor can then be revised based on such reflection and data analysis.

4 Development Time and Use

The previous description illustrates that Pseudo Tutors are relatively easy to develop and do not require AI programming expertise. In this section we focus on the development time of Pseudo Tutors, comparing it to estimates for other types of computer-based learning environments. Estimates for the development time of intelligent tutoring systems have varied from 100-1000 hours of development per hour of instruction [2, 8, p. 254]. Estimates for the development of CAI vary even more widely [15 , p. 830]. One of our own estimates for the development of Cognitive Tutors, which comes from the initial 3-year project to create the Algebra Cognitive Tutor [16], is about 200 hours per one hour of instruction. We developed the original Cognitive Tutor Algebra in roughly 10,000 hours and this provided approximately 50 hours of instruction. While we have not, as yet, collected formal data on the development and instructional use of Pseudo Tutors, we do have some very encouraging informal data from 4 projects that have built Pseudo Tutors with our technology.

- *The Economics Project:* Part of the Open Learning Initiative (OLI) at Carnegie Mellon University, the Economics Project has a goal of supplementing an on-line introductory college-level microeconomics course with tutors.
- *The Math Assistments Project*: A four-year project funded by the Department of Education, the Assistments Project is intended to provide web-based assessments that provide instructional assistance while they assess.
- *The LSAT Project*: A small project aimed at improving the performance of students taking the law school entrance examination on analytic problems.
- *The Language Learning: Classroom Project*: Four students in a Language Technologies course at CMU used the Pseudo Tutor technology to each build two prototype Pseudo Tutors related to language learning.

In order to estimate the development time to instructional time ratio, we asked the authors on each project, after they had completed a set of Pseudo Tutors, to estimate the time spent on design and development tasks and the expected instructional time of the resulting Pseudo Tutors (see Table 1). Design time is the amount of time spent selecting and researching problems, and structuring those problems on paper. Development time is the amount of time spent with the tools, including creating a GUI, the behavior diagrams, hints, and error messages. Instructional time is the time it would likely take a student, on average, to work through the resulting set of Pseudo Tutors. The final column is a ratio of the design and development time to instructional time for each project's Pseudo Tutors. The average Design/Development Time to Instructional Time ratio of about 23:1, though preliminary, compares favorably to the corresponding estimates for Cognitive Tutors (200:1) and other types of instructional technology given above. If this ratio stands up in a more formal evaluation, we can claim significant development savings using the Pseudo Tutor technology.

Table 1. Data on Pseudo Tutor Development and Instructional Use (in Minutes)

	# Of Pseudo Tutors	Design Time	Dev. Time	Instructional Time	Design/Dev to Instr.
Economics	11	3600	2190	180	**32.2**
Math Assistments	20	810	1170	98	**20.2**
LSAT	3	240	3000	180	**18.0**
Language Learning	8	210	575	50	**15.7**
Totals		*4860*	*6935*	*508*	*23.2*

Aside from the specific data collected in this experiment, this study also demonstrates how we are working with a variety of projects to deploy and test Pseudo Tutors. In addition to the projects mentioned above, the Pseudo Tutor authoring tools have been used in an annual summer school on Intelligent Tutoring Systems at CMU and courses at CMU and WPI. The study also illustrates the lower skill threshold needed to develop Pseudo-Tutors, compared to typical intelligent tutoring systems: None of the Pseudo Tutors mentioned were developed by experienced AI programmers. In the Language Learning Classroom Project, for instance, the students learned to build Pseudo Tutors quickly enough to make it worthwhile for a single homework assignment.

Preliminary empirical evidence for the instructional effectiveness of the Pseudo-Tutor technology comes from a small evaluation study with the LSAT Analytic Logic Tutor, involving 30 (mostly) pre-law students. A control group of 15 students was given 1 hour to work through a selection of sample problems in paper form. After 40 minutes, the correct answers were provided. The experimental group used the LSAT Analytic Logic Tutor for the same period of time. Both conditions presented the students with the same three "logic games." After their respective practice sessions, both groups were given a post-test comprised of an additional three logic games. The results indicate that students perform significantly better after using the LSAT Analytic

Logic Tutor (12.1 ± 2.4 v. 10.3 ± 2.3, $t(28) = 2.06$, $p < .05$). Additionally, pre-questionnaire results indicate that neither group of students had a significant difference in relevant areas of background that influence LSAT test results. Thus, the study provides preliminary evidence that Pseudo Tutors are able to support student learning in complex tasks like analytic logic games.

5 Comparing Pseudo Tutors and Full Cognitive Tutors

In principle, Pseudo Tutors and full Cognitive Tutors exhibit identical behavior in interaction with students. Both perform model tracing, provide context-sensitive instruction in the form of hints and error feedback messages, and are flexible to multiple possible solution strategies and paths. Authoring for this flexibility is different. In the case of a full Cognitive Tutor, such flexibility is modeled by a production system that generalizes across problem solving steps within and between problems. In a Pseudo Tutor, such flexibility is modeled by explicit demonstration of alternative paths in each problem. Authors face challenges in both cases. Writing production rules that work correctly across multiple situations requires significant skill and inevitable cycles of testing and debugging. On the other hand, demonstrating alternative solutions may become increasingly tedious as the number of problems increases and the complexity of alternative paths within problems increases.

To illustrate this contrast, we consider what it might take to re-implement a real Cognitive Tutor unit as a Pseudo Tutor. Consider the Angles Unit in the Geometry Cognitive Tutor [17]. This unit has about 75 problems. At first blush, the thought of developing 75 Pseudo Tutor behavior graphs may not seem daunting. It could be done by someone without AI programming expertise and might seem that it would take less time than developing the corresponding production rule model.

While alternative inputs can be handled by Pseudo Tutors, as described above, it can be time consuming to provide them, requiring separate links in the behavior diagram. For example, in the Angles unit of the Geometry Cognitive Tutor, students give reasons for their answers. Although there is always only a single correct solution for a numeric answer step, there may be different reasons for the step, at least in the more complex problems. Currently, those alternative correct reasons need to be represented with alternative links in a behavior diagram, which in itself is not a problem, except that the part of the diagram that is "downstream" from these links would have to be duplicated, leading to a potentially unwieldy diagram if there were multiple steps with alternative inputs. At minimum, a way of indicating alternative correct inputs for a given link would be useful. We are currently working on generalization features within Pseudo Tutor, one form of which is to allow authors write simple spreadsheet-like formulas to check student inputs.

While possible in principle, other behaviors are difficult in practice to replicate in Pseudo Tutors. For example, the Geometry Cognitive Tutor imposes some subtle constraints on the order in which students can go through the steps in a problem. These constraints are hard to express within Pseudo Tutors. To recreate this tutor's behavior, one would have to be able to (1) require students to complete a given answer-reason pair before moving on to the next answer-reason pair (i.e., if you give a numeric answer, the next thing you need to do is provide the corresponding reason - and vice versa) and (2) require students to complete a step only if the pre-requisites for that step have been completed (i.e., the quantities from which the step is derived). To implement these requirements with current Pseudo Tutor technology would require a huge behavior diagram. In practice, Pseudo Tutors often compromise on expressing such subtle constraints on the ordering of steps. Most of the Pseudo Tutors developed so far have used a "commutative mode", in which the student can carry out the steps in any order. We are planning on implementing a "partial commutativity" feature, which would allow authors to express that certain groups of steps can be done in any order, whereas others need to be done in the order specified in the behavior graph.

Despite some limitations, Pseudo Tutors do seem capable of implementing useful interactions with students. As we are building more Pseudo Tutors, we are become more aware of their strengths and limitations. One might have thought that it would be an inconvenient limitation of Pseudo Tutors that the author must demonstrate all reasonable alternative paths through a problem. However, in practice, this has not been a problem. But, these questions would best be answered by re-implementing a Cognitive Tutor unit as a Pseudo Tutor. We plan to do so in the future.

6 Conclusions

We have described a method for authoring tutoring systems that exhibit intelligent behavior, but can be created without AI programming. Pseudo Tutor authoring opens the door to new developers who have limited programming skills. While the Pseudo Tutor development time estimates in Table 1 compare favorably to past estimates for intelligent tutor development, they must be considered with caution. Not only are the these estimates rough, there are differences in the quality of the tutors produced where most Pseudo Tutors to date have been ready for initial lab testing (alpha versions) and past Cognitive tutors have been ready for extensive classroom use (beta+ versions). On the other hand, our Pseudo Tutor authoring capabilities are still improving.

In addition to the goal of Pseudo Tutor authoring contributing to faster and easier creation of working tutoring systems, we also intend to encourage good design practices, like cognitive task analysis [5] and to facilitate fast prototyping of tutor design ideas that can be quickly tested in iterative development. If desired, full Intelligent Tutors can be created and it is a key goal that Pseudo Tutor creation is substantially "on path" to doing so. In other words, CTAT has been designed so that almost all of the work done in creating a Pseudo Tutor is on path to creating a Cognitive Tutor.

Pseudo Tutors can provide support for learning by doing and can also be flexible to alternative solutions. CTAT's approach to Pseudo-Tutor authoring has advantages over other authoring systems, like RIDES [3], that only allow a single solution path. Nevertheless, there are practical limits to this flexibility. Whether such limits have a significant affect on student learning or engagement is an open question. In future experiments, we will evaluate the effects of limited flexibility by contrasting student learning from a Pseudo Tutor with student learning from a full Cognitive Tutor. The Pseudo Tutor approach may be impractical for scaling to large intelligent tutoring systems where students are presented a great of number of problem variations. In full tutors, adding new problems is arguably less effort because only the machine-readable problem specification needs to be entered and the production rules take care of computing alternative solution paths. Adding new problems in Pseudo Tutors is arguably more costly because solution paths must be demonstrated anew. Future research should check these arguments and, more importantly, provide some guidance for when it might make sense to author an intelligent tutor rather than a Pseudo Tutor.

References

1. Corbett, A. T., Koedinger, K. R., & Hadley, W. H. (2001). Cognitive Tutors: From the research classroom to all classrooms. In Goodman, P. S. (Ed.) Technology Enhanced Learning: Opportunities for Change, (pp. 235-263). Mahwah, NJ: Lawrence Erlbaum.
2. Murray, T. (1999). Authoring intelligent tutoring systems: An analysis of the state of the art. International Journal of Artificial Intelligence in Education, 10, pp. 98-129.
3. Murray, T., Blessing, S., & Ainsworth, S. (Eds.) (2003). Authoring Tools for Advanced Technology Learning Environments: Towards cost-effective adaptive, interactive and intelligent educational software. Dordrecht, The Netherlands: Kluwer.
4. Lovett, M. C. (1998). Cognitive task analysis in service of intelligent tutoring system design: A case study in statistics. In Goettl, B. P., Halff, H. M., Redfield, C. L., & Shute, V. J. (Eds.) Intelligent Tutoring Systems, Proceedings of the Fourth Int'l Conference. (pp. 234-243). Lecture Notes in Comp. Science, 1452. Springer-Verlag.
5. Schraagen, J. M., Chipman, S. F., Shalin, V. L. (2000). *Cognitive Task Analysis*. Mawah, NJ: Lawrence Erlbaum Associates.
6. Koedinger, K. R., Aleven, V., & Heffernan, N. (2003). Toward a rapid development environment for Cognitive Tutors. In U. Hoppe, F. Verdejo, & J. Kay (Eds.), *Artificial Intelligence in Education, Proc. of AI-ED 2003* (pp. 455-457). Amsterdam, IOS Press.
7. Anderson, J. R., Corbett, A. T., Koedinger, K. R., & Pelletier, R. (1995). Cognitive tutors: Lessons learned. *The Journal of the Learning Sciences, 4 (2)*, 167-207.
8. Anderson, J. R. (1993). *Rules of the Mind.* Mahwah, NJ: Lawrence Erlbaum.
9. Corbett, A.T. & Anderson, J.R. (1995). Knowledge tracing: Modeling the acquisition of procedural knowledge. *User modeling and user-adapted interaction, 4*, 253-278.
10. Newell, A., & Simon, H. A. (1972). *Human problem solving*. Englewood Cliffs, NJ: Prentice-Hall.
11. Reiser, B. J., Tabak, I., Sandoval, W. A., Smith, B. K., Steinmuller, F., & Leone, A. J. (2001). BGuILE: Strategic and conceptual scaffolds for scientific inquiry in biology classrooms. In S. M. Carver & D. Klahr (Eds.), *Cognition and instruction: Twenty-five years of progress* (pp. 263-305). Mahwah, NJ: Erlbaum.
12. Rittle-Johnson, B. & Koedinger, K. R. (submitted). Context, concepts, and procedures: Contrasting the effects of different types of knowledge on mathematics problem solving. Submitted for peer review.

13. Lajoie, S. P., Azevedo, R., & Fleiszer, D. M. (1998). Cognitive tools for assessment and learning in a high information flow environment. *Journal of Educational Computing Research, 18*, 205-235.
14. Shute, V.J. & Glaser, R. (1990). A large-scale evaluation of an intelligent discovery world. *Interactive Learning Environments, 1*: p. 51-76.
15. Eberts, R. E. (1997). Computer-based instruction. In Helander, M. G., Landauer, T. K., & Prabhu, P. V. (Ed.s) *Handbook of Human-Computer Interaction*, (pp. 825-847). Amsterdam, The Netherlands: Elsevier Science B. V.
16. Koedinger, K. R., Anderson, J. R., Hadley, W. H., & Mark, M. A. (1997). Intelligent tutoring goes to school in the big city. *International Journal of Artificial Intelligence in Education, 8*, 30-43.
17. Aleven, V.A.W.M.M., & Koedinger, K. R. (2002). An effective metacognitive strategy: Learning by doing and explaining with a computer-based Cognitive Tutor. *Cognitive Science, 26*(2).

Acquisition of the Domain Structure from Document Indexes Using Heuristic Reasoning

Mikel Larrañaga, Urko Rueda, Jon A. Elorriaga, and Ana Arruarte

Department of Languages and Information Systems,
University of the Basque Country. P.K. 649
20080 Donostia, Basque Country
{jiplaolm, jibrumou, jipelarj, jiparlaa}@si.ehu.es

Abstract. Domain Module is essential for many different kinds of Technology Supported Learning Systems. Some authors have pointed out the need of tools that may develop the domain module in an automatic or semi-automatic way. Nowadays, a lot of information of any domain, which can be used as the source for the target domain module, can be easily found in different formats. The work here presented describes a domain independent method based on Natural Language Processing techniques and heuristic reasoning to acquire the domain module from documents and their indexes.

1 Introduction

The rapid advance in the Education Technology area during the last years makes it possible to evolve education at different levels: from personal interaction with a teacher in a classroom to computer assisted learning, from written textbooks to electronic documents. Different kinds of approaches (Intelligent Tutoring Systems, e-learning systems, collaborative learning systems...) profit from new technologies in order to educate different kinds of students. These Technology Supported Learning Systems (TSLSs) have proved to be very useful in many learning situations such as distance learning and training. TSLSs require the representation of the domain to be learnt. However, the development of the domain module is not easy because of the amount of data that must be represented. Murray [10] pointed out the need of tools that facilitate the construction of the domain module in a semi automatic way.

Electronic documents constitute a source of information that can be used in TSLSs for this purpose. However, electronic documents require a transformation process before incorporating them in a TSLS due to their different features. Vereoustre and McLean [14] present a survey of current approaches in the area of technologies for electronic documents that are used for finding, reusing and adapting documents for learning purposes. They describe how research in structured documents, document representation and retrieval, semantic representation of document content and relationships, learning objects and ontologies, could be used to provide solutions to the problem of reusing education material for teaching and learning.

J.C. Lester et al. (Eds.): ITS 2004, LNCS 3220, pp. 175–186, 2004.

In fact, in the past 5-7 years there have been considerable efforts in the computer-mediated learning field towards standardization of metadata elements to facilitate a common method for identifying, searching and retrieving learning objects [11]. Learning objects are reusable pieces of educational material intended to be strung together to form larger educational units such as activities, lessons or whole courses [4]. A Learning Object (LO) has been defined as any entity, digital or non-digital, which can be used, re-used or referenced during technology supported learning [7]. In 2002, LOM (Learning Object Metadata), the first standard for Learning Technology was accredited. Learning Object Metadata (LOM) is defined as the attributes required to fully/adequately describe a Learning Object [7]. The standard will focus on the minimal set of attributes needed to allow these LOs to be managed, located, and evaluated but lacks the instructional design information for the decision-making process [15]. Recently, a number of efforts have been initiated with the aim of adding didactical information in the LO description [5][15][13][12]. So far, there has not been any significant work in automating the discovery and packaging of LOs based on variables such as learning objectives and learning outcomes [9]. As a conclusion, it is clear that some pedagogical knowledge has to guide the sequence of the LOs presented to the student for both open learning environments and more classical ITSs.

The final aim of the project here presented is to extract the domain knowledge of a TSLS from existing documents in order to lighten its development cost. It uses Artificial Intelligence methods and techniques like Natural Language Processing (NLP) and heuristic reasoning to achieve this goal. However, the acquisition of this knowledge still requires the collaboration of instructional designers in order to get an appropriate representation of the Domain Module. The system here presented is aimed at identifying the topics included in documents, to establish the pedagogical relationships among them, and to cut the whole document into LOs categorizing them according to the pedagogical purpose and, thus, tagging them with the corresponding metadata. Three basic features are essential in representing the domain module in TSLSs: 1) Learning units that represent the teaching/learning topics, 2) relationships among contents, and 3) learning objects or didactic resources.

Once the electronic document that is going to be the source of the domain knowledge has been selected, the process of preparing the learning material to be included in the domain module of a TSLS involves the following three steps [6]:

- Identifying the relevant topics included in the document.
- Establishing the pedagogical and sequential relationships between the contents.
- Identifying the Learning Objects.

This paper focuses on the identification of the relevant topics of the document and the discovery of pedagogical and sequential relationships between them. Concretely, the structure of the domain is extracted just by analysing the index of a document. In a similar direction, Mittal et al. [8] present a system where the input is the set of slides for a course in PowerPoint and the output are a concept tree and a relational tree. Their approach is based on rules for the identification of relationships (class of, applied to, prerequisite) between concepts and the identification of objects (definition, example, figure, equation…) in a concept. However, rules are specific to computer science and mathematics like-courses. The solution presented here is domain independent and has been proved with a wide set of subject matters.

This paper starts with a description of the analysis of the indexes of the documents. Next, the heuristics to identify the pedagogical relationships among topics are presented and also the results of their application in a wide set of subject matters. Finally, some conclusions and future work are pointed out.

2 Index Analysis

Indexes are useful sources of information for acquiring the domain module in a semi-automatic way because they are usually well-structured and contain the main topics of the domain. Besides, they are quite short so a lot of useful information can be extracted in a low cost process. The documents' authors have previously analysed the domain and decided how to organise the content according to pedagogical principles. They use the indexes as the basis for structuring the subject matter. Therefore, the main implicit pedagogical relations can be inferred from the index by using NLP techniques and a collection of heuristics.

Fig. 1 illustrates the index analysis process that is described next:

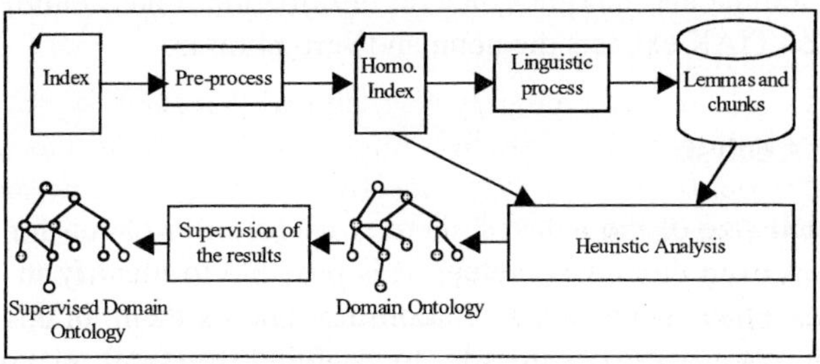

Fig. 1. Index analysis process

2.1 Index Pre-process

The indexes are usually human made text files and therefore, they may contain different numbering formats and some inconsistencies such as typographic errors, format errors, etcetera. In order to run an automatic analysis process the indexes must be error-free, so they have to be corrected and homogenized before the analysis.

In the pre-process step, performed automatically, the numbering of the index items is filtered and replaced by tabulations with the aim of sharing the same index structure. However, the correction of inconsistencies can hardly be performed automatically. Hence, this task is performed manually by the users. The result of this step is a text file in which each title of section is in one line (index item) and the level of nesting of the title is defined by the number of tabulations.

2.2 Linguistic Process

In this process the index is analysed using NLP tools. Due to the differences between languages, specific tools are needed. The work here presented has been performed with documents written in Basque language. Basque is an agglutinative language, i.e., for the formation of words the dictionary entry takes each of the elements needed for the different functions (syntactic case included). More specifically, the affixes corresponding to the determiner, number and declension case are taken in this order independently of each other. As prepositional functions are realised by case suffixes inside word-forms, Basque presents a relative high power to generate inflected word-forms. This characteristic is particularly important because the words in Basque contain much more part-of-speech information than words in other languages. These characteristics make morphosyntactic analysis very important for Basque. Thus, for the index analysis, the lemmas of the words must be extracted so as to the gather correct information. This process is carried out using EUSLEM [2], a lemmatizer/tagger for the Basque. Noun phrases, verb phrases and multiword terms are detected by ZATIAK [1]. The result of this step is the list of lemmas and the chunks of the index items. These lemmas and chunks constitute the basis of the domain ontology that will be completed in the analysis of the whole document.

The morphosyntactic analysis is performed by EUSLEM, which annotates each word with the lemma and morphosyntactic information. Later, entities, postpositions are extracted. ZATIAK extracts the noun and verb phrases.

2.3 Heuristic Analysis

Despite the small size of the indexes, there is useful information for the TSLSs that can be extracted from them. Concretely, it is possible to identify the main topics of the domain (BLUs) and pedagogical relationships among them. In this step the system makes use of a set of heuristics in order to establish structural relationships between topics (*Is-a* and *Part-of*) and sequential relationships (*Prerequisite* and *Next*). The next section goes deeper into this analysis.

2.4 Supervision of the Results

The results of the analysis are presented to the user in a graphical way by means of concept maps using the CM-ED tool [3]. CM-ED (Concept Map EDitor) is a general-purpose tool for editing concept maps. The results of the analysis may not fit what the users expect or they may want to adapt the structure of the domain to some particular needs. These modifications can be performed on the concept maps by adding, removing or modifying both concepts and relations. The nodes represent the domain topics and the labelled arcs represent the relations.

3 Heuristic Analysis

As mentioned above, the indexes contain both the main topics of the domain as well as the implicit pedagogical relations among them. In this task the structure of the domain is gathered using a set of heuristics from the homogenized index. This analysis is domain independent.

The process starts assuming an initial structure that later on is refined. In this approach, each index item is considered as a domain topic (BLU). Regarding the relationships, two kinds of pedagogical relationships are detected: structural and sequential. Structural relations are inferred between an item and its sub-items (nested items). A sub-item of a general topic is used to explain a part of that issue or a particular case of it. Sequential relations are inferred among concepts of the same nesting level. The order of the items establishes the sequence of the contents in the learning process. The obtained initial domain structure is refined using a set of heuristics.

The following procedure was carried out to define the heuristics that are described in this section:

1. A small set of indexes related to Computer Science has been analysed in order to detect some patterns that may help in the classification of relationships.
2. This heuristics have been tested in a wide set of indexes related to different domains. As a result of this experiment the relationships implicit in the indexes have been inferred.
3. The results of the heuristics have been contrasted with the real relationships (identified manually).
4. After analysing the results paying special attention to the detected lacks in the heuristics, some new heuristics have been defined.
5. The performance of the improved set of heuristic has also been measured.

Next the sets of heuristics are described and the results of the experiments presented and discussed.

3.1 Heuristics Set 1

Pedagogical relationships structure the didactic material. This information can be used in TSLS in different ways, for example to plan the learning sessions. Two types of pedagogical relationships are considered in this work: structural and sequential relationships. Structural relationships define the BLU taxonomy in terms of parts of learning units (*Part-of* relationship) and cases of a particular BLU (*Is-a* relationship). Sequential relationships represent the order in which the topics should be learned. The *Next* relationship is used to tell what is the normal continuation for a BLU whereas the *prerequisite* relationship is used to inform that a particular BLU has to be learned before another one. Both relationships can be combined to decide the appropriate sequence of BLUs. As said before, the initial structure of the domain uses only abstract pedagogical relationships, i.e. structural or sequential relationship. However, relations must be refined into *part-of*, *is-a*, *prerequisite* and *next*. Following the heuristics that are applied to refine the Structural and Sequential relations are detailed.

Even though the work has been conducted with Basque language, the examples will be presented in both Basque and English[1] for a better understanding.

Heuristics for Structural relationships. The first analysis of the document indexes (step 1 in the above procedure) has proved that the most common structural relation is the *Part-of* relation. Therefore, by default, the structural relations will be classified into *part-of*. In addition, some heuristics have been identified to detect the *is-a* relation or to reinforce the hypothesis that the structural relation is describing a *part-of* relation. This heuristics are applied to know the structural relationship between an index item and the sub-items included in it. However, the empirical analysis showed that index items do not always share the same linguistic structure. Therefore, different heuristics may apply in the same set of index sub-items. The system combines the information provided by the heuristics that can be applied in order to refine the pedagogical relationships. If the percentage of sub-items that satisfy the heuristics' preconditions goes beyond a predefined *threshold*, the relations are classified into the corresponding relationship. In addition this percentage is considered the *level of certainty*.

- **MultiWord Heuristic (MWH):** MultiWord Terms may contain information to infer the *is-a* relation. This relation can be inferred in sub-items with the following patterns: noun + adjective, noun + noun phrase, etcetera. If the noun that appears in these patterns (*agente* or *agent*) is the same of the general item (*agenteak* or *agents*), *is-a* relationship is more plausible (Table 1).

Table 1. Fragment of an index on which the MWH can be applied

3.4.2. *Agenteak*	3.4.2. *Agents*
3.4.2.1. *Agente* mugikorrak	3.4.2.1. Mobile *Agents*
3.4.2.2. *Agente* estatikoak	3.4.2.2. Stationary *Agents*
...	...

- **Entity Name Heuristic (ENH):** Entity names are used to identify examples of a particular entity. When the sub-items contain entity names, the relation between the item and the sub-items can be considered as the *is-a* relation. In Table 2, *Palm Os*, *Windows CE (Pocket PC)* and *Linux Familiar 0.5.2 distribuzioa* correspond to entity names.

Table 2. Fragment of an index on which the ENH can be applied

3.7. Laguntzaile Pertsonal Digitalak (PDA-ak)	3.7. Personal Digital Assistants (PDA)
3.7.1. *Palm OS*	3.7.1. *Palm OS*
3.7.2. *Windows CE (Pocket PC)*	3.7.2. *Windows CE (Pocket PC)*
3.7.3. *Linux Familiar 0.5.2 distribuzioa*	3.7.3. *Linux Familiar 0.5.2 distribution*

- **Acronyms Heuristic (AH):** When the sub-items contain just acronyms, the structural relations may be the *is-a* relation. In Table 3, the *XUL* and *jXUL* acronyms

[1] In some examples, there may be some information lost in the English translations

represent the names of some examples of languages for designing graphical interfaces.

Table 3. Fragment of an index on which the AH can be applied

4.2.3. Interfaze grafikoak sortzeko lengoaiak 4.2.3.1. *XUL* 4.2.3.2. *jXUL* ...	4.2.3. Languages for building graphical interfaces 4.2.3.1. *XUL* 4.2.3.2. *jXUL* ...

Table 4. Example on an index fragment on which the PGH1 can be applied

4.5. Inplementazioa *4.5*.1. Aplikazio*aren* inplementazioa *4.5*.2. Agente*en* inplementazioa ...	4.5. Implementation *4.5*.1. Implementation *of* the application *4.5*.2. Implementation *of* the agents ...

- **Possessive Genitives Heuristic for Structural relations (PGH1):** Possessive Genitives (*-en* suffix in Basque, *of* preposition in English) contain references to other contents. They are used to describe just parts of the content so *part-of* relations can be reinforced by analysing items with possessive genitives that make references to the general topic (Table 4).

Heuristics for Sequential Relationships. The analysis of document indexes has proved that the most common sequential relation is the *next* relation. Therefore, by default, any sequential relation is traduced into *next*. However, the *prerequisite* relation can be also found in the indexes. Following some heuristics that are used to infer the *prerequisite* relation are described:

- **Reference Heuristic (RH):** References to previous index items are used to detect *prerequisite* relations (Table 5).
- **Possessive Genitives Heuristic for Sequential relations (PGH2):** Possessive genitives between index items of the same nesting level can be used to identify *prerequisite* relations (Table 6).

Table 5. Example of a fragment of an index on which the RH can be applied

4. *Sarrera/irteera* .... 6. Eraginkortasun altuko *sarrera/irteera*	4. *Input/Output* .... 6. High Performance *Input/Output*

Table 6. Example of a fragment of an index on which the PGH2 can be applied

3.5.2. *Agenteak* ... 3.5.3. *Agenteen* exekuzio eredua	3.5.2. *Agents* ... 3.5.3. *Agent* execution paradigm

3.2 Evaluation of the Performance of the Heuristic Set 1

The above-described heuristics have been tested with 150 indexes related to a wide variety of domains such as Economy, Philosophy, Pedagogy, and so on. These indexes have been analysed manually to know the real relationships. As a result of this process, 7231 relationships have been identified in these indexes (3935 structural relationships and 3296 sequential relationships). As Table 7 illustrates, the most frequent relationships are *Part-Of* (93.29% of structural relationships) and *Next* (85.83% of sequential relationships) relationships. Therefore, it has been confirmed that the initial hypothesis which establishes the *Part-of* as the default structural relationship and the *Next* as the default sequential relationship is sound.

Table 7. Percentage of relations

STRUCTURAL RELATIONSHIPS		SEQUENTIAL RELATIONSHIPS	
PART-OF	IS-A	NEXT	PREREQUISTE
3671	264	2829	467
93.2909784%	6.7090216%	85.8313107%	14.1686893%

The same set of indexes has been analysed using the heuristics set 1. Table 8 describes the heuristics' precision (i.e. success rate when they are triggered) obtained in this empirical study. The first three columns show the performance of the heuristics that refine the *Is-a* relationship, whereas the forth column describes the results of the heuristic that confirm *Part-of* relationship, and the last two refer to the Prerequisite refinement. The first row measures how many times a heuristic has triggered correctly and the second one counts the wrong activations. The third row presents the percentage of correct activations. As mentioned above, the ENH heuristic triggers when the sub-item contains an entity name, which usually represents a particular case or an example. The AH is triggered when the sub-item entails just an acronym, which also refers to an example. As it can be observed in Table 8, the precision of these heuristics is 100%. Sub-items that form multiword terms based on the super-item activate MWH. Multiword terms are very usual in Basque language, and they usually represent a particular case of the original term. This heuristic has a tested precision of 92.59%. The heuristics that classify prerequisite relationship, i.e. RH and PGH2, also have a high precision (93.333% for RH and 96.15% for PGH2).

Table 9 shows a comparison between the real relationships and those identified using the heuristic set 1. It illustrates the recall of each heuristic (first row), i.e. the number of relationships correctly identified compared with the numbers obtained in the manual analysis, as well as the recall of the heuristics all together (second row). In order to better illustrate the performance of the method, the data for *Part-of* and *Next* relationships, corresponding to default reasoning, are also included in the table. *Part-of* relationships are classified by default (94,5%) and reinforced by the PGH1 heuristic, which is fired in 0.735% of *Part-of* relationships. Although the outcome of this heuristic is not good, it may help the system to determine *Part-of* relationships when *Is-a* is also plausible. The combination of the PGH1 and by-default classification of *Part-of* results in 95.27% correctly classified *Part-of* relationships. The by-default classification of *Next* relationships also provides a high success rate (97.85%). In addition, the combination of RH and PGH2 correctly classifies 80.09% of prerequisites, which is a good result for a domain independent method. However, as it can be appreciated in Table 9, the heuristics that classify *Is-a* relationships, all combined, only succeed in 28.79% of the cases despite their high precision.

Table 8. Precision of the heuristics

	IS-A			Part-Of	Prerequisite	
	MWH	ENH	AH	PGH1	RH	PGH2
Correct	25	38	13	27	224	150
Incorrect	2	0	0	0	16	6
%	92,593%	100%	100%	100%	93,333%	96,154 %

Table 9. Recall of the used heuristics

	IS-A			Part-Of		Prerequisite		Next
	MWH	ENH	AH	PGH 1	Default	RH	PGH 2	Default
Gath-ered (%)	9.469697	14.39 7	4.924	0.735	94.53769491	47.966	32.12	97.84587379
	28.7878788%			95.27318933%		80.0856531%		97.84587379%

3.3 Heuristic Set 2

Even though 80% of prerequisites and almost 29% of the *Is-a* relations are detected, the results have not been as satisfying as expected. The indexes have been manually analysed again in order to know the reasons of the low recall for the *Is-a* refining heuristics. The study showed that, on the one hand, the *Is-a* relationship is used to express examples and particular cases of a topic and it is difficult to infer whether a BLU entails an example or just a part of the upper BLU without Domain Knowledge. On the other hand, indexes related to Computer Sciences (the initial set of indexes) are quite schematic, whereas other domains use implicit or contextual knowledge as well as synonyms, metaphors and so on. Considering that the aim of this work is to infer the relations in a domain independent way, specific knowledge cannot be used in order to improve the results. This second study was carried out in order to detect other domain independent methods that may improve the results. Firstly, a set of keywords that usually introduce example sub-items has been identified. These keywords facilitate *Is-a* relationship recognition. Table 10 shows an example of the **Keywords Based Heuristic (KBH)**.

In addition, the problem of the implicit or contextual knowledge has to be overcome. Therefore, new heuristics have been defined in order to infer *Is-a* and *Prerequisite* relationships. The heuristic set 1 is triggered when the whole super-item is included in the sub-item, e.g the MWH triggers when it finds a super-item such as *agenteak* (agents) and a set of sub-items like *agente mugikorrak* (mobile agents). However, in many

Table 10. Keywords based heuristic

Heuristic	Example	
KBH: *motak* (kinds), *Aplikazioak* (applications), *tresnak* (tools),…	Tresnak Osziloskopia …	Tools Oscilloscope …

cases contextual knowledge is used to refer to the topic presented in the super-item or in a previous item. The heuristic set 2 is an improved version of the initial set taking into account contextual knowledge. Two main ways of using contextual knowledge have been identified in the analysis. The first one entails the use of the head of the phrase of a particular item to refer to that item, e.g. authors may refer using the term *karga* (charge) to refer to the *karga elektrikoa* (electric charge) topic. The second one entails the use of acronyms to refer to the original item. In some index sub-items, the acronym corresponding to an item is added at the end of the item between brackets and later that acronym is used to reference the whole topic represented by the index item.

Regarding the structural relationships the heuristics to detect *Is-a* relationships have been improved. **Head of the phrase + MultiWord Heuristic (He+MWH)** is fired when the head of the phrase of an item is used to form multiword terms in the sub-items. **Acronyms + MultiWord Heuristic (A+MWH)** is triggered when the acronyms corresponding to an item is used by the sub-items to form multiword terms. **Common Head + MultiWord Heuristic (CHe+MWH)** is activated when a set of sub-items share a common head of phrase and form multiword terms based on it; this heuristic does not look at the super-item.

Concerning the sequential relationships, the initial set of heuristics uses the references to the whole item and possessive genitives with the whole item to detect prerequisites. In order to deal with the contextual knowledge problem the new heuristics work as follows. **Head of the phrase + Reference Heuristic (He+RH)** is activated by references to the head of a previous index item while **Acronym + Reference Heuristic (A+RH)** is triggered when the acronym corresponding to a previous index item is referenced. The possessive genitive is also used by the new heuristics to detect prerequisites. **Head of the phrase + Possessive Genitive Heuristic (He+PGH2)** is activated by items entailing possessive genitives based on the head of a previous index item whereas possessive genitives using the acronym of a previous index item trigger **Acronym + Possessive Genitive Heuristic (A+PGH2)**.

3.4 Evaluation of the Performance of the Heuristic Set 2

Fig. 2 shows the performance of the proposed method using both the initial heuristic set and the enhanced one. 99.33% of *Part-of* relationships and 99.47% of *Next* relationships are correctly detected. As mentioned above, these relationships are classified by default. The erroneous cases are due to undetected *Is-a* and *Prerequisite* relationships, which need domain information to be detected. As it can be observed in Fig. 2, the performance has raised to 65,53% for *Is-a* relationship and to 88% for *Prerequisite*. These results look promising, taking into account that this method is domain independent. However, it has been observed that the heuristics have not triggered in some cases because of the use of synonyms and other related terms. Adapting the heuristics to deal with synonyms may improve the performance even more.

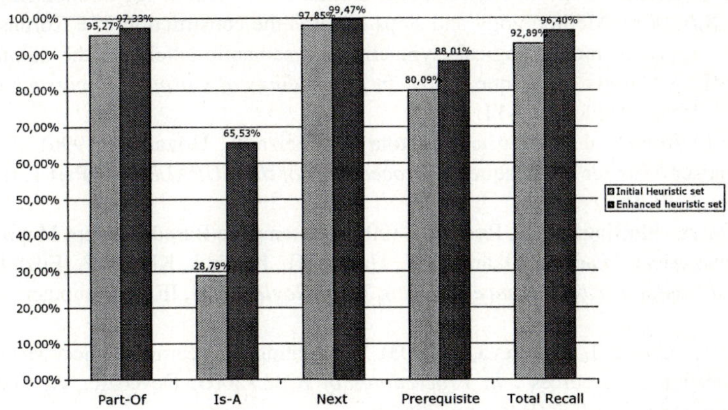

Fig. 2. Comparison of the performance of the initial and the enhanced heuristic set

4 Conclusions and Future Work

The aim of this work is to facilitate the building process of Technology Supported Learning Systems (TSLS) by acquiring the Domain Module from textbooks and other existing documents. The semi-automatic acquisition of the domain knowledge will significantly reduce the instructional designers' workload when building the TSLSs. This paper has presented a domain independent system for generating the domain module structure from the analysis of indexes of textbooks. The domain module structure includes the topics of the domain and the pedagogical relationships among them. The system performs the analysis using NLP tools and Heuristic Reasoning. Some heuristics have been implemented in order to identify pedagogical relations between topics. These heuristics provide additional information about the type of the pedagogical relations. The performance of the heuristics has been measured and after analysing the results an improved set of heuristics has been designed and tested.

Next phases of this work will include the analysis of the whole documents in order to extract the Didactic Resources to be used in the TSLS and also to create the ontology of the domain. In addition, the system will profit from linguistic ontologies with the aim of enriching both the domain ontology and the domain module structure (second level topics, related topic of other domains, new pedagogical relations, etc).

Acknowledgements. This work is funded by the University of the Basque Country (UPV00141.226-T-14816/2002), the Spanish CICYT (TIC2002-03141) and the *Gipuzkoa* Council in an European Union program.

References

1. Aduriz I., Aranzabe M. J., Arriola J.M., Ezeiza N., Gojenola K., Oronoz M., Soroa A., Urizar R. (2003). Methodology and steps towards the construction of a Corpus of written Basque tagged in morphological, syntactic, and semantic levels for the automatic processing (IXA Corpus of Basque, ICB). *In proceedings of Corpus Llinguistics 2003*. Lancaster. United Kingdom, 10-11.
2. Aduriz I., Aldezabal I., Alegria I., Artola X., Ezeiza N., Urizar R. (1996). EUSLEM: A Lemmatiser / Tagger for Basque. *In Proceedings of the EURALEX'96*, Part 1. Gothemburg (Sweden) , 17-26.
3. Arruarte, A., Elorriaga, J. A., Rueda, U. (2001). A template Based Concept Mapping tool for Computer-Aided Learning. Okamoto, T., Hartley, R., Kinshuk, Klus, J. P. (Eds), IEEE *International Conference on Advance Learning Technologies 2001*, IEEE Computer society, 309-312.
4. Brooks, C., Cooke, J., Vassileva, J. (2003). "Evaluating the Learning Object Metadata for K-12 Educational Resources". *In Proceedings of ICALT2003*, Devedzic, V., Spector, J.M., Sampson, D.G., Kinshuk (Eds.), pp. 296-297.
5. CANDLE. www.candle.eu.org
6. Larrañaga, M. (2002). Enhancing ITS building process with semi-automatic domain acquisition using ontologies and NLP techniques. *In Proceedings of the Young Researches Track of the Intelligent Tutoring Systems (ITS 2002).* Biarritz (France).
7. LTSC. (2001). IEEE P1484.12 Learning Object Metadata Working Group homepage [Online]. http://ltsc.ieee.org/wg12/
8. Mittal, A., Dixit, S., Maheshwari, L.K. (2003). "Enhanced Understanding and Retrieval of E-learning Documents through Relational and Conceptual Graphs". *In Supplementary Proceedings of AIED2003*, Aleven, V., Hoppe, U., Kay, J., Mizoguchi, R., Pain, H., Verdejo, F. and Yacef, K. (Eds.), pp. 645-652.
9. Mohan, P. and Brooks, C. (2003). "Learning Objects on the Semantic Web". In Proceedings of ICALT2003, Devedzic, V., Spector, J.M., Sampson, D.G., Kinshuk (Eds.), pp. 195-199.
10. Murray, T. (1999). Authoring Intelligent Tutoring Systems: an Analysis of the State of the Art. *International Journal of Artificial Intelligence in Education*, 10, 98-129.
11. Polsani, PR. (2003). "Use and Abuse of Reusable Learning Objects". *Journal of Digital Information*, Vol. 3, Issue 4.
12. Redeker, G.H.J. (2003). "An Educational Taxonomy for Learning Objects". *In Proceedings of ICALT2003*, Devedzic, V., Spector, J.M., Sampson, D.G., Kinshuk (Eds.), pp. 250-251.
13. Sampson, D. and Karagiannidis, C. (2002). "From Content Objects to Learning Objects: Adding Instructional Information to Educational Meta-Data". *In Proceedings of 2nd IEEE Computer Society International Conference on Advanced Learning Technologies (ICALT 02)*, pp. 513-517.
14. Vereoustre, A. and McLean, A. (2003). "Reusing Educational Material for Teaching and Learning: Current Approaches and Directions". *In Supplementary Proceedings of AIED2003*, Aleven, V., Hoppe, U., Kay, J., Mizoguchi, R., Pain, H., Verdejo, F. and Yacef, K. (Eds.), pp. 621-630.
15. Wiley, D.A. (2002). "Connecting Learning Objects to Instructional Design Theory: A Definition, a Metaphor, and a Taxonomy". Wiley, D.A. (Eds.), *The Instructional Use of Learning Objects*, pp. 3-23

Role-Based Specification of the Behaviour of an Agent for the Interactive Resolution of Mathematical Problems

Miguel A. Mora, Roberto Moriyón, and Francisco Saiz

E.P.S, Universidad Autónoma de Madrid, Cantoblanco, 28049 Madrid, Spain
{Miguel.Mora, Roberto.Moriyon, Francisco.Saiz}@uam.es

Abstract. In this paper we describe how a computer system, which includes an authoring tool for teachers and an execution tool for students, is able to generate interactive dialogs in a Mathematics teaching application. This application is named ConsMath, and allows students to learn how to solve problems of Mathematics that involve symbolic calculations. This is done by means of an agent that is in charge of delivering the dialogs to students. The design process entails the dynamic generation of the user interface intended for learners with the insertion of decision points. During the execution, a tracking agent matches students' actions with the ones previously associated to decision points by the designer, thereby activating dynamic modifications in the interface by using a hierarchy of production rules. Students can use ConsMath both at their own pace or in a collaborative setting.

1 Introduction

There are nowadays many computer systems that can be used when learning Mathematics like Computer Algebra Systems (CASs), [3], [11], [12], that can be used as cognitive tools in a learning environment, but that lack the interactivity necessary for a more direct participation of teachers and students in the learning process. Some learning environments, like [2] [6] [1], present a variety of learning materials that include motivations, concepts, elaborations, etc, and have a bigger level of interactivity. Additionally, demonstrating alternative solution paths to problems, e. g. the behavior recorder mechanism used in [6], provides tutors with specification methods for some kind of interactivity. MathEdu, [5], provides a rich interaction capacity built on a CAS like Mathematica. Still, there exists a need of more intelligent systems with bigger capacity of interaction with the student.

The final interactivity of many teaching applications consists of dialogs between learners and applications where they have to answer to questions from an application. In this context, it turns out that the design of user interfaces is a complex process and it usually requires the creation of code. However, teachers are not usually prepared for this. Authoring tools are therefore very appropriate in order to simplify this process for tutors. Besides, it would be desirable to have WYSIWYG authoring and execution tools where students and teachers use similar environments.

Authoring tools for building learning applications allow tutors to get involved in the generation of the software to be delivered to students. For instance, it is usual to find a scenario where teachers are able to add their own controls (buttons, list boxes,

J.C. Lester et al. (Eds.): ITS 2004, LNCS 3220, pp. 187–196, 2004.

etc) that will form the final application, and even to specify the behavior of such controls when students interact with them. Nonetheless, those authoring tools do not usually give support to specify the feedback to be given to students depending on their actions.

As a consequence of that, models of authoring tools that allow the design of tutoring applications that interact more completely with the students, performing a dialog with them, are desirable. A dialog between a student and a tutoring application involves the existence of moments where the student has to make choices or give information to the system. It can be modeled by means of a tree structure that represents the different paths the dialog can follow, where the nodes represent abstract decision points, which can be used to control the dialogs that take place when solving different problems. This structure is simple enough as to allow teachers to create it interactively, without the need to use any programming language, and it is still powerful enough to represent interesting dialogs from the didactic point of view.

In this paper we present a role-based mechanism of specification of the model for the interaction with the student that is part of the ConsMath computer system, [7], [8], which allows the construction of interactive applications with which students can learn how to solve problems of Mathematics that involve symbolic computations.

ConsMath includes both a WYSIWYG authoring tool and an execution tool written in Java. Teachers design interactive tutoring applications for the resolution of problems using the authoring tool in an intuitive and simple way, since the development environment looks exactly like the students' working environment, except for the availability of some additional functionality, and at each instant the designer has in front of him the same contents and dialog components the student will have at a specific point during the resolution of the problem with the execution tool. The design process is possible in this simple setting thanks to the use of techniques of programming by demonstration, [4], an active research area within the field of Human-Computer Interaction.

ConsMath supports a methodology by which an interactive application for the resolution of sets of problems can be built in a simple way starting from a static document that shows a resolution of a particular problem, and adding to it different layers of interactivity. The initial document can be created by the designer using an editor of scientific texts or it can come from a different source, like Internet.

ConsMath includes a tracking agent that deals with the application being executed by students and matches their operations with the model created by the teacher. Thus, the agent owns all the information necessary for determining the exact state of the interaction. ConsMath has been built using a collaborative framework, [9], so it can also be used in a collaborative setting. For example, students can learn collaboratively, and the tutor can interactively monitor their progress, on the basis of the dialog model previously created.

The rest of the paper is structured as follows: in the next section we shall describe ConsMath from the perspective of a user. After that, we shall describe the mechanisms related to the tracking agent, together with the recursive uses of the model in case the resolution of a problem is reduced to the resolution of one or more simpler subproblems. Finally, we will explain the main conclusions of our work.

2 Interactive Design and Resolution of Exercises of Mathematics

As we have explained in the previous section, ConsMath exercises can be designed by means of a design tool, and they can be solved by means of an execution tool. Both processes are done in a WYSIWYG user interface, without the need of any programming. The development environment looks exactly like the students' working environment, except for the availability of some additional functionality, and at each instant the designer has in front of him the same contents and dialog components the student will have at a corresponding point during the resolution of the problem.

In order to design a problem, the designer specifies a sort of movie that includes a description of how the problem can be solved interactively, together with other movies that describe possible ways that do not lead to the resolution of the exercise, including the appropriate feedback for the student. Just like movie players act by behaving as the persons they are representing are supposed to do, ConsMath designers accomplish their task by imitating alternatively the behaviour of the students when solving the exercises posed to them, including actions that correspond to conceptual or procedural mistakes, and the behaviour of the system in response to their actions.

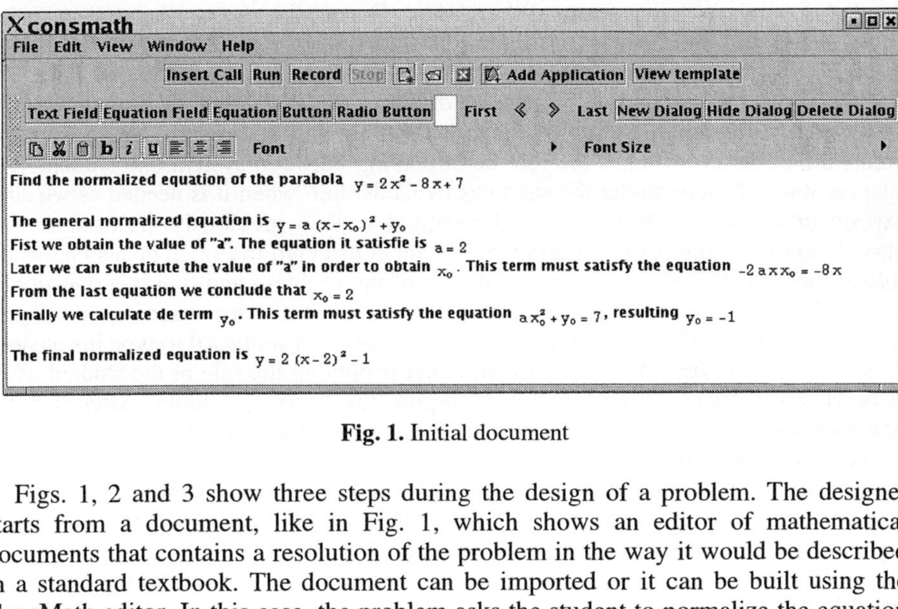

Fig. 1. Initial document

Figs. 1, 2 and 3 show three steps during the design of a problem. The designer starts from a document, like in Fig. 1, which shows an editor of mathematical documents that contains a resolution of the problem in the way it would be described in a standard textbook. The document can be imported or it can be built using the ConsMath editor. In this case, the problem asks the student to normalize the equation of a parabola, putting it under the form (1),

$$y = \alpha\,(x - x_0)^2 + y_0 \tag{1}$$

in terms of its degree of aperture α and the coordinates of its vertex (x0 , y0). After this, in a first step, the designer generalizes the problem statement and its resolution by introducing generic variables in the formulae that appear in the statement, and defining constraints among the formulae that appear in the resolution of the problem, in a spreadsheet style. For example, the designer can give names A, B and C to the coefficients in the equation of the parabola, and he can also specify the different formulae that appear in the resolution of the problem in terms of these coefficients. These steps give rise to an interactive document that allows a student to change the equation to be normalized, and the document is updated automatically.

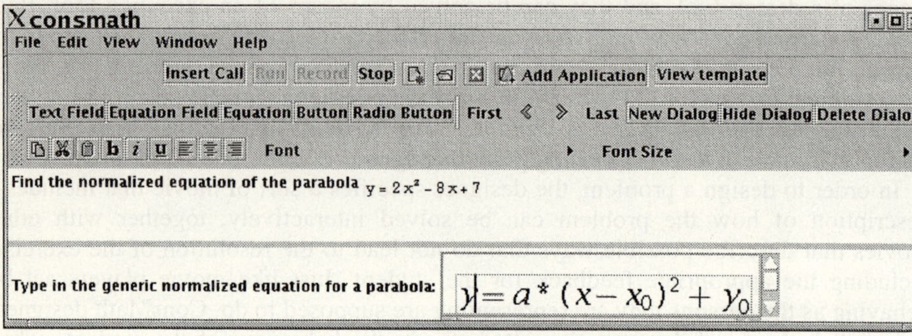

Fig. 2. Designer entering the correct answer

Once a generalized interactive document has been specified, the designer describes the dialog between the system and the student. During this dialog, the student makes choices and gives information to the system, and the system gives the student feedback and asks for new decisions to be taken for the resolution of the problem. The teacher specifies the dialog by means of the ConsMath editor of mathematical documents, using some additional functionality that will be described next. At some points the designer switches the role he is playing between system and student. The change of role is done under the shadows by ConsMath when it is needed as we shall explain in the next section. During the steps described previously the designer has played the role of the system. Before the instant considered in Fig. 2, he also plays the role of the system, hiding first the resolution of the problem and typing a question to be posed to the student, where he is asked for the general normalized second degree equation. After this, he enters a field where the student is supposed to type his answer. At the instant considered in Fig. 2 the designer is playing the role of the student when answering the question. He does it by typing the correct formula. After that the designer starts playing again the role of the system. First he gives a name to the formula introduced by the student, then he erases the part of the editing panel where the last question and the answer appear, and finally he poses a new question to the student asking which of the coefficients in the general normalized second degree equation will be calculated first. This is shown in Fig. 3.

In order to create the interactive dialogs, the designer can write text using the WYSIWYG editor, and can insert ConsMath components, like text fields, equation fields, simple equations, buttons, etc. Also, other Java components can be used in the dialogs, importing these components to the ConsMath palette. Each component has a name and a set of properties. The designer can specify the value of a property using a mathematical expression that can contain mathematical and ConsMath functions. These functions allow us to define variables, to evaluate expressions and to create constraints between variables or components. It is important to notice that when the designer erases parts of the document, although they disappear from the editor pane, they are not deleted, since formulae can still reference variables defined in them.

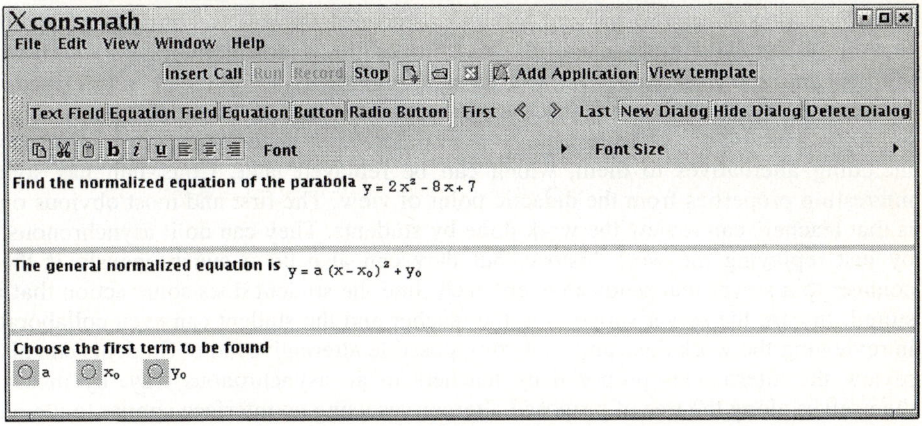

Fig. 3. Designer specifying a multiple-choice question

At any time the designer can return to any of the previous states where he is playing the role of the student, and start working again as before. This can be done by means of buttons included in the user interface that allow him to go back and forth. When he is back at one of these points, the designer can continue working as before, and ConsMath interprets automatically that he is specifying a different path to be followed in case the answer of the student doesn't fit the one specified before. In this way, a tree of alternatives that depend on the students actions is specified. The rest of the design process follows a similar pattern.

Once the design is finished, it can be saved. After this, the execution process can start at any moment. There are two ways in which a student can start solving a problem: either the statement is completely specified or the system is supposed to generate a random version of a given class of problem to be solved. The first situation can arise either because the tutor or the tutoring system that controls the knowledge of the student decides the specific problem the student has to solve, or because the student is asked to introduce the specific formulae that appear in the statement. There is a third possibility that takes place when a problem is solved as part of the resolution of another one. During the resolution of a problem, the parts of the movie created by the designer where he has played the role of the system are played automatically, while the ones where the designer plays the role of the student are used as patterns to be matched against his actions during the interactive resolution of the problem. Each decision of the student directs the performance of the movie towards one of the alternative continuations. Hence, for example, if the general normalized equation typed by the student in the first step is incorrect, the system will show him a description of the type of equation that is needed.

The above paragraphs are a description of the way ConsMath interacts with designers and students. In order to achieve this interactivity, the design and resolution tools must be able to represent interaction activities in a persistent way, with the possibility to execute them and undo them at any moment from scratch. Moreover, the following operations are possible: activities can bifurcate, in the sense that at any point of any activity an alternative can be available, and the actions accomplished by the users determines which of the existing alternatives is executed at each moment. Besides these functional requirements, an editor of mathematical documents that include constraints among parts of formulae is needed, as well as editing functionality that allows the dynamic change of the structure of the document, hiding parts of it that are kept in the background. The way these requirements are satisfied is described in the next section. Now we shall discuss some consequences of the satisfaction of them.

As a consequence of being able to store interaction histories in a persistent way, including alternatives to them, which can be replayed later, ConsMath has some interesting properties from the didactic point of view. The first and most obvious one is that teachers can review the work done by students. They can do it asynchronously by just replaying the work history, but they can also do it synchronously if they connect to a server that sends an event each time the student does some action that is stored. In case the server supports it, the teacher and the student can even collaborate in reviewing the work done and analyzing possible alternatives to it. Students can also review the alternatives proposed by teachers in an asynchronous way, by moving themselves along the tree of proposed alternatives using an interface similar to the one available to course designers.

3 Description of the Tracking Agent

In this section we describe the mechanisms used to implement the behaviour of ConsMath described in the previous section. The main concepts involved are the following ones: a design tree, where the necessary information is stored, a set of production rules contained in the designed tree, which are used in order to decide the actions to be taken by the system at each moment, and a tracking agent, which creates and interprets dynamically the information included in the design tree and activates the rules in order to help the student solve problems interactively.

The tracking agent is the component in charge of the high level interaction aspects in ConsMath. This agent has two main functions: firstly, to interpret the tutor intentionality when the tutor is designing the interaction that takes place during the resolution of the problem being designed using programming by example techniques, and, secondly, to interpret the student actions, comparing these actions with the ones previously exemplified by the tutor or course designer, and replaying the scenario designed by the tutor in response to those student actions. The tracking agent can be controlled be the designer by using a control panel to refine the interactive rules that are being designed, but when the agent is used by the students to execute a previously designed course, the agent interprets the student's actions using the information stored during the design phase, reacting in a proactive way.

The actions exemplified by the tutor are modeled by a design tree with two different interlaced zones, see fig. 4, namely decision zones and performance zones. The design tree represents the conceptual tree of alternative paths that the resolution of a problem can follow depending on the students' actions, described in the previous section. For example, the different answers that can be produced by a student in the example of the fig.3 can be modeled by a decision zone with two alternatives, one for the correct answer and other for the incorrect one. Each alternative is connected with a performance sequence of actions, one performance sequence to show the student an error dialog, and the other to continue with the problem resolution.

Decision zones are subtrees of the design tree that are formed by one node, which marks the starting point of the decision zone, and its children. The tracking agent stores in them the information to discriminate the different situations that can be produced by the student's actions. More specifically, each descendant node represents one of these alternatives and is linked to one performance zone, forming a decision rule. A decision rule is fired when it is enabled and its head, which is the descendant node of the corresponding decision zone, matches an action from the student. Students' actions give rise to events produced by the user interface. These events form the descendant nodes in decision zones.

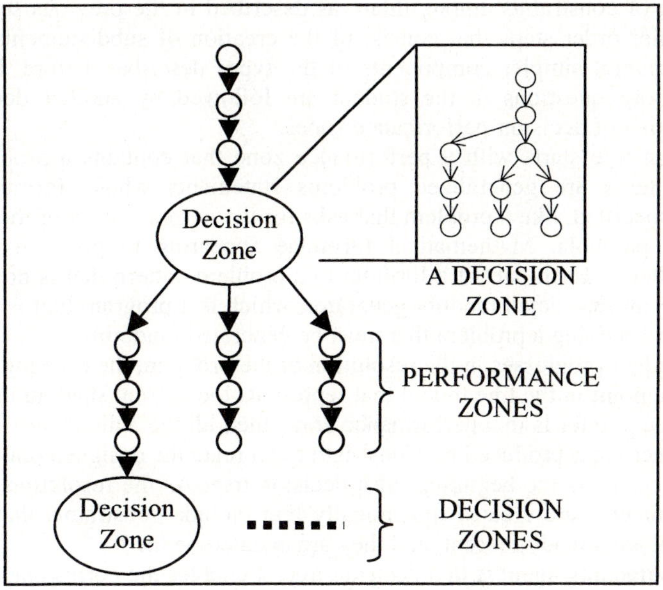

Fig. 4. Structure of a design tree

The designer specifies these events interactively emulating the students' actions. In case these events are produced within a performance zone, the tracking agent automatically starts a decision tree. The specification of these events is accomplished as follows:

- Button and multiple-choice events are generated directly by clicking on these components after they are created.
- Conditional events are produced by the evaluation of a condition that corresponds to a formula, like a comparison between two mathematical expressions. When the designer creates a condition, he types its corresponding formula in a field, including dependencies with respect to previous formulae that appear in the document. The designer simulates the action of the students that generates the event by entering a value in one of the input controls on which the condition depends. The tracking agent enters this elaborated event in the decision tree.
- Matching events are produced by the evaluation of a pattern matching condition between a formula typed by the student and a pattern specified by the designer, like a pattern of trigonometric polynomials. Similarly to the previous case, the designer has to create a pattern by entering the expression that specifies it, and he must

simulate the action of the students that generates the corresponding event by entering a value in the input control associated to this pattern.

Performance zones are sequences of execution steps, previously designed by the tutor or designer, which manipulate dynamically the document and can pose the student a new question. The steps that form performance zones can be of the following types: insert text, create random generator, insert or change formula, insert input component, etc. The creation and modification of formulae involves also the creation and modification of constraints among them, as described in the previous section. There are also higher order steps that consist of the creation of subdocuments, which are formed by several simpler components of the types described before. Performance zones that pose questions to the student are followed by another decision zone, forming the tree of decision-performance zones.

The design tree starts with a performance zone that contains a problem pattern. Problem patterns are generalized problems statements whose formulae are not completely specified, like a problem that asks for the normalization of the equation of an arbitrary parabola. Mathematical formulae appearing in problem patterns are formulae patterns. Each part of a formula in a problem pattern that is not completely specified has an associated random generator, which is a program that is called when a student starts solving a problem that must be generated randomly.

As the student progresses in the resolution of the problem, the tracking agent keeps a pointer to a point in the tree model that represents the current stage in the resolution process. If the pointer is in a performance zone, then all the actions previously stored by the designer are reproduced by ConsMath to recreate the designed dialog, stopping when the agent finds the beginning of a decision tree. As the resolution goes ahead, new subdocuments are created dynamically that include constraints that depend on formulae that are already present, and they are updated on the fly.

When the tracking agent is in a decision tree, it enables the corresponding decision rules, and waits until the user generates an action that fires one of them. Then, it enters the corresponding performance zone. This iterative process ends when the agent arrives to the end of a branch in the tree model. When this happens, in case a subproblem is being solved, the resolution of the original problem continues as we will see in the next subsection.

4 Using Calls to Sub-models

The models created with the tracking agent can be stored in the server, creating a library of reusable problems. This is done at design time using a button to insert a call to a subproblem. At run time, when the agent arrives to the call, it pushes the new model in the execution stack, and begins the execution of the new model until its end. The whole execution ends when the execution stack is empty once the agent arrives to the end of the first model in the stack.

For example, if we want to create a model to teach how to compute limits using L'Hôpital rule, we can create a problem pattern that can be used to compute (2),

$$\lim_{x->c} \frac{f(x)}{g(x)} \tag{2}$$

where “f”, “c” and “g” are the input variables of the problem pattern. In our example we can create a first dialog showing to the student the problem to solve and asking him which method he is going to use to solve that problem. For example we can ask him to choose among several methods for the computation of limits, including L’Hôpital rule and the direct computation of the limit.

Each time the student chooses one of the options, the system has to check that his decision is correct. In case it is not, the designer must have specified how the system will respond. Each time the student chooses L’Hôpital rule the system makes a recursive call to the same subproblem with new values for the initial variables “f” and “g”. Finally, when the student chooses to give directly the solution the recursion ends.

5 Evaluation

We have tested how ConsMath can be used for the design of interactive sets of problems. These tests have been performed by two math teachers. A collection of problems from the textbook [10] on ordinary differential equations has been designed. The teachers found that the resulting interactive problems are useful from the didactic point of view, the use of the tool is intuitive and simple, and they could not have developed anything similar without ConsMath. The teachers have also warned us that before using the system on a larger scale with less advanced users like students, the behaviour of the editor of math formulae should be refined. Since this editor is a third-party component, we are planning to replace it by our own equation editor in a future release.

Also, we have done an initial evaluation of previously designed problems in a collaborative setting, where two experts try to collaborate in order to solve a problem and another one, using the teacher role, supervises and collaborates with them. In these tests the experts with the role of students were collaborating synchronously, while the teacher was mainly in an asynchronous collaborative session, joining the synchronous session just to help the students. The first results helped us to improve some minor usability problems that we plan to fix in the next months in order to shortly carry out tests with the students enrolled in a course.

6 Conclusions

We have described a mechanism to design the interaction between students and a computer system in a learning environment using Programming by Example techniques which allow the designer to create highly interactive applications without any programming knowledge. This mechanism includes the specification of rules that define the actions students have to make during the resolution of problems. Teachers define these rules by means of a role-based process where they act based on the assumption that sometimes they play the role of instructors and other times they act as real students. ConsMath allows the design of collections of problems related to different subjects in Mathematics like elementary Algebra and Calculus.

Acknowledgements. The work described in this paper is part of the Ensenada and Arcadia projects, funded by the National Plan of Research and Development of Spain, projects TIC 2001-0685-C02-01 and TIC2002-01948 respectively.

References

1. Beeson, M.: "Mathpert, a computerized learning environment for Algebra, Trigonometry and Calculus", Journal of Artificial Intelligence in Education, pp. 65-76, 1990.
2. Büdenbender, J., Frischauf, A., Goguadze, G., Melis, E., Libbrecht, P., Ullrich, C.: "Using Computer Algebra Systems as Cognitive Tools", pp. 802-810, 6th International Conference, ITS 2002, LNCS 2363, Springer 2002, ISBN 3-540-43750-9.
3. Char, B.W., Fee, G.J., Geddes, K.O., Gonnet, G.H., Monagan, M.B."A tutorial introduction to MAPLE". Journal of Symbolic Computation, 2(2):179–200, 1986.
4. Cypher, A.: "Watch what I do. Programming by Demonstration", ed. MIT Press (Cambridge, MA), 1993.
5. Diez, F., Moriyon, R.: "Solving Mathematical Exercises that Involve Symbolic Computations"; in "Computing in Science and Engineering, pp. 81-84, vol. 6, n. 1, 2004.
6. Koedinger, K.R., Anderson, J.R., Hadley, W.H., Mark, M. A.: "Intelligent tutoring goes to school in the big city". Int. Journal of Artificial Intelligence in Education, 8, 1997.
7. Mora, M., A., Moriyón, R., Saiz, F.: "Mathematics Problem-based Learning through Spreadsheet-like Documents", proc. International Conference on the Teaching of Mathematics, Crete, Greece, 2002, http://www.math.uoc.gr/~ictm2/
8. Mora, M., A., Moriyón, R., Saiz, F.: "Building Mathematics Learning Applications by Means of ConsMath " in Proceedings of IEEE Frontiers in Education Conference, pp. F3F1-F3F6, November 2003, Boulder, CO.
9. Mora, M., A., Moriyón, R., Saiz, F.: "Developing applications with a framework for the analysis of the learning process and collaborative tutoring". International Journal Cont. Engineering Education and Lifelong Learning, Vol. 13, Nos. 3/4, 2003268-279, pp. 268-279, 2003, USA
10. Simmons, G. F.: "Differential equations: with applications and historical notes", ed. McGraw-Hill, 1981.
11. Sorgatz, A., Hillebrand, R.: "MuPAD". Linux Magazin, (12/95), 1995.
12. Wolfram, S.: "The Mathematica Book", ed. Cambridge University Press (fourth edition), 1999.

Lessons Learned from Authoring for Inquiry Learning: A Tale of Authoring Tool Evolution

Tom Murray, Beverly Woolf, and David Marshall

University of Massachusetts, Amherst, MA
tmurray@cs.umass.edu

Abstract. We present an argument for ongoing and deep participation by subject matter experts (SMEs, i.e. teachers and domain experts) in advanced learning environment (LE) development, and thus for the need for highly usable authoring tools. We also argue for the "user participatory design" of involving SMEs in creating the authoring tools themselves. We describe our experience building authoring tools for the Rashi LE, and how working with SMEs lead us through three successive authoring tool designs. We summarize lessons learned along they way about authoring tool usability.[1]

1 Introduction

Despite many years of research and development, intelligent tutoring systems and other advanced adaptive learning environments have seen relatively little use in schools and training classrooms. This can be attributed to several factors that most of these systems have in common: high cost of production, lack of widespread convincing evidence of the benefits, limited subject matter coverage, and lack of buy-in from educational and training professionals. Authoring tools are being developed for these learning environments (LEs) because they address all of these areas of concern [1]. Authoring tools can reduce the development time, effort, and cost; they can enable reuse and customization of content; and they can lower the skill barrier and allow more people to participate in development and customization ([2], [3]). And finally, they impact LE evaluation and evolution by allowing alternative versions of a system to be created more easily, and by allowing greater participation by teachers and subject matter experts.

Most papers on LE authoring tools focus on how the features of an authoring tool facilitate building a tutor. Of the many research publications involving authoring tools, extremely few document the use of these tools by subject matter experts (SMEs, which includes teachers in our discussion) not intimately connected with the research group to build tutors that are then used by students in realistic settings (exceptions include work described in [2] and [3]). A look at over 20 authoring systems (see [1]) shows them to be quite complex, and it is hard to imaging SMEs using them without significant ongoing support. Indeed, tutoring systems are complex, and de-

[1] We gratefully acknowledge support for this work from the U.S. Department of Education, FPISE program (#P116B010483) and NSF CCLI (# 0127183).

J.C. Lester et al. (Eds.): ITS 2004, LNCS 3220, pp. 197–206, 2004.

signing them is a formidable task even with the burden of writing computer code removed. More research is needed determine how to match the skills of the target SME user to the design of authoring tools so that as a field we can calibrate our expectations about the realistic benefits of these tools. Some might say that the role of SMEs can be kept to a minimum--we disagree. Principles from human-computer interaction and participatory design theory are unequivocal in their advocacy for continuous, iterative design cycles using authentic users ([4], [5]). This leads us to two conclusions. First, LE usability requires the participation of SMEs (with expertise in the domain and with teaching). LE evaluations by non-SMEs may be able to determine that a given feature is not usable, that learners are overwhelmed or not focusing on the right concepts, or that a particular skill is not being learned; but reliable insights about *why* things are not working and how to improve the system can only come from those with experience teaching in the domain. The second conclusion is that, since authoring tools do indeed need to be usable by SMEs, then SMEs need to be highly involved in the formative stages of designing the authoring tools themselves, in order to insure that these systems can in fact be used by an "average" (or even highly skilled) SME.

This paper provides case study and strong anecdotal evidence for the need for SME participation in LE design and in LE authoring tool design. We describe the Rashi inquiry learning environment, and our efforts to build authoring tools for Rashi. In addition to illustrating how the design of the authoring tool evolved as we worked with SMEs (college professors), we argue for the importance of SME involvement and describe some lessons learned about authoring tools design. First we will describe the Rashi LE.

2 The Rashi Inquiry Environment for Human Biology

Learning through sustained inquiry activities requires a significant amount of reflection, planning, and other metacognitive and higher level skills, yet these very skills are lacking in many students ([6],[7]). Thus it is crucial to support, scaffold, and teach these skills. This support includes providing "cognitive tools" [8] that relieve some of the cognitive load through reminding, organizational aides, and visualizations; and providing coaching or direct feedback on the inquiry process. Our project, called Rashi, aims to address these issues by providing a generic framework for supporting inquiry in multiple domains.

A number of educational software projects have addressed the support of inquiry learning in computer based learning environments and collaborative environments (for example: Inquiry Island [9], SimQuest [10], Bio-World [11], Belvedere [12], CISLE [13]). These projects have focused on various aspects of inquiry, including: providing rich simulation-based learning environments for inquiry; providing tools for the gathering, organization, visualization, and analysis of information during inquiry, and – the main focus of our work – directly supporting and scaffolding the various stages of inquiry. Our work advances the state of the art by providing a generic framework for LE tools for: searching textual and multimedia recourses, using

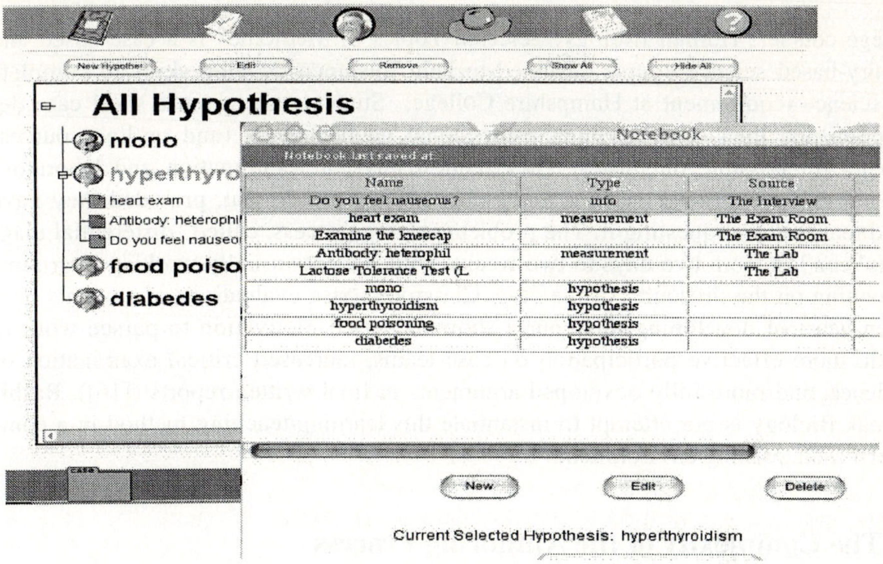

Fig. 1. A&B: Rashi Hypothesis Editor and Inquiry Notebook

case-based visualization and measurement, supporting organization and metacognition within opportunistic inquiry data gathering and hypothesis generation. The project also breaks new ground in its development of authoring tools for such systems--SimQuest is the only inquiry-based system that includes authoring tools, and its focus is more on authoring equation-centric models than on case-based inquiry.

Students use Rashi to accomplish the following tasks in a flexible opportunistic order ([14] [15]):

- Make observations and measurements using a variety of tools
- Collect and organize data in an "Inquiry Notebook"
- Pose hypotheses and create evidential relationships between hypothesis and data using a "Hypothesis Editor"
- Generate a summary of their final arguments with the Report Generator.

Figure 1 show the Rashi Hypothesis Editor (A) and Inquiry Notebook (B). Students use a variety of tools (not shown) to gather data which they store and organize in the Inquiry Notebook. They use the Hypothesis editor to create argument trees connecting data to hypotheses. Rashi also includes an intelligent coach [14], requiring the SMEs to enter not only the case data that the student accesses, but the evidential relationships leading to an acceptable hypothesis. Domain knowledge which must be authored in Rashi consists of cases (e.g. the patient Janet Stone), data (e.g. "temperature is 99.1"), inferences (e.g. "patient has a fever"), hypotheses (e.g. patient has hyperthyroidism), evidential relationships (e.g. fever supports hyperthyroidism), and principles (references to general knowledge or rules, as in text books).

Rashi is being used in several domains (including Human Biology, environmental engineering (water quality), geology (interpreting seismic activity), and forest ecology (interpreting a forest's history), and in this paper we focus on our most fully developed project, in the Human Biology domain, which is based on a highly successful college course. "Human Biology: Selected Topics in Medicine" is a case-based and inquiry-based science course designed to help freshmen develop skills to complete the science requirement at Hampshire College. Students are given a short case description and then scour through professional medical texts (and on-line sources) looking for possible diagnoses. They request physical examination and laboratory tests from the instructor, who gives them this data piece-meal, provided they have good reasons for requesting it. The problem solving process, called "differential diagnosis" can last from two days to two weeks, with students usually working in groups, depending on the difficulty of the case. Classroom-base evaluations of students over seven years of developing this course show increased motivation to pursue work in depth, more effective participation on case teams, increased critical examination of evidence, and more fully developed arguments in final written reports ([16]). Rashi-Human Biology is our attempt to instantiate this learning/teaching method in a computer-based learning environment.

3 The Complexity of the Authoring Process

In this section we will describe some of what is involved in developing a case-based tutorial for Rashi-Human-Biology, and in so doing we will illustrate both the need for SME participation and the task complexity that the authoring tool needs to support. The complexity of the Rashi LE and of authoring content in Rashi is comparable to that of most other LEs and LE authoring systems. For Rashi-Human-Biology our experts are two college biology professors skilled in using case-based learning and problem-based learning (CBL/PBL, see [17]) methods in the classroom (one of them does the bulk of the work with us, and we will usually refer to her as "the" expert). Given the relative complexity of the data objects involved in designing a case, the expert assists with the following tasks: develop medical diagnosis rules (inferential argument links), create descriptive scenarios and patient signs/symptoms for cases, articulate the details of a problem-based inquiry learning pedagogy, identify primary and secondary sources that students may go to for medical information, and inform us about the expected level of knowledge of the target audience. Our expert also helped us set up formative (clinical and in-class) evaluative trials of the system, and was critical in the analysis of trial results to determine whether students understood the system, whether they were using the system as expected, and whether they were engaged and learning in ways consistent with her goals for classroom CBL. The creation and sequencing of cases that introduce new concepts and levels of difficulty requires significant expertise. This involves setting values for the results of dozens of patient exams and laboratory tests, some of which are normal (for the age, gender, etc. of the patient) and some abnormal. Data must be authored not only for the acceptable hypothesis, but also to anticipate other alternative hypotheses and tests that the students may propose. Student behavior in complex LEs can never be anticipated, and a number of iterative trials are needed to create a satisfactory knowledge base for a give case.

The author uses the Rashi authoring tools to enter the following into the knowledge base:

- Propositions and hypotheses such as "has a fever", "has diabetes"
- Inferential relationships between the propositions such as "high fever supports diabetes"
- Cases with case specific values: Ex: the "Janet Stone Case" has values including "temperature is 99.1" "White blood cell count is 5.0 x 10^3 "

For the several cases we have authored so far there are many hundreds of propositions, relationships, and case values. Each of these content objects has several attributes to author. The authoring complexity comes in large part from the sheer volume of information and interrelationships to maintain and proof-check. The authoring tools assist with this task but can not automate it, as too much heuristic judgment is involved.

The above gives evidence for the amount of participation that can be required of a domain expert when building novel LEs. Also, it should be clear that deep and on-going participation is needed by the SME. We believe this to be the case for all almost all adaptive LE design. Since our goal is not to produce one tutor for one domain, but tutors for multiple domains and multiple cases, and to enable experts to continue to create new cases and customize existing cases in the future, we see the issues of authoring tool usability as critical and perennial. The greater the complexity of the LE, the greater the need for authoring tools. In designing an authoring tool there are tradeoffs involved in how much of the complexity can be exposed to the author and made a) inspectable, and b) authorable or customizable [4].

The original funding for Rashi did not include funds for authoring tool construction, and the importance of authoring tools was only gradually appreciated. Because of this, initial attempts to support SMEs were focused on developing tools of low complexity and cost. In the next section we describe a succession of three systems built to support authors in managing the propositions and evidential relationships in Rashi. Each tool is very different as we learned more in each iteration about how to schematically and visually represent the content. In one respect, the three tools illustrate the pros and cons of three representational formalisms for authoring the network of evidential relationships comprising the domain expertise (network, table-based, and form-based). In addition, each successive version added new functionality as the need for it was realized.

4 Lessons Learned from Three Authoring Tools

A Network-based representation. At first, the most obvious solution to the authoring challenge seemed to be to create a semantic network tool for linking propositions. The domain knowledge can be conceptualized as a semantic network of evidential relationships (supports, strongly supports, refutes, is consistent with, etc.). We built such a tool, shown in Figure 2 that allowed us to create, delete, and move nodes in the network("propositions"). Nodes could be "opened" and their attributes edited. Nodes of different types (e.g. data, hypotheses, principle) are color-coded. Such a network-

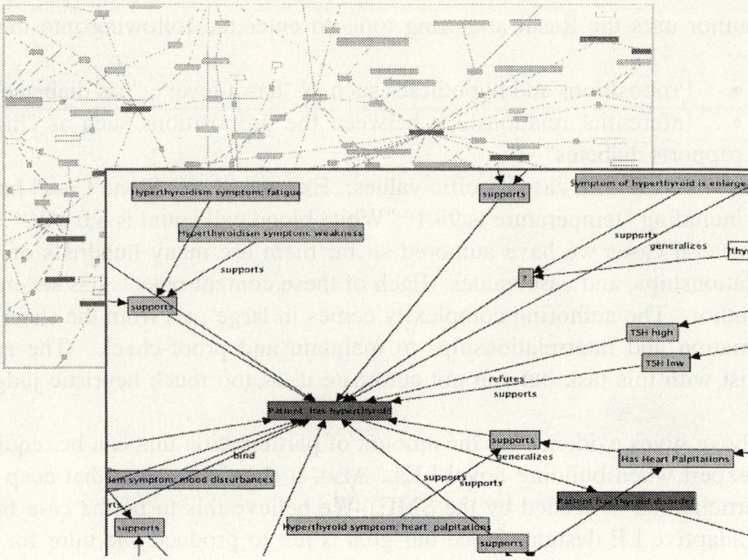

Fig. 2. Network-based authoring tool

style model seemed to fit well with the mental model of the argument structure that we wanted the expert to have. However, in working with both the biology professor and the environmental engineering professor (for a Rashi tutor in another domain), as the size of the networks began to grow, the network became spaghetti-like and the interface became unwieldy. The auto-layout feature was not sufficient and the author needed to constantly reposition nodes manually to make way for new nodes and links. The benefits of the visualization were overcome by the cognitive load of having to deal with a huge network, and more and more the tool was used exclusively by the programming and knowledge engineering team, and not by the domain experts/teachers. We realized that the expert only needed to focus on the local area of nodes connected to the node being focused on, and that in this situation the expert did not benefit much from the big picture view of the entire network (or a region of it) that the tool provided. We concluded that it would require less cognitive load if the authors just focused on each individual relationship: X support/refutes Y, and we moved to an authoring tools which portrayed this in a tabular format.

A table-based representation. The second tool was build using macros and other features available in Microsoft Excel (see Figure 3). The central piece of the tool was a table allowing the author to create Data->RelationshipType->Inference triplets (e.g. "high-temperature supports mono") (Figure 3A). For ease of authoring it was essential that the author choose from pop-up menus in creating relationships (which can be easily accomplished in Excel). In order to flexibly support the pop-ups, data tables were created with all of the options for each item in the triplet (Figure 3B). The same item of data (proposition) or inference (hypothesis) can be used many times, i.e. relationship is a many-to-many mapping. Authors could add new items to the tables in Figure 3B and to the list of relationships in Figure 3A (A and B are different worksheets in the Excel data file). Using the Excel features the author can sort by any of the columns to see, for example, all of the hypotheses connected to an observation; or all of the observations connected to a hypothesis; or all of the "refutes" relationships together. This method worked well for a while. But as the list of items grew in length the pop-up-menus became unwieldy. Our solution to this was to segment them into parts where the author chooses *one* from list A, B, C, or D and *one* from list X, Y, or Z (this modified interface is not shown). The complexity increased as we began to deal with intermediate inferences which can participate in both the antecedent *and* the consequent of relationships, so these items needed to show up in both right hand and left hand pop up menus. As we began to add authoring of case-values to the tool, the need to maintain unique identifiers for all domain "objects" was apparent, and the system became even more unwieldy.

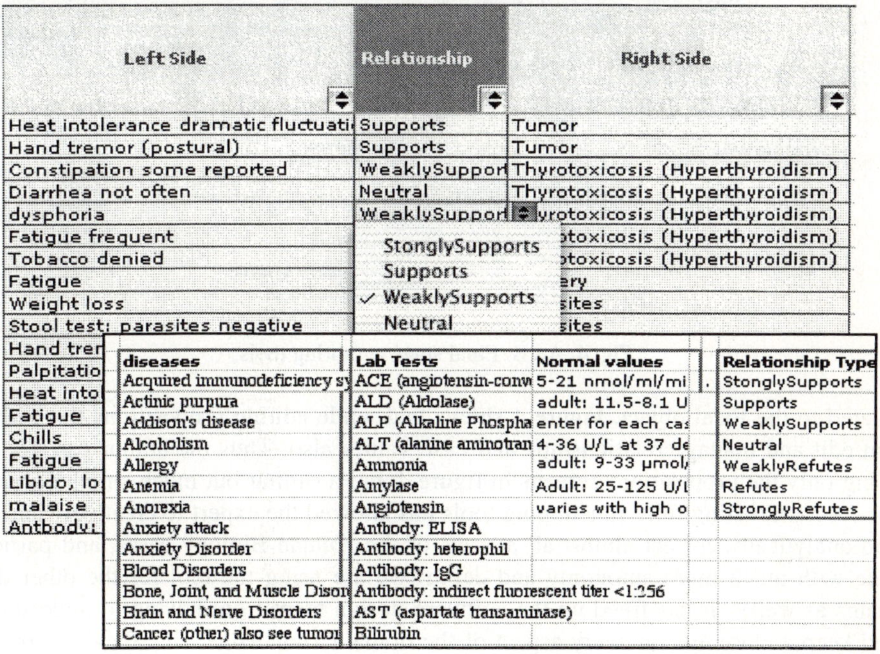

Fig. 3. A&B: Table-base authoring tool

A form-based representation. Eventually we conceded that we needed to invest in building a "real" full fledged authoring tool. Our data model of objects, attributes, and relationships is best conceptualized in terms of relational database tables. Because of its abilities in rapid prototyping of user interfaces we used FileMaker Pro. Figure 4 shows some of the screens from the resulting authoring tool, which we have been successfully using over the last year with SMEs. The figure shows the form view and the list view for the propositions database. We have similar screens for the other objects: cases, relationships, and case values. We are able to add "portal" views so that while inspecting one type of object you can see and edit objects of other types that are

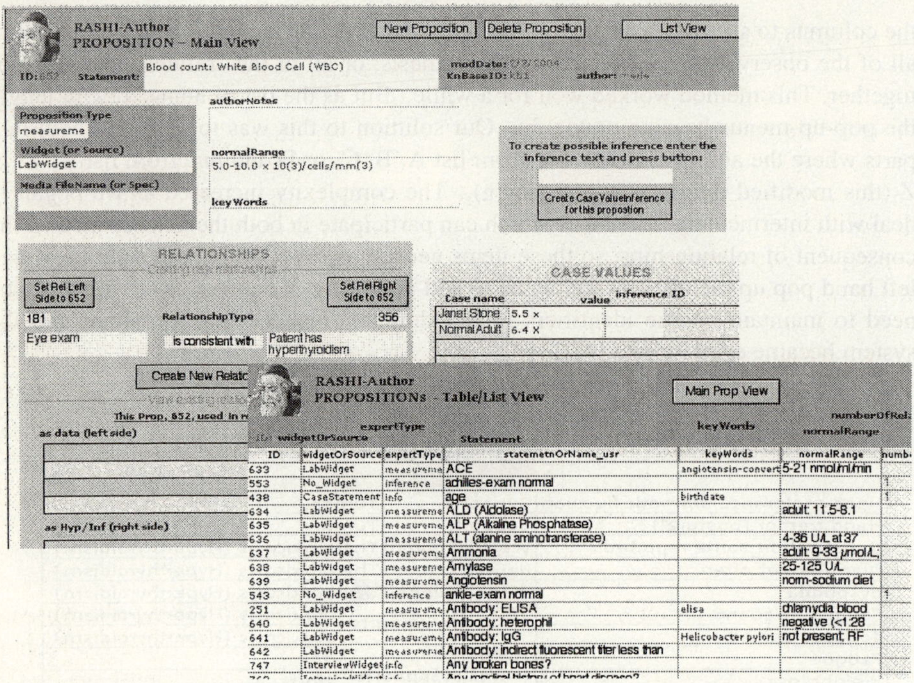

Fig. 4. A&B: Final stage authoring tools

related to the focal object. Figure 4 shows that while editing propositions the author can edit and manage relationships and case values also. Thus the author can get by using only the propositions screens in figure 4 and a similar but much simpler screen for cases. Creating fully functioning tools has allowed the expert to creatively author and analytically correct almost all aspects of the Human Biology cases, and participate with much more autonomy and depth (we are using the tool for the other domains as well). It has freed up the software design team from having to understand and keep a close eye on every aspect of the domain knowledge, and alleviates much of the time it took to maintain constant communication between the design team and the domain expert on the details of the content.

5 Discussion

Why did we bother to describe three versions of authoring tools when it was only the final one that was satisfactory? Stories of lessons learned from software development are rare, but the trial and error process can illustrate important issues. In our case this process has illustrated the importance of having SMEs involved in authoring tool design, and the importance of finding the right external representation for the subject matter content.

Comparison with other authoring tool projects. The Rashi authoring tools are relatively unique in that there is only one other project that deals with authoring tools for adaptive inquiry learning environments, the SimQuest/SMILSE project [10]. SimQuest takes a very different approach to authoring inquiry learning environments than Rashi. SimQuest focuses on runnable mathematical models, and supports students in learning science principles through experimentation. The SimQuest authoring environment supports the authoring of equations, graphical portrayals of situations, and the tasks and feedback messages needed in instruction. Rashi focuses on teaching inquiry skills and non-mathematical (symbolic) knowledge (as in biology and geology), and on case-based and rule-based expertise (the evidential relationships are simple rules). Thus the Rashi authoring tools show the application of authoring tools to a new type of domain. However, the elemental methods and interface features used by the Rashi authoring tools does not advance the state of the art beyond other systems (see [18]). However, as mentioned above, the vast majority of authoring tool projects do not focus on what it takes to create tools that can be used generally by SMEs, as we do. Other than this work, only in the Redeem project ([2] and other papers by Ainsworth) includes analyses of not only the successes, but also the ubiquitous problems encountered when employing SMEs to help build adaptive LEs. Redeem studies deal mostly with authoring instructional strategies, vs. our focus on complex subject matter content.

External Representations. We have also seen evidence that the representational formalism used in the authoring tool can affect its usability. The visual representations must match the deep structure of the knowledge in the tutor, must match the cognitive demands of authoring for the intended author characteristics, and msut scale up to large content knowledge bases. Studies by Suthers et al. and Ainsworth et al. ([19] [20]) have shown that different external representations facilitate different tasks and internal representations for students using LEs. Similarly, our work has illustrated, albeit anecdotally, the differential effects of three external representations (network, table, and from-based) in knowledge acquisition tools.

References

[1] Murray, T. (2003). An Overview of Intelligent Tutoring System Authoring Tools: Updated analysis of the state of the art. Chapter 17 in Murray, T., Blessing, S. & Ainsworth, S. (Eds.). *Authoring Tools for Advanced Technology Learning Environments.* Kluwer Academic Publishers, Dordrecht.

[2] Ainsworth, S., Major, N., Grimshaw, S., Hayes, M., Underwood, J., Williams, B. & Wood, D. (2003). REDEEM: Simple Intelligent Tutoring Systems from Usable Tools. Chapter 8 in Murray, T., Blessing, S. & Ainsworth, S. (Eds.). *Authoring Tools for Advanced Technology Learning Environments.* Kluwer Academic Publishers, Dordrecht.

[3] Halff, H, Hsieh, P., Wenzel, B., Chudanov, T., Dirnberger, M., Gibson, E. & Redfield, C. (2003). Requiem for a Development System: Reflections on Knowledge-Based, Generative Instruction, Chapter 2 in Murray, T., Blessing, S. & Ainsworth, S. (Eds.). *Authoring Tools for Advanced Technology Learning Environments.* Kluwer Academic Publishers, Dordrecht.

[4] Shneiderman, B. (1998). *Designing the User Interface* (Third Edition). Addison-Wesley, Reading, MA, USA.

[5] Norman, D. (1988). *The Design of Everyday Things.* Doubleday, NY.

[6] Mayer, R. (1998). Cognitive, metacognitive, and motivational aspects of problems solving. Instructional Science vol. 26, p. 49-63.

[7] Duell, O.K. & Schommer-Atkins, M. (2001). Measures of people's belief about knowledge and learning. Educational psychology review 13(4) 419-449.

[8] Lajoie, S. (Ed), 2000. *Computers as Cognitive Tools Volume II.* Lawrence Erlbaum Inc.: New Jersey

[9] White, B., Shimoda, T., Frederiksen, J. (1999). Enabling students to construct theories of collaborative inquiry and reflective learning: computer support for metacognitive development. *International J. of Artificial Intelligence in Education* Vol. 10, 151-1182.

[10] van Joolingen, W., & de Jong, T. (1996). Design and Implementation of Simulation Based Discovery Environments: The SMILSE Solution. *Jl. of Artificial Intelligence in Education* 7(3/4) p 253-276.

[11] Lajoie, S., Greer, J., Munsie, S., Wikkie, T., Guerrera, C., Aleong, P. (1995). Establishing an argumentation environment to foster scientific reasoning with Bio-World. Proceedings of the International Conference on Computers in Education, pp. 89-96. Charlottesville, VA: AACE.

[12] Suthers, D. & Weiner, A. (1995). Groupware for developing critical discussion skills. *Proceedings of CSCL '95, Computer Supported Collaborative Learning*, Bloomington, Indiana, October 1995.

[13] Scardamalia, Marlene, and Bereiter, Carl (1994). Computer Support for Knowledge-Building Communities. The Journal of the Learning Sciences, 3(3), 265-284.

[14] Woolf, B.P., Marshall, D., Mattingly, M., Lewis, J. Wright, S. , Jellison. M., Murray, T. (2003). Tracking Student Propositions in an Inquiry System. Proceedings of Artificial Intelligence in Education, July, 2003, Sydney, pp. 21-28.

[15] Murray, T., Bruno, M., Woolf, B., Marshall, D., Mattingly, M., Wright, S. & Jellison, M. (2003). A Coached Learning Environment for Case-Based Inquiry Learning in Human Biology. Proceedings of E-Learn 2003. Phoenix, Arizona, November 2003, pp. 654-657. AACE Digital Library, www.AACE.org.

[16] Bruno, M.S. & Jarvis, C.D. (2001). It's Fun, But is it Science? Goals and Strategies in a Problem-Based Learning Course. J. of Mathematics and Science: Collaborative Explorations.

[17] Kolodner, J.L, Camp, P.J., D., Fasse, B. Gray, J., Holbrook, J., Puntambekar, S., Ryan, M. (2003). Problem-Based Learning Meets Case-Based Reasoning in the Middle-School Science Classroom: Putting Learning by Design(tm) Into Practice. *Journal of the Learning Sciences*, October 2003, Vol. 12: 495-547.

[18] Murray, T., Blessing, S. & Ainsworth, S. (Eds) (2003). *Authoring Tools for Advanced Technology Learning Environments: Toward cost-effective adaptive, interactive, and intelligent educational software.* Kluwer Academic Publishers, Dordrecht

[19] Suthers, D. & Hundhausen, C. (2003). An empirical study of the effects of representational guidance on collaborative learning. *J. of the Learning Sciences* 12(2), 183-219.

[20] Ainsworth, S. (1999). The functions of multiple representations. *Computers & Education* vol. 33 pp. 131-152.

The Role of Domain Ontology in Knowledge Acquisition for ITSs

Pramuditha Suraweera, Antonija Mitrovic, and Brent Martin

Intelligent Computer Tutoring Group
Department of Computer Science, University of Canterbury
Private Bag 4800, Christchurch, New Zealand
{psu16, tanja, brent}@cosc.canterbury.ac.nz

Abstract. There have been several attempts to automate knowledge acquisition for ITSs that teach procedural tasks. The goal of our project is to automate the acquisition of domain models for constraint-based tutors for both procedural and non-procedural tasks. We propose a three-phase approach: building a domain ontology, acquiring syntactic constraints directly from the ontology, and engaging the author in a dialog, in order to induce semantic constraints using machine learning techniques. An ontology is arguably easier to create than the domain model. Our hypothesis is that the domain ontology is also useful for reflecting on the domain, so would be of great importance for building constraints manually. This paper reports on an experiment performed in order to test this hypothesis. The results show that constraints sets built using a domain ontology are superior, and the authors who developed the ontology before constraints acknowledge the usefulness of an ontology in the knowledge acquisition process.

1 Introduction

Intelligent Tutoring Systems (ITS) are educational programs that assist students in their learning by adaptively providing pedagogical support. Although highly regarded in the research community as effective teaching tools, developing an ITS is a labour intensive and time consuming process. The main cause behind the extreme time and effort requirements is the knowledge acquisition bottleneck [9].

Constraint based modelling (CBM) [10] is a student modelling approach that somewhat eases the knowledge acquisition bottleneck by using a more abstract representation of the domain compared to other common approaches [7]. However, building constraint sets still remains a major challenge. In this paper, we propose an approach to automatic acquisition of domain models for constraint-based tutors. We believe that the domain ontology can be used as a starting point for automatic acquisition of constraints. Furthermore, building an ontology is a reflective task that focuses the author on the important concepts of the domain. Therefore, our hypothesis is that ontologies are also important for developing constraints manually.

To test this hypothesis we conducted an experiment with graduate students enrolled in an ITS course. They were given the task of composing the knowledge base

J.C. Lester et al. (Eds.): ITS 2004, LNCS 3220, pp. 207–216, 2004.

for an ITS for adjectives in the English language. We present an overview of our goals and the results of our evaluation in this paper.

The remainder of the paper is arranged into five sections. The next section presents related work on automatic knowledge acquisition for ITSs, while Section 3 gives an overview of the proposed project. Details of enhancing the authoring shell WETAS are given in Section 4. Section 5 presents the experiment and its results. Conclusions and future work are presented in the final section.

2 Related Work

Research attempts at automatically acquiring knowledge for ITSs have met with limited success. Several authoring systems have been developed so far, such as KnoMic (Knowledge Mimic)[15], Disciple [13, 14] and Demonstr8 [1]. These have focussed on acquiring procedural knowledge only.

KnoMic is a learning-by-observation system for acquiring procedural knowledge in a simulated environment. The system represents domain knowledge as a generic hierarchy, which can be formatted into a number of specific representations, including production rules and decision trees. KnoMic observes the domain expert carrying out tasks within the simulated environment, resulting in a set of observation traces. The expert annotates the points where he/she changed a goal because it was either achieved or abandoned. The system then uses a generalization algorithm to learn the conditions of actions, goals and operators. An evaluation conducted to test the accuracy of the procedural knowledge learnt by KnoMic in an air combat simulator revealed that out of the 140 productions that were created, 101 were fully correct and 29 of the remainder were functionally correct [15]. Although the results are encouraging, KnoMic's applicability is restricted to simulated environments.

Disciple is a shell for developing personal agents. It relies on a semantic network that describes the domain, which can be created by the author or imported from a repository. Initially the shell has to be customised by building a domain-specific interface, which gives the domain expert a natural way of solving problems. Disciple also requires a problem solver to be developed. The knowledge elicitation process is initiated by a proble-solving example provided by the expert. The agent generalises the given example with the assistance of the expert and refines it by learning from experimentation and examples. The learned rules are added to the knowledge base.

Disciple falls short of providing the ability for teachers to build ITSs. The customisation of Disciple requires multiple facets of expertise including knowledge engineering and programming that cannot be expected from a typical domain expert. Furthermore, as Disciple depends on the problem solving instances provided by the domain expert, they should be selected carefully to reflect significant problem states.

Demonstr8 is an authoring tool for building model-tracing tutors for arithmetic. It uses programming by demonstration to reduce the authoring effort. The system provides a drawing tool like interface for building the student interface of the ITS. The system automatically defines each GUI element as a working memory element (WME), while WMEs involving more than a single GUI element must be defined manually. The system generates production rules by observing problems being solved by an expert. Demonstr8 performs an exhaustive search in order to determine the problem-solving procedure used to obtain the solution. If more than one such procedure exists, then the user would have to select the correct one. Domain experts must have significant knowledge of cognitive science and production systems in order to be able to specify higher order WMEs and validate production rules.

3 Automatic Constraint Acquisition

Existing approaches to knowledge acquisition for ITSs acquire procedural knowledge by recording the expert's actions and generalising recorded traces using machine learning algorithms. Even though these systems are well suited to simulated environments where goals are achieved by performing a set of steps in a specific order, they fail to acquire knowledge for non-procedural domains. Our goal is to develop an authoring system that can acquire procedural as well as declarative knowledge.

The authoring system will be an extension of WETAS [4], a web-based tutoring shell. WETAS provides all the domain-independent components for a text-based ITS, including the user interface, pedagogical module and student modeller. The pedagogical module makes decisions based on the student model regarding problem/feedback generation, whereas the student modeller evaluates student solutions by comparing them to the domain model and updates the student model. The main limitation of WETAS is its lack of support for authoring the domain model.

WETAS is based on Constraint based modelling (CBM), proposed by Ohlsson [10] which is a student modelling approach based on his theory of learning from performance errors [11]. CBM uses constraints to represent the knowledge of the tutoring system [6, 12], which are used to identify errors in the student solution. CBM focuses on correct knowledge rather than describing the student's problem solving procedure as in model tracing [7]. As the space of false knowledge is much grater than correct knowledge, in CBM knowledge is modelled by a set of constraints that identify the set of correct solutions from the set of all possible student inputs. CBM represents knowledge as a set of ordered pairs of relevance and satisfaction conditions. The relevance condition identifies the states in which the constraint is relevant, while the satisfaction condition identifies the subset of the relevant states in which the constraint is satisfied.

Manually composing a constraint set is a labour intensive and time-consuming task. For example, SQL-Tutor contains over 600 constraints, each taking over an hour to produce [5]. Therefore, the task of composing the knowledge base of SQL-Tutor would have taken over 4 months to complete. Since WETAS does not provide any assistance for developing the knowledge base, typically a knowledge base is composed using a text editor. Although the flexibility of a text editor may be powerful for knowledge engineers, novices tend to be overwhelmed by the task.

Our goal is to significantly reduce the time and effort required to generate a set of constraints. We see the process of authoring a knowledge base as consisting of three phases. In the first phase, the author composes the domain ontology. This is an interactive process where the system evaluates certain aspects of the ontology. The expert may choose to update the ontology according to the feedback given by the system. Once the ontology is complete, the system extracts certain constraints directly from it, such as cardinality restrictions for relationships or domains for attributes. The second stage involves learning from examples. The system learns constraints by generalising the examples provided by the domain expert. If the system finds an anomaly between the ontology and the examples, it alerts the user, who corrects the problem. The final stage involves validating the generated constraints. The system generates examples to be labelled as correct or incorrect by the domain expert. It may also present the constraints in a human readable form, for the domain expert to validate.

4 Enhancing WETAS: Knowledge Base Generation via Ontologies

We propose that the initial authoring step be the development of a domain ontology, which will later be used to generate constraints automatically. An ontology describes the domain, by identifying all domain concepts and relationships between them. We believe that it is highly beneficial for the author to develop a domain ontology even when the constraint sets is developed manually, because this helps the author to reflect on the domain. Such an activity would enhance the author's understanding of the domain and therefore be a helpful tool when identifying constraints. We also believe that categorising constraints according to the ontology would assist the authoring process.

To test our hypothesis, we built a tool as a front-end for WETAS. Its main purpose is to encourage the use of domain ontology as a means of visualising the domain and organising the knowledge base. The tool supports drawing the ontology, and composing constraints and problems. The ontology front end for WETAS was developed as a Java applet. The interface (Fig. 1a) consists of a workspace for developing a domain ontology (*ontology view*) and editors for syntax constraints, semantic constraints, macros and problems. As shown in Fig. 1a, concepts are represented as rectangles, and sub-concepts are related to concepts by arrows. The concept details such as attributes and relationships can be specified in the bottom section of the ontology view. The interface also allows the user to view the constraints related to a concept.

The ontology shown in Fig. 1a conceptualises the Entity Relationship (ER) data model. *Construct* is the most general concept, which includes *Relationship*, *Entity, Attribute* and *Connector* as sub-concepts. *Relationship* is specialized into *Regular* and *Identifying* ones. *Entity* is also specialized, according to its types, into *Regular* and *Weak* entities. *Attribute* is divided in to two sub-concepts of *Simple* and *Composite* attributes. The details of the *Binary Identifying relationship* concept are depicted in Fig. 1. It has several attributes (such as *Name* and *Identified-participation*), and three relationships (Fig. 1b): *Attributes* (which is inherited from *Relationship*), *Owner*, and *Identified-entity*. The interface allows the specification of restrictions of these relationships in the form of cardinalities. The relationship between *Identifying relationship* and *Regular entity* named *Owner* has a minimum cardinality of 1. The interface also allows the author to display the constraints for each concept (Fig. 1c). The constraints can be either directly entered in the ontology view interface or in the syntax/semantic constraints editor.

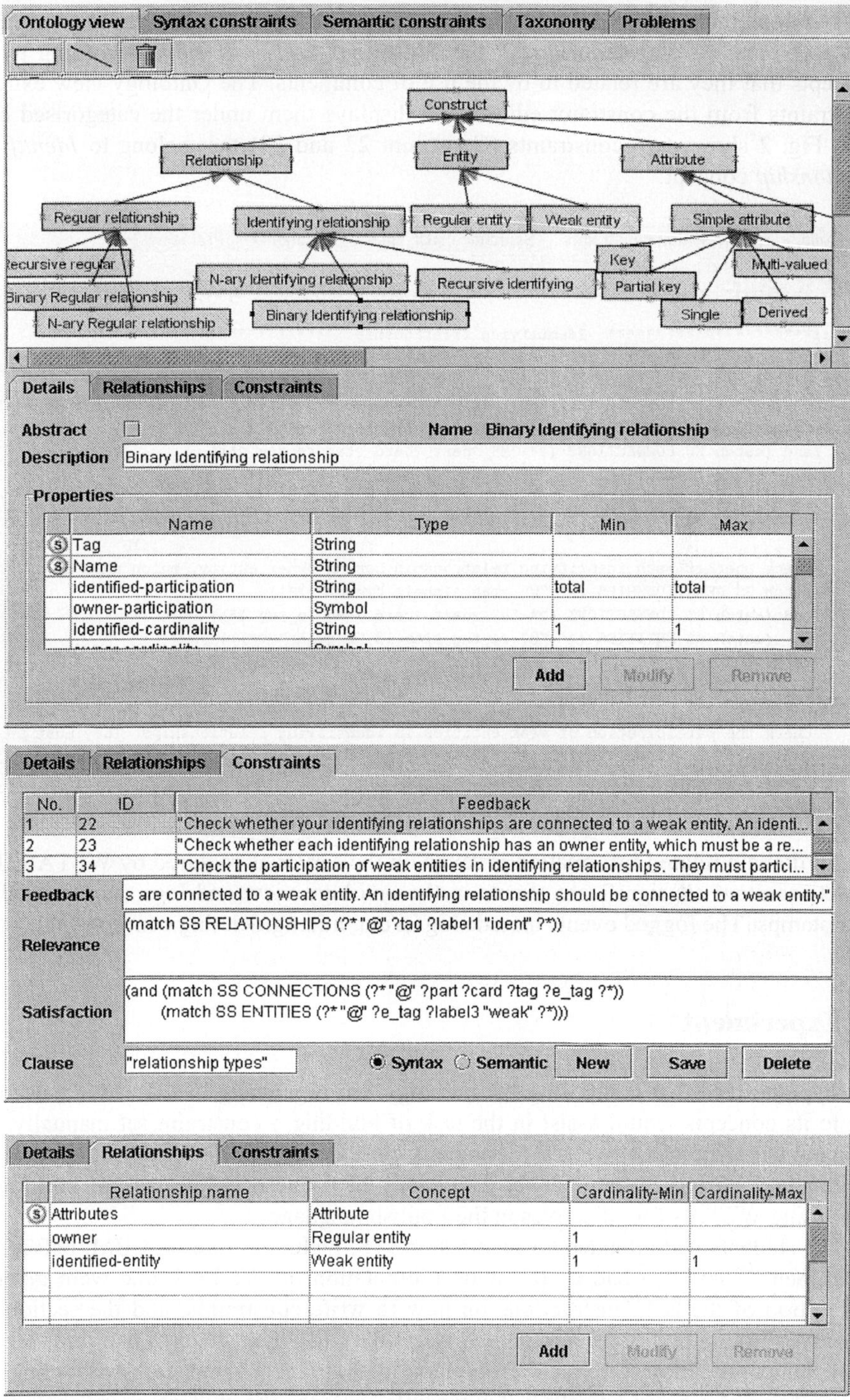

Fig. 1. Ontology for ER data model

The constraint editors allow authors to view and edit the entire list of constraints and problems. As shown in Fig. 2, the constraints are categorised according to the concepts that they are related to by the use of comments. The Ontology view extracts constraints from the constraint editors and displays them under the categorised concept. Fig. 2 shows two constraints (Constraint 22 and 23) that belong to *Identifying relationship* concept.

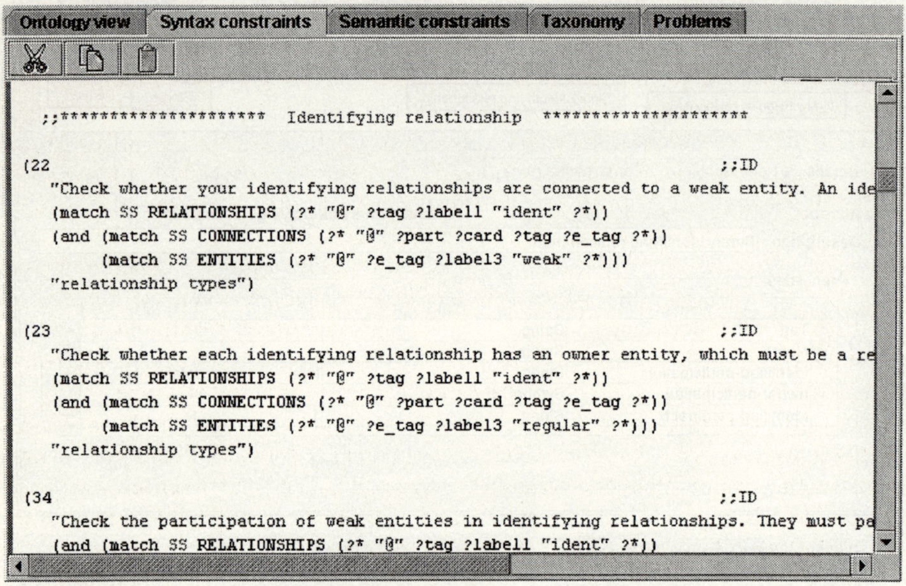

Fig. 2. Syntax constraints editor

All domain related information is saved on the server as required by WETAS. The applet monitors all significant events in the ontology view and logs them with their time stamps. The logged events include log in/out, adding/deleting concepts etc.

5 Experiment

We hypothesized that composing the ontology and organising the constraints according to its concepts would assist in the task of building a constraint set manually. To evaluate our hypothesis, we set 18 students enrolled in the 2003 graduate course on Intelligent Tutoring Systems at the University of Canterbury the task of building a tutor using WETAS for adjectives in the English language.

The students had attended 13 lectures on ITS, including five on CBM, before the experiment. They also had a 50 minute presentation on WETAS, and were given a description of the task, instructions on how to write constraints, and the section on adjectives from a text book for English vocabulary [2]. The students had three weeks to implement the tutor. A typical problem is to complete a sentence by providing the correct form of a given adjective. An example sentence the students were given was: "My sister is much ________ than me (wise)."

The students were also free to explore LBITS [3], a tutor developed in WETAS that teaches simple vocabulary skills. The students were allowed to access the "last two letters" puzzles, where the task involved determining a set of words that satisfied the clues, with the first two letters of each word being the same as the last two letters of the previous one. All domain specific components, including its ontology, the constraints and problems, were available.

Seventeen students completed the task satisfactorily. One student lost his entire work due to a system bug, and this student's data was not included in the analysis. The same bug did not affect other students, since it was eliminated before others experienced it. Table 1 gives some statistics about the remaining students, including their interaction times, numbers of constraints and the marks for constraints and ontology.

The participants took 37 hours to complete the task, spending 12% of the time in the ontology view. The time in the ontology view varied widely, with a minimum of 1.2 and maximum of 7.2 hours. This can be attributed to different styles of developing the ontology. Some students may have developed the ontology on paper before using the system, whereas others developed the whole ontology online. Furthermore, some students also used the ontology view to add constraints. However, the logs showed that this was not a popular option, as most students composed constraints in the constraint editors. One factor that contributed to this behaviour may be the restrictiveness of the constraint interface, which displays only a single constraint at a time.

WETAS distinguishes between semantic and syntactic constraints. In the domain of adjectives, it is not clear as to which category the constraints belong. For example, in order to determine whether a solution is correct, it is necessary to check whether the correct rule has been applied (semantics) and whether the resulting word is spelt correctly (syntax). This is evident in the results for the total number of constraints for each category. The averages of both categories are similar (9 semantic constraints and 11 syntax constraints). Some participants have included most of their constraints as semantic and others vice versa. Students on average composed 20 constraints in total.

We compared the participants' solution to the "ideal" solution. The marks for these two aspects are given under *Coverage* (the last two columns in Table 1). The ideal knowledge base consists of 20 constraints. The *Constraints* column gives the number of the ideal constraints that are accounted for in the participants' constraint sets. Note that the mapping between the ideal and participants' constraints is not necessarily 1:1. Two participants accounted for all 20 constraints. On average, the participants covered 15 constraints. The quality of constraints was high generally.

The ontologies produced by the participants were given a mark out of five (the *Ontology* column in Table 1). All students scored high, as expected because the ontology was straightforward. Almost every participant specified a separate concept for each group of adjectives according to the given rules [2]. However, some students constructed a flat ontology, which contained only the six groupings corresponding to the rules (see Fig. 3a). Five students scored full marks for the ontology by including the degree (comparative or superlative) and syntax such as spelling (see Fig. 3b).

Even though the participants were only given a brief description of ontologies and the example ontology of LBITS, they created ontologies of a reasonable standard. However, we cannot make any general assumptions on the difficulty of constructing ontologies since the domain of adjectives is very simple. Furthermore, the six rules for determining the comparative and superlative degree of an adjective gave strong hints on what concepts should be modelled.

Table 1. Results

	Time (hours)		Number of constraints			Coverage	
	Total	Ontology view	Semantic	Syntax	Total	Constraints	Ontology
S1	38.16	4.57	27	3	30	20	5
S2	51.55	7.01	3	10	13	19	4
S3	10.22	1.20	14	1	15	17	4
S4	45.25	2.54	30	4	34	18	5
S5	48.96	4.91	11	5	16	20	4
S6	44.89	4.66	24	1	25	18	5
S7	18.97	2.87	1	15	16	17	4
S8	22.94	4.99	3	18	21	15	3
S9	34.29	4.30	11	4	15	18	5
S10	33.90	7.23	0	14	14	18	3
S11	55.76	3.28	16	1	17	17	5
S12	30.46	2.84	0	16	16	10	3
S13	60.94	3.47	1	15	16	13	3
S14	32.42	1.96	1	17	18	12	3
S15	33.35	4.04	1	14	15	11	3
S16	29.60	6.24	0	30	30	4	5
Mean	36.98	4.13	8.94	10.50	19.44	15.44	4.00
S.D.	13.66	1.72	10.47	8.23	6.60	4.37	0.89

Fourteen participants categorised their constraints according to the concepts of the ontology as shown in Fig. 2. For these participants, there was a significant correlation between the ontology score and the constraints score (0.679, $p<0.01$). However, there was no significant correlation between the ontology score and the constraints score when all participants were considered. This strongly suggests that the participants used the ontology to write constraints developed better constraints.

An obvious reason for this finding may be that more able students produced better ontologies and also produced a complete set of constraints. To test this hypothesis, we determined the correlation between the participant's final grade for the course (which included other assignments) and the ontology/constraint scores. There was indeed a strong correlation (0.840, $p<0.01$) between the grade and the constraint score. However, there was no significant correlation between the grade and the ontology score. This lack of a relationship can be due to a number of factors. Since the task of building ontologies was novel for the participants, they may have found it interesting and performed well regardless of their ability. Another factor is that the participants had more practise at writing constraints (in other assignments for the same course) than on ontologies. Finally, the simplicity of the domain could also be a contributing factor.

a.

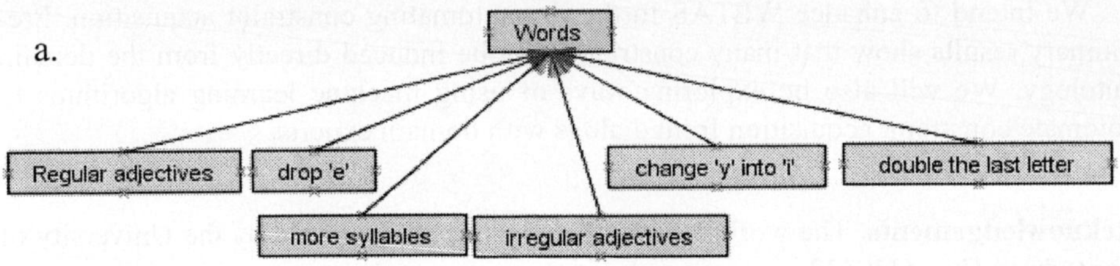

b.

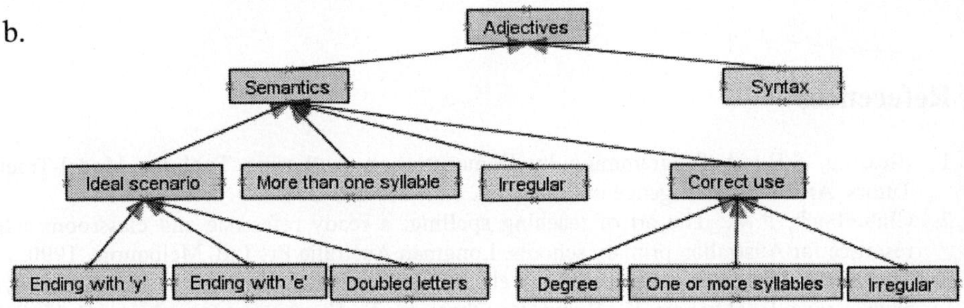

Fig. 3. Ontologies constructed by students

The participants spent 2 hours per constraint (sd=1 hour). This is twice the time reported in [8], but the participants are neither knowledge engineers nor domain experts, so the difference is understandable. The participants felt that building an ontology made constraint identification easier. The following comments were extracted from their reports: "*Ontology helped me organise my thinking;*" "*The ontology made me easily define the basic structure of this tutor;*" "*The constraints were constructed based on the ontology design;*" "*Ontology was designed first so that it provides a guideline for the tasks ahead.*"

The results indicate that ontologies do assist constraint acquisition: there is a strong correlation between the ontology score and the constraints score for the participants who organised the constraints according to the ontology. Subjective reports confirmed that the ontology was used as a starting point when writing constraints. As expected, more able students produced better constraints. In contrast, most participants composed good ontologies, regardless of their ability.

6 Conclusions

We performed an experiment to determine whether the use of domain ontologies would assist manual composition of constraints for constraint-based ITSs. The WETAS authoring shell was enhanced with a tool that allowed users to define a domain ontology and use it as the basis for organizing constraints. We showed that constructing a domain ontology indeed assisted the creation of constraints. Ontologies enable authors to visualise the constraint set and to reflect on the domain, assisting them to create more complete constraint bases.

We intend to enhance WETAS further by automating constraint acquisition. Preliminary results show that many constraints can be induced directly from the domain ontology. We will also be exploring ways of using machine learning algorithms to automate constraint acquisition from dialogs with domain experts.

Acknowledgements. The work reported here has been supported by the University of Canterbury Grant U6532.

References

1. Blessing, S.B.: A Programming by Demonstration Authoring Tool for Model-Tracing Tutors. Artificial Intelligence in Education, 8 (1997) 233-261
2. Clutterbuck, P.M.: The art of teaching spelling: a ready reference and classroom active resource for Australian primary schools. Longman Australia Pty Ltd, Melbourne, 1990.
3. Martin, B., Mitrovic, A.: Authoring Web-Based Tutoring Systems with WETAS. In: Kinshuk, Lewis, R., Akahori, K., Kemp, R., Okamoto, T., Henderson, L. and Lee, C.-H. (eds.) Proc. ICCE 2002 (2002) 183-187
4. Martin, B., Mitrovic, A.: WETAS: a Web-Based Authoring System for Constraint-Based ITS. Proc. 2nd Int. Conf on Adaptive Hypermedia and Adaptive Web-based Systems AH 2002, Springer-Verlag, Berlin Heidelberg New York, pp. 543-546, 2002.
5. Mitrovic, A.: Experiences in Implementing Constraint-Based Modelling in SQL-Tutor. In: Goettl, B.P., Halff, H.M., Redfield, C.L. and Shute, V.J. (eds.) Proc. 4th Int. Conf. on Intelligent Tutoring Systems, San Antonio, (1998) 414-423
6. Mitrovic, A.: An intelligent SQL tutor on the Web. Artificial Intelligence in Education, 13, (2003) 171-195
7. Mitrovic, A., Koedinger, K. Martin, B.: A comparative analysis of cognitive tutoring and constraint-based modeling. In: Brusilovsky, P., Corbett, A. and Rosis, F.d. (eds.) Proc. UM2003, Pittsburgh, USA, Springer-Verlag, Berlin Heidelberg New York (2003) 313-322
8. Mitrovic, A., Ohlsson, S.: Evaluation of a Constraint-based Tutor for a Database Language. Artificial Intelligence in Education , 10(3-4) (1999) 238-256
9. Murray, T.: Expanding the Knowledge Acquisition Bottleneck for Intelligent Tutoring Systems. Artificial Intelligence in Education, 8 (1997) 222-232
10. Ohlsson, S.: Constraint-based Student Modelling. Proc. Student Modelling: the Key to Individualized Knowledge-based Instruction, Springer-Verlag (1994) 167-189
11. Ohlsson, S.: Learning from Performance Errors. Psychological Review, 103 (1996) 241-262
12. Suraweera, P., Mitrovic, A.: KERMIT: a Constraint-based Tutor for Database Modeling. In: Cerri, S., Gouarderes, G. and Paraguacu, F. (eds.) Proc. 6th Int. Conf on Intelligent Tutoring Systems ITS 2002, Biarritz, France, LCNS 2363 (2002) 377-387
13. Tecuci, G.: Building Intelligent Agents: An Apprenticeship Multistrategy Learning Theory, Methodology, Tool and Case Studies. Academic press, 1998.
14. Tecuci, G., Keeling, H.: Developing an Intelligent Educational Agent with Disciple. Artificial Intelligence in Education, 10 (1999) 221-237
15. van Lent, M., Laird, J.E.: Learning Procedural Knowledge through Observation. Proc. Int. Conf. on Knowledge Capture, (2001) 179-186

Combining Heuristics and Formal Methods in a Tool for Supporting Simulation-Based Discovery Learning

Koen Veermans[1] and Wouter R. van Joolingen[2]

[1] Faculty of Behavioral Sciences University of Twente, PO Box 217
7500 AE Enschede, The Netherlands
veermans@edte.utwente.nl

[2] Graduate school of teaching and learning, University of Amsterdam, Wibautstraat 2-4
1091 GM Amsterdam, The Netherlands
wouter@ilo.uva.nl

Abstract. This paper describes the design of a tool to support learners in simulation-based discovery learning environments. The design redesigns and extents a previous tool to overcome issues that came up in a classroom learning setting. The tool focuses on supporting learners with experimentation to identify or test hypotheses. The aim is not only to support learning domain knowledge, but also learning discovery learning skills. For this purpose the tool uses heuristics and formal methods to assess the learners experimenting behavior, and translates this assessment into feedback directed at improving the quality of the learners discovery learning behavior. The tool is designed to be part of an authoring environment for designing simulation-based learning environments, which put some constraints on the design, but also ensures that the tool can be reused in different learning environments. After describing the design, a learning scenario is used to serve as an illustration of the tool, and finally some concluding remarks, evaluation results, and potential extensions for the tool are presented.

1 Introduction

Discovery learning or Inquiry Learning has a long history in education [1, 4] and has regained popularity over the last decade as a result of changes in the field of education that put more emphasis on the role of the learner in the learning process. Zachos, Hick, Doane, and Sargent [19] define discovery learning as "the self-attained grasp of a phenomenon through building and testing concepts as a result of inquiry of the phenomenon" (p. 942). The definition emphasizes that it is the learner who builds concepts, that the concepts need to be tested, and that building and testing of concepts are part of the inquiry of the phenomenon. Computer simulations have rich potential to provide learners with opportunities to build and test concepts, and learning with these computer simulations is also referred to as simulation-based discovery learning.

Like in discovery learning, the idea of simulation-based discovery learning is that the learner actively engages in a process. In an unguided simulation-based discovery environment learners have to set their own learning goals. At the same time they have to find and apply the methods that help to achieve these goals, which is not always easy. Two main goals can be associated with simulation-based discovery learning; development of knowledge about the domain of discovery, and development of skills

J.C. Lester et al. (Eds.): ITS 2004, LNCS 3220, pp. 217–226, 2004.

that facilitate development of knowledge about the domain (i.e., development of skills related to the process of discovery).

This paper describes a tool that combines support for learning the domain knowledge with specific attention for learning discovery learning skills. Two constraints had to be taken into account in the design of the tool. The first constraint is related to the exploratory nature of discovery learning. To maintain the exploratory nature of the environment, the tool may be *directive*, should try to be *stimulating* and must be *non-obligatory*, leaving room for exploration to the learner. The second constraint is related to the context in which the tool should be operating, SIMQUEST [5], an authoring environment for the design and development of simulation-based learning environments. Since SIMQUEST allows the designer to specify the model, the domain will not be known in advance, and therefore, the support cannot rely on domain knowledge.

2 Learning Environments

At the core of SIMQUEST learning environments are one or more simulation models; visualized to learners through representations of the model (numerical, graphical, animated, etc.) in simulation interfaces. SIMQUEST includes templates for assignments (f.i. exercises that provide a learner with a subgoal), explanations (f.i. background information or feedback on assignments) and several tools (f.i. experiment storage tool). These components can be used to design a learning environment that supports learners. The control mechanism determines when the components present themselves to the learner and allows the designer to specify the balance between system control and learner control in the interaction between learning environment and learner.

This framework allows authors to design and develop simulation-based learning environments, and to some extent support for learners working with these learning environments. However, it does not provide a way of assessing of and providing individualized support on the learners' experimentation with a simulation. This was the starting point for the design of a tool called the 'monitoring tool' [16]. It supported experimenting by learners based on a formal analysis of their experimentation in relation to hypotheses (these hypotheses had to be specified by the designer in assignments). A study [17] showed positive results, but also highlighted two important problems with the monitoring tool.

The first problem is that one of the strengths of the monitoring tool is also one of its weaknesses. The monitoring tool did not rely on domain knowledge for the analysis of the learners' experimentation. The strength of this approach is that it is domain independent, the weakness that it can not use knowledge about the domain to correct learners when this might be needed. This might lead to incorrect domain knowledge, and incorrect self-assessment of the exploration process, because the outcome of the exploration process serves as a benchmark for learners in assessing the exploration process [2]. In the absence of external feedback, learners have to rely on their own assessment of the outcome of the process. If this assessment is incorrect, the resulting assessment of the exploration might also be incorrect.

The second problem is that the design of the tool was based primarily on formal principles related to induction and deduction. This had the shortcoming that it could only give detailed feedback about experimentation in combination with certain categories of hypothesis, like for instance semi-quantitative hypotheses (f.i. *"If the velocity becomes twice as large then kinetic energy becomes four times as large")*. In more common language this hypothesis might be expressed as: "*There is a quadratic relation between velocity and kinetic energy*", but this phrasing has no condition part that can be used to make a formal assessment of experiments.

As a solution for this second problem the tool is extended with less formal, i.e. heuristic assessment of the experimentation. The heuristics that were used for this purpose originate from an inventory [12] of literature [4, 7, 8, 9, 10, 11, 13, 14, 15] about problem solving, discovery learning, simulation-based learning, and machine discovery, in search for heuristics that could prove useful in simulation-based discovery learning. A set of heuristics (Table 1) related to experimentation and hypothesis testing was selected from this inventory for the present purpose.

Table 1. Heuristics that were incorporated in the tool

Keep track	Keep records of what you are doing. [7,9]
Simple values	Design experiments giving characteristic results. [8] Choose special cases, set any parameter to 1,2,3. [13]
Votat	If a variable is not relevant for the hypothesis under, test then hold that variable constant, or vary one thing at a time (VOTAT), or If not varying a variable, then pick the same value as used in the previous experiment [4, 7, 14, 15]
Identify Hypothesis	Generate a small amount of data and examine for a candidate rule or relation. [4]
Equal increments	If choosing a third value for a variable, then choose an equal increment as between first and second values. Or if manipulating a variable, then choose simple, canonical manipulations. [14]
Confirm Hypothesis	Generate several additional cases in an attempt to either confirm or disconfirm the hypothesized relation. [4]
Extreme values	Try some extreme values to see if there are limits on the proposed relationship.[14]
Inductive discovery heuristics	-If you have recorded a set of values for X and a set of values for Y, and the values of X and Y are have a constant ratio of increments, then infer that a linear relation exists between X and Y -If you have recorded a set of values for X and a set of values for Y, and the absolute value of X increases and the absolute value of Y increases, and these values are not linearly related, Then consider the ratio of X and Y -If you have recorded a set of values for X and a set of values for Y, and the absolute value of X increases and the absolute value of Y decreases, and these values are not linearly related, then consider the product of X and Y [10, 11]

Heuristic assessment of the experimentation will allow the tool to provide feedback on experimentation without needing specific hypotheses as input for the process of evaluating the learners' experiments. Consequently, the hypotheses in the assignments can now be stated in "normal" language, which makes it easier for the learners not only to investigate, but also to conceptualize them. If the hypothesis in the assignment is no longer used as input for the analysis of the learners' experimentation, it is also no longer needed to connect the experimentation feedback to assignments. This means that feedback on the correctness of the hypothesis can be given in the assignment, thus, solving the first problem. The feedback on experimentation can be moved to the tool in which the experiments are stored; a more logical place to provide feedback on experimentation. Moving the feedback to this tool requires it to be redesigned, and this was the starting point for a redesign of the tool.

3 Redesign of the Experiment Storage Tool

Originally the experiment storage tool was only a storage place for experiments. If the tool should provide feedback on experimenting it means there should be a point at which this feedback is communicated to the learner, preferable not disrupting the learner. It was decided to extend the experiment storage tool with a facility to draw graphs, and combine the feedback with the learner-initiated action of drawing a graph. Figure 1gives an overview of the position of the new tool within the system.

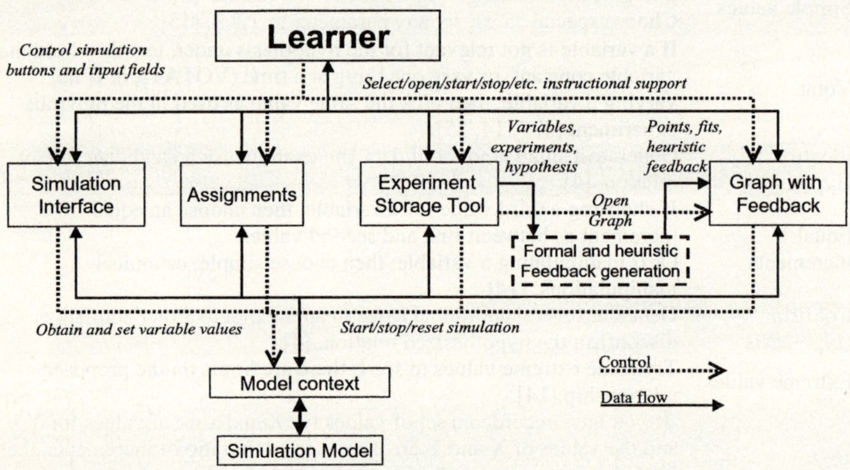

Fig. 1. The structure of control and information exchange between a learner and a SimQuest learning environment with the new experiment storage tool with graphing and heuristic support

Drawing a graph is not a trivial task and has been the object of instruction in itself [6]. It was therefore decided to let the tool take care of drawing the graph, but to provide feedback related to drawing and interpreting graphs to the learner, as well as, feedback related to experimenting. The learner has to do is to select a variable for the x-axis, and a variable for the y-axis, which provides the tool with important information that can be used for generating feedback. Through the choice of variables the learner expresses interest in a certain relation.

Learners can ask the tool to fit a function on the experiments along with drawing a graph. Basic qualitative functions (monotonic increase and monotonic decrease), and quantitative functions (constant, linear, quadratic, and reciprocal) are provided to the learners. More functions could of course be provided, but it was decided to restrict the set of functions to the functions first, because too many possibilities might overwhelm learners. Fitting a function is optional, but when a learner selects this option it provides the tool with valuable extra information for the analysis of the experimentation.

Learners can also construct new variables based on existing variables. New variables can be constructed using basic simple arithmetic functions add, subtract, divide, and multiply. Whenever the learner creates a new variable, a new column will be added to the experiment storage tool, and this column will also be updated for new experiments. The learner can compare these values to other values in the table to see how the newly constructed variable relates to the variables that were already listed in the monitoring tool. The redesigned version of the monitoring tool with its new functionality is shown in Figure 2.

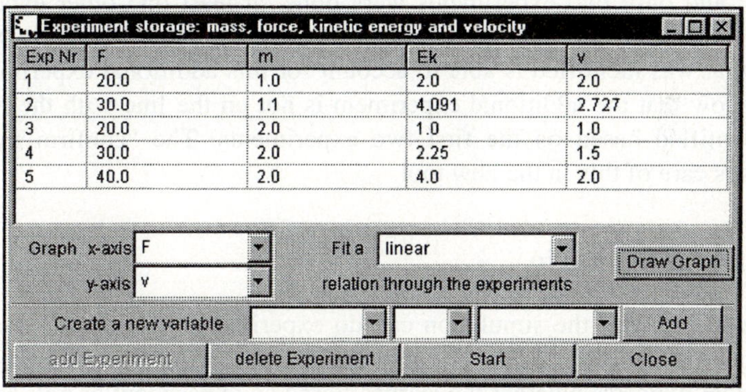

Fig. 2. The experiment storage tool.

4 Providing Heuristic Support

The previous section described the basic functions of the experiment storage tool. This section describes how the tool will provide support for the learner. Three different parts can be distinguished in the support: drawing the data points, calculating and drawing a fit, and providing feedback based on the heuristics from Table 1 The first two parts are rather straightforward, and will therefore not be described in detail.

The heuristics from Table 1 were divided into general heuristics and specific heuristics. General heuristics include heuristics that are valuable for experimenting regardless of the context of application. A heuristic like "keep track of your experiments" is, for instance, always important. Specific heuristics include heuristics that are dependent on the context of application. "Choosing equal increments" between experiments, for instance, depends on the kind of hypothesis that the learner is looking for. It is a valuable heuristic when you are looking for a quantitative relation between variables, but when you are looking for a qualitative relation between variables it is not really necessary to use this heuristic. In this case it might be more useful to look at a range of values, also including some extreme values, than to concentrate on using "equal increments".

The division between general and specific heuristics is reflected in the feedback that is given to the learners when they draw a graph. General heuristics are always used to assess the learner's experiments, and can always generate feedback. Specific heuristics are only be used to assess the learner's experiments if the learner fits a function on the experiments. Which of the specific heuristics are be used, depends on the kind of function. For instance, the 'equal increments' heuristic will not be used if the learner fits a qualitative function on the experiments.

The specific heuristics "identify hypothesis" can be said to represent the formal analysis that of the experiments that was used in the first version of the tool [16]. The first version of the tool checked whether the hypothesis could be identified based on the experimental evidence that was generated by the learner. It also checked whether this identification was proper. It did not check if the experimental evidence could also confirm the hypothesis. For instance, if the hypothesis is that two variables are linearly related, and only two experiments were done, at least one other experiment is needed for confirming this hypothesis. This extra experiment could show that the hypothesis that was identified is able to account for this additional experiment, but it could also show that the additional experiment is not on the line with the hypothesis that was identified based on the first two experiments. The "confirm hypothesis" heuristic takes care of this in the new tool.

5 A Learning Scenario

A learner working with the simulation can do experiments, decide whether to store the experiment in the tool or not. The tool keeps track of all these experiments and keeps a tag that indicates whether the learner stored an experiment or not. At a certain moment, the learner decides to draw a graph. The learner has to select a variable for the x-axis and for the y-axis, and press the button to draw a graph for these variables. At this point, the tool checks what 'type' of variables the learner is plotting, and based on this check the tool can stop without drawing a graph and present feedback to the learner, or proceed with drawing the graph. The first will happen if a learner tries to draw a graph with two input variables, since this does not make sense. Input variables are independent, and any relation that might show in a graph will therefore be the result of the changes that were made by the learner, and not of a relation between the variables. The tool will not draw a graph either when a student tries to draw a graph with an input variable on the y-axis, and an output variable on the x-axis. Unlike with the two input variables this could make sense, but it is common practice to plot the variables the other way around. In both cases the learner will receive feedback that explains why no graph was drawn, and what they could change in order to draw a graph that will provide more insight on relations in the domain.

If the learner selects an input variable on the x-axis, and an output variable on the y-axis, or two output variables the tool will proceed with drawing a graph, and will generate feedback based on the heuristics.

First, the general experimenting heuristics evaluate the experiments that the learner has performed. Each of the heuristics will compare the learner's experiments with the pattern (for an example see Table 2) that was defined for the heuristic. If necessary the heuristic can ask the tool to filter the experiments (f.i. only stored experiments). The feedback text is generated based on the result of this comparison, and returned to the tool. The tool temporarily stores the feedback until it will be presented to the learner.

Table 2. Example patterns for the 'equal increments' heuristic

Equal increments	If in a set of experiments in which the value for input variable on the x-axis changes, and the other input variables are kept the same There is no set of experiments in which the increment between the first and the second experiment is equal to the increment between the second and the third experiment Then remind the learner of the equal increment heuristic

The next step will be that the tool analyses the experiments using the same principles that were described in Veermans & van Joolingen [16]. Based on these principles the tool identifies sets of experiments that are informative for the relation between the input variable on the x-axis and the variable on the y-axis. For this purpose the experiments are grouped into sets in which all input variables other than the variable o the x-axis are kept constant. This will result in one or more sets of experiments that will be sent to the specific experiment heuristics, which will compare them with their heuristic pattern, and, if necessary, generate feedback text.

At this point the tool will draw the graph (see for example Figure 3). Together with the plots the tool will now present the feedback that was generated by the general experimenting heuristics. The feedback consists of the name of the heuristic, the outcome of the comparison with the heuristic pattern, an informal text that says that it could be useful to set up experiments according to this heuristic. The tool will provide information on each of the experiment sets that consists of the values of the input variables in this set and the feedback on the specific experiment heuristics.

If the learner decides to plot two output variables, it is not possible to divide the experiments formally into separate sets of informative experiments. Both output variables are dependent on one or more input variables, and it is not possible to say what kind of values for the input variables make up a set that can be used to see how the output variables are co-varying given the different values for the input variables. Some input variables might influence both output variables, and some only one of them. This makes it impossible to assess the experiments and the relation between the outputs formally. This uncertainty is communicated to the learners, warning them that they should be careful with drawing conclusions based on such a graph. It is accompanied by the suggestion to remove some experiments to get a set of experiments in which only one input variable is varied that than is the one that causes variation in the output variables. This feedback is combined with the feedback that was generated by the general experiment heuristics.

Learners can also decide to fit a function through their experiments, and if possible, a fit will be calculated for each of the experiment sets. These fits will be added to the graph, and additional feedback will be generated and presented to the learner. This additional feedback consists of a calculated estimation of the fit and more elaborate feedback from the specific experiment heuristics. The estimation of the fit

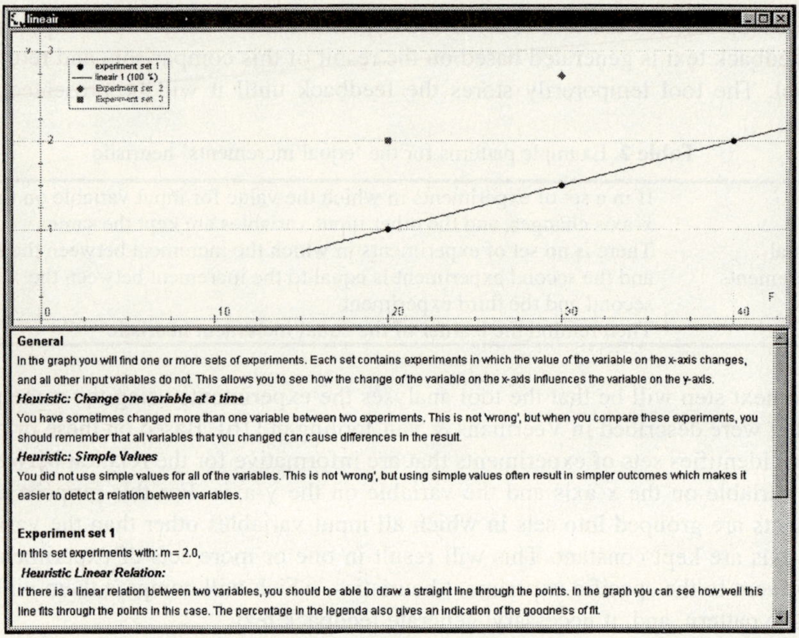

Fig. 3. Example of a graph with heuristic feedback based on the experiments in Figure 2

is expressed with a value on a scale ranging from 0% to 100%, with 0% denoting no fit at all, and 100% a perfect fit. The feedback that is generated by the specific experiment heuristics can be more elaborate when the learner fits a function, because the function can be seen as a hypothesis. This hypothesis allows a more detailed specification of the specific experimentation heuristics. The minimum number of experiments that is needed to be able to identify a function through the experiments can be compared with the actual number of experiments in each of the experiment sets. If the actual number is smaller than the required number this is used to generate feedback. The minimum number to confirm a hypothesis is the minimum number that can identify the hypothesis, plus one extra experiment that can be used for confirmation. Learners are also suggested to look at both the graph and the estimation of the fit to guide their decision on the correctness of the fit. At the same time one of the inductive discovery heuristic is used to suggest the learner to create a new variable that could help to establish a firm conclusion on the nature of the relationship.

6 Concluding Remarks About the Design of the Tool

The previous sections described the design of the tool for supporting hypothesis testing. The tool uses both formal and heuristic methods to analyze the experiments that learners perform in the process of testing a hypothesis, and, based on the result of the analysis, draws conclusions about the quality of the learners' hypothesis testing process. A learning scenario illustrated how the tool can support learners. It is not a learner-modeling tool, in the sense that keeps and updates a persistent model of the learner's knowledge, but is in the sense that it interprets the behavior of the learner, and uses this interpretation to provide individualized and contextualized feedback to the learner. The fact that tool uses both formal and heuristic methods, makes it broader in its scope than a purely formal tool.

In relation to the goal for the tool and the constraints it can be concluded that:

1. *The tool can support testing hypotheses and drawing conclusions.* Sorting the experiments into sets that are informative for the relation in the graph, drawing these sets as separate plots, generating feedback on experimentation, and generating feedback that can help the learner in the design and analysis of the experiments, supports hypothesis testing. Drawing separate plots, and presenting an estimated fit for a fitted function supports drawing conclusions.
2. *It leaves room for the learners to explore.* The tool leaves learners free to set up their own experiments, to draw graphs, and to fit relations through these graphs, thus leaving room for the learners to explore the relation between variables in the simulation.
3. *It is able to operate within the context of the authoring environment.* The tool is designed as a self-standing tool, and can be used as such. It does not have dependencies other than a dependency on the central manager of the simulation model.

7 Evaluation and Possible Extensions of the Tool

The tool described in this paper has been implemented and used in a simulation environment on the physics domain of collisions. This environment has first been evaluated in a small usability study with four high school students, and later with 46 high school students from two schools. Only a few results related to the tool will be highlighted here, a more elaborate description can be found in [18]. The results show among others that use of heuristics in the learning environment lead to higher learning outcomes compared to the environment with the previous version of the tool. It also showed that learner's were able to set up proper experimentation with the support in the environment; that using graphs with the feedback correlated positively with learning outcomes, but also that some learners felt quickly ready to be without the feedback. A possible extension could therefore be to allow more freedom to the learner related to presentation of feedback about heuristics and to selection of experiments that should be included in analyses. Especially for proficient learners it might work better if they can decide that they don't need certain feedback anymore. What could also prove to be of additional value is to make the tool less domain independent. One could think of the possibility to allow for instance assignments to communicate to the experiment storage tool which heuristics should be used in analyses, and set parameters for the patterns of these heuristics. This would allow the designer to tailor the heuristics and the patterns more to the domain, and/or to learners that are going to work with the learning environment.

References

1. Bruner, J. S. (1961).The act of discovery. Harvard Educational Review, 31, 21-32.
2. Butler, D. L., & Winne, P. H. (1995). Feedback and self-regulated learning: A theoretical synthesis. Review of Educational Research, 65, 245-281.
3. Dewey, J. (1938). Logic: the theory of inquiry. New York: Holt and Co.
4. Glaser, R., Schauble, L., Raghavan, K., & Zeitz, C. (1992). Scientific reasoning across different domains. In E. De Corte, M. Linn, H. Mandl, & L. Verschaffel (Eds.), Computer-based learning environments and problem solving (pp. 345-373). Berlin: Springer-Verlag.
5. Joolingen, W. R. van, & Jong, T. de (2003). SimQuest: Authoring educational simulations. In T. Murray, S. Blessing & S. Ainsworth (Eds.), Authoring Tools for Advanced Technology Educational Software: Toward cost-effective production of adaptive, interactive, and intelligent educational software. Lawrence Erlbaum
6. Karasavvidis, I. (1999). Learning to solve correlational problems. A study of the social and material distribution of cognition. PhD Thesis. Enschede, The Netherlands: University of Twente.
7. Klahr, D., & Dunbar, K. (1988). Dual space search during scientific reasoning. Cognitive Science, 12, 1-48.
8. Klahr, D., Fay, A. L., & Dunbar, K. (1993), Heuristics for scientific experimentation: A developmental study. Cognitive Psychology, 25, 111-146.
9. Kulkarni, D., & Simon, H. A. (1988). The processes of scientific discovery: The strategy of experimentation. Cognitive Science, 12, 139-175.
10. Langley, P. (1981). Data-Driven discovery of physical laws. Cognitive Science, 5, 31-54.
11. Qin, Y., & Simon, H. A. (1990). Laboratory replication of scientific discovery processes. Cognitive Science, 14, 281-312.
12. Sanders, I., Bouwmeester, M., & Blanken, M. van (2000). Heuristieken voor experimenteren in ontdekkend leeromgevingen. Unpublished report.
13. Schoenfeld, A. (1979). Can heuristics be taught? In J. Lochhead & J. Clement (Eds.), Cognitive process instruction (pp. 315-338). Philadelphia: Franklin Institute Press.
14. Schunn, C. D., & Anderson, J. R. (1999). The generality/specificity of expertise in scientific reasoning. Cognitive Science, 23, 337-370.
15. Tsirgi, J. E. (1980). Sensible reasoning: A hypothesis about hypotheses. Child Development, 51, 1-10.
16. Veermans, K., & Joolingen, W. R. van (1998). Using induction to generate feedback in simulation-based discovery learning environments. In B. P. Goetl, H. M., Halff, C. L. Redfield, & V. J. Shute (Eds.), Intelligent Tutoring Systems, 4th International Conference, San Antonio, TX USA (pp. 196-205). Berlin: Springer-Verlag.
17. Veermans, K., Joolingen, W. R. van, & Jong, T. de (2000). Promoting self directed learning in simulation based discovery learning environments through intelligent support. Interactive Learning Environments 8, 229-255.
18. Veermans, K., Joolingen, W. R. van, & Jong, T. de (submitted). Using Heuristics to Facilitate Discovery Learning in a Simulation Learning Environment in a Physics Domain.
19. Zachos, P., Hick, L. T., Doane, W. E. J., & Sargent, S. (2000). Setting theoretical and empirical foundations for assessing scientific inquiry and discovery in educational programs. Journal of Research in Science Teaching. 37, 938-962.

Toward Tutoring Help Seeking
Applying Cognitive Modeling to Meta-cognitive Skills

Vincent Aleven, Bruce McLaren, Ido Roll, and Kenneth Koedinger

Human-Computer Interaction Institute, Carnegie Mellon University
{aleven, bmclaren}@cs.cmu.edu, {idoroll, koedinger}@cmu.edu

Abstract. The goal of our research is to investigate whether a Cognitive Tutor can be made more effective by extending it to help students acquire help-seeking skills. We present a preliminary model of help-seeking behavior that will provide the basis for a *Help-Seeking Tutor Agent*. The model, implemented by 57 production rules, captures both productive and unproductive help-seeking behavior. As a first test of the model's efficacy, we used it off-line to evaluate students' help-seeking behavior in an existing data set of student-tutor interactions, We found that 72% of all student actions represented unproductive help-seeking behavior. Consistent with some of our earlier work (Aleven & Koedinger, 2000) we found a proliferation of hint abuse (e.g., using hints to find answers rather than trying to understand). We also found that students frequently avoided using help when it was likely to be of benefit and often acted in a quick, possibly undeliberate manner. Students' help-seeking behavior accounted for as much variance in their learning gains as their performance at the cognitive level (i.e., the errors that they made with the tutor). These findings indicate that the help-seeking model needs to be adjusted, but they also underscore the importance of the educational need that the Help-Seeking Tutor Agent aims to address.

1 Introduction

Meta-cognition is a critical skill for students to develop and an important area of focus for learning researchers. This, in brief, was one of three broad recommendations in a recent influential volume entitled "How People Learn," in which leading researchers survey state-of-the-art research on learning and education (Bransford, Brown, & Cocking, 2000). A number of classroom studies have shown that instructional programs with a strong focus on meta-cognition can improve students' learning outcomes (Brown & Campione, 1996; Palincsar & Brown, 1984; White & Frderiksen, 1998). An important question therefore is whether instructional technology can be effective in supporting meta-cognitive skills. A small number of studies have shown that indeed it can. For example, it has been shown that self-explanation, an important metacognitive skill, can be supported with a positive effect on the learning of domainspecific skills and knowledge (Aleven & Koedinger, 2002; Conati & VanLehn, 2000; Renkl, 2002; Trafton & Tricket, 2001).

This paper focuses on a different meta-cognitive skill: help seeking. The ability to solicit help when needed, from a teacher, peer, textbook, manual, on-line help system, or the Internet may have a significant influence on learning outcomes. Help seeking has

J.C. Lester et al. (Eds.): ITS 2004, LNCS 3220, pp. 227–239, 2004.

been studied quite extensively in social contexts such as classrooms (Karabenick, 1998). In that context, there is evidence that better help seekers have better learning outcomes, and that those who need help the most are the least likely to ask for it (Ryan et. al, 1998).

Help seeking has been studied to a lesser degree in interactive learning environments. Given that many learning environments provide some form of on-demand help, it might seem that proficient help use would be an important factor influencing the learning results obtained with these systems. However, there is evidence that students tend not to effectively use the help facilities offered by learning environments (for an overview, see Aleven, Stahl, Schworm, Fischer & Wallace, 2003). On the other hand, there is also evidence that when used appropriately, on-demand help can have a positive impact on learning (Renkl, 2000; Schworm & Renkl, 2002; Wood, 2001; Wood & Wood, 1999) and that different types of help (Dutke & Reimer, 2000) or feedback (McKendree, 1990; Arroyo et al., 2001) affect learning differently.

Our project focuses on the question of whether instructional technology can help students become better help seekers and, if so, whether they learn better as a result. Luckin and Hammerton (2002) reported some interesting preliminary evidence with respect to "meta-cognitive scaffolding." We are experimenting with the effects of computer-based help-seeking support in the context of Cognitive Tutors. This particular type of intelligent tutor is designed to support "learning by doing" and features a cognitive model of the targeted skills, expressed as production rules (Anderson, Corbett, Koedinger, & Pelletier, 1995). Cognitive Tutors for high-school mathematics have been highly successful in raising students' test scores and are being used in 1700 schools nationwide (Koedinger, Anderson, Hadley, & Mark, 1997).

As a first step toward a Help-Seeking Tutor Agent, we are developing a model of the help-seeking behavior that students would ideally exhibit as they work with the tutor. The model is implemented as a set of production rules, just like the cognitive models of Cognitive Tutors. The Help-Seeking Tutor Agent will use the model, applying its model-tracing algorithm at the meta-cognitive level to provide feedback to students on the way they use the tutor's help facilities. In this paper, we present an initial implementation of the model. We report results of an exploratory analysis, aimed primarily at empirically validating the model, in which we investigated, using an existing data set; to what extent students' help-seeking behavior conforms to the model and whether model conformance is predictive of learning.

2 Initial Test Bed: The Geometry Cognitive Tutor

Although our help-seeking model is designed to work with any Cognitive Tutor, and possibly other intelligent tutors as well, we are initially testing it within the Geometry Cognitive Tutor, shown in Figure 1.

The Geometry Cognitive Tutor was developed in our lab as an integrated component of a full-year geometry high-school curriculum. It is currently in routine use in 350 schools around the country. The combination of tutor and curriculum has been shown to be more effective than classroom instruction (Koedinger, Corbett, Ritter, & Shapiro, 2000). Like other Cognitive Tutors, the Geometry Cognitive Tutor uses a cognitive model of the skills to be learned. It uses an algorithm called model tracing to evaluate the student's solution steps and provide feedback (Anderson et al., 1995).

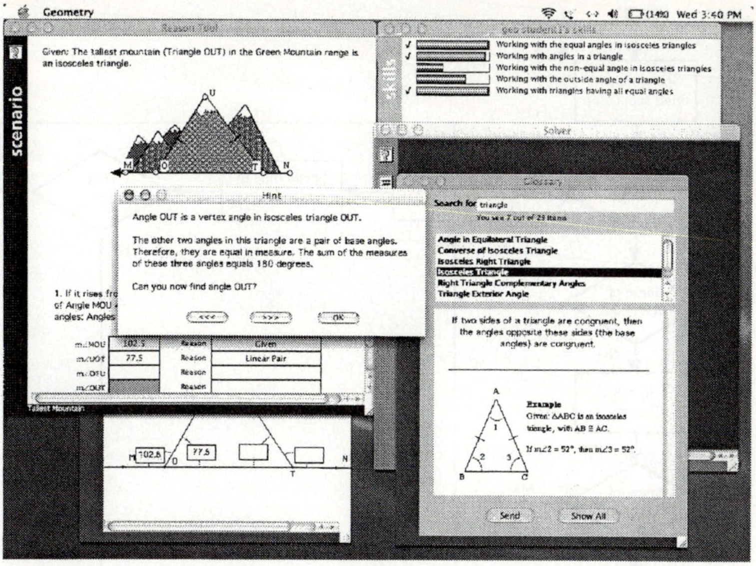

Fig. 1. The Geometry Cognitive Tutor

The Geometry Cognitive Tutor offers two different types of help on demand. At the student's request, context-sensitive hints are provided at multiple levels of detail. This help is tailored toward the student's specific goal within the problem at hand, with each hint providing increasingly specific advice. The Geometry Cognitive Tutor also provides a less typical source of help in the form of a de-contextualized Glossary. Unlike hints, the Glossary does not tailor its help to the user's goals; rather, at the student's request, it displays information about a selected geometry rule (i.e., a theorem or definition). It is up to the student to search for potentially relevant rules in the Glossary and to evaluate which rule is applicable to the problem at hand.

Cognitive Tutors keep track of a student's knowledge growth over time by means of a Bayesian algorithm called knowledge tracing (Corbett & Anderson, 1995). At each problem-solving step, the tutor updates its estimates of the probability that the student knows the skills involved in that step, according to whether the student was able to complete the step without errors and hints. A Cognitive Tutor uses the estimates of skill mastery to select problems and make pacing decisions on an individual basis. These estimates also play a role in the model of help seeking, presented below.

3 A Model of Desired Help-Seeking Behavior

3.1 Design

As part of our investigation into the help-seeking behavior of students, we have designed and developed a preliminary model of ideal help-seeking behavior, shown in Figure 2. This model shares some general traits with models of social help seeking put forward by

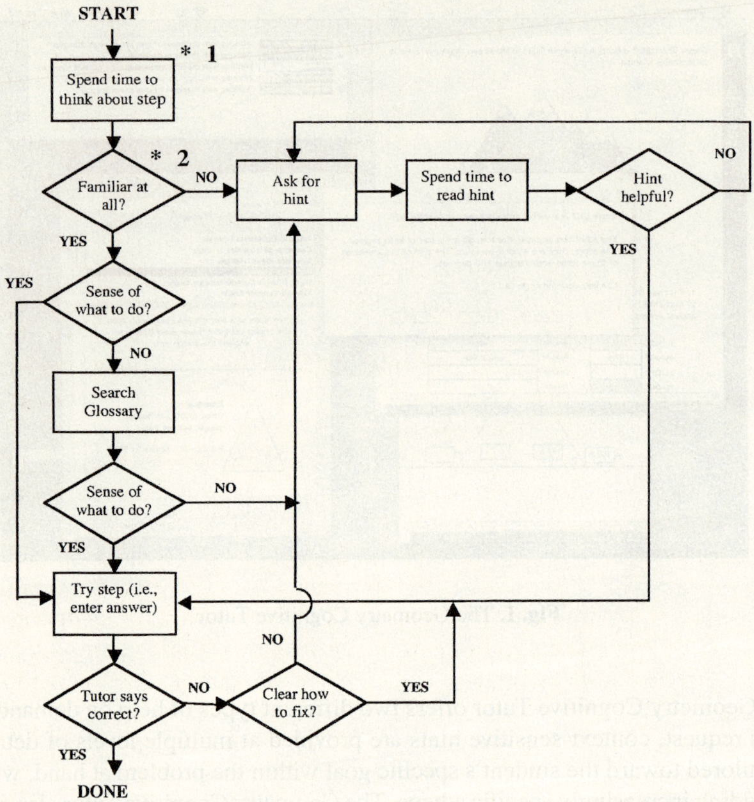

Fig. 2. A model of help-seeking behavior (The asterisks "*" indicate examples of where violations of the model can occur. To be discussed later in the paper.)

Nelson-LeGall's (1981) and Newman's (1994). We believe our model is a contribution to the literature on help seeking because it is more fine-grained than existing models and will eventually clarify poorly understood relations between help seeking and learning.

According to the model, the ideal student behaves as follows: If, after spending some time thinking about a problem-solving step, a step does not look familiar, the student should ask the tutor for a hint. After reading the hint carefully, she should decide whether a more detailed hint is needed or whether it is clear how to solve the step. If the step looks familiar from the start, but the student does not have a clear sense of what to do, she should use the Glossary to find out more. If the student does have a sense of what to do, she should try to solve it. If the tutor feedback indicates that the step is incorrect, the student should ask for a hint unless it was clear how to fix the problem. The student should think about any of her actions before deciding on her next move.

For implementation, we had to refine and make concrete some of the abstract elements of the flowchart. For example, the self-monitoring steps *Familiar at all?* and *Sense of what to do?* test how well a particular student knows a particular skill at a particular point in time. Item response theory (Hambleton & Swaminathan, 1985) is not a suitable way to address this issue, since it does not track the effect of learning over time. Instead, as a starting point to address these questions, we use the estimates of an individual student's skill mastery derived by the Cognitive Tutor's knowledge- tracing algorithm. The tests *Familiar at all?* and *Sense of what to do?* compare these estimates against pre-defined thresholds. So, for instance, if a student's current estimated level for the skill involved in the given step 0.4, our model assumes *Familiar at all?* = YES, since the threshold for this question is 0.3 . For *Sense of what to do?*, the threshold is 0.6. These values are intuitively plausible but need to be validated empirically. One of the goals of our experiments with the model, described below, is to evaluate and refine the thresholds.

The tests *Clear how to fix?* and *Hint helpful?* also had to be rendered more concrete. For the *Clear how to fix?* test, the help-seeking model prescribes that a student with a higher estimated skill level (for the particular skill involved in the step, at the particular point in time that the step is tried), should re-try a step after missing it once, but that mid or lower skilled students should ask for a hint. In the future we plan to elaborate *Clear how to fix?* by using heuristics that catch some of the common types of easy-to-fix slips that students make. Our implementation of *Hint Helpful?* assumes that the amount of help a student needs on a particular step depends on their skill level for that step. Thus, a high-skill student, after requesting a first hint, is predicted to need 1/3 of the available hint levels, a mid-skill student 2/3 of the hints, and a low-skill student all of the hints. However, this is really a question of reading comprehension (or self-monitoring thereof). In the future we will use basic results from the reading comprehension literature and also explore the use of tutor data to estimate the difficulty of understanding the tutor's hints.

3.2 Implementation

We have implemented an initial version of the help-seeking model of Figure 2. The current model consists of 57 production rules. Thirty-two of the rules are "bug rules," which reflect deviations of the ideal help-seeking behavior and enable the help-seeking tutor to provide feedback to students on such deviations. The model is used to evaluate two key pieces of information each time it is invoked in the process of model-tracing at the meta-cognitive level: (1) whether the student took sufficient time to consider his or her action, (2) whether the student appropriately used, or did not use, the tutor's help facilities at the given juncture in the problem-solving process. As an example, let us consider a student faced with an unfamiliar problem-solving step in a tutor problem. Without spending much time thinking about the step, she ventures an answer and gets it wrong. In doing so, the student deviates from the help-seeking model in two ways: she does not spend enough time thinking about the step (a meta-cognitive error marked as "* 1" in Figure 2) and in spite of the fact that the step is not familiar to her, she does not ask for a hint (marked as "* 2"). The students' errors will match bug rules that capture unproductive help-seeking behavior, allowing the tutor to provide feedback.

Figure 3 shows the tree of rules explored by the model-tracing algorithm as it searched for rules matching the student's help-seeking behavior (or in this situation, lack thereof). Various paths in the tree contain applicable rules that did not match the student's behavior (marked with "***"), including most notably a rule that represents the "ideal" meta-cognitive behavior in the given situation ("think-about-step-deliberately").

The rule chain that matched the students' behavior is highlighted. This chain includes an initial rule that starts the meta-cognitive cycle ("start-new-metacog-cycle"), a subsequent bug rule that identifies the student as having acted too quickly ("bug1-think-about-step-quickly"), a second bug rule that indicates that the student was not expected to try the step, given her low mastery of the skill at that point in time ("bug1-try-step-low-skill"), and, finally, a rule that reflects the fact that the student answered incorrectly ("bug-tutor-says-step-wrong"). The feedback message in this case, compiled from the two bug rules identified in the chain, is: "Slow down, slow down. No need to rush. Perhaps you should ask for a hint, as this step might be a bit difficult for you." The bug rules corresponding to the student acting too quickly and trying the step when they should not have are shown in Figure 4.

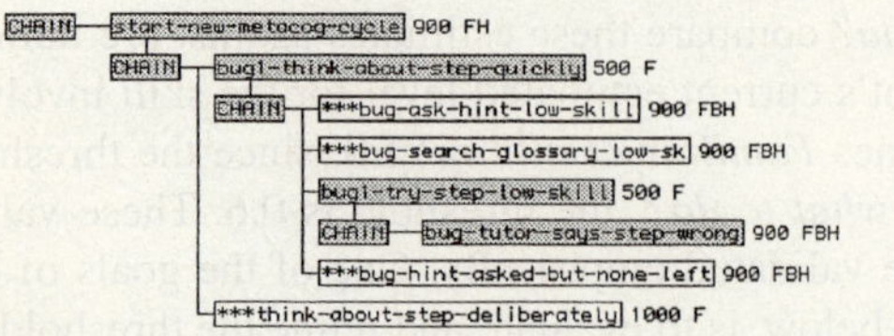

Fig. 3. A chain of rules in the Meta-Cognitive Model

The fact that the student got the answer wrong is not in itself considered to be a meta-cognitive error, even though it is captured in the model by a bug rule ("bug-tutor-says-step-wrong"). This bug rule merely serves to confirm the presence of bugs captured by other bug rules, when the student's answer (at the cognitive level) is wrong. Further, when the student answer is correct, (at the cognitive level) no feedback is given at the meta-cognitive level, even if the student's behavior was not ideal from the point of view of the help-seeking model.

The help-seeking model uses information passed from the cognitive model to perform its reasoning. For instance, the skill involved in a particular step, the estimated mastery level of a particular student for that skill, the number of hints available for that step, and whether or not the student got the step right, are passed from the cognitive to the meta-cognitive model. Meta-cognitive model tracing takes place after cognitive model tracing. In other words, when a student enters a value to the tutor, that value is first evaluated at the cognitive level before it is evaluated at the meta-cognitive level. An important consideration in the development of the Help-Seeking Tutor was to make it modular and useable in conjunction with a variety of Cognitive Tutors. Basically, the Help-Seeking Tutor Agent will be a plug-in agent applicable to a range of Cognitive Tutors with limited customization. We have attempted to create rules that are applicable to any Cognitive Tutor, not to a specific tutor. Certainly, there will be some need for customization, as optional supporting tools (of which the Glossary is but one example) will be available in some tutors and not others.

4 A Taxonomy of Help-Seeking Bugs

In order to compare students' help-seeking behavior against the model, we have created a taxonomy of errors (or bugs) in students' help-seeking behavior, shown in Figure 5. The taxonomy includes four main categories. First, the "Help Abuse" category covers situations in which the student misuses the help facilities provided by the Cognitive Tutor. This occurs when a student spends too little time with a hint ("Clicking Through Hints"), when a student requests hints (after some deliberation) when they are knowledgeable

Rule: Bug1-think-about-step-quickly
If the student is engaged in a meta-cognitive problem
And the current subgoal is to think about the step
And the student spent less than *min-thinking-time* to think about the step
Then
Remove the subgoal (next subgoal is to decide what action to take)

Bug message: "Slow down, slow down. No need to rush."

Rule: Bug1-try-step-low-skill
If the student is engaged in a meta-cognitive problem
And the current subgoal is to decide what action to take
And the students' estimated mastery level for the skill involved in the current step is less than *min-familiarity-level*
And the student has not seen all the hints yet for the current step
Then
Try step
Set a subgoal to evaluate the result

Bug message: "Perhaps you should ask for a hint, as this step might be a bit difficult for you."

Fig. 4. Example bug rules matching unproductive help-seeking behavior.

enough to either try the step ("Ask Hint when Skilled Enough to Try Step") or use the Glossary ("Ask Hint when Skilled Enough to Use Glossary"), or when a student overuses the Glossary ("Glossary Abuse"). Recall from the flow chart in Figure 2 that a student with high mastery for the skill in question should first try the step, a student with medium mastery should use the Glossary, and a student with low mastery should ask for a hint.

Second, the category "Try-Step Abuse" represents situations in which the student attempts to hastily solve a step and gets it wrong, either when sufficiently skilled to try the step ("Try Step Too Fast") or when less skilled ("Guess Quickly when Help Use was Appropriate").

Third, situations in which the student could benefit from asking for a hint or inspecting the Glossary, but chose to try the step instead, are categorized as "Help Avoidance". There are two bugs of this type – "Try Unfamiliar Step Without Hint Use" and "Try Vaguely Familiar Step Without Glossary Use."

Finally, the category of "Miscellaneous Bugs" covers situations not represented in the other high-level categories. The "Read Problem Too Fast" error describes hasty reading of the question, when first encountered followed by a rapid help request. "Ask for Help Too Fast" describes a similar situation in which the student asks for help too quickly after making an error. The "Used All Hints and Still Failing" bug represents situations in which the student has seen all of the hints, yet cannot solve the step (i.e., the student has failed more than a threshold number of times). In our implemented model, the student is advised to talk to the teacher in this situation.

In general, if the student gets the step right at the cognitive level, we do not consider a meta-cognitive bug to have occurred, regardless of whether the step was hasty or the student's skill level was inappropriate.

5 Comparing the Model to Students' Actual Meta-cognitive Behavior

We conducted an empirical analysis to get a sense of how close the model is to being usable in a tutoring context and also to get a sense of students' help-seeking behavior. We replayed a set of logs of student-tutor interactions, comparing what actually happened in a given tutor unit (viz., the Angles unit of the Geometry Cognitive Tutor), without any tutoring on help seeking, with the predictions made by the help-seeking model. This methodology might be called "model tracing after the fact" – it is not the same as actual model tracing, since one does not see how the student might have changed their behavior in response to feedback on their help-seeking behavior. We determined the extent to which students' help-seeking behavior conforms to the model. We also determined the frequency of the various categories of meta-cognitive bugs described above. Finally, we determined whether students' help-seeking behavior (that is, the degree to which they follow the model) is predictive of their learning results.

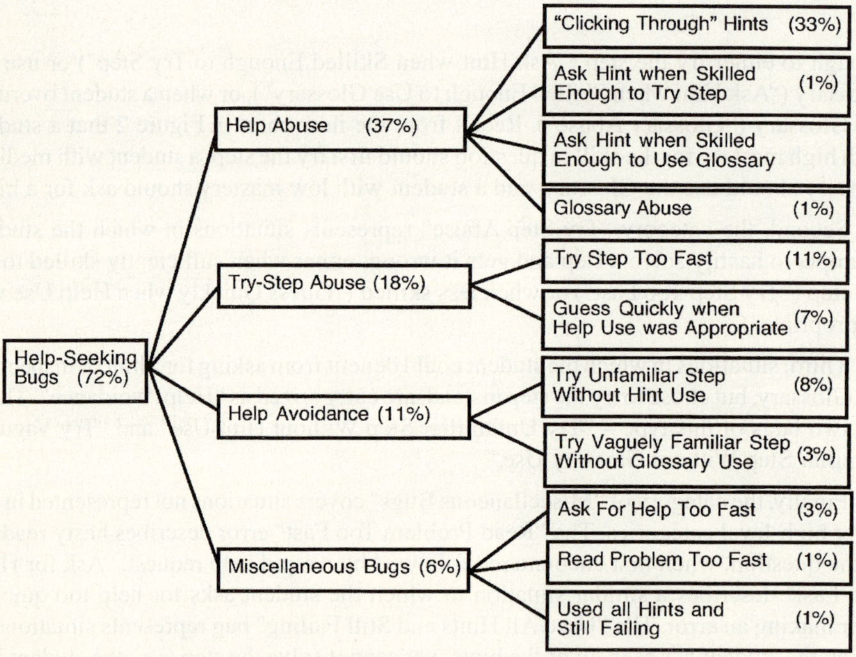

Fig. 5. A taxonomy of help-seeking bugs. The percentages indicate how often each bug occurred in our experiment.

The data used in the analysis were collected during an earlier study in which we compared the learning results of students using two tutor versions, one in which they explained their problem-solving steps by selecting the name of the theorem that justifies it and one in which the students solved problems without explaining (Aleven &

Koedinger, 2002). For purposes of the current analysis, we group the data from both conditions together. Students spent approximately 7 hours working on this unit of the tutor. The protocols from interaction with the tutor include data from 49 students, 40 of whom completed both the Pre- and Post-Tests. These students performed a total of approximately 47,500 actions related to skills tracked by the tutor.

The logs of the student-tutor interactions where replayed with each student action (either an attempt at answering, a request for a hint, or the inspection of a Glossary item) checked against the predictions of the help-seeking model. Actions that matched the model's predictions were recorded as "correct" help-seeking behavior, actions that did not match the model's predictions as "buggy" help-seeking behavior. The latter actions were classified automatically with respect to the bug taxonomy of Figure 5, based on the bug rules that were matched. We computed the frequency of each bug category (shown in Figure 5) and each category's correlation with learning gains. The learning gains (LG) were computed from the pre- and post-test scores according to the formula (LG = (Post - Pre) / (1 - Pre), mean 0.41; standard deviation 0.28).

The overall ratio of help-seeking errors to all actions was 72%; that is, 72% of the students' actions did not conform to the help-seeking model. The most frequent errors at the meta-cognitive level were Help Abuse (37%), with the majority of these being "Clicking Through" hints (33%). The next most frequent category was Try Step Abuse (18%), which represents quick attempts at answering steps. Help Avoidance – not using help at moments when it was likely to be beneficial – was also quite frequent (11%), especially if "Guess quickly when help was needed" (7%), arguably a form of Help Avoidance as well as Try-Step Abuse, is included in both categories.

Table 1. Correlation between the bug categories and Learning Gain

	Help Abuse	Try-Step Abuse	Help Avoidance	Misc. Bugs	Total Meta-cognitive Bugs
Learning Gain	-0.46	0.02	-0.10	-0.47	-0.61

The frequency of help-seeking bugs was correlated strongly with the students' overall learning ($r = -0.61$ with $p < .0001$), as shown in Table 1. The model therefore is a good predictor of learning gains – the more help-seeking bugs students make, the less likely they are to learn. The correlation between students' frequency of success at the cognitive level (computed as the percentage of problem steps that the student completed without errors or hints from the tutor) and learning gain is about the same ($r = .58$, $p = .0001$) as the correlation between help-seeking bugs and learning. Success in help seeking and success at the cognitive level were highly correlated ($r = .78$, $p < .0001$). In a multiple regression, the combination of help-seeking errors and errors at the cognitive level accounted only for marginally more variance than either one alone. We also looked at how the bug categories correlated with learning (also shown in Table 1). Both Help Abuse and Miscellaneous Bugs were negatively correlated with learning with $p < 0.01$. These bug categories have in common that the students avoid trying to solve the step. On the other hand, Try Step Abuse and Help Avoidance were not correlated with learning.

6 Discussion

Our analysis sheds light on the validity of the help-seeking model and the adjustments we must make before we use it for "live" tutoring. The fact that some of the bug categories of the model correlate negatively with learning provides some measure of confidence that the model is on the right track. The correlation between Hint Abuse and Miscellaneous Bugs and students' learning gain supports our assumption that the help-seeking model is valid in identifying these phenomena. On the other hand, the model must be more lenient with respect to help-seeking errors. The current rate of 72% implies that the Help-Seeking Tutor Agent would intervene (i.e., present a bug message) in 3 out of every 4 actions taken by a student. In practical use, this is likely to be quite annoying and distracting to the student. Another finding that may lead to a change in the model is the fact that Try-Step Abuse did not correlate with learning. Intuitively, it seems plausible that a high frequency of incorrect guesses would be negatively correlated with learning. Perhaps the threshold we used for "thinking time" is too high; perhaps it should be depend on the student's skill level. This will require further investigation. Given that the model is still preliminary and under development, the findings on students' help seeking should also be regarded as subject to further investigation.

The finding that students often abuse hints confirms earlier work (Aleven & Koedinger, 2000; Aleven, McLaren, & Koedinger, to appear; Baker, Corbett, & Koedinger, in press). The current analysis extends that finding by showing that help abuse is frequent relative to other kinds of help-seeking bugs and that it correlates negatively with learning. However, the particular rate that was observed (37%) may be inflated somewhat because of the high frequency of "Clicking Through Hints" (33%). Since typically 6 to 8 hint levels were available, a single "clicking-through" episode – selecting hints until the "bottom out" or answer hint is seen – yields multiple actions in the data. One would expect to see a different picture if the clicking episodes were clustered into a single action.

Several new findings emerged from our empirical study. As mentioned, a high help-seeking error rate was identified (72%). To the extent that the model is correct, this suggests that students generally do not have good help-seeking skills. We also found a relatively high Help Avoidance rate, especially if we categorize "Guess Quickly when Help Use was Appropriate" as a form of Help Avoidance (18% combined). In addition, since the frequency of the Help Abuse category appears to be inflated by the high prevalence of Clicking Through Hints, categories such as Help Avoidance are correspondingly deflated. The significance of this finding is not yet clear, since Help Avoidance did not correlate with learning. It may well be that the model does not yet successfully identify instances in which the students should have asked for help but did not. On the other hand, the gross abuse of help in the given data set is likely to have lessened the impact of Help Avoidance. In other words, given that the Help Avoidance in this data set was really Help Abuse avoidance, the lack of correlation with learning is not surprising and should not be interpreted as meaning that help avoidance is not a problem or has no impact on learning. Future experiments with the Help-Seeking Tutor Agent may cast some light on the importance of help avoidance, in particular if the tutor turns out to reduce the Help Avoidance rate.

It must be said that we are just beginning to analyze and interpret the data. For instance, we are interested in obtaining a more detailed insight into and understanding of Help Avoidance. Under what specific circumstances does this occur? We also intend to investigate in greater detail how students so often get a step right even when they answer too quickly, according to the model. Finally, how different would the results look if clicking through hints is considered a single mental action?

7 Conclusion

We have presented a preliminary model of help seeking which will form the basis of a Help-Seeking Tutor Agent, designed to be seamlessly added to existing Cognitive Tutors. To validate the model, we have run it against pre-existing tutor data. This analysis suggests that the model is on the right track, but is not quite ready for "live" tutoring, in particular because it would lead to feedback on as much as three-fourths of the students' actions, which is not likely to be productive. Although the model is still preliminary, the analysis also sheds some light on students' help-seeking behavior. It confirms earlier findings that students' help-seeking behavior is far from ideal and that help-seeking errors correlate negatively with learning, underscoring the importance of addressing help-seeking behavior by means of instruction.

The next step in our research will be to continue to refine the model, testing it against the current and other data sets, and modifying it so that it will be more selective in presenting feedback to students. In the process, we hope to gain a better understanding, for example, of the circumstances under which quick answers are fine or under which help avoidance is most likely to be harmful. Once the model gives satisfactory results when run against existing data sets, we will use it for live tutoring, integrating the Help-Seeking Tutor Agent with an existing Cognitive Tutor. We will evaluate whether students' help-seeking skill improves when they receive feedback from the Help-Seeking Tutor Agent and whether they obtain better learning outcomes. We will also evaluate whether better help-seeking behavior persists beyond the tutor units in which the students are exposed to the Help-Seeking Tutor Agent and whether students learn better in those units as a result. A key hypothesis is that the Help- Seeking Tutor Agent will help students to become better learners.

Acknowledgments. The research reported in this paper is supported by NSF Award No. IIS-0308200.

References

Aleven V. & Koedinger, K. R. (2002). An effective meta-cognitive strategy: Learning by doing and explaining with a computer-based Cognitive Tutor. *Cognitive Science*, 26(2), 147-179.

Aleven, V., & Koedinger, K. R. (2000). Limitations of Student Control: Do Student Know when they need help? In G. Gauthier, C. Frasson, & K. VanLehn (Eds.), *Proceedings of the 5th International Conference on Intelligent Tutoring Systems, ITS 2000* (pp. 292-303). Berlin: Springer Verlag.

Aleven, V., McLaren, B. M., & Koedinger, K. R. (to appear). Towards Computer-Based Tutoring of Help-Seeking Skills. In S. Karabenick & R. Newman (Eds.), *Help Seeking in Academic Settings: Goals, Groups, and Contexts*. Mahwah, NJ: Erlbaum.

Aleven, V., Stahl, E., Schworm, S., Fischer, F., & Wallace, R.M. (2003). Help Seeking in Interactive Learning Environments. *Review of Educational Research*, 73(2), 277-320.

Anderson, J. R., Corbett, A. T., Koedinger, K. R., & Pelletier, R. (1995). Cognitive tutors: Lessons learned. *The Journal of the Learning Sciences*, 4, 167-207.

Arroyo, I., Beck, J. E., Beal, C. R., Wing, R., & Woolf, B. P. (2001). Analyzing students' response to help provision in an elementary mathematics intelligent tutoring system. In R. Luckin (Ed.), Papers of the AIED-2001 Workshop on Help Provision and Help Seeking in Interactive Learning Environments (pp. 34-46).

Baker, R. S., Corbett, A. T., & Koedinger, K. R. (in press). Detecting Student Misuse of Intelligent Tutoring Systems. In *Proceedings of the 7th International Conference on Intelligent Tutoring Systems. ITS 2004*.

Bransford, J. D., Brown, A. L., & Cocking, R. R. (Eds.) (2000). *How People Learn: Brain, Mind, Experience, and School.* Washington, CD: National Academy Press.

Brown, A. L., & Campione, J. C. (1996). Guided Discovery in a Community of Learners. In K. McGilly (Ed.), *Classroom Lessons: Integrating Cognitive Theory and Classroom Practice* (pp. 229-270). Cambridge, MA: The MIT Press.

Conati C. & VanLehn K. (2000). Toward computer-based support of meta-cognitive skills: A computational framework to coach self-explanation. *International Journal of Artificial Intelligence in Education*, 11, 398-415.

Corbett, A. T. & Anderson, J. R. (1995). Knowledge tracing: Modeling the acquisition of procedural knowledge. *User Modeling and User-Adapted Interaction*, 4, 253-278.

Dutke, S., & Reimer, T. (2000). Evaluation of two types of online help information for application software: Operative and function-oriented help. *Journal of Computer-Assisted Learning*, 16, 307-315.

Hambleton, R. K. & Swaminathan, H. (1985). *Item Response Theory: Principles and Applications.* Boston: Kluwer.

Karabenick, S. A. (Ed.) (1998). *Strategic help seeking. Implications for learning and teaching.* Mahwah: Erlbaum.

Koedinger, K. R., Anderson, J. R., Hadley, W. H., & Mark, M. A. (1997). Intelligent tutoring goes to school in the big city. *International Journal of Artificial Intelligence in Education*, 8, 30-43.

Koedinger, K. R., Corbett, A. T., Ritter, S., & Shapiro, L. (2000). Carnegie Learning's Cognitive Tutor^{TM}: Summary Research Results. White paper. Available from Carnegie Learning Inc., 1200 Penn Avenue, Suite 150, Pittsburgh, PA 15222, E-mail: info@carnegielearning.com, Web: http://www.carnegielearning.com

Luckin, R., & Hammerton, L. (2002). Getting to know me: Helping learners understand their own learning needs through meta-cognitive scaffolding. In S. A. Cerri, G. Gouardères, & F. Paraguaçu (Eds.), *Proceedings of Sixth International Conference on Intelligent Tutoring Systems, ITS 2002* (pp. 759- 771). Berlin: Springer.

McKendree, J. (1990). Effective feedback content for tutoring complex skills. *Human Computer Interaction*, 5, 381-413.

Nelson-LeGall, S. (1981). Help-seeking: An understudied problem-solving skill in children. *Developmental Review*, 1, 224-246.

Newman, R. S. (1994). Adaptive help seeking: a strategy of self-regulated learning. In D. H. Schunk & B. J. Zimmerman (Eds.), *Self-regulation of learning and performance: Issues and educational applications* (pp. 283-301). Hillsdale, NJ: Erlbaum.

Palincsar, A. S., & Brown, A. L. (1984). Reciprocal teaching of comprehension-fostering and comprehension monitoring activities. *Cognition and Instruction*, 1, 117-175.

Renkl, A. (2002). Learning from worked-out examples: Instructional explanations supplement selfexplanations. *Learning and Instruction*, 12, 529-556.

Ryan, A. M., Gheen, M. H. & Midgley, C. (1998), Why do some students avoid asking for help? An examination of the interplay among students' academic efficacy, teachers' social-emotional role, and the classroom goal structure. *Journal of Educational Psychology*, 90(3), 528-535.)

Schworm, S. & Renkl, A. (2002). Learning by solved example problems: Instructional explanations reduce self-explanation activity. In W. D. Gray & C. D. Schunn (Eds.), *Proceeding of the 24th Annual Conference of the Cognitive Science Society* (pp.816-821). Mahwah, NJ: Erlbaum.

Trafton, J.G., & Trickett, S.B. (2001). Note-taking for self-explanation and problem solving. *Human- Computer Interaction*, 16, 1-38.

White, B., & Frederiksen, J. (1998). Inquiry, modeling, and metacognition: Making science accessible to all students. Cognition and Instruction, 16(1), 3-117.

Wood, D. (2001). Scaffolding, contingent tutoring, and computer-supported learning. *International Journal of Artificial Intelligence in Education*, 12.

Wood, H., & Wood, D. (1999). Help seeking, learning and contingent tutoring. *Computers and Education*, 33, 153-169.

Why Are Algebra Word Problems Difficult? Using Tutorial Log Files and the Power Law of Learning to Select the Best Fitting Cognitive Model

Ethan A. Croteau[1], Neil T. Heffernan[1], and Kenneth R. Koedinger[2]

[1] Computer Science Department
Worcester Polytechnic Institute
Worcester, MA. 01609, USA
{ecroteau, nth}@wpi.edu

[2] School of Computer Science
Carnegie Mellon University
Pittsburgh, PA. 15213, USA
koedinger@cmu.edu

Abstract. Some researchers have argued that algebra word problems are difficult for students because they have difficulty in comprehending English. Others have argued that because algebra is a generalization of arithmetic, and generalization is hard, it's the use of variables, per se, that cause difficulty for students. Heffernan and Koedinger [9] [10] presented evidence against both of these hypotheses. In this paper we present how to use tutorial log files from an intelligent tutoring system to try to contribute to answering such questions. We take advantage of the Power Law of Learning, which predicts that error rates should fit a power function, to try to find the best fitting mathematical model that predicts whether a student will get a question correct. We decompose the question of "Why are Algebra Word Problems Difficult?" into two pieces. First, is there evidence for the existence of this articulation skill that Heffernan and Koedinger argued for? Secondly, is there evidence for the existence of the skill of "composed articulation" as the best way to model the "composition effect" that Heffernan and Koedinger discovered?

1 Introduction

Many researchers had argued that students have difficulty with algebra word-problem *symbolization* (writing algebra expressions) because they have trouble comprehending the words in an algebra word problem. For instance, Nathan, Kintsch, & Young [14] "claim that [the] symbolization [process] is a highly *reading-oriented* one in which poor *comprehension* and an inability to access relevant long term knowledge leads to serious errors." [emphasis added]. However, Heffernan & Koedinger [9] [10] showed that many students can do *compute* tasks well, whereas they have great difficulty with the *symbolization* tasks [See Table 1 for examples of *compute* and *symbolization* types of questions]. They showed that many students could comprehend the words in the problem, yet still could not do the symbolization. An alternative explanation for "Why Are Algebra Word Problems Difficult?" is that the key is the use of

J.C. Lester et al. (Eds.): ITS 2004, LNCS 3220, pp. 240–250, 2004.

variables. Because algebra is a generalization of arithmetic, and it's the variables that allow for this generalization, it seems to make sense that it's the variables that make algebra symbolization hard.

However, Heffernan & Koedinger presented evidence that cast doubt on this as an important explanation. They showed there is hardly any difference between students' performance on *articulation* (see Table 1 for an example) versus *symbolization* tasks, arguing against the idea that the hard part is the presence of the variable per se.

Instead, Heffernan & Koedinger hypothesized that a key difficulty for students was in articulating arithmetic in the "foreign" language of algebra. They hypothesized the existence of a skill for articulating one step in an algebra word problem. This articulation step requires that a student be able to say (or "articulate") how it is they would do a computation, without having to actually do the arithmetic. Surprising, the found that is was easier for a student to actually do the arithmetic then to articulate what they did in an expression. To successfully articulate a student has to be able to write in the language of algebra. Question 1 for this paper is "Is there evidence from tutorial log files that support the conjecture that the *articulate* skill really exists?"

In addition to conjecturing the existence of the skill for articulating a single step, Heffernan & Koedinger also reported what they called the "composition effect" which we will also try to model. Heffernan & Koedinger took problems requiring two mathematical steps and made two new questions, where each question assessed each of the steps independently. They found that the difficulty of the one two-operator problem was much more than the combined difficulty of the two one-operator problems taken together. They termed this the composition effect. This led them to speculate as to what the "hidden" difficulty was for students that explained this difference in performance. They argued that the hidden difficulty included knowledge of *composition of articulation*. Heffernan & Koedinger attempted to argue that the composition effect was due to difficulties in articulating rather than on the task of comprehending, or at the symbolization step when a variable is called for. In this paper we will compare these hypotheses to try to determine the source of the composition effect originates. We refer to this as Question 2.

Heffernan & Koedinger's arguments were based upon two different samplings of about 70 students. Students' performances on different types of items were analyzed. Students were not learning during the assessment so there was no need to model learning. Heffernan & Koedinger went on to create an intelligent tutoring system, "Ms Lindquist", to teach student how to do similar problems. In this paper we attempt to use tutorial log file data collected from this tutor to shed light on this controversy. The technique we present is useful for intelligent tutoring system designers as it shows a way to use log file data to refine the mathematical models we use in predicting whether a student will get an item correct. For instance, Corbett and Anderson describe how to use "knowledge tracing" to track students performance on items related to a particular skill, but all such work is based upon the idea that you know what skills are involved already. But in this case there is controversy [15] over what are the important skills (or more generally, *knowledge components*). Because Ms Lindquist selects problems in a curriculum section randomly, we can learn what the knowledge components are that are being learned. With out problem randomization we would have no hope of separating out the effect of problem ordering with the difficulty of individual questions.

In the following sections of this paper we present the investigations we did to look into the existence of both the skills of *articulation* as well as *composition of articulation*. In particular, we present mathematically predictive models of a student's chance of getting a question correct. It should be noted, such predicative models have many other uses for intelligent tutoring systems, so this methodology has many uses.

1.1 Knowledge Components and Transfer Models

As we said in the introduction, some [14] believed that comprehension was the main difficulty in solving algebra word problems. We summarize this viewpoint with our three skill transfer model that we refer to as the "Base" model.

The *Base Model* consists of arithmetic knowledge component (KC), comprehension KC, and using a variable KC. The transfer model indicates the number of times a particular KC has been applied for a given question type. For a two-step "compute" problem the student will have to *comprehend* two different parts of the word problem (including but not limited to, figuring out what operators to use with which literals mentioned in the problem) as well as using the *arithmetic* KC twice. This model can predict that symbolization problems will be harder than the articulation problems due to the presence of a variable in the symbolization problems. The *Base Model* suggests that computation problems should be easier than articulation problems, unless students have a difficult time doing arithmetic.

The KC referred to as "*articulating one-step*" is the KC that Heffernan & Koedinger [9] [10] conjectured was important to understanding what make algebra problems so difficult for students. We want to build a mathematical model with the *Base Model* KCs and compare it what we call the "*Base+Model*", that also includes the *articulating one-step* KC.

So Question 1 in this paper compares the *Base Model* with a model that adds in the *articulating one-step* KC. Question 2 goes on to try to see what is the best way of adding knowledge components that would allow the model to predict the composition effect. Is the composition during the articulation, comprehension, articulation, or the symbolization? Heffernan and Koedinger speculated that there was a composition effect during articulation, suggesting that knowing how to treat an expression the same way you treat a number would be a skills that students would have to learn if they were to be good at problems that involved two-step articulation problems. If Heffernan & Koedinger's conjecture was correct, we would expect to find that the *composition of articulation* KC is better (in combination with one of the two Base Model variants) at predicting students difficulties than any of the other composition KCs.

1.2 Understanding How We Use This Model to Predict Transfer

Qualitatively, we can see that a our transfer model predicts that practice on one-step computation questions should transfer to one-step articulation problems only to the degree that a student learns (i.e., receives practice at employing) the *comprehending one-step* KC. We can turn this qualitative observation into a quantified prediction method by treating each knowledge component as having a *difficulty* parameter and a *learning* parameter. This is where we take advantage of the Power Law of Learning, which is one of the most robust findings in cognitive psychology. The power law says that the performance of cognitive skills improve approximately as a power function of practice [16] [1]. This has been applied to both error rates as well as time to complete a task, but our use here will be with error rates. This can be stated mathematical as follows:

$$\text{Error Rate}(x) = b * x^{-d} \tag{1}$$

Where x represents the number of times the student has received feedback on the task, b represents a *difficulty* parameter related to the error rate on the first trail of the task, and d represents a *learning* parameter related to the learning rate for the task. Tasks that have large b values represent tasks that are difficult for students the first time they try it (could be due to the newness of the task, or the inherit complexity of the task). Tasks that have a large d coefficient represent tasks where student learning is fast. Conversely, small values of d are related to tasks that students are slow to improve[1].

The approach taken here is a variation of "learning factors analysis", a semi-automated method for using learning curve data to refine cognitive models [12]. In this work, we follow Junker, Koedinger, & Trottini [11] in using logistic regression to try to predict whether a student will get a question correct, based upon both item factors (like what knowledge components are used for a given question, which is what we are calling *difficulty* parameters), student factors (like a students pretest score) and factors that depend on both students and items (like how many times this particular students has practiced their particular knowledge component, which is what we are calling *learning* parameters.) Corbett & Anderson [3], Corbett, Anderson & O'Brien [4] and Draney, Pirolli, & Wilson [5] report results using the same and/or similar methods as described above. There is also a great deal of related work in the psychometric literature related to item response theory [6], but most of it is focused on analyzing test (e.g., SAT or GRE) rather than student learning.

1.3 Using the Transfer Model to Predict Transfer in Tutorial Log Files

Heffernan [7] created Ms. Lindquist, an intelligent tutoring system, and put it online (***www.algebratutor.org***) and collected tutorial log files for all the students learning to symbolize. For this research we selected a data set for which Heffernan [8] had previously reported evidence that students were learning during the tutoring sessions. Some 73 students were brought to a computer lab to work with Ms. Lindquist for two class periods totaling an average of about 1 hour of time for each student. We present

---

[1] All *learning* parameters are restricted to be positive otherwise the parameters would be modeling some sort of forgetting effect.

data from students working only on the second curriculum section, since the first curriculum was too easy for students and showed no learning. (An example of this dialog is shown in Table 2 and will be discussed shortly). This resulted in a set of log files from 43 students, comprising 777 rows where each row represents a student's first attempt to answer a given question.

Table 1. Showing a made-up tutor log file and how it uses the *Base+Model* Transfer Model

	1	2	3	4	5	6	7	8	9	10	11	12	13	14	15	16
						Example Question	Outcomes		**Knowledge Components: *Difficulty* Parameters**				**Knowledge Components: *Learning* Parameters**			
	Scenario Identifier	**Factor: *Task directions***	**Factor: *Steps***	**Attempt at question type**	**First Attempt in sequence**		**Response Time (Seconds)**	**Response (Correct or not)**	**Arithmetic**	**Comprehending One-Step**	**Using a Variable**	**Articulating One-Step**	**Arithmetic**	**Comprehending One-Step**	**Using a Variable**	**Articulating One-Step**
1	1	S	2	1	T	**Scenario 1:** Anne is rowing a boat in a lake and is 800 yards from the dock from which she started. She rows back towards the dock at 40 yards per minute for "m" minutes and stops to rest. How far is she from the dock now? **Tutor**: Please write an expression for the distance Anne has left to row.			**0**	**2**	**1**	**2**	**0**	**0**	**0**	**0**
2						**Student**:8-40/m	**130**	**N**								
3	1	C	2	1	T	**Tutor**: Hmm. No. We will come back to the distance Anne has left to row. Let me try to break this down for you. Please compute the distance Anne has left to row if the number of minutes rowing was 3 minutes?						**0**	**0**	**0**	**0**	**0**
4						**Student**:580	**38**	**N**								
5	1	C	1	1	T	**Tutor**: Hmm. No. Let me ask you a different question. Please compute the distance rowed so far if the number of minutes rowing was 3 minutes?			**1**	**1**	**0**	**0**	**0**	**0**	**0**	**0**
6						**Student**:12	**19**	**N**								
7	1	C	1	2	F	**Tutor**: Hmm. No. Try again please. Please compute the distance rowed so far if the number of minutes rowing			**1**	**1**	**0**	**0**	**0**	**0**	**0**	**0**

						was 3 minutes? Hint: Use the fact that her speed rowing is 40 yards per minute and the number of minutes rowing is 3 minutes.										
8						**Student**: 120	**9**	**Y**								
9	1	C	2	2	T	**Tutor**: Correct. Now, lets try this question again: Please compute the distance Anne has left to row if the number of minutes rowing was 3 minutes?			**~~2~~ 1**	**~~2~~ 1**	**0**	**0**	**1**	**1**	**0**	**0**
10						**Student**: 680	**24**	**Y**								
11	1	A	2	1	T	**Tutor**: Correct. Using only 800, 40, and 3 write an expression for the distance Anne has left to row			**0**	**~~2~~ 0**	**0**	**2**	**~~3~~ 2**	**~~3~~ 2**	**0**	**0**
12						**Student:** 120-800	**18**	**N**								
13	1	A	1	1	T	**Tutor:** No. Your answer of "120-800" equals "-680", but you wanted to write an expression that equaled "680". But that is only because you didn't say where the 120 came from. What math did you do to get the 120?			**0**	**~~1~~ 0**	**0**	**1**	**~~3~~ 2**	**~~3~~ 2**	**0**	**0**
14						**Student:** 3*40	**22**	**Y**								
15	1	A	2	2	T	**Tutor:** Correct. Now, lets try this question again: Using only 800, 40, and 3 write an expression for the distance Anne has left to row.				**~~2~~ 0**	**0**	**~~2~~ 1**	**~~3~~ 2**	**~~4~~ 2**	**0**	**1**
16						**Student**: 800-40*3	**18**	**Y**								
17	1	S	2	2	T	**Tutor**: Correct. Now use "m" instead of 3 to again express the distance Anne has left to row.			**0**	**~~2~~ 0**	**1**	**~~2~~ 0**	**~~3~~ 2**	**~~6~~ 2**	**0**	**~~3~~ 2**
18						**Student**:800-40*m	**9**	**Y**								
19						**Tutor**: Correct. Lets do a new problem.										
20	2	S	2	1	T	**Scenario 2:** Michael works as a waiter. Saturday he worked "h" hours. The restaurant pays him an hourly wage of $3 an hour. He also made $40 dollars in tips. Write an expression for the total amount he earned Saturday Night. **Tutor:** Write an expression for the total amount he earned Saturday Night.			**0**	**2**	**1**	**2**	**~~3~~ 2**	**~~8~~ 2**	**1**	**~~5~~ 2**

Table 1 shows an example of the sort of dialog Ms. Lindquist carries on with students (this is with "made-up" student responses). Table 1 starts by showing a student working on scenario identifier #1 (Column 1) and only in the last row (Row 20) does the scenario identifier switch. Each word-problem has a single *top-level* question which is always a *symbolize* question. If the student fails to get the top level question correct, Ms. Lindquist steps in to have a dialog (as shown in the 6th column) with the student, asking questions to help break the problem down into simpler questions. The combination of the second and third column indicates the question type. The second column is for the *Task Direction* factor, where S=Symbolize, C=Compute and A=Articulate. By crossing *task direction* and *steps,* there are six different question types. The 4th column defines what we call the *attempt* at a question type. The number appearing in the attempt column is the number of times the problem type has been presented during the scenario. For example, the first time one of the six question types is asked, the attempt for that question will be "1". Notice how on row 7, the attempt is "2" because it's the second time a *one-step compute* question has been asked for that scenario identifier. For another example see rows 3 and 7. Also notice that on line 20 the attempt column indicates a first attempt at a two-step symbolize problem for the new scenario identifier.

Notice that on row 5 and 7, the same question is asked twice. If the student did not get the problem correct at line 7, Ms Lindquist would have given a further hint of presenting six possible choices for the answer. For our modeling purposes, we will ignore the exact number of attempts the student had to make at any given question. Only the first attempt *in a sequence* will be included in the data set. For example, this is indicated in Table 1, in the 7th row of the 5th column, where the "F" for false indicates that row will be excluded from the data set.

The 6th column has the exact dialog that the student and tutor had. The 7th and 8th columns are grouped together because they are both outcomes that we will try to predict.[2] Columns 9-16 show what statisticians call the *design matrix*, which maps the possible observations onto the fixed effect (independent) coefficients. Each of these columns will get a coefficient in the logistic regression. Columns 9-12 show the *difficulty* parameters, while columns 13-16 show the *learning* parameters. We only list the four knowledge components of the *Base+ Model*, and leave out the four different ways to deal with composition. The *difficulty* parameters are simply the knowledge components identified in the transfer model. The *learning* parameter is calculated by counting the number of previous attempts a particular knowledge component has been learned (we assume learning occurs each time the system gives feedback on a correct answer). Notice that these learning parameters are strictly increasing as we move down the table, indicating that students' performance should be monotonically increasing.

Notice that the question asked of the student on row 3 is the same as the one on row 9, yet the problem is easier to answer after the system has given feedback on "the distance rowed is 120". Therefore the difficulty parameters are adjusted in row 9, column 9 and 10, to reflect the fact that if the student had already received positive feedback on those knowledge components. By using this technique we make the credit-blame assignment problem easier for the logistic regression because the number of knowledge components that could be blamed for a wrong answer had been reduced. Notice that because of this method with the difficulty parameters, we also had to adjust the learning parameters, as shown by the crossed out learning parame-

[2] Currently, we are only predicting whether the response was correct or not, but later we will do a Multivariate logistic regression to take into account the time required for the student to respond.

ters. Notice that the learning parameters are **not** reset on line 20 when a new scenario was started because the learning parameters extend across all the problems a student does.

1.4 How the Logistic Regression Was Applied

With some minor changes, Table 1 shows a snippet of what the data set looked like that we sent to the statistical package to perform the logistic regression. We performed a logistic regressions predicting the dependent variable *response* (column 8) based on the independent variables on the knowledge components (i.e., columns 9-16). For some of the results we present, we also add a student specific column (we used a student's pretest score) to help control for the variability due to students differing incoming knowledge.

2 Procedure for the Stepwise Removal of Model Parameters

This section discusses how a fit model is made parsimonious by a stepwise elimination of extraneous coefficients. We only wanted to include in our models those variables that were reasonable and statistically significant. The first criterion of reasonableness was used to exclude a model that had "negative" learning curves that predict students would do worse over time. The second criterion of being statistically significant was used to remove, in a stepwise manner, coefficients that were not statistically significant (those coefficients with t-values between 2 and –2 is a rule of thumb used for this). We choose, somewhat arbitrarily, to first remove the learning parameters before looking at the difficulty parameters. We made this choice because the learning parameters seemed to be, possibly, more contentious. At each step, we chose to remove the parameter that had the least significance (i.e., the smallest absolute t-value).

A systematic approach to evaluating a model's performance (in terms of error rate) is essential to comparing how well several models built from a training set would perform on an independent test set.

We used two different was of evaluating the resulting models: BIC and a k-holdout strategy. The Bayesian Information Criterion is one method that is used for model selection [17] that tries to balance goodness of fit with the number of parameters used in the model. Intuitively, BIC, penalizes models that have more parameters. Differences in BIC greater than 6 between models are said to be strong evidence while differences of greater than 10 is said to be very strong (See [2] for another example of cognitive model selection using BIC for model selection in this way.)

We also used a k-holdout strategy that worked as follows. The standard way of predicting the error rate of a model given a single, fixed sample is to use a stratified k-fold cross-validation (we choose k=10). Stratification is simply the process of randomly selecting the instances used for training and testing. Because the model we are trying to build makes use of a student's successive attempts, it seemed sensible to randomly select whole students rather than individual instances. Ten fold implies the training and testing procedure occurs ten times. The stratification process created a testing set by randomly selecting one-tenth of the students not having appeared in a prior testing set. This procedure was repeated ten times in order to have included each student in a testing set exactly once.

A model was then constructed for each of the training sets using a logistic regression with the student response as the dependent variable. Each fitted model was used to predict the student response on the corresponding testing set. The prediction for each instance can be interpreted as the model's fit probability that a student's response was correct (indicated by a "1"). To associate the classification with the bivariate class attribute, the prediction was rounded up or down depending if it was greater or less than 0.5. The predictions were then compared to the actual response and the total number of correctly classified instances were divided by the total number of instances to determine the overall classification accuracy for that particular testing set.

3 Results

We summarize the results of our model construction, with Table 2 showing the results of models we attempted to construct. To answer Question 1, we compared the *Base Model* to the *Base+ Model* that added the *articulate one-step* KC. After applying our criterion for eliminating non-statistically significant parameters we were left with just two difficulty parameters for the *Base Model* (all models in Table 2 also had the very statistically significant pretest parameter).

Table 2. Models Computed: BIC and K-holdout evaluation, and the KC in each unique model

	Models	
Name	Base	Base +
Model #	0	1
BIC	2508.9	2493.7
Overall Evaluation	59.6%	64.3%
KCs	Comprehending one-step	Articulating-one-step
	Articulating variable	Articulating variable
		Arithmetic

It turned out that the *Base+ Model* did a better statistically significant better job (smaller BIC are better) than the *Base Model* in terms of BIC (the difference was great than 10 BIC points suggesting a statistically significant difference). The *Base+ Model* also did better when using the K-holdout strategy (59.6% vs 64.3%). We see from Table 2 that the *Base+ Model* eliminated the *comprehending one-step* KC and added instead the *articulating one-step* and *arithmetic* KCs suggesting that "articulating" does a better job than comprehension as the way to model what is hard about word problems.

So after concluding that there was good evidence for *articulating one-step*, we then computed Models 2-4. We found that two of the four ways of trying to model composition resulted in models that were inferior in terms of BIC and not much different in terms of the K-holdout strategies. We found that models 4 and 5 were reduced to the *Base+ Model* by the step-wise elimination procedure. We also tried to calculate the effect of combining any two of the four composition KCs but all such attempts were reduced by the step-wise elimination procedure to already found models. This suggests that for the set of tutorial log files we used, there was not sufficient evidence to argue for the *composition of articulation* over other ways of modeling the composition effect.

It should be noted that while none of the learning parameters of any of the knowledge components were in any of the final models (thus creating models that predict no learning over time) we should note that on models 4 and 5, the last parameter that was eliminated was a *learning* parameters that both had t-test values that were within a very small margin of being statistically significant (t=1.97 and t=1.84). It should also be noted that in Heffernan [8] the learning within Experiment 3 was only close to being statistically significant. That might explain why we do not find any statistically significant learning parameters.

We feel that Question 1 ("Is there evidence from tutorial log files that support the conjecture that the *articulating one-step* KC really exists?") is answered in the affirmative, but Question 2 ("What is the best way to model the composition effect") has not been answered definitely either way. All of the models that tried to explicitly model a composition KC did not lead to significantly better models. So it is still an open question of how to best model the composition effect.

4 Conclusions

This paper presented a methodology for evaluating models of transfer. Using this methodology we have been able to compare different plausible models. We think that this method of constructing transfer models and checking for parsimonious models against student data is a powerful tool for building cognitive models.

A limitation of this techniques is that the results depend on what curriculum (i.e., the problems presented to students, and the order in which that happened) the students were presented with during their course of study. If students were presented with a different sequence of problems, then there is no guarantee of being able to draw the same conclusions.

We think that using transfer models could be an important tool to use in building and designing cognitive models, particularly where learning and transfer are of interest. We think that this methodology makes a few reasonable assumptions (the most important being the Power Law of Learning). We think the results in this paper show that this methodology could be used to answer interesting cognitive science questions.

References

1. Anderson, J. R., & Lebiere, C. (1998). *The Atomic Components of Thought.* Lawrence Erlbaum Associates, Mahwah, NJ.
2. Baker, R.S., Corbett, A.T., Koedinger, K.R. (2003) Statistical Techniques for Comparing ACT-R Models of Cognitive Performance. Presented at 10th Annual ACT-R Workshop.
3. Corbett, A. T. and Anderson, J. A. (1992) Knowledge tracing in the ACT programming tutor. In: Proceedings of 14-th Annual Conference of the Cognitive Science Society.
4. Corbett, A. T., Anderson, J. R., & O'Brien, A. T. (1995) Student modeling in the ACT programming tutor. Chapter 2 in P. Nichols, S. Chipman, & R. Brennan, *Cognitively Diagnostic Assessment.* Hillsdale, NJ: Erlbaum.
5. Draney, K. L., Pirolli, P., & Wilson, M. (1995). A measurement model for a complex cognitive skill. In P. Nichols, S. Chipman, & R. Brennan, *Cognitively Diagnostic Assessment.* Hillsdale, NJ: Erlbaum.
6. Embretson, S. E. & Reise, S. P. (2000) Item Response Theory for Psychologists Lawrence Erlbaum Assoc.
7. Heffernan, N. T. (2001). *Intelligent Tutoring Systems have Forgotten the Tutor: Adding a Cognitive Model of an Experienced Human Tutor.* Dissertation & Technical Report. Carnegie Mellon University, Computer Science, http://www.algebratutor.org/pubs.html.
8. Heffernan, N. T. (2003) *Web-Based Evaluations Showing both Cognitive and Motivational Benefits of the Ms. Lindquist Tutor* 11th International Conference Artificial Intelligence in Education. Syndey. Australia.
9. Heffernan, N. T., & Koedinger, K. R.(1997) The composition effect in symbolizing: the role of symbol production versus text comprehension. In *Proceeding of the Nineteenth Annual Conference of the Cognitive Science Society* (pp. 307-312). Hillsdale, NJ: Lawrence Erlbaum Associates.
10. Heffernan, N. T., & Koedinger, K. R. (1998) A developmental model for algebra symbolization: The results of a difficulty factors assessment. *Proceedings of the Twentieth Annual Conference of the Cognitive Science Society*, (pp. 484-489) Hillsdale, NJ: Lawrence Erlbaum Associates.
11. Junker, B., Koedinger, K. R., & Trottini, M. (2000). Finding improvements in student models for intelligent tutoring systems via variable selection for a linear logistic test model. Presented at the Annual North American Meeting of the Psychometric Society, Vancouver, BC, Canada. http://lib.stat.cmu.edu/~brian/bjtrs.html
12. Koedinger, K. R. & Junker, B. (1999). Learning Factors Analysis: Mining student-tutor interactions to optimize instruction. Presented at Social Science Data Infrastructure Conference. New York University. November, 12-13, 1999.
13. Koedinger, K.R., & MacLaren, B. A. (2002). Developing a pedagogical domain theory of early algebra problem solving. CMU-HCII Tech Report 02-100. Accessible via http://reports-archive.adm.cs.cmu.edu/hcii.html.
14. Nathan, M. J., Kintsch, W. & Young, E. (1992). A theory of algebra-word-problem comprehension and its implications for the design of learning environments. *Cognition & Instruction* 9(4): 329-389.
15. Nathan, M. J., & Koedinger, K. R. (2000). Teachers' and researchers' beliefs about the development of algebraic reasoning. *Journal for Research in Mathematics Education*, 31, 168-190.
16. Newell, A., & Rosenbloom, P. (1981) Mechanisms of skill acquisition and the law of practice. In Anderson (ed.), *Cognitive Skills and Their Acquisition.*, Hillsdale, NJ: Erlbaum.
17. Raftery, A.E. (1995) Bayesian model selection in social research. *Sociological Methodology* (Peter V. Marsden, ed.), Cambridge, Mass.: Blackwells, pp. 111-196 .

Towards Shared Understanding of Metacognitive Skill and Facilitating Its Development

Michiko Kayashima[1], Akiko Inaba[2], and Riichiro Mizoguchi[2]

[1] Tamagawa University, 6-1-1 Tamagawagakuen, Machida, Tokyo, 194-8610 Japan
kayasima@lit.tamagawa.ac.jp

[2] I.S.I.R., Osaka University, 8-1 Mihogaoka, Ibaraki, Osaka, 567-0047 Japan
{ina, miz}@ei.sanken.osaka-u.ac.jp
http://www.ei.sanken.osaka-u.ac.jp/

Abstract. Our research objective is to organize existing learning strategies and systems to support the development of learners' metacognitive skill. It is difficult to organize them because the term metacognition itself is mysterious and ambiguous. In order to achieve the objective, we first organize activities in cognitive skill and metacognitive skill. It enables us to reveal what activity existing learning strategies and systems support as metacognitive skill or what activity they do not support. Next, we simplify existing learning strategies and systems by ontology. It helps us to understand what of learning strategies and support systems is respectively different, and what of them is respectively similar. It will contribute to a part of an instructional design process.

1 Introduction

Recently many researchers who are convinced that metacognition has relevance to intelligence [1,26], are shifting their attention from the theoretical to practical educational issues. As a result of this shift, researchers are designing a number of effective learning strategies [15,16,23,24,25] and computer based learning systems [5,6,8,20] to facilitate the development of learners' metacognition.

However, there is one critical problem encountered in these strategies and systems: the concept of metacognition is ambiguous and mysterious [2,4,18]. There are several terms currently used to describe the same basic phenomenon (e.g., self-regulation, executive control). The varied phenomena that have been subsumed under the term, metacognition, are described. Also cognitive and metacognitive functions are often used interchangeably in the literature [2,4,7,15,16,17,18,19,22,27]. The ambiguity mainly comes from the following three reasons: (1)it is difficult to distinguish metacognition from cognition; (2)metacognition has been used to refer to two distinct area of research: knowledge about cognition and regulation of cognition; and (3)there are four historical roots to the inquiry of metacognition [2].

With this ambiguous definition of "metacognition", we cannot answer the crucial questions concerning existing learning strategies or systems: what they have supported, or not; what is difficult for them to support; why it is difficult; and essentially what is the distinction between cognition and metacognition. In order to answer these questions, we first should clarify how many concepts are subsumed

J.C. Lester et al. (Eds.): ITS 2004, LNCS 3220, pp. 251–261, 2004.

under the term metacognition and how each of these concepts depend upon each other. This clarification enable us to consider the goals for learning strategies, and systems to support the development of learners' metacognition; what and why it is difficult to achieve each of these goals; and how we eliminate difficulties in achieving each of the goals using strategies and support systems.

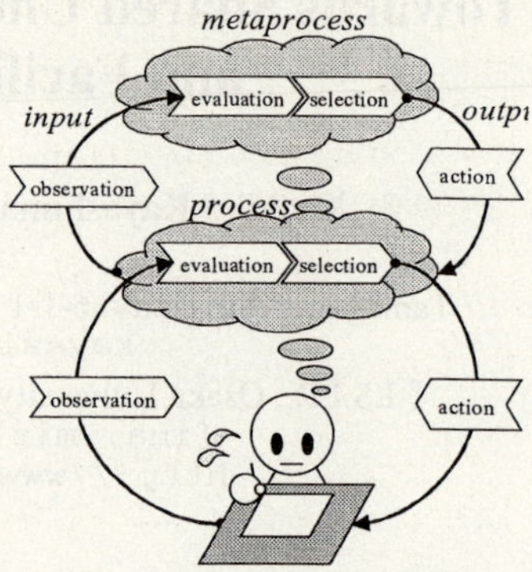

Fig. 1. Double Loop Model

Our research objective is to organize existing learning strategies and systems to facilitate the development of learners' metacognition which is not knowledge about cognition, but regulation of cognition that we call metacognitive skill. In this paper, we organize activities in cognitive skill and metacognitive skill for the understanding of metacognitive skill, with correspondence to all of the varied and diverse activities that have been subsumed under the heading of metacognition. By giving target activities of each existing learing strategies and systems a label corresponding to the organized activities, we can share the understanding of them each other. Existing strategies and systems adopt mainly collaborative learning or interaction with computer systems as a learning style. Moreover, we simplify existing learning strategies and systems by using the frame of Inaba's "Learning Goal Ontology" [9,10]. It helps us to understand what of learning strategies and support systems is respectively different, and what of them is respectively similar. For example, one strategy may have the same goal as another strategy but supporting methods may differ.

2 Activities in Cognitive Skill and Metacognitive Skill

We organize activities in cognitive skill and metacognitive skill based on a *double loop model* which we propose to define activities of metacognitive skill and cognitive skill in a similar manner using two layers of mind: the cognitive and metacognitive layers as seen in Fig. 1[11,12,13,14]. Within these two layers of mind and the outside world, we integrate activities of the layers into two kinds of activities: input of information from the external layer and output of it to the internal layer; and the processing of information at the internal layer.

In terms of the two kinds of activities and the target of the activity, we categorize activities of cognitive skill and metacognitive skill as seen in Table 1. Each of the skills is subdivided into two activities: we regard the cognitive skill as Basic Cognition and Cognitive Activity; the metacognitive skill as Basic Metacognition and Metacognitive Activity. Basic cognition and basic metacognition respectively include "Observation", basic cognition and basic metacognition respectively encompass "Evaluation", "Selection", and "Action/Output" as an activity.

Table 1. Activities in Cognitive Skill and Metacognitive Skill

Activity	Definition of activity	Target of activity	Denomination	Skill
Observation	To input information from the external layer and output it to the internal layer.	Information at the external layer	Basic cognition	Cognitive skill
			Basic Metacognition	Metacognitive skill
Evaluation	To process information at the internal layer.	Information at the internal layer	Cognitive activity	Cognitive skill
Selection			Metacognitive activity	Metacognitive skill
Output				

Observation as basic cognition is to take information from the outside world into working memory (WM) at the cognitive layer. As a result, a state or a sequence of states is generated in WM at the cognitive layer. Evaluation and Selection as cognitive activity is to evaluate the sequence of states in WM, select actions from a knowledge base, and create an action-list. Consequently, a state or a sequence of states in WM at the cognitive layer is transformed. Output as cognitive activity is to output actions in an action-list as behavior. Observation as basic metacognition is to take information of cognitive activities and information in WM at the cognitive layer into WM at the metacognitive layer. As a result, a state or a sequence of states in WM at the metacognitive layer is transformed. Evaluation and Selection are to evaluate states in WM at the metacognitive layer, select actions from a knowledge base, and form actions to regulate cognitive activities at the cognitive layer as an action-list. In this way, a state or a sequence of states in WM at the metacognitive layer is transformed. Output as metacognitive activity is to perform actions in an action-list to regulate cognitive activities at the cognitive layer. As a result, cognitive activities at the cognitive layer are changed.

We clarify the target activities of learning strategies and systems by consideration of the correspondence of organized activities in Table 1 to target activities. Consider a learner's activity with Error-Based Simulation (we abbreviate it as EBS) [8] and the Reflection Assistant (we abbreviate it as RA) [5, 6]. EBS is a behavior simulation generated from an erroneous equation for mechanics problems. The strange behavior in an EBS makes the error in the equation clear and gives the learner a motivation to reflect, and provides opportunities that a learner monitors his/her previous cognitive activity objectively. RA consists of three phases to help learners do three reflective activities; understanding of goals and given facts of the problem; recalling previous knowledge; organizing the problem, and thinking about strategies to solve the problem. These reflective activities allow learners to identify knowledge about problem solving; strategically encode the nature of the problem and form a mental representation of its elements; select appropriate strategies depending on the mental representation. Based on the organized activities in cognitive skill and metacognitive skill, RA facilitates learners' basic cognition and cognitive activities while EBS facilitates metacognitive activities.

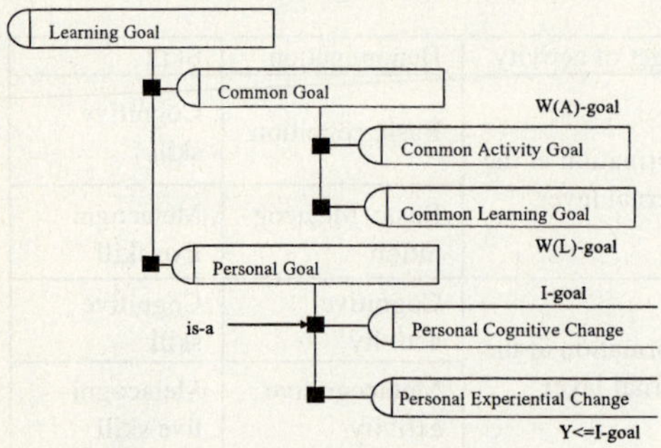

Fig. 2. Learning Goal Ontology

We should consider support systems and methods to facilitate learners' mastering activities of metacognitive skills in light of the target of the activity and how the activity is performed, because these would influence the weight of the cognitive load of the activity, and the difficulty to master the activity [12,13,14]. Concerning cognitive load, it would increase in the following order: basic cognition, cognitive activity, basic metacognition, and metacognitive activity. The cognitive load of basic cognition would read (Observation) only, while cognitive activity would read, operate, and write. The cognitive load of basic metacognition and metacognitive activity would be higher, because the activities are involved in complicated activities: allocating one's mental resources for the activities of basic cognition, cognitive activity, basic metacognition, or metacognitive activity while engaging basic cognition or cognitive activity. Clarifying target activities within organized activities in Table 1 is important in understanding the difficulty in mastering skills, and to select appropriate learning strategies.

3 Learning Goal Ontology for Metacognitive Skill

In this section, we represent concepts of learning strategies and support systems which support the development of metacognitive skills. The concepts are described using the frame of Inaba's "Learning Goal Ontology." Utilizing the ontology and approximate models for representing the learning theories, we can simplify learning strategies and support systems, helping in their understanding. Of course, this understanding is partial and rough in comparison with the knowledge base of learning strategies and systems. However, it would be useful for understanding difference between strategies, which strategies are effective for development of a learner's metacognitive skill, etc.

First, we describe briefly Inaba's "Learning Goal Ontology" [9, 10]. As Fig.2 shows, "Learning Goal" is divided into two kinds of goals: "common goal" relates to the group as a whole, and "personal goal" refers to the individual learner's goal. The "personal goal" is also subdivided into two types of goals: the goal represented as a change of learner's knowledge/cognitive states (I-goal), and the goal attained by interaction with others (Y<=I-goal). Similarly, the "common goal" is subdivided into two kinds of goals: activity goal for the whole group (W(A)-goal), and learning development goal for the whole group (W(L)-goal).

We pick up four learning strategies; two from the strategies and two from learning support systems which help the development of learners' metacognitive skills: ASK to THINK–TEL WHY (we abbreviate as AT) [15,16], reciprocal teaching (we abbreviate as RT)[23], RA [5,6] and EBS [8].

Table 2. I-goals

I-goal		Definition	Source
Development of Cognitive Skill	Other regulation	To infer others' cognitive activities from their behaviors, evaluate them, and ask a question or advise others on how to regulate their cognitive activities.	[15,16,23, 24]
	Reference	To refer to similar problems and strategies, solve, and verify the solution.	[5, 6]
Development of Metacognitive Skill	Awareness	To be aware of one's own mistakes.	[8]

Table 3. Y<=I-goals

Y<=I goal	Definition	Source
Learning by Trial and Error	Learning by applying various knowledge or skill to other learners and guiding the learners.	[15, 16]
Learning. by Self-expression	Learning by externalizing self-thinking process, such as self-explanation and presentation.	[15, 16]
Learning by Awareness	Learn by being aware of one's own mistakes.	[8]
Learning by Practice	Learn by demonstrating knowledge or skill to other learners and guiding the learner.	[23, 24]
Learning by Discussion	Learn by demonstrating knowledge or skill to other learners.	[23, 24]
Learning by Referring	Learn by referring to similar problems	[5, 6]

Table 4. W(L)-goals

W(L)-goal	Definition	Source
Comprehension	Setting up the situation for comprehending expository text.	[15,16,23,24]
Problem-Solving	Setting up the situation for solving some problem.	[5, 6, 8]

We identify goals for these learning strategies and systems for each of the four categories: I-goal, Y<=I-goal, W(A)-goal, and W(L)-goal. For I-goal, we adopt Inaba's classification of I-goals for collaborative learning: acquisition of content specific knowledge, development of cognitive skills, development of metacognitive skills, and development of skill for self-expression. Each I-goal has a developmental stage. The I-goal "acquisition of content specific knowledge" has three phases of learning: accretion, tuning, and restructuring. Each I-goal of skill learning has three stages: cognitive stage, associative stage, and an autonomous stage.

Table 5. W(A)-goals

W(Activity)-goal	Definition	Source
Setting up the situation for ASK to THINK–TEL WHY	Setting up the situation where a learner is assigned a "Questioner" role and the other learner is assigned a "Teller" role.	[15, 16]
Setting up the situation for reciprocal teaching	Setting up the situation where a learner is assigned a "Dialogue Leader" role and a teacher is assigned a "Facilitator" role.	[23, 24]
Setting up the situation for using Reflection Assistant	Setting up the situation where learners interact with the Reflection Assistant.	[5, 6]
Setting up the situation for using EBS	Setting up the situation where learners can interact with the EBS.	[8]

We identify the concept of development of cognitive skill and metacognitive skill in detail based on our organized activities in Table 1. As Table 2 shows, in the two learning theories and two support systems for development of metacognitive skills, there are three I-goals: "Other regulation", "Reference" and "Awareness". Our organized activities reveal that "Other regulation" and "Reference" are cognitive skills while "Awareness" is a metacognitive skill, which is explained below.

"Other regulation" infers others' cognitive activities from their behaviors, evaluates them, and asks a question or advises others on how to regulate their cognitive activities. The target of the activity is other learners' cognitive activities, that is, it is the world outside of the person. The activity is to observe the outside world, encode its result into the WM at the cognitive layer, evaluate the state, select what to do next, and perform it. "Other regulation" is thus classified as basic cognition and cognitive activity.

"Reference" refers to problems in which a given problem is similar, solved with referring to similar problems and verifying the solution by a learner him/herself. For "Reference", the target of the activity is the outside world. The activity is to observe a given problem, encode its result into the WM at the cognitive layer, refer to similar problems and their answer which are presented by a support system, apply them, and check the answer by a learner him/herself. For "Reference", the activities are to form knowledge like a schema, that is, to acquire meta-knowledge. These are classified as basic cognition and cognitive activities.

The difference between "Other regulation" and "Reference" can be explained by our organized activities. There are four activities: observation, evaluation, selection and output as parts of cognitive skill. Although the observation and evaluation of "Other regulation" and "Reference" are almost alike, the selection of "Other regulation" is different from the selection of "Reference." The former is to select activities to regulate other's cognitive activities; while the latter is to select activities to reform a learner's own knowledge.

"Awareness" is to be aware of one's own mistakes, and hopefully to trace one's own cognitive activities back to their causes. According to our organized activities, "Awareness" is a trigger to provoke the observation state in WM and cognitive activities at the cognitive layer. So, we categorize "Awareness" as a metacognitive skill.

To achieve I-goals, a learner is expected to achieve at least one of Y<=I-goals. Y<=I-goals are achieved through interaction with other learners, a teacher or computer systems based on learning strategies and learning systems. Table 3 shows Y<=I-goals. For example, to achieve the I-goal "Other regulation (Associative stage)", some learners could follow the Y<=I-goal "Learning by Practice", while some learners could take Y<=I-goals "Learning by Trial and Error" to achieve the I-goal "Other regulation (Cognitive stage)." Table 4 shows the W(L)-goals, and Table 5 shows W(A)-goals. To achieve Y<=I-goals, a learner is expected to achieve W(A)-goals with W(L)-goals. AT and RT have text comprehension as W(L)-goal, while RA and EBS have problem-solving as W(L)-goal.

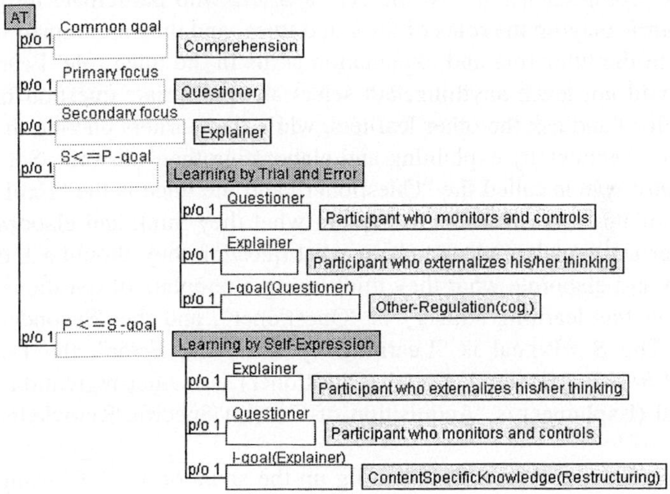

Fig. 3. ASK to THINK–TEL WHY (AT)

4 Conceptual Structure of W(A)-Goal

Two learning strategies: both AT and RT provide learners with support not only to comprehend a text but also to develop their metacognitive skills. Using the structure shown in Fig. 2, we show what these strategies support; the difference between the strategies; and the commonalities of the strategies.

Fig. 3 represents the W(A)-goal "Setting up the situation for AT" using the structure shown in Fig. 2. W(A)-goal basically consists of a common goal, a Primary focus, and a Secondary focus, S<=P-goal and P<=S-goal. The conceptual structure of W(A)-goal does not contain all elements representing learning strategies and systems, but rather essential elements to make the learning session effective. W(A)-goal represents an activity within the whole group: i.e. what activity the group performs. The common goal is a W(L)-goal which is the common learning goal every member shares. The Primary focus and Secondary focus are specific to role-players in the group. The P<=S-goal and S<=P-goal are interaction goals among group members, that is, a type of Y<=I-goal. The S<=P-goal is the goal of the person who participates in the learning session as the Primary focus to interact with the learners who play a role as Secondary focus, while P<=S-goal is the goal of the person who plays a Secondary focus role to interact with the learners who play a Primary focus role. Y<=I–goal consists of three parts: "I-role", "You-role" and "I-goal". I-role is a role to attain the Y<=I-goal. A member who plays I-role (I-member) is expected to attain his/her I-goal by attaining the Y<=I-goal. You-role means a role as a partner for the I-member. I-goal (I) is an I-goal which defines what the I-member attains. (For more details, please see [9,10])

The AT has been used to comprehend science and social studies material. Its W(L)-goal is "Comprehension." At the AT, learners who participate in the learning session take turns playing the roles of tutor and tutee, and they are trained in question-asking skills in the tutor role and explanation skills in the tutee role. Learners in the tutor role should not teach anything, but select an appropriate question from a template of questions and ask the other learners, while the learners playing the tutee role respond to the questions by explaining and elaborating their answers. So, the learner playing the tutor role is called the "Questioner" and the tutee is the "Explainer". The questioner regulates other learners to explain what they think and elaborate upon it. The questioner acquires knowledge about what question they should ask other learners to explain and elaborate what they think using a template of questions. The "Primary focus" in this learning strategy is "Questioner", and the "Secondary Role" is "Explainer". The S<=P-goal is "Learning by Trial and Error", the P<=S-goal is "Learning by Self-Expression." I-goal (Questioner) is "Other-regulation (Cognitive stage)", I-goal (Explainer) is "Acquisition of Content Specific Knowledge (Restructuring)."

Fig. 4 represents the W(A)-goal "Setting up the situation for RT" using the structure shown in Fig. 2. The RT has been used to understand an expository text. Its W(L)-goal is also "Comprehension." At the RT, members in a group take turns in leading a dialogue concerning sections of a text, and generate summaries and predictions and in clarifying misleading or complex sections of the text. Initially, the teacher demonstrates activities as a dialogue leader, and then provides each learner who plays a role of a dialogue leader with guidance and feedback at the appropriate level. The learner who plays the role mimics teacher's activities, that is, a leader practices what he learned through observing the teacher's demonstration. Other members in the group discuss about questions of a dialogue leader and the gist of what has been read. In the form of discussion, members' thinking is externalized. So, the form of discussion helps a dialogue leader to monitor other members' comprehension, and also promotes other members to elaborate their comprehension each other. Thus, a member who leads a dialogue is called the "Dialogue Leader" and other members in a group are the "Discussant." A dialogue leader promotes others' comprehensive monitoring and regulation. The discussants promote their comprehension. The "Primary focus" in this learning strategy is "Dialogue Leader", and the"Secondary Role" is "Discussant". The S<=P-goal is "Learning by Practice", the P<=S-goal is "Learning by Discussion". I-goal (Dialogue Leader) is "Other-Regulation (associative stage)" and I-goal (Discussant) is "Acquisition of Content

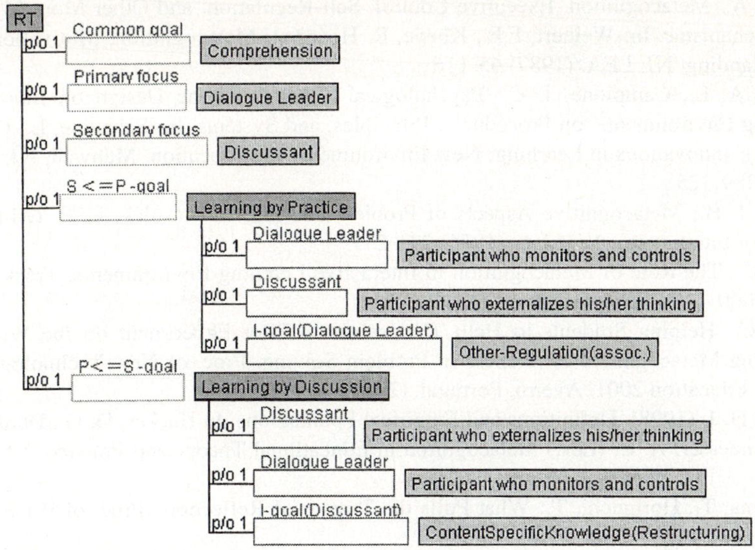

Fig. 4. Reciprocal Teaching (RT)

Specific Knowledge (Restructuring)." Based on the conceptual structure of a W(A)-goal, the distinction between AT and RT is made clear. Also it is clear that what activity both AT and RT support is not learners' metacognitive skill but cognitive skill.

5 Conclusion

The ambiguity of the term metacognition raises issues in support of the development of a learners' metacognitive skill. To clarify this ambiguity, we have organized activities that cover a variety of activities pertaining to metacognitive skill. Based on the organized activities, we can clarify what activity learners master by using learning strategies and support systems. In this paper, we show that the activity which some computer-based systems support, which has been subsumed under the heading metacognition, is actually cognitive activity. Also, we explained existing learning strategies and support systems which support the development of learners' metacognitive skill in relationship to Learning Goal Ontology.

In the future, we would like to identify learning goals that are proposed in other existing learning strategies and learning support systems using the organized activities in cognitive skill and metacognitive skill, and represent them with the Learning Goal Ontology.

References

1. Borkowski, J., Carr, M., & Pressely, M.: "Spontaneous" Strategy Use: Perspectives from Metacognitive Theory. Intelligence, vol. 11. (1987) 61-75

2. Brown, A.: Metacognition, Executive Control, Self-Regulation, and Other More Mysterious Mechanisms. In: Weinert, F.E., Kluwe, R. H. (eds.): Metacognition, Motivation, and Understanding. NJ: LEA. (1987) 65-116
3. Brown, A. L., Campione, J. C.: Psychological Theory and the Design on Innovative Learning Environments: on Procedures, Principles, and Systems. In: Schauble, L., Glaser, R. (eds.): Innovations in Learning: New Environments for Education. Mahwah, NJ: LEA. (1996) 289-325
4. Flavell, J. H.: Metacognitive Aspects of Problem-Solving. In: Resnick, L. B. (ed.): The Nature of Intelligence. NJ: LEA. (1976) 231-235
5. Gama, C.: The Role of Metacognition in Interactive Learning Environments, Track Proc. of ITS2000 – Young Researchers. (2000)
6. Gama, C.: Helping Students to Help Themselves: a Pilot Experiment on the Ways of Increasing Metacognitive Awareness in Problem Solving. Proc. of New Technologies in Science Education 2001. Aveiro, Portugal. (2001)
7. Hacher, D. J. (1998). Definitions and Empirical Fpundations. In Hacker, D. G., Dunlosky, J. and Graesser, A. C. (Eds.) Metacogniton in Educational Theory and Practice. NJ:LEA. 1-23.
8. Hirashima, T., Horiguchi, T.: What Pulls the Trigger of Reflection? Proc. of ICCE2001. (2001)
9. Inaba, A., Supnithi, T., Ikeda, M., Mizoguchi, R., Toyoda, J.: How Can We Form Effective Collaborative Learning Groups? – Theoretical Justification of "Opportunistic Group Formation" with Ontological Engineering. Proc. of ITS2000. (2000)
10. Inaba, A., Supnithi, T., Ikeda, M., Mizoguchi, R., Toyoda, J.: Is a Learning Theory Harmonious With Others? Proc. of ICCE2000. (2000)
11. Kayashima, M., Inaba, A.: How Computers Help a Learner to Master Self-Regulation Skill? Proc. of Computer Support for Collaborative Learning 2003. (2003)
12. Kayashima, M., Inaba, A.: Difficulties in Mastering Self-Regulation Skill and Supporting Methodologies. Proc. of the International AIED Conference 2003. (2003)
13. Kayashima, M., Inaba, A.: Towards Helping Learners Master Self-Regulation Skills. Supplementary Proc. of the International AIED Conference, 2003. (2003)
14. Kayashima, M., Inaba, A.: The Model of Metacognitive Skill and How to Facilitate Development of the Skill. Proc. of ICCE Conference 2003. (2003)
15. King, A.: ASK to THINK-TEL WHY: a Model of Transactive Peer Tutoring for Scaffolding Higher Level Complex Learning. Educational Psychologist. 32(4). (1997) 221-235
16. King, A.: Discourse Patterns for Mediating Peer Learning. In: O'Donnell A.M., King, A. (eds.): Cognitive Perspectives on Peer Learning. NJ: LEA. (1999) 87-115
17. Kluwe, R. H.: Cognitive Knowledge and Executive Control: Metacognition. In: Griffin, D. R. (ed.): Animal Mind - Human Mind. New York: Springer-Verlag. (1982) 201-224
18. Livingston, J. A.: Metacognition: an Overview. http://www.gse.buffalo.edu/fas/shuell/cep564/Metacog.htm. (1997)
19. Lories, G., Dardenne, B., Yzerbyt, V. Y.: From Social Cognition to Metacognition. In: Yzerbyt, V. Y., Lories, G., Dardenne, B. (eds.): Metacognition. SAGE Publications Ltd. (1998) 1-15
20. Mathan, S. & Koedinger, K. R.: Recasting the Feedback Debate: Benefits of Tutoring Error Detection and Correction Skills. Proc. of the International AIED Conference 2003. (2003)
21. Mizoguchi, R., Bourdeau, J.: Using Ontological Engineering to Overcome Common AI-ED Problems. IJAIED, vol. 11. (2000)

22. Nelson, T. O. & Narens, L.: Why Investigate Metacognition? In: Metcalfe, J., Shimamura, A.P. (eds.): Metacognition. MIT Press. (1994). 1-25.
23. Palincsar, A. S., Brown, A.: Reciprocal Teaching of Comprehension - Fostering and Comprehension Monitoring Activities. Cognitive and Instruction. 1(2). (1984) 117-175
24. Palincsar, A.S., Herrenkohl, L.R.: Designing Collaborative Contexts: Lessons from Three Research Programs. In: O'Donnell, A. M., King, A. (eds.): Cognitive Perspectives on Peer Learning. Mahwah, NJ: LEA. (1999) 151-177
25. Schoenfeld, A. H.: What's All the Fuss about Metacognition? In: Shoenfeld, A. H. (ed.): Cognitive Science and Mathematics Education. LEA. (1987) 189-215
26. Sternberg, R. J.: Inside Intelligence. American Scientist, 74. (1986) 137-143.
27. Yzerbyt, V. Y., Lories, G., Dardenne, B.: Metacognition: Cognitive and Social Dimension. London: SAGE. (1998)

Analyzing Discourse Structure to Coordinate Educational Forums

Marco Aurélio Gerosa, Mariano Gomes Pimentel, Hugo Fuks, and Carlos Lucena

Computer Science Department, Catholic University of Rio de Janeiro (PUC-Rio)
R. M. S. Vicente, 225, Rio de Janeiro, Brazil - 22453-900
{gerosa, mariano, hugo, lucena}@inf.puc-rio.br

Abstract. In this paper, aspects related to discourse structure like message chaining, message date and categorization are used by teachers to coordinate educational forums in the AulaNet environment. These aspects can be computationally analyzed without having to inspect the content of each message. This analysis could be applied to forums in other educational environments.

1 Introduction

As an asynchronous communication tool, a forum makes it possible for learners to participate at their own pace while allowing them more time to think. However, educational environments still do not offer computational aids that are appropriate for coordinating forums. The majority of the environments present a typical implementation that does not take into account educational aspects and it remains up to the teacher (without specific computational support) to collect and analyze the information that is necessary to coordinate group discussion.

Coordination is the effort needed to organize a group to enable it to work as a team in a manner that channels communication and cooperation towards the group's objective [8]. When coordinating a group discussion in a forum, among other factors the teacher must be prepared to ensure that all of the learners are participating, that the contributions add value to the discussion, that the conversation does not go off on non-productive tangents and that good contributions are encouraged.

This article focuses on message chaining, categorization and timestamp. These message attributes help in the coordination of educational forums without the teacher inspecting the content of individual messages and in a manner that allows computational support for this

In a forum, where messages are structured hierarchically (tree), it is possible to obtain indications about the depth of the discussion and the level of interaction by observing the form of this tree. Measurements such as the average depth level and percentage of leaves provide indications about how a discussion is going. Message categorization can also help to identify the types of messages, making a separate analysis of each message type possible. By analyzing the date that messages were sent, among other factors it is possible to identify the amount of time between the

J.C. Lester et al. (Eds.): ITS 2004, LNCS 3220, pp. 262–272, 2004.

sending of messages, the day of the week and the hour expected for messages to be sent. Comparing this data also makes it possible to obtain other information, such as the type of message expected per level, how fast the tree grows, which types of messages are answered more quickly, etc. Based upon these aspects, the course coordinator can evaluate how a discussion is evolving, giving him enough time to redirect the discussion and, for example, to check up on the effects of his interventions.

The AulaNet environment supports the creation of educational forums, as presented in Section 2. The Information Technology Applied to Education (ITAE) course, which provided the data for the analyses presented in this article, also is discussed in this section. Section 3 shows the analyses about discourse structure. Section 4 concludes the article.

2 The Conferences Service in the AulaNet Environment

The AulaNet is an environment based on a groupware approach for teaching-learning via the Web that has been under development since June 1997 by the Software Engineering Laboratory of the Catholic University of Rio de Janeiro (PUC-Rio). The AulaNet is freeware and is available in Portuguese, English and Spanish versions at groupware.les.inf.puc-rio.br and www.eduweb.com.br.

The Information Technology Applied to Education (ITAE) course has been taught since 1998 on the Computer Science Department of PUC-Rio. This course is being taught entirely at a distance through the AulaNet environment. Its objective is to get learners to collaborate using information technology, becoming Web-based educators [2]. The course seeks to build a learning network [5] where the group learns, mainly, through the interaction of its participants in collaborative learning activities.

The ITAE is organized by subject, with one topic discussed per week. Learners read selected content relating to the topic, conduct research to expand their knowledge and participate in a discussion about specific questions of the subject being studied. The discussion is carried out over three consecutive days using the AulaNet's Conferences service.

In the ITAE, the role of transmitting information and leading the discussion, which generally is an attribute of course mediators, is shared with learners. A learner is selected in each conference to play of the role of the *seminar leader*, being responsible for preparing a seminar message followed by three questions, used by group members to develop their argumentation. During this phase, the seminar leader is responsible for keeping the discussion going and maintaining the conference's dynamics.

Each Conference message is evaluated and commented upon individually by the course's mediators in order to provide guidance to learners about how to build knowledge and prepare their texts; the idea is to avoid the sending in of contributions that do not add value to the group. The problems that are encountered in the contributions are commented upon in the message itself, generally in a form that is visible to all participants, so that the learners better understand where they can improve and what they have gotten right.

3 Coordination of Educational Forums

Analyses about message chaining, categorization and timestamp are presented in this section, showing how these factors can help in the coordination of educational forums. The data and examples were collected from five editions of the ITAE course.

3.1 Message Chaining

Communication tools have different ways of structuring messages: linear (list), hierarchical (tree) or network (graph), as can be seen in Figure 1. Despite the fact that a list is a specific case of a tree, and this is a particular type of graph, no one structure is always better than another. Linear structuring is appropriate for communication in which chronological order is more important than any eventual relationships between the messages, such as the sending of notices, reports and news. Hierarchical structuring is appropriate for viewing the width and the depth of the discussion, making it possible to structure messages sharing the same subject on the same branch. However, since there is no way to link a message between one branch and another, the tree can only grow and, thus, the discussion takes place in diverging lines [9]. Network structuring can be used to seek convergence of the discussion.

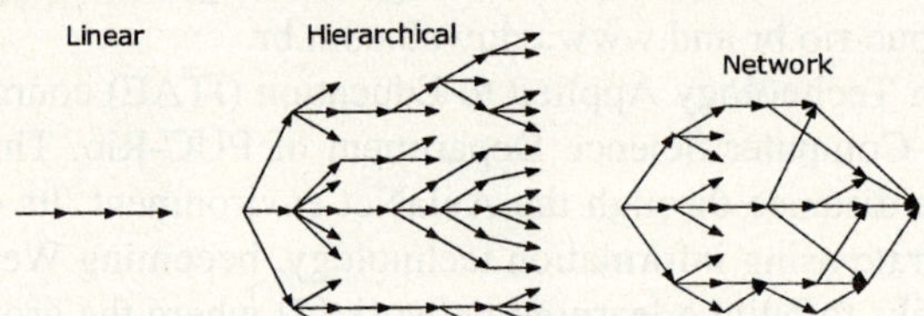

Fig. 1. Examples of discussion structure

The forum has a hierarchical structure. In the ITAE, the forum, based on the Conferences service, is used for the in-depth discussion of the course's subject matter. The AulaNet makes it possible for the author of the message, at the moment he or she is preparing it, to select a category from a set that have been previously defined by the course coordinator [3]. The available categories available in the ITAE course, used to identify the message type, are *Seminar*, *Question*, *Argumentation*, *Counter-Argumentation* and *Clarification*, originally based on the IBIS' node types [1]. According to the dynamics of the course, at the beginning of each week a previously selected learner posts a message from the *Seminar* category to serve as the root of the discussion, as well as three messages from the *Question* category. During the following 50 hours, all learners answer to and discuss these questions.

The format of the resulting tree indicates the depth of the discussion, thus, the level of interaction [7]. For example, a tree that has only three levels indicates that there was almost no interaction, given that level zero is the seminar, level one comprises the questions and level two comprises the answers to the questions. That means the learners only answered the questions without discussing the ideas with each other. The trees extracted from the conferences of the five editions of the ITAE course are shown in Figure 2.

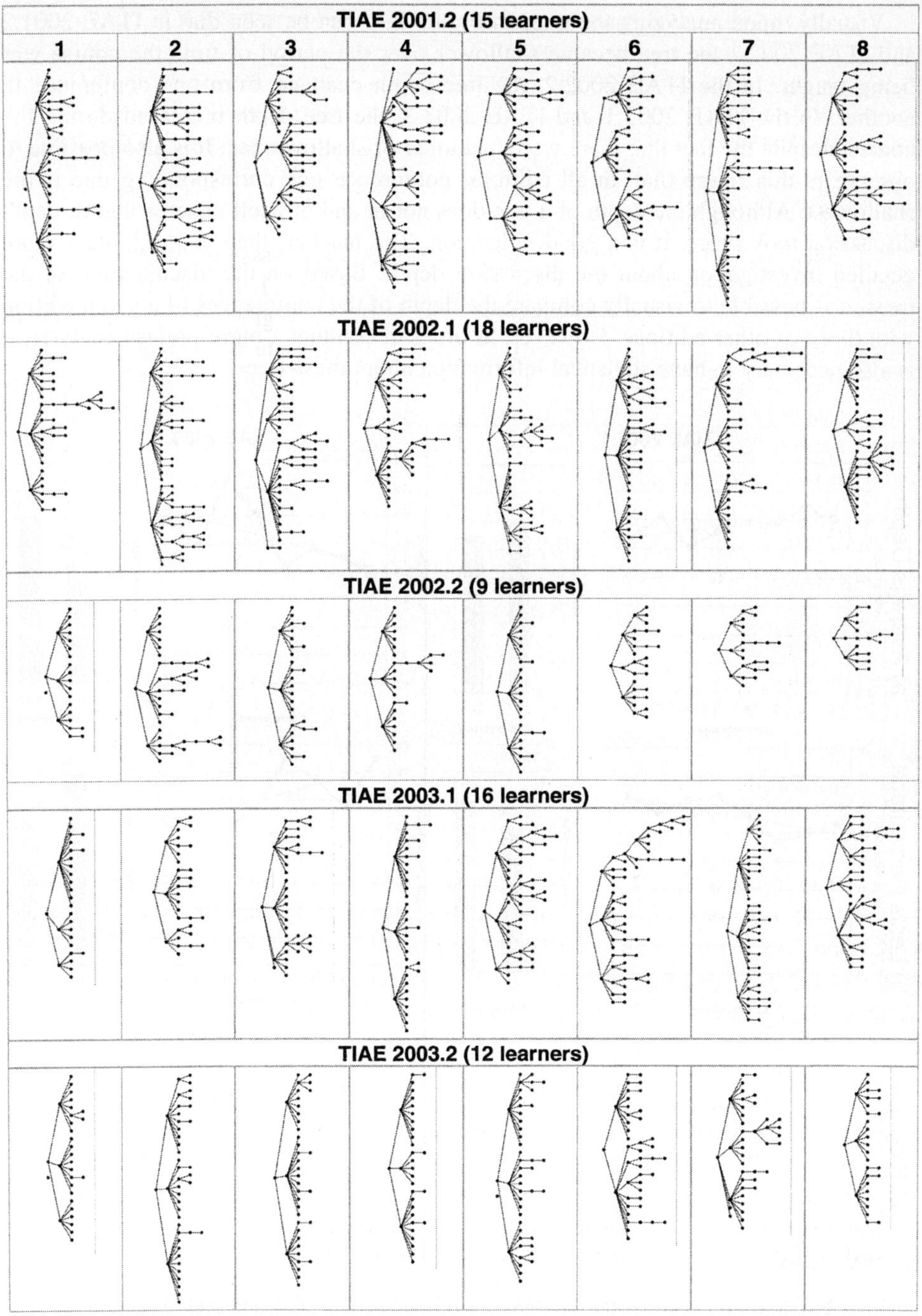

Fig. 2. Trees extracted from the Conferences of the five editions of the ITAE course

Visually, upon analyzing the trees in Figure 2, it can be seen that in ITAE 2001.2 and ITAE 2002.1 the tree became shallower over the period of time the course was being taught. In the ITAE 2002.2, the tree depth changed from one conference to another. In the ITAE 2003.1 and ITAE 2003.2, the tree depth increased during the course, despite the fact that there were a number of shallow trees. It is also possible to observe in this figure that, in all editions, conference one corresponding tree is the shallowest. Although the depth of a tree does not in and of itself ensures that in-depth discussion took place, it is a good indication. The teacher, then, can initiate a more detailed investigation about the discussion depth. Based on the visualization of the trees, it is possible to visually compare the depth of the conferences of a given edition with those of other editions. However, in order to conduct a more precise analysis, it is also necessary to have statistical information about these trees.

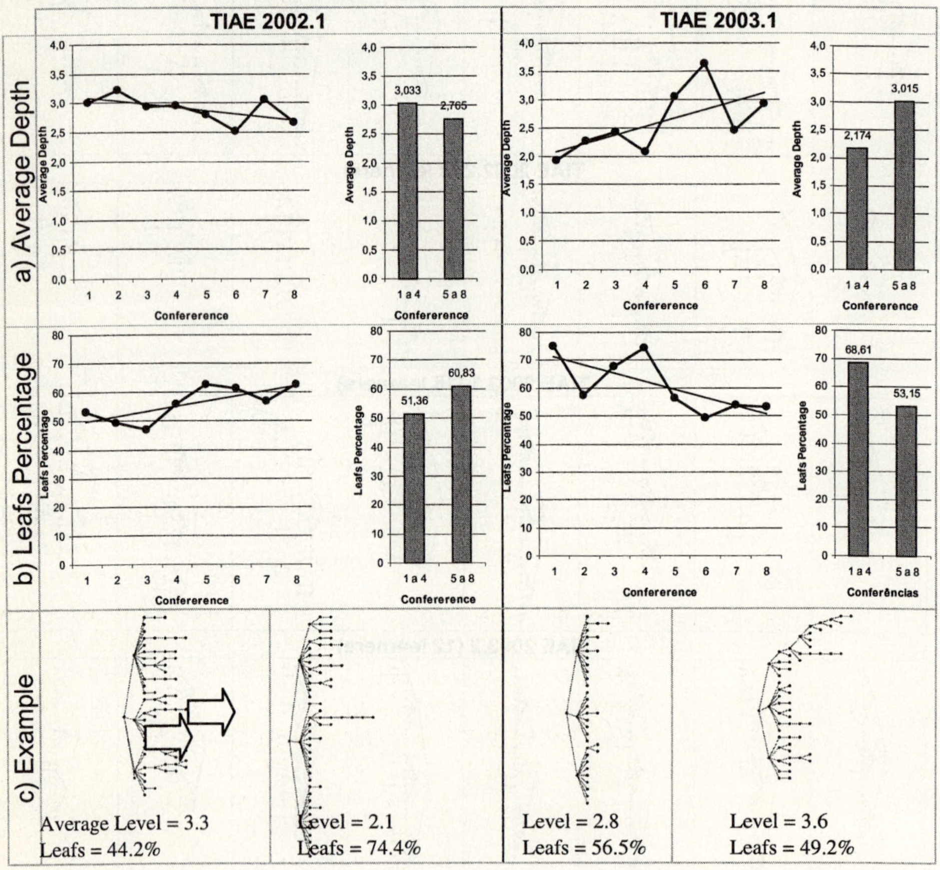

Fig. 3. Comparison of the Conferences of the ITAE 2002.1 and 2003.1 editions

It can be seen in Figure 3 that the average depth of the tree in the ITAE 2002.1 edition declined while the percentage of messages without answers (leaves) increased, which indicates that learners were having diminishing interaction as the course advanced. In this edition, in the first four Conferences the average level of the tree was 3.0 and the percentage of messages without answers was 51%; in the last four Conferences, the average tree level was 2.8 and the leaves were 61%. For its part, in the ITAE 2003.1, learners interacted more over the course of the conferences: the tree corresponding to the discussion was getting deeper while the percentage of messages without answers was decreasing. The average level was 2.2 in the first four Conferences, increasing to 3.0 in the last four Conferences, while the percentage of messages without answers went from 69% in the first four Conferences to 53% in the last four. Figure 3 also presents a comparison between a conference at the beginning and another at the end of each one of these editions, emphasizing their difference. The trees shown in Figure 2 and the charts in Figure 3 indicate that the interaction on ITAE 2002.1 edition declined over the course of the conferences, while the interaction on ITAE 2003.1 edition increased.

All of this data was obtained without having to inspect the content of the messages. Comparing the evolution of the form and of the information about the trees in the course allows teachers to intervene when they perceive that the level of interaction has fallen or when the Conference is not reaching the desired depth level. Next in Figure 4 is shown the expected quantity of messages per level.

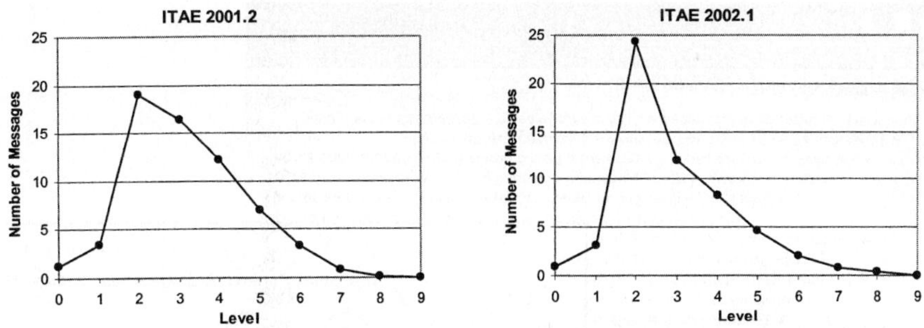

Fig. 4. Average quantity of messages per tree level corresponding to the conferences

A peak in the average quantity of messages at level 2 can be seen in Figure 4. In level 0, where just a seminar message is expected (sent by a learner at the beginning of the week), there is an average of one message in each tree of the course editions analyzed. In level 1, there is an average of 3 messages, which are the three questions proposed by the seminar leader. In level 2, where the arguments are sent in response to the questions, there is a peak in the quantity of messages. In level 3 and thereafter if the quantity of messages of the tree in any given Conference departs significantly from this standard, the teacher should investigate to check what is happening.

3.2 Message Categorization

Upon preparing a message, the author chooses the category that is most appropriate to the content being developed, providing a semantic aspect to the relationship between the messages. The AulaNet does not force the adoption of fixed sets of categories.

The coordinating teacher—the one who plans the course—can adjust the category set to the objectives and characteristics of the group and the tasks.

Upon viewing the messages of a Conference, participants immediately realize the category to which the message belongs (between brackets) together with its title, author and date. Thus, it is possible to estimate how the discussion is progressing and what is the probable content of the messages. The AulaNet also implements reports about the utilization of the categories per participant, in order to facilitate the future refining of the category set and to obtain indications about the characteristics of the participants and their compliance with tasks. Categorization also helps organize the discussion in a manner that favors decision making and maintenance of communication memory [2].

The categories adopted in the ITAE Conferences reflect the course dynamics. They are: *Seminar*, for the root message of the discussion, posted by the seminar leader at the beginning of the week; *Question*, to propose discussion topics, also posted by the seminar leader; *Argumentation*, to answer the questions, offering the author's point of view in the message subject line and the arguments for it in the body of the message; *Counter-Argumentation*, to be used when the author states a position that is contrary to an argument; and finally, *Clarification*, to request or clarify doubts about a specific message.

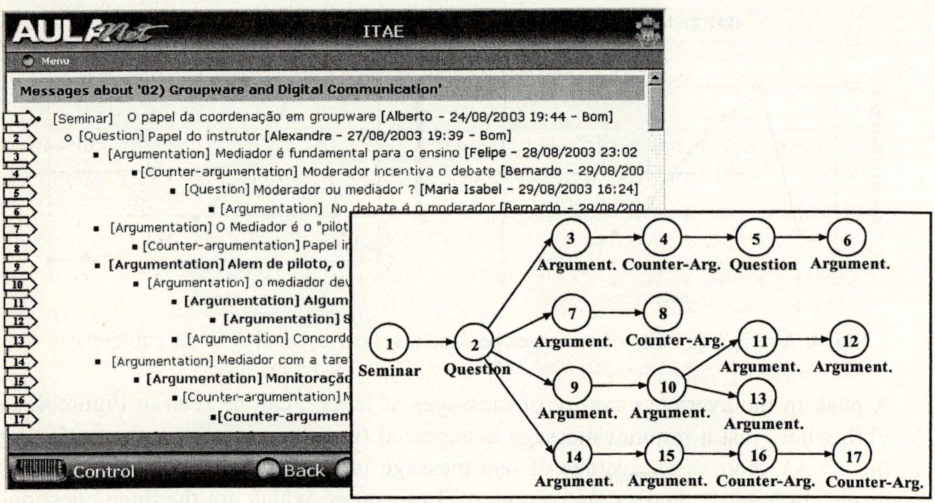

Fig. 5. Tree derived from a Conference

Figure 5 presents a portion of dialogue from a Conference with numbered messages and a tree equivalent of this portion. Looking at the categories, it is possible to perceive the semantics of the relationships between these messages. For example, message 4 is a counter-argument to message 3; 5 questions 4; 6 answers to the question posted by 5 through an argument; and so forth.

It is also possible to identify the differences between messages of different categories. For example, in this article, level three categories were analyzed taking into account their grades and quantity of characters.

As previously explained, the *Seminar* category is used in the first message of the Conference (level 0); next, three messages from the *Question* category are associated with level 1; and the answers to the *Argumentation* category appear on level 2. As of level 3, messages from all of the categories can appear, with the exception of the *Seminar* category. Figure 6 presents the percentage of messages of each category on the different tree levels of the ITAE course edition. As expected, one can observe that on level 0 (the tree root), the predominant category is *Seminar*, on level 1 it is *Question*, and on level 2 it is *Argumentation*. The *Counter-Argumentation* category begins to appear on level 3; the use of the *Clarification* category begins to appear as of level 1 (it is possible to clarify a seminar or a question). Those messages whose relationship between the category and the level differ from what has been described, normally, derive from choosing the wrong category.

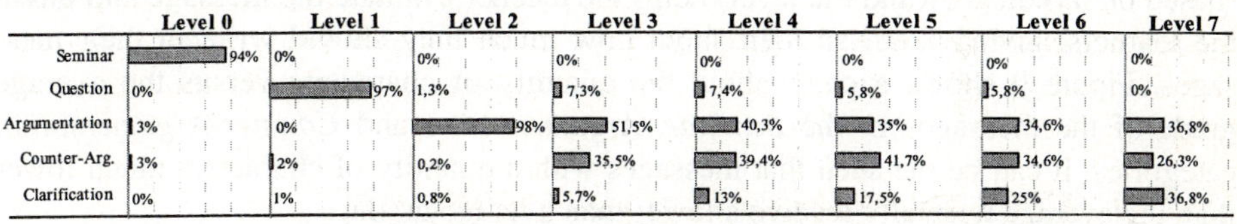

Fig. 6. Percentage of utilization of the categories per tree level

Message size also has a different expected value for each one of the categories, given that each category has its own objectives and semantic. Figure 7 presents the average values of characters for its category and average deviations. In this figure one can see that the *Seminar* category is the one having the largest messages, followed by *Argumentation* and *Counter-Argumentation.* The shortest messages are those in the *Question* and *Clarification* categories.

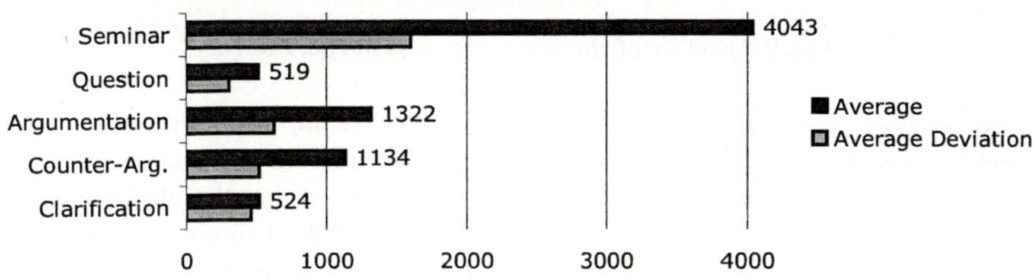

Fig. 7. Quantity of characters per category

At some point, during the course, one of the ITAE learners said: "When we counter-argue we can be more succinct, since the subject matter already is known to all." This statement is in keeping with the chart in Figure 7. If the subject is known to all (it was presented during the previous messages) the author can go directly to the point that interests him or her. Somehow, this also can be noted in the chart in Figure 8, which presents a decline in the average quantity of the characters per level in the *Argumentation* (correlation = -80%) and *Counter-Argumentation* (correlation = -93%) categories.

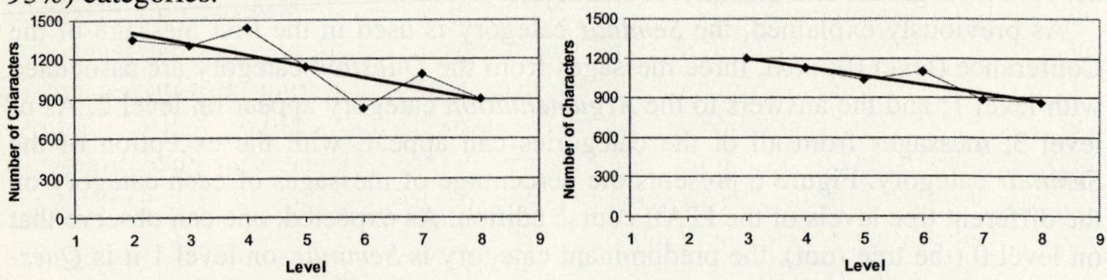

a) Argumentation Category

b) Conter-Argumentation Category

Fig. 8. Quantity of characters in the messages per level

Knowing in advanced the quantity of characters expected for a given message (based on its category and the level) helps the teacher evaluate the message and orient the learners, giving them an idea about how much they should write in their messages. Figure 9 shows a chart about the quantity of characters versus the average grade of the messages in the *Seminar*, *Argumentation* and *Counter-Argumentation* categories. It can be the seen that messages with a quantity of characters much lower than the average normally receive a lower than average grade.

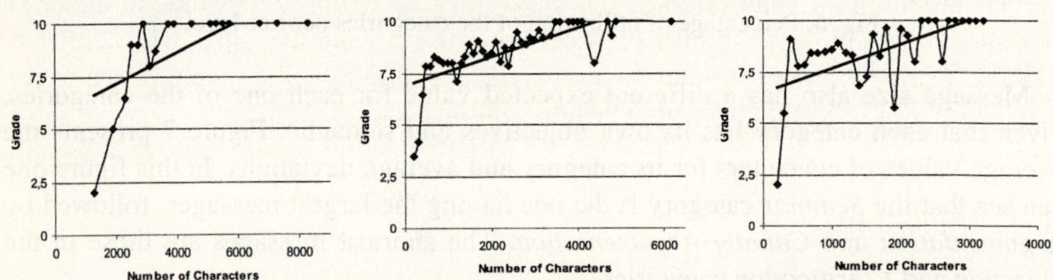

a) Seminar

b) Argumentation

c) Conter-Argumentation

Fig. 9. Quantity of characters versus grade per category

The category also helps to identify the direction that the discussion is taking. For example, in a tree or a branch only containing argumentation messages, there is probably no idea confrontation taking place. It is expected that the clashing of ideas helps to involve more participants into the discussion, thus, bringing up confronting points of view. Similarly, excessive counter-argumentation should attract mediator's attention. The group might be getting too involved into a controversy or, even worst, there may be interpersonal conflicts taking place.

3.3 Message Timestamp

On the ITAE course, the Conference takes place over 50 hours: from 12 noon Monday to 2 p.m. Wednesday. Over the course of these hours, learners post messages answering questions and arguments and counter-arguments to previous messages.

Figure 10 presents the frequency of the messages sent during the Conferences of the ITAE 2003.2 edition. On this edition, it can be seen that almost half of the message total was sent during the last five hours of the Conference. This phenomenon of students waiting until the last moment possible to carry out their tasks is well known and has been dubbed "Student Syndrome" [4].

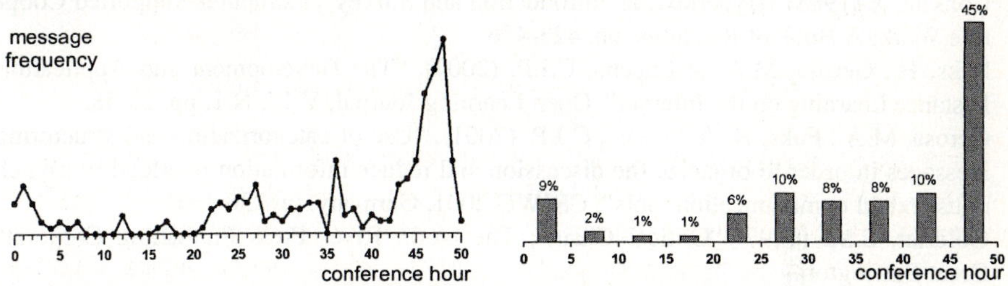

Fig. 10. Frequency of messages over the course of the conferences of the ITAE 2003.2 edition

The last-minute behavior observed in Figure 10 reminds the teacher to encourage earlier sending in of contributions. The act of sending contributions near to the deadline disturbs an in-depth discussion, given that last-minute messages will neither be graded during the discussion nor be answered. This might be the reason for an excessive amount of leaves on the trees in some conferences.

4 Conclusion

Message chaining, categorization and message timestamp are factors that help in the coordination of educational forums within ITAE. Based upon the form established by message chaining, it is possible to infer the level of interaction among course participants. Message categorization provides semantics to the way messages are connected, helping to identify the accomplishment of tasks, identification of incorrectly message nesting and the direction the discussion is taking. The analysis of message timestamp makes it possible to identify the Student Syndrome phenomenon, which gets in the way of the development of an in-depth discussion and the orientation provided by an evaluation of the messages.

By analyzing the characteristics of the messages, teachers are able to better coordinate learners, knowing when to intervene in order to keep the discussion from moving in an unwanted direction. Furthermore, these analyses could be used to develop filter for intelligent coordination and mechanisms for error reduction. It should be emphasized that these quantitative analyses provide to the teachers indications and alerts about situations where problems exist and where the discussion is going well. However, final decision and judgment are still up to the teacher.

Finally, discourse structure and message categorization also help to organize the recording of the dialogue, facilitating its subsequent recovery. Based upon the tree form, with the help of the categories, it is possible to obtain visual information about the structure of the discussion [6]. Teachers using collaborative learning environments to carry out their activities should take these factors into account for the better coordination of educational forums.

References

1. Conklin, J. (1988) "Hypertext: an introduction and Survey", Computer Supported Cooperative Work: A Book of Readings, pp. 423-476
2. Fuks, H., Gerosa, M.A. & Lucena, C.J.P. (2002), "The Development and Application of Distance Learning on the Internet", Open Learning Journal, V.17, N.1, pp. 23-38.
3. Gerosa, M.A., Fuks, H. & Lucena, C.J.P. (2001), "Use of categorization and structuring of messages in order to organize the discussion and reduce information overload in asynchronous textual communication tools", CRIWG 2001, Germany, pp 136-141.
4. Goldratt, E.M. (1997) "Critical Chain", The North River Press Publishing Corporation, Great Barrington.
5. Harasim, L., Hiltz, S. R., Teles, L., & Turoff, M. (1997) "Learning networks: A field guide to teaching and online learning", 3rd ed., MIT Press, 1997.
6. Kirschner, P.A., Shum, S.J.B. & Carr, C.S. (eds), Visualizing Argumentation: Software Tools for Collaborative and Educational Sense-Making, Springer, 2003.
7. Pimentel, M. G., Sampaio, F. F. (2002) "Comunicografia", Revista Brasileira de Informática na Educação - SBC, v. 10, n. 1. Porto Alegre, Brasil.
8. Raposo, A.B. & Fuks, H. (2002) "Defining Task Interdependencies and Coordination Mechanisms for Collaborative Systems", Cooperative Systems Design, IOS Press, 88-103.
9. Stahl, G. (2001) "WebGuide: Guiding collaborative learning on the Web with perspectives", Journal of Interactive Media in Education, 2001.

Intellectual Reputation to Find an Appropriate Person for a Role in Creation and Inheritance of Organizational Intellect

Yusuke Hayashi and Mitsuru Ikeda

School of Knowledge Science, Japan Advanced Institute of Science and Technology
1-1 Asahidai, Tatsunokuchi, Nomi, Ishikawa, 9231211, Japan
{yusuke, ikeda}@jaist.ac.jp

Abstract. Humans act collaboratively in a community with mutual understanding of others' roles in the context of an activity. Collaboration is not productive when mutual understanding is insufficient. This paper proposes "Intellectual Reputation" as a recommendation that is useful to find a right person for a right role in the creation and inheritance of organizational intellect. Intellectual reputation defines what is expected of an organization member to fully satisfy a role in the organizational intellect formation process. It can provide valuable awareness information for organization members to find an appropriate person for a given role in the creation and inheritance of organizational intellect. This paper explains the concept of intellectual reputation and the way to generate it. First, this paper describes requirements to generate Intellectual reputation and introduce models filling the requirements. Then, it explains a generation mechanism of intellectual reputation and how the models work in the mechanism.

1 Introduction

In daily life, humans act collaboratively in a community with mutual understanding of others' roles in the context of that activity. Nevertheless, that collaboration is not productive when mutual understanding is insufficient.

As Hood pointed out [6], we mutually realize others' roles in a community from activities they have engaged in. Perception is important to perform mutual collaboration. Perception and estimation of roles can be called "Reputation." Carter et al. [2] discuss the concept of "reputation" in the field of multi-agent systems, referring to Goffman's analogy of identity management to the dramatic world of the theater [3]. The audience has certain expectations of roles for actors. Reputation is constructed based on the audience's belief that the actors have fully satisfied their roles. If the audience judges that actors have met their roles, they are rewarded with positive reputation.

In this study, along similar lines of thought, reputation defines what is expected of an organization member to fully satisfy a role in the formative process of the organizational intellect. Reputation can constitute valuable awareness information for

J.C. Lester et al. (Eds.): ITS 2004, LNCS 3220, pp. 273–284, 2004.

finding an appropriate person for a given role in organizational intellect creation and inheritance.

There is growing concern with IT support for community members to share the context of collaborative activity and to manage it successfully. Ogata et al. defined awareness of one's own or another's knowledge as "Knowledge awareness" and developed Sherlock II, which supports group formation for collaborative learning based on learners' initiatives with knowledge awareness [11]. The ScholOnt project by Buckingham et al. aims at supporting an academic community [1]. They clarify norms of academic exchange and have been developing an information system to raise mutual awareness of roles in academic activity. Such awareness information indicates others' behaviors to document in document sharing or claim-making.

This research is intended to provide more valuable awareness information based on an interpretation of the user's behavior in terms of a model of organizational intellect for creation and inheritance This paper proposes "Intellectual Reputation, (IR)," which is a recommendation to find an appropriate person for a given role in the creation and inheritance of organizational intellect.

This paper is organized as the following. Section 2 introduces the framework of organizational memory as the basis of considering IR. Section 3 describes the concept of IR. Section 4 presents a definition and mechanism of IR with an example. Section 5 summarizes this paper.

2 Organizational Memory

Figure 1 shows a rough sketch of the organizational memory concept. In an organization, there are organization members with their intellect and vehicles stored in the vehicle repository. A vehicle, e.g. document, learning contents, and bulletin board, and so on, represents intellect and mediates it among people. Communicating with each other through vehicles, the organizational members create and inherit organizational intellects in organizational activity.

The essential idea of this study is that such a support system is composed not only of information systems, but also of organizational members. The concept emphasizes that having an intellect means not only merely knowing something, but also digesting it through creation or practical use. It also means that the intellect cannot be separated from a person because it includes skill and competency. For those reasons, it is difficult to manage intellect directly, even though we would like to do so. To reach that solution, this study aims to support creation and inheritance of organizational intellect by managing information concerning the intellect.

We can communicate intellect with narrow limits, for example, what kind of intellect is there, or who or which vehicle is related to an intellect. These correspond to *Member profile*, *Intellect profile*, and *Vehicle profile* in Fig. 1. This study proposes models to connect persons, intellects and vehicles and use of the models for awareness information to increase accessibility to intellect even if we can not externalize them at all.

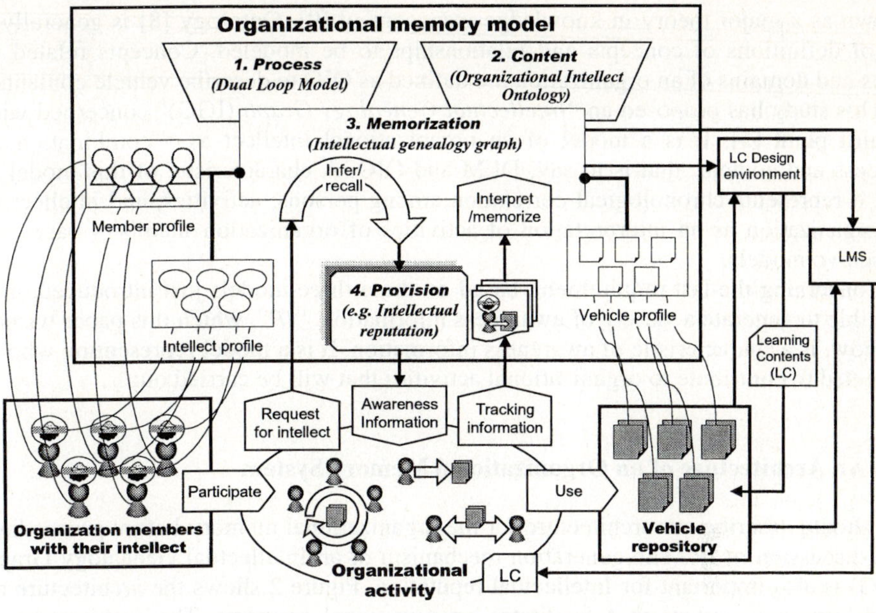

Fig. 1. An overview of an organizational memory

2.1 Models for Observing and Helping the Formative Process of Organizational Intellect

We must consider models that satisfy the following requirements to achieve the goal stated above.

1. Models must set a desirable process for each organization from abstract to concrete activities. The desirable process can be a guideline for members to ascertain the way they should behave in the organization and can form the basis of design for information systems that are aware of the process.
2. Models must establish the basis for each organization member to understand intellect in the organization. The basis arranges mutual understanding among the members and support system in addition to the members.
3. Models must memorize intellect in terms not only of meaning, but also in terms of the formative process. The formative process is important information to understand, manage, and use intellects appropriately in the organization.
4. Models must provide information for organization members to be aware of organizational intellect. That helps members to make decisions about planning activities.

This study has proposed models addressing the first three points so far.

"*Dual loop model* (DLM)" and "*Organizational intellect ontology* (OIO)" address the first and second points, respectively [4]. Simply put, DLM describes an ideal process of creation and inheritance of an organizational intellect from both viewpoints of the 'individual' as the substantial actor in an organization, and the 'organization' as the aggregation of individuals. This model is based on the SECI model and is well known as a major theory in knowledge management [9]. Ontology [8] is generally a set of definitions of concepts and relationships to be modeled. Concepts related to tasks and domains of an organization are defined as OIO to describe vehicle contents.

This study has proposed an "*Intellectual Genealogy Graph* (IGG)" concerned with a third point [5]. It is a model of an organizational intellect as a combination of process and content; that is to say, DLM and OIO. A characteristic of this model is that it represents chronological correlation among persons, activities, and intellect in an organization as an interpretation of activities of organization members based on these two models.

Concerning the last requirement, based on these three models just introduced, it is possible to generate a variety of awareness information. "*IR*", which this paper wishes to show, is a characteristic of awareness information. It is a model representing who is expected to contribute to organizational activities that will be carried out.

2.2 An Architecture of an Organizational Memory System

We should describe our architecture for the organizational memory before proceeding to a discussion of IR. The generation mechanism of an Intellectual Genealogy Graph (IGG) is also important for Intellectual reputation. Figure 2 shows the architecture of an information system that facilitates organizational memory. The architecture is presumed to consist of a server and clients. The server manages information about organizational intellect. The organization members get information needed for their activity from the server through user interfaces. As an embodiment of this architecture, we have developed a support environment for the creation and inheritance of organizational intellect: Kfarm. For details of that support environment, please see references [4, 9, 10]. Herein, we specifically address the generation and use of the IGG and IR.

The middle of Fig. 2 presents the IGG. That graph has the following three levels:

- *Personal level* (PL) describes interpersonal activity and the status of intellect concerned with it.
- *Interaction level* (IL) describes interaction among members and their roles in that interaction using PL description.
- *Organizational level* (OL) describes the activity and status of intellect in terms of organization using PL and IL description.

The input for generation of IGG is a time-series of vehicle level activities tracked through user interfaces. That time-series is a series of actions: e.g., drawing up a document, having a discussion with it and then revising it. Vehicles used in the activities are stored in the vehicle repository. The vehicle level data are transformed to IGG by the reasoning engine, which is indicated on the right of Fig. 2. The reasoning engine has three types of rule bases corresponding to the three levels of IGG. The rule bases are developed based on *DLM ontology*, which is a conceptualization of DLM. The rule base for the personal level (PLRB) is based on Personal Loop in DLM. The rule bases for the interaction level and the organizational level (ILRB and OLRB) are based on the organizational loop in DLM. Each model level is generated by applying the rules to the lower level of a model or models. For example, the organizational level model is generated from the personal level one and interactive level one. The IGG is modeled based on these rule bases.

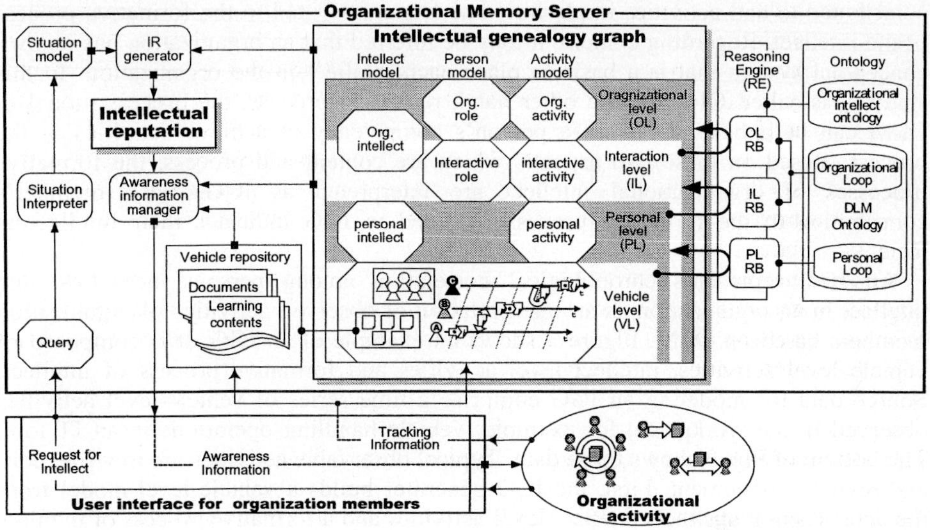

Fig. 2. Architecture of an information system for the organizational memory

The left of Fig. 2 represents IR as one way to use the IGG. The next chapter contains a more complete discussion of that process along with the concept of IR.

3 Intellectual Reputation

This section presents discussion of how to meet the fourth requirement mentioned in the previous section. The essential concept is IR, which is recommendation by organizational memory. The IR provides supportive evidence to identify a person who can play a suitable role to the current context.

We next introduce the "Intellectual Role", which is a conceptualization of actors who carry out important activities in the formative process of organizational intellect. Two reasons exist for considering Intellectual Role. One is to form a basis for describing each member and vehicle's contribution to the formative process of an organizational intellect at the abstract level. The other is to establish criteria for estimating which person can fill a role in an activity that will be carried out in an organization. First, this section explains IGG in terms of the former significance and then discusses the concept of IR in terms of the latter.

3.1 Intellectual Genealogy Graph as the Basis of Generation of Intellectual Reputation

In this study, Intellectual Roles each member played in the past are extracted from records of their activities based on DLM. One characteristic is that the performance of the formative process of organizational intellect can be viewed as having two aspects: contents and activities. Contents imply which field of work that person has contributed to and activities imply how one has contributed to the formative process of the intellect. Regarding content, it may be inferred that an organization has its own conceptual system that is a basis to place each intellect in the organization. In this study, it is called OIO. On the other hand, regarding process, the process model of DLM can be a basis to assess a person's competency to achieve activities in the process. Based on these two aspects, which are content and process, the formative processes of organizational intellect are interpreted as IGG. Each member's contribution to the formative process recorded in IGG indicates their Intellectual Role.

An IGG represents chronological correlation among persons, activities, and intellect in an organization as an interpretation of observed activities of organization members based on DLM. Figure 3 shows an example of an IGG. It is composed of vehicle level activities, intellect level activities and formative process of intellect. Source data for modeling an IGG comprise a time series of vehicle-level activities observed in the workplace, for example, vehicle handling operations in an IT tool. The bottom of Fig. 3 shows those data. Typical observable activities are to write, edit, and review a document. First, the IGG generator builds a vehicle-level model from the data. Then, it abstracts intellect level activities and a formative process of intellect from the vehicle level based on DLM.

IGG offers the following three types of interpretation for generating IR:

- *Interpretation of content and status of intellect:* The content and status of intellect are shown as formative process of intellect at the upper left of Fig. 3. Organizational intellect ontology is a representation of an organization's own conceptual system which each organization possesses either implicitly or

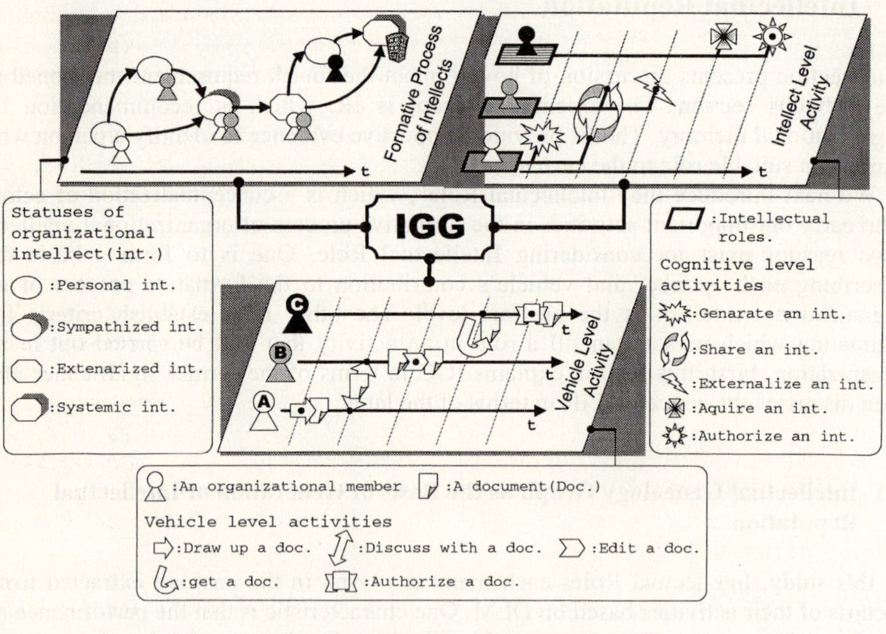

Fig. 3. Intellectual genealogy graph.

explicitly. The importance of an intellect in the organization is clarified in terms of the ontology. The aggregation of the intellects that are possessed by a person serves to show their special field of work in the organization.

- *Hierarchical interpretation of activity*: This hierarchy is shown as intellect level activities at the upper right of Fig. 3. According to DLM, the organizational intellect memory interprets members' vehicle-level activities at three intellect-levels of activities: personal, interactive, and organizational. Consequently, accumulation of interpreted activities represents roles that the actor played in the formative process of the organizational intellect.
- *Chronological interpretation*: It is important to note that the importance of an intellect and an activity are determined not only by themselves, but also by performance of the actor through the entire formative process. The IGG records the progress of each member's activity and transitions of intellects caused by the activity in chronological order.

3.2 Definition of Intellectual Reputation

This study defines Intellectual Reputation as an Intellectual Role expected to be filled in the future activity. As mentioned above, the Intellectual Role filled by each member in the formative process of the organizational intellect is recorded in IGG. The IR of a person is estimated from the individual's record and indicates whether that person can serve in a required role or not. For example, a person of high reputation for an activity means the person expected to able to fill a role required in the activity based on that person's past records.

This conceptualization may not always concur with the usual meaning of "reputation." IR does not resemble an accumulation of subjective interpretations of past activities. Instead, it is a model-based interpretation. A common point is that both are clues for searching for people expected to contribute in a context.

Figure 4 depicts an overview of IR generation. IR is provided as the result of comparison between the actual situation in the organization and IGG in the organizational memory. The input for IR generation is an activity planned to carry out in the organization, for example, shown at the bottom right of Fig. 4. First, the situation of activity is interpreted to a required intellectual role based on DLM in the same way as IGG generation. The situation is described in the subject domain and the intellectual role required in the activity. The situation interpreter, shown in the middle left of Fig. 2, makes this description. Secondly, the situation is compared with each member's subject domain and Intellectual Roles recorded in IGG. The IR generator, shown above left of Fig. 2, performs this comparison. Finally, the outputs are members expected to contribute to the activity. In the case of Fig. 4, based on the records of persons A, B, and C in IGG shown at the left of Fig. 4, person A is selected as a person of high reputation for the required role for the situation. The output is provided for organization members through an organizational intellect creation and inheritance support environment.

One notable feature of IR generation is that a comparison is made between the situation and not only each member's recorded Intellectual Roles, but also their expected Intellectual Roles. The expected Intellectual Role means that the member

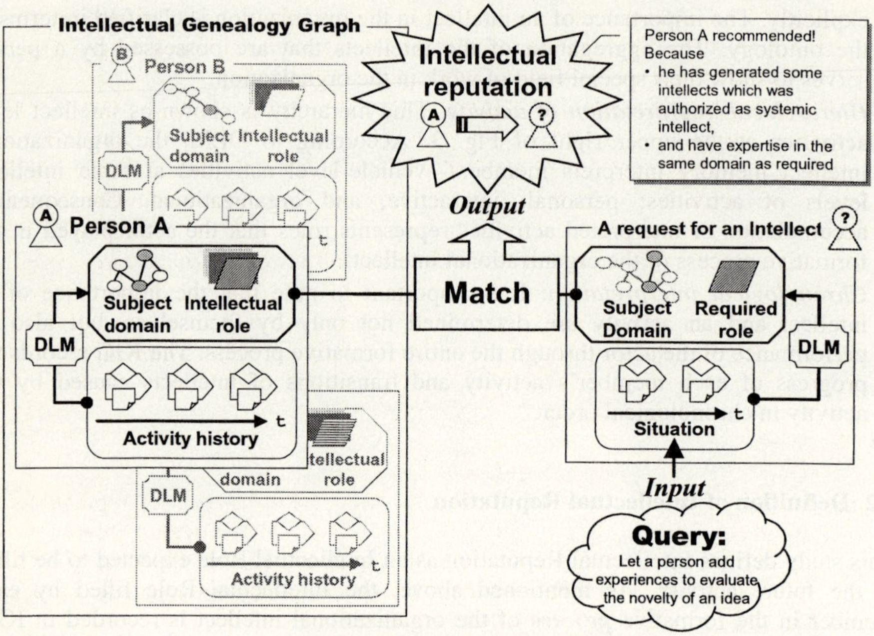

Fig. 4. Intellectual reputation

did not fill the role actually. The member's recorded activities and roles imply that the member can fill the role. This study defines relations among activities, competency and intellectual roles and the expected Intellectual Roles are derived from IGG based on the relations. An example of that is shown in the right panel of Fig. 4. The reason says that person A has not served in a reviewer role, but has served in a creator role. The creator role is that the creator generates unique ideas and has been authorized to use the ideas as systemic intellect in the organization. Assuming that such a capacity that is related to creativity is necessary to serve in a reviewer role, the record of filling the creator role can be the basis of IR derivation.

4 Generation of Intellectual Reputation

This chapter explains how IR is generated from IGG, taking the query "Who is competent to review my proposal of 'ontology-aware authoring tool' from an organizational viewpoint?" as an example.

In DLM terms, the query is interpreted "Who can review my intellect as a systemic intellect in our organization?" The interpretation is done by the query interpreter module. A 'systemic' intellect means that the organization accepts the value of the intellect to be shared and inherited among organization members.

The context of a query is represented by the two elements shown below.

- *Type_of_activity* represents a type of vehicle-level activity that the querist wants to perform. *Type_of_activity* in the example query is 'to review the intellect as a systemic intellect.'

- *Object_of_activity* represents the vehicle-level object of the activity. Object content is described in a conceptual index. *Object_of_activity* in the example query is 'ontology-aware authoring tool.'

The matchmaking module finds a person who can contribute to the query context from an IGG in an organizational intellect memory. Each member is compared with the following requirements derived from the context.

- *Intellect* is an intellect similar to the intellect represented in the vehicle referred by the *object_of_activity*.
- *Role* is the intellectual role fulfilled by the person in the formative process of the *intellect*.
- *Result* is a current state of the *intellect*.

We will elaborate these three aspects of the requirement in the following.

4.1 Intellects

As mentioned before, in an IGG, the importance of the intellect is represented in terms of the organization's own ontology. The IR generator searches the organizational intellect memory for intellects which are closely related to the *object_of_activity* based on the ontology. In the example, the retrieved intellects should be related to 'ontology-aware authoring tool'.

4.2 Roles

Roles that one plays in the formative process of an intellect are extracted from IGG as mentioned in the previous section. Table 1 shows some typical roles.

For example, the typical intellect-level activities of a person `P` who plays a role `originator(I,P)` are `pa_construct` and `pa_publish`, which mean that the person creates a personal intellect and publishes it to others.

Table 1. Roles in the process of creation and inheritance of organizational intellect (partial)

Type	Explanation
`Originator(I,P)`	Person `P` proposed the original idea of intellect `I`.
`Sympathized_person(I,V,P)`	Person `P` sympathized (understood and accepted) with a version `V` of intellect `I`.
`Externalizer(I,V,P)`	Person `P` externalized (made explicit) a version `V` of intellect `I`.
`Reviewer(I,V,P)`	Person `P` reviewed a version `V` of intellect `I`.
`Authorizer(I,V,P)`	Person `P` authorized a version `V` of intellect `I` as an important one for the organization.
`Disseminator(I,V,P)`	Person `P` disseminated a version `V` of intellect `I` among organization members.

4.3 Results

In grasping the importance of an activity that formed an intellect, it is important to know the descendants of the intellect and to evaluate their importance. Using IGG, all descendant intellects from an intellect are identified along the formative process. Table 2 shows categories to show the importance of an ancestral intellect based on the growth level of descended intellects. The levels of intellects correspond to the statuses of intellect in Nonaka's SECI model.

Table 2. The growth level of descendant intellects (partial)

Type	Explanation
`grow_sympathized_intellect(I)`	A descendant intellect of `I` has been sympathized by organization members.
`grow_conceptual_intellect(I)`	A descendant intellect of `I` has been externalized clearly in terms of the organization's own ontology.
`grow_systemic_intellect(I)`	A descendant intellect of `I` has been authorized as an important one by the organization.
`derived_personal_intellect(I)`	Authorized intellect `I` has been spread among organization members.

4.4 Examples of Intellectual Reputation

An ideal person to meet requirements imposed by the query, "Who is competent to review my idea about 'ontology-aware authoring tool' as a systemic intellect?", is one who has many experiences playing important roles in the formative processes of systemic intellects related to 'ontology-aware authoring tool.' In addition, it is desirable that an individual has reviewed others' intellects. The IR Generator searches IGGs for such a person by extracting intellects, roles, and results.

Figure 5 shows IRs of two persons: `P1` and `P2`. Both `P1` and `P2` have reputations for intellect `I1` and `I2`, respectively. In this case, `I2` is closer to the required intellect than `I1`. In addition, `P1` has experience in reviewing the intellect `I1` and has authorized `I1` as a systemic intellect. On the other hand, `P2` does not have experience in reviewing others' intellect, but has experience in playing important roles of originator and externalizer in the formative process of intellect `I2`, whose descendant has also been authorized as a systemic intellect.

Though we can expect that `P1` and `P2` have expertise for the required activity, what is expected for each person is different: e.g., `P1` is expected to appropriately review by taking advantage of one's own experience in reviewing a similar idea. On the other hand, `P2` is expected to appreciate the originality of the idea because that individual has practical experience in creating a similar idea through their own effort. These candidates are selected by rules based on the required conditions of intellectual roles.

Figure 5 shows that, to support finding the right person who meets the requirement for the context, IR shows abstract information of Intellect, Role, and Result, which are interpreted and recorded as IGG in organizational intellect memory, in addition to specific information regarding vehicle-level activity and the vehicle.

Generally, users browse IR information shown in Fig. 4 using graphical user interfaces (GUIs) provided with a user environment. Our study continues to develop a user environment, Kfarm, as a client of the IR generator. Kfarm provides users with an easy-to-use GUI to browse IR. Most entities that constitute IR, e.g., persons, intellects, vehicles, and IGGs, are represented as GUI icons. A user can view vehicle contents by double-clicking the vehicle icon to review the intellect represented in the vehicle.

```
(1) Intellectual Reputation of person(P1) for intellect(I1)-------
   Vehicle-level activity: va_review(P1, V1)
   Vehicle: vehicle(V1)
   File: "toward_the_ontological_engineering.doc"
   Index: "ontology"
   Intellect-level activity: oa_review(P1, I1)
   Intellect: intellect(I1)
   Role: reviewer(I1, P1)
   Result: grow_systemic_intellect(I1)
(2) Intellectual Reputation of person(P2)for intellect(I2)-------
   Vehicle-level activity: va_represent(P2, V2), va_sort(P2, V2)
   Vehicle: vehicle(V2)
   File: "An_ontology-aware_authoring_tool.doc"
   Index: "ontology", "authoring tool"
   Intellect-level activity: pa_construct(P2, I2), oa_create(P2,
     I2), oa_externalize(P2, I2)
   Intellect: intellect(I2)
   Role: originator(I2, P2), externalizer(I2, P2)
   Result: grow_systemic_intellect(I2)
```

Fig. 5. Examples of IRs

5 Conclusion

This paper presented discussion of the role and importance of intellectual reputation as awareness information. Organization members should understand individuals' roles in the formative process of organizational intellect to create and inherit organizational intellect. Intellectual reputation is helpful information to find an appropriate person for a right role in the creation and inheritance of organizational intellect.

This study will expand the IR concept into vehicles in the future. For example, it is useful to know how a learning content contributes to which process or scene in the creation or inheritance of organizational intellect. Grasping situations to which each learning content contributes will allow management of learning contents, which more effectively correspond to the organizational intellect formation process.

References

1. Buckingham Shum, S., Motta, E., Domingue, J.: ScholOnto: An Ontology-Based Digital Library Server for Research Documents and Discourse", Int. J. Digit. Libr., 3 (3) (2000) 237–248
2. Carter J., Bitting E., Ghorbani, A. A.: Reputation formalization for an information sharing multiagent system, Comp. Intell., Vol. 18, No. 4 (2002) 515–534
3. Goffman, Erving. The Presentation of Self in Everyday Life. Doubleday: Garden City, New York, (1959)
4. Hayashi, Y., Tsumoto, H., Ikeda, M., Mizoguchi, R.: "Toward an Ontology-aware Support for Learning-Oriented Knowledge Management", Proc. of the 9th Int. Conf. on Comp. in Educ. (ICCE'2001), (2001) 1149–1152

5. Hayashi, Y., Tsumoto, H., Ikeda, M., Mizoguchi, R.: "An Intellectual Genealogy Graph - Affording a Fine Prospect of Organizational Learning-", Proc. of the 6th International Conference on Intelligent Tutoring Systems (ITS 2002), (2002) 10–20
6. Hood, L., McDermott, R.P., Cole, M.: Let's try to make it a good day: Some not so simple ways, Disc. Proc., 3 (1980) 155–168
7. Nonaka, I., Takeuchi, H.: The Knowledge-Creating company: How Japanese Companies Create the Dynamics of Innovation, Oxford University Press, (1995)
8. Mizoguchi R., Bourdeau J.: Using Ontological Engineering to Overcome AI-ED Problems, Int. J. of Art. Intell. in Educ., Vol.11, No.2 (2000) 107–121
9. Takeuchi, M., Odawara, R., Hayashi, Y., Ikeda, M., Mizoguchi, R.: A Collaborative Learning Design Environment to Harmonize Sense of Participation, Proc. of the 10th Int. Conf. on Comp. in Education ICCE'03 (2003) 462–465
10. Tsumoto, H., Hayashi, Y., Ikeda, M., Mizoguchi, R.: "A Collaborative-learning Support Function to Harness Organizational Intellectual Synergy"□Proc. of the 10th Int. Conf. on Comp. in Education ICCE'02 (2002) 297–301
11. Ogata H., Matsuura K., Yano Y.: "Active Knowledge Awareness Map: Visualizing Learners' Activities in a web Based CSCL Environment", Proc. of NTCL2000 (2000) 89–97

Learners' Roles and Predictable Educational Benefits in Collaborative Learning

An Ontological Approach to Support Design and Analysis of CSCL

Akiko Inaba and Riichiro Mizoguchi

ISIR, Osaka University, 8-1 Mihogaoka, Ibaraki, Osaka, 567-0047 Japan
{ina, miz}@ei.sanken.osaka-u.ac.jp
http://ww.ei.sanken.osaka-u.ac.jp/

Abstract. To facilitate shared understandings of several models of collaborative learning, and collect rational models of effective collaborative learning, we have been constructing a system of concepts to represent collaborative learning sessions relying on existing learning theories. We call the system of concepts Collaborative Learning Ontology, and have been extracting and representing models inspired by the theories with the ontology. In this paper, as a part of the ontology, we concentrated on clarifying behavior and roles for learners in collaborative learning sessions, conditions to assign appropriate roles for each learner, and predictable educational benefits by playing the roles. The system of concepts and models will be beneficial to both designing appropriate groups for collaborative learning sessions, and interaction analysis among learners to assess educational benefits of the learning session.

1 Introduction

In the last decade, many researchers have contributed to development of the research area "Computer Supported Collaborative Learning" (CSCL) [e.g., 3, 8-15, 19, 24, 26], and advantages of collaborative learning over individual learning have been well known. The collaborative learning, however, is not always effective for every learner in a learning group. Educators sometimes argue that it is essential for collaborative learning and its advantage that learners take turns to play some roles; for example, tutor, tutee, helper, assistant, and so on. Of course, in collaborative learning, the learners not only learn passively, but also interact with others actively, and they share their knowledge and develop their skills through it. Educational benefits that a learner gets through the collaborative learning process depend mainly on interaction among learners, that is, the educational benefits depend on what roles the learner plays in the collaborative learning. Moreover, the relationship between a role in a group and a learner's knowledge and/or cognitive states when the learner begins to play the role is critical. If the learner performs a role which is not appropriate for his/her knowledge and/or cognitive state, his/her efforts would be in vain. So, designers and educators should consider carefully the relationship among learners' states, experiences, and conditions for role assignment; and the synergistic and/or harmful effect of a

J.C. Lester et al. (Eds.): ITS 2004, LNCS 3220, pp. 285–294, 2004.

combination of more than one role; when they form learning groups and design learning processes. To realize this, we need to organize models and rules for role assignments the designers and educators can refer to, and construct a system of concepts to facilitate shared understanding of them.

Our research objectives include constructing a collaborative learning support system that detects appropriate situation for a learner to join in a collaborative learning session, forms a collaborative learning group appropriate for the situation, and monitors and supports the learning processes dynamically. To fulfill these objectives, we have to consider the following:

1. How to detect appropriate situations to start collaborative learning sessions and to set up learning goals for the group and members of the group,
2. How to form an effective group which ensures educational benefits to each members of the group, and
3. How to analyze interaction among learners and facilitate desired interaction in the learning group.

We have discussed item 1 in our previous papers [8, 9], and have been constructing a support system for analyzing interaction for item 3 [13, 14]. We also have been discussing item 2, especially, concentrated on extracting educational benefits expected to acquire through collaborative learning (i.e., learning goals), and constructing a system to support group formation represented as a combination of the goals [11, 26].

This paper focuses on learners' behavior, roles, conditions to assign appropriate roles for learners, and predictable educational benefits of the roles referring to learning theories, as a remaining part of the item 2. First, we overview our previous work, that is, the system of concepts to represent collaborative learning session: we call it "Collaborative Learning Ontology", especially we describe "Learning Goal Ontology" which is a part of the Collaborative Learning Ontology. Next, we pick up learners' behavior and roles from learning theories. Then, we discuss conditions of role assignments and predictable benefits by playing the roles.

2 Learning Theories and Collaborative Learning Ontology

There are many theories to support the advantage of collaborative learning. For instance, Observational learning [2], Constructivism [20], Self-regulated learning [21], Situated learning [16], Cognitive apprenticeship [5], Distributed cognition [23], Cognitive flexibility theory [25], Sociocultural Theory [28], Zone of proximal development [27, 28], and so on. If learners learn in compliance with strategies based on the theories, we can expect some educational benefits for the learners with the strong support of the theory. So, we have been constructing models referring to these theories. However, there is a lack of common vocabulary to describe the models. Therefore, we have been constructing the "Collaborative Learning Ontology" which is a system of concepts to represent collaborative learning sessions proposed by these learning theories [10, 11, 26]. Here, we focus on the "Learning Goal Ontology". The concept "Learning Goal" is one of the most important concepts for forming a learning group because each learner joins in a collaborative learning session in order to attain a

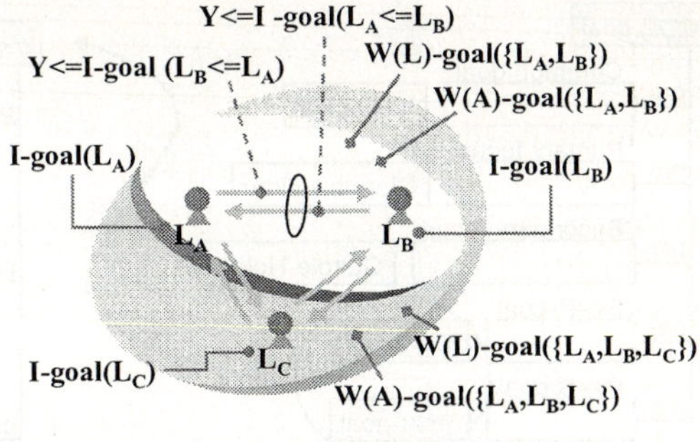

Fig. 1. Learning Goals in a Collaborative Learning Session

learning goal. The Ontology will be able to make it easier to form an effective learning setting and to analyze the educational functions of a learning group. [17, 18]

We have extracted common features of phenomena, such as development of learning community, interaction among learners and educational benefits for a learner, from the learning theories. The learning theories account for such phenomena, and a designer or a learner can regard the phenomena as goals. So, we use the term "learning goal" to represent such phenomena. Namely, we call the goal of development of learning community W(L)-goal, the goal of group's activity W(A)-goal, the goal of interaction among learners Y<=I-goal, and the goal of educational benefits for a learner I-goal.

Fig.1 represents learning goals in a group where three learners: L_A, L_B and L_C are participating. Learner L_A has an I-goal that is attained through this collaborative learning session and this goal is described in Fig.1 as I-goal (L_A). Both L_B and L_C also have I-goals, and they are represented as I-goal (L_B) and I-goal (L_C) respectively. Y<=I-goal (L_B<=L_A) is a Y<=I-goal between L_A and L_B observed from L_A's viewpoint. In other words, it means the reason why L_A interacts with L_B. Concerning this interaction between L_A and L_B, there is also a Y<=I-goal observed from L_B's viewpoint. That is, it is the reason why L_B interacts with L_A. This Y<=I-goal is represented as Y<=I-goal (L_A<=L_B). Both I-goal (L_A) and Y<=I-goal (L_B<=L_A) are personal goals of L_A. Both W(L)-goal ({L_A, L_B}) and W(A)-goal ({L_A, L_B}) are goals of the learning group ({L_A, L_B}). Similarly, W(L)-goal ({L_A, L_B, L_C}) and W(A)-goal ({L_A, L_B, L_C}) are goals of the learning group ({L_A, L_B, L_C}).

We have identified goals for collaborative learning for each of the four categories with justification based on learning theories. We have identified four kinds of I-goals and three phases for each of them, such as 'acquisition of content-specific knowledge (phase: accretion, tuning, and restructuring)' [22], 'development of cognitive skill (phase: cognitive stage, associative stage, and autonomous stage)' [1, 7], and so on. The learner is expected to achieve these I-goals through interaction with other learners. We have pick up ten kinds of Y<=I-goals, such as 'learning by teaching' [6], 'learning by observation' [2], 'learning by self-expression' [25], and so on. The examples of W(L)-goals are 'knowledge sharing' [23], 'creating a solution' [20], 'spread of skills' [5, 16] and so on. The W(A)-goals mean activities accomplished by learning groups; for example, the learning activity where a new comer to the community learns something by his/her own practice, mentioned in the theory of LPP [16], the learning activity where a knowledgeable learner teaches something to a poor learner, mentioned in the theory of Peer Tutoring [6] (For whole set of the goals, see [10, 11]).

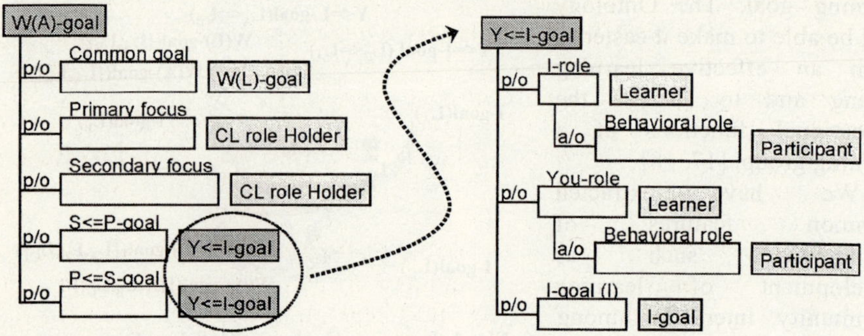

Fig.2. Conceptual Structure of a W(A)-goal and a Y<=I-goal

Each W(A)-goal provides the rationale justified by specific learning theory. That is, the W(A)-goal specifies a rational arrangement of learning goals and a group formation. Fig.2 shows a typical representation for the structure of a W(A)-goal. The W(A)-goal consists of five concepts: Common goal, Primary Focus, Secondary Focus, S<=P-goal, and P<=S-goal. The Common Goal is a goal of the whole group, and the entity of the Common goal refers to the concepts defined as W(L)-goal ontology. Both Primary Focus and Secondary Focus are learners' roles in a learning group. A learning theory generally argues the process that learners, who play a specific role, can obtain educational benefits through interaction with other learners who play other roles. The theories have common characteristics to argue effectiveness of a learning process focusing on a specific role of learners. So, we represent the focus in the theories as Primary Focus and Secondary Focus. S<=P-goal and P<=S-goal are interaction goals between Primary focused learner (P) and Secondary focused learner (S) from P's viewpoint and S's viewpoint, respectively. The entities of these goals refer to the concepts defined as Y<=I-goals. The conditions, which are proper to each W(A)-goal, can be added to the concepts, if necessary. Each of the Y<=I-goals referred to by S<=P-goal and P<=S-goal consists of three concepts as follows:

I-role: a role to attain the Y<=I-goal. A member who plays I-role (I-member) is expected to attain his/her I-goal by attaining the Y<=I-goal.

You-role: a role as a partner for the I-member.

I-goal (I): an I-goal that means what the I-member attains.

We have described detailed discussion of the goals in our previous papers [10, 11, 26]. In the remains of this paper, we concentrate on identifying behavior and roles, clarifying conditions to assign a role for a learner, and connecting the roles with predictable educational benefits.

3 Learners' Roles and Behavior in Collaborative Learning Inspired by Learning Theories

Table 1 shows learners' behavior and roles in collaborative learning sessions inspired by the learning theories. There are nine types of behavior and thirteen types of roles.

As we describe in the previous section, we represent each model of learning theory as two roles for learners, interaction goals between the role-holders, and common goal for both role-holders. Learning models which have more than three role-holders can be represented as a composite of models which have two role-holders. So, we represent each model as a simplified two-role model. For example, the model of the theory 'Cognitive Apprenticeship' has Master and Apprentice, and the model of 'Sociocultural Theory' has Client and Diagnoser. It is just the same to any N-tupple relation is composed of binary relations.

The effect of externalization is one of the main advantages of collaborative learning, and the behaviors *presenting* and *tutoring* aim at the effect. The three roles, Problem holder, Panelist, and Client, have the same behavior: *presenting*. The *presenting* is to externalize something in a learner's mind, that is, the learner creates it originally, while the *tutoring* is to externalize what he/she already listened or was taught from others. The behaviors *imitating* and *observing* aim at the effect of modeling other learners, and it regards the other learners as good examples for some behavior. By *observing*, we mean only seeing someone's behavior, and by *imitating*, we mean seeing and doing. The behaviors *advising* and *guiding* aim at developing a learner's cognitive skill such as diagnosing, and it regards the other learners as case-holders. By *advising*, we mean to monitor the other learners, diagnose their problems, and give some advice to them. By *guiding*, we mean that a learner demonstrates something to other learners, observes the other learners do it, and advises on it. The

Table 1. Behavior and Roles of Learners in Collaborative Learning Sessions

Behavior	Definition	Role	Src.
Advising	To diagnose problems and give some advice to other learners	Anchored instructor Diagnoser	[4, 27, 28]
Guiding	To demonstrate something to other learners and then guide the learners' behavior	Master	[5]
Imitating	To imitate other learners' behavior	Apprentice	[5]
Observing	To observe other learners' behavior	Observer	[2]
Passive learning	To be taught something new from other learners	Peer tutee	[6]
Presenting	To explain something in his/her mind to other learners	Problem holder, Panelist, Client	[4, 25, 27, 28]
Problem solving	To solve problems	Peripheral participant, Full participant	[16, 20, 23]
Reviewing	To compare and review other learners' opinions and his/her thinking process	Audience	[25]
Tutoring	To explain something he/she already knows to other learners	Peer tutor	[6]

reviewing expects a learner to reflect his/her thinking process by opinions of other learners, the *problem solving* expects learners to share knowledge and create new ones. The both regard the other learners as stimuli.

4 Who Can Play the Role and Who Is Appropriate?

To design effective learning processes and form appropriate groups for learners, it is important to assign an appropriate role to each learner. As we described, educational benefits depend on how learners interact with each other: what roles they play in collaborative learning. For example, teaching something to other learners is effective for the learner, who already knows it but does not have experience in using the knowledge. Since the learner has to explain it in his/her words in order to teach it to others, he/she is expected to comprehend it more clearly. On the other hand, the same role is not effective for the learner who already understands it well, uses it many times, and teaches it to other learners again and again. In such a case, it is effective not for the learner who teaches it, but only for learners who are taught it. So, to clarify the conditions for role assignments is necessary to support design processes of learning sessions.

Table 2. Roles, Conditions for role assignments, and Predictable educational benefits

Role	Condition	Predictable benefits	Src.
Anchored instructor	* having the target knowledge * knowing how to diagnose others - not having experience in diagnosing others	Acquisition of content specific knowledge (tuning) Development of cognitive skill (associative stage)	[4]
Apprentice	- not having the knowledge how to use the target skill - not having the experience to use the target skill	Development of cognitive and/or metacognitive skill (cognitive stage & associative stage)	[5]
Audience	* having the target knowledge * having experience in using the knowledge * having related knowledge in the domain	Acquisition of content specific knowledge (restructuring)	[25]
Client	* knowing how to use the target metacognitive skill	Development of the meta- cognitive skill (associative stage)	[27,28]
Diagnoser	* knowing how to use the target cognitive skill	Development of the cognitive skill	[27,28]

		(associative stage)	
Full participant	* having the target knowledge * having experience in using the knowledge * having related knowledge in the domain * knowing how to use the target cognitive skill * having experience in using the cognitive skill * having how to use target metacognitive skill * having experience in using the metacognitive skill	Acquisition of content specific knowledge (restructuring) Development of the cognitive skill (autonomous stage) Development of meta-cognitive skill (autonomous stage)	[16, 20, 23]
Master	* knowing how to use target cognitive skill * having experience in using the cognitive skill * having how to use target meta-cognitive skill * having experience in using the meta-cognitive skill	Development of cognitive and/or metacognitive skill (autonomous stage)	[5]
Observer	- not having the target knowledge - not having the knowledge how to use the target skill	*depending on what to observe*	[2]
Panelist	* knowing how to use a skill for self-expression * having his/her own opinion - not having experience in using the skill for self-expression	Development of skill for self-expression (associative stage)	[25]
Peer tutee	- not having the target knowledge	Acquisition of content specific knowledge (accretion)	[6]
Peer tutor	* having the target knowledge - not having experience in using the knowledge - misunderstanding the knowledge	Acquisition of content specific knowledge (tuning)	[6]
Peripheral participant	* knowing how to use the target cognitive skill * knowing how to use the target meta-cognitive skill - not having experience in using the cognitive skill	Development of cognitive skill (associative stage) Development of meta-cognitive skill (associative stage)	[16]

	- not having experience in using the metacognitive skill		
Problem (Anchor) holder	* having a problem - having related knowledge to solve the problem	Acquisition of conter specific knowledge (tuning)	[4]

Table 2 shows the roles which appear in collaborative learning sessions inspired by the learning theories we have referred to, conditions for each role, and predictable educational benefits by playing each role. This prediction is based on the theories. There are two types of conditions: *necessary conditions* and *desired conditions*. The *necessary conditions* are essential for the role: if a learner does not satisfy the conditions, the learner cannot play the role. On the other hand, the *desired conditions* should be satisfied to enable a learner to get full benefits of the role: if a learner does not satisfy the conditions, the learner can play the role, but educational benefits may not be ensured. In Table 2, the conditions marked with '*' are the *necessary conditions*, and the conditions marked with '-' are the *desired conditions*. For example, any learner can play the role 'Peer tutor' as long as the learner has target knowledge to teach other learners. If the learner misunderstood the knowledge and/or he/she did not have experience in using the knowledge, it is a good opportunity for the learner to play the role 'Peer tutor', because to externalize his/her knowledge in his/her words facilitates re-thinking of the knowledge, and gives an opportunity to notice the misunderstanding [6].

By clarifying the conditions to assign learners some roles like this, it would be possible for designers who are not experts of learning theories and even if computer systems to assign appropriate roles for each learner, to form groups for effective collaborative learning, and to predict educational benefits that each learner will get through the learning session in compliance with learning theories. It will be useful not only to support design processes for collaborative learning sessions, but also to analyze processes for them.

5 Conclusion

We have been constructing a system of concepts to represent collaborative learning sessions. To facilitate shared understandings of several models of collaborative learning, and collect rational models of effective collaborative learning, we have been relying on existing learning theories. We have been extracting models inspired by the theories and constructing Collaborative Learning Ontology. In this paper, we concentrated on clarifying behavior and roles for learners, conditions to assign appropriate roles for each learner, and predictable educational benefits by playing the roles, as a part of the ontology. By specifying these conditions, roles, and predictable educational benefits, we can select easily appropriate roles for each learner, and construct a feasible system to support group formation which searches appropriate learners for each role when a collaborative learning begins [11].

As our next steps, we will consider the possibilities of combination of some roles. We should consider carefully the synergistic and/or harmful effect of a combination of more than one role. Moreover, we plan to extract heuristics to assign roles for learners. For example, according to the theory 'Peer tutoring', a learner who has a misunderstanding is appropriate for the role 'Peer tutor'. However, there is a risk: if a learner who plays 'Peer tutee' does not know the knowledge, the learner would believe what the peer tutor teaches and the peer tutee would also have the misunderstanding. It is caused by characteristics of the theory: the theory 'Peer tutoring', primary focus is 'Peer tutor' and his/her benefits, and the theory gives little attention to benefits of 'Peer tutee'. We will also describe the risks like this with the theory-based conditions for role assignments. Then, we will consider order of recommendations of roles, and implement the mechanism how to recommend the roles in a collaborative learning support system [14], and supporting environment for instructional design process for CSCL [12]. At this stage, we have been collecting supportive theories for collaborative learning, that is, all theories we referred to describe positive effects of collaborative learning, because we would like to collect effective models of collaborative learning as reference models to design collaborative learning. Of course, collaborative learning also has negative effect, and the negative models are useful to avoid designing such learning sessions. It will also be included in our future work.

References

1. Anderson, J. R. Acquisition of Cognitive Skill, Psychological Review, 89(4), 369-406 (1982)
2. Bandura, A. "Social Learning Theory", New York: General Learning Press (1971)
3. Barros, B., & Verdejo, M.F. Analysing student interaction processes in order to improve collaboration. The DEGREE approach, IJAIED, 11 (2000)
4. Cognition and Technology Group at Vanderbilt. Anchored instruction in science education, In: R. Duschl & R. Hamilton (Eds.), "Philosophy of science, cognitive psychology, and educational theory and practice." Albany, NY: SUNY Press. 244-273 (1992)
5. Collins, A. Cognitive apprenticeship and instructional technology, In: Idol, L., & Jones, B. F. (Eds.) "Educational values and cognitive instruction: Implications for reform." Hillsdale, N.J.: LEA (1991)
6. Endlsey, W. R. "Peer tutorial instruction", Englewood Cliffs, NJ: Educational Technology (1980)
7. Fitts, P. M. Perceptual-Motor Skill Learning, In: Melton, A. W. (Ed.), "Categories of Human Learning", New York: Academic Press. 243-285 (1964)
8. Ikeda, M., Hoppe, U., & Mizoguchi, R. Ontological issue of CSCL Systems Design, Proc. of AIED95, 234-249 (1995)
9. Ikeda, M., Go, S., & Mizoguchi, R. Opportunistic Group Formation, Proc. of AIED97, 166-174 (1997)
10. Inaba, A., Ikeda, M., Mizoguchi, R., & Toyoda, J. http://www.ei.sanken.osaka-u.ac.jp/~ina/LGOntology/ (2000)
11. Inaba, A., Supnithi, T., Ikeda, M., Mizoguchi, R., & Toyoda, J. How Can We Form Effective Collaborative Learning Groups? -Theoretical justification of "Opportunistic Group Formation" with ontological engineering, Proc. of ITS2000, 282-291 (2000)

12. Inaba, A., Ohkubo, R., Ikeda, M., Mizoguchi, R., & Toyoda, J. An Instructional Design Support Environment for CSCL - Fundamental Concepts and Design Patterns, Proc. of AIED-2001, 130-141 (2001)
13. Inaba, A., Ohkubo, R., Ikeda, M., & Mizoguchi, R. Models and Vocabulary to Represent Learner-to-Learner Interaction Process in Collaborative Learning, Proc. of ICCE2003, 1088-1096 (2003)
14. Inaba, A., Ohkubo, R., Ikeda, M., & Mizoguchi, R. An Interaction Analysis Support System for CSCL - An Ontological Approach to Support Instructional Design Process, Proc. of ICCE2002 (2002)
15. Katz, A., O'Donnell, G., & Kay, H. An Approach to Analyzing the Role and Structure of Reflective Dialogue, IJAIED, 11 (2000)
16. Lave, J. & Wenger, E. "Situated Learning: Legitimate peripheral participation", Cambridge University Press (1991)
17. Mizoguchi, R., & Bourdeau, J. Using Ontological Engineering to Overcome Common AI-ED Problems, IJAIED, 11 (2000)
18. Mizoguchi, R., Ikeda, M., & Sinitsa, K. Roles of Shared Ontology in AI-ED Research, Proc. of AIED97, 537-544 (1997)
19. Muhlenbrock, M., & Hoppe, U. Computer Supported Interaction Analysis of Group Problem Solving, Proc. of CSCL99, 398-405 (1999)
20. Piaget, J., & Inhelder, B. "The Psychology of the Child", New York: Basic Books (1971)
21. Resnick, M. Distributed Constructionism, Proc. of the International Conference on the Learning Science (1996)
22. Rumelhart, D.E., & Norman, D.A. Accretion, Tuning, and Restructuring: Modes of Learning, In: Cotton, J.W., & Klatzky, R.L. (Eds.) "Semantic factors in cognition." Hillsdale, N.J. : LEA, 37-53 (1978)
23. Salomon, G. "Distributed cognitions", Cambridge University Press (1993)
24. Soller, A. Supporting Social Interaction in an Intelligent Collaborative Learning System, IJAIED, 12 (2001)
25. Spiro, R. J., Coulson, R., L., Feltovich, P. J., & Anderson, D. K. Cognitive flexibility: Advanced knowledge acquisition ill-structured domains, Proc. of the Tenth Annual Conference of Cognitive Science Society, Hillsdale, NJ, LEA, 375-383 (1988)
26. Supnithi, T., Inaba, A., Ikeda, M., Toyoda, J., & Mizoguchi, R. Learning Goal Ontology Supported by Learning Theories for Opportunistic Group Formation, Proc. of AIED99 (1999)
27. Vygotsky, L.S. The problem of the cultural development of the child, Journal of Genetic Psychology, 36, 414-434 (1929)
28. Vygotsky,L.S. "Mind in Society: The development of the higher psychological processes", Cambridge, MA: Harvard University Press (1930, Re-published 1978)

Redefining the Turn-Taking Notion in Mediated Communication of Virtual Learning Communities

Pablo Reyes and Pierre Tchounikine

LIUM-CNRS FRE 2730, Université du Maine Avenue Laënnec,
Le Mans, 72085 Le Mans cedex 9, France
{Pablo.Reyes, Pierre.Tchounikine}@lium.univ-lemans.fr

Abstract. In our research on social interactions taking place in forum-type tools that virtual learning communities use, we have found that the users have the following particular temporal behavior: they answer generally some messages situated in different threads in a very short time period, in a digest-like way. This paper shows this work pattern through a quantitative study and proposes an integration of this work pattern in a Forum-type tool developed for supporting the interactions of virtual learning communities through the creation of a new structure we will name Session. This structure allows the turn-taking of threaded conversations in an orderly fashion to become visible.

1 Introduction

This work takes place in a research project that aims to contribute to a better understanding of interactions within virtual learning communities, in the context of computer-based tools. We design, implement and test innovative tools to provide data that will enable us to progress in our conceptualization of our research domain and phenomena.

Network technologies have enabled web-learning activities based on the emergence of virtual learning communities (VLC). In the VLC the collaborative learning activities are realized mainly through a conversational asynchronous environment, which we call forum-type tools. The expression forum-type tools (FTT) designate a mainly text-based and asynchronous, electronic conferencing system that makes use of a tree hierarchical data structure of enchained messages called threads. These FTT are tools widely used for communication and learning throughout Internet and e-learning platforms. These tools have opened the possibility of creating virtual learning communities in which students discuss a great variety of subjects, and in different depth levels, through a threaded conversation structure.

This paper proposes a change of the turn-taking notion in distributed and collaborative learning environments that use FTT. Here, we take charge of a set of issues described in the literature that make reference to turn-taking difficulties in virtual environments. Concretely, we propose a redefinition of the turn-taking concept in threaded conversations that take place in VLC. The new turn-taking concept in the FTT context is characterized as a new temporal structure that we call *session*. The session structure is a mechanism for the turn-taking management of threaded conversations.

J.C. Lester et al. (Eds.): ITS 2004, LNCS 3220, pp. 295–304, 2004.

The new turn-taking notion stems from a quantitative study in temporary aspects of the behavior of the users using FTT in their VLC, paying particular attention to the work practices of these users. This choice is inspired by ethnographic and Scandinavian participatory design approaches [1]. This method emphasizes the informatics' systems construction, which represents the actual work practice in the communities to whom this system is directed.

We suggest that this change can be an element that enhances and facilitates the emergence and development of learning interactions that take place in FTT as written learning conversations. The learning conversations are the ones that "go further than just realizing information exchange; rather, they allow participants to make connections between previously unrelated ideas, or to see old ideas in a new way. They are conversations that lead to conceptual change" [2].

Our approach has a clearly differing view than the research on turn-taking issues which focus, as a main factor, on the consequences of delay in the communication tools as forums and chat's (e.g., [3,4]).

This paper is organized as follows: First comes an overview of turn-taking in virtual environments. We next describe a quantitative study of temporal behavior of participants of a VLC. Then, we present the session structure and the implementation of a prototype that reifies these ideas. Finally, we present some preliminary results from an empirical study.

2 Turn-Taking in Virtual Environments

Turn-taking in spoken conversations deals with the alternating turns for communicating between participants. This process takes place in an orderly fashion: in each turn each participant speaks and then the other responds and so forth. In this way, the conversations are oriented in a series of successive steps or "turns" and the turn-taking's become the basic mechanism of conversation organization (e.g., [5]).

Nevertheless, the application of the same turn-taking concept in the CMC context (written conversations, principally) is not correct: "The turn-taking model does not adequately account for this mode of interaction" [6]. Actually, the nature of the communication medium changes the nature of the turn-taking concept. Consequently, the turn-taking system in CMC tools is substantially different to the face-to-face interactions (e.g., [7,6] or [8]).

The communication that takes place in these tools follows a multidimensional sequential pattern (e.g., a conversation with parallel threads), rather than a linear sequential pattern, with complex interactions that result "inlayered topics, multiple speech acts and interleaved turns" [6]. In synchronous communication tools, e.g. chats, the turn-taking has a confused meaning: generally the dyadic exchanges are interleaved with others dyadic exchanges [3]. In this way, and in these tools, the message exchanges are highly overlapped. The same overlap problem is distinguished in asynchronous tools [3] (generally FTT). In asynchronous communications (newsgroup type communication through FTT) everybody holds the floor at any time what breaks the traditional concept of turn-taking. In this way, all participants can produce messages independently and simultaneously. We found that the development of face-to-face conversations is basically a linear process of alterning turns. But in the FTT this linearity is destroyed by the generation of multiples threads in a parallel way. In this way, the on-line conversation grows in a dispersed way with a blurred notion of turn-taking. This situation generates deterrents that have direct consequences on collaborative learning and the learning conversations on which it is based: a dispersed conversation prevents the participants building their own "adequate mental representation of the virtual space and time within which they interact" [9]. So students have a weaker perception of the global discussion, since "in order to communicate and learn collaboratively in such an environment, participants need to engage in what they can perceive as a normal discussion" [9], what is not obvious to obtain in the actual FTT.

The importance of turn-taking, and the turn management for the learning conversations is stated by several authors: The turn management in distance groups can influence the performance of groups [10]; In a collaborative problem solving activity the students build sequentially the solutions through the alterning turns [11]; The turn-taking represents the rhythm of a conversation; Expliciting the rhythm of communication patterns can help improve the coordination of the interactions [12]; The turn-taking is essential for a good understanding of conversations [5].

3 Mining Temporal Work Patterns Through a Quantitative Study

3.1 Introduction to This Quantitative Study

In order to understand some temporal work practice in the VLC, we studied a collection of Usenet newsgroups. The research has shown that some newsgroups can be considered a community [13].

The objective of this empirical study is to analyze participant's actions, in order to find *recurrent sequences of work practices* (work patterns) [14]. The work practices are the starting point for the technical solutions that facilitate the work patterns found.

A quantitative approach to data collection has been pursued for finding the temporal work practices. We analyze the temporal behavior of participants. Particularly, their participation on the threaded conversations, and how the way of participating denotes a specific time management pattern of users of FTT.

For this research, we selected data from a collection of threaded conversations belonging to some open access newsgroups. The process of selection is realized in two steps: First, the detection of newsgroups with the characteristics of interactivity of a VLC. Particularly, we take in account the length of threads and the activity of groups. Next, the detection and selection of threaded conversations in these newsgroups where there are deepened exchanges. The newsgroups that have the role of a dynamic FAQ (a question and one or two answers) are far from the notion of learning community that we sustain, where exists a complex and rich exchange of interactions in relation to topics of interest of a particular community.

3.2 Newsgroup's Detection

We selected a number of eight newsgroups[1] that are particularly active and have a number of threaded conversations that largely exceed the average length of the threads. This analysis covers roughly 50.000 messages through a 4-month time span in these 8 newsgroups. The mean volume per month of sent messages (1628 messages) of the selected newsgroups is very high compared with the monthly mean of the newsgroups, such as has been noted by Butler (50 messages) [15].

In relation to the thread's length, the thread's length mean in the newsgroups is 2.036 messages [15]. The selected newsgroups in this work exceed largely these mean (13.25). Quantitatively, these newsgroups have an active and in-depth communication among their members. This fact indicates how engaged people are with the community. This selection ensures we are looking at conversations in communities that have *a very high amount of on-topic discussion*. The thread's length reveals a more in-depth commentary relating to a specific topic. Also, the length of threads is recognized as a measurement of the interactivity [16].

3.3 Selection of Threads

The second stage of selection corresponds to the selection of threads from a minimal threshold length in the selected newsgroups in order to look at the work patterns in threads with a high complexity and interactivity. This selection better focuses this quantitative study: a discussion with only three or four messages does not enable us to discover these work patterns. Thus, we consider that this process of detection and filter does not decrease the validity of our results, but it focuses the research in the field of our interest. Our interest is providing new tools for better managing discussions which have complex interactions (highly intertwined conversations) in VLCs.

We set the minimal limit of the length of threads to 10 messages. In this way we analyse only the threaded conversations with a 10 or more messages. With this approach, we leave away only 20% of the messages (that is, the messages that belong to threads having less than 10 messages).

3.4 Results and Findings

The results of the quantitative study are focused on the temporal behavior of the users in the delivery of their messages. First, we pay attention to an interesting work pattern, which is repeated throughout the threads analyzed in our study: the participants answer messages in a great percentage in a buffer or digest way (they send several messages during a short time). The analyses show that a fraction of messages (25%) in the selected newsgroup is sent in a consecutive way by a specific participant answering different branches on different threads.

In a deeper analysis of the consecutive messages, we found that the mean of the period between these messages is 14 minutes. This period confirms the notion of these

---

[1] comp.ai.philosophy, humanities.lit.authors.shakespeare, humanities.philosophy.objectivism, sci.anthropology.paleo, soc.culture.french, talk.origins, talk.philosophy.humanism, talk.politics.guns.

consecutive messages being sent in a digest-like way by the participants. Moreover, the distribution of the period between adjacent messages can be understood (and well characterized) through a log-normal distribution.

This quantitative study illustrated a particular work practice: users do not send messages in a regular frequency, but users answer generally in a buffer-like way. They successively concentrate their activity of sending messages in a short duration of time and thus they bring up to date their interventions in the conversation. In these actualizations, sometimes they answer two (70% of cases), three (22% of cases) or more (8% of cases) messages in different threads. This work pattern has been also distinguished by [7]. Nevertheless, is not possible to be easily aware of this work pattern in the traditional FTT. Figure 1 shows a traditional interface of newsgroups. The left side of figure 1 shows 10 messages in a temporal order. The right side figure 1 shows the same 10 messages in a threaded order. We pay attention that the two temporally consecutive messages sent by "Rober" are situated in different threads. We note that the FTT doesn't have a temporal structure that shows this temporal behavior. Consequently, the interventions of users are dislocated and distributed. This fact entails a blurred notion of traditional turn-taking rules. The importance of a clear structure of turn-taking in conversations has been stated in section 2.

Thus, we consider the introduction of a new temporal structure in FTT (section 4.1) that will become the new turn-taking unity in threaded conversations as explained further in section 4.3.

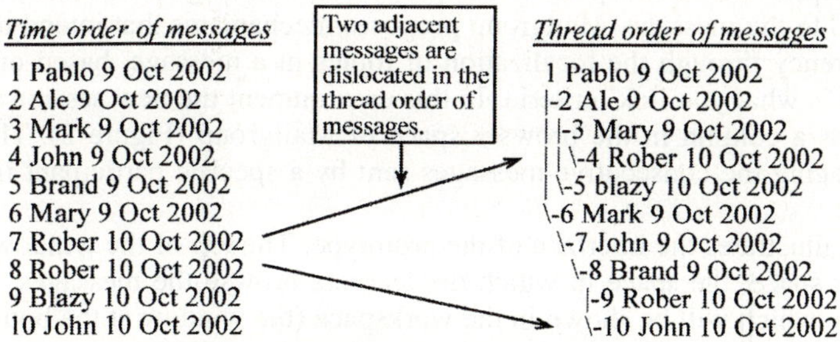

Fig. 1. Messages in a temporal order and thread order view in actual FTTs

4 The Implementation of Session in the "Mailgroup" Forum Type Tool

4.1 Session Structure

We propose the creation of a structure called session. This structure intends to model the turn-taking behavior and make visible the particular rhythm of answers that is an existing work practice. A session is "a period of time (…) for carrying out a particular activity" [17]. In our context, a session corresponds to a group of messages sent consecutively in a short duration of time by the same participant. That is, a new structure that sticks together the messages sent at almost the same time.

The introduction of the session structure in FTT changes the concept of turn-taking in the threaded conversations given that communication turns are now visually realized from sessions (packaged messages) and not from the individual messages.

We implement this structure in a FTT as columns (Figure 2) that package the messages in a parallel and linear view.

4.2 Prototype Implementation

The session structure is integrated in a FTT called 'Mailgroup' [18]. Mailgroup is an electronic tool that allows communication for an electronic learning community. In this environment, the participants can maintain a discussion by exchanging messages structured by sessions that permit the packaging of these messages in an ordered manner. Nevertheless, Mailgroup does not aim to change the temporary organization of threaded conversations, but only to make salient this organization, that remains implicit in other FTT.

Mailgroup has been designed according to the global objective of supporting learning conversations taking place in forums. In this perspective, Mailgroup also introduces mechanisms to overcome an already identified situation which discourage the emergence of the learning conversations [18]: 'Interactional incoherence': threads of messages only denote the relation between the messages, without taking into account the 'topics' that correspond to the parts of the message selected by the student that respond to the message. Mailgroup proposes mechanisms that intend to surmount this incoherency through the localization of topics in a message, based on the 'what you answer is what you link' criteria. In this environment the new session structure is visualized as a column in the browser space of Mailgroup (Figure 2). The columns allow packaging the consecutive messages sent by a specific participant in a parallel view.

Figure 2 illustrates the interface of the prototype. The top of the window display is the browser space, the space in which the learners browse the messages, ordered by the sessions, which will be shown in the workspace (the window at the bottom). In the workspace, learners inspect, reply and create messages. The system generates the graphical visualization from the answers and new topics created by the users.

The browser space shows the whole of the discussion represented by a graph: Vertexes (the circles in figure 2) correspond to the topics of a conversation, and the edges correspond to the links between the topics. The lines placed between the vertexes of different columns correspond to links explicitly created by the users between these two topics. All of the messages (circles) situated in a one column correspond to a single session. The new sessions are positioned to the right of previous ones. The tree structures of the browser space are interactive, since users can click on the vertexes and look at the topics contents in the working space.

Figure 2 shows the graph corresponding to the same structure of messages as figure 1. In this graph visualization, users can observe that threads structure grows in a linear and consecutive way. Moreover, if there are two or more threads, they can visualize them in a parallel way thanks to the implementation of the session notion. If a user contributes in a session with more than one message, their messages are placed in the same column. This way, users can perceive the time order and thread order of messages in a single visualization. With this visualization users can be more aware of structure of interactions of their community.

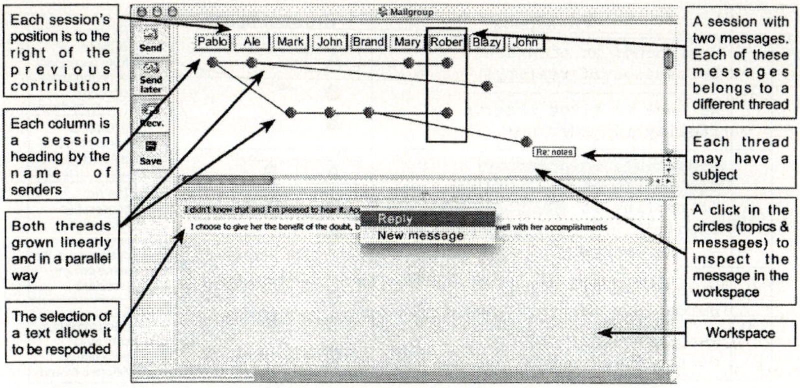

Fig. 2. The Interface of "Mailgroup"

The dynamics of a session's construction in a threaded conversation. The construction of a session is a very simple and transparent process for the users. The users only must write their new messages or answers of other messages, and then they must send the whole of messages with the send button. The messages sent in this way are displayed only in one column (Figure 2).

In this way, the threaded conversation development is shaped and structured by the sessions. The users only must look at the columns to be graphically aware of the activity of the other participants. Now, the messages are positioned in an orderly fashion and the threaded conversation grows linearly.

Figure 3 illustrates the relationship between the actions of the participants in the workspace, and the representation of their actions in the browser space. Figure 3 represents a situation where a user (participant A) creates two messages in a session. The user B answers to one of these messages, and a third user (participant C) answers two messages of different threads in the same session. Figure 3.(1) shows the participant A's message contents as all users see them in the workspace. The two messages are displayed in the browser space just as a vertex placed at the lower part of the sender name. The messages are placed in a column that represents the first session of this conversation. Figure 3.(2) illustrates: First, an action of participant B who reacts to one message of participant A by answering through a contextual menu (in workspace); Second, the effect of this action in the browser space. As a result, a new session (column) is added to the right-hand side, with a link between the two messages. Figure 3.(3) shows a new session created by the participant C who has written two messages (answers, in this case) in their session. Each answer reacts to different threads. The workspace of figure 3.(3) shows the two answers of participant C.

In this way, we preserve, through the session integration, in threaded conversations the linearity of face-to-face conversations, and the users can be better aware of the interventions that take place in the group.

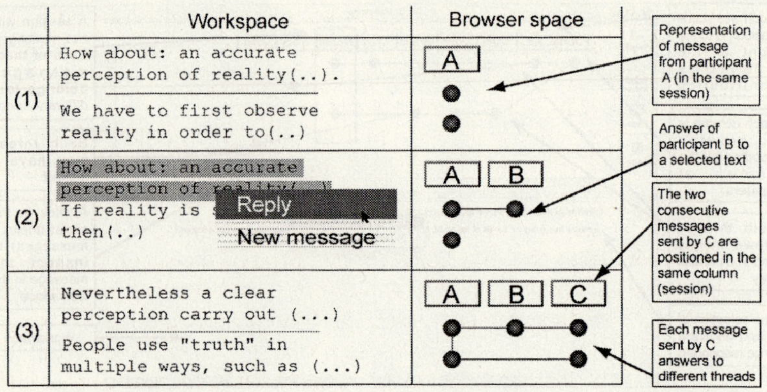

Fig. 3. The dynamics of the construction of three sessions in Mailgroup

4.3 Sessions as Turn-Taking Element in Threaded Conversations

We state that the session structure represents a turn-taking element in CMC environments. We propose that the turn-taking in threaded conversations is not the message, but that the whole of messages that each participant answers in each branch of conversation is the equivalent in the threaded conversations to face-to-face turn taking. In the FTT we must interpret the turn-taking in another level of granularity, and no longer think that each intervention in a thread is a turn in the conversation, but the group of messages (each one in different threads) sent in an intervention is now the turn.

With the use of this session element, the users obtain a clearer notion of the turn-taking that takes place in threaded conversations, the non-linearity of threaded conversations disappears and the turn-taking in CMC becomes the alterning turns of sessions. This session structure tries to clarify the turn-taking in threaded conversations for better coordination, cooperation and collaboration given that users can situate and contextualize better the interventions of participants. Also, this structure allows management and parallel visualization of different threads in a multithread conversation, which are normally visualized in a dispersed way (e.g., figure 1): The session structure encompasses the messages that are normally disperse in different threads.

In this way, this structure overcomes an observed dissociation in threaded conversations between the temporal order of messages and the thread order of messages [19,3]. This dissociation has important consequences on participants, which often fail to follow the development of a multithread debate [19].

5 Preliminary Empirical Results

An empirical study was designed in order to collect feedback on the actual characteristics of our prototype from the user's perspective. In this study, 15 participants were recruited. The participants were teachers, who carried out, during one month and a half, a distance collaborative activity as part of a training course on information and communication technologies (ICT). During this study, the tool was used just as a medium of communication and discussion, not as a point of concern in itself. The participants' activity objective was, actually, to carry out a collaborative analysis of integration and utilization of ICT in the educational milieu.

The discussion contributions were studied in order to examine the impact of the new thread visualization in the threaded conversations of the participants in a learning context. More, students' impressions of the use and value of the proposed tool and its potentials for learning enhancement were collected with a questionnaire.

The experience has showed that the introduction of the session construct in VLC does not generate a significant change in the temporal behavior of participants (between 20% and 30% of the messages are still consecutive messages). Nevertheless, we have eliminated these consecutive messages as serials events converting them into parallel events through the construction of sessions that contain two or more messages.

The questionnaire findings confirm the benefits of using this visualization for the threaded conversations. The participants consider in a high number (75%) that the proposed visualization and organization of messages allows them to better follows the development of conversations.

Another remarkable result is that the participants consider in a high proportion (75%) that Mailgroup permits an effective visualization of participant's exchanges. This fact improves the navigation through the contributions, which "is a key usability issue for online communities; particularly communities of practice which involve a large amount of information exchange" [20].

6 Conclusions

This paper attempts to connect the turn-talking issues found in the literature and empirical findings with some practical propositions.

We propose in this paper the introduction of a new element in the forum-type tools that make certain work practices of participants in a VLC explicit. The forum-type tools have become, together with email, the basic tools for realizing collaborative learning activities.

This work is framed by our objective of creating new artifacts that make collaborative learning environments more flexible and give new possibilities of communication, coordination and action. The introduction of a session structure redefines the concept of turn-taking in threaded conversations. With the session construct these conversations become the alterning turns as the face-to-face conversations.

The introduction of the session construct allows make salient a temporal behavior of participants of a VLC that actually the technology hides. We conjecture that expliciting these behaviors can be an element to improve the management of threads learning conversations. This way, this structure gives a more coherent visualization of turn-taking. More, The session can be conceptualized as a type of representational guidance [21] element for the students or participants. That is, a representation (as graphs or pictures) that helps to promote collaborative interactions of users through a direct perception of participant's turns.

The origins of the FFT were mainly the distribution of news, and were not an environment for interactive communication. In this context, we try to fix up these tools to obtain the better and perfectible environments for group communications. And this, based on the tenet that making the structures of interactions more coherent with our communication patterns contributes to facilitate the communication in the VLC.

References

1. Bødker, K., F. Kensing, and J. Simonsen, *Changing Work Practices in Design*, in *Social Thinking - Software Practice*, Y.e.a. Dittrich, Editor. 2002, MIT Press.
2. Bellamy, R., *Support for Learning Conversations*. 1997.
3. Herring, S. *Interactional Coherence in CMC*. in *32nd Hawai'i International Conference on System Sciences*. 1999. Hawai: IEEE Computer Society Press.
4. Pankoke-Babatz, U. and U. Petersen. *Dealing with phenomena of time in the age of the Internet*. in *IFIP WWC 2000*. 2000.
5. Sacks, H., E. Schegloff, and G. Jefferson, *A simplest systematics for the organisation of turn-taking in conversation*. Language, 1974. **50**.
6. Murray, D.E., *When the medium determines turns: Turn-taking in computer conversation*, in *Working with language*, H. Coleman, Editor. 1989, Mouton de Gruyter: Berlín - Nueva York. p. 319-337.
7. McElhearn, K., *Writing conversation : an analysis of speech events en e-mail mailing lists*. Revue Française De Linguistique Appliquée, 2000. **5**(1).
8. Warschauer, M., *Computer-mediated collaborative learning: Theory and practice*. Modern Language Journal, 1997. **81**(3): p. 470-481.
9. Pincas, A. *E-learning by virtual replication of classroom methodology*. in *The Humanities and Arts higher education Network, HAN*. 2001.
10. McKinlay, A. and J. Arnott. *A Study of Turn-taking in a ComputerSupported Group Task*. in *People and Computers, HCI'93 Conference*. 1993: Cambridge University Press.
11. Teasley, S. and J. Roschelle, *Constructing a joint problem space*, in *Computers as cognitive tools.*, S. Lajoie and S. Derry, Editors. 1993, Lawrence Erlbaum: Hillsdale, NJ.
12. Begole, J., et al. *Work rhythms: Analyzing visualizations of awareness histories of distributed groups*. in *Proceedings of CSCW 2002*. 2002: ACM Press.
13. Roberts, T.L. *Are newsgroups virtual communities?* in *CHI'98*. 1998.
14. Singer, J. and T. Lethbridge. *Studying work practices to assist tool design in software engineering*. in *6th International Workshop on Program Comprehension (WPC'98)*. 1998. Ischia, Italy.
15. Butler, B.S., *When is a Group not a Group : An Empirical Examination of Metaphors for Online Social Structure*. 1999, Graduate School of Business, University of Pittsburgh.
16. Rafaeli, S. and F. Sudweeks, *Networked interactivity*. Journal of Computer-Mediated Communication, 1997. **2**(4).
17. Cambrige Dictionary, *Cambridge Dictionary Online*. n.d., Cambridge University.
18. Reyes, P. and P. Tchounikine. *Supporting Emergence Of Threaded Learning Conversations Through Augmenting Interactional And Sequential Coherence*. in *CSCL Conference*. 2003.
19. Davis, M. and A. Rouzie, *Cooperation vs. Deliberation: Computer Mediated Conferencing and the Problem of Argument in International Distance Education*. International Review of Research in Open and Distance Learning, 2002. **3**(1).
20. Preece, J., *Sociability and usability: Twenty years of chatting online*. Behavior and Information Technology Journal, 2001. **20**(5): p. 347-356.
21. Suthers, D., *Towards a Systematic Study of Representational Guidance for Collaborative Learning Discourse*. Journal of Universal Computer Science, 2001. **7**(3).

Harnessing P2P Power in the Classroom

Julita Vassileva

Department of Computer Science, MADMUC Lab
University of Saskatchewan, 1C101 Engineering Bldg,
57 Campus Drive, Saskatoon, S7N 5A9 CANADA
jiv@cs.usask.ca
http://www.cs.usask.ca/faculty/julita

Abstract. We have implemented a novel peer-to-peer based environment called Comtella, which allows students to contribute and share class-related resources. This system has been implemented successfully in a fourth year undergraduate course on Ethics and IT. The intermediate results of the ongoing experiment show a significant increase in participation and contribution in the test version in comparison with a previous offering of the class where students contributed class-related resources via their own personal web-sites. Our ongoing and future work focuses on motivating higher levels of participation and getting students involved in the quality control of the contributions aiming at a self-organizing virtual learning community.

1 Introduction

The Computer Science Department at the University of Saskatchewan offers a fourth year undergraduate class called "Ethics and Information Technologies" which discusses broader social issues related to the development and deployment of IT in the real world, including privacy, freedom of speech, intellectual property, computer crime and security, workplace issues and professionalism. One week of classes and discussion is dedicated to each of these themes. Much of the content of the class involves legal cases, which are often ongoing and not yet resolved. The class has a strong communication component, involving class discussions and requiring students to summarize popular magazine articles related to the issues. For the class discussion, it is important to read and analyze the different viewpoints presented in the media and it is impossible to rely only on the textbook as a source of up-to-date cases and controversial viewpoints in discussion. Most newspapers and magazines, professional and public organizations have websites that represent their viewpoints on current controversial issues and cases. News about the development of lawsuits, new stories related to the use of IT appear constantly. Therefore, the Internet is an ideal resource of readings related to the class and can be used to create a repository for students' use. However, keeping current in the stream of news on such a wide variety of topics and locating appropriate resources for each week is an overwhelming task for the instructor.

J.C. Lester et al. (Eds.): ITS 2004, LNCS 3220, pp. 305–314, 2004.

Therefore, one of the class activities involves the students in the process of creating and maintaining of such a repository. Students are required to find on a weekly basis web-links to articles related to the issues discussed during the week and post them on their personal websites dedicated to the class. The instructor reviews these websites and selects from them several links to post on the class website. The students need to write a one-page summary - discussion for one of these selected articles.

The process described above is quite laborious both for the students and for the instructor. The students need to create and maintain personal class-websites on which to post the links they find. The instructor needs to review frequently differently organized student websites, to see which students have found links to new articles, to read and evaluate the articles and add selected good papers to the official class website where the students can pick an article to summarize. This process takes time and usually can be done only in the end of the week, therefore the students can only write summaries for the articles on the topic discussed during the previous week, which makes it impossible to focus all activities of the students to the currently discussed topic. Another disadvantage of this process is that the selected by the instructor articles posted on the class website reflect the instructor's subjective interests in the area; the students may prefer to summarize different articles than those selected by the instructor.

The process of sharing class related articles, selection of articles and summarization can be supported much better by using a peer-to-peer (P2P) file-sharing technology. Therefore we decided to deploy in the "Ethics and IT" class Comtella, a P2P system developed at the MADMUC lab of the Computer Science Department for sharing academic papers among researchers in a group, lab or department. The next section introduces briefly the area of P2P file-sharing. Section 3 describes the Comtella system. Section 4 explains how Comtella was applied to support the Ethics and IT class. Section 5 presents the first encouraging evaluation results.

2 P2P Files-Sharing Systems

Peer to Peer (P2P) file-sharing systems have been around for 5 years and have enjoyed enormous popularity as free tools for downloading music (.mp3) files and movies. They have also gained a lot of public attention due to the controversial lawsuit that the RIAA launched against Napster and the ensuing on-going public debate about copyright protection. RIAA initially claimed that P2P technologies are used mainly to violate copyright and argued unsuccessfully for banning them. It succeeded in closing Napster, which used a centralized index of the files shared by all participants to facilitate the search. However, the widely publicized decision spurred a bunch of new entirely distributed and anonymous file-sharing applications relying on protocols such as Gnutella or FreeNet, which make it very hard to identify and prosecute file-sharers. Up to now, with the exceptions of P2P applications aimed at sharing CPU cycles (e.g. SETI@home which harnesses the CPU power of the participating peers' PCs to compute data from telescopes to search for signs of extraterrestrial intelligence and several projects like the Intel Philanthropic Peer-to-Peer project using

P2P technology to harness computer power for medical research), instant messaging applications like Jabber and AVAKI, and collaboration applications like Groove, the most widely used P2P applications are used for illegal file-sharing (e.g. KaZaA, BearShare, E-Donkey) of copyrighted music, films, or pornographic materials. Most recently, there have been initiatives to put P2P file-sharing for better use, e.g. MS Sharepoint or Nullsoft's Waste which serves a small private network of friends.

We see a huge potential for P2P file-sharing to tap the individual efforts of instructors, teaching assistants and learners in creating and sharing learning materials. These materials can be specially developed instructional modules or learning objects as in EDUTELLA (Neidl et al, 2002), or in the Ternier, Duval & Neven's (2001) proposal for a P2P based learning object repository. However, any kind of files can be shared in a P2P way, including PowerPoint files presenting lecture notes, web-based notes or references, research papers (used as teaching materials in graduate classes or during graduate student supervision). We propose a P2P system enabling learners to bring in and share course-related materials, called Comtella. The system is described in the next section. Section 4 presents results of an ongoing experiment with the system in the Ethics and IT course and compares the amount of student contributions using Comtella with the contributions of students taking the same class in the previous year, using their own websites to post links to the resources found.

3 The Comtella System

The Comtella system (Vassileva, 2002) was developed at the MADMUC lab at the Computer Science Department to support graduate students in the laboratory to share research papers found on-line. Comtella uses an extension of the Gnutella protocol, and is fully distributed. Each user needs to download a client application (called "servent") which allows sharing new papers with the community (typically, pdf files, but it can be easily extended for all kinds of files) and searching for papers shared by oneself and by the other users. The shared papers need to be annotated with respect to their content as belonging to a subject category (an adapted subset of the ACM subject index). The user searches by specifying a category and receives a list of all own papers and papers shared by others related to this category. From the list of results, the user can download the desired papers and view them in a browser.

While the research papers shared by users are not necessarily their own papers, but written by other authors, there is a copyright issue. However, these papers are typically found on the Web anyway (Comtella supports the user to seamlessly save and share pdf files that are viewed in the browser as that are typically found on the Web using search tools, such as Google or CiteSeer). Storing a local copy of the paper may be considered as a violation of copyright. However, users typically store local copies of viewed papers for personal use anyway, since they can not rely that they will find the file if they search again later (the average lifetime of a document on the web is approximately three months). Saving a copy for backup purpose is generally considered fair use. The sharing of papers happens on a small scale, among people interested in the same area within a research group or department, typically 5-10 people.

Lending a book to a friend or colleague is normally considered fair use and in academic environment supervisors and graduate students typically share articles both electronically or printed on paper. Therefore, we believe that this type of sharing can not be considered copyright violation, since it has educational use and stimulates the flow of ideas, research information and assists the generation of new ideas.

In addition to facilitating the process of sharing papers, Comtella supports the development of a shared group repository of resources, by synergizing the efforts of all participating users. It allows users to rate the papers they share and add comments, which can yield a global ranking of the papers with respect to their quality and/or popularity within the group. Thus an additional source of information is generated automatically, that can be very useful for newcomers to the lab (e.g. new students) to get initial orientation in the assembled paper repository.

Comtella has been used on experimental basis with some interruptions and various successes for nearly one year in the MADMUC lab and for about three months across the Computer Science Department. We identified a number of technical issues related to instability of servents caused by Java-related memory leaks, and communicating across firewalls (so that the users could use the system from home), which have been mostly resolved. There were logistics issues, related to the fact that the system was fully distributed: a user who wanted to use the system both from home and from the office had to always leave his/her servents running on both machines, so that s/he can access from work his/her own papers shared by the servent at home and to access from home the papers shared at the work computer. In fact, Comtella considers the user's servents at home and at work as servents of two different users, with different ids, lists of shared papers etc.

In order to access the papers shared by another user, the other user has to be on-line. This proved to be a problem, because users typically switch off their home computers when they are at work. In addition, the users tend to start their servents only when they want to search for papers and to quit it afterwards. This leads to very few servents being on-line simultaneously, and therefore there are very few (if any) results to a query. It is very important to ensure a critical mass of on-line servents to maintain an infrastructure that guarantees successful searches and attracts more users to keep on-line their servents. Various solutions have been deployed in the popular file-sharing systems like KaZaA and LimeWire, for example, switching off the servent can be made particularly hard.

Finally, even when most of the users keep their servents running all the time, the system quickly reaches a "saturation" point, when all users download all the files in which they are interested from other users during their first successful searches. If there are no new resources injected into the system (by users bringing in and sharing new papers), very soon it makes no sense for a user to search in his/her main area of interest since there is nothing new. Ultimately, the system reaches equilibrium where everyone has all papers that everyone else has. In order to achieve a dynamic and useful system, the users have to share new papers regularly and thus contribute to the growing repository rather to behave as lurkers (Nonnecke & Preece, 2000). Motivating users to contribute is an important problem and we have researched a motivational strategy based on rewards in terms of quality of service and community visualization of contributions (Bretzke & Vassileva, 2003).

Since Comtella provides exactly the infrastructure allowing users to bring in and share resources with each other, we decided to deploy it in the "Ethics in IT" course to support students in sharing and rating on-line papers related to the topics of the course. We expected to have a higher participation and contribution rate than in the case where Comtella is used to share research papers within a lab, since within a class, the students are required to put a concerted effort scheduled by the class curriculum (weekly topics) to summarize papers and to contribute new papers to get a participation mark. We wanted to see also how the contribution level when students use Comtella will differ from the level in the previous offering of the class, when students had to add the links to their own class website. Finally, we wanted to experiment with some of our motivational strategies to see if they actually lead to increase in participation compared to a system with no motivational strategies.

4 Applying Comtella in the Ethics in IT Course

The first problem that had to be dealt with was ensuring a critical number of servents running at any given time, so that queries were guaranteed to yield some results. Our previous experience with peer-help systems shows that otherwise the users are unlikely to query again, and the usage of the system quickly winds down to zero. However, while in a research lab graduate students tend to leave their office computers running permanently, it is unrealistic to expect that undergraduate students will have a permanently running computer at home where they can keep running their Comtella client. Therefore, we had to make a compromise with the distributed P2P architecture, and move all servents to two server machines. We split the user interface (UI) part of the servent from the backend part (BE) that processes and forwards queries, pings and pongs to other peers and maintains the list of files shared by the user. The UI part is a jar file that students can download and run on their local machine to log into their own BE, which runs constantly on the server. Thus all queries by other users are served by the BE which is available all the time, even when the user is not on-line. Users log into their BE only when they need to search for papers or to share new papers. In this way, we also restricted the access to allow only class members and imposed unambiguous user identification through username and password. This is important since we need to keep track of users' contribution to reward it fairly with participation marks.

The next change to the Comtella architecture was necessitated by two factors:

- shared files by the servent of each user occupy a lot of disk space. Since now the BE on a central server, the disk space required may exceed the availability and become prohibitive.
- the files shared for the class are mostly from web-magazines and their format is varied. Some are html, xml, xhtml, some contain flash. Saving a copy of the file on disk is not trivial and depends on the browser and the settings. Sometimes a file can be associated with a directory of images, ad banners etc.

For these two reasons, we decided to modify the standard Gnutella servent functionality and instead of sharing the actual files, only their URLs are shared. To share a paper from the Web, the user needs to copy and paste the URL into the Comtella "Share" window, to copy and paste the title of the article from the browser, and finally to select the category (topic) of the article, which is indicated by the week of the class it relates to (see Figure 1). The shared paper in this way consists of: title, URL, category, and optionally, rating and comment, if the user decides to provide them.

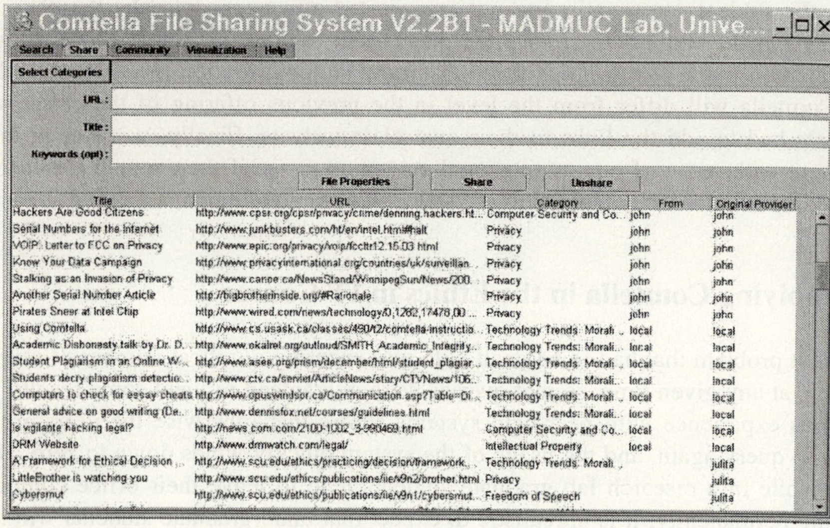

Fig. 1. Sharing new links in Comtella

Users who decide to search for papers related to the topic of a given week have to specify the topic from the category list in the "Search" window. The servent sends the query to its neighbour servents residing on the server and they forward the query to their neighbours. If any of the servents that receive the query share some papers about this topic, the results are sent back to the querying peer using the standard Gnutella protocol. In other words, the protocol for search is not changed; the only change is the physical location of the BE of the servents that reside now on two server machines.

Students can view and read the papers that were yielded as results of the search by clicking on the "Visit" button without actually downloading the paper (see Figure 2). Clicking "Visit" starts the default browser with the URL of the paper and the student can view the paper in the browser. The student can also view the comments of the user who shares the paper and his/her rating of the paper. If the student likes the paper and decides to share it him/herself, to comment on it or rate it, s/he can download it, by clicking on the "download" button. This initiates a download process between the servents (which follows again the standard Gnutella protocol). Rather than the actual paper, the title and URL are downloaded, while the comment and rating that the sharing user entered are not. In this way, each user who shares a paper has to provide his/her own comment and rating.

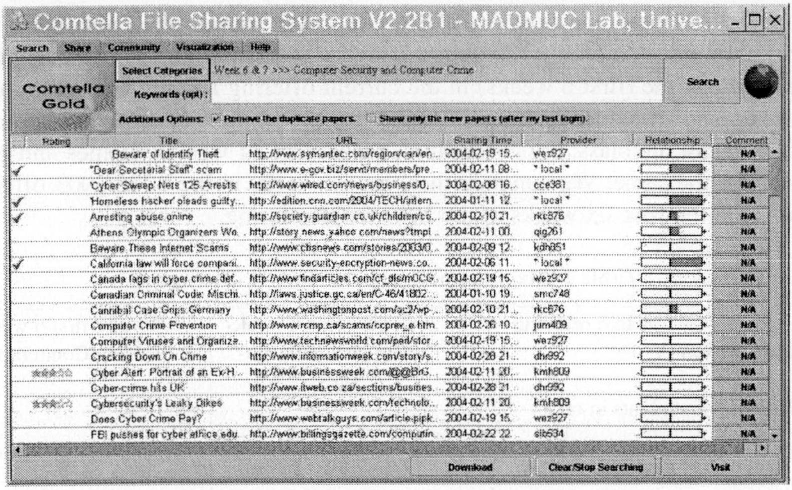

Fig. 2. Searching for papers about a given topic (category).

The ratings of the papers indicate the quality of the paper and the level of interest the students who downloaded the paper have in the topic of the paper. The students were instructed to select for their weekly summary a paper that was rated highly by two or more students of those who share the paper. The students could enter their weekly summary through Comtella too, by entering a summary for a selected paper from their shared papers.

If two students disagreed in their rating of a paper, their relationship strength decreases. The relationship between the student who does the search and each student who shares a paper is shown in the search results (see Figure 2). In this way, students can find other students who judge papers in a similar way, since the relationship value serves as a measure of trust that the student has in the papers provided by the other student.

Comtella became a focal point of all weekly course activities. The instructor did not need to find and share any new articles since the students provided an excessive number of materials, which were immediately accessible for anyone who wanted to search for papers with the same topic (category). It became also unnecessary for the instructor to review all contributed papers and select those appropriate to be summarized, since the ratings of the papers indicated the good papers and those in which the students were interested.

5 Evaluation

The deployment of Comtella in the Ethics and IT course is ongoing at the time of writing. The planned evaluation of the system includes data collected through system use (e.g. statistics on numbers of contributed papers, numbers of downloaded papers, ratings and summaries written, average time spent on line, frequency of logging in) and data from student questionnaires. However, even though the experiment is only half-way through, comparing the average levels of student contributions during the same period of time (first 6 weeks) in the current offering and the last year's offering of the class shows evidence for the success of the system. In both cases the same instructor taught the class; the curriculum, scheduling of weekly themes and grading scheme were the same. We compare the first six weeks in the 2002/2003 offering of the class with the first six weeks of the 2003/2004 offering.

Table 1. Main characteristics of the two offerings.

\ Class offering **Parameters **	2002/03 - first 6 weeks (using personal web-sites)	2003/04 - first 6 weeks (using Comtella)
Number of students in class:	25	35
Total contributed links:	51	334
Average number of new links contributed per person (average from only those who contributed):	4.63	11.52
Number of students who didn't contribute at all:	14 or 56% of the class	6 or 17% of the class
Percentage of links contributed by the top five (5) students:	78% of all the contributed links	39% of all contributed links

Table 1 summarizes the student and participation data in each class. We can see that the average number of contributed new links per person in the 2003/2004 class where students used Comtella was nearly three times higher than in the 2002/2003 class. The bulk (nearly 80%) of contributions in the 2002/2003 class was done by five students, while in the 2003/2004 class the top five students contributed approximately 40% of the links and the contributions were spread more equally (see also Figure 3, which compares the distribution of contributions among the students in the two class offerings). We can see that 56% of the students in the 2002/2003 class did not contribute, versus only 17% in the 2003/04 class. Figure 4 shows how regularly students contributed over the course of the first six weeks of the experiment. As can be seen more students contributed regularly in the 2003/2004 class than in the 2002/2003 class.

One reason for these encouraging results is that it is much easier for the students to add new links in Comtella than to maintain a website and add links there. Another reason is that searching for relevant links with Comtella is much more convenient than visiting the websites of each student in the class, so the students tended to use the system much more often. They visited links shared by others in Comtella and when viewing these articles they found new relevant articles (since often Web-magazine articles have a sidebar field "Related Stories" or "Related Links") and shared them in Comtella "on the go".

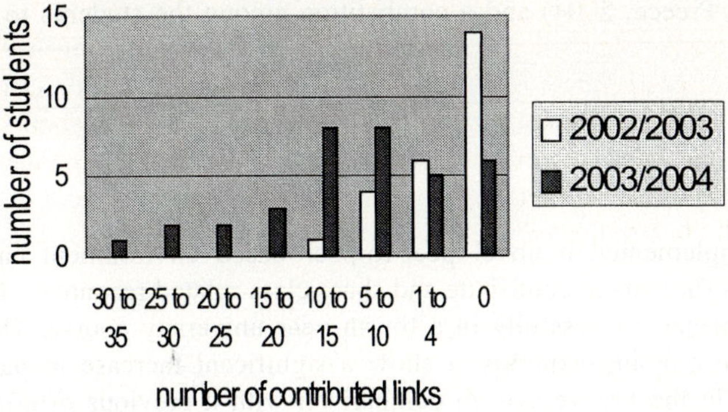

Fig. 3. Number of new contributions: comparing the first weeks of the two courses.

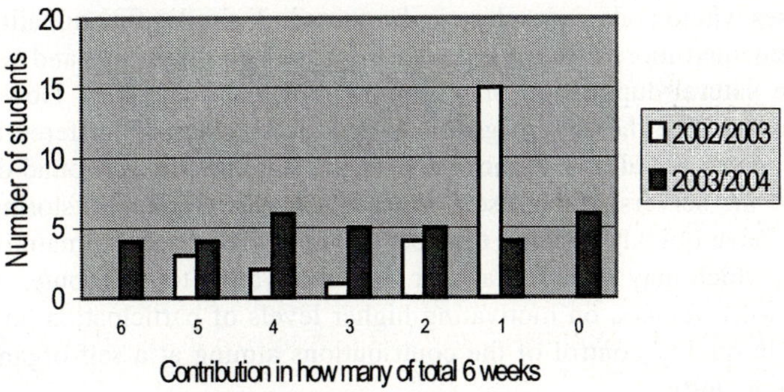

Fig. 4. Regularity of contributions.

While in the beginning the instructor had to evaluate the links added and to rate them, from the third week on the students started giving ratings to the articles themselves and the system became self-organized. Of course, monitoring is still necessary, since currently nothing prevents students from sharing links that are not related to the contents of the course or offensive materials. In our experiment, such an event has not happened to date, possibly, since the students are senior students in their last year before graduation. Yet, it would be good to incorporate tools that would allow the community of students to have a say on the postings of the colleagues and thus achieve an automatic quality control by the community of users, similar to Slashdot.

In the remaining six weeks of the course, we will experiment a three level "membership" in the Comtella community based on the level of contribution: bronze, silver and gold, that will give certain privileges for members who have contributed on regular basis papers that have been downloaded and rated highly by other students. This newer version contains also a visualization of the community showing the contribution level of each individual member, information about whether s/he is on-line at the moment in line with the motivation visualization described in (Bretzke & Vassileva, 2003). The goal is to create a feeling of community (Smith & Kollock, 1999,

De Souza & Preece, 2004) and a competition among the students to find more and better links.

6 Conclusions

We have implemented a novel peer-to-peer based environment called Comtella, which allows students to contribute and share class-related resources. This system has been implemented successfully in a fourth year university course. The intermediate results of the ongoing experiment show a significant increase in participation and contribution in the test version in comparison with a previous offering of the class where students contributed class-related resources via their own personal web-sites. We believe that the system can be applied to support a wide range of courses requiring intensive reading of on-line resources, e.g. in the humanities, or even programming courses where code-examples can be shared. A similar functionality could have been implemented more efficiently using a centralized repository and search engine, without the natural duplication of resources implied by Gnutella. However, we did not want to sacrifice the advantages of logical decentralization offered by a P2P architecture, since they allows to move any of the servents freely around depending on the load on the servers. If the users were sharing actual papers, storing them on a server may have quickly become too costly. The shared papers remain in the control of the user, which may be important for their motivation to contribute. Our ongoing and future work focuses on motivating higher levels of participation and student involvement in quality control of the contributions aiming at a self-organizing virtual learning community.

References

1. Bretzke H., Vassileva J.: Motivating Cooperation in Peer to Peer Networks, Proceedings User Modeling UM03, Johnstown, PA, Lecture Notes in Computer Science, Vol. 2702. Springer-Verlag, Berlin Heidelberg New York, 218-227 (2003).
2. Comtella © 2002-2004 available from http://bistrica.usask.ca/madmuc/peer-motivation.htm
3. De Souza, C., Preece, J. A framework for analyzing and understanding online communities. Interacting with Computers. 16 (3), 579-610 (2004).
4. Nejdl, W., Wolf B. et al.: EDUTELLA : A P2P Networking Infrastructure Based on RDF, WWW2002, May 7 -11, Honolulu, Hawaii, USA (2002).
5. Nonnecke, B., Preece, J., Lurker Demographics: Counting the Silent. Proceedings of ACM CHI'2000, Hague, The Netherlands, 73–80 (2000).
6. Smith, M.A. and Kollock, P., 1999. Communities in Cyberspace. , Routledge, London.
7. Ternier, S., Duval, E., and Vandepitte P. LOMster: Peer-to-Peer Learning Object Metadata. Proceedings of EdMedia-2002, AACE: Blacksburg, 1942-1943 (2002).
8. Vassileva J.: Supporting Peer-to-Peer User Communities, in R. Meersman, Z. Tari et al. (Eds.) Proc. CoopIS, DOA, and ODBASE, LNCS 2519, Springer: Berlin, 230-247 (2002).

Analyzing Online Collaborative Dialogues: The *OXEnTCHÊ–Chat*

Ana Cláudia Vieira, Lamartine Teixeira, Aline Timóteo, Patrícia Tedesco, and Flávia Barros

Universidade Federal de Pernambuco
Centro de Informática
Recife - PE Brasil
Phone: +55 8121268430
{achv, lat2, alt, pcart, fab}@cin.ufpe.br

Abstract. Internet-based virtual learning environments allow participants to refine their knowledge by interacting with their peers. Besides, they offer ways to escape from the isolation seen in the CAI and ITS systems. However, simply allowing participants to interact is not enough to eliminate the isolation feeling and to motivate students. Recent research in Computer Supported Collaborative Learning has been investigating ways to minor the above problems. This paper presents the *OXEnTCHÊ–Chat*, a chat tool coupled with an automatic dialogue classifier which analyses on-line interaction and provides just-in-time feedback to both instructors and learners. Feedback is provided through reports, which can be user-specific or about the whole dialogue. The tool also counts on a chatterbot, which plays the role of an automatic coordinator. The implemented prototype of *OXEnTCHÊ–Chat* has been evaluated and the obtained results are very satisfactory.

1 Introduction

Since the 1970's, research in the area of Computing in Education has been looking for ways to improve learning rates with the help of computers [1]. Until the mid 1990's, computational educational systems focused on offering individual assistance to students (e.g., Computer Assisted Instruction (CAI), and early Intelligent Tutoring Systems (ITS)). As a consequence, the students could only work in isolation, frequently feeling unmotivated to spend long hours in this task.

Currently, the available information and communication technologies (ICTs) provide means for the development of group work/learning virtual systems [2] at considerably low costs. This scenario has favoured the emergence of virtual learning environments (VLE) on the Internet (e.g., WebCT [3]). One of the benefits of group work is that the participants can refine their knowledge by interacting with the others. Besides, it offers ways to escape from the isolation seen in the CAI and ITS systems.

However, simply offering technology for interactions between VLE participants is not enough to eliminate the isolation feeling. The students are not able to see their peers, and to feel that they are part of a "community". This way, they tend to become unmotivated [4], and drop out of on-line courses fairly frequently.

J.C. Lester et al. (Eds.): ITS 2004, LNCS 3220, pp. 315–324, 2004.

Recent research in Computer Supported Collaborative Learning (CSCL) [5] has been investigating ways of helping users to: (1) feel more motivated; and (2) achieve better performances in collaborative learning environments. One way to tackle problem (1) is to provide the interface with an animated agent that interacts with the students. In fact, studies have shown that these software agents facilitate human computer interaction, and are able to influence users' behavior [6]. Regarding issue (2), one possibility is to monitor the collaboration process, analyzing it and providing feedback to the users on how to better participate in the interaction. Besides, the system should also keep the instructor informed about the interaction (so that s/he can decide if, when and how to intervene or change pedagogical practices).

In this light, we developed the *OXEnTCHÊ–Chat*, a tool that tackles the above problems by monitoring the interaction process and offering feedback to users. The system provides a chat tool coupled with an automatic dialogue classifier which analyses on-line interaction and provides just-in-time feedback reports to both instructors and learners. Two different reports are available: (1) general information about the dialogue (e.g. chat duration, number of users); and (2) specific information about one user's participation, how to improve it. The system also counts on a chatterbot [7], which plays the role of an automatic coordinator (helping to maintain the dialogue focus, and trying to motivate students to engage in the interaction). The tool was evaluated with two groups, and the obtained results are very satisfactory.

The remainder of this paper is organised as follows. Section 2 presents a brief review of the state of the art in systems that analyse collaboration. Section 3 describes the *OXEnTCHÊ–Chat* tool, and section 4 discusses experiments and results. Finally, section 5 presents conclusions and suggestions for further work.

2 Collaborative Learning Systems That Monitor the Interaction

In order to be able to foster more productive interactions, current collaborative learning systems that monitor the participants' interaction typically focus their analysis on one of two levels: (1) the participant's individual actions; or (2) the interaction as a whole. Of the five systems discussed in this section, the first two focus on (1), whereas the other three focus on (2).

LeCS (Learning from Case Studies) [8] is collaborative learning environment for case studies. In order to solve their case, participants follow a methodology consisting of seven steps. At the end of each step, the group should send a partial answer to the system. An interface agent monitors the solution development, as well as user's participation. This agent sends messages to the students reminding them that they have forgotten given step, and to encourage remiss students to participate more.

COLER (*COllaborative Learning Environment for Entity-Relationship modelling*) [9] is an Internet-based collaborative learning environment. Students first work individually (in a private workspace) and then collaborate to produce an Entity- Relationship (E-R) model. Each student has an automated coach. It gives feedback to the student whenever a difference between his/her individual E-R models and the one built by the group is detected.

DEGREE (*Distance Environment for GRoup ExperiencEs*) [10] monitors the interaction of distant learners in a discussion forum in order to support its pedagogical decisions. The system sends messages to the students with the aim of helping them reflect about the solution-building process, as well as about the quality of their collaboration. It also provides feedback about the group performance.

COMET (*A Collaborative Object Modelling Environment*) [11] is a system developed so that teams can collaboratively solve object-oriented design problems, using the Object Modelling Technique (OMT). The system uses sentence openers (e.g. I think, I agree) in order to analyse the ongoing interaction. The chat log stores information about the conversation, such as date, day of the week, time of intervention, user login and sentence openers used. COMET uses Hidden Markov Models to analyse the interaction and assess the quality of knowledge sharing.

MArCo (*Artificial Conflict Mediator* – in Portuguese) [12] counts on an artificial conflict mediator that monitors the dialogue, giving tips on how to better proceed when a conflict is detected to the participants.

Apart from DEGREE, current systems that monitor on-line collaboration tend to either concentrate their feedback on the users' specific actions or on the whole interaction. On the one hand, by concentrating only on particular actions, systems can miss opportunities for improving group performance. On the other hand, by concentrating on the whole interaction, systems can miss opportunities for engaging students into the collaborative process, and thus not properly motivating them.

3 The *OXEnTCHÊ–Chat*

The *OXEnTCHÊ–Chat* is a tool that tackles the problems of lack of motivation and low group performance by providing feedback to individual users as well as to the group. The system provides a chat tool coupled with an automatic dialogue classifier which analyses the on-line interaction and provides just-in-time feedback to instructors/teachers and learners. Teachers receive feedback reports on both the group and on individual students (and thus can evaluate students and change pedagogical practices), whereas students can only check their individual performance. This combination of automated dialogue analysis and just-in-time feedback for teachers and students constitutes a novel approach. The *OXEnTCHÊ–Chat* is an Internet-based tool, implemented in Java. Its architecture is explained in details in section 3.1.

3.1 Tool's Architecture

OXEnTCHÊ–Chat adopts a client-server architecture (Fig. 1). The system consists of two packages, chat and analysis. Package chat runs on the client machines, and contains the chat interfaces. When users make a contribution to the dialogue (which can be either a sentence or a request for feedback), it is sent to package *analysis*.

Package *analysis* runs on the server, and is responsible for classifying the ongoing dialogue and for generating feedback. This package counts on five modules: Analysis Controller; Subject Classifier; Feature Extractor; Dialogue Classifier; and Report Generator. There are also two databases: Log, which stores individual users' logs and the whole dialogue log; and Ontology, which stores the ontologies for various subject domains. Package *analysis* also counts on the Bot Agent.

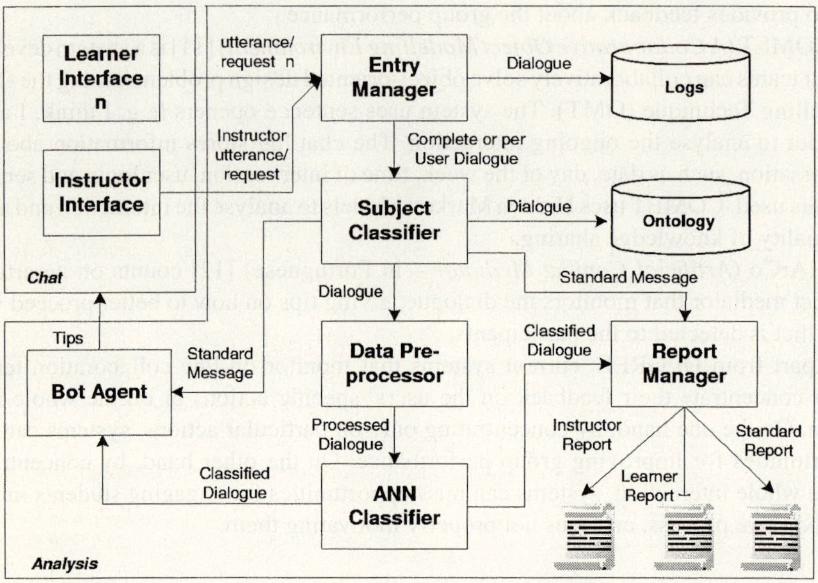

Fig. 1. The System's Architecture

The *Analysis Controller* (AC) performs three functions: to receive users' contributions to the dialogue; to receive requests for feedback; and to send relevant messages to the Bot. When the AC receives a contribution to the dialogue, it stores this contribution in the whole dialogue log, as well as in the corresponding user's log. When the AC receives a student's request for feedback, it retrieves the corresponding user's log, and sends it to the *Subject Classifier* (SC). If the request is from the teacher, the AC retrieves the whole dialogue log as well as any individual logs requested. The retrieved logs are then sent to the SC. The AC forwards to the Bot all messages directed to it (e.g., a query about a concept definition).

The SC analyses the dialogue and identifies whether or not participants have discussed the subject the teacher proposed for that chat. This analysis is done by querying the relevant domain ontology (stored in the Ontology database). Currently, there are six ontologies available: Introduction to Artificial Intelligence, Intelligent Agents, Multi-Agent Systems, Knowledge Representation, Machine Learning and Project Management. When the SC verifies that the students are really discussing the proposed subject, it sends the dialogue log to the *Feature Extractor* (FE) for further analysis. If not, the SC sends a message to the *Report Manager* (RM), asking it to generate a Standard report. The SC also informs the Bot Agent about the subject under discussion, so that it can provide relevant web links to the participants.

The FE computes the number of collaborative skills [13] individually employed by each user and the total number of skills used in the complete dialogue. It also counts the total number of dialogue utterances, number of participants and total chat time. These results are then sent to the *Dialogue Classifier* (DC).

The DC classifies the dialogue as effective or non-effective. Dialogues are considered effective when there is a significant use of collaborative skills (e.g. creative conflict) that indicate user's reflection on the subject. Currently, the DC uses either a MLP neural network or a Decision tree. In order to train these classifiers, we have manually tagged a corpus of 200 dialogues collected from the Internet, and then used 100 dialogues for training, 50 for testing, and 50 for cross-validation. The DC sends its classification to the RM, which composes the final analysis report.

The RM produces three reports: *Instructor, Learner* and *Standard*. The *Instructor* report presents information about the whole dialogue (number of users present, total number of contributions, chat duration, collaborative skills used). The *Learner* report presents specific information about the student's participation (time spent in chat, number and type of collaborative skills used). This report can also be accessed by the teacher, allowing him/her to verify specific details about a student's performance. The *Standard* report informs that the subject proposed for the current chat session has not been discussed and, consequently, that the dialogue was classified as non-effective.

The Bot Agent is a pro-active chatterbot[1] that plays the role of an automatic dialogue coordinator. As such, it has two main goals. First of all, it must help maintain the dialogue focus, interfering in the chat whenever a change of subject is detected by the SC. Three actions can be performed here: (1) the Bot simply writes a message on the environment calling the students back to the subject of discussion; and/or (2) it presents some links to Web sites related to the subject under discussion, in order to bring new insights to the conversation.

Another goal of this agent is to motivate absent students to engage in the conversation (the dialogue log will provide the information on who is actively participating in the chat session). Here, the Bot may act by sending a private message to each absent student inviting them back, or by writing in the chat window asking all students to participate and collaborate in the discussion. Finally, the Bot Agent may also be answer students' simple questions based on (pre-stored) information about the current subject (acting as a FAQ-bot[2]). The idea of using a chatterbot in this application comes from the fact that, besides facilitating the process of human computer interaction, chatterbots are also able to influence the user's behavior [6].

In order to facilitate users' communication, the chat interface (Fig. 2) presents a similar structure to other chats found on the Internet. Chat functionalities include: user identification, change of nickname, change of text colour, automatic scrolling, emoticons, and help. The *OXEnTCHÊ–Chat*'s interface is divided into four regions: (1) top bar, containing generic facilities; (2) chat area; (3) message composition facilities; and (4) list of logged-on users. In (1) there are four buttons: exit chat, change nick, request feedback, and help. In (2) (indicated by ❶ in Fig. 2) the user can follow the group

[1] Chatterbots are software agents that communicate with people in natural language.

[2] A FAQ-bot is a chatterbot whose aim is to answer Frequent Asked Questions.

interaction. The facilities found in (3) allow participants to talk in private, change font colour and insert emoticons to express their feelings.

By clicking on button ❷ participants choose which *sentence openers* [13] they want to use. *OXEnTCHÊ–Chat* provides a list of collaborative sentence openers in Portuguese, compiled during the tool's development. This list is based on available linguistics studies [16], as well as on an empirical study of our dialogue corpus (used to train the MLP and Decision Tree classifiers). We carefully analysed the corpus, labelling participants' utterances according to the collaborative skills they indicated. The final list of sentence openers was based both on their frequency in the dialogue corpus as well as on our studies about linguistics and about collaborative dialogues (e.g. [14]).

Arrow ❸ points to the Agent Bot's name in the logged users window. We have decided to show the Bot as a logged user (Billy) to encourage participants to interact with it. The Bot can answer user's questions based on pre-stored concept definitions, send messages to users that are not actively contributing to the dialogue, or play the role of an automated dialogue coordinator.

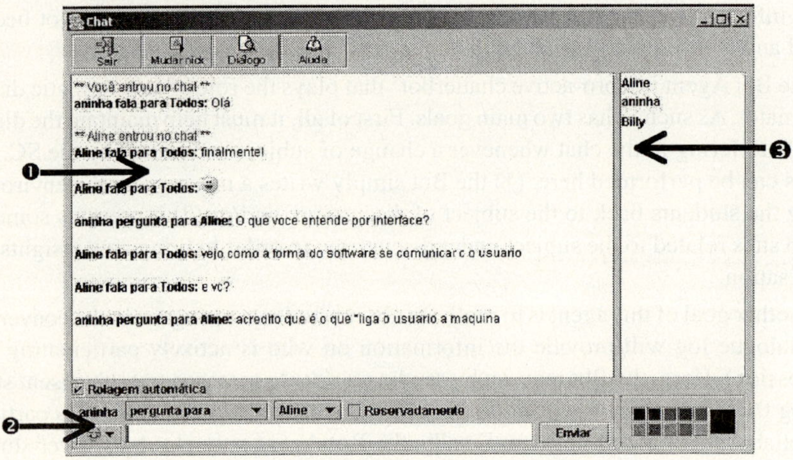

Fig. 2. *OXEnTCHÊ–Chat*'s Interface

Fig. 3 presents the window showed to the teacher when s/he requests feedback. In ❶ the teacher can see which individual dialogue logs are available. In ❷ the instructor can choose between analysing the complete dialogue, or the individual performances. The teacher can do so by clicking on the buttons labelled "Analisar diálogo completo" (Analyze the complete dialogue) and "Analisar conversa selecionada" (Analyze the selected dialogue), respectively. Item ❸ shows the area where feedback reports are presented. This particular example shows an *Instructor Report*. It contains the following information: total chat duration, number of user's contributions, number of participants, number of collaborative skills used, SC analysis and final classification (effective, in this case).

We have also developed an add-in that allows the instructor to access the dialogue analysis even if s/he is not online during the interaction. In order to get feedback reports, the teacher should select the relevant dialogue logs, and click on the corresponding interface buttons to obtain Instructor and/or Learner reports.

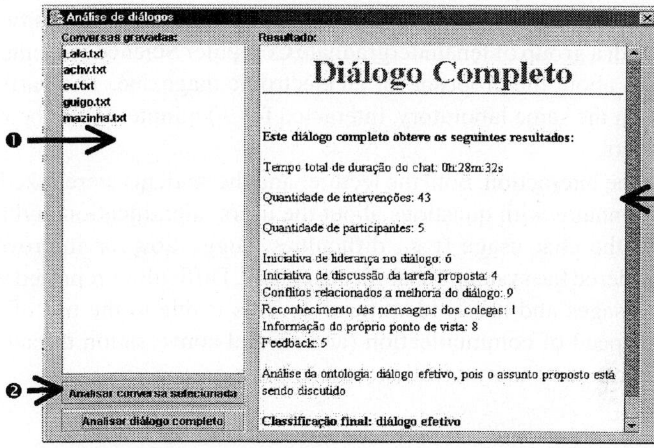

Fig. 3. Instructor's Online Feedback Report

3.2 Implementation Details

The *OXEnTCHÊ–Chat* was implemented in Java. This choice was due to Java's support for distributed applications, its portability, and the built-in multithreading mechanism. In order to achieve a satisfactory message-exchange performance, we used Java Sockets to implement the client-server communication.

The FE module is a parser based on a grammar which defines the collaborative sentence openers and their variations. This grammar was written in JavaCC, a parser generator that reads a grammar specification and converts it to a Java program. The ontologies used by the DC were defined in XML, due to its seamless integration with Java and the easy representation of hierarchical data structures.

4 Evaluating the *OXEnTCHÊ–Chat*

In order to evaluate the *OXEnTCHÊ–Chat*, we carried out two experiments. First, a usability test was performed, in order to ensure communication via the interface. The tool was refined based on the results of this experiment, and a second experiment was carried out. This time, the goal was to assess the quality of the feedback provided by the tool. At the time of the experiments, the *OXEnTCHÊ–Chat* did not count on the Bot Agent yet. It was integrated later, as a refinement suggested by the results obtained. The experiments and their results are described below.

4.1 Evaluating the Tool's Usability

In order to assess the tool's usability, we first tested the *OXEnTCHÊ–Chat*'s performance with nine users. All participants commented that the system was fairly easy to use. However, they suggest some interface improvements. All suggestions were considered, and the resulting interface layout is shown in Fig. 2.

Following, we conducted a usability test at the Federal Rural University of Pernambuco (UFRPE) with a group of ten undergraduate Computer Science students. They used the tool to discuss about the proposal for an electronic magazine. The participants and their lecturer, all in the same laboratory, interacted for 90 minutes while being observed by three researchers.

At the end of the interaction, both the lecturer and the students were asked to fill in an evaluation questionnaire with questions about the users' identification and background as well as about the chat usage (e.g., difficulties, suggestion for improvement). All participants considered the system's usability excellent. Difficulties reported were related to reading of messages and user's identification. This is due to the use of nicknames, as well as to the speed of communication (and several conversation threads) that is so common in synchronous communication.

4.2 Evaluating the Quality of the Feedback Provided

In order to assess the quality of the *feedback* provided, we carried out an evaluation experiment with two groups of participants. The main objective was to validate the feedback and the dialogue classification provided by the *OXEnTCHÊ–Chat*.

The first experiment was performed at UFRPE, with the same group that participated in the usability test. This time, learners were asked to discuss about a face-to-face class ministered by the lecturer. Initially, the observers explained how participants could obtain the tool's feedback. Participants and the lecturer interacted for forty minutes. Participants requested individual feedback during and after the interaction. The lecturer requested the *Instructor Report* and also accessed several *Learner Reports*.

At the end of the test, the participants filled in a questionnaire, and remarked that the chat was enjoyable, since the tool was easy to use and provided interesting *just-in-time* feedback. They pointed out that a more detailed feedback, including tips on how to improve their participation would be useful. Nine out of the ten students rated the feedback as good, while one rated it as regular, stating that it was too general.

The second experiment was carried out at UFPE. Five undergraduate Computer Science students (with previous background on Artificial Intelligence) participated in it. The participants were asked to use *OXEnTCHÊ–Chat* to discuss about Intelligent Agents. Participants interacted for twenty-five minutes. The lecturer was not present during the experiment, and thus used the off-line feedback add-in in order to obtain the *Instructor* and *Learner* reports. She assessed the quality of the feedback provided by analysing the dialogue logs and comparing them to the system's reports.

At the end of their dialogue, participants filled in the same evaluation questionnaire that was distributed at UFRPE. Out of the five participants, two rated the feedback as excellent, two rated it as good, and one rated it as weak.

Participants in the two experiments suggested several improvements to the *OX-EnTCHÊ–Chat*. In particular, they suggested that the feedback reports should include specific tips on how to improve one's participation in the collaborative dialogue. The lecturers agreed with the system's feedback report, and remarked that such tool would be very helpful for teachers to assess their students and to reflect on their pedagogical practices. Table 1 summarises the tests and the results obtained.

The results obtained indicated that the tool had achieved its main goal, both helping teachers and students to better understand how the interaction was evolving, and helping students to get a better picture of their participation. Thus, the results obtained were considered to be very satisfactory. They did, however, bring to light the need for more specific feedback, and also for other ways of motivating students to collaborate more actively. As a consequence of these findings, the Bot Agent was developed and integrated to our tool.

Table 1. Summary of Tests and their Results

Test	Local	Number of Participants	Duration	Teacher's Presence	Result
Preliminary	UFPE	9	30 min	No	Good usability, tips for refinement
Usability	UFRPE	10	90 min	Yes	Excellent usability
Feedback 1	UFRPE	10	40 min	Yes	Good(9), Regular(1)
Feedback 2	UFPE	5	25 min	No	Excellent (2), Good(2), Weak (1)

5 Conclusions and Further Work

Recent research in CSCL has been investigating ways to mitigate the problems of student's feeling of isolation and lack of motivation, common to Virtual Learning Environments. In order to tackle these issues, several Collaborative Learning Environments monitor the interaction and provide feedback specific to users actions or to the whole interaction.

In this paper, we presented the *OXEnTCHÊ–Chat*, a tool that tackles the above problems. It provides a chat tool coupled with an automatic dialogue classifier which analyses on-line interaction and provides just-in-time feedback to both teachers and learners. The system also counts on a chatterbot to automatically coordinate the interaction. This combination of techniques and functionalities is a novel one. *OXEnTCHÊ–Chat* has been evaluated with two different groups, and the obtained results are very satisfactory, indicating that this approach should be taken further.

At the time of writing, we are working on improving the Bot Agent by augmenting its domain knowledge and skills, as well as on evaluating its performance. In the near future we intend to improve *OXEnTCHÊ–Chat* in three different aspects: (1) to include other automatic dialogue classifiers (e.g. other neural network models); (2) to improve the feedback provided to teachers and learners, making it more specific; and (3) to improve the Bot capabilities, so that it can contribute more effectively to the dialogue, by, for example, playing a given role (e.g. tutor) in the interaction.

References

1. Wenger, E. Artificial Intelligence and Tutoring Systems: Computational and Cognitive Approaches to the Communication of Knowledge. Ed: Morgan Kaufmann (1987) 486p
2. Wessner, M. and Pfister, H.: Group Formation in Computer Supported Collaborative Learning. In Proceedings of Group´01, ACM Press, (2001) 24-31
3. Goldberg, M.W. Using a Web-Based Course Authoring Tool to Develop Sophisticated Web-based Course. Available at WWW in: http://www.webct.com/service/ViewContent?contentID=11747. Accessed in 15/09/2003
4. Issroff, K., and Del Soldato, T., Incorporating Motivation into Computer-Supported Cooperative Learning. In Brna, P. Paiva, A. and Self, J. (eds.) *Proceedings of the European Conference on Artificial Intelligence in Education*, Edições Colibri, (1996) 284-290
5. Dillenbourg P. Introduction: What do you mean by Collaborative Learning? In Dillenbourg, P. (ed.) *Collaborative Learning: Cognitive and Computational Approaches.* Elsevier Science, (1999) 1-19
6. Chou C. Y.; Chan T. W.; Lin C. J.: Redefining the learning companion: the past, present, and future of educational agents Computers & Education 40, Elsevier Science (2003) 255-269
7. Galvão, A.; Neves, A.; Barros, F. "Persona-AIML: Uma Arquitetura para Desenvolver Chatterbots com Personalidade". In.: IV Encontro Nacional de Inteligência Artificial. Anais do XXIII Congresso SBC. v.7. Campinas, Brazil, (2003) 435- 444
8. Rosatelli, M. and Self, J. A Collaborative Case Study System for Distance Learning, International Journal of Artificial Intelligence in Education, 12, (2002) 1-25
9. González M. A. C. e Suthers D. D.: Coaching Collaboration in a Compute-Mediated learning Environment. (2002) Available at http://citeseer.nj.nec.com/514195.html. Accessed in 12/12/2003
10. Barros, B. e Verdejo, M. F.: Analysing student interaction processes in order to improve collaboration. The Degree Approach. *International Journal of Artificial Intelligence in Education*, 11, (2000) 221-241
11. Soller A.; Wiebe J.; Lesgold A.: A Machine Learning Approach to Assessing Knowledge Sharing During Collaborative Learning Activities. *Proceedings of Computer Support for Collaborative Learning 2002*, (2002) 128-137.
12. Tedesco, P. MArCo: Building an Artificial Conflict Mediator to Support Group Planning Interactions, *International Journal of Artificial Intelligence in Education*, 13, (2003) 117-155
13. MacManus, M. M. e Aiken, R. M.: Monitoring Computer-Based Collaborative Problem Solving. *Journal of Artificial Intelligence in Education*, 6(4), (1995) 307-336
14. Marcuschi, L. A.: Análise da Conversação. Editora Ática, (2003)

A Tool for Supporting Progressive Refinement of Wizard-of-Oz Experiments in Natural Language

Armin Fiedler[1], Malte Gabsdil[2], and Helmut Horacek[1]

[1] Department of Computer Science
Saarland University, P.O. Box 15 11 50
D-66041 Saarbrücken, Germany
{afiedler,horacek}@cs.uni-sb.de
[2] Department of Computational Linguistics
Saarland University, P.O. Box 15 11 50
D-66041 Saarbrücken, Germany
gabsdil@coli.uni-sb.de

Abstract. *Wizard-of-Oz* techniques are an important method for collecting data about the behavior of students in tutorial dialogues with computers, especially when the interaction is done in natural language. Carrying out such experiments requires dedicated tools, but the existing ones have some serious limitations for supporting the development of systems with ambitious natural language capabilities. In order to better meet such demands, we have developed DiaWoZ, a tool that enables the design and execution of *Wizard-of-Oz* experiments to collect data from dialogues and to evaluate components of dialogue systems. Its architecture is highly modular and allows for the progressive refinement of the experiments by both designing increasingly sophisticated dialogues and successively replacing simulated components by actual implementations. A first series of experiments carried out with DiaWoZ has confirmed the need for elaborate dialogue models and the incorporation of implemented components for subsequent experiments.

1 Introduction

Natural language interaction is considered a major hope for increasing the effectiveness of tutorial systems, since [7] has empirically demonstrated the necessity of natural language dialogue capabilities for the success of tutorial sessions. Moreover, *Wizard-of-Oz (WOz)* techniques proved to be an appropriate approach to collect data about dialogues in complex domains [3]. In a WOz experiment subjects interact with a system that is feigned by a human, the so-called *wizard*. Thus, WOz experiments generally allow one to capture the idiosyncrasies of human-machine as opposed to human-human dialogues [5,4]. Hence, these techniques are perfectly applicable for collecting data about the behavior of students in tutorial dialogues with computers.

Carrying out WOz experiments in a systematic and motivated manner is expensive and requires dedicated tools. However, existing tools have serious limitations for supporting the development of systems with ambitious natural language capabilities. In order to meet the demands of testing tutorial dialog systems in their development, we have designed and implemented DiaWoZ, a tool that enables setting up and executing

J.C. Lester et al. (Eds.): ITS 2004, LNCS 3220, pp. 325–335, 2004.

of WOz experiments to collect dialogue data. Its architecture is highly modular and allows for the progressive refinement of the experiments by both modelling increasingly sophisticated dialogues and successively replacing simulated components of the system by actual implementations. Our investigations are part of the DIALOG project [1] [1]. Its goal is to (i) empirically investigate the use of flexible natural language dialogue in tutoring mathematics, and (ii) develop an experimental prototype system gradually embodying the empirical findings. The system will conduct dialogues in written natural language to help a student understand and construct mathematical proofs. In contrast to most existing tutorial systems, we envision a modular design, making use of the powerful proof system ΩMEGA [9]. This design enables a detailed reasoning about the student's action and enables elaborate system responses.

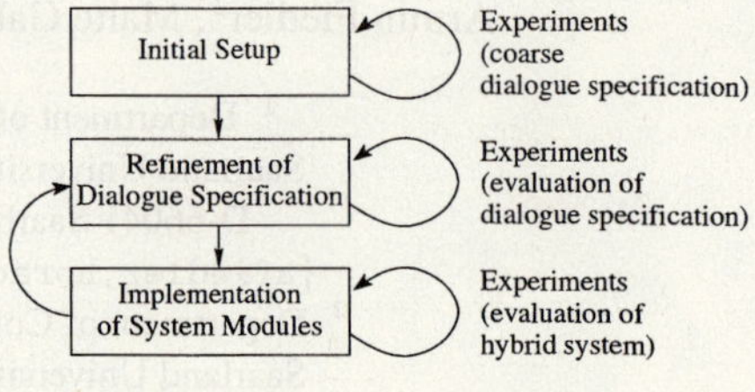

Fig. 1. Progressive Refinement Cycles.

In Section 2, we motivate our approach in more detail. Section 3 is devoted to the architecture of DiaWoZ and Section 4 discusses the dialogue specification for a short example dialogue. We conclude the paper by discussing experience gained from the first experiments carried out with DiaWoZ and sketch future developments.

2 Motivation

In our approach, we first want to collect initial data on tutoring mathematics, as well as a corpus of the associated dialogues, similar to what human tutors do when tutoring in the domain. This is particularly important in our domain of application, due to the notorious lack of empirical data about mathematical dialogues, as opposed to the vast host of textbooks. In these "classical" WOz experiments, the tutor is free to enter utterances without much restriction. Refinement at this stage merely means to define subdialogues or topics the wizard has to address during the dialogue, but without committing him to any predefined sequence of actions.

In addition, we plan to *progressively refine* consecutive WOz experiments as depicted in Figure 1. This concerns two aspects:

- We aim at setting up experiments where the dialogue specifications are spelled out in increasing detail, thereby limiting the choices of the wizard. These experiments will enable us to formulate increasingly finer-grained hypotheses about the tutoring dialogue, and to test these hypotheses in the next series of experiments.
- We want to evaluate already existing components of the dialogue system before other components have been implemented. For example, if the dialogue manager and the natural language generation component are functional, but natural language analysis is not, the wizard has to take care of natural language understanding. Since we expect that the inclusion of system components will have an effect on the dialogues that

[1] The DIALOG project is part of the Collaborative Research Center on *Resource-Adaptive Cognitive Processes* (SFB 378) at Saarland University.

can be performed, the dialogue specification ought to be refined again whenever a new system component is added.

3 The Architecture of DiaWoZ

The architecture of DiaWoZ (cf. Figure 2) and its dialogue specification language are designed to support the progressive refinement of experiments as discussed in Section 2. We assume that the task of authoring a dialogue to be examined in a WOz experiment is usually performed distinct in time and place from the task of performing the corresponding WOz experiment. To reflect on this distinction, we decided to divide DiaWoZ into two autonomous subcomponents, which can run independently: the ***Dialogue Authoring*** and the ***Dialogue Execution*** components. In order to handle communication, both the tutoring system and wizard utterances are presented to the subject via the *Subject Interface*, which also allows the subject to enter text. To enable subsequent examination by the experimenter, the *Logging Module* structures and stores relevant information of the dialogue.

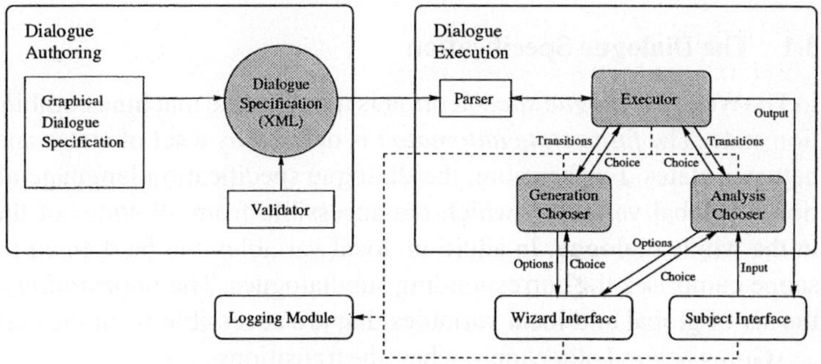

Fig. 2. The architecture of DiaWoZ.

The Dialogue Authoring component is a tool for specifying the dialogues to be examined in a WOz experiment. Using the *Graphical Dialogue Specification* module, which allows for drag-and-drop construction of the dialogue specification, the experimenter can assemble a finite state automaton augmented with information states as the specification of a dialogue. A *Validator* ensures that the dialogue specification meets certain criteria (e.g., every state is reachable from the start state, and the end state can be reached from every state). The complete dialogue specification is passed to the Dialogue Execution component.

The Dialogue Execution component first parses the dialogue specification and constructs an internal representation of it. This representation is then used by the *Executor* to execute the automaton. The Executor determines which state is the currently active one and which transitions are available. Depending on the dialogue turn these transitions are passed to a chooser. The *Generation Chooser* receives the possible transitions that, in turn, generate the tutor's next utterance. The *Analysis Chooser* receives possible transitions that analyze the subject's utterances. Both choosers may delegate the task of choosing a transition to specialized modules, such as an intelligent tutoring system to determine the next help message or a semantic analysis component that analyzes the subject's utterance. Moreover, both choosers may also inform the wizard of the available options via the *Wizard Interface* and thus allow the wizard to pick a transition.

DiaWoZ is devised as a distributed system, such that the Dialogue Authoring and the Dialogue Execution components, the Wizard and Subject Interfaces, and the Logging Module each can be run on different machines. The components are implemented in Java and the communication is via sockets using an XML interface language. Since XML parsers are available for almost every all languages, new modules can be programmed in any programming language and added to the system. In the remainder of this section, we discuss the main components of DiaWoZ in some more detail.

3.1 The Dialogue Specification

In DiaWoZ, a *dialogue specification* is a finite state machine combined with an information state. The *finite state automaton* is defined by a set of states and a set of transitions between states. Furthermore, the dialogue specification language allows for the definition of global variables, which are accessible from all states of the automaton, hence in the whole dialogue. In addition, local variables can be defined for each state, whose scope comprises the corresponding subdialogues. The *information state* is conceived as the set of global and local variables that are accessible from the current state.

Going beyond other approaches, the transitions are associated with preconditions and effects. The *preconditions* are defined in terms of variables in the information state and restrict the set of applicable transitions for the current state dependent on the information state. The *effects* can both change the information state by setting its variables to different values and result in a function call, triggering an observable event such as an utterance. In particular, transitions can be parameterized in terms of the variables of the information state and the values to which they are changed in the transitions' effects. The dialogue specification language is defined in XML, which makes it rather clumsy to read, but easy to validate.

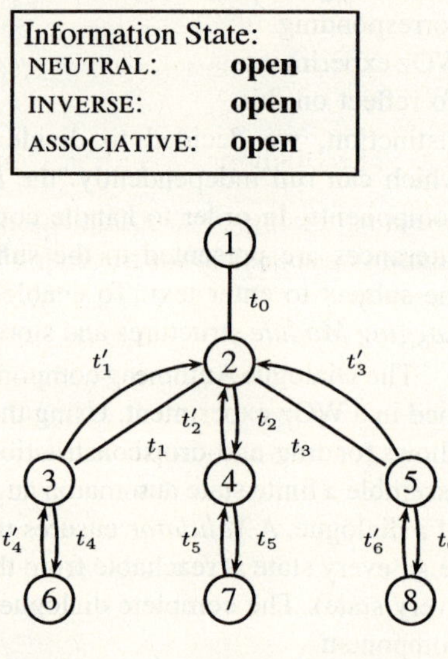

Fig. 3. An example dialogue specification.

Adding an information state to a finite state automaton renders the dialogue specification very flexible and allows us to define a wide range of dialogue models: from models that are purely finite-state by leaving the information state empty to the information-state–based dialogue modeling approach proposed in the TRINDI project (cf., e.g., [11]) by defining a degenerated automaton that consists of only one state and arbitrarily many recursive transitions. It is also possible to define a single state with one recursive transition without any preconditions and effects that allows for arbitrary input by the wizard. This last setting is used for conducting "classical" WOz experiments. The combination of finite state automata with information states gives us the advantages of both approaches without committing to their respective drawbacks. This allows us to devise non-trivial dialogues that can still be handled appropriately by the wizard.

As an example consider the following task from algebra: An algebraic structure $(S, \circ)$, where S is a set and $\circ$ an operator on S, should be classified. $(S, \circ)$ is a group if (i) there is a neutral element in S with respect to $\circ$, (ii) each element in S has an inverse element with respect to $\circ$, and (iii) $\circ$ is associative. In a tutorial dialogue, the tutor must ensure, that the student addresses all three subtasks to conclude that a structure is a group. An appropriate dialogue specification is given in Figure 3. The initial information state is displayed on the left side, while the finite-state automaton is shown on the right side. State 1 is the start state. In State 2, there are three transitions t_1, t_2, and t_3, which lead to parts of the automaton that represent subdialogues about the neutral element (States 3 and 6), the inverse elements (States 4 and 7), and associativity (States 5 and 8), respectively. The information state consists of three global variables NEUTRAL, INVERSE, and ASSOCIATIVE capturing whether their corresponding values have been solved. The preconditions of the transitions are the following:

t_1: NEUTRAL = **open**
t_2: INVERSE = **open**
t_3: ASSOCIATIVE = **open**
The remaining transitions are always applicable.

The effects of the transitions t'_1, t'_2, and t'_3 change the value of NEUTRAL, INVERSE, and ASSOCIATIVE, respectively, to **done**. Moreover, each transition produces an utterance in the dialogue. We will give more detail about the utterances in Section 4.

3.2 The Dialogue Execution Components

The main dialogue execution components are the executor and the choosers. The Executor is responsible for traversing the finite-state part of the dialogue specification. In particular, the Executor keeps track of the current state of the finite-state automaton and of the current information state. It calculates the set of applicable transitions in the current state based on the transitions' preconditions and the information state.

For example, if State 2 is the current state and the value of NEUTRAL is **done**, t_1 is not applicable. When a transition has been chosen, the Executor applies the transition, that is, it calculates the new state of the finite-state automaton and updates the information state as defined by the effects of the chosen transition. For example, when leaving State 3 by applying t'_1, NEUTRAL is set to **done**.

The executor is linked to two transition choosers in the architecture depicted in Figure 2. The Analysis Chooser manages the transitions that are responsible for analyzing the subject's utterances. The task of the Generation Chooser is to choose the next action that should be performed by the system. We decided to make a clear-cut distinction between the two choosers in our architecture for two reasons. First, it prevents us from intermingling the transitions that encode the turns of the tutoring system with those that encode the subject's turns, and thus supports a clearly modular design. Second, it allows us to add newly implemented subcomponents of the tutoring system that can provide the chooser with enough information to automatically choose a transition. For example, it should be possible to add to the Generation Chooser a software component that generates help messages without affecting other subcomponents of the Generation Chooser or the

Analysis Chooser. Thus, the choosers allow for the progressive refinement of consecutive experiments. In general, the transition picked by the chooser can be presented to the wizard to confirm or overrule this choice.

3.3 The Wizard and Subject Interfaces

The Wizard Interface (cf. Figure 4) includes a frame that displays the whole dialogue at every point as well as a split window, which displays both the options provided by the Generation Chooser (indicated by *Tutor Choices*) and the options provided by the Analysis Chooser (indicated by *Subject Choices*) in two distinct frames. At each point in time only one of the choosers is enabled depending on the dialogue turn. Figure 4 shows the situation, where the subject entered an utterance, which the wizard analyzes by choosing entries in pull-down menus. Note that the Generation Chooser is disabled, since we are in the subject's dialogue turn. The disabled chooser still shows the options from the previous dialogue turn. To allow for parameterized transitions we use pull-down menus that facilitate the wizard's task substantially. Other options may be displayed as simple buttons or edit fields.

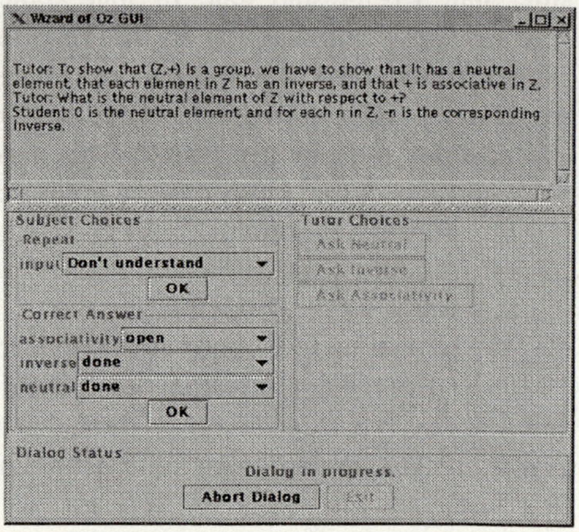

Fig. 4. The Wizard Interface window.

The subject interface is rather simple. Although a multi-modal interface is desirable, DiaWoZ currently allows only for text output and input.

4 An Example Dialogue

To show how DiaWoZ works, let us come back to the example dialogue specification given in Figure 3. It covers the following example dialogue (where Z denotes the set of integers):

(U1) **Tutor:** To show that $(Z, +)$ is a group, we have to show that it has a neutral element, that each element in Z has an inverse, and that $+$ is associative in Z.

(U2) **Tutor:** What is the neutral element of Z with respect to $+$?

(U3) **Student:** 0 is the neutral element, and for each n in Z, $-n$ is the corresponding inverse.

(U4) **Tutor:** That leaves us to show associativity.

Let us now examine the dialogue in detail. Starting in State 1, there is only one transition that can be picked, namely t_0. It leads to State 2 and outputs utterance (U1). In State 2, all three transitions t_1, t_2, and t_3 can be picked, because their preconditions are fulfilled. The wizard chooses t_1, which leads to State 3 and produces the tutor's utterance (U2). Now, the student enters utterance (U3). Note that the student not only answers the tutor's question, but also gives the solution for the second subtask about the inverse elements. Since there is no natural language understanding component included in the system in our example setting, the wizard has to analyze the student's utterance. To allow for that, DiaWoZ presents the window depicted in Figure 4 to the wizard, where the field titled "Repeat" stands for transition t_4, while the field titled "Correct Answer" denotes transition t'_1. The wizard instantiates the parameters of t'_1 by choosing the value **done** for the variables NEUTRAL and INVERSE of the information state to be set by the effect of t'_1. Note that this choice reflects the fact that the student overanswered the tutor's question. Moreover, note that due to the overanswering the tutor should not choose the subtask about the inverse elements in the next dialogue turn, but instead proceed with the remaining problem about associativity. With clicking OK in the "Correct Answer" field, transition t'_1 is selected. Thus, the Executor updates the information state by setting the values of NEUTRAL and INVERSE to **done** and brings us back to State 2. This time, only transition t_3 is applicable, which justifies the production of utterance (U4) through extra linguistic knowledge.

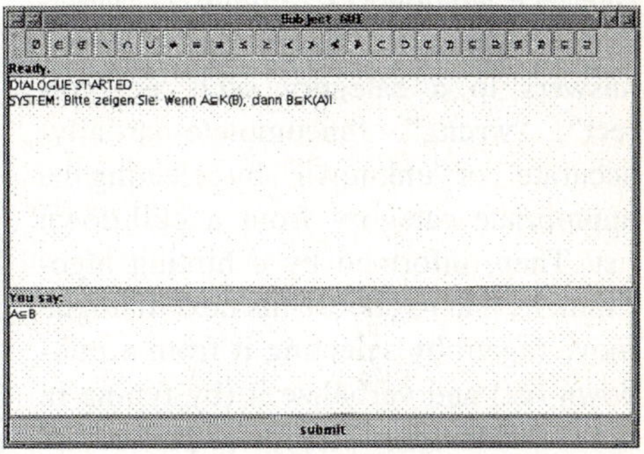

Fig. 5. The Subject Interface window.

5 DiaWoZ in Use

In the DIALOG project, we aim at a tutorial dialogue system for mathematics [1]. Via a series of WOz experiments, we follow the progressive refinement approach described in this paper. The first experiment has already been conducted and reported on [2]. It aimed primarily at collecting a corpus of tutorial dialogues on naive set theory. We shall describe how we used DiaWoZ in this experiment and discuss the lessons learned.

5.1 A First Experiment

In the experiment, subjects and wizard were located in different rooms. The subjects were told that they should work with a tutorial system for mathematics and evaluate it later. They were provided with the Subject Interface that allowed them to read the dialogue as it had developed so far in the window's upper frame and to enter their dialogue contributions in its lower frame (cf. Figure 5).

The wizard was able to see the dialogue model in a separate window (cf. Figure 6). Since the major aim of the experiment was to collect a corpus of tutorial dialogues in mathematics, a very simple dialogue model with three states and five transitions served this purpose. State 1 is the state, where the system produces an utterance, whereas State 2 is the state, where the subject is supposed to enter his dialogue contribution. State 3, finally, is the end state, which indicates the end of the dialogue. The transition labeled *ask* corresponds to the system asking the subject for an answer. The transition *answer* corresponds to the subject's answer. Both transitions hand over the turn to the interlocutor. The *reflexive* transitions, in contrast, allow the tutor and the subject, respectively, to utter something and keep the turn. The transition *end-dialogue*, finally, results in the end state and thus ends the dialogue. The wizard can scrutinize the dialogue model by clicking on states and transitions, which are then described in more detail in the lower part of the window.

In every state of the dialogue, the wizard had to choose the next transition to be applied, both when he or the subject made a dialogue move by manipulating the Wizard Interface window (cf. Figure 7). Moreover, he had to assign the subjects' answers to a category such as "correct", "wrong", "incomplete-partially-accurate", or "unknown", by selecting the appropriate category from a pull-down list. Then, informed by a hinting algorithm, he had to choose his next dialogue move (again by selecting it from a pull-down list) and verbalize it (by typing in his verbalization). The lower part of the interface window allowed the wizard to type in standard utterances he wanted to reuse by copy and paste. These utterances could be stored in a file.

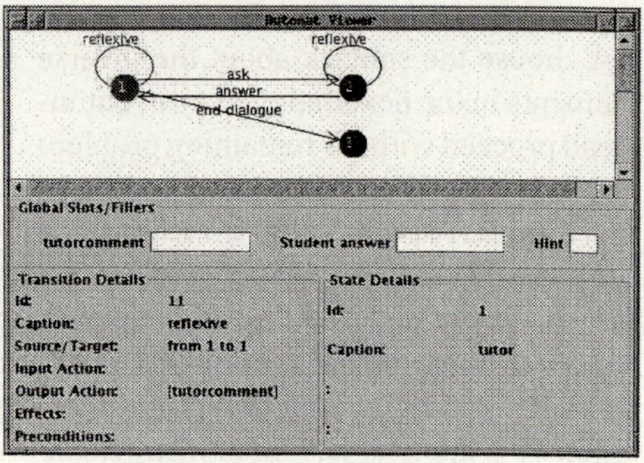

Fig. 6. The example dialogue model.

Both the subjects and the wizard could make use of mathematical symbols provided as buttons in both interfaces. A resource file, which is accessible by the experimenter, defines which symbols are provided, such that the buttons can be tailored to the domain of the dialogue. The Logging Module logged information about selected transitions, reached states, chosen answer categories and dialogue moves, and utterances typed in by the subjects and the wizard along with time stamps of all actions. To analyze the data collected during the experiment, we built a log file viewer that allows for searching the log file for information, hiding and revealing of information, and printing of revealed information.

Carrying out WOz experiments in a systematic and motivated manner is expensive and requires dedicated tools. DiaWoZ is inspired by different existing dialogue building and WOz systems. MDWOZ [8] and SUEDE [6] are two examples of systems for designing and conducting WOz experiments. MDWOZ features a distributed client-server architecture and includes modules for database access as well as visual graph drawing and inspection. SUEDE provides a sophisticated GUI for drawing finite-state diagrams, a browser-like environment for running experiments, and an "analysis mode" in which the experimenter can easily access and review the collected data. The drawback of these systems, however, is that they only allow for finite-state dialogue modeling, which is restricted in its expressiveness. Conversely, development environments like the CSLU toolkit [10], offer more powerful dialogue specifications (e.g., by attaching program code to states or transitions), but do not support the WOz technique.

In the experiments, the students evaluated working with the simulated system rather positively, which is some evidence for the good functionality of DiaWoZ. By and large, the dialogue specifications were reasonable for the first experiment, except from one problem. Namely the need for a time limit had not been foreseen. Our initial dialogue model did not have reflexive transitions, such that the turn was given to the subject when the wizard had entered his utterance. If the subject did not answer, the wizard could not take the initiative anymore. To remedy this problem, we introduced reflexive transitions to allow the wizard keeping the turn for as long as the the subject had not typed in his answer. We are currently investigating how to solve this problem generally in diawoz by providing the wizard with the means of seizing the turn at any point. Altogether, we have gained experience from this first series of experiments in three major respects:

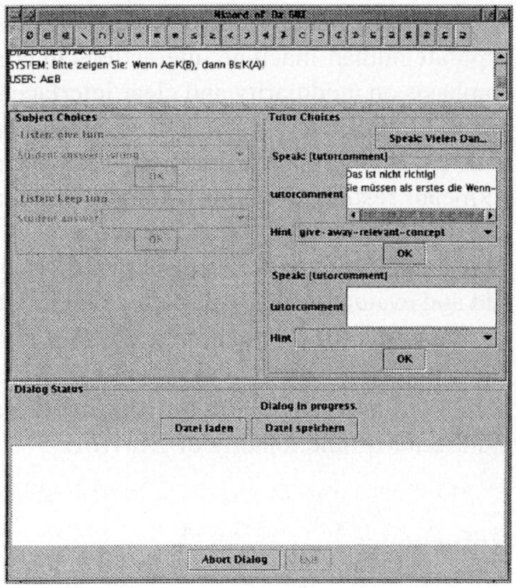

Fig. 7. The Wizard Interface window.

The design of the interface. Some subjects suggested having hot keys to access the symbol buttons and the submit button without using the mouse, which is likely to be significantly faster. Another source for easing and speeding-up the communication on behalf of the subjects lies in the use of cut-and-paste facilities. A few experienced subjects found out how to exploit these features, but no indication about this was given in the interface. Moreover, one subject suggested an acoustic signal to indicate that the system has generated an utterance.

The quality of the hints. In order to determine the wizard's reaction, we have made use of an elaborate hinting algorithm. We have varied hinting strategies systematically, the *socratic* strategy being the most ambitious one. However, contrary to our expectations, this strategy did not turn out to be superior to the others, which led us to analyze more deeply the method by which the content of the hints was generated.

The flexibility of natural language interaction. In the experiments, it turned out that the subjects used fragments of natural language text and mathematical formulas in a freely intertwined way, much more than we had expected. Some of the utterances they produced required very cooperative reasoning on behalf of the wizard to enable a proper interpretation. In order to obtain a natural corpus, which was a main goal in the first series of experiments, applying this high degree of cooperativity was beneficial, but it is unrealistic for interpretation by a machine.

For the next series of experiments we will undertake modifications in the student interface that incorporate the suggestions made by the experiment subjects. Moreover, we have also enhanced our hinting algorithm to include abstractions and new perspectives, thus extending the repertoire of that module according to the experimental results. We plan to make this module accessible to DiaWoZ as a software component for the next series of experiments. Finally, we have to restrict communication in natural language intertwined with formulas, so that the degree of fragmentation is manageable by the analysis component we are developing. In terms of DiaWoZ, this will lead to a more detailed dialogue structure to be spelled out by the means the tool offers.

6 Conclusion

We presented the architecture of DiaWoZ, a Wizard-of-Oz tool which can be used to simulate human-machine interactions in complex domains. In the design, we put great emphasis on modularity and clear interface specifications. To define dialogues, we augmented finite-state approaches of dialogue modeling with information states. This enables great flexibility in designing dialogue specifications. Hence, the architecture is by no means restricted to tutorial dialogues. One of the main features of the architecture is that it allows for the progressive refinement of consecutive WOz experiments: It is possible both to refine the dialogue specification between experiments and to successively add and evaluate already implemented modules of the tutoring system.

We have also reported on a series of experiments with DiaWoZ, to explore tutorial dialogues in the area of mathematics. Our experience from the first series has led to a number of insights. which we will incorporate in subsequent series, thereby exploiting the extended functionality of DiaWoZ.

References

1. C. Benzmüller, A. Fiedler, M. Gabsdil, H. Horacek, I. Kruijff-Korbayová, M. Pinkal, J. Siekmann, D. Tsovaltzi, B. Vo, and M. Wolska. Tutorial dialogs on mathematical proofs. In *Proceedings of the IJCAI Workshop on Knowledge Representation and Automated Reasoning for E-Learning Systems*, pages 12–22, Acapulco, 2003.
2. C. Benzmüller, A. Fiedler, M. Gabsdil, H. Horacek, I. Kruijff-Korbayová, M. Pinkal, J. Siekmann, D. Tsovaltzi, B. Vo, and M. Wolska. A Wizard-of-Oz experiment for tutorial dialogues in mathematics. In V. Aleven, U. Hoppe, J. Kay, R. Mizoguchi, H. Pain, F. Verdejo, and K. Yacef, editors, *AIED2003 Supplementary Proceedings*, volume VIII: Advanced Technologies for Mathematics Education, pages 471–481, Sydney, Australia, 2003. School of Information Technologies, University of Sydney.
3. N.O. Bernsen, H. Dybkjær, and L. Dybkjær. *Designing Interactive Speech Systems — From First Ideas to User Testing*. Springer, 1998.
4. N. Dahlbäck, A. Jönsson, and L. Ahrenberg. Wizard of Oz Studies — Why and How. *Knowledge-Based Systems*, 6(4):258–266, 1993.
5. N. M. Fraser and G. N. Gilbert. Simulating speech systems. *Computer Speech and Language*, 5:81–99, 1991.
6. S. R. Klemmer, A. K. Sinha, J. Chen, J. A. Landay, N. Aboobaker, and A. Wang. SUEDE: A Wizard of Oz Prototyping Tool for Speech User Interfaces. In *CHI Letters, The 13th Annual ACM Symposium on User Interface Software and Technology*, volume 2, pages 1–10, 2000.

7. J. Moore. What makes human explanations effective? In *In Proceedings of the Fifteenth Annual Conference of the Cognitive Science Society*, pages 131–136. Hillsdale, NJ. Earlbaum, 2000.
8. C. Munteanu and M. Boldea. MDWOZ: A Wizard of Oz Environment for Dialog Systems Development. In *Proceedings 2nd International Conference on Language Resources and Evaluation — LREC*, 2000.
9. J. Siekmann, C. Benzmüller, V. Brezhnev, L. Cheikhrouhou, A. Fiedler, A. Franke, H. Horacek, M. Kohlhase, A. Meier, E. Melis, M. Moschner, I. Normann, M. Pollet, V. Sorge, C. Ullrich, C-P Wirth, and J. Zimmer. Proof development with ΩMEGA. In A. Voronkov, editor, *Automated Deduction — CADE-18*, number 2392 in LNAI, pages 144–149. Springer Verlag, 2002.
10. S. Sutton and R. Cole. Universal Speech Tools: the CSLU Toolkit. In *Proceedings of the International Conference on Spoken Language Processing (ICSLP)*, pages 3221–3224, 1998.
11. D. Traum, J. Bos, R. Cooper, S. Larsson, I. Lewin, C. Matheson, and M. Poesio. A Model of Dialogue Moves and Information State Revision. Technical Report Deliverable D2.1, TRINDI, 1999.

Tactical Language Training System: An Interim Report

W. Lewis Johnson[1], Carole Beal[1], Anna Fowles-Winkler[2], Ursula Lauper[2], Stacy Marsella[1], Shrikanth Narayanan[3], Dimitra Papachristou[1], and Hannes Vilhjálmsson[1]

[1] Center for Advanced Research in Technology for Education (CARTE), USC / Information Sciences Institute, 4676 Admiralty Way, Marina del Rey, CA 90292 USA
{Johnson, CBeal, Marsella, Dimitrap, Hannes}@isi.edu

[2] Micro Analysis & Design, 4949 Pearl East Circle, Suite 300, Boulder, CO 80301 USA
{AWinkler, ULauper}@maad.com

[3] Speech Analysis and Interpretation Laboratory, 3740 McClintock Avenue, Room EEB 430 Los Angeles, CA 90089 2564
Shri@sipi.usc.edu

Abstract. Tactical Language Training System helps learners acquire basic communicative skills in foreign languages and cultures. Learners practice their communication skills in a simulated village, where they must develop rapport with the local people, who in turn will help them accomplish missions such as post-war reconstruction. Each learner is accompanied by a virtual aide who can provide assistance and guidance if needed, tailored to each learner's individual skills. The aide can also act as a virtual tutor as part of an intelligent tutoring system, giving the learners feedback on their performance. Learners communicate via a multimodal interface, which permits them to speak and choose gestures on behalf of their character in the simulation. The system employs video game technologies and design techniques, in order to motivate and engage learners. A version for Levantine Arabic has been developed, and versions for other languages are in the process of being developed.

1 Introduction

The Tactical Language Training System helps learners acquire communicative competence in spoken Arabic and other languages. An intelligent agent coaches the learners through lessons, using innovative speech recognition technology to assess their mastery and provide tailored assistance. Learners then practice particular missions in an interactive story environment, where they speak and choose appropriate gestures in simulated social situations populated with autonomous, animated characters. We aim to provide effective language training both to high-aptitude language learners and to learners with low confidence in their language abilities. We hypothesize that such a learning environment will be more engaging and motivating than traditional language instruction and yield rapid skill acquisition and greater learner self-confidence.

J.C. Lester et al. (Eds.): ITS 2004, LNCS 3220, pp. 336–345, 2004.

2 Motivations

Current foreign language instruction is heavily oriented toward a small number of common languages. For example, in the United States, approximately ninety-one percent of Americans who study foreign languages in schools, colleges, and universities choose Spanish, French, German, or Italian, while very few choose such commonly spoken languages such as Chinese, Arabic, or Russian [18]. Arabic, the sixth most widely spoken language in the world, accounts for less than 1% of US college foreign language enrollment [17]. Moreover, many such courses can be very time consuming, because learners often must cope with unfamiliar writing systems as well as differing cultural norms. This can be a significant barrier for students who want to acquire basic communication skills so that they can function effectively overseas.

The Tactical Language Training System (TLTS) provides integrated training in foreign spoken language and culture. It employs a task-based approach, where the learner acquires the skills needed to accomplish particular communicative tasks [4]. It focuses on authentic tasks of particular relevance to the learners, involving social interactions with (simulated) native speakers. Written language is omitted, to emphasize basic spoken communication. Vocabulary is limited to what is required for specific situations, and is gradually expanded through a series of increasingly challenging situations that comprise a story arc or narrative. Grammar is introduced only as needed to enable learners to generate and understand a sufficient variety of utterances to cope with novel situations. Nonverbal gestures (both "dos" and "don'ts") are introduced, as are cultural norms of etiquette and politeness, to help learners accomplish the social interaction tasks successfully. We are developing a toolkit to support the rapid creation of new task-oriented language learning environments, thus making it easier to support less commonly taught languages. preliminary version of a training system has been developed for Levantine Arabic, and a new version for Iraqi Arabic is under development.

Although naturalistic task-oriented conversation has the advantage of encouraging learning by doing, such conversations by themselves do not ensure efficient learning [4], [14]. Learners also benefit from form feedback (i.e., corrective feedback on the form of their utterances) when they make mistakes. But since criticism can be embarrassing and face-threatening [2], native speakers may avoid criticizing learner speech in social situations. Language instructors are more willing to critique learner language; however the language classroom is an artificial environment that easily loses the motivational benefits of authentic task-oriented dialog. The TLTS addresses this problem by providing learners with two closely coupled learning environments with distinct interactional characteristics. The Mission Skill Builder (MSB) incorporates a pedagogical agent that provides continual form feedback. The Mission Practice Environment (MPE) provides authentic practice in social situations, accompanied by an aide character who can offer help if needed. This approach combines task orientation, form feedback, and scaffolding to maximize learning efficiency and effectiveness. The MSB builds on previous work with socially intelligent pedagogical agents [10], [11], while the MPE build on work on interactive pedagogical dramas [15].

The Mission Practice Environment is built using computer game technology, and exploits game design techniques, in order to promote learner engagement and motivation. Although there is significant interest in the potential of game technology to promote learning [6], there are some important outstanding questions about how to exploit this potential. One is *transfer* – how does game play result in the acquisition of skills that transfer outside of the game? Another is how best to exploit *narrative structure* to promote learning? Narrative structure can make learning experiences more engaging and meaningful, but can also discourage learners from engaging in learning activities such as exploration, study, and practice that do not fit into the story line. By combining learning experiences with varying amounts of narrative structure, and by evaluating transfer to real-world communication, we hope to develop a deeper understanding of these issues.

The TLTS builds on ideas developed in previous systems involving microworlds (e.g., FLUENT, MILT) [7],[9], conversation games (e.g., Herr Kommissar) [3], speech pronunciation analysis [23], learner modeling, simulated encounters with virtual characters (e.g., Subarashii, Virtual Conversations, MRE) [1], [8], [20]. It extends this work by providing rich form feedback, by separating game interaction from form feedback, and by supporting a wide range of spoken learner inputs, in an implementation that is robust and efficient enough for ongoing testing and use on commodity computers. The use of speech recognition for tutoring purposes is particularly challenging and innovative,since speech recognition algorithms tend not to be very reliable on learner speech.

3 Example

The following scenario illustrates how the TLTS is used. To appreciate the learner's perspective, imagine that you are a member of an Army Special Forces unit assigned to conduct a civil affairs mission in Lebanon.[1] Your unit will need to enter a village, establish rapport with the people, make contact with the local official in charge, and help carry out post-war reconstruction. To prepare for your mission, you go into the Mission Skill Builder and practice your communication skills, as shown in Figure 1. Here, for example, you learn a common greeting in Lebanese Arabic, "marHaba." You practice saying "marHaba" into your headset microphone. Your speech is automatically analyzed for errors, and your virtual tutor, Nadiim, gives you immediate feedback. If you mispronounce the pharyngeal /H/ sound, as native English speakers commonly do, you receive focused, supportive feedback. Meanwhile, a learner model keeps track of the phrases and skills you have mastered. When you feel that you are ready to give it a try, you enter the Mission Practice Environment. Your character in the game, together with a non-player character acting as your aide, enters the village. You enter a café, and start a conversation with a man in the café, as shown in Figure 2

[1] Lebanon was initially chosen because Lebanese native speakers and speech corpora are widely available. This scenario is typical of civil affairs operations worldwide, and does not reflect actual or planned US military activities in Lebanon.

(left). You speak for your character into your microphone, while choosing appropriate nonverbal gestures. In this case you choose a respectful gesture, and your interlocutor, Ahmed, responds in kind. If you encounter difficulties, your aide can help you, as shown in Figure 2 (right). The aide has access to your learner model, and therefore knows what Arabic phrases you have mastered. If you had not yet mastered Arabic introductions the aide would provide you with a specific phrase to try. You can then go back to the Skill Builder and practice further.

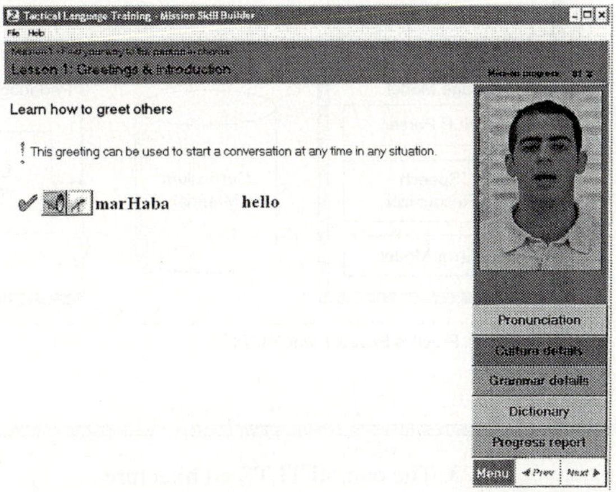

Fig. 1. A coaching section in the Mission Skill Builder

Fig. 2. Greeting a Lebanese man in a café

4 Overall System Architecture

The TLTS architecture must support several important internal requirements. A Learner Model supports run-time queries and updates by both the Skill Builder and the Practice Environment. Learners need to be able to switch back and forth easily between the Skill Builder and the Practice Environment, as they prefer. The system must support rapid authoring of new content by teams of content experts and game developers. The system must also be flexible enough to support modular testing and integration with the DARWARS architecture, which is intended to provide any-time, individualized cognitive training to military personnel. Given these requirements, a distributed architecture makes sense (see Figure 3). Modules interact using content-based messaging, currently implemented using the Elvin messaging service.

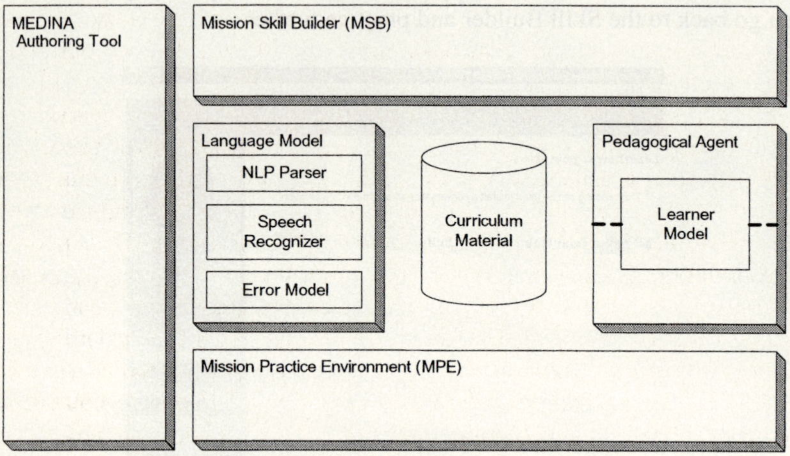

Fig. 3. The overall TLTS architecture

The Pedagogical Agent monitors learner performance, and uses performance data both to track the learner's progress in mastering skills and to decide what type of feedback to give to the learner. The learner's skill profile is recorded in a Learner Model, which is available as a common resource, and implemented as a set of inference rules and dynamically updated tables in an SQL database. The learner model keeps a record of the number of successful and unsuccessful attempts for each action over the series of sessions, as well as the type of error that occurred when the learner is unsuccessful. This information is used to estimate the learner's mastery of each vocabulary item and communicative skill, and to determine what kind of feedback is most appropriate to give to the learner in a given instance. When a learner logs into either the Skill Builder or the Practice Environment, his/her session is immediately associated with a particular profile in the learner model. Learners can review summary reports of their progress, and in the completed system instructors at remote locations will be able to do so as well.

To maintain consistency in the language material, such as models of pronunciation, vocabulary and phrase construction, a single Language Model serves as an interface to the language curriculum. The Language Model includes a speech recognizer that both applications can use, a Natural Language Parser that can annotate phrases with structural information and refer to relevant grammatical explanations and an Error Model which detects and analyzes syntactic and phonological mistakes.

While the Language Model can be thought of as a view of and a tool to work with the language data, the data itself is stored in a separate Curriculum Materials database. This database contains all missions, lessons and exercises that have been constructed, in a flexible Extensible Markup Language (XML) format, with links to media such as sound clips and video clips. It includes exercises that are organized in a recommended sequence, and tutorial tactics that are employed opportunistically by the pedagogical agent in response to learner actions. The database is the focus of the authoring activity. Entries can be validated using the tools of the Language Model. The Medina authoring tool (currently under development) consolidates this process into a single interface where people with different authoring roles can view and edit different views of the curriculum material while overall consistency is ensured.

Since speech is the primary input modality of the TLTS, robustness and reliability of speech processing are of paramount concern. The variability of learner language makes robustness difficult to achieve. Most commercial automated speech recognition (ASR) systems are not designed for learner language [13], and commercial computer aided language learning (CALL) systems that employ speech tend to overestimate the reliability of the speech recognition technology [22]. To support learner speech recognition in the TLTS, our initial efforts focused on acoustic modeling for robust speech recognition especially in light of limited domain data availability [19]. In this case, we bootstrapped data from English and modern standard Arabic and adapted it to Levantine Arabic speech and lexicon. Dynamic switching of recognition grammars was also implemented, as were recognition confidence estimates, used by the pedagogical agent to decide how to give feedback. The structures of the recognition networks are distinct for the MSB and the MPE environments. In the MSB mode, the recognition is based on limited vocabulary networks with pronunciation variants and hypothesis rejection. In the MPE mode, the recognizer supports less constrained user inputs, focusing on recognizing the learner's intended meaning.

4.1 Mission Skill Builder Architecture

The Mission Skill Builder (MSB) is a one-on-one tutoring environment which helps the learner to acquire mission-oriented vocabulary, pronunciation training and gesture recognition knowledge. In this learning environment the learner develops the necessary skills to accomplish specific missions. A virtual tutor provides personalized feedback to improve and accelerate the learning process. In addition, a progress report generator generates a summary of skills the learner has mastered, which is presented to the learner in the same environment.

The Mission Skill Builder user interface is implemented in SumTotal's ToolBook, augmented by the pedagogical agent and speech recognizer. The learner initiates speech input by clicking on a microphone icon, which sends a "start" message to the automated speech recognition (ASR) process. Clicking the microphone icon again sends a "stop" message to the speech recognition process, which then analyzes the speech and sends the recognized utterance back to the MSB. The recognized utterance, together with the expected utterance, is passed to the Pedagogical Agent, which in turn passes this information to the Error Model (part of the Language Model), to analyze and detect types of mistakes. The results of the error detection are then passed back to the Pedagogical Agent, which decides what kind of feedback to choose, depending on the error type and the learner's progress. The feedback is then passed to the MSB and is provided to the learner via the virtual tutor persona, realized as a set of video clips, sound clips, and still images. In addition the Mission Skill Builder informs the learner model about several learner activities with the user interface, which help to define and extend the individual learner profile.

4.2 Mission Practice Environment Architecture

The Mission Practice Environment (MPE) is responsible for realizing dramatically and visually engaging 3D simulations of social situations, in which the learner can interact with non-player characters by speaking and choosing gestures. Most of the MPE work is done in two modules: The Mission Engine and the Unreal World (see Figure 4). The former controls what happens while the latter renders it on the screen and provides a user interface.

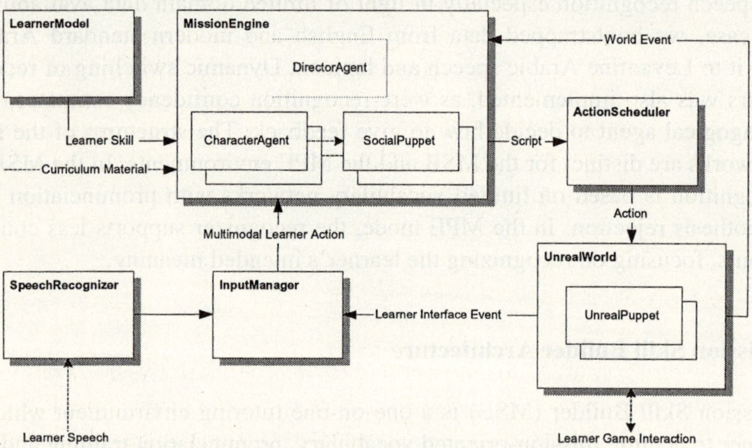

Fig. 4. The Mission Practice Environment architecture

The Unreal World uses the Unreal Tournament 2003 game engine where each character, including the learner's own avatar, is represented by an animated figure called an Unreal Puppet. The motion of the learner's puppet is for the most part driven by input from the mouse and keyboard, while the other puppets receive action requests from the Mission Engine through the Unreal World Server, which is an extended version of the Game Bots server [12]. In addition to relaying action requests to puppets, the Unreal World Server sends information about the state of the world back to the Mission Engine. Events from the user interface, such as mouse button presses, are first processed in the Input Manager, and then handed to the Mission Engine where a proper reaction is generated. The Input Manager also invokes the Speech Recognizer, when the learner presses the right mouse button, and sends the recognized utterance, with information about the chosen gesture, to the Mission Engine.

The Mission Engine uses a multi-agent architecture where each character is represented as an agent with its own goals, relationships with other entities (including the learner), private beliefs and mental models of other entities [16]. This allows the user to engage in a number of interactions with one or more characters that each can have their own, evolving attitude towards the learner. Once the character agents have chosen an action, they pass their communicative intent to corresponding Social Puppets that plan a series of verbal and nonverbal behavior that appropriately carry out that intent in the virtual environment. We plan to incorporate a high-level Director Agent that influences the character agents, to control how the story unfolds and to ensure that pedagogical and dramatic goals are met. This agent exploits the learner model to know what the learners can do and to predict what they might do. The director will use this information as a means to control the direction of the story by manipulating events and non-player characters as needed, and to regulate the challenges presented to the student.

A special character that aides the learners during their missions uses an agent model of the learner to suggest what to say next when the learner asks for help or when the learner seems to be having trouble progressing. When such a hint is given, the Mission Engine consults the Learner Model to see whether the learner has mastered the skills involved in producing the phrase to be suggested. If the learner does not have the required skill set, the aide spells out in transliterated Arabic exactly what needs to be said, but if the learner should know the phrase in Arabic, the aide simply provides a hint in English such as "You should introduce yourself."

5 Evaluation

System and content evaluation is being conducted systematically, in stages. Usability and second language learning experts have evaluated and critiqued the learner interface, content organization, and instructional methods. Learner speech data are being collected, to inform and train the speech recognition models. Learners at the US Military Academy and at USC have worked through the first set of lessons and scenes and provided feedback. A formative evaluation study with eight beginning learners was performed in Spring 2004. Learners worked with the Tactical Language Training System in one 2-hour session. The subjects found the MPE game to be fun and interesting, and were generally confident that with practice, they would be able to master the game. This supports our hypothesis that the TLTS will enable a wide range of learners, including those with low levels of confidence, to acquire communication skills in difficult languages such as Arabic. However, the learners were generally reluctant to start playing the game, because they were afraid that they would not be able to communicate successfully with the non-player characters. To address this problem, we are modifying the content in the MSB to give learners more conversational practice and encourage learners to enter the MPE right away.

The evaluation also revealed problems in the MSB Tutoring Agent's interaction. The agent applied a high standard for pronunciation accuracy, which beginners found difficult to meet. At the same time, inaccuracies in the speech analysis algorithms caused the agent in some cases to reject utterances that were pronounced correctly. The algorithm for scoring learner pronunciation has since been modified, to give higher scores to utterances that are pronounced correctly but slowly; this eliminated most of the problems of correct speech being rejected. We have also adjusted the feedback selection algorithm to avoid criticizing the learner when speech recognition confidence is low. This revised feedback mechanism is scheduled to be evaluated in further tests with soldiers in July 2004 at Ft. Bragg, North Carolina.

6 Conclusions and Future Work

The Tactical Language Training System project has been active for a relatively brief period, yet it has already made rapid progress in combining pedagogical agent, pedagogical drama, speech recognition, and game technologies in support of language learning. Once the system design is updated based upon the results of the formative evaluations, the project plans the following tasks:

- integrate the Medina authoring tool to facilitate content development,
- incorporate automated tracking of learner focus of attention, to detect learner difficulties and provide proactive help,
- construct additional content to cover a significant amount of spoken Arabic,
- perform summative evaluation of the effectiveness of the TLTS in promoting learning, and analysis of the contribution of TLTS component features to learning effectiveness, and
- support translingual authoring – adapting content from one language to another, in order to facilitate the creation of similar learning environments for a range of less commonly taught languages.

Acknowledgments. The project team includes, in addition to the authors, CARTE members Catherine M. LaBore, David V. Pynadath, Nicolaus Mote, Shumin Wu, Ulf Hermjakob, Mei Si, Nadim Daher, Gladys Saroyan, Hartmut Neven, Chirag Merchant and Brett Rutland. From the US Military Academy COL Stephen Larocca, John Morgan and Sherri Bellinger. From the USC School of Engineering Shrikanth Narayanan, Naveen Srinivasamurthy, Abhinav Sethy, Jorge Silva, Joe Tepperman and Larry Kite. From the USC School of Education Harold O'Neil and Sunhee Choi, and from UCLA CRESST Eva Baker. Thanks to Lin Pirolli for her editorial comments. This project is part of the DARWARS initiative sponsored by the US Defense Advanced Research Projects Agency (DARPA).

References

1. Bernstein, J., Najmi, A. & Ehsani, F.: Subarashii: Encounters in Japanese Spoken Language Education. CALICO Journal 16 (3) (1999) 361-384

2. Brown, P. & Levinson: *Politeness: Some universals in language use*. Cambridge University Press, New York (1987)
3. DeSmedt, W.H.: Herr Kommissar: An ICALL conversation simulator for intermediate German. In V.M. Holland, J.D. Kaplan, & M.R. Sams (Eds.), *Intelligent language tutors: Theory shaping technology*, 153-174. Lawrence Erlbaum, Mahwah, NJ (1995)
4. Doughty, C.J. & Long, M.H.: Optimal psycholinguistic environments for distance foreign language learning. Language Learning & Technology 7(3), (2003) 50-80
5. Gamper, G. & Knapp, J.: A review of CALL systems in foreign language instruction. In J.D. Moore et al. (Eds.), Artificial Intelligence in Education, 377-388. IOS Press, Amsterdam (2001)
6. Gee, P.: What video games have to teach us about learning and literacy. Palgrave Macmillan, New York (2003)
7. Hamberger, H.: Tutorial tools for language learning by two-medium dialogue. In V.M. Holland, J.D. Kaplan, & M.R. Sams (Eds.), Intelligent language tutors: Theory shaping technology, 183-199. Lawrence Erlbaum, Mahwah, NJ (1995)
8. Harless, W.G., Zier, M.A., and Duncan, R.C.: Virtual Dialogues with Native Speakers: The Evaluation of an Interactive Multimedia Method. CALICO Journal 16 (3) (1999) 313-337
9. Holland, V.M., Kaplan, J.D., & Sabol, M.A.: Preliminary Tests of Language Learning in a Speech-Interactive Graphics Microworld. CALICO Journal 16 (3) (1999) 339-359
10. Johnson, W.L.: Interaction tactics for socially intelligent pedagogical agents. IUI 2003, 251-253. ACM Press, New York (2003)
11. Johnson, W.L.,& Rizzo, P.: Politeness in tutoring dialogs: "Run the factory, that's what I'd do." ITS 2004, in press (2004)
12. Kaminka, G.A., Veloso, M.M., Schaffer, S., Sollitto, C., Adobbati, R., Marshall, A.N., Scholer, A. and Tejada, S.: GameBots: A Flexible Test Bed for Multiagent Team Research. Communications of the ACM, 45 (1) (2002) 43-45
13. LaRocca, S.A., Morgan, J.J., & Bellinger, S.: On the path to 2X learning: Exploring the possibilities of advanced speech recognition. CALICO Journal 16 (3) (1999) 295-310
14. Lightbown, P.J. & Spada, N.: How languages are learned. Oxford University Press, Oxford (1999)
15. Marsella, S., Johnson, W.L. and LaBore, C.M.: An interactive pedagogical drama for health interventions. In Hoppe, U. and Verdejo, F. eds., Artificial Intelligence in Education. IOS Press, Amsterdam (2003)
16. Marsella, S.C. & Pynadath, D.V.: Agent-based interaction of social interactions and influence. Proceedings of the Sixth International Conference on Cognitive Modelling, Pittsburgh, PA (2004)
17. Muskus, J.: Language study increases. Yale Daily News, Nov. 21, 2003
18. NCOLCTL: National Council of Less Commonly Taught Languages. http://www.councilnet.org (2003)
19. Srinivasamurthy, N. and Narayanan: ``Language-adaptive Persian speech recognition", Proc. Eurospeech (Geneva,Switzerland) (2003)
20. Swartout, W.,Gratch, J., Johnson, W.L., et al. : Towards the Holodeck: Integrating graphics, sound, character and story. Proceedings of the Intl. Conf. on Autonomous Agents,409-416. ACM Press, New York (2001)
21. Swartout, W. & van Lent: Making a game of system design. CACM 46(7) (2003) 32-39
22. Wachowicz, A. and Scott, B.: Software That Listens: It's Not a Question of Whether, It's a Question of How. CALICO Journal 16 (3), (1999) 253-276
23. Witt, S. & Young, S.: Computer-aided pronunciation teaching based on automatic speech recognition. In S. Jager, J.A. Nerbonne, & A.J. van Essen (Eds.), Language teaching and language technology, 25-35. Swets & Zeitlinger, Lisse (1998)

Combining Competing Language Understanding Approaches in an Intelligent Tutoring System

Pamela W. Jordan, Maxim Makatchev, and Kurt VanLehn

Learning Research and Development Center, Intelligent Systems Program and Computer Science Department, University of Pittsburgh, Pittsburgh PA 15260
{pjordan,maxim,vanlehn}@pitt.edu

Abstract. When implementing a tutoring system that attempts a deep understanding of students' natural language explanations, there are three basic approaches to choose between; symbolic, in which sentence strings are parsed using a lexicon and grammar; statistical, in which a corpus is used to train a text classifier; and hybrid, in which rich, symbolically produced features supplement statistical training. Because each type of approach requires different amounts of domain knowledge preparation and provides different quality output for the same input, we describe a method for heuristically combining multiple natural language understanding approaches in an attempt to use each to its best advantage. We explore two basic models for combining approaches in the context of a tutoring system; one where heuristics select the first satisficing representation and another in which heuristics select the highest ranked representation.

1 Introduction

Implementing an intelligent tutoring system that attempts a deep understanding of a student's natural language (NL) explanation is a challenging and time consuming undertaking even when making use of existing NL processing tools and techniques [1,2,3]. A motivation for attempting a deep understanding of an explanation is so that a tutoring system can reason about the domain knowledge expressed in the student's explanation in order to diagnose errors that are only implicitly expressed [4] and to provide substantive feedback that encourages further self-explanation [5]. To accomplish these tutoring system tasks, the NL technology must be able to map typical student language to an appropriate domain level representation language. While some NL mapping approaches require relatively little domain knowledge preparation there is currently still a trade-off with the quality of the representation produced especially as the complexity of the representation language increases.

Although most NL mapping approaches have been rigorously evaluated, the results may not scale-up or generalize to the tutoring system domain. First it may not be practical to carefully prepare large amounts of domain knowledge in the same manner as may have been done for the evaluation of an NL approach. This is especially a problem for tutoring systems since they need to cover a large

J.C. Lester et al. (Eds.): ITS 2004, LNCS 3220, pp. 346–357, 2004.

amount of domain knowledge to have an impact on student learning. Second, acceptable performance results may vary across applications if the requirements for representation fidelity vary. For example, a document retrieval application may not require a deep understanding of every sentence in the document to be successful whereas providing tutorial feedback to students on the content of what they write may. Finally, while one approach may be more promising than another for providing a better quality representation, the time required to prepare the domain knowledge to achieve the desired fidelity is not yet reliably predictable. For these reasons, it may be advisable to include multiple approaches and to re-examine how the approaches are integrated within the tutoring system as the domain coverage expands and improves over time.

Our goal in this paper is to examine ways in which multiple language mapping approaches can be integrated within one tutoring system so that each approach is used to its best advantage relative to a particular time-slice in the life-cycle of the knowledge development for the tutoring system. At a given time-slice, one approach may be functioning better than another but we must anticipate that the performances may change when there is a significant change in the domain knowledge provided. Our approach for integrating multiple mapping approaches, each with separate evolving knowledge sources, is to set up a competition between them and allow a deliberative process to decide for every student sentence processed which representation is the best one to use. This approach is similar to what is done in multi-agent architectures [6]. We will experimentally explore a variety of ways of competitively combining three types of NL understanding approaches in the context of the Why2-Atlas tutoring system; 1) symbolic, in which sentence strings are parsed using an NL lexicon and grammar 2) statistical, in which a corpus is used to train a text classifier and 3) hybrid, in which rich symbolic features are used to supplement the training of a text classifier.

First we will describe the Why2-Atlas tutoring domain and representation language to give an impression of the difficulty of the NL mapping task. Next we will characterize the expected performance differences of the individual approaches. Next we will describe how we measure performance and discuss how to go about selecting the best configuration for a particular knowledge development time-slice. Next we will describe two types of competition models and their selection heuristics where the heuristics evaluate representations relative to typical (but generally stated) representation failings we anticipate and have observed for each approach. Finally, we will examine the performance differences for various ways of combining the NL understanding approaches and compare them to two baselines; the current best single approach and tutoring on all possible topics.

2 Overview of the Why2-Atlas Domain and Representation Language

The Why2-Atlas system covers 5 qualitative physics problems on introductory mechanics. For each problem the student is expected to type an answer and explanation which the system analyzes in order to identify appropriate elicita-

Table 1. Slots for one body vector quantities with examples of slot filler constants.

Description	Slot sorts (examples of slot filler constants)
quantity	`Quantity1b` (velocity, acceleration)
identifier	`Id` (ID100)
body (or two bodies in case of `force`)	`Body` (pumpkin, man)
axial component or not	`Comp` (horizontal, vertical)
qualitative derivative of the magnitude	`D-mag` (constant, increase, decrease)
quantitative derivative of the magnitude	`D-mag-num` (*none*)
zero or non-zero magnitude	`Mag-zero` (zero, nonzero)
quantitative magnitude	`Mag-num` (*none*)
sign for axial component	`Dir` (pos,neg)
qualitative derivative of the direction	`D-dir` (constant, nonconstant)
beginning of time interval	`Time` (*problem specific*)
end of time interval	`Time` (*problem specific*)

tion, clarification and remediation tutoring goals. The details of the Why2-Atlas system are described in [1] and only the mapping of an isolated NL sentence to the Why2-Atlas representation language will be addressed in this paper. In this section we give an overview of the rich domain representation language that the system uses to support diagnosis and feedback.

The Why2-Atlas ontology is strongly influenced by previous qualitative physics reasoning work, in particular [7], but makes appropriate simplifications given the subset of physics the system is addressing. The Why2-Atlas ontology comprises bodies, states, physical quantities, times and relations. The ontology and representation language are described in detail in [4].

For the sake of simplicity, most bodies in the Why2-Atlas ontology have the semantics of point-masses. Body constants are problem specific. For example the body constants for one problem covered by Why2-Atlas are `pumpkin` and `man`.

Individual bodies can be in *states* such as `freefall`. Being in a particular state implies respective restrictions on the forces applied on the body. There is also the special state of `contact` between two bodies where `attached` bodies can exert mutual forces and the positions of the two bodies are equal, `detached` bodies do not exert mutual forces, and `moving-contact` bodies can exert mutual forces but there is no conclusion on their relative positions. The latter type of contact is introduced to account for point-mass bodies that are capable of pushing/pulling each other for certain time intervals (a non-impact type of contact), for example the man pushing a pumpkin up.

Physical quantities are represented as one or two body vectors. The one body vector quantities are `position`, `displacement`, `velocity`, `acceleration`, and `total-force` and the only two body one in the Why2-Atlas ontology is `force`. The single body scalar quantities are `duration`, `mass`, and `distance`.

Every physical quantity has slots and respective restrictions on the sort of a slot filler as shown in Table 1, where examples of slot filler constants of the proper sorts are shown in parentheses. Note that the sorts `Id`, `D-mag`, and `D-mag-num` do not have specific constants. These slots are used only for cross-referencing between different propositions.

Time instants are basic primitives in the Why2-Atlas ontology and a time interval is a pair (t_i, t_j) of instants. This definition of time intervals is sufficient for implementing the semantics of *open time intervals* in the context of the mechanics domain.

Some of the multi-place relations in our domain are `before`, `rel-position` and `compare`. The relation `before` relates time instants in the obvious way. The relation `rel-position` provides the means to represent the relative position of two bodies with respect to each other, independently of the choice of a coordinate system—a common way to informally compare positions in NL. The relation `compare` is used to represent the ratio and difference of two quantities' magnitudes or for quantities that change over time, magnitudes of the derivatives.

The domain propositions are represented using order-sorted first-order logic (FOL) (see for example [8]). For example, "force of gravity acting on the pumpkin is constant and nonzero" has the following representation in which the generated *identifier* constants `f1` and `ph1` appear as arguments in the `due-to` relation predicate (sort information is omitted):

```
(force f1 ?body1 pumpkin ?comp constant ?d-mag-num nonzero ?mag-num ?dir
  ?d-dir ?t1 ?t2)
(due-to d1 f1 ph1)
(phenomenon ph1 gravity)
```

There is no explicit negation so a negative student statement such as "there is no force" is represented as the force being zero. The version of the system currently under development is extending the knowledge representation to cover disjunctions, conditional statements and other types of negations.

3 Overview of the Language Understanding Approaches

In general, symbolic approaches are expected to yield good coverage and accuracy if sufficient knowledge of the domain can be captured and efficiently utilized. Whereas statistical and hybrid approaches are much easier to develop for a domain than symbolic ones and can provide just as good of coverage, those that use little more than a text corpus are expected to provide less accurate representations of what the student meant than pure symbolic approaches (once the knowledge engineering problem is adequately addressed).

Although there are many tools available for each type of approach, we developed Why2-Atlas domain knowledge sources for the symbolic approach Carmel [9], the statistical approach Rainbow [10] and the hybrid symbolic and statistical approach Rappel [11]. The knowledge development for each approach is still ongoing and at different levels of completeness, yet the system has been successfully used by students in two tutoring studies. Below we describe each of the approaches, as well as the tools we use, in more detail. We use the theoretical strengths and weaknesses of each general type of approach as the basis for our hand-coded selection heuristics.

3.1 Symbolic Approach

The traditional approach for mapping NL to a knowledge representation language is symbolic; sentence strings are parsed using an NL lexicon and grammar. There are many practical and robust sentence-level syntactic parsers available for which wide coverage NL lexicons and grammars exist [12,13,9], but syntactic analysis can only canonicalize relative to syntactic aspects of lexical semantics [14]. For example, the similarity of "I baked a cake for her" and "I baked her a cake" is found but their similarity to "I made her a cake" is not.[1] The latter sort of canonicalization is typically provided by semantic analysis. But there is no general solution at this level because semantic analysis falls into the realm of cognition and mental representations [15] and must be engineered relative to the domain of interest.

CARMEL provides combined syntactic and semantic analysis using the LCFlex robust syntactic parser, a broad coverage grammar, and semantic constructor functions that are specific to the domain to be covered [9]. Given a specification of the desired representation language, it then maps the resulting analysis to the domain representation language. Until recently, semantic constructor functions had to be completely hand-generated for every lexical entry. Although tools to facilitate and expedite this level of knowledge representation are currently being developed [16,17], it is still a significant knowledge engineering effort.

Because the necessary lexical-level knowledge engineering is difficult and time consuming and it is unclear how to predict when such a task will be sufficiently completed, there may be unexpected gaps in the semantic knowledge. Also robust parsing techniques can produce partial analyses and typically have a limited ability to self-evaluate the quality of the representation into which it maps a student sentence. So the ability to produce partial analyses in conjunction with gaps in the knowledge sources suggest that symbolic approaches will tend to undergenerate representations for sentences that weren't anticipated during the creation of their knowledge sources.

3.2 Statistical Approach

More recent approaches for processing NL are statistical; a corpus is used to train a wide variety of approaches for analyzing language. Statistical approaches are popular because there is relatively little effort involved to get such an approach working, if a representative corpus already exists. The most useful of these approaches for intelligent tutoring systems has been text classification in which a subtext is tagged as being a member of a particular class of interest and uses just

[1] The need to distinguish the semantic differences between "bake" and "made" depends on the application for which the representation will be used.

the words in the class tagged corpus for training a classifier. This particular style of classification is called a *bag of words* approach because the meaning that the organization of a sentence imparts is not considered. The classes themselves are generally expressed as text as well and are at the level of an exemplar of a text that is a member of the class. With this approach, the text can be mapped to its representation by looking up a hand-generated propositional representation for the exemplar text of the class identified at run-time.

RAINBOW is one such *bag of words* text classifier; in particular it is a Naive Bayes text classifier. The classes of interest must first be decided and then a training corpus developed where subtexts are annotated with the class to which it belongs. For the Why2-Atlas training, each sentence was annotated with one class. During training RAINBOW computes an estimate of the probability of a word in a particular class relative to the class labellings for the Why2-Atlas training sentences. Then when a new sentence is to be analyzed at run-time, RAINBOW calculates the posterior probabilities of each class relative to the words in the sentence and selects the class with the highest probability [10].

Like most statistical approaches, the quality of RAINBOW's analysis depends on the quality of its training data. Although good annotator agreement is possible for the classes of interest for the Why2-Atlas domain [18], we found the resulting training set for a class sometimes includes sentences that depend on a particular context for the full meaning of that class to be licensed. In practice the necessary context may not be present for the new sentence that is to be analyzed. This suggests that the statistical approach will tend to overgenerate representations. It is also possible for a student to express more than one key part of an explanation in a single sentence so that multiple class assignments would be more appropriate. This suggests that the statistical approach will also sometimes undergenerate since only the best classification is used. However, we expect the need for multiple class assignments to happen infrequently since the Why2-Atlas system includes a sentence segmenter that attempts to break up complex sentences before sentence understanding is attempted by any of the approaches.

3.3 Hybrid Approach

Finally, there are hybrids of symbolic and statistical approaches. For example, syntactic features can be used to supplement the training of a text classifier. Although the syntactic features often are obtained via statistical parsing methods, they are sometimes obtained via symbolic methods instead since the resulting feature set is richer [18]. With text classification, the classes are still generally defined via an exemplar of the class so the desired propositional representation must still be obtained via a look-up according to the class identified at run-time.

RAPPEL is a hybrid approach that uses symbolically-derived syntactic dependency features (obtained via MINIPAR [13,19]) to train for classes that are defined at the representation language level [11] instead of at an informal text level. There is a separate classifier for each type of proposition in the knowledge representation language. Each classifier indicates whether a proposition of the type it recognizes is present and if so, which class it is. The class indicates which slots are filled with which slot constants. There is then a one-to-one correspondence between a class and a proposition in the representation language. To arrive at the representation for a single sentence, RAPPEL applies all of the trained classifiers and then combines their results during a post-processing stage.

For Why2-Atlas we trained separate classifiers for every physics quantity, relation and state for a total of 27 different classifiers. For example, there is a separate classifier for `velocity` and another for `acceleration`. Bodies are also handled by separate classifiers; one for one body propositions and another for two body propositions. The basic approach for the body classifiers is similar to that used in statistical approaches to reference resolution (e.g. [20,21]). The number of classes within each classifier depend on the number of slot constant filler combinations possible. For example, the class *v_h* encodes the proposition (velocity id1 horizontal ?body ?var$_1$ ... ?var$_n$) and the class *v_hip* encodes the proposition (velocity id2 horizontal ?body increase ?mag-zero ?mag-num pos ?t1 ?t2) where *v* represents the predicate `velocity`, *h* represents the slot constant `horizontal`, *i* represents the slot constant `increase` and *p* represents the constant `pos`.

Having a large number of classifiers and classes requires a larger, more comprehensive set of training data than is needed for a typical text classification approach. And just as with the preparation of the training data for the statistical approach, the annotator may still be influenced by the context of a sentence. However, we expect the impact of contextual dependencies to be less severe since the representation-defined classes are more formal and finer-grained than text-defined classes. For example, annotators may still resolve intersentential anaphora and ellipsis but the content related inferences needed to select a class are much finer-grained and therefore a closer fit to the actual meaning of the sentence.

Although we have classifiers and classes defined that cover the entire Why2-Atlas representation language, we have not yet provided training for the full representation language. Given the strong dependence of this approach on the completeness of the training data, we expect this approach to sometimes undergenerate just as an incomplete symbolic approach would and sometimes to overgenerate because of overgeneralizations during learning, just as with any statistical approach.

4 Computing and Comparing Performances

To measure the overall performance of the Why2-Atlas system when using different understanding approach configurations, we use a test suite of 35 held-out multi-sentence student essays (235 sentences total) that are annotated for the elicitation and remediation topics that are to be discussed with the student. Elicitation topics are tagged when prescribed, critical physics principles are missing from the student's explanation and remediation topics are tagged when the essay implicitly or explicitly exhibits any of a small number of misconceptions or errors that are typical of beginning students. From a language analysis perspective, the representation of the essay must be accurate enough to detect when physics principles are both properly and improperly expressed in the essay.

For the entire test suite we compute the number of true positives (TP), false positives (FP), true negatives (TN) and false negatives (FN) for the elicitation topics selected by the system relative to the elicitation topics annotated for the test suite essays. From this we compute recall = TP/(TP+FN), precision = TP/(TP+FP), and false alarm rate = FP/(FP+TN).

As a baseline measure, we compute the recall, precision and false alarm rate that results if all possible elicitations for a physics problem are selected. For our 35 essay test suite the recall is 1, precision is .61 and false alarm rate is 1. Although NL evaluations compute an F-measure (the harmonic average of recall and precision) in order to arrive at one number for comparing approaches, it does not allow errors to be considered as fully as with other analysis methods such as receiver operating characteristics (ROC) areas [22] and d' [23]. These measures are similar in that they combine the recall and the false alarm rates into one number but allow for error skewing [22]. Rather than undertaking a full comparison of the various NL understanding approach configurations for this paper, we will instead look for those combinations that result in a high recall and a low false alarm rate. Error skewing depends on what costs we need to attribute to false negatives and false positives. Both potentially have negative impacts on student learning in that the former leaves out important information that should have been brought to the student's attention and the latter can confuse the student or cause lack of confidence in the system.

5 The Selection Heuristics

Although an NL understanding approach is not strictly an agent in the sense of [24] (e.g. it doesn't reason about goals or other agents) it can be treated architecturally as a service agent in the sense of [25] as has been done in many dialogue systems (e.g. [26,3]). Generally the service agents supply slightly different information or are relevant in slightly different contexts so that the evaluator or coordinator decides which single service agent will be assigned a particular task. For example, [26] describes a system architecture that includes competing discourse strategy service agents and an evaluator that rates the competing strategies and selects the highest rated strategy agent to perform the communication task.

However, in the case of competing NL understanding approaches, an evaluator would need to predict which approach will provide the highest quality analysis of a sentence that needs to be processed in order to decide which one should be assigned the task. Because such a prediction would probably require at least a partial analysis of the sentence, we take the approach of assigning the task to all of the available language understanding approaches and then assessing the quality of the results relative to the expected typical accuracy faults of each approach.

The first competition model tries each approach in a preferred sequential ordering, stopping when a representation is acceptable according to a general filtering heuristic and otherwise continuing. The filtering heuristic estimates which representations are over or undergenerated and excludes those representations so that it appears that no representation was found for the sentence. A representation for a sentence is undergenerated if any of the word stems in a sentence are constants in the representation language and none of those are in the representation generated or if the representation produced is too sparse. For Why2-Atlas, it is too sparse if 50% of the propositions in the representation for a sentence have slots with less than two constants filling them. Most propositions in the representation language contain six slots which can be filled with constants. Propositions that are defined to have two or fewer slots that can be filled with constants are excluded from this assessment (e.g. the relations before and rel-position are excluded). Representations are overgenerated if the sentences are shorter than 4 words since in general the physics principles to be recognized cannot be expressed in fewer words.

For the sequential model, we use a preference ordering of symbolic, statistical and hybrid in these experiments because of the way in which Why2-Atlas was originally designed and our expectations for which approach should produce the highest quality result at this point in the development of the knowledge sources. We also created some partial sequential models as well to look at whether the more expensive understanding approaches add anything significant at this point in their development.

The other competition model requests an analysis from all of the understanding approaches and then uses the filtering heuristic along with a ranking heuristic (as described below) to select the best analysis. If all of the analyses for either competition model fail to meet the selection heuristics then the sentence is regarded as uninterpretable. The run-time difference between the two competition models are nearly equivalent if each understanding approach in the second model is run in parallel using a distributed multi-agent architecture such as OAA [25].

The ranking heuristic again focuses on the weaknesses of all the approaches. It computes a score for each representation by first finding the number of words in the intersection of the constants in the representation and the word stems in the sentence (*justified*), the number of word stems in the sentence that are constants in the representation language that do not appear in the representation (*undergenerated*) and the number of constants in the representation that are not word stems in the sentence (*overgenerated*). It then selects the one with the highest score, where the score is; $justified - 2 * undergenerated - .5 * overgenerated$. The weightings reflect both the importance and approximate nature of the terms.

The main difference between the two models is that the ranking approach will choose the better representation (as estimated by the heuristics) as opposed to one that merely suffices.

6 Results of the Combined Competing Approaches

The top part of Table 2 compares the baseline of tutoring all possible topics and the individual performances of the three understanding approaches when each is used in isolation from the others. We see that only the statistical approach lowers the false alarm rate but does so by sacrificing recall. The rest are not significantly different from tutoring all topics. However, the results of the statistical approach are clearly not good enough.

Table 2. Performance of language understanding approaches for actions taken in the Why2-Atlas system

approach	recall	precision	false alarm rate
baseline1 (tutor all topics)	1.0	.61	1.0
symbolic	1.0	.61	1.0
statistical (baseline2)	.60	.93	.07
hybrid	.94	.59	1.0
all (satisficing)	.67	.80	.26
hybrid + statistical (satisficing)	.70	.78	.31
symbolic + statistical (satisficing)	.69	.80	.26
all (highest ranked)	.73	.76	.36

The bottom part of Table 2, shows the results of combining the NL approaches. The satisficing model that includes all three NL mapping approaches performs better than the individual models in that it modestly improves recall but at the sacrifice of a higher false alarm rate. The satisficing model checks each representation in order 1) symbolic 2) statistical 3) hybrid, and stops with the first representation that is acceptable according to the filtering heuristic. We also see that both of the satisficing models that include just two understanding approaches perform better than the model in which all approaches are combined; with the symbolic + statistical model being the best since it increases recall without further increasing the false alarm rate. Finally, we see that the model, which selects the best representation from all three approaches, provides the most balanced results of the combined or individual approaches. It provides the largest increase in recall and the false alarm rate is still modest compared to the baseline of tutoring all possible topics. To make a final selection of which combined approach one should use, there needs to be an estimate of which errors will have a larger negative impact on student learning. But clearly, selecting a combined approach will be better than selecting a single NL mapping approach.

7 Discussion and Future Work

Although none of the NL mapping approaches adequately represent the physics content covered by the Why2-Atlas system at this point in their knowledge development, they can be combined advantageously by estimating representations that are over or undergenerated.

We are considering two future improvements. One is to automatically learn ranking and filtering heuristics using features that represent differences between annotated representations and the representations produced by the understanding approaches. The heuristics can then be tuned to the types of representations that the approaches are producing at a particular time-slice in the domain knowledge development. The second future improvement is to add reference resolution to the heuristics in order to canonicalize words and phrases to their body constants in the representation language. Although we could try canonicalizing other lexical items to their representation language constants, this might not be as fruitful. While a physics expert could use *push* and *pull* and know that this implies that forces are involved, this is not a safe assumption for introductory physics students.

Acknowledgments. This research was supported by ONR Grant No. N00014-00-1-0600 and by NSF Grant No. 9720359.

References

1. VanLehn, K., Jordan, P., Rosé, C., Bhembe, D., Böttner, M., Gaydos, A., Makatchev, M., Pappuswamy, U., Ringenberg, M., Roque, A., Siler, S., Srivastava, R.: The architecture of Why2-Atlas: A coach for qualitative physics essay writing. In: Proceedings of Intelligent Tutoring Systems Conference. Volume 2363 of LNCS., Springer (2002) 158–167
2. Aleven, V., Popescu, O., Koedinger, K.: Pilot-testing a tutorial dialogue system that supports self-explanation. In: Proceedings of Intelligent Tutoring Systems Conference. Volume 2363 of LNCS., Springer (2002) 344
3. Zinn, C., Moore, J.D., Core, M.G.: A 3-tier planning architecture for managing tutorial dialogue. In: Proceedings of Intelligent Tutoring Systems Conference (ITS 2002). (2002) 574–584
4. Makatchev, M., Jordan, P., VanLehn, K.: Abductive theorem proving for analyzing student explanations and guiding feedback in intelligent tutoring systems. Journal of Automated Reasoning: Special Issue on Automated Reasoning and Theorem Proving in Education (2004) to appear.
5. Aleven, V., Popescu, O., Koedinger, K.R.: A tutorial dialogue system with knowledge-based understanding and classification of student explanations. In: Working Notes of 2nd IJCAI Workshop on Knowledge and Reasoning in Practical Dialogue Systems. (2001)
6. Sandholm, T.W.: Distributed rational decision making. In Weiss, G., ed.: Multiagent Systems: A Modern Approach to Distributed Artificial Intelligence. The MIT Press, Cambridge, MA, USA (1999) 201–258
7. Ploetzner, R., VanLehn, K.: The acquisition of qualitative physics knowledge during textbook-based physics training. Cognition and Instruction **15** (1997) 169–205
8. Walther, C.: A many-sorted calculus based on resolution and paramodulation. Morgan Kaufmann, Los Altos, California (1987)

9. Rosé, C.P.: A framework for robust semantic interpretation. In: Proceedings of the First Meeting of the North American Chapter of the Association for Computational Linguistics. (2000) 311–318
10. McCallum, A., Nigam, K.: A comparison of event models for naive bayes text classification. In: Proceeding of AAAI/ICML-98 Workshop on Learning for Text Categorization, AAAI Press (1998)
11. Jordan, P.W.: A machine learning approach for mapping natural language to a domain representation language. in preparation (2004)
12. Abney, S.: Partial parsing via finite-state cascades. Journal of Natural Language Engineering **2** (1996) 337–344
13. Lin, D.: Dependency-based evaluation of MINIPAR. In: Workshop on the Evaluation of Parsing Systems, Granada, Spain (1998)
14. Levin, B., Pinker, S., eds.: Lexical and Conceptual Semantics. Blackwell Publishers, Oxford (1992)
15. Jackendoff, R.: Semantics and Cognition. Current Studies in Linguistics Series. The MIT Press (1983)
16. Rosé, C., Gaydos, A., Hall, B., Roque, A., VanLehn, K.: Overcoming the knowledge engineering bottleneck for understanding student language input. In: Proceedings of of AI in Education 2003 Conference. (2003)
17. Dzikovska, M., Swift, M., Allen, J.: Customizing meaning: building domain-specific semantic representations from a generic lexicon. In Bunt, H., Muskens, R., eds.: Computing Meaning. Volume 3. Academic Publishers (2004)
18. Rosé, C., Roque, A., Bhembe, D., VanLehn, K.: A hybrid text classification approach for analysis of student essays. In: Proceedings of HLT/NAACL 03 Workshop on Building Educational Applications Using Natural Language Processing. (2003)
19. Lin, D., Pantel, P.: Discovery of inference rules for question answering. Journal of Natural Language Engineering **Fall-Winter** (2001)
20. Strube, M., Rapp, S., Müller, C.: The influence of minimum edit distance on reference resolution. In: Proceedings of Empirical Methods in Natural Language Processing Conference. (2002)
21. Ng, V., Cardie, C.: Improving machine learning approaches to coreference resolution. In: Proceedings of Association for Computational Linguistics 2002. (2002)
22. Flach, P.: The geometry of ROC space: Understanding machine learning metrics through ROC isometrics. In: Proceedings of 20th International Conference on Machine Learning. (2003)
23. MacMillan, N., Creelman, C.: Detection Theory: A User's Guide. Cambridge University Press, Cambridge, UK (1991)
24. Franklin, S., Graesser, A.: Is it an agent, or just a program?: A taxonomy for autonomous agents. In: Proceedings of the Third International Workshop on Agent Theories, Architectures, and Languages, Springer-Verlag (1996)
25. Cheyer, A., Martin, D.: The open agent architecture. Journal of Autonomous Agents and Multi-Agent Systems **4** (2001) 143–148
26. Jokinen, K., Kerminen, A., Kaipainen, M., Jauhiainen, T., Wilcock, G., Turunen, M., Hakulinen, J., Kuusisto, J., Lagus, K.: Adaptive dialogue systems - interaction with interact. In: Proceedings of the 3rd SIGdial Workshop on Discourse and Dialogue. (2002)

Evaluating Dialogue Schemata with the Wizard of Oz Computer-Assisted Algebra Tutor

Jung Hee Kim[1] and Michael Glass[2]

[1] Dept. Computer Science
North Carolina A&T State Univ.
Greensboro, NC 27411
jungkim@ncat.edu
[2] Dept. Math & CS
Valparaiso University
Valparaiso, IN 46383
michael.glass@valpo.edu

Abstract. The Wooz tutor of the North Carolina A&T algebra tutorial dialogue project is a computer program that mediates keyboard-to-keyboard tutoring of algebra problems, with the feature that it can suggest to the tutor canned structures of tutoring goals and canned sentences to insert into the tutoring dialogue. It is designed to facilitate and record a style of tutoring where the tutor and student collaboratively construct an answer in the form of an equation, a style often attested in natural tutoring of algebra. The algebra tutoring dialogue project collects and analyzes these dialogues with the aim of describing tutoring strategies and language with enough rigor that they may be evaluated and incorporated in machine tutoring. By plugging our analyzed dialogues into the computer-suggested tutoring component of the Wooz tutor we can evaluate the fitness of our dialogue analysis.

1 Introduction

Tutorial dialogues are often structurally analyzed for purposes of constructing tutoring systems and understanding the tutorial process. However there are not many ways for validating the analysis of a dialogue, either for verifying that the analysis matches the structure that a human would use, or for verifying that the analysis is efficacious. In the algebra tutorial dialogue project at North Carolina A&T State University we use a machine-assisted human tutor to evaluate our analysis of elementary college algebra tutoring dialogues. The project has collected transcripts of human tutoring using an interface that provides an enhanced chat-window environment for keyboard to keyboard tutoring of algebra problems [1]. These transcripts of tutorial dialogue are annotated based on the tutor's intentions and language. From these annotations we have created structured tutoring scenarios which we import into an enhanced computer-mediated tutoring interface: the Wooz tutor. In subsequent tutoring sessions, the tutor has the option of selecting language from the canned scenario, edited or ignored as the tutor sees fit, for tutoring some of the problems. The resulting transcripts are then analyzed to evaluate the fitness of our scenarios for tutoring, based on measures

J.C. Lester et al. (Eds.): ITS 2004, LNCS 3220, pp. 358–367, 2004.

such as pre- and post-test scores and the number of times that the tutor deviated from the script.

The algebra tutorial dialogue project captures tutoring of high school and college algebra problems with several goals in mind: 1) cataloging descriptions of tutoring behavior from both tutor and student, using where possible enough rigor that they might be useful for dialogue-based computerized tutoring, 2) evaluating the effectiveness of various tutoring behaviors as they are originally observed, and 3) describing these computer-mediated human educational dialogue interactions in general, as being of use to the educational dialogue and cognitive psychology communities. The Wooz tutor is a useful tool for partially evaluating our success in these endeavors.

2 Environment and Procedure

2.1 Computer-Mediated Tutoring Environment

The tutoring dialogues we captured consist of a tutor and a student working problems collaboratively. The dialogue model is of a tutor and student conversing, with both the problem statement and the equation being worked on being visible to both parties. We analyze typed communication because first, this is the mode most tractable for computerization and second, we can capture all the communication between student and tutor, there are no gaze, gesture, prosodic features, and so on to capture and annotate. Thus the computer-supported tutoring environment affords the following:

1. The statement of the problem currently being worked on is always on display in a dedicated window.
2. The equations being developed while solving the problem are displayed in a dedicated window, there is a tool bar for equation editing.
3. Typed tutorial dialogue appears, interleaved, in a chat-window.

Additionally there is some status information, e.g. which party has the current turn, and the tutor has some special controls, such as a menu of problem statements to pick from. One feature of this software environment is that the equation editor toolbar is customized for each problem, so extraneous controls not needed for solving the problem under discussion are not displayed.

A phenomenon annotated in other transcripts of algebra tutoring is deixis [2, 3], in particular pointing at equations or parts of equations. Although our interface has the capability to display and edit several equations at the same time in its equation area, it has no good referring mechanism for the participants to use. So far, we have not noticed this to be an issue in the dialogues we have collected.

Regarding our experience with the program, we have collected transcripts from 50+ students to date, each comprised of about one hour of tutoring, for a total of approximately 3000 turns and 300 problems. Students and tutors receive brief instruction before use, they have had little difficulty learning to use the application, including constructing equations.

2.2 Dialogue Collection

These problem-oriented tutoring dialogues are similar in form to those studied extensively by the ITS community, e.g. [3, 4, 5], whose salient features were summarized by [6]. An extract from a typical dialogue is illustrated in Figure 1.

Problems solved during these tutoring sessions include both symbolic manipulation problems and word problems, viz:

1. Please factor $3x^2 - 11x + 6$.
2. Bob drove "m" miles from Denver to Fargo. Normally this trip takes "n" hours, but on Tuesday there was good weather and he saved 2 hours. Write an equation for his driving speed "s".

Students solve an average of between 5 and 6 problems in an hour session.

One feature of our tutoring data collection protocol is that the student's performance on the pre-test determines which categories of problems will be tutored. The tutor gives priority to problems similar to the ones the student answered incorrectly on the pre-test, but did not leave totally blank. These are the areas where we judge that the student is likely most ready to benefit from tutoring. The post-test then covers only the problem areas that were tutored, so that any learning gains we measure are specifically measuring learning for the particular tutoring that occurred. For data analysis purposes the students are coded with an achievement level, on a scale of 1 (lowest) to 5. The achievement judgment is derived from the teacher of the student's algebra class, based on previous academic performance in the class.

The NC A&T dialogue project has accumulated 51 one-hour transcripts in this way. The students are all recruited from the first year basic algebra classes. About 24 of the transcripts were taught by an expert tutor, a professor of mathematics with extensive experience tutoring algebra, 16 are divided approximately evenly between experienced tutors, two people with extensive experience but no formal mathematics education background, and 11 were taught by a novice tutor, an upper-level mathematics student.

Students exhibit a learning gain of 0.35 across all tutoring sessions, calculated as:

$$(\text{posttest} - \text{pretest}) / (1 - \text{pretest})$$

where the test scores range from 0.0 to 1.0. The expert tutor's sessions exhibit a learning gain of 0.41, the experienced tutors' learning gain is 0.33, and the novice tutor's learning gain is 0.24. These data show that the dialogues do, in fact, record learning events. Furthermore it also indicates that even though novice tutors can be successful, additional tutoring experience seems to improve tutoring outcomes.

2.3 Dialogue Analysis

Figure 1 shows an extract from a relatively short dialogue where the student solved one multiplication problem. (In printed transcripts, the evolving equation in the equation window is interpolated into the dialogue every time the equation changes.) Even though the student performed perfectly in solving the problem, it illustrates the most prominent tutoring strategy used by our tutors: ensuring that the student can state the type of problem (multiplying polynomials in this case) and a technique to solve it (a mnemonic device in this case) before proceeding with a solution. Rarely do the tutors skip these steps. This tactic can also be seen in the transcripts of [2]. This tactic alone is often enough to get the student to solve the problem, as illustrated, even when the student failed to solve similar problems on the pre-test. Getting the student to explicitly state the problem and method is consistent with the view that learning mathematics often invokes metacognitive processes [7].

	Problem: (3x-2) (x+5)
Tu:	*What operation do you need to apply here?*
St:	*Factoring.*
Tu:	*No, Not factoring.*
Tu:	*The expression is already factored.*
Tu:	*What is the opposite of factoring?*
St:	*Distributing.*
Tu:	*You can say distributing.*
Tu:	*But we are multiplying here.*
Tu:	*Now, what process do we use when we are multiplying two binomials.*
St:	*Foil.*
Tu:	*Excellent, You use FOIL.*
Tu:	*What does FOIL stand for?*
St:	*First Outer Inner Last.*
	$3x^2 + 15x - 3x^2 - 10$
Tu:	*Good, Now go ahead and use FOIL to multiply the two binomials together.*
	$3x^2 + 15x - 2x - 10$
St:	
St:	
	$3x^2 + 13x - 10$
St:	
Tu:	*Excellent.*

Fig. 1. Typical Tutorial Dialogue

We annotate our transcripts according to a hierarchy of the tutor's dialogue and tutorial goals. For purposes of constructing a mechanical tutor that models human dialogue behaviors, this style of rigorously annotated human dialogues has provided the data which inform several intelligent tutoring system projects, e.g. the CIRCSIM-Tutor baroreceptor reflex tutor [8, 9, 10], the Auto-Tutor computer literacy tutor [11], and the Ms. Lindquist algebra word problem tutor [12]. Our annotation scheme is similar to the CIRCSIM-Tutor scheme [10].

The model underlying this style of markup is that tutoring consists of a set of verbal gambits, whereby: 1) a gambit potentially spans multiple turns of dialogue, 2) each gambit addresses a particular tutorial goal, and 3) goals and subgoals are hierarchically organized, meaning there are gambits within gambits. We call a sequence of goals a schema, each subtree can also be a schema. This view of dialogue is motivated by current computer models of dialogue planning. Our schemata do not, in themselves, attempt to describe domain or pedagogical reasoning. For example we have a tutorial goal called obtain-factors which occurs as part of larger pedagogical gambits, but we do not record how the tutor finds factors. The result of this annotation process is that we identify tutoring schemata, common patterns of dialogue goals that the tutors employ, without identifying the domain or pedagogical reasoning that may explain those schemata. In consequence, many of our schemata are quite problem-specific. The fact that this assemblage of goals and schemata is imputed from text by the researchers, and not derived in a principled way, makes evaluating them more important.

The Atlas-Andes tutor [13] guides the student through problem-solving tasks where the main tutorial mode consists of model tracing guided by physics reasoning. Our markup would be unable to capture and our Wooz tutor would be unable to evaluate such dialogues. However Atlas-Andes also includes, as an adjunct method of tutoring, dialogue schemata similar to our own called Knowledge Construction Dialogues. These dialogues would seem to be amenable to Wooz tutor evaluation.

A reason this style of analysis is possible is that our tutors do not teach much algebraic reasoning. Instead they emphasize applying problem-solving methods previously learned in class, along with teaching the metacognitive skills to know how to apply these methods.

Figure 2 shows the evolving trace of tutorial goals from one of our typical dialogues, as affected by student errors and retries. The three prominent goals discussed above are labeled identify-operation, identify-approach and solve-problem in this annotation scheme.

We abstract general schemata from many instances of tutoring such as Figure 2. The quite general-purpose schema of identify-problem, identify-approach, and solve-problem usually involves problem-specific sub-schemata. For example, to satisfy solve-problem in the trinomial factoring domain, we have a schema of make-binomials and confirm-factoring. If that fails, solve-problem might be satisfied by an alternate

Goal Hierarchy	*Comment*
IDENTIFY OPERATION	Operation is factoring
TUTOR OPERATION	Elicit the operation from the student, 1st attempt
TUTOR EXPRESSION	Student did not recognize it is an expression, this is a fixup
TUTOR OPERATION	2nd attempt
IDENTIFY APPROACH	Solution approach is trial-and-error factoring
TUTOR TRIAL-AND-ERROR	Elicit from or inform the student to factor by trial-and-error
SOLVE PROBLEM	
MAKE BINOMIALS	Ask the student to produce both binomial terms all at once.
OBTAIN FACTORS	Student failed, obtain terms one at a time, 1st attempt
OBTAIN FIRST FACTOR	
OBTAIN SECOND FACTOR	
CONFIRM FACTORING	
CHECK-VIA-FOIL	Confirm by multiplying back The student made an error.
OBTAIN FACTORS	2nd attempt
OBTAIN SECOND FACTOR	Correct the one term the student got wrong
(CONFIRM FACTORING)	Student did this without the tutor prompting

Fig. 2. Tutorial Goals in a Typical Dialogue

IDENTIFY THE PROBLEM
What are we doing with this expression?
We are factoring.
INTRODUCE THE TRAIL-ERROR APPROACH.
What method can we use to factor this?
Let's use the trial and error method.
SOLVE PROBLEM
SOLVE VIA MAKING BINOMIALS
MAKE BINOMIALS
So you set up your 2 sets of parentheses and fill them in with factors of the first term and the last.
This trinomial will factor into 2 binomials.
CONFIRM FACTORING
Now how do we check our factors.
Now use FOIL to check this
MAKE FIRST TERM
What are the two factors of 2x squared?
Ok, x squared factors into x and x, right?
etc.
SOLVE VIA CORRECTING FACTORS
etc.

Fig. 3. Extract From Sentences For Each Goal as Presented to the Wooz Tutor

schema of obtain-factors, (which itself is composed of the goals obtain-first-factor and obtain-second-factor) followed by confirm-factoring.

2.4 Wooz Tutor

The tutorial schemata are then evaluated by using them in tutorial dialogues with students, via the Wooz Tutor[1]. Running in Wooz Tutor mode, the computer-mediated communication software presents the human tutor with an additional menu of tutoring goals and a set of associated sentences for each goal. The tutor can optionally select and edit a sentence, then send it to the dialogue.

Note that since the Wooz tutor is a superset of our normal computer-mediated tutoring interface, it is possible to conduct tutoring dialogues where some of the problems are mechanically assisted and some are produced entirely from the human tutor.

Following the identification of schemata, we collect examples of language used for each goal. The sets of goals and associated sentences are then collected together, one set for each problem, illustrated in Figure 3. Some of the sentences are simple templates where the variable slots can be filled in with the student's name or problem-specific information. On the Wooz tutor interface, the goals hierarchy appears as an

[1] Wooz comes from Wizard of Oz. The public face of the tutor, including its language and goals, comes from the machine, while there is a human intelligence pulling the strings. The name is a bit of a misnomer, as we do not try to fool the students.

expandable tree of nodes, where expanding a leaf node exposes the sentences that can be picked. Mouse-over of a goal node shows the first sentence that can be used for expressing that goal, enabling the tutor to peer inside the tree more readily. Figure 4 shows the Wooz tutor as the tutor sees it.

From the transcripts we can then evaluate how much of the dialogue came from the canned sentences, edited sentences, or entirely new sentences. We can also tell when the tutor left the goal script. This gives us an indication of the effectiveness and completeness of our isolated tutoring schemata and language.

The intelligence for understanding and evaluating student input, and deciding when and where to switch tutorial goals, still resides in the human tutor. The schemata we isolate and test with this method do not specify all that is needed for mechanizing the tutoring process with an ITS. However the tradeoff for leaving the decisions in the hands of a human tutor is that the simple evaluation of schemata is quite cheap.

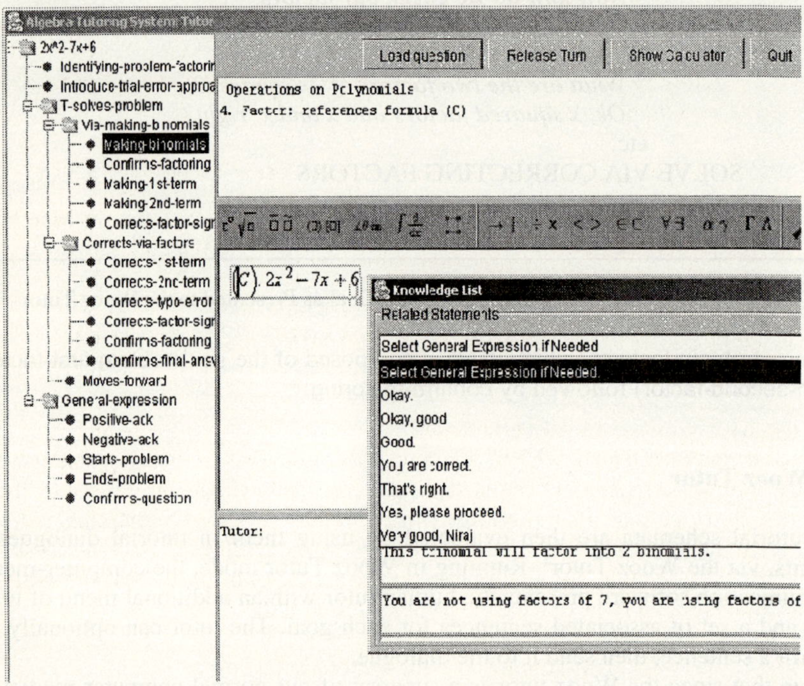

Fig. 4. Wooz Tutor Computer-Mediated Tutoring Interface, Tutor's Screen

3 Results and Discussion

We have 6 tutoring sessions where the expert tutor utilized the Wooz structured scenario for the trinomial factoring problem. Thus we have no estimates of statistical significance. The other problems in the same tutoring session were tutored by normal means. We have 15 examples of tutoring this problem without benefit of the structured scenario. The learning gains were 0.75 for the Wooz-assisted sessions and -0.14

(a loss) for the non-assisted sessions. The Wooz-assisted tutoring sessions had only lower achievement (levels 1 through 3) students, while the non-assisted sessions had a more mixed population. Considering only the students at the lower achievement levels gives a learning gain of 0.75 for Wooz and 0.0 for the unassisted tutors. Note also that the Wooz-assisted gains compare favorably to the 0.35 gain over all problems in all transcripts. These results point toward Wooz-assisted tutoring producing superior learning gains, but the numbers are so small that we do not have statistical significance.

Comparing the number of turns to tutor one problem (both tutor and student combined) and clock time to tutor one problem for Wooz vs. non-Wooz for the same problem, we see that Wooz is a trifle slower and less wordy in the achievement matched group, and a much slower and a trifle more wordy overall. Table 1 shows these results. We would have expected the Wooz assisted dialogue to be faster because of less typing, but this does not seem to be the case.

In the Wooz-assisted dialogues, the tutors almost always followed the suggested tutorial goal schemata. This suggests that we have the goal structure correct. We have not tried the computer-suggested goal structure and dialogue with novice tutors to see whether it affects their tutoring.

Table 1. Statistics for Wooz-Assisted vs. Manual Dialogues on One Problem

	Wooz-Assisted Dialogues	All Manual Dialogues	Achievement-Matched Manual Dialogues
Learning Gain	0.75	-0.14	0.00
Avg. Turns	21.83	20.13	25.30
Avg. Time	18:52	14:05	18:04
n	6	15	10

Of the tutor turns in the Wooz-assisted dialogue, 70% were extracted from the database of canned sentences with no change, 6% were edits of existing sentences, and 24% were new sentences. There is little difference between the edits and the new sentences, it seems that once the tutor started editing a sentence she changed almost the whole thing. The new and changed sentences almost always respond to specifics of student utterances that did not appear in the attested transcripts used in building the sentence database. Here is an example of a modified turn:

St:	I'm going to use the quadratic formula.
Tu (original):	Is this an equation?
Tu (edited):	We use the quadratic formula for quadratic equations. Is this an equation?

This phenomenon, the human tutor responding to specific variations in the student responses, would seem to reduce the Wooz tutor's evaluative probity. When a tutor changes a sentence, we have no way to know whether the unchanged sentence would have worked just as well. Nevertheless, with experience we should build up knowledge of what rates of sentence modifications to reasonably expect. Forcing the tutor to follow Wooz tutor's suggestions would mean that discovering gaps in schemata would become more difficult, making it less useful as an evaluative tool.

Wooz bears a familial similarity to the snapshot analysis technique for evaluating intelligent tutoring systems, for example [14], whereby at various points in the tutorial session the choices of experienced tutors are compared with the choices of the machine tutor. In an ITS project, Wooz could function as a cheap way to partially evaluate the same schemata before they are incorporated into the machine tutor.

The Wooz tutor does not evaluate the completeness or the reliability of coding. It is thus not a substitute for traditional evaluation measures such as inter-rater reliability. But by evaluating whether schemata imputed from transcripts are complete and efficacious it could provide an additional measure of evaluation to a dialogue annotation project. In particular a high inter-rater reliability shows that the analysis is reproducible, not that it is useful. This technique can help fill that gap.

4 Conclusions

The technique of providing canned tutoring goals structure and sentences to the human tutor in keyboard-to-keyboard tutoring seems to work well for our purpose of evaluating whether we have analyzed dialogue in a useful manner. We can evaluate whether the tutoring language and goal structure are actually complete enough for real dialogues and actually provide effective tutoring.

The input understanding and decision making structures that would be necessary for building an ITS are not evaluated here. The positive result is that Wooz tutor evaluation is cheap and easy, since you do not have to do all the work to commit to working tutoring software. Furthermore you can evaluate only a few small dialogues by mixing them in with ordinary un-assisted tutoring. Compared to techniques for evaluating transcript annotation such as inter-rater reliability measurement, Wooz tutoring provides the advantage that it tests the final transcript analysis in real dialogues.

We have no evidence, partly because of a small number of test cases and partly because we do not force the tutor to follow the machine's suggestions, that the artificial assist to the tutor speeds up the tutoring process or improves learning outcomes.

Acknowledgements. The Wooz tutor and ancillary applications were developed by a hard-working inspired group of NC A&T students that included Niraj Patel, Oliver Hinds, Kevin Purrington, and Jie Zhao. The idea for computer-assisted human tutoring was suggested by Kurt van Lehn, and the algebra tutorial dialogue project was suggested by Martha Evens.

This work was supported by the Cognitive Science Program, Office of Naval Research, under grant N00014-02-1-0164, to North Carolina A&T State University. The content does not reflect the position or policy of the government and no official endorsement should be inferred.

References

1. Patel, Niraj, Michael Glass, and Jung Hee Kim. 2003. "Data Collection Applications for the NC A&T State University Algebra Tutoring Dialogue (Wooz Tutor) Project," Fourteenth Midwest Artificial Intelligence and Cognitive Science Conference (MAICS-2003), Cincinnati, 2003.
2. Heffernan, Neil T. 2001. *Intelligent Tutoring Systems are Forgotten the Tutor: Adding a Cognitive Model of Human Tutors*. Ph.D. diss,. Computer Science Department, School of Computer Science, Carnegie Mellon University. Technical Report CMU-CS-01-127.
3. McArthur, David, Cathleen Stasz, and Mary Zmuidzinas. 1990. "Tutoring Techniques in Algebra," *Cognition and Instruction*, vol. 7, pp. 197-244.
4. Fox, Barbara. 1993. *The Human Tutorial Dialogue Project*, Lawrence Erlbaum Associates.
5. Graesser, Arthur C., Natalie K. Person, and Joseph P. Magliano. 1995. "Collaborative Dialogue Patterns in Naturalistic One-to-One Tutoring," *Applied Cognitive Psychology*, vol. 9, pp. 495-522.
6. Person, Natalie and Arthur C. Graesser. 2003. "Fourteen Facts about Human Tutoring: Food for Thought for ITS Developers." In H.U. Hoppe, M.F. Verdejo, and J. Kay, *Artificial Intelligence in Education* (Eleventh International Conference, AIED-2003, Sidney, Australia), IOS Press.
7. Carr, Martha and Barry Biddlecomb 1998. "Metacognition in Mathematics from a Constructivist Perspective." In Hacker, Douglas, John Dunlosky, and Arthur C. Graesser, Metacognition in Educational Theory and Practice, Mahwah, NJ: Lawrence Erlbaum, pp. 69-91.
8. Kim, Jung Hee, Reva Freedman, Michael Glass, and Martha W. Evens. 2004. "Annotation of Tutorial Goals for Natural Language Generation," in preparation.
9. Freedman, Reva, Yujian Zhou, Michael Glass, Jung Hee Kim, and Martha W. Evens. 1998a. "Using Rule Induction to Assist in Rule Construction for a Natural-Language Based Intelligent Tutoring System," Twentieth Annual Conference of the Cognitive Science Society, Madison, pp. 362-367.
10. Freedman, Reva, Yujian Zhou, Jung Hee Kim, Michael Glass, and Martha W. Evens. 1998b. "SGML-Based Markup as a Step toward Improving Knowledge Acquisition for Text Generation," *AAAI 1998 Spring Symposium: Applying Machine Learning to Discourse Processing. Stanford*: AAAI Press, pp. 114117.
11. Person, Natalie K., Arthur C. Graesser, Roger J. Kreuz, Victoria Pomeroy, and the Tutoring Research Group. 2001. "Simulating Human Tutor Dialog Moves in AutoTutor," *International Journal of Artificial Intelligence in Education*, vol. 12, pp. 23-39.
12. Heffernan, Neil T. and Kenneth R. Koedinger, 2002. "An Intelligent Tutoring System Incorporating a Model of an Experienced Human Tutor," *Intelligent Tutoring Systems, Sixth International Conference, ITS-2002, Biarritz*, Springer Verlag.
13. Rosé, Carolyn P., Pamela Jordan, Michael Ringenberg, Stephanie Siler, Kurt VanLehn, and Anders Weinstein. 2001. "Interactive Conceptual Tutoring in Atlas-Andes." In J. Moore, C. L. Redfield, and W. L. Johnson, *Artificial Intelligence in Education* (Tenth International Conference, AIED-2001, San Antonio) IOS Press, pp. 256-266.
14. Mostow, Jack, Cathy Huang, and Brian Tobin. 2001. "Pause the Video: Quick but Quantitative Expert Evaluation of Tutorial Choices in a Reading Tutor that Listens." In J. Moore, C. L. Redfield, and W. L. Johnson, *Artificial Intelligence in Education* (Tenth International Conference, AIED-2001, San Antonio) IOS Press, pp. 243-253.

Spoken Versus Typed Human and Computer Dialogue Tutoring

Diane J. Litman[1], Carolyn P. Rosé[2], Kate Forbes-Riley[1], Kurt VanLehn[1], Dumisizwe Bhembe[1], and Scott Silliman[1]

[1] Learning Research and Development Center, University of Pittsburgh, 3939 O'Hara St., Pittsburgh, PA 15260
{litman,vanlehn}@cs.pitt.edu

[2] Language Technologies Institute/Human-Computer Interaction Institute, Carnegie Mellon University, Pittsburgh, PA 15260
{rosecp,forbesk,bhembe,scotts}@pitt.edu

Abstract. While human tutors typically interact with students using spoken dialogue, most computer dialogue tutors are text-based. We have conducted 2 experiments comparing *typed* and *spoken* tutoring dialogues, one in a human-human scenario, and another in a human-computer scenario. In both experiments, we compared spoken versus typed tutoring for learning gains and time on task, and also measured the correlations of learning gains with dialogue features. Our main results are that changing the modality from text to speech caused large differences in the learning gains, time and superficial dialogue characteristics of human tutoring, but for computer tutoring it made less difference.

1 Introduction

It is widely believed that the best human tutors are more effective than the best computer tutors, in part because [1] found that human tutors could produce a larger difference in the learning gains than current computer tutors (e.g., [2,3,4]). A major difference between human and computer tutors is that human tutors use face-to face spoken natural language dialogue, whereas computer tutors typically use menu-based interactions or typed natural language dialogue. This raises the question of whether making the interaction more natural, such as by changing the modality of the tutoring to spoken natural language dialogue, would decrease the advantage of human tutoring over computer tutoring.

Three main benefits of spoken tutorial dialogue with respect to increasing learning have been hypothesized. One is that spoken dialogue may elicit more student engagement and knowledge construction. [5] found that students who were prompted for self-explanations produced more when the self-explanations were spoken rather than typed. Self-explanation is just one form of student cognitive activity that is known to cause learning gains [6,7,8]. If it can be increased by using speech, perhaps other beneficial thinking can also be elicited as well.

A second hypothesis is that speech allows tutors to infer a more accurate student model, including long-term factors such as overall competence and motivation, and short-term factors such as whether the student really understood

J.C. Lester et al. (Eds.): ITS 2004, LNCS 3220, pp. 368–379, 2004.

the tutor's utterance. Having a more accurate understanding of the students should allow the tutor to adapt the instruction to the student so as to accelerate the student's learning. In other work we have shown that the prosodic and acoustic information of speech can improve the detection of speaker states such as confusion [9], which may be useful for adapting tutoring to the student.

A third hypothesis is that learning will be enhanced in computational environments that prime a more social interpretation of the teaching situation, as when an animated agent talks, and responds contingently (as in dialogue) to a learner. While [10] found that the use of a dialogue agent improved learning, there was no evidence that output media impacted learning. In [11], an interactive pedagogical agent using speech rather than text output improved student learning, while the visual presence or absence of the agent did not impact performance.

It is thus important to test whether a move to spoken dialogues is likely to cause higher learning gains, and if so, to understand why it accelerates learning. It is particularly important given that natural language tutoring systems are becoming more common. Although a few use spoken dialogues [12], most still use typed dialogues (e.g. [13,14,15]), although as shown by our work it is technically feasible to convert a tutor from typed dialogue tutor to spoken dialogue. While the details of this conversion are not covered in this paper, it took about 9 person-months of effort. Thus, many developers may be wondering whether they should aim for a spoken or a typed dialogue tutoring system.

It is also important to study the difference between spoken and typed dialogue in two contexts: human tutoring and computer tutoring. Given the current limitations of both speech and natural language processing technologies, computer tutors are far less flexible than human tutors, and also make more errors. The use of human tutors provides a benchmark for estimating the performance of an "ideal" computer system with respect to speech and natural language processing performance. We thus conducted two experiments. Both used qualitative physics as the task domain, similar pretests and posttests, and similar training sequences. However, one experiment used an experienced human tutor who communicated with students either via speech or typing. The other used the Why2-Atlas tutoring system [16] with either its original typed dialogue or a new spoken dialogue user interface. The new system is called ITSPOKE [9].

2 The Common Aspects of the Experiments

In both experiments, the students learned how to solve qualitative physics problems, which are physics problems that can be answered without doing any mathematics. A typical problem is, "If a massive truck and a lightweight car have a head-on collision, and both were going the same speed initially, which one suffers the greater impact force and the greater change in motion? Explain your answer." The answer to such a problem is a short essay.

The experimental procedure was as follows. Students who have not taken any college physics were first given a pretest measuring their knowledge of physics.

Next, students read a short textbook-like pamphlet, which described the major laws (eg., Newton's first law) and the major concepts. Students then worked through a set of up to 10 training problems with the tutor. Finally, students were given a posttest that was isomorphic to the pretest; both consisted of 40 multiple choice questions. The entire experiment took no more than 9 hours per student, and was usually performed in 1-3 sessions. Subjects were University students responding to ads, and were compensated with money or course credit.

The interface used for all experiments was basically the same. The student first typed an essay answering a qualitative physics problem. The tutor then engaged the student in a natural language dialogue to provide feedback, correct misconceptions, and to elicit more complete explanations. At key points in the dialogue, the tutor asked the student to revise the essay. This cycle of instruction and revision continued until the tutor was satisfied with the student's essay, at which point the tutor presented the ideal essay answer to the student.

For the studies described below, we compare characteristics of student dialogues with both typed and spoken computer tutors (Why2-Atlas and ITSPOKE, respectively), as well as with a single human tutor performing the same task as the computer tutor for each system. Why2-Atlas is a *text-based* intelligent tutoring dialogue system [16], developed in part to test whether deep approaches to natural language processing (e.g., sentence-level syntactic and semantic analysis, discourse and domain level processing, and finite-state dialogue management) elicit more learning than shallower approaches. ITSPOKE (Intelligent Tutoring SPOKEn dialogue system) [9] is a *speech-enabled* version of Why2-ATLAS. Student speech is digitized from microphone input and sent to the Sphinx2 recognizer. The most probable "transcription" output by Sphinx2 is sent to the Why2-Atlas natural language processing "back-end". Finally, the text response produced by Why2-Atlas is sent to the Cepstral text-to-speech system.

3 Human-Human Tutoring: Experiment 1

3.1 Experimental Procedure

Experiment 1 compared typed and spoken tutoring, using the same *human* tutor in both conditions. In the typed condition, the interaction was in the form of a *typed* dialogue between the student and tutor, where the human tutor performed the same task that Why2-Atlas was designed to perform. A text-based chat web interface was used, with student and tutor in separate rooms; students knew that the tutor was human. In the spoken condition, the interaction was in the form of a *spoken* dialogue, where the human tutor performed the same task that ITSPOKE was designed to perform. (While the dialogue was changed to speech, students still typed the essay.) The tutor and student spoke through head-mounted microphones, allowing all speech to be digitally recorded to the computer. The student and tutor were in the same room (due to constraints of speech recording), but separated by a partition. The same web interface was used as in the typed condition, except that no dialogue history was displayed (this would have required manual transcription of utterances). In the typed condition

Excerpt from 2 minutes into a *typed* dialogue:

Tutor: You have correctly said the balls are in free fall. What do you conclude from this fact?

Student: There is no air resistance and the balls' accelerations are constant in regards to one another

Tutor: Right, so the conclusion is that they both have the same acceleration, the free fall acceleration. Now you have to show that time taken by them to reach the ground will be the same. How do you do that?

Student: F (net forces) / mass = f/m because F = m*a therefore ratio should equal one another

Tutor: But that does not tell you anything about the time taken. What physical quantities will determine the time taken. Will the initial velocity of the balls matter?

Student: yes, assuming starting at rest? sorry, kind of at a loss at the moment

Excerpt from 8.3 minutes into a *spoken* dialogue:

Tutor: So the accel- the- both the balls will have same acceleration G is that right?

Student: Yeah.

Tutor: Ok. So now, can you uh argue about the time?

Student: Yeah. Uh the reason the two balls hit the ground at exactly the same instant is because the net forces acting on it, which is acceleration due to gravity, are equal.

Tutor: Force is gravity and acceleration is the same, ok, and what else?

Student: Um -(sniff)

Tutor: What other factors determine the time taken are the same?

Student: Uh, the height at which they're dropped -

Tutor: mm-hm

Student: Uh, the the acceleration due to gravity. Uh -

Fig. 1. Excerpts from Human-Human Dialogues

strict turn-taking was enforced, while in the spoken condition interruptions and overlapping speech were permitted. This was because we plan to add "bargein" to ITSPOKE, which will enable students to interrupt ITSPOKE. Sample dialogue excerpts from both conditions are displayed in Figure 1.

Pre and posttest items were scored as right or wrong, with no partial credit. Students who were not able to complete all 10 problems due to lack of time took the posttest after only working through a subset of the training problems.

Experiment 1 resulted in two human tutoring corpora. The *typed* dialogue corpus consists of 171 physics problems with 20 students, while the *spoken* dialogue corpus consists of 128 physics problems with 14 students. In subsequent analyses, a "dialogue" refers to the transcript of one student's discussion of one problem with the tutor.

3.2 Results

Table 1 presents the means and standard deviations for two types of analyses, learning and training time, across conditions. The pretest scores were not reliably different across the two conditions, $F(33) = 1.574$, $p = 0.219$, $MSe = 0.009$. In

Table 1. Learning and Time: Human Tutoring Spoken (14) and Typed (20) Conditions

Dependent Measure	Human Spoken	Human Typed
Pretest Mean (standard deviation)	.42 (.10)	.46 (.09)
Posttest Mean (standard deviation)	.72 (.11)	.67 (.13)
Adjusted Posttest Mean (standard deviation)	.74 (.11)	.66 (.11)
Dialogue Time (standard deviation)	166.58 (45.06)	430.05 (159.65)

an ANOVA with condition by test phase factorial design, there was a robust main effect for test phase, F(67) = 90.589, p = 0.000, MSe = 0.012, indicating that students in both conditions learned a significant amount during tutoring. However, the main effect for condition was not reliable, F(33) = 1.823, p = 0.186, MSe = 0.014, and there was no reliable interaction. In an ANCOVA, the adjusted posttest scores show a strong trend of being reliably different, F(1,33)=4.044, p=0.053, MSe = 0.01173. Our results thus suggest that the human speech tutored students learned more than the human text tutored students; the effect size is 0.74. With respect to training time, students in the spoken condition completed their dialogue tutoring in less than half the time than in the typed condition, where dialogue time was measured as the sum over the training problems of the number of minutes between the time that the student was shown the problem text and the time that the student was shown the ideal essay. The extra time needed for both the tutor and the student to type (rather than speak) each dialogue turn in the typed condition was a major contributor to this difference. An ANOVA shows that the difference in means across the two conditions was reliably different, with F(33) = 35.821, p = 0.00, MSe = 15958.787. For human tutoring, our results thus support our hypothesis that spoken tutoring is indeed more effective than typed tutoring, for both learning and training time.

It is important to understand why the change in modality (and interruption policy) increased learning. Table 2 presents the means for a variety of measures characterizing different aspects of dialogue, to determine which aspects differ across conditions, and to examine whether different dialogue characteristics correlate with learning across conditions (although the utility of correlation analysis might be limited by our small subject pool). For each dependent measure (explained below), the second through fourth columns present the means (across students) for the spoken and typed conditions, along with the statistical significance of their differences. The fifth through eighth columns present a Pearson's correlation between each dialogue measure and raw posttest score. However, in the spoken condition, the pre and posttest scores are highly correlated (R=.72, p =.008); in the typed condition they are not (R=.29, p=.21). Because of the spoken correlation, the last four columns show the correlation between posttest and the dependent measure, after the correlation with pretest is regressed out.

The measures in Table 2 were motivated by previous work suggesting that learning correlates with increased student language production. In pilot studies of the typed corpus, average student turn length was found to correlate with learning. We thus computed the average length of student turns in words (Ave.

Table 2. Dialogue Aspects & Learning: Human Spoken (14) & Typed (20) Conditions

Dependent Measure	Spoken mean	Typed mean	p	Zero Order Correlations				Controlled for Pre-Test Correlations			
				Spoken		Typed		Spoken		Typed	
				R	p	R	p	R	p	R	p
Tot. Stud. Words	2322.43	1569.30	.03	-.473	.09	.065	.78	-.261	.39	.013	.96
Tot. Stud. Turns	424.86	109.30	.00	-.340	.24	-.148	.53	-.016	.96	-.213	.38
Ave. Stud. Wds/Turn	5.21	14.45	.00	-.167	.57	.491	.03	-.209	.49	.515	.03
Slope: Stud. Wds/Trn	-.01	-.05	.04	-.275	.34	-.375	.10	.379	.20	-.291	.23
Int: Stud. Wds/Trn	6.51	16.39	.00	-.176	.55	.625	.00	-.441	.13	.593	.01
Tot. Tut. Words	8648.29	3366.30	.00	-.482	.08	.027	.91	-.164	.59	-.034	.89
Tot. Tut. Turns	393.21	122.90	.00	-.436	.12	-.171	.47	-.110	.72	-.239	.32
Ave. Tut. Wds/Turn	23.04	28.23	.01	-.139	.64	.496	.03	-.086	.78	.536	.02
S-T Tot. Wds Ratio	.27	.45	.00	.067	.82	.275	.24	-.202	.51	.268	.27
S-T Wd/Trn Ratio	.25	.51	.00	.026	.93	.283	.23	-.237	.44	.277	.25

Stud. Wds/Turn), as well as the total number of words and turns per student, summed across all training dialogues (Tot. Stud. Words, Tot. Stud. Turns). We also computed these figures for the tutor's contributions (Ave. Tut. Wds/Turn, Tot. Tut. Words, Tot. Tut. Turns). The slope and intercept measures will be explained below. Similarly, the studies of [17] examined student language production relative to tutor language production, and found that the percentage of words and utterances produced by the student positively correlated with learning. This led us to compute the number of students words divided by the number of tutor words (S-T Tot. Wds Ratio), and a similar ratio of student words per turn to tutor words per turn (S-T Wd/Trn Ratio).

Table 2 shows interesting differences between the spoken and typed corpora of human-human dialogues. For every measure examined, the means across conditions are significantly different, verifying that the style of interactions is indeed quite different. In spoken tutoring, both student and tutor take more turns on average than in typed tutoring, but these spoken turns are on average shorter. Moreover, in spoken tutoring both student and tutor on average use more words to communicate than in typed tutoring. However, in typed tutoring, the ratio of student to tutor language production is higher than in speech.

The remaining columns attempt to uncover which aspects of tutorial dialogue in each condition were responsible for its effectiveness. Although the zero order correlations are presented for completeness, our discussion will focus only on the last four columns, which we feel present the more valid analysis.

In the typed condition, as in its earlier pilot study, there is a positive correlation between average length of student turns in words and learning (R=.515, p = .03). We hypothesize that longer student answers to tutor questions reveal more of a student's reasoning, and that if the tutor is adapting his interaction to the student's revealed knowledge state, the effectiveness of the tutor's instruction might increase as average student turn length increases. Note that there is no correlation between total student words and learning; we hypothesize that how much a student explains (as estimated by turn length) is more important than how many questions a student answers (as estimated by total word production). There is also a positive correlation between average length of tutor turn and learning (R=.536, p=.02). Perhaps more tutor words per turn means that the tutor is explaining more or giving more useful feedback. A deeper coding of our data would be needed to test all of these hypotheses. Finally, as in the typed pilot study [18], student words per turn usually decreased gradually during the sessions. In speech, turn length decreased from an average of 6.0 words/turn for the first problem to 4.5 words/turn by the last problem. In text, turn length decreased from an average of 14.6 words for the first problem to 10.7 words by the last problem. This led us to fit regression lines to each subject and compare the intercepts and slopes to learning. These measures indicate roughly how verbose a student was initially and how quickly the student became taciturn. Table 2 indicates a reliable correlation between intercept and learning (R=.593; p=.01) for the typed condition, suggesting that inherently verbose students (or at least those who initially typed more) learned more in typed human dialogue tutoring.

Since there were no significant correlations in the the spoken condition, we have begun to examine other measures that might be more relevant in speech. For example, the mean number of total syntactic questions per student is 35.29, with a trend for a negative correlation with learning (R=-.500, p=.08). This result suggests, that as with our text-based correlations, our current surface level analyses will need to be enhanced with deeper codings before we can fully interpret our results (e.g., by manually coding non-interrogative form questions, and by distinguishing question types).

4 Human-Computer Tutoring: Experiment 2

4.1 Experimental Procedure

Experiment 2 compared typed and spoken tutoring using the Why2-Atlas and ITSPOKE *computer* tutors, respectively. The experimental procedure was the same as for Experiment 1, except that students worked through only 5 physics problems, and the pretest was taken after the background reading (allowing us to measure gains caused by the experimental manipulation, without confusing them with gains caused by background reading). Strict turn-taking was now enforced in both conditions as bargein had not yet been implemented in ITSPOKE.

While Why2-Atlas and ITSPOKE used the same web interface, during the dialogue, Why2-Atlas students typed while ITSPOKE students spoke through a head-mounted microphone. In addition, the Why2-Atlas dialogue history contained what the student actually typed, while the ITSPOKE history contained the potentially noisy output of ITSPOKE's speech recognizer. The speech recognizer's hypothesis for each student utterance, and the tutor utterances, were not displayed until after the student or ITSPOKE had finished speaking.

Figure 2 contains excerpts from both Why2-Atlas and ITSPOKE dialogues. Note that for ITSPOKE, the output of the automatic speech recognizer (the

Excerpt from 3.0 minutes into a *typed* dialogue:

Why2-Atlas: You have answered the problem correctly except that what you have in your essay is not a sufficient explanation. Before the release, what is the relationship between the man's velocity and the keys' velocity?

Student: They are the same

Why2-Atlas: Uh huh. If gravity is the only force acting on an object, will it be moving or staying still?

Student: Moving

Why2-Atlas: Good. Not only are the person, keys, and elevator moving, they have only gravitational forces acting on them. When an object is falling and has only gravitational force on it, it is said to be in what?

Student: Free fall

Excerpt from 11.1 minutes into *spoken* dialogue:

ITSPOKE: If you push on the same box with three times the force, what happens to the acceleration of the box?

Student: it increases (ASR: it increases)

ITSPOKE: Terrific. OK, what is the box's acceleration when you are pushing three times relative to its acceleration when you were only pushing with one-third the force?

Student: it decreases (ASR: it decreases since)

ITSPOKE: Could you please repeat that?

Student: it increases (ASR: it increases)

Fig. 2. Excerpts from Why2-Atlas and ITSPOKE Dialogues

ASR annotations) sometimes differed from what the student actually said. Thus, ITSPOKE dialogues contained rejection prompts (when ITSPOKE was not confident of what it thought the student said, it asked the student to repeat, as in the third ITSPOKE turn). On average, ITSPOKE produced 1.4 rejection prompts per dialogue. ITSPOKE also misrecognized utterances; when ITSPOKE heard something different than what the student said but was confident in its hypothesis, it proceeded as if it heard correctly. While the ITSPOKE word error rate was 31.2%, semantic analysis based on speech recognition versus perfect transcription differed only 7.6% of the time. Semantic accuracy is more relevant for dialogue evaluation, as it does not penalize for unimportant word errors.

Experiment 2 resulted in two computer tutoring corpora. The *typed* Why2-Atlas dialogue corpus consists of 115 problems (dialogues) with 23 students, while the ITSPOKE *spoken* corpus consists of 100 problems (dialogues) with 20 students.

4.2 Results

Table 3 presents the means and standard deviations for the learning and training time measures previously examined in Experiment 1. The pre-test scores were not reliably different across the two conditions, $F(42) = 0.037$, $p = 0.848$, $MSe = 0.036$. In an ANOVA with condition by test phase factorial design, there was a

Table 3. Learning and Time: Computer Tutoring Spoken (20) and Typed (23)

Dependent Measure	Computer Spoken	Computer Typed
Pretest Mean (standard deviation)	.48 (.17)	.49 (.20)
Posttest Mean (standard deviation)	.69 (.18)	.70 (.16)
Adjusted Posttest Mean (standard deviation)	.69 (.13)	.69 (.13)
Dialogue Time (standard deviation)	97.85 (32.8)	68.93 (29.0)

robust main effect for test phase, F(85) = 29.57, p = 0.000, MSe = 0.032, indicating that students learned during their tutoring. The main effect for condition was not reliable, F(42)=0.029, p=0.866, MSe=0.029, and there was no reliable interaction. In an ANCOVA of the multiple-choice test data, the adjusted post-test scores were not reliably different, F(1,42)=0.004, p=0.950, MSe=0.01806. Thus, the Why-Atlas tutored students did not learn reliably more than the ITSPOKE tutored students. With respect to training time, students in the spoken condition took more time to complete their dialogue tutoring than in the typed condition. In the spoken condition, extra utterances were needed to recover from speech recognition errors; also, listening to tutor prompts often took more time than reading them, and students sometimes needed to both listen to, then read, the prompts. An ANOVA shows that this difference was reliable, with F(42)=9.411, p=0.004, MSe=950.792. In sum, while adding speech to Why2-Atlas did not yield the hoped for improvements in learning, the degradation in tutor understanding due to speech recognition (and potentially in student understanding due to text-to-speech) also did not decrease student learning. A separate analysis showed no correlation between word error or semantic degradation (discussed in Section 4.1) with learning or training time.

Table 4. Dialogue & Learning: Computer Spoken (20) & Typed (23) Conditions

Dependent Measure	Spoken mean	Typed mean	p	Zero Order Correlations				Controlled for Pre-Test Correlations			
				Spoken		Typed		Spoken		Typed	
				R	p	R	p	R	p	R	p
Tot. Student Words	296.85	238.17	.12	.043	.86	-.354	.10	.394	.10	.050	.82
Tot. Student Turns	116.75	87.96	.02	-.093	.70	-.549	.01	.210	.39	-.168	.46
Ave. Student Words/Turn	2.42	2.77	.29	.061	.80	.167	.45	.119	.63	.202	.37
Slope: Student Wds/Trn	-.02	.00	.02	-.179	.45	-.084	.70	-.287	.23	-.102	.65
Intercept: Stud. Wds/Trn	3.21	2.88	.40	.246	.30	.250	.25	.321	.18	.281	.21
Tot. Tutor Words	6314.90	4972.61	.03	-.100	.68	-.576	.00	.283	.24	-.159	.48
Tot. Tutor Turns	148.20	110.22	.01	-.061	.80	-.529	.01	.252	.30	-.133	.56
Ave. Tutor Words/Turn	42.11	44.33	.06	-.261	.27	-.565	.01	-062	.80	-.164	.47
Stud-Tut Tot. Word Ratio	.05	.05	.57	.219	.35	.238	.27	.281	.25	.201	.37
Stud-Tut Wds/Trn Ratio	.06	.06	.64	.089	.71	.278	.20	.094	.70	.212	.35
Tot. Subdial/KCD	3.29	1.98	.01	-.304	.19	-.732	.00	-.018	.94	-.457	.03

Table 4 presents the means for the measures used in Experiment 1 to characterize dialogue, as well as for a new "Tot. Subdialogues per KCD" measure for our computer tutors. A Knowledge Construction Dialogue (KCD) is a line of questioning targeting a specific concept (such as Newton's Third Law). When students answer questions incorrectly, the KCDs correct them through a "subdialogue", which may involve more interactive questioning or simply a remedial statement. Thus, subdialogues per KCD is the number of student responses treated as wrong. We hypothesized that this measure would be higher in speech, due the previously noted degradation in semantic accuracy.

Compared to Experiment 1, Table 4 shows that there are less differences between spoken and typed *computer* tutoring dialogues. The total words produced by students, the average length of turns and initial verbosity, and the ratios of student to tutor language production are no longer reliably different across conditions. As hypothesized, Tot. Subdialogues per KCD is reliably different (p=.01). Finally, the last four columns show a significant negative correlation between Tot. Subdialogues per KCD and posttest score (after regressing out pretest) in the typed condition. There is also a trend for a positive correlation with total student words in the spoken condition, consistent with previous results on learning and increased student language production.

5 Discussion and Current Directions

The main results of our study are that changing the modality from text to speech caused large differences in the learning gains, time and superficial dialogue characteristics of human tutoring, but for computer tutoring it made less difference. Experiment 1 on human tutoring suggests that spoken dialogue (allowing interruptions) is more effective than typed dialogue (prohibiting interruptions), with mean adjusted posttest score increasing and training time decreasing. We also find that typed and spoken dialogues are very different for the surface measures examined, and for the typed condition we see a benefit for longer turns (evidenced by correlations between learning and average and initial student turn length and average tutor turn length). While we do not see these results in speech, spoken utterances are typically shorter than written sentences (and in our experiment, turn length was also impacted by interruption policy), suggesting that other measures might be more relevant. However, we plan to investigate whether spoken phenomena such as disfluencies and grounding might also explain the lack of correlation.

The results of Experiment 2 on computer tutoring are less conclusive. On the negative side, we do not see any evidence that replacing typed dialogue in Why2-Atlas with spoken dialogue in ITSPOKE improves student learning. However, on the positive side, we also do not see any evidence that the degradation in understanding caused by speech recognition decreases learning. Furthermore, compared to human tutoring, we see less difference between spoken and typed computer dialogue interactions, at least for the dialogue aspects measured in our experiments. One hypothesis is that simply adding a spoken "front-end", without also modifying the tutorial dialogue system "back-end", is not enough to change how students interact with a computer tutor. Another hypothesis is that the limitations of the particular natural language technologies used in Why2-Atlas (or the expectations that the students had regarding such limitations) are inhibiting the modality differences. Finally, if there were differences between conditions, perhaps the shallow measures used in our experiments and/or our small number of subjects prevented us from discovering them. In sum, while the results of human tutoring suggest that spoken tutoring is a promising approach for enhancing learning, more exploration is required to determine how to productively incorporate speech into computer tutoring systems.

By design, the modality change left the content of the computer dialogues completely unchanged – the tutors said nearly the same words and asked nearly the same questions, and the students gave their usual short responses. On the other hand, the content of the human tutoring dialogues probably changed considerably when the modality changed. This suggests that modality change makes a difference in learning only if it also facilitates content change. We will investigate this hypothesis in future work by coding for content and other deep features.

Finally, we had hypothesized that the spoken modality would encourage students to become more engaged and to self-construct more knowledge. Although a deeper coding of the dialogues would be necessary to test this hypothesis, we can get a preliminary sense of its veracity by examining the total number of words uttered. Student verbosity (and perhaps engagement and self-construction) did not increase significantly in the spoken computer tutoring experiment. In the human tutoring experiment, the number of student words did significantly increase, which is consistent with the hypothesis and may explain why spoken human tutoring was probably more effective than typed human tutoring. However, the number of tutor words also significantly increased, which suggests that the human tutor may have "lectured" more in the spoken modality. Perhaps these longer explanations contributed to the benefits of speaking compared to the text, but it is equally conceivable that they reduced the amount of engagement and knowledge construction, and thus limited the gains. This suggests that although we considered how the modality might effect the student, we neglected to consider how it might effect the tutor, and how that might impact the students' learning. Clearly, these issues deserve more research. Our goal is to use such investigations to guide the development of future versions of Why2-Atlas and ITSPOKE, by modifying the dialogue behaviors in each system to best enhance the possibilities for increasing learning.

Acknowledgments. This research is supported by ONR (N00014-00-1-0600, N00014-04-1-0108).

References

1. Blom, B.S.: The 2 Sigma problem: The search for methods of group instruction as affective as one-to-one tutoring. Educational Researcher **13** (1984) 4–16

2. Anderson, J.R., Corbett, A.T., Koedinger, K.R., Pelletier, R.: Cognitive tutors: Lessons learned. The Journal of the Learning Sciences **4** (1995) 167–207
3. VanLehn, K., Lynch, C., Taylor, L., Weinstein, A., Shelby, R.H., Schulze, K., Treacy, D.J., Wintersgill, M.C.: Minimally invasive tutoring of complex physics problem solving. In: Proc. Intelligent Tutoring Systems (ITS), 6th International Conference. (2002) 367–376
4. Graesser, A.C., Wiemer-Hastings, K., Wiemer-Hastings, P., Kreuz, R.: Autotutor: A simulation of a human tutor. Journal of Cognitive Systems Research **1** (1999)
5. Hausmann, R., Chi, M.: Can a computer interface support self-explaining? The International Journal of Cognitive Technology **7** (2002)
6. Chi, M., Leeuw, N.D., Chiu, M., Lavancher, C.: Eliciting self-explanations improves understanding. Cognitive Science **18** (1994) 439–477
7. Renkl, A.: Learning from worked-out examples: A study on individual differences. Cognitive Science **21** (1997) 1–29
8. Chi, M.T.H., Siller, S.A., Jeong, H., Yamauchi, T., Hausmann, R.G.: Learning from human tutoring. Cognitive Science (2001) 471–477
9. Litman, D.J., Forbes-Riley, K.: Predicting student emotions in computer-human tutoring dialogues. In: Proc. Association Computational Linguistics (ACL). (2004)
10. Graesser, A.C., Moreno, K.N., Marineau, J.C., Adcock, A.B., Olney, A.M., Person, N.K.: Autotutor improves deep learning of computer literacy: Is it the dialog or the talking head? In: Proc. AI in Education. (2003)
11. Moreno, R., Mayer, R.E., Spires, H.A., Lester, J.C.: The case for social agency in computer-based teaching: Do students learn more deeply when they interact with animated pedagogical agents. Cognition and Instruction **19** (2001) 177–213
12. Schultz, K., Bratt, E.O., Clark, B., Peters, S., Pon-Barry, H., Treeratpituk, P.: A scalable, reusable spoken conversational tutor: Scot. In: AIED Supplementary Proceedings. (2003) 367–377
13. Michael, J., Rovick, A., Glass, M.S., Zhou, Y., Evens, M.: Learning from a computer tutor with natural language capabilities. Interactive Learning Environments (2003) 233–262
14. Zinn, C., Moore, J.D., Core, M.G.: A 3-tier planning architecture for managing tutorial dialogue. In: Proceedings Intelligent Tutoring Systems, Sixth International Conference (ITS 2002), Biarritz, France (2002) 574–584
15. Aleven, V., Popescu, O., Koedinger, K.R.: Pilot-testing a tutorial dialoque system that supports self-explanation. In: Proc. Intelligent Tutoring Systems (ITS): 6th International Conference. (2002) 344–354
16. VanLehn, K., Jordan, P., Rosé, C., Bhembe, D., Böttner, M., Gaydos, A., Makatchev, M., Pappuswamy, U., Ringenberg, M., Roque, A., Siler, S., Srivastava, R., Wilson, R.: The architecture of Why2-Atlas: A coach for qualitative physics essay writing. In: Proc. Intelligent Tutoring Systems (ITS), 6th International Conference. (2002)
17. Core, M.G., Moore, J.D., Zinn, C.: The role of initiative in tutorial dialogue. In: Proc. 11th Conf. of European Chapter of the Association for Computational Linguistics (EACL). (2003) 67–74
18. Rose, C.P., Bhembe, D., Siler, S., Srivastava, R., VanLehn, K.: The role of why questions in effective human tutoring. In: Proc. AI in Education. (2003)

Linguistic Markers to Improve the Assessment of Students in Mathematics: An Exploratory Study

Sylvie Normand-Assadi[1], Lalina Coulange[1,2], Élisabeth Delozanne[3], and Brigitte Grugeon[1,4]

[1]IUFM de Créteil, Rue Jean Macé, 94861 BONNEUIL Cedex, France
{sylvie.normand,lalina.coulange,elisabeth.delozanne}@creteil.iufm.fr
[2]DIDIREM - Paris VII, 2, Place Jussieu, 75 251 PARIS Cedex 05, France
[3]CRIP5 - Paris V, 45-46 rue des Saints-Pères, 75 006 PARIS, France
[4]IUFM d'Amiens 49, boulevard de Châteaudun 80044 AMIENS CEDEX, France
brigitte.grugeon@amiens.iufm.fr

Abstract. We describe an exploratory empirical study to investigate whether some linguistic markers can improve the assessment of students when they answer questions in their own words. This work is part of a multidisciplinary project, the Pépite project, that aims to give math teachers software support to assess their students in elementary algebra. We first set this study within the context of the project and we compare it with related work. Then we present our methodology, the data analysis and how we have linked linguistic markers to discursive modes and then these discursive modes to levels of development in algebra thinking. The conclusion opens onto promising perspectives.

1 Introduction

In this paper we present an exploratory empirical study to improve the diagnosis of students' answers in the Pépite system when answers are articulated in students' language[1]. In previous papers [6, 9] we presented the Pépite project that aims to provide math teachers with software support to assess their students in elementary algebra. We basically assume that students' answers to a set of well-chosen problems show not only errors but also coherences in students' algebra thinking. Like in [12], we are not only interested in detecting errors but also in detecting students' conceptions that produce these errors. We have adopted an iterative design methodology. Our study is the beginning of the second iteration.

At the first design stage, it was important for the educational researchers in our team to have the students answer in their own words even if the software was not able to analyze and understand them completely. So far Pépite software analyses MCQ and answers to open questions when they are expressed using algebraic expressions [6,9].

[1] This research was partially funded by the "Programme Cognitique, école et sciences cognitives, 2002-2004" from the French Ministry of Research and by the IUFM of Créteil. Numerous colleagues from the IUFM of Créteil and teachers are acknowledged for testing Pépite in their classes.

J.C. Lester et al. (Eds.): ITS 2004, LNCS 3220, pp. 380–389, 2004.

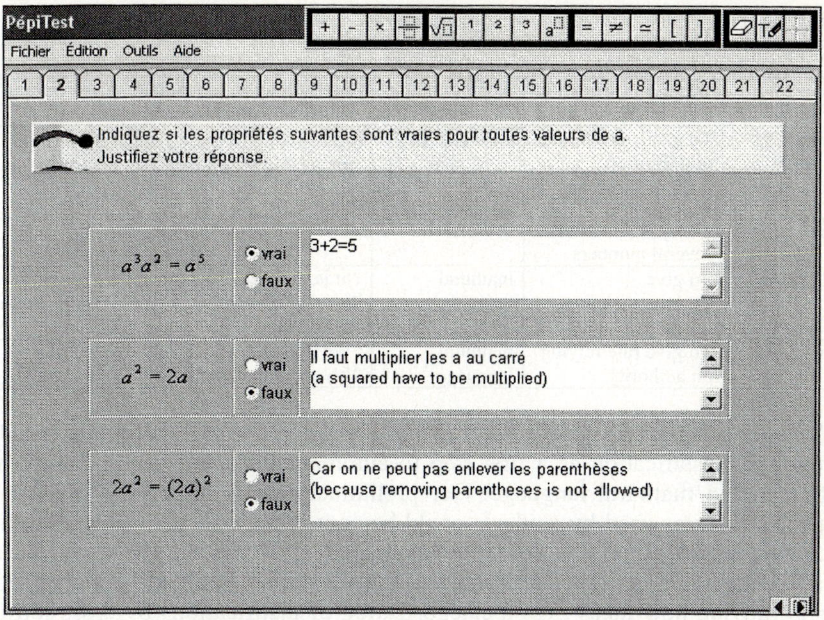

Fig. 1. Juliette's answers to exercise 2 in Pépite

Therefore, in order to have a full diagnosis, the system needs the teacher's assessment for answers expressed in "mathural" language such as in Figure 1. By "mathural", we mean a language created by students that combines mathematical language and natural language. The formulations produced by students in this language are often incorrect or not completely correct from a mathematical point of view. But we assume that they demonstrate an early level of comprehension of mathematical notions.

Table 1 shows the example of what the educational researchers in our team diagnosed in students' justifications [3, 8]. The diagnosis is based on a classification of justifications like in other research work [1, 10, 13]. Pépite implements this analysis and first diagnoses whether the justification is algebraic, numerical or expressed in mathural language. Then it assesses whether numerical or algebraic answers are correct. For "mathural" answers it only detects automatically that students rely on "school authority" by using markers like "il faut" (it is necessary), "on doit" (you have to), "on ne peut pas" (it is not allowed). In other words, for these students mathematics consist in respecting formal rules without having to understand them.

Workshop and classrooms experiments with teachers showed that, except in very special occasions, they need a fully automated diagnosis to get a quick and accurate overview of the student's competencies [6]. Thus, one of our research targets is to enhance the diagnosis software by analyzing answers expressed in "mathural" language in a more efficient way. We also noticed that our first classification (Cf. Table 1) was too specific to a high school level and that teachers were more tolerant than Pépite toward mathural justifications. For instance for the following answer "the product of two identical numbers with different exponents is this same number but with both exponents added, thus a to the power 2+3", Pépite does not consider it as an algebraic proof when human assessors do.

Table 1. Current Pepite's analysis of some students' justifications when stating that "$a^2 * a^3 = a^5$" is true for every a.

Proof by …	Type of justification	Representation mode	Examples of students' justifications
algebra	To give correct rule or definition	algebraic	$a^3\ a^2 = a \times a \times a \times a \times a = a^5$ $a^2\ a^3 = a^{2+3}$ $a^n\ a^p = a^{n \times p}$
numerical example	To try with one or several numbers	numerical	$2^3 \times 2^2 = 32$
explanation	To give explanations	mathural language	"it is true because both exponents are added" "in multiplications with powers, exponents are added
school authority	To give rule relying on authority	mathural language	"We must never multiply exponents" "It's a fundamental law"

We assumed that a linguistic study of our corpus might give important insights to improve the classification as a first step to automatically analyze the quality of the justifications in mathural language. Our preliminary study aimed to point out how linguistic structures used by students could be connected with their algebra thinking. Hence we adopted a dual point of view: linguistic and didactical. The study was made up of five steps: (1) an empirical analysis from a purely linguistic point of view in order to provide new ideas ; (2) a categorization of justifications by cross fertilizing the first and second authors' linguistic and didactical points of view; (3) a review of this categorization in a workshop with teachers, educational researchers, psychological ergonomists, Pépite designers and a linguist (the first author); (4) a final categorization refined by the four authors and presented here; (5) a validation of the categorization set up by the Pépite team. In the following sections we present our methodology, the final categorization and the data analysis. The paper ends with a discussion of the results and with perspectives: first to confirm these early results with other data and then to use these results to build systems that understand some open answers uttered in "mathural" language in a more efficient way.

2 Methodology

This study is based on an empirical analysis of linguistic productions given by 168 students (aged 15 – 16) from French secondary schools while solving algebraic tasks using 'PépiTest'. We focused on a specific task (exercise 2, Figure 1) where students were asked to say if some algebraic properties are true or false and to justify their statements in their own words. The exercise is made up of three *questions* and for each question the student's *answer* is composed of a *choice* (between true or false) and a *justification* (the arguments students give to justify their choice between true or false). These justifications are various: no justification, only algebraic or numerical expressions, "mathural language" statements. In the following sections we focus only on students who gave at least one justification expressed in "mathural language" (52 students).

The statements written by students were studied as speech acts [16] performed by students in the context of the task. We aimed to connect what students said (locutionary act), what they meant (illocutionary act) and what they performed (perlocutionary act) [4]. Speech acts performed by students were conditioned by context (here to justify their choices). At a pragmatic level, we assessed the illocutionary strength of students' statements in relation with the objective of the utterances: the task they were asked to perform ("validate or invalidate an algebraic equality and justify this choice"). Our approach is situated within the Integrated Pragmatic Framework [5]. We pointed out different formal linguistic markers expressed by students. We interpreted these markers as providing a specific orientation to the statement. In our opinion this orientation characterizes a discourse mode. Discourse produced in an assessment context is a very specific written dialog between one student and an unknown reader who will judge him/her. The contract for the writer is very different from a conversational dialog as studied in [11] or from Socratic Dialog as studied in ITS community [1, 2, 7, 10]. But as in some of these studies [12, 13] we are looking for a classification of the quality of students' justifications and criteria to classify these justifications.

Table 2. Classifications of the students' justifications

Correctness	Discursive mode	Level of development in algebra thinking
CC	*Argumentative:* Students use connections between their arguments to articulate their justifications (consequence, restriction, opposition)	*Conceptual:* Students handle concepts
CC or CP	*Descriptive:* Students describe some elements from the context set by the given equality	*Contextual:* Students select some elements that make sense in the context
CP, II	*Explanatory:* Students require causality often with wrong arguments.	*Formal or school authority:* Students apply or mention formal rules or malrules
CP, II	*Legal:* Students base their justifications on legal or authoritative arguments.	

We first distinguished two groups of students' answers according to the correctness of their choices: Group 1: Students who gave right choices « true/false » to the three questions (24 students), Group 2: Students who gave, at least, one wrong choice to one of the three questions (28 students). Then, for each question we codified: correct choice / correct justification (CC), correct choice / partial justification (CP), correct choice / incorrect justification (CI) ; incorrect choice / incorrect justification (II). Secondly, for each question, we started by highlighting the features of the equality from a mathematical point of view. Then, for each category of coded answers, we pointed out specific linguistic forms used by students and we proposed a typology of justifications from a discursive point of view. So we obtained a quantitative analysis of the corpus that linked students' performance level on the task (correctness) to four discursive modes: argumentative, descriptive, explanatory and legal. Thirdly, from a didactic point of view, we *a priori* hypothesized that these different discursive modes were closely linked with different levels of development in the students' algebra thinking that we qualify as: conceptual, contextual and formal (or school authority). Table 2 summarizes the categorization and the next section describes its application to the corpus we studied.

3 Data Analysis

In this section, we present how we characterized each question from a mathematical point of view and how we classified students answer according to (i) performance on the task, (ii) discursive mode, (iii) level of development in algebra thinking.

3.1 Question 1: $a^3 a^2 = a^5$

From a mathematical point of view, this equality has three main features. First, this equality is true. Second, it is very similar to an algebraic rule ($a^m a^n = a^{m+n}$) that is found in every textbook and teacher' courses as part of the curriculum. Third, the both members of the equality can be developed ($a^3 a^2$ = (a×a×a) × a×a et a^5= a×a×a×a×a). For this questions we determined five categories..

CC (Correct choice/correct justification), argumentative mode (consequence, restriction), conceptual level :3 students from Group 1
Students use coordinating conjunctions such as: « donc » (thus) , « mais » (but) to establish relationship such as *consequence* or *restriction*. Thus, we assumed that their discourse was *argumentative* and that through their arguments their algebra thinking was situated on a *conceptual level*. For instance:
« Le produit de deux nombres identiques à exposants différents est ce même nombre mais avec leurs exposants ajoutés tous deux, donc a puissance 2+3 » (the product of two identical numbers with different exponents is this same number but with both exponents added, thus a to the power 2+3).

CC (Correct choice/correct justification) descriptive mode, contextual level: 5 students , 1 from Group 1, 4 from Group 2
Students use a complex sentence, including a main clause and a situating subordinate clause: these clauses are juxtaposed or embedded. The main clause defines the action (« on ajoute, on additionne »: one adds, one adds up). The second clause indicates the *context* which is defined by students and which is necessary for the action (« lors d'une multiplication », « dans une multiplication »: when multiplying, in a multiplication). Their discourses are *descriptive* and their arguments reflect a *contextual* level. Specific linguistic forms are used such as: « lorsque » (when), « quand » (when), « dans » (in). For instance:
« quand on multiplie des mêmes nombres avec des puissances, on adition les puissances et le nombre reste inchangé » (when you multiply numbers with powers, you add the power and the number remains unchanged)

CP (Correct choice/partial justification), descriptive mode and contextual level: 15 students, 12 from Group 1, 3 from Group 2
Students use a complex sentence similar to the previous one. Nevertheless, the justification is coded as partial because students do not mention every condition required for the application of the general mathematical rule. In fact, students often forget the following condition: variable a, which is exponentiated, has to be the same. Students focus on the components of the equality that change from the first member

to the second member: exponents 3, 2 and 5. They overlook a, the stable component. So we classified these justifications as situated on the *contextual* level. Specific linguistic forms are used such as: « lorsque » (when), « quand » (when) « dans » (in). For instance: (i) « Dans les multiplication à puissances, on additionne les exposants » (in multiplications with powers, exponents are added), (ii) « quand on multiplie des nombres avec des puissances il faut additionner les puissances » (When numbers with powers are multiplied, it is necessary to add up the powers).

CP (Correct choice/partial justification), explanatory and legal mode, school authority level: 6 students from Group 2
Like in the previous type of answer, students focus only on changing features from left member to right member of the equality. But instead of setting a context, students require *causality*, beginning an explanation with connectors such as « car » (it's true because, as). Some of them use *modal verbs* expressing feasibility, possibility or obligation such as « il faut » (it is necessary, you have to). Through the usage of such linguistic forms, we qualify these discourses as *explanatory*. Moreover, as they formulate only partially the rule without mentioning its context of validity we assume that students in that case give a *legal dimension* to their explanations. In other words, they feel this equality respects « formal laws » in algebraic calculus. Thus we classified their algebra thinking in a "*school authority*" category. For example:
(i) « car il faut additionner les puissants » (because it is necessary to add the powers), (ii) « c'est vrai car on additionne les 2exposent » (it is true because both exponents are added).

II (Incorrect choice/Incorrect justification), legal mode, school authority level: 4 students from Group 2
Student use *modal verbs*, such as « falloir » (« il faut», it is necessary) or « devoir » (to have to) to justify their wrong choice. In our opinion by using such verbs they situate their discourse in a *legal dimension*. Here the formal law is implicit or sometimes explicit malrule (such as $a^m a^n = a^{mn}$). For example: (i) « on doit faire une soustraction entre les deux chiffres du haut » (a subtraction between the two upper digits has to be made), (ii) « il ne faut pas additionné les puissances mais les multiplier » (we are not allowed to add up the powers but we have to multiply them).

3.2 Question 2: $a^2 = 2a$

The given equality ($a^2 = 2a$) is false. Furthermore, as it is not similar to any classical rule given in algebra courses, students cannot evoke such a rule.[2] Each algebraic expression of this equality can be developed - in (a×a) and (a + a) or (2×a)-. We defined three categories of students' answers.

---

[2] In that, it is different of other false equalities: as $a^3 a^2 = a^6$ which is similar to the form of the rule $a^m a^n = a^{m+n}$.

CC, argumentative mode (opposition), conceptual level: 11 students, 9 from Group 1, 2 from Group 2
Students use a complex sentence, including a main clause and a subordinate clause: linked by a *conjunctive locution* marking an *opposition* between the two members of the equality: « tandis que » or « alors que » (while/whereas), « et non pas » (and not). Their discourse is *argumentative,* and reflects a *conceptual level*. For example: (i) « a^2 signifie a×a alors que 2a signifie a×2 » (a squared means a×a while 2a means a×2), (ii) « L'expression a^2 équivaut à a×a, et non pas à 2×a » (the expression a^2 is equivalent to a×a, and not 2×a) .

CC, argumentative mode (coordination), conceptual level: 9 students, 5 from Group 1, 4 from Group 2
As previously, students use a complex sentence but main and subordinate clauses are linked by a *coordinating conjunction*: « et » (and). The link between the two clauses is established, but not specified, contrary to the previous case where students expressed an opposition. For such justifications the conjunction « et » (and) is used. For example: (i) « car le premier ça fait a fois a et le deuxième ça fait 2 fois a » (because the first results in a times a and the second results in 2 times a), (ii) « a^2 = a×a et 2a = 2×a » (a^2 = a×a and 2a = 2×a).

CP, descriptive mode, contextual level: 5 students, 3 from Group 1, 2 from Group 2
In this category, the connection with the second member has become implicit: only one member of the equality is considered. Students describe some algebraic expressions equivalent to this member and introduced their justification by « c'est » « ça fait » (it is, that results in). Their discourse is *descriptive* and the level *contextual.* For example: (i) « ça fait a×a. » (it results in a×a), (ii) « c'est « a+a » qui est égal à 2a. » (it is « a+a » who is equal to 2a).

II, explanatory mode, school authority level: 6 students from Group 2
Students require causality, beginning their justification with connectives such as « car » (because, as) or « c'est vrai car » (it's true because). Their discourse is explanatory using wrong arguments. For example: (i) « car le a au carré vaut bien deux fois a» (because the value of a squared is actually twice a), (ii) « c'est vrai car la lettre a qui est élevé au carré donne 2a (a×a = 2a). » (it is true because the squared letter a results in 2a (a×a = 2a).

3.3 Question 3: $2a^2 = (2a)^2$

The given equality ($2a^2 = (2a)^2$) is false. Like the previous equality, it is not similar to any classical rules given in algebra courses. Each member can be developed ($2a^2$ = 2×a×a, $(2a)^2$ = 2×a×2×a). The right part of the equality contains parentheses: mathematics teachers often underline the role of parentheses in numerical and algebraic calculus. For this question we have obtained five categories.

CC, argumentative mode(opposition), conceptual level: 14 students, 12 from Group 1, 2 from Group 2
As for previously, students use complex sentence including a main clause and a subordinate clause. These clauses are linked by a *conjunctive locution* which marks the *opposition* between the two members of the equality (focusing on the role of parentheses): « tandis que » or « alors que » (while/whereas), « et non pas » (and not). Their discourse is argumentative and their argument conceptual. For example: (i) « Dans la première partie de l'équation, seul a est au carré alors que dans la deuxième, le produit de 2a est au carré » (In the first part of the equation, only a is squared while in the second part, the product of 2a is squared), (ii) « $2a^2 = 2 \times a^2$ et non pas $(2a)^2$ car ce serait égal à $4a^2$. » (« $2a^2 = 2 \times a^2$ and not $(2a)^2$ because it would be equal to $4a^2$).

CC, argumentative mode (coordination), conceptual level: 5 students, 3 from Group 1, 2 from Group 2
Students use a complex sentence, similar to the previous one but the main and subordinate clauses are linked by a *coordinating conjunction*: « et » (and). Some juxtapose two main clauses, considering each member separately. Students do not mark explicit opposition or explicit links between the clauses. For example: (i) « car $2a^2$, c'est a qui est au carré. Et $(2a)^2$, c'est 2a qui est au carré. » (because $2a^2$, it is a that is squared. And $(2a)^2$, it is 2a that is squared), (ii) «$2a^2 = 2 \times a^2$: il n'y a que le a qui est au carré. $(2a)^2 = 4a^2$: le tout est au carré. » ($2a^2 = 2 \times a^2$: only a is squared. $(2a)^2 = 4a^2$: the whole is squared)

CP, descriptive mode (restriction), contextual level: 4 students, 2 from Group 1, 2 from Group 2
The connection with the second member is implicit. Only one member (the right one) of the equality is considered by students. They focus on the right member, introducing their description by « c'est » (that is), thus underlining the restrictive function of the square which concerns only variable a (because of the absence of parentheses) by « juste », « seulement » (only). Their discourse is descriptive and the level contextual. For example: (i) « c'est juste le a qui est au carré. » (only a is squared), (ii) « comme il n'y a pas de parenthèses, c'est seulement la valeur « a » que l'on multiplie par elle-même.» (as there is no parentheses, only value a is to be multiplied by itself).

II, legal mode, school authority level: 2 students from Group 2
Students frequently use modal verbs such as « pouvoir » (can) or « avoir le droit » (be allowed to) to justify their wrong choice, focusing on the importance of parentheses. By using such verbs, they situate their discourse on a legal dimension. For instance: (i) « on a le droit de mettre des parenthèses à un chiffre » (we are allowed to put parentheses to a digit), (ii) « on peut mettre une parenthese, cela ne change rien sauf lors d'un calcul, quand il y a des prioritées. » (we can put a parenthesis, it does not change anything except when you have priorities in a calculation).

II, explanatory mode, school authority level: 2 students from Group 2
Students use causality beginning their justification with *connectives* such as « car » (because, as). Their discourse is an explanation using wrong arguments.. For instance:

(i) « car on multiplie de gauche à droite » (because we multiply from left to right), (ii) « car les deux résultats sont égaux. » (because both results are equal).

4 Results and Perspectives

This study is exploratory but offers some significant results and promising perspectives. We a priori hypothesized links between the discursive modes and the level of development in students' algebra thinking. This empirical study allowed us to define a classification of the students' answers based on these links. Applying it systematically to our data did not invalidate our a priori hypothesis. So this study takes an important step in our project to improve the automatic assessment of students' "mathural" answers.

Our first perspective is to validate this hypothesized correlation in the two following ways. First it remains to be confirmed by systematically triangulating performance (correctness), level in algebra thinking (classification with linguistic markers) and students' profile (built by PepiTest with the whole test), this for every single student in the corpus we studied here. We began to testing our categorization, on some students. We compared their level of development in algebra thinking (as described in this paper by classifying their answer to this specific exercise) with their cognitive profile established by Pépite (by analyzing their answers along the whole test). We noticed that, even in group 1 (correct choices for the three questions), the distinction between school authority/contextual/conceptual levels we derived from linguistic markers is relevant from a cognitive point of view. As suggested by Grugeon [8], students situated in school authority level have difficulties in other exercises to interpret algebraic expressions and often invoke malrules when they make algebraic calculations. Moreover, students adopting argumentative discourse at a conceptual level obtain good results to the whole test. Concerning the contextual category, the interpretation of data seems to be more complex. In particular we hypothesize that the mathematical features of the equality may influence the discourse mode and we will have to investigate that. Second, we will test our typology on other corpora to assess its robustness. We have built a new set of questions based on the same task (to validate or invalidate the equality of two algebraic expressions) but modulating the variables pointed out in this study (true or false equality, features of the expression. We expect to shade light on the nature of partial justifications and contextual level.

Our second perspective is to study how using those linguistic patterns can improve the diagnosis system of Pépite. The current diagnosis system assesses students' choices. Then it distinguishes whether the justification is numerical, algebraic or "mathural". It can both analyze most algebraic or numerical expressions and detect some modal auxiliaries to diagnose a "school authority" level. But so far it has been unable to assess the correctness of justifications in "mathural" language. Once our categorization is validated we will be able to implement a system that links linguistic markers and a level in algebra thinking. The correctness of justification cannot be always automatically derived but (i) an argumentative level is likely to be linked to a correct justification, (ii) a contextual level to a correct or partial (iii) a legal level to a partial or incorrect. Moreover, we will investigate whether the level assigned by this study can be useful to implement an adaptive testing system.

References

1. V. Aleven, K. Koedinger, O. Popescu, A Tutorial Dialog System to Support Self-explanation: Evaluation and Open Questions, Artificial Intelligence in Education (2003) 39-46.
2. V. Aleven, O. Popescu, A. Ogan, K. Koedinger, A Formative Classroom Evaluation of a Tutorial Dialog System that Supports Self-explanation: Workshop on Tutorial Dialog Systems, Supplementary Proceedings of Artificial Intelligence in Education (2003) 303-312.
3. M. Artigue, T. Assude, B. Grugeon, A. Lenfant, Teaching and Learning Algebra : approaching complexity through complementary perspectives, Proceedings of 12 th ICMI Study Conference, Melbourne, December 9-14 (2001) 21-32.
4. J.L. Austin, How to do the things with words. Cambridge, Cambridge University Press (1962)
5. O. Ducrot, Le dire et le dit, Paris, Minuit (1984)
6. É. Delozanne, D. Prévit, B. Grugeon, P. Jacoboni, Supporting teachers when diagnosing their students in algebra, Workshop Advanced Technologies for Mathematics Education, Supplementary Proceedings of Artificial Intelligence in Education (2003) 461-470.
7. A. Graesser, K. Moreno, J. Marineau, A. Adcock, A. Olney, N. Person, Auto-Tutor Improves Deep Learning of Computer Literacy: Is it the Dialog or the Talking Head ? Artificial Intelligence in Education (2003) 47-54.
8. B. Grugeon, Etude des rapports institutionnels et des rapports personnels des élèves à l'algèbre élémentaire dans la transition entre deux cycles d'enseignement : BEP et Première G, thèse de doctorat, Université Paris VII (1995).
9. S. Jean, E. Delozanne, P. Jacoboni, B. Grugeon, A diagnostic based on a qualitative model of competence in elementary algebra, Artificial Intelligence in Education (1999) 491-498
10. P. Jordan, S. Siler, Student Initiative and Questioning Strategies in Computer-Mediated Human Tutoring Strategies, on Empirical Methods for Tutorial Dialog Systems, International Conference on Intelligent Tutoring Systems, 2002.
11. M. M. Louwerse, H. H. Mitchell, Towards a Taxonomy of a Set of Discourse Markers in Dialog: A Theoritical and Computational Linguistic Account, *Discourse Processes, 35*(3) (2004) 199-239.
12. C. P. Rosé, A. Roque, D. Bhembe, K. VanLehn, 2003, A Hybrid Text Classification Approach for Analysis of Student Essays, Proceedings of the HLT-NAACL 03 Workshop on Educational Applications of NLP (2003).
13. C. P. Rosé, A. Roque, D. Bhembe, K. VanLehn, Overcoming the Knowledge Engineering Bottleneck for Understanding Student Language Input, Artificial Intelligence in Education, (2003) 315-322.
14. J. R. Searle, Speech Acts, An essay in the Philosophy of Language, Cambridge, CUP (1969)

Advantages of Spoken Language Interaction in Dialogue-Based Intelligent Tutoring Systems

Heather Pon-Barry, Brady Clark, Karl Schultz, Elizabeth Owen Bratt, and Stanley Peters

Center for the Study of Language and Information
Stanford University
210 Panama Street
Stanford, CA 94305-4115, USA
{ponbarry, bzack, schultzk, ebratt, peters}@csli.stanford.edu

Abstract. The ability to lead collaborative discussions and appropriately scaffold learning has been identified as one of the central advantages of human tutorial interaction [6]. In order to reproduce the effectiveness of human tutors, many developers of tutorial dialogue systems have taken the approach of identifying human tutorial tactics and then incorporating them into their systems. Equally important as understanding the tactics themselves is understanding how human tutors decide which tactics to use. We argue that these decisions are made based not only on student actions and the content of student utterances, but also on the meta-communicative information conveyed through spoken utterances (e.g. pauses, disfluencies, intonation). Since this information is less frequent or unavailable in typed input, tutorial dialogue systems with speech interfaces have the potential to be more effective than those without. This paper gives an overview of the Spoken Conversational Tutor (SCoT) that we have built and describes how we are beginning to make use of spoken language information in SCoT.

1 Introduction

Studies of human-to-human tutorial interaction have identified many dialogue tactics that human tutors use to facilitate student learning [13], [18], [11]. These include tactics such as pumping the student for more information, giving a concrete example, and making reference to the dialogue history. Furthermore, transcripts have been analyzed in order to understand patterns between the category of a student utterance (e.g. partial answer, request for clarification) and the category of a tutor response (e.g. positive feedback, leading question) [23]. However, since the majority of dialogue-based ITS rely on typed student input, information from the student utterance is limited to the content of what the student typed. Human tutors have access not only to the words uttered by the student, but also to meta-communicative information such as timing, or the way a response is delivered; they use this information to diagnose the student and to choose appropriate tactics [12]. This suggests that in order for a dia

J.C. Lester et al. (Eds.): ITS 2004, LNCS 3220, pp. 390–400, 2004.

logue-based ITS to tailor its choice of tactics in the way that humans do, the student utterances must be spoken rather than typed.

Intelligent tutoring systems that have little to no natural language interaction have been deployed in public schools and have been shown to be more effective than classroom instruction alone [19]. However, the effectiveness of both expert and novice human tutors [3], [9] suggests that there is more room for improvement. Current results from dialogue-based tutoring systems are promising [22], [24] and suggest that dialogue-based tutoring systems may be more effective than tutoring systems with no dialogue. However, most of these systems use either keyboard-to-keyboard interaction or keyboard-to-speech interaction (where the student's input is typed, but the tutor's output is spoken). This progression towards human-like use of natural language suggests that tutoring systems with speech-to-speech interaction might be even more effective. The current state of speech technology has allowed researchers to build successful spoken dialogue systems in domains ranging from travel planning to in-car route navigation [1]. There is reason to believe that spoken dialogue tutorial systems can be just as successful.

Also, recent evidence suggests that spoken tutorial dialogues are more effective than typed tutorial dialogues. A study of self-explanation (the process of explaining solution steps in the student's own words) has shown that spontaneous self-explanation is more frequent in spoken rather than typed tutorial interactions [17]. In addition, a comparison of spoken vs. typed human tutorial dialogues showed that the spoken dialogues contained a higher proportion of student words to tutor words, which has been shown to correlate with student learning [25].

There are many ways an ITS can benefit from spoken interaction. One idea currently being explored is that prosodic information from the speech signal can be used to detect emotion, allowing developers to build more responsive tutoring systems [21]. Another advantage is that speech allows the student to use their hands to gesture while speaking (e.g. pointing to objects in the workspace). Finally, spoken input contains meta-communicative information such as hedges, pauses, and disfluencies, which can be used to make inferences about the student's understanding. These features of spoken language are all things that human tutors have access to when deciding which tactics to use, and that are also available to intelligent tutoring systems with spoken, multi-modal interfaces (although some are more feasible to detect than others). In this paper, we describe how an ITS can take advantage of spoken interaction, how we have begun to do this in SCoT, and the challenges we have faced.

2 Advantages of Spoken Dialogue

Spoken dialogue contains many features that human tutors use to gauge student understanding and student affect. These features include:

- hedges (e.g. "I guess I just thought that was right")
- disfluencies (e.g. "um", "uh", "What-what is in this space?")
- prosodic features (e.g. intonation, pitch, energy)
- temporal features (e.g. pauses, speech rate)

Studies in psycholinguistics have shown that when answering questions, speakers produce hedges, disfluencies, and rising intonation when they have a lower "feeling-of-knowing" [26] and that listeners are sensitive to these phenomena [4]. However, it is not entirely clear whether these generalizations apply to tutorial dialogue, and if they are present, how human tutors respond to them. In a Wizard-of-Oz style comparison of typed vs. spoken communication (to access an electronic mail system), the number of disfluencies was found to be significantly higher in speech than in typing [17]. There are no formal analyses comparing the relative frequencies of hedges, however, a rough comparison (by the author) of data from typed dialogues [2] and transcripts of spoken tutoring [10] suggests that some hedges (e.g. "I guess") are significantly more frequent in speech, while other hedges (e.g. "I think") are equally frequent in both speech and typing.

Human tutors may use the dialogue features listed above in assessing student confidence or uncertainty and in tailoring the discussion to the student's needs. In building an ITS, many of these features of spoken language can be detected, and used both in selecting the most appropriate tutoring tactic and in updating the student model.

Another benefit of spoken interaction is the ability to coordinate speech with gesture. Compared to keyboard input, spoken input has the advantage of allowing the student to use their hands to gesture (e.g. to point to objects in the workspace) while speaking. Studies have shown that speech and direct manipulation (i.e. mouse-driven input) have reciprocal strengths and weaknesses which can be leveraged in multimodal interfaces [14]. For certain types of tutoring (i.e. tutoring where the student is doing a lot of pointing and placing), spoken input and direct manipulation together may be better than just speech or just direct manipulation. Furthermore, allowing the student to explain their reasoning while pointing to objects in the GUI creates a *common workspace* between the participants [8] which helps contextualize the dialogue and facilitate a mutual understanding between the student and tutor, making it easier for the tutor to know if the student is understanding the problem correctly.

3 Overview of SCoT

Our approach is based on the assumption that the activity of tutoring is a joint activity[1] where the content of the dialogue (language and other communicative signals) follows basic properties of conversation but is also driven by the activity at hand [8]. Following this hypothesis, SCoT's architecture separates conversational intelligence (e.g. turn management, construction of a structured dialogue history, use of discourse markers) from the activity that the dialogue accomplishes (in this case, reflective tutoring). SCoT is developed within the Conversational Intelligence Architecture [20], a general purpose architecture which supports multi-modal, mixed-initiative dialogue.

[1] A joint activity is an activity where participants coordinate with one another to achieve both public and private goals [8]. Moving a desk, playing a duet, and shaking hands are all examples of joint activities.

SCoT-DC, the current instantiation of our tutoring system, is applied to the domain of shipboard damage control. Shipboard damage control refers to the task of containing the effects of fires, floods, and other critical events that can occur aboard Navy vessels. Students carry out a reflective discussion with SCoT-DC after completing a problem-solving session with DC-Train [5], a fast-paced, real-time, multimedia training environment for damage control. The fact that problem-solving in damage control occurs in real-time makes reflective tutorial dialogue more appropriate than tutorial dialogue during problem-solving. Because the student is not performing problem-solving steps during the dialogue, it is important for the tutor to get as much information as possible from the student's utterances. In other words, having access to both the meaning of an utterance as well as the manner in which it was spoken will help the tutor assess how well the student is understanding the material.

SCoT is composed of many separate components. The two most relevant for this discussion are the dialogue manager and the tutor. They are described in sections 3.1 and 3.2. A more detailed system description is available in [7].

3.1 Dialogue Manager

The dialogue manager handles aspects of conversational intelligence (e.g. turn management, construction of a structured dialogue history, use of discourse markers) in order to separate purely linguistic aspects of the interaction from tutorial aspects. It contains multiple dynamically updated components—the two main components are the *dialogue move tree*, a structured history of dialogue moves, and the *activity tree*, a hierarchical representation of the past, current, and planned activities initiated by either the tutor or the student. For SCoT, each activity initiated by the tutor corresponds to a tutorial goal; the decompositions of these goals are specified by activity recipes contained in the recipe library (see section 3.2).

3.2 Tutor

The tutor component contains the tutorial knowledge necessary to plan and carry out a flexible and coherent tutorial dialogue. The tutorial knowledge is divided between a *planning and execution system* and a *recipe library* (see Figure 1).

The **planning and execution system** is responsible for selecting initial dialogue plans, revising plans during the dialogue, classifying student utterances, and deciding how to respond to the student. All of these tasks rely on external knowledge sources such as the knowledge reasoner, the student model, and the dialogue move tree (collectively referred to as the *Information State*). The planning and execution system "executes" tutorial activities by placing them on the activity tree, where they get interpreted and executed by the dialogue manager. By separating tutorial knowledge from external knowledge sources, this architecture allows SCoT to lead a flexible dialogue and to continually re-assess information from the Information State in order to select the most appropriate tutorial tactic.

The **recipe library** contains activity recipes that specify how to decompose a tutorial activity into other activities and low-level actions. An activity recipe can be thought of as a tutorial goal and a plan for how the tutor will achieve the goal. The recipe library contains a large number of activity recipes for both low-level tactics (e.g. responding to an incorrect answer) and high-level strategies (e.g. specifications for initial dialogue plans). The recipes are written in a scripted language [15] allowing for automatic translation of the recipes into system activities. An example activity recipe will be shown in section 4.2.

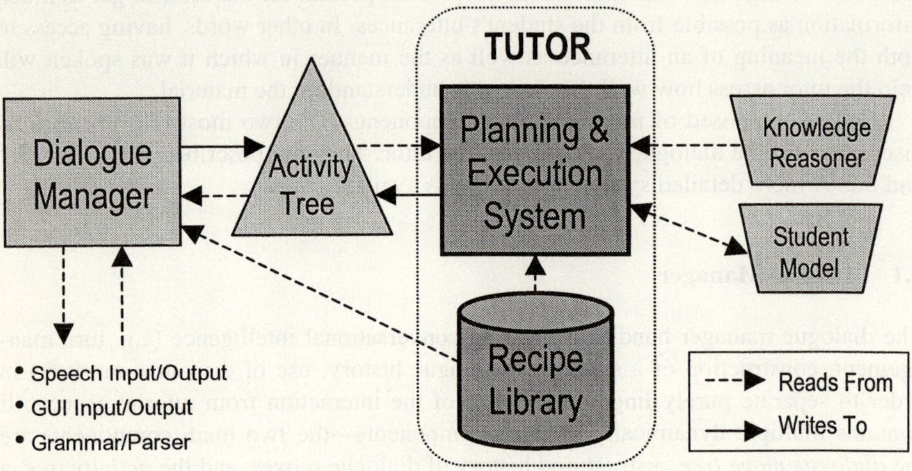

Fig. 1. Subset of SCoT architecture

Other components that the tutor makes use of are the **knowledge reasoner** and the **student model**. The knowledge reasoner provides a domain-general interface to domain-specific information; it provides the tutor with procedural, causal, and motivational explanations of domain-specific actions. The student model uses a Bayesian network to characterize the causal connections between pieces of target domain knowledge and observable student actions. It can be dynamically updated both during the problem solving session and during the dialogue.

4 Taking Advantage of Spoken Language in SCoT

4.1 Observations from Human Tutoring

Because spoken language interaction in tutoring systems is a relatively unexplored area, it is not clear which features of spoken language human tutors pay attention to in deciding when to use various tutorial tactics. As part of an ongoing study, we have been analyzing transcripts of human tutorial dialogue from multiple domains in order to make observations and form hypotheses about how human tutors use these features of spoken dialogue. Two such observations are described below.

One observation we have made is that if the student hedges a correct answer, the tutor will frequently paraphrase what the student said. This seems plausible because by paraphrasing, the tutor is grounding the conversation [8] while attempting to eliminate the student's uncertainty. An example of a hedged answer followed by paraphrasing is shown in Figure 2 below.

Tutor:	Now, the question is what determines stroke volume, and you told me contractility, and what else?
Student:	Well, I guess if the right atrial pressure were a lot higher, then there would be more of an impetus for the blood to go into the right ventricle, and that would increase that somewhat.
Tutor:	So right atrial pressure represents one of the determinants.
Student:	Yes.
Tutor:	OK.

Fig. 2. Excerpt from CIRCSIM corpus of human keyboard-to-keyboard dialogues [10]

Another observation we have made is that human tutors frequently refer back to past dialogue following an incorrect student answer with hedges or mid-sentence pauses. This seems plausible because referring back to past dialogue helps students integrate new information with existing knowledge, and promotes reflection, which has been shown to correlate with learning [6]. An example of an incorrect answer with mid-sentence pauses followed by a reference to past dialogue is shown in Figure 3 (each colon ':' represents a 0.5 sec pause).

Student:	600-30+20 divided by :::::::::::::: two :::::::: no this parts wrong ::: [writes 600-(30+20)/2 and then scratches out the 600-]
Tutor:	Right.
Tutor:	That [points at (30+20)/2] looks great but it doesn't work. OK You would think it would, you are just averaging, but it doesn't work. What did we define average speed as earlier?

Fig. 3. Dialogue excerpt from Algebra corpus of spoken tutorial interaction [18]

4.2 Activity Recipes

The division of knowledge in the tutor component (between the recipe library and the planning and execution system) allows us to independently evaluate hypotheses such as the ones in section 4.1 (i.e. test whether their presence or absence affects the effectiveness of SCoT). Each hypothesis is realized by a combination of activity recipes, and the planning and execution system ensures that a coherent dialogue will be produced regardless of which activities are put on the activity tree.

An activity recipe corresponding to the tutorial goal ***discuss problem solving sequence*** is shown below. A recipe contains three primary sections: *DefinableSlots*, *MonitorSlots*, and *Body*. The *DefinableSlots* specify what information is passed in to the recipe, the *MonitorSlots* specify which parts of the Information State are used in determining how to execute the recipe, and *Body* specifies how to decompose the activity into other activities or low-level actions. The recipe below decomposes the activity of discussing a problem solving sequence into either three or four other activities (depending on whether the problem has already been discussed). The tutor places these activities on the activity tree, and the dialogue manager begins to execute their respective recipes.

```
Activity <discuss_problem_solving_sequence> {

    DefinableSlots {
        currentProblem;
    }

    MonitorSlots {
        currentProblem.alreadyDiscussed;
    }

    Body {
        if (!currentProblem.alreadyDiscussed) {
            situate_problem_context;
        }
        state_review_purpose;
        state_correct_steps;
        elicit_missing_steps;
    }
}
```

All activity recipes have this same structure. The modular nature of the recipes helps us test our hypotheses by making it easy to alter the behavior of the tutor. Furthermore, the tutorial recipes are not particular to the domain of damage control; through our testing of various activity recipes we hope to get a better understanding of domain-independent tutoring principles.

4.3 Multi-modality

Another way that SCoT takes advantage of the spoken interface is through multi-modal interaction. Both the tutor and the student can interactively perform actions in an area of the graphical user interface called the *common workspace*. In the current version of SCoT-DC, the common workspace consists of a 3D representation of the ship which allows either party to zoom in or out and to select (i.e. point to) compartments, regions, and bulkheads (lateral walls of a ship). This is illustrated below in Figure 4, where the common workspace is the large window in the upper left corner.

The tutor can contextualize the problems being discussed by highlighting compartments in specific colors (e.g. red for fire, gray for smoke) to indicate the type and location of the crises. Because the dialogue in SCoT is spoken rather than typed, the student also has the ability to coordinate his/her speech with gesture. This latter coordination is an area we are currently working on, and we hope to soon support interchanges such the one in Figure 5 below, where both the tutor and student coordinate their speech with actions in the common workspace.

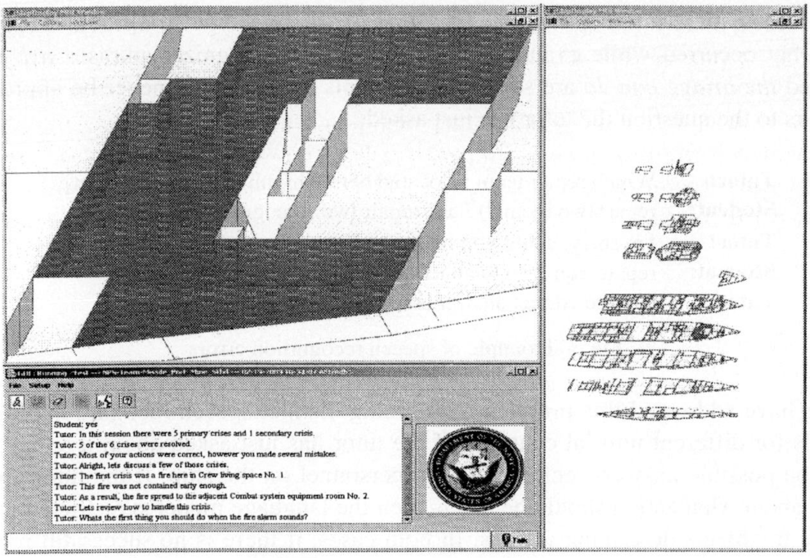

Fig. 4. Screen shot of SCoT-DC

Tutor:	If there is a fire here [highlights compartment], in compartment 1-126-0-A, which bulkheads should you set fire boundaries on?
Student:	I should set primary boundaries here [selects bulkhead], and here [selects other bulkhead]...

Fig. 5. Example of coordinating speech with gesture

4.4 What We Have Learned

Although using spoken language in an intelligent tutoring system can bring about many of the benefits described above, it has also raised some challenges which ITS developers should be aware of.

Student affect. Maintaining student motivation is a challenge for all intelligent tutoring systems. We have observed issues relating to student affect, possibly stemming from the spoken nature of the dialogue. For example, in a previous version of SCoT, listeners remarked that repeated usage of phrases such as *You made this mistake more than once* and *We discussed this same mistake earlier* made the tutor seem overly critical. Other (non-spoken) tutorial systems give similar types of feedback (e.g. [11]), yet none have reported this sort feedback to cause such negative affect. This suggests that users have different reactions when listening to, rather than reading, the tutor's output, and that further work is necessary to better understand this difference.

Improving Speech Recognition. We are currently running an evaluation of SCoT, and preliminary results show speech recognition accuracy to be fairly high (see section 5). However, we have learned that small recognition errors can greatly reduce the effectiveness of a tutoring session. Figure 6 shows one type of speech recognition error that occurred while evaluating SCoT-DC. The recognized phrases *ask repair two* and *the bridge can do* are sentence fragments which would never be appropriate answers to the question the tutor has just asked.

Tutor:	Which repair team is located here? [highlights compartment]
Student:	repair two (actual) / ask repair two (recognized)
Tutor:	I'm sorry, could you rephrase that?
Student:	repair team two (actual) / the bridge can do (recognized)
Tutor:	No, the correct answer is repair team two.

Fig. 6. Example of speech recognition errors

We have addressed this problem by defining distinct speech recognition language models for different tutorial contexts. If the tutor has just asked about a repair team, then the possible answers are restricted to personnel on the ship. If the tutor has just asked about what action should be taken, then the language model is restricted to verb phrase fragments describing actions. In both cases, if there is no successful recognition in the small, tailored grammar, we then back off to the whole grammar. Adapting the language model to the dialogue context in this way appears to be aiding our recognition performance significantly, in line with an 11.5% error rate reduction found in other dialogue systems [27]. Misrecognitions not only prevent the tutor from properly assessing the student's knowledge, they also cause the student to distrust information coming from the tutor, which makes it difficult to facilitate learning. Thus, taking advantage of the tutorial and dialogue context to constrain the language model can substantially benefit the overall system.

5 Conclusions and Current Evaluation of SCoT

In this paper, we argued that spoken language interaction is an integral part of human tutorial dialogue and that information from spoken utterances is very useful in building dialogue-based intelligent tutors that understand and respond to students as effectively as human tutors. We described the Spoken Conversational Tutor we have built, and described how SCoT is beginning to take advantage of features of spoken language. We do not yet understand exactly how human tutors make use of spoken language features such as disfluencies and pauses, but we are building a tutorial framework that allows us to test various hypotheses, and in time reach a better understanding of how to take advantage of spoken language in intelligent tutoring systems.

We are currently evaluating the effectiveness of SCoT-DC (a version that does not yet make use of meta-communicative information or include a student model) with students at Stanford University. Preliminary quantitative results suggest that interacting with SCoT improves student learning (measured by performance in DC-Train and on a written test). Qualitatively, naïve users have found the system fairly easy to interact with, and speech recognition has not been a significant problem—preliminary results show very high recognition accuracies. Excluding out-of-grammar utterances (e.g. "request the, uh...shoot" or "oops my bad"), which account for approximately 12% of the total utterances, recognition accuracy has been approximately 0.79, or approximately 0.98 ignoring minor misrecognitions (i.e. singular vs. plural forms and *a* ↔ *the*) that do not affect the tutor's classification of the utterance. Further results will be available by the time of the conference. In addition, we are planning on running evaluations of the new version of SCoT in the near future to test the effectiveness of hypotheses about spoken language along the lines of those described in section 4.1.

Acknowledgements. This work is supported by the Office of Naval Research under research grant N000140010660, a multidisciplinary university research initiative on natural language interaction with intelligent tutoring systems. Further information is available at http://www-csli.stanford.edu/semlab/muri.

References

1. Belvin, R., Burns, R., & Hein, C. (2001). Development of the HRL Route Navigation Dialogue System. In *Proceedings of the First International Conference on Human Language Technology Research,* Paper H01-1016
2. Bhatt, K. (2004). Classifying student hedges and affect in human tutoring sessions for the CIRCSIM-Tutor intelligent tutoring system. Unpublished M.S. Thesis, Illinois Institute of Technology.
3. Bloom, B.S. (1984). The 2 sigma problem: The search for methods of group instruction as effective one-on-one tutoring. *Educational Researcher, 13,* 4-16.
4. Brennan, S. E., & Williams, M. (1995). The feeling of another's knowing: Prosody and filled pauses as cues to listeners about the metacognitive states of speakers. *Journal of Memory and Language, 34,* 383-398.
5. Bulitko, V., & Wilkins., D. C. (1999). Automated instructor assistant for ship damage control. In *Proceedings of AAAI-99.*
6. Chi, M.T.H., Siler, S., Jeong, H., Yamauchi, T., & Hausmann, R.G. (2001). Learning from tutoring. Cognitive Science, 25:471-533.
7. Clark, B., Lemon, O., Gruenstein, A., Bratt, E., Fry, J., Peters, S., Pon-Barry, H., Schultz, K., Thomsen-Gray, Z., & Treeratpituk, P. (In press). A General Purpose Architecture for Intelligent Tutoring Systems. In *Natural, Intelligent and Effective Interaction in Multimodal Dialogue Systems.* Edited by Niels Ole Bernsen, Laila Dybkjaer, and Jan van Kuppevelt. Dordrecht: Kluwer.
8. Clark, H.H. (1996). *Using Language.* Cambridge: University Press.
9. Cohen, P.A., Kulik, J.A., & Kulik, C.C. (1982). Educational outcomes of tutoring: A meta-analysis of findings. *American Educational Research Journal, 19,* 237-248.
10. Transcripts of face-to-face and keyboard-to-keyboard tutorial dialogues, between physiology professors and first-year students at Rush Medical College (received from M. Evens).
11. Evens, M., & Michael, J. (Unpublished manuscript). *One-on-One Tutoring by Humans and Machines.* Computer Science Department, Illinois Institute of Technology.
12. Fox, B. (1993). *Human Tutorial Dialogue.* New Jersey: Lawrence Erlbaum.

13. Graesser, A.C., Person, N.K., & Magliano J. P. (1995). Collaborative dialogue patterns in naturalistic one-to-one tutoring sessions. *Applied Cognitive Psychology, 9,* 1-28.
14. Grasso, M.A., & Finin, T.W. (1997). Task Integration in Multimodal Speech Recognition Environments. *Crossroads, 3(3),* 19-22.
15. Gruenstein, A. (2002). Conversational Interfaces: A Domain-Independent Architecture for Task-Oriented Dialogues. Unpublished M.S. Thesis, Stanford University.
16. Hausmann, R. & Chi, M.T.H. (2002). Can a computer interface support self-explaining? *Cognitive Technology, 7(1),* 4-15.
17. Hauptmann, A.G. & Rudnicky, A.I. (1988). Talking to Computers: An Empirical Investigation. *International Journal of Man-Machine Studies 28(6),* 583-604
18. Heffernan, N. T. (2001). Intelligent Tutoring Systems have Forgotten the Tutor: Adding a Cognitive Model of Human Tutors. Dissertation. Computer Science Department, School of Computer Science, Carnegie Mellon University. Technical Report CMU-CS-01-127.
19. Koedinger, K. R., Anderson, J.R., Hadley, W.H., & Mark, M. A. (1997). Intelligent tutoring goes to school in the big city. *International Journal of Artificial Intelligence in Education, 8,* 30-43.
20. Lemon, O., Gruenstein, A., & Peters, S. (2002). Collaborative activities and multitasking in dialogue systems. In C. Gardent (Ed.), *Traitement Automatique des Langues (TAL, special issue on dialogue), 43(2),* 131-154.
21. Litman, D., & Forbes, K. (2003). Recognizing Emotions from Student Speech in Tutoring Dialogues. In *Proc. of the IEEE Automatic Speech Recognition and Understanding Workshop (ASRU).*
22. Person, N.K., Graesser, A.C., Bautista, L., Mathews, E., & the Tutoring Reasearch Group. (2001). Evaluating student learning gains in two versions of AutoTutor. In J. D. Moore, C. L. Redfield, & W. L. Johnson (Eds.) *Proceedings of Artificial intelligence in education: AI-ED in the wired and wireless future*, 286-293.
23. Person, N.K., & Graesser, A.C. (2003). Fourteen facts about human tutoring: Food for thought for ITS developers. In *Proceedings of the AIED 2003 Workshop on Tutorial Dialogue Systems: With a View Towards the Classroom.*
24. Rosé, C., Jordan, P., Ringenberg, M., Siler, S., VanLehn, K., & Weinstein, A. (2001). Interactive Conceptual Tutoring in Atlas-Andes. In *Proc. of AI in Education 2001*.
25. Rosé, C.P., Litman, D., Bhembe, D., Forbes, K., Silliman, S., Srivastava, R., & VanLehn, K. (2003). A Comparison on Tutor and Student Behavior in Speech Versus Text Based Tutoring. In *Proc. of the HLT-NAACL 03 Workshop on Educational Applications of NLP.*
26. Smith, V. L., & Clark, H. H. (1993). On the course of answering questions. *Journal of Memory and Language, 32,* 25-38.
27. Xu, W. & Rudnicky, A. (2000). Language modeling for dialog system. In *Proceedings of ICSLP 2000*. Paper B1-06.

CycleTalk: Toward a Dialogue Agent That Guides Design with an Articulate Simulator

Carolyn P. Rosé[1], Cristen Torrey[1], Vincent Aleven[1], Allen Robinson[1], Chih Wu[2], and Kenneth Forbus[3]

[1] Carnegie Mellon University, 5000 Forbes Ave., Pittsburgh PA, 15213
{cprose,ctorrey,aleven}@cs.cmu.edu, alr@andrew.cmu.edu

[2] US Naval Academy, 121 Blake Rd., Annapolis MD, 21402-5000
wu@usna.edu

[3] Northwestern University, 1890 Maple Ave., Evanston IL, 60201
forbus@cs.northwestern.edu

Abstract. We discuss the motivation for a novel style of tutorial dialogue system that emphasizes reflection in a design context. Our current research focuses on the hypothesis that this type of dialogue will lead to better learning than previous tutorial dialogue systems because (1) it motivates students to explain more in order to justify their thinking, and (2) it supports students' metacognitive ability to ask themselves good questions about the design choices they make. We present a preliminary cognitive task analysis of design exploration tasks using CyclePad, an articulate thermodynamics simulator [10]. Using this cognitive task analysis, we analyze data collected in two initial studies of students using CyclePad, one in an unguided manner, and one in a Wizard of Oz scenario. This analysis suggests ways in which tutorial dialogue can be used to assist students in their exploration and encourage a fruitful learning orientation. Finally, we conclude with some system desiderata derived from our analysis as well as plans for further exploration.

1 Introduction

Tutorial dialogue is a unique, intensely dynamic form of instruction that can be highly adaptive to the individual needs of students [15] and provides opportunities for students to make their thinking transparent to a tutor. In this paper we introduce early work to develop a novel tutorial dialogue agent to support guided, exploratory learning of scientific concepts in a design scenario. Current tutorial dialogue systems focus on leading students through directed lines of reasoning to support conceptual understanding [16], clarifying procedures [21], or coaching the generation of explanations for justifying solutions [19], problem solving steps [1], predictions about complex systems [9], or computer literacy [11]. Thus, to date tutorial dialogue systems have primarily been used to support students in strongly directed types of task domains. We hypothesize that in the context of creative design activities the adaptivity of

J.C. Lester et al. (Eds.): ITS 2004, LNCS 3220, pp. 401–411, 2004.

dialogue has greater impact on learning than the impact that has been demonstrated in previous comparisons of tutorial dialogue to challenging alternative forms of instruction such as an otherwise equivalent targeted "mini-lesson" based approach (e.g., [12]) or a "2nd-generation" intelligent tutoring system with simple support for self-explanation (e.g., [1]).

We are conducting our research in the domain of thermodynamics, using as a foundation the CyclePad articulate simulator [10]. CyclePad offers students a rich, exploratory learning environment in which they apply their theoretical thermodynamics knowledge by constructing thermodynamic cycles, performing a wide range of efficiency analyses. CyclePad has been in active use in a range of thermodynamics courses at the Naval Academy and elsewhere since 1996 [18]. By carrying out the calculations that students would otherwise have to do by more laborious means (e.g., by extrapolation from tables), CyclePad makes it possible for engineering students to engage in design activities earlier in the curriculum than would otherwise be possible. Qualitative evaluations of CyclePad have shown that students who use CyclePad have a deeper understanding of thermodynamics equations and technical terms [4].

In spite of its very impressive capabilities, it is plausible that CyclePad could be made even more effective. First, CyclePad supports an unguided approach to exploration and design. While active learning and intense exploration have been shown to be more effective for learning and transfer than more highly directed, procedural help [7,8] pure exploratory learning has been hotly debated [3,13,14]. In particular, scientific exploratory learning requires students to be able to effectively form and test hypotheses. However, students experience many difficulties in these areas [13]. Guided exploratory learning, in which a teacher provides some amount of direction or feedback, has been demonstrated to be more effective than pure exploratory learning in a number of contexts [14].

Second, CyclePad is geared towards explaining its inferences to students, at the student's request. It is likely to be more fruitful if the students do more of the explaining themselves, assisted by the system. Some results in the literature show that students learn better when producing explanations than when receiving them [20]. Thus, a second area where CyclePad might be improved is in giving students the opportunity to develop their ability to think through their designs at a functional level and then explain and justify their designs.

A third way in which CyclePad's pedagogical approach may not be optimal is that students typically do not make effective use of on-demand help facilities offered by interactive learning environments (for a review of the relevant literature, see [2]). That is, students using CyclePad may not necessarily seek out the information provided by the simulator, showing for example how the second law of thermodynamics applies to the cycle that they have built, with a possibly detrimental effect on their learning outcomes. Thus, students' experience with CyclePad may be enhanced if they were prompted at key points to reflect on how their conceptual knowledge relates to their design activities.

We argue that engaging students in natural language discussions about the pros and cons of their design choices as a highly interactive form of guided exploratory learning is well suited to the purpose of science instruction. In the remainder of the paper, we present a preliminary cognitive task analysis of design exploration tasks using CyclePad. We present an analysis of data collected in two initial studies of students using CyclePad, one in an unguided manner, and one in a Wizard of Oz scenario. We present preliminary evidence from this analysis that suggests how tutorial dialogue can be used to assist students in their exploration. Finally, we conclude with some system desiderata derived from our analysis as well as plans for further exploration.

2 CycleTalk Curriculum

A thermodynamic cycle processes energy by transforming a working fluid within a system of networked components (condensers, turbines, pumps, and such). Power plants, engines, and refrigerators are all examples of thermodynamic cycles. In its initial development, the CycleTalk curriculum will emphasize the improvement of a basic thermodynamic cycle, the simple Rankine cycle. Rankine cycles of varying complexities are used in steam-based power plants, which generate the majority of the electricity in the US.

At a high level, there are three general modifications that will improve the efficiency of a Rankine cycle:

Adjusting the temperature and pressure of the fluid in the boiler will increase efficiency, up to the point where the materials cannot withstand the extreme conditions.

Adding a reheat cycle reheats the working fluid before sending it through a second turbine. This requires extra energy to the second heater, but it is balanced by the work done by the second turbine.

Adding a regenerative cycle sends some of the steam leaving the turbine back to the water entering the boiler, which decreases the energy required to heat the water in the boiler.

These modifications can be combined, and multiple stages of reheat and regeneration are often used to optimize efficiency, though the cost of additional parts must be weighed against the gains in efficiency.

3 Exploratory Data Collection

We have begun to collect data related to how CyclePad is used by students who have previously taken or are currently taking a college-level thermodynamics course. The goal of this effort is to begin to assess how tutorial dialogue can extend CyclePad's effectiveness and to refine our learning hypotheses in preparation for our first controlled experiment. In particular we are exploring such questions as: (1) To what extent are students making use of CyclePad's on-demand help? (2) What exploratory strategies are students using with CyclePad? Are these strategies successful or are students floundering? Do students succeed in improving the efficiency of cycles? (3)

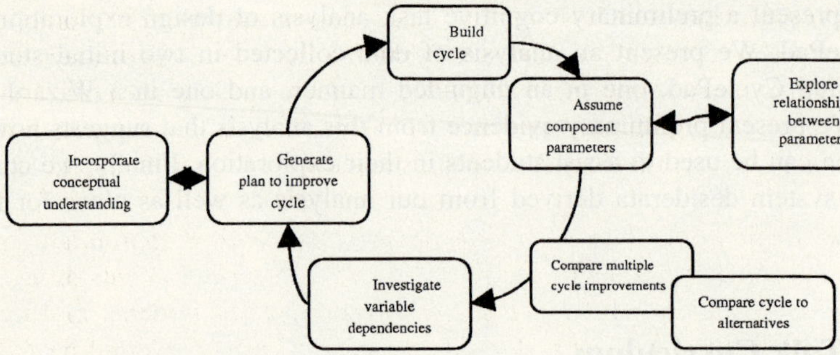

Fig. 1. Task analysis of exploring a design space with CyclePad

To what extent are student explorations of the design space correlated with their observed conceptual understanding, as evidenced by their explanation behavior?

At present, we have two forms of data. We have collected the results of a take-home assignment administered to mechanical engineering students at the US Naval Academy, in which students were asked to improve the efficiency of a shipboard version of a Rankine cycle. These results are in the form of written reports, as well as log files of the student's interactions with the software. In addition, we have directly observed several Mechanical Engineering undergraduate students at Carnegie Mellon University working with CyclePad on a problem involving a slightly simpler Rankine cycle. These students were first given the opportunity to work in CyclePad independently. Then, in a Wizard of Oz scenario, they continued to work on the problem while they were engaged in a conversation via text messaging software with a graduate student in Mechanical Engineering from the same university. For these students we have collected log files and screen movies of their interactions with CyclePad as well as transcripts of their typed conversation with the human tutor.

We have constructed a preliminary cognitive task analysis (See Fig. 1) describing how students might use CyclePad in the type of scenario they encountered during these studies (i.e., to improve a simple Rankine cycle).

Creating the cycle and defining key parameters. When creating a thermodynamic cycle according to the problem description, or modifying a given thermodynamic cycle, students must select and connect components. Further, they must provide a limited number of assumed parameter values to customize individual cycle components and define the cycle state. CyclePad will compute as many additional parameters as can be derived from those assumptions. When each parameter has a value, either given or inferred, CyclePad calculates the cycle's efficiency. In order to be successful, students must carefully select and connect components and be able to assume values in ways that acknowledge the relationships between the components.

Investigating Variable Dependencies. Once the cycle state has been fully defined (i.e., the values of all parameters have been set or inferred), students can use CyclePad's sensitivity analysis tool to study the effect of possible modifications to these values. With this tool, students can plot one variable's effect on another variable.

These analyses may have implications for their redesign strategy. For example, when a Rankine cycle has been fully defined, students can plot the effect of the pressure of the output of the pump on the thermal efficiency of the cycle as a whole. The sensitivity analysis will show that up to a certain point, increasing the pressure will increase efficiency. The student can then adjust the pressure to its optimum level.

Exploring Relationships among Cycle Parameters. Setting appropriate assumptions given a specific cycle topology can be difficult for novice students of thermodynamics. For any specific cycle topology, it is important for students to understand which parameters must be given and which parameters can be inferred based on the given values. In order to help in this regard, CyclePad allows students to request explanations that articulate the relationships between parameters, moving forward from a given parameter to conclusions or backward to assumptions. For example, CyclePad will answer questions such as "Why does P(S2) = 10,000 kPa?" or "What follows from P(S2) = 10,000 kPa?". Here, P(S2) specifies the pressure of the working substance at a particular stage in the cycle.

Comparing Multiple Cycle Improvements. Students can create their redesigned cycles, and, once the cycle states are fully defined, students can compute the improved cycle efficiency. Comparing cycle efficiencies of different redesigns lets students explore the problem space and generate the highest efficiency possible. Suppose a student began improving the efficiency of the Rankine cycle by including a regenerative cycle. It would then be possible to create an alternative design which included a reheat cycle (or several reheat cycles) and to compare the effects on efficiency before combining them. By comparing alternatives, the student has the potential to gain a deeper understanding of the design space and underlying thermodynamics principles and is likely to produce a better redesign.

3.1 Defining Cycle State

Despite CyclePad's built-in help functionality, we have observed that a number of students struggle when defining the state of each of the components in the cycle. On the take-home assignment, 19 students were asked to improve the efficiency of a shipboard version of a Rankine cycle. The work of only 11 students resulted in the ability to compute the efficiency of their improved cycle using CyclePad, even though these students had two weeks to complete the assignment and ample access to the professor. Of the 11 students who were able to fully define their improved cycle, 3 students created impractical or unworkable solutions and 3 other students did not improve the efficiency of the cycle in accordance with the problem statement. From the efforts of these students, we have seen that implementing one's redesign ideas in the CyclePad environment should not be considered trivial.

Because we only have the artifacts of these students' take-home assignments, it is difficult to speculate as to exactly what these students found difficult about fully defining each state of their improved cycle. It seems likely however that the greater complexity of the redesigned cycles that students constructed (on average, the redesigned cycles had 50% more components than the cycle that the students started out with) made it more difficult for students to identify the key parameters whose values must be assumed. We have informally observed that our expert tutor is capable of defining the state of even complicated cycles in CyclePad without much, if any, trial and error. Perhaps he quickly sees a deep structure, as opposed to novice students who may be struggling to maintain associations when the number of components increases (see e.g., [5]). As we continue our data collection, we hope to investigate how student understanding of the relationships between components affects their ability to fully define a thermodynamic cycle.

We did observe the complexity of implementing a redesigned cycle directly through several Wizard-of-Oz-style studies where the student worked first alone, then with a tutor via text-messaging software. In unguided work with CyclePad, we saw students having difficulty setting the assumptions for their improved cycle. One student was working for approximately 15 minutes on setting the parameters of a few components, but he encountered difficulty because he had not ordered the components in an ideal way. The tutor was able to help him identify and remove the obstacle so that he could quickly make progress. When the tutoring session began, the tutor asked the student to explain why he had set up the components in that particular way.

Student: I just figured I should put the exchanger before the htr

[The student is using "htr" to refer to the heater.]

Tutor: How do you think the heat exchanger performance/design will vary with the condition of the fluid flowing through it? What's the difference between the fluid going into the pump and flowing out of it?

Student: after the pump the water's at a high P

[P is an abbreviation for pressure.]

Tutor: Good! So how will that affect your heat exchanger design?

Student: if the exchanger is after the pump the heating shouldn't cause it to change phase because of the high pressure

…

Tutor: But why did you put a heat exchanger in?

Student: I was trying to make the cycle regenerative

…

Tutor: OK, making sure you didn't waste the energy flowing out of the turbine, right?

After the discussion with the tutor about the plan for the redesign, the student was able to make the proposed change to the cycle and define the improved cycle completely without any help from the tutor. Engaging in dialogue forces students to think through their redesign and catches errors that seem to be difficult for students to detect on their own. By initiating explanation about the design on a functional level, the tutor was able to elicit an expression of the student's thinking and give the student a greater chance for success in fully defining the improved cycle.

3.2 Exploring Component Relationships

As mentioned, in order to gain an understanding of how cycle parameters are related (crucial to fully defining the state of a cycle) students can ask CyclePad to explain the relations in which a given parameter takes part. Without guidance from a tutor, however, students tended not to take advantage of this facility, consistent with results from other studies [1]. Investigation of the log files from the take-home assignment reveals very limited use of CyclePad's explanation features. Only one log file indicated that a student had used the functionality more than ten times, and the log files of 8 of 19 students contained no evidence that the functionality was ever used. (We cannot rule out the possibility that students used the explanation features on CyclePad files they did not turn in or that they chose to ask their professor for help instead.) Similarly, in our direct observation of students working independently with CyclePad, we saw that students often set parameter values that contradict one another, causing errors that must be resolved before continuing. One student encountered numerous contradictions on a single parameter over a short length of time, but still did not ask the system to explain how that parameter could be derived.

By contrast, students working with the tutor did seek out CyclePad's explanations, for example when the tutor asked them a question to which they could not respond.

Tutor: What does your efficiency depend on?

…

Student asks CyclePad for "What equations mention eta-Carnot?"

(eta-Carnot refers to the hypothetical efficiency of a completely reversible heat engine. The student is asking a theoretical question about how efficiency would be determined under ideal conditions.)

CyclePad displays eta-Carnot(CYCLE) = 1 – [Tmin(CYCLE)/Tmax(CYCLE)]

Student: the definition of carnot efficiency

Tutor: What can you deduce from that?

Student: that the lower Tmin/Tmax, the higher the efficiency of the cycle; ie, the greater the temperature difference in the cycle the more efficient

Tutor: Is there any way you can modify your cycle accordingly?

The challenges faced by students working with CyclePad could be opportunities for learning. CyclePad has the capacity to explain how the cycles are functioning, but students do not seem to utilize CyclePad's articulate capacities spontaneously. When students are prompted to explain themselves and they receive feedback on their explanations, they are more likely to utilize CyclePad's helpful features in productive ways. Furthermore, as part of the discussion, the tutor may explicitly direct the student to seek out explanations from CyclePad.

3.3 Investigating Variable Dependencies

One of the most useful tools that CyclePad offers students is the sensitivity analysis. A sensitivity analysis will plot the relationship between one variable (such as pressure or temperature) and a dependent variable (such as thermal efficiency). Information like this can be very useful in planning one's approach to a redesign.

There were two students who performed large numbers of sensitivity analyses, as evidenced from their log files, but the comments from the professor on these students' written reports were critical of their process. They did not seem to document a well-reasoned path to their solution. From the relatively large numbers of sensitivity analyses in quick succession, one could speculate that these students' use of the sensitivity analysis tool was not purposeful. Rather, these students appeared to take a blanket approach in the hope that something useful might turn up. In contrast, we observe the tutor assisting students to interpret sensitivity analyses and apply those interpretations to their designs in a systematic way, as illustrated in the following dialogue:

Student: I have recreated the basic cycle and am now in the sensitivity analysis
Tutor: Go ahead. Let's stick to eta-thermal
[student sets up the efficiency analysis in CyclePad]
Tutor: So what does this tell you?
Student: the higher the temperature to which the water is heated in the heater, the higher the thermal efficiency
Tutor: So do you want to try changing the peak temperature?
Student: to improve the efficiency, yes

3.4 Comparing Multiple Cycle Improvements

CyclePad makes it relatively easy for students to try alternative design ideas and thereby to generate high-quality designs. However, students working independently with CyclePad tended not to explore the breadth of the design space, even if they seemed to be aware of design ideas that would improve their design. Although students who did the take-home assignment were aware of both the reheat and regenerative strategies through course materials, only 8 of these 19 students incorporated both strategies into their redesigned cycles. Also, in the written report associated with the take-home assignment, the students were asked to explain the result of each strategy on the efficiency of the cycle. 15 of 19 students correctly explained that regeneration would improve the efficiency of the cycle. However, only 10 of 19 students used a regeneration strategy in their redesigned cycle.

In contrast, students working with the tutor are prompted to consider as many alternative approaches as they can and they are encouraged to contrast these alternatives with one another on the basis of materials and maintenance cost, in addition to cycle efficiency. This explicit discussion of alternatives with the tutor should produce an optimal design. Here is an example dialogue where the tutor is leading the student to consider alternative possibilities:

Tutor: Yes, very good. How do you think you can make it better? i.e. how will you optimize the new component?
Student: we could heat up the water more
Tutor: That's one, try it out. What do you learn?

Student: the efficiency increases pretty steadily with the increased heating - should i put the materials limitation on like there was earlier? or are we not considering that right now

Tutor: OK, how about other parameters? Obviously this temperature effect is something to keep in mind. Include the material effect when you start modifying the cycle

Student: ok

Tutor: What else can you change?

Student: pump pressure

Tutor: So what does the sensitivity plot with respect to pump pressure tell you?

Student: so there's kind of a practical limit to increasing pump pressure, after a while there's not much benefit to it

Tutor: Good. What other parameters can you change?

Student: exit state of the turbine

Tutor: Only pressure appears to be changeable, let's do it. What's your operating range?

Student: 100 to 15000. right?

Tutor: Do you want to try another range? Or does this plot suggest something?

Student: we could reject even lower, since its a closed cycle

Tutor: Good!

4 System Desiderata

Our exploratory data collection illustrates that CyclePad's significant pedagogical potential tends to be underutilized when students do not receive tutorial guidance beyond what CyclePad itself can offer. Our data suggests that the goals of CyclePad are realized more effectively when students have the opportunity to engage in tutorial dialog. In particular, we see a need for a tutorial dialogue agent to engage students in learning activities including (1) thinking through their designs at a functional level, (2) seeking out explanations from CyclePad, (3) reflecting on implications of sensitivity analysis and efficiency measurements for their designs, and (4) weighing trade-offs between alternative choices.

In order to fulfill these objectives, we have designed CycleTalk as a tutorial dialogue agent that monitors a student's interactions with CyclePad in search of opportunities to engage them in the four learning activities just mentioned. This tutor agent will contain a detailed knowledge base of domain-specific pedagogical content knowledge as well as mechanisms that allow it to build up detailed student models. We plan to reuse much of the functionality that has been developed in the context of previous CyclePad help systems such as the RoboTA [10]. As the student is interacting with CyclePad to build thermodynamic cycles and perform sensitivity analyses, the tutor agent will monitor the student's actions, building a detailed student model that keeps track of which portions of the space of design choices the student has already explored, which analyses have already been performed, and what the student is likely to have learned from them. When the tutor agent determines based on its observations or by detecting a request from the student that a dialogue with the student is necessary, it formulates a dialogue goal that takes into consideration the student model and the state of the student's design. The latter information is maintained by CyclePad's truth maintenance system.

5 Conclusions and Current Directions

In this paper we have presented an analysis of a preliminary data collection effort and its implications for the design of the CycleTalk tutorial dialogue agent. We have argued in favor of natural language discussions as a highly interactive form of guided discovery learning. We are currently gearing up for a controlled study in which we will test the hypothesis that exploratory dialogue leads to effective learning. During the study, students will work on a similar design scenario as the ones presented in this paper. On a pre/post test we will evaluate improvement of students' skill in creating designs, in understanding design trade-offs, and in conceptual understanding of thermodynamics, as well as their acquisition of meta-cognitive skills such as self-explanation. In particular we will assess the value of the dynamic nature of dialogue by contrasting a Wizard-of-Oz version of CycleTalk with a control condition in which students are lead in a highly scripted manner to explore the design space, exploring each of the three major efficiency enhancing approaches in turn through step-by-step instructions

Acknowledgments. This project is supported by ONR Cognitive and Neural Sciences Division, Grant number N000140410107.

References

1. Aleven V., Koedinger, K. R., & Popescu, O.: A Tutorial Dialogue System to Support Self-Explanation: Evaluation and Open Questions. Proceedings of the 11th International Conference on Artificial Intelligence in Education, AI-ED (2003).
2. Aleven, V., Stahl, E., Schworm, S., Fischer, F., & Wallace, R.M.: Seeking and Providing Help in Interactive Learning Environments. Review of Educational Research, 73(2), (2003) pp 277-320.
3. Ausubel, D.: Educational Psychology: A Cognitive View, (1978) Holt, Rinehart and Winston, Inc.
4. Baher, J.: Articulate Virtual Labs in Thermodynamics Education: A Multiple Case Study. Journal of Engineering Education, October (1999). 429-434.
5. Chi, M. T. H.; Feltovich, P. J.; & Glaser, R.: Categorization and Representation of Physics Problems by Experts and Novices. Cognitive Sciencs 5(2): 121-152, (1981).
6. Core, M. G., Moore, J. D., & Zinn, C.: The Role of Initiative in Tutorial Dialogue, Proceedings of the 10th Conference of the European Chapter of the Association for Computational Linguistics, (2003), Budapest, Hungary.
7. Dutke, S.: Error handling: Visualizations in the human-computer interface and exploratory learning. Applied Psychology: An International Review, 43, 521-541, (1994).
8. Dutke, S. & Reimer, T.: Evaluation of two types of online help for application software, Journal of Computer Assisten Learning, 16, 307-315, (2000).
9. Evens, M. and Michael, J.: One-on-One Tutoring by Humans and Machines, Lawrence Earlbaum and Associates (2003).

10. Forbus, K. D., Whalley, P. B., Evrett, J. O., Ureel, L., Brokowski, M., Baher, J., Kuehne, S. E.: CyclePad: An Articulate Virtual Laboratory for Engineering Thermodynamics. Artificial Intelligence 114(1-2): 297-347, (1999).
11. Graesser, A., Moreno, K. N., Marineau, J. C.: AutoTutor Improves Deep Learning of Computer Literacy: Is It the Dialog or the Talking Head? Proceedings of AI in Education (2003).
12. Graesser, A., VanLehn, K., the TRG, & the NLT.: Why2 Report: Evaluation of Why/Atlas, Why/AutoTutor, and Accomplished Human Tutors on Learning Gains for Qualitative Physics Problems and Explanations, LRDC Tech Report, (2002) University of Pittsburgh.
13. de Jong, T. & van Joolingen, W. R.: Scientific Discovery Learning With Computer Simulations of Conceptual Domains, Review of Educational Research, 68(2), pp 179-201, (1998).
14. Mayer, R. E.: Should there be a three-strikes rule against pure discovery learning? The Case for Guided Methods of Instruction, American Psychologist 59(1), pp 14-19, (2004).
15. Nückles, M., Wittwer, J., & Renkl, A.: Supporting the computer experts'' adaptation to the client's knowledge in asynchronous communication: The assessment tool. In F. Schmalhofer, R. Young, & G. Katz (Eds.). Proceedings of EuroCogSci 03. The European Cognitive Science Conference (2003) (pp. 247-252). Mahwah, NJ: Erlbaum.
16. Rosé, C. P., Jordan, P., Ringenberg, M., Siler, S., VanLehn, K., & Weinstein, A.: Interactive Conceptual Tutoring in Atlas-Andes, In J. D. Moore, C. L. Redfield, & W. L. Johnson (Eds.), Artificial Intelligence in Education: AI-ED in the Wired and Wireless Future, Proceedings of AI-ED 2001 (pp. 256-266). (2001) Amsterdam, IOS Press.
17. Rosé, C. P., Gaydos, A., Hall, B. S., Roque, A. & VanLehn, K:. Overcomming the Knowledge Engineering Bottleneck for Understanding Student Language Input , Proceedings of the 11th International Conference on Artificial Intelligence in Education, AI-ED (2003).
18. Tuttle, K., Wu, Chih.: Intelligent Computer Assisted Instruction in Thermodynamics at the U.S. Naval Academy, Proceedings of the 15th Annual Workshop on Qualitative Reasoning, (2001) San Antonio, Texas.
19. VanLehn, K., Jordan, P., Rosé, C. P., and The Natural Language Tutoring Group.: The Architecture of Why2-Atlas: a coach for qualitative physics essay writing, Proceedings of the Intelligent Tutoring Systems Conference, (2002) Biarritz, France.
20. Webb, N. M.: Peer Interaction and Learning in Small Groups. International Journal of Education Research, 13, 21-39, (1989).
21. Zinn, C., Moore, J. D., & Core, M. G.: A 3-Tier Planning Architecture for Managing Tutorial Dialogue. In S. A. Cerri, G. Gouardères, & F. Paraguaçu (Eds.), Proceedings of the Sixth International Conference on Intelligent Tutoring Systems, ITS 2002 (pp. 574-584). Berlin: Springer Verlag, (2002).

DReSDeN: Towards a Trainable Tutorial Dialogue Manager to Support Negotiation Dialogues for Learning and Reflection

Carolyn P. Rosé and Cristen Torrey

Carnegie Mellon University, 5000 Forbes Ave., Pittsburgh PA, 15213
{cprose,ctorrey}@cs.cmu.edu

Abstract. This paper introduces the DReSDeN[1] tutorial dialogue manager, which adopts a similar Issues Under Negotiation approach to that presented in Larsson [20]. Thus, the information state that is maintained in DReSDeN represents the items that are currently being discussed as well as their interrelationships. This representation provides a structure for organizing the representation for the interwoven conversational threads [26] out of which the negotiation dialogue is composed. We are developing DReSDeN in the context of the CycleTalk tutorial dialogue system that supports the development of critical thinking and argumentation skills by engaging students in negotiation dialogues. We describe the role of DReSDeN in the CycleTalk tutorial dialogue system, currently under development. We then give a detailed description of DReSDeN's underlying algorithms and data structures, illustrated with a working example. We conclude with some early work in using machine learning techniques to adapt DReSDeN's behavior.

1 Introduction

Current tutorial dialogue systems focus on a wide range of application contexts including leading students through directed lines of reasoning to support conceptual understanding [27], clarifying procedures [33], or coaching the generation of explanations for justifying solutions [32], problem solving steps [1], predictions about complex systems [10], or descriptions of computer architectures [13]. Formative evaluation studies of these systems demonstrate that state-of-the-art computational linguistics technology is sufficient for building tutorial dialogue systems that are robust enough to be put in the hands of students and to provide useful learning experiences for them. In this paper we introduce DReSDeN, a new tutorial dialogue planner as an extension of the APE tutorial dialogue planner [12]. This work is motivated by lessons learned from the first generation of tutorial dialogue systems, with a focus on Knowledge Construction Dialogues [27,16] that were developed using the APE framework.

---

[1] DReSDeN stands for Debate-Remediate-Self-explain-for-Directing-Negotiation-dialogues.

J.C. Lester et al. (Eds.): ITS 2004, LNCS 3220, pp. 412–422, 2004.

The DReSDeN tutorial dialogue planner was developed in the context of the CycleTalk thermodynamics tutoring project [29] that aims to cultivate self-monitoring skills by training students to ask themselves valuable questions about the choices they make in a design context as they work with the CyclePad articulate simulator [11]. The CycleTalk system is meant to do this by engaging students in negotiation dialogues in natural language as they design thermodynamic cycles, such as the Rankine Cycle displayed in Figure 1. A thermodynamic cycle processes energy by transforming a working fluid within a system of networked components (condensers, turbines, pumps, and such). Power plants, engines, and refrigerators are all examples of thermodynamic cycles. In its initial development, the CycleTalk curriculum will emphasize the improvement of the simple Rankine cycle. Rankine cycles of varying complexities are used in steam-based power plants, which generate the majority of the electricity in the US.

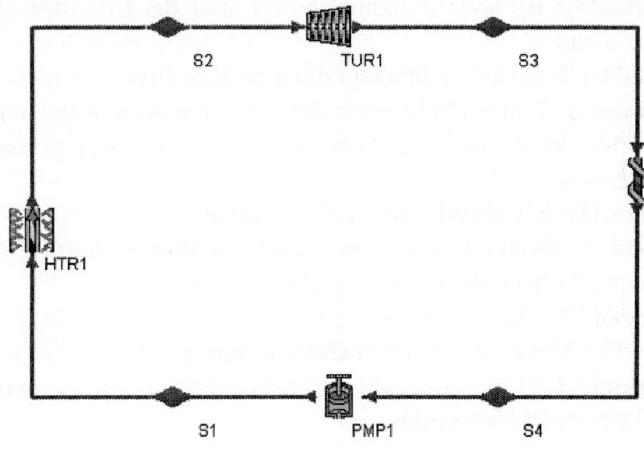

Fig. 1. A Simple Rankine Cycle

Beyond understanding thermodynamics concepts and how and why individual factors can affect the efficiency of a cycle, design requires students to weigh and balance alternative choices in order to accomplish a particular purpose. Furthermore, design requires not only a theoretical understanding of the underlying science concepts but also a practical knowledge of how these concepts are manifest in the real world under non-ideal circumstances. Because of the intense demands that design places on students, we hypothesize that design problems will provide the ultimate environment in which students will be stimulated to construct knowledge actively for themselves. Figure 2 contains an example dialogue between a human tutor and a student discussing design trade-offs in connection with a rankine cycle. This is an actual dialogue extracted from a corpus of dialogues between Carnegie Mellon University Mechanical Engineering graduate students (as tutors) and Mechanical Engineering undergrads (as students) while working together on a Rankine cycle optimization task, although some details have been omitted for simplicity.

Notice that in the dialogue in Figure 2. the student and tutor are negotiating the pros, cons, hows, and whys of alternative design choices. Negotiation dialogues are

(1) Tutor(thread0): What parameters do you think cycle efficiency depends on?
(2) Student(thread0): It depends on the pressure differential
(3) Tutor(thread0): OK, get a cycle T-S diagram. So now we need to maximize work output, right?
(4) Student(thread0): So you want the inside of the 'box' to be as large as possible with as little wasted energy at the bottom.
(5) Tutor(thread0): Perfect! So how can we do it? We need to minimize heat lost while maximizing work output.
(6) Student(thread1): That's what I was trying to do with the heat-exchanger
(7) Tutor(thread2): Right, but how can you make the lower portion go down? You can go to lower condensor pressures.
(8) Student(thread2): But then you have to worry about a 2-phase mixture
(9) Tutor(thread2): OK, but there are ways to solve this problem. **(thread3)** You could bring in reheat.
(10) Student(thread3): By adding another boiler after the first turbine and then running it through a second?
(11) Tutor(thread4): Wait, let's talk about other options first.
(12) Student(thread4): You could increase the initial pressure of the pump.
(13) Tutor(thread4): Well, that's the same as higher condensor pressures. **(thread5)** Can you superheat steam?
(14) Student(thread5): It's already superheated partially
(15) Tutor(thread5): Would that improve steam quality at turbine exit? **(thread0)** Let's check these points from the sensitivity plots.
(16) Student(thread0): OK.
(17) Tutor(thread3): Make plots of eta thermal vs boiler T.
(18) Student(thread3): So that is roughly a linear increase, but the maximum temp of the materials will eventually be reached…

Fig. 2. Example Negotiation Dialogue

composed of multiple, interwoven threads, each addressing a single proposal under negotiation [26]. The dialogue in Figure 2 begins with a single thread that addresses the general topic of factors that affect cycle efficiency. In turn (6), the student introduces a subordinate thread (i.e., thread 1) that addresses one specific way to increase cycle efficiency. Next, the tutor introduces a second subordinate thread (thread 2), parallel with thread 1, that introduces a second method for improving cycle efficiency. In turn (9), the tutor builds on this by further elaborating the proposal in thread 2. Thus, the resulting thread 3 is subordinate to thread 2. Two additional parallel threads are introduced in turns (11) and (13) respectively. In turn (15), the focus shifts back to the original more general topic, and then returns to subordinate thread 3. Notice that this dialogue proceeds in a mixed-initiative fashion, with both the tutor and the student taking the initiative to introduce proposals for consideration. This is significant since our ultimate goal is to provide only as much support as students need, while encouraging them to take more and more leadership in the exploration process as their ability increases [7]. This is not typical with state-of-the-art tutorial dialogue systems that normally behave in a highly directed fashion. Thus, one of our challenges has been to develop a dialogue manager that can support this type of interaction. Note that our focus is not to encourage the students to take initiative in the dialogue [8], but in the exploratory task itself. Allowing the student to take initiative at the dialogue level is simply one means to that end.

In the remainder of the paper, we outline the theoretical motivation for the DReSDeN tutorial dialogue manager. We then describe how it is used in the CycleTalk tutorial dialogue system, currently under development. We then give a detailed description of DReSDeN's underlying algorithms and data structures, illustrated with a working example. We conclude with some early work in using machine learning techniques to adapt DReSDeN's behavior.

2 Motivation

The development of the DReSDeN tutorial dialogue manager was guided by concerns specifically related to supporting negotiation and reflection in a tutorial dialogue context. The role of DReSDeN in CycleTalk is to support student exploration of the design space, encourage students to consciously reflect on the design choices they are making, and to offer feedback on their ideas.

The idea of using negotiation dialogue for instruction is not new. For example, Pilkington et al. (1992) argue the need for computer based tutoring systems to move to more flexible types of dialogues that involve challenging and defending arguments to support students' information gathering processes. When students participate in the argumentation process, they engage higher-order mental processes, including reasoning, critical thinking, evaluative assessment of argument and evidence, all of which are forms of core academic practice [24]. Negotiation provides a context in which students are encouraged to adopt an evaluative epistemology [18], where judgments are evaluated using criteria and evidence in order to weigh alternatives against one another. Baker (1994) argues that negotiation is an active and interactive approach to instruction that is an effective mechanism for achieving coordination of both problem solving and communicative actions between peer learners, or between a learner and a tutor. It keeps both conversational participants equally active and engaged throughout the process. Nevertheless, the potential for using negotiation as a pedagogical tool within a tutorial dialogue system has not been thoroughly explored. While much has been written about the potential for negotiation dialogue for instruction, very few controlled experiments have compared its effectiveness to that of alternative forms of instruction, and no current tutorial dialogue system that has been evaluated with students fully implements this capability.

On a basic level, the DReSDeN flavor of negotiation shares many common features with the types of negotiation modelled previously. For example, all types of negotiations involve agents making proposals that can either be accepted or rejected by the other agent or agents. Some models, such as [5,15,9], also provide the means for modeling justifications for choices as well as the ability to modify a proposal in the light of objections received from other agents. Nevertheless, at a deep level, the DReSDeN flavor of negotiation is distinctive. In particular, previous models of negotiation are primarily adversarial in that the primary goal of the dialogue participants is to agree on a proposal or even to convince the other party of some specific view. The justifications and elaborations that are part of the conversation are in service to the goal of convincing the other party to adopt a specific view, or at least a mutually acceptable view. In the DReSDeN flavor of negotiation, on the other hand, the main objective is to explore the space and to reflect upon the justifications. Thus, the underlying goals and motivation of the tutor agent are quite different from previously modeled negotiation style conversational agents and may lead to interesting differences in information presentation and discourse structure. In particular, while the negotiation dialogues DReSDeN is designed to engage students in shares many surface features with previously explored forms of negotiation, the underlying goal is not to convince the student to adopt a particular decision or even to come to an agreement, but instead to motivate the student to reason through the alternatives, to ask himself reflective questions, and to make a choice with understanding that thoughtfully takes other alternatives into consideration.

Much prior work on managing negotiation dialogues outside of the intelligent tutoring community is based on dialogue game theory [22] and the information state update approach to dialogue management [31,19]. Larsson (2002a, 2002b) presents an information state update approach to managing negotiations with plans to implement it in the GoDiS dialogue framework [4]. The information state in his model is a representation of Issues Under Negotiation, that explicitly indicates what has been decided so far and which alternative possible choices for as yet unmade decisions are currently on the table. Lewin (2001) presents a dialogue manager for a negotiative type of form filling dialogue where users negotiate the contents of a database query, including both which pieces of information are required as well as the values of those particular pieces. The DReSDeN tutorial dialogue manager adopts a similar Issues Under Negotiation approach to that presented in Larsson (2002b). Thus, the information state that is maintained in DReSDeN represents the items that are currently being discussed as well as their relationships to one another. This representation provides a structure for organizing the representation for the interwoven conversational threads [26] out of which the negotiation dialogue is composed.

We build on the foundation of our prior work building and evaluating Knowledge Construction Dialogues (KCDs) [27]. KCDs were motivated by the idea of Socratic tutoring. KCDs are interactive directed lines of reasoning that are each designed to lead students to learn as independently as possible one or a small number of concepts, thus implementing a preference for an "Ask, don't tell" strategy. When a question is presented to a student, the student types a response in a text box in natural language. The student may also simply click on Continue, and thus neglect to answer the question. If the student enters a wrong or empty response, the system will engage the student in a remediation sub-dialogue designed to lead the student to the right answer to the corresponding question. The system selects a subdialogue based on the content of the student's response, so that incorrect responses that provide evidence of an underlying misconception can be handled differently than responses that simply show ignorance of correct concepts. Once the remediation is complete, the KCD returns to the next question in the directed line of reasoning.

KCDs have a very simple underlying dialogue management mechanism, specifically a finite state push down automaton. Thus, they do not make full use of the reactive capabilities of the APE tutorial dialogue manager. They make use of very simple shallow semantic parsing grammars to analyze student input, classifying it into one of a small number of pre-defined answer classes. A set of accompanying authoring tools [16] makes it possible for domain experts to author the lines of reasoning underlying the KCDs. These authoring tools have been used successfully by domain experts with no technical or linguistic background whatsoever. KCDs invite students to enter freeform natural language responses to tutor questions. These tools make KCD development fast and easy. The most time consuming aspect of developing a knowledge construction dialogue is taking the time to thoughtfully design a line of reasoning that will be compelling enough to facilitate student understanding and student learning. Thus, the simplicity of the KCD technology allows developers to invest the majority of their time and energy on pedagogical concerns.

Thus, KCDs are a means for directly encoding the pedagogical content knowledge that is required to teach a concept effectively. Nevertheless, while KCDs have proved themselves robust enough to stand up to evaluations with real students, they fall short of the ideal of human tutorial dialogue. For example, KCDs are designed to lead students through a predetermined directed line of reasoning. While they have the ability to engage students in subdialogues when they answer questions incorrectly, they are designed to keep the student from straying too far away from the main line of reasoning. In order to do this, they respond to a wide range of responses that do not express the correct answer to questions in the same way. The DReSDeN tutorial dialogue manager provides a level of dialogue management above the level of individual KCDs. The goal is to build on what was valuable in the KCD approach while enabling a more flexible dialogue management approach that makes it practical to support mixed initiative and multi-threaded negotiation dialogues.

3 Dialogue Management in DReSDeN

In this section we discuss the main data structures and control mechanisms that are part of the implemented DReSDeN dialogue manager and present a working example that uses toy versions of the required knowledge sources. Further developing these knowledge sources is one of our current directions. DReSDeN has four main data structures that guide its performance. First, it has access to a library of handwritten KCDs. We also plan to generate some KCDs on the fly using a data structure called an ArgumentMap that encodes domain information to provide the foundation for the negotiation or discussion. The KCD library contains lines of reasoning used for exploring pros and cons of typical design scenarios and for remediating deficits in conceptual understanding that are related to issues under negotiation. The KCD library also contains generic KCDs for eliciting explanations and design decisions from students. Next, there is a threaded discourse history, generated in the course of a conversation, which is a graph with parent-child relationships between threads. Each thread of the discourse is managed separately with its own KCD like structure. The flexibility in DReSDeN comes from the potential for multiple threads to be managed in parallel. The final data structure, the discourse model describes the rules that determine how control is passed from one thread to the next.

Each dialogue begins with a single thread, initiated with a single KCD goal. With the initiation of this thread, a tutor text is produced in order for the dialogue system to introduce the topic of discussion. When the student responds, the system must decide whether the student's text addresses the currently in focus thread, a different thread, or begins a new thread. This decision is made using the discourse model, which is a finite state machine. Each state is associated with rules for determining how to relate the student's turn to the discourse history as well as rules for determining what the tutor's next move should be. For example, part of this decision is whether the tutor should continue on the currently in focus thread, shift to a different existing thread, or create a new thread. Currently the conditions on the rules are implemented in terms of a small number of predicates implemented in Lisp. In the next section we discuss how we have begun experimenting with machine learning techniques to learn the conditions that determine how to relate student turns to the discourse history.

Figure 4 presents a sample working example. This example was produced using a discourse model that favors exploring alternative proposals in parallel. In its KCD library, it has access to a small list of lines of reasoning each exploring a different proposal as well as a thread for comparing proposals. It's discourse model implements a state machine that first elicits proposals from the student until the student has articulated the list that it is looking for. Each proposal is maintained on its own thread, which is created when the student introduces the proposal. After all proposals are elicited, the discourse model causes the focus to shift from parallel thread to parallel thread on each turn in a round robin manner until each proposal has been explored. It then calls for the introduction of a final thread that compares proposals and elicits a final decision.

See Figure 3 for a dialogue created using this dialogue model. First a thread is introduced into the discourse in turn (1) for the purpose of negotiating design choices about improving the efficiency of a rankine cycle. Next, two separate threads, each representing a separate design choice suggested by the student in response to a tutor request are introduced in turns (2) and (4) and processed in turn using a general elicitation KCD construct. Both of these threads are related to the initial thread via a design-possibility relation. Control passes back and forth between threads as different aspects of the proposal are explored. Note the alternating thread labels. After the final design choice elicitation thread is processed, an additional thread, which is subordinate to the two parallel threads just completed, is introduced in order to encourage the student to compare the two proposals and make a final choice, to which the student responds by suggesting the addition of a reheat cycle, a preference observed among the students in our data collection effort. The system responds by offering an alternative suggestion. As noted, with an alternative discourse model, this dialogue could have been processed using a different strategy in which each alternative proposal was completely explored in isolation, in such a way that we would not observe the thread switching phenomenon observed in Figure 3.

(1) Tutor(thread 0): How do you think you could make the simple Rankine cycle more efficient?
(2) Student(thread 1): you could add a reheat cycle
(3) Tutor(thread 2): What is something else you could try?
(4) Student(thread 2): you could try heating up the water more so that it's hotter when it exits the boiler
(5) Tutor(thread 1): Adding a reheat cycle is a good idea. Can you explain why?
(6) Student(thread 1): It rejects less heat to the environment. Also, it lowers the pressure of the steam before it enters the compressor.
(7) Tutor(thread 2): Sounds good. Superheating the water is a good idea. Can you explain how it would help the efficiency?
(8) Student(thread 2): it causes the phase change of the liquid to occur at a lower level
(9) Tutor(thread 1): Okay. How would you implement a reheat cycle?
(10) Student(thread 1): add an extra heater and an extra turbine
(11) Tutor(thread 2): Fine. Can you explain how you would implement your super heated water solution?
(12) Student(thread 2): Just crank up the heater
(13) Tutor(thread 3): Fine. Which of these options would you choose?
(14) Student(thread 3): i think reheat I would pick the reheat option.
(15) Tutor(thread 3): I would choose superheating the fluid because it is the simplest choice, and keeping it simple is good.

Fig. 3. Example DReSDeN Dialogue about Rankine Cycle Design Possibilities

4 Machine Learning Techniques for Adapting DReSDeN's Behavior

Our learning hypothesis is that negotiation dialogue will prove to be a highly effective form of tutorial dialogue. Within that framework, however, there exist a multiplicity of more specific research questions about how this expansive vision is most productively implemented in tutorial dialogue. Many local decisions must be made in the course of a negotiation that influence the direction that negotiation will take. Examples include which evidence to select as supporting evidence, which alternative design choice or prediction to argue in favor of, or when to challenge a student versus when to let the student move on. When the goal is to encourage exploration of a space of alternatives rather than to lead the student to a pre-determined conclusion, then there are many potential answers to all of these questions. Thus, we will explore the relative pedagogical effectiveness of alternative strategies for using negotiation in different contexts. Part of our immediate plans for future work is to explore this space using a machine learning based optimization approach such as reinforcement learning a [30] or Genetic Programming [17]. The learned knowledge will be encoded in the discourse model that guides the management of DReSDeN's multi-threaded discourse history.

In the KCD approach to dialogue management [27], student answers that do not express a correct answer to a tutor query are treated as wrong answers. Thus, one challenge in expanding from a highly directed, tutor dominated approach to dialogue management to a mixed-initiative one is to distinguish the cases where the student is taking the initiative from the cases where the student's answer is wrong. Thus, we began our explorations of machine learning approaches to adapting DReSDeN's behavior by addressing the problem of distinguishing between student answers to tutor questions and student initiatives. We used as data the complete transcripts from 5 students' corresponding with human tutors over a typed, chat interface, while working on a rankine cycle optimization problem. Altogether, the corpus contains 484 student contributions, 59 of which were marked as student initiatives by a human coder. We considered as student initiatives unsolicited observations, predictions, suggestions, and questions (apart from hedges [3]).

We used Ripper [6] as a classification algorithm to learn rules for distinguishing student initiatives from direct answers based on the bag of words present in the student contribution. The initial results were discouraging, yielding only a 10% reduction in error rate over the initial baseline error rate of 12.2% that would be obtained by consistently assigning the majority class. However, we noticed that the difficulty seemed to arise from trouble learning rules to distinguish hedges from true questions. Thus, in a second round of experimentation, we used Ripper again to distinguish student contributions that were either initiatives or hedges from other contributions. This time there was a 17.6% baseline error rate. In a 10 fold cross-validation evaluation, Ripper was able to learn rules to reduce this error rate to 5.8%, roughly one third of the baseline error rate. Furthermore, a simple heuristic of considering complete sentences to be true questions and fragments to be hedges yielded an accuracy of 82% over all student questions, and 87% over the full set of initiatives+hedges. Our encouraging preliminary results demonstrate that very simple techniques can make significant headway towards solving this important problem. We expect to be able to achieve better performance than this in practice since students tend not to use hedges with tutorial dialogue systems [3], and since the dialogue context normally provides strong expectations for student answers that can be used to unambiguously determine that correct answers constitute direct answers rather than initiatives.

5 Conclusion and Current Directions

In this paper we have introduced the DReSDeN tutorial dialogue manager as an extension to the APE tutorial dialogue planner used in our previous research. We currently have a working prototype implementation of the DReSDeN. We are continuing to collect Wizard-of-Oz data in the thermodynamics domain, which we plan to use as the foundation for building our domain specific knowledge sources and for continued machine learning experiments as described.

Acknowledgements. This project is supported by ONR Cognitive and Neural Sciences Division, Grant number N000140410107.

References

1. Aleven V., Koedinger, K. R., & Popescu, O.: A Tutorial Dialogue System to Support Self-Explanation: Evaluation and Open Questions. Proceedings of the 11th International Conference on Artificial Intelligence in Education, AI-ED (2003).
2. Baker, M.: A Model for Negotiation in Teaching-Learning Dialigues, International Journal of AI in Education, 5(2), pp 199-254, (1994).
3. Bhatt, K., Evens, M. & Argamon, S.: Hedged Responses and Expressions of Affect in Human/Human and Human/Computer Tutorial Interactions, Proceedings of the Cognitive Science Society (2004).
4. Bohlin, P., Cooper, R., Engdahl, E., Larsson, S.: Information states and dialogue move engines. In Alexandersson, J. (Ed.) IJCAI-99 Workshop on Knowledge and Reasoning in Practical Dialogue Systems, (1999) pp 25-32.
5. Chu-Carroll, J., Carberry, S.: Conflict resolution in collaborative planning dialogues. *International Journal of Human-Computer Studies*, 53(6):969-1015. (2000)
6. Cohen, W.: Fast Effective Rule Induction. *Machine Learning: Proceedings of the Twelfth International Conference.* (1995)
7. Collins, A., Brown, J. S., Newman, S. E.: Cognitive Apprenticeship: Teaching the Crafts of Reading, Writing, and Mathematics, in L. B. Resnick (Ed..) *Knowing, Learning, And Instruction: Essays in Honor of Robert Glaser*, (1989) Hillsdale: Lawrence Earlbaum Associates.
8. Core, M. G., Moore, J. D., & Zinn, C.: The Role of Initiative in Tutorial Dialogue, in *Proceedings of the 10th Conference of the European Chapter of the Association for Computational Linguistics.* (2003)
9. Di Eugenio, B., Jordan, P., Thomason, R., Moore, J.: The Acceptance Cycle: An empirical investigation of human-human collaborative dialogues, *International Journal of Human Computer Studies.* 53(6), (2000) 1017-1076.
10. Evens, M. and Michael, J.: *One-on-One Tutoring by Humans and Machines*, (2003) Lawrence Earlbaum and Associates.
11. Forbus, K. D., Whalley, P. B., Evrett, J. O., Ureel, L., Brokowski, M., Baher, J., Kuehne, S. E.: CyclePad: An Articulate Virtual Laboratory for Engineering Thermodynamics. Artificial Intelligence 114(1-2): (1999) 297-347.
12. Freedman, R.: Using a Reactive Planner as the Basis for a Dialogue Agent, *Proceedings of FLAIRS 2000*, (2000) Orlando.
13. Graesser, A., Moreno, K. N., Marineau, J. C.: AutoTutor Improves Deep Learning of Computer Literacy: Is It the Dialog or the Talking Head? *Proceedings of AI in Education* (2003)
14. Graesser, A., VanLehn, K., the TRG, & the NLT: *Why2 Report: Evaluation of Why/Atlas, Why/AutoTutor, and Accomplished Human Tutors on Learning Gains for Qualitative Physics Problems and Explanations*, LRDC Tech Report, (2002) University of Pittsburgh.
15. Heeman, P. and Hirst, G.: Collaborating on Referring Expressions. Computational Linguistics, 21(3), (1995) 351-382.
16. Jordan, P., Rosé, C. P., & VanLehn, K.: Tools for Authoring Tutorial Dialogue Knowledge. In J. D. Moore, C. L. Redfield, & W. L. Johnson (Eds.), Artificial Intelligence in Education: AI-ED in the Wired and Wireless Future, Proceedings of AI-ED 2001 (pp. 222-233). (2001) Amsterdam, IOS Press.
17. Koza, J.: *Genetic Programming: On the programming of computers by means of natural selection*, (1992) Bradford Books.

18. Kuhn, D.: A developmental model of critical thinking. *Educational Researcher*. 28(2), (1999) pp 16-26.
19. Larsson, S. & Traum, D.: Information state dialogue management in the trindi dialogue move engine toolkit. NLE Special Issue on Best Practice in Spoken Language Dialogue Systems Engineering, (2000) pp 323-340.
20. Larsson, S.: Issue-based Dialogue Management, PhD Dissertation, Department of Linguistics, Goeteberg University, Sweden (2002)
21. Larsson, S.: Issues Under Negotiation, Proceedings of SIGDIAL 2002.
22. Levin, J. A. ; Moore, J. A.: 'Dialogue-Games: Meta-communication Structures for Natural Language Interaction'. Cognitive Science, 1 (4), (1980) 395-420.
23. Lewin, I.: Limited Enquiry Negotiation Dialogues, Proceedings of Eurospeech (2001).
24. McAlister, S. R.: Argumentation and a Design for Learning, CALRG Report No. 197, (2001) The Open University
25. Pilkington, R. M., Hartley, J. R., Hintze, D., Moore, D.: Learning to Argue and Arguing to Learn: An interface for computer-based dialogue games. International Journal of Artificial Intelligence in Education, 3(3), (1992) pp 275-85.
26. Rosé, C. P., Di Eugenio, B., Levin, L. S., Van Ess-Dykema, C.: Discourse Processing of Dialogues with Multiple Threads, Proceedings of the Association for Computational Linguistics (1995).
27. Rosé, C. P., Jordan, P., Ringenberg, M., Siler, S., VanLehn, K., & Weinstein, A.: Interactive Conceptual Tutoring in Atlas-Andes, In J. D. Moore, C. L. Redfield, & W. L. Johnson (Eds.), Artificial Intelligence in Education: AI-ED in the Wired and Wireless Future, Proceedings of AI-ED 2001 (pp. 256-266). (2001) Amsterdam, IOS Press.
28. Rosé, C. P., Roque, A., Bhembe, D., VanLehn, K.: A Hybrid Text Classification Approach for Analysis of Student Essays, Proceedings of the HLT-NAACL 03 Workshop on Educational Applications of NLP (2003).
29. Rosé, C. P., Aleven, V. & Torrey, C.: CycleTalk: Supporting Reflection in Design Scenarios With Negotiation Dialogue, CHI Workshop on the Designing for the Reflective Practitioner (2004).
30. Sutton, R. S., & Barto, A. G.: Reinforcement Learning: An Introduction. (1989) The MIT Press: Cambridge, MA.
31. Traum, D., Bos, R., Cooper, R., Larsson, S., Lewin, I, Mattheson, C., & Poesio, M.: A model of dialogue moves and information state revision. (2000) Technical Report D2.1, Trindi.
32. VanLehn, K., Jordan, P., Rosé, C. P., and The Natural Language Tutoring Group: The Architecture of Why2-Atlas: a coach for qualitative physics essay writing, Proceedings of the Intelligent Tutoring Systems Conference, (2002) Biarritz, France.
33. Zinn, C., Moore, J. D., & Core, M. G.: A 3-Tier Planning Architecture for Managing Tutorial Dialogue. In S. A. Cerri, G. Gouardères, & F. Paraguaçu (Eds.), Proceedings of the Sixth International Conference on Intelligent Tutoring Systems, ITS 2002 (pp. 574-584). Berlin: Springer Verlag, (2002).

Combining Computational Models of Short Essay Grading for Conceptual Physics Problems

M.J. Ventura, D.R. Franchescetti, P. Pennumatsa, A.C. Graesser, G.T. Jackson, X. Hu, Z. Cai, and the Tutoring Research Group

Institute for Intelligent Systems
Memphis, TN 38152, (901) 678-2364,
{mventura,dfrncsch,ppenumts,a-graesser,gtjackn,xhu,zcai}
@memphis.edu
http://www.iismemphis.org

Abstract. The difficulties of grading essays with natural language processing tools are addressed. The present project investigated the effectiveness of combining multiple measures of text similarity to grade essays on conceptual physics problems. Latent semantic analysis (LSA) and a new text similarity metric called Union of Word Neighbors (UWN) were used with other measures to predict expert grades. It appears that the best strategy for grading essays is to use student derived ideal answers and statistical models that accommodate inferences. LSA and the UWN gave near equivalent performance in predicting expert grades when student derived ideal answers served as a comparison for student answers. However, if ideal expert answers are used, explicit symbolic models involving word matching are more suitable to predict expert grades. This study identified some computational constraints on models of natural language processing in intelligent tutoring systems.

1 Introduction

Traditional measures of user modeling in intelligent tutoring systems have not depended on an analysis of the meaning of natural language and discourse. However, natural language understanding has progressed dramatically in recent years with the development of automated essay graders [5] and tutorial dialogue in natural language [6], [8].

One challenge in building natural language understanding modules has been the extension of mainstream representational systems to capture text similarity and the correctness of the text with respect to some ideal rubric. One framework that has been successful in meeting this challenge is Latent Semantic Analysis [10], [13]. Latent Semantic Analysis (LSA) is a statistical language understanding technique that constructs relations among words from the analysis of a large corpus of written text. Word meanings are represented as vectors whereas sentence or essay meanings are linear combinations of the word vectors. Similarity between two texts is measured by the cosine between the corresponding two vectors. The input to LSA is a corpus that is segmented into documents, which are typically paragraphs or sentences. A large word-document matrix is formed from the corpus, based on the occurrences of the

J.C. Lester et al. (Eds.): ITS 2004, LNCS 3220, pp. 423–431, 2004.

words in the documents. Singular value decomposition, a technique similar to factor analysis, then builds relationships between words that were not directly captured in the original texts. The metrics of similarity between words (A and B) are not derived by simple contiguity frequencies between A and B, by co-occurrence counts between A and B in the documents, or by correlations in usage, but instead depend on dimensionality reduction to "infer" deeper relations [12], [13].

The fact that LSA can handle such large amounts of information helps give it the capability to represent semantic meaning and world knowledge. One of its salient successes is that it can be used to grade essays with performance equal to human professionals [5]. It has been shown that LSA-based essay graders assign grades as reliably as experts in composition, even when the essays are not well-formed grammatically or semantically [5]. Foltz et al [5] and Landauer et al. [13] analyzed essays covering several topics (the heart, introductory psychology, the Panama Canal, and tolerance of diversity in America) and reported that that the correlation between LSA's score and an average human score was no different from the inter-rater reliability between human scorers. Foltz has taken this process one step further by having students write essays using the web and having LSA grade the submitted essays. If the student was not satisfied with the grade, LSA provided feedback on the type of information that was lacking so the student could rewrite the essay for a better grade. The students' first essays had an average grade of 85% while their final revision's average grade was 92%. Thus, Foltz's intelligent essay grader using LSA was able to detect what information was absent when compared with an ideal essay, to provide feedback, and to accurately assess the improved essay [5]. These results suggest that LSA is able to capture some representation of meaning and that this representation has some correspondence to human graders.

LSA metrics have also performed a reasonable job in tracking the coverage of expectations and the identification of misconceptions in AutoTutor, a tutoring system that interacts with learners with conversational dialogue in natural language [8], [10]. LSA has not only proven successful for user modeling during the dynamic, turn by turn dialogue of AutoTutor, but also for essay grading during post-test evaluation [16].

Although LSA has shown impressive performance for long essays of 200 or more words, the performance on shorter essays has been somewhat problematic [13]. Correlations generally increase as the length of the text increases, showing correlations as high as .73 in research conducted at other labs [5]. Conversely, we found the correlation between LSA and expert raters to range from r = .31 to .50 in our analysis of short essay grading for conceptual physics problems [6] and answers to questions about computer literacy [16]. In light of the challenges of grading short essays, the present study examined a variety of methods to evaluate the correctness of student essays on conceptual physics problems.

1.1 Convergent Measures to Evaluate Essay Correctness for Physics

What do humans do when grading essays and how might different natural language understanding tools model these processes? Consider the following example:

STUDENT ANSWER: *The egg will land behind where the unicycle touches the ground. The force of gravity and air resistance will slow the egg down.*

EXPERT ANSWER: *The egg will land beside the wheel, which is the point where the unicycle touches the ground. The egg has the same horizontal velocity as the unicycle when it is released.*

Many of the same words appear in both answers, yet a human expert grader assigned this particular answer an F for being too ambiguous. The correct answer says that the egg will land beside the wheel whereas the student answer incorrectly says it lands behind the wheel. Therefore, word similarity can only solve part of the puzzle. In order to properly evaluate correctness, a human or computer system needs to consider the relationship between the two passages beyond their word similarities, to consider the surrounding context of each individual word, and to consider combinations of words.

We need to address several questions when measuring how well the content of the student answer matches the correct answer. Two questions are particularly under focus in the present research. One question is what comparison benchmark to use when grading essays. The vocabulary used by experts may be somewhat different from students, so we examined both expert answers and good student answers as comparison gold standards. The second question is whether it is worthwhile to combine different natural language understanding metrics of similarity in an attempt achieve more accurate prediction of expert grades. Multiple measures of text quality and similarity may yield a better approximation of the contextual meaning of an essay.

The primary techniques we investigated in the present study were LSA, an alternative corpus-based model called the Union of Word Neighbors (UWN) model, and word overlap between essay and answer. It is conceivable that simple word overlap (including all words) may be superior to LSA. The high frequency words may be extremely important in judging correctness. For instance, if the correct answer is *"the pumpkin will land behind the runner"* and the student answers is *"the pumpkin will land beside the runner"*, LSA and UWN will judge this comparison to be quit high because *behind* and *beside* are highly related in LSA; however, simple word matching will identify no relationship between these two words. On the other hand, LSA and UWN can abstract information inferentially from the essay, so they provide relevant information beyond word matching.

2 Union of Word Neighbors (UNW)

In the UNW model, semantic information for any given word *w* is the pooled words that co-occur with that word *w* in the set of sentences with word *w* in the corpus. This pool of words is called the *neighborhood* set; it includes all words that co-occur with the target word *w*. These words are assumed to be related to the target word and serve as the basis for all associations. The neighborhood intersection is the relation that occurs when two target words share similar co-occurrences with other words. Similar to LSA, two words (A and B) become associated by virtue of their occurrence with many of the same third-party words. For example, *food* and *eat* may become associated because they both occur with words such as *hungry* and *table*. Therefore, the neighborhood set ***N*** for any word *w* is the only information we have, based on the exemplar sentences for words in the corpus.

2.1 Neighbor Weights

The neighborhood set for any word is intended to represent the meaning of a word from a corpus. But there were several theoretical challenges that arose when we developed the model. One challenge was how to differentially weight neighborhood words. We assigned *neighborhood weights* to each neighborhood word *n* of word *w* according to Equation (1).

$$\lambda_{n|w} = \frac{f(n \mid w)}{\sqrt{f(w)f(n)}} \tag{1}$$

The expression $f(n|w)$ designates the frequency of occurrence of the neighbor word *n* to target word *w*. Additionally, $f(n)$ is the total frequency of the neighbor word *n*, and $f(w)$ is the total frequency of the target word *w*. This formula essentially restricts the weights for the neighbor words as being between 0 and 1 in most cases. It follows that the weighting function was aimed at giving more importance to words that consistently co-occur and less importance to words that occur frequently in the corpus. Additionally, rare co-occurrences may be given low weights because they do not consistently co-occur with the target word. Each occurrence of a neighbor to a target word is also weighted by an inverse proportion of its physical distance to the target word position in each sentence; this assumption is similar to the Hyperspace Analogue for Language (HAL) [3]. Weightings are calculated by the inverse of the difference between the cardinal position of the target word from the position of the neighbor. For example, if a neighbor is 3 words away from a target word in a sentence, the calculation would be 1/3.

Some assumptions had to be made in order to build relevant associations to target words. The next section will explain the procedures of the algorithm written to perform these operations.

2.2 Neighborhood Intersection Algorithm

In order to construct the neighborhood set for a word, we explored an algorithm that pooled all words *N* that co-occurred with the target word *w*. Our subject matter was conceptual physics so we used a corpus consisting of the textbook *Conceptual Physics* [11]. Each sentence in the corpus served as the context for direct co-occurrence. So for the entire set of sentences $(s_1 ... s_C)$ that contain target word *w*, every unique word in sentences $(s_1 ... s_C)$ was pooled into the neighborhood set *N*. For example, the neighborhood of *velocity* included *force, acceleration,* and *mass* because these words frequently occur in the same sentences that *velocity* occurs in. This represents the neighborhood *N* of each target word *w*. Each word in the set $(n_1 ... n_K)$ of *N* is weighted by the function described in Equation 1.

Combining word neighbors to capture essay meanings. In order to capture the meaning of the essay, a neighborhood is formed that is a linear combination of individual word neighbors that get pooled into *N*. To evaluate the relation between any two essays N_1 and N_2, we applied the following algorithmic procedure:

1. Pool neighborhood sets for each word w in each essay, computing the weights for all the neighbors for each word in an essay using Equation 1.
2. Add all neighbors' weights for each word in each essay into N_1 (i.e. pooled neighbors for essay 1) and N_2 (i.e. pooled neighbors for essay 2).
3. Calculate neighborhood intersection as in Equation 2.

$$\frac{\sum_{n\in N_1 \cap N_2}\left(\lambda_{n|w_1} + \lambda_{n|w_2}\right)}{\sum_{n\in N_1 \cup N_2}\left(\lambda_{n|w_1} + \lambda_{n|w_2}\right)} \tag{2}$$

The numerator is the summation of neighbor weights over the intersection of the neighborhood sets (N_1 and N_2) whereas the denominator is the summation of neighbor weights over the union of the two neighborhood sets (i.e., λ is equal to the neighbor weight in each essay). This formula produces a value between 0 and 1. In the next section we will discuss the performance of this model on essay grading.

3 AutoTutor and Essays

AutoTutor is a learning environment that tutors students by holding a conversation in natural language [6], [8]. AutoTutor has been developed for Newtonian qualitative physics and computer literacy. AutoTutor's design was inspired by explanation-based constructivist theories of learning [2], [14] intelligent tutoring systems that adaptively respond to student knowledge [1], [15] and empirical research on dialogue patterns in tutorial discourse [4], [9]. AutoTutor presents challenging problems (formulated in questions) from a curriculum script and then engages in mixed initiative dialogue that guides the student in building an answer. It provides feedback to the student on what the student types in (positive, neutral, negative feedback), pumps the student for more information, prompts the student to fill in missing words, gives hints, fills in missing information with assertions, identifies and corrects erroneous ideas, answers the student's questions, and summarizes answers. AutoTutor has produced learning gains of approximately .70 sigma for deep levels of comprehension [6].

AutoTutor may be viewed as a conversational coach to guide students in preparing essays that solve physics problems or answer questions. Essays are also used to evaluate AutoTutor's learning gains. One of the challenges of evaluating learning gains is how to grade these essays that are created either during the course AutoTutor instruction or during the posttest evaluation. We have previously used experts to grade essays, but our goal is shifting towards automated essay grading to provide immediate feedback to users.

4 Method

The essay questions consisted of 16 deep-level physics problems that tapped various conceptual physics principles. All essays (n = 344) were graded by one physics expert, whose grades were used as the gold standard to evaluate the various measures.

Each essay question had two ideal answers, one created by the expert and one taken randomly from all the student answers that were given an A grade by the expert for each particular problem. The reason why we used ideal student answers was to evaluate the effect of expert versus student wording on grading performance. Although both LSA and UWN build semantic relations beyond the words, it is possible that wording plays an important role in evaluating correctness. Expert wording is somewhat stilted in an academic style whereas student wording is more vernacular.

Additional measures were collected and assessed as possible predictors of essay grades. These included summed verbosity of essay and answer (measured as number of words), word overlap, and the adjective incidence score for each student answer. The adjective incidence score is the number of adjectives per 1000 words, which was measured by Coh-Metrix [7]. Coh-Metrix is a web facility that analyzes texts on approximately 200 measures of language, world knowledge, cohesion and discourse. The adjective incidence score was the only measure in Coh-Metrix that significantly correlated with expert grades and was not redundant with our other measures (i.e., LSA, UWN, verbosity, word overlap). The adjective incidence score captures the extent to which the student precisely refers to noun referents. The verbosity measure was included because there is evidence that longer essays receive higher grades [5]. Word overlap captures the extent to which the verbatim articulation of the ideal information is captured in the student essay. The word overlap score is a proportion of words shared by the ideal and student essay divided by the total number of words in both the ideal essay and the student essay.

4.1 Results and Discussion

Tables 1 and 2 show correlation matrices for the different measures using student ideal essays versus expert essays. The variables in each correlation matrix were UWN, LSA, word overlap, verbosity, and adjective incidence score. All correlations of .13 or higher were statistically significant at $p < .05$, two tailed.

A number of trends emerged in the data analysis. Use of the ideal student answers yielded somewhat better performance than the ideal expert answers for both LSA and UWN. LSA, UWN, and word overlap all performed relatively the same in predicting expert grades when using ideal student answers, $r \approx .42$ (.44, .43, and .41 for UWN, LSA, and keyword, respectively). UWN and LSA correlations decreased when using ideal expert answers. There also were large correlations between LSA, UWN, and word overlap, which suggests that theses measures explain much of the same variance of the expert ratings. Multiple regression analyses were conducted to assess the significance of each individual measure and their combined contributions. Table 3 shows two forced-entry multiple regression analyses performed with all measures on ideal expert answers and ideal student answers. The two multiple regression equations were statistically significant, with $R^2 = .20$ of the variance explained for expert answers and $R^2 = .33$ for ideal student answers. As can be seen in these tables of results, word overlap and adjective incidence were significant when ideal expert answers served as the comparison benchmark, whereas LSA, UWN, verbosity, and adjective incidence were significant when the ideal student answers served as the comparison benchmark. Therefore, it appears that LSA and UWN are not appropriate measures when comparing student essays to expert ideal answers. Expert answers are apparently more abstract, precise, and stilted than the students. Experts express principles of physics (e.g., According to Newton's third law...) with words that can not be easily substituted in student answers (i.e., no other word can be used to describe "Newton's third law"). However, when ideal student essays are used as a benchmark, LSA and UWN more accurately predict grades perhaps because of the more vernacular wording or because of the possible substitutability of words in ideal student answers. Therefore, it apparently is easier for LSA and UWN to detect isomorphically correct answers using student ideal essays than ideal expert answers.

Table 1. Correlations Using Student Essays and Ideal Expert Answers.

	Rating	Word overlap	Verbosity	LSA	UWN
Word overlap	.40				
Verbosity	.18	.27			
LSA	.36	.75	.23		
UWN	.30	.67	.45	.46	
Adjective incidence	.29	.37	.10	.31	.26

Table 2. Correlations Using Student Essays and Ideal Student Answers.

	Rating	Word overlap	Verbosity	LSA	UWN
Word overlap	.42				
Verbosity	.32	.14			
LSA	.43	.75	.13		
UWN	.46	.73	.33	.59	
Adjective incidence	.29	.17	.04	.26	.23

Table 3. Regression Betas for all measures using Ideal Expert and Student Answers to predict grades.

	Standardized Coefficients (Expert answers)	*t*-value	Standardized Coefficients (Student answers)	*t*-value
	Beta		Beta	
(Constant)		.471		-2.182 *
Word overlap	.223	2.461 *	.090	1.020
Verbosity	.080	1.440	.227	4.658 *
UWN	.014	.186	.174	2.406 *
LSA	.119	1.632 *	. 184	2.470 *
Adjective incidence	.168	3.155 *	.196	4.120 *

5 General Discussion

Our analysis of student physics essays revealed that the amount of variance explained by our multiple measures of quality was modest, but statistically significant. However, given the difficulties of the predicting correctness of short essays [5], [13] we are encouraged by the results. When inferred semantic similarity plays only a small role in the correctness of an answer, other metrics are needed that can detect similarities and differences between benchmark ideal answers and student answers. This is where word overlap and frequency counts of adjectives become useful; they are sensitive to high frequency words and characteristics of a text that are independent of content words. For example, ideal answers in physics contain specific prepositions (e.g., *behind, beside, across, in*), common polysemous verbs (e.g., *land, fall*), and many adjectives and adverbs (e.g., *greater, less, farther, horizontal, vertical*) that play a large role in the correctness of an essay. The meanings of these words in LSA or UWN may be inaccurate because of their high frequency and similarity of word contexts in the corpus they appear. Conversely, when content words do play a role in the answer (e.g., *net force, mass, acceleration*), similar words can be substituted (e.g., *force, energy, speed*). LSA and UWN are sometimes able to inferentially abstract and relate words that are substitutable to determine similarity.

We explored the importance of using different benchmarks to score essays. This has implications for essay grading as well as the curriculum templates to use in AutoTutor's interactive dialogues. For example, we use LSA to compare student dialogue turns to expert written expectations when we evaluate the correctness of student answers. The results of this study support the conclusion that the use of expert answers alone may not be the best strategy for accurately evaluating student correctness. Instead of only using expert derived answers, it might be more suitable to use student derived explanations, given that the multiple regression model using student ideal answers predicted essay grades more accurately.

Finally, it appears that the UWN model did a moderately good job in predicting grades, on par with LSA. While UWN did not do well when expert ideal answers served as the benchmark, it was a good predictor when ideal student answers served as the benchmark. UWN identifies related words at the sentence level in a corpus, whereas LSA identifies word meanings and relations at the paragraph level in a corpus; so UWN is not be able to abstract all of the relevant information to compare to an ideal expert answer. Nevertheless there are two important benefits of UWN. First, it is a word meaning estimation metric that can create a score online, with no preprocessing needed to calculate word meanings. In the context of intelligent tutor systems, this enables one to add any relevant feedback from students to the corpus that the UWN is using to derive word meanings. This could improve performance of UWN because specific key terms will be given additional meaning from student input. This advantage would be difficult with LSA since the statistical computations require a nontrivial amount of time to derive word meanings. Any added information to the corpus would result in a new analysis. Therefore, UWN warrants more investigation as a metric for text comparison because of its dynamic capability of updating its representation, as AutoTutor learns from experience.

Acknowledgments. This research was supported by the National Science Foundation (REC 0106965, ITR 0325428), the Department of Defense Multidisciplinary University Research Initiative (MURI) administered by ONR under grant N00014-00-1-0600, and the Institute for Education Sciences (IES R3056020018-02). Any opinions, findings, and conclusions or recommendations expressed in this material are those of the authors and do not necessarily reflect the views of NSF, DoD, ONR, or IES.

References

1. Anderson, J. R., Corbett, A. T., Koedinger, K. R., & Pelletier, R. (1995). Cognitive tutors: Lessons learned. *The Journal of the Learning Sciences, 4,* 167-207.

2. Aleven V. & Koedinger, K. R. (2002). An effective metacognitive strategy: Learning by doing and explaining with a computer-based Cognitive Tutor. *Cognitive Science, 26*. 147-179.
3. Burgess, C. (1998). From simple associations to the building blocks of language: Modeling meaning in memory with the HAL model. *Behavior Research Methods, Instruments, & Computers, 30,* 188 - 198.
4. Chi, M. T. H., Siler, S. A., Jeong, H., Yamauchi, T. & Hausmann, R. G. (2001). Learning from human tutoring. *Cognitive Science*, *25*, 471-533.
5. Foltz, P.W., Gilliam, S., & Kendall, S. (2000). Supporting content-based feedback in online writing evaluation with LSA. *Interactive Learning Environments, 8*, 111-128.
6. Graesser, A.C., Lu, S., Jackson, G.T., Mitchell, H., Ventura, M., Olney, A., & Louwerse, M.M. (in press). AutoTutor: A tutor with dialogue in natural language. *Behavioral Research Methods, Instruments, and Computers.*
7. Graesser, A.C., McNamara, D.S., Louwerse, M.M., & Cai, Z. (in press). Coh-Metrix: Analysis of text on cohesion and language. *Behavioral Research Methods, Instruments, and Computers.*
8. Graesser, A.C., Person, N., Harter, D., & TRG (2001). Teaching tactics and dialog in AutoTutor. *International Journal of Artificial Intelligence in Education*, 12, 257-279.
9. Graesser, A.C., Person, N.K., & Magliano, J.P. (1995). Collaborative dialogue patterns in naturalistic one-on-one tutoring. *Applied Cognitive Psychology*, 9, 359-387.
10. Graesser, A.C., Wiemer-Hastings, P., Wiemer-Hastings, K., Harter, D., Person, N., & Tutoring Research Group (2000). Using latent semantic analysis to evaluate the contributions of students in AutoTutor. *Interactive Learning Environments*, *8*, 129-148.
11. Hewitt, P.G. (1998). *Conceptual physics* (8th edition). Reading, MA: Addison-Wesley.
12. Landauer, T. K., & Dumais, S. T. (1997) A solution to Plato's problem: The latent semantic analysis theory of acquisition, induction, and representation of knowledge. *Psychological Review, 104*, 211-240.
13. Landauer, T.K., Foltz, P.W., & Laham, D. (1998). An introduction to latent semantic analysis. *Discourse Processes*, 25, 259-284.
14. VanLehn, K., Jones, R. M. & Chi, M. T. H. (1992). A model of the self- explanation effect. *Journal of the Learning Sciences, 2*(1), pp. 1-60.
15. VanLehn, K., Lynch, C., Taylor, L.,Weinstein, A., Shelby, R., Schulze, K., Treacy, D., & Wintersgill, M. (2002). In S. A. Cerri, G. Gouarderes, & F. Paraguacu (Eds.), *Intelligent Tutoring Systems 2002* (pp. 367-376). Berlin, Germany: Springer.
16. Wiemer-Hastings, P., Wiemer-Hastings, K., and Graesser, A. (1999). Improving an intelligent tutor's comprehension of students with Latent Semantic Analysis. In S.P. Lajoie and M. Vivet, *Artificial Intelligence in Education* (pp. 535-542). Amsterdam: IOS Press.

From Human to Automatic Summary Evaluation

Iraide Zipitria[1,2], Jon Ander Elorriaga[2], Ana Arruarte[2], and Arantza Diaz de Ilarraza[2]

[1] Developmental and Educational Psychology Department
[2] Languages and Information Systems Department
University of the Basque Country (UPV/EHU)
649 P.K., E-20080 Donostia
{iraide,elorriaga,arruarte,jipdisaa}@si.ehu.es

Abstract. One of the goals remaining in Intelligent Tutoring Systems is to create applications to evaluate open-ended text in a human-like manner. The aim of this study is to produce the design for a fully automatic summary evaluation system that could stand for human-like summarisation assessment. In order to gain this goal, an empirical study has been carried out to identify underlying cognitive processes. The studied sample is compound by 15 expert raters on summary evaluation with different professional backgrounds in education. Pearson's correlation has been calculated to see inter-rater agreement level and stepwise linear regression to observe predicting variables and weights. In addition, interviews with subjects provided qualitative information that could not be acquired numerically. Based on this research, a design of a fully automatic summary evaluation environment has been described.

1 Introduction

One of the goals remaining in Intelligent Tutoring Systems (ITSs) is to create applications that are able to evaluate open-ended text in a human-like manner. But, is it really possible? In the context of ITSs, human knowledge evaluation has traditionally been measured using close-ended methods. Based on a pre-established answer system, this evaluation has the advantage of being countable, hence assures the possibility of a more objective assessment. Nonetheless, it involves a greater probability of scoring by chance and restricts the richness of students' responses. Therefore, it produces a pre-established and limited student-tutor communication.

Moreover, open-ended evaluation methods assess free text or text written in natural language. Open-ended methods provide the sort of information that is not possible to detect in the previous scenario. Free text contains more accurate information on students' real knowledge. But unfortunately it is not countable and it is hard to produce an inter-rater homogeneous evaluation. There are environments that allow assessment of open-ended written communication. Those are very flexible and offer the possibility of a richer answer; dialogue systems, free text assessment, etc. But, due to the complexity of reproducing teachers' domain knowledge it is complicated to evaluate free text automatically. Recent developments in NLP (Natural Language Processing) make possible domain dependant free text assessment [1,2,3,11,12,13,15].

J.C. Lester et al. (Eds.): ITS 2004, LNCS 3220, pp. 432–442, 2004.

The work here presented adds further efforts in automatic free text evaluation with the design of a model to evaluate summaries automatically. A first step has been working towards the development of a model of summarisation evaluation based on expert knowledge that could stand for almost any users. In order to gain this goal, a cognitive study of teacher and lecturer's evaluation procedure has been run. This study has taken into consideration three main problem groups on summary evaluation: second language (L2), immature and mature summarisers. Finally, once human cognition has been observed and taking into account needs of experts in different contexts, we have placed the basis of the design of the automatic summary evaluation environment

The paper starts with a brief description of related work. Then, there are insights and data analysis of human summary evaluation. Next, design issues of LEA, as an automatic summary evaluation environment are presented. Finally, the paper closes with conclusions and future perspectives.

2 Related Work

Summary is the most common method to evaluate human comprehension on a given theme or text. Thus far, there are two systems that have been able to assess summaries automatically: SS, Summary Street [5] and SEE, Summary Evaluation Environment [8].

Summary Street [5], is a summary assessment tool to train students in summarisation abilities. It is focused on human evaluation and provides global scores and feedback on coherence, cohesion and reiteration. It does not intend to substitute teachers, but to provide a working environment to students that want to gain summarisation skills. The system is created to give immediate feedback on summaries. It provides measures on: spelling, summary length, overall score, section coverage, etc. SS is a good environment for students to train their summarisation abilities once and again, obtaining instant feedback. It is mainly thought for children.

SEE [8], is a summary evaluation system that provides scores in grammaticality, coherence and cohesion. The smallest unit of evaluation is the sentence. Evaluation metrics are calculated in terms of recall, coverage, retention and weighted retention and precision and pseudo precision. Content coverage is analysed using N-gram models to predict oncoming words based on the previous word co-occurrence history [10]. For each document or document set an ideal summary is created. In addition, there are various baseline summaries. NIST (National Institute of Standards & Technology) used SEE to provide an interface to judge content and quality of automatically produced summaries. The final goal was to measure grammaticality, cohesion and coherence categorizing as all, most, some, hardy any or none (equivalent to 100%, 80%, 60%, 40%, 20% and 0% in DUC 2001).

SEE is mainly focused on the evaluation of automatically generated summaries and produce little information on summarisers' performance. According to [8], it seems clear that automatic evaluation should match human assessment. But how do humans evaluate summaries? The next study was run to answer this question.

3 Data and Insights from Human Summary Evaluation

The roots of this study are placed on the experience of teacher and lecturers in practice. The final goal is to be able to provide a system that matches as much as possible the requirements on summarisation evaluation of our experts. The requirement, on one hand, was to identify the environments where summarisation assessment occurs, and on the other, the behaviour that summary raters show when evaluating.

3.1 Subjects

Overall, there were 15 experts on summary evaluation: five secondary school teachers, five second language (L2) teachers of Basque and five university lecturers. Most of them were working in different educational contexts and did not know each other.

3.2 Methodology

The experiment included a booklet of five summaries to be evaluated and an interview on evaluation procedure. Booklet summaries were previously obtained from primary, secondary, L2 and university students. Finally, five of them were chosen for evaluation purposes. The first summary (S1) was written by a secondary education student who had produced the summary selecting several sentences of the read text. The second summary (S2) was written by a L2 student of Basque, the third (S3) was summarised by another secondary education student, the forth (S4) was produced by a university student and finally the fifth (S5) by another L2 student of Basque. Raters did not have any information on the summary writer's background or identity.

Summaries were rated on a 0 to 10 scale producing measures on overall score and partial scores in cohesion, coherence, language, adequacy and comprehension. Those partial evaluation measure variables were chosen as a consequence of the interviews with experts, and taking into account reports on teaching and evaluation procedure of free text in Basque primary and secondary education [4]. In addition, subjects had the chance of writing comments in the text or explaining any further information that they found relevant and could not express otherwise.

3.3 Results and Discussion

Results show that S4 was overall rated highest and S2 lowest. S2, S3 and S5 showed a very similar overall evaluation and S1 were rated highest among the non-mature summarisers. A graphic representation of overall and partial score means can be seen in figure 1. Lowest scores in language are produced by the two L2 student summaries (S2, S5). An underlying score is found in S2 that is the lowest score in language and highest in comprehension.

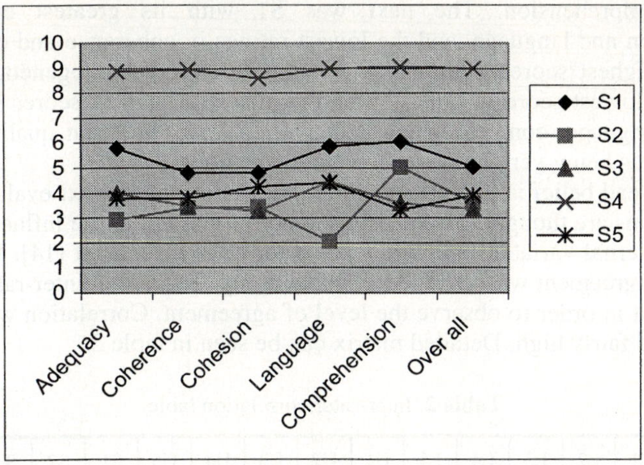

Fig. 1. Summary score mean graph.

The subjects found out that S1 was copied from the text. Some of them even suggested that they scored the summary far too high for a plagiarized summary. Therefore, the result is very much influenced by the rater's kindness in the given moment. Further comments in each summary ratings can be seen in table 1.

Table 1. Summary of qualitative evaluation.

	Primary & secondary education teachers	L2 learning teachers	University lecturers
S1 (Secondary School)	It lacks objectivity. Copies from the reading.	Copies unconnected sentences from the text.	Sentences taken from the text. It has been copied.
S2 (L2)	Seems to understand but produces poor language.	Very poor. Expression is so poor that its value is reduced.	Many orthography errors. It shows very bad writing.
S3 (Secondary School)	Information missing. Low comprehension. Reiteration and unfinished sentences.	Does not understand the text and could not write a good summary. Information missing.	Too short. Reiterated sentences. Many ideas missing.
S4 (University.)	Good text comprehension and text structure. Too long sentences and some reiterations.	Well understood and expressed. Good.	Good.
S5 (L2)	He/she seems to understand but shows great language difficulties.	Poor.	Ungrammatical sentences. It seems a free interpretation.

Overall, S1 got a score-mean of 5.4, S2 produced an overall score mean of 3.4, S3 scored 3.7, S4 got a score of 8.9 and finally S5 got a score of 3.9. The lowest score was produced by S2, having the lowest evaluation in language and highest in comprehension. This result was followed by S3 with the lowest score in cohesion and highest in language. Then, S5 had its greatest values in cohesion and language and worst in comprehension. The next was S1 with its greatest evaluations in comprehension and language, and the lowest ratings in coherence and cohesion. And finally, the highest scored summary was S4 with a very homogeneous evaluation, obtaining its lowest score in cohesion and similar and highest scores for adequacy, coherence, language, comprehension and overall score. Its main quality apart from high scores was being very homogeneous in evaluations.

A well spread belief is that there is little agreement on free text evaluation. Due to this, evaluations are thought to be highly subjective and under the influence of a great amount of external variables and with little inter-rater agreement [14]. We wanted to see if this disagreement was to be found in our study. Therefore, inter-rater correlation was calculated in order to observe the level of agreement. Correlation was significant ($P < 0.01$) and fairly high. Detailed matrix can be seen in table 2.

Table 2. Inter-rater correlation table.

	L1	L2	L3	L4	L5	U1	U2	U3	U4	U5	S1	S2	S3	S4	S5
L1	1	0.814	0.844	0.887	0.877	0.618	0.925	0.715	0.939	0.618	0.555	0.397	0.695	0.697	0.917
L2	0.814	1	0.756	0.83	0.805	0.602	0.874	0.781	0.825	0.59	0.665	0.614	0.756	0.738	0.746
L3	0.844	0.756	1	0.766	0.966	0.478	0.787	0.699	0.831	0.52	0.438	0.444	0.661	0.646	0.82
L4	0.887	0.83	0.766	1	0.826	0.572	0.908	0.865	0.923	0.74	0.786	0.633	0.781	0.809	0.862
L5	0.877	0.805	0.966	0.826	1	0.472	0.837	0.736	0.859	0.546	0.476	0.461	0.66	0.676	0.87
U1	0.618	0.602	0.478	0.572	0.472	1	0.718	0.516	0.638	0.584	0.613	0.519	0.725	0.6	0.393
U2	0.925	0.874	0.787	0.908	0.837	0.718	1	0.8	0.907	0.688	0.711	0.611	0.826	0.781	0.817
U3	0.715	0.781	0.699	0.865	0.736	0.516	0.8	1	0.752	0.714	0.802	0.784	0.84	0.749	0.74
U4	0.939	0.825	0.831	0.923	0.859	0.638	0.907	0.752	1	0.688	0.64	0.527	0.756	0.798	0.9
U5	0.618	0.59	0.52	0.74	0.546	0.584	0.688	0.714	0.688	1	0.695	0.591	0.698	0.59	0.65
S1	0.555	0.665	0.438	0.786	0.476	0.613	0.711	0.802	0.64	0.695	1	0.843	0.843	0.755	0.477
S2	0.397	0.614	0.444	0.633	0.461	0.519	0.611	0.784	0.527	0.591	0.843	1	0.832	0.652	0.384
S3	0.695	0.756	0.661	0.781	0.66	0.725	0.826	0.84	0.756	0.698	0.843	0.832	1	0.739	0.603
S4	0.697	0.738	0.646	0.809	0.676	0.6	0.781	0.749	0.798	0.59	0.755	0.652	0.739	1	0.674
S5	0.917	0.746	0.82	0.862	0.87	0.393	0.817	0.74	0.9	0.65	0.477	0.384	0.603	0.674	1

Contrary to the common belief on free text evaluation, our experts showed a very high level of agreement. L2 teachers (L) agreed among themselves producing significant correlations that vary from r=0.75 to r=0.96. University lecturers (U) agreed from r=0.51 to r=0.9. Finally, secondary school teachers (S) agreed with r=0.47 to r=0.84. It appeared to be a very high level of agreement that might show underlying stable variables that would enable us to reproduce stable human like evaluation measures. It also needs to be pointed out again that raters in some cases came from different backgrounds and had no connection whatsoever with each other.

In order to observe underlying predicting variables, stepwise multiple linear regression was calculated. Overall score was chosen as the dependant variable and coherence, cohesion, language, adequacy and comprehension were chosen as independent variables. Results explained 89% of the variance as it produced a standardised R^2 =0.89 and showed to be significant $F(1,71)=199.9$; $p< 0.01$. Then, three of the variables were chosen as general predictors by the model: COHERENCE, COMPREHENSION and LANGUAGE. Adequacy and cohesion were excluded. Beta values were 0.47 for coherence, 0.38 for comprehension and 0.16 for language. As a consequence of this modelling, nearly half of the overall score's weight would be given by coherence, more than one third by comprehension and 16% by language.

In addition to quantitative data, qualitative information was taken into account. Different feedback requirements were observed in the studied three groups. These groups were considered for the design of this experiment and for the identification of the context where summary evaluation occurs. After having interviewed our experts, it was concluded that:

Primary & secondary education students go through a stepwise methodology to acquire summarisation strategies. The main goal is to learn how to abstract main concepts from text and at the same time produce the required language abilities to create an acceptable summary. Then, evaluation becomes another step in the process together with summarisation instruction. Assessment is given gradually during the summarisation instruction process itself.

During this assessment process, they use several tools that support summarisation. Important tools are concept maps and schemas that allow selection of main ideas from text. The use of them is considered good training in learning to identify relevant ideas. Additionally, they are also aided with theoretical material on connectors, input in reiteration, input in plagiarism, coherence, cohesion, adequacy, grammar, etc. Teaching is mainly instructive, although cooperative learning, peer-evaluation and self-evaluation are also integrated in the learning process. Assessment is produced stepwise where teachers/instructors will define the evaluation criterion at the beginning and then, students will work to gain this goal by trial and error. Finally, students produce a report about the whole process. This report includes concept maps, schema, connectors, prepositions, etc.

Second language learning students are often mature summarisers that have a lack of language ability in the target language, but good strategies in summarisation methodology. Several studies have shown that second language learners produce poor summaries in the language they are studying but produce mature summaries in their own language [9]. In this case, the problem is different and learning and evaluation strategies vary from the previous case.

When evaluating, the interviewed L2 teachers affirm that first of all they look at main idea identification and then language competence. They distinguish the relevance of these parameters according to ability and language level of students. They have rarely observed any plagiarism among L2 students.

Student support is based on the use of dictionaries, theory of grammar, and concept maps in some cases. Nevertheless, the use of concept maps, in this case, depended on personal criteria. While some of them tend to find this support helpful, other students prefer to rely on their working memory capacity. Furthermore, the use of aid tools vary depending on second language ability, the more proficient the students the closer to native mature summarisers needs. In summary, lower levels focus mainly in grammar while higher levels are more focused in comprehension and style.

In **University** it is assumed that students have proficient language abilities and are mature summarisers. There is not specific training on summarisation at this level. Aid tools are used by students according to their own criteria. Their work is evaluated including summarisation ability but there is no training whatsoever on summarisation.

Thus, these three groups showed different needs in summary production and evaluation. In early stages there is a training period where summarisation methodology is acquired practicing the individual requirements that a summary has through a stepwise process. Then, primary education students learn text comprehension strategies, main idea identification, use of connectors, text transformation, etc. In summary, they gain discursive and abstraction competence.

The L2 group tends frequently to be more heterogeneous. Here, their summarisation abilities depend upon their previous literacy on one hand, and language proficiency on the other. But this second group also requires specific training that does not necessarily match the requirements of the previous group. Finally, the university group does not obtain any instructive training at all. Training, if any, become a more individual matter.

A summary of the support tools used by those groups is shown in table 3.

Table 3. Aid tools on summarisation.

	Primary & secondary education	L2 learning	University
Dictionaries	Sometimes. They often ask unknown terms.	Often. They also ask unknown terms.	Often.
Concept map & schemas	Often used as part of the training process on.	Its use depends on the learner's criteria.	Its use depends on the learner's criteria.
Theory of grammar	Rarely. They tend to ask when confused.	Often in low levels.	Just when certain rules change.
Theory on summarisation	Teachers offer support handouts and lecture-notes on cohesion, coherence, adequacy, etc.	Sometimes support handouts and lecture-notes on cohesion, coherence, adequacy, etc.	None
Sample summaries	Sometimes, they do peer-evaluation exercises and study right and wrongs in summary writing.	Some teachers offer sample summaries as a baseline for students to produce their own ones.	None

In conclusion, despite their diverse background and ignorance on summary writer's details, subjects showed a fairly high level of agreement. Moreover, summary evaluation required assessment strategies that not always matched the profile they were used to. Thus, in spite of the differences, there seems to be a common tendency when evaluating summaries. It seems that behind the level of subjectivity that any decision on free text evaluation may have, there is a high level of inter-rater agreement. Moreover, higher dispersion levels where found on L2 summaries, but according to subjects written reports this behaviour had much to do with different opinions on the level of text comprehension and summarisation abilities on those summaries. Bearing in mind the target group we are facing, this might mean that further studies need to be done on this specific group in order to identify the requirements that would adjust or at least explain this level of dispersion.

4 LEA: An Automatic Summary Evaluation Environment

Based on previous findings, this section aims to settle the bases of a summary evaluation environment.

The previously described study on summary evaluation modelling and the analysis of past studies on summarisation and summary assessment have been considered to place the basis of the design of an automatic summary evaluation environment -LEA, *Laburpen Ebaluaketa Automatikoa*-. It takes evaluation decisions based on human expertise modelling, resembling human responses. LEA is addressed to two types of users: teachers and students. On one hand, teachers will be able to manage summarisation exercises and inspect student's responses. On the other hand, immature, mature or L2 students might create their own summaries.

The main difference from SS is that LEA is designed for virtually any user. Moreover, this design is aimed not only to train students in summarisation skills but also to assess human summary evaluation performance. In addition to coherence, content coverage and cohesion LEA also gives feedback in use of language and adequacy.

The full architecture of LEA can be seen in figure 2. Next, each component is briefly described.

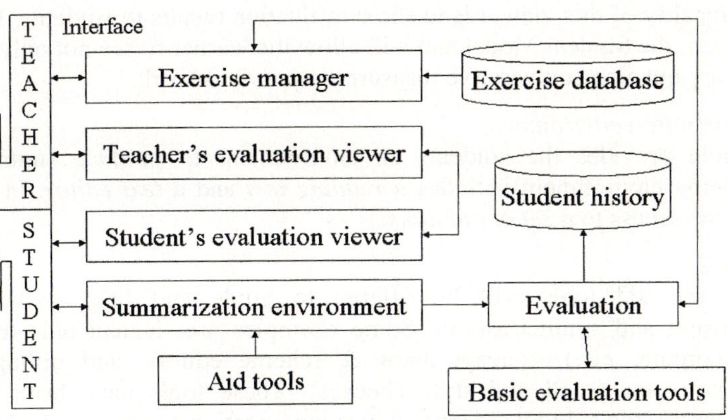

Fig. 2. Design for automatic summary evaluation.

LEA has two kinds of user: students/learners and instructors. Therefore, it is organised in two areas. The teacher area includes facilities to manage exercises and inspect student data. The student area, allows learners to read a text, write a summary and obtain feedback on it.

o *Exercise manager*

This is the module in charge of exercise and reading text management. The instructor is normally the one that defines the summarisation scenario. Knowing roughly the learner's summarisation abilities, an adequate text, aid tools and feedback will be selected. In addition, evaluation parameters are settled and weights on each parameter will be balanced according to the summarisers' profiles.

o *Evaluation module*
This module is responsible for producing global scores based on partial scores in cohesion, coherence, adequacy, use of language and comprehension. Global score decisions will be taken either automatically, based on modelling considerations -see section 3-, or customised by the teacher. Partial scores will be obtained from the *basic evaluation tools*.

o *Basic evaluation tools*
This set of tools provides measures on domain knowledge and summarisation skills, using Latent Semantic Analysis, LSA [7] and Natural Language Processing (NLP) techniques. LSA is a paradigm that allows to show human cognitive competence by means of performing text similarity measures [6]. The set of NLP tools includes a lemmatiser, spell and style checkers, etc. The combination of these tools will feed results on coherence, cohesion, comprehension, language and adequacy.

o *Teacher's evaluation viewer*
The teacher's evaluation viewer allows instructors to inspect the student models. This is the place where lecturers will find all the information obtained by the system. For each student, it will show not only data on the last summary but also comparative measures to previous performance.

o *Student's evaluation viewer*
The functionality of this viewer is to show evaluation results to students. Data will be obtained from the Student Model and will allow the learner to see not only data on the last summary but also comparative measures to previous work.

o *Summarisation environment*
This module provides the students an environment to produce summaries. The summarisation environment includes *a reading text* and a *text editor*. In addition, it facilitates the access to *a set of aid tools*.

o *Aid tools*
Summarisation aid tools will be offered to guide and help students in text comprehension and summarisation. Some examples are: lexical aids (dictionaries, wordnet, corpora, etc.), concept maps & scheme editors, and orthography and grammar corrector (spell and style checker). These tools have been selected to virtually emulate the aid tools identified in summarisation practice (see table 3).

o *Exercise database*
This database contains all the exercise collection with specific details on each reading text.

o *Student history*
It keeps student history; previous summarisation exercises and their corresponding evaluations, and student general details.

5 Conclusions

Against the common belief of subjectivity on free text evaluation criterion, a global tendency in summarisation assessment has been observed among our subjects. It is clear that there is an inter-rater common criterion when rating those summaries. Even if subject's background is very heterogeneous, it seems clear that they all had a similar expectation of what a summary should account for in this experiment. Then, their mental summary or text-macrostructure seems to have many features in common to gain this common agreement. Their criterion points out coherence, comprehension and language as predictors of the overall score in summary evaluation.

The design here presented has been the result of a global study of requirements in human summary evaluation. It provides all the required tools and specifications that we have detected thus far. It takes into account the observed needs on primary, secondary, L2 and university education. Evaluation can be fully automatic, but it also gives the chance to configure certain features according to instructors' requirements. Finally, in addition to instructional assessment, it can be used as a self-learning/self-evaluation environment. Previous work in summarisation evaluation has focused the attention on immature summariser training and automatic summary evaluation. In this case, we deal with a design that takes into consideration mature, immature and L2 summariser's evaluation. Hence, it is thought for almost any user.

Furthermore, instead of being a disadvantage, one of the warranties of any automatic design is that it produces stable assessment criteria that will keep stable from one to the next session/student. This is not the case in human assessment that is under the influence of many environmental extrinsic and intrinsic variables. Stability of evaluation criteria is lower but human raters assert that they are able to evaluate values that no machine could (e.g. student's motivation). Likewise, the system cannot produce assessment on calligraphy, opinion, elegance, novelty level, etc. Nonetheless, this assessment is difficult for humans as well and it is subject to be biased.

It has been concluded that an automatic summary evaluation system should produce an overall score, and measure in comprehension, cohesion, coherence, adequacy and language. Whether this evaluation measures would finally be shown to students or not, has been left to instructors' consideration. Nonetheless, the model points out text coherence as the main predictor of overall score in summarisation followed by comprehension and language ability.

The inclusion of *aid tools* has shown to be necessary for certain target users. For instance, grammar theory of Basque and summarisation instruction theory have shown to be valuable tools in teaching environments. Basque grammar theory has been reported as valuable for L2 learners of Basque and summarisation instruction theory has been identified as a necessary tool in early or immature summarisation.

Bearing in mind the modelling study, we have tried to adapt the design to our subject's current working procedure. It has been intended to give them a complete tool to produce the routine task that they are used to, on a different environment and independently, providing all the required elements. As is known, for many reasons this task requires continuous teacher supervision. This way, students would be able to obtain similar feedback independently. Moreover, it can be included in automated tutoring environments as a complementary evaluation to close ended tasks. According to our teachers' reports, many times they are not able to assess all the summaries one by one, and they tent to assess one anonymously to let students know success and failures in the given summary. This would provide an alternative evaluation in these cases.

Future work is directed at the complexion of the automatic summary evaluation system. It consists on refining this model with greater data and further statistical calculations. Further statistical analysis of the data is being performed in order to find the optimum modelling strategy. In addition, full implementations of the presented design and system testing in the target educational contexts have been planned.

Acknowledgements. This work is funded by the University of the Basque Country (UPV00141.226-T-14816/2002, UPV/EHU PIE12-1-2004), Spanish CICYT (TIC2002-03141) and the Gipuzkoa Council in a European Union program.

References

1. Aleven, V., Koedinger, K.R., Popescu, O. A Tutorial Dialog System to Support Self-Explanation: Evaluation and Open Questions. In: Kay, J., editor. Artificial Intelligence in Education. Sydney, Australia: IOS Press; (2003). p. 35-46.
2. Foltz, P.W., Gilliam, S., Kendall, S. Supporting content-based feedback in online writing evaluation with LSA. In: Interactive Learning Environments; (2000).
3. Graesser, A., Wiemer-Hastings, P., Wiemer-Hastings, K., Harter, D., Person, N, the Tutoring Research Group. Using Latent Semantic Analysis to evaluate the contributions of students in Auto-Tutor. In: Interactive Leraning Environments; (2000). p. 129-148.
4. Ikastolen_Elkartea. OSTADAR DBH-1 Euskara eta Literatura Irakaslearen Gida 3. zehaztapen maila. In: Ikastolen Elkartea; (2003).
5. Kintsch, E., Steinhart, D., Stahl, G., the LSA research group. Developing summarisation skills through the use of LSA-based feedback; (2000).
6. Landauer, T.K., Dumais, S.T. A solution to Plato's problem: The latent semantic analysis theory of acquisition, induction and representation of knowledge. In: Psychological Review; (1997). p. 211-240.
7. Landauer, T.K., Foltz, P.W., Laham, D. Introduction to Latent Semantic Analysis. In: Discourse Processes; (1998). p. 259-284.
8. Lin, C.-Y., Hovy, E. Automatic Evaluation of Summaries Using N-gram Co-occurrence Statistics. In: Human Technology Conference. Edmonton-Canada; (2003). p. 150-157.
9. Long, J., Harding-Esch, E. Summary and recall of text in first and second languages. In: Gerver, D., editor. Language Interpretation and Communication: Plenum Press; (1978). p. 273-287.
10. Manning, C., Schutze, H. Foundations of Statistical Natural Language Processing. In: The MIT Press; (1999).
11. Rickel, J., Lesh, N., Rich, C., Sidner, C.L., Gertner, A. Collaborative Discourse Theory as a Foundation for Tutorial Dialogue. In: International Conference on Intelligent Tutoring Systems, ITS; (2002). p. 542-551.
12. Robertson, J., Wiemer-Hastings, P. Feedback on Children's Stories Via Multiple Interface Agents. In: International Conference on Intelligent Tutoring Systems, ITS. Biarritz-San Sebastian; (2002).
13. Rosé, C.P., Gaydos, A., Hall, B.S., Roque, A., VanLehn, K. Overcoming the Knowledge Engineering Bottelneck for Understanding Student Language Input. In: Kay, J., editor. Artificial Intelligence in Education. Sydney, Australia: Amsterdam: IOS Press; (2003).
14. Sherrard, C. Teaching students to summarize: Applying textlinguistics. In: Systems; (1989). p.1-11.
15. VanLehn, K., Jordan, P.W., Rose, C.P., Bhembe, D., Bottner, D., Gaydos, A., et al. The Architecture of Why2 Atlas: A Coach for Qualitative Physics Essay Writing. In: International Conference on Intelligent Tutoring Systems, ITS. Biarritz-San Sebastian; (2002).

Evaluating the Effectiveness of a Tutorial Dialogue System for Self-Explanation

Vincent Aleven, Amy Ogan, Octav Popescu, Cristen Torrey, Kenneth Koedinger

Human Computer Interaction Institute, Carnegie Mellon University
5000 Forbes Ave, Pittsburgh, PA 15213, USA
+1 412 268 5475
aleven@cs.cmu.edu, {octav,koedinger}@cmu.edu
{aeo,ctorrey}@andrew.cmu.edu,

Abstract. Previous research has shown that self-explanation can be supported effectively in an intelligent tutoring system by simple means such as menus. We now focus on the hypothesis that natural language dialogue is an even more effective way to support self-explanation. We have developed the Geometry Explanation Tutor, which helps students to state explanations of their problem-solving steps in their own words. In a classroom study involving 71 advanced students, we found that students who explained problem-solving steps in a dialogue with the tutor did not learn better overall than students who explained by means of a menu, but did learn better to state explanations. Second, examining a subset of 700 student explanations, students who received higher-quality feedback from the system made greater progress in their dialogues and learned more, providing some measure of confidence that progress is a useful intermediate variable to guide further system development. Finally, students who tended to reference specific problem elements in their explanations, rather than state a general problem-solving principle, had lower learning gains than other students. Such explanations may be indicative of an earlier developmental level.

1 Introduction

A self-explanation strategy of learning has been shown to improve student learning [1]. It has been employed successfully in intelligent tutoring systems [2, 3]. One approach to supporting self-explanation in such a system is to have students provide explanations by means of menus or templates. Although simple, that approach has been shown to improve students' learning [2]. It is likely, however, that students learn even better when they explain their steps in their own words, aided by a system capable of providing feedback on their explanations. When students explain in their own words, they are likely to pay more attention to the crucial features of the problem, causing them to learn knowledge at the right level of generality. They are also more likely to reveal what they know and what they do not know, making it easier for the system to provide detailed, targeted feedback. On the other hand, in comparison to

J.C. Lester et al. (Eds.): ITS 2004, LNCS 3220, pp. 443–454, 2004.

explaining by means of a menu or by filling out templates, free-form explanations require more time and effort by the students. Free-form explanations require that students formulate grammatical responses and type them in. Further, templates or menus may provide extra scaffolding that is helpful for novices but missing in a natural language dialogue. Indeed, menus have been shown to be surprisingly effective in supporting explanation tasks [2, 4, 5], although it is not clear whether menus help in getting students to learn to *generate* better explanations. Whether on balance the advantages of dialogue pay off in terms of improved learning is thus an empirical question.

To answer that question, we have developed a tutorial dialogue system, the Geometry Explanation Tutor, that engages students in a natural language dialogue to help them state good explanations [6, 7]. Tutorial dialogue systems have recently come to the forefront in AI and Education research [6, 8, 9, 10, 11]. The Geometry Explanation Tutor appears to be unique among tutorial dialogue systems in that it focuses on having students explain and provides detailed (but undirected) feedback on students' explanations. A number of dialogue systems have been evaluated with real students, some in real classrooms (e.g., [12]). Some success has been achieved, but it is fair to say that tutorial dialogue systems have not yet been shown to be definitively better than the more challenging alternatives to which they have been compared.

The current paper reports on the results of a classroom study of the Geometry Explanation Tutor, which involved advanced students in a suburban junior high school. As reported previously, there was little difference in the learning outcomes of students who explained in their own words and those who explained by means of a menu [12], as measured by a test that involved problem-solving items, explanation items, and various transfer items. Yet even if there were no significant differences in students' overall learning gains, it is still possible that students who explained in a dialogue with the system may have acquired better geometry communication skills. Further, the result does not explain why there was no overall difference between the conditions, how well the system's natural language and dialogue components functioned, and whether one might reasonably expect that improvements in these components would lead to better learning on the part of the students. Finally, the result does not illuminate how different students may have employed different strategies to construct explanations in a dialogue with the system and how those strategies might correlate to their learning outcomes. Answers to those questions will help to obtain a better understanding of the factors that determine the effectiveness of a tutorial dialogue system that supports self-explanation. We address each in turn.

2 The Geometry Explanation Tutor

The Geometry Explanation Tutor was developed by adding dialogue capabilities to the Geometry Cognitive Tutor, which is part of a geometry curriculum currently being taught in approximately 350 high schools across the country. The combination of tutor and curriculum has been shown to improve on traditional classroom instruction

Student: the two angles add up to 180 degrees
Tutor: Yes, the sum of the angle measures is 180. But you have to be more specific. In general, the sum of what kind of angles is 180?
Student: The two angles add up to 180 degrees so the angles are supplimentary
Tutor: [accepts explanation by means of implicit feedback]

Fig. 1. A student dialog with the tutor, attempting to explain the Separate Supplementary Angles rule

[2]. The Geometry Cognitive Tutor focuses on geometry problem solving: students are presented with a diagram and a set of known angle measures and are asked to find certain unknown angles measures. Students are also required to explain their steps. We are investigating the effect of two different ways of supporting self-explanation: In the menu-based version of the system, students explain each step by typing in, or selecting from an on-line Glossary, the name of a geometry definition or theorem that justifies the step. By contrast, in the dialogue-based version of the system (i.e., the Geometry Explanation Tutor), students explain their quantitative answers in their own words. The system engages them in a dialogue designed to improve their explanations. It incorporates a knowledge-based natural language understanding unit that interprets students' explanations [7]. To provide feedback on student explanations, the system first parses the explanation to create a semantic representation [13]. Next, it classifies the representation according to a hierarchy of approximately 200 explanation categories that represent partial or incorrect statements of geometry rules that occur commonly as novices try to state explanation rules. After the tutor classifies the response, its dialogue management system determines what feedback to present to the student, based on the classification of the explanation. The feedback given by the tutor is detailed yet undirected, without giving away too much information. The student may be asked a question to elicit a more accurate explanation, but the tutor will not actually provide the correction. There are also facilities for addressing errors of commission that suggest that the student remove an unnecessary part of an explanation.

An example of a student-tutor interaction is shown in Fig. 1. The student is focusing on the correct rule, but does not provide a complete explanation on the first attempt. The tutor feedback helps the student in fixing his explanation.

3 Effect of Dialogue on Learning Results

A classroom study was performed with a control group of 39 students using the menu-based version of the tutor, and an experimental group of 32 students using the dialogue version (for more details, see [12]). The results reported here focus on 46 students in three class sections, 25 in the Menu condition and 21 in Dialogue condition, who had spent at least 80 minutes on the tutor and were present for the pre-test and post-test. All student-tutor interactions were recorded for further evaluation. The

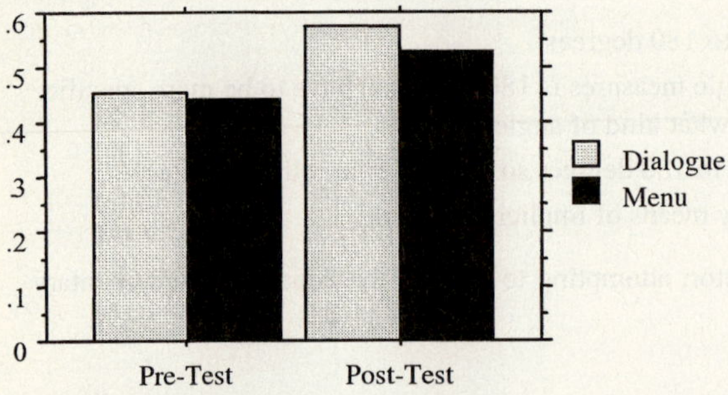

Fig. 2. Overall Pre/Post Test Score (proportion correct)

students completed a pre-test to measure prior knowledge and a post-test after the study.

A 2x2 repeated-measures ANOVA on the test scores, with test time (Pre/Post) as an independent factor (as in Fig. 2), revealed no significant difference between the conditions (F(1,44) = .578, p > .4), consistent with the result reported in [12]. The high pre-test scores (Dialogue .47, Menu .43) may explain in part why no significant differences were found in learning gains. However, a significant difference emerged when focusing on the Explanation items, that is, items that ask for an explanation of a geometry rule used to find the angle measure in the previous step (see Fig. 3). These items were graded with a scheme of .33 points for giving the correct name of the rule to justify their answer, .67 points for attempting to provide a statement of the correct rule but falling short of a complete and correct statement, and a full point for a complete statement of the correct rule[1]. A repeated-measures ANOVA revealed a significant difference in learning gains between the conditions. Even with an initial advantage in Explanation score for the students in the Dialogue condition ($F(1,44) = 4.7, p < .05$), they had significantly greater learning gains on Explanation items compared to the Menu condition ($F(1,44) = 18.8, p < .001$). It may appear that the grading scheme used for Explanation items favors students in the Dialogue condition, since only complete and correct rule statements were given full credit and only students in the Dialogue condition were required to provide such explanations in their work with the tutor. However, even with a scheme that awards full credit for any attempt at explaining that references the right rule, regardless of whether it is a complete statement, there is no significant advantage for the Menu group. No significant difference was found between the two conditions on the other item types.

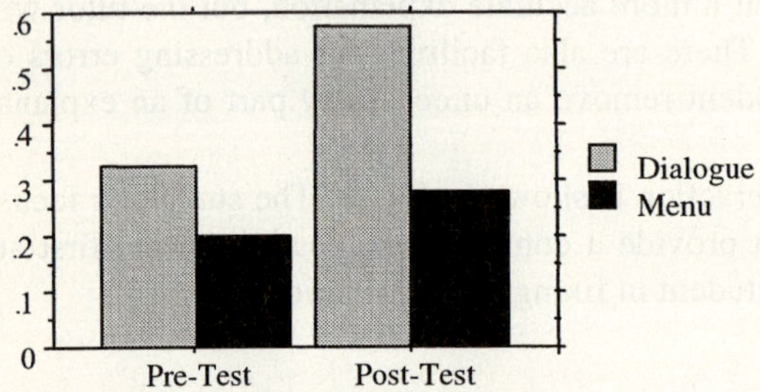

Fig. 3. Score on explanation items (proportion correct).

[1] In a previously-published analysis of these data [3], a slightly different grading scheme was used for Explanation items: half credit was given both for providing the name of a correct rule name and for providing an incomplete statement of a rule. The current scheme better reflects both standards of math communication and the effort required to provide an explanation.

A closer look at the Explanation items shows distinct differences in the type and quality of explanations given by students in each condition (see Fig. 4). In spite of written directions on the test to give full statements of geometry rules, students in the Menu condition only attempted to give a statement of a rule 29% of the time, as opposed for example to merely providing the name of a rule or not providing any explanation. The Dialogue condition, however, gave a rule statement in 75% of their Explanation items. When either group did attempt to explain a rule, the Dialogue condition focused on the correct rule more than twice as often as the Menu group (Dialogue .51 ± .27, Menu .21 ±.24; $F(1,44) = 16.2$, $p < .001$), and gave a complete and correct statement of that rule almost seven times as often (Dialogue .44 ± .27 Menu .06 ± .14; $F(1,44) = 37.1$, $p < .001$). A selection effect in which poorer students follow instructions better cannot be ruled out but seems unlikely. The results show no difference for correctness in answering with rule names (Dialogue .58, Menu .61), but the number of explanations classified as rule names for the Dialogue group (a total of 12) is too small for this result to be meaningful.

To summarize, in a student population with high prior knowledge, we found that students who explained in a dialogue learned better to state high-quality explanations than students who explained by means of a menu, at no expense for overall learning. Apparently, for students with high prior knowledge, the explanation format affects communication skills more than that it affects students' problem-solving skill or understanding, as evidenced by the fact that there was no reliable difference on problem-solving or transfer items.

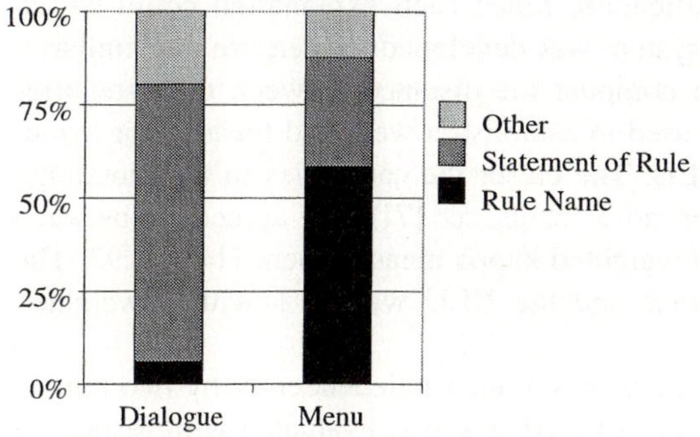

Fig. 4. Relative frequency of different explanation types at the post-test

4 Performance and Learning Outcomes

In order to better understand how the quality of the dialogues may have influenced the learning results, and where the best opportunities for improving the system might be, we analyzed student-tutor dialogues collected during the study. A secondary goal of the analysis was to identify a measure of dialogue quality that correlates well with learning so that it could be used to guide further development efforts.

The analysis focused on testing a series of hypothesized relations between the system's performance, the quality of the student/system dialogues, and ultimately the students' learning outcomes. First, it is hypothesized that students who tend to make progress at each step of their dialogues with the system, with each attempt closer to a complete and correct explanation than the previous, will have better learning results than students who do not. Concisely, *greater progress* → *deeper learning*. Second, we hypothesize that students who receive better feedback from the tutor will make greater progress in their dialogues with the system, or *better feedback → greater progress → deeper learning.* Finally, before this feedback is given, the system's natural language understanding (NLU) unit must provide an accurate classification of the student's explanation. With a good classification, the tutor is likely to provide better, more helpful feedback to the student. The complete model we explore is whether *better NLU → better feedback → greater progress → deeper learning.*

To test the hypothesized relations in this model, several measures were calculated from a randomly-selected subset of 700 explanations (each a single student explanation attempt-tutor feedback pair) out of 3013 total explanations. Three students who did not have at least 10% of their total number of explanations included in the 700 were removed because the explanations included might not represent an accurate picture of their performance.

First, the quality of the system's performance in classifying student explanations was measured as the extent to which two human raters agreed with the classification provided by the NLU. Each rater classified the 700 explanations by hand with respect to the system's explanation hierarchy and then their classifications were compared to each other and to the system's classification. Since each explanation could be assigned a set of labels, a partial credit system was developed to measure the similarity between sets of labels. A formula to compute the distance between the categories within the explanation hierarchy was used to establish a weighted measure of agreement between the humans and the NLU. The closer the categories in the hierarchy, the higher the agreement was rated (for more details, see [7]). The agreement between the two human raters was 94% with a weighted kappa measurement [14] of .92. The average agreement between the humans and the NLU was 87% with a weighted kappa of .81.

Second, the feedback given by the tutor was graded independently by two human raters. On a one-to-five scale, the quality of feedback was evaluated with respect to the student's response and the correct geometry rule. Feedback to partial explanations was placed on the scale based on its appropriateness in assisting the student with correcting his explanation, with 1 being totally unhelpful and 5 being entirely apropos. Explanations that were complete yet were not accepted by the tutor, as well as explanations that were not correct yet were accepted as such, were given a rating of one. Responses where the tutor correctly acknowledged a complete and correct explanation were given a five. The two raters had a weighted agreement kappa of .75, with 89% agreement.

Finally, the progress made by the student within a dialogue was assessed. Each of the 700 explanations was paired with its subsequent student explanation attempt in the dialogue and two human raters independently evaluated whether the second explanation in each pair represented progress towards the correct explanation, compared to the first. The raters were blind with respect to the tutor's feedback that occurred in between the two explanations. (That is, the feedback was not shown and thus could not have influenced the ratings.) Responses were designated "Progress" if the student advanced in the right direction (i.e., improved the explanation). "Progress & Regression" applied if the student made progress, but also removed a crucial aspect of the geometry rule or added something incorrect. If the explanation remained identical in meaning, it was designated "Same". The final category was "Regression," which meant that the second explanation was worse than the first. The two raters had an agreement of 94% in their assessment, with a kappa of .55.

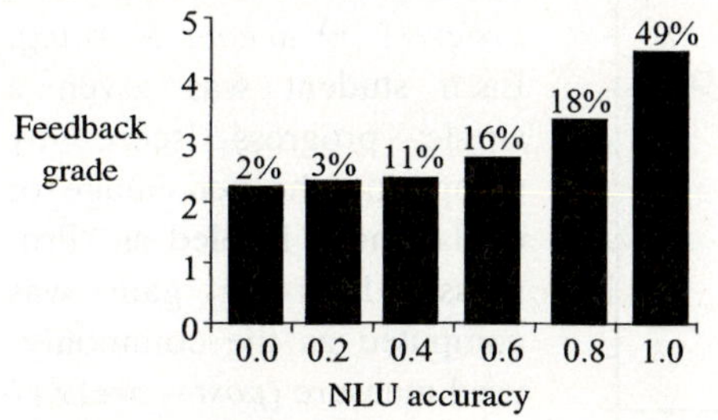

Fig. 5. Average feedback grade as a function of NLU accuracy. The percentages shown above the bars indicate the frequency of the accuracy scores.

Having established the three measures, we tested whether there was (correlational) evidence for the steps in the model. First, we looked at the relation *better NLU → better feedback.* A chi-square test shows that the correlation is significant ($\chi^2(12) = 262.8$, $p < .0001$). Fig. 5 refers to the average feedback grade for a particular range of agreement with the NLU. In the figure, frequency of each accuracy score is listed above the column. A higher NLU rating is indicative of a higher feedback grade.

Table 1. Progress toward a correct and complete explanation as a function of the quality of the system feedback received

Feedback Grade	Regres-sion	Same	Progress & Regression	Progress	N
1	20.5%	67.1%	2.3%	10.2%	88
2	16.0%	41.3%	9.3%	33.3%	75
3	19.1%	29.2%	9.0%	42.7%	89
4	13.5%	18.3%	19.2%	49.0%	104
5	3.9%	26.9%	7.7%	61.5%	78

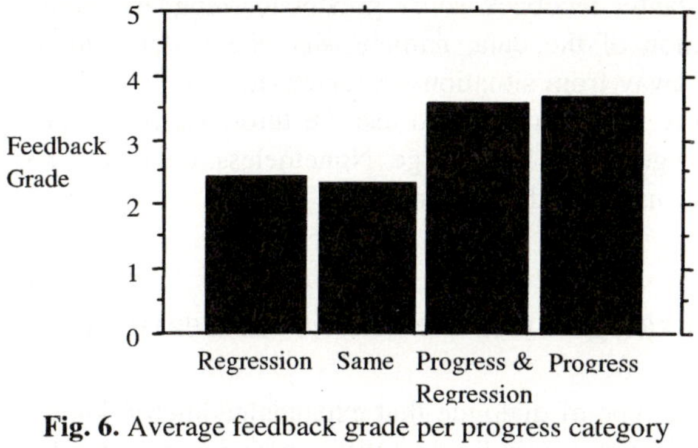

Fig. 6. Average feedback grade per progress category

We tested the relation *better feedback → greater progress* by looking at the relative frequency of the progress categories following feedback of any given grade (1 through 5). As shown in Table 1, the higher the feedback rating, the more likely the student is to make progress (i.e., provide an improved explanation). The lower the feedback grade, the more likely it is that the student regresses. A chi-square test shows that the correlation is significant ($\chi^2(12) = 92.7$, $p < .0001$). Fig. 6 is a condensed view that shows the average feedback grade for each category, again illustrating that better feedback was followed by greater progress.

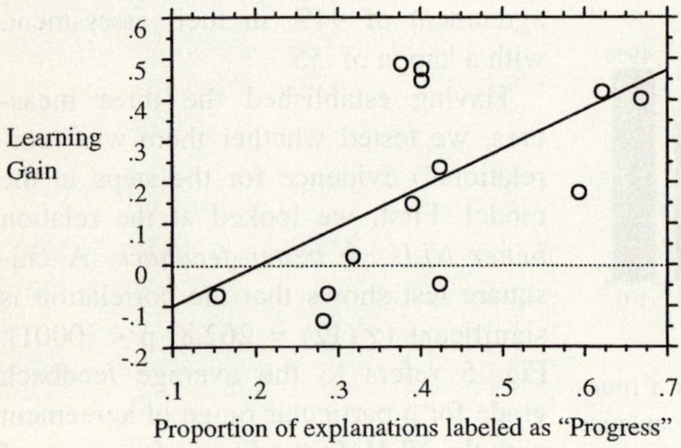

Fig. 7. Best Fit Progress vs. Learning Gain

Finally, we looked at the last step in our model, *greater progress → deeper learning.* Each student was given a single progress score by computing the percentage of explanations labeled as "Progress." Learning gain was computed as the commonly-used measure *(post – pre) / (1 – pre)*. While the relation between learning gain and progress was not significant (r = .253, p > .1), we hypothesized that this may in part be a result of greater progress by students with high pre-test scores, who may have had lower learning gains because their scores were high to begin with. This hypothesis was confirmed by doing a median split that divided the students at a pre-test score of .46. This correlation was significant within the low pre-test group (r = .588, p < .05) as seen in Fig. 7, but not within the high pre-test group (r = .031, p > .9). We also examined the relation *better feedback → deeper learning,* which is a concatenation of the last two steps in the model. The relation between learning gain and feedback grade was statistically significant (r = .588, p < .01).

Merging the results of these separate analyses, we see that each step in the hypothesized chain of relations, *better NLU → better feedback → greater progress → deeper learning,* is supported by means of a statistically significant correlation. We must stress, however, that the results are correlational, not causal. While it is tempting to conclude that better NLU and better feedback *cause* greater learning, we cannot rule out an alternative interpretation of the data, namely, that the better students somehow were better able to stay away from situations in which the tutor gives poor feedback. They might more quickly figure out how to use the tutor, facilitated perhaps by better understanding of the geometry knowledge. Nonetheless, the results are of significant practical value, as discussed further below.

5 Students' Explanation Strategies and Relation with Learning

In order to get a better sense of the type of dialogue that expands geometric knowledge, we investigated whether there were any individual differences in students' dialogues with the tutor and how such differences relate to students' learning outcomes. First we conducted a detailed study of the dialogues of four students in the Dialogue condition. Two students were randomly selected from the quarter of students with the highest learning gains, two from the quarter with the lowest learning gains. In reviewing these case studies, we observed that the low-improvement students often referred to specific angles or specific angle measures in their explanations. For example, one student's first attempt at explaining the Triangle Sum rule is as follows: "I added 154 to 26 and got 180 and that's how many degrees are in a triangle." In contrast, both high-improvement students often began their dialogue by referring to a single problem feature such as "isosceles triangle." In doing so, students first confirmed the correct feature using the feedback from the tutor, before attempting to express the complete rule.

Motivated by the case-study review, the dialogues of all students in the Dialogue condition were coded for the occurrence of these phenomena. An explanation which referred to the name of a specific angle or a specific angle measure was labeled "problem-specific" and an explanation which named only a problem feature was labeled "incremental." The sample of students was ordered by relative frequency of problem-specific instances and split at the median to create a "problem-specific" group and a "no-strategy" group. The same procedure was done again, on the basis of the frequency of incremental instances, to create an "incremental" group and a "no-strategy" group.

The effect of each strategy on learning gain was assessed using a 2X2 repeated-measures ANOVA with the pre- and post-test scores as repeated measure and strategy frequency (high/low) as independent factor (see Fig. 8). The effect of the incremental strategy was not significant. However, the effect of the problem-specific strategy on learning gain was significant ($F(2,23) = 4.77$, $p < .05$). Although the problem-specific group had slightly higher pre-test scores than the no-strategy group, the no-strategy group had significantly higher learning gains.

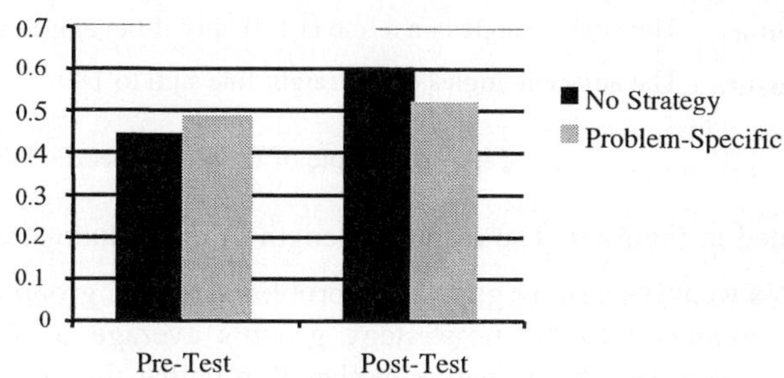

Fig. 8. Overall test scores (proportion correct) for frequent and infrequent users of the problem-specific strategy

It was surprising that the incremental strategy, which was used relatively frequently by the two high-improving students in the case studies, was not related with learning gain in the overall sample. Apparently, incremental explanations are not as closely tied to a deep understanding of geometry as expected. Perhaps some students use this strategy to "game" the system, guessing at keywords until they receive positive feedback, but this cannot be confirmed from the present analysis.

On the other hand, students who used the problem-specific strategy frequently ended up with lower learning gains. One explanation of this phenomenon may be that the dialogues that involved problem-specific explanations tended to be longer, as il-

Student: angles lgh and tgh are supplementary

Tutor: Yes, the angles are supplementary. You need to state a geometry rule that explains why the angles are supplementary.

Student: angles lgh and tgh are supplementary, because when you have 180 and subtraction the one angle, you get the second angle

Tutor: Can you state a rule that says that certain types of angles are supplementary?

Student: angles lgh and tgh are supplementary, the sum of their angles is 180

Tutor: In this problem, you have two adjacent angles. Can you state a general rule that says that those kinds of angles are supplementary?

Student: angles lgh and tgh are supplementary, because they are on a straight line the sum of their angles is 180

Tutor: Yes. And what do you know about the angle measures? If angles form a line, their measures must...

Student: the angles on a straight line sum to 180

Tutor: You are very very close. But not ALL angles on a line add up to 180.

Student: the angles on a straight line sum to 180

Tutor: The sum of angles on a line is 180 only if the angles are adjacent.

Student: The adjacent angles on a straight line sum to 180

Fig. 9. Example of Problem-Specific Dialogue

lustrated in Figure 9. The extended length of these dialogues may be resulting in this group's weaker learning gains. The problem-specific group averaged only 52.5 problems, compared to the no-strategy group's average of 71 problems in the same amount of time. An alternative explanation is that the problem-specific group could be less capable, in general, than the no-strategy group, although the pre-test scores revealed no difference. Problem-specific explanations might reveal an important aspect of student understanding. Their reliance on superficial features might indicate a weakness in their understanding of geometric structures, in their ability to abstract. Possibly, they illustrate the fact that students at different levels of geometric understanding "speak different languages" [15]. While the implications for the design of the Geometry Explanation Tutor are not fully clear, it is interesting to observe that students' explanations reveal more than their pre-test scores.

6 Conclusion

The results of a classroom study show an advantage for supporting self-explanation by means of dialogue, as compared to explaining by means of a menu: Students who explain in a dialogue learn better to provide general explanations for problem-solving steps, in terms of geometry theorems and definitions. However, there was no overall difference between the learning outcomes of the students in the two conditions, possibly because the students in the sample were advanced students, as evidenced by high pre-test scores, and thus there was not much room for improvement. It is possible also that the hypothesized advantages of explaining in one's own words did not materialize simply because it takes much time to explain.

Investigating relations between system functioning and student learning, we found correlational evidence for the hypothesized chain of relations, *better NLU → better feedback → greater progress → deeper learning,* Even though these results do not show that the relations are causal, it is reasonable to concentrate further system development efforts on the variables that correlate with student learning, such as progress in dialogues with the system. Essentially, progress is a performance measure and is easier to assess than students' learning gains (no need for pre-test and post-test and repeated exposure to the same geometry rules).

Good feedback correlates with students' progress through the dialogues and with learning. This finding suggests that students do utilize the system's feedback and can extract the information they need to improve their explanation. On the other hand, students who received bad feedback regressed more often. From observation of the explanation corpus, other students recognized that bad feedback was not helpful and tended to enter the same explanation a second time. Generally, students who (on average) received feedback of lesser quality had longer dialogues than students who received feedback of higher quality ($r = .49$, $p < .05$). A study of the 10% longest dialogues in the corpus revealed a recurrent pattern: stagnation (i.e., the repeated turns in a dialogue in which the student did not make progress) followed either by a "sudden jump" to the correct and complete explanation or by the teacher's indicating to the system that the explanation was acceptable (using a system feature added especially for this purpose). This analysis suggests that the tutor should be able to recover better from periods of extended stagnation. Clearly, the system must detect stagnation – relatively straightforward to do using its explanation hierarchy [6] – and provide very directed feedback to help students recover.

The results indicate that accurate classification by the tutor's NLU component (and here we are justified in making a causal conclusion) is crucial to achieving good, precise feedback, although it is not sufficient– the system's dialogue manager must also keep up its end of the bargain. Efforts to improve the system focus on areas where the NLU is not accurate and areas where the NLU is accurate but the feedback is not very good, as detailed in [7, 12].

Finally, an analysis of the differences between students with better/worse learning results found strategy differences between these two groups of students. Two specific strategies were identified, an incremental strategy that focused on using system feedback first to get "in the right ballpark" with minimal effort, and then to expand the explanation. A second strategy was a problem-specific strategic in which students referred to specific problem elements. Students who used the problem-specific explanation strategy more frequently had lower learning gains. Further investigations are needed to find out whether the use of the problem-specific strategy provides additional information about the student that is not apparent from their numeric answers to problems and if so, how a tutorial dialogue system might take advantage of that information.

Acknowledgements. The research reported in this paper has been supported by NSF grants 9720359 and 0113864. We thank Jay Raspat of North Hills JHS for his inspired collaboration.

References

1. Chi, M. T. H. (2000). Self-Explaining Expository Texts: The Dual Processes of Generating Inferences and Repairing Mental Models. In R. Glaser (Ed.), *Advances in Instructional Psychology*, (pp. 161-237). Mahwah, NJ: Erlbaum.
2. Aleven V., Koedinger, K. R. (2002). An Effective Meta-cognitive Strategy: Learning by Doing and explaining with a Computer-Based Cognitive Tutor. *Cog Sci,* 26(2), 147-179.
3. Conati C., VanLehn K. (2000). Toward Computer-Based Support of Meta-Cognitive Skills: a Computational Framework to Coach Self-Explanation. *Int J Artificial Intelligence in Education,* 11, 398-415.
4. Atkinson, R. K., Renkl, A., Merrill, M. M. (2003). Transitioning from studying examples to solving problems: Combining fading with prompting fosters learning. *J Educational Psychology*, 95, 774-783.
5. Corbett, A., Wagner, A., Raspat, J. (2003). The Impact of Analysing Example Solutions on Problem Solving in a Pre-Algebra Tutor. In U. Hoppe et al. (Eds.), *Proc 11th Int Conf on Artificial Intelligence in Education* (pp. 133-140). Amsterdam: IOS Press.
6. Aleven V., Koedinger, K. R., Popescu, O. (2003). A Tutorial Dialog System to Support Self-Explanation: Evaluation and Open Questions. In U. Hoppe et al. (Eds.), *Proc 11th Int Conf on Artificial Intelligence in Education* (pp. 39-46). Amsterdam: IOS Press.
7. Popescu, O., Aleven, V., & Koedinger, K. R. (2003). A Knowledge-Based Approach to Understanding Students' Explanations. In V. Aleven, et al. (Eds.), *Suppl Proc 11th Int Conf on Artificial Intelligence in Education, Vol. VI* (pp. 345-355). School of Information Technologies, University of Sydney.
8. Evens, M. W. et al. (2001). CIRCSIM-Tutor: An intelligent tutoring system using natural language dialogue. *Twelfth Midwest AI and Cog. Sci. Conf*, MAICS 2001 (pp. 16-23).
9. Graesser, A. C., VanLehn, K., Rosé, C. P., Jordan, P. W., Harter, D. (2001). Intelligent tutoring systems with conversational dialogue. *AI Magazine, 22*(4), 39-51.
10. Rose C. P., Siler, S., VanLehn, K. (submitted). Exploring the Effectiveness of Knowledge Construction Dialogues to Support Conceptual Understanding.
11. Rose C. P., VanLehn, K. (submitted). An Evaluation of a Hybrid Language Understanding Approach for Robust Selection of Tutoring Goals.
12. Aleven V., Popescu, O., Ogan, A., Koedinger, K. R. (2003). A Formative Classroom Evaluation of a Tutorial Dialog System that Supports Self-Explanation. In V. Aleven et al. (Eds.), *Suppl Proc 11th Int Conf on Artificial Intelligence in Education, Vol. VI* (pp. 345-355). School of Information Technologies, University of Sydney.
13. Rosé, C. P., Lavie, A. (1999). LCFlex: An Efficient Robust Left-Corner Parser. User's Guide, Carnegie Mellon University.
14. Carletta, J. (1996). Assessing Agreement on Classification Tasks: The Kappa Statistic. *Computational Linguistics*, 22(2):249-254.
15. Schoenfeld, Alan H. "On Having and Using Geometric Knowledge." In *Conceptual and Procedural Knowledge: The Case of Mathematics,* J. Hiebert (Ed.), 225-64. Hillsdale, N.J: Lawrence Erlbaum Associates, 1986.

Student Question-Asking Patterns in an Intelligent Algebra Tutor

Lisa Anthony, Albert T. Corbett, Angela Z. Wagner, Scott M. Stevens, and Kenneth R. Koedinger

Human Computer Interaction Institute, Carnegie Mellon University, 5000 Forbes Avenue, Pittsburgh, PA 15217, USA
{lanthony, corbett, awagner, sms, koedinger}@cs.cmu.edu
http://www.cs.cmu.edu/~alps/

Abstract. Cognitive Tutors are proven effective learning environments, but are still not as effective as one-on-one human tutoring. We describe an environment (ALPS) designed to engage students in question-asking during problem solving. ALPS integrates Cognitive Tutors with Synthetic Interview (SI) technology, allowing students to type free-form questions and receive pre-recorded video clip answers. We performed a Wizard-of-Oz study to evaluate the feasibility of ALPS and to design the question-and-answer database for the SI. In the study, a human tutor played the SI's role, reading the students' typed questions and answering over an audio/video channel. We examine the rate at which students ask questions, the content of the questions, and the events that stimulate questions. We found that students ask questions in this paradigm at a promising rate, but there is a need for further work in encouraging them to ask deeper questions that may improve knowledge encoding and learning.

1 Introduction

Intelligent tutoring environments for problem solving have proven highly effective learning environments [2,26]. These environments present complex, multi-step problems and provide the individualized support students need to complete them: step-by-step accuracy feedback and context-specific problem-solving advice. Such environments have been shown to improve learning one standard deviation over conventional classrooms, roughly a letter grade improvement. They are two or three times as effective as typical human tutors, but only half as effective as the best human tutors [7].

While intelligent problem-solving tutors are effective active *problem-solving* environments, they can still become more effective active *learning* environments by engaging students in active knowledge construction. In problem solving, students can set shallow *performance* goals, focusing on getting the right answer, rather than *learning* goals, focusing on developing knowledge that transfers to other problems (*c.f.*, [10]). Some successful efforts to foster deeper student learning have explored plan scaffolding [18], and self-explanations of problem-solving steps [1]. We are developing an environment intended to cultivate active learning by allowing students to ask open-ended questions. Encouraging students to ask deep questions during problem solving may alter their goals from performance-orientation toward learning-

J.C. Lester et al. (Eds.): ITS 2004, LNCS 3220, pp. 455–467, 2004.

orientation, perhaps ultimately yielding learning gains. Aleven & Koedinger [1] showed that getting students to explain what they *know* helps learning; by extension, getting students to explain what they *don't know* may also help.

In this project, we integrate Cognitive Tutors, a successful problem-solving environment, with Synthetic Interviews, a successful active inquiry environment, to create ALPS, an "Active Learning in Problem Solving" environment. Synthetic Interviews simulate face-to-face question-and-answer interactions. They allow students to type questions and receive video clip answers. While others [4,12,13,21] are pursuing various tutorial dialogue approaches that utilize natural language processing technology, one advantage of Synthetic Interviews over these methods is that their creation may be simpler. A long-term summative goal in this line of research is whether or not this strategy is as pedagogically-effective as it is cost-effective. Before addressing this goal, however, we first must address two important formative system-design goals, which have not been explored in detail in the context of computer tutoring environments: to what extent will students, when given the opportunity, ask questions of a computer tutor to aid themselves in problem solving, and what is the content of these questions? This paper briefly describes the ALPS environment and then focuses on a Wizard-of-Oz study designed to explore these formative issues.

1.1 Cognitive Tutors

Cognitive Tutors are intelligent tutoring systems designed based on cognitive psychology theory and methods, that pose complex, authentic problems to students [2]. In the course of problem solving, students represent the situation algebraically in the worksheet, graph the functions, and solve equations with a symbol manipulation tool. Each Cognitive Tutor is constructed around a cognitive model of the knowledge students are acquiring, and can provide step-by-step accuracy feedback and help. Cognitive Tutors for mathematics, in use in over 1400 US schools, have been shown to raise student achievement one standard deviation over traditional classroom instruction [8].

Cognitive Tutors provide a help button, which effectively answers just one question during problem solving: "What do I do next?" The tutor provides multiple levels of advice, typically culminating in the actual answer. This help mechanism is sufficient for students to solve problems successfully, but may limit student opportunities to engage in active learning. In fact, students can abuse this help system. For instance, Aleven & Koedinger [1] found that 85% of students' help-seeking events in one geometry tutor unit consisted of quickly "drilling down" to the most specific hint level without reading intermediate levels. Answer-seeking behavior like requesting these "bottom-out" hints may be characteristic of an orientation toward near-term performance rather than long-term learning [3].

Cognitive Tutors might be even more effective if they provided the same "learning by talking" interactions as effective human tutors, by supporting active-learning activities like making inferences, elaborating, justifying, integrating, and predicting [6]. The ALPS environment employs *active inquiry* Synthetic Interview technology to open a channel for students to ask questions as the basis of such active-learning activities.

1.2 Synthetic Interviews

The Synthetic Interview (SI) [25] is a technology that provides an *illusion* of a face-to-face interaction with an individual: users ask questions as if they were having a conversation with the subject of the interview. For example, SIs have been created for asking Albert Einstein about relativity and for asking medical professionals about heart murmurs. This simulated dialogue effect is achieved by indexing videotaped answers based on the types of questions one can expect from the users of that particular SI. Users type a question, and the Synthetic Interview replies with a video clip of the individual answering this question. The SI performs this mapping from query to answer via an information retrieval algorithm based on "TFIDF" (term-frequency, inverse document frequency, *e.g.*, [23]). Question-matching occurs statistically based on relative word frequency in the database of known questions and in the user query, rather than through knowledge-based natural-language processing (NLP). Systems using knowledge-based NLP often suffer an implementation bottleneck due to the knowledge engineering effort required to create them [20]. Unlike the reliance of such NLP systems on *explicit* domain knowledge authoring, SIs possess *implicit* domain knowledge via what questions are answered and how. Any given answer has many question formulations associated with it. Several rounds of data collection may be required to obtain a sufficient query-base for the SI algorithm; past SIs have had up to 5000 surface-form-variant questions associated with 200 answers. This need for multiple rounds of data collection is similar to that needed to create other textual classification systems, and on the whole, purely statistical approaches (like Synthetic Interviews) still require less development effort than NLP systems [20].

1.3 ALPS: Active Learning in Problem Solving

The ALPS environment is an adaptation of the Cognitive Tutor to include a Synthetic Interview. The current version is a high school Algebra I lesson covering linear function generation and graphing. In addition to the normal Cognitive Tutor windows, the student sees a web browser pointing to the Synthetic Interview server. This browser shows the video tutor's face at all times, with a text box in which the student may type in a question for the tutor. We hypothesize that formulating questions rather than just pressing a hint button can help engage students in learning and self-monitoring.

This paper describes a design study employing a Wizard-of-Oz simulation of the ALPS environment in which a human tutor plays the Synthetic Interview. The study examines how students take advantage of the opportunity to ask open-ended questions in a computer-based problem solving environment, by looking at the following issues: the rate at which students ask questions; the contexts in which students ask questions; the extent to which tutor prompting elicits questions; and the content of student questions with respect to learning- or performance-orientation. These results will help guide design of question-scaffolding in the ALPS environment. The study also serves to collect student questions to populate the ALPS question and answer databases.

2 Student Questions in Other Learning Environments

Past research on question-asking rates in non-computer environments provides reasonable benchmarks for gauging ALPS' usability and effectiveness. Graesser and Person [14] report that, in conventional classroom instruction, the rate of questions per student per hour is 0.11. This extremely low number is due to the fact that students share access to the teacher with 25 to 30 other students, and is also due to the lecture format of typical classroom instruction. At the other extreme, in one-on-one human tutoring, students ask questions at the average rate of 26.5 questions per hour [14]. Of these, 8.5 questions per hour are classified as deep-reasoning questions.

The nature of student questions in *intelligent tutoring systems* is largely unexplored. ITSs that allow natural language student inputs generally embody Socratic tutorial dialogues (*c.f.*, AutoTutor [13], CIRCSIM-Tutor [12], Atlas [11]). By nature, Socratic dialogues are overwhelmingly driven by questions from the tutor. Although there are problem-solving elements in many of these systems, the tutor-student dialogue is both the primary activity and the primary mode of learning. Because Socratic dialogues are tutor-controlled, students in these systems tend to ask relatively few questions. Therefore, these ITSs vary in how fully they attempt to process student questions and question rate and content are largely unreported. A few studies have examined student questions in *computer-mediated* Socratic tutoring, however, in which the student and human tutor communicate through a textual computer interface. In a study by Jordan and Siler [16], only about 3% of (typed) student utterances were questions, and in Core et al [9], only 10% of student moves were questions. Shah et al [24] found that only about 6% of student utterances were questions; students asked 3.0 questions per hour, well below that of human face-to-face tutoring.

In contrast to such tutor-controlled dialogues, the study reported in this paper examines student question-asking in the Cognitive Tutor, a mathematics problem-solving environment with greater *learner* control. The student, not the tutor, is in control of his progress; students work through the problem-solving steps at their own pace. The program provides accuracy feedback for each problem-solving step, but the students must request advice when they encounter impasses. Therefore, we expect that student question-asking rates will be higher in ALPS than in the systems reported above.

Graesser and Person [14], in a study on human tutoring, found a positive correlation between final exam scores and the proportion of student questions during tutoring sessions that were classified as "knowledge-deficit" or "deep-reasoning" utterances. Therefore, we believe that getting students to ask questions, *to the extent that they are asking deep-reasoning questions*, may alter student goals, and yield learning gains.

3 Wizard-of-Oz Design Study

In the Wizard-of-Oz (WOZ) study, a human played the role of the Synthetic Interview while students worked in the Cognitive Tutor. The students were able to type questions in a chat window and receive audio/video responses from the human tutor (Wizard). Our research questions concerned several characteristics of the questions students might ask: (1) **Frequency**—at what rate do students ask questions to deepen their knowledge; (2) **Prompting & Timing**—what elicits student questions most; and (3) **Depth**—what learning goals are revealed by the content of student questions.

3.1 Methods

Participants. Our participants were 10 middle school students (nine seventh graders, one eighth grader; eight males, two females) from area schools. Two students had used the standard Cognitive Tutor algebra curriculum in their classrooms that year, three students had been exposed to Cognitive Tutors in a previous class session, and five had never used Cognitive Tutors before.

Procedure. The study took place in a laboratory setting. The students completed algebra and geometry problems in one session lasting one and a half hours. During a session, the student sat at a computer running the Cognitive Tutor with a chat session connected to the Wizard, who was sitting at a computer in another room. The students were instructed to direct all questions to the Wizard in the other room via the chat window. In a window on his own computer screen, the Wizard could see the student's screen and the questions the student typed. The Wizard responded to student questions via a microphone and video camera; the student heard his answer through the computer speakers and saw the Wizard in a video window onscreen. Throughout problem solving, if the student appeared to be having difficulty (e.g., either he made a mistake on the same problem-solving action two or more times, or he did not perform any problem-solving actions for a prolonged period), the Wizard prompted the student to ask a question by saying "Do you want to ask a question?"

Measures. The data from the student sessions were recorded via screen capture software. All student mouse and keyboard interactions were captured, as well as student questions in the chat window and audio/video responses from the Wizard. The sessions were later transcribed from the captured videos. All student actions were marked and coded as "correct," "error," "typo," or "interrupted" (when a student began typing in a cell but interrupted himself to ask a question). Student utterances were then separately coded by two of the authors along three dimensions based on the research questions mentioned above: initiating participant (student or tutor); question timing in the context of the problem-solving process (*i.e.*, before or after errors or actions); and question depth. After coding all 10 sessions along the three criteria, the two coders met to resolve any disagreements. Out of 431 total utterances, disagreement occurred in 12.5% of items; the judges discussed these to reach consensus.

3.2 Qualitative Results and Discussion

We classified each problem-solving question at one of the following three depths: answer-oriented, process-oriented, or principle-oriented. Answer-oriented questions can be thought of as "what" questions. The student is asking about the problem-solving process for a particular problem, usually in very specific terms and requesting a very specific answer (*e.g.*, "what is the area of this triangle [so I can put it in the cell]?"). Process-oriented questions can be thought of as "how" questions. The student is asking how to perform a procedure in order to solve a particular problem, but the question represents a more general formulation of the request than simply asking for the answer (*e.g.*, "how do I figure out the area of this triangle?"). Principle-oriented questions can be thought of as "why" questions and are of the most general type. The student is asking a question about a mathematical concept or idea which he is trying to understand (*e.g.*, "Why is the area of a triangle 1/2*b*h?") These three categories form a continuum of question depth, with answer-oriented lying at the shallow end of knowledge-seeking, principle-oriented lying at the deep end, and process-oriented lying somewhere in the middle. We include here an illustrative example from the WOZ of interaction sequences from each category. In each example, input from the student is denoted with **S** and the Wizard, with **W**.

Answer-oriented: These questions ask about the answer to a problem step or about a concrete calculation by which a student may try to get the answer. The following interaction occurred in a problem asking about the relationship among pay rate, hours worked and total pay. An hourly wage of "$5 per hour" was given in the global problem statement, and the student was answering the following question in the worksheet: "You normally work 40 hours a week, but one particular week you take off 9 hours to have a long weekend. How much money would you make that week?" The student correctly typed "31" for the number of hours worked, but then typed "49" (40 + 9) for the amount of money made. When the software turned this answer red, indicating an error, the student asked, "Would I multiply 40 and 9?" The Wizard asked the student to think about why he picked those numbers. The student answered, "Because they are the only two numbers in the problem."

Asking "Would I multiply 40 and 9?" essentially asks "Is the answer 360?" The student wants the Wizard to tell him if he has the right answer, betraying his performance-orientation. The student is employing a superficial strategy: trying various operators to arithmetically combine the two numbers ("40" and "9") that appear in the question. After the first step in this strategy (addition) fails, he asks the Wizard if multiplication will yield the correct answer (he likely cannot calculate this in his head). Rather than ask how to reason about the problem, he asks for the answer to be given to him.

Process-oriented: These student questions on how to find an answer frequently take the form of "how do I find…" or "how do I figure out…" The following occurred when a student was working on a geometry problem involving the area of a 5-sided figure composed of a rectangle plus a triangle. He had already identified the given information in the problem and was working on computing each subfigure's area. He typed "110" for the area of the rectangle and asked, "How do you find the area of a triangle?" The Wizard told him the general formula. In this case, the student correctly understood what he was supposed to compute, but did not know the formula. He is not asking to be told the answer, but instead *how to find* it. The Wizard's general answer can then help the student on future problems.

Principle-oriented: General principle-oriented questions show when the student is moving beyond the current problem context and reasoning about the general mathematical principles involved. We saw only one example of this type of question. It took place after the student had finished computing the area and perimeter of a square of side length 8 (area = 64, perimeter = 32). The student did not need help from the Wizard while solving this problem. He typed "2s+2s" for the formula of a square's perimeter, and typed "s*s" for the formula of a square's area. He then asked, "Is area always double perimeter?" The student's question signified a reflection on his problem-solving activities that prompted him to make a potential hypothesis about mathematics. A future challenge is to encourage students to ask more of these kinds of questions, actively engaging them in inquiry about domain principles.

3.3 Quantitative Results and Discussion

Figures 1, 2, and 3 show the results from the analysis along three dimensions: initiating participant, question timing, and question depth. Error bars in all cases represent the 95% confidence interval. Figure 1 shows the mean number of utterances per student per hour that are prompted, unprompted, or part of a dialogue. "Unprompted" (M=14.44, SD=7.07) means the student asked a question without an explicit prompt by the tutor. "Prompted" (M=3.49, SD=1.81) means the student asked after the Wizard prompted him, as in by saying "Do you want to ask a question?" "Dialogue response" (M=11.80, SD=12.68) means the student made an utterance in direct response to a question or statement by the Wizard, and "Other" (M=8.23, SD=5.04) includes statements of technical difficulty or post-problem-solving discussions initiated by the Wizard. The latter two categories are not included in further analyses.

Figure 1 shows that students asked questions at a rate of 14.44 unprompted questions per hour. Students ask approximately four times more unprompted than prompted questions ($t(18)=4.74$, $p<.01$). The number of prompted questions is bounded by the number of prompts from the Wizard, but note that the number of Wizard prompts per session (M=9.49, SD=2.65) significantly outnumbers the number of prompted questions ($t(18)=5.92$, $p<.01$). Even when the Wizard *explicitly* prompts students to ask questions, they often do not comply. This suggests that a question-encouraging strategy in ALPS simply consisting of prompting will not be sufficient.

Figure 2 shows question timing with respect to the student's problem-solving actions. "Before Action" (M=8.62, SD=6.26) means the student asked the question about an action he was about to perform. "After Error" (M=8.46, SD=2.55) means the student asked about an error he had just made or was in the process of resolving. "After Correct Action" (M=0.85, SD=1.26) means the student asked about a step he had just answered correctly. The graph shows that students on average ask significantly fewer questions after having gotten a step right than in the other two cases ($t(28)$=5.09, p<.01), revealing a bias toward treating the problem-solving experience as a performance-oriented task. Once they obtain the right answer, students do not generally reflect on what they have done. This suggests that students might need encouragement after having finished a problem to think about what they have learned and how the problem relates to other mathematical concepts they have encountered.

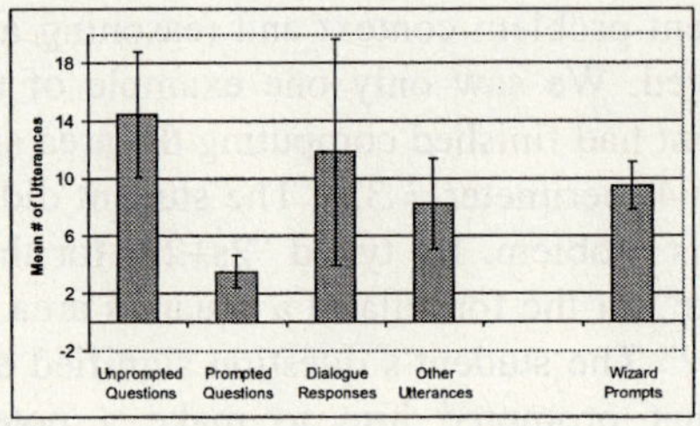

Fig. 1. Mean number of utterances per hour

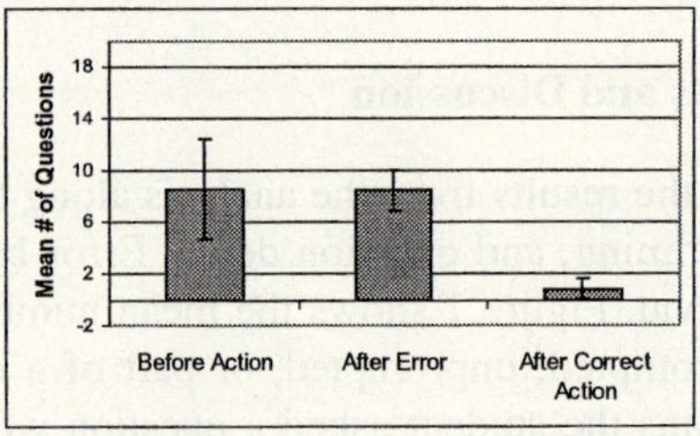

Fig. 2. Mean number of unprompted and prompted questions per hour by question timing

Figure 3 shows the mean number of questions grouped by question topic. "Interface" (M=10.21, SD=5.60) means the question concerned how to accomplish something in the software interface or how to interpret something that happened in the software. "Definition" (M=0.97, SD=1.09) questions asked what a particular term meant. "Answer" (M=4.98, SD=3.58), "Process" (M=1.68, SD=1.60), and "Principle" (M=0.07, SD=0.23) questions are defined above. Figure 3 shows an emphasis on interface questions; although one might attribute the high proportion of student interface questions to the fact that half the participants were students who had not used the Cognitive Tutor software before, the data show no reliable difference between the two groups in question rate or content. Yet even among non-interface questions, one can see that students still focus on "getting the answer right," as shown by the large proportion of answer-oriented questions. The difference between the number of "shallow" questions (answer-oriented) and the number of "deep" questions (process-oriented plus principle-oriented) is significant ($t(28)$=4.55, p<.01).

While Figure 2 shows that students on average ask questions before actions and after errors at about the same rate, the type of question asked varies across the two contexts. The distinction between the distributions of these two question contexts may be revealing: asking a question before performing an action may imply forethought and active problem solving, whereas asking only after an error could imply that the student was not thinking critically about what he understood. Figure 4 displays a breakdown of the interaction between question timing and the depth or topic. Based on the data, when students ask questions before performing an action, they are most likely to be asking about how to accomplish some action in the interface which they are intending to perform. When they ask questions after an error, they are most often asking about how to get the answer they could not get right on their own. The one principle-oriented question was asked after a correct action and is not represented in Figure 4.

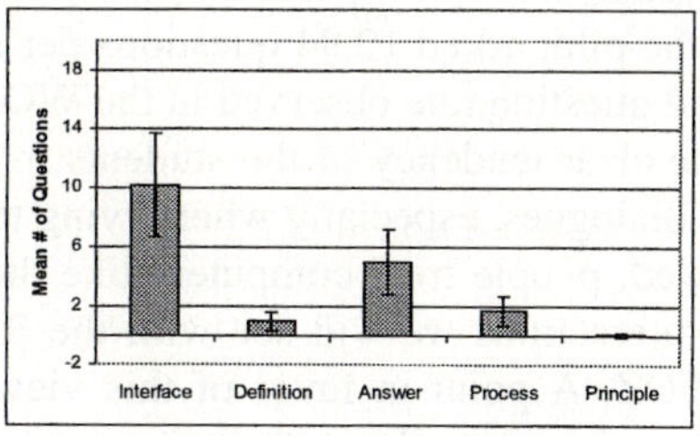

Fig. 3. Mean number of unprompted or prompted questions per hour by perceived depth

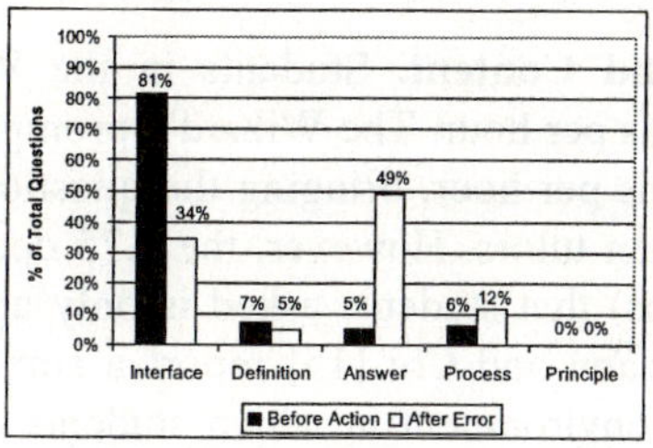

Fig. 4. Comparison of distributions of "Before Action" and "After Error" questions based on question depth. "After Correct Action" is not included due to low frequency of occurrence

Additional analysis shows that, of the questions that are "After Error" (102 total), 100% are directly about the error that the student has just made or is in the process of resolving (*i.e.*, through several steps guided by the Wizard). Of those that are "After Correct Action" (9 total), 4 (44%) are requests for feedback about progress (*e.g.*, "am I doing ok so far?"), 4 (44%) are clarifications about how the interface works (*e.g.*, "can I change my answers after I put them in?") and only one (11%) is a process- or principle-oriented query about general mathematics (*e.g.*, "is area always double perimeter?"). Thus it seems that, although students do take the opportunity to ask questions, they do not generally try to elaborate their knowledge by asking deep questions.

4 Current and Future Work

Database Seeding: A Preliminary ALPS Pilot. The Wizard-of-Oz study was also designed to populate the ALPS question and answer databases. The ten students generated 208 total questions variations, for which we recorded 47 distinct video clip answers. Recently we conducted a preliminary pilot of the ALPS environment in which five middle school students used ALPS at home. The Synthetic Interview technology processed student questions and presented video clip answers. The five students asked 23 total questions in about 100 minutes total use; all are effectively "unprompted," as the pilot system was not capable of prompts like those in the Wizard-of-Oz study. Students in the pilot asked 12.94 questions per student per hour, slightly lower than the unprompted question rate observed in the WOZ.

A concern has been the clear tendency of the students in the WOZ toward engaging the human Wizard in dialogues, especially when trying to repair errors. However, as Nass and Reeves showed, people treat computers like they treat people [19], implying that the kinds of interactions we will see with the SI-enabled system will be similar to those in the WOZ. A point in favor of this view is that the unprompted question-asking rates reported in our pilot with the computer SI, are similar to those in the WOZ with the human Wizard. Therefore, we do not believe that applying the results from the WOZ to the SI is problematic.

Question-Asking Rate and Content. Students in the Wizard-of-Oz study asked 14.44 unprompted questions per hour. The Wizard's prompts to ask questions yielded an additional 3.49 questions per hour, bringing the question-asking rate to about 2/3 of that observed with human tutors. However, the 1.75 deep questions (process- and principle-oriented questions) that students asked is only about 1/5 the rate observed with human tutors. Hausmann and Chi [15] report a similar result for a computer-mediated self-explanation environment in which students read instructional text and typed self-explanations of the text as they read. In this environment students typed superficial paraphrases of the text sentences at a far higher rate than deeper self-explanations of the sentences, and self-explanations were generated at a far lower rate than in earlier studies of spoken self-explanations [5].

Increasing the rate of deep questions in the ALPS environment is an important challenge. Hausmann and Chi suggest that the additional cognitive load of typing versus spoken input may inhibit students' self-explanation rate. They did succeed in raising students' self-explanation rate somewhat in the computer-mediated environment with content-free prompts designed to elicit explanations, for instance, "Could you explain how that works?" By analogy the first step in raising the rate of deep questions in the ALPS environment may be to replace the generic Wizard prompt ("Do you want to ask a question") with an analogous prompt designed to elicit deeper questions, such as "Do you want to ask how to find this answer?" In the long run, the integration of a speech recognizer that allows students to ask questions orally may be necessary to achieve the highest rate of deep questions, but we plan first to explore several types of question scaffolding strategies.

First, prior instruction on how to structure deep questions can be designed. It has been shown that training students to self-explain text when working on their own by asking themselves questions improves learning [22]. By analogy, training students on how to ask questions of a tutor may be effective in ALPS. Second, it may be possible to progressively scaffold question-asking by initially providing a fixed set of appropriate questions in menu format, and later providing direct feedback and advice on the questions students ask. It may also be possible to capitalize on shallow questions students ask as raw material for these scaffolds; the system could suggest several ways in which a student question is shallow and could be generalized. Finally, it may be useful to emphasize post-problem review questions as well as problem-solving questions. Katz and Allbritton [17] report that human tutors often employ post-problem discussion to deepen understanding and facilitate transfer. Since students do not have active performance goals at the conclusion of problem solving, it may be an opportune time not just to invite, but to actively encourage and scaffold deeper questions.

5 Conclusions

The Wizard-of-Oz study allowed us to evaluate ALPS' viability and identify design challenges in supporting active learning via student-initiated questions. The study successfully demonstrated that students ask questions in the ALPS environment at a rate approaching that of one-on-one human tutoring. However, based on student question content, we can conclude that students are still operating with performance goals rather than learning goals. It may be that the students did not know how to ask deep questions, or that the question-asking experience was too unstructured to encourage deep questions. There may be ways in which we can promote learning goals, including using prompts specifically designed to elicit deeper questions, implementing various deep-question scaffolds, encouraging reflective post-problem discussions, and adding a speech recognizer to reduce cognitive load.

Acknowledgments. Supported in part by National Science Foundation (NSF) Grant EIA0205301 "ITR: Collaborative Research: Putting a Face on Cognitive Tutors: Bringing Active Inquiry into Active Problem Solving." Thanks for support and effort: Brad Myers, Micki Chi, Sharon Lesgold, Harry Ulrich, Chih-Yu Chao; Timm Mason, Pauline Masley, Heather Frantz, Jane Kamneva, Dara Weber; Alex Hauptmann; Carolyn Penstein Rosé, Nathaniel Daw and Ryan Baker. Thanks very much to our ALPS video tutor Bill Hadley.

References

1. Aleven, V.A.W.M.M., Koedinger, K.R.: An Effective Metacognitive Strategy: Learning by Doing and and Explaining with a Computer-Based Cognitive Tutor. Cognitive Science 26 (2002) 147–149

2. Anderson, J.R., Corbett, A.T., Koedinger, K.R., Pelletier, R.: Cognitive Tutors: Lessons Learned. Journal of the Learning Sciences 4 (1995) 167 –207
3. Baker, R.S., Corbett, A.T., Koedinger, K.R., Wagner, A.Z.: Off-task Behavior in the Cognitive Tutor Classroom: When Students "Game the System." Proc. CHI (2004) to appear
4. Carbonell, J.R.: AI in CAI: Artificial Intelligence Approach to Computer Assisted Instruction. IEEE Trans. on Man-Machine Systems 11 (1970) 190–202
5. Chi, M.T.H., DeLeeuw, N., Chiu, M.-H., LaVancher, C.: Eliciting Self-explanations Improves Understanding. Cognitive Science 18 (1994) 439–477
6. Chi, M.T.H., Siler, S.A., Jeong, H., Yamauchi, T., Hausmann, R.G.: Learning from Human Tutoring. Cognitive Science 25 (2001) 471–533
7. Corbett, A.T.: Cognitive Computer Tutors: Solving the Two-Sigma Problem. Proc. User Modeling (2001) 137–147
8. Corbett, A.T., Koedinger, K.R., Hadley, W.H.: Cognitive Tutors: From the Research Classroom to All Classrooms. In: P. Goodman (ed.): Technology Enhanced Learning: Opportunities for Change. L. Erlbaum, Mahwah New Jersey (2001) 235–263
9. Core, M.G., Moore, J.D., Zinn, C.: Initiative in Tutorial Dialogue. ITS Wkshp on Empirical Methods for Tutorial Dialogue Systems (2002) 46–55
10. Elliott, E.S., Dweck, C.S.: Goals: An Approach to Motivation and Achievement. Journal of Personality and Social Psychology 54 (1988) 5–12
11. Freedman, R.: Atlas: A Plan Manager for Mixed-Initiative, Multimodal Dialogue. AAAI Wkshp on Mixed-Initiative Intelligence (1999)
12. Freedman, R.: Degrees of Mixed-Initiative Interaction in an Intelligent Tutoring System. AAAI Symposium on Computational Models for Mixed-Initiative Interaction (1997)
13. Graesser, A., Moreno, K.N., Marineau, J.C., Adcock, A.B., Olney, A.M., Person, N.K.: AutoTutor Improves Deep Learning of Computer Literacy: Is it the Dialog or the Talking Head? Proc. AIEd (2003) 47–54
14. Graesser, A.C., Person, N.K.: Question Asking During Tutoring. American Educational Research Journal 31 (1994) 104–137
15. Hausmann, R.G.M., Chi, M.T.H.: Can a Computer Interface Support Self-explaining? Cognitive Technology 7 (2002) 4–14
16. Jordan, P., Siler, S.: Student Initiative and Questioning Strategies in Computer-Mediated Human Tutoring Dialogues. ITS Wkshp on Empirical Methods for Tutorial Dialogue Systems (2002)
17. Katz, S., Allbritton, D.: Going Beyond the Problem Given: How Human Tutors Use Post-Practice Discussions to Support Transfer. Proc. ITS (2002) 641–650
18. Lovett, M.C.: A Collaborative Convergence on Studying Reasoning Processes: A Case Study in Statistics. In: Carver, S., Klahr, D. (eds.): Cognition and Instruction: Twenty-five Years of Progress. L. Erlbaum, Mahwah New Jersey (2001) 347–384
19. Reeves, B., Nass, C.: The Media Equation: How People Treat Computers, Television, and New Media Like Real People and & Places. Cambridge University Press, Cambridge UK (1996)
20. Rosé, C.P., Gaydos, A., Hall, B.S., Roque, A., VanLehn, K.: Overcoming the Knowledge Engineering Bottleneck for Understanding Student Language Input. Proc. AIEd (2003) 315–322
21. Rosé, C.P., Jordan, P., Ringenberg, M., Siler, S., VanLehn, K., Weinstein, A.: Interactive Conceptual Tutoring in Atlas-Andes. Proc. AIEd (2001) 256–266
22. Rosenshine, B., Meister, C., Chapman, S.: Teaching Students to Generate Questions: A Review of the Intervention Studies. Review of Educational Research 66 (1996) 181–221

23. Salton, G., Buckley, C.: Term Weighting Approaches in Automatic Text Retrieval. Technical Report #87-881, Computer Science Dept, Cornell University, Ithaca, NY (1987)
24. Shah, F., Evens, M., Michael, J., Rovick, A.: Classifying Student Initiatives and Tutor Responses in Human Keyboard-to-Keyboard Tutoring Sessions. Discourse Processes 33 (2002) 23–52
25. Stevens, S.M., Marinelli, D.: Synthetic Interviews: The Art of Creating a 'Dyad' Between Humans and Machine-Based Characters. IEEE Wkshp on Interactive Voice Technology for Telecommunications Applications (1998)
26. VanLehn, K., Lynch, C., Taylor, L., Weinstein, A., Shelby, R., Schulze, K., Treacy, D., Wintersgill, M.: Minimally Invasive Tutoring of Complex Physics Problem Solving. Proc. ITS (2002) 367–376

Web-Based Intelligent Multimedia Tutoring for High Stakes Achievement Tests

Ivon Arroyo[1], Carole Beal[2,3], Tom Murray[1], Rena Walles[2], and Beverly P. Woolf[1]

[1] Computer Science Department, University of Massachusetts Amherst
{ivon, tmurray, bev}@cs.umass.edu

[2] Department of Psychology, University of Massachusetts Amherst
{cbeal, rwalles}@psych.umass.edu

[3] Information Sciences Institute, University of Southern California
cbeal@isi.edu

Abstract. We describe Wayang Outpost, a web-based ITS for the Math section of the Scholastic Aptitude Test (SAT). It has several distinctive features: help with multimedia animations and sound, problems embedded in narrative and fantasy contexts, alternative teaching strategies for students of different mental rotation abilities and memory retrieval speeds. Our work on adding intelligence for adaptivity is described. Evaluations prove that students learn with the tutor, but learning depends on the interaction of teaching strategies and cognitive abilities. A new adaptive tutor is being built based on evaluation results; surveys results and students' log files analyses.

1 Introduction

High stakes achievement tests have become increasingly important in the past years in the United States, and a student's performance on such tests can have a significant impact on his or her access to future educational opportunities. At the same time, concern is growing that the use of high stakes achievement tests, such as the Scholastic Aptitude Test (SAT)-Mathematics exam and others (e.g., the MCAS exam) simply exacerbates existing group differences, and puts female students and those from traditionally underrepresented minority groups at a disadvantage. Studies have shown that women generally perform less well than men on the SAT-M although their academic performances in college are similar (Wainer&Steiberg, 1992). Student's performance on SAT has a significant impact on students' access to future educational opportunities such as admission to universities and scholarships. New approaches are required to help all students perform to the best of their ability on high stakes tests.

Computer-based intelligent tutoring systems (ITS) provide one promising option for helping students prepare for high stakes achievement tests. Research on intelligent tutoring systems has clearly shown that users of tutoring software can make

J.C. Lester et al. (Eds.): ITS 2004, LNCS 3220, pp. 468–477, 2004.

rapid progress and dramatically improve their performance in specific content areas. Evaluation studies of ITS for school mathematics showed the benefits to student users in school settings (Arroyo, 2003).

This paper describes "Wayang Outpost", an Intelligent Tutoring System to prepare students for the mathematics section of the SAT, an exam taken by students at the end of high school in the United States. Wayang Outpost provides web-based access to tutoring on SAT-Math (http://wayang.cs.umass.edu). Wayang Outpost is an improvement over other tutoring systems in several ways. First, although they can provide effective instruction, few ITS have really taken advantage of the instructional possibilities of multimedia techniques in the help component, in terms of sound and animation. Second, this paper describes our work on incorporating intelligence to improve teaching effectiveness in various parts of the system: problem selection, hint selection and student engagement. Third, although current ITS model the student's knowledge on an ongoing basis to provide effective help, there have been only preliminary attempts to incorporate knowledge of student group characteristics (e.g., profile of cognitive skills, gender) into the tutor and to use this profile information to guide instruction (Shute, 1995; Arroyo et al., 2000). Wayang Outpost addresses factors that have been shown to cause females to score lower than males in these tests. It is suspected that cognitive abilities such as spatial abilities and math fact retrieval are important determinants of the score in these standardized tests. Math Fact retrieval is a measure of a student's proficiency with math facts, the probability that a student can rapidly retrieve an answer to a simple math operation from memory. In some studies, math fact retrieval was found to be an important source of gender differences in math problems (Royer et al., 1999). Other studies found that when mental rotation ability was statistically adjusted for, the significant gender difference in SAT-M disappeared (Casey et al, 1995).

2 System Description

Wayang Outpost was designed as a supplement to high school geometry courses. Its orientation is to help students learn to solve math word problems typical of those on high stakes achievement tests, which may require the novel application of skills to tackle unfamiliar problems. Wayang Outpost provides web-based instruction. The student begins a session by logging into the site and receiving a problem. The setting is an animated classroom based in a research station in Borneo, which provides rich real world content for mathematical problems. Each math problem (a battery of SAT-Math problems provided by the College Board) is presented as a flash movie, with decisions about problem and hint selection made on the server (the tutor's "brain"). If the student answers incorrectly, or requests help, step-by-step guidance is provided in the form of Flash animations with audio (see figure 1). The explanations and hints provided in Wayang Outpost therefore resemble what a human teacher might provide when explaining a solution to a student, e.g., by drawing, pointing, highlighting critical parts of geometry figures, and talking, in contrast to previous ITS that relied heavily on static text and images.

Cognitive skills assessment. Past research suggests that the assessment of cognitive skills is relevant to selecting teaching strategies or external representations that yield best learning results. For instance, a study of students' level of cognitive development in AnimalWatch suggested that hints that use concrete materials in the explanations yield higher learning than those which explain the solution with numerical procedures for students at early cognitive development stages (Arroyo et al., 2000). Thus, Wayang Outpost also functions as a research test bed to investigate the interaction of gender and cognitive skills in mathematics problem solving, and in selecting the best pedagogical approach. The site includes integrated on-line assessments of component cognitive skills known to correlate with mathematics achievement, including an assessment of the student's proficiency with math facts, indicating the degree of fluency (accuracy and speed) of arithmetic computation (Royer et al., 1999), and spatial ability, as indicated by performance on an standard assessment of mental rotation skill (Vandenberg et al., 1978). Both tests have captured gender differences in the past.

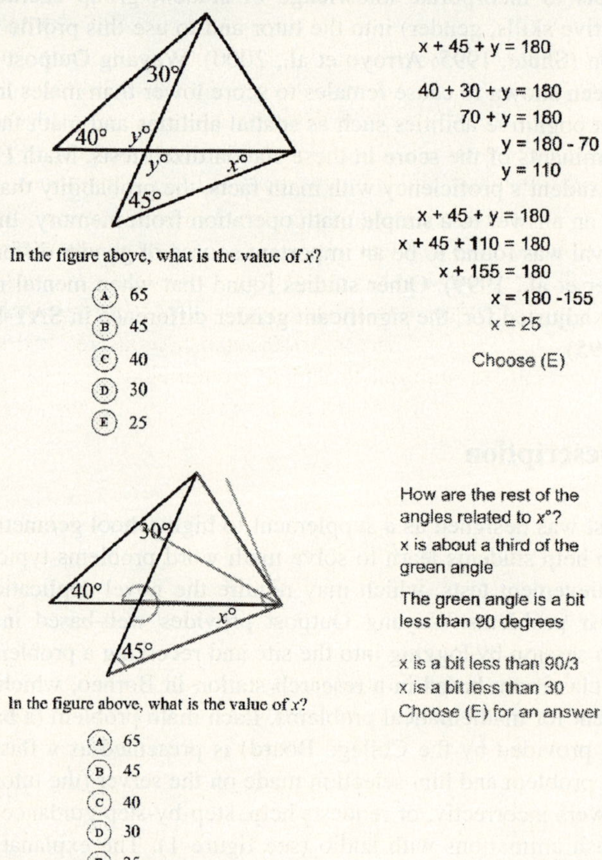

Fig. 1. The computational (top) and visual (bottom) teaching strategies

Help in Wayang Outpost. Each geometry problem in Wayang is linked to two alternative types of hints, following different strategies to solving the problem: one strategy provides a computational and numeric approach and the second provides spatial transformations and visual estimations, generally encompassing a spatial "trick" that makes the problem simpler to solve. An example is shown in Figure 1. The choice of hint type should be customized for individual students on the basis of their cognitive profile, to help them develop strategies and approaches that may be more effective for particular problems. For example, students who score low on the spatial ability assessment might receive a high proportion of hints that emphasize mental rotation and estimation, approaches that students of poor spatial ability may not apply even though they are generally more effective in a timed testing situation. This is a major hypothesis we have evaluated, and the findings are described in the evaluation section.

Adventures: fantasy component. Wayang Outpost includes measures of transfer via performance on challenging multi-step math problems integrated into virtual adventures. Animated characters based on real female scientists (who serve as science, technology, engineering and mathematics role models) lead the virtual adventures. Thus the fantasy component is female-friendly and uses female role models. For example, the character based on Anne Russon (orangutan researcher, University of Toronto) takes the student across the rainforest to rescue orangutans trapped in a fire. Within the fantasy adventure, students are provided hints and shown SAT problems that are similar to the problem being solved within the adventure. The Lori Perkins character (Zoo Atlanta, Georgia) leads the "illegal logging" adventure involving the over-harvesting of rainforest teakwood, leading to flooding and loss of orangutan habitat. Students are asked to calculate a variety of items: discrepancies between the observed and permitted areas of harvest; orangutan habitat area lost to the resulting floods; perimeter distances required to detour around flooded areas; and how far to travel to reach areas with emergency cell phone access using cone models of satellite coverage.

3 Intelligence for Adaptive Tutoring

As the student works through a problem, performance data (e.g., latency, answer choice, hints requested) are stored in a centralized database. This raw data about student interactions with the system feed all our intelligent modules, to select problems at the appropriate level of challenge, to chooses hints that will be helpful for the student, to detect negative attitudes towards help and the tutoring system in general.

Major difficulties in building a student model for standardized testing include the fact that we start without a clear idea of either problem difficulty or which skills should be taught. Skills are sparse across problems, so there is a high degree of uncertainty in the estimation of students' knowledge. This is different from the design of most other tutoring systems: generally, the ITS designer knows the topics to be taught, and then needs to create the content and pedagogy. In the case of standardized testing, the content is given, without a clear indication of the underlying skills. The only clear goal is to have students improve their achievement in these types of problems. Despite clear indicators of learning have been observed, a more effective Wayang Outpost is being built by adapting the tutor's decisions in various parts of the system. We are adding artificial intelligence for adaptivity in the following tutoring decisions:

Problem selection. Problems in Wayang are expensive to build, as the help is sophisticated (using animations and sound), and each problem is extremely different from each other, thus making it hard to show a problem more than twice with different arguments, without having students get the impression that it is "the same problem again". The result is that we cannot afford the construction of hundreds or thousands of problems, so that certain problems can be used and others discarded. Because Wayang Outpost currently contains 70 distinct problems, the reality is that a sophisticated algorithm that uses skill mastery levels to determine the appropriate skills that a problem should contain is not necessary at this stage. However, we believe some form of intelligent problem selection would be beneficial. We have thus implemented an algorithm to optimize word problem "ordering", a pedagogical agent whose goal is to show a problem where the student will behave slightly worse than the average behavior expected for the problem (in terms of mistakes made and hints seen). Expected values of behavior at a problem computed from log files from prior users of the system (which used random problem selection). The agent keeps a "desired problem difficulty" factor for the next problem. The next problem selected is the one that has the closest difficulty to the desired difficulty, which changes after every solved problem: when the student behaves better than what is expected for the problem (based on log files' data of past users), the "desired problem difficulty" factor increases. Otherwise, it decreases, and thus the next problem will be easier.

Level of information in hints. When the student seeks for help, a hint explains a step in the solution. Sequences of hints explain the full solution to the problem when students keep clicking for help. However, hints have been designed to be "skipped", in that each hint contains a summary of the previous steps. Thus, skipping a hint implies providing minimal information about the step (e.g. if a student clicks for help and the first hint is skipped, the second hint shown will provide a short static summary of the first step and the full explanation for the second step in the solution using multimedia). Martin&Arroyo (2004) present the results of experiments with simulated students, which showed how a Reinforcement Learning agent can learn how to "skip" hints that don't seem useful. A more efficient Wayang Outpost will be built by providing only those hints that seem "useful". The agent learns the usefulness of hints by rewarding highly those hints that lead the student to an answer and punishing those hints that lead to incorrect answers or make the students ask for more help.

Attitudes inference. There is growing evidence that students may have non-optimal help seeking behaviors, and that they seek and react to help depending on student motivation, gender, past experience and other factors (Aleven et al, 2003). We found that students' negative attitudes towards help and the system are detrimental to learning, and that these attitudes are correlated to specific behaviors with the tutor such as time spent on hints, problems seen per minute, hints seen per problem, standard deviation of hints asked per problem, etc. We created a Bayesian Network from students' log files and surveys about attitudes towards the system, with the purpose of making inferences of students' attitudes and beliefs *while* students use the system, and we proposed remedial actions when specific attitudes are detected (Arroyo et al., 2004).

Teaching strategy selection. Evaluation studies described in section 8 try to capture the link between the spatial and computational teaching strategies described in section 4, and different cognitive abilities (spatial ability and memory retrieval of math facts), with the idea of "macro-adapting" teaching strategies to cognitive abilities, which are diagnosed at pretest time, by selecting one teaching strategy over the other one for the whole tutoring session. Results in section 8 provide guidelines for strategy selection depending on cognitive abilities, which will be implemented and tested in schools in fall 2005.

4 Evaluation Studies

We tested the relevance of students' cognitive strengths (e.g., math fact retrieval speed and mental rotation abilities) to the effective selection of pedagogies described in previous sections, to evaluate the worth of adapting help strategy selection to basic cognitive abilities of each student. As described in the previous sections, two help strategies were provided by the tutor, emphasizing either spatial or computational approaches to the solution. The question that arises immediately is whether the help component should *capitalize* or *compensat*e for a student's cognitive strengths. Is the spatial approach effective for students with high spatial ability (because it capitalizes on their cognitive strengths) or for those with low spatial ability (because it compensates for their cognitive weaknesses)? Is the computational help better for students with high mathematics facts accuracy and retrieval speed from memory (because it capitalizes on the fast retrieval of arithmetic facts), or is it better for students with low speed of math fact retrieval (because it trains them in the retrieval of facts)? Given a specific cognitive profile, what type of help should be provided to the student?

4.1 Experiment Design

Two studies were carried out in rural and urban area schools in Massachusetts. In each of the studies, students were randomly assigned to two different versions of the system: one providing spatial help, the other providing computational help. Students took a computer-based mental rotation test and also a computer-based test that assessed a student's speed and accuracy in determining whether simple mathematics facts were true or false (Royer et al., 1999).

In the first study, 95 students were involved, 75% females. There was no pre and post-test data, so learning was captured with a *'Learning Factor'* that describes how students decrease their need for help in subsequent problems during the tutoring session, on average. This measure should be higher when students learn more. See a description of this measure (which can be higher than 100%) in (Arroyo et al., 2004). Students used Wayang Outpost for about 2 hours. Students also used the *adventures* of the system for about an hour. After that, students were given a survey asking for feedback about the system and evaluating their willingness to use the system again. The second study involved 95 students in an urban area school in Massachusetts, who used the tutoring system in the same way for about the same amount of time. These students were also given the cognitive skills pretest and a post-tutor survey asking about perceptions of the system.

4.2 Results

In the first study, we found a significant gender differences in spatial ability, specifically a significant difference in the number of correct responses (independent samples t-test, t=2, p=0.05), females having significantly less correct answers than males. Females also spent more time in each test item, though not significantly more. We did not find differences for the math fact retrieval test in this experiment, neither for accuracy nor speed. In the second study, we found a significant gender difference in math fact accuracy (females scoring higher than males). We did not find, however, a gender difference in retrieval speed in any of the two studies, differences that other authors have found (Royer, 1999). We created a variable that combined accuracy and speed to generate an overall score of math fact retrieval ability and spatial ability. By classifying students into high and low spatial and math fact retrieval ability (by splitting at the median score), we established a 2x2x2 design to test the impact of hints and cognitive abilities on students' learning, with a group size of 11-15 students.

In the Fall 2003 study, significant interaction effects were found between cognitive abilities and teaching strategies in predicting learning, based on an ANOVA (R^2=0.68). An interaction effect between mental rotation and the type of help was found (F=3.5, p=0.06, figure 2, table 1). The means in this study suggest that hints capitalize on students' mental rotation: when a student has low spatial abilities, learning is higher with computational help, and when the student has high spatial ability, hints that teach with spatial transformations produce the most learning.

Table 1. Learning as an average percent reduction of help requests in subsequent problems

	Low spatial		High Spatial	
	Spatial help	Comp. help	Spatial help	Comp. Help
Low retrieval	-10%	**47%**	**43%**	-13%
High retrieval	-9%	**325%**	**18%**	-15%

Table 2. Average percent improvement from pre to posttest (pencil and paper)

	Low spatial		High Spatial	
	Spatial help	Comp. help	Spatial help	Comp. Help
Low retrieval	**83%**	43%	**23%**	19%
High re-trieval	12%	**19%**	19%	**26%**

In the second study, pre and posttest improvements were used as a measure of learning. A significant overall difference in percentage of questions answered correctly from pre- to post-test was found, $F(1,95)=20.20$, $p=.000$. Students showed an average 27% increase of their pre-test score at post-test time after 2 hours of using the tutor. An ANOVA revealed an interaction effect between type of hint, gender and math fact retrieval in predicting pre to posttest score increase ($F(1,73)=4.88$, $p=0.03$), suggesting that girls are the ones who are prone to capitalize on their math fact retrieval ability while boys are not (table 2). Girls of low math fact retrieval do not improve their score when exposed to computational hints, while they do improve when exposed to spatial hints. A similar ANOVA just for boys gave no significant interaction effect between hint type and math fact retrieval, while another one just for girls showed a stronger effect ($F(1,41)=5.0$, $p=0.03$). The effect is described in figure 3.

In the first study, the spatial dimension was more relevant than the math fact retrieval dimension, while in the second study, math fact retrieval was more important than spatial abilities, despite the fact that students had similar scores on average in the two studies. Despite these disparities, both results are consistent in that that the system should provide teaching strategies that capitalize on the students' cognitive strengths whenever there is one cognitive ability that is stronger than the other one.

Fantasy component. A second goal in our evaluation studies was to find whether the fantasy component in the adventures had differential effects on the motivation of girls and boys to use the system, given the female-friendly characteristics of the fantasy context and the female role models. After using the plain tutor with no fantasy component, we asked students whether they would want to use the system again. Students then used the adventures (SAT problems embedded in adventures with narratives about orangutans and female scientists) after using the plain tutor and we then asked them again whether they would want to use the system. In both occasions, students were asked how many more times they would like to use the Wayang system (1 to 5 scale), from would not use it again (1) to as many times as possible (5).

In the first study, we found a significant gender difference in willingness to return to use the fantasy component of the system (independent samples t-test, $t=2.2$, $p=0.04$), boys willing to return to the "adventures" less than girls. This effect was repeated in the second study (t-test, $t=2.2$, $p=0.03$). This suggests that girls enjoyed the adventures more than boys did, possibly because girls may have felt more identified with female characters, as there is no significant difference in willingness to return to the plain tutor section with no fantasy component. Again, the adventures section seems to capture females' attention more than males, while the plain tutor attracts both genders equaly. However, significant independent samples t-tests indicated that girls liked the overall system more, took it more seriously, thought the help was useful more than males, heard the audio in the explanations more.

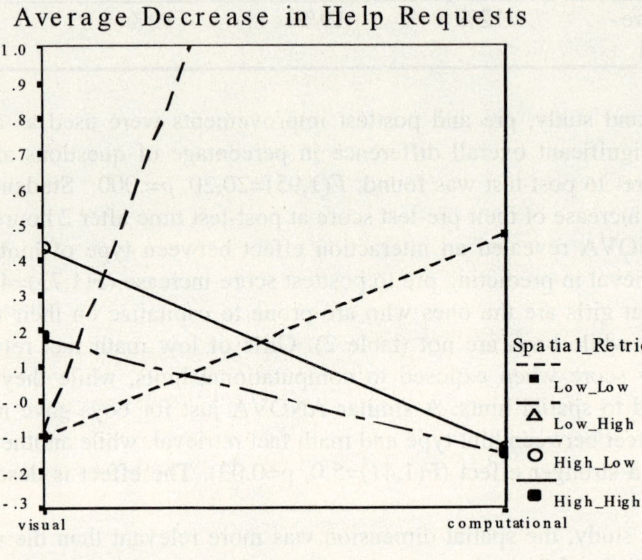

Fig. 2. Learning with two different teaching strategies in the Fall 2003 study.

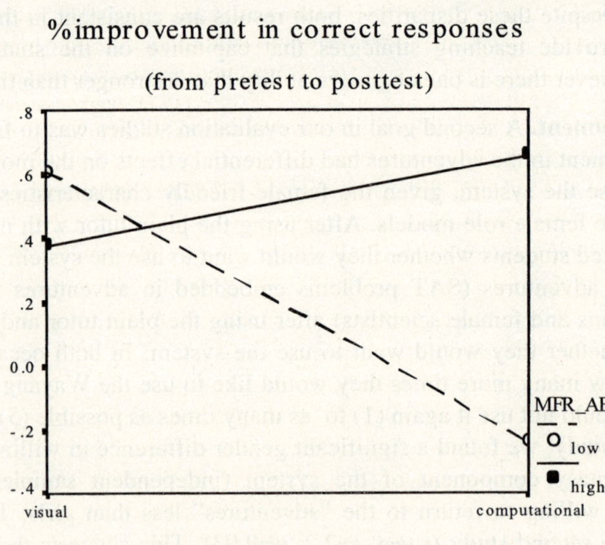

Fig. 3. Learning with two different teaching strategies in the 2004 study (girls only).

5 Summary

We have described Wayang Outpost, a tutoring system for the mathematics section of the SAT (Scholastic Aptitude Test). We described how we are adding intelligence for adaptive behavior in different parts of the system. Girls are especially motivated to use the *fantasy* component. The tutor was beneficial for students in general, with high improvements from pre to posttest. However, results suggest that adapting the provided hints to students' cognitive skills yields higher learning. Students with low-spatial and high-retrieval profiles learn more with computational help (using arithmetic, formulas and equations), and students with high-spatial and low-retrieval profiles, learn more with spatial explanations (spatial tricks and visual estimations of angles and lengths). These abilities may be diagnosed with pretests before starting to use the system. Future work involves evaluating the impact of cognitive skills training on students' achievement with the tutor, and evaluating the intelligent adaptive tutor.

Acknowledgements. We gratefully acknowledge support for this work from the National Science Foundation, HRD/EHR #012080. Any opinions, findings, conclusions or recommendations expressed in this material are those of the authors and do not necessarily reflect the views of the granting agencies.

References

Arroyo, I.; Beck, J.; Woolf, B.; Beal., C; Schultz, K. (2000) Macroadapting Animalwatch to gender and cognitive differences with respect to hint interactivity and symbolism. Proceedings of the Fifth International Conference on Intelligent Tutoring Systems.

Arroyo, I. (2003). Quantitative evaluation of gender differences, cognitive development differences and software effectiveness for an elementary mathematics intelligent tutoring system. Doctoral dissertation. UMass Amherst.

Arroyo, I., Murray, T., Woolf, B.P., Beal, C.R. (2004) Inferring unobservable learning variables from students' help seeking behavior. This volume.

Casey, N.B.; Nuttall, R.; Pezaris, E.; Benbow, C. (1995). The influence of spatial ability on gender differences in math college entrance test scores across diverse samples. Developmental Psychology, 31, 697-705.

Royer, J.M., Tronsky, L.N., Chan, Y., Jackson, S.J., Merchant, H. (1999). Math fact retrieval as the cognitive mechanism underlying gender differences in math test performance. Contemporary Educational Psychology, 24.

Shute, V. (1995). SMART: Student Modeling Approach for Responsive Tutoring. In *User Modeling and User-Adapted Interaction.* 5:1-44.

Martin, K., Arroyo, I. (2004). AgentX: Using Reinforcement Learning to Improve the Effectiveness of Intelligent Tutoring Systems. This volume.

Vandenberg, G. S., & Kuse, R. A. (1978). Mental Rotations, A Group Test of Three-Dimensional Spatial Visualization. Perceptual and Motor Skills 47, 599-604

Wainer, H.; Steiberg, L. S. Sex differences in performance on the mathematics section of the Scholastic Aptitude Test: a bidirectional validity study, Harvard Educational Review 62 no. 3 (1992), 323-336.

Can Automated Questions Scaffold Children's Reading Comprehension?

Joseph E. Beck, Jack Mostow, and Juliet Bey[1]

Project LISTEN (www.cs.cmu.edu/~listen)
Carnegie Mellon University
RI-NSH 4213, 5000 Forbes Avenue, Pittsburgh, PA 15213-3890, USA
Telephone: 412-268-1330 voice / 412-268-6436 FAX
{Joseph.Beck, Jack.Mostow}@cs.cmu.edu

Abstract. Can automatically generated questions scaffold reading comprehension? We automated three kinds of multiple-choice questions in children's assisted reading:

1. *Wh-* questions: ask a generically worded *What/Where/When* question.
2. Sentence prediction: ask which of three sentences belongs next.
3. Cloze: ask which of four words best fills in a blank in the next sentence.

A within-subject experiment in the spring 2003 version of Project LISTEN's Reading Tutor randomly inserted all three kinds of questions during stories as it helped children read them. To compare their effects on story-specific comprehension, we analyzed 15,196 subsequent cloze test responses by 404 children in grades 1-4.

- *Wh-* questions significantly raised children's subsequent cloze performance.
- This effect was cumulative over the story rather than a recency effect.
- Sentence prediction questions probably helped ($p = .07$).
- Cloze questions did not improve performance on later questions.
- The rate of hasty responses rose over the year.
- Asking a question less than 10 seconds after the previous question increased the likelihood of the student giving a hasty response.

The results show that a computer can scaffold a child's comprehension of a given text without understanding the text itself, provided it avoids irritating the student.

1 Introduction: Problem and Approach

In 2000, the National Reading Panel [10] sifted through the reading research literature to identify interventions whose efficacy is supported by scientifically rigorous evidence. We focus here on a type of intervention found to improve children's comprehension skills when performed by humans: asking questions. "Teachers ask students questions during or after reading passages of text. [...] A question focuses the student on particular content and can facilitate reasoning (e.g., answering why or how)." [10]

---

[1] Now at University of Southern California Law School, Los Angeles, CA 90089.

J.C. Lester et al. (Eds.): ITS 2004, LNCS 3220, pp. 478–490, 2004.

Can such interventions be automated? Are the automated versions effective? How can we tell?

We investigate these questions in the context of Project LISTEN's Reading Tutor, which listens to children read aloud, and helps them learn to read [7]. During the 2002-2003 school year, children used the Reading Tutor daily on some 180 Windows™ computers in nine public schools.

The aspect of the 2002-2003 version relevant to this study was its ability to insert questions when children read. The Reading Tutor presented text incrementally, adding one sentence (or fragment) at a time. Before doing so, it could interrupt the story to present a multiple-choice question. It displayed a prompt and a menu of choices, and read them both aloud to the student using digitized human speech, highlighting each menu item in turn. The student chose a response by clicking on it. The Reading Tutor then continued, giving the student spoken feedback on whether the answer was correct, at least when it could tell. We tried to avoid free response typed input since, aside from difficulties in scoring responses, students using the Reading Tutor are too young to be skilled typists. In other experiments students average 30 seconds to type a single word. Requiring typed responses would be far too time-consuming.

This paper investigates three research issues:

- What kinds of automated questions assist children's reading comprehension?
- Are their benefits within a story cumulative or transient?
- At what point do questions frustrate students?

Section 2 describes the automated questions. Section 3 describes our methodology and data. Section 4 reports results for the three research issues. Section 5 concludes.

2 Interventions: Automated Question Insertion

First we had to generate comprehension questions. Good questions should help student comprehension. Skilled personnel might write good questions by hand. However, this approach would be labor-intensive and text-specific. The Reading Tutor has hundreds of stories, totaling tens of thousands of words. Writing good questions for every story, let alone every sentence, would take considerable time, and the questions would not be reusable for new stories.

Natural language understanding might be used to generate questions based on understanding the text. Although this approach might in principle provide good questions for any text, it would require non-trivial development effort to achieve high quality output, efficient performance, and robustness to arbitrary text.

Instead, we eschewed both the "brute force" and "high tech" approaches, and took a "low tech" approach. That is, we looked for ways to generate comprehension questions automatically, but without relying on technology to understand the text.

2.1 Generic wh-Questions

Teachers can improve children's reading comprehension by training them to generate questions [10], especially generic *wh-* (e.g. *wh*at, *wh*ere, *wh*en) questions [11]. Accordingly, we developed a few generic questions that we could reuse in (virtually) any context: *Who? What? When? Where? Why? How? So?* Each of these questions is almost always applicable, and very often useful. The last question, short for *So what?*, was suggested by Al Corbett, as a short way to ask the larger significance of the current sentence. Not only should asking these questions stimulate comprehension, but also asking them enough might train students to ask them themselves.

First we had to make the questions usable. Our initial attempts failed, in informative ways. Our first thought was to insert one-word questions to elicit free-form spoken responses, which we would not attempt to recognize; their purpose was to stimulate comprehension, not to assess it. However, not every w*h*- question makes sense in every context. We feared that asking nonsensical questions would confuse children.

We tried to overcome this problem by asking the meta-question, *Click on a question you can answer, or click Back to reread the sentence*: *Who? What? When? Where? Why? How? So?* This approach was a step in the direction of training students to generate questions and would hopefully stimulate children's metacognition.

However, when we "kid-tested" this meta-question at a July 2002 reading lab, children found it too confusing, as evidenced by prolonged inaction or by asking the lab monitor for help. We attributed these difficulties to several problems, which we addressed as follows. To avoid cognitive overload caused by the number of questions, we abandoned the meta-question approach and had the Reading Tutor randomly choose which question to ask. The task was too hard for young children with poor comprehension, so we restricted questions to stories at a grade 3 level or harder; comprehension interventions seldom start before grade 3 [10]. The one-word questions were too short to map clearly to the context, so we rephrased the prompts to make them more explicit, at the suggestion of LISTENer June Sison. The questions were too open-ended to suggest answers, so we changed them to be multiple-choice instead of free-form. Usability testing at an August 2002 reading lab indicated that children understood the revised questions:

What part of the story are you reading now? the end; the beginning; the middle

What has happened so far? a problem has been solved; a mistake; a problem; a problem is being solved; a meeting; an introduction; facts were given; nothing yet; I don't know

Has this happened to you? It happens to me sometimes; It has happened to someone I know; It has never happened to me; This is a silly question!

What could you learn from this? How not to do something; Some new words; How to solve a problem; How to do something; New facts about a subject; A new way of saying something; I don't know

When does this take place? in the present; in the future; in the past; It could happen in the past; I can't tell

Where does this take place? in an apartment; in a house; in an ancient kingdom; anywhere; in outer space; indoors; in a forest; nowhere; on a farm; in the water; outdoors; I can't tell

We also added questions limited to particular genres, e.g., *Who* for fiction. We didn't think of any good generic multiple choice *Why* questions.

2.2 Sentence Prediction Questions

One way to stimulate or test comprehension of a text is to ask the reader to unscramble it. We operationalized this idea as a sentence prediction task in the form of the multiple-choice question *Which will come next?* The three response choices were the next three sentences of the story, in randomized order.

The sentence prediction task had an advantage over the generic *wh-* questions in that the Reading Tutor knew which answer was correct. This information enabled it to give immediate feedback by saying (in recorded human speech) either *Way to go!* or *Not quite.*

2.3 Cloze Questions

A third kind of multiple-choice question was a "cloze" (fill-in-the-blank) prompt generated from a story sentence by deleting a word, e.g. *Resources such as fish are renewable, as long as too many are not taken or ______. coral; damage; market; destroyed.* The choices consisted of the missing word plus three distractor words chosen randomly from the same story, but so as to have the same general type as the correct word:

- "sight" words (the most frequent 225 words in a corpus of children's stories)
- "easy" words (the top 3,000 except for sight words)
- "hard" words (the next 22,000 words), and
- "defined" words (words explicitly annotated with explanations).

The Reading Tutor automatically generated, inserted, and scored such multiple choice cloze questions [8]. The 2002 study had used these automatically generated questions to assess comprehension. Students' performance on such questions predicted their performance on the vocabulary and comprehension subtests of the Woodcock Reading Mastery Test with correlations better than 0.8.

This study also found careless guessing, indicated by responding sooner than 3 seconds after the prompt. In an attempt to reduce guessing, we modified cloze questions to provide explicit feedback on correctness: *Alright, good job!* or *I don't think so.*

Brandão & Oakhill [4] asked children *Do you know why?* to probe – and stimulate – their comprehension. We adapted this question to follow up cloze questions on "defined" words. After a correct answer, the Reading Tutor added, *That's right! Do you know why?* If not, or after an incorrect answer, it asked, *Which phrase fits better in the sentence?* The two choices were short definitions of the correct word and a distractor.

3 Methodology: Experimental Design, Data, and Analysis

The next problem was how to tell if asking automated questions improved students' comprehension. We couldn't simply test whether their comprehension improved over time, because we expected it to improve as a consequence of their regular classroom instruction. A conventional between-subjects experiment would have compared two versions of the Reading Tutor, one with the questions and one without, in terms of their impact on students' gains in comprehension skills. However, such experiments are costly in time, personnel, and participants.

Project LISTEN had previously addressed this difficulty by embedding within-subject experiments in the Reading Tutor to evaluate various tutorial interventions. For example, one experiment evaluated the effect of vocabulary assistance by randomly explaining some words but not others, and administering multiple choice questions the next day to see if students did better on the explained words [1]. These experiments assumed that instruction on one word was unlikely to affect performance on another word – i.e., that vocabulary knowledge can be approximated as a collection of separately learned atomic pieces of knowledge that do not transfer to each other.

In contrast, instruction on a general comprehension skill violates this non-transfer assumption. We therefore decided to look for *scaffolding* effects instead of *learning* effects. Students who are ready to benefit from comprehension strategies but have not yet internalized them should comprehend better with the intervention than without it. We therefore look for a difference between assisted and unassisted performance.

As in [8], we segmented student-tutor interaction sequences into episodes with measurable local outcomes. We hypothesized that if the intervention were effective, students would perform better on cloze questions for awhile thereafter – for how long, we didn't know; perhaps the next few sentences.

3.1 Within-Subject Randomized-Dosage Experimental Manipulation

The question-asking experiment operated as follows. Before each sentence, the Reading Tutor randomly decided whether to insert a question, and if so, of what kind. Thus the number and kinds of questions varied randomly from one story reading to another. The Reading Tutor inserted questions only in new stories, not in stories students were rereading, where they might therefore remember answers based on prior exposure.

The three kinds of questions differed slightly in when they could occur. Such differences between experimental conditions can introduce bias if not properly controlled. To avoid confusing poor readers, the Reading Tutor inserted *wh-* questions, sentence prediction questions, and "defined word" cloze questions only in stories at and above level C (roughly grade 3). However, it asked other cloze questions in stories at all levels. Also, some *wh-* questions were genre-specific. For example, the Reading Tutor inserted *Who* questions in fiction, which it could assume had one or more characters, but not in non-fiction and poetry, which can violate that assumption.

To avoid sample bias we needed to compare data generated under the same conditions. For example, it would be unfair to compare fiction-specific *wh-*questions to null interventions in other genres. We therefore excluded data from stories below level C and genre-specific *wh-* questions, leaving "3W": *what, when,* and *where.*

3.2 Data Set

The data set for this paper came from eight public schools that used the Reading Tutor throughout the 2002-2003 school year, located in four Pittsburgh-area school districts, urban and suburban, low-income and affluent, African-American and Caucasian. Reading Tutors at each school used a shared database on a server at that school. Each night these servers sent the day's transactions back via the Internet to our lab to update a single aggregated database. We mapped research questions onto MySQL queries as described in [9]. We used SPSS and Excel to analyze and visualize query results. A bug in the Reading Tutor's mechanism for assigning students to appropriate story levels affected data for fall 2002 [3], so we restricted our data set to the 2003 data.

Of 404 users the Reading Tutor logged as having read stories at level C or higher in 2003, 252 students had moderate usage – that is, at least one hour and at least 10 sentences. There were 56 first-graders, 96 second-graders, 50 third-graders, 17 fourth-graders, and 33 students for whom we did not know their grade.

The data set includes a total of 23,372 questions, consisting of 6,720 3W questions, 1,865 sentence prediction questions, and 15,187 cloze questions. Table 1 shows the mean and maximum number of questions of each kind seen by each student. The minimum is not shown because it was zero for each kind. While reading new stories at levels C-G (approximately grades 3-7), students were asked a 3W, prediction, or cloze question about once every 4 minutes or 10 sentences, on average.

Table 1. Questions asked (per-student mean and maximum)

	Number		**Per minute**		**Per sentence**	
	Mean	Max	Mean	Max	Mean	Max
3W	24.9	164	0.0865	0.60	4%	19%
Prediction	7	40	0.0235	0.12	1%	6%
Cloze	35.7	278	0.1232	0.60	5%	24%
All	67.7	472	0.2332	1.20	10%	40%

3.3 Cloze Performance as Outcome Variable

To measure students' fluctuating comprehension of stories as they read, we used available data – their responses to the inserted questions. We did not know which answers to the *wh-* questions were correct, some questions can have multiple correct answers, and some questions could not even be scored by a human rater (e.g. *Has this happened to you?*).

The sentence prediction and cloze questions were both machine-scorable. In fact the Reading Tutor gave students immediate feedback on responses to them. But did they really measure comprehension?

To make sure, we validated students' performance on each kind of question against their Passage Comprehension pretest scores. Performance on sentence prediction questions averaged only 41% correct. To test their validity as a measure of comprehension, we correlated this percentage against students' posttest Passage Comprehension, excluding students with fewer than 10 non-hasty sentence prediction responses. The correlation was only 0.03, indicating that they were not a valid test of comprehension. In contrast, Mostow *et al.* [8] had already shown that performance on automated cloze questions in the 2001-2002 version of the Reading Tutor predicted Passage Comprehension at R=.5 for raw % correct, and at R=0.85 in a model that included the effects of item difficulty of story level and word type. We didn't regenerate such a model for the 2003 data, but we confirmed that it showed a similar correlation of raw cloze performance to test scores.

Note that the same cloze question operated both as an intervention that might scaffold comprehension, and as a local outcome measure of the preceding interventions. We use the terms "cloze intervention" and "test question" to distinguish these roles.

Fig. 1 shows the number of recent interventions before 15,196 cloze test items. We operationalize "recent" as "within the past two minutes," based on our initial analysis, which suggested a two-minute window for effects on cloze performance.

3.4 Logistic Regression Model

To test the effects of 3W, prediction, and cloze interventions on students' subsequent comprehension, we constructed a logistic regression model [6] in SPSS to predict the correctness of their responses to test questions.

To control for differences between students, we included student identity as a factor in the model. Omitting student identity would ignore statistical dependencies among the same student's performance on different items. Including student identity as a factor accounts for statistical dependencies among responses by the same student, subject to the assumption that responses are independent given the ability of the student and the difficulty of the item. This "local independence" assumption is justified by the fact that each test question was asked only once, and was unlikely to affect the student's answers to other test questions. We neglect possible dependency among test responses caused by a common underlying cause such as story difficulty.

To control for differences in difficulty of test questions, the model included the type of cloze question, according to the type of word deleted -- "sight," "easy," "hard," or "defined". An earlier study [8] had previously found that word type significantly affected cloze performance.

To represent cumulative effects of different types of questions, our model included as separate covariates the number of 3W, prediction, and cloze interventions, since the start of the current story. Our initial analysis had suggested that cloze performance was higher for two minutes after a 3W question. To model such recency effects we added similar covariates for the number of 3W and cloze interventions in the two minutes preceding the current test question.

However, we treated recent sentence prediction questions differently, because they revealed the next three sentences, thereby giving away the answer to test questions on those sentences. To exclude such contamination, we screened out from the data set any test response closely preceded by a sentence prediction question. Consequently, our model had no covariate for the number of recent sentence prediction questions, because it was always zero.

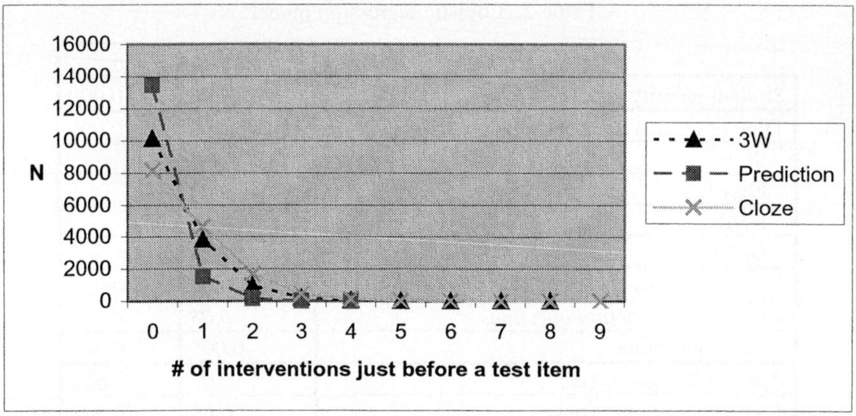

Fig. 1. Histogram of # recent interventions

The model included three covariates to represent possible temporal effects at different scales. To model improvement over the course of the year, we included the month when the question was asked. To model changes in comprehension over the course of the story, we included the time elapsed since the story started. To model effects of interruption, we included the time since the most recent Reading Tutor question.

4 Results

Table 2 shows which predictor variables in the logistic regression model affected cloze test performance. As expected, student identity and test question type were highly significant. The beta value for a covariate shows how an increase of 1 in the value of the covariate affects the log odds of the outcome. Thus the increasingly negative beta values for successive test question types reflect their increasing difficulty. These beta values are not normalized and hence should not be compared to measure effect size. The p values give the significance of each predictor variable after controlling for the other predictors.

4.1 What Kinds of Questions Assisted Children's Reading Comprehension?

According to the logistic regression model, 3W questions had a positive effect (beta = .05, p = .023) and sentence prediction had a possible effect (beta = .08, p = *.072*). Cloze interventions had no effect (beta = -.005, p = .765), lending credence to our local independence assumption. These results cannot be credited simply to the time spent so far reading the story, which had a *negative* though insignificant effect (beta = -.013, p = .137) on cloze performance. We conclude that *3W questions boosted comprehension enough to outweigh the cost of disrupting reading.*

Table 2. Logistic regression model

	Beta	p
Student identity	.	0.000
Type of (cloze) test question	0	0.000
Sight	0	
Easy	-0.03	
Hard	-0.19	
Defined	-1.04	
# 3W questions	0.05	0.023
# sentence prediction questions	*0.08*	*0.072*
# cloze questions	-0.005	0.765
# recent 3W questions	*-0.07*	*0.074*
# recent cloze questions	0.02	0.548
Time of year (month)	-0.01	0.551
Time since start of story (minutes)	-0.013	0.137
Time since last intervention (sec)	-0.001	0.036

Generic questions force readers to carry more of the load than do text-specific questions. Is this extra burden on the student's working memory worthwhile [5] or a hindrance [2]? Generic 3W questions, which let students figure out how a question relates to the current context, had a positive effect. Cloze interventions, which are sentence-specific and more explicitly related to the text, did not.

What about feedback? One might expect questions to help more when students are told if their answers are correct. One reason is cognitive: the feedback itself may improve comprehension by flagging misconceptions. Another reason is motivational: students might consider a question more seriously if they receive feedback.

Despite the lack of such feedback, 3W questions bolstered comprehension of later sentences. Despite providing such feedback, cloze interventions did not help. Evidently the advantages of 3W questions sufficed to overcome their lack of feedback.

4.2 Were the Benefits Within a Story Cumulative or Transient?

We had previously [3] considered only the effect of an intervention on the very next test item. Our logistic regression model now revealed the effect of recent 3W questions was actually negative, and only marginally significant. Recent cloze interventions had no effect. In summary, the *benefits of 3W questions were cumulative.*

Fig. 2 shows how cloze performance varied with the number of preceding questions of each type. To reduce noise, cases with fewer than 30 observations are omitted. The *y* values are raw % correct, not adjusted for any of the logistic regression variables, so they must be interpreted with caution, but suggest that 3W beats cloze after 4 questions.

4.3 At What Point Did Questions Frustrate Students?

The temporal portion of the logistic regression model shows that cloze performance fell over the year, over the story, and (significantly) right after an intervention. Why?

Fig. 3 shows how the blowoff rate changed after any Reading Tutor intervention. The *x*-axes show the time in seconds since the previous question. As the axis labels reflect, we binned into 2-second intervals. The blowoff rate spiked at nearly 90% for cloze questions asked too soon. Within 20 seconds, the blowoff rate decayed back to an asymptotic level of about 12%.

We analyzed how often students avoided answering questions. The "blowoff rate" measured the percentage of hasty responses. Prior analysis of cloze questions [8] had shown that students who responded in less than 3 seconds performed at or near chance level and were probably not seriously considering the question. The blowoff rates in 2003 were 23% for 3W questions, 12% for sentence prediction, and 11% for cloze (computed not just on the subset used in the logistic regression). The higher blowoff rate for 3W questions might be due to their lack of immediate feedback. As Table 3 shows, the overall percentage of hasty cloze responses rose over time.

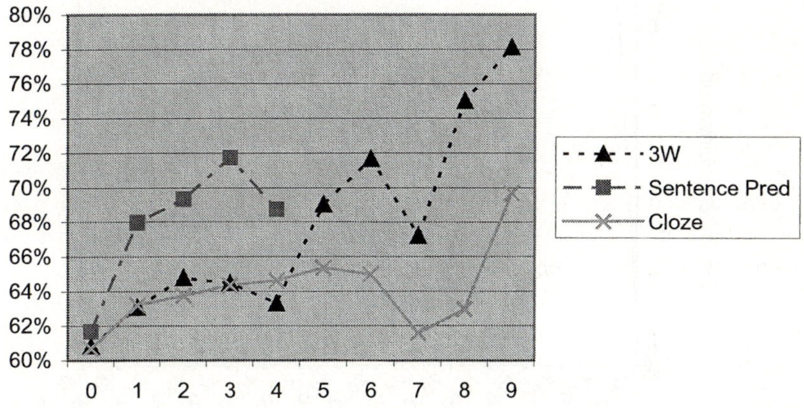

Fig. 2. Cloze performance versus number of preceding questions of each type

Table 3. Changing rate of hasty cloze responses in spring 2003

Month	Blowoff rate	# test items
Jan	9.9%	3255
Feb	11.4%	3224
Mar	16.0%	3889
Apr	15.7%	3120
May	18.7%	1612

In summary, *frustration with inserted questions, as measured by how often students responded too hastily to give them careful thought, rose over the course of the year and spiked when one question followed another by less than 10 seconds.*

5 Conclusion: Contributions and Lessons

This paper contributes interventions, evaluation, and methodology.

We reported three automatic ways to ask multiple-choice comprehension questions. Developing these methods involved adapting, user-testing, and generalizing methods used by human teachers. Generic *wh-* questions adapt a method found effective by the National Reading Panel. Sentence prediction questions resemble manually created unscrambling tasks. We augmented a previously reported method [8] for cloze question generation, adding feedback and *Do you know why?* follow-up probes.

We evaluated the effect of these questions on student comprehension as measured by subsequent cloze test questions. The 3W questions we evaluated had a significant positive effect, which was cumulative rather than a recency effect. The sentence prediction questions had a probable effect, and the cloze questions had no effect. Future work should study how effects vary by student level, text difficulty, and question type.

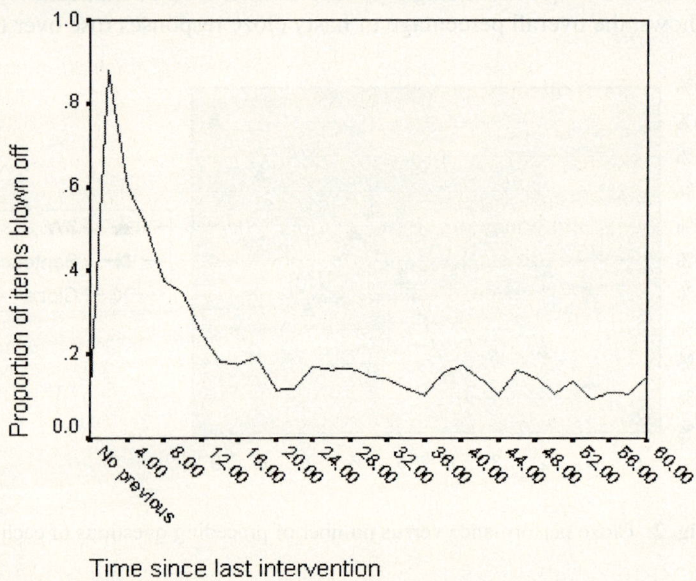

Fig. 3. Blowoff rate versus time (in seconds) since previous question

We analyzed student frustration as shown by hasty responses. Such avoidance behavior was likelier when less than 10 seconds elapsed between questions.

Our evaluation methodology incorporated an interesting approach to the challenge of evaluating the effects of alternative tutorial interventions. The within-subject design avoided the sample size reduction incurred by conventional between-subjects designs. The randomized dosage explored the effects of different amounts of each intervention. The logistic regression model controlled for variations in students, item difficulty, and time.

Our analyses illustrate some advantages of networked tutors and storing student-tutor interactions in a database. The ability to easily combine data from many students and analyze information as recent as the previous day is very powerful. Capturing interactions in a suitable database representation makes them easier to integrate with other data and to analyze [9].

One theme of this research is to focus the AI where it can help the most, starting with the lowest-hanging fruit. Rather than trying to generate sophisticated questions or understand children's spoken answers, we instead focused on when to ask simpler, generic questions. What stories are most appropriate for question asking? What is an opportune time to ask questions? There are many ways to apply language technologies to reading comprehension, some of which may turn out to be feasible and beneficial. However, what ultimately matters is the student's reading comprehension, not the computer's. The Reading Tutor cannot evaluate student answers to some types of questions it asks, but by asking them can nevertheless assist students' comprehension. Using the analysis methods presented here may one day enable it to measure in real-time the effects of those questions.

Acknowledgements. This work was supported by the National Science Foundation, ITR/IERI Grant No. REC-0326153. Any opinions, findings, and conclusions or recommendations expressed in this publication are those of the authors and do not necessarily reflect the views of the National Science Foundation or the official policies, either expressed or implied, of the sponsors or of the United States Government. We thank the students and educators at the schools where Reading Tutors recorded data, and other members of Project LISTEN who contributed to this work.

References

1. Aist, G., *Towards automatic glossarization: Automatically constructing and administering vocabulary assistance factoids and multiple-choice assessment.* International Journal of Artificial Intelligence in Education, 2001. **12**: p. 212-231.
2. Anderson, J.R., *Rules of the mind.* 1993, Hillsdale, NJ: Lawrence Erlbaum Associates.
3. Beck, J.E., J. Mostow, A. Cuneo, and J. Bey. *Can automated questioning help children's reading comprehension?* in *Proceedings of the Tenth International Conference on Artificial Intelligence in Education (AIED2003).* 2003.p. 380-382 Sydney, Australia.
4. Brandão, A.C.P. and J. Oakhill. *"How do we know the answer?" Children's use of text data and general knowledge in story comprehension.* in *Society for the Scientific Study of Reading 2002 Conference.* 2002.p. The Palmer House Hilton, Chicago.
5. Kashihara, A., A. Sugano, K. Matsumura, and T. Hirashima. *A Cognitive Load Application Approach to Tutoring.* in *Proceedings of the Fourth International Conference on User Modeling.* 1994.p. 163-168.
6. Menard, S., *Applied Logistic Regression Analysis.* Quantitative Applications in the Social Sciences, 1995. **106**.
7. Mostow, J. and G. Aist, *Evaluating tutors that listen: An overview of Project LISTEN*, in *Smart Machines in Education*, K. Forbus and P. Feltovich, Editors. 2001, MIT/AAAI Press: Menlo Park, CA. p. 169-234.

8. Mostow, J., J. Beck, J. Bey, A. Cuneo, J. Sison, B. Tobin, and J. Valeri, *Using automated questions to assess reading comprehension, vocabulary, and effects of tutorial interventions.* Technology, Instruction, Cognition and Learning, to appear. 2.
9. Mostow, J., J. Beck, R. Chalasani, A. Cuneo, and P. Jia. *Viewing and Analyzing Multimodal Human-computer Tutorial Dialogue: A Database Approach.* in *Proceedings of the Fourth IEEE International Conference on Multimodal Interfaces (ICMI 2002).* 2002.p. 129-134 Pittsburgh, PA: IEEE.
10. NRP, *Report of the National Reading Panel. Teaching children to read: An evidence-based assessment of the scientific research literature on reading and its implications for reading instruction.* 2000, National Institute of Child Health & Human Development: Washington, DC.
11. Roshenshine, B., C. Meister, and S. Chapman, *Teaching students to generate questions: A review of the intervention studies.* Review of Educational Research, 1996. **66**(2): p. 181-221.

Web-Based Evaluations Showing Differential Learning for Tutorial Strategies Employed by the Ms. Lindquist Tutor

Neil T. Heffernan and Ethan A. Croteau

Computer Science Department
Worcester Polytechnic Institute
Worcester, MA. 01609, USA
{nth, ecroteau}@wpi.edu

Abstract. In a previous study, Heffernan and Koedinger [6] reported upon the Ms. Lindquist tutoring system that uses dialog and Heffernan conducted a web-based evaluation [7]. The previous evaluation considered students coming from three separate teachers and analyzed the individual learning gains based on the number of problems completed depending on the tutoring strategy provided. This paper examines a set of new web-based experiments. One set of experiments is targeted at determining if a differential learning gain exists between two of the tutoring strategies provided. Another set of experiments is used to determine if student motivation is dependent on the tutoring strategy. We replicate some findings from [7] with regard to the learning and motivation benefits of Ms Lindquist's intelligent tutorial dialog. These experiments related to learning report on over 1,000 participants contributing at most 20 minutes each, for a grand total of over 200+ combined student hours.

1 Introduction

Several groups of researchers are working on incorporating dialog into tutoring systems: for instance, CIRCSIM-tutor [3], AutoTutor [4], the PACT Geometry Tutor [1], and Atlas-Andes [8]. The value of dialog in learning is still controversial because dialog takes up precious time that might be better spent telling students the answer and moving on to another problem.

In previous work, Heffernan and Koedinger [6] reported upon the Ms. Lindquist tutoring system that uses dialog and Heffernan conducted a web-based evaluation [7] using the students from one classroom teacher. This paper reports upon some additional web-based evaluations using the students from multiple teachers. Ms. Lindquist was the first model-tracing tutor that had both a model of student thinking and a model on tutorial planning [5]. The Ms. Lindquist tutoring system helps students become proficient in writing expressions for algebra word problems. This system is of the "coached practice" variety that does not offer explicit instruction (i.e., long web pages or lectures), but instead is meant to scaffold "learning by doing" while students practice their problem solving skills. An assumption in the development of this system was that students would learn more if they could have an intelligent dialog rather

J.C. Lester et al. (Eds.): ITS 2004, LNCS 3220, pp. 491–500, 2004.

then simply being told the answer. In earlier work [5] we showed that students learned more when they engaged in a dialog with the Ms. Lindquist tutoring system, but did not investigate if it was worth the extra time spent. Later we reported some web-based results [7] that suggested a motivation benefit as some learning benefits might come from using these more intelligent dialogs that Ms Lindquist provided, but the evidence was not unequivocal.

This paper reports the latest results of experiments that were conducted with students using the tutor via the internet (at *www.AlgebraTutor.org*). Each student who visits the web site is informed that they are taking part in an experiment. Then they are randomly assigned to a condition in the experiment. There are several experimental conditions in these experiments, each of them representing different types of "intelligent" feedback that involve a tutorial dialog. These tutorial strategies are based upon the observation of an experienced tutor [5]. For instance, the "Concrete Articulation" strategy conducts a dialog based upon the idea of using a concrete instance. The following dialog is a necessarily-short dialog example of the Concrete Articulation Strategy:

Tutor: In the marching band there are 7 fewer flute players than drummers. If the number of drummers is "x", write an expression for the total number of flute players and drummers.
Student: 7-x+x {Correct answer is x+(x-7)}
Tutor: No. We will come back to the total number of flute players and drummers. Let me try to break this down for you. Please compute the number of flute players if the number of drummers was 10 drummers? {Note: Ms Lindquist notices that the student computed the number of drummers wrong, so she focuses in on that subgoal.}
Student: 10-7
Tutor: Correct. Now use "x" instead of 10 to again express the number of flute players.
Student: x-7
Tutor: Correct. Now, lets try this question again: Please write an expression for the total number of flute players and drummers.
Student: x-7+x
Tutor: Correct. Let us go onto the next problem.

The next example will illustrate the "Verbal" strategy that Ms. Lindquist uses based on the idea that students are more accustomed to expressing ideas in English than in algebraic expressions. It makes sense to first ask the student to explain in English how to achieve a goal and then to ask them how to do it using algebraic symbols afterwards. The following dialog illustrates the Verbal Strategy:

Tutor: Anne is rowing a boat in a lake and is 800 yards from the dock from which she started. She rows back towards the dock at 40 yards per minute for "m" minutes and stops to rest. How far is she from the dock now?
Student: 40*m {Correct answer is 800-40*m}

Tutor: Hmm. No. We will come back to the distance Anne has left to row. Let me try to break this down for you. Can you explain how you would find the distance rowed so far? The distance rowed so far is equal to:

A menu is displayed with three drop-down boxes containing the following items:

[Phrase]	[Operator]	[Phrase]
her speed rowing the distance Anne has left to row the distance rowed so far the distance she started from the dock the distance she started from the dock	Plus Minus Times Divided by	her speed rowing the distance Anne has left to row the distance rowed so far the distance she started from the dock the distance she started from the dock

Student: The distance rowed so far is equal to the number of minutes rowing times the distance Anne has left to row.
Tutor: Correct. Now, follow that up by writing an expression for the distance rowed so far.
Student: 40*m
Tutor: Correct. Now, lets try this question again: Please write an expression for the distance Anne has left to row.
Student: 800-40*m
Tutor: Correct. A new problem is needed.

The experiments reported upon in this paper mainly pertain to the Concrete Articulation Strategy, but the Ms. Lindquist tutoring system is quite complicated and has several different pedagogical strategies. Please see [6] for more information on Ms. Lindquist including other more interesting dialog examples.

The control condition in all of these experiments is to simply tell the student the correct answer if they make a mistake (i.e., "No. A correct answer is 5m-100. Please type that.") If a student does not make an error on a problem, and therefore receives no corrective feedback of any sort, then the student has not participated in either the control condition or the experimental condition for that problem. For each experiment "time on task" is controlled, whereby a student is given problems until a timer has gone-off and then is advanced to a posttest after completing the problem they are currently working on.

The Ms. Lindquist's curriculum is composed of five sections, starting with relatively easy one-operator problems (i.e., "5x"), and progressing up to problems that need four or more mathematical operations to correctly symbolize (i.e., "5x+7*(30-x)"). Few students make it to the fifth section, so the experiments we report on are only in the first two curriculum sections. At the beginning of each curriculum section, a tutorial feedback strategy is selected that will be used throughout the exercise whenever the student needs assistance. Because of this setup, each student can participate in five separate experiments, one for each curriculum section. We would like to learn which tutorial strategy is most effective for each curriculum area.

Since its inception in September 2000, over 17,000 individuals have logged into the tutoring system via the website, and hundreds of individuals have stuck around long enough (e.g., 30 minutes) to provide potentially useful data. The system's architecture is constructed in such a way that a user download a web page with a Java applet on it, which communicates to a server located at Carnegie Mellon University. Students' responses are logged into files for later analysis. Individuals are asked to identify themselves as a student, teacher, parent or researcher. We collect no identifying information from students. Students are asked to make up a login name that is used to identify them if they return at a later time. Students are asked to specify how much math background they have. We anticipate that some teachers will log in and pretend to be a student, which will add additional variance to the data we collect, thereby making it harder to figure out what strategies are most effective; therefore, we also ask at the end of each curriculum section if we should use their data (i.e., did they get help from a teacher, or are they really not a student). Such individuals are removed from any analyses. We recognize that there will probably be more noise in web based experiments due to the fact that individuals will vary far more than would normally occur in individual classroom experiments (Ms. Lindquist is used by many college students trying to brush up on their algebra, as well as by some students just starting algebra), nevertheless, we believe that there is still the potential for conducting experiments studying student learning. Even though the variation between individuals will be higher, thus introducing more noise into the data, we will be able to compensate for this by generalizing over a larger number of students than would be possible in traditional laboratory studies.

In all of the experiments described below, the items within a curriculum section were randomly chosen from a set of problems for that section (usually 20-40 such problems per section). The posttest items (which are the exact same as the pretest items) were fixed (i.e., all students received the same two-item posttest for the first section, as well as the same three-item posttest for the second section, etc.) We will now present the experiments we performed.

2 Experiments: Differential Learning

Thirteen experiments were conducted to see if there was a difference in learning gain (measured by the difference in posttest and pretest score) according to the tutoring strategy provided by the tutor. To determine if the difference in learning gain between the tutoring strategies was statistically significant an ANOVA was conducted. The measure of learning gain was considered to be a "lightweight" evaluation due to the brevity of the pretest and posttest.

Each experiment involved two tutoring strategies given at random to a group of students. Each student participating in the experiment answered at least one problem incorrectly during the curriculum section, causing the tutor to intervene. Students receiving a perfect pretest were eliminated from some of the experiments in an attempt to eliminate the "ceiling effect" caused by the shortness of the pretest and the large number of students scoring perfectly.

The experiments can be divided into two groups, the first examining the difference between the Inductive Support (IS) and Cut-to-the-chase (Cut) strategy and the second examining the difference between the IS and Verbal strategy. If students reported that they were students and were required to use the tutor, they were given either the IS or Cut strategy (we consider these students to be in the "forced" group). If students reported that they were students and were not required to use the tutor, they were given either the IS or Verbal strategy (these students are referred to as the "non-forced" group). Each experiment was conducted over a single curriculum section. In some cases there were multiple experiments for the same curriculum section and strategy comparison, which was made possible by having several large but distinct sets of students coming from different versions of the tutor where time on task had been modified. The thirteen experiments, which are indicated in table 1, will now be described along with their results.

2.1 Experiment 1 and 2 (Section 1, Verbal Versus Cut)

An early version of the tutor provided the Verbal and Cut strategies on Section 1 to forced students, so these two experiments are based on those students. In experiment 1, 64 students received Verbal, whereas 87 students received Cut. Since approximately 2/3 of these students obtained a perfect pretest, experiment 2 was conducted with the same students, but removing those students receiving a perfect pretest. The reason for keeping the first experiment is that reporting on overall learning is only possible if all students taking the pretest are accounted for even if they received a perfect score. Due to the large number of students receiving a perfect pretest, it is obvious that a longer pretest would have helped eliminate this problem, but may also have reduced the number of students completing the entire curriculum section.

2.2 Results for Experiment 1 and 2

The first experiment showed no evidence of a differential learning gain between the Verbal and Cut strategies with the learning gain for Verbal being 13% and for Cut being 14%. This was not surprising since 2/3 of the students had received a perfect pretest, which was our motivation for creating experiment 2, having those students eliminated. For the second experiment, there was also no evidence of a differential learning gain, although the learning gain for Verbal was 41% and Cut was 35%. For each of these experiments the number of problems solved by strategy was statistically different ($p<.0001$). This is not particularly surprising as the Cut strategy simply provides the correct answer, whereas the Verbal strategy is more time consuming by using menus and intelligent dialog, which results in fewer problems being completed on average. Another observation is that the time on task for each strategy was statistically different ($p<.0001$). This is explained by a design decision to allow students to finish the problem they are working on before advancing to the posttest, which means more time consuming tutoring strategies result in a slightly longer average time on task.

2.3 Experiment 3 (Section 1, IS Versus Cut)

For the first section forced students, the IS and Cut strategies were provided on the latest version of the tutor. Although the number of forced students was substantially less than non-forced students (due to the tutor being available online rather than used just in a classroom setting), both experimental conditions had over 60 students. Only enough data was available for a single experiment on the first section involving the IS and Cut strategies since the tutor previously provided the Verbal and Cut strategies on that section as seen in Experiments 1 and 2.

2.4 Results for Experiment 3

For this experiment, a differential learning gain between the IS and Cut strategy was observed as being statistically significant (P=.0224). Students with the IS strategy had a learning gain of 53% and those with the Cut strategy 36%. The pretest scores were surprising in that those students given the IS strategy had a lower score, on average 22% correct with those given the Cut strategy having on average 34% correct. Interestingly, the students given the IS strategy not only had lower performance on the pretest, but also had a higher performance on the posttest, which explains the statistically significant learning gain observed.

2.5 Experiment 4 and 5 (Section 2, IS Versus Cut)

On the second curriculum section, the IS and Cut strategies were given to the forced students. Two experiments were conducted using a set of students that were controlled for time. The students in Experiment 5 were given twice as much time as those in Experiment 4 (1200 seconds vs. 600 seconds).

2.6 Results for Experiment 4 and 5

Both Experiment 4 and 5 showed no evidence of differential learning by tutoring strategy. For Experiment 4, the learning gain was 18% for IS and 14% for Cut. This is confounded by the learning gain on Experiment 5, which was 19% for IS and 23% for Cut. Since both experiments contained relatively few students in each condition, it is not surprising that the results from Experiment 4 and 5 would be contradictory.

2.7 Experiment 6–11 (Section 1, IS Versus Verbal)

These six experiments compared differential learning for the IS and Verbal strategies on the first section, which were given to non-forced students. It was noticed for Experiment 6 that approximately 2/3 of the students received a perfect pretest. To prevent a ceiling effect of student's not demonstrating learning, those students receiving a perfect pretest were removed to produce Experiment 7. Experiment 8 involved a much smaller group of students (approximately 30 per condition) receiving the same amount of time on Section 1 as those in the previous experiment. Although the students in Experiment 8 had very high pretest scores, those students receiving a perfect score were not removed due to the much smaller sample size. Experiments 9 and 10 both involved separate groups of students who had those students receiving a perfect pretest removed from the sample. Experiment 11 was the combination of the students from Experiments 9 and 10, as both of those experiments provided the same time on task.

2.8 Results for Experiment 6–11

Experiments 6-11 all showed that students given the IS strategy as having a higher learning gain than those receiving the Verbal strategy. Experiment 8 had a p-value suggesting the difference in learning gain was not statistically significant, which could partially be explained by the small sample size (approximately 30 students given each condition) and due to the high pretest scores (75% for IS and 84% for Cut), which resulted in a ceiling-effect. Looking at the posttest scores, those given IS received 89% correct, whereas those given Cut received 93% correct. It should be noted that Experiment 11, which was the combination of students from Experiments 9 and 10 increased the statistical significance for learning gain from (P=0.1030) and (P=0.0803) consecutively to (P=0.0210).

2.9 Experiments 12 and 13 (Section 2, IS Versus Verbal)

These two experiments compared differential learning for the IS and Verbal strategies on the second section, which were given to non-forced students. Both experiments involved a separate group of students having a different time on task. In Experiment 12 the average problem solving time was approximately 700 seconds, whereas in Experiment 13 the average problem solving time was approximately 1200 seconds. The sample size used for experiment 13 (having approximately 100 students) contained almost twice as many students as that used for experiment 13.

2.10 Results for Experiment 12 and 13

Experiments 12 and 13, which are both on the second curriculum section did not show statistical evidence of differential learning gain. For Experiment 12 the learning gain of those students given the IS strategy, which was 22% was slightly higher than those students given the Cut strategy, which was 18%. The results of Experiment 13, which had twice the number of students and double the amount of time on task had a learning gain of 30% for those given the IS strategy and 33% for those given the Cut strategy. Although the difference in learning gain was insignificant for both of these experiments, it was odd that such a large number of students would show nothing significant after 20 minutes of problem solving. It was observed that the pretest score between condition in Experiment 13 was statistically significant (P=.0465), which indicates that the lightweight evaluation method may be partially responsible.

3 Experiments: Student Motivation

Four experiments were conducted to determine if there was a difference in student motivation determined by the tutorial strategy (either IS or Verbal) offered by the tutor. For the first experiment, students received either the IS or Verbal strategy on the first section and all students were given the Cut strategy on the second section. We were not particularly interested in student motivation involving the Cut strategy as we already examined this [7] found that if students were given Cut they left the web site at much higher rates. For the second experiment, students received the same tutorial strategy (either IS or Verbal) on both the first and second sections. In this experiment, only students completing the first section and starting work on the second section were analyzed for their completion rate on the second section. The third experiment looked at only those students working on the first section to determine if there was a difference in completion rate for that section. The fourth and final experiment looked at those students skipping the first section due to getting a perfect pretest and starting work on the second section.

The number of students within each control condition is indicated in the *count* column of table 1. Experiment 3 has the largest number of students, because it included those students starting work on section 1, which is the majority of students. Experiment 4 also contains a large number of students, which results from a large number of students skipping the first section due to a perfect pretest. An ANOVA was conducted for each of the four experiments to see if the difference in motivation (section completion rate) by tutorial strategy was statistically significant.

3.1 Results of Student Motivation

For the first experiment, with approximately 150 students in each condition, the percent of students completing the second section was 50% and 49% for IS and Verbal consecutively which was not statistically different. For the second experiment, with approximately 65 students in each condition, the section completion rate was 55% and 65% for IS and Verbal consecutively, which was also not statistically different. The third and four experiments contained an even larger number of students, but for both of these experiments no difference in motivation was seen for the given tutorial strategy. The motivation experiments are summarized in the following table:

From these four experiments, it would appear that student motivation is not influenced by giving either the IS or Verbal strategy. Possibly student motivation is not seen, because students starting the second section after finishing the first have nearly the same motivation. It would be interesting to see if student motivation on the

Table 1. Experiments on Student Motivation

Experiment	Count IS	Count Verbal	Section Completed (%) IS	Section Completed (%) Verbal	P-Value
1	189	121	50	49	.6166
2	73	60	55	65	.2362
3	697	428	61	59	.6005
4	275	187	47	51	.4123

first section was dependent on strategy given, which will most likely be looked at in a future study.

4 Discussion: Web-Based Experiments

However, these results should be taken with a grain of salt given that students are taking a two or three item pretest and posttest, which is due to our decision to provide only a lightweight evaluation as previously mentioned. Web-based evaluation for the most part makes this lightweight evaluation useful given the large collection of data that is produced.

5 Conclusion

In earlier work [5] presented evidence that suggested that students learned more when they engaged in a dialog with the Ms. Lindquist tutoring system, but did not investigate if it was worth the extra time spent. Later we reported some web-based results [7] that suggested that the Cut to the chase strategy was inferior to the IS strategy in terms of learning gain.

From the experiments reported in this work conducted on differential learning by tutorial strategy, it appears that the benefit to using one strategy over another is sometimes seen on the first curriculum section. In particular, experiment three is something of a replication of the work from [7]. This could partially be explained by the tutorial dialogs on the second section being longer and requiring more time to read. It should be noted that a student can spend a great deal of time on a single problem, and these results are making us consider setting a time cut-off for a dialog so that students don't spend too much time on any one dialog.

Next we turn to comparing IS with Verbal. It appears that providing the IS strategy is a better choice than Verbal on the first curriculum section as seen by the significant difference in learning gain on experiment 7, 9, 10 and 11. We were pleasantly surprised that we could detect differences in learning rates in only 8-10 minutes suing such crude (2 item pre and posttests).

The strong evidence for the IS strategy being better than the Cut strategy was not particularly surprising. Heffernan [7] previously reported seeing a similar result, but this was for students working on the second curriculum section. We have to study this further to better understand these results.

Finally, it should be reiterated that no differences in motivation could be found between the IS and Verbal strategies. This could possibly be explained by both of these strategies being advanced, in that they keep a participant more involved than the naïve Cut strategy. This results is also consistent with [7] that reported the same thing. Given that students seemed to learn a little better with the IS strategy than the Verbal strategy, we thought we might see a motivation benefit for the IS strategy but we did not.

References

1. Aleven V., Popescu, O. & Koedinger, K. R. (2001). Towards tutorial dialog to support self-explanation: Adding natural language understanding to a cognitive tutor. In Moore, Redfield, & Johnson (Eds.), *Proceedings of Artificial Intelligence in Education 2001*. Amsterdam: IOS Press.
2. Birnbaum, M.H. (Ed.). (2000). "Psychological Experiments on the Internet." San Diego: Academic Press. http://psych.fullerton.edu/mbirnbaum/web/IntroWeb.htm
3. CIRCSIM-Tutor (2002). (See http://www.csam.iit.edu/~circsim/)
4. Graesser, A.C., Wiemer-Hastings, P., Wiemer-Hastings, K., Harter, D., Person, N., & the TRG (in press). Using latent semantic analysis to evaluate the contributions of students in AutoTutor. *Interactive Learning Environments*.
5. Heffernan, N. T. (2001). *Intelligent Tutoring Systems have Forgotten the Tutor: Adding a Cognitive Model of an Experienced Human Tutor*. Dissertation & Technical Report. Carnegie Mellon University, Computer Science, http://www.algebratutor.org/pubs.html.
6. Heffernan, N. T., & Koedinger, K. R. (2002) An intelligent tutoring system incorporating a model of an experienced human tutor. *Sixth International Conference on Intelligent Tutoring Systems*.
7. Heffernan, N. T. (2003). Web-Based Evaluations Showing both Cognitive and Motivational Benefits of the Ms. Lindquist Tutor. *11th International Conference Artificial Intelligence in Education. Sydney*, Australia.
8. Rosé, C., Jordan, P., Ringenberg, M, Siler, S., VanLehn, K. and Weinstein, A. (2001) Interactive conceptual Tutoring in Atlas-Andes. In *Proceedings of AI in Education 2001 Conference*.

The Impact of Why/AutoTutor on Learning and Retention of Conceptual Physics

G. Tanner Jackson, Matthew Ventura, Preeti Chewle, Art Graesser, and the Tutoring Research Group

Institute for Intelligent Systems, University of Memphis,
38152 Memphis, Tennessee
{gtjacksn, mventura, pchewle, a-graesser}@memphis.edu
http://www.iismemphis.org

Abstract. Why/AutoTutor is an intelligent tutoring system for conceptual physics that guides learning through tutorial dialog in natural language. It adapts to student contributions within dialog turns in both a conversationally appropriate and pedagogically effective manner. It uses an animated agent with synthesized speech to engage the student and provide a human-like conversational partner. Why/AutoTutor serves as a learning scaffold throughout the tutoring session and facilitates active knowledge construction on the part of the student. Why/AutoTutor has recently been compared with an ideal information delivery system in order to assess differences in learning gains, the factors that contribute to those gains, and the retention of that knowledge.

1 Introduction

Why/AutoTutor is the fourth in a series of tutoring systems built by the Tutoring Research Group at the University of Memphis. Why/AutoTutor is an intelligent tutoring system that uses an animated pedagogical agent to converse in natural language with students. This recent version was designed to tutor students in Newtonian conceptual physics, whereas all previous versions were designed to teach introductory computer literacy. The architecture of AutoTutor has been described in previous publications [1], [2], [3], [4], so only an overview is provided here before we turn to some empirical tests of Why/AutoTutor on learning gains.

1.1 AutoTutor Overview

AutoTutor is a tutoring system with natural language dialog that simulates the discourse patterns and pedagogical strategies of a typical human tutor. The dialog mechanisms of AutoTutor were designed to incorporate naturalistic conversation patterns from real tutoring sessions [5] as well as theoretically ideal strategies for promoting learning gains. The primary goal of the AutoTutor project has been to build an intelligent agent that can deliver conversational dialog that is both pedagogically effective and engaging. AutoTutor is more than an information delivery system. It is a collaborative scaffold that uses natural language conversation to assist students in actively constructing knowledge.

Why/AutoTutor is a complex system with a number of semi-autonomous computational modules. A dialog manager coordinates the conversation that occurs between

J.C. Lester et al. (Eds.): ITS 2004, LNCS 3220, pp. 501–510, 2004.

the learner and the pedagogical agent. Subject matter content and general world knowledge are represented with both a structured curriculum script and with latent semantic analysis (LSA), as discussed below [6], [7]. LSA and surface language features determine the assessment metrics of the quality of learners' contributions. AutoTutor makes use of an animated conversational agent with facial expressions, synthesized speech, and rudimentary gestures. Although it is acknowledged that the conversational dialog will probably never be as dynamic and adaptive as human-to-human conversation, we do believe that AutoTutor's conversational skills are as good as or better than other pedagogical agents. Evaluations of the dialog fidelity have supported the conclusion that AutoTutor can respond to the vast majority of student contributions in a conversationally and pedagogically appropriate manner [8], [9].

AutoTutor's architecture includes a set of permanent databases that do not get updated during the course of tutoring. The first is a curriculum script database, which contains a complete set of tutoring materials including: tutoring questions, ideal answers, answer expectations (specific components necessary for a complete answer), associated misconceptions, corrections of misconceptions, and other dialog moves with related content. A second permanent database is an indexed copy of the *Conceptual Physics* textbook [10]. When a student asks AutoTutor a question, the tutor uses a question answering facility to pull a plausible answer from the textbook, or another relevant document. In a similar manner, AutoTutor makes use of the glossary from the *Conceptual Physics* textbook as a third permanent database. Fourth, the server contains a set of lexicons, syntactic parsers, and other computational linguistics modules that support information extraction, analyze student contributions, and help AutoTutor proceed appropriately through a tutoring session. Fifth, the server houses a space for latent semantic analysis (LSA).

LSA is a core component for representing semantic world knowledge about conceptual physics, curriculum content, or any other subject matter [6], [11]. LSA is a high-dimensional, statistical representation that assigns vector quantities to words and documents on the basis of co-occurrence constraints in a large corpus of documents. These vectors are used to calculate the conceptual similarity of any two segments of text, which could be as small as a word or as large as a complete document [7], [12], [13]. We use LSA in AutoTutor as a semantic matching operation that compares the student contributions to expected good answers and to possible misconceptions.

In a normal session, Why/AutoTutor begins with a two-minute introduction and overview, and then launches into the appropriate learning session. Why/AutoTutor typically covers five conceptual physics problems in a single session. After the introduction, it starts the conversation by posing a problem and prompting the student for an answer. A conversation ensues as the tutor and student attempt to collaboratively cover the material necessary to answer the question completely. For example, one of the questions is "Suppose a boy is in a free-falling elevator and he holds his keys motionless right in front of his face and then lets go. What will happen to the keys? Explain why". Below is an excerpt from the middle of a dialog between Why/AutoTutor and an actual student.

TUTOR-1: What about this? The boy and his keys free fall in the elevator starting with the same vertical __________?

STUDENT-1: acceleration
TUTOR-2: Sort of … vertical position.
TUTOR-3: Moving on, and another thing, objects starting from the same position, and having the same velocity will have the same displacement.
TUTOR-4: What happens when two objects start at the same position with same acceleration?
STUDENT-2: they have the same velocity
TUTOR-5: OK.
TUTOR-6: The displacement of the keys and the boy's face should be_____?
STUDENT-3: equal
TUTOR-7: Yep, you are absolutely right! The same.

This example demonstrates several distinct tutoring features that are common in Why/AutoTutor. The system (a) prompts the student for specific information missing from a previous response (TUTOR-1, TUTOR-6), (b) inserts correct information into an erroneous or incomplete student turn (TUTOR-2), (c) provides a summary of relevant information and then gives a hint with a related question (TUTOR-3 & TUTOR-4), (d) "understands" and assesses natural language contributions, including semantically similar statements (STUDENT-2, STUDENT-3), (e) provides feedback to the student on the student's previous turn (TUTOR-2, TUTOR-5, TUTOR-7), and (f) maintains coherence from previous turns while it adapts to student contributions (STUDENT-2 content excludes specific required information about "equal displacement" so the TUTOR-6 turn asks a question related to this required information). Research on naturalistic tutoring [5], [14], [15], [16] provided some of the guidance in designing these dialog moves and tutoring behaviors.

1.2 AutoTutor Evaluations

The primary evaluation of all versions of AutoTutor has been the extent to which it successfully produces learning gains. Learning gains from AutoTutor have been evaluated in several experiments on the topics of computer literacy [2], [17] and conceptual physics [1], [18]. In most of the studies, participants take a pretest, followed by a tutoring treatment, and ending in a posttest. AutoTutor has been compared with many different types of comparison (control) conditions in approximately a dozen experiments. The comparison conditions vary for each experiment because colleagues differ in their opinion of a suitable control for AutoTutor. Post-test scores resulting from AutoTutor have been compared with (a) pretest scores (*Pretest*) and with posttest scores in a variety of comparison conditions: (b) student reads nothing (*Read-nothing*), (c) student reads relevant chapters from the course textbook (*Textbook*), (d) student reads excerpts from the textbook only if they are directly relevant to the content during training by AutoTutor (*Textbook-reduced*), (e) student reads text prepared by the experimenters that succinctly describes the content covered in the curriculum script of AutoTutor (*Script-content*), (f) intelligent tutoring systems from the University of Pittsburgh (*Why/Atlas*), (g) information delivery of ideal text, with summaries, examples, and misconception remediation (*Minilesson*), (h) expert human tutors communicating with students completely via computer (*Human computer mediated*), and (i) expert human tutors communicating with students via phone and computer (*Human phone mediated*).

A number of outcomes have been drawn from previous analyses, but only a few are mentioned here. First, AutoTutor is effective at promoting learning gains, especially at deep levels of comprehension (the effect size, $d \cong 0.70$) [1], [2], when compared with: the ecologically valid situation where students read nothing, baseline rates at pretest, or reading the textbook for a controlled amount of time (equivalent to time spent with AutoTutor). Second, reading the textbook is not much different from doing nothing. These two results together support the claim that a tutor is needed to encourage the learner to focus on the appropriate content and to comprehend it at deeper levels.

2 Why/AutoTutor Evaluation Methods in Present Study

The current study was specifically designed to explore the relation between two learning conditions (*Minilesson* vs. *Why/AutoTutor*) and their possible impacts on learning gains, knowledge retention, and transfer of knowledge.

2.1 Participants

As in our previous experiments on Newtonian physics, students were enrolled in introductory physics courses, and received extra credit for their participation. Students were recruited for the experiment after having completed the related material in the physics course. In total, 70 students participated in the experiment. Due to incomplete data for some students, 67 participants were included in the analyses for the multiple choice data, and only 56 participants were included in the analyses for the essay data.

2.2 Procedure

Participation in the experiment consisted of two sessions, one week apart, each involving two testing phases. In the first session (approximately 2.5 to 3 hours) participants took a pretest, interacted with one of the tutors in a training session, and took an immediate posttest. During the second session (approximately 30 minutes to 1 hour), which was one week later, participants took a retention test and a far transfer test. The pretest consisted of three conceptual physics essay questions. During the training sessions, participants interacted with one of the tutors in an attempt to answer five conceptual physics problems. The immediate posttest and the retention test were counterbalanced, both forms consisting of three conceptual physics essays and 26 multiple choice questions. The far transfer task involved answering seven essay questions that were designed to test the transfer of knowledge (at deep conceptual levels, not surface similarities) from the training session.

2.3 Materials

The posttest and retention test both included a counterbalanced set of 26 multiple choice questions that were extracted from or similar to those in the Force Concept Inventory (FCI). The FCI is a widely used test of Newtonian physics [19]. An example problem is provided below in Table 1. The multiple choice questions in previous studies were counterbalanced between the pretest and posttest (there was no retention test). One concern with this procedure is that the participants could possibly become sensitized to the content of the multiple choice test questions during the pretest, and would thereby perform better during the posttest phase; the potential pretest sensitization would confound the overall learning gains. The graded essays correlated highly (r=.77) with the multiple choice scores in previous studies, so the multiple choice section was pushed to after the training, and essays alone served as the pretest measure.

All testing phases included open-ended conceptual physics essay questions that were designed by experienced physics experts. Each essay question required approximately a paragraph for a complete answer; an example question is illustrated in Table 1. All essay questions were evaluated (blind to condition) by accomplished physics experts both holistically (an overall letter grade) and componentially (by identifying specific components of an ideal answer, called expectations, and misconceptions associated with the problem). When grading holistically, the physics experts read each student essay answer and graded it according to a conventional letter grade scale (i.e., A, B, C, D, or F). This grade was later translated into numerical form for analysis purposes, with higher scores corresponding to better grades. Essays were also graded in a componential manner by grading each expectation and misconception associated with each essay on an individual basis. The expectations and misconceptions were graded as explicitly present, implicitly present, or absent. To be considered explicitly present, an expectation/misconception would have to be stated in an overt, obvious manner. An implicitly present expectation/misconception would be counted if the participant seemed to have the general idea, but did not necessarily express it completely. An expectation/misconception would be considered absent if there were no signs of direct or indirect inclusion, or if it was obviously excluded.

At the end of the second session, participants answered 7 far transfer essay questions. The far transfer essays were designed to test knowledge transfer from the training and testing set to a new set and style of questions that covered the same underlying physics principles. Table 1 shows one of the example questions. The far transfer questions were also graded both holistically and componentially by the physics experts.

The two learning conditions in this experiment were *Why/AutoTutor*, as previously described, and *Minilesson*. The *Minilesson* is an automated information delivery system which covers the same physics problems as AutoTutor. The Minilessons provided relevant and informative summaries of Newton's laws, along with examples that demonstrated both good principles and common misconceptions. Students were presented text by the *Minilesson* and clicked a "Next" button to continue through the material (paragraph by paragraph). The following is a small excerpt from the *Miniles-*

son, using the same elevator-keys problem as before, "As you know, displacement can be defined as the total change in position during the elapsed time. The man's displacement is the same as that of his keys at every point in time during the fall. So, we can conclude..." The *Minilesson* condition was designed to convey the information necessary for an ideal answer to the posed problems. It is considered to be an ideal text for covering all aspects of each problem.

Table 1. Examples of testing materials.

Test	Example
Multiple Choice	A long-jumper runs at full speed, jumps from the take-off point, and a second later lands in the sand. While he is in the air during his jump, in which direction is his acceleration due to the earth's gravitational force? a) vertically downward, b) both vertically downward and horizontally in the direction he is moving in, c) only horizontally in the direction he is moving in, d) he is not accelerating due to the earth's gravity while he is in the air
Essay	A clown is riding a unicycle in a straight line. She accidentally drops an egg beside her as she continues to move with constant velocity. Ignoring air resistance, where will the egg land relative to the point where the unicycle touches the ground? Explain.
Far Transfer	Suppose you toss a baseball straight up in a vacuum. As it rises, but before it reaches the top, what forces (if any) act on the baseball? Which forces (if any) are constant, which are decreasing and which are increasing? Explain your answers.

3 Results

We conducted several analyses that investigated differences between training conditions across different testing phases. The results from the multiple choice and essay data confirmed a previously held hypothesis that the students' prior knowledge level may be inversely related to proportional learning gains. This hypothesis is discussed briefly in the conclusion section of this paper (see also [18]).

Table 2 presents effect sizes (*d*) for *Why/AutoTutor*, as well as means and standard deviations from the multiple choice and holistic essay grades. When considering the effect sizes for *Why/AutoTutor* alone, it significantly facilitated learning compared with the pretest baseline rate. For the posttest immediately following training, *Why/AutoTutor* showed an effect size of 0.97 sigma compared to the pretest. That means, on average, participants who interacted with *Why/AutoTutor* scored almost a full standard deviation (approximately a full letter grade) above their initial pretest score. This large learning gain also persisted through a full week delay when the same participants took the retention test (d=0.93) and the far transfer test (d=1.41). It should be noted that these students had already finished covering the related material in class sometime before taking the pretest, so they rarely, if ever, covered the material again during subsequent class exposure, i.e., between the pre- and posttests. Thus, any significant knowledge retention can probably be attributable to the training rather than intervening relearning. Similarly, *Why/AutoTutor* had a positive effect size for almost all comparisons with the *Minilesson* performance: multiple choice retention scores (d=0.34), holistic retention grades (d=0.14), and holistic far transfer grades (d=0.38). *Why/AutoTutor* had only one negative effect size (d=-0.10) when compared with the *Minilesson* condition at the immediate posttest performance. Unfortunately, however, most of these comparisons with Minilessons were not statistically significant.

A statistical analysis of the holistic essays revealed that participants performed significantly higher in all subsequent tests than in the pretest, $F(1,54) = 27.80$, $p < .001$, $MS_{error} = 0.38$, so there was significant learning in both conditions. However, an ANOVA on the holistically graded essays, across all testing occasions, found no significant differences between *Why/AutoTutor* and *Minilesson* participants, $F(1,54) = 1.27$, $p = .27$, $MS_{error} = 2.911$. A one-way ANOVA on the multiple choice test also indicated that the participants in the *Why/AutoTutor* condition did not significantly differ from those in the *Minilesson* condition, $F(1,65) = 2.32$, $p = .13$, $MS_{error} = 0.050$. Analyses of the detailed expectation/misconception assessments demonstrated similar trends as the previous analyses. In these assessments, we computed the proportion of expectations (or anticipated misconceptions) that were present in the essay according to the expert judges. Remember that each essay was graded in a componential manner by grading each expectation and misconception as explicitly present, implicitly present, or absent. The analyses included here used a lenient grading criteria, meaning that expectations are considered covered if they are either explicitly or implicitly present in a student's essay. Misconceptions used a similar lenient grading criteria during analysis. Effect sizes for expectations were favorable when comparing pretestperformance in AutoTutor to all respective subsequent posttest phases (d=0.52, d=0.31, d=0.73, respectively). Similarly, when compared to pretest scores, effect sizes for the analysis on the misconceptions were favorable for *Why/AutoTutor* (d=-0.48, d=-0.56, d=-0.20, in respective order). Having fewer misconceptions is considered good, so lower numbers and negative effects are better. When *Why/AutoTutor* was compared to the *Minilesson*, each effect size was in a favorable direction (expectations: d=0.24, d=0.16, d=0.33, and misconceptions d=-0.03, d=-0.17, d=-0.24, respectively).

A repeated measures analysis on the expectations revealed that in both conditions participants expressed significantly more correct expectations in all subsequent tests than in the pretest, $F(1,54) = 21.99$, $p < .001$, $MS_{error} = 0.036$. A repeated measures analysis of the misconceptions similarly revealed that students expressed significantly fewer misconceptions in the posttest and retention test than in the pretest, $F(1,54) = 13.68$, $p < .001$, $MS_{error} = 0.005$. A one-way ANOVA on the expectations resulted in non-significant differences between test phases of *Why/AutoTutor* ($\overline{x} = .460$,

Table 2. Multiple Choice and Essay Results. Proportion Means with Standard Deviations in Parentheses (SD). Effect Size$_m$ = Effect Size for AutoTutor Using the Minilesson group. Effect Size$_p$ = Effect Size for AutoTutor Using the Pretest.

	Multiple Choice		Holistic Essay Grades			
	Posttest	Retention	Pretest	Posttest	Retention	Far Transfer
AutoTutor	.708 (.14)	.686 (.22)	.137 (.09)	.224 (.11)	.221 (.14)	.264 (.17)
Minilesson	.656 (.18)	.607 (.23)	.116 (.06)	.240 (.16)	.200 (.15)	.211 (.14)
Effect Size$_m$		.34		-.10	.14	.38
Effect Size$_p$		--		.97	.93	1.41

$\bar{x} = .601$, $\bar{x} = .545$, $\bar{x} = .657$) and *Minilesson* ($\bar{x} = .384$, $\bar{x} = .535$, $\bar{x} = .496$, $\bar{x} = .574$, respectively), $F(1,54) = 1.38$, $p = .25$, $MS_{error} = 0.188$. An ANOVA on the misconceptions also revealed non-significant differences between test phases of *Why/AutoTutor* ($\bar{x} = .094$, $\bar{x} = .056$, $\bar{x} = .049$, $\bar{x} = .078$) and *Minilesson* ($\bar{x} = .091$, $\bar{x} = .058$, $\bar{x} = .059$, $\bar{x} = .095$, respectively), $F(1,54) = .34$, $p = .56$, $MS_{error} = 0.007$.

4 Discussion and Conclusion

The good news for Why/AutoTutor was the overall significant learning gains between pretest and posttest phases and the consistently favorable effect sizes for AutoTutor, even when compared with the Minilesson condition. Eighteen out of nineteen effect sizes were favorable for AutoTutor. These results support the conclusion that Why/AutoTutor is effective at promoting learning. The bad news is that the differences between Why/AutoTutor and the Minilesson conditions were not quite statistically significant. On average, students in the Why/AutoTutor condition improved a whole letter grade on all tests after the pretest (*d*'s varied from .93 to 1.41). Why/AutoTutor's comparisons to the Minilesson conditions were more modest, averaging $d = .38$. The positive retention and far transfer results lend support to the initial claim that AutoTutor is targeted to tutor students at deeper levels of comprehension which persist longer than surface levels of information.

The null results between conditions are less surprising than one might expect. The *Minilesson* condition was considered an ideal information delivery system. Its content was the best content possible for students to use as a study aid; it is a condition with ideal content that is yoked to the content of Why/AutoTutor. Interestingly, AutoTutor actually covers less content than the *Minilesson.* AutoTutor does not go over expected good answers that it infers the student knows, whereas the *Minilesson* explicitly covers every expected good answer. However, the overall performance of Why/AutoTutor was still equal to or better than the *Minilesson* condition.

There were similar trends in a previous study that had no retention component [18]. There were overall significant learning gains for each condition, but no differences between the conditions. Both studies used students currently enrolled in physics courses, which made the participants “physics intermediates”. Since all previous studies involved participants with intermediate physics knowledge, subsequent analyses were conducted that examined only those students with a pretest score lower than forty percent, called “physics novices”. These post hoc analyses on physics novices indicated that students with lower pretest scores had higher learning gains and showed different trends than the higher pretest students. Specifically, low knowledge students may benefit the most from interacting with these learning tools. A study in progress has been specifically designed to have physics novices interact with the systems in an attempt to provide more discriminating assessments of potential learning differences.

Several questions remain unanswered from the available research. What is it about these systems that facilitates learning, and under what conditions? Is it the mode of content delivery, the content itself, or some complex interaction? Do motivation and emotions play an important role, above and beyond the cognitive components? One of the goals in our current AutoTutor research is to further explore what exactly leads to these learning gains, and to determine how different learning environments produce such similar effects. Our current and future studies have been designed to address these questions directly. Even though a detailed answer may yet be unknown, the fact still remains that students learn significantly from interacting with AutoTutor and this transferable knowledge is acquired at a level that persists over time.

Acknowledgements. The Tutoring Research Group (TRG) is an interdisciplinary research team comprised of researchers from psychology, computer science, physics, and education (visit **http://www.autotutor.org**). This research was supported by the National Science Foundation and the DoD Multidisciplinary University Research Initiative administered by ONR. Any opinions, findings, and conclusions or recommendations expressed in this material are those of the authors and do not necessarily reflect the views of DoD, ONR, or NSF. Kurt VanLehn, and others at the University of Pittsburgh collaborated with us in preparing AutoTutor materials on conceptual physics.

References

1. Graesser, A.C., Jackson, G.T., Mathews, E.C., Mitchell, H.H., Olney, A.,Ventura, M., Chipman, P., Franceschetti, D., Hu, X., Louwerse, M.M., Person, N.K., & TRG: Why/AutoTutor: A test of learning gains from a physics tutor with natural language dialog. In R. Alterman and D. Hirsh (Eds.), Proceedings of the 25th Annual Conference of the Cognitive Science Society. Boston, MA: Cognitive Science Society. (2003) 1-6
2. Graesser, A.C., Lu, S., Jackson, G.T., Mitchell, H., Ventura, M., Olney, A., & Louwerse, M.M.: AutoTutor: A tutor with dialog in natural language. Behavioral Research Methods, Instruments, and Computers. (in press)

3. Graesser, A.C., Wiemer-Hastings, K., Wiemer-Hastings, P., Kreuz, R., & TRG: AutoTutor: A simulation of a human tutor. Journal of Cognitive Systems Research, 1, (1999) 35-51
4. Graesser, A.C., VanLehn, K., Rose, C., Jordan, P., & Harter, D.: Intelligent tutoring systems with conversational dialogue. AI Magazine, 22, (2001) 39-51
5. Graesser, A. C., Person, N. K., & Magliano, J. P. : Collaborative dialog patterns in naturalistic one-to-one tutoring. Applied Cognitive Psychology, 9, (1995) 1-28
6. Graesser, A.C., Wiemer-Hastings, P., Wiemer-Hastings, K., Harter, D., Person, N., and the TRG: Using latent semantic analysis to evaluate the contributions of students in AutoTutor. Interactive Learning Environments, 8, (2000) 129-148
7. Landauer, T.K., Foltz, P.W., Laham, D.: An introduction to latent semantic analysis. Discourse Processes, 25, (1998) 259-284
8. Jackson, G. T., Mueller, J., Person, N., & Graesser, A.C.: Assessing the pedagogical effectiveness and conversational appropriateness in three versions of AutoTutor. In J.D. Moore, C.L. Redfield, and W.L. Johnson (Eds.) Artificial Intelligence in Education: AI-ED in the Wired and Wireless Future. Amsterdam: OIS Press. (2001) 263-267
9. Person, N.K., Graesser, A.C., Kreuz, R.J., Pomeroy, V., & TRG: Simulating human tutor dialog moves in AutoTutor. International Journal of Artificial Intelligence in Education, 12, (2001) 23-39
10. Hewitt, P.G. Conceptual physics (8th edition). Reading, MA: Addison-Wesley. (1992)
11. Olde, B. A., Franceschetti, D.R., Karnavat, Graesser, A. C. & the TRG: The right stuff: Do you need to sanitize your corpus when using latent semantic analysis? Proceedings of the 24th Annual Conference of the Cognitive Science Society. Mahwah, NJ: Erlbaum. (2002) 708-713
12. Foltz, P.W., Gilliam, S., & Kendall, S.: Supporting content-based feedback in on-line writing evaluation with LSA. Interactive Learning Environments, 8, (2000) 111-127
13. Kintsch, W.: Comprehension: A paradigm for cognition. Cambridge, MA: Cambridge University Press. (1998)
14. Chi, M. T. H., Siler, S., Jeong, H., Yamauchi, T., & Hausmann, R. G.: Learning from human tutoring. Cognitive Science, 25, (2001) 471-533
15. Fox, B.: The human tutorial dialog project. Hillsdale, NJ: Erlbaum. (1993)
16. Moore, J.D.: Participating in explanatory dialogs. Cambridge, MA: MIT Press. (1995)
17. Graesser, A.C., Moreno, K., Marineau, J., Adcock, A., Olney, A., & Person, N.: AutoTutor improves deep learning of computer literacy: Is it the dialog or the talking head? In U. Hoppe, F. Verdejo, and J. Kay (Eds.), Proceedings of Artificial Intelligence in Education. Amsterdam: IOS Press. (2003) 47-54
18. VanLehn, K. & Graesser, A. C.: Why2 Report: Evaluation of Why/Atlas, Why/AutoTutor, and accomplished human tutors on learning gains for qualitative physics problems and explanations. Unpublished report prepared by the University of Pittsburgh CIRCLE group and the University of Memphis Tutoring Research Group. (2002)
19. Hestenes, D., Wells, M., & Swackhamer, G.: Force Concept Inventory. The Physics Teacher, 30, 141-158.

ITS Evaluation in Classroom: The Case of AMBRE-AWP

Sandra Nogry, Stéphanie Jean-Daubias, and Nathalie Duclosson

LIRIS
Université Claude Bernard Lyon 1 - CNRS
Nautibus, 8 bd Niels Bohr, Campus de la Doua
69622 Villeurbanne Cedex
FRANCE
{Sandra.Nogry,Stephanie.Jean-Daubias,
Nathalie.Guin-Duclosson}@liris.cnrs.fr

Abstract. This paper describes the evaluation of an Intelligent Tutoring System (ITS) designed within the framework of the multidisciplinary AMBRE project. The aim of this ITS is to teach abstract knowledge based on problem classes thanks to the Case-Based Reasoning paradigm. We present here AMBRE-AWP, an ITS we designed following this principle for additive word problems domain and we describe how we evaluated it. We conducted first a pre-experiment with five users. Then we conducted an experiment in classroom with 76 eight-year-old pupils using comparative methods. We present the quantitative results and we discuss them using results of qualitative analysis.

Keywords: Intelligent Tutoring System evaluation, learning evaluation, additive word problems, teaching methods, Case-Based Reasoning

1 Introduction

This paper describes studies conducted in the framework of the AMBRE project. The purpose of this project is to design Intelligent Tutoring Systems (ITS) to teach methods. Derived from didactic studies, these methods are based on a classification of problems and solving tools. The AMBRE project proposes to help the learner to acquire a method following the steps of the Case-Based Reasoning (CBR) paradigm. We applied this principle to the additive word problems domain. We implemented the AMBRE-AWP system and evaluated this system with eight-year-old pupils in different manners.
In this paper, we first present the AMBRE principle. Then, we describe its application to additive word problems and two experiments carried out with eight-year-old pupils in laboratory and in classroom to evaluate the AMBRE-AWP ITS.

2 The AMBRE Project

The purpose of the AMBRE project is to design an ITS to help learners to acquire methods using Case-Based Reasoning [4].

J.C. Lester et al. (Eds.): ITS 2004, LNCS 3220, pp. 511–520, 2004.

The methods we want to teach in the AMBRE project were suggested by mathematic didactic studies [12] [15]. In a small domain, a method is based on a classification of problems and of solving tools. The acquisition of this classification enables the learner to choose the solving technique that is best suited to a given problem to solve. However, in some domains, it is not possible to explicitly teach problem classes and solving techniques associated with those classes. So, the AMBRE project proposes to enable the learner to build his own method using the case-based reasoning paradigm.
Case-Based Reasoning [7] can be described as a set of sequential steps (elaborate a target case, retrieve a source case, adapt the source to find the target case solution, revise the solution, store the case). The CBR paradigm is a technique that has already been used in various parts of ITS (e.g. learner model, diagnosis). The closest application to our approach is Case-Based Teaching [1] [9] [13]. Systems based on this learning strategy present a close case to the learner when (s)he encounters difficulties in solving a problem, or when (s)he faces a problem (s)he never came across before (in a new domain or a new type).
In the AMBRE project, CBR is not used by the system, but proposed to the learner as a learning strategy. Thus, in order to help the learner to acquire a method, we propose to present him a few typical worked-out examples (serving as case base initialization). Then, the learner is assisted in solving new problems. The environment guides the learner's solving of the problem by following each step of the CBR cycle (Fig. 1): the learner reformulates the problem in order to identify problem structure features (elaboration of the CBR cycle). Then, (s)he chooses a typical problem (retrieval). Next, (s)he adapts the typical problem solution to the problem to solve (adaptation). Finally, (s)he classifies the new problem (storing). The steps are guided by the system, but done by the learner. In the AMBRE ITS, revision is included as a diagnosis of learner responses in each step of the cycle.

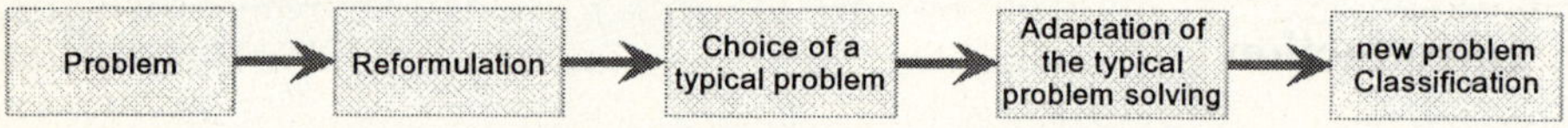

Fig. 1. The CBR cycle adapted to the AMBRE project.

The design process adopted in the AMBRE project is iterative, it is based on the implementation of prototypes that are tested and then modified This design satisfied the preoccupation with validating multidisciplinary design choices and detecting problems of use as early as possible.
Before the AMBRE design, the SYRCLAD solver [5] was designed to be used in ITS. SYRCLAD solves problems according to the methods we want to teach.
To begin the AMBRE design, we specified the objective of the project (to learn methods) and the approach to be used (CBR approach). Then we developed a first simple prototype (AMBRE-counting) for the numbering problems domain (final scientific year level, 18 year-old students). This prototype implemented the AMBRE principle with a limited number of problems, and limited functionalities (the Artificial Intelligence modules were not integrated). This prototype was evaluated in classroom using experimental method of cognitive psychology to assess the impact of the CBR paradigm on method learning. The results did not show significant learning improvement using the AMBRE ITS. Nevertheless, we identified difficulties experienced by learners during the system use [4]. These results and complementary

studies of cognitive psychology moved us to propose recommendations and new specifications.

After that, we implemented a system for additive word problem solving (AMBRE-AWP) taking into account the previous recommendations and specifications. This system includes a new interface, the SYRCLAD solver, and help and diagnosis functionalities.

This system was evaluated by developers and teachers, and used by children in laboratory. Then it was used by pupils in classroom.

In next sections, we present in more details AMBRE-AWP and we describe the evaluation of the system.

3 AMBRE-AWP: An ITS to Solve Additive Word Problems

AMBRE-AWP is an ITS for additive word problem solving based on the AMBRE principle. We chose additive word problems domain because this difficult domain for children is suitable to AMBRE principle. Learners have difficulties to visualize the problem situation [3]. Didactic studies proposed additive word problems classes [17] identifying problem type (add, change, compare) and the place of the unknown that can help learners to visualize the situation. Nonetheless, it is not possible to teach these classes explicitly. AMBRE principle might help the learner to identify the problem's relevant features (the problem class).

These problems are studied in primary school. Thus we adapted the system to be used individually in classroom in primary school by eight-year-old pupils.

According to the AMBRE principle, AMBRE-AWP presents examples to learner and then guides him following the steps described below.

Reformulation of the problem: once the learner has read the problem to solve (e.g. "Julia had 17 cookies in her bag. She ate some of them during the break. Now, she has 9 left. How many cookies did Julia eat during the break?"), the first step consists in reformulating the problem. The learner is asked to build a new formulation of the submitted problem identifying its relevant features (i.e. problem type and unknown place). We chose to represent problem classes by diagrams that we adapted from didactic studies [17] [18]. The reformulation no longer has most of the initial problem's surface features, and becomes a reference for the remainder of the solving.

Choice of a typical problem: the second step of the solving consists for the learner in comparing the problem to be solved with the typical problems by identifying differences and similarities in each case. Typical problems are represented by their wording and their reformulation. The learner should choose the problem that seems the nearest to the problem to be solved, such nearness being based on reformulations. By choosing a typical problem, the learner implicitly identifies the class of the problem to be solved.

Adaptation of the typical problem solution to the problem to be solved: in order to write the solution, the learner should adapt the solution of the typical problem he chose in the previous step to the problem to be solved (Fig. 2). The solution writing consists first in establishing the equation corresponding to the problem. Then, the learner writes how to calculate the solution and then calculates it. Finally, (s)he constructs a sentence to answer the question. If the learner uses the help functionality,

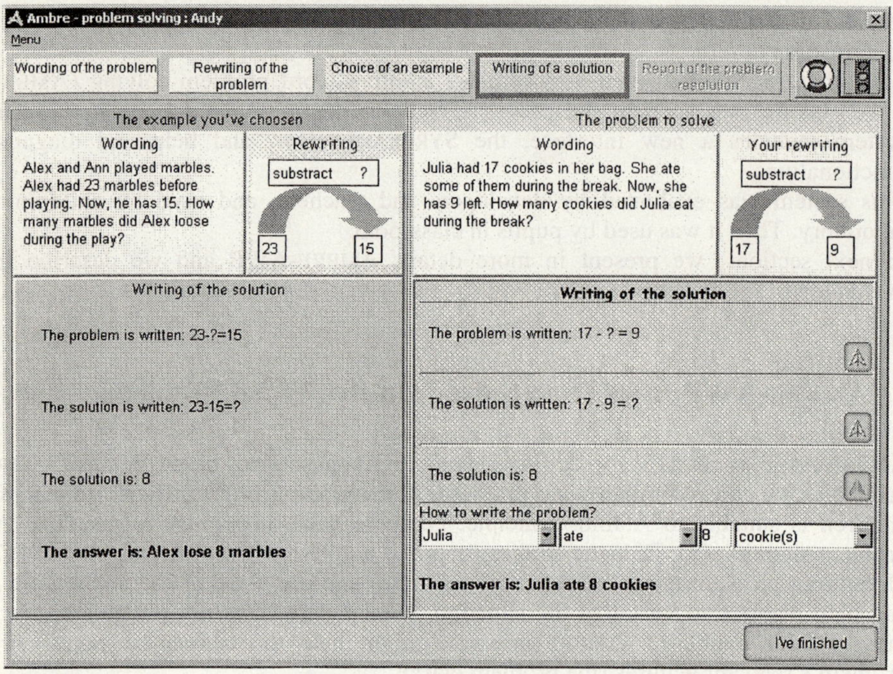

Fig. 2. Adaptation step in AMBRE-AWP (English translation of the French interface).

the system can assist the adaptation by outlining with colors similarities between the typical problem (Fig. 2: left side) and the problem to solve (Fig. 2: right side).

Classification of the problem: first, the learner can read the report of the problem solving. Then, he has to classify the new problem by associating it with a typical problem that represents a group of existing problems of the same class. During that step, the learner should identify the group of problems associated with the solved problem.

4 AMBRE-AWP Evaluation with Eight-Year-Old Pupils

After the implementation, AMBRE-AWP was evaluated with pupils. To evaluate a system, Senach [16] distinguishes two aspects: the usability and the utility of the system. Usability concerns the capacity of the software to allow the user to reach his objectives easily. Utility deals with the adequacy of the software to the high level objectives of the customer. In the case of ITS, the user is the learner and the customer is the teacher or the "educational system". So, we must take into account learner specificity in the usability evaluation. The high level objective of ITS is learning. So, the evaluation of the system utility concerns the evaluation of the learning. In our case, we have to evaluate the method learning. If usability can be evaluated with classical methods developed in Human Computer Interaction (HCI) domain, learning evaluation requires specific methods.

In this section, we present the AMBRE-AWP evaluation with eight-year-old children. We first describe a pre-experiment in laboratory, which enabled us to evaluate usability. This pre-experiment moved us to modify of the system. Then, we present evaluation of AMBRE-AWP utility in classroom.

4.1 Pre-experiment in Laboratory

We evaluated AMBRE-AWP in a pre-experiment in order to observe the appropriateness of the system to the learners and to identify usability problems.

Due to the specificity of the learners (young children, beginner readers, not very familiar with computer), we chose to use one to one testing [8]: we observed individually eight-year-old learners using AMBRE-AWP in order to detect the main usability problems. They had to solve two additive word problems with the system during 45 minutes. During the use of the system, we observed interactions between the children and the system and we recorded what users said. Then, learners filled up a short questionnaire that let us to know if they liked mathematics, if they are familiar with computer use and their satisfaction.

In order to evaluate AMBRE-AWP usability, we referred to existent ergonomic criteria. Among these criteria we chose seven criteria proposed by Bastien & Scapin [2], Nielsen [11] and Schneiderman [14] that are adapted [6] to observe ITS usability: Learnability (how do users understand the system use?), general understanding (do users understand the software principle?), effectiveness (are there some interface elements that lead to systematic errors?), error management (are there ergonomic problems which lead to errors?), help management (do users use the help functionality?), cognitive load and satisfaction

We observed five users; all were familiar with computer use (regular use at school or at home) and liked mathematics. Some of them were poor readers.

First, as we expected, observations showed that users passed a lot of time to discover interface elements (e.g.: list-box). Although users encountered difficulties to use the system during the first problem resolution, these difficulties disappeared during the second problem resolution. So, the interface use seemed to be time consuming but well understood. The general understanding of the system seemed to be difficult: users did not understand well the AMBRE principle and the link between solving steps. Moreover, we observed cognitive overload during the worked-out examples presentation and the adaptation step. Furthermore, in the adaptation step (Fig. 2), learners had difficulties to write how to calculate the solution. Teachers confirmed that this sub-step was not adapted to the arithmetical knowledge of the target users.

The observation of the help functionality use showed that help was often used. Nevertheless, children did not well understand help and error messages.

Finally, the questionnaire analysis showed that four users among five were satisfied and consider AMBRE-AWP pleasant to use.

We take into account these results to adapt AMBRE-AWP to eight-year-old users capabilities, modifying the system. For example, in order to facilitate the system learnability, we chose to replace the tutorial with a demonstration explaining the AMBRE principle and showing how to use the interface during the first session; to reduce cognitive load, we modified the examples presentation. Moreover, we deleted the adaptation sub-step, which was not adapted to learners of this age.

4.2 Learning Evaluation

After the pre-experiment, we evaluated the utility of the modified system measuring the impact of AMBRE-AWP on method learning for additive word problems.
More precisely, we were interested in knowing if AMBRE-AWP has an impact on the learner ability to identify the class of a problem and if the expected impact of AMBRE-AWP is due to CBR approach or if it is only due to problem reformulation with diagram.
For that, we used experimental method [8]. We compared AMBRE-AWP use with the use of two control prototypes. The experiment was conducted in classroom with 76 eight-year-old pupils divided in six groups in order to reproduce actual use conditions. During six weeks, each group worked in computer classroom and used the software during half an hour per week. Each child used individually the software. We measured the learning outcomes with different tasks and we completed these data with a qualitative approach.

4.3 Evaluation Paradigm

We compared three systems: the AMBRE-AWP ITS and two control systems. The whole system, AMBRE-AWP, guides the solving toward the CBR cycle according to the AMBRE principle.
The first control system, the "reformulation and solving system" presents worked-out examples and guides the learner to solve the problem. The learner reformulates the problem and then writes the solution. Finally, he can read the problem report. In contrast with AMBRE-AWP, this system does not propose to choose and to use a prototypical example. The aim of this control system is to verify the impact of reformulation with diagrams on learning.
The second control system, the "simple solving system", proposes to find the problem solution directly. Once the learner has read the worked-out examples and the problem to be solved, he writes the solution. Finally, he can read the problem report. Contrary to the AMBRE-AWP ITS, there is no reformulation and the step of the choice of typical problem. As this system has fewer steps than the others, learners have to make another task after problem solving so that all groups solve an equivalent number of problems. This task consists in reading a problem wording and finding pertinent information in this text (a number) to answer a question.
In each of the three pupils classes, one group uses AMBRE-AWP and the other group uses of the other control systems. Learners are assigned to groups according to their mathematical level so that groups are equivalent. In order to measure the learning outcomes, we use a "structure features detection task", a problem solving task and an "equation writing task".
"Structure features detection task" consists in reading a first problem, and then choosing between two problems the one that is solved like the first problem. In this task, we manipulate unknown place, problem type and surface features. This task enables to evaluate the learner ability to identify two problems that have the same structure features whatever the surface features and the difficulty of the problem are.
Problem solving task is a paper and pencil task. It consists in solving six problems: two problems close to problems presented by the system ("easy problems") and four problems that content non pertinent data for the resolution ("difficult problems"). This

task enables to evaluate the impact of the system on paper and pencil task with simple and difficult problems.
In the "Equation writing task" we presented a diagram representing a problem class. The learner task consisted in typing the equation corresponding to the diagram (filling up boxes with numbers and operation). This task allows us to test the learner ability to associate the corresponding equation with the problem class (represented by diagrams). This task is realized only by groups that made the reformulation step (the AMBRE-AWP group and the "Reformulation and solving system" group).
The experimental design we adopt is an *interrupted-time series design*: we present the problem solving task as pre-test, after the fourth system use, as post-test and as delayed post-test one month after the last system use. The "structure features detection task" is presented after each system use; the "equation writing task" is presented after the fifth system use and as post-test.
In order to complete these data, we adopt a qualitative approach [8]. Before the experiment, we made an "a priori" analysis in order to highlight the various strategies usable by learners who solve problems with AMBRE-AWP. During the system use, we noticed all questions asked. Moreover, we observed the difficulties encountered by learners, the interactions between the learners and the interactions between the learners and the persons that supervise the sessions. In post-test, the learners filled up a questionnaire in order to take into account their satisfaction and remarks. Finally, we analysed the use traces in order to identify the strategies used by learners, to highlight the most frequent errors and to identify the steps that cause difficulties to learners. With these methods, we would like to identify difficulties encountered by learners and want to take into account the complexity of the situation.

4.4 Results

In this section, we present the quantitative results and we discuss these results using qualitative results.
With the problem solving task, we performed an analysis of variance on performances with groups (AMBRE-AWP, simple solver system, Reformulation and solving system) and tests (4 tests) as variables. Performances in pre-test are significantly lower than performance of the other tests ($F(3,192)=18.1$; $p<0.001$). There is no significant difference between tests performed after the fourth system use, as post-test and as delayed post-test one month after the last system use. There is no significant differences between groups ($F(2,64)=0.12$; $p=0.89$) and no interaction between group and sessions ($F(6,192)=1.15$; $p=0.33$). With the "structure features detection task", there is no significant difference between the AMBRE-AWP group and the other groups (Chi^2 ($dl=1$)$=0.21$; $p= 0.64$). Even at the end of the experiment, surface features interfere with structure feature in problem choice. The "equation writing task" shows that learners that use AMBRE-AWP and "Reformulation and solving system" are both able to write the right equation corresponding to a problem class represented by a diagram in fifty percent of the cases. Thus there is no difference between the results of the AMBRE-AWP group and the control groups for each task. The three systems equally improve learning outcomes. Results of "structure feature detection task" and "equation writing task" do not show method learning. So, these results do not validate the AMBRE principle.

The qualitative analysis allows explaining these results. First, pupils did not use AMBRE-AWP as we expected. The observation shows that when they wrote the solution, they did not adapt the typical problem to solve the problem. Secondly, learners solved each problem very slowly (means 15 minutes). As they are beginner readers, they had difficulties to read instructions and messages, and were discouraged sometimes to read them. Besides, they met difficulties during reformulation and adaptation steps because they did not identify well their mistakes and they did not master arithmetic techniques. Thirdly, the comparison between "simple solving system" and AMBRE-AWP is questionable. Indeed, despite the additional task, the "simple solving system" group resolved significantly more problems than the AMBRE-AWP group (means 9 problems vs. 14 problems during the 6 sessions, $F(1, 45) = 9.7$; $p<0.01$). Moreover assistance required by pupils and given by persons that supervised sessions varied with groups. With AMBRE-AWP, questions and assistance often consisted in reformulating help and diagnosis messages. Whereas, in the simple solving system it consisted in giving mathematic helps sometimes comparable to AMBRE-AWP reformulation. So, even if AMBRE principle has an impact on learning, the difference between number of problems solved by AMBRE-AWP group and "simple solving system" group and the difference of assistance could partly explain that these two groups have similar results.

Thus, the quantitative results (no difference between groups) can be explained by three reasons. First, pupils did not use prototypical problems to solve their problem. As we expected that the choice and adaptation of a typical problem could facilitate analogy between problems and favour method learning, it is not surprising that we do not observe method learning. Secondly, learners solved each problem slowly and they were confronted with a lot of difficulties (reading, reformulation, solution calculating) all over the AMBRE cycle. These difficulties probably disrupt their understanding of the AMBRE principle. Third, there are methodological issues due to the difficulty to use comparison method in real word experiments because it is not possible to control all factors. A pre-test of the control system should decrease these difficulties but not suppress them. These methodological issues confirm our impression that it is necessary to complete experimental method with qualitative approach to evaluate an ITS in real word [10].

These qualitative results show that AMBRE-AWP is not well adapted for eight-year-old pupils. However, questionnaire and interviews showed that a lot of pupils were enthusiastic to use AMBRE-AWP (more than the "simple solver system"); they appreciated to reformulate the problem with diagrams.

5 Conclusions and Prospects

The framework of the study described in this paper is the AMBRE project. This project relies on the CBR solving cycle to have the learner acquire a problem solving method based on a classification of problems. We implemented a system based on the AMBRE principle for additive word problems solving (AMBRE-AWP). We evaluated it with eight-year-old pupils. In the first experiment, we observed five children in laboratory, in order to identify some usability problems and to verify the adequacy of the system with this type of users. Then, we realized an experiment in classroom during six week with 76 pupils. We compared the system with two control systems to assess the impact of the AMBRE principle on method learning. Results show performances improvement between pre-test and post-test but no difference between the AMBRE-AWP group and the other groups. Thus the AMBRE-AWP system improves learning outcomes but not more than other systems. These results cannot allow us to validate the AMBRE principle. The qualitative results show that learners did not use the system like we expected it. They construct the solution without adapting the typical problem solution. Moreover, they had difficulties like reading, and calculating that slowed down the problem solving.

This experiment leads us to modify some aspects of the system. We modified the diagnosis messages so that they are more understandable for primary school pupils. Moreover, in order to reduce the difficulties due to reading, we consider integrating to AMBRE-AWP a text-to-speech synthesis system in order to present the diagnosis messages and instructions.

Furthermore, as that AMBRE-AWP is too complex for eight-year-old pupils, we are trying to identify learners for whom AMBRE-AWP is more appropriate. At present, we are testing the system with twenty nine-year-old pupils in order to evaluate if they have less difficulties than eight-year-old pupils and if problems are adapted to them. If this pre-test is positive, we will evaluate the AMBRE principle with them.

Besides, in collaboration with teachers, we design simpler activities preparatory to AMBRE-AWP within the reach of young pupils in order to acquire capabilities used in AMBRE-AWP. For example, we propose activities that develop the capability to identify relevant features in the problem wording. We also develop activities that highlight the links between the wording of the problem, its reformulation and its solving showing how a modification on the wording acts on its reformulation, how a modification on the reformulation acts on its wording, and what are the consequences of these modifications on the solving.

Finally, we propose two long-term prospects. We study the possibility to propose AMBRE-AWP to adults within a literacy context, using new story types in the wordings problems. We are also designing an environment for teachers enabling them to customize the AMBRE-AWP environment and to generate the problems they wish their pupils to work on with the system.

Acknowlegments. This research has been supported by the interdisciplinary program STIC-SHS «Société de l'Information» of CNRS

References

1. Aleven, V. & Ashley, K.D.: Teaching Case-Based Argumentation through a Model and Examples - Empirical Evaluation of an Intelligent Learning Environment. Artificial Intelligence in Education, IOS Press (1997), 87-94.
2. Bastien, C. & Scapin, D.: Ergonomic Criteria for the Evaluation of Human-Computer Interfaces. In RT n°156, INRIA, (1993).
3. Greeno, J.G. & Riley, M.S.: Processes and development of understanding. In metacognition, motivation and understanding, F.E. Weinert, R.H. Kluwe Eds (1987), Chap 10, 289-313.

4. Guin-Duclosson, N., Jean-Daubias, S. & Nogry, S.: The AMBRE ILE: How to Use Case-Based Reasoning to Teach Methods. In proceedings of ITS, Biarritz, France: Springer (2002), 782-791.
5. Guin-Duclosson, N.: SYRCLAD: une architecture de résolveurs de problèmes permettant d'expliciter des connaissances de classification, reformulation et résolution. Revue d'Intelligence Artificielle, vol 13-2, Paris : Hermès (1999), 225-282
6. Jean, S.: Application de recommandations ergonomiques : spécificités des EIAO dédiés à l'évaluation. In proceedings of RJC IHM 2000 (2000), 39-42
7. Kolodner, J.: Case Based Reasoning. San Mateo, CA: Morgan Kaufmann Publishers (1993).
8. Mark, M. A., & Greer, J. E.: Evaluation methodologies for intelligent tutoring systems. Journal of Artificial Intelligence in Education, vol 4.2/3 (1993), 129-153.
9. Masterton, S.: The Virtual Participant: Lessons to be Learned from a Case-Based Tutor's Assistant. Computer Support for Collaborative Learning, Toronto (1997), 179-186.
10. Murray, T.: Formative Qualitative Evaluation for "Exploratory" ITS research. Journal of Artificial Intelligence in Education, vol 4(2/3, (1993), 179-207.
11. Nielsen, J.: Usability Engineering, Academic Press (1993).
12. Rogalski, M.: Les concepts de l'EIAO sont-ils indépendants du domaine? L'exemple d'enseignement de méthodes en analyse. Recherches en Didactiques des Mathématiques, vol 14 n° 1.2 (1994), 43-66.
13. Schank, R. & Edelson, D.: A Role for AI in Education: Using Technology to Reshape Education. Journal of Artificial Intelligence in Education, vol 1.2 (1990), 3-20.
14. Schneiderman, B.: Designing the User Interface: Strategies for Effective Human-Computer Interaction. Reading, MA : Addison-Wesley (1992).
15. Schoenfeld, A.: Mathematical Problem Solving. New York: Academic Press (1985).
16. Senach, B.: L'évaluation ergonomique des interfaces homme-machine. L'ergonomie dans la conception des projets informatiques, Octares editions (1993), 69-122.
17. Vergnaud, G.: A classification of cognitive tasks and operations of the thought involved in addition and substraction problems. Addition and substraction: A cognitive perspective, Hillsdale: Erlbaum (1982), 39-58.
18. Willis, G. B. & Fuson, K.C.: Teaching children to use schematic drawings to solve addition and subtraction word problems. Journal of Educational Psychology, vol 80 (1988), 190-201.

Implicit Versus Explicit Learning of Strategies in a Non-procedural Cognitive Skill

Kurt VanLehn[1], Dumiszewe Bhembe[1], Min Chi[1], Collin Lynch[1],
Kay Schulze[2], Robert Shelby[3], Linwood Taylor[1], Don Treacy[3], Anders Weinstein[1],
and Mary Wintersgill[3]

[1] Learning Research & Development Center, University of Pittsburgh, Pittsburgh, PA, USA
{VanLehn, Bhembe, mic31, collinl, lht3, andersw}@pitt.edu

[2] Computer Science Dept., US Naval Academy, Annapolis, MD, USA
schulze@artic.nadn.navy.mil

[3] Physics Department, US Naval Academy, Annapolis, MD, USA
{treacy, mwinter}@artic.nadn.navy.mil

Abstract. University physics is typical of many cognitive skills in that there is no standard procedure for solving problems, and yet a few students still master the skill. This suggests that their learning of problem solving strategies is implicit, and that an effective tutoring system need not teach problem solving strategies as explicitly as model-tracing tutors do. In order to compare implicit vs. explicit learning of problem solving strategies, we developed two physics tutoring systems, Andes and Pyrenees. Pyrenees is a model-tracing tutor that teaches a problem solving strategy explicitly, whereas Andes uses a novel pedagogy, developed over many years of use in the field, that provides virtually no explicit strategic instruction. Preliminary results from an experiment comparing the two systems are reported.

1 The Research Problem

This paper compares methods for tutoring non-procedural cognitive skills. A *cognitive* skill is a task domain where solving a problem requires taking many actions, but the challenge is not in the physical demands of the actions, which are quite simple ones such as drawing or typing, but in deciding which actions to take. If the skill is such that at any given moment, the set of acceptable actions is fairly small, then it is called a *procedural* cognitive skill. Otherwise, let us call it a *non-procedural* cognitive skill. For instance, programming a VCR is a procedural cognitive skill, whereas developing a Java program is a non-procedural skill because the acceptable actions at most points include editing code, executing it, turning tracing on and off, reading the manual, inventing some test cases and so forth. Roughly speaking, the sequence of actions matters for procedural skills, but for non-procedural skills, only the final state matters. However, skills exists at all points along the continuum between procedural and non-procedure. Moreover, even in highly non-procedural skills, some sequences

J.C. Lester et al. (Eds.): ITS 2004, LNCS 3220, pp. 521–530, 2004.

of actions may be unacceptable, such as compiling an error-free Java program twice in a row without changing the code or the compiler settings.

Tutoring systems for procedural cognitive skills can be quite simple. At every point in time, because there are only a few actions that students should take, the tutor can give positive feedback when the student's action matches an acceptable one, and negative feedback otherwise. When the student gets stuck, the tutor can pick an acceptable next action and hint it. Of course, in order to give feedback and hints, the tutor must be able to calculate at any point the set of acceptable next actions. This calculation is often called "the ideal student model," the "expert model." Such tutors are often called *model tracing* tutors.

It is much harder to build a tutoring system for non-procedural cognitive skills. Several techniques have been explored. The next few paragraphs review three of them.

One approach to tutoring a non-procedural skill is to teach a specific problem-solving procedure, method or strategy. The strategy may be well-known but not ordinarily taught, or the strategy may be one that has been invented for this purpose. For instance, the CMU Lisp tutor (Corbett & Bhatnagar, 1997) teaches a specific strategy for programming Lisp functions that consists of first inferring an algorithm from examples, then translating this algorithm into Lisp code working top-down and left-to-right. The basic idea of this approach is to convert a non-procedural cognitive skill into a procedural one. This allows one to use a model tracing tutor. Several model tracing tutors have been developed for non-procedural cognitive skills (e.g., Reiser, Kimberg, Lovett, & Ranney, 1992; Scheines & Sieg, 1994).

A second approach is to simply ignore the students' actions and look only at the product of those actions. Such tutoring systems act like a grader in a course, who can only examine the work submitted by a student, and has no access to the actions taken while creating it. Such tutors are usually driven by a knowledge base of condition-advice pairs. If the condition is true of the product, then the advice is relevant. Recent examples include tutors that critique a database query (Mitrovic & Ohlsson, 1999) or a qualitative physics essay (Graesser, VanLehn, Rose, Jordan, & Harter, 2001). Let us call this approach *product critiquing*.

Instead of critiquing the product, a tutoring system can critique the process even if it doesn't understand the process completely. Like product critiquing tutors, such a tutor has a knowledge base of condition-advice pairs. However, the conditions are applied as the student solves the problem. In particular, after each student action, the conditions are matched against the student's action and the state that preceded it. For instance, in the first tutoring system to use this technique (Burton & Brown, 1982), students played a board game. If they made a move that was significantly worse than the best available move, the tutor would consider giving some advice about the best available more. Let us call this approach *process critiquing*.

The distinctions between a process critiquing tutor and a model tracing tutor are both technical and pedagogical. The technical distinction is that a model tracing tutor has rules that recognize *correct* actions, whereas the process critiquing tutor has rules that recognize *incorrect* actions. Depending on the task domain, it may be much easier to author one kind of rule than the other. The pedagogical distinction is that model tracing tutors are often used when learning the problem solving strategy is an instructional objective. The strategy is usually discussed explicitly by the tutor in its hints, and presented explicitly in the texts that accompany the tutor. In contrast, the process critiquing tutors rarely teach an explicit problem solving strategy.

All three techniques have advantages and disadvantages. Different ones are appropriate for different cognitive skills. The question posed by this paper is which one is best for a specific task domain, physics problem solving. Although the argument concerns physics, elements of it may perhaps be applied to other task domains as well.

2 Physics Problem Solving

Physics problem solving involves building a logical derivation of an answer from given information. Table 1 uses a two-column proof format to illustrate a derivation. Each row consists of a proposition, which is often an equation, and its justification. A justification refers to a domain principle, such as Newton's second law, and to the propositions that match the principle's premises. The tradition in physics is to display only the major propositions in a derivation. The minor propositions, which are often simple equations such as *a_x=a*, are not displayed explicitly but instead are incorpo-

Table 1. A derivation of a physics problem

Problem: A motorboat cruises slowly to the mouth of the harbor, covering 230 m in 460 s at a constant velocity. It then speeds up to a cruising speed of 5 m/s in 60 seconds. What is its average acceleration while speeding up? Assume it always travels in a straight line. Let time 1 be when the motorboat starts the 230 m journey; let time 2 be when it starts speeding up; and let time 3 be when it reaches cruising speed.

	Proposition	**Justification**
1	d12_x = 230 m	Given (where d12 is the displacement of the motorboat from time 1 to 2, the x-axis is horizontal, and d12_x is the x-component of d12)
2	t12 = 460 s	Given (where t12 is the duration from time 1 to 2)
3	t23 = 60 s	Given (where t23 is the duration from time 2 to 3)
4	v3_x = 5 m/s	Given (where v3 is the motorboat's velocity at time 3)
5	v12_x = d12_x / t12	Definition of average velocity applied over the time interval from time 1 to time 2 (where v12 is the average velocity of the motorboat during time 1 to 2)
6	v12_x = 0.50 m/s	Algebraically solve 1, 2, 5 for v12_x
7	a23_x = (v3_x-v2_x)/t23	Definition of average acceleration applied over the time interval from time 2 to 3 (where a23 is the average acceleration of the motorboat during time 2 to 3, and v2 is the velocity of the motorboat at time 2)
8	v2_x = v12_x	Constant velocity
9	a23_x = a23	Projection
10	a23 = 0.075	Algebraically solve 3, 6, 7, 8, 9 for a23

rated algebraically into the main propositions. The justifications are almost never displayed by students or instructors, although textbook examples often mention a few major justifications. Such proof-like derivations are the solution structures of many other non-procedural skills, including geometry theorem proving, logical theorem proving, algebraic or calculus equation solving, etc.

Although AI has developed many well-defined procedures for deductive problem solving, such as forward chaining and backwards chaining, they are not explicitly taught in physics. Explicit strategy teaching is also absent in many other non-procedure cognitive skills.

Although no physics problem solving procedures are taught, some students do manage to become competent problem solvers. Although it could be that only the most gifted students can learn physics problem solving strategies implicitly, two facts suggest otherwise. First, for simpler skills than physics, many experiments have demonstrated that people can learn implicitly, and that explicit instruction sometimes has no benefit (e.g., Berry & Broadbent, 1984). Second, the Cascade model of cognitive skill acquisition, which features implicit learning of strategy, is both computationally sufficient to learn physics and an accurate predictor of student protocol data (VanLehn & Jones, 1993; VanLehn, Jones, & Chi, 1992).

If students really are learning how to select principles from their experience, as this prior work suggests, perhaps a tutoring system should merely expedite such experiential learning rather than replace it with explicit teaching/learning. One way to do that, which is suggested by stimulus sampling and other theories of memory, is to ensure that when students attempt to retrieve an experience that could be useful in the present situation, they draw from a pool of *successful* problem solving experiences. This in turn suggests that the tutoring system should just keep students on successful solution paths. It should prevent floundering, generation of useless steps, traveling down dead end paths, errors and other unproductive experiences. This pedagogy has been implemented by Andes, a physics tutoring system (VanLehn et al., 2002). The pedagogy was refined over many years of evaluation at the United States Naval Academy. The next section describes Andes' pedagogical method.

3 The Andes Method for Teaching a Non-procedural Skill

Andes does not teach a problem solving strategy, but it does attempt to fill students' episodic memory with appropriate experiences. In particular, whenever the student makes an entry on the user interface, Andes colors it red if it is incorrect and green if it is correct. Students almost always correct the red entries immediately, asking Andes for help if necessary. Thus, their memories should contain either episodes of green, correct steps or well-marked episodes of red errors and remediation.

The most recent version of Andes does present a small amount of strategy instruction in one special context, namely, when students get stuck and ask for help on what to do next. This kind of help is called "next-step help" in order to differentiate it from asking what is wrong with a red entry. Andes' next-step help suggests applying a major principle whose equation contains a quantity that the problem is seeking. Even if there are other major principles in the problem's solution, it prefers one that is contains a sought quantity. For instance, suppose a student were solving the problem shown in Table 1, had entered the givens and asked for next-step help. Andes would elicit *a23* as the sought quantity and the definition of average velocity (shown on line 7 of Table 1) as the major principle.

Andes' approach to tutoring non-procedural skills is different from product critiquing, process critiquing and model tracing. Andes gives feedback during the problem solving process, so it is not product critiquing. Like a model-tracing tutor, it uses rules to represent correct actions, but like a process-critiquing tutor, it does not explicitly teach a problem solving strategy. Thus, is pedagogically similar to a process-critiquing system and technically similar to a model-tracing system.

Andes is a highly effective tutoring system. In a series of real-world (not laboratory) evaluations conducted at the US Naval Academy, effect sizes ranged from 0.44 to 0.92 standard deviations (VanLehn et al., 2002).

However, there is still room for improvement, particularly in getting students to follow more sensible problem solving strategies. Log files suggest that students sometimes get so lost that they ask for Andes' help on almost every action, which suggests that they have no "weak method" or other general problem solving strategy to fall back upon when their implicit memories fail to show them a way to solve a problem. Students often produce actions that are not needed for solving the problem, and they produce actions in an order that conforms to no recognizable strategy. The resulting disorganized and cluttered derivation makes it difficult to appreciate the basic physics underlying the problem's solution.

We tried augmenting Andes' next-step help system to explicitly teach a problem solving strategy (VanLehn et al., 2002). This led to such long, complex interactions that students generally refused to ask for help even when they clearly needed it. The students and instructors both felt that this approach was a failure.

It seems clear in retrospect that a general problem solving strategy is just too complex and too abstract to teach in the context of giving students hints. It needs to be taught explicitly. That is, it should be presented in the accompanying texts, and students should be stepped carefully through it for several problems until they have mastered the procedural aspects of the strategy. In other words, students may learn even better than Andes if taught in a model-tracing manner.

4 An Experiment: Andes Versus Pyrenees

This section describes an experiment comparing two tutoring systems, a model tracing tutor (Pyrenees) with a tutor that encourages implicit learning of strategies (Andes). Pyrenees teaches a form of backward chaining called the Target Variable Strategy. It is taught to the students briefly using the instructions shown in the appendix. Although Pyrenees uses the same physics principles and the same physics problems as Andes, its user interface differs because it explicitly teaches the Target Variable Strategy.

4.1 User Interfaces

Both Andes and Pyrenees have the same 5 windows, which display:

- The physics problem to be solved
- The variables defined by the student
- Vectors and axes
- The equations entered by the student
- A dialogue between the student and the tutor

In both systems, equations and variable names are entered via typing, and all other entries are made via menu selections. Andes uses a conventional menu system (pull down menus, pop-up menus and dialogue boxes), whereas Pyrenees uses teletype-style menus.

For both tutors, every variable defined by the student is represented by a line in the Variables window. The line displays the variable's name and definition. However, in Pyrenees, the window also displays the variable's state, which is one of these:

- *Sought*: If a value for the variable is currently being sought, then the line displays, e.g., "mb = SOUGHT: the mass of the boy."
- *Known*: If a value has been given or calculated for a variable, then the line displays the value, e.g., "mb = 5 kg: the mass of the boy."
- *Other*: If a variable is neither Sought nor Known, then the line displays only the variables name and definition, e.g., "mb: the mass of the boy."

The Target Variable Strategy's second phase, labeled "applying principles" in the Appendix, is a form of backwards chaining where Sought variables serve as goals. The student starts this phase with some variables Known and some Sought. The student selects a Sought variable, executes the Apply Principle command, and eventually changes the status of the variable from Sought to Other. However, if the equation produced by applying the principle has variables in it that are not yet Known, then the student marks them Sought. This is equivalent to subgoaling in backwards chaining. The Variables window thus acts like a bookkeeping device for the backwards chaining strategy; it keeps the current goals visible.

As an illustration, suppose a student is solving the problem of Table 1 and has entered the givens already. The student selects *a23* as the sought variable, and it is marked Sought in the Variable window. The student executes the Apply Principle command, selects "Projection" and produces the equation shown on line 9 of Table 1, *a23_x=a23*. This equation has an unknown variable in it, *a23_x*, so it is marked Sought in the Variable window. The Sought mark is removed from *a23*. Now the cycle repeats. The student executes the Apply Principle command, selects "definition of average acceleration," produces the equation shown on line 7 of Table 1, removes the Sought mark from *a23_x*, and adds a Sought mark to *v2_x*. This cycle repeats until no variables are marked Sought. The resulting system of equations can now be solved algebraically, because it is guaranteed to contain all and only the equations required for solving the problem.

In Andes, students can type any equation they wish into the Equation window, and only the equation is displayed in the window. In Pyrenees, equations are entered only by applying principles in order to determine the value of a Sought variable, so its equation window displays the equation plus the Sought variable and the principle application, e.g., "In order to find *W*, we apply the weight law to the boy: $W = mb*g$."

Some steps, such as defining variables for the quantities given in the problem statement, are repeated so often that students master them early and find them tedious thereafter. Both Andes and Pyrenees relieve students of some of these tedious steps. In Andes, this is done by predefining certain variables in problems that appear late in the sequence of problems. In Pyrenees, steps in applying the Target Variable Strategy, shown indented in the Appendix, can be done by either the student or the tutor. When students have demonstrated mastery of a particular step by doing it correctly the last 4 out of 5 times, then Pyrenees will take over executing that step for the student. Once it has taken over a step, Pyrenees will do it 80% of the time; the student must still do the step 20% of the time. Thus, student's skills are kept fresh. If they make a mistake when it is their turn, then Pyrenees will stop doing the step for them until they have re-demonstrated their competence.

4.2 Experimental Subjects, Materials, and Procedures

The experiment used a two-condition, repeated measures design with 20 students per condition. Students were required to have competence in high-school trigonometry and algebra, but to have taken no college physics course. They completed a pre-test, a multi-session training, and a post-test.

The training had two phases. In phase 1, students learned how to use the tutoring system. In the case of Pyrenees, this included learning the target variable strategy. During Phase 1, students studied a short textbook, studied two worked example problems, and solved 3 non-physics algebra word problems. In phase 2, students learned the major principles of translational kinematics, namely, the definition of average velocity $v=d/t$, the definition average acceleration $a=(vf-vi)/t$, the constant-acceleration equation $v=(vi+vf)/2$ and freefall acceleration equation, $a=g$. They studied a short textbook, studied a worked example problem, solved 7 training problems on their tutoring system and took the post-test.

4.3 Results

The post-test consisted of 4 problems similar to the training problems. Students were not told how their test problems would be scored. They were free to show as much work as they wished. Thus, we created two scoring rubrics for the tests. The "Answer rubric" counted only the answers, and the "Show work" rubric counted only the derivations leading up to the answers but not including the answers themselves. The Show-work rubric gave more credit for writing major principles' equations than minor ones. It also gave more credit for defining vector variables than scalar variables.

Table 2 presents the results. Scores are reported as percentages. A one-way ANOVA showed that the pre-test means were not significantly different. When students post-tests were scored with the Answer rubric, their scores were not significantly different according to both an one-way Anova ($F(29)=.888$, $p=.354$) and an

Ancova with the pre-test as the covariate ($F(28)=2.548$, $p=.122$). However, when the post-test were scored with the Show-work rubric, the Pyrenees students scored reliably higher than the Andes students according to both an Anova ($F(29)=6.076$, $p=.020$) and an Ancova with the pre-test as the covariate ($F(28)=5.527$, $p=.026$).

5 Discussion

Pyrenees requires students to focus on applying individual principles, whereas Andes requires only that students write equations. Moreover, Andes allows students to combine several principle applications algebraically into one equation. Thus, the Andes students may have become used to deriving answers while showing less work. This would explain why they had lower Show-work scores.

However, having learned an explicit problem solving strategy did not seem to help Pyrenees students derive correct answers. This may be due to a floor effect—three of the four test problems were too difficult for most students regardless of which training they received. Also, during the test, students had to do their own algebraic manipulations, while during training, the tutors handled all the algebraic manipulations for them so that they could concentrate on learning physics.

This was the first laboratory evaluation of Andes and of Pyrenees, so we learned a great deal about how to improve such evaluations. In the next experiment in this series, we plan to pace the instruction more slowly and to give students more examples. We need to devise a testing method that doesn't require students to do their own algebra. Most importantly, we need a way to measure floundering, which we expect Pyrenees will reduce, and across-chapter transfer, which we expect Pyrenees will increase.

Although this experimental results should be viewed with caution due to the many improvements that could be made to the evaluation methods, the results are consistent with our hypothesis that Andes students learn problem solving strategies implicitly, which limits their generality and power relative to an explicitly taught strategy. When Pyrenees taught a problem solving strategy explicitly, its students employed a qualitatively better strategy on post-tests, but this did not suffice to raise their Answer score relative to the Andes students.

Table 2. Means and Standard Errors

	Andes	**Pyrenees**	**p (2-tailed)**
N	17	14	
Pretest	39.9 (4.99)	44.4 (5.62)	.555
Posttest Show-work	30.4 (2.71)	40.1 (2.84)	.020
Posttest Answer	35.3 (6.45)	26.8 (6.13)	.354
Adjusted Show-work	30.8 (2.54)	39.7 (2.80)	.026
Adjusted Answer	36.8 (4.94)	25.0 (5.44)	.122

Acknowledgements. This research was supported by the Cognitive Science Program of the Office of Naval Research under grant N00014-03-1-0017 to the University of Pittsburgh and grant N0001404AF00002 to the United States Naval Academy.

References

1. Berry, E. C., & Broadbent, D. E. (1984). On the relationship between task performance and associated verbalizable knowledge. *The Quarterly Journal of Experimental Psychology, 36A*, 209-231.
2. Burton, R. R., & Brown, J. S. (1982). An investigation of computer coaching for informal learning activities. In D. Sleeman & J. S. Brown (Eds.), *Intelligent Tutoring Systems*. New York: Academic Press.
3. Corbett, A. T., & Bhatnagar, A. (1997). Student modeling in the ACT programming tutor: Adjusting a procedural learning model with declarative knowledge, *Proceedings of the Sixth International Conference on User Modeling*.
4. Graesser, A. C., VanLehn, K., Rose, C. P., Jordan, P. W., & Harter, D. (2001). Intelligent tutoring systems with conversational dialogue. *AI Magazine, 22*(4), 39-51.
5. Lesgold, A., Lajoie, S., Bunzo, M., & Eggan, G. (1992). Sherlock: A coached practice environment for an electronics troubleshooting job. In J. H. a. C. Larkin, R.W. (Ed.), *Computer Assisted Instruction and Intelligent Tutoring Systems: Shared Goals and Complementary Approaches* (pp. 201-238). Hillsdale, NJ: Lawrence Erlbaum Associates.
6. Mitrovic, A., & Ohlsson, S. (1999). Evaluation of a constraint-based tutor for a database language. *International Journal of Artificial Intelligence and Education, 10*, 238-256.
7. Reiser, B. J., Kimberg, D. Y., Lovett, M. C., & Ranney, M. (1992). Knowledge representation and explanation in GIL, an intelligent tutor for programming. In J. H. Larkin & R. W. Chabay (Eds.), *Computer Assisted Instruction and Intelligent Tutoring Systems: Shared Goals and Complementary Approaches* (pp. 111-150). Hillsdale, NJ: Lawrence Erlbaum Associates.
8. Scheines, R., & Sieg, W. (1994). Computer environments for proof construction. *Interactive Learning Environments, 4*(2), 159-169.
9. VanLehn, K., & Jones, R. M. (1993). Learning by explaining examples to oneself: A computational model. In S. Chipman & A. Meyrowitz (Eds.), *Cognitive Models of Complex Learning* (pp. 25-82). Boston, MA: Kluwer Academic Publishers.
10. VanLehn, K., Jones, R. M., & Chi, M. T. H. (1992). A model of the self-explanation effect. *The Journal of the Learning Sciences, 2*(1), 1-59.
11. VanLehn, K., Lynch, C., Taylor, L., Weinstein, A., Shelby, R., Schulze, k., Treacy, D., & Wintersgill, M. (2002). Minimally invasive tutoring of complex physics problem solving. In S. A. Cerri & G. Gouarderes & F. Paraguacu (Eds.), *Intelligent Tutoring Systems 1001: Proceedings of the 6th International Conference* (pp. 158-167). Berlin: Springer-Verlag.

Appendix: The Target Variable Strategy

The Target Variable Strategy is has three main phases, each of which consists of several repeated steps. The strategy is:

1 *Translating the problem statement*. For each quantity mentioned in the problem statement, you should:

1.1 define a variable for the quantity; and

1.2 give the variable a value if the problem statement specifies one, or mark the variable as "Sought" if the problem statement asks for its value to be determined. The tutoring system displays a list of variables that indicates which are Sought and which have values.

2 *Applying principles*. As long as there is at least one variable marked Sought in the list of variables, you should:

2.1 choose one of the Sought variables (this is called the "target" variable);

2.2 select a principle application such that when the equation for that principle is written, the equation will contain the target variable;

2.3 define variables for all the undefined quantities in the equation;

2.4 write the equation, replacing its generic variables with variables you have defined

2.5 (optional) rewrite the equation by replacing its variables with algebraic expressions and simplifying

2.6 remove the Sought mark from the target variable; and

2.7 mark the other variables in the equation Sought unless those variables are already known or were marked Sought earlier.

3 *Solving equations*. As long as there are equations that have not yet been solved, you should:

3.1 pick the most recently written equation that has not yet been solved;

3.2 recall the target variable for that equation;

3.3 replace all other variables in the equation by their values; and

3.4 algebraically manipulate the equation into the form V=E where V is the target variable and E is an expression that does not contain the target variable (usually E is just a number).

On simple problems, the Target Variable Strategy may feel like a simple mechanical procedure, but on complex problems, choosing a principle to apply (step 2.2) requires planning ahead. Depending on which principle is selected, the derivation of a solution can be short, long or impossible. Making an appropriate choice requires planning ahead, but that is a skill that can only be mastered by solving a variety of problems. In order to learn more quickly, students should occasionally make inappropriate choices, because this lets them practice detecting when an inappropriate choice has been made, going back to find the unlucky principle selection (use the Backspace key to undo recent entries), and selecting a different principle instead.

Detecting Student Misuse of Intelligent Tutoring Systems

Ryan Shaun Baker, Albert T. Corbett, and Kenneth R. Koedinger

Human-Computer Interaction Institute, Carnegie Mellon University,
5000 Forbes Avenue, Pittsburgh, PA, 15217, USA
{rsbaker, corbett, koedinger}@cmu.edu

Abstract. Recent research has indicated that misuse of intelligent tutoring software is correlated with substantially lower learning. Students who frequently engage in behavior termed "gaming the system" (behavior aimed at obtaining correct answers and advancing within the tutoring curriculum by systematically taking advantage of regularities in the software's feedback and help) learn only 2/3 as much as similar students who do not engage in such behaviors. We present a machine-learned Latent Response Model that can identify if a student is gaming the system in a way that leads to poor learning. We believe this model will be useful both for re-designing tutors to respond appropriately to gaming, and for understanding the phenomenon of gaming better.

1 Introduction

There has been growing interest in the motivation of students using intelligent tutoring systems (ITSs), and in how a student's motivation affects the way he or she interacts with the software. Tutoring systems have become highly effective at assessing what skills a student possesses and tailoring the choice of exercises to a student's skills [6,14], leading to curricula which are impressively effective in real-world classroom settings [7]. However, intelligent tutors are not immune to the motivational problems that plague traditional classrooms. Although it has been observed that students in intelligent tutoring classes are more motivated than students in traditional classes [17], students misuse intelligent tutoring software in a way that suggests less than ideal motivation [1,15]. In one recent study, students who frequently misused tutor software learned only 2/3 as much students who used the tutor properly, controlling for prior knowledge and general academic ability [5]. Hence, intelligent tutors which can respond to differences in student motivation as well as differences in student cognition (as proposed in [9]) may be even more effective than current systems.

Developing intelligent tutors that can adapt appropriately to unmotivated students depends upon the creation of effective tools for assessing a student's motivation. Two different visions of motivation's role in intelligent tutors have resulted in two distinct approaches to assessing motivation. In the first approach, increased student motivation is seen as an end in itself, and the goal is to create more empathetic, enjoyable,

J.C. Lester et al. (Eds.): ITS 2004, LNCS 3220, pp. 531–540, 2004.

and motivating intelligent tutoring systems. In order to do this, it is desirable to have the richest possible picture of a student's current motivational state – for instance, de Vicente and Pain have developed a model that classifies a student's motivational state along 9 axes [8].

An alternate approach focuses on motivation as a factor which affects learning; improving motivation is viewed primarily as a means to improving learning. Investigating motivation in this fashion hinges upon determining which motivation-related behaviors most strongly affect learning, and then understanding and assessing those specific behaviors and motivations. For instance, Mostow and his colleagues have identified that some students take advantage of learner-control features of a reading tutor to spend the majority of their time playing rather than working, or to repeatedly re-read stories they already know by heart [15]. Another motivation-related behavior is "help abuse", where a student quickly and repeatedly asks for help until the tutor gives the student the correct answer, often before the student attempts the problem on his or her own [18]. Aleven and Koedinger have determined that seeking help before attempting a problem on one's own is negatively correlated to learning, and have worked to develop a model of student help-seeking that can be used to give feedback to students on how to use help more effectively [1].

In [5], we presented a study on a category of strategic behavior, termed "gaming the system", which includes some of the motivation-related behaviors discussed above. Gaming the system is behavior aimed at performing well in an educational task by systematically taking advantage of properties and regularities in the system used to complete that task, rather than by thinking about the material. Students in our study engaged in two types of gaming the system: help abuse and systematic trial-and-error. We investigated these phenomena by observing students for two class periods as the students used a tutor lesson on scatterplot generation, using methods adapted from past quantitative observational studies of student off-task behavior in traditional classrooms [cf. 12]. Each student's behavior was observed a number of times during the course of each class period. The students were observed in a specific order determined before the class began in order to prevent bias towards more interesting or dramatic events. In each observation, each student's behavior was coded as being one of the following categories: working in the tutor, talking on-task, talking off-task, silently off-task (for instance, surfing the web), inactive (for instance, asleep), and gaming the system.

We found that a student's frequency of gaming was strongly negatively correlated with learning, but was *not* correlated with the frequency of other off-task behavior; nor was other off-task behavior significantly correlated with learning, suggesting that not all types of low motivation are equivalent in their effects on student learning with ITSs. The evidence from this study was neutral as to whether gaming was harmful in and of itself (by hampering the learning of the specific skills gamed) or whether it was merely symptomatic of non-learning goals [cf. 3].

Understanding why students game the system will be essential to deciding how the system should respond. Ultimately, though, whatever remediation approach is chosen, it is likely to have costs as well as benefits. For instance, preventive approaches, such as changing interface widgets to make them more difficult to game or delaying successive levels of help to prevent rapid-fire usage[1], may reduce gaming, but at the cost of making the tutor more frustrating and less time-efficient for other students. Since many students use help effectively [18] and seldom or never game the system [5], the costs of using such an approach indiscriminately may be higher than the rewards. Whichever approach we take to remediating gaming the system, the success of that approach is likely to depend on accurately and automatically detecting which students are gaming the system and which are not.

In this paper, we report progress towards this goal: we present and discuss a machine-learned Latent Response Model (LRM) [13] that is highly successful at discerning which students frequently game the system in a way that is correlated with low learning. Cross-validation shows that this model should be effective for other students using the same tutor lesson. Additionally, this model corroborates the hypothesis in Baker et al 2004 that students who game the system (especially those who show the poorest learning) are more likely to do so on the most difficult steps.

2 Methods

2.1 Data Sources

In order to develop an algorithm to detect that a student is gaming the system, we combined three sources of data on student performance and behavior in a cognitive tutor lesson teaching about scatterplot generation [4]. All data was drawn from a group of 70 students using that cognitive tutor lesson as part of their normal mathematics curricula.

The first source of data was a log of every action each student performed while using the tutor. Each student performed between 71 and 478 actions within the tutor. For each action, we distilled 24 features from the log files. The features were:

- The tutoring software's assessment of the action – was the action correct, incorrect and indicating a known bug (procedural misconception), incorrect but not indicating a known bug, or a help request[2]? (represented as 3 binary variables)
- The type of interface widget involved in the action – was the student choosing from a pull-down menu, typing in a string, typing in a number, plotting a point, or selecting a checkbox? (represented as 4 binary variables)
- The tutor's assessment, post-action, of the probability that the student knew the skill involved in this action, called "pknow" (derived using the Bayesian knowledge tracing algorithm in [6]).
- Was this the student's first attempt to answer (or get help) on this problem step?
- "Pknow-direct", a feature drawn directly from the tutor log files (the previous two features were distilled from it). If the current action is the student's first at-

[1] A modification currently in place in the commercial version of Cognitive Tutor Algebra.

[2] Due to an error in tutor log collection, we only obtained data about entire help requests, not about the internal steps of a help request.

tempt on this problem step, then pknow-direct is equal to pknow, but if the student has already made an attempt on this problem step, then pknow-direct is -1. Pknow-direct allows a contrast between a student's first attempt on a skill he/she knows very well and a student's later attempts.
- How many seconds the action took (both the actual number of seconds, and the standard deviations from the mean time taken by all students on this problem step across problems.)
- How many seconds were spent in the last 3 actions, or 5 actions. (two variables)
- How many seconds the student spent on each opportunity to practice this skill, averaged across problems.
- The total number of times the student has gotten this specific problem step wrong, across all problems. (includes multiple attempts within one problem)
- The number of times the student asked for help or made errors at this skill, including previous problems.
- How many of the last 5 actions involved this problem step.
- How many times the student asked for help in the last 8 actions.
- How many errors the student made in the last 5 actions.

The second source of data was the set of human-coded observations of student behavior during the lesson. This gave us the approximate proportion of time each student spent gaming the system, $G_0 \ldots G_{69}$.

Since it is not clear that all students game the system for the same reasons or in exactly the same fashion, we used student learning outcomes as a third source of data. We divided students into three sets: a set of 53 students never observed gaming the system, a set of 9 students observed gaming the system who were not obviously hurt by their gaming behavior, having either a high pretest score or a high pretest-posttest gain (this group will be referred to as GAMED-NOT-HURT), and a set of 8 students observed gaming the system who were apparently hurt by gaming, scoring low on the post-test (referred to as GAMED-HURT). It is important to distinguish GAMED-HURT students from GAMED-NOT-HURT students, since these two groups may behave differently (even if an observer sees their actions as similar), and it is more important to target interventions to the GAMED-HURT group than the GAMED-NOT-HURT group. This sort of distinction has been found effective for developing algorithms to differentiate cheating from other categories of behavior [11].

2.2 Data Modeling

Using these three data sources, we trained a density estimator to predict how frequently an arbitrary student gamed the system. The algorithm we chose was forward-selection [16] on a set of Latent Response Models (LRM) [13]. LRMs provide two prominent advantages for modeling our data: First, they offer excellent support for integrating multiple sources of data, including both labeled and unlabeled data. Secondly, an LRM's results can be interpreted much more easily by humans than the results of most neural network, support vector machine, or decision tree algorithms, facilitating thought about design implications.

The set of possible parameters was drawn from linear effects on the 24 features discussed above (parameter*feature), quadratic effects on those 24 features (parameter*feature^2), and 23x24 interaction effects between features (parameter* feature$_A$*feature$_B$). During model selection, the potential parameter was added that most reduced the mean absolute deviation between our model predictions and the original data, using iterative gradient descent to find the best value for each candidate parameter. Forward-selection continued until no parameter could be found which appreciably reduced the mean absolute deviation. The best-fitting model had 4 parameters, and no model considered had more than 6 parameters.

Given a specific model, the algorithm first predicted whether each individual tutor action was an instance of gaming the system or not. Given a set of n parameters across all students and actions, with each parameter α_i associated with feature X_i (or X_i^2, or $X_i Y_i$), a prediction P_m as to whether action m was an instance of gaming the system was computed as $P_m = \alpha_0 X_0 + \alpha_1 X_1 + \alpha_2 X_2 + \ldots + \alpha_n X_n$. Each prediction P_m was then thresholded using a step function, such that if $P_m \leq 0.5$, $P'_m = 0$, otherwise $P'_m = 1$. This gave us a classification P'_m for each action within the tutor. We then determined, for each student, what proportion of that student's actions P'_m were classified as gaming, giving us a set of values $G'_0 \ldots G'_{69}$. By comparing the values $G'_0 \ldots G'_{69}$ to the observed proportions of time each student spent gaming the system, $G_0 \ldots G_{69}$, we computed each candidate model's deviation from the original data. These deviations were used during iterative gradient descent and model selection, in order to find the best model parameters.

Along with finding the best model for the entire data set, we conducted Leave One Out Cross Validation (LOOCV) to get a measure of how effectively the model will generalize to students who were not in the original data set (the issue of how well the model will generalize to different tutor lessons will be discussed in the Future Work section). In doing a LOOCV, we fit to sets of 69 of the 70 students, and then investigated how good the model was at making predictions about the 70th student.

2.3 Classifier

For the purpose of assigning interventions, we developed a classifier to identify which students are gaming and in need of an intervention. We did so by setting a threshold on how often the model perceives a student is gaming. Any student above this threshold is considered to be gaming, and all other students are considered not gaming. Given different possible thresholds, there is a tradeoff between correctly identifying gaming students (hits) and incorrectly identifying non-gaming students as gaming students (false positives), shown in the Receiver Operating Characteristic (ROC) curve in Figure 1. The classifier's ability to distinguish gaming is assessed with an A' value, which gives the probability that if the model is given one gaming student and one non-gaming student, it will accurately identify which is which [10].

3 Results

3.1 Our Classifier's Ability to Detect Gaming Students

In this section, we discuss our classifier's ability to detect which students game. All discussion is with reference to the cross-validated version of our model/classifier, in order to assess how well our approach will generalize to the population in general, rather than to just our sample of 70 students.

Since most potential interventions will have side-effects and costs (in terms of time, if nothing else), it is important both that the classifier is good at correctly identifying the GAMED-HURT students who are gaming and not learning, and that it rarely assigns an intervention to students who do not game.

If we take a model trained to treat both GAMED-HURT and GAMED-NOT-HURT students as gaming, it is significantly better than chance at classifying the GAMED-HURT students as gaming (A' =0.82, $p<0.001$). At the threshold value with the highest ratio between hits and false positives, this classifier correctly identifies 88% of the GAMED-HURT students as gaming, while only classifying 15% of the non-gaming students as gaming. Hence, this model can be reliably used to assign interventions to the GAMED-HURT students. By contrast, the same model is not significantly better than chance at classifying the GAMED-NOT-HURT students as gaming (A' =0.57, p=0.58).

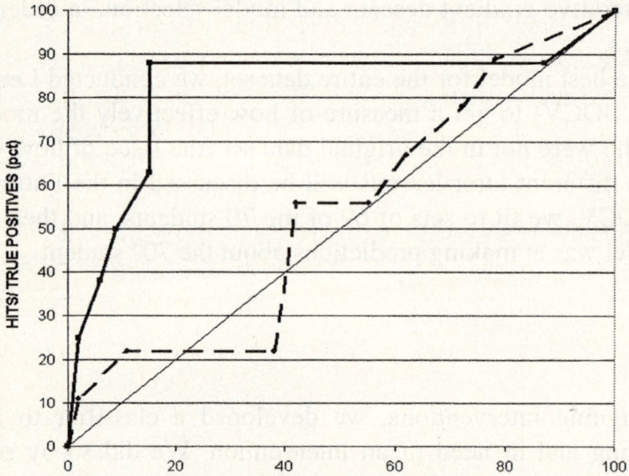

Fig. 1. Empirical ROC Curves showing the trade-off between true positives and false positives, for the cross-validated model trained on both groups of gaming students.

Since it is more important to detect GAMED-HURT students than GAMED-NOT-HURT students, it is conceivable that there may be extra leverage gained from training a model only on GAMED-HURT students. In practice, however, a model trained only on GAMED-HURT students (A' =0.77) does no better at identifying the GAMED-HURT students than the model trained on both groups of students. Thus, in our further research, we will use the model trained on both groups of students to identify GAMED-HURT students.

It is important to note that although gaming is negatively correlated to post-test score, our classifier is not just classifying which students fail to learn. Our model is not better than chance at classifying students with low post-test scores (A' =0.60, p=0.35) or students with low learning (low pre-test *and* low post-test) (A' =0.56, p=0.59). Thus, our model is not simply identifying all gaming students, nor is it identifying all students with low learning – it is identifying the students who game *and* have low learning: the GAMED-HURT students.

3.2 Describing Our Model

At this point, our primary goal for creating a model of student gaming has been achieved – we have developed a model that can accurately identify which students are gaming the system, in order to assign interventions. Our model does so by first predicting whether each of a student's actions is an instance of gaming. Although the data from our original study does not allow us to directly validate that a specific step is an instance of gaming, we can investigate what our model's predictions imply about gaming, and whether those predictions help us understand gaming better.

The model predicts that a specific action is an instance of gaming when the expression shown in Table 1 is greater than 0.5.

Feature F_0,"ERROR-NOW, MANY-ERRORS-EACH-PROBLEM", identifies a student as more likely to be gaming if the student has already made at least one error on this problem step within this problem, and has also made a large number of errors on this problem step in previous problems. It identifies a student as less likely to be gaming if the student has made a lot of errors on this problem step in the past, but now probably understands it (and has not yet gotten the step wrong in this problem).

Table 1. How the model predicts whether a specific action is an instance of gaming

Name	Coefficient	Feature
F_0: "ERROR-NOW, MANY-ERRORS-EACH-PROBLEM"	-0.0375	pknow-direct * number of errors the student has made on this problem step (across all problems)
F_1: "QUICK-ACTIONS-AFTER-ERROR"	+ 0.094	pknow-direct * time taken, in SD above (+) or below (-) the mean time for all students, on this problem step (across all problems)
F_2: "MANY--ERRORS-EACH-PROBLEM-POPUP"	+ 0.231	number wrong on this problem step (across all problems), if the problem step uses a popup menu
F_3: "SLIPS-ARE-NOT-GAMING"	- 0.225	pknow * how many errors the student made on last 5 actions

Feature F_1,"QUICK-ACTIONS-AFTER-ERROR", identifies a student as more likely to be gaming if he or she has already made at least one error on this problem step within this problem, and is now making extremely quick actions. It identifies a student as less likely to be gaming if he or she has made at least one error on this problem step within this problem, but works slowly during subsequent actions, or if a student answers quickly on his or her first opportunity (in a given problem step) to use a well-known skill.

Feature F_2,"MANY-ERRORS-EACH-PROBLEM-POPUP", indicates that making many errors across multiple problems is even more indicative of gaming if the problem-step involves a popup menu. In the tutor studied, popup menus are used for multiple choice questions where the responses are individually lengthy; but this enables a student to attempt each answer in quick succession.

Feature F_3,"SLIPS-ARE-NOT-GAMING", identifies that if a student has a high probability of knowing a skill, the student is less likely to be gaming, even if he or she has made many errors recently. Feature F_3 counteracts the fact that features F_0 and F_1 do not distinguish well-known skills from poorly-known skills, if the student has already made an error on the current problem step within the current problem.

The model discussed above is trained on all students, but is highly similar to the 70 models generated during cross-validation. Features F_0, F_2 and F_3 appear in over 97% of the cross-validated models, and feature F_1 appears in 71% of those models. No other feature was used in over 10% of the cross-validated models.

One surprising aspect of this model is that none of the features involve student use of help. We believe that this is primarily an artifact of the tutor log files we obtained; current research in identifying help abuse relies upon considerable data about the timing of each internal step of a help request (cf. [2]). Despite this limitation, it is interesting that a model can accurately detect gaming without directly detecting help abuse. One possibility is that students who game the system in the ways predicted by our model also game the system in the other fashions observed in our original study.

3.3 Further Investigations with Our Model

One interesting aspect of our model is how it predicts gaming actions are distributed across a student's actions. 49% of our model's 21,520 gaming predictions occurred in clusters where at least 2 of the nearest 4 actions were also instances of gaming. To determine the chance frequency of such clusters, we ran a Monte Carlo simulation where each student's instances of predicted gaming were randomly distributed across that student's 71 to 478 actions. In this simulation, only 5% (SD=1%) of gaming predictions occurred such clusters. Hence, our model predicts that substantially more gaming actions occur in clusters than one could expect from chance.

Our model also suggests that there is at least one substantial difference between when GAMED-HURT and GAMED-NOT-HURT students choose to game – and this difference may explain why the GAMED-HURT students learn less. Compare the model's predicted frequency of gaming on "difficult skills", which the tutor estimated the student had under a 20% chance of knowing (20% was the tutor's estimated probability that a student knew a skill upon starting the lesson), to the frequency of gaming on "easy skills", which the tutor estimated the student had over a 90% chance of knowing. The model predicted that students in the GAMED-HURT group gamed significantly more on difficult skills (12%) than easy skills (2%), $t(7)=2.99$, $p<0.05$ for a two-tailed paired t-test. By comparison, the model predicted that students in the GAMED-NOT-HURT group did not game a significantly different amount of the time on difficult skills (2%) than on easy skills (4%), $t(8)=1.69$, $p=0.13$. This pattern of results suggests that the difference between GAMED-HURT and GAMED-NOT-HURT students may be that GAMED-HURT students chose to game exactly when it will hurt them most.

4 Future Work and Conclusions

At this point, we have a model which is successful at recognizing students who game the system and show poor learning. As it has good results under cross-validation, it is likely that it will generalize well to other students using the same tutor.

We have three goals for our future work. The first goal is to study this phenomena in other middle school mathematics tutors, and to generalize our classifier to those tutors. In order to do so, we will collect observations of gaming in other tutors, and attempt to adapt our current classifier to recognize gaming in those tutors. Comparing our model's predictions about student gaming to the recent predictions about help abuse in [2] is likely to provide additional insight and opportunities. The second goal is to determine more conclusively whether our model is actually able to identify exactly when a student is gaming. Collecting labeled data, where we can link the precise time of each observation to the actions in a log file, will assist us in this goal. The third goal is to use this model to select which students receive interventions to reduce gaming. We have avoided discussing how to remediate gaming in this paper, in part because we have not completed our investigations into *why* students game. Designing appropriate responses to gaming will require understanding why students game.

Our long-term goal is to develop intelligent tutors that can adapt not only to a student's knowledge and cognitive characteristics, but also to a student's behavioral characteristics. By doing so, we may be able to make tutors more effective learning environments for all students.

Acknowledgements. We would like to thank Tom Mitchell, Rachel Roberts, Vincent Aleven, Lisa Anthony, Joseph Beck, Elspeth Golden, Cecily Heiner, Amy Hurst, Brian Junker, Jack Mostow, Ido Roll, Peter Scupelli, and Amy Soller for helpful suggestions and assistance. This work was funded by an NDSEG Fellowship.

References

1. Aleven, V., Koedinger, K.R. Investigations into Help Seeking and Learning with a Cognitive Tutor. In R. Luckin (Ed.), Papers of the AIED-2001 Workshop on Help Provision and Help Seeking in Interactive Learning Environments (2001) 47-58
2. Aleven, V., McLaren, B., Roll, I., Koedinger, K. Toward Tutoring Help Seeking: Applying Cognitive Modeling to Meta-Cognitive Skills. To appear at Intelligent Tutoring Systems Conference (2004)
3. Arbreton, A. Student Goal Orientation and Help-Seeking Strategy Use. In S.A. Karabenick (Ed.), Strategic Help Seeking: Implications For Learning And Teaching. Mahwah, NJ: Lawrence Erlbaum Associates (1998) 95-116
4. Baker, R.S., Corbett, A.T., Koedinger, K.R. Learning to Distinguish Between Representations of Data: a Cognitive Tutor That Uses Contrasting Cases. To appear at International Conference of the Learning Sciences (2004)
5. Baker, R.S., Corbett, A.T., Koedinger, K.R., Wagner, A.Z. Off-Task Behavior in the Cognitive Tutor Classroom: When Students "Game the System". Proceedings of ACM CHI 2004: Computer-Human Interaction (2004) 383-390
6. Corbett, A.T. & Anderson, J.R. Knowledge Tracing: Modeling the Acquisition of Procedural Knowledge. User Modeling and User-Adapted Interaction Vol. 4 (1995) 253-278
7. Corbett, A.T., Koedinger, K.R., & Hadley, W. S. Cognitive Tutors: From the Research Classroom to All Classrooms. In P. Goodman (Ed.), Technology Enhanced Learning: Opportunities For Change. Mahwah, NJ : Lawrence Erlbaum Associates (2001) 235-263
8. de Vicente, A., Pain, H. Informing the Detection of the Students' Motivational State: an Empirical Study. In S. A. Cerri, G. Gouarderes, F. Paraguacu (Eds.), Proceedings of the Sixth International Conference on Intelligent Tutoring Systems (2002) 933-943
9. del Soldato, T., du Boulay, B. Implementation of Motivational Tactics in Tutoring Systems. Journal of Artificial Intelligence in Education Vol. 6(4) (1995) 337-376
10. Donaldson, W. Accuracy of d' and A' as Estimates of Sensitivity. Bulletin of the Psychonomic Society Vol. 31(4) (1993) 271-274.
11. Jacob, B.A., Levitt, S.D. Catching Cheating Teachers: The Results of an Unusual Experiment in Implementing Theory. To appear in Brookings-Wharton Papers on Urban Affairs.
12. Lloyd, J.W., Loper, A.B. Measurement and Evaluation of Task-Related Learning Behavior: Attention to Task and Metacognition. School Psychology Review vol.15(3)(1986) 336-345.
13. Maris, E. Psychometric Latent Response Models. Psychometrika vol.60(4) (1995) 523-547.
14. Martin, J., vanLehn, K. Student Assessment Using Bayesian Nets. *International* Journal of Human-Computer Studies vol. 42 (1995) 575-591
15. Mostow, J., Aist, G., Beck, J., Chalasani, R., Cuneo, A., Jia, P., Kadaru, K. A La Recherche du Temps Perdu, or As Time Goes By: Where Does the Time Go in a Reading Tutor that Listens? Sixth International Conference on Intelligent Tutoring Systems (2002) 320-329
16. Ramsey, F.L., Schafer, D.W. The Statistical Sleuth: A Course in Methods of Data Analysis. Belmont, CA: Duxbury Press (1997) Section 12.3
17. Schofield, J.W. Computers and Classroom Culture. Cambridge, UK: Cambridge University Press (1995)
18. Wood, H., Wood, D. Help Seeking, Learning, and Contingent Tutoring. *Computers and Education* vol.33 (1999) 153-159

Applying Machine Learning Techniques to Rule Generation in Intelligent Tutoring Systems

Matthew P. Jarvis, Goss Nuzzo-Jones, and Neil T. Heffernan

Computer Science Department
Worcester Polytechnic Institute, Worcester, MA, USA
{mjarvis,goss,nth}@wpi.edu

Abstract. The purpose of this research was to apply machine learning techniques to automate rule generation in the construction of Intelligent Tutoring Systems. By using a pair of somewhat intelligent iterative-deepening, depth-first searches, we were able to generate production rules from a set of marked examples and domain background knowledge. Such production rules required independent searches for both the "if" and "then" portion of the rule. This automated rule generation allows generalized rules with a small number of sub-operations to be generated in a reasonable amount of time, and provides non-programmer domain experts with a tool for developing Intelligent Tutoring Systems.

1 Introduction and Background

The purpose of this research was to develop tools that aid in the construction of Intelligent Tutoring Systems (ITS). Specifically, we sought to apply machine learning techniques to automate rule generation in the construction of ITS. These production rules define each problem in an ITS. Previously, authoring these rules was a time-consuming process, involving both domain knowledge of the tutoring subject and extensive programming knowledge. Model Tracing tutors [12] have been shown to be effective, but it has been estimated that it takes between 200 and 1000 hours of time to develop a single hour of content. As Murray, Blessing, & Ainsworth's [3] recent book has reviewed, there is great interest in figuring out how to make useful authoring tools. We believe that if Intelligent Tutoring Systems are going to reach their full potential, we must reduce the time it takes to program these systems. Ideally, we want to allow teachers to use a programming by demonstration system so that no traditional programming is required. This is a difficult problem. Stephen Blessing's Demonstr8 system [3]had a similar goal of inducing production rules. While Demonstr8 attempted to induce simple production rules from a single example by using the analogy mechanism in ACT-R, our goal was to use multiple examples, rather than just a single example.

We sought to embed our rule authoring system within the Cognitive Tutor Authoring Tools [6] (CTAT, funded by the Office of Naval Research), generating JESS (an expert system language based on CLIPS) rules. Our goal was to automatically generate generalized JESS (Java Expert System Shell) rules for a problem, given background knowledge in the domain, and examples of the steps needed to complete the procedure. This example-based learning is a type of Programming by Demonstration

J.C. Lester et al. (Eds.): ITS 2004, LNCS 3220, pp. 541–553, 2004.

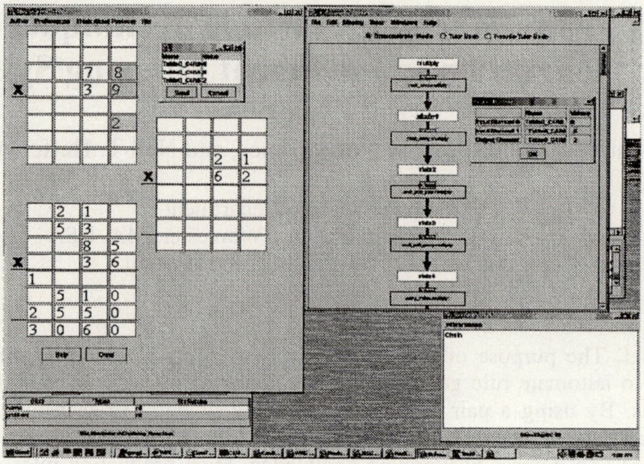

Fig. 1. Example Markup and Behavior Recorder

[5] [8]. Through this automated method, domain experts would be able to create ITS without programming knowledge. When compared to tutor development at present, this could provide an enormous benefit, as writing the rules for a single problem can take a prohibitive amount of time.

The CTAT provide an extensive framework for developing intelligent tutors. The tools provide an intelligent GUI builder, a Behavior Recorder for recording solution paths, and a system for production rule programming. The process starts with a developer designing an interface in which a subject matter expert can demonstrate how to solve the problem. CTAT comes with a set of recordable and scriptable widgets (buttons, menus, text-input fields, as well as some more complicated widgets such as tables) (shown in Figure 1) as we will see momentarily. The GUI shown in Figure 1 shows three multiplication problems on one GUI, which we do just to show that this system can generalize across problems; we would not plan to show students three different multiplication problems at the same time.

Creating the interface shown in Figure 1 involved dragging and dropping three tables into a panel, setting the size for the tables, adding the help and "done" buttons, and adding the purely decorative elements such as the "X" and the bold lines under the fourth and seventh rows. Once the interface is built, the developer runs it, sets the initial state by typing in the initial numbers, and clicks "create start state". While in "demonstrate mode", the developer demonstrates possibly multiple sets of correct actions needed to solve the problems. The Behavior Recorder records each action with an arc in the behavior recorder window. Each white box indicates a state of the interface. The developer can click on a state to put the interface into that state. After demonstrating correct actions, the developer demonstrates common errors, and can write "bug" messages to be displayed to the student, should they take that step. The developer can also add a hint message to each arc, which, should the student click on the hint button, the hint sequence would be presented to the student, one by one, until the student solved the problem. A hint sequence will be shown later in Figure 4. At this point, the developer takes the three problems into the field for students to use. The purpose of this is to ensure that the design seems reasonable. His software will work only for these three problems and has no ability to generalize to another multiplication problem. Once the developer wants to make this system work for any multiplication problem instead of just the three he has demonstrated, he will need to write a set of production rules that are able to complete the task. At this point, programming by demonstration starts to come into play. Since the developer already wanted to demonstrate several steps, the machine learning system can use those demonstrations as positive examples (for correct student actions) or negative examples (for expected student errors) to try to induce a general rule.

In general, the developer will want to induce a set of rules, as there will be different rules representing different conceptual steps. Figure 2 shows how the developer could break down a multiplication problem into a set of nine rules. he developer must then mark which actions correspond to which rules. This process should be relatively easy for a teacher. The second key way we make the task feasible is by having the developer tell us a set of inputs for each rule instance. Figure 1 shows the developer click in the interface to indicate to the system that the greyed cells containing the 8 and 9 are inputs to the rule (that the developer named "mult_mod") that should be able to generate the 2 in the A position (as shown in Figure 2). The right hand side of Figure 2 shows the six examples of the "mult_mod" rule with the two inputs being listed first and the output listed last. These six examples correspond to the six locations in Figure 1 where an "A" is in one of the tables.

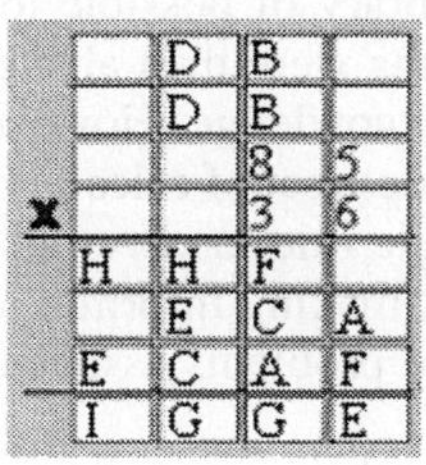

Rule Label	Rule Action
A	Multiply, Mod 10
B	Multiply, Div 10
C	Multiply, Add Carry, Mod 10
D	Multiply, Add Carry, Div 10
E	Copy Value
F	Mark Zero
G	Add, Add Carry, Mod 10
H	Add, Add Carry, Div 10
I	Add

Rule A Examples	
Inputs	Outputs
8, 9	2
8, 3	4
1, 2	2
1, 6	6
5, 6	0
5, 3	5

Fig. 2. Multiplication Rules

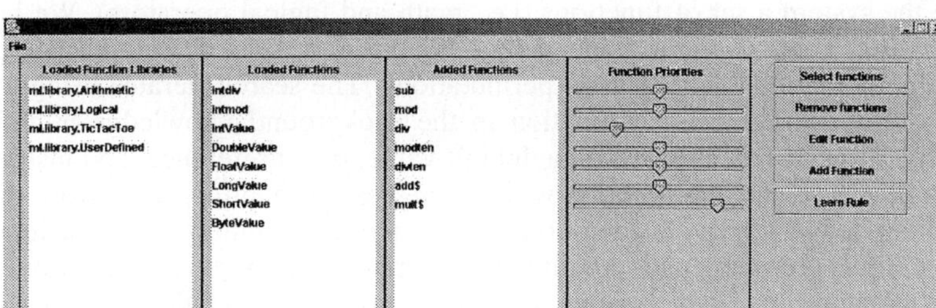

Fig. 3. Function Selection Dialog

These two hints (labeling rules and indicating the location of input values) that the developer provides for us help reduce the complexity of the search enough to make some searches computationally feasible (inside a minute). The inputs serve as "islands" in the search space that will allow us to separate the right hand side and the left hand side searches into two separate steps. Labeling the inputs is something that the CTAT did not provide, but without which we do not think we could have succeed at all.

The tutoring systems capable of being developed by the CTAT are composed of an interface displaying each problem, the rules defining the problem, and the working memory of the tutor. Most every GUI element (text field, button, and even some entities like columns) have a representation in working memory. Basically, everything that is in the interface is known in working memory. The working memory of the tutor stores the state of each problem, as well as intermediate variables and structures associated with any given problem. Working memory elements (JESS facts) are operated upon by the JESS rules defining each problem. Each tutor is likely to have its own unique working memory structure, usually a hierarchy relating to the interface elements. The CTAT provide access and control to the working memory of a tutor during construction, as well as possible intermediate working memory states. This allows a developer to debug possible JESS rules, as well as for the model-tracing algorithm [4] [1] of the Authoring Tools to validate such rules.

2 Right-Hand Side Search Algorithm

We first investigated the field of Inductive Logic Programming (ILP) because of its similar problem setup. ILP algorithms such as FOIL [11], FFOIL [10], and PROGOL [9] were given examples of each problem, and a library of possible logical relations that served as background knowledge. The algorithms were then able to induce rules to cover the given examples using the background knowledge. However, these algorithms all use information gain heuristics, and develop a set of rules to cover all available positive examples. Our problem requires a single rule to cover all the examples, and partial rules are unlikely to cover any examples, making information gain metrics ineffective. ILP also seems to be geared towards the problems associated with learning the left-hand side of the rule.

With the unsuitability of ILP algorithms, we then began to pursue our own rule-generation algorithm. Instead of background knowledge as a set of logical relations, we give the system a set of functions (i.e., math and logical operators). We began by implementing a basic iterative-deepening, depth-first search through all possible function combinations and variable permutations. The search iterates using a declining probability window. Each function in the background knowledge is assigned a probability of occurrence, based on a default value, user preference, and historical usage. The search selects the function with the highest probability value from the background knowledge library. It then constructs a variable binding with the inputs of a given example problem, and possibly the outputs from previous function/variable bindings. The search then repeats until the probability window (depth limit) is reached. Once this occurs, the saved ordering of functions and variable bindings is a rule with a number of sub-operations equal to the number of functions explored. We define the length of the rule as this number of sub-operations. Each sub-operation is a function chosen from the function library (see Figure 3), where individual function probabilities can be initially set (the figure shows that the developer has indicated that he thinks that multiplication is very likely compared to the other functions). The newly generated rule is then tested against the example it was developed from, all other positive examples, and negative examples if available. Should the rule not describe all of the positive examples, or incorrectly predict any negative examples, the last function/variable binding is removed, the probability window is decreased, and the search continues until a function/variable binding permutation meets with success or the search is cancelled.

This search, while basic in design, has proven to be useful. In contrast to the ILP methods described earlier, this search will specifically develop a single rule that covers all examples. It will only consider possible rules and test them against examples once the rule is "complete," or the rule length is the maximum depth of the search. However, as one would expect, the search is computationally prohibitive in all but the simple cases, as run time is exponential in the number of functions as well as the depth of the rule. This combinatorial explosion generally limits the useful depth of our search to about depth five, but for learning ITS rules, this rule length is acceptable since one of the points of intelligent tutoring systems is to create very finely grained rules. The search can usually find simple rules of depth one to three in less than thirty seconds, making it possible that as the developer is demonstrating examples, the system is using background processing time to try to induce the correct rules. Depth four rules can generally be achieved in less than three minutes. Another limitation of the search is that it assumes entirely accurate examples. Any noise in the examples or background knowledge will result in an incorrect rule, but this is acceptable as we can rely on the developer to accurately create examples.

While we have not altered the search in any way so as to affect the asymptotic efficiency, we have made some small improvements that increase the speed of learning the short rules that we desire. The first was to take advantage of the possible commutative properties of some background knowledge functions. We allow each function to be marked as commutative, and if it is, we are able to reduce the variable binding branching factor by ignoring variable ordering in the permutation.

We noted that in ITSs, because of their educational nature, problems tend to increase in complexity inside a curriculum, building upon themselves and other simpler problems. We sought to take advantage of this by creating support for "macro-operators," or composite rules. These composite rules are similar to the macro-operators used to complete sub-goals in Korf's work with state space searches [7]. Once a rule has been learned from the background knowledge functions, the user can choose to add that new rule to the background knowledge. The new rule, or even just pieces of it, can then be used to try to speed up future searches.

3 Left-Hand Side Search Algorithm

The algorithm described above generates what are considered the right-hand side of JESS production rules. JESS is a forward-chaining production system, where rules resemble first-order logical rules (given that there are variables), with a left and right hand side. The left-hand side is a hierarchy of conditionals which must be satisfied for the right-hand side to execute (or "fire" in production system parlance) [4]. As previously mentioned, the tutoring systems being constructed retain a working memory, defining the variables and structures for each problem in the tutor being authored. The left-hand side of a production rule being activated in the tutoring system checks its conditionals against working memory elements. Each conditional in the hierarchy checks against one or more elements of working memory; each element is known as a fact in working memory. Within each conditional is pattern-matching syntax, which defines the generality of the conditional. As we mentioned above, working memory elements, or facts, often have a one-to-one correspondence with elements in the interface. For instance, a text field displayed on the interface will have a corresponding working memory element with its value and properties. More complex interface elements, such as tables, have associated working memory structures, such as columns and rows. A developer may also define abstract working memory structures, relating interface elements to each other in ways not explicitly shown in the interface.

To generate the left-hand side in a similarly automated manner as the right-hand side, we must make create a hierarchy of conditionals that generalizes the given examples, but does not "fire" the right-hand side inappropriately. Only examples listed as positive examples can be used for the left-hand side search, as examples denoted as negative are incorrect in regard to the right-hand side only. For our left-hand side generation, we make the assumption that the facts in working memory are connected somehow, and do not loop. They are connected to form "paths" (as can be seen in the Figure 4) where tables point to lists of columns which in turn point to lists of cells which point to given cell which has a value.

To demonstrate how we automatically generate the left-hand side, we will step through an example JESS rule, given in Figure 4. This "Multiply, Mod 10" rule occurs in the multi-column multiplication problem described below. Left-hand side generation is conducted by first finding all paths searching from the "top" of working memory (the "?factMAIN_problem1" fact in the example) to the "inputs" (that the developer has labeled in the procedure shown in Figure 1) that feed into the right-hand side search (in this case, the cells containing the values being operated on by the right-hand side operators.) This search yields a set of paths from the "top" to the values themselves. In this multiplication example, there is only one such path, but in Experiment #3 we had multiple different paths from the "top" to the examples. Even with the absence of multiple ways to get from "top" to an input, we still had a difficult problem.

Once we combine the individual paths, and there are no loops, the structure can be best represented as a tree rooted at "top" with the inputs and the single output as leaves in the tree. This search can be conducted on a single example of working memory, but will generate rules that have very specific left-hand sides which assume the inputs and output locations will always remain fixed on the interface. This assumption of fixed locations is violated somewhat in this example (the output for A moves and so does the second input location) and massively violated in tic-tac-toe. Given that we want parsimonious rules, we bias ourselves towards short rules but risk learning a rule that is too specific unless we collect multiple examples.

One of these trees would be what would come about if we were only looking at the first instance of rule A, as shown in Figure 2, where you would tend to assume that the two inputs and the output will always be in the same last column as shown graphically in Figure 5.

A different set of paths from top to the inputs occurs in the second instance of rule A that occurs in the 2nd column, 7th row. In this example we see that the first input and second input are not always in the same column, but the 2nd input and the output are in the same column as shown in Figure 5.

One such path is the series of facts given in the example rule, from problem to table, to two possible columns, to three cells within those columns. Since this path branches and contains no loops, it can best be represented as a tree. This search can be conducted on a single example of working memory, but will generate a very specific

```
;; define a rule called mult_mod (see Multi-Column Multiplication problem for details)

(defrule mult_mod
        ;; begin left-hand side ("if")
        (addition (problem ?factMAIN__problem1 ))
        ;; select any table from working memory
        ?factMAIN__problem1 <- (problem
                (interface-elements $? ?factMAIN__tableAny1 $? ))
                ; ;bind an interface element ?factMAIN__tableAny1

                ;; and if that element is a table then...
                ;; [going to first get the top input that is always on the far right]
                ?factMAIN__tableAny1 <- (table
                        (columns ? ? ? ?factMAIN__column4  $? ))
                        ;;then select the 4th  (right most) column from that table
                        ?factMAIN__column4 <- (column
                                (cells ? ? ?factMAIN__cell3  $? ))
                                ;; select the cell in the 3rd row of the fourth column
                                ;;and bind the value in that cell to ?v#0#1, while also ;;checking that its not
                                nil
                                ?factMAIN__cell3 <- (cell
                                        (value ?v#0#1  &  ~nil))
                                        ;bind and check not nil
                                        ;; from that same table, select any column
                ?factMAIN__tableAny1 <- (table
                        (columns $? ?factMAIN__columnAny1 $? ))
                        ;; select any cell from that  column
                        ?factMAIN__columnAny1 <- (column
                                (cells $? ?factMAIN__cellAny1 $? ))

                                ;; select the name of any cell in any column of the
                                ;; selected table. Check to make sure this cell is empty,
                                ;; as it is the output cell
                                ?factMAIN__cellAny1 <- (cell
                                        (name ?sai_name) (value nil))

                        ;; select the 4th cell from that column
                        ?factMAIN__columnAny1 <- (column
                                (cells ? ? ? ?factMAIN__cell4  $? ))

                                ;; select the value of the 4th  cell of the any column of
                                ;; the selected table. This cell is required to be in the
                                ;; same column as the above cell (cell1).  Check to make
                                ;; sure that cell is not empty
                                ?factMAIN__cell4 <- (cell
                                        (value ?v#0#0&~nil))

        ?selection-action-input <- (selection-action-input)
        ;this line indicates it's a correct rather than buggy rule
        ;; end left-hand side
=>
        ;; begin right-hand side ("then")
        ;; Execute right-hand side operations on selected arguments
        (bind ?v#1#0 ((new ml.library.Arithmetic) mult$
                (new java.lang.Integer (integer ?v#0#0))
                (new java.lang.Integer (integer ?v#0#1))))

        (bind ?v#1#1 ((new ml.library.Arithmetic) modten
                (new java.lang.Integer (integer ?v#1#0))))

        ;; output computed value to appropriate cell and update working memory
        (modify ?factMAIN__cellAny1 (value ?v#1#1))
        (modify ?selection-action-input
        ;these lines related to model tracing and are not discussed herein
                (selection ?sai_name)
                (action "UpdateTable")
                (input ?v#1#1)))
```

Fig. 4. An actual JESS rule that we learned. The order of the conditionals on the left hand side has been changed, and indentation added, to make the rule easier to understand

left-hand side. To create a generalized left-hand side, we need to conduct this path search over multiple examples.

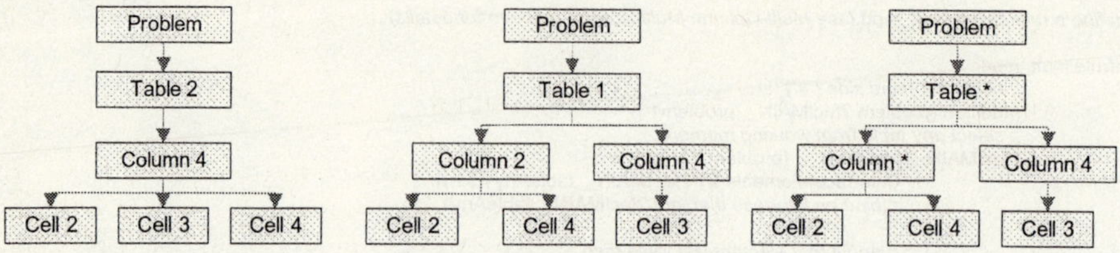

Fig. 5. Left-hand side trees

Despite the obvious differences in the two trees shown above, they represent the left-hand side of the same rule, as the same operations are being performed on the cells once they are reached. Thus, we must create a general rule that applies in both cases. To do this, we merge the above trees to create a more general tree. This merge operation marks where facts are the same in each tree, and uses wildcards (*) to designate where a fact may apply in more than one location. If a fact cannot be merged, the tree will then split. A merged example of the two above trees is show in Figure 5.

In this merged tree (there are many possible trees), the "Table 1" and "Table 2" references have been converted to a wildcard "Table *." This generalizes the tree so that the wildcard reference can apply to any table, not a single definite one. Also the "Column 2" reference in the first tree has been converted to a wildcard. This indicates that that column could be any column, not just "Column 2". This allows this merged tree to generalize the second tree as well, for the wildcard could be "Column 4." This is one possible merged tree resulting from the merge operation, and is likely to be generalized further by additional examples. However, it mirrors the rule given in Figure 4, with the exception that "Cell 2" is a wildcard in the rule.

We can see the wildcards in the rule by examining the pattern matching operators. For instance, we select any table by using:

```
?factMAIN__problem1 <- (problem
        (interface-elements $? ?factMAIN__tableAny1 $? ))
```

The "$?" operators indicate that there may be any number of interface elements before or after the "?factMAIN_tableAny1" that we select. To select a fact in a definite position, we use the "?" operator, as in this example:

```
?factMAIN__tableAny1 <- (table
        (columns ? ? ? ?factMAIN__column4 $? ))
```

This selects the 4th column by indicating that there a three preceding facts (three "?'s") and any number of facts following the 4th ("$?").

We convert the trees generated by our search and merge algorithm to JESS rules by applying these pattern matching operations. The search and merge operations often generate more than one tree, as there can be multiple paths to reach the inputs, and to maintain generality, many different methods of merging the trees are used. This often leads to more than one correct JESS rule being provided.

We have implemented this algorithm and the various enhancements noted in Java within the CTAT. This implementation was used in the trials reported below, but remains a work in progress. Following correct generation of the desired rule, the algorithm outputs a number of JESS production rules. These rules are verified for consistency with the examples immediately after generation, but can be further tested using the model trace algorithm of the authoring tools [4].

4 Methods/Experiments

4.1 Experiment #1: Multi-column Multiplication

The goal of our first experiment was to try to learn all of the rules required for a typical tutoring problem, in this case, Multi-Column Multiplication. In order to extract the information that our system requires, the tutor must demonstrate each action required to solve the problem. This includes labeling each action with a rule name, as well as specifying the inputs that were used to obtain the output for each action. While this can be somewhat time-consuming, it eliminates the need for the developer to create and debug his or her own production rules.

For this experiment, we demonstrated two multiplication problems, and identified nine separate skills, each representing a rule that the system was asked to learn (see Figure 2). After learning these nine rules, the system could automatically complete a multiplication problem. These nine rules are shown in Figure 2.

The right-hand sides of each of these rules were learned using a library of Arithmetic methods, including basic operations such as add, multiply, modulus ten, among others. Only positive examples were used in this experiment, as it is not necessary (merely helpful) to define negative examples for each rule. The left-hand side search was given the same positive examples, as well as the working memory state for each example.

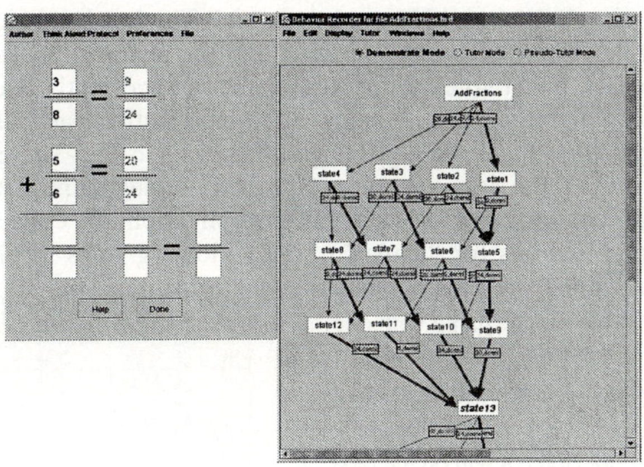

Fig. 6. Fraction Addition Problem

4.2 Experiment #2: Fraction Addition

Our second experiment was to learn the rules for a solving a fraction addition problem. These rules were similar to the multiplication rules in the last experiment, but had a slightly different complexity. In general, the left-hand side of the rules was simpler, as the interface had fewer elements and they were organized in a more definite way. The right-hand-side of the rules were of similar complexity to many of the rules in multiplication.

We demonstrated a single fraction addition problem using the Behavior Recorder and identified the rules shown in Figure 7. The multiple solution paths that are displayed in the Behavior Recorder allow the student to enter the values in any order they wish.

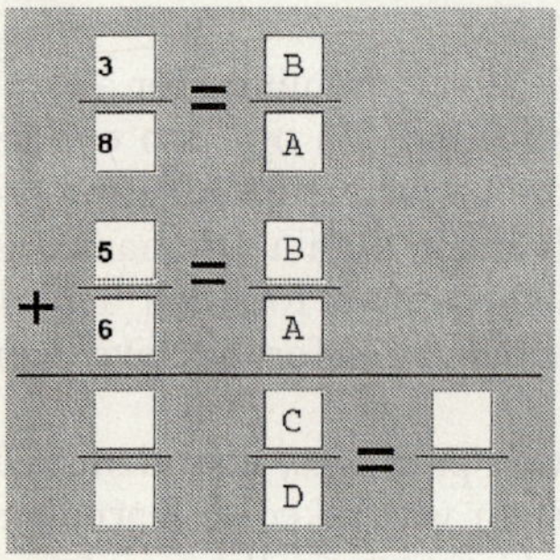

Rule B Examples	
Inputs	**Outputs**
8,6,3	9
6,8,5	20

Rule Label	Rule Action
A	Least Common Multiple
B	Least Common Multiple, Divide, Multiply
C	Add Numerators
D	Copy Value

Fig. 7. Fraction Addition Rules

4.3 Experiment #3: Tic-Tac-Toe

In this experiment, we attempted to learn the rules for playing an optimal game of Tic-Tac-Toe (see Figure 8). The rules for Tic-Tac-Toe differ significantly from the rules of the previous problem. In particular, the right-hand side of the rule is always a single operation, simply a mark "X" or a mark "O." The left-hand side is then essentially the entire rule for any Tic-Tac-Toe rule, and the left-hand sides are more complex than either of the past two experiments. In order to correctly learn these rules, it was necessary to augment working memory with information particular to a Tic-Tac-Toe game. Specifically, there are eight ways to win a Tic-Tac-Toe game: one of the three rows, one of the three columns, or one of the two diagonals. Rather than simply grouping cells into columns as they were for multiplication, the cells are grouped into these winning combinations (or "triples"). The following rules to play Tic-Tac-Toe were learned using nine examples of each:

- Rule #1: Win (win the game with one move)
- Rule #2: Play Center (optimal opening move)
- Rule #3: Fork (force a win on the next move)
- Rule #4: Block (prevent an opponent from winning)

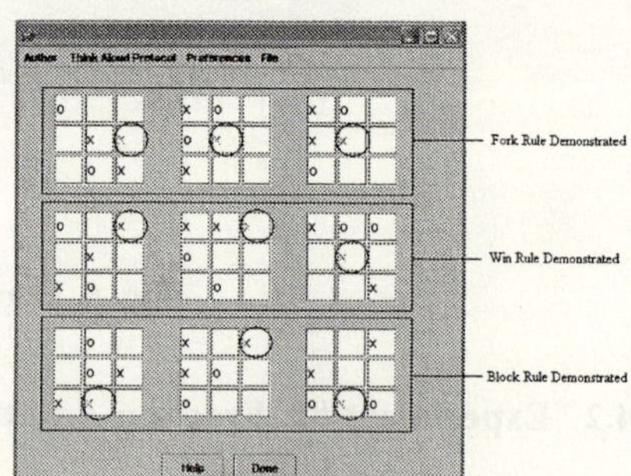

Fig. 8. Tic-Tac-Toe Problem

5 Results

These experiments were performed on a Pentium IV, 1.9 GHz with 256 MB RAM running Windows 2000 and Java Runtime Environment 1.4.2. We report the time it takes to learn each rule, including both the left-hand-side search and the right-hand-side search.

5.1 Experiment #1: Multi-column Multiplication

Rule Label	Rule Learned	Time to Learn (seconds)	Number of Steps
A	Multiply, Mod 10	0.631	2
B	Multiply, Div 10	0.271	2
C	Multiply, Add Carry, Mod 10	20.249	3
D	Multiply, Add Carry, Div 10	18.686	3
E	Copy Value	0.190	1
F	Mark Zero	0.080	1
G	Add, Add Carry, Mod 10	16.354	3
H	Add, Add Carry, Div 10	0.892	3
I	Add	0.160	1
	Total Time:	57.513	

5.2 Experiment #2: Fraction Addition

Rule Label	Rule Learned	Time to Learn (seconds)	Number of Steps
A	LCM	0.391	1
B	LCM, Divide, Multiply	21.461	3
C	Add	2.053	1
D	Copy Value	0.060	1
	Total Time:	**23.965**	

5.3 Experiment #3: Tic-Tac-Toe

Rule Learned	Time to Learn (seconds)	Number of Steps
Win	1.132	1
Play Center	1.081	1
Fork	1.452	1
Block	1.102	1
Total Time:	**4.767**	

6 Discussion

6.1 Experiment #1: Multi-column Multiplication

The results from Experiment #1 show that all of the rules required to build a Multi-Column Multiplication tutor can be learned in a reasonable amount of time. Even some longer rules that require three mathematical operations can be learned quickly using only a few positive examples. The rules learned by our algorithm will correctly fire and model-trace within the CTAT. However, these rules often have over general left-hand sides. For instance, the first rule learned, "Rule A", (also shown in Figure 4), may select arguments from several locations. The variance of these locations within the example set leads the search to generalize the left-hand side to select multiple arguments, some of which may not be used by the rule. During design of the left-hand side search, we intentionally biased the search towards more general rules. Despite these over-generalities, this experiment presents encouraging evidence that our system is able to learn rules that are required to develop a typical tutoring system.

6.2 Experiment #2: Fraction Addition

The rules for the Fraction Addition problem had, in general, less complexity than the Multi-Column Multiplication problem. The right hand sides were essentially much simpler, and the total number of rules employed much lower. The left-hand sides did not suffer from the over-generality experience in Multi-Column Multiplication, as the number of possible arguments to the rules was much fewer. This experiment provides a fair confirmation of the capabilities of both the left and right hand side searches with regard to the Multi-Column Multiplication problem.

6.3 Experiment #3: Tic-Tac-Toe

To learn appropriate rules for Tic-Tac-Toe, we employed abstract working memory structures, relating the interface elements together. Specifically, we created working memory elements relating each "triple" or set of three consecutive cells together. These triples are extremely important when creating a "Win" or "Block" rule. With these additions to working memory, our left-hand side search was able to create acceptably general rules for all four skills listed. However, as in the case of Multi-Column Multiplication, some rules were over-general, specifically the "Fork" rule, with which our search is unable to recognize that the output cell is always the intersection of two triples. This observation leads to the most optimal rule; our search generates working but over-general pattern matching. Nonetheless, this experiment demonstrates an encouraging success in regard to generating complex left-hand sides of JESS rules.

7 Conclusions

Intelligent tutoring systems provide an extremely useful educational tool in many areas. However, due to their complexity, they will be unable to achieve wide usage without a much simpler development process. The CTAT [6] provide a step in the right direction, but to allow most educators to create their own tutoring systems, support for non-programmers is crucial. The rule learning algorithm presented here provides a small advancement toward this goal of allowing people with little or no programming knowledge to create intelligent tutoring systems in a realistic amount of time. While the algorithm presented here has distinct limitations, it provides a significant stepping-stone towards automated rule creation in intelligent tutoring systems.

7.1 Future Work

Given that we are trying to learn rules with a brute force approach, our search is limited to short rules. We have experimented with allowing the developer to control some of the steps in our algorithm while allowing the system to still do some search. The idea is that developers can do some of the hard steps (like the RHS search), while the system can be left to handle some of the details (like the LHS search). In order to use machine learning effectively, we must get the human computer interaction "correct" so that the machine learning system can be easily controlled by developers. We believe that this research is a small step toward accomplishing this larger goal.

Acknowledgements. This research was partially funded by the Office of Naval Research (ONR) and the US Department of Education. The opinions expressed in this paper are solely those of the authors and do not represent the opinions of ONR or the US Dept. of Education.

References

1. Anderson, J. R. and Pellitier, R. (1991) A developmental system for model-tracing tutors. In Lawrence Birnbaum (Eds.) *The International Conference on the Learning Sciences*. Association for the Advancement of Computing in Education. Charlottesville, Virginia (pp. 1-8).
2. Blessing, S.B. (2003) A Programming by Demonstration Authoring Tool for Model-Tracing Tutors. In Murray, T., Blessing, S.B., & Ainsworth, S. (Ed.), Authoring Tools for Advanced Technology Learning Environments: Toward Cost-Effective Adaptive, Interactive and Intelligent Educational Software. (pp. 93-119). Boston, MA: Kluwer Academic Publishers
3. Choksey, S. and Heffernan, N. (2003) An Evaluation of the Run-Time Performance of the Model-Tracing Algorithm of Two Different Production Systems: JESS and TDK. Technical Report WPI-CS-TR-03-31. Worcester, MA: Worcester Polytechnic Institute
4. Cypher, A., and Halbert, D.C. Editors. (1993) Watch what I do : Programming by Demonstration. Cambridge, MA: The MIT Press.
5. Koedinger, K. R., Aleven, V., & Heffernan, N. T. (2003) Toward a rapid development environment for cognitive tutors. 12th Annual Conference on Behavior Representation in Modeling and Simulation. Simulation Interoperability Standards Organization.
6. Korf, R. (1985) Macro-operators: A weak method for learning. Artificial Intelligence, Vol. 26, No. 1.
7. Lieberman, H. Editor. (2001) Your Wish is My Command: Programming by Example. Morgan Kaufmann, San Francisco
8. Muggleton, S. (1995) Inverse Entailment and Progol. New Generation Computing, Special issue on Inductive Logic Programming, 13.
9. Quinlan, J.R. (1996). Learning first-order definitions of functions. Journal of Artificial Intelligence Research. 5. (pp 139-161)
10. Quinlan, J.R., and R.M. Cameron-Jones. (1993) FOIL: A Midterm Report. Sydney: University of Sydney.
11. VanLehn, K., Freedman, R., Jordan, P., Murray, C., Rosé, C. P., Schulze, K., Shelby, R., Treacy, D., Weinstein, A. & Wintersgill, M. (2000). Fading and deepening: The next steps for Andes and other model-tracing tutors. *Intelligent Tutoring Systems: 5th International Conference,* Montreal, Canada. Gauthier, Frasson, VanLehn (eds), Springer (Lecture Notes in Computer Science, Vol. 1839), pp. 474-483.

A Category-Based Self-Improving Planning Module

Roberto Legaspi[1], Raymond Sison[2], and Masayuki Numao[1]

[1] Institute of Scientific and Industrial Research, Osaka University
8-1 Mihogaoka, Ibaraki, Osaka, 567-0047, Japan
{roberto,numao}@ai.sanken.osaka-u.ac.jp
[2] College of Computer Studies, De La Salle University – Manila
2401 Taft Avenue, Malate Manila, 1004, Philippines
sisonr@ccs.dlsu.edu.ph

Abstract. Though various approaches have been used to tackle the task of instructional planning, the compelling need is for ITSs to improve their own plans dynamically. We have developed a Category-based Self-improving Planning Module (CSPM) for a tutor agent that utilizes the knowledge learned from automatically derived student categories to support efficient on-line self-improvement. We have tested and validated the learning capability of CSPM to alter its planning knowledge towards achieving effective plans for various student categories using recorded teaching scenarios.

1 Introduction

Instructional planning is the process of sequencing teaching activities to achieve a pedagogical goal. Its use in tutoring, coaching, cognitive apprenticeship, or Socratic dialogue can provide consistency, coherence, and continuity to the teaching process [20], in addition to achieving selected teaching goals [10].

Though ITSs are generally adaptive, few are capable of self-improvement despite the identification and reiteration of several authors of the need for this capability (e.g., [7, 14, 12, 9, 5, 6]). A self-improving tutor is capable of revising instructional plans and/or learning new ones in response to any perceived inefficiencies in existing plans. O'Shea's quadratic tutor [12], for example, could change instructional plans by backward-reasoning through a set of causal teaching rules, chaining from a desired change in a teaching "variable" (e.g., the time a student needs to learn a skill) to executable actions. However, it does not follow that this and similar tutors (e.g., [9, 5, 6]) can self-improve efficiently.

Machine learning techniques have been successfully applied in computerized tutors in various ways: to infer student models (as reviewed in [16]); to optimize teaching responses to students [3, 11]; and to evaluate a tutor and understand how learning proceeds through simulated students [19, 3]. We innovatively utilize an information-theoretic metric called *cohesion*, and *matching* and *sampling* heuristics to assist a *Q-learning* algorithm in developing and improving plans for different student categories. The result is a learning process that enables the tutor of an ITS to efficiently self-improve on-line with respect to the needs of different categories of learners. We have implemented the learning process in a Category-based Self-improving Planning Module (CSPM) within an ITS tutor agent. As an agent, the tutor becomes capable of learning and performing on its own during on-line time-constrained interactions.

J.C. Lester et al. (Eds.): ITS 2004, LNCS 3220, pp. 554–563, 2004.

In the rest of this paper, we first provide an overview of CSPM and describe the methodology used to test and validate its learning capabilities using real-world data. We then expound the learning approaches of CSPM, and for each approach, we report and discuss selected experimental results that demonstrate its viability. Finally, we give our concluding remarks and future direction.

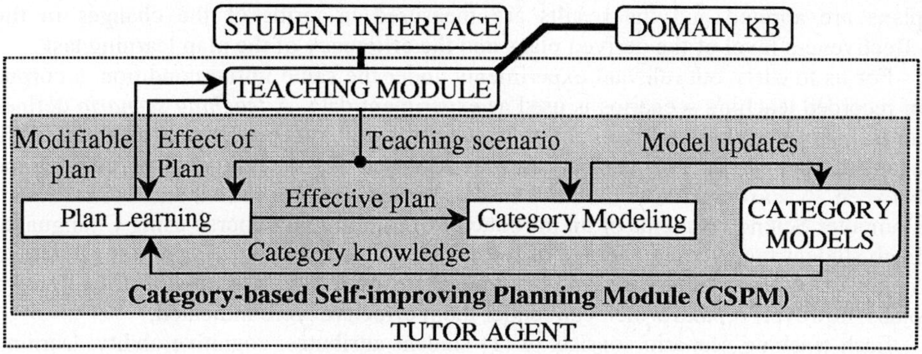

Fig. 1. The functional view of CSPM as well as its external relationships with the other components of the Ist

2 The CSPM's Functional Design

Fig. 1 shows the functional design of CSPM as configured in an ITS.

CSPM reasons using high level of abstraction, i.e., it only decides the sequence of activities to execute based on its category knowledge, and leaves the fine-grained kind of implementation to the Teaching Module (TM). The TM takes each teaching activity and maps it to a procedural knowledge that selects the appropriate domain content and implements the activity. Both procedural and content knowledge are stored in one domain knowledge base.

CSPM automatically learns models of different student categories. A *category model* is an incremental representation of its members' learning characteristics (such as capability, weaknesses, and learning style), current knowledge state, and the plans that are likely to work best for these members. For every student who interacts with the tutor, CSPM either classifies the student to one of the existing category models or to a new model. Depending on his progress, the student may be re-classified.

Utilizing its category knowledge, CSPM derives a modifiable plan. The TM executes this plan and assesses its effectiveness. Based on this assessment, CSPM self-improves accordingly. Eventually, CSPM exploits the plan it deems effective. A plan is effective if at the end of it the set teaching goal is achieved.

3 Experimentation Methodology

By segregating architecturally the components for pedagogic decision making and delivery, we can test the learning capability of CSPM with minimal influence from the other ITS components. This kind of testing follows a layered evaluation framework [8,

4] and opens CSPM to the benefits of an ablative evaluation approach to direct any future efforts to improve it [2].

Experimentation is performed in three stages. An initial set of category models is derived and their usefulness is observed in the first stage. In the second, category knowledge is utilized to construct a map that will serve as source of candidate plans. The third one simulates the development of the same teaching scenario as different plans are applied and the results are measured in terms of the changes in the effectiveness level of the derived plans and the efficiency of the plan learning task.

For us to carry out relevant experiments under the same initial condition, a corpus of recorded teaching scenarios is used as experiment data. A *teaching scenario* defines an instructional plan and the context in which it will succeed. These scenarios were adapted from [13]'s 105 unique cases of recorded verbal protocols of interactions between 26 seasoned tutors (i.e., two instructors and 24 peer tutors) and 120 freshman Computer Science students of an introductory programming course using C language. Each student received an average of three instructional sessions. Each case contained a plan, effective or otherwise, and the context in which it was applied. For ineffective plans, however, repairs which can render them effective were indicated.

Each teaching scenario consists of (1) student attributes: cognitive ability, learning style, knowledge scope, and list of errors committed; (2) session attributes: session goal and topic to be discussed; and (3) the corresponding effective plan. The cognitive abilities of the tutees were measured in terms of their performance in tests and problem-solving exercises conducted in class prior to their initial tutorial session, and their learning styles were determined using an assessment instrument. The *knowledge scope* attribute indicates until where in the course syllabus has the student been taught.

All in all, this method permits us to do away with the expensive process of evaluating CSPM while in deployment with all the other ITS components.

4 Learner Categorization and Instructional Planning

Learners should be categorized along certain attributes only if it makes difference in learning (as exemplified by [1]). We selected pairs of scenarios that differ in only one student attribute, and observed how such difference produced different plans (refer to Table 1 in the next page). With different cognitive ability levels, treatment differed in terms of difficulty level of activity objects (i.e., example, problem exercise, etc.) and pace of delivery. When numeric (N_1) and non-numeric (N_2) data types were introduced, low-level learners were taught gradually using easy to comprehend objects as opposed to simultaneously discussing both topics for the high-level learner using difficult objects. [Note: "Ex" means example] The visual student benefited from the use of illustration while the auditory student learned through more oral explanations when the concept of 2-dimensional arrays (2dA) was introduced. Depending on what errors have been committed before iterative constructs (IC) were reviewed, either differentiation of usage (Plan 1) or of syntax and semantics (Plan 2) of the constructs was carried out. Lastly, plans depended on how much domain content has been taken by the student prior to the tutorial session. When students' knowledge about variables (V) and constants (C) were assessed (discussion about C immediately succeeds that of V in the course syllabus), Plan 1 defined first the syntax of both constructs before familiarization was implemented since no knowledge yet about C has been given, while Plan 2 already included a test since both topics have been covered already.

Table 1. Different plans resulted from differences in student features. Each plan is an ordered list of teaching activities each of the form A (TO, LS, DL [,LE]) where: A–activity name; TO–topic; LS–learning style; DL–object's difficulty level; and LE –pointer to the student's error list

Feature 1 – Instructional Plan 1	Feature 2 – Instructional Plan 2
Low cognitive ability	*High cognitive ability*
presentDefinition(N_1,visual,easy)	giveGeneralSummary(N_1&N_2,visual,difficult)
giveDivergentEx(N_1,visual,easy,(&err))	differentiateConcepts(N_1&N_2,visual,difficult)
presentDefinition(N_2,visual,easy)	giveGeneralEx(N_1&N_2,visual,difficult,(&err))
giveDivergentEx(N_2,visual,easy,(&err))	giveDivergentEx(N_1&N_2,visual,difficult,(&err))
Visual	*Auditory*
defineRules(2dA,visual,easy)	presentIntro(2dA,visual,easy)
showPicture(2dA,visual,easy)	explainRelevance(2dA,visual,easy)
rephraseDefinition(2dA,visual,easy)	presentDefinition(2dA,visual,easy)
givePrototypicEx(2dA,visual,easy,(&err))	reviewPre-Requisite(2dA,visual,easy,(&err))
	givePrototypicEx(2dA,visual,easy, (&err))
Error = Misuse of looping constructs	*Error = Incorrect loop exit implementation*
differentiateConcepts(IC,visual,easy)	defineRules (IC,visual,easy)
giveSimulatedPractice(IC,visual,easy,(&err))	rephraseDefintions(IC,visual,easy)
	giveExercise(IC,visual,easy,(&err))
Knolwedge_scope = variables (V)	*Knolwedge_scope = constants (C)*
defineRules(V&C,visual,easy)	explainContext(V&C,visual,easy)
giveDistributedPractice(V&C,visual,easy,(&err))	giveEnd-pointPre-test(V&C,visual,easy,(&err))
giveExercise(V&C,visual,easy,(&err))	

Fig. 2 shows the category model structure as as a tree of depth four:

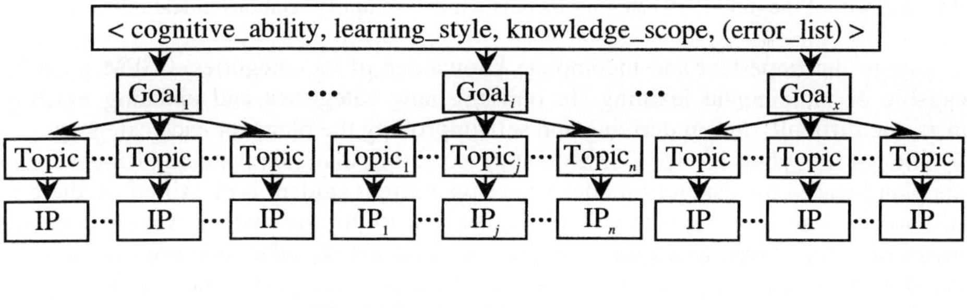

Fig. 2. Category Model Structure

Given this structure, category membership is a conjunction of student attribute values (i.e., common features). A path from the root to one of the leaf nodes specifies the plan that is supposed to work best for the context specified by the path. When categorization was automatically performed on the 105 teaching scenarios, 78 initial category models were formed.

The representation is rather straightforward since we wanted to acquire a comprehensible explanation of the relationship between learner features and instructional plans. This relationship is depicted in Fig. 3. With the low-level learners of A, support comes through easy to grasp examples, exercises, and explanations, and with the tutor providing sufficient guidance through feedback, advice, and motivation. With B's moderate-level learners, the tutor can minimize supervision while increasing the difficulty level of the activity objects. Transition to a new topic (discussion on FOR construct precedes that of the WHILE and DO-WHILE) is characterized by plans that preteach vocabulary, integrate new knowledge, contextualize instruction, and test current knowledge (A1, A2, and A4); while reference to a previous topic may call for summarization and further internalization (B1).

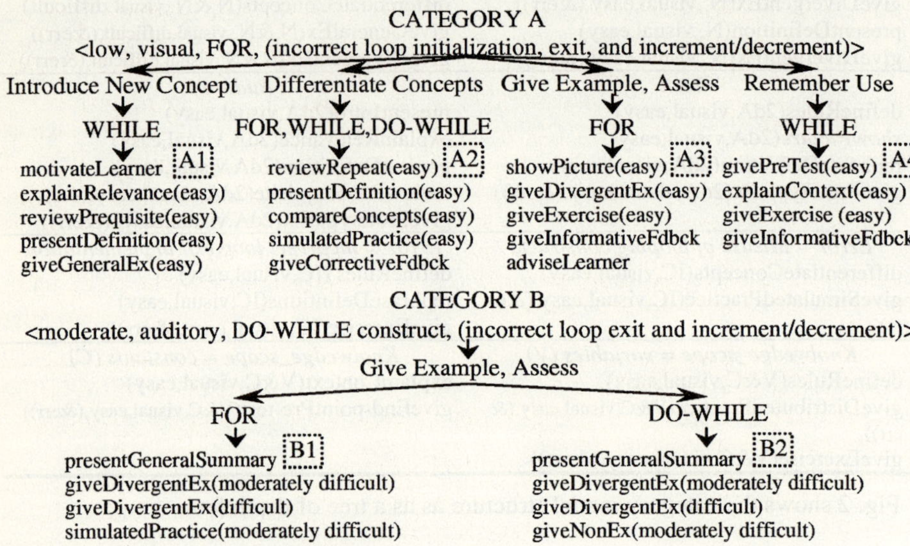

Fig. 3. Two [of the initial] 78 category models which exemplify relations in features and plans

Due to the imperfect and incomplete knowledge of its categories, CSPM must be capable of incremental learning. In building new categories and updating existing ones, the difficulty lies in deriving and self-improving the plans for each category.

Though it is plausible for CSPM to start expecting that the plan being sought for is the plan local to the category model where the current student is classified to, there is still no guarantee that the plan will immediately work for the student. A more accurate behavior is for CSPM to acquire that plan but then slowly adapt and improve it to fit the student. But if the student is classified to a new category, where and how can CSPM derive this plan? CSPM demonstrates these two requisite intelligent behaviors – find an initial plan, and then adapt and improve it – by utilizing unsupervised machine learning techniques and heuristics for learning from experience.

5 Provision for an Initial Modifiable Plan

In the absence of a local plan, it is plausible to find the solution in the *nearest category*, i.e., the category least distant to the new one in terms of learner features. To find this category, CSPM uses an information-theoretic measure called *cohesion* and applies it on the student attribute values. Unlike a Euclidean distance metric that sums the attribute values independently, cohesion is a distance measure in terms of relations between attributes. (For an elaborate analysis and discussion of this metric, we refer the reader to [18]). Briefly, *cohesion* (C_C) is defined as $C_C = W_C/O_C$ where W_C represents the average distance between the members of category C and O_C represents the average distance between C and all other categories. The category that is most cohesive is the one that best maximizes the similarity among its members while concurrently minimizing its similarity with other categories. CSPM pairs the new category to one of the existing categories and treats this pair as one category, say NE. Cohesion score can now be computed for NE and the rest of the existing categories ($C_{NE} = W_{NE}/O_{NE}$). The computation is repeated, pairing each time the new category with another existing one, until the cohesion score has been computed for all possible pairs. The existing category in the pair that yields the highest C_{NE} is the nearest.

Once CSPM learns the nearest category, it immediately seeks the branches whose goal and topic are identical to, or if not, resemble most (i.e., most similar in terms of subgoals that comprise the goal, and in terms of syntax, semantics, and/or purpose that describe the topic's construct), those of the new category. CSPM finally adopts the plan of the selected branch. Fig. 4 illustrates an outcome of this process. The new model in (4a) was derived using a teaching scenario that is not among the initial ones.

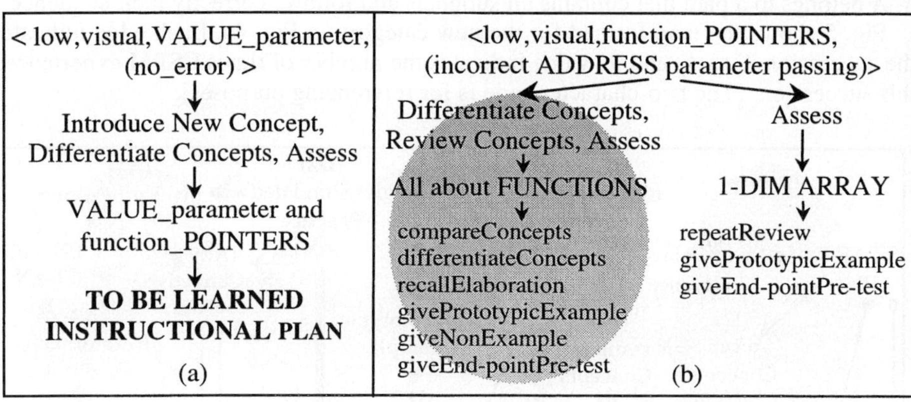

Fig. 4. The figure in (b) describes the *nearest* category model learned by CSPM for the *new* model in (a). CSPM adopts as initial modifiable plan the one in the selected branch or path (as indicated by the shaded portion) of the nearest category

To alter the acquired initial plan – be it from the nearest category or from an already existing one – towards an effective version, CSPM learns a map of alternative plans which it will intelligently explore until it exploits the one it learned as effective.

6 Provision for an Intelligent Exploration

The *map* of alternative plans (or, interchangeably, possible versions of a plan), is a directed graph of related teaching activities that need to be carried out in succession. CSPM initially forms this as a union of effective plans from categories having goals that are similar to, or form the subgoals of, the current session's goal. This is because the way by which activities should be sequenced is explicitly seen in the goal. Naturally, however, not all activities in this initial map will apply to the current student. Thus, CSPM prunes the map by retaining an activity *A* if only if:

1. *A* is in the set of activities $S_{effective} = S_{topic} \cap S_{learner}$. Given that *f(attribute_value)* returns the set of activities that are effective (as gathered from the existing categories) for the given attribute value of the current session, then:
   - S_{topic} = union of all $f(topic_j | j=1..m)$. The *m* topics include the current topic and all other topics that belong to its class (e.g., class of C iterative constructs, which includes FOR, WHILE, and DO-WHILE).
   - $S_{learner}$ = union of all $f(student\_attribute_k | k=1..p)$. Excluding $S_{learner}$ points back to the learner-insensitive classroom instruction that is motivated by achieving the goal for the topic while remaining incognizant of the student's state.
2. *A* follows certain tutorial norms. For example, when the activity "giveEnd-pointPre-Test" results to a failing score, "giveInformativeFeedback" or "give CorrectiveFeedback" should be among the succeeding activities.
3. *A* belongs to a path that contains all subgoals and follows correctly their sequence.

Fig. 5 shows the map formed for the new category in Fig. 4a. Each edge indicates the succession A_i to A_j, and its value indicates the number of times CSPM experienced this succession. [The two-character code is for referencing purposes].

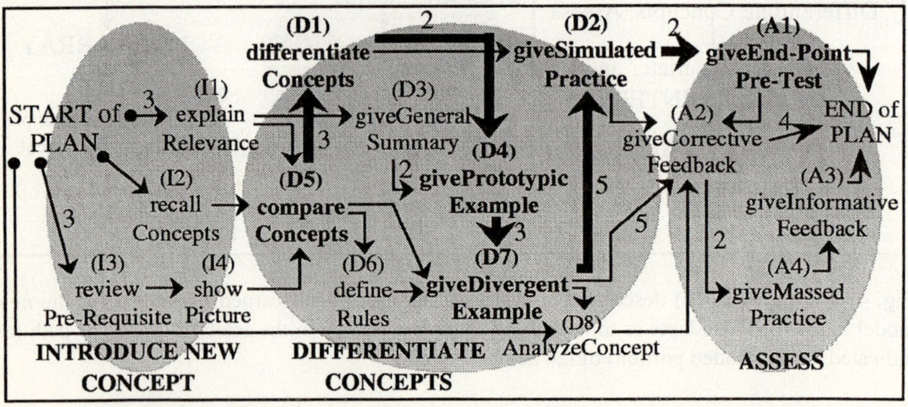

Fig. 5. The map of alternative plans for the new category model in Fig. 4a

Given the map, CSPM must intelligently explore it to mitigate the effect of random selection. Intuitively, the best path is the one that resembles most the initial modifiable plan. Using a *plan-map matching heuristic*, CSPM selects the subpath that preserves most the initial plan's activities and their sequence. With this exploration becomes focused. Afterwards, the selected subpath is augmented with the other necessary activities. CSPM follows the *sampling heuristic* of selecting first the most frequent successions since they worked well in many, if not most, situations. With this, exploration becomes prioritized. The category-effected subpath and the heuristic values provide a guided exploration mechanism based on experience.

We demonstrate this learning task using the initial plan from Fig. 4b and the map in Fig. 5. Executing the plan-map matching heuristic, CSPM selects the subpath D5,D1,D4,D7,D2,A1. Notice that "recallElaboration" in the initial plan is removed automatically, which is valid since reviewing the concepts is no longer among the subgoals, and "giveNonExample" can be replaced with "giveDivergentExample(D7)" since both can be used to discriminate between concepts. To determine which activities are appropriate for the first subgoal, CSPM will heuristically sample the successions. Once sampled, the edge value becomes zero to give way to other successions. Lastly, depending on the student's score after A1 is carried out, CSPM directs the TM to A2 in case the student fails or to end the session if otherwise.

7 Provision for Self-Improvement

To perform various plan modifications and evaluate the effectiveness of each, CSPM utilizes *Q-learning* [21]. As a reinforcement learning [17] method, it is able to process on-line an experience generated from interaction with minimal amount of computation. More importantly, evidences show that Q-learning becomes more efficient when provided with background knowledge [15].

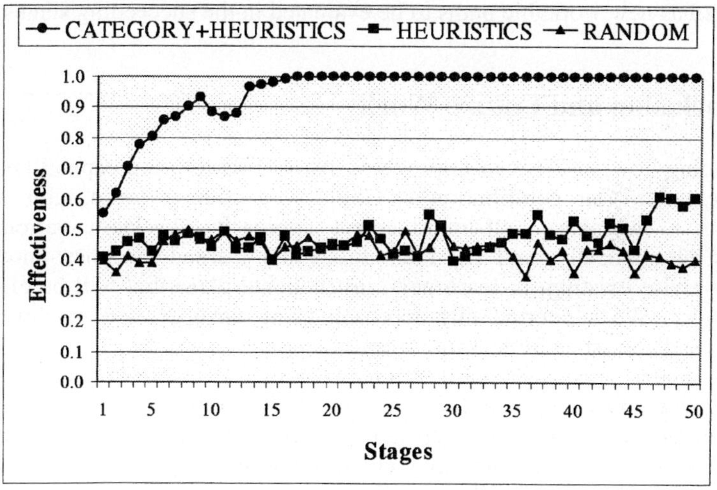

Fig. 6. The CSPM's learning performance

Specifically, CSPM's Q-learning algorithm, or Q-learner, derives a version of the plan by exploring the map and relays this to the TM which in turn executes it. The TM reports the outcome as being effective, neutral (or no effect), or ineffective. With this feedback the Q-learner improves the plan as needed. The Q-learner uses an internal $\in$-greedy policy. This means that a certain percentage of the time, $\in$, it chooses another version of the plan rather than the one it thought was best. This helps prevent the Q-learner from getting stuck to a sub-optimal version. Over time, $\in$ is gradually reduced and the Q-learner begins to exploit the plan it evaluates as optimal.

We run the Q-learner using new teaching scenarios as test cases differing in their level of required learning tasks. We want to know (1) if and when CSPM can learn the effective plans expected for these scenarios, (2) if it can self-improve efficiently, and (3) if category knowledge is at all helpful in deriving the effective plans.

This last experiment has three different set-ups: (1) category knowledge and heuristics are utilized; (2) category knowledge is removed and only heuristic is used; and (3) CSPM randomly selected among possible successions. Each set-up simulates the development of the same scenario for 50 successive stages; each stage is characterized by a version of CSPM's plan. Each version is evaluated vis-à-vis the effective plan in the test scenario. CSPM's learning performance is the mean effectiveness in every stage across all test scenarios.

Analogous to a teacher improving and perfecting his craft, Fig. 6 (next page) shows how CSPM's learning performance becomes effective [asymptotically] over time. It took so much time to learn an effective plan using heuristics alone, worst random selection. When category knowledge is infused, however, CSPM acquired the effective plans at an early stage. It can be expected that as more category background knowledge are constructed prior to system deployment, and/or learned during on-line interactions, a better asymptotic behavior can be achieved. Lastly, CSPM was able to discover new plans, albeit without new A_i to A_j successions since it learned the new plans using existing ones. However, this can be addressed by providing other viable sources of new successions, for example, appropriate learner's feedback which can be incorporated as new workable paths to be evaluated in the succeeding stages.

8 Conclusion and Future Work

Understanding how an ITS can improve on its own its tutoring capabilities is a rich area of research. Our contribution is CSPM – a planner for a tutor agent that implements a two-phase self-improvement approach: (1) learn various student categories automatically, and (2) then utilize the learned category knowledge to efficiently revise existing, or learn new, instructional plans that will be effective for each category. We supported this approach using unsupervised machine learning techniques and heuristics for learning from experience.

Various improvements can augment this work. A very interesting study is to find a relation between polymorphous (i.e., some features are not common) categories and instructional planning. Another, as previously mentioned, is to include in the planning process learner's feedback which may enhance the planning knowledge. Lastly, it is inevitable for CSPM to be tested in actual ITS-student tutorial interactions.

References

1. Arroyo, I., Beck, J., Beal, C., Woolf, B., Schultz, K.: Macroadapting AnimalWatch to gender and cognitive differences with respect to hint interactivity and symbolism. Proceedings of the Fifth International Conference on Intelligent Tutoring Systems (2000) 574-583

2. Beck, J.: Directing Development Effort with Simulated Students, In: Cerri, S.A., Gouardes, G., Paraguacu, F. (eds.). Lecture Notes in Computer Science, 2363 (2002) 851-860
3. Beck, J.E., Woolf, B.P., Beal, C.R.: ADVISOR: A machine learning architecture for intelligent tutor construction. Proceedings of the Seventeenth National Conference on Artificial Intelligence (2000) 552-557
4. Brusilovsky, P., Karagiannidis, C., Sampson, D.: The Benefits of Layered Evaluation of Adaptive Applications and Services. 8th International Conference on User Modelling, Workshop on Empirical Evaluations of Adaptive Systems (2001) 1-8
5. Dillenbourg, P.: The design of a self-improving tutor: PROTO-TEG. Instructional Science, 18(3) (1989) 193-216
6. Gutstein, E.: SIFT: A Self-Improving Fractions Tutor. PhD thesis, Department of Computer Sciences, University of Wisconsin-Madison (1993)
7. Hartley, J.R., Sleeman, D.H.: Towards more intelligent teaching systems. International Journal of Man-machine Studies, 5 (1973) 215-236
8. Karagiannidis, C., Sampson, D.: Layered Evaluation of Adaptive Applications and Services. Proceedings on International Conference on Adaptive Hypermedia and Adaptive Web-Based Systems (2000) 343-346
9. Kimball, R.: A self-improving tutor for symbolic integration. In: Sleeman, D.H., and Brown, J.S. (eds): Intelligent Tutoring Systems, London Academic Press (1982)
10. MacMillan, S.A., Sleeman, D.H.: An Architecture for a Self-improving Instructional Planner for Intelligent Tutoring Systems. Computational Intelligence, 3 (1987) 17-27
11. Mayo, M., Mitrovic, A.: Optimising ITS Behaviour with Bayesian Networks and Decision Theory. International Journal of Artificial Intelligence in Education, 12 (2001) 124-153
12. O'Shea, T.: A self-improving quadratic tutor. International Journal of Man-machine Studies, 11 (1979) 97-124. Reprinted in: Sleeman, D.H., and Brown, J.S. (eds): Intelligent Tutoring Systems, London Academic Press (1982)
13. Reyes, R.: A Case-Based Reasoning Approach in Designing Explicit Representation of Pedagogical Situations in an Intelligent Tutoring System. PhD thesis, College of Computer Studies, De La Salle University, Manila (2002)
14. Self, J.A.: Student models and artificial intelligence. Computers and Education, 3 (1977) 309-312
15. Singer, B., Veloso, M.: Learning state features from policies to bias exploration in reinforcement learning. Proceedings of the Sixteenth National Conference on Artificial Intelligence (1999) 981
16. Sison, R., Shimura, M.: Student modeling and machine learning. International Journal of Artificial Intelligence in Education, 9 (1998) 128-158
17. Sutton, R., Barto, A.: Reinforcement Learning: An Introduction. Cambridge, MA: MIT Press (1998)
18. Talmon, J.L., Fonteijn, H., Braspenning, P.J.: An Analysis of the WITT Algorithm. Machine Learning, 11, (1993) 91-104
19. VanLehn, K., Ohlsson, S., Nason, R.: Applications of simulated students: An exploration. Journal of Artificial Intelligence in Education, 5(2) (1994) 135-175
20. Vassileva, J., Wasson, B.: Instructional Planning Approaches: from Tutoring towards Free Learning. Proceedings of Euro-AIED '96 (1996) 1-8
21. Watkins, C.J.C.H., Dayan, P.: Q-learning. Machine Learning, 8, (1992) 279-292

AgentX: Using Reinforcement Learning to Improve the Effectiveness of Intelligent Tutoring Systems

Kimberly N. Martin and Ivon Arroyo

Department of Computer Science University of Massachusetts 140 Governors Drive Amherst, MA 01003 {kmartin,ivon}@cs.umass.edu

Abstract. Reinforcement Learning (RL) can be used to train an agent to comply with the needs of a student using an intelligent tutoring system. In this paper, we introduce a method of increasing efficiency by way of customization of the hints provided by a tutoring system, by applying techniques from RL to gain knowledge about the usefulness of hints leading to the exclusion or introduction of other helpful hints.

Students are clustered into learning levels and can influence the agents method of selecting actions in each state in their cluster of affect. In addition, students can change learning levels based on their performance within the tutoring system and continue to affect the entire student population. The RL agent, AgentX, then uses the cluster information to create one optimal policy for all students in the cluster and begin to customize the help given to the cluster based on that optimal policy.

1 Introduction

The cost of tracing knowledge when students ask for help is high, as students need to be monitored after each step of the solution. The ITS requires a special interface to have the student interact with the system at each step, or explain to the tutoring system what steps have been done. Such is the case of ANDES [6] or the CMU Algebra tutor [8]. While trying to reduce the cost of Intelligent Tutoring Systems, one possibility is to try to infer students flaws based on the answers they enter or the hints they ask for. However, if students steps in a solution are not traced by asking the student after each step of the solution, and the student asks for help, how do we determine what hints to provide? One possibility is to show hints for the first step, and then for the second step if the student keeps asking for help and so on. However, the assumption cannot be made that the students seeking utility from the ITS are all at the same level when in fact even within a single classroom, students will show a range of strengths and weaknesses. Some students may need help with the first step, others may be fine with a summary of the first step and need help on the second one. Efficiency could be improved by skipping hints that aid on skills that the student already knows. In an ITS that gives hints to a student in order to assist the student in reaching a correct solution, the hints are ordered by the ITS developer and may not reflect the true nature of the help needed by the student. Though feedback may be gathered through formative evaluations after the student has used the system for future enhancements, traditional tutoring systems get no feedback on the usefulness of the hints while the student is using the system.

J.C. Lester et al. (Eds.): ITS 2004, LNCS 3220, pp. 564–572, 2004.

Reinforcement Learning (RL) is a technique for learning actions in stochastic environments. While ITSs are becoming more adaptive, much of the customization is done based on student models that are built based on prior knowledge about what implies mastery. An improvement can be found in imploring RL, as optimal actions can be learned for each student, producing student and pedagogical models that self-modify themselves while learning how to teach. By combining techniques from RL with information from testing loaded a priori, the individual student adaptation is dynamic and the need for a pre-customized system is reduced.

In this paper, we will introduce a method of increasing the efficiency of hint sequencing and student performance by adding a RL agent to an ITS. In the agent, a policy is updated through policy iteration with each problem completed. The reward is calculated at the end of the problem and propagates back to all of the skills used in the problem updating the overall usefulness of hints of this skill type to the student currently using the system. With a state-value being associated with each possible trajectory of hint types, useful sequences begin to emerge and policy iteration produces an updated, more suitable policy.

2 Related Work

There exist intelligent tutoring systems that have implored techniques from Machine Learning (ML) in order to reduce the amount of knowledge engineering done at development [1, 3, 4, 5, 7]. These systems are modified so that the configurability of the system is done on the fly, making the system more adaptive to the student and simplifying the need for rigid constructs at development. ADVISOR [3] is an ML agent developed to simplify the structure of an ITS. ADVISOR parameterizes the teaching goals of the system so that they rely less on expert knowledge a priori and can be adjusted as needed. CLARISSE [1] is an ITS that uses Machine Learning to initialize the student model by way of classifying the student into learning groups. ANDES [7] is a Newtonian physics tutor that uses a Bayes Nets approach to create a student model to decide what type of help to make available to the student by keeping track of the students progress within a specific physics problem, their overall knowledge of physics and their abstract goals for solving the problem.

Our goal is to combine methods of clustering students and predicting the type and amount of help that is more useful to the student to boost overall efficiency of the ITS.

3 Reinforcement Learning Techniques

Reinforcement Learning [10] is used for learning how to act in a stochastic environment by interaction with the environment. When a student interacts with an ITS, there is no completely accurate method for predicting the students actions (answering) at each time step, so designing an agent that will learn the strengths and weaknesses of the student as they forge through each problem will assist in exposing helpful elements of the system that can then be exploited in order to make the students use of the ITS more productive. A policy, Π, defines the behavior of the agent at a given time and is a mapping from perceived states of the environment to actions to be taken when in those states. The state space is then made up of all possible states that the agent can perceive and the set of actions being all actions available to the agent from a perceived state, thus a reward function maps perceived states of the environment to a single number, a reward, indicating the intrinsic desirability of the state. The value of a state, $V(s)$, is the total amount of reward the agent can expect to accumulate over the future starting from that state. So, a policy is said to be optimal if the value for all states in the state space are optimal and the policy leads an agent from its current state through states that will lead it to the state with the highest expected return, R.

3.1 Calculating State Values

We use the Bellman equation (Equation 1) to assign the expected return from the best action from a state based on the current (optimal) policy to that state. It is written as

$$\sum_{s'} P_{ss'}^{\Pi(s)}[R_{ss'}^{\Pi(s)} + \gamma V(s') \tag{1}$$

where $P_{ss'}^{\Pi(s)}$ is the transition probability, $R_{ss'}^{\Pi(s)}$ is the reward and γ is a discount rate.

3.2 Policy Iteration

Since AgentX interacts with the environment, it sees rewards often making it impractical to compute an optimal policy only once. Instead, we use a policy iteration technique that improves the policy after each time step. Policy iteration is the process combining policy evaluation, updating the value of the policy, and policy improvement, obtaining the best policy available. Policy iteration behaves like an anytime algorithm since it allows us to have some policy for each problem at all times and continues to check for a better policy. Figure 1 shows the policy iteration algorithm.

4 Experimental Design

The experiments and setup referred to in this paper are based on theWayang Outpost [2] web-based intelligent tutoring system. A simplified overview of the architecture of the Wayang system is as follows: A problem is associated with a set of skills related to the problem. A problem has hints (that aid on a skill associated with the problem) for which order is significant. For the purpose of AgentX, the skills have been mapped to distinct letters $A, B, \ldots, P$ and the hints are then $A_1, A_2, \ldots, A_n, B_1, B_2, \ldots, B_n, \ldots, P_1, P_2, \ldots, P_n$ where the order of the hints are preserved by their appearance in any problem (i.e., A_4 can never follow A_6).

4.1 State Space Reduction

Initially, the state space was comprised of every distinct path from the beginning of a problem to the end of the problem for all problems. Where a path is a sequence of hints that are seen and the end of a problem is the point at which a correct solution is provided

1. Initialization
   $V(s) \in R$ and $\Pi(s) \in A(s)$ arbitrarily for all $s \in S$
2. Policy Evaluation
   Repeat
   $\Delta \leftarrow 0$
   For each $s \in S$:
      $v \leftarrow V(s)$
      $V(s) \leftarrow \sum_{s'} P_{ss'}^{\Pi(s)}[R_{ss'}^{\Pi(s)} + \gamma V(s')]$
      $\Delta \leftarrow max(\Delta, |vV(s)|)$
   until $\Delta < \theta$ (a small positive number)
3. Policy Improvement
   policy-stable $\leftarrow$ *true*
   For each $s \in S$:
      $b \leftarrow \Pi(s)$
      $\Pi(s) \leftarrow argmax_a \sum_s P_{ss'}^{\Pi(s)}[R_{ss'}^{\Pi(s)} + \gamma V(s')]$
   If $b \neq \Pi(s)$ then *policy-stable* $\leftarrow$ *false*
   If *policy-stable*, then stop; else go to 2

Where S is the complete state space, s is the current state, $s\prime$ is the next state and $A(s)$ is the set of all actions available from state s.

Fig. 1. Policy Iteration Algorithm.

or all hints for the problem have been shown. In order to reduce the complexity of the state space, we consider a distinct path to be a sequence of skills. This reduction speeds up the learning rate because it reduces the number of distinct states needed to be seen in optimizing the policy since the set of skills is small. If in solving a problem, the student could see hints that aid on the following sequence of skills $A \rightarrow A \rightarrow K \rightarrow D \rightarrow F$ (as arriving at the solution to this problem involves steps that imply the use of these skills), or some subsequence of this sequence, then Figure 2 shows all of the states associated with this problem. Any subsequence of skills can be formed by moving up and to the right (zero or more spaces) in the tree.

4.2 Using Pretest Information

Wayang has the option that students take a computer-based pretest before using the ITS. The pretest uncovers the students strengths and weaknesses as they relate to problems in the system. With the computer-based pretest, information is easily accessible, and we can reduce the state space even further by excluding hints from skills where the student excels. In addition to the exclusion of the would be superfluous hints, we are able to use information about the weaknesses the student exhibits by initializing the value of the states that include skills of weakness with greater expected rewards, making the state more desirable to the agent instead of initializing each state with the same state-value.

An action in this system can be seen as moving from state to state where a state is a specific skill sequence containing skills that are related to the problem. Rewards occur

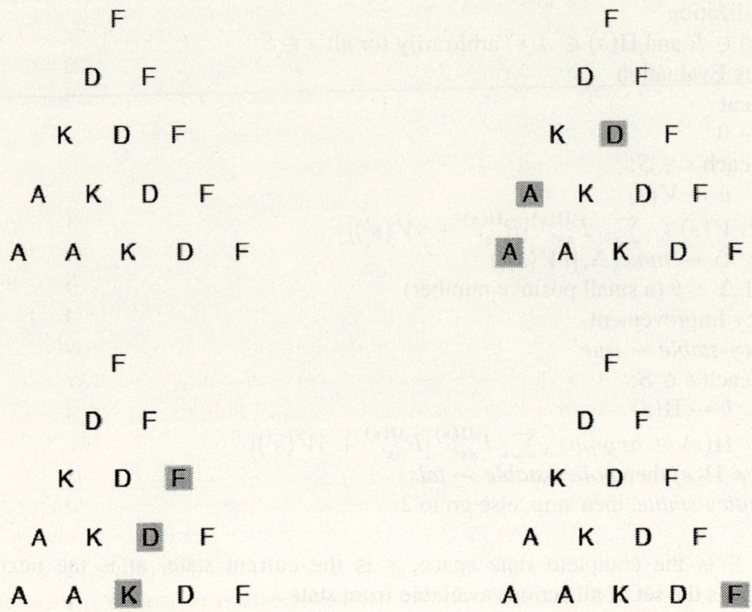

Fig. 2. Possible skill trajectories from the state subspace for problem P.

only at the end of each problem, then propagate back to all states which are sub-states of the skill sequence.

Table 1. AgentX reward structure.

Action	Reward
correct answer	+10 hints seen
incorrect answer	- hints seen
no answer	+(1 / hints seen)

4.3 Rewards

In acting in the system, the agent seeks states that will lead to greater rewards, then updates the value of each state effected by the action at the end of the problem. In order to guide the agent toward more desirable states, developing a reward structure that makes incorrect answers worse as the student receives more hints and correct answers better as students receive less hints allows us to shape the behavior of the action selection process at each state (Table 1). The reward for each problem is then the sum of the rewards given after each hint is seen. By influencing the agents with a reward [9] structure such as this, getting at correct answers sooner seems most desirable and speed up the process of reinforcement learning. The agent updates affected by the problem as it moves through the problem. An example shows that if the agent chooses state $A \rightarrow A \rightarrow K \rightarrow D \rightarrow F$ for the problem because its state value is the largest out of all eligible next states, then after the first hint from skill A is seen, state A is updated with the proper reward, after the second hint from skill A is seen, $A \rightarrow A$ is updated with the proper reward, etc.

4.4 Student Models

By sorting students into learning levels through clustering and re-clustering, student models can be used to speed up the policy iteration process for an individual student. Each problem completed by one student affects a cluster of students, diminishing the need for each problem to be seen by each student in order to judge the usefulness of help of a certain type to that student. Because theWayang system is web-based and students use it all at the same time in classroom mode, a whole cluster of students that have a similar proficiency level or similar characteristics may be updating the shared value of a state. In the case where a student stays within their original cluster, all problems that this student completes will apply to the policy iteration process done on this specific process. In the case where a students learning level changes, they no longer have the ability to affect their former student cluster but are now re-classified into a new cluster, which is now their region of affect. They retrieve the state values and optimal policy of the new cluster and begin to have an effect on that cluster of students, thus making it possible to effect the entire population if they continue to change learning levels. Figure 3 shows the overall architecture of the system.

5 Experimental Setup

In creating the learning agent, we randomly generate student data for a student population of 1000. The random data is in the form of pre-test evaluation scores that allows the student to answer correctly, incorrectly, and not at all with different probabilities based on the data generated from the pre-test evaluation (Equation 2).

$$P(correct) + P(incorrect) + P(no\_answer) = 1 \qquad (2)$$

As the student learns a skill, the probabilities are shifted away from answering incorrectly. Also, as the students actions are recorded the agent, the percentages for giving no answer and incorrect answers are able to effect the probability weightings. The students are first sorted. The randomized pretest produces a numerical score for each of the skills utilized in the entire tutoring system, then we can use the harmonic mean of all scores to sort students into the multiple learning levels. Learning levels are created by the students expected success after having pretest results recorded and measured in percentiles. Table 2 shows the learning levels. Any student with no pretest data available is automatically placed into learning level L4 since it contains the students who perform in the 50th percentile. Once the clusters are formed, after a short period of question answering (after x problems are attempted, where x is a small number such as 3 or 4), the students are able to change clusters based on their success within the tutor. The current success is measured by actions in percentages as seen in Equation 3.

$$currentsuccess = \#correct/(\#total\_hints\_seen \;-\; \#noanswer) \qquad (3)$$

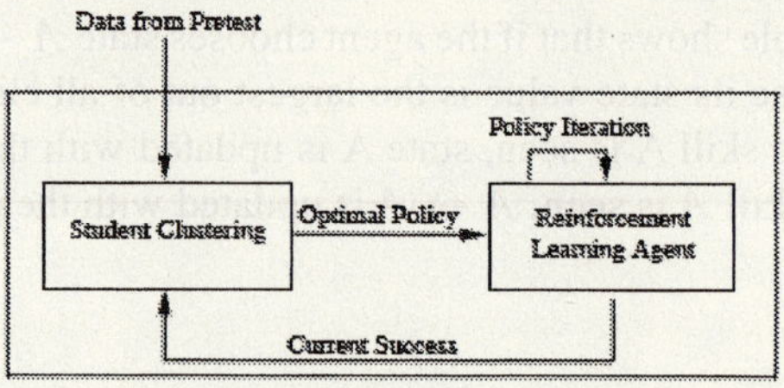

Fig. 3. AgentX architecture.

Table 2. Learning levels for clustering students and their success measures.

Level	Expected	Current	Level	Expected	Current
L_1	90th percentile	90 - 100%	L_4	45th percentile	40 - 59%
L_2	80th percentile	80 - 89%	L_5	25th percentile	20 - 39%
L_3	65th percentile	60 - 79%	L_6	0th percentile	0 - 19%

So, answering correctly after each hint seen is 100% success and answering correctly after two hints are seen is 50% if the student answers incorrectly after the first hint and 100% if the student does not answer after the first hint.

While the learning levels are meant to achieve a certain amount of generalization over students, it is true that students who are in L_1 will perform better over all skills than that of any other grouping of students, which is why it is sufficient to use these learning levels even though the students may have different strengths. By the time students attain L_1, they will be good at most skills and need fewer hints. While students in the middle levels will show distinctive strengths and weaknesses, but at different degrees of success, allowing the learning levels to properly sort them based on success. This clarifies a goal of the system to be able to cluster all students into L_1. Figure 4 shows the initial population of students within learning levels.

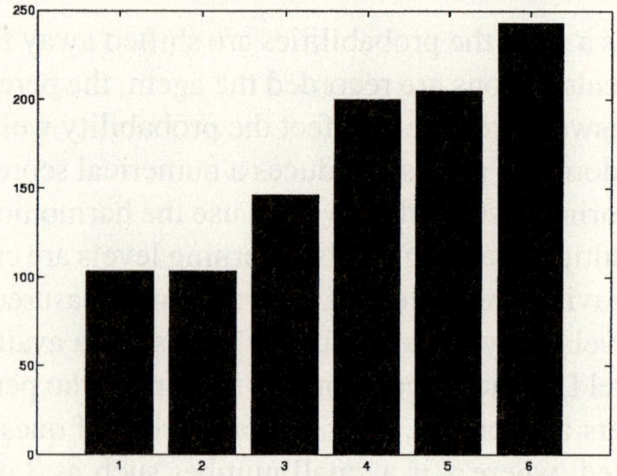

Fig. 4. Student population in learning levels before any problems are attempted.

6 Results

In experimenting with different RL agents, we used an ϵ-greedy agent with different ϵ thresholds and a softmax agent. Figure 5a, 5b, and 5c shows the population of students in each learning level after 15 problems have been attempted by all students where the RL agent is ϵ-greedy with 10% exploration ($\epsilon = 0.1$), softmax, and no RL agent respectively. Using the RL agent shifts the majority of the students towards the learning levels with success greater than 50% while the system without an RL agent maintains a slightly more normal (Gaussian) distribution of students about the learning level that includes 50% success. The average number of hints being shown in L_1 after 15 problems is reduced to 3.6 (three or four hints) as opposed to showing all hints (five).

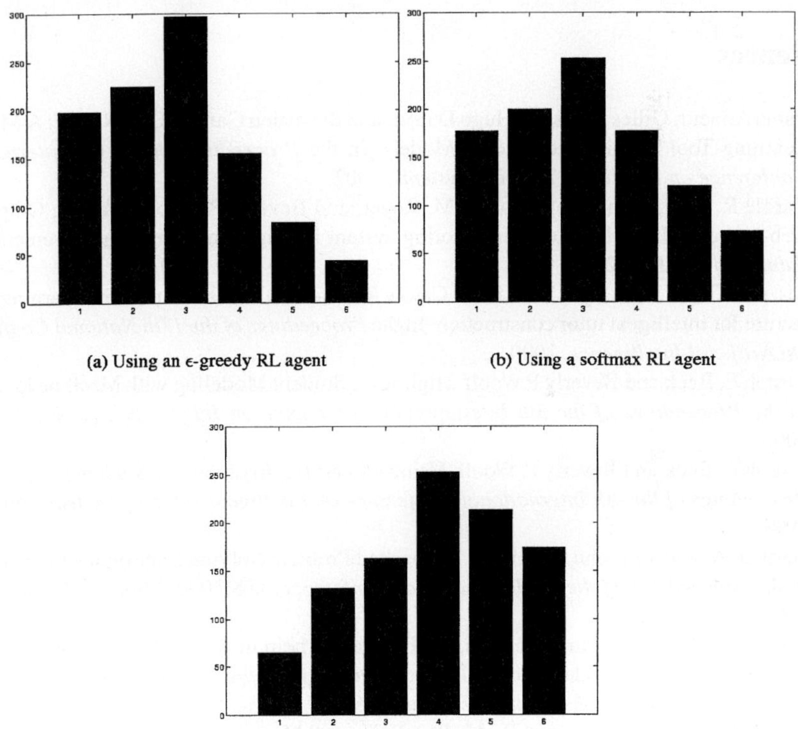

(a) Using an ϵ-greedy RL agent

(b) Using a softmax RL agent

(c) Using no RL agent

Fig. 5. Student population in learning levels after each student has attempted 15 problems.

7 Conclusions

Using Reinforcement Learning agents can help to dynamically customize ITSs. In this paper we have shown that it is possible to boost student performance and a method for increasing the efficiency of an ITS after a small number of problems have been seen by incorporating a student model that allows the system to cluster students into learning levels and by choosing subsequences of all possible hints for a problem instead of simply showing all possible hints available to that problem. Defining a reward structure based on a students progress within a problem and allowing their response to affect a region of other, similar students reduces the need to see more distinct problems in creating a policy for how to act when faced with new skill sets and the need to solicit student feedback after each hint. With the goal to increase membership in learning level L1 (90–100% success), which directly relates to the notion of increasing the efficiency of the system, we have shown that using an RL agent within an ITS can accomplish this.

References

[1] Esma Aimeur, Gilles Brassard, Hugo Dufort, and Sebastien Gambs. CLARISSE: A Machine Learning Tool to Initialize Student Models. In the *Proceedings of the 6th International Conference on Intelligent Tutoring Systems*. 2002.

[2] Carole R. Beal, Ivon Arroyo, James M. Royer, and Beverly P. Woolf. Wayang Outpost: A web-based multimedia intelligent tutoring system for high stakes math achievement tests. *Submitted to AERA* 2003.

[3] Joseph E. Beck, Beverly P. Woolf, and Carole R. Beal. ADVISOR: A machine learning architecture for intelligent tutor construction. In the *Proceedings of the 17th National Conference On Artificial Intelligence.* 2000.

[4] Joseph E. Beck and Beverly P.Woolf. High-level Student Modeling with Machine Learning. In the *Proceedings of the 5th International Conference on Intelligent Tutoring Systems.* 2000.

[5] Joseph E. Beck and Beverly P. Woolf. Using a Learning Agent with a Student Model. In the *Proceedings of the 4th International Conference on Intelligent Tutoring Systems.* pp. 6-15. 1998.

[6] Gertner, A. and VanLehn, K. Andes: A Coached Problem Solving Environment for Physics. In the *Proceedings of the 5th International Conference*, ITS 2000, Montreal Canada, June 2000.

[7] Gertner, A, Conati, C, and VanLehn, K.. Procedural help in Andes: Generating hints using a Bayesian network student model. In the *Proceedings of the 15th National Conference on Artificial Intelligence*. Madison, Wisconsin. 1998.

[8] Koedinger, K. R., Anderson, J.R., Hadley, W.H., and Mark, M . A. Intelligent tutoring goes to school in the big city. *International Journal of Artificial Intelligence in Education*, 8, 30-43. 1997.

[9] Adam Laud and Gerald DeJong. The Influence of Reward on the Speed of Reinforcement Learning. In the *Proceedings of the 20th International Conference on Machine Learning (ICML-2003)*. 2003.

[10] R.S. Sutton and A.G. Barto. Reinforcement Learning: An Introduction. MIT Press, Cambridge, MA. 1998.

An Intelligent Tutoring System Based on Self-Organizing Maps – Design, Implementation and Evaluation

Weber Martins[1] and Sirlon Diniz de Carvalho[2]

[1] Federal Univ of Goias, Electrical and Computer Engineering,
Praça Universitária s/n
Catholic University of Goias, Department of Psychology,
Av. Universitária 1.440
Goiânia, Goiás, Brazil
{weber@eee.ufg.br)

[2] Faculdades Alves Faria, Department of Information System
Av. Perimetral Norte, 4129 - Vila João Vaz - 74445-190
Goiânia, Goiás, Brazil
{sirlon@pireneus.eee.ufg.br}

Abstract. This work presents the design, implementation and evaluation of an Intelligent Tutorial System based on Self-Organizing Maps (neural networks), which is able to adapt, react, and offer customized and dynamic tuition. The implementation was realized in web environment (and technology). On the instructional design, the content, source of knowledge to be learned, has been modeled in an original way and is adequate to neural control. At the evaluation, two user groups have been compared. The first one (the control group) moves freely in the content, while the other group (the experimental group) is guided by the decision of neural networks previously trained from the most successful free interactions. Therefore, the control group serves not only as reference but also as source of good examples. Statistical techniques were employed to analyze the significance of sample differences between the two groups. Results from the interaction time have shown significant differences in favor of the guided tutor. All users guided by the intelligent control have performed as well as the best ones which had freedom to navigate through the content.

1 Introduction

Since 1950, the computer has been employed in Education as an auxiliary tool towards successful learning [1] with Computer-Assisted Instruction (CAI). The inclusion of (symbolic) intelligent techniques has introduced the Intelligent Computer-Assisted Instruction (ICAI) or Intelligent Tutoring Systems (ITS). The adaptation to the personal user features is one of the main characteristics of this new paradigm [2].

Despite the evolution of ICAI systems, the tutoring methods are basically defined by the expert conceptual knowledge and by the user learning behavior during the

J.C. Lester et al. (Eds.): ITS 2004, LNCS 3220, pp. 573–579, 2004.

tutoring process. Besides, the development of such systems is limited to the field of symbolic Artificial Intelligence (AI).

In this article, the use of the widest spread subsymbolic model, artificial neural networks, is proposed with an original methodology of content engineering (instructional design). Additionally, some experiments are reported in order to compare the proposed system with another system where content navigation is decided by the user free-will. These navigations are evaluated and the best ones are extracted to build the neural training set. Alencar [3] has introduced this idea with no empirical evidence. He has shown that multilayer perceptrons (MLP) networks [6] could find important patterns for the development of dynamic lesson generation (automatic guided content navigations). Our work employs a different neural model, self organizing maps (SOM), which adaptively builds topological ordered maps with reduction of dimensionality.

The main difference between this proposal and traditional ICAI systems is related to the need of expert knowledge. No expert knowledge is required in our work.

1.1 Self-Organizing Maps

Self-organizing maps were introduced by Teuvo Kohonen [4]. They have biological plausibility since similar maps have been found in the brain. After the training has taken place, neurons with similar functions are situated at the same region. The distance between neurons shows the difference of their responses. Similar stimuli are recognized (lead to highest responses) by the same set of neurons which are at the same region of the topological ordered map.

Self-organizing maps are composed basically by one layer (if it is not considered the input layer, where each input is perceived by one neuron), see Fig. 1. Training implements competitive learning: neurons compete to respond to specific input patterns, the ones that are more similar with their own prototypes (which are realized by the synaptic weights). Neurons are locally connected by a soft scheme. Not only is the most excited neuron involved at the adaptation process but also the ones in his neighborhood. Therefore, not just one neuron learns to respond more specifically but the entire region nearby.

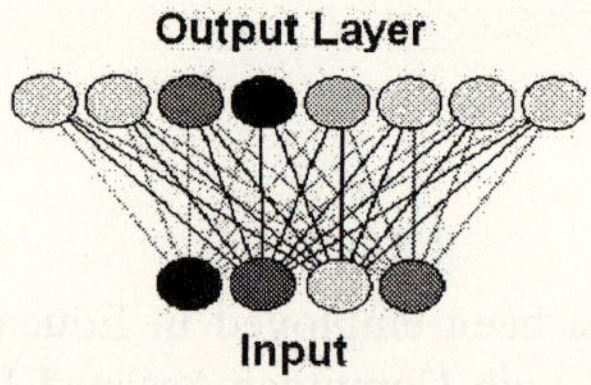

Fig. 1. Example of a self-organizing map

The specification of the winner neuron is performed typically by using the Euclidian distance between the neuron prototype and the current input pattern [5]. Fig. 2 shows and example of topological map built to order a set of colors (represented by red, green and blue components). At the end of the training, neurons at the same region are focused at similar colors. Two distant neurons respond better to very different colors.

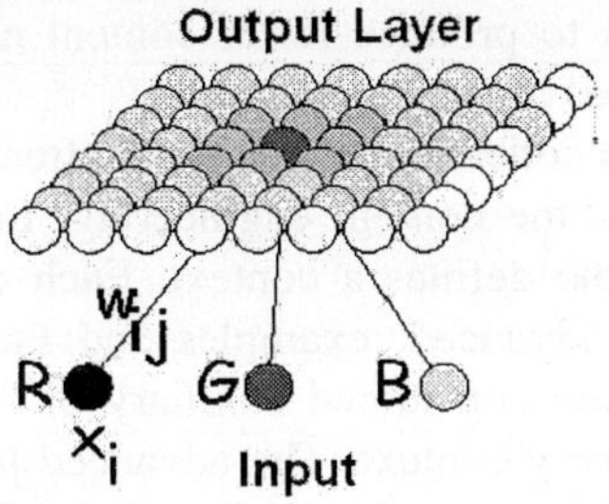

Fig. 2. Weights associated to each input

The initialization of neurons prototypes are done at random. Sometimes, this tactic is abandoned if the examples are not very spread in the input space (for instance, the colors are all redish). An alternative is the use of randomly chosen samples from the training set. SOM training is conducted in two phases. The first one is characterized by global ordering and fast decreasing of neighborhood while the second one does local and minor adjustments [8].

The definition of the winner neuron in Self-Organizing Maps could be done by using several metrics. The commonest procedure is the identification of the neuron that has the smallest Euclidian distance in relation to the presented input [4]. This distance can be calculated as shown below.

$$D_{i,j} = \sum_{i=1}^{n} \| x_i - w_{ji} \| \tag{1}$$

where:

$D_{i,j}$ is the distance between the j-th neuron and n-dimensional input pattern

x_i is the i-th dimension of the input pattern

w_{ji} is the conexion weight of the neuron related to the i-th dimension of the input pattern.

2 Proposed System

The idea of creating an intelligent tutoring system, capable of dynamic lesson generation, based on neural networks has been originated from the interest of developing a system able to decide without expert advice. Such constraint is commonly found in the literature [7].

In the proposed system, neural networks are responsible for the decision making. They are trained to imitate the best content navigations that have been encountered when users have been guided by their free-will. Notice that the control group is also the source of knowledge needed to train the neural networks employed in the experimental group. Our target is to produce faster content navigation with performance similar to the best occurrences in free navigation.

The first phase is the data collection originated by free navigation. Fig. 3 shows its dynamics and, in particular, the content engineering. Lessons are organized in sequences of topics. Each topic defines a context. Each context is expressed in five levels: intermediary, easy, advanced, examples and faq (frequent answered questions). The last two levels are considered auxiliary of the others. The intermediary level is the entry point of every context. The advanced level includes extra information in order to keep the interest of advanced students. The easy level, on the other hand, simplifies the intermediary context in an attempt to reach the student comprehension. The example level is intended to students that perceive things by concrete situations. The faq level tries to anticipate questions commonly found in the process of learning that specific content.

After the contact with each level (in all contexts), learners face a multiple-choice exercise. Before the lesson starts, there is a need to introduce aspects of the environment to the learner and to implement an initial evaluation. After the lesson, there is a final test in order to measure the resulting retention of information (that will serve as an estimate of the learning efficiency).

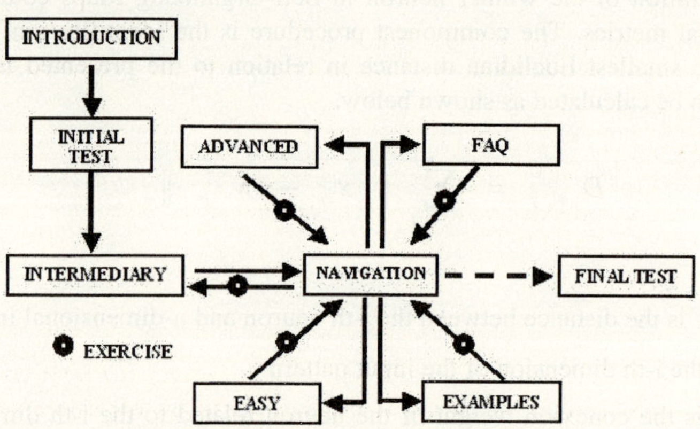

Fig. 3. Structure of navigation

At the second phase, the navigation is guided by neural networks specifically trained to imitate the decisions of the best users at each point. Therefore, there is one distinct SOM for each level of every context. At the end of the interaction with the "theoretical" content and the following exercise, a SOM is fed with the current state in order to decide to where the user should be sent (a different level of the same context or the intermediary level of the next context).

2.1 Implementation

Despite the typical use of two-dimensional SOM, we have opted in favor of uni-dimensional SOM disposed at a ring topology (with 10 neurons each). The training of each SOM was completed after 5,400 cycles. Each SOM was evaluated for global ordering and accuracy. To force SOMs to decide on destinations within the tutor, there is a need to label each neuron. This labeling was carried out by a simple ranking rule where the neuron responds the destiny to which it was more similar (in the sense of average Euclidian distance) at the training set. If a neuron has been more responsive to situations where the next destiny is the next context so this is its label, its decision when it is the most excited neuron of the map (refer to [9] for details).

2.2 Experiments

Students (randomly chosen) from the first year of Computer Engineering and Information Systems from the State University of Goiás were taken to test our hypotheses. Some instruction was given to the students to explain how the system works. Individual sessions were kept below one hour. The experimental design has involved, therefore, two independent samples. Initial and final tests were composed by 11 questions each. The level of correctness and the time latency were recorded throughout the student session.

Twenty two students have been submitted to the free navigation. One of them was discarded because he has shown no improvement (by the comparison of final and initial evaluations).

The subject of the tutor was "First Concepts in Informatics" and was structured in 11 contexts (with 5 levels each). As a consequence, 55 SOM networks were trained. The visits to these contexts and exercises have produced 1,418 records.

2.3 Results

With respect to session duration, a relevant aspect in every learning process (particularly in web training), we have performed the comparison between control and experimental groups by taking out initial and final tests. Fig. 4 shows average session duration at each group. By applying the t-test, we have confirmed the hypothesis of significant less time spent by the experimental group (an approximately 10-minute difference has occurred in average).

The application of the t-test has resulted in an observed t of 2.65. By using level of significance of 5% and degree of freedom (df) of 39, the critical t is 1.68. Therefore, the observed t statistic is within the critical zone and the null hypothesis (that states no significant differences) should be rejected in favor of the experimental hypothesis.

With respect to the improvements shown by means of the initial and final tests, we have compared the control and experimental groups by employing the t-test again. By doing so, we have tried to assess the learning efficiency of both methods.

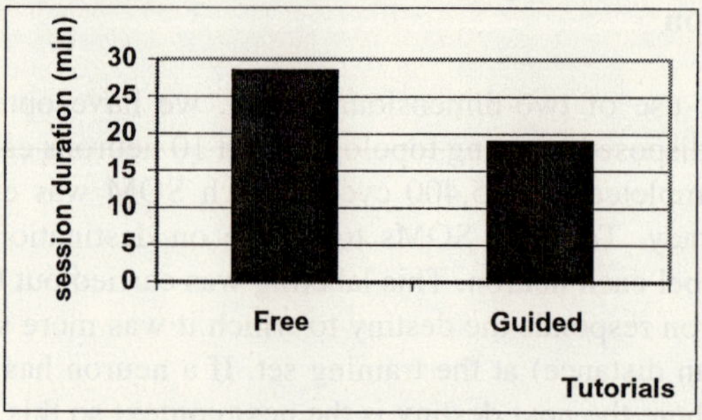

Fig. 4. Average section duration

Fig. 5 shows the average of corrected answers in both tests. One can see that the control group has produced slightly better averages. In fact, these differences are not significant when inferential statistics are employed. The observed value of the t was 1.55. As before, the critical t is 1.68 and there are 39 degrees of freedom when a level of significance of 5% is used. In this situation, the observed value is outside the critical zone and the null hypothesis should not be rejected based on this empirical evidence. Therefore, we should not reject the hypothesis that observed differences have occurred by chance (and/or sample error). Furthermore, one should notice the occurrence of relevant improvement in both groups. In the end, students have more than doubled their corrected answers. We should remind that each test is composed of 11 questions (one question for each one of the contexts).

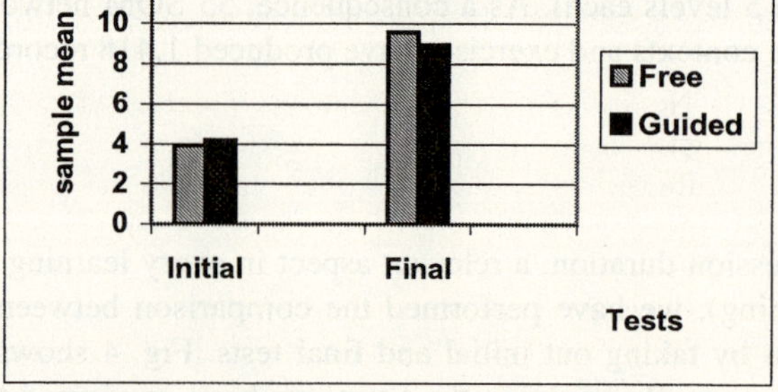

Fig. 5. Average of corrected answers in tests

3 Conclusion

This article has formalized the proposal of an intelligent tutoring system based on self-organizing maps (also known as Kohonen maps) without any use of expert knowledge. Additionally, we have implemented this proposal in web technology and tested it with two groups in order to contrast free and intelligent navigation. The control (free navigation) group is also the source of examples for SOM training.

The content is organized in a sequence of contexts. Each context is expressed in 5 levels: intermediary, easy, advanced, examples and frequent answered questions. The subject of the implemented tutor was "First Concepts in Informatics" and was structured in 11 contexts. This structure is modular and easily applied to other subjects which is an important feature of the proposed system.

Results from experimental work have shown significant differences on session duration with no loss of learning. This work contributes in the sense of presenting a new model for the creation of intelligent tutoring systems. We are not claiming its superiority but its right for consideration in specific situations or in the design of hybrid systems.

References

1 Chaiben, H. Um Ambiente Computacional de Aprendizagem Baseado em Redes Semânticas. Curitiba, 1996. Dissertação (Mestrado em Ciências) - CEFET-PR - Centro Federal de Educação Tecnológica do Paraná, Brazil (in Portuguese)

2 Giraffa, L.M.M & VIccarI, R.M. The Use of Agents Techniques on Intelligent Tutoring Systems. Instituto de Informática-PUC/RS. Porto Alegre, Brazil, 1997.

3 Alencar, W.S. Sistemas Tutores Inteligentes Baseados em Redes Neurais. MSc dissertation, Federal University of Goiás, Brazil, 2000. (in Portuguese)

4 Kohonen T. (1982). Analysis of a Simple Self-Organizing Process. Biological Cybernetics 44:135-140. Springer.

5 Silva, J.C.M. "Ranking" de Dados Multidimensionais Usando Mapas Auto-Organizáveis e Algoritmos Genéticos. MSc dissertation, Federal University of Goiás, Brazil, 2000. (in Portuguese)

6 Haykin, S. S.; Redes Neurais Artificiais - Princípio e Prática. 2ª Edição, Bookman, São Paulo, 2000. (in Portuguese)

7 Viccari, R.M. & Giraffa, L.M.M, Sistemas Tutores Inteligentes: Abordagem Tradicional vrs. Abordagem de Agentes. XII Simpósio Brasileiro de Inteligência Artificial. Curitiba, Brazil, 1996. (in Portuguese)

8 Kohonen, T. Self-Organizing Maps. Berlin: Springer, 2001.

9 Martins, W. & Carvalho, S. D. "Mapas Auto-Organizáveis Aplicados a Sistemas Tutores Inteligentes". Anais do VI Congresso Brasileiro de Redes Neurais, pp. 361-366, São Paulo, Brazil, 2003.(in Portuguese)

Modeling the Development of Problem Solving Skills in Chemistry with a Web-Based Tutor

Ron Stevens[1], Amy Soller[2], Melanie Cooper[3], and Marcia Sprang[4]

[1] IMMEX Project, UCLA, 5601 W. Slauson Ave, #255, Culver City, CA. 90230
immex_ron@hotmail.com
[2] ITC-IRST, Via Sommarive 18, 38050 Povo, Trento, Italy,
soller@itc.it
[3] Department of Chemistry, Clemson University, Clemson, SC. 29634
cmelani@clemson.edu
[4] Placentia-Yorba Linda Unified School District, 1830 N. Kellogg Drive, Anaheim, CA 92807
msprang@pylusd.k12.ca.us

Abstract. This research describes a probabilistic approach for developing predictive models of how students learn problem-solving skills in general qualitative chemistry. The goal is to use these models to apply active, real-time interventions when the learning appears less than optimal. We first use self-organizing artificial neural networks to identify the most common student strategies on the online tasks, and then apply Hidden Markov Modeling to sequences of these strategies to model learning trajectories. We have found that: strategic learning trajectories, which are consistent with theories of competence development, can be modeled with a stochastic state transition paradigm; trajectories differ across gender, collaborative groups and student ability; and, these models can be used to accurately (>80%) predict future performances. While we modeled this approach in chemistry, it is applicable to many science domains where learning in a complex domain can be followed over time.

1 Introduction

Real-time modeling of how students approach and solve scientific problems is important for understanding how competence in scientific reasoning develops, and for using this understanding to improve all students' learning. Student strategies, whether successful or not, are aggregates of multiple cognitive processes [1], [2] including comprehending the material, searching for other relevant information, evaluating the quality of the information, drawing appropriate inferences from the information, and using self-regulation processes to help keep the student on track [3], [4], [5], [6], [7]. While it is unreasonable to expect students to become domain experts, models of domain learning suggest that students should at least be expected to make significant progress marked by changes in knowledge, and strategic processing [8].

Documenting student strategies at various levels of detail can provide evidence of a student's changing understanding of the task, as well as the relative contributions of different cognitive processes to the strategy [9]. Given sufficient detail, such

J.C. Lester et al. (Eds.): ITS 2004, LNCS 3220, pp. 580–591, 2004.

descriptions can provide a framework for providing feedback to the student to improve learning, particularly if the frameworks developed had predictive properties. Our long-term goal has been to develop online problem-solving systems, collectively called IMMEX (Interactive Multi-Media Exercises) to better understand how strategies are developed during scientific problem solving [10], [11]. IMMEX problem solving follows the hypothetical-deductive learning model of scientific inquiry [12], [13] where students need to frame a problem from a descriptive scenario, judge what information is relevant, plan a search strategy, gather information, and eventually reach a decision that demonstrates understanding (http://www.immex.ucla.edu). Over 100 IMMEX problem sets have been created by teams of educators, teachers, and university faculty that reflect disciplinary learning goals, and meet state and national curriculum objectives and learning standards.

In this study, the problem set we used to model strategic development is termed *Hazmat*, and provides evidence of student's ability to conduct qualitative chemical analyses (Figure 1). The problem begins with a multimedia presentation, explaining that an earthquake caused a chemical spill in the stockroom and the student's challenge is to identify the chemical. The problem space contains 22 menu items for accessing a Library of terms, the Stockroom Inventory, or for performing Physical or Chemical Testing. When the student selects a menu item, she is asked to confirm the test requested and is then shown a multimedia presentation of the test results (e.g. a precipitate forms in the liquid or the light bulb switches on suggesting an electrolytic compound). When students feel they have gathered adequate information to identify the unknown they can attempt to solve the problem. The IMMEX database collects timestamps of each student selection.

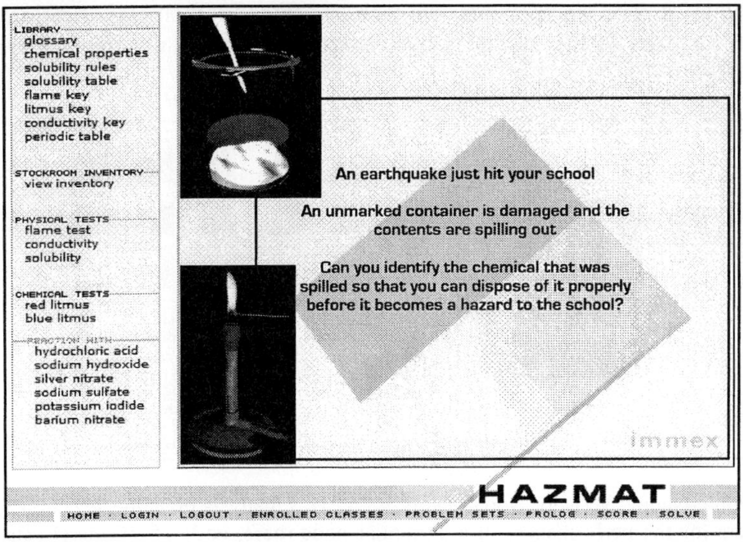

Fig. 1. ***HAZMAT*** This composite screen shot of *Hazmat* illustrates the challenge to the student and shows the menu items on the left side of the screen. Also shown are two of the test items available. The item in the upper left corner shows the result of a precipitation reaction and the frame at the lower left is the result of flame testing the unknown

To ensure that students gain adequate experience, this problem set contains 34 cases that can be performed in class, assigned as homework, or used for testing. These cases are of known difficulty from item response theory analysis (IRT [14]), helping teachers select "hard" or "easy" cases depending on their student's ability [15]. Developing learning trajectories from these sequences of intentional student actions is a two-stage process. First, the strategies used on individual cases of a problem set are identified and classified with artificial neural networks (ANN) [16], [15], [17], [18]. Then, as students solve additional problems, the sequences of strategies are modeled into performance states by Hidden Markov Modeling (HMM) [19].

1.1 Identifying Strategies with Artificial Neural Network Analysis

The most common student approaches (i.e. strategies) to solving *Hazmat* are identified with competitive, self-organizing artificial neural networks (SOM) using the student's selections of menu items as they solve the problem as input vectors [15], [17]. Self-organizing maps learn to recognize groups of similar performances in such a way that neurons near each other in the neuron layer respond to similar input vectors [20]. The result is a topological ordering of the neural network nodes according to the structure of the data where geometric distance becomes a metaphor for strategic similarity. Often we use a 36-node neural network and train with between 2000-5000 performances derived from students with different ability levels (i.e. regular, honors and AP high school and university freshmen) and where each student performed at least 6 problems of the problem set. Selection criteria for the numbers of nodes, the different architectures, neighborhoods, and training parameters have been described previously [17]. The components of each strategy in this classification can be visualized for each of the 36 nodes by histograms showing the frequency of items selected (Figure 2).

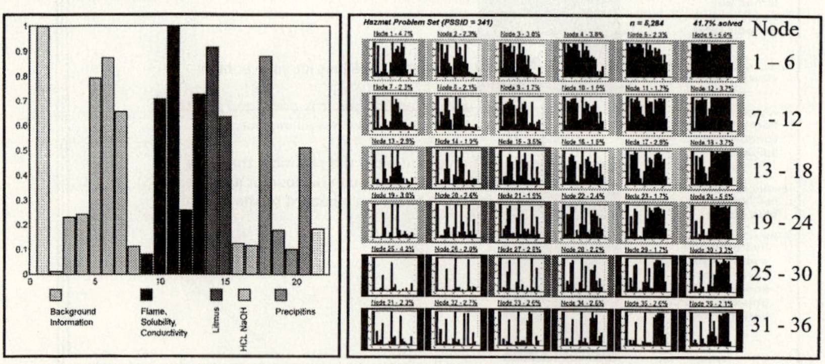

Fig. 2. Sample Neural Network Nodal Analysis. **A.** This analysis plots the selection frequency of each item for the performances at a particular node (here, node 15). General categories of these tests are identified by the associated labels. This representation is useful for determining the characteristics of the performances at a particular node, and the relation of these performances to those of neighboring neurons. **B.** This figure shows the item selection frequencies for all 36 nodes following training with 5284 student performances

Most strategies defined in this way consist of items that are always selected for performances at that node (i.e. those with a frequency of 1) as well as items that are ordered more variably. For instance, all Node 15 performances shown in Figure 2 A contain the items 1 (Prologue) and 11 (Flame Test). Items 5, 6, 10, 13, 14, 15 and 18 have a selection frequency of 60 - 80% and so any individual student performance would contain only some of these items. Finally, there are items with a selection frequency of 10-30%, which we regard more as background noise.

Figure 2 B is a composite ANN nodal map, which illustrates the topology generated during the self-organizing training process. Each of the 36 graphs in the matrix represents one node in the ANN, where each individual node summarizes groups of similar students problem solving performances automatically clustered together by the ANN procedure. As the neural network was trained with vectors representing the items students selected, it is not surprising that a topology developed based on the quantity of items. For instance, the upper right hand of the map (nodes 6, 12) represents strategies where a large number of tests have been ordered, whereas the lower left corner contains strategies where few tests have been ordered.

A more subtle strategic difference is where students select a large number of Reactions and Chemical Tests (items 15-21), but no longer use the Background Information (items 2-9). This strategy is represented in the lower right hand corner of Figure 2 B (nodes 29, 30, 34, 35, 36) and is characterized by extensive selection of items mainly on the right-hand side of each histogram. The lower-left hand corner and the middle of the topology map suggest more selective picking and choosing of a few, relevant items. In these cases, the SOM's show us that the students are able to solve the problem efficiently, because they know and select those items that impact their decision processes the most, and which other items are less significant.

Once ANN's are trained and the strategies represented by each node defined, then new performances can be tested on the trained neural network, and the node (strategy) that best matches the new performance can be identified. Were a student to order many tests while solving a *Hazmat* case, this performance would be classified with the nodes of the upper right hand corner of Figure 2 B, whereas a performance where few tests were ordered would be more to the left side of the ANN map. The strategies defined in this way can be aggregated by class, grade level, school, or gender, and related to other achievement and demographic measures. This classification is an observable variable that can be used for immediate feedback to the student, serve as input to a test-level scoring process, or serve as data for further research.

1.2 Hidden Markov Model Analysis of Student Progress

This section describes how we can use the ANN performance classification procedure described in the previous section to model student learning progress over multiple problem solving cases. Here students perform multiple cases in the 34-case *Hazmat* problem set, and we then classify each performance with the trained ANN (Table 1). Some sequences of performances localize to a limited portion of the ANN topology map like examples 1 or 3, suggesting only small shifts in strategy with each new performance. Other performance sequences, like example 2 show localized activity on the topology activity early in the sequence followed by large topology shifts indicating more extensive strategy shifts. Others illustrate diverse strategy shifts moving over the entire topology map (i.e. examples 4, 5).

Table 1. Student Learning Sequences. The sequence of the ANN node classifications of student performances are traced for 5 students. By mapping these sequences to the performance characteristics at each node of the trained ANN, a description of each student's progress can be generated. By examining the topology of strategy change, trajectories can be classified as *localized* (i.e. confined to a contiguous region of Figure 2 B), *progressive* (i.e. moving across the ANN topology map), or *shifting* (i.e. making larger jumps across the map)

Example	Strategy Sequence	Description	Trajectory
1	32 33 28 33 33	Limited test selections, few background resources	Localized
2	12 18 24 20 1	Many tests becoming fewer with progress.	Progressive
3	5 24 6 18	Many test selections.	Localized
4	4 22 33 33	Resource extensive going to data.	Shifting
5	4 6 14 25 30 19	Shifts between data rich and data lean strategies.	Shifting

While informative, manual inspection and mapping of nodes to strategies is a time-consuming process. One approach for dynamically, and automatically modeling this information would be to probabilistically link the strategic transitions. However, with 1296 possible transitions in a 36-neuron map, full probabilistic models would likely lack predictive power.

By using HMMs we have been able to aggregate the data and model the development and progression of generalized performance characteristics. HMM's are used to model processes that move stochastically through a series of predefined states [19]. These methods had been used successfully in previous research efforts to characterize sequences of collaborative problem solving interaction, leading us to believe that they might show promise for also understanding individual problem solving [21], [22].

In our HMMs for describing student strategy development, we postulate, from a cognitive task analysis, between 3-5 states that students may pass through as competence develops. Then, many exemplars of sequences of strategies (ANN node classifications) are repeatedly presented to the HMM modeling software to model progress. These models are defined by a transition matrix that shows the probability of transiting from one state to another and an emission matrix that relates each state back to the ANN nodes that best represent that state. (Murphy, K. http://www.ai.mit.edu/~murphyk/Software/HMM/hmm.html). Recall from the previous section that each of these nodes characterizes a particular problem solving strategy. The transitions between the 5 states describe the probability of students transitioning between problem solving strategies as they perform a series of IMMEX cases. While the emission matrices associated with each state provides a link between student performances (ANN node classification) and progress (HMM states), the transition matrix (describing the probability of moving from each state in the HMM to each other state) can be used for analyzing / predicting subsequent performances.

Both of these features are shown in Figure 3 with the transitions between the different states in the center, and the ANN nodes representing each state at the periphery. States 1, 4, and 5 appear to be absorbing states as these strategies once used are likely to be used again. In contrast, students adopting State 2 and 3 strategies are less likely to persist with those states but are more likely to transit to another state. When the emission matrix of each state was overlaid on the 6 x 6 neural network grid, each state (Figure 3), represented topology regions of the neural network that were often contiguous (with the exception of State 4).

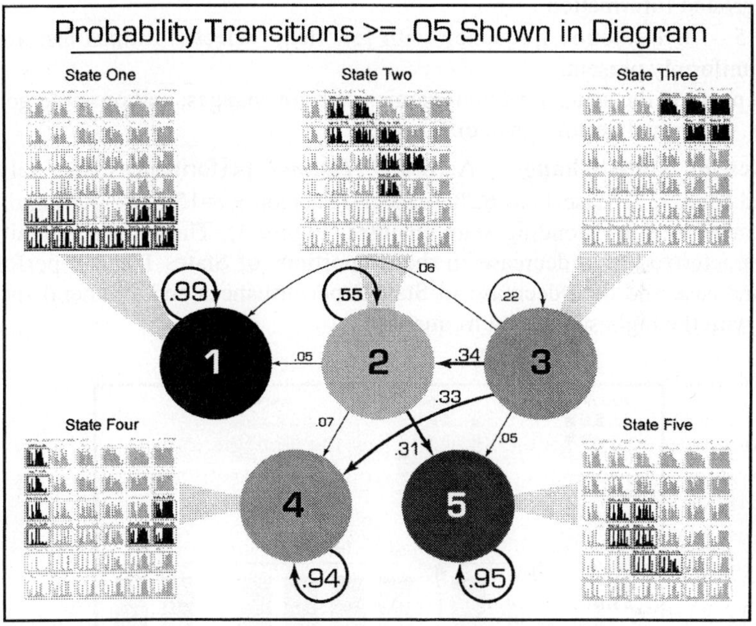

Fig. 3. Mapping the HMM Emission and Transition Matrices to Artificial Neural Network Classifications. The five states comprising the HMM for *Hazmat* are indicated by the central circles with the transitions between the states shown by the arrows. Surrounding the states are the artificial neural network nodes most closely associated with each state

2 Results

As we wish to use the HMM to determine how students strategic reasoning changes with time, we performed initial validation studies to determine 1) how the state distribution changes with the number of cases performed, 2) whether these changes reflect learning progress, and, 3) whether the changes over time 'make sense' from the perspective of novice/expert cognitive differences.

The overall solution frequency for the *Hazmat* dataset (N= 7630 performances) was 56%, but when students' performance was mapped to their strategy usage as mapped by the HMM states these states revealed the following quantitative and qualitative characteristics:

- State 1 – 55% solution frequency showing variable numbers of test items and little use of Background Information;
- State 2 – 60% solution frequency showing equal usage of Background Information as well as action items; little use of precipitation reactions.
- State 3 – 45% solution frequency with nearly all items being selected.
- State 4 – 54% solution frequency with many test items and limited use of Background Information.
- State 5 – 70% solution frequency with few items selected Litmus test and Flame tests uniformly present.

We next profiled the states for the dynamics of state changes, and possible gender and group vs. individual performance differences.

Dynamics of State Changes. Across 7 *Hazmat* performances the solved rate increased from 53% (case 1) to 62% (case 5) (Pearson $\chi^2 = 15.5$, $p=.008$) and this was accompanied by corresponding state changes (Figure 4). These longitudinal changes were characterized by a decrease in the proportions of States 1 and 3 performances and an increase and then decrease in State 2 performances and a general increase in State 5 (with the highest solution frequency).

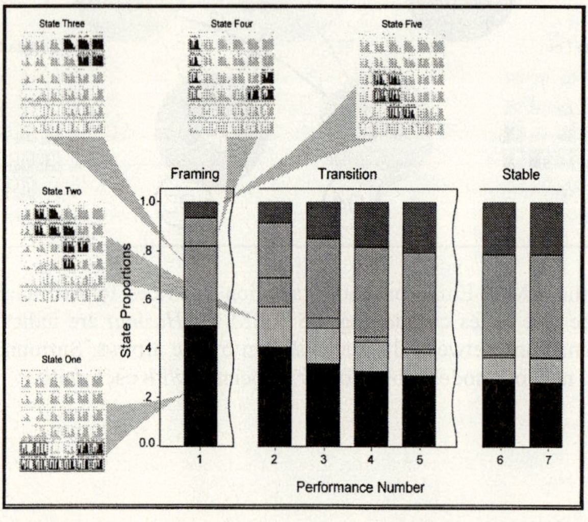

Fig. 4. Dynamics of HMM State Distributions with Experience and Across Classrooms. The bar chart tracks the changes in all student strategy states (n=7196) across seven *Hazmat* performances. Mini-frames of the strategies in each state are shown for reference

Group vs. Individual Performance. In some settings the students worked on the cases in teams of 2-3 rather than individually. Group performance significantly increased the solution frequency from a 51% solve rate for individuals to 63% for the students in groups. Strategically, the most notable differences were the maintenance of State 1 as the dominant state, the nearly complete lack of performances in States 2 and 3, and the more rapid adoption of State 4 performances by the groups (Figure 5).

In addition, the groups stabilized their performances faster, changing little after the third performance whereas males and females stabilized only after performance 5. This makes sense because states 2 and 3 represent transitional phases that students pass through as they develop competence. Collaborative learners may spend less time in these phases if group interaction indeed helps students see multiple perspectives and reconcile different viewpoints [23].

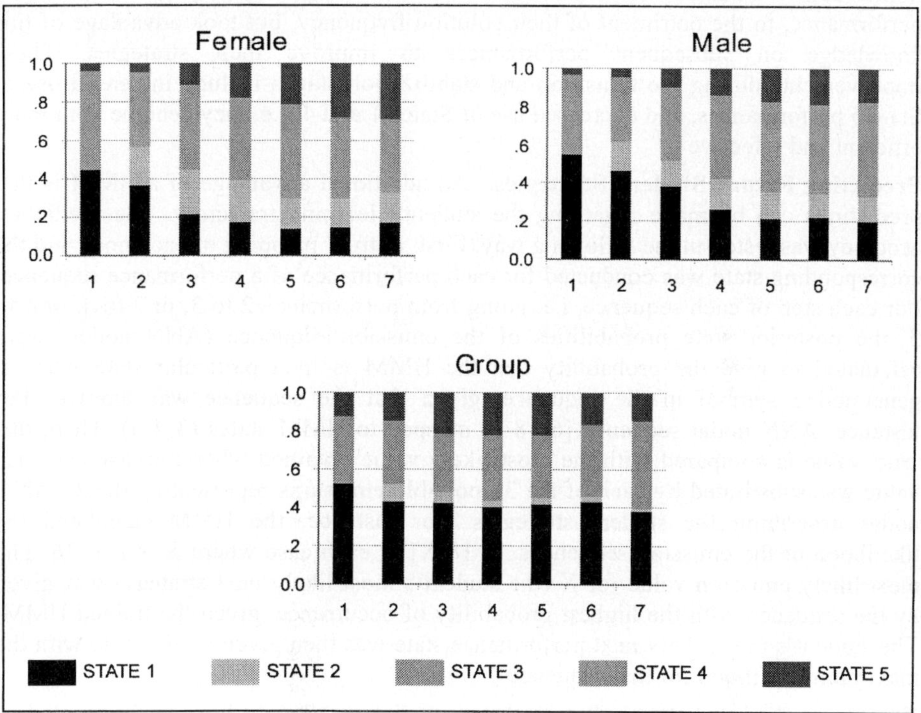

Fig. 5. State Distributions for Individuals and Groups

Also, shown in Figure 5 are the differences in the state distribution of performances across males and females ((Pearson $\chi^2 = 31.2$, $p<0.000$). While there was a steady reduction in State 1 performances for both groups, the females entered State 2 more rapidly and exited more rapidly to State 5. These differences became non-significant at the stable phase of the trajectories (performances 6 and 7). Thus males and females have different learning trajectories but appear to arrive at similar strategy states.

Ability and State Transitions. Learning trajectories were then developed according to student ability as determined by IRT. For these studies, students were grouped into high (person measure = 72-99, n = 1300), medium (person measure 50-72, n = 4336) and low (person measure 20-50, n = 1994) abilities. As expected from the nature of IRT, the percentage solved rate correlated with student ability. What was less expected was that when the solved rate by ability was examined for the sequence of performances, the students with the lowest ability had not only the highest solved rate on the first performance, but also one that was significantly better than the highest ability students (57% vs 44% n = 866, p< 0.00). Predictably, this was rapidly reversed on subsequent cases. To better understand these framing differences a cross-tabulation analysis was conducted between student ability and neural network nodal classifications on the first performances. This analysis highlighted nodes 3, 4, 18, 19, 25, 26, and 31 as having the highest residuals for the low ability students, and nodes 5, 6, 12, and 17 for the highest ability students. From this data, it appeared that the higher ability students more thoroughly explored the problem space on their first performance, to the detriment of their solution frequency, but took advantage of this knowledge on subsequent performances to improve their strategies. These improvements during the transition and stabilization stages include increased use of State 5 performances, and decreased use of States 1 and 4; i.e. they become both more efficient and effective

Predicting Future Student Strategies. An additional advantage of a HMM is that predictions can be made regarding the student's learning trajectory. The prediction accuracy was tested in the following way. First, a 'true' mapping of each node and the corresponding state was conducted for each performance of a performance sequence. For each step of each sequence, i.e. going from performance 2 to 3, or 3 to 4, or 4 to 5, the posterior state probabilities of the emission sequence (ANN nodes) were calculated to give the probability that the HMM is in a particular state when it generated a symbol in the sequence, given that the sequence was emitted. For instance, ANN nodal sequence [6 18 1] mapped to HMM states (3 4 4). Then, this 'true' value is compared with the most likely value obtained when the last sequence value was substituted by each of the 36 possible emissions representing the 36 ANN nodes describing the student strategies. For instance, the HMM calculated the likelihood of the emission sequences, [6 18 X] in each case where X = 1 to 36. The most likely emission value for X (the student's most likely next strategy) was given by the sequence with the highest probability of occurrence, given the trained HMM. The student's most likely next performance state was then given by the state with the maximum likelihood for that sequence.

Comparing the 'true' state values with the predicted values estimated the predictive accuracy of the model at nearly 90% (Table 2). As the performance sequence increased, the prediction rate also increased, most likely reflecting that by performances 4, 5 and 6, students are repeatedly using similar strategies.

Table 2. Prediction of Future Performances

Performance #	1	2	3	4	5	6
% Correct Predictions	67	75	83	88	86	91

3 Discussion

The goal of this study was to explore the use of HMMs to begin to model how students gain competence in domain-specific problem solving. The idea of 'learning trajectories' is useful when thinking about how students progress on the road to competence [24]. These trajectories are developed from the different ways that novices and experts think and perform in a domain, and can be thought of as defining stages of understanding of a domain or discipline [4]. During early learning, students' domain knowledge is limited and fragmented, the terminology is uncertain and it is difficult for them to know how to properly frame problems. In our models, this first strategic stage is best represented by State 3 where students extensively explore the problem space and select many of the available items. As expected, the solved rate for such a strategy was poor. This approach is characteristic of surface level strategies or those built from situational (and perhaps inaccurate) experiences. From the transition matrix in Figure 4, State 3 is not an absorbing state and most students move from this strategy type on subsequent performances.

With experience, the student's knowledge base becomes qualitatively more structured and quantitatively deeper and this is reflected in the way competent students, or experts approach and solve difficult domain-related problems. In our model States 2 and 4 would best represent the beginning of this stage of understanding. State 2 consists of an equal selection of background information and test information, suggesting a lack of familiarity of the nature of the data being observed. State 4 on the other hand shows little/no selection of background information but still extensive and non-discriminating test item selection. Whereas State 2 is a transition state, State 4 is an absorbing state - perhaps one warranting intervention for students who persist with strategies represented by this state.

Once competence is developed students would be expected to employ both effective and efficient strategies. These are most clearly shown by our States 1 and 5. These states show an interesting dichotomy in that they are differentially represented in the male and female populations with males having a higher than expected number of State 1 strategies and females higher than expected State 5 strategies.

The solution frequencies at each state provide an interesting view of progress. For instance, if we compare the earlier differences in solution frequencies with the most likely state transitions from the matrix shown in Figure 4, we see that most of the students who enter State 3, having the lowest problem solving rate (45%), will transit either to State 2 or 4. Those students who transit from State 3 to 2 will show on average a 15% performance increase (from 45% to 60%) and those students who transit from States 3 to 4 will show on average a 9% performance increase (from 45% to 54%). The transition matrix also shows that students who are performing in State 2 (with a 60% solve rate) will tend to either stay in that state, or transit to State 5, showing a 10% performance increase (from 60% to 70%). This analysis shows that students' performance increases as they solve science inquiry problems through the IMMEX Interactive Learning Environment, and that by using ANN and HMM methods, we are able to track and understand their progress.

When given enough data about student's previous performances, our HMM models performed at over 90% accuracy when tasked to predict the most likely problem solving strategy the student will apply next. Knowing whether or not a student is likely to continue to use an inefficient problem solving strategy allows us to determine whether or not the student is likely to need help in the near future. Perhaps more interestingly, however, is the possibility that knowing the distribution of students' problem solving strategies and their most likely future behaviors may allow us to strategically construct collaborative learning groups containing heterogeneous combinations of various behaviors such that intervention by a human instructor is required less often [25].

Finally, our studies provide some information on the effects of collaborative learning when students perform the cases. In particular, collaborative problem solving appeared to reduce the use of strategies in States 2 and 3, which are the most transitory states. In this regard, one effect of the collaboration may be to help groups more rapidly establish stable patterns of problem solving. A question of interest would be whether or not these states persist once students engage again in individual problem solving.

Acknowledgments. Supported in part by grants from the National Science Foundation (ROLE 0231995, DUE 0126050, ESE 9453918), the PT^3 Program of the U.S. Department of Education (P342A-990532), and the Howard Hughes Medical Institute Precollege Initiative.

References

1. Anderson, J.D.,(1980). Cognitive psychology and its implications. San Francisco: W.H. Freeman
2. Chi, M. T. H., Glaser, R., and Farr, M.J. (eds.), (1988). The Nature of Expertise, Hillsdale, Lawrence Erlbaum, pp 129-152
3. Chi, M. T. H., Bassok, M., Lewis, M. W., Reinmann, P., and Glaser, R. (1989). Self-Explanations: how students study and use examples in learning to solve problems. Cognitive Science, 13, 145-182
4. VanLehn, K., (1996). Cognitive Skill Acquisition. Annu. Rev. Psychol 47: 513-539
5. Schunn, C.D., and Anderson, J.R. (2002). The generality/specificity of expertise in scientific reasoning. Cognitive Science
6. Corbett, A. T. & Anderson, J. R. (1995). Knowledge tracing: Modeling the acquisition of procedural knowledge. User Modeling and User-Adapted Interaction, 4, 253-278
7. Schunn, C.D., Lovett, M.C., and Reder, L.M. (2001). Awareness and working memory in strategy adaptivity. Memory & Cognition, 29(2); 254-266
8. Haider, H., and Frensch, P.A. (1996). The role of information reduction in skill acquisition. Cognitive Psychology 30: 304-337
9. Alexander, P., (2003). The development of expertise: the journey from acclimation to proficiency. Educational Researcher, 32: (8), 10-14
10. Stevens, R.H., Ikeda, J., Casillas, A., Palacio-Cayetano, J., and S. Clyman (1999). Artificial neural network-based performance assessments. Computers in Human Behavior, 15: 295-314
11. Underdahl, J., Palacio-Cayetano, J., and Stevens, R., (2001). Practice makes perfect: assessing and enhancing knowledge and problem-solving skills with IMMEX software. Learning and Leading with Technology. 28: 26-31
12. Lawson, A.E. (1995). Science Teaching and the Development of Thinking. Wadsworth Publishing Company, Belmont, California
13. Olson, A., & Loucks-Horsley, S. (Eds). (2000). Inquiry and the National Science Education Standards: A guide for teaching and learning. Washington, DC: National Academy Press
14. Linacre, J.M. (2004). WINSTEPS Rasch measurement computer program. Chicago. Winsteps.com

15. Stevens, R.H., and Najafi K. (1993). Artificial neural networks as adjuncts for assessing Medical students' problem-solving performances on computer-based simulations. Computers and Biomedical Research 26(2), 172-187
16. Rumelhart, D. E., & McClelland, J. L. (1986). Parallel distributed processing: Explorations in the Microstructure of Cognition. Volume 1: Foundations. Cambridge, MA: MIT Press
17. Stevens, R., Wang, P., Lopo, A. (1996). Artificial neural networks can distinguish novice and expert strategies during complex problem solving. JAMIA vol. 3 Number 2 p 131-138
18. Casillas, A.M., Clyman, S.G., Fan, Y.V., and Stevens, R.H. (1999). Exploring alternative models of complex patient management with artificial neural networks. Advances in Health Sciences Education 1: 1-19, 1999
19. Rabiner, L., (1989). A tutorial on Hidden Markov Models and selected applications in speech recognition. Proc. IEEE, 77: 257-286
20. Kohonen, T., 2001. Self Organizing Maps. 3rd extended edit. Springer, Berlin, Heidelberg, New York
21. Soller, A. (2004). Understanding knowledge sharing breakdowns: A meeting of the quantitative and qualitative minds. Journal of Computer Assisted Learning (in press)
22. Soller, A., and Lesgold, A. (2003). A computational approach to analyzing online knowledge sharing interaction. Proceedings of Artificial Intelligence in Education, 2003. Australia, 253-260
23. Lesgold, A., Katz, S., Greenberg, L., Hughes, E., & Eggan, G. (1992). Extensions of intelligent tutoring paradigms to support collaborative learning. In S. Dijkstra, H. Krammer, & J. van Merrienboer (Eds.), Instructional Models in Computer-Based Learning Environments. Berlin: Springer-Verlag, 291-311
24. Lajoie, S.P. (2003). Transitions and trajectories for studies of expertise. Educational Researcher, 32: 21-25
25. Giordani, A., & Soller, A. (2004). Strategic Collaboration Support in a Web-based Scientific Inquiry Environment. European Conference on Artificial Intelligence, "Workshop on Artificial Intelligence in Computer Supported Collaborative Learning", Valencia, Spain

Pedagogical Agent Design: The Impact of Agent Realism, Gender, Ethnicity, and Instructional Role

Amy L. Baylor and Yanghee Kim

Pedagogical Agent Learning Systems (PALS) Research Laboratory
Department of Educational Psychology and Learning Systems
307 Stone Building
Florida State University
United States
850-644-5203
baylor@coe.fsu.edu

Abstract. In the first of two experimental studies, 312 students were randomly assigned to one of 8 conditions, where agents differed by ethnicity (Black, White), gender (male, female), and image (realistic, cartoon), yet had identical messages and computer-generated voice. In the second study, 229 students were randomly assigned to one of 12 conditions where agents represented different instructional roles (expert, motivator, and mentor), also differing by ethnicity (Black, White), and gender (male, female). Overall, it was found that students had greater transfer of learning when the agents had more realistic images and when agents in the "expert" role were represented non-traditionally (as Black versus White). Results also generally confirmed prior research where agents perceived as less intelligent lead to significantly improved self-efficacy. The presence of motivational messages, as employed through the motivator and mentor agent roles, led to enhanced learner self-regulation and self-efficacy. Results are discussed with respect to social cognitive theory.

1 Introduction

Pedagogical agent design has recently been placing greater emphasis on the importance of the agent as an actor rather than as a tool (Persson, Laaksolahti, & Lonnqvist, 2002), thus focusing on the agent's implicit social relationship with the learner. The social cognitive perspective in teaching and learning emphasizes the importance that social interaction (e.g., Lave & Wenger, 2001; Vygotsky, Cole, John-Steiner, Scribner, & Souberman, 1978) plays in contributing to motivational outcomes such as learner self-efficacy (Bandura, 2000) and self-regulation (Zimmerman, 2000).

According to Bandura (1997), attribute similarities between a social model and a learner, such as gender, ethnicity, and competency, often have predictive significance for the learner's efficacy beliefs and achievements. Similarly, pedagogical agents of the same gender or ethnicity or similar competency as learners' might be viewed as more affable and could instill strong efficacy beliefs and behavioral intentions to

J.C. Lester et al. (Eds.): ITS 2004, LNCS 3220, pp. 592–603, 2004.

learners. Learners may draw positive judgments about their capabilities when they observe agents who demonstrate successful performance.

Even so, while college students were not more likely to choose to work with an agent of the same gender (Baylor, Shen, & Huang, 2003), in a between-subjects study they were more satisfied with their performance and reported that the agent better facilitated self-regulation if it was male (Baylor & Kim, 2003). Similarly, Moreno and colleagues (2002) revealed that learners applied gender stereotypes to animated agents, and this stereotypic expectation affected their learning. With respect to the ethnicity of pedagogical agents, empirical results do not provide consistent results. In both a computer-mediated communication and an agent environment, participants who had similar-ethnicity partners than those with different-ethnicity partners presented more persuasive and better arguments; elicited more conformity to the partners' opinions; and perceived their partners as more attractive and trustworthy (Lee & Nass, 1998). In a more recent study, Baylor and Kim (2003b) examined the impact of pedagogical agents' ethnicity on learners' perception of the agents. Undergraduate participants who worked with pedagogical agents of the same ethnicity rated the agents as more credible, engaging, and affable than those who worked with agents of different ethnicity. However, Moreno and colleagues (2002) indicated that the ethnicity of pedagogical agents did not influence students' stereotypic expectations or learning.

Given their function for supporting learning, pedagogical agents must also represent different instructional roles, such as expert, instructor, mentor, or learning companion. These roles also may interact with the agent's gender and ethnicity given that human social relationships influence their perceptions and understanding in general (Dunn, 2000). In a similar fashion, the instructional roles of the pedagogical agents may influence the perceptions or expectations of and the social bonds with learners. Along this line, Baylor and Kim (2003c, in press) showed that distinct roles for pedagogical agents—as expert, motivator, and mentor—significantly influenced the learners' perceptions of the agent persona, self-efficacy, and learning.

Lastly, Norman (1994; 1997) expressed concerns about human-like interfaces. If an interface is anthropomorphized too realistically, people tend to form unrealistic expectations. That is, a too realistic human-like appearance and interaction can be deceptive and misleading by implying promises of functionality that can be never reached. On the other hand, socially intelligent agents are of "no virtual difference" from humans (Vassileva, 1998) and can provoke "illusion of life" (Hays-Roth & Doyle, 1998), thus impressing the learners interacting with a "living" virtual being (Rizzo, 2000). So, we may inquire how realistic agent images should be to establish social relations to learners. Norman argues that people will be more accepting of an intelligent interface when their expectation matches with its real functionality. What extent of agent realism will match learners' expectations with agent functionality is an open question, however.

Consequently, the relationships among pedagogical agent gender, ethnicity, instructional role, and realism seem to play a role to enhance learner motivation (e.g., self-efficacy), self-regulation, and learning. The purpose of this research was to examine these relationships through two controlled experiments. Experiment I examined the impact of agent gender, ethnicity, and realism; Experiment II examined the impact of agent gender, ethnicity, and instructional role.

2 Experiment I: Agent Realism, Gender, Ethnicity

2.1 Agent Design

Eight agent images were designed by a graphic artist based on the same basic face, but differing by gender, ethnicity, and realism. The animated agents were then developed using a 3D character design tool, Poser 5, and Microsoft Agent Character Builder. Next, the agents were incorporated into the web-based research application, MIMIC (Multiple Intelligent Mentors Instructing Collaboratively) (Baylor, 2002). To control confounding effects, we used consistent parameters and matrices to delineate facial expression, mouth movement, and overall silhouettes across the agents. Also, except for image, the agents had identical scripts, voice, animation, and emotion. For voice, we used computer-generated male and female voices. For animation, blinking and mouth movements were included. Emotion was expressed using the scripts together with facial expression, such as smiling. Figure 1 presents the images of the eight agents used in the study.

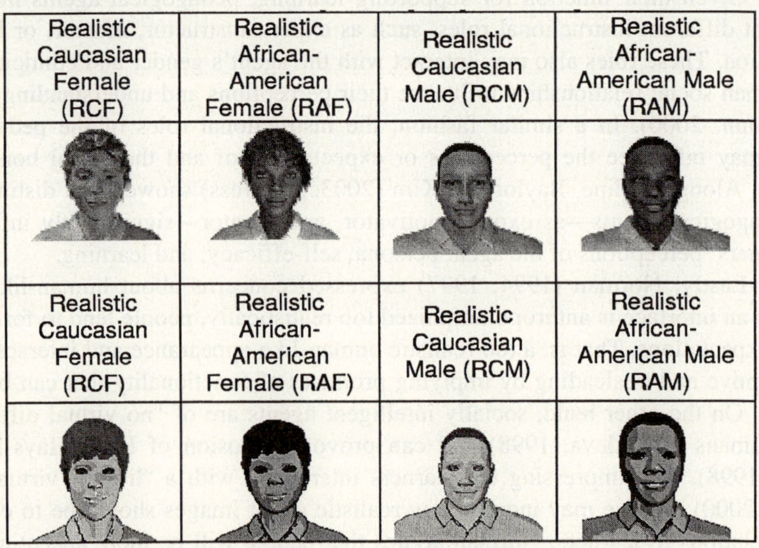

Fig. 1. Images of eight agents in Experiment I

Validation. In a controlled between-subjects study with 83 undergraduates, we validated that each agent effectively represented the intended gender, ethnicity, and degree of realism.

2.2 Method

Dependent Variables. Dependent variables included self-regulation, self-efficacy, and learning and were identical for both Experiment I and II.

Self-regulation. Learners' self-regulation was assessed through three Likert-scale items: 1) I stopped to think over what I was learning and doing; 2) I kept track of my progress; and 3) I evaluated the quality of my lesson plan. The students rated their self-regulation on a five-point scale ranging from 1 (*Strongly disagree*) to 5 (*Strongly agree*). Item reliability was evaluated as $\alpha = 0.85$.

Self-efficacy. Learners' self-efficacy beliefs about the learning tasks were measured with a one-item question developed according to the guidelines of Bandura and Schunk (1981) for specificity. The guidelines emphasize that self-efficacy is the degree to which one feels capable of performing a particular task at certain designated levels (Bandura, 1986). The participants answered the question, "How sure are you that you can write a lesson plan?" on a scale ranging from 1 (*Not at all sure*) to 5 (*Extremely sure*) after the intervention.

Learning. Learning was assessed by an open-ended question where the participants had to transfer their knowledge to a new situation. The participants were asked to write a brief instructional plan with the following prompt:

> Applying what you've learned, develop an instructional plan for the following scenario: Imagine that you are a sixth grade teacher of a mathematics class. Your principal informs you that a member of the president's advisory committee will be visiting next week and wants to see an example of your instruction about multiplication of fractions.

The overall quality of a the answers were evaluated by two instructional designers, who scored the students' answers with a detailed scoring rubric on a scale ranging from 1 (*very poor*) to 5 (*excellent*). Inter-rater reliability was evaluated as Cohen's *Kappa* = 0.95.

Sample. Participants included 312 pre-service teachers enrolled in an introductory educational technology class in two large southeast universities in the United States. Approximately 30% of the participants were male and 70% were female; 53% of the participants were Caucasian, 33% were African-American, and 14% were others. The average age of the participants was 20.54 years (SD=2.63).

Procedure. The experiment was conducted during a regular session of an introductory educational technology course. The participants were randomly assigned to one of the eight agent conditions. They logged on the web site loading MIMIC (Multiple Intelligent Mentors Instructing Collaboratively), which was designed to help the students develop instructional planning. The participants were given as much time as they needed to finish each phase of the tasks. The entire session took about an hour with individual variations.

Design and Analysis. The study employed a 2 × 2 × 2 design, including agent gender (Male vs. Female), agent ethnicity (Caucasian vs. African-American), and agent realism (realistic vs. cartoon-like) as the factors. For self-regulation, a MANOVA (multivariate analysis of variance) was conducted. For self-efficacy and learning, analysis of variance (ANOVA) was conducted. The significance level was set as $\alpha = 0.5$.

2.3 Results

Self-regulation. MANOVA revealed a significant main effect for agent gender, Wilks' Lambda = .97, $F(3, 287) = 3.45$, $p = .01$, where the presence of a male agent led to significantly more reported self-regulatory behavior than the presence of a female agent. Follow-up post-hoc univariate analyses (ANOVA) revealed significant main effects for each of the three sub-measures (all $p<.05$).

Self-efficacy. ANOVA indicated a significant main effect for agent gender where the presence of the male agent led to increased self-efficacy, $F(1, 289)=4.20$, $p<.05$. Analysis of additional Likert items revealed that students perceived the male agents as significantly more interesting, intelligent, useful, and leading to greater satisfaction than the female agents.

Learning. For all students (male and female) ANOVA revealed a marginally significant main effect for agent realism on learning, $F(1, 289) = 4.2$, $p =.09$. Overall, students who worked with the realistic agents ($M = 3.13$, $SD = 1.05$) performed marginally better than students who worked with the cartoon-like agents ($M = 2.94$, $SD = 1.1$). Interestingly, a post-hoc ANOVA indicated a significant main effect for agent realism where males working with realistic agents ($M=3.50$) learned more than males working with cartoon agents ($M=2.51$, $F(1,84) =6.50$, $p=.01$. For female students, the main effect for agent realism was not significant.

3 Experiment II: Agent Role, Ethnicity, and Gender

3.1 Agent Design

For the second study, a different set of twelve agents, differing by gender, ethnicity, and role, were designed using a 3D character design tool, Poser 5 and Mimic Pro 2. These agents were richer than those in Experiment I, where the focus was on the agent image. Consequently, to establish distinct instructional roles, it was important to consider a set of media features that influence agent "persona," including image, animation, affect, and voice. Image is a key factor in affecting learners' perception of the computer-based agent as credible (Baylor & Ryu, 2003b) and motivating (Baylor

& Kim, 2003a; Baylor, Shen, & Huang, 2003; Kim, Baylor, & Reed, 2003). Animation includes body movements such as hand gestures, facial expression, and head nods, which can convey information and draw students' attention (Cassell, 1998; Johnson, Rickel, & Lester, 2000; McNeill, 1992; Roth, 2001). Affect, or emotion, is also an integral part of human intellectual and cognitive functioning (Kort, Reilly, & Picard, 2001; Picard, 1997) and thus was deemed as critical for facilitating the social relationship with learners and affecting their emotional development (Saarni, 2001). Finally, voice is a powerful indicator of social presence (Nass & Steuer, 1993), and so the human voices were recorded to match the voices with the gender, ethnicity, and roles of each agent and with their behaviors, attitudes, and language. Figure 2 shows the images of the twelve agents.

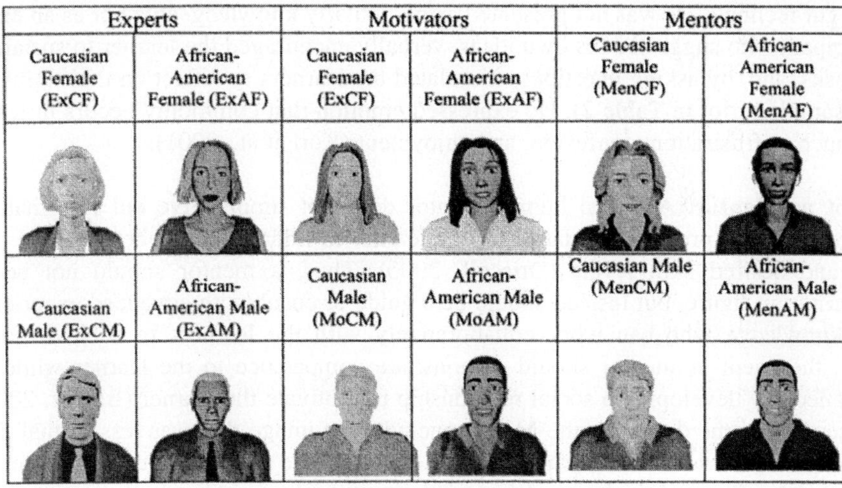

Fig. 2. Images of twelve agents in Experiment II

The agent-student dialogue was pre-defined to control for agent functionality across students. Given that people tend to apply the same social rules and expectations from human-human interaction to computer-human interaction (Reeves & Nass, 1996), we referred to research on human instructors for implications for the agent role design.

Agent as Expert. The design of the Expert was based on research that shows that the development of expertise in humans requires years of deliberate practice in a domain (Ericsson, Krampe, & Tesch-Romer, 1993) and that experts exhibit mastery or extensive knowledge and perform better than the average within a domain (Ericsson, 1996; Gonzales, Burdenski, Stough, & Palmer, 2001). Also, experts will be confident and stable in performance and not swayed emotionally by instant internal or external stimulation. Based on this, we operationalized the expert agent through the image of a professor in forties. His animation was limited to deictic gestures, and he spoke in a formal and professional manner, with authoritative speech. Being emotionally detached from the learners, his function was to provide accurate information in a succinct way (see sample script in Table 2).

Agent as Motivator. The design of the Motivator was based on social modeling research dealing with learners' efficacy beliefs, a critical component of learner motivation. According to Bandura (1997), attribute similarity between the learner and social model significantly affects the learners' self-efficacy beliefs. In other words, learning and motivation are enhanced when learners observed a social model of the same age (Schunk, 1989). Further, verbal encouragement in support of the learner performing a task facilitates learners' self-efficacy beliefs. Thus, we operationalized a motivator agent with a peer-like image of a casually-dressed student in his twenties, considering that our target population was college students. Given that expressive gestures of pedagogical agents may have a strong motivating effects (Johnson et al., 2000), the agent gestures were expressive and highly-animated. He spoke enthusiastically and energetically, while sometimes using colloquial expressions, e.g., 'What's your gut feeling?' He was not presented as particularly knowledgeable but as an eager participant who suggested his own ideas, verbally encouraged the learner to sustain at the tasks, and, by asking questions, stimulated the learners to reflect on their thinking (see sample script in Table 2). He expressed emotion that commonly occurs in learning, such as frustration, confusion, and enjoyment (Kort et al., 2001).

Agent as Mentor. An ideal human mentor does not simply give out information; rather, a mentor provides guidance for the learner to bridge the gap between the current and desired skill levels (Driscoll, 2000). Thus, a mentor should not be an authoritarian figure, but instead should be a guide or coach with advanced experience and knowledge who can work collaboratively with the learners to achieve goals. Thus, the agent as mentor should demonstrate competence to the learner while simultaneously developing a social relationship to motivate the learner (Baylor, 2000). Consequently, the design of the Mentor included an image that was less formal than the Expert, yet older than the peer-like Motivator. The Mentor's gestures were designed to be identical to the Motivator, incorporating both deictic and emotional expressions. His voice was friendly and approachable, yet more professional and confident than the Motivator. We operationalized the Mentor's functionality to incorporate the characteristics of both the Expert and Motivator, (i.e., to provide information and motivation); thus, his script was a concatenation of the content of the Expert and Motivator scripts.

Validation. We initially validated that each agent was effectively representing the intended gender, ethnicity, and roles with 174 undergraduates in a between-subjects design. The results indicated successful instantiations of the twelve agents.

3.2 Method

Dependent variables were identical to those employed in Experiment I and included self-regulation, self-efficacy, and learning.

Sample. Participants included 229 undergraduates enrolled in a computer literacy course in a large university in the Southeastern United States. Approximately 39% of the participants were male and 61% were female; 70% of the participants were Caucasian, 10% were African-American, and 20% were others. Approximately 39% of the participants were male and 61% were female. The average age of the participants was 19.39 (SD=1.64).

Procedure. The experiment was conducted during a regular session of a computer literacy class. The participants were randomly assigned to one of the twelve agent conditions. They logged on the web site loading a modified version of MIMIC (Multiple Intelligent Mentors Instructing Collaboratively), which was designed to help the students develop instructional planning for e-Learning. The participants were given as much time as they needed to finish each phase of the tasks. The entire session took about an hour with individual variations.

Design and Analysis. The study employed a 2 × 2 × 3 design, including agent gender (Male vs. Female), agent ethnicity (White vs. Black), and agent role (expert vs. motivator vs. mentor) as the factors. For self-regulation, a MANOVA (multivariate analysis of variance) was conducted. For self-efficacy and learning, analysis of variance (ANOVA) was conducted. The significance level was set as $\alpha = 0.5$.

3.3 Results

Self-regulation. MANOVA revealed a significant main effect for agent role on self-regulation, Wilks' Lambda = .94, $F(6, 430) = 2.22$, $p < .05$. Overall, students who worked with the mentor or motivator agents rated their self-regulation significantly higher than students who worked with the expert agent. MANOVA also revealed a main effect for agent ethnicity on self-regulation where Black agents led to increased self-regulation as compared to White agents, Wilks' Lambda =.96, $F(3, 205) = 2.90$, $p < .05$.

Self-efficacy. There was a significant main effect for agent gender on self-efficacy, $F(1, 217) = 6.90$, $p < .05$. Students who worked with the female agents (M = 2.36, SD = 1.16) showed higher self-efficacy beliefs than students who worked with the male agents (M = 2.01, SD = 1.12). Analysis of additional Likert items revealed that students perceived the female agents as significantly less knowledgeable and intelligent than the male agents. There was also a significant main effect for agent role on self-efficacy, $F(2, 217) = 4.37$, $p = .01$. Students who worked with the motivator (M = 2.37, SD = 1.2) and mentor agents (M = 2.32, SD = 1.2) showed higher self-efficacy beliefs than students who worked with the expert agent (M = 1.86, SD = 0.94).

Learning. There was a significant interaction of agent role and agent ethnicity on learning, $F(2, 214) = 3.36$, $p < .05$. Post hoc t-tests of the cell means indicated that there was a significant difference between the Black (M = 2.61, SD =.75) and White

Experts (M = 2.13 , SD =.84, p<.01), indicating that the Black agents were significantly more effective in the role of Expert than the White agents. This interaction is illustrated in Figure 3. Additional analysis of Likert items regarding the level to which students paid attention during the program revealed that students with the Black Experts better "focused on the relevant information" ((M = 3.03, SD =1.08 vs. M = 2.42, SD =1.11) and "concentrated" (M = 2.70, SD = .95 vs. M = 2.23, SD = 1.10).

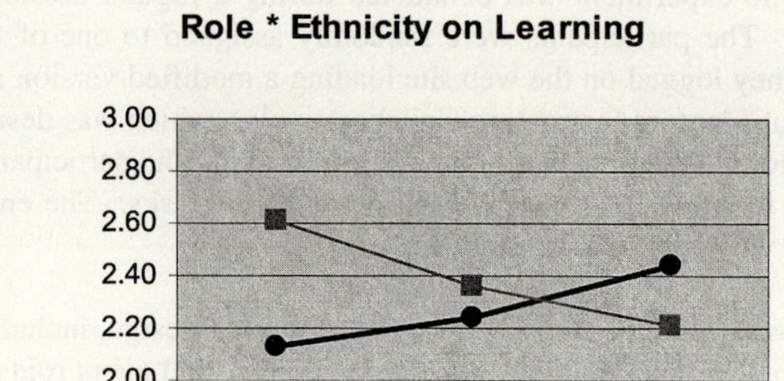

	Expert	Motivator	Mentor
White	2.13	2.24	2.44
Black	2.61	2.36	2.21

Fig. 3. Interaction of Role * Ethnicity on Learning

4 Discussion

Results from Experiment I highlight the potential value of more realistic agent images (particularly for male students) to positively affect transfer of learning. This supports the value in designing pedagogical agents to best represent the live humans that they attempt to simulate (e.g., Hays-Roth & Doyle, 1998; Rizzo, 2000). Even so, a variety of permutations of agents with different levels of realism needs to be examined to more fully substantiate this finding.

In Experiment II, the Black agents in the role of expert led to significantly improved learning as compared to the White agents as experts, even though both had identical messages. Students working with the Black experts also reported enhanced concentration and focus, which could be explained by the fact that they perceived the agents as more novel (and thereby more worthy of paying attention to) than the White experts. Similarly, Black agents overall (in all roles) led to enhanced learner self-regulation in the same experiment, perhaps because they also warranted greater attention and focus. In support of this explanation (i.e., that students pay more attention to agents that represent non-traditional roles), we recently found that a female agent acting as a non-traditional engineer (e.g., outgoing, highly attractive) significantly enhanced student interest in engineering as compared to a more stereotypical "nerdy" version (e.g., introverted, homely) (Baylor, 2004).

The importance of the agent message was demonstrated in Experiment II, where the presence of motivational messages (as delivered through the motivator and mentor agent instructional roles) led to greater learner self-regulation and self-efficacy. This finding is supported by Bandura (1997), who suggests that such verbal persuasion leads to positive motivational outcomes.

Our prior research has indicated that agents that are perceived as *less* intelligent lead to greater self-efficacy (Baylor, 2004; Baylor & Kim, in press). This was replicated in Experiment II since the female agents (who were perceived as significantly less intelligent than the males) led to enhanced self-efficacy. Similarly, the finding that the motivator and mentor agents led to greater self-efficacy could be attributed to the fact that they were validated to be perceived as significantly less expert-like (i.e., knowledgeable, intelligent) than the expert agents. While results from Experiment I initially seem contradictory because the agents rated as most intelligent (males) also led to improved self-efficacy, this can be attributed to an overall positive student bias toward the male agents in this particular study (e.g., they were rated as more useful, interesting, and leading to overall more satisfaction and self-regulation).

Overall, while the agent message is undoubtedly important, results support the conclusion that a seemingly superficial interface feature like pedagogical agent image plays a very important role in impacting learning and motivational outcomes. The image is key because it directly impacts how the learner perceives it as a human-like instructor; consequently, pedagogical agent designers must take great care in choosing how to represent the agent's gender, ethnicity, and realism.

Acknowledgments. This work was sponsored by National Science Foundation Grant # IIS-0218692

References

Arroyo, I., Beck, J. E., Woolf, B. P., Beal, C. R., & Schultz, K. (2000). Macroadapting animalwatch to gender and cognitive differences with respect to hint interactivity and symbolism. In *Intelligent Tutoring Systems, Proceedings* (Vol. 1839, pp. 574-583).

Arroyo, I., Murray, T., Woolf, B. P., & Beal, C. R. (2003). *Further results on gender and cognitive differences in help effectiveness.* Paper presented at the The International Conference of Artificial Intelligence in Education, Sydney, Australia.

Bandura, A. (1997). *Self-efficacy: The exercise of control.* New York: W. H. Freeman.

Bandura, A. (Ed.). (2000). Self-Efficacy: The Foundation of Agency. Mahwah, NJ: Lawrence Erlbaum Associates, Inc.

Baylor, A. L. (2000). Beyond butlers: intelligent agents as mentors. *Journal of Educational Computing Research, 22*(4), 373-382.

Baylor, A. L. (2004). *Encouraging more positive engineering stereotypes with animated interface agents.* Unpublished manuscript.

Baylor, A. L., & Kim, Y. (2003a). *The Role of Gender and Ethnicity in Pedagogical Agent Perception.* Paper presented at the E-Learn (World Conference on E-Learning in Corporate, Government, Healthcare, & Higher Education), Phoenix, Arizona.

Baylor, A. L., & Kim, Y. (2003b). *The role of gender and ethnicity in pedagogical agent perception.* Paper presented at the E-Learn, the Annual Conference of Association for the Advancement of Computing in Education., Phoenix, AZ.

Baylor, A. L., & Kim, Y. (2003c). *Validating Pedagogical Agent Roles: Expert, Motivator, and Mentor.* Paper presented at the International Conference of Ed-Media, Honolulu, Hawaii.

Baylor, A. L. & Kim, Y. (in press). The effectiveness of simulating instructional roles with pedagogical agents. *International Journal of Artificial Intelligence in Education.*

Baylor, A. L., & Ryu, J. (2003a). *The API (Agent Persona Instrument) for assessing pedagogical agent persona.* Paper presented at the International Conference of Ed-Media, Honolulu, Hawaii.

Baylor, A. L., & Ryu, J. (2003b). Does the presence of image and animation enhance pedagogical agent persona? *Journal of Educational Computing Research, 28*(4), 373-395.

Baylor, A. L., Shen, E., & Huang, X. (2003). *Which Pedagogical Agent do Learners Choose? The Effects of Gender and Ethnicity.* Paper presented at the E-Learn (World Conference on E-Learning in Corporate, Government, Healthcare, & Higher Education), Phoenix, Arizona.

Cassell, J. (1998). A Framework For Gesture Generation And Interpretation. In A. Pentland (Ed.), *Computer Vision in Human-Machine Interaction.* New York: Cambridge University Press.

Cooper, J., & Weaver, K. D. (2003). *Gender and Computers: Understanding the Digital Divide*: NJ: Lawrence Erlbaum Associates.

Driscoll, M. P. (2000). *Psychology of Learning for Instruction*: Allyn & Bacon.

Dunn, J. (2000). Mind-reading, emotion understanding, and relationships. *International Journal of Behavioral Development, 24*(2), 142-144.

Ericsson, K. A. (1996). The acquisition of expert performance: an introduction to some of the issues. In K. A. Ericsson (Ed.), *The Road to Excellence: The Acquisition of Expert Performance in the Arts, Sciences, Sports, and Games* (pp. 1-50). Hillsdale, NJ: Erlbaum.

Ericsson, K. A., Krampe, R. T., & Tesch-Romer, C. (1993). The role of deliberate practice in the acquisition of expert performance. *Psychological Review, 100*(3), 363-406.

Gonzales, M., Burdenski, T. K., Jr., Stough, L. M., & Palmer, D. J. (2001, April 10-14). *Identifying teacher expertise: an examination of researchers' decision-making.* Paper presented at the American Educational Research Association, Seattle, WA.

Hays-Roth, B., & Doyle, P. (1998). Animate Characters. *Autonomous Agents and Multi-Agent Systems, 1*, 195-230.

Johnson, W. L., Rickel, J. W., & Lester, J. C. (2000). Animated pedagogical agents: face-to-face interaction in interactive learning environments. *International Journal of Artificial Intelligence in Education, 11*, 47-78.

Kim, Y., Baylor, A. L., & Reed, G. (2003). *The Impact of Image and Voice with Pedagogical Agents.* Paper presented at the E-Learn (World Conference on E-Learning in Corporate, Government, Healthcare, & Higher Education), Phoenix, Arizona.

Kort, B., Reilly, R., & Picard, R. W. (2001). An affective model of interplay between emotions and learning: reengineering educational pedagogy-building a learning companion. *Proceedings IEEE International Conference on Advanced Learning Technologies*, 43-46.

Lave, J., & Wenger, E. (2001). *Situated learning: legitimate peripheral participation*: Cambridge University Press.

Lee, E., & Nass, C. (1998). *Does the ethnicity of a computer agent matter? An experimental comparison of human-computer interaction and computer-mediated communication.* Paper presented at the WECC Conference, Lake Tahoe, CA.

McCrae, R. R., & John, O. P. (1992). An introduction to the fve factor model and its applications. *Journal of Personality, 60*, 175-215.

McNeill, D. (1992). *Hand and mind: what gestures reveal about thought*. Chicago: University of Chicago Press.

Moreno, K. N., Person, N. K., Adcock, A. B., Eck, R. N. V., Jackson, G. T., & Marineau, J. C. (2002). *Etiquette and Efficacy in Animated pedagogical agents: the role of stereotypes*. Paper presented at the AAAI Symposium on Personalized Agents, Cape Cod, MA.

Nass, C., & Steuer, J. (1993). Computers, voices, and sources of messages: computers are social actors. *Human Communication Research, 19*(4), 504-527.

Norman, D. A. (1994). How might people interact with agents? *Communications of the ACM, 37*(7), 68-71.

Norman, D. A. (1997). How might people interact with agents. In J. M. Bradshaw (Ed.), *Software agents* (pp. 49-55). Menlo Park, CA: MIT Press.

Passig, D., & Levin, H. (2000). Gender preferences for multimedia interfaces. *Journal of Computer Assisted Learning, 16*(1), 64-71.

Persson, P., Laaksolahti, J., & Lonnqvist, P. (2002). Understanding social intelligence. In K. Dautenhahn, A. H. Bond, L. Canamero & B. Edmonds (Eds.), *Socially intelligent agents: Creating relationships with computers and robots*. Norwell, MA: Kluwer Academic Publishers.

Piaget, J. (1962). *Play, dreams, and imitation in childhood*. New York: Norton.

Piaget, L. (1995). *Sociological studies* (I. Smith, Trans. 2nd ed.). New York: Routledge.

Picard, R. (1997). *Affective Computing*. Cambridge: The MIT Press.

Reeves, B., & Nass, C. (1996). *The Media Equation: How people treat computers, television, and new media like real people and places*. Cambridge: Cambridge University Press.

Rizzo, P. (2000). Why should agents be emotional for entertaining users? A critical analysis. In A. M. Paiva (Ed.), *Affective interaction: Towards a new generation of computer interfaces* (pp. 166-181). Berlin: Springer-Verlag.

Roth, W.-M. (2001). Gestures: their role in teaching and learning. *Review of Educational Research, 71*(3), 365-392.

Saarni, C. (2001). Emotion communication and relationship context. *International Journal of Behavioral Development, 25*(4), 354-356.

Schunk, D. H. (1989). Social cognitive theory and self-regulated learning. In B. J. Zimmerman & D. H. Schunk (Eds.), *Self-regulated learning and academic achievement: Theory, research, and practice* (pp. 83-110). New York: Springer-Verlag.

Vassileva, J. (1998). *Goal-based autonomous social agents: Supporting adaptation and teaching in a distributed environment*. Paper presented at the 4th International Conference of ITS 98, San Antonio, TX.

Vygotsky, L. S., Cole, M., John-Steiner, V., Scribner, S., & Souberman, E. (1978). *Mind in society*. Cambridge, Massachusetts: Harvard University Press.

Zimmerman, B. J. (2000). Attaining self-regulation: A social cognitive perspective. In M. Boekaerts, P. Pintrich & M. Zeidner (Eds.), Self-Regulation: Theory, Research and Application (pp. 13-39). Orlando, FL: Academic Press.

Designing Empathic Agents: Adults Versus Kids

Lynne Hall[1], Sarah Woods[2], Kerstin Dautenhahn[2], Daniel Sobral[3], Ana Paiva[3], Dieter Wolke[4], and Lynne Newall[5]

[1] School of Computing & Technology, University of Sunderland, UK,
lynne.hall@sunderland.ac.uk

[2] Adaptive Systems Research Group, University of Hertfordshire, UK, s.n.woods,
k.dautenhahn@herts.ac.uk

[3] Instituto Superior Technico & INESC-ID, Porto Salvo, Portugal
ana.paiva@inesc-id.pt

[4]Jacobs Foundation, Zurich, Switzerland, dieter.wolke@jacobsfoundation.org

[5]Northumbria University, Newcastle, UK, lynne.newell@unn.ac.uk

Abstract. An evaluation study of a Virtual Learning Environment populated by synthetic characters for children to explore issues surrounding bullying behaviour is presented. This 225 participant evaluation was carried out with three stakeholder groups, (children, teachers and experts) to examine their attitudes and empathic styles about the characters and storyline believability. Results revealed that children expressed the most favourable views towards the characters and the highest levels of believability towards the bullying storyline. Children were more likely to have an empathic response than adults and found the synthetic characters more realistic and true-to-life.

1 Introduction

Virtual Learning Environments (VLEs) populated with animated characters offer children a safe environment where they can explore and learn through experiential activities [5, 8]. Animated characters offer a high level of engagement, through their use of expressive and emotional behaviours [6], making them intuitively applicable for exploring personal and social issues. However, the design and implementation of VLEs populated with animated characters are complex tasks, involving an iterative development process with a range of stakeholders.

The VICTEC (Virtual ICT with Empathic Characters) project uses synthetic characters and Emergent Narrative as an innovative means for children aged 8-12 years to explore issues surrounding bullying behaviour. FearNot (Fun with Empathic Agents to Reach Novel Outcomes in Teaching), the application being developed in VICTEC, is a 3D VLE featuring a school populated by 3-D self-animated agents representing various character roles involved in bullying behaviour through improvised dramas.

The main focus of this paper is to consider the different perspectives and empathic reactions of adult and child populations in order to optimise the design and ultimately usage of a virtual world to tackle bullying problems. The perspective that we have taken is that if children empathise with characters a deeper exploration and understanding of bullying issues is possible [3]. Whilst it is less critical for other stakeholder groups, such as teachers, to exhibit similar empathic reactions to children,

J.C. Lester et al. (Eds.): ITS 2004, LNCS 3220, pp. 604–613, 2004.

the level of empathy and its impact on agent believability [9] has strong implications for teacher's usage of such applications for classroom-based teaching. As relatively few teachers have exposure to sophisticated, innovative educational environments they may have inappropriately low or high expectations of an unknown technology. To offer an alternative perspective, the views and empathic reactions of discipline-specific experts were also obtained to enable us to gain the view of stakeholders who were "early adopters" of VLEs and synthetic characters.

The main questions we are seeking to answer in this paper are: Are there differences in the views, opinions and attitudes of children and adults? And, if there are differences, what are their design implications? In the first section we discuss development and technical issues for our early prototype. In the second section we discuss our approach to using this prototype. We then present the results and discuss our findings.

2 FearNot: Technical and Development Issues

FearNot is an interactive 3D environment that allows children to interact and influence the events happening in a story featuring bullying scenarios.

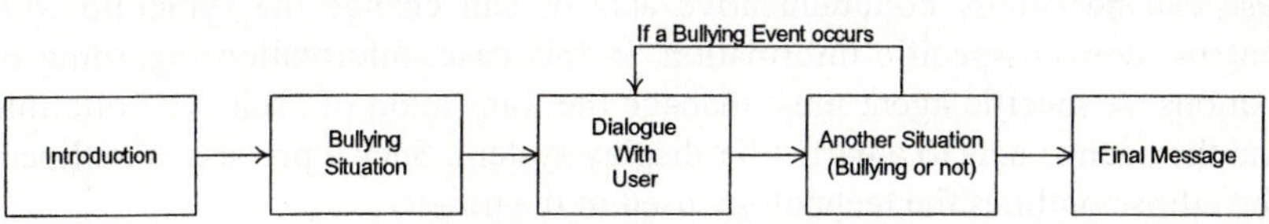

Fig. 1. Interacting with FearNot

Fig. 1. presents a schematic view of the episodes of an interaction with FearNot. After each of these, the victim starts a dialogue probing for user help. This dialogue concludes with the selection of a coping strategy which influences the course of the events in the episodes ahead. The episodes are not pre-scripted, and arise from the actions of the characters in the story that act autonomously, performing their roles in character (as a bully, a victim, a bystander or a bully-victim).

2.1 The FearNot Trailer Approach

Fig. 1. identifies how interaction will occur with the final version of FearNot. However, we needed to gain feedback from users and stakeholders at an early stage in the lifecycle when there was no stable version of the final product and where development emerges as a response to research findings. Recognising this as an issue early in the design of FearNot prompted the creation of the trailer approach which is a snapshot vision of the final product, similar to the trailers seen for movies, where the major themes of a film are revealed. Also similar to a movie trailer using real movie clips, our trailer used a technology closely resembling the final application.

The trailer depicts a physical bullying episode containing 3 characters, Luke the bully, John the victim and Martina the narrator. The trailer begins with an introduction to the main characters, Luke and John and subsequently shows Luke knocking John's pencil case off the table and then kicking him to the floor. John then asks the user what he should do to try and stop Luke bullying him and arrives at 3 possible choices: 1) Ignore Luke, 2) Fight back, 3) Tell someone that he trusts such as his teacher or parents.

Developmental constraints of the application did not allow us to include the dialogue phase in the first trailer developed. Nonetheless, the importance of the dialogue phase for the overall success of the application required us to include it. As an advance, we built a dialogue phase between the bullying situation and the final message. We are using the Wizard of OZ technique [1] to iterate on our dialogue system and adjust the user interaction during this stage.

2.2 Re-using the Trailer Technology for FearNot

The re-use of the trailer technology in the final application is possible due to the agent-based approach [14] we adopted for the FearNot application, as depicted in Fig. 2. Several Agents share a virtual symbolic world where they can perform high-level acts. These can be simply communicative acts or can change the symbolic world, which contains domain-specific information, in this case, information regarding bullying situations. A specific agent must manage the translation of such symbolic information and the agents' acts to a particular display system. Such a process is outlined in Fig. 2. (the ellipse outlines the technology used in the trailer).

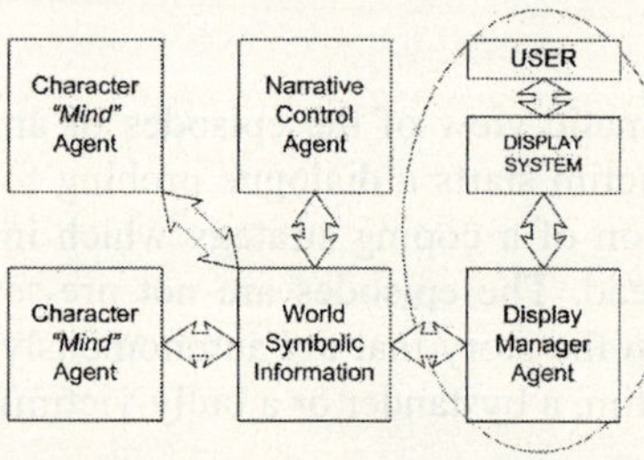

Fig. 2. FearNot Agent-Based Approach

Popular approaches to implementing environments with self-animated characters suffer from being too low-level (e.g. [4]), solely focusing on a realistic display of character behaviour and directly connecting character architecture and display system. Although PAR [2] constitutes an example of a higher-level approach, this is a humanoid-dependent language and too complex for our needs. Flexible Improv [7] systems are becoming the de facto standards in the field, however, current implementations make it impossible to achieve rich high-level character behaviour. Therefore, the approach we have chosen has two different levels: 1) the higher-level act and 2) the lower-level view-action (which then renders to a specific display system).

The modular agent-based approach enables us to work in parallel on components. Whilst defining the act ontology which coordinates agent communication, we were able to focus on the lower-level graphical language definition that was used to implement the trailer. This consists of a scripted sequence of view-actions, depicting the situation and emulating the character acts. For this approach to integrate high-level acts and low level view-actions we assumed a simple trailer-bounded ad-hoc high-level language. Yet, the trailer served equally as a validating tool for our approach.

The trailer was implemented as a Java applet running inside a browser, as demonstrated in Fig. 3. A simple View Manager was developed which emulated character acts and ran a sequence of view actions to a display system, implemented with the use of a proprietary game engine. These provide excellent tools for prototyping, and were sufficiently stable and robust to fully implement the FearNot application. The view action language aims to minimize the effort required to change other displays.

Fig. 3. A screenshot of the FearNot Trailer, Displaying a Physical Bullying Situation.

3 The Trailer Experiment

The trailer was evaluated using a questionnaire applicable for children and adults and focused on character attributes (voice believability, likeableness, conversation content, movement) storyline (believability), character preferences and empathy (sorrow and anger). Measurement was predominantly by a 5 point Likert scale.

225 trailer questionnaires were completed by 128 children from schools in England and Portugal (57%), 54 experts (24%) and 43 teachers / educationalists (19%). Table 1 illustrates the gender and age distribution of the sample.

Table 1. Gender and Age Distribution of the Sample

Gender / Age	Frequency	%
Male child	64	29
Female child	63	28
Male adult	49	22
Female adult	46	21

Teachers in the sample were from a wide range of primary and secondary schools in the South of England. They were predominantly female (90%), aged between 25 to 56. The children, aged from 8-13 (x=9.83, SD=1.04), were from primary schools located in urban and rural areas of Hertfordshire, UK (47%) and Cascais, Portugal (53%). The experts were attendees at the Intelligent Virtual Agents workshop in Kloster Irsee, Germany and were predominantly male (80%) and under 35 (67%). Table 2 illustrates the procedure used for showing the FearNot trailer and completion of the trailer questionnaire.

Table 2. FearNot Demonstration and Questionnaire Completion

Sample	Procedure
Experts	Trailer shown and questionnaire explained to whole audience. Completed as part of conference workshop.
Teachers	Trailer shown and questionnaire explained to whole audience and completed as part of a teacher workshop, Germany, and a teacher seminar, Bristol, UK.
Children	Trailer shown and questionnaire distributed to all children. The questionnaire was explained to the whole class and the researcher then guided the children through each question ensuring that they understood each question.

4 Results

Frequency distributions were examined using histograms for questions that employed Likert scales to ensure that the data was normally distributed. Chi-square tests in the form of cross-tabulations were calculated to determine relationships between different variables for categorical data. One way analysis of variance (ANOVA) using Scheffe's post-hoc test were carried out to examine mean differences between the 3 stakeholder groups according to questionnaire responses using the Likert scale.

4.1 Character Attributes

There were significant differences between the stakeholder groups and views of the believability (F=6.16, (225, df=2), p=0.002), realism F=9.16, (225, df=2), p=0.00) and smoothness (F=12.96, (224, df=2), p=0.00) of character movement with children finding character movement more believable, realistic and smooth compared to adults, see table 3. No significant gender differences were revealed for the believability or smoothness of character movement. An independent samples T-test revealed significant gender differences for the realism of character movement (t=2.91, 225, df=220, p=0.004). Females (m=3.17) found character movement significantly more realistic than males (m=3.63).

Significant differences were found for the believability (F=11.82, (224, df=2), p=0.00) and likeability (F=9.35, (221, df=2), p=0.00) of character voices, with teachers finding voices less believable and likeable. An independent samples T-test revealed significant differences between gender and believability of voices (t=-2.65, 221, df = 219, p=0.01). Females (m=2.53) found the character voices less believable than males (m=2.15).

Table 3. Mean Group Values for Character Movement

Mean values for character movement (1 = positive, 5 = negative)	Child	Teacher	Expert
Believable	3.04	3.77	3.31
Realistic	3.11	3.81	3.76
Smooth	2.82	3.88	3.17

4.2 Storyline

No significant differences were found between children, teachers and experts or gender for the believability of character conversation and interest levels of character conversation. Significant differences were found in the views of the storyline believability (F=10.17, (224, df=2), p=0.00) and the true-to-lifeness of both the character conversation (F=6.45, (223, df=2), p=0.002) and the storyline (F=14.08, (225, df=2), p=0.00), with children finding the conversation and storyline more true to life and believable.

There were significant differences between child, expert and teacher views in relation to the match between the school environment and the characters (F=10.40, (220, df=2), p=0.00). Children were significantly more positive towards the match between the school environment and characters compared to teachers (Fig. 4.). Children were also more positive about the School appearance (F=22.08, (224, df=2), p=0.00)

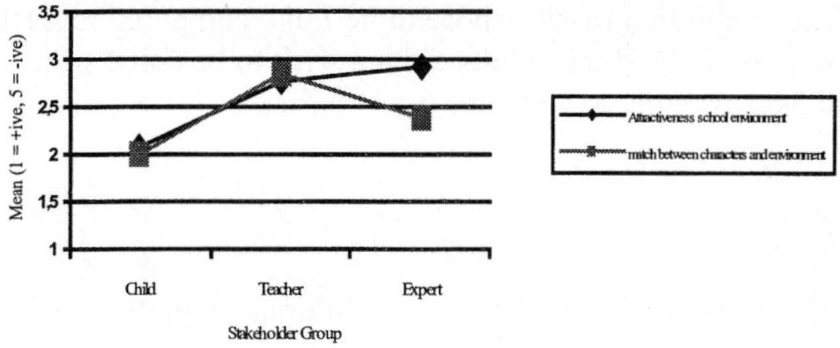

Fig. 4. Mean Group Differences for the Attractiveness of the Virtual School Environment and the Match between Characters and the School Environment.

4.3 Character Preferences

Significant gender differences were found for children only when character preference was considered, (x=20.46, N=195, df = 2, p=0.000) indicating no overall gender preferences for John (the victim) but that significantly more female children preferred

Martina (the narrator), and significantly more male children preferred Luke (the bully).

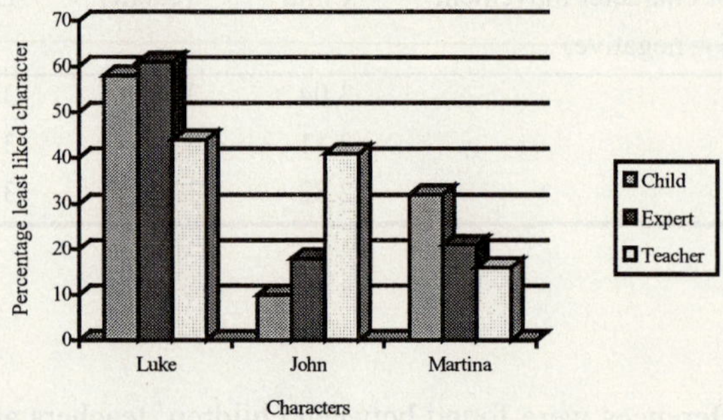

Fig. 5. Percentages for Least Liked Characters According to Children, Experts and Teachers.

Significant differences were revealed between teachers, children and experts for the least liked character (x=18.35, N=201, DF=4, p=0.001) (Fig. 5). Significantly more teachers least liked John (the victim), compared to children and experts. Female adults disliked John (the victim) more than children and experts (37%), and male children disliked Martina the most (52%). 78% of female children disliked Luke the most closely followed by the male adults, 60% of whom disliked Luke the most.

There were no significant differences between children, teachers and experts in which of the characters they would like to be. However, significant differences emerged when gender and age were taken into account. 40% of male children chose to be John and 88% of female children, followed by 73% of female adults chose to be Martina. No female children (n=59) chose to be Luke compared to 44% of male children who chose to be Luke. Male adults did not wish to be John, with 51% wishing to be Martina and 34% wanting to be Luke.

4.4 Empathy

Significant differences were found between children, experts and teachers for expressing sorrow (x=10.33, N=216, df=2, p=0.006) and anger (x=26.13, N=213, df=2, p=0.000). Children were most likely to feel sorry or angry, see table 4, however, whilst most children felt sorry for the victim, significantly more experts felt sorry for Luke (the bully) compared to teachers and children (x=13.60, N=175, df = 2, p=0.001). Significant age and gender differences emerged, (x=27.42, N=210, df=3, p=0.000) where more female children expressed anger towards the characters compared to adults. This anger was almost exclusively directed at Luke (90%).

Table 4. Empathic Responses to Characters

	Luke (Bully)	John (Victim)	Martina (Narrator)
% Felt sorry for characters			
Child	5.0	95.0	0.0
Expert	27.0	74.0	0.0
Teacher	7.0	93.0	0.0
% anger towards characters			
Child	85.0	13.0	2.0
Expert	70.0	30.0	0.0
Teacher	73.0	9.0	18.0

5 Discussion

The main aims of this paper were to consider whether there were any differences in the opinions, attitudes and empathic reactions of children and adults towards FearNot, and whether differences uncovered offer important design implications for VLEs addressing complex social issues such as bullying.

A summary of the main results revealed that (1) Children were more favourable towards the appearance of the school environment, character voices, and character movement compared to teachers who viewed these aspects less positively. (2) Children, particularly male children found the conversation and storyline most believable, realistic and true-to-life. (3) No significant differences were revealed between children and adults for most-liked character, although teachers disliked 'John' the victim character the most compared to children and experts. (4) Children preferred same-gender children, with male characters disliking the female narrator character; female children disliking the male bully; and children choosing to be same-gender characters. (5) Children, particularly females, expressed more empathic reactions (feeling sorry and/or angry for the characters) compared to adults.

Throughout the results, a recurrent finding was the more positive attitude and perspective of children towards the FearNot trailer in terms of the school environment, character appearance, character movement, conversation between the characters and engagement with the storyline. Children's views expressed were typically within the positive range under 3 (scale 1 to 5). Children's engagement and high level of empathic reactions to the trailer are encouraging as they indicate the potential for experiential learning with children clearly having a high level of belief and comprehension of a physical virtual bullying scenario.

The opposite trend seems to have emerged from the teacher responses, where teachers clearly have high expectations that are not met or possibly are unable to engage effectively with such a novel system such as FearNot. Experts were positive about the technical issues of FearNot such as the physical representation of the characters. However, they failed to engage with the educational theme of bullying and applied generic criteria ignoring the underlying domain. Thus, whilst character movement and voices were rated highly, limited levels of empathy were seen with experts taking a somewhat voyeuristic approach.

We consider that self-animated characters bring richness to the interaction essential to obtain believable interactions. Nevertheless, danger of unbelievable "schizophrenic" behaviour [10] is real, and enormous technical challenges emerge. To overcome these, constant interaction between agent developers and psychologists is crucial. Furthermore, the use of a higher-level narrative control arises as another technical challenge that is being explored, towards the achievement of story coherence that characters are ineffective, on their own, to attain. The use of a cartoon style offers a technical safety net that hinders some jerkiness natural to experimental software. Furthermore, the cartoon metaphor already provides design decisions that most cartoon-viewing children accept naturally.

6 Conclusion

The trailer approach described in this paper enabled us to obtain a range of viewpoints and perspectives from different stakeholder groups. Further, the re-use of the technology for the trailer within the final application highlights the benefits of adopting an agent-based approach, allowing the development of a mid-tech prototype that can evolve into the final application. Input from a range of stakeholders is essential for the development of an appropriate application. There must be a balance between true to life and acceptable (by teachers and parents) behaviours and language. The use of stereotypical roles (e.g. typical bully) can bias children's understanding and simple design decisions can influence the children's perception of a character (e.g., Luke looks a lot "cooler" than John). The educational perspective inhibits the applicability of the «game» label to the application, which most of the time children instantly apply to an application like this. Achieving a balance between the expectations of all stakeholders involved may be the hardest goal to achieve over and above technical challenges.

References

1. Anderson, G., Höök, K., Paiva, A., & Costa, M. (2002). Using a Wizard of Oz study to inform the design of SenToy. Paper presented at the Designing Interactive Systems.
2. Badler, N., Philips, C., & Webber, B. (1993). Simulating humans. Paper presented at the Computer graphics animation and control, New York.
3. Dautenhahn, K. (2002). Design spaces and niche spaces of believable social robots. Paper presented at the International Workshop on Robots and Human Interactive Communication.
4. Magnenat-Thalmann, N., & Thalmann, D. (1991). Complex models for animating synthetic actors. Computer Graphics and Applications, 11, 32-44.
5. Moreno, R., Mayer, R. E., Spires, H. A., & Lester, J. C. (2001). The Case for Social Agency in Computer-Based Teaching: Do Students Learn More Deeply When They Interact With Animated Pedagogical Agents. Cognition and Instruction, 19(2), 177-213.

6. Nass, C., Isbister, K., & Lee, E. (2001). Truth is beauty: researching embodied conversational agents. Cambridge, MA: MIT Press.
7. Perlin, K., & Goldberg, A. (1996). Improv: A system for scripting interactive actors in virtual worlds. Paper presented at the Computer Graphics, 30 (Annual Conference Series).
8. Pertaub, D.-P., Slater, M., & Barker, C. (2001). An Experiment on Public Speaking Anxiety in Response to Three Different Types of Virtual Audience. Presence: Teleoperators and Virtual Environments,, 11(1), 68-78.
9. Prendinger, H., & Ishizuka, M. (2001). Let's talk! Socially intelligent agents for language conversation training. IEEE Transactions on Systems, Man, and Cybernetics - Part A: Systems and Humans, 31(5), 465-471.
10. Sengers, P. (1998). Anti-Boxology: Agent Design in Cultural Context. PhD Thesis, Technical Report CMU-CS-98-151, Carnegie Mellon University.
11. Wooldridge, M. (2002). An Introduction to Multiagent Systems. London: John Wiley and Sons Ltd.

RMT: A Dialog-Based Research Methods Tutor With or Without a Head

Peter Wiemer-Hastings[1], David Allbritton[2], and Elizabeth Arnott[2]

[1] School of Computer Science, Telecommunications, and Information Systems
peterwh@cs.depaul.edu
[2] Department of Psychology {dallbrit|earnott}@depaul.edu
DePaul University
243 South Wabash Avenue
Chicago, Illinois, 60604, USA

Abstract. RMT (Research Methods Tutor) is a dialog-based tutoring system that has a dual role. Its modular architecture enables the interchange and evaluation of different tools and techniques for improving tutoring. In addition to its research goals, the system is intended to be integrated as a regular component of a term-long Research Methods in Psychology course. Despite the significant technical challenges, this may help reduce our knowledge gap about how such systems can help students with long-term use. In this paper, we describe the RMT architecture and give the results of an initial experiment that compared RMT's animated agent "talking head" with a text-only version of the system.

1 Introduction

Research on human to human tutoring has identified one primary factor that influences learning: the cooperative solving of example problems [1]. Typically, a tutor poses a problem (selected from a relatively small set of problems that they frequently use), and gives it to the student. The student attempts to solve the problem, one piece at a time. The tutor gives feedback, but rarely gives direct negative feedback. The tutor uses pumps (e.g. "Go on."), hints, and prompts (e.g. "The groups would be chosen ...") to keep the interaction going. The student and tutor incrementally piece together a solution for the problem. Then the tutor often offers a summary of the final solution [1]. This model of tutoring has been adopted by a number of recent dialog-based intelligent tutoring systems.

Understanding natural language student responses has been a major challenge for ITS's. Approaches have ranged from encouraging one-word answers [2] to full syntactic and semantic analysis of the responses [3,4,5]. Unfortunately, it can take man-years of effort to develop the specialized lexical, syntactic, and conceptual knowledge to make such language-analysis successful which limits how far these approaches can spread.

The AutoTutor system took a different approach to the natural language processing problem. AutoTutor uses a mechanism called Latent Semantic Analysis (LSA, described more completely below) which is automatically derived from

J.C. Lester et al. (Eds.): ITS 2004, LNCS 3220, pp. 614–623, 2004.

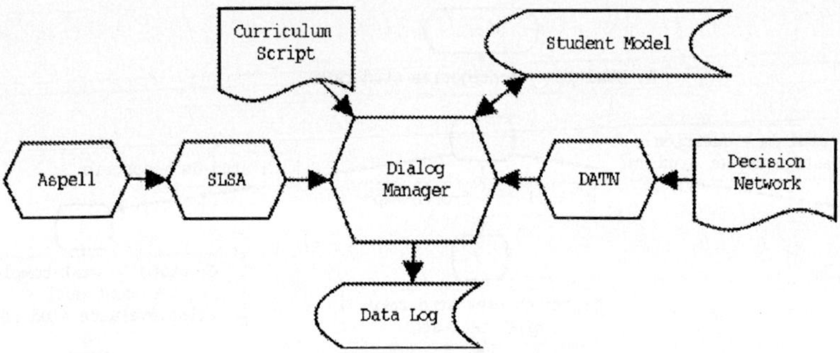

Fig. 1. RMT Architecture

a large corpus of texts, and which gives an approximate but useful similarity metric between any two texts [6]. Student answers are evaluated by comparing them to a set of expected answers with LSA. This greatly reduces the knowledge acquisition bottleneck for tutoring systems. AutoTutor's tutoring style is modeled on human tutors. It maintains only a simple model of the student, and uses the same dialog moves mentioned above (prompts and pumps, for example) to do constructive, collaborative problem solving with the student. AutoTutor has been shown to produce learning gains of approximately one standard deviation unit compared to reading a textbook [7], been ported to a number of domains, and has been integrated with another tutoring system: Why/AutoTutor [7].

This paper describes RMT (Research Methods Tutor) which is a descendant of the AutoTutor system. RMT uses the same basic tutoring style that AutoTutor does, but was developed with a modular architecture to facilitate the study of different tools and techniques for dialog-based tutoring. One primary goal of the project is to create a system which can be integrated into the Research Methods in Psychology classes at DePaul University (and potentially elsewhere). We describe here the basic architecture of RMT, our first attempts to integrate it with the courses, and the results of an experiment that compares the use of an animated agent with text-only tutoring.

2 RMT Architecture

As mentioned above, RMT is a close descendant of the AutoTutor system. While AutoTutor incorporates a wide variety of artificial intelligence techniques, RMT was designed as a lightweight, modular system that would incorporate only those techniques required to provide educationally beneficial tutoring to the student. This section gives a brief description of RMT's critical components.

2.1 Dialog Manager

As shown in figure 1, the dialog manager (DM) is the central controller of the system. Because RMT is a web-based system, each tutoring session has its own

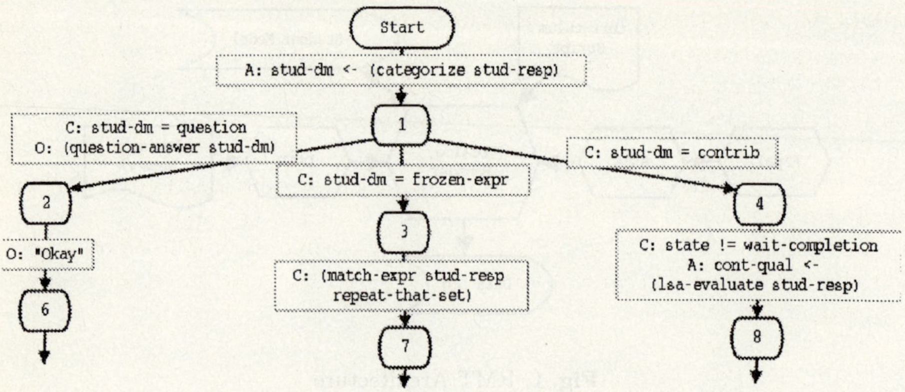

Fig. 2. A partial decision network

dialog manager, and the DM maintains information about the parameters of the tutoring session and the current state of the dialog. The DM reads student responses as posts from a web page, and then asks the Dialog Advancer Transition Network (DATN) to compute an appropriate tutor response.

Each tutor "turn" can perform three different functions: evaluate the student's previous utterance (e.g. "Good!"), confirm or add some additional information (e.g. "The dependent variable is test score."), and produce an utterance that keeps the dialog moving. Like AutoTutor, RMT uses pumps, prompts, and hints to try to get the student to add information about the current topic. RMT also asks questions, summarizes topics, and answers questions.

The DATN determines which type of response the tutor will give using a decision network which graphically depicts the conditions, actions and system outputs. Figure 2 shows a segment of RMT's decision network. For every tutor turn, the DATN begins processing at the Start state. The paths through the network eventually join back up at the Finish state, not shown here. On the arcs, the items marked C are the conditions for that arc to be chosen. The items labeled A are actions that will be performed. For example, on the arc from the start state, the DATN categorizes the student response. The items marked O are outputs — what the tutor will say next. Because this graph-based representation controls utterance selection, the tutor's behavior can be modified by simply modifying the graph.

2.2 Understanding Student Contributions

RMT uses Latent Semantic Analysis (LSA) to evaluate student contributions. LSA was first developed for information retrieval — selecting query-relevant texts from a database. LSA has also been shown to perform well at finding synonyms, suggesting appropriate texts for students to read, and even grading student essays [8]. AutoTutor was the first system to use LSA to "understand" student responses in an interactive tutoring system [6], and it has subsequently been incorporated or evaluated for use by several other systems [3,2, for example].

LSA evaluates a student response by comparing it to a set of expected answers. This works well in the tutoring setting because the tutor asks most of the questions and knows what types of answers (good and bad) the student is likely to produce. Due to space constraints, a complete description of LSA in a tutoring task is not included here. For more detail, please see [6]. One current research direction in the RMT project is to explore different applications of LSA, including segmenting input sentences into subject, verb, and object parts and comparing each separately.

2.3 Additional Functionality

Logging. For data collection purposes, RMT borrows a piece of wisdom from a very successful reading tutor called Project LISTEN, "Log everything" [9]. As it interacts with a student, RMT stores information about each interaction in a database. The database collects and relates the individual utterances and a variety of other variables, for example, the type and quality of a student response. The database also contains information about the students and the tutoring conditions that they are assigned to. Thus, in addition to providing data for the experiments described below, we will be able to perform *post hoc* analyses by selecting relevant tutoring topics. (For example, "Is there a difference in student response quality on Mondays and Fridays?")

Talking Heads. As AutoTutor does, RMT uses an animated agent with synthesized speech to present the tutor's utterances to the student. In principle, this allows the system to use multiple modes of communication to deliver a richer message. For example, the tutor can avoid face-threatening direct negative feedback, but still communicate doubt about an answer with a general word like "Well" with the proper intonation. Furthermore, in relation to text-only tutoring, the student is more likely to "get the whole message" because they can not simply skim over the text.

Curriculum Script. A number of studies have shown that human tutors use a "curriculum script", or a rich set of topics which they plan to cover during a tutoring session [1]. RMT's curriculum script serves the same function. It is the repository of the system's knowledge about the tutoring domain. In particular, it contains the topics that can be covered, the questions that the tutor can ask, the answers that it expects it might get from the students, and a variety of dialog moves to keep the discourse going. RMT's curriculum script currently contains approximately 2500 items in 5 topics. We believe that this gives us a reasonable starting point for using the tutoring system throughout a significant portion of a quarter-long class.

2.4 Pilot Testing and Results

We are currently preparing RMT for full-scale introduction into research methods classes at DePaul University. In Fall, 2003, we performed a pilot test of the system to ensure that there were no major glitches with it, that students would understand how to interact with it using a web browser, and to determine student attitudes toward the system.

Three versions of RMT were pilot tested with 26 volunteers enrolled in Introductory Psychology: a text-only interface (N = 8) and two versions using synthesized speech with animated agents, "Merlin" (N = 9) and "Miyako" (N = 9). Merlin is a cartoon-like character with many animations. Miyako is more human-like figure, but has limited movement. Each student completed one module on the topic of research validity, then answered both open-ended and Likert-scaled questions about the tutor interface, tutorial content, and tutor effectiveness.

Student responses to open-ended questions included positive comments about several specific aspects of the tutor's pedagogical design, including: the feedback the tutor provided about their answers; receiving hints and prompts that lead the student to the right answer; and having multiple chances to provide the correct answer to a question.

Although the pilot data does not speak to the actual effectiveness of the tutor in terms of objective measures of student learning, we did obtain student ratings of the effectiveness of both the curriculum script content and the tutor as a whole. The three conditions (text-only, Merlin, Miyako) did not differ in students' ratings of the tutorial content, but did differ in ratings of overall tutor effectiveness. On six-point scales, students indicated they expected to learn more from the text-only version of the tutor (mean = 2.5) than from the Merlin (mean = 3.7, $p = 0.09$ by LSD paired comparisons) or Miyako (mean = 3.9, $p < .05$) versions. As found in [10], these results suggest that more research is needed in the area of likeability and pedagogical effectiveness of agents.

In Winter Term 2004, we made the system available to the students in the research methods classes for the first time. The delivered system used the Miyako agent instead of Merlin because we were concerned that the students would not take the cartoonish Merlin character seriously. We used a different speech engine (Lernout & Hauspie British English) because it produced less irritating speech. Approximately 100 students signed up to voluntarily use the system. Unfortunately, they had to wait to use the system for about a week after they signed up while we registered them with the system. We believe that that delay along with the lack of any overt incentive for the students to use the system led to a disappointing outcome: only 6 students ever logged into the system even one time. In the Spring term, we offered extra credit to students who used the system, and 4 students completed all the requirements. In the future we plan to integrate the tutoring system more closely with the curriculum and have the teachers be more involved in promoting the system. In the next section, we present the results of a study that we performed using Intro Psych subject pool participants.

3 Experiment

Our design was a 2 x 2 factorial, with agent (the Miyako head vs. text only) and task version (traditional tutoring task vs. simulated employment as a research assistant, described in more detail below) as between-subjects factors. Students were randomly assigned to the conditions except that participation in the agent conditions required the ability to install software on their Windows-based computer. As a result, more students interacted with the text-only presentation rather than the Miyako animated agent. 101 participants took the pretest. 23 were assigned to the "Miyako" agent, 78 to text-only presentation. 59 were assigned to the research assistant task version, and 42 to the tutor task version.

Each participant had one or two modules available (experimental design, reliability) to be completed.[1] We first reviewed the transcripts to code whether each participant had completed each module. We discarded data from participants who were non-responsive or who had technical difficulties.

Many students appeared to have difficulty installing the speech and agent software and getting it to work properly. A 2 x 2 between-subjects ANOVA comparing the number of modules completed (0, 1 or 2) for the four conditions in the study also suggested that there were significant technical issues with the agent software. Although there was no significant difference in the number of modules completed by participants in the two task versions (RA = .69; tutor = .81 modules completed), participants in the Miyako agent condition completed significantly fewer modules (.47) than those in the text-only condition (1.0), $F(1,97) = 8.57, p < .01$.

Our primary dependent measure was gain score, defined as the difference between the number correct on a 40-question multiple-choice post-test and an identical pre-test. All analyses of gain scores included pre-test score as a covariate, an analysis which is functionally equivalent to analyzing post-test scores with pre-test scores as a covariate [11].

We first examined whether completion of the tutor modules was associated with greater gain scores compared to students who took the pre- and post-tests but did not successfully complete the modules. Of the 75 participants who completed both the pre-test and the post-test, 28 completed both modules, 26 completed one module, and 21 did not satisfactorily complete either module before taking the post-test. In a one-way ANCOVA, gain scores were analyzed with number of modules completed as the independent variable and pre-test score as the covariate. The main effect of number of modules was significant, $F(2,71) - 9.50, p < .001$. Although the mean pre-test to post-test gain score for those completing two modules (4.4 on a 40-item multiple-choice test) was greater than that for those who completed no modules (2.4), participants who completed only one module showed no gain at all (gain = -.3). Only the difference between the mean gain for one module (-.3) versus 2 modules (4.4) was statistically significant, as indicated by non-overlapping 95% confidence intervals.

[1] One week into the experiment, we found that students were completing the first topic too quickly, so we added another.

Breaking down the effects on gain scores for each of the two modules, it appeared that the "reliability" module significantly improved learning, but the "experimental design" module did not. Students who completed the reliability module had higher gain scores (4.4) than those who did not (0.9), and this difference was significant in an ANCOVA in which pre-test score was entered as the covariate, $F(1,72) = 14.17, p < .001$. A similar analysis for the experimental design module revealed non-significantly lower gain scores for students who completed the experimental design module than those who did not, with mean gains of 2.1 vs. 2.4 respectively, $F(1,72) < 1$.

The reliability module was considerably longer than the experimental design module, so time on task may be partly responsible for the differences in effectiveness between the two modules.

We next examined the effects of our two primary independent variables, agent and task version, on gain scores. For these analyses we included only participants who had successfully completed at least one module after taking the pre-test and before taking the post-test. Of the 54 participants who completed at least one module, 6 interacted with the Miyako agent and 48 used the text-only interface. Students were more evenly divided between the two task versions, with 25 in the tutor and 29 in the research assistant version.

Gain scores were entered into a 2 x 2 ANCOVA with agent and task version as between-subjects factors and pre-test score as the covariate. Gain scores were greater for students using the text-only interface (mean = 2.6, N = 48) than for those interacting with the Miyako agent (mean = -1.5, N = 6), $F(1,49) = 3.70, p = .06$. Neither the main effect of task version nor the agent * task version interaction was significant, $Fs < 1$.

Because of the low number of participants interacting with the animated agent the effect of agent in the this analysis must be interpreted with caution, but it is consistent with our other findings indicating that students had difficulty with the Miyako agent. We suspect that technical difficulties may have been largely responsible.

4 Discussion

In this section, we describe some of the aspects of the system that may have contributed to the results of the experiment. In particular, we look at the the tutoring modules that were used, the animated agent, and the task version.

Modules. We initially included only one module in the experiment because we thought it would take the participants somewhere between 30 and 60 minutes to complete it. We chose the "experimental design" module because we thought it would be accessible to intro psych students. Because we added the second module, "reliability", partway through the experiment and because the two modules are significantly different, we can not say whether the gain difference for the number of modules completed was caused by the amount of interaction with the tutor, or due to some effects of the particular modules.

It could also be the case that the subject pool students had enough familiarity with the experimental design material that they performed better on the pretest, and therefore had less opportunity for gain.

The Agent. There were two significant weakness of the agent used here that may have affected our results. First, there may have been software installation difficulties. The participants were using the system on their own computers in their homes, and had to install the agent software if they were assigned to the agents version. The underlying agent technology that we used, Microsoft Agents, requires three programs to be installed from a Microsoft server. The participants could have had difficulty following the instructions for downloading the software or could have been nervous about installing software that they did not search out for themselves.

Second, the particular animated agent that we used was rather limited. A good talking head should be able not just to tap into the social dynamics present between a human tutor and student, but also provide an additional modality of communication: prosody. In particular, human tutors are known to avoid giving explicit negative feedback because that could cause the student to "lose face" and make her nervous about offering further answers. Instead, human tutors tend to respond to poor student answers with vague verbal feedback ("well" or "okay") accompanied by intonation that makes it clear that the answer could have been better [12].

Unfortunately, the agent that we used was essentially a shareware agent that had good basic graphics, but relatively no additional animations that might display the tutor's affect that goes along with the verbal feedback. Furthermore, the text-to-speech synthesizer that we used (Lernout & Hauspie British English) was relatively comprehensible, but we have not yet tackled the difficult task of trying to make the speech engine produce the type of prosodic contours that human tutors use. Thus, all of the tutor utterances are offered in a relatively detached, stoic conversational style.

Despite these limitations, we had hypothesized that the agent version would have an advantage over text-only for at least one reason: in the text-only version, the students might well just scan over the feedback text to find the next question. With audio feedback, the student is essentially forced to listen to the entire feedback and question before entering the next response. Of course, this may have also contributed to the lower completion rate of students in the agent version because they may have become frustrated by the relatively slow pace of presentation of the agent's synthesized speech.

Task Version. As mentioned above, we tested two different task versions, the traditional tutor and a simulated research assistant condition. In the former, the tutor poses questions,[2] the student types in an answer, and the dialog continues with both parties contributing further information until a relatively complete

[2] As in human-human tutoring, students may ask questions, but rarely do [12].

answer has been given. In the research assistant condition, the basic "rules of the game" are the same with one subtle, but potentially significant difference: instead of a tutor, the system is assuming the role of an employer who has hired the student to work on a research project. As previous research has shown, putting students into an authentic functional role — even when it is simulated — can greatly increase their motivation to perform the task, and thereby also increase their learning [13].

Unfortunately, in the current version of RMT, our simulation of the research advisor role is rather minimal. The only difference is in the initial "introduction" that the agent gives to the student. In the traditional tutor condition, the agent (or text) describes briefly how the tutoring session will progress with the student typing their responses into the browser window. In the research assistant version, the agent starts with an introduction that is intended to establish the social relationship between the research supervisor and student/research assistant. Unfortunately, there are no continuing cues to enforce this relationship. We intend to develop this aspect of the system further, but for the current evaluation we needed to focus on getting the basic mechanisms of the tutor in place along with the research methods tutoring content.

5 Conclusions

Because RMT is designed to be used in conjunction with classes on an everyday basis, there are obviously significant technical issues to overcome. In addition to the issues mentioned in the previous section, we plan on focusing on the natural language understanding mechanism to incorporate a variety of syntactic and discourse mechanisms in order to improve the system's understanding of the student replies.

We feel that in the long run, this type of system will be shown to be a valuable adjunct to classroom instruction. With a dialog-based tutoring system, the student can interact in a natural way using their own words. The process of constructing responses to the tutor's questions can in itself help the students "firm up the ideas" in their heads. However, it is also clear based on our experience that the tutoring system can not just be offered to the students. It must be an integrated component of the course.

While the results of our current experiment indicate that the use of an animated agent "talking head" does not increase learning (and in fact, appeared to lead to degradation of the students' knowledge), we feel that further research is warranted on this topic. The limitations of our current agent may have interfered with the student's attention to the material under discussion.

In any case, RMT has been shown to help students learn the rather difficult material covered in Psychology research methods classes. As we continue to develop and refine the system, we hope that it can eventually become another standard mechanism for augmenting the students' education.

References

1. Graesser, A.C., Person, N.K., Magliano, J.P.: Collaborative dialogue patterns in naturalistic one-to-one tutoring. Applied Cognitive Psychology **9** (1995) 359–387
2. Glass, M.: Processing language input in the CIRCSIM-tutor intelligent tutoring system. In Moore, J., Redfield, C., Johnson, W., eds.: Artificial Intelligence in Education, Amsterdam, IOS Press (2001) 210–221
3. Rosé, C., Jordan, P., Ringenberg, M., S. Siler and, K.V., Weinstein, A.: Interactive conceptual tutoring in Atlas-Andes. In: Proceedings of AI in Education 2001 Conference. (2001)
4. Aleven, V., Popescu, O., Koedinger, K.R.: Towards tutorial dialog to support self-explanation: Adding natural language understanding to a cognitive tutor. In: Proceedings of the 10th International Conference on Artificial Intelligence in Education. (2001)
5. Zinn, C., Moore, J.D., Core, M.G., Varges, S., Porayska-Pomsta, K.: The be&e tutorial learning environment (beetle). In: Proceedings of the Seventh Workshop on the Semantics and Pragmatics of Dialogue (DiaBruck 2003). (2003) Available at http://www.coli.uni-sb.de/diabruck/.
6. Wiemer-Hastings, P., Graesser, A., Harter, D., the Tutoring Research Group: The foundations and architecture of AutoTutor. In Goettl, B., Halff, H., Redfield, C., Shute, V., eds.: Intelligent Tutoring Systems, Proceedings of the 4th International Conference, Berlin, Springer (1998) 334–343
7. Graesser, A., Jackson, G., Mathews, E., Mitchell, H., Olney, A., Ventura, M., Chipman, P., Franceschetti, D., Hu, X., Louwerse, M., Person, N., TRG: Why/autotutor: A test of learning gains from a physics tutor with natural language dialog. In: Proceedings of the 25th Annual Conference of the Cognitive Science Society, Mahwah, NJ, Erlbaum (2003)
8. Landauer, T.K., Laham, D., Rehder, R., Schreiner, M.E.: How well can passage meaning be derived without using word order? a comparison of Latent Semantic Analysis and humans. In: Proceedings of the 19th Annual Conference of the Cognitive Science Society, Mahwah, NJ, Erlbaum (1997) 412–417
9. Mostow, J., Aist, G.: Evaluating tutors that listen. In Forbus, K., Feltovich, P., eds.: Smart Machines in Education. AAAI Press, Menlo Park, CA (2001) 169–234
10. Moreno, K., Klettke, B., Nibbaragandla, K., Graesser, A.: Perceived characteristics and pedagogical efficacy of animated conversational agents. In Cerri, S., Gouarderes, G., Paraguacu, F., eds.: Proceedings of the 6th Annual Conference on Intelligent Tutoring Systems, Springer (2002) 963–972
11. Werts, C.E., Linn, R.L.: A general linear model for studying growth. Psychological Bulletin **73** (1970) 17–22
12. Person, N.K., Graesser, A.C., Magliano, J.P., Kreuz, R.J.: Inferring what the student knows in one-to-one tutoring: The role of student questions and answers. Learning and Individual Differences **6** (1994) 205–229
13. Schank, R., Neaman, A.: Motivation and failure in educational simulation design. In Forbus, K., Feltovich, P., eds.: Smart machines in education. AAAI Press, Menlo Park, CA (2001) 37–69

Using Knowledge Tracing to Measure Student Reading Proficiencies

Joseph E. Beck[1] and June Sison[2]

[1] Center for Automated Learning and Discovery
[2] Language Technologies Institute
School of Computer Science, Carnegie Mellon University
Pittsburgh, PA 15213. USA.
{joseph.beck, sison}@cs.cmu.edu
Phone: +1 412 268 5726

Abstract. Constructing a student model for language tutors is a challenging task. This paper describes using knowledge tracing to construct a student model of reading proficiency and validates the model. We use speech recognition to assess a student's reading proficiency at a subword level, even though the speech recognizer output is at the level of words. Specifically, we estimate the student's knowledge of 80 letter to sound mappings, such as *ch* making the sound /K/ in "chemistry." At a coarse level, the student model did a better job at estimating reading proficiency for 47.2% of the students than did a standardized test designed for the task. Our model's estimate of the student's knowledge on individual letter to sound mappings is a significant predictor of whether he will ask for help on a particular word. Thus, our student model is able to describe student performance both at a coarse- and at a fine-grain size.

1 Introduction

Project LISTEN's Reading Tutor [8] is an intelligent tutor that listens to students read aloud with the goal of helping them learn how to read English. Target users are students in first through fourth grades (approximately 6- through 9-year olds). Students are shown one sentence (or fragment) at a time, and the Reading Tutor uses speech recognition technology to (try to) determine which words the student has read incorrectly. Much of the Reading Tutor's power comes from allowing children to request help and from detecting some mistakes that students make while reading. It does not have the strong reasoning about the user that distinguishes a classic intelligent tutoring system, although it does base some decisions, such as picking a story at an appropriate level of challenge, on the student's reading proficiency.

We have constructed models that assess a student's overall reading proficiency [2], but have not built a model of the student's performance on various skills in reading. Much of the difficulty comes from the inaccuracies inherent in speech recognition. Providing explicit feedback based only on student performance on one attempt at reading a word is not viable since the accuracy at distinguishing correct from incorrect reading is not high enough [13]. Due to such problems, student modeling has not

J.C. Lester et al. (Eds.): ITS 2004, LNCS 3220, pp. 624–634, 2004.

received as much attention in computer assisted language learning systems as in classic ITS [5], although there are exceptions such as [7].

Our goal is to use speech recognition to reason about students' proficiency at a finer grain-size. Even if it is not possible to provide immediate feedback for student mistakes, it may be possible to collect enough data over time to estimate a student's proficiency at various aspects of reading. Such a result would be helpful for other tutors that use speech input, particularly language tutors. Our approach is to use knowledge tracing to assess student reading skills.

2 Knowledge Tracing

Knowledge tracing [4] is an approach for estimating the probability a student knows a skill given observations of him attempting to perform the skill. First we briefly discuss the parameters used in knowledge tracing, then we describe how to modify the approach to work with speech recognition.

2.1 Parameters in Knowledge Tracing

For each skill in the curriculum, there is a P(k) representing the probability the student knows the skill, and there are also two learning parameters:

- P(L0) is the initial probability a student knows a skill
- P(t) is the probability a student learns a skill given an opportunity

However, student performance is a noisy reflection of his underlying knowledge. Therefore, there are two performance parameters for each skill:

- P(slip) = P(incorrect | know skill), i.e., the probability a student gives an incorrect response even if he has mastered the skill. For example, hastily typing "32" instead of "23."
- P(guess) = P(correct | didn't know skill), i.e. the probability a student manages to generate a correct response even if he has not mastered the skill. For example, a student has a 50% chance of getting a true/false question correct.

When the tutor observes a student respond to a question either correctly or incorrectly, it uses the appropriate skill's performance parameters (to discount guesses and slips) to update its estimate of the student's knowledge. A fuller discussion of knowledge tracing is available in [4].

2.2 Accounting for Speech Recognizer Inaccuracies

Although knowledge tracing updates its estimate of the student's internal knowledge on the basis of observable actions, this approach is problematic with the Reading Tutor since the output of automated speech recognition (ASR) is far from trustworthy. Fig. 1 shows how both student and interface characteristics mediate student performance. In standard knowledge tracing, there is no need for the intermediate nodes or their transitions to the observed student performance. However, since our observations of the student are noisy, we need additional possible transitions. FA stands for the probability of a False Alarm and MD stands for the probability of Miscue Detection. A false alarm is when the student reads a word correctly but the word is rejected by the ASR; a detected miscue is when the student misreads a word and it is scored as incorrect by the ASR. In a perfect environment, FA would be 0 and MD would be 1, and there would therefore be no need for the additional transitions. Overall in the Reading Tutor, FA ≈ 0.04 and MD ≈ 0.25 (only counting cases where the student said some other word, the tutor is much better at scoring silence as incorrectly reading a word).

All we are able to observe is whether the student's response is scored as being correct, and the tutor's estimate of his knowledge. Given these limitations, any path that takes the student from knowing a skill to generating an incorrect response is considered a slip; it does not matter if the student actually slipped, or if his response was observed as incorrect due to a false alarm. Similarly, a guess is any path from the student not knowing the skill to an observed correct performance. Therefore, can define two additional variables slip' and guess' to account for both paths:

slip' = slip * MD + (1-slip) * FA

guess' = guess * (1-FA) + (1-guess) * (1-MD)

Since we expect ASR performance to vary based on the words being read, it is not appropriate to use a constant MD and FA for all words. Therefore, when we observe a slip, while it would be informative to know whether it was caused by the student or the ASR, there is no good way of knowing which is at fault. As a result, we do not try to infer the FA, MD, slip, and guess parameters. Instead, we directly estimate the slip' and guess' parameters for each skill directly from data (see Section 3.4).

For simplicity, we henceforth refer to guess' and slip' and guess and slip. However, note that the semantics of P(slip) and P(guess) change when using knowledge tracing in this manner. These parameters now model both the student and the method for scoring the student's performance. However, the application of knowledge tracing and the updating of student knowledge remain unchanged.

3 Method for Applying Knowledge Tracing

We now describe how we applied knowledge tracing to our data. First we describe the data collected, next we describe the reading skills we modeled, then we describe how to determine which words the student attempted to read, and finally discuss the knowledge tracing parameter estimates.

3.1 Description of Data

Our data come from 284 students who used the Reading Tutor in the 2002-2003 school year. The students using the Reading Tutor were part of a controlled study of learning gains, so were pre- and post-tested on several reading tests. Students were administered the Woodcock Reading Mastery Test [14], the Test of Written Spelling [6], the Gray Oral Reading Test [12], and the Test of Word Reading Efficiency [11]. All of these tests are human administered and scored.

Students' usage ranged from 27 seconds to 29 hours, with a mean of 8.6 hours and a median of 5.9 hours. The 27 seconds of usage was anomalous, as only four other users had less than one hour of usage.

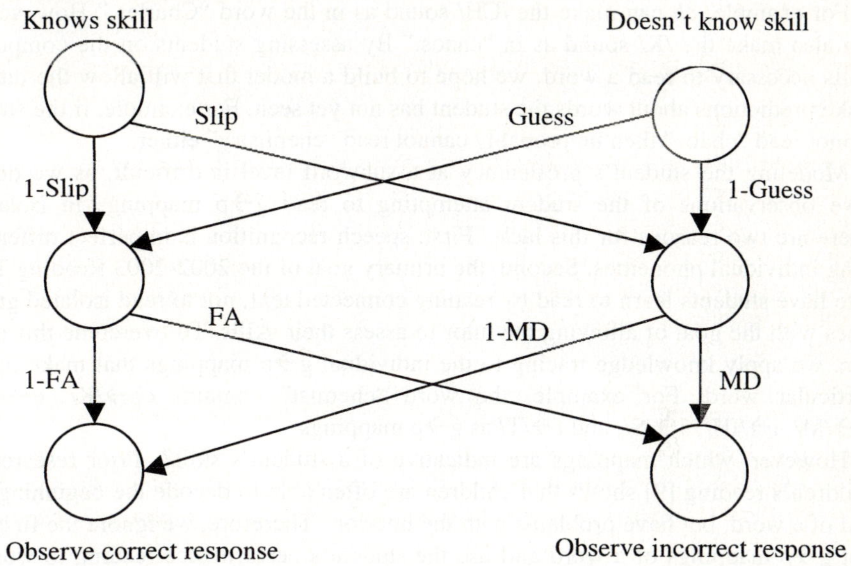

Fig. 1. Knowledge tracing with imperfect scoring of student responses.

While using the Reading Tutor, students read from 3 words to 35102. The mean number of words read was 8129 and the median was 5715. When students read a sentence, their speech was processed by the ASR and aligned against the sentence [10]. This alignment scores each word of the sentence as either being accepted (heard by the ASR as read correctly), rejected (the ASR heard and aligned some other word), or skipped. In Table 1, the student was supposed to read "The dog ran behind the house." The bottom row of the table shows how the student's performance would be scored by the tutor.

Table 1. Example alignment of ASR output to sentence

Sentence	The	dog	ran	behind	the...
ASR output	The	the	ran		
Scoring	Accept	Reject	Accept	Skipped	Skipped

3.2 What Reading Skills to Assess?

Given the ASR's judgment of the student's reading, we must decide which reading skills we wish to assess. We could measure the student's competency on each word in the English language, but such a model would suffer from sparse data problems and would not generalize to new words the student encounters. Instead, we assess a student's knowledge of grapheme→phoneme (g→p) mappings. A grapheme is a group of letters in a word that produces a particular phoneme (sound). So our goal is to assess the student's knowledge these g→p mappings.

For example, *ch* can make the /CH/ sound as in the word "Charles." However, *ch* can also make the /K/ sound as in "chaos." By assessing students on the component skills necessary to read a word, we hope to build a model that will allow the tutor to make predictions about words the student has not yet seen. For example, if the student cannot read "chaos" then he probably cannot read "chemistry" either.

Modeling the student's proficiency at a subword level is difficult, as we do not have observations of the student attempting to read g→p mappings in isolation. There are two reasons for this lack. First, speech recognition is imperfect differentiating individual phonemes. Second, the primary goal of the 2002-2003 Reading Tutor is to have students learn to read by reading connected text, not to read isolated graphemes with the goal of allowing the tutor to assess their skills. To overcome this problem, we apply knowledge tracing to the individual g→p mappings that make up the particular word. For example, the word "chemist" contains ch→/K/, e→/EH/, m→/M/, i→/IH/, s→/S/, and t→/T/ as g→p mappings.

However, which mappings are indicative of a student's skill? Prior research on children's reading [9] shows that children are often able to decode the beginning and end of a word, but have problems with the interior. Therefore, we ignore the first and last g→p mappings of a word and use the student's performance reading to word to update the tutor's estimate of the student's knowledge of the interior g→p mappings. In the above example we would update the student's knowledge on e→/EH/, m→/M/, i→/IH/, and s→/S/. Words with fewer than three graphemes do not adjust the estimate of the student's knowledge.

3.3 Which Words to Score?

When students read a sentence in the Reading Tutor, sometimes they do not attempt to read all of the words in the sentence. If the student pauses in his reading, the ASR will score what the student has read so far. For example, in Table 1, the student appears to have gotten stuck on the word "behind" and stopped reading. It is reasonable to infer the student could not read the word "behind." However, the scoring of "the" and "house" depends on what skills are being assessed. If the goal is to measure the student's overall reading competency, then counting those words as read incorrectly will provide a better estimate since stronger readers will need to pause fewer times. Informal experiments on our data bear out this idea.

However, our goal is not to assess a student's overall reading proficiency, but to estimate his proficiency at particular g→p mappings. For this goal, the words "the" and "house" provide no information about the student's competency on the mappings that make up those words. Therefore we do not apply knowledge tracing to those words.

More formally, we estimate the words a student attempted as follows:

1. i = Find the first word in the sentence that was accepted
2. j = Last word in the sentence that was accepted
3. Apply knowledge tracing to sentence words $i \ldots j+1$

In the example in Table 1, $i=1$ and $j=3$, and the words 1-4 would be scored ("The dog ran behind"). This heuristic assumes the reason the student stopped reading was because he could not read the next word in the sentence.

3.4 Parameter Estimation

We have described how to take the aligned ASR output and to use a heuristic to determine which words to score, and which g→p mappings in the words to model. The next step is to estimate the four knowledge tracing parameters (L0, t, guess, slip) for the set of data collected from students.

There are 429 distinct g→p mappings that occur in at least one word in our dictionary. We used the student's performance on words containing those mappings as input to an optimization algorithm[1] to fit the four knowledge tracing parameters for each g→p using our students' performance data. We then restricted the set of mappings to those with at least 1000 attempts combined from all students. We also removed mappings that fit the knowledge tracing model poorly; we required an R^2 of 0.20. These restrictions limited the set to 80 mappings.

The optimization code required some modification since it was designed for more traditional knowledge tracing. For example, the code restricted the number of "exercises" where students get to apply a particular skill to be less than 100. In our case, an exercise is a student attempting to read a word containing a particular g→p mapping. Some students encounter a particular mapping thousands of times. Another restriction is that P(guess) was forced to be less than 0.3 and P(slip) to be less than 0.1. For our task, such a restriction is inappropriate as mappings with at least 10,000 observations had an average P(guess) of 0.71 and P(slip) of 0.13.

The reason P(guess) is so high is that the Reading Tutor is biased towards hearing the student read the sentence correctly in order to reduce frustration from novices having correct reading scored as incorrect. These data demonstrate that with current speech recognition technology, a tutor cannot provide the same type of immediate feedback as a tutor with typed input due to the uncertainty in whether the student was correct. With such a high guess parameter, many observations are required for a student to be considered proficient in a skill. Fortunately, students read hundreds of words each day they use the Reading Tutor, so the bandwidth should be sufficient to estimate the student's proficiencies.

Once the above steps have been performed, we have a set of knowledge tracing parameter estimates for 80 g→p mappings. By taking the aligned output of the ASR of the student's reading, we can apply the knowledge tracing model to estimate the student's proficiency on each skill. This process results in a probability estimate as to whether the student knows each of the 80 reading skills in our model.

---

[1] Source code is courtesy of Albert Corbett and Ryan Baker and is available at http://www.cs.cmu.edu/~rsbaker/curvefit.tar.gz

4 Validation

We now discuss validating our model of the student's reading proficiency. First we demonstrate that, overall, it is a good model of how well students can identify words. Then we show that the individual g→p estimates have predictive power.

4.1 Performance at Predicting Word ID Scores

If we run knowledge tracing over the student's Reading Tutor performance for the year, we get a set of 80 probabilities that estimate the student's proficiency at each g→p mapping. To validate the accuracy of these probabilities, we use them to predict the student's Word Identification (WI) post test score from the Woodcock Reading Mastery Test [14]. The posttest occurred near the end of the school year. For the WI test, a human presents words for the student to read and records whether the student read the word correctly or not, and terminates the test when the student gets four words in a row incorrect. The WI test is a good test for validating the overall accuracy of our g→p mappings since it presents students with a series of words; the student then either recognizes the word on sight or segments the words into graphemes and produces the appropriate phonemes.

The goal is to use the estimates of the student's knowledge of the 80 g→p mappings to predict his grade equivalent WI post test score. Grade equivalent scores are of the form grade.month, for example 3.4 corresponds to a third grader in the fourth month of school. The month portion range from 0 to 9, with summer months excluded.

Grade equivalent can be misleading. For example, a math test of simple addition may show that a first-grader had a score of 5.3. This result does **not** mean the student has the math proficiency of a fifth grader, rather it means that he scored as well as a fifth grader might be expected to do on that test (so the student is quite skilled at addition, but the score says nothing about his knowledge of other math skills a fifth grader would be expected to know, such as fractions).

In contrast, many reading tests are designed for grades K-12 (roughly ages 5 through 17). For example, in WI, the test starts with easy words such as "red" and "the." For a student to receive a score of 5.3, the student would have to read words such as "temporal" or "gruffly." If a first grader can read such words (and the preceding words on the test), it is not unreasonable to say he can identify words as well as a fifth grader (although his other reading skills may be lacking). As a target for building a model of the student, the grade equivalent scale is a reasonable choice due to its interpretability by researchers. This use of grade equivalent scores follows guidelines [1] for when their use is appropriate.

We expect different g→p mappings to be predictive for students in different grades since skills that students have mastered in prior grades are unlikely to remain predictive in later grades. Therefore, we constructed a model for each grade. We entered terms into the regression model until the change in R^2 was less than 0.01 for grades one and two and less than 0.05 for grades three and four (there were fewer students in grades 3 and 4). This process resulted in ten mappings entering the model for grade one, 25 mappings for grade two, five mappings for grade three, and four mappings for grade four.

The resulting regression model for WI scores had, using a leave-one-out cross validation, an overall correlation of 0.88 with the WI test. It is reasonable to conclude that our model of students' word identification abilities is in reasonable agreement with a well-validated instrument for measuring the skill. We examined the case where our model's error from the student's actual WI was greatest: a fourth grader whose pretest WI score was 3.9, her posttest was 3.3, and our model's prediction was 6.1. It is unlikely the student's proficiency declined by 0.6 grade levels over the course of the year, and it was unclear whether we should believe the 3.3 or the 6.1. Perhaps our model is more trustworthy than the gold standard against which we validated it? There are a variety of reasons not to trust a single test measurement, including that it was administered on a particular day. Perhaps the student was feeling ill or did not take the test seriously? Also, we would like to know if our measure is better than WI. To get around these limitations, we looked at an alternate method of measuring word identification.

4.2 Alternate Measure of Word Identification

To find an alternate method of measuring word identification, we examined our battery of tests we administer to students to find a set of tests that are most similar to WI:

1. The Accuracy score from the Gray Oral Reading Test (GORT) measures how many mistakes students make reading connected text. It correlates with WI at 0.76.
2. Sight Word Efficiency (SWE) from Test Of Word Reading Efficiency (TOWRE) measures how quickly students can decode common words. It correlates with WI at 0.80.
3. The Test of Written Spellling (TWS) is the opposite of word identification as students are presented a sound and asked to generate the proper letters, but is related to word identification [3]. It correlates with WI at 0.86.

None of these measures perfectly matches the construct of word identification, but they measure closely related constructs. We took the mean of these three tests as a proxy for the students' word identification proficiency. These tests were sometimes administered on different days and usually by different testers. The mean of the three tests correlates with WI at 0.87. Furthermore, the mean of the 3 scores (hereafter called WI3) does not suffer nearly as badly as WI from students dropping several months in proficiency from pre- to post-test. Given the stability of the WI3 measure, its being composed of constructs closely related to word identification, and its statistical correlation with WI, we feel it is a good measure of the students "true' word identification score.

Returning to the student whose WI posttest score deviated from the model. Her WI score was 3.3 her predicted score was 6.1, and her WI3 score was 5.1. Perhaps our model did a better job for this student than the WI test? To evaluate the accuracy of our model, we compared our model and the WI score to see how often each was closer to the WI3 score. The WI test was closer to the WI3 score 52.8% of the time, while our model was closer 47.2% of the time. An alternate evaluation is to examine the mean absolute error (MAE) between each estimate and WI3. WI had an MAE of 0.71 (SD of 0.56), while our model had an MAE of 0.77 (SD of 0.67), a difference of only 0.06 GE (roughly three weeks). So our model was marginally worse than the WI test at assessing (a proxy for) a student's word identification abilities. However, the WI test is a well-validated instrument, and to come with 0.06 GE of it is an accomplishment. Although marginally worse than the paper test, the knowledge tracing model can estimate the student's proficiency at any time throughoutthe school year, and requires no student time to generate an assessment.

4.3 Predicting Help Requests

To validate whether our model's estimates of the student's knowledge of individual g→p mappings were accurate, we predicted whether the student would ask for help on a word. We used help requests rather than the student's performance at reading words since we already extracted considerable data about student reading performance to build our model. Thus using it to confirm our model would be circular.

To measure whether knowledge of g→p mappings would help predict whether the student would ask for help, we examined every word the student encountered and noted whether he asked for help or not. We excluded words composed of fewer than three graphemes (since our model is based on student performance on interior g→p mappings). Approximately 79% of English tokens in children's reading materials are composed of 3 or more graphemes. The above restrictions limited us to 288,614 sentence word tokens the students encountered during their time using the Reading Tutor.

We constructed a logistic regression model to predict whether a student would ask for help on a word. This model had several components:

1. The identity of the student was a factor. Adding the student to the model controls for overall student ability, student differences in help-seeking behavior (in the past, student help request rates have differed by two orders of magnitude in the Reading Tutor).
2. The difficulty of the word (on a grade equivalent scale) was a covariate. Presumably students are more likely to ask for help on difficult words.
3. The position of the word in the sentence was a covariate. In the Reading tutor, students sometimes do not read the entire sentence. Therefore, we suspected that words earlier in the sentence are more likely to be clicked on for help.
4. The average knowledge of the 80 g→p for the student at the point in time when he encountered the word was a covariate. This term modeled the changes in the student's knowledge over the course of the year.
5. The student's average knowledge of the g→p mappings that composed the word, excluding the first and last mappings. For our data, of words with 3 or more graphemes, the modal number of graphemes was 3 and the median was 4. Therefore, there are generally only one or two interior

g→p mappings, so the student's average knowledge of the mappings in a word was not a broad description of the student's competencies, but is a focused description of his knowledge of the components of this word.

Logistic regression generates Beta coefficients to determine each variable's influence on the outcome. The Beta coefficients were 0.48 for word difficulty, -0.96 for the student's overall ability, -0.38 for the student's mean proficiency of the g→p mappings in the word, and -0.035 for the word's position in the sentence. If a variable has a positive Beta coefficient, then as the variable's value increases the student's probability of asking for help increases. Conversely, a negative Beta implies as the value increases, the student's probability of requesting help decreases. All of the Beta values were significant at $P<0.001$, and all point in the intuitive direction: as students become more proficient at reading they ask for help less, if a student has a higher estimated knowledge of the g→p mappings in this particular word, even after controlling for word difficulty, then the student is less likely to ask for help. It is important to note that the Beta values are not normalized in logistic regression, thus it is not appropriate to order the various features by how much predictive power they have.

These results provide evidence that individual estimates of the student's proficiency on g→p mappings are meaningful indicators of proficiency.

5 Conclusions and Future Work

This paper demonstrates that it is possible to apply classic student modeling techniques to language learning tutors that use speech recognition. While it is true the data are extremely noisy, it is possible to account for the noise and model student proficiency on subword skills, in our case g→p mappings, of reading. This model of proficiency is accurate in the aggregate since it is able to assess a student's word identification proficiency nearly as well as a paper test designed for the task. Furthermore, the individual estimates of the student's knowledge are also useful, since they predict whether a student requests help on a word.

Next steps for this work include a better model of credit assignment for words that are accepted or rejected. If the ASR believes the student made a mistake, it may not be fair to blame all of the interior g→p mappings, the blame should be spread probabilistically. Similarly, a student may generate correct reading without knowing all of the g→p mappings in a word.

Similarly, we will investigate a better model of how children decode words. For example, although early readers tend to understand the first part of a word, students who are just starting to read may struggle at this step. A model of children's reading that treats each component of the word as a separate skill would account for this problem.

Acknowledgements. This work was supported by the National Science Foundation, ITR/IERI Grant No. REC-0326153. Any opinions, findings, and conclusions or recommendations expressed in this publication are those of the authors and do not necessarily reflect the views of the National Science Foundation or the official policies, either expressed or implied, of the sponsors or of the United States Government. We also acknowledge members of Project LISTEN who contributed to the design and development of the Reading Tutor, and the students who used the tutor.

References

1. *Canadian Psychological Association: Guidelines for Educational and Psychological Testing*. 1996: Also available at: http://www.acposb.on.ca/test.htm.
2. Beck, J.E., P. Jia, and J. Mostow. *Assessing Student Proficiency in a Reading Tutor that Listens*. in *Ninth International Conference on User Modeling*. 2003.p. 323-327 Johnstown, PA.
3. Carver, R.P., *The highly lawful relationship among pseudoword decoding, word identification, spelling, listening, and reading*. Scientific Studies of Reading, 2003. **7**(2): p. 127-154.
4. Corbett, A. and J. Anderson, *Knowledge tracing: Modeling the acquisition of procedural knowledge*. User modeling and user-adapted interaction, 1995. **4**: p. 253-278.
5. Heift, T. and M. Schulze, *Student Modeling and ab initio Language Learning*. System, the International Journal of Educational Technology and Language Learning Systems, 2003. **31**(4): p. 519-535.
6. Larsen, S.C., D.D. Hammill, and L.C. Moats, *Test of Written Spelling*. fourth ed. 1999, Austin, Texas: Pro-Ed.
7. Michaud, L.N., K.F. McCoy, and L.A. Stark. *Modeling the Acquisition of English: an Intelligent CALL Approach"*. in *Eighth International Conference on User Modeling*. 2001.p.: Springer-Verlag.
8. Mostow, J. and G. Aist, *Evaluating tutors that listen: An overview of Project LISTEN*, in *Smart Machines in Education*, K. Forbus and P. Feltovich, Editors. 2001, MIT/AAAI Press: Menlo Park, CA. p. 169-234.
9. Perfetti, C.A., *The representation problem in reading acquisition*, in *Reading Acquisition*, P.B. Gough, L.C. Ehri, and R. Treiman, Editors. 1992, Lawrence Erlbaum: Hillsdale, NJ. p. 145-174.
10. Tam, Y.-C., J. Beck, J. Mostow, and S. Banerjee. *Training a Confidence Measure for a Reading Tutor that Listens*. in *Proc. 8th European Conference on Speech Communication and Technology (Eurospeech 2003)*. 2003.p. 3161-3164 Geneva, Switzerland.
11. Torgesen, J.K., R.K. Wagner, and C.A. Rashotte, *TOWRE: Test of Word Reading Efficiency*. 1999, Austin: Pro-Ed.
12. Wiederholt, J.L. and B.R. Bryant, *Gray Oral Reading Tests*. 3rd ed. 1992, Austin, TX: Pro-Ed.
13. Williams, S.M., D. Nix, and P. Fairweather. *Using Speech Recognition Technology to Enhance Literacy Instruction for Emerging Readers*. in *Fourth International Conference of the Learning Sciences*. 2000.p. 115-120: Erlbaum.
14. Woodcock, R.W., *Woodcock Reading Mastery Tests - Revised (WRMT-R/NU)*. 1998, Circle Pines, Minnesota: American Guidance Service.

The Massive User Modelling System (MUMS)

Christopher Brooks[1], Mike Winter[1], Jim Greer[2], and Gordon McCalla[2]

[1] Department of Computer Science, University of Saskatchewan,
57 Campus Drive, Saskatoon, SK, S7N 5A9, Canada
{cab938, mfw127}@mail.usask.ca

[2] Department of Computer Science, University of Saskatchewan,
57 Campus Drive, Saskatoon, SK, S7N 5A9, Canada
{greer, mccalla}@cs.usask.ca

Abstract. Effective distributed user modelling in intelligent tutoring systems requires the integration of both pedagogical and domain applications. This integration is difficult, and often requires rebuilding applications for the specific e-learning environment that has been deployed. This paper puts forth both an architecture and an implementation prototype for achieving this integration. It focuses on providing platform and language neutral access to services, without commitment to any particular ontology.

1 Introduction

A recent trend within intelligent tutoring systems and related educational technologies research is to move away from monolithic tutors that deal with individual learners, and instead favour "adaptive learning communities" that provide a related variety of collaborative learning services for multiple learners [9]. An urgent challenge facing this new breed of tutoring systems is the need for precise and timely coordination that facilitates effective adaptation in all constituent components. In addition to supporting collaboration between the native parts of a tutoring system, an effective inter-component communication system is required to provide the ability to know of and react to learner actions in external applications. For example, consider the kinds of errors a student encounters when trying to solve a Java programming problem. If the errors are syntactical, a tutor may find it useful to intervene directly within the development environment that student is using. If the errors are related to the higher level course concepts, the tutor may instead find it useful to dynamically assemble and deliver external resources (learning objects) to the student. Finally, if an appropriate solution can not be found that helps the student to resolve their errors, the tutor may find it useful to refer the user to a domain expert or peer who has had success at similar tasks.

To provide this level of adaptation, the tutor must be able to form a coherent model of students as they work with different domain applications. The tutor must be able to collect, understand, and respond to user modelling "events" in both real time and on an archival basis. These needs can be partially addressed by integrating intelligent tutoring system functionality within larger web-based e-learning systems including

J.C. Lester et al. (Eds.): ITS 2004, LNCS 3220, pp. 635–645, 2004.

learning management systems such as WebCT [28] and Blackboard [3] or e-learning portals like uPortal [26]. These applications provide an array of functionality meant to directly support learning activities including social communication, learner management, and content delivery functions. An inherent problem with these e-learning systems is that they are often unable to capture interaction between a learner and other applications the learner may be using to complete their learning task. While a potential solution to this problem is to integrate all possible external applications that may be used by the student within an e-learning system, this task is difficult at best due to proprietary API's and e-learning system homogeneity.

In [27] we proposed a method of integrating various e-learning applications using a multi-agent architecture, where each application was represented by an agent that negotiated with other agents to provide information about learners using the system. A learner using the system was then able to see portions of this information by interacting with a personal agent, who represented the tutor of the system. In this system, the tutor's sole job was to match learners with one another based on learner preferences and competencies. This system was useful at a conceptual level, but suffered from the drawbacks of being difficult to implement and hard to scale-up. The integration of agent features (in particular reasoning and negotiation) within every application instance required high computational power forcing the user into a more centralized computing environment. To further provide the performance and reliability required, agents had to be carefully crafted using a proprietary protocol for communication. This hindered both agent interoperability and system extensibility.

This paper presents a framework and prototype specifically aimed at supporting the process of collecting and disseminating user information to software components interested in forming user models. This framework uses both semantic web and web service technologies to encourage interoperability and extensibility at both the semantic and the syntactic levels. The organization of this paper is as follows: Section 2 describes the framework at a conceptual level. Section 3 follows with an outline of the environment we are using to prototype the system, with a particular emphasis on the integration of our modelling framework with the legacy e-learning applications we are trying to support. Section 4 contrasts our work with similar work in the semantic web community. Finally, Section 5 concludes with a look at future goals.

2 The MUMS Framework

We present the Massive User Modelling System (MUMS) framework, which is inspired by traditional event systems such as CORBA [20] and JINI [25]. The principle artefact within MUMS is the modelling opinion being expressed. We adopt the definition of an opinion as a *temporally grounded codification of a fact about a set of users from the perspective of a given event producer.* Opinions are passed between three independent entities in the framework:

1. Evidence Producers: observe user interaction with an application and publish opinions about the user. These opinions can range from direct observations of the interaction that has taken place, to beliefs about the user's knowledge, desires, and

intentions. While the opinions created can be of any size, the focus is on creating brief contextualized statements about a user, as opposed to fully modelling the user.

2. Modellers: are interested in acting on opinions about the user, usually by reasoning over these to create a user model. The modeller then interacts with the user (or the other aspects of the system, such as learning materials) to provide adaptation. Modellers may be interested in modelling more than one user, and may receive opinions from more than one producer. Further, modellers may be situated and perform purpose-based user modelling by restricting the set of opinions they are interested in receiving.
3. Broker: acts as an intermediary between producers and modellers. The broker receives opinions from producers and routes them to interested modellers. Modellers communicate with the broker using either a publish/subscribe model or a query/response model. While the broker is a logically centralized component, different MUMS implementations may find it useful to distribute and specialize the services being provided for scalability reasons.

While the definition of an opinion centers on human users, it does not restrict the producer from describing other entities and relationships of interest. For instance, an evidence producer embedded within an integrated software development environment might not just express information about the particular compile-time errors a student receives, but may also include the context of the student's history for this programming session, as well as some indication of how the tutor should provide treatment for the problem. The definition also allows for evidence producers to have disagreeing opinions about users, and for the opinion of a producer can change over time.

This three-entity system purposefully supports the notion of active learner modelling [17]. In the active learning modelling philosophy, the focus is on creating a learner model situated for a given purpose, as opposed to creating a complete model of the learner. This form of modelling tends to be less intensive than traditional user modelling techniques, and focuses on the just-in-time creation and delivery of models instead of the storage and retrieval of models. The MUMS architecture supports this by providing both a stream-based publish/subscribe and an archival query/response method of obtaining opinions from a broker. Both of these modes of event delivery require that modellers provide a semantic query for the opinions they are interested in, as opposed to the more traditional event system notions of channel subscription and producer subscription. This approach decouples the producers of information from the consumers of information, and leads to a more easily adaptable system where new producers and modellers can be added in an as-needed fashion. The stream-based method of retrieving opinions allows modellers to provide just-in-time reasoning, while the archival method allows for more resource-intensive user modelling to occur. All opinions transferred within the MUMS system include a timestamp indicating when they were generated, allowing modellers to build up more complete or historical user models using the asynchronous querying capabilities provided by the broker.

By applying the adaptor pattern [8] to the system, a fourth entity of interest can be derived, namely the filter.

4. Filters: act as broker, modeller, and producer of opinions. By registering for and reasoning over opinions from producers, a filter can create higher level opinions. This offloads the amount of work done by a modeller to form a user model, but maintains the more flexible decentralized environment. Filters can be chained together to provide any amount of value-added reasoning that is desired. Finally, filters can be specialized within a particular instance of the MUMS framework by providing domain specific rules that govern the registration of, processing of, and creation of opinions.

Interactions between the entities are shown in Fig. 1. Some set of evidence producers publish opinions based on observations with the user to a given broker. The broker routes these opinions to interested parties (in this case, both a filter and the modeller towards the top of the diagram). The filter reasons over the opinions, forms derivative statements, and publishes these new opinions back to the broker and any modellers registered with the filter. Lastly, modellers interested in retrieving archival statements about the user can do so by querying any entity which stores these opinions (in this example, the second modeller queries the broker instead of registering for real time opinion notification).

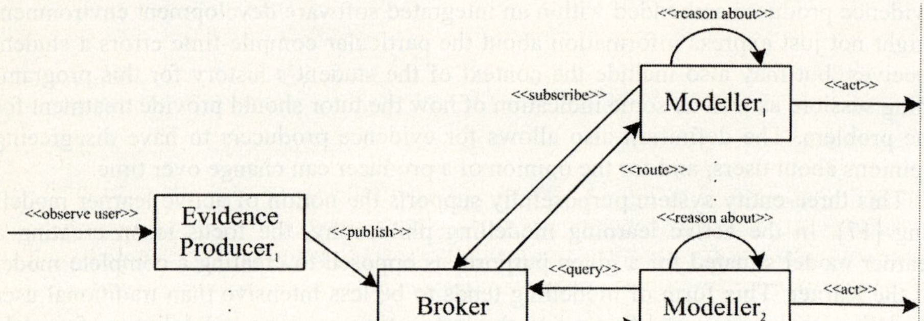

Fig. 1. A logical view of the MUMS architecture

The benefits of this architecture are numerous. First, the removal of reasoning and negotiation abilities from the producers of opinions greatly decreases the complexity when creating new producer types. Instead of being rebuilt from scratch with user modelling in mind, existing applications (be they applications explicitly meant to support the learning process, or domain-specific applications) can be easily extended and added to the system. Second, the decoupling between the producers and the modellers serves to increase both the performance and the extensibility of the system. By adding more physical brokers to store and route messages, a greater number of producers or modellers can be supported. This allows for a truly distributed system, where modelling is done on different physical machines throughout the network. Third, the semantic querying and decoupling between modellers and producers allows for the dynamic addition of arbitrary numbers of both types of application to the MUMS system. Once these entities have joined in the system, their participation can increase the expressiveness of the user models created, without requiring modifications to existing producers and modellers. Finally, the logical centralization the broker allows for the setting of administration policies, such as privacy rules and the maintenance of data integrity, through the addition of filters.

All of these benefits address key challenges for adaptive learning systems. These systems must allow for the integration of both existing domain applications as well as learning management specific applications. This integration must be able to take place with a minimal amount of effort to accommodate the various stakeholders within an institution (e.g. administrators, researchers, instructional designers), and must be able to be centrally managed to provide for privacy of user data. Last, the system must be able to scale not just to the size of a single classroom, but to the needs of a whole department or institution.

3 Implementation Prototype

The MUMS architecture is currently being prototyped within the distributed e-learning environment in the Department of Computer Science at the University of Saskatchewan. This environment has been created over a number of years and involves applications from a variety of different research projects. While initially aimed at garnering research data, these applications are all currently deployed in a support fashion within some of our computer science courses. There are four main applications:

1. A content delivery system, which deploys IMS content packaging [15] formatted learning objects to students using a web browser.
2. A web based forum discussion system built around the notions of peer help (I-Help Public Discussions [11]).
3. An instant messaging and chat application (I-Help Instant Messenger).
4. A quizzing system which deploys IMS QTILite [14] formatted quizzes and records evaluations of students

We are currently in the process of adding new applications to this list. These applications include development environments, e-learning portals, and web browsers. Each of these systems contribute to and benefit from models of the user and hence require a flexible user modelling environment. To accommodate this, we have implemented the MUMS architecture with three clear goals in mind: scalability, interoperability and extensibility. The technical solutions we are using to achieve these goals will be addressed in turn.

3.1 Interoperability

With the goal of distributing the system to as many domain specific applications as is necessary, interoperability is a key concern. To this end, all opinion publishing from producers is done using our implementation of the Web Services Events (WS-Events) [5] infrastructure specification. This infrastructure defines a set of data types and rules for passing events using web services. These rules include administrative information about the producer or modeller (e.g. contact information, quality of service, etc), a payload that contains the semantics of the opinion, and information on managing advertising and subscriptions. Using this infrastructure helps to protect entities from future changes in the way opinion distribution is handled. Further, modellers can either subscribe to events using WS-Events (publish/subscribe), or can query the broker directly using standard web service technologies (query/response). This allows for both the real-time delivery of new modelling information, as well as the ability to access archived information from the past in a manner independent of platform and programming language.

We enhance semantic interoperability by expressing the payload of each event using the Resource Description Framework (RDF) [16]. This language provides a naturally extensible and ontology-neutral method for describing modeling information in a format that is easily computer readable. It has become the lingua franca of the semantic web, and a number of toolkits (notably, Jena [13] and Drive [24]) have arisen to make RDF graph manipulation easier. When registering for events, modellers provide patterns to match using the RDF Data Query Language (RDQL) [23].

Finally, design time interoperability is achieved by maintaining a separate ontology database which authors can inspect when creating new system components. This encourages the reuse of previously deployed ontologies, while maintaining the flexibility of opinion routing independent of ontology.

3.2 Extensibility

Besides the natural extensibility afforded by the use of the RDF as a payload format, the MUMS architecture provides for distributed reasoning through the use of filters. In general, a filter is a component that masquerades as any combination of producer, modeller, or broker of events. There are at least two specialized instances of a filter:

1. Reasoners: register or query for events with the goal of being able to produce higher level derivative events. For instance, one might create a reasoner to listen for events related to message sending from the web-based discussion and instant messenger producers, and then create new opinions which indicate the changing social structure amongst peers in the class.
2. Blockers: are placed between producers and modellers with the goal of modifying or restricting events that are published. Privacy filters are an example of a blocker. These filters can anonymize events or require that a modeller provide special authentication privileges when subscribing.

While the system components in our current implementation follow a clear separation between those that are producers and consumers of information, we expect most future components will aim at value adding the network by reasoning over data sources before producing opinions. Thus we imagine that the majority of the network will be made up of reasoner filters chained together with a few blockers to implement administrative policies.

3.3 Scalability

Early lessons learned from testing the implementation prototype indicated that there are two main factors involved in slowing down the propagation of opinions:

1. Message serialization: The deserialization of SOAP messages into native data types is an expensive process. This process is especially important to the broker, which shares a many-to-one relationship with producers.
2. Subscription evaluation: Evaluating RDF models against a RDQL query is a time consuming operation. This operation grows with the complexity of the models, the complexity of the query, and the number of queries (number of modeller registrations) that a broker has.

To counteract this, the MUMS architecture can be extended to include the notion of domain brokers. A domain broker is a broker that is ontology aware, and can provide enhanced quality of service because of this awareness. This quality of service usually comes in the form of more efficient model storage, and thus faster query resolution. Further, brokers are free to provide alternative transport mechanisms which may lead to faster data transfers (e.g. a binary protocol which compresses RDF messages could be used for mobile clients with error-prone connections, while a UDP protocol describing RDF using N-Triples [10] could be used to provide for the more real-time delivery of events). The use of domain brokers can be combined with reasoners and blockers to meet the performance, management, and expressability requirements of the system.

Finally, the architectural notion of a broker as a centralized entity is a logical notion only. Physically we distribute the load of the broker amongst a small cluster of machines connected to a single data store to maintain integrity.

An overview of the prototype, including the technologies in use, is presented in Fig. 2. Evidence producers are written in a variety of languages, including a Java producer for the course delivery system, a C# producer for the public discussion system and a C++ producer (in the works) for the Mozilla web browser. The broker is realized through a cluster of Tomcat web application servers running an Apache Axis application which manage subscriptions and semantic routing. This application uses a PostreSQL database to store both subscription and archival information. Subscriptions are stored as a tuple indicating the RDQL pattern that should be matched, and the URL at which the modeller can be contacted. At this moment there is one Java-based modeller which graphically displays aggregate student information for instructors from the I-Help public forums. Besides a description of student posting frequency, this modeller displays statistics for a whole forum, as well as a graphical picture of student interaction. In addition there are two other applications under development including a pedagogical content planner and a peer help matchmaker.

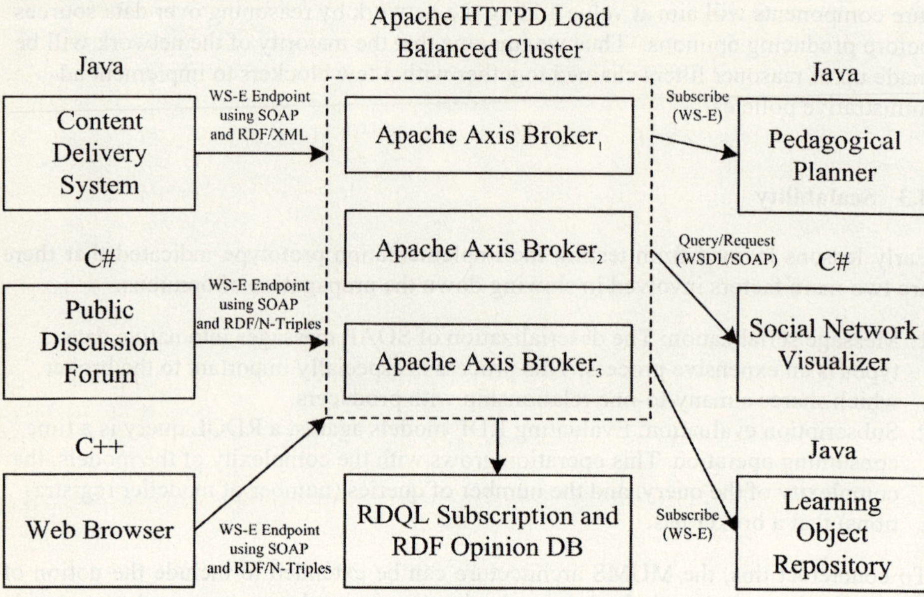

Fig. 2. Prototype implementation of the MUMS architecture

4 Related Work

While inspired by the needs for distributed intelligent tutoring systems, we see this work overlapping three distinct fields of computer science; distributed computing, the semantic web, and learner modelling. Related research in each of these fields will be addressed in turn.

The distributed systems field is a mature field that has provided a catalyst for much of our work. Both general and specific kinds of event systems are described throughout the literature, and a number of mature specifications, such as the Java RMI and the CORBA, exist. Unlike MUMS, these event systems require the consumers of events (modellers) to subscribe to events (opinions) based on the expected event producer or the channel (subject) the events will arrive on. This increases the coupling between entities in the system, requiring that either the consumer is aware of a given producer, or that they share a strict messaging ontology. In [4], Carzaniga et al. describe a model for content-based addressing and routing at the network level. We build upon this model by applying similar principles in the application layer, allowing the modellers of opinions to register for those opinions which match some semantic pattern. This allows for the ad hoc creation and removal of both evidence producers and modellers within the system.

While the semantic web as a research area has been growing quickly for a number of years, the focus of this area has been on creating formalisms for knowledge management representation. The general approach with sharing data over the semantic web is to consider it just "an extension of the current web" [2], and to follow a query/response communication model. Thus, a fair amount of work has been done in conjunction with database research to produce efficient mechanisms for storing (e.g. [22] [12]) and querying data (e.g. [23]), but new methods for transmitting this data have largely been unexplored. For instance, the HP Joseki project [1] and the Nokia URI Query Agent Model [19]provide methods for publishing, updating, and retrieving RDF data models using HTTP. This approach is useful for large centralized models where data transfer uses more resources than data querying; however, it provides poor support for the real-time delivery of modeling information. Further, it supports the notion of a single model per user which is formed through consensus between producers, as opposed to the more lightweight situated user modeling suggested by active modeling researchers. We instead provide a method which completely decouples producers from one another, and offload the work in forming user modellers to the consumers of opinions.

The work done by Nejdl et al. in [18] and Dolog and Nejdl in [7] and [6] marries the idea of the semantic web with learner modelling. In these works the authors describe a network of learning materials set up in a peer-to-peer fashion. Resources are described in RDF using both general pedagogical metadata (in particular the IEEE Learning Object Metadata specification) and learner specific metadata (such as the IMS LIPS or PAPI). The network is searchable by end-users through the use of personal learning assistants who can query peers in the network for learning resource metadata, then filter the results based on a user model. While this architecture distributes the responsibility for user modeling, it also limits communication to the query/response model. Thus, personal learning agents must continually query data sources to discover new information about the student they are modelling. In addition, by arranging data sources in a peer network the system loses its ability to effectively centrally control these sources. For instance, an institution would need to control all of the peers in the network to provide for data integrity or privacy over the data being shared.

5 Conclusions and Future Work

As cited by Picard et al., the ITS working group of 1995 described tutoring systems as:

> "…hand-crafted, monolithic, standalone applications. They are time-consuming and costly to design, implement, and deploy. Each development teams must redevelop all of the component functionalities needed. Because these components are so hard and costly to build, few tutors of realistic depth and breadth ever get built, and even fewer ever get tested on real students." [21]

Despite research invested into providing agent based architectures for tutoring systems, tutors remain largely centralized in deployment. These tutors are generally domain specific, and are unable to easily interface with the various legacy applications that students may be using to augment their learning. When such interfacing is available, it comes with a high cost to designers, as integration requires both a shared ontology to describe what the student has done, as well as considerable low level software integration work. MUMS provides an alternative architecture where producers can be readily associated with legacy applications and where modellers and reasoners can readily produce useful learner modelling information.

This paper has presented both a framework and a prototype to support the just-in-time production and delivery of user modelling information. It provides a general architecture for e-learning applications to share user data, as well as details on a specific implementation for this architecture, which builds on technologies being used within the web services and semantic web communities. It provides an approach to student modelling that is platform, language, and ontology independent. Further, this approach allows for both the just-in-time delivery of modelling information, as well as the archival and retrieval of past modelling opinions.

Our immediate future work involves further integration of domain specific applications within this framework. We will use this new domain specific information to provide for more accurate resource suggestions to the learner, including both the acquisition of learning objects from learning object repositories as well as expertise location through peer matchmaking. Tangential to this, we are interested in pursuing the use of user defined filters through personal learning agents. These agents can act as a "front-end" for the learner to have input over the control and dissemination rights of their learner information. Finally, we are examining the issue of design time interoperability through ontology sharing using the Web Ontology Language (OWL).

Acknowledgements. We would like to thank the reviewers for their valuable recommendations. This work has been conducted with support from a grant funded by the Natural Science and Engineering Research Council of Canada (NSERC) for the Learning Object Repositories Network (LORNET).

References

1. Joseki : The Jena RDF Server. Available online at http://www.joseki.org/. Last accessed March 22, 2004.
2. Berners-Lee, T., Hendler, J., and Lassila, O., The Semantic Web *Scientific American*, May, 2001. Scientific American, Inc.
3. Blackboard Inc. blackboard. Available online at http://www.blackboard.com/. Last accessed March 22, 2004.
4. Carzanigay, A., Rosenblumz, D. S., and Wolfy, A. L. Content-Based Addressing and Routing: A General Model and its Application. In *Technical Report CU-CS-902-00* .
5. Catania, N., et al. Web Services Events (WS-Events) Version 2.0. Available online at http://devresource.hp.com/drc/specifications/wsmf/WS-Events.pdf. Last accessed March 22, 2004.
6. Dolog, P. and Nejdl, W. Challenges and Benefits of the Semantic Web for User Modelling. In *Workshop on Adaptive Hypermedia and Adaptive Web-Based Systems 2003, Held at WWW 2003*.
7. Dolog, P. and Nejdl, W. Personalisation in Elena: How to cope with personalisation in distributed eLearning Networks. In *International Conference on Worldwide Coherent Workforce, Satisfied Users - New Services For Scientific Information*. Oldenburg, Germany.
8. Gamma, E., Helm, R., Johnson, R., and Vlissides, J. (eds) *Design Patterns*, 1st edition. Addison-Wesley, 1995.

9. Gaudioso, E. and Boticario, J. G. Towards Web-based Adaptive Learning Communities. In *Artificial Intelligence in Education 2003*.
10. Grant, J. and Beckett, D. RDF Test Cases. Available online at http://www.w3.org/TR/2004/REC-rdf-testcases-20040210/. Last accessed March 22, 2004.
11. Greer, J., McCalla, G., Vassileva, J., Deters, R., Bull, S., and Kettel, L. Lessons Learned in Deploying a Multi-Agent Learning Support System: The I-Help Experience. In *Artificial Intelligence in Education 2001*. San Antonio, TX, USA.
12. Harris, S. and Gibbins, N. 3store: Efficient Bulk RDF Storage. In *Workshop on Semantic Web Storage and Retrieval 2003*. Vrije Universiteit, Amsterdam, Netherlands.
13. Hewlett-Packard Development Company, L.P. Jena 2 - A Semantic Web Framework. Available online at http://www.hpl.hp.com/semweb/jena.htm. Last accessed March 22, 2004.
14. IMS Global Learning Consortium Inc. IMS Question & Test Interoperability Lite Specification, Version 1.2. 2002.
15. IMS Global Learning Consortium Inc. IMS Content Packaging Specification version 1.1.3. 2003.
16. Klyne, G. and Carroll, J. J. Resource Description Framework (RDF): Concepts and Abstract Syntax. Available online at http://www.w3.org/TR/2004/REC-rdf-concepts-20040210/. Last accessed March 22, 2004 .
17. McCalla, G., Vassileva, J., Greer, J., and Bull, S. Active Learner Modelling.
18. Nejdl , W., Wolpers, M., Siberski, W., Schmitz, C., Schlosser, M., Brunkhorst, I., and Lser, A. Super-peer-based routing and clustering strategies for rdf-based peer-to-peer networks. In *12th International World Wide Web Conference*. Budapest, Hungary.
19. Nokia. URIQA: The Nokia URI Query Agent Model. Available online at http://sw.nokia.com/uriqa/URIQA.html. Last accessed March 22, 2004.
20. Object Management Group. Common Object Request Broker Architecture (CORBA/IIOP).
21. Picard, R. W., Kort, B., and Reilly, R. Affective Learning Companion Project Summary: Exploring the Role of Emotion in Propelling the SMET Learning Process. Available online at http://affect.media.mit.edu/AC_research/lc/nsf1.html.
22. Reggiori, A., van Gulik, D.-W., and Bjelogrlic, Z. Indexing and retrieving Semantic Web resources: the RDFStore model. In *Workshop on Semantic Web Storage and Retrieval 2003*. Vrije Universiteit, Amsterdam, Netherlands.
23. Seaborne, Andy. RDQL - A Query Language for RDF: W3C Member Submission.
24. Singh, R. Drive - An RDF Parser for the .NET Platform. Available online at http://www.driverdf.org/. Last accessed March 22, 2004.
25. Sun Microsystems, Inc. Jini Technology Core Platform Specification.
26. uPortal. uPortal by JA-SIG. Available online at http://uportal.org/. Last accessed March 22, 2004.
27. Vassileva, J., McCalla, G., and Greer, J. Multi-Agent Multi-User Modeling in I-Help. *User Modeling and User-Adapted Interaction: Special Issue on User Modelling and Intelligent Agents*, 13(1):1-31, 2002
28. WebCT. WebCT.com. Available online at http://www.webct.com/. Last accessed March 22, 2004.

An Open Learner Model for Children and Teachers: Inspecting Knowledge Level of Individuals and Peers

Susan Bull and Mark McKay

Electronic, Electrical and Computer Engineering, University of Birmingham,
Edgbaston, Birmingham B15 2TT, UK
s.bull@bham.ac.uk

Abstract. This paper considers research on open learner models, which are usually aimed at adult learners, and describes how this has been applied to an intelligent tutoring system for 8-9 year-old children and their teachers. We introduce Subtraction Master, a learning environment with an open learner model for two and three digit subtraction, with and without adjustment (borrowing). It was found that some children were quite interested in their learner model and in a comparison of their own progress to that of their peers, whereas others did not demonstrate such interest. The level of interest and engagement with the learner model did not clearly relate to ability.

1 Introduction

There have been several investigations into open learner models (OLM). One of the aims of opening the learner model to the individual modelled, is to encourage students to reflect on their learning. For example, Mr Collins [1] and STyLE-OLM [2] employ a negotiation mechanism whereby the student can debate the contents of their model with the learning environment, if they disagree with the representations of their beliefs. This process is intended to help improve the accuracy of the learner model while also promoting learner reflection on their understanding, as users are required to justify any changes they wish to make to their model, before these are incorporated.

Mitrovic and Martin argue that self-assessment is important in learning, and this might be facilitated by providing students access to their learner model [3]. Their system employs a simpler skill meter to open the model, to consider whether even with a simple learner model representation, self-assessment can be enhanced. They suggest their open learner model may be especially helpful for less able students.

The above examples are for use by university students, who can be expected to understand the role of reflection in learning. Less research has been directed at children's use of OLMs, and whether children might benefit from their availability. One example is Zapata-Rivera and Greer, who allowed 10-13 year-old children in different experimental conditions to browse their learner model, changing it if they felt this to be appropriate [4]. They argue that children of this age can perform self-assessment and undertake reflection on their knowledge in association with an OLM. In contrast, Barnard and Sandberg found that secondary school children did not look at their learner model when this was available optionally [5].

J.C. Lester et al. (Eds.): ITS 2004, LNCS 3220, pp. 646–655, 2004.

Another set of users who have received some attention, are instructors - i.e. tutors can access the representations of the knowledge of those they teach. For example, in some systems the instructor can use their students' learner models as a source of information to help them adapt their teaching to the individual or group [6], [7].

Kay suggests users might want to see how they are doing compared to others in their cohort [8]. Linton and Schaefer display a learner's knowledge in skill meter form against the combined knowledge of other user groups [9]. Bull and Broady show co-present pairs their respective learner models, to prompt peer tutoring [10].

Given the interest in the use of various forms of OLM to promote reflection by university students, both by showing them their own models and in some cases, the models of peers; and work on showing learner models to instructors, it would be interesting to extend this approach to children and teachers. Some work has been undertaken with children [4], [5], but we wish to consider the possibilities for younger students. We therefore use a simple learner model representation.

We introduce Subtraction Master, an intelligent tutoring system (ITS) for mathematics for use by 8-9 year olds. Subtraction Master opens its learner model to the child, including a comparison of their progress against the general progress of their peers; and opens individual and average models to the teacher. The aim is to investigate whether children of this age will sufficiently understand a simple OLM and, moreover, whether they will want to use it. If so, do they wish to view information about their own understanding, and/or about how they relate to others in their class? Will they want to try to improve if their knowledge is shown to be weak?

2 Subtraction Master

Subtraction Master is an ITS with an OLM, for 8-9 year-olds. The aim of developing the system was to investigate the potential of OLMs for teachers and children at a younger age than previously investigated. The domain of subtraction was chosen as there is comprehensive research on children's problems in this area [11], [12].

Subtraction Master is a standard ITS, comprising a domain model, learner model and teaching strategies. The teaching strategies are straightforward, selected based on a child's progress, with random questions of appropriate difficulty according to their knowledge. Questions also elicit further information about misconceptions if it is inferred that these may exist. Additional help can be consulted at any time, and can also be recommended by the system. Help is adaptive, related to the question and question type the child is currently attempting, and is presented in the format most suitable for the individual. This section provides an overview of the system.

2.1 The Subtraction Master Domain

The domain is based on the U.K. National Numeracy Strategy [13], incorporating common calculation errors and misconceptions. The domain covers 2 and 3 digit subtraction, ranging from 2 digit no adjustment (borrow), to 3 digit hundreds to tens adjustment, tens to units adjustment. Specifically, the following are considered:

- two digit subtraction (no adjustment) e.g. 23-12
- two digit subtraction (adjustment from tens to units) e.g. 76-28

- three digit subtraction (no adjustment) e.g. 459-234
- three digit subtraction (adjustment from tens to units) e.g. 574-359
- three digit subtraction (adjustment from hundreds to tens and tens to units) e.g. 364-175

2.2 The Subtraction Master Learner Model

The learner model contains representations of knowledge of the types of subtraction given above, and misconceptions of the individual user, drawn from a misconceptions library. The possible misconceptions modelled by the system are:

- misconception - *commutative*: 5-7 is treated the same as 7-5 (the smaller number is always subtracted from the larger. Thus 23-18=15)
- misconception - *place value*: borrowing from the wrong column (in 410-127, 4 is decreased to 3 and 1 is inserted at the head of the units column; then 3 is decreased to 2 and 1 is inserted at the head of the tens column)
- misconception - *zero has no effect*: 0-5 is treated the same as 5-0 (similar to commutative, but occurs only with zero. 13-5 would be answered correctly)
- bug - *addition completed rather than subtraction*: 7-5=12
- bug - *place value incorrect due to incorrect transcription of calculation*: working out the answers on paper, children transcribe figures incorrectly

As stated above, the primary aim is to investigate the potential of open learner models for children. Thus the focus of Subtraction Master is not as complex as would be suggested by investigations such as those of Brown and Burton [11] and Burton [12]. OLMs will be investigated in the context of more complex ITSs if this seems warranted after the initial investigations with simpler environments.

In addition to explicit misconceptions, representations of skill level are as follows:

- question type: level 1 (question type not attempted, or no correct answers, or incorrect responses outweighing correct answers)
- question type: level 2 (question type attempted, at least one correct, no misconceptions)
- question type: level 3 (below 40%, some correct, little evidence of misconceptions)
- question type: level 4 (40%-50% correct, little evidence of misconceptions)
- question type: level 5 (above 50% correct, little evidence of misconceptions)

'Question type' refers to the kind of question (e.g. two digit subtraction, no adjustment). The 'level' indicates the child's proficiency in that question type, with 5 being the most advanced. The definitions of level are arbitrary at this stage - the intention is to provide encouraging feedback through the OLM, in accordance with classroom teaching practice. Thus progression through levels can be achieved reasonably easily.

Level 1 indicates that a question type has either not been attempted, that the child has not answered any of those questions correctly, or that their incorrect answers and misconceptions outweigh their correct responses. For level 2 the learner must have answered at least one question correctly, and displayed no misconceptions. This allows a more positive representation (than level 1) for a learner without misconceptions, but who has not yet answered enough questions to reach level 3 (i.e. there is insufficient evidence to place them at level 3). In subsequent levels (3-5) it is possible that the child will have exhibited a misconception; however, their correct responses will outweigh any misconceptions. The data in the learner model is associated with a degree of certainty, depending on the extent of evidence available to support it.

2.3 The Subtraction Master Teaching Strategies

The subtraction explanations are animations of the standard decomposition method where figures are crossed out and decreased for 'borrowing', and expanded decomposition where figures are broken into tens and units, to reinforce place value (e.g. 47 is written as 40 and 7). A number square (a square of numbers from 1-100) is used if a child is unsuccessful with the decomposition methods. The form of explanation is that inferred most suitable to help a learner overcome a problem. The target is the standard decomposition method, as this is achievable by children of this age (i.e. it is currently taught by the teacher). Help screens are available for consultation at any time. Where the system detects the child is having difficulty, it prompts them to use help.

The questions offered increase in difficulty as the child progresses successfully. Where there are problems, the system guides the child through the subtraction process. If a possible misconception is detected, further questions are selected to elicit data on the likelihood of the child holding that misconception.

3 The Subtraction Master Open Learner Model

This section presents the open learner model as seen by children and teachers.

3.1 The Subtraction Master Open Learner Model for Children

The OLM can be accessed as a means to raise children's awareness of their progress, using a menu or buttons. These are labelled: 'see how you are doing' and 'compare yourself to children of your age'. The individual learner model is displayed in Fig. 1.

The children have not yet learnt about graphs, therefore the learner model data cannot be presented in that form. Instead, images are used, that correspond to the skill levels for each question type:

- (level 1: *no image*, not attempted / none correct / weak performance)
- level 2: *tick*, satisfactory
- level 3: *smiling face*, good
- level 4: *grinning face*, very good
- level 5: *'cool' grinning face with sunglasses*, fantastic

Weak performances are not shown. A blank square might mean the child has not attempted questions of that type, or they have performed badly. This avoids demotivating children by showing negative information. Their aim is to 'achieve faces'.

If the child chooses 'compare yourself to children of your age', they can view the model of themselves compared to the 'average peer', as in Fig. 2. In this example, the child is doing extremely well compared to their peers in the first question type, indicated by the grinning face with sunglasses; and very well with the second and third

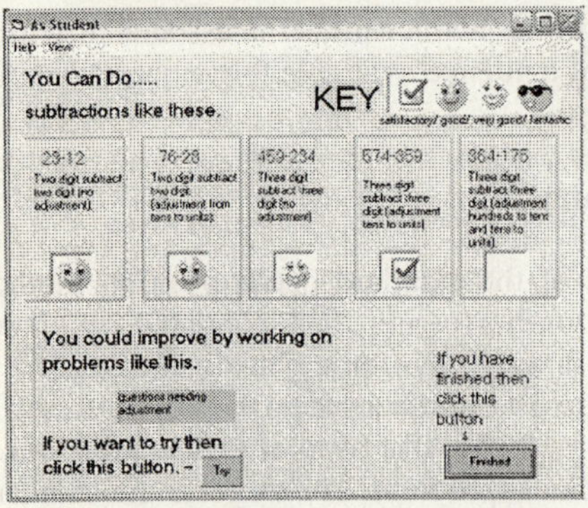

Fig. 1. The individual learner model

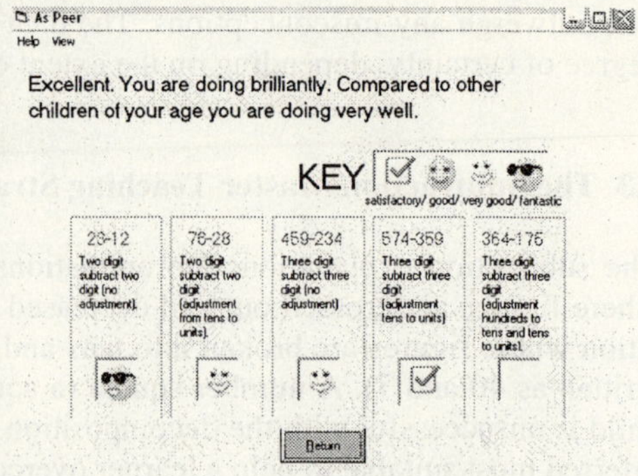

Fig. 2. Comparison to the average peer

types. They are performing in line with others in the fourth. However, in the final type, there is no representation. In this case this is because the child, and the class as a whole, have not yet attempted many questions of this kind. Where a child was not doing well compared to others, there would also be no representation. The aim is that the child will want to improve after making this comparison to their peers.

After 20 questions, the child is presented with their individual learner model and offered the chance to improve specific areas if these have been assessed as weak (bottom left of Fig. 1). This may be simply where they are having most difficulty, or where misconceptions are inferred, or it might be where the system is less certain of its representations. This is in part to encourage those who have not explored their learner model, to do so, and in part to guide learners towards areas that they could improve. While guidance occurs during individualised tutoring, this prompting within the OLM explicitly alerts learners of where they might best invest their effort.

In systems for use by adults, an approach of negotiating the learner model has been used [1], [2], to allow learners to try to persuade the system that their perception of their understanding is correct, if they disagree with the system's representations in the model. One way in which they can do this is to request a short test to prove their point. Since negotiation with a system over one's knowledge state is quite a complex procedure, this may not be appropriate for younger children. Thus the idea of a brief test to provoke change in the model if a child disagrees with it, is maintained in Subtraction Master, but the possibilities for adjusting the model are suggested by the system. The child can take up the challenge of a test if they believe they can improve the representation in their learner model; or they can accept the test while at the same time working through further examples to improve their skills in their weaker areas. The former quick method of correcting the model is useful, for example, if a child suddenly understands their problem. This can be illustrated with an example from one of the children in the study (see section 4), who showed misconceptions about commutative laws. On viewing help, she exclaimed 'I got it, I keep changing the numbers around instead of borrowing'. The student's learner model contained a history of the problem. When offered a test to change the model contents, she accepted and managed to remove the problem area from her model. She therefore did not have to complete a longer series of questions in order for the model to reflect this progress.

3.2 The Subtraction Master Open Learner Model for Teachers

Teachers can access the models of individuals, or they can view the average model of the group. Figs. 3 and 4 show the teacher's view, that can be accessed while they are with the child during the child's interaction, or later at their own PC. Teachers can edit the model of any individual if they believe it to have become incorrect (such as when a child has suddenly grasped a concept during coaching by the teacher, or if new results from paper-based testing are available, etc.). I.e. teachers can update the model to improve its accuracy, in order that the system continues to adapt appropriately to meet children's needs if they have been learning away from Subtraction Master.

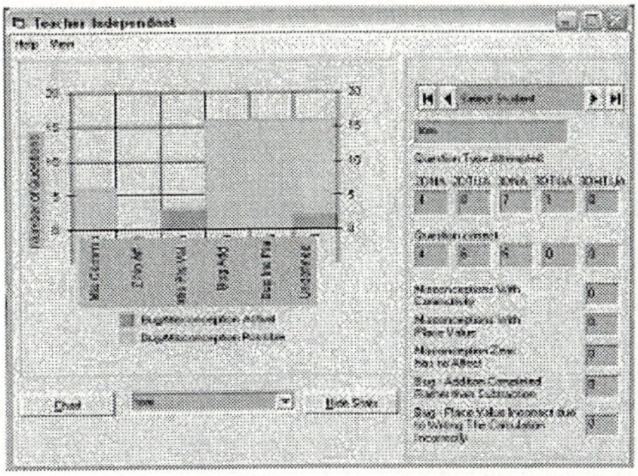

Fig. 3. The teacher's view of the individual

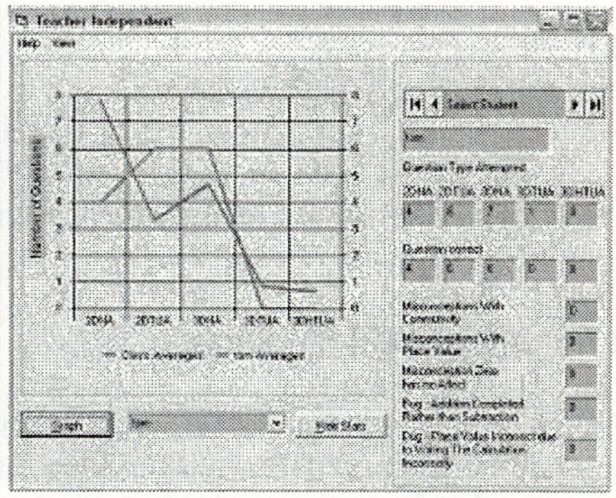

Fig. 4. The teacher's view of the individual compared to the group

Children are not shown misconceptions. However, this may be useful data for teachers. Figs. 3 and 4 show the learner model of Tom. Fig. 3 illustrates areas in which he could have shown misconceptions given the questions attempted (shaded light), and the misconceptions that were observed (shaded dark). The last column shows 'undefined' errors. In the above example, from a possible 15 undefined errors (15 questions were attempted), 2 undefined errors were exhibited. 3 incorrect responses suggest a likely place value misconception, out of 3 questions attempted, where this problem could be manifested (column 3). The first column shows Tom answered 6 questions where he could have shown a commutative error, but did not.

The upper portion of the right side of the screen shows Tom's performance across question types (number attempted, number correct). Below this is the strength of evidence for the five types of misconception or bug. As can be seen by the figure for place value being 0, the teacher has edited the model to reflect the fact that Tom no longer holds this misconception after help from the teacher.

Fig. 4 shows Tom's performance against the average achievement of the group. The group data can also be presented without comparison to a specific individual. Thus teachers can also investigate where the group is having most difficulty.

4 Benefits of a Simple Individual and Peer OLM for Children

We here present an overview of a study of potential benefits of the Subtraction Master OLM for children. The following questions were of particular interest:

- Would children want to view their learner model?
- Would children want to view the peer comparison model?
- Would children be able to interpret their learner model?
- Would children be able to interpret the peer comparison model?
- Would children find the open learner model useful?

4.1 Subjects

Subjects were 11 8-9 year-olds at a Birmingham school, selected by the Head Teacher to represent high achievers (4), average (2), low achievers (5); with 6 boys and 5 girls spread quite evenly in the high and low groups. Both average pupils were boys.

4.2 Materials and Method

Audio recordings were made while children used Subtraction Master. They were sometimes prompted for further information. Written notes were made to provide contextual information. Additional information was obtained by structured interview after the interaction. Sessions lasted around half an hour.

4.3 Results

Table 1 shows use of the open learner model by children. Students are listed in sequence as ranked for ability by the Head Teacher, from lowest to highest.

Table 1. Use of the open learner model by children

Use of OLM	Low Achievers					Average		High Achievers			
	S1	S2	S3	S4	S5	S6	S7	S8	S9	S10	S11
little or none		x		x	x				x		
spontaneous	x		x			xx	x	x		xx	x

Four children made little or no use of their OLM after the first inspection, while 7 returned to it spontaneously - 2 using it extensively (S6 and S10). There is no clear relationship between ability and preference for viewing the learner model, though in general it appears that the higher ranked students tend to be more interested. However, the lowest ranked child did use their model, and the third highest did not.

Transcripts of children's comments while using the OLM suggest many understand and benefit from it, illustrated by the following. (E=experimenter, S=subject.)

E: [Asks about the open learner model]
S1: Well at first that little face and then afterwards the big face was there.
E: And what did that mean to you?

S1: That I know my maths better.

S10: [Of the peer model] They are very good. I know they are both good because I have only had one of those ones and I had one of those other ones.
E: Can you think of a reason why you have one of those?
S10: Because other people have done more and they did it more times than me at the moment, and I have only done one ... So mine would go up when the next person gets one of them wrong.
......
E: You kept checking the models of yourself compared to others and perhaps compared to a test if you were taking a test. Why did you keep doing that?
S10: To see how I was doing.

S11: How good am I doing [compared] to the other pupils?
......
S11: The average people have got this face on, and that's a bit over average, and that's really over average, and that's less than average a bit.
E: [Asks about the peer model]
S11: Encourage me to do better actually, see how people are getting on, try to work hard, improve on last year or if we have to do another test ... I liked that.

The more able pupils (S10, S11) are better able to articulate their understanding of the OLM, and appreciate what is represented, even by the peer model. S1, ranked lowest, also used the OLM. It was harder to get S1 to freely express his views, but the excerpt shows he understood the individual model, as revealed upon prompting.

A chance occurrence further demonstrated a child's appreciation of the meaning of his learner model. Whilst S6 ('average') was working, his mother (a classroom assistant) asked how he was getting on. He looked at his learner model and replied 'great'.

4.4 Discussion

Our aim was not to develop a full ITS, but rather to investigate the potential for using OLMs with 8-9 year olds. Hence the system is relatively simple. We recognise that using only 11 subjects, our results are merely suggestive. It does seem, however, that the issue of using OLMs with children of this age, is worth investigating further.

We return to the questions raised earlier: Would children want to view their learner model? Would children want to view the peer comparison model? Would children be able to interpret their learner model? Would children be able to interpret the peer comparison model? Would children find the open learner model useful?

There appears to be a difference between children in their interest in the OLM. Seven children chose to use their model on more than one occasion, with 2 using it extensively. These two kept referring back to their model to monitor their progress. For them, the OLM was clearly motivating. One was high ability, and the other, medium ability. Thus the OLM can be a motivating factor for at least these two levels of student. The remaining 5 children who used their learner model spontaneously were two low-achievers, the other medium-level student, and two further high-achievers. The model therefore appears of interest to children of all abilities, though in general the higher level children had a greater tendency to refer to their learner models.

Of the 4 children who did not use their learner model, 2 were also disinterested in learning with computers generally (S2 and S5). Thus it may be this factor rather than the learner model itself, that is the basis of their lack of use of their learner model.

In addition to observations of students returning to their models, the transcript excerpts from low and high ability children demonstrate that 8-9 year olds can understand simple learner model representations. S1, the child with most difficulties, articulated his views only after prompting, but nevertheless showed an understanding of the learner model, albeit at a simple level. S10 and S11, high ability students, gave spontaneous explanations. The excerpts given, show their views of the comparative peer model. Both wanted to check their progress relative to others. S11 spontaneously asked how other children were doing before viewing the peer model. When the peer model was then shown to him, he became particularly interested in it. S6, an average student, referred to his learner model in order to report his progress to his mother.

The above questions can be answered positively for over half the children, as noted in the structured interview and student comments while using Subtraction Master. There was a tendency for higher- and medium-ability children to show greater interest, but two of the five lower-ability children also used their learner model.

We do not know to what extent the results are influenced by the novelty of the approach to the children, and the fact that they were selected for 'special treatment'. This needs to be followed up with a longer study with a greater number of subjects, which also considers learning gains. (A short pre- and post-test were administered, showing an average 16% improvement across subjects, but due to the limited time with the children, extended use of the system and delayed post-test were not possible.)

5 Summary

This paper introduced Subtraction Master, an ITS for subtraction for 8-9 year-olds. It was designed as a vehicle for investigating the potential of simple individual OLMs and comparison of the individual to peers, to enhance children's awareness of their progress. The children demonstrated an understanding of their learner model, and 7 of the 11 showed an interest in using it. These had a range of abilities. The next step is to allow children to use the system longer-term, to discover whether this level of interest is maintained over time, and if so, to develop a more complex ITS and investigate further open learner modelling issues with a larger number of children.

Acknowledgement. We thank Keith Willetts, Head Teacher of Paganel Junior School, Birmingham, and the children and teachers involved in the study.

References

1. Bull, S. & Pain, H. (1995). 'Did I say what I think I said, and do you agree with me?': Inspecting and Questioning the Student Model, Proceedings of World Conference on Artificial Intelligence in Education, Association for the Advancement of Computing in Education (AACE), Charlottesville, VA, 1995, 501-508.

2. Dimitrova, V., Self, J. & Brna, P. (2001). Applying Interactive Open Learner Models to Learning Technical Terminology, User Modeling 2001: 8th International Conference, Springer-Verlag, Berlin Heidelberg, 148-157.
3. Mitrovic, A. & Martin, B. (2002). Evaluating the Effects of Open Student Models on Learning, Adaptive Hypermedia and Adaptive Web-Based Systems, Proceedings of Second International Conference, Springer-Verlag, Berlin Heidelberg, 296-305.
4. Zapata-Rivera, J.D. & Greer, J.E. (2002). Exploring Various Guidance Mechanisms to Support Interaction with Inspectable Learner Models, Intelligent Tutoring Systems: 6th International Conference, Springer-Verlag, Berlin, Heidelberg, 442-452.
5. Barnard, Y.F. & Sandberg, J.A.C. (1996). Self-Explanations, do we get them from our students?, Proceedings of European Conference on AI in Education, Lisbon, 115-121.
6. Bull, S. & Nghiem, T. (2002). Helping Learners to Understand Themselves with a Learner Model Open to Students, Peers and Instructors, Proceedings of Workshop on Individual and Group Modelling Methods that Help Learners Understand Themselves, International Conference on Intelligent Tutoring Systems 2002, 5-13.
7. Zapata-Rivera, J-D. & Greer, J.E. (2001). Externalising Learner Modelling Representations, Proceedings of Workshop on External Representations of AIED: Multiple Forms and Multiple Roles, International Conference on Artificial Intelligence in Education 2001, 71-76.
8. Kay, J. (1997). Learner Know Thyself: Student Models to Give Learner Control and Responsibility, Proceedings of ICCE, AACE, 17-24.
9. Linton, F. & Schaefer, H-P. (2000). Recommender Systems for Learning: Building User and Expert Models through Long-Term Observation of Application Use, User Modeling and User-Adapted Interaction 10, 181-207.
10. Bull, S. & Broady, E. (1997). Spontaneous Peer Tutoring from Sharing Student Models, Artificial Intelligence in Education, IOS Press, Amsterdam, 143-150.
11. Brown, J.S. & Burton, R.R. (1978). Diagnostic Models for Procedural Bugs in Basic Mathematical Skills, Cognitive Science 2, 155-192.
12. Burton, R.R. (1982). Diagnosing Bugs in a Simple Procedural Skill, Intelligent Tutoring Systems, Academic Press, 157-183.
13. Department for Education and Skills (2004). The Standards Site: The National Numeracy Strategy, http://www.standards.dfes.gov.uk/numeracy.

Scaffolding Self-Explanation to Improve Learning in Exploratory Learning Environments

Andrea Bunt, Cristina Conati, and Kasia Muldner

Department of Computer Science, University of British Columbia
201-2366 Main Mall
Vancouver, British Columbia, V6T 1Z4
(604)822-4632

Abstract. Successful learning though exploration in open learning environments has been shown to depend on whether students possess the necessary meta-cognitive skills, including systematic exploration, hypothesis generation and hypothesis testing. We argue that an additional meta-cognitive skill crucial for effective learning through exploration is self-explanation: spontaneously explaining to oneself available instructional material in terms of the underlying domain knowledge. In this paper, we describe how we have expanded the student model of ACE, an open learning environment for mathematical functions, to track a learner's self-explanation behaviour and how we use this model to improve the effectiveness of a student's exploration.

1 Introduction

Several studies in Cognitive Science and ITS have shown the effectiveness of the learning skill known as *self-explanation*, i.e., spontaneously explaining to oneself available instructional material in terms of the underlying domain knowledge [6]. Because there is evidence that this learning skill can be taught (e.g., [2]), several computer-based tutors have been devised to provide explicit support for self-explanation. However, all these tutors focus on coaching self-explanation during fairly *structured* interactions targeting problem-solving skills (e.g., [1], [7, 8] and [10]). For instance, The SE-Coach [7][8] is designed to model and trigger students' self-explanations as they study examples of worked out solutions for physics problems. The Geometry Explanation Tutor [1] and Normit-SE [10] support self-explanations of problem-solving steps, in geometry theorem proving and data normalization respectively. In this paper, we describe how we are extending support for self-explanation to the type of *less structured* pedagogical interactions supported by open learning environments.

Open learning environments place less emphasis on supporting learning through structured, explicit instruction and more on allowing the learner to freely explore the available instructional material [11]. In theory, this type of active learning should enable students to acquire a deeper, more structured understanding of concepts in the

J.C. Lester et al. (Eds.): ITS 2004, LNCS 3220, pp. 656–667, 2004.

domain [11]. In practice, empirical evaluations have shown that open learning environments are not always effective for all students. The degree of learning from such environments depends on a number of student-specific features, including activity level, whether or not the student already possesses the meta-cognitive skills necessary to learn from exploration and general academic achievement (e.g., [11] and [12]).

To improve the effectiveness of open learning environments for different types of learners, we have been working on devising adaptive support for effective exploration. The basis of this support is a student model that monitors the learners' exploratory behaviour and detects when they need guidance in the exploration process. The model is implemented in the Adaptive Coach for Exploration (ACE), an open learning environment for mathematical functions [3, 4]. An initial version of this model integrated information on both student domain knowledge and the *amount* of exploratory actions performed during the interaction to dynamically assess the effectiveness of student exploration. Empirical studies showed that hints based on this model helped students learn from ACE. However, these studies also showed that the model sometimes overestimated the learners' exploratory behaviour, because it always interpreted a large number of exploratory actions as evidence of good exploration. In other words, the model was not able distinguish between learners who merely performed actions in ACE's interface and learners who *self-explained* those actions.

In this paper, we describe 1) how we modified ACE's student model to assess a student's self-explanation behaviour, and 2) how ACE uses this assessment to improve the effectiveness of a student's exploration through tailored scaffolding for self-explanation. ACE differs from Geometry Explanation Tutor and the Normit-SE not only because it supports self-explanation in a different kind of educational activity, but also because these systems do not model a student's need or tendency to self-explain. The Geometry Explanation Tutor prompts students to self-explain *every* problem-solving step, Normit-SE prompts students to self-explain every *new* or *incorrect* problem-solving step. Neither of these systems considers whether it is dealing with a self-explainer who would have initiated the self-explanation regardless of the coach's hints, even though previous studies on self-explanations have shown that some students do self-explain spontaneously [6]. Thus, these approaches are too restrictive for an open learning environment, because they may force spontaneous self-explainers to perform unnecessary interface actions, contradicting the idea of interfering as little as possible with students' free exploration. Our approach is closer to the SE-Coach's, which prompts for self-explanation only when its student model assesses that the student actually needs the scaffolding [9]. However, the SE-Coach mainly relies on the time spent on interface actions to assess whether or not a student is spontaneously self-explaining. In contrast, ACE also relies on the assessment of a student's self-explanation tendency, including how this tendency evolves as a consequence of the interaction with ACE. Using this richer set of information, ACE can provide support for self-explanation in a more timely and tailored manner.

In the rest of the paper, we first describe ACE's interface, and the general structure of its student model. Next, we illustrate the changes made to the interface and the model to provide explicit guidance for self-explanation. Finally, we illustrate the model's behaviour based on sample simulated scenarios.

2 The ACE Open Learning Environment

ACE is an adaptive open learning environment for the domain of mathematical functions. ACE's activities are divided into units, which are collections of exercises. Figure 1 shows the main interaction window for two of ACE's units: the *Machine Unit* and the *Plot Unit*. Ace's third unit, the *Arrow Unit*, is not displayed for brevity.

The Machine and the Arrow Units allow a learner to explore the relation between input and output of a function. In the Machine Unit, the learner can drag the inputs displayed at the top of the screen to the tail of the "machine" (the large arrow shown in Fig. 1, left), which then computes the corresponding output. The Arrow Unit allows the learner to match a function's inputs and outputs, and is the only unit within ACE that has a clear definition of correct behaviour. The Plot Unit (Fig. 1, right), allows the learner to explore the relationship between a function's graph and its equation by manipulating one entity, and then observing the corresponding changes in the other.

To support the exploration process, ACE includes a coaching component that provides tailored hints when ACE's student model assesses that students have difficulties exploring effectively. For more detail on ACE's interface and coaching component see [4]. In the next section, we describe the general structure of ACE's student model.

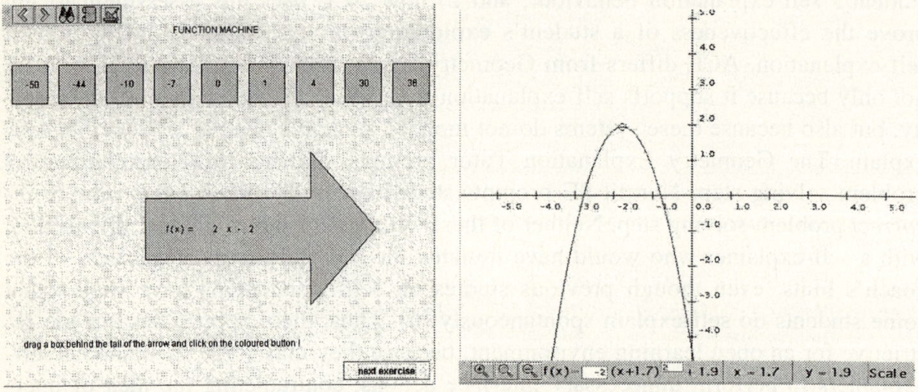

Fig. 1. Machine Unit (Right) and Plot Unit (Left)

3 General Structure of ACE's Student Model

ACE's student model uses Bayesian Networks to manage the uncertainty inherent to assessing students' exploratory behaviour. The main cause of this uncertainty is that both exploratory behaviour and the related meta-cognitive skills are not easily observable unless students are required to make them explicit. However, forcing students to articulate their exploration steps would clash with the unrestricted nature of open learning environments.

The structure of ACE's student model derives from an iterative design process [3] that gave us a better understanding of what defines effective exploration. Figure 2 shows a high-level description of this structure, which comprises several types of nodes used to assess exploratory behaviour at different levels of granularity:

- *Relevant Exploration Cases*: the exploration of individual exploration cases in an exercise (e.g., dragging the number 3, a small positive input, to the back of the function machine in the Machine Unit).
- *Exploration of Exercises*: the exploration of individual exercises.
- *Exploration of Units*: the exploration of individual units.
- *Exploration of Categories*: the exploration of groups of relevant exploration cases that appear across multiple exercises (e.g., all the cases involving a positive slope in the Plot unit).
- *Exploration of General Concepts*: the exploration of general domain concepts (e.g., the input/output relation for different types of functions).

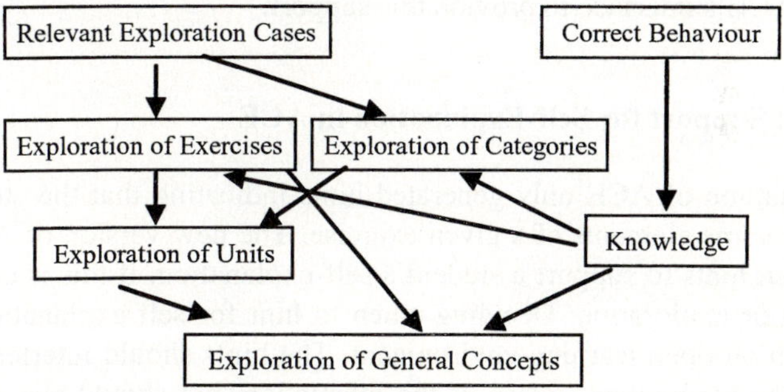

Fig. 2. High-Level Structure of ACE's Student Model

The links among the different types of exploration nodes represent how they interact to define effective exploration. Exploration nodes have binary values representing the probability that the learner has sufficiently explored the associated item.

ACE's student model also includes binary nodes representing the probability that the learner understands the relevant domain knowledge (summarized by the node *Knowledge* in Fig. 2). The links between knowledge and exploration nodes represent the fact that the degree of exploration needed to understand a concept depends on how much knowledge of that concept a learner already has. Knowledge nodes are updated only through actions for which there is a clear definition of correctness (e.g., linking inputs and outputs in the Arrow Unit).

4 Extending ACE to Track and Support Self-Explanation

As we mentioned in the introduction, initial studies on ACE generated encouraging evidence that the system could help students learn better from exploration [3, 4].

However, these studies also showed that sometimes ACE overestimated students' exploratory behaviour (as indicated by post-test scores).

We believe that a likely cause of this problem was that ACE considered a student's interface actions to be sufficient evidence of good exploratory behaviour, without taking into account whether s/he was *self-explaining* the outcome of these actions. To understand how self-explanation can play a key role in effective exploration, consider a student who quickly moves a function graph around the screen in the Plot unit, without reflecting on how these movements change the function equation. Although this learner is performing many exploratory actions, s/he can hardly learn from them because s/he is not self-explaining their outcomes. We observed this exact behaviour in a number of our subjects who tended to spend little time on exploratory actions, and who did not learn the associated concepts (as demonstrated by pre-test / post-test differences).

To address this limitation, we decided to extend ACE's interface and student model to provide tailored support for self-explanation. We first describe modifications made to ACE's interface to provide this support.

4.1 Tailored Support for Self-Explanation in ACE

The original version of ACE only generated hints indicating that the student should further explore some elements of a given exercise. The new version of ACE can also generate tailored hints to support a student's self-explanation, if this is detected to be the cause of poor exploration. Deciding when to hint for self-explanation is a challenging issue in an open learning environment. The hints should interfere as little as possible with the exploratory nature of the interaction, but should also be timely so that even the more reluctant self-explainers can appreciate their relevance. Thus, ACE hints to self-explain individual actions are provided as soon as the model predicts that the student is not self-explaining their outcomes when s/he should be.

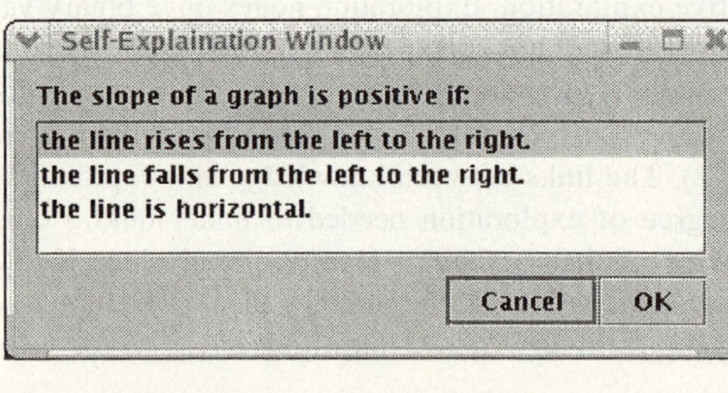

Fig. 3. Example of a Self-Explanation Tool for the Plot Unit.

The first of these hints is a generic suggestion to slow down and think a little more about the outcome of the performed actions. Following the approach of the SE-Coach [7, 8], ACE provides further support for those students who cannot spontaneously self-explain by suggesting the usage of interface tools, designed to help students generate relevant self-explanations. One type of hint targets self-explanations related to the outcome of specific actions, or *exploration cases*. For instance, Figure 3 shows a dialogue box involved in eliciting a self-explanation for an exploration case associated with a linear function in the Plot Unit. The multiple-choice approach is used here to avoid dealing with parsing of free text explanations, although this is something that we may change in future versions of the system, following [1]. After the student selects one of the statements, the coach provides feedback for correctness. Providing feedback for correctness is consistent with the view adopted by other approaches to coaching for self-explanation: although incorrect self-explanation can still be beneficial for learning [5], helping students to generate correct self-explanations further increases the efficacy of this meta-cognitive skill [1][2] [7][10]. ACE also provides hints to self-explain an exercise as a whole (e.g., the behaviour of a constant function in the machine unit), which are generated when a student tries to leave that exercise. We now describe the changes made to ACE's student model to support the hinting behaviour just described.

5 New Model for Self-Explanation

Obtaining information on a student's self-explanation behaviour in an open learning environment is a difficult challenge. The tools presented in the previous section can provide *explicit* evidence that a student is self-explaining, but because ACE does not force students to use these tools, the model must also try to assess whether or not the learner is self-explaining *implicitly*, i.e., without any tool usage. The only evidence that can be used toward this end is time a student spends on each exploratory action. Unfortunately, this evidence is clearly ambiguous, since a long time spent on an action does not necessarily mean reflection on that action. Similarly, a sequence of actions performed very quickly could be either due to a low self-explanation (SE) tendency, or to a student's desire to experiment with the interface before starting to explore the exercise more carefully. Without any further information on the student's general SE tendency, the latter ambiguity can be solved only by waiting until the student asks to leave the exercise (as the SE-Coach does, for instance [7, 8]). This, however, misses the opportunity to generate hints in context, when they can be best appreciated by the student.

Therefore, to improve its evaluation of students' exploration behaviour, ACE's student model includes an assessment of a student's SE tendency. In addition to assessing SE tendency, the model also assesses how it evolves during the interaction with ACE, to model the finding that SE tendency can be improved through explicit coaching [2]. To represent this evolution, we moved from a Bayesian Network that was mostly static [3] to a full Dynamic Bayesian Network. In this network, a new time slice is created after each student exploratory or SE action. These are described below.

5.1 Implicit Self-Explanation Slices

In the absence of explicit SE actions, the model tries to assess whether the student is implicitly self-explaining each exploratory action. Figure 4 shows two time slices created after two exploratory actions. Since the remainder of the exploration hierarchy (see Fig. 2) has not undergone significant change, we omit it for clarity. In this figure, the learner is currently exploring exercise 0 (node e_0 in Fig. 4), which has three relevant exploration cases (e_0Case_0, e_0Case_1 and e_0Case_2 in Fig. 4). At time T, the learner performed an action corresponding to the exploration of e_0Case_2; at time T+1, the action corresponded to e_0Case_1. Nodes representing the assessment of self-explanation are shaded grey. All nodes in the model are binary, except for *time*, which has values *Low/Med/High*. We now describe each type of self-explanation node:

- *Implicit SE:* represents the probability that the learner has self-explained a case implicitly, without using the interface tools. The factors influencing this assessment include the time spent exploring the case and the stimuli that the learner has to self-explain. Low time on action is always taken as negative evidence for implicit explanation. The probability that self-explanation happened with longer time depends on whether there is a stimulus to self-explain.
- *Stimuli to SE:* represents the probability that the learner has stimuli to self-explain, either from the learner's general SE tendency or from a coach's explicit hint.
- *SE Tendency:* represents the model's assessment of a student's SE tendency. The prior probability for this node will be set using either default population data or, when possible, data for a specific student. In either case, the student model's belief in that student's tendency will subsequently be refined by observing her behaviour with ACE. More detail on this assessment is presented in section 5.3.
- *Time:* represents the probability that the learner has spent a sufficient time covering the case. We use time spent as an indication of effort (i.e., the more time spent the greater the potential for self-explanation). Time nodes are observed to low, medium and high according to the intervals between learner actions.
- *Coach Hint to SE:* indicates whether or not the learner's self-explanation action was preceded by a prompt from the coach.

We now discuss the impact of the above nodes on the model's assessment of the learner's exploratory behaviour. Whether or not a learner's action implies effective exploration of a given case (e.g., e_0Case_2) depends on the probability that: 1) the student self-explained the action and 2) s/he knows the corresponding concept, as assessed by the set of knowledge nodes in the model (summarized in Fig. 4 by the node *Knowledge*). In particular, the CPT for a case exploration node is defined so that low self-explanation with high knowledge generates an assessment of adequate exploration and, thus, does not trigger a Coach hint. This accounts for the fact that a student with high knowledge of a concept does not need to dwell on the related case to improve her understanding [3]. Note that the assessment of *implicit SE* is independent from the student's knowledge. We consider implicit self-explanation to have occurred regardless of correctness, consistent with the original definition of self-explanation [6].

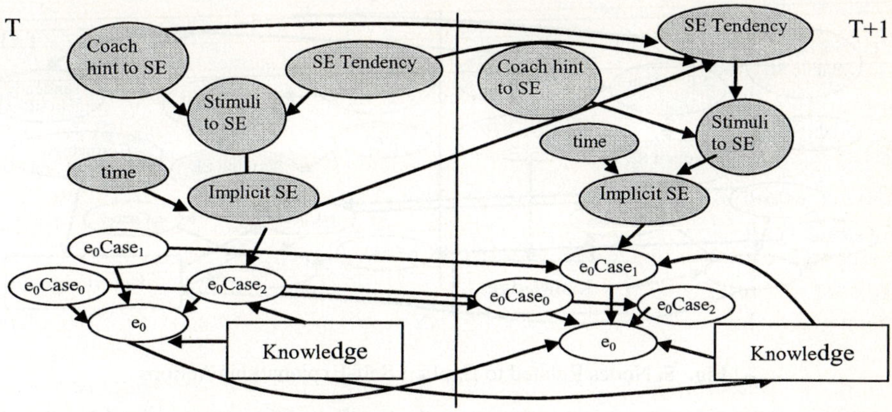

Fig. 4. Nodes Related to Implicit Self-Explanation Actions

5.2 Explicit Self-Explanation Slices

Usage of ACE's SE tools provides the model with additional information on the student's self-explanation behaviour. Self-explanation actions using these tools generate explicit self-explanation slices; two such slices are displayed in Figure 5. Compared to implicit SE slices, explicit SE slices include additional evidence nodes representing: 1) the usage of the SE tool (*SE Action* node in Fig. 5), and 2) the correctness of this action (*Correctness* node in Fig. 5). The *SE Action* node, together with the time the student spent on this action, influences the assessment of whether an explicit self-explanation actually occurred (*Explicit SE* node in Fig. 5). As was the case for the implicit SE slices, correctness of the SE action does not influence this assessment. However, correctness does influence the assessment of the student's corresponding knowledge, since it is a form of explicit evidence. Consequently, if the explicit SE action is correct, the belief that the student effectively explored the corresponding case is further increased through the influence of the corresponding knowledge node(s).

5.3 Assessing Self-Explanation Tendency

One novel aspect of ACE's student model is its ability to assess how a student's tendency to self-explain evolves during the interaction with the system. In particular, the model currently represents the finding that explicit coaching can improve SE tendency [2]. Fig. 5 shows how the model assesses this tendency in the explicit SE slices.

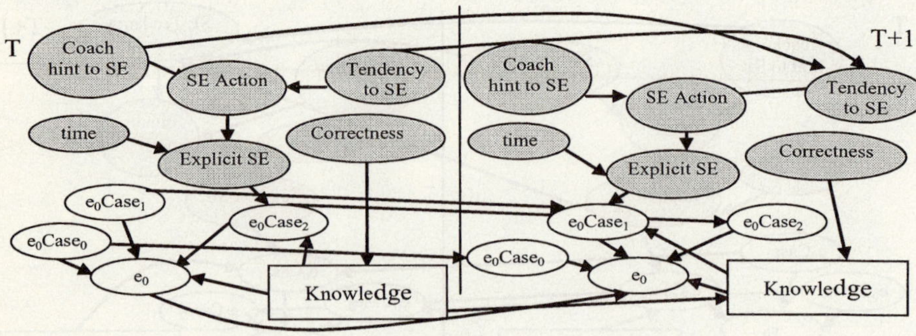

Fig. 5. Nodes Related to Explicit Self-Explanations Actions

This assessment consists of two stages. In the first stage, represented by the slice created in response to a student's explicit SE action (slice T in Fig. 5), evidence of a Coach hint to self-explain allows the model to refine its assessment of the student's SE tendency *before* s/he performed the SE action. The CPT for a *SE Action* node is designed so that the amount of credit for the SE action that goes to the student's *SE Tendency* in slice T depends upon whether the action was preceded by a hint. The occurrence of such a hint *explains away* much of the evidence, limiting the increase in the belief that the student's *SE Tendency* was the cause of the SE action.

The second stage models how a student's SE tendency evolves as a result of a Coach's hint to self-explain. A *Coach hint to SE* node at time *T* is linked to a *SE tendency* node at time *T+1*, so that the probability that the tendency is high increases after the hint occurs. The magnitude of this increase is currently set to be quite conservative, but we plan to refine it by performing user studies. A similar mechanism is used to assess *SE Tendency* in implicit SE slices.

6 Sample Assessment

We now illustrate the assessment generated by our model with two sample scenarios.

Scenario 1: Explicit SE Action. Suppose a student, assessed to have a low initial knowledge and a fairly high SE tendency, is exploring an exercise in the Plot Unit. She first performs an exploratory action, and then chooses to self-explain explicitly using the SE tools. Figure 6 (Top) illustrates the model's assessment of the relevant knowledge, SE tendency, and case exploration for the first three slices of the interaction. Slice 1 shows the model's assessment prior to any student activity. Slice 2 shows the assessment after one exploratory action with medium time has been performed, but not explicitly self-explained. Since the student's SE tendency is fairly high and medium time was spent performing the action, the assessment of case exploration increases. Slice 3 shows the assessment after the student performed an explicit SE action (corresponding to the same exploration case). Since the action was performed without a Coach hint, the appraisal of her SE tendency increases in that time slice. The self-explanation action was correct, which increases knowledge of the related concept. Finally, case exploration increases in Slice 3 because 1) the learner spent enough time self-explaining and 2) has provided direct evidence of her knowledge.

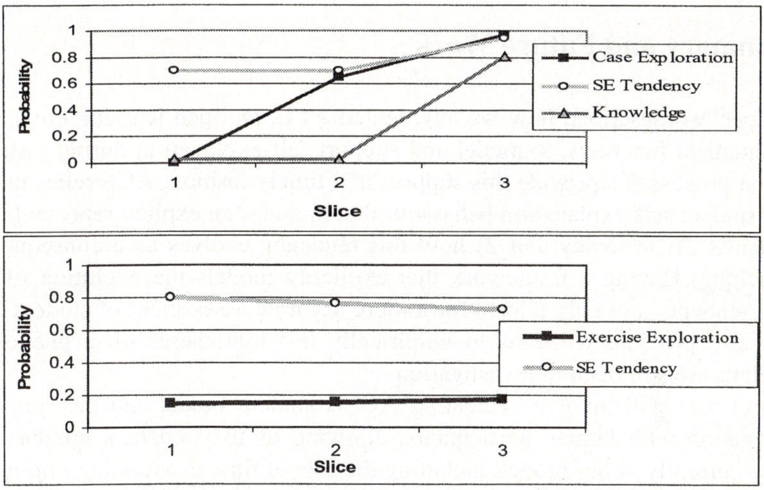

Fig. 6. Scenario 1 (Top) and Scenario 2 (Bottom)

Scenario 2: Insufficient Time. Let's now suppose that our student moves on to a Plot Unit exercise involving the linear function, and that she has low knowledge of this function's behaviour. Our student tries various configurations of the function in the interface, but does each action quickly, leaving little time for self-explanation. Figure 6 (Bottom) illustrates the model's assessment of the exercise and SE tendency nodes for the first three slices of this interaction. With each quick action performed by the student, the model's belief in the student having explored the exercise adequately increases very slightly to indicate that actions were performed, but were not sufficiently self-explained. This belief is based on the model's assessment of the explored case nodes, for which the belief would be low in this scenario (since each action corresponds to a different case, we did not show case probabilities in the graph to avoid cluttering the figure). After these three actions, the exercise exploration is low, but the student's tendency to self-explain remains fairly high to account for the possibility that the student will eventually engage in self-explanation. This will lead the Coach to believe that although the student has not explored the exercise well so far, s/he may do so prior to moving on to a new one. The Coach remains silent unless the student actually tries to leave the exercise without providing any further evidence of self explanation. On the other hand, had the model assessed the student's SE tendency to be low, the Coach would have intervened as soon as a lack of self-explanation was detected.

The low probability for adequate exercise exploration illustrates the difference between this version of the model and the original ACE model [3]. The old model took into account only coverage of exploratory actions, without assessing whether the student had self-explained the implications of those actions. Thus, that model would have assessed our student to have adequately explored the cases covered by her actions.

7 Summary and Future Work

In this paper, we described how we augmented ACE, an open learning environment for mathematical functions, to model and support self-explanation during a student's exploration process. To provide this support in a timely fashion, ACE relies on a rich model of student self-explanation behaviour that includes an explicit representation of 1) a student's SE tendency and 2) how this tendency evolves as a consequence of ACE coaching. Having a framework that explicitly models the evolution of a student's SE tendency not only allows for a more accurate assessment of student behaviour, but also provides a means to empirically test hypotheses on a phenomenon whose details are still open to investigation.

The next step will involve evaluating ACE's student model and the support for self-explanation with human participants, allowing us to validate a number of assumptions currently in our model, including the role of time in assessing implicit self-explanation and the impact coach hints on self-explanation tendency. In addition, we plan to investigate the most appropriate interface options for presenting the self-explanation hints and tools. We are also examining ways to improve the assessment of implicit SE through the use of eye tracking to track students' attention.

References

1. Aleven, V. and K.R. Koedinger, An Effective Meta-cognitive Strategy: Learning by Doing and Explaining with a Computer-Based Cognitive Tutor. Cognitive Science, 2002. **26**(2): p. 147-179.
2. Bielaczyc, K., P. Pirolli, and A.L. Brown, Training in Self-Explanation and Self-Regulation Strategies: Investigating the Effects of Knowledge Acquisition Activities on Problem-Solving. Cognition and Instruction, 1995. **13**(2): p. 221-252.
3. Bunt, A. and C. Conati. Probabilistic Student Modelling to Improve Exploratory Behaviour. Journal of User Modeling and User-Adapted Interaction, 2003. **13**(3): p.269-309.
4. Bunt, A., C. Conati, M. Huggett, and K. Muldner, On Improving the Effectiveness of Open Learning Environments through Tailored Support for Exploration. in AIED 2001, 10th World Conference of Artificial Intelligence and Education. 2001. San Antonio, TX.
5. Chi, M.T.H., Self-Explaining Expository Texts: The Dual Processes of Generating Inferences and Repairing Mental Models. In Advances in Instructional Psychology, 2000, p. 161-237.
6. Chi, M.T.H., M. Bassok, M. Lewis, P. Reimann and R. Glaser, Self-Explanations: How Students Study and Use Examples in Learning to Solve Problems. Cognitive Science, 1989. **15**: p. 145-182.

7. Conati, C., J. Larkin, and K. VanLehn, A Computer Framework to Support Self-Explanation, in Proceedings of the Eighth World Conference of Artificial Intelligence in Education. 1997.
8. Conati, C. and K. VanLehn, Toward Computer-based Support of Meta-cognitive Skills: A Computational Framework to Coach Self-Explanation. International Journal of Artificial Intelligence in Education, 2000. **11**.
9. Conati, C. and K. VanLehn. Providing Adaptive Support to the Understanding of Instructional Material. in IUI 2001, International Conference on Intelligent User Interfaces. 2001. Santa Fe, NM, USA.
10. Mitrovic, A. Supporting Self-Explanation in a Data Normalization Tutor. in Supplementary proceedings, AIED 2003. 2003.
11. Shute, V.J. and R. Glaser, A Large-Scale Evaluation of an Intelligent Discovery World. Interactive Learning Environments, 1990. **1**: p. 51-76.
12. van Joolingen, W.R. and T. de Jong, Supporting Hypothesis Generation by Learners Exploring an Interactive Computer Simulation. Instructional Science, 1991. **20**: p. 389-404.

Metacognition in Interactive Learning Environments: The Reflection Assistant Model

Claudia Gama

Federal University of Bahia, Department of Computer Science
Salvador(BA), Brazil
www.dcc.ufba.br
claudiag@ufba.br

Abstract. Computers have a lot of potential as metacognitive tools, by recording and replaying some trace of the learners' activities to make them reflect on their actions. This paper describes research[1] that created generic metacognition model called the Reflection Assistant (RA) that explores new instructional designs for metacognition instruction in problem solving environments. Three metacognitive skills are explicitly trained: knowledge monitoring, strategies planning, and evaluation of learning experience.

As part of this research we built the MIRA system, a problem solving environment for algebra word problems, which incorporated the RA model. We expected that through interactions with the reflective activities, students would be encouraged to becoming more conscious about their learning processes and skills. To investigate the effectiveness of the RA model for metacognition training, we conducted an empirical study with MIRA. The results suggest the reflective activities helped students improve their performance, time management skills, and knowledge monitoring ability.

1 Introduction

Metacognition is a form of cognition, a second or higher order thinking process which involves active control over cognitive processes [1]. Sometimes it is simply defined as thinking about thinking or as a person's cognition about cognition.

Extensive research suggests that metacognition has a number of concrete and important effects on learning, as it produces a distinctive awareness of the processes, as well as the results of the learning endeavour [1]. Recently, many studies have examined ways in which theories of metacognition can be applied to education, focusing on the fundamental question *"Can explicit instruction of metacognitive processes facilitate learning?"*. The literature points to several successful examples (see [2], for instance).

Research also indicates that metacognitively aware learners are more strategic and perform better than unaware learners [3]. One explanation is that metacognitive awareness enables individuals to plan, sequence, and monitor their

[1] This research was supported by grant No. 200275-98.4 from CNPq-Brazil.

J.C. Lester et al. (Eds.): ITS 2004, LNCS 3220, pp. 668–677, 2004.

learning in a way that directly improves performance [4]. However, not all students engage spontaneously in metacognitive thinking unless they are explicitly encouraged to do so through carefully designed instructional activities [5].

Hence it is important to do research on effective ways to include metacognitive support in the design of natural and computer-based learning environments. Some attempts have been made to incorporate metacognition training into interactive learning environments (ILEs) and Intelligent Tutoring Systems (ITSs), mostly in the form of embedded reflection on the learning task or processes.

Researchers in this area have recognized the importance of incorporating metacognitive models into ILE design [6]. However the lack of an operational model of metacognition makes this task a difficult one. Thus, the development of models or frameworks that aim to develop metacognition, cognitive monitoring, and regulation in ILEs is an interesting and open topic of investigation.

This paper describes a framework called the Reflection Assistant (RA) Model for metacognition instruction. This model was implemented into an ILE called MIRA. The model and some illustrations of the MIRA environment are presented, together with the results of an empirical evaluation performed.

2 Metacognitive Training in Interactive Learning Environments

Designing metacognitive activities in ILEs that focus on improvements at the domain and metacognitive level is a theoretical and practical challenge. Most ILEs and ITSs have regarded metacognition training as a by-product, sometimes addressing the issue of metacognition in a tangential way, providing embedded reflection tools, but not overtly targeting metacognitive development or analysing the impacts of such tools on students' metacognition and attitudes towards learning.

Very few attempts have been made to design explicit metacognitive models into ILEs. One example is MIST, a system that helps students to actively monitor their learning when studying from texts [7]. Its design follows a process-based intervention and uses collaboration, and questioning as tutorial strategies to facilitate students' planning and monitoring skills. MIST was rather simple from a computational point of view, but demonstrated success in bringing about some changes to the learning activities of students. Another interesting example is the SE-Coach system [8]; it supports students learning from examples through self-explanations. In SE-Coach a student model integrates information about the students actions with a model of correct self-explanations and the students domain knowledge.

Major instructional and design issues arise when learning systems intend to promote metacognition. The criteria used to decide what is the most suitable combination of the possible options can vary from domain to domain and depend on the kind of task proposed. But there are nonetheless two basic requirements which the designer should always follow: *(i)* to be careful not to increase the student's cognitive load; and *(ii)* to get students to recognize the importance of the metacognitive activities to the learning process.

3 The Reflection Assistant Model

The RA Model puts forth the notion that focusing on metacognitive skills as object of reflection triggers the development of these skills and has the potential to improve learning. Hence, it intends to make students aware of the importance of metacognition for the success of the learning endeavour [9].

While the RA Model is dedicated to the metacognitive aspects of learning, it has been designed to be used in conjunction with problem-solving learning environments. So it acts as an assistant to the learning process. The goals of this new *integrated* environment are:

1. Elicit a connection in the student's mind between her metacognitive skills and her domain-level actions, as well as the products or results she generates.
2. Emphasize the importance of having an accurate judgment of the understanding of the problems to be solved as a means to improve attention and to allocate cognitive resources appropriately.
3. Demonstrate to the student means to assess, reflect on, and improve her problem solving process.

3.1 Theoretical Basis

We have adopted Tobias & Everson's model of metacognition as the theoretical foundation for the RA model [10]. They have investigated largely the monitoring aspect of metacognition, based on the assumption that accurate monitoring is crucial in learning and training contexts where students have to master a great deal of new knowledge [11]. Their model assumes that the ability to differentiate between what is known and unknown is a prerequisite for the effective self-regulation of learning. This skill is called *knowledge monitoring* and it supports the development of other metacognitive skills, such as comprehension monitoring, help seeking, planning, and revising.

Following their formulation of an interdependent and hierarchic relation between metacognitive skills, the RA Model proposes an incremental focus on metacognition training in the same order they propose. Thus, primarily the RA is directed to learners' improvement of *knowledge monitoring*. Supported by this, it focuses on *evaluation of the learning process*; then on top of those two, it works on the *selection of metacognitive strategies*, i.e. general heuristics or strategies that are loosely connected to the domain and the task.

3.2 The RA Model and the Problem Solving Domain

The problem solving activity can be divided into three conceptual stages: (a) preparation to solve the problem or familiarization stage, (b) production stage, and (c) evaluation or judgement stage [12]. The RA is organized around these stages, matching specific metacognition instruction to the characteristics of each of these stages as shown in Fig.1.

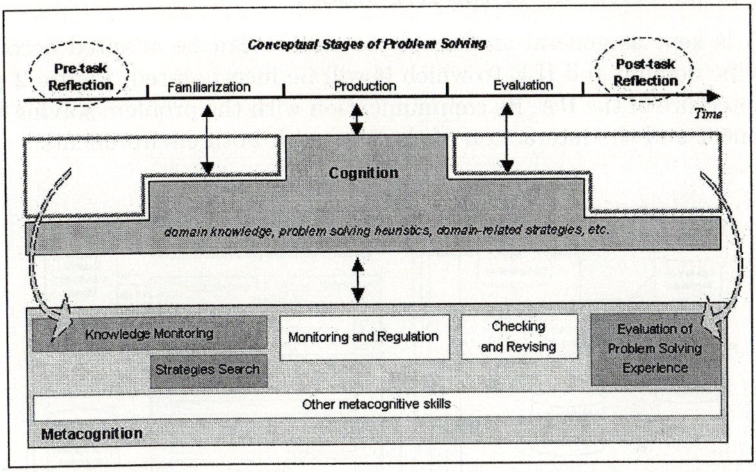

Fig. 1. Problem solving conceptual stages and the RA Model.

At the top of the diagram is a timeline representing a typical problem solving episode broken down into conceptual stages. The layer in the middle of the diagram shows the cognitive skills that are brought to bear on the process as time goes by. The layer at the bottom represents the metacognitive skills which are active along the way. Considering these conceptual stages, we have set specific moments where each of the metacognitive skills selected shall be trained. As such, *knowledge monitoring* and *strategies selection* are mainly explored in the familiarization stage, when the learner should naturally spend some time understanding the nature of the problem, recognizing the goals, and identifying the givens of the problem.

We believe that cognitive load is higher at the production stage. Therefore, the design of the RA Model does not include any major interference during the production stage. Instead, two new conceptual stages in problem solving were created, which are called *pre-task reflection* and *post-task reflection*.

At these new stages the cognitive load is lower, because the student is not engaged in actually solving the problem, but still has the problem fresh on her mind. Thus, the RA Model uses this "cognitive space" to promote reflection on knowledge monitoring and evaluation of the problem solving experience.

The ***Pre-task reflection stage*** covers the metacognitive aspects necessary to start the new problem; it provides suitable conditions for the student to become aware of useful general strategies, resources available, and also the degree of attention necessary to succeed in solving the problem.

The ***Post-task reflection stage*** creates a space where the student thinks about her actions during the past problem solving activity, comparing them with her reflections expressed just before the beginning of that problem.

3.3 The Architecture of the RA Model

The RA is kept as general as possible so that it can be adapted according to the specific domain and ILE to which it will be incorporated. Figure 2 presents the architecture of the RA, its communication with the problem solving learning environment and the interaction of the user with both environments.

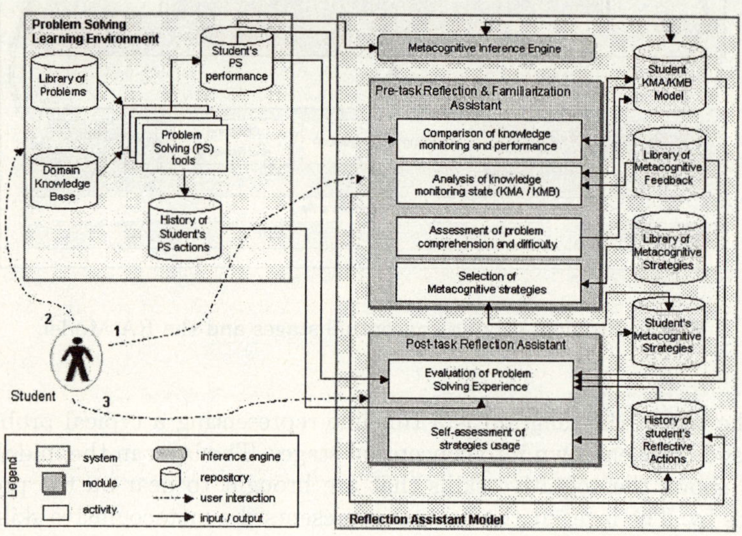

Fig. 2. Architecture of the Reflection Assistant Model.

The RA is divided into two main modules: *pre-task reflection and familiarization assistant* and *post-task reflection assistant.*

The *pre-task reflection and familiarization assistant* aims at preparing the student for the problem solving activity, promoting reflection on knowledge monitoring, assessment of the understanding of the problem to be attempted, and awareness of useful metacognitive strategies.

The *post-task reflection assistant* presents activities related to the evaluation of problem solving and takes place just after the student finishes a problem.

Besides the modules, the RA includes an inference engine to assess students' level of metacognition. Finally, the RA incorporates a series of data repositories, which contain either general knowledge about metacognition or information about students' demonstrated or inferred metacognition.

From the user's perspective the interaction takes place in the following sequence: (1) the student starts by performing the first two activities proposed in the pre-task and familiarization assistant, then the ILE presents a new problem and she proceeds to the other two activities of the same assistant; (2) she solves the problem with the aid of the problem solving tools provided by the ILE; and (3) after finishing the problem, she performs the activities proposed by the post-task reflection assistant.

3.4 The RA Metacognitive Inference Engine

Tobias & Everson have also developed an empirically validated instrument for measuring knowledge monitoring accuracy (KMA) [11]. This instrument was adapted and augmented for the purposes of our model and is the basis for the inference engine which infers only one metacognitive skill: knowledge monitoring.

The student's knowledge monitoring ability is inferred from the ILE (using the student's performance on problem solving) and from the RA (using the student's own prediction of her understanding of problems and ability to solve them). The inference mechanism is applied every time the student attempts a new problem and the student model is updated as a result. Two aspects of knowledge monitoring ability are inferred: knowledge monitoring accuracy (KMA) and knowledge monitoring bias (KMB).

Knowledge Monitoring Accuracy (KMA) refers to how skillful a student is at predicting how she will perform on a learning task; it reflects her awareness of the knowledge she possesses.

Knowledge Monitoring Bias (KMB) provides a statistical measure of any tendency or bias in the learner's knowledge monitoring ability.

3.5 Measuring Knowledge Monitoring Accuracy (KMA)

Tobias & Everson's original instrument evaluated the learner's knowledge monitoring accuracy by first asking her whether she was able to solve a problem and later asking her to solve that problem. The KMA resulted from the match between these two pieces of information. By collecting a significant number of elementary assessments for the same student, their instrument produced a statistical profile of the student's awareness of her own knowledge.

To build our version of the KMA measure we expanded their formula. We allowed both prediction and performance to take a third value representing some intermediary state. In the dimension of prediction, we added the possibility for the student to predict that she would partially solve the problem or that she partially understood it. In the dimension of performance, we now treat partially correct answers as a meaningful case.

The mean of the KMA scores over all problems solved so far yields the *current KMA state* of the student. The more the student interacts with the environment, the more reliable becomes the RA's assessment of her KMA. The score inferred for the KMA is shown to students in the reflective activities. For this purpose the numeric values are converted into qualitative ones. The classification summarizes scores by mapping them in three categories: low KMA, average KMA, and high KMA.

3.6 Measuring Knowledge Monitoring Bias (KMB)

The KMB measure was created since the KMA does not provide a detailed account about the type of inaccuracies the student may show. For example, imagine a student that was assigned a low KMA profile, because she is constantly predicting that she will solve the problems correctly, but her problem solutions are invariably wrong. This case is different from the one of another student that tends to estimate that she will not solve the problems completely correct, but then most of the time she reaches a correct solution.

The KMB takes into account the way student deviate from an accurate assessment of her knowledge monitoring. If there is no deviation, we say that the student is accurate in her assessment of her knowledge or *realistic* about it. Otherwise, three cases are possible: *(i)* the student often predicts she will solve the problems but she does not succeed, demonstrating through this an *optimistic* assessment of her knowledge; *(ii)* the student often predicts she will not solve the problems, but then she succeeds in solving them, demonstrating through this a *pessimistic* assessment of her knowledge; and *(iii)* she is sometimes optimistic in her assessment of her knowledge as she is pessimistic, in a *random* pattern.

A classification of student's *current KMB state* in respect to her predictions deviations is made based on the mean of KMB scores over all problems solved so far.

3.7 The RA Reflective Activities and the MIRA System

A system called MIRA (Metacognitive Instruction using a Reflection Approach) was built and it incorporated the RA reflective activities and metacognition assessment mechanism. Below we detail some of the reflective activities in the RA model and give an illustration of how they were implemented in MIRA.

Activity 1: Comparison of Knowledge Monitoring and Performance. This activity aims to trigger reflection on student's trend and progress of her knowledge monitoring ability. It focuses on past problems, showing to the student her previous performance and comparing them to her judgements of her knowledge and understanding of those problems. Figure 3 shows part of this activity in MIRA. It depicts bar-type graphs showing the self-assessment of problem understanding next to performance for all past problems. Textual explanations are also used to provoke appropriate interpretations of the graphs, also asking students to look for trends.

Activity 2: Analysis of Knowledge Monitoring State. This activity also focuses on knowledge monitoring ability. It refers to problem solving in general and presents the RA's inferred assessment of student's level of KMA and KMB. In this way, it aims to foster accuracy of knowledge monitoring by raising awareness of knowledge monitoring ability overtly. Graphical widgets called *reflectometers* indicate the KMA and the KMB (Fig.4).

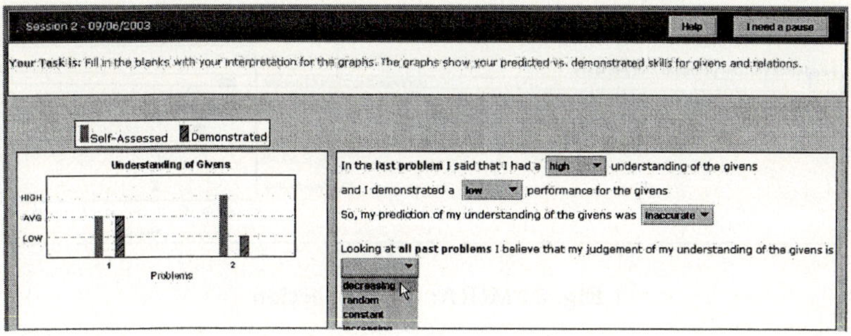

Fig. 3. MIRA: reflection on predicted and demonstrated knowledge skills.

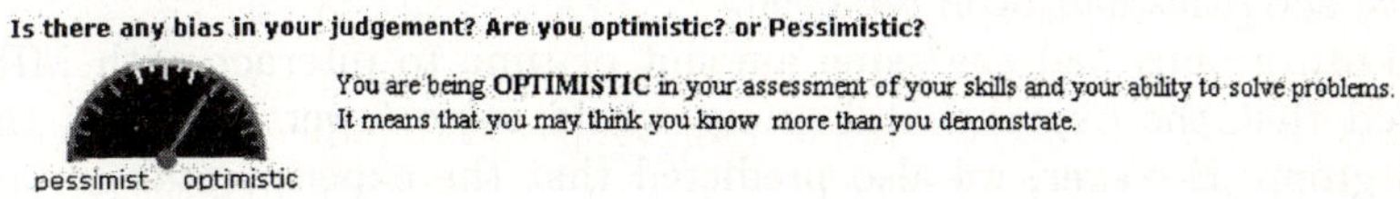

Fig. 4. Reflectometer with KMB assessment.

Activity 3: Self-assessment of the Problem Comprehension and Difficulty. This activity is related to the self-assessment of the current problem still to be solved. It aims to make the student reflect on her understanding of the concepts and components of the problem and on her confidence to solve it correctly.

Activity 4: Selection of Metacognitive Strategies. The goal of this activity is to make students reflect on three types of metacognitive strategies that can be useful to solve the problem at hand: monitoring understanding, monitoring progress and controlling errors, and revising solution paths. Thus, this activity helps students to select of relevant strategies, their purposes and appropriate moments to apply them.

Activity 5: Evaluation of Problem Solving Experience. This activity aims to give an opportunity to the student to review her most recent experience. The focus is on helping her to reflect on her use of resources, and other time management issues. In so doing she can develop a better understanding of her problem solving practice. We have developed a graphical reification of the student's interaction with the problem solving activity (Fig.5).

4 Evaluation of the RA Model

An empirical study was conducted with 25 undergraduate students who used MIRA in three one-hour sessions. They were divided in two groups: *experimental group*, that interacted with MIRA to solve problems *and* performed reflective

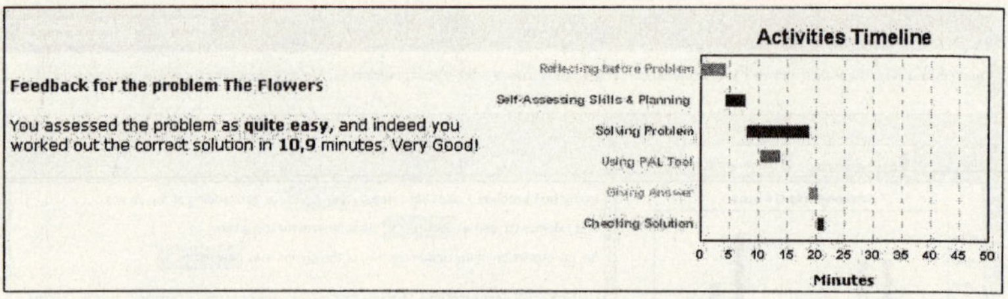

Fig. 5. MIRA: post reflection.

activities; and *control group*, that interacted with a version of MIRA where all reflective activities had been removed.

As both groups had the same amount of time to interact with MIRA, we predicted that the experimental group would solve fewer problems than the control group. However, we also predicted that the experimental group would perform better.

Indeed, the number of problems attempted by the experimental group (N=112) was highly significantly smaller (Mann-Whitney U test, z=2.56, p=0.005$< \alpha =$ 0.01) than that of the control group (N=136). At the same time, the experimental group had a significantly better performance in MIRA than the control group: the number of correct answers per total of problems attempted was significantly greater than that of the control group (z=1.66, p (1-tailed)=0.048). It was also the case for the number of answers almost correct (with minor errors) per total of problems attempted (z=1.82, p (1-tailed)=0.04).

At the metacognitive level, there was a higher increase of KMA in the experimental group than in the control group. However, this difference was not statistically significant. So, even though we have some evidence of the benefits on students' knowledge monitoring skill, we can not make strong claims about the validity of the RA model for knowledge monitoring development.

5 Conclusions

The Reflection Assistant model is a generic framework that can be tailored and used together with different types of problem solving environments. All the elements can be adjusted and augmented according to the objectives of the designers and the requirements of the domain. The interface has to be designed according to the ILE as it was done in the MIRA System presented. The ultimate goal is to create a comprehensive problem solving environment that provides activities that serve to anchor new concepts into the learner's existing cognitive knowledge to make them retrievable.

One important innovation introduced by the RA Model is the idea that it is necessary to conceive specific moments and activities to promote awareness of aspects of the problem solving process. Therefore, the RA is designed as a separate component from the problem solving environment with specialized activities. Therefore, two new stages in problem solving activity are proposed:

pre-task reflection stage and post-task reflection stage. During these stages the student interacts uniquely with the reflective activities proposed in the RA Model, which focus on the her metacognitive skills and reflection on her problem solving experience.

As the evaluation of MIRA demonstrated a shift from quantity to quality was an interesting consequence of the inclusion of the RA model in MIRA. As seen in the experiment, the quantity of problems performed did not lead to better performance.

Another experiment with a bigger number of subjects is necessary to draw more definite conclusions about the influence and benefits of the Reflection Assistant model proposed here.

References

1. Flavell, J.H.: Metacognition and cognitive monitoring. a new area of cognitive-developmental inquiry. American Psychologist **34** (1979) 906–911
2. Hacker, D.J., Dunlosky, J., Graesser, A.C., eds.: Metacognition in Educational Theory and Practice. Hillsdale, NJ: Lawrence Erlbaum Associates (1998)
3. Pressley, M., Ghatala, E.S.: Self-regulated learning: Monitoring learning from text. Educational Psychologist **25** (1990) 19–33
4. Schraw, G., Dennison, R.S.: Assessing metacognitive awareness. Contemporary Educational Psychology **19** (1994) 460–475
5. Lin, X.D., Lehman, J.D.: Supporting learning of variable control in a computer-based biology environment: Effects of prompting college students to reflect on their own thinking. Journal of Research in Science Teaching **36** (1999) 837–858
6. Aleven, V., Koedinger, K.R.: Limitations of student control: Do students know when they need help? In Gauthier, G., C., F., VanLehn, K., eds.: 5th International Conference on Intelligent Tutoring Systems - ITS 2000, Berlin: Springer Verlag (2000) 292–303
7. Puntambekar, S.: Investigating the effect of a computer tool on students' metacognitive processes. PhD thesis, University of Sussex (1995)
8. Conati, C., Vanlehn, K.: Toward computer-based support of meta-cognitive skills: a computational framework to coach self-explanation. International Journal of Artificial Intelligence in Education **11** (2000) 398–415
9. Gama, C.: Metacognition and reflection in its: increasing awareness to improve learning. In Moore, J.D., ed.: Proceedings of the Artificial Intelligence in Education Conference, San Antonio, Texas, IOS Press (2001) 492–495
10. Tobias, S., Everson, H.T.: Knowing what you know and what you don't: further research on metacognitive knowledge monitoring. College Board Research Report 2002-3, College Entrance Examination Board: New York (2002)
11. Tobias, S., Everson, H.T., Laitusis, V., Fields, M.: Metacognitive Knowledge Monitoring: Domain Specific or General? Paper presented at the Annual meeting of the Society for the Scientific Study of Reading, Montreal (1999)
12. Artzt, A.F., Armour-Thomas, E.: Mathematics teaching as problem solving: A framework for studying teacher metacognition underlying instructional practice in mathematics. Instructional Science **26** (1998) 5–25

Predicting Learning Characteristics in a Multiple Intelligence Based Tutoring System

Declan Kelly [1] and Brendan Tangney [2]

[1] National College of Ireland, Dublin, Ireland
dkelly@ncirl.ie
[2] University of Dublin, Trinity College, Ireland
tangney@tcd.ie

Abstract. Research on learning has shown that students learn differently and that they process knowledge in various ways. EDUCE is an Intelligent Tutoring System for which a set of learning resources has been developed using the principles of Multiple Intelligences. It can dynamically identify user learning characteristics and adaptively provide a customised learning material tailored to the learner. This paper introduces the predictive engine used within EDUCE. It describes the input representation model and the learning mechanism employed. The input representation model consists of input features that describe how different resources were used and inferred from fine-grained information collected during student computer interactions. The predictive engine employs the Naive Bayes classifier and operates online using no prior information. Using data from a previous experimental study, a comparison was made between the performance of the predictive engine and the actual behaviour of a group of students using the learning material without any guidance from EDUCE. Results indicate correlation between student's behaviour and the predictions made by EDUCE. These results suggest that the concept of learning characteristics can be modelled using a learning scheme with appropriately chosen attributes.

1 Introduction

Research on learning has shown that students learn differently, that they process and represent knowledge in different ways, that it is possible to diagnose a student's learning style and that some students learn more effectively when taught with preferred methods [1, 2].

Individual learning characteristics could be used as the basis of selecting material but, identifying learning characteristics can be difficult. Furthermore it is not clear which aspects of learning characteristics are worth modelling, how the modelling can take place and what can be done differently for users with different learning styles in a computer based environment [3].

Typically questionnaires and psychometric tests are used to assess and diagnose learning characteristics [4] but these can be time-consuming, require the student to be

J.C. Lester et al. (Eds.): ITS 2004, LNCS 3220, pp. 678–688, 2004.

explicitly involved in the process and may not be accurate. Once the profile is generated, it is static and does not change regardless of user interactions. What is desirable, is a learning environment that has the capacity to develop and refine the profile of the student's learning characteristics whilst the student is engaged with the computer

Several system adapting to the individual's learning characteristic have been developed [5],[6]. In attempts to build a model of student's learning characteristics, information from the student is obtained using questionnaires, navigation paths, answers to questions, link sorting, stretch text viewing and explicit updates by the user to their own student model. Machine learning techniques offer a solution in the quest to develop and refine a model of learning characteristics [7], [8]. Typically these systems contain a variety of instructional types such as explanations or example and fragments of different media types representing the same content, with the tutoring system choosing the most suitable for the learner. Another approach is to compare the student's performance in tests to that of other students, and to match students with instructors who can work successfully with that type of student [9]. Other systems try to model learning characteristics such as logical, arithmetic and diagrammatic ability [10].

EDUCE[11] is an Intelligent Tutoring System that uses a predictive engine, built using machine learning techniques, to identify and predicts learning characteristics online in order to provide a customised learning path. It uses a pedagogical model based on Gardner's Multiple Intelligence(MI) concept [12] to classify content, model the student and deliver material in diverse ways. In EDUCE[13] four different intelligences are used to develop four categories of content: verbal/linguistic, visual/spatial, logical/mathematical and musical/rhythmic intelligences. Currently, science is the subject area for which content has been developed.

This paper describes the predictive engine within EDUCE. The predictive engine is based upon the assumption that students do exhibit patterns of behaviour appropriate to their particular learning characteristics and it is possible to describe those patterns. Through observations of the student, it builds an individual predictive model for each learners and allows EDUCE to adapt the presentation of content.

The input representation model to the learning scheme consists of fine-grained features that describe the student's interest in and use of different resources available. The predictive engine employs the Naive Bayes algorithm [14]. It operates online using no prior information, develops a predictive model for each individual student and continues to refine that model with further observations of the student. At the start of each learning unit predictions are made as to what the learners preferred resource is and when will it be used.

The paper outlines how, using data from a previous experimental study, an evaluation was made on the predictive accuracy of the adaptive engine and the appropriateness of the input features chosen. The results suggest that that the concept of learning characteristics can be modelled using a learning scheme with appropriately chosen attributes.

2 EDUCE Architecture

EDUCE's architecture consists of a student model , a domain model, a pedagogical model, a predictive engine and a presentation model. The MI concept inspires the student model in EDUCE. Gardner identifies eight intelligences involved in solving problems, in producing material such as compositions, music or poetry and other educational activities. EDUCE uses four of these intelligences in modelling the student: Logical/Mathematical intelligence (LM), Verbal/Linguistic (VL), Visual/ Spatial (VS) and Musical/Rhythmic (MR).

EDUCE builds a model of the student's learning characteristics by observing, analysing and recording the student's choice of MI differentiated material. Other information also stored in the student model includes the navigation history, the time spent on each learning unit, answers to interactive questions and feedback given by the student on navigation choices.

The domain model is structured in two hierarchical levels of abstraction, concepts and learning units. Concepts in the knowledge base are divided into section and sub-sections. Each section consists of learning units that explain a particular concept. Each learning unit is composed of a number of panels that correspond to key instructional events. Learning units contain different media types such as text, image, audio and animation. Within each unit, there are multiple resources available to the student for use. These resources have been developed using the principles of Multiple Intelligences. Each resource uses pre-dominantly the one intelligence and is used to explain or introduce a concept in a different way. The resources were developed using content experts in the area and validated by experienced Multiple Intelligence practitioners.

In the teaching of a concept, key instructional events are the elements of the teaching process in which learners acquire and transfer new information and skills. The EDUCE presentation model has four key instructional events:

- *Awaken*: The main purpose of this stage is to attract the learner's attention, Fig. 1.
- *Explain*: Different resources reflecting MI principles are used to explain or introduce the concept in different ways.
- *Reinforce*: This stage reinforces the key message in the lesson
- *Transfer*: Here learners convert memories into actions by answering interactive questions

At the Awaken stage, to progress onto the next panel, the learner chooses one from four different options. Each choice will lead to a different resource that predominately reflects the principles of one intelligence. At the Reinforce and Transfer stage the learner has the option of going back to view alternative resources.

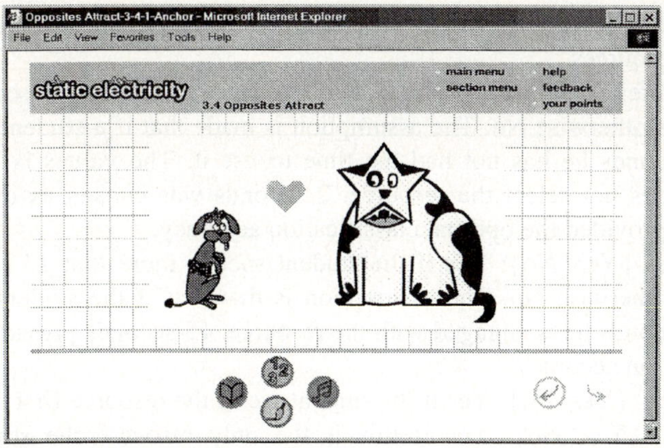

Fig. 1. The Awaken stage of "Opposites Attract" with four options for different resources

3 Predictive Engine

In EDUCE predictions are made about which resource a student prefers. Being able to predict student behaviour provides the mechanism by which instruction can be adapted and by which to motivate a student with appropriate material. As the student progresses through a tutorial, each leaning unit offers four different types of resources. The student has the option to view only one, view them all or to repeatedly view some. The prediction task is to identify at the start of each learning unit which resource the student would prefer, this is referred to as the predicted preferred resource. Fig. 2 illustrates the main phases of the prediction process and their implementation within EDUCE.

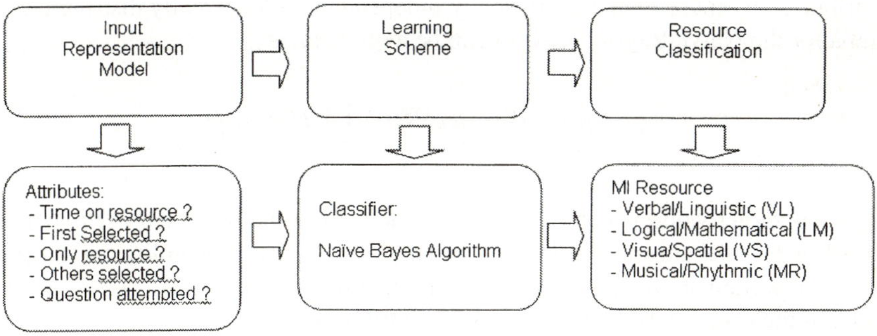

Fig. 2. The different stages in the predictive engine and their implementation within EDUCE.

Instead of modelling the static features of the learning resources themselves, a set of dynamic features describing the usage of the different resources has been identified. The following attributes have been chose to reflect how the student uses the different resources.

- NormalTime {Yes, No}: Yes if students spent more that 2 seconds viewing aresources otherwise No. The assumption is made that if a student has spent less than 2 seconds he has not had the time to use it. The values is also No if the student does not select the resource. 2 seconds was chosen as in experimental studies it provided the optimal classification accuracy.
- LongTime {Yes, No}: Yes if the student spends more that 15 seconds on the resource otherwise No. The assumption is that that if the student spends more that 15 seconds he is engaged with the resource. 15 seconds provided the optimal classification accuracy.
- FirstChoice {Yes, No}: Yes if the student views the resource first otherwise No
- OnlyOne {Yes, No}: Yes if this is the only resource the student looks at otherwise No
- Repeat {Yes, No}: Yes if the student looks at the resource more than once otherwise No
- QuestAtt {Yes, No}: Yes if the student looks at the resource and attempts a question otherwise No.
- QuestRight {Yes, No}: Yes if the student looks at the resource and gets the question right otherwise no.
- Resource {VL, LM, VS, MR}: The name of the resource: Verbal/Linguistic, Logical/Mathematical, Visual/Spatial and Musical/Rhythmic. This is the feature the learning scheme will classify.

The goal is to construct individual user models based upon the user's own data. However this results in only a small number of training instances per user. The other requirement is that the classifier may have no prior knowledge of the user. With these requirements in mind, the learning mechanism chosen was the Naïve Bayes algorithm as it works well with sparse datasets [14]. Naïve Bayes works on the assumption that all attributes are uncorrelated, statistically independent and normally distributed. The formula for the Naïve Bayes classifier can be expressed as

$$v_{NB} = \underset{v_j \epsilon V}{\text{argmax}} P(v_j) \prod_i P(a_i|v_j)$$

v_{NB} is the target value which can be any value v_j from the finite set V. $P(a_i|v_j)$ is the probability of the attribute a_i for the given class v_j. The probability for the target value of a particular instance, or of observing the conjunction a_1, a_2 .. a_n , is the product of the probabilities of the individual attributes.

During each learning unit observations are made about how different resources are used. At the end of the learning unit, one instance is created for each target class value For example, the instances generated for one student after the interaction with one particular learning unit and four resources are given in Table 1.

Table 1. Example instances after interaction with one learning unit.

Normal Time	Long Time	First Choice	Only One	Repeat	Quest Att	Quest Right	Resource
Yes	Yes	Yes	No	No	Yes	Yes	VS
Yes	No	No	No	Yes	Yes	Yes	VL
Yes	Yes	No	No	No	Yes	Yes	MR
No	No	No	No	No	No	No	LM

Table 2. The instance classified against each resource.

Normal Time	Long Time	First Choice	Only One	Repeat	Quest Att	Quest Right	Resource
Yes	Yes	Yes	Yes	Yes	Yes	Yes	?

The training data is updated with these new instances. The entire training data set for each student consists of all the instances generated, with equal weighting, from the learning units that have been used. At the start of each learning unit the predictive engine is asked to classify the instance that describes what the student spends time on, what he views first, what he repeatedly views and what helps him to answer questions, namely the instance illustrated in Table 2.

The range of target values is {VL, LM, VS, MR} one for each class of resource. For each possible target value the Naive Bayes classifier calculates a probability on the fly. The probabilities are obtained by counting the frequency of various data combinations within the training examples. The target class value chosen is the one with the highest probability. Figure 3 illustrates the main steps in the algorithm of the predictive engine.

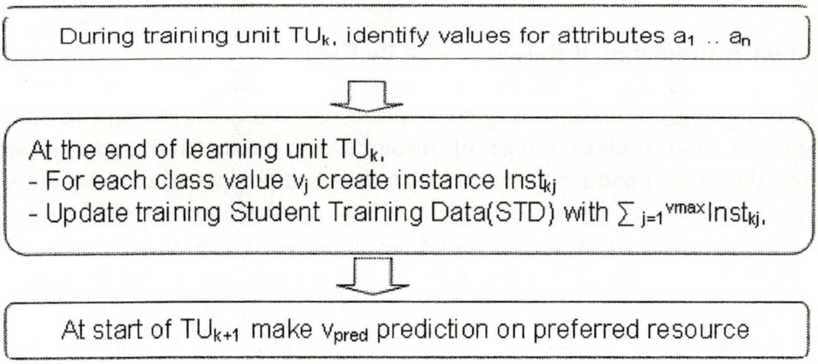

Fig. 3. The algorithm describing how instances are created and predictions made.

4 Evaluation

Data involving 25 female students from a previous experimental research study [15] was used to evaluate the accuracy of the predictive engine. Each student interacted with EDUCE for approximately 40 minutes giving a total of 3381 observations over the entire group. 840 of these interactions were selections for a particular type of resource. In each learning unit students had a choice of four different modes of instruction: VL, VS, MR, LM. As no prior knowledge of student preference is available, the first learning unit experienced by the student was ignored when doing the evaluation.

For individual modeling, one approach is to load all of the student's data at the end of a session and evaluate the resultant classifier against individual selections made. The other approach is to evaluate the classifier predictions against user choices made only using data up to the point the user's choice was made. This approach simulates the real behaviour of the classifier when working with incomplete profiles of the student. The second approach was used as this reflects the real performance when dynamically making predictions in an online environment

A number of different investigations were made to determine answers to the following questions

- Is it possible to predict if the student will use a resource in a learning unit ?
- Is it possible to predict when the student will use a resource in a learning unit ?
- What range of resources did students use ?
- How often did the prediction of students preferred type of resource change ?
- Can removing extreme cases where there is no discernable pattern of behaviour help in the prediction the preferred resource ?

Evaluation 1: Predicting if Resource Will Be Used

Each learning unit has up to four types of resources to use. At the start of each unit, the student's most preferred type of resource was predicted based on previous selections the student had made. After the student had completed the learning unit, it was investigated to see if the student had used the predicted preferred resource. In 75 % of cases the prediction was correct and the student had used the resource. In other words EDUCE was able to predict with 75 % accuracy that a student will use the predicted preferred resource. The results suggest that there is a pattern of behaviour when choosing among a range of resources and that students will continually use their preferred resource.

Evaluation 2: Predicting When Resource Will Be Used

In each learning unit, the student can determine the order in which resources can be viewed. Is it possible to know at what stage the student will use his preferred resource? When inspecting the learning units where the predicted preferred resource was used, it was found that in 78 % of cases the predicted preferred resource was used first, i.e. in the 75% of cases where the prediction was correct the predicted resource was visited first 78% of the time. The results suggest that it is a challenging classification to predict the first resource a student will use in a learning unit. However when the student does use the predicted preferred resource, it will with 78 % accuracy be the first one used. Figure 4 illustrates these results. The analogy is that of shooting an arrow at a target. 75 % of the time the target is hit and when the target is hit, 78 % of the time it is a bulls-eye!.

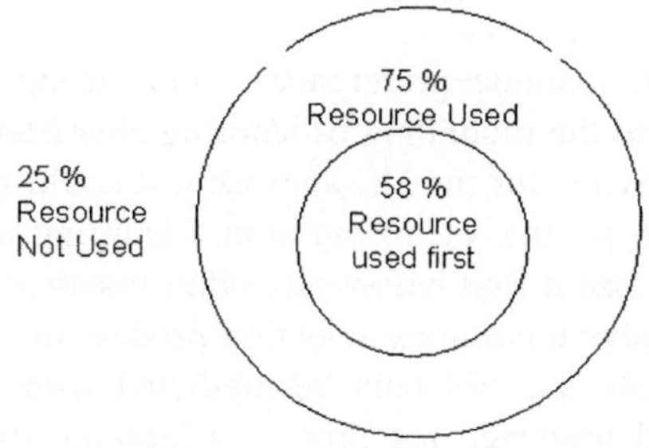

Fig. 4. Classification accuracy of predicted preferred resource.

Evaluation 3: Number of Changes in Predicted Preferred Resource

To determine the extent of how stable the predicted preferred resource is, an analysis was made of the number of times the prediction changed. The average number of changes in the preferred resource was 1.04. The results suggest that as student's progress throughout a tutorial they identify quite quickly which type of resource they prefer as the predicted resource will on average change once per student.

Evaluation 4: The Range of Resources Used

Did students use all available resources or just a subset of those resources ? By performing an analysis of the resources selected from those available in each unit, it was found that students on average used 40 % of the available resources. This result suggests that students identified for themselves a particular subset of resources which appealed to them and ignored the rest. But did all students choose the same subset ? To determine which subset, a breakdown of the resources used against each class of resource was calculated. Table 3 displays the results.

The even breakdown across all resources suggests that each student chose a different subset of resources. (If all students chose the same subset of VL and LM resources, VS and MR would be 0 %). It is interesting to note that the MR approach appeals to the most number of students and the LM approach appeals to the least number of students. Taking this into account, each class of resource is appealing to different students groups of roughly equal size.

Table 3. Breakdown of resources used

VL	LM	VS	MR
25 %	16 %	27 %	33 %

Evaluation 5: Modelling Learning Approaches Without Extreme Cases

Inspecting students with extreme preferences, very strong and very weak reveals some further insights, into the modelling of learning characteristics. With one student with a very strong preference for the VL approach, it could be predicted with 100 % accuracy that she would use the VL resource in a learning unit, and that with 92 % accuracy that she would use it first before any other resources. On the other extreme, some students seem to have a complex selection process not easily recognisable. For example with one student, it could only be predicted with 33 % accuracy that she would use her predicted preferred resource in a learning unit and only with 11 % accuracy that she would used first. In this particular case, the results suggest that she was picking a different resource in each unit and not looking at alternatives.

Some students will not display easily discernable patterns of behaviour and these outliers can be removed to get a clearer picture of the prediction accuracy for students with strong patterns of behaviour. After removing the 5 students with the lowest prediction rates the prediction accuracy for the rest of group was recalculated. This resulted in an accuracy of 84 % that the predicted preferred resource will be used and in an accuracy of 65 % that the predicted preferred resource will be used first in a learning unit. The suggests that strong predictions can be made about the preferred class of resource. However predicting what will be used first is still a difficult classification task.

5 Conclusions

In this paper the predictive engine in EDUCE was described. The prediction task was defined as the resource students prefer to use. The input representation model is a fine-grained set of features that describe how the resource is used. On entry to a particular unit, the learning scheme predicts which resource the student will use.

A number of evaluations were carried out and the performance of the predictive engine was compared against the real behaviour of students. The purpose of the evaluation was to determine whether it is possible to model a concept such as learning characteristics. The results suggest that strong predictions can be made about the students preferred resource. It can be determined with a relatively high degree of probability that the student will use the predicted preferred resource in a learning unit. However to determine if the preferred resource will be used first is more difficult task. The results also suggest that predictions about the preferred resource are relatively stable, that students only use a subset of resources and that different students use different subsets. Combing the results together suggest that there is a concept such as learning characteristics that is different for alternative groups of students and that it is possible to model this concept.

Currently empirical studies are taking place to examine the reaction of students to the predictive engine in EDUCE. The study is examining two instructional strategies, that is giving students content they like to see and content they do not like to see. The purpose of these studies is to examine the relationship between instructional strategy and learning performance.

Future work with the predictive engine involves further analysis in order to identify the relevance of different features. Other work will involve generalizing the adaptive engine to use different categories of resources. Here the range of categories is based on the Multiple Intelligence concept, however that can be easily be replaced with another set of resources based on a different learning theory.

References

1. Riding, R. & Rayner. S, (1997): Cognitive Styles and learning strategies. David Fulton. .
2. Rasmussen, K. L. (1998): Hypermedia and learning styles: Can performance be influenced? Journal of Multimedia and Hypermedia, 7(4).
3. Brusilovsky, P. (2001): Adpative Hypermedia. User Modeling and User-Adapted Instruction, Volume 11, Nos 1-2. Kluwer Academic Publisher
4. Riding, R. J. (1991): Cognitive Styles Analysis, Learning and Training Technology, Birmingham.
5. Carver, C., Howard, R., & Lavelle, E. (1996): Enhancing student learning by incorporating learning styles into adaptive hypermedia. 1996 ED-MEDIA Conference on Educational Multimedia and Hypermedia. Boston, MA.
6. Specht, M. and Oppermann, R. (1998): ACE: Adaptive CourseWare Environment, New Review of HyperMedia & MultiMedia 4,
7. Stern, M & Woolf. B. (2000): Adaptive Content in an Online lecture system. In: Proceedings of the First Adpative Hypermedia Conference, AH2000.
8. Castillo, G., Gama, J., Breda, A. (2003): Adaptive Bayes for a Student Modeling Prediction Task based on Learning Styles. Proceedings of the User Modeling Conference, Johnstown, PA, USA, 2003.
9. Gilbert, J. E. & Han, C. Y. (1999): Arthur: Adapting Instruction to Accommodate Learning Style. In: Proceedings of WebNet'99, World Conference of the WWW and Internet, Honolulu, HI.
10. Milne, S. (1997): Adapting to Learner Attributes, experiments using an adaptive tutoring system. Educational Pschology Vol 17 Nos 1 and 2, 1997
11. Kelly, D. & Tangney, B. (2002): Incorporating Learning Characteristics into an Intelligent Tutor. In: Proceedings of the Sixth International on ITSs, ITS2002.
12. Gardner H. (1983) Frames of Mind: The theory of multiple intelligences. New York. Basic Books.

13. Kelly, D. (2003). A Framework for using Multiple Intelligences in an ITS. Proceedings of EDMedia'03, World Conference on Educational Multimedia, Hypermedia & Telecommunications, Honolulu, HI.
14. Duda, R. & Hart, P. (1973). Pattern Classification and Scene Analysis. Wiley, New York.
15. Kelly, D. & Tangney, B. (2003). Learner's responses to Multiple Intelligence Differentiated Instructional Material in an ITS. Proceedings of the Eleventh International Conference on Artificial Intelligence in Education, AIED'2003.

Alternative Views on Knowledge: Presentation of Open Learner Models

Andrew Mabbott and Susan Bull

Electronic, Electrical and Computer Engineering, University of Birmingham, Edgbaston, Birmingham, B15 2TT, UK
{axm891, s.bull}@bham.ac.uk

Abstract. This paper describes a study in which individual learner models were built for students and presented to them with a choice of view. Students found it useful, and not confusing to be shown multiple representations of their knowledge, and individuals exhibited different preferences for which view they favoured. No link was established between these preferences and the students' learning styles. We describe the implications of these results for intelligent tutoring systems where interaction with the open learner model is individualised.

1 Introduction

Many researchers argue that open learner modelling in intelligent tutoring systems may enhance learner reflection (e.g. [1], [2], [3], [4]), and a range of externalisations for learner models have been explored. In Mr Collins [1], learner and system negotiate over the system's representation of the learner's understanding. Vismod [4] provides a learner with a graphical view of their Bayesian learner model. STyLE-OLM [2] works with the learner to generate a conceptual representation of their knowledge. ELM-ART's [5] learner model is viewed via a topic list annotated with proficiency indicators. These examples demonstrate quite varied interaction and presentation mechanisms, but in any specific system, the interaction style remains constant.

It is accepted that individuals learn in different ways and much research into learning styles has been carried out (e.g. [6], [7]). This suggests not all learners may benefit equally from all types of interaction with an open learner model. Ideally, the learner's model may be presented in whatever form suits them best and they may interact with it using the mechanism most appropriate to them. In discussion of learner reflection, Collins and Brown [8] state: "Students should be able to inspect their performance in different ways", concluding that multiple representations are helpful. However, there has been little research on offering a learner model with a choice of representations or interaction methods. Some studies [9], [10], suggest benefit in tailoring a learning environment to suit an individuals learning style, so it may be worth considering learning style as a basis for adapting interaction with an open learner model.

J.C. Lester et al. (Eds.): ITS 2004, LNCS 3220, pp. 689–698, 2004.

This paper describes a study in which we use a short web-based test to construct simple learner models, representing students' understanding of control of flow in C programming. Students are offered a choice of representations of the information in their model. We aim to assess whether this is beneficial, or if it causes information overload. We investigate whether there is an overall preference for a particular view, or whether individuals have particular preferences, and if so, whether it is possible to predict these from information about their learning style. We also consider other ways of individualising the interaction with an open learner model, such as negotiation between learner and system, and comparing individual learner models with those of peers or for the group as a whole. The system employed is not intended to be a complete intelligent tutoring system, and consists of only those aspects associated with presenting the learner model. Such an arrangement would not normally be used in isolation, but is useful for the purpose of investigating the issues described above.

2 The Learner Model

The system's domain is control of flow in C Programming, and is based on an MSc module for Electronic, Electrical, and Computer Engineering students entitled "Introduction to Procedural Programming and Software Design".

2.1 Building the Learner Model

The domain is divided into nine basic concepts plus some higher-level concepts formed by aggregating these. A thirty-question multiple-choice test provides data for the learner model. Each question offers up to nine alternatives, plus an "unsure" option, and is associated with one or more concepts. Choosing the correct answer adds points to the scores for these concepts. In some cases, points may be deducted from concepts not related to the question, if a student's response demonstrates a lack of understanding of this area too. Sufficient time was allowed to answer all of the questions, so unanswered questions are assumed to show a lack of understanding. The overall knowledge for a concept is calculated as a fraction of the possible score.

The model also includes information about six possible misconceptions a learner may hold. Some questions were designed such that they included incorrect answers that would be likely to be chosen by a student who has a given misconception.

2.2 Presenting the Learner Model

Learners are offered four representations of their model's contents. If they favour different views from each other then they may each have a potentially different experience interacting with their model. Thus it is important that the learner can obtain relevant information about their knowledge using any view in isolation, so while the views differ structurally, the same information is available. Kay [3] identifies four questions learners may seek to answer when viewing their model: "*What do I know?*", "*How well do I know topic X?*", "*What do I want to know?*", and "*How can I best learn X?*". For effective reflection on knowledge, the learner must be able to answer these questions easily, particularly the first two. Thus a simple and intuitive system was used where the learner's knowledge on a topic is represented by a single coloured node on a scale from grey, through yellow to green, with bright green indicating complete knowledge and grey indicating none. Where a misconception is detected, this overrides and the topic is coloured red. This simplicity means that learners should require little time to familiarise themselves with the environment.

Figures 1 to 4 illustrate the four views available to the learner. Tabs above the model allow navigation between views, with misconceptions listed above this.

The *lectures* view (Fig. 1) lists topics according to the order they were presented in the lecture course. This may aid integration of knowledge gained from using the system with knowledge learned from the course, and help students who wish to locate areas of poor understanding to revise from the lecture slides. Factors such as conceptual difficulty and time constraints may affect decisions on the ordering of lecture material, such that related topics are not always covered together. The *related concepts* view (Fig. 2) shows a logical, hierarchically structured grouping of subject matter. This allows a topic to be easily located and may correspond better to a stu-

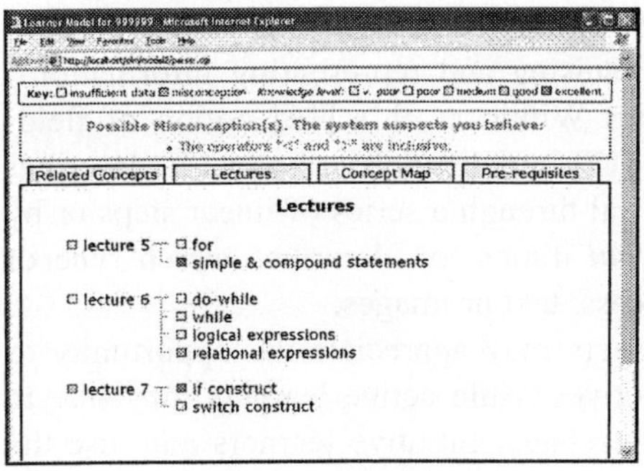

Fig. 1. Lectures view

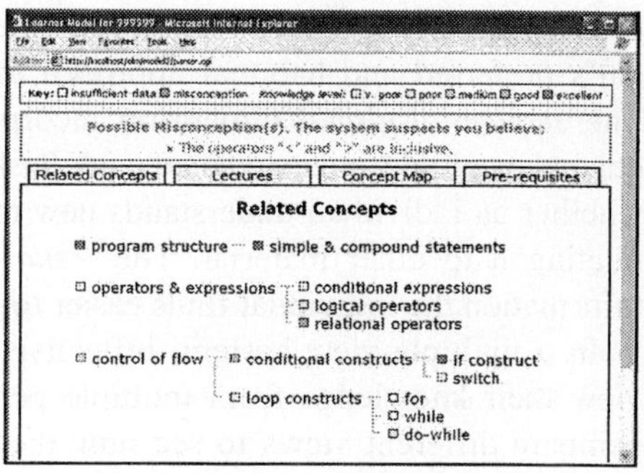

Fig. 2. Related concepts view

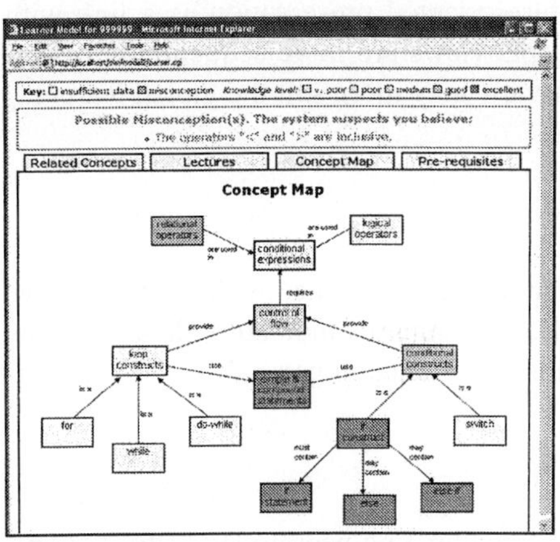

Fig. 3. Concept map view

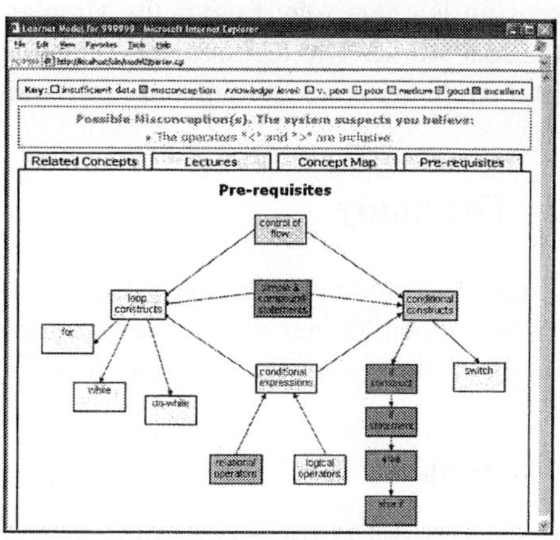

Fig. 4. Pre-requisites view

dent's mental representation of the course. The *concept map* view (Fig. 3) presents the conceptual relationship between the topics. To date, research combining concept maps (or similar) with open learner models has focused on learner constructed maps [2], [11], but in the wider context of information presentation, arguments have been made for the use of pre-constructed concept maps, or the similar *knowledge maps* [12], [13]. Finally, the *pre-requisites* view (Fig. 4) shows a suggested order for studying topics, similar to Shang et al's [14] annotated dependency graph.

A student's choice of view may not be based purely on task, but also preference. If differences in learning style contribute to these preferences, the Kolb [6] and Felder-Silverman [7] learning style models may have relevance in the design of the views. According to these models, learning involves two stages: reception, and subsequent processing, of information. In terms of reception, Felder and Silverman's use of the terms *sensing* and *intuitive* is similar to Kolb's use of *concrete* and *abstract*. Sensing learners prefer information taken in through the senses, while intuitive learners prefer information arising introspectively. Both models label learners' preferences for processing using the terms *active* or *reflective*. Active learners like to do something active with the information while reflective learners prefer to think it over.

The Felder-Silverman model has two further dimensions, sometimes referred to as dimensions of cognitive style, and defined by Riding & Rayner [15] as "an individual's preferred and habitual approach to organising and representing information". The *sequential-global* dimension incorporates Witkin et al.'s [16] notion of field-dependence/field-independence and Pask's [17] serialist/holist theory. It describes whether an individual understands new material through a series of linear steps or by relating it to other material. The *visual-verbal* dimension describes which type of information the individual finds easier to process: text or images.

In a multiple-view system, reflective learners may appreciate the opportunity to view their knowledge from multiple perspectives while active learners may like to compare different views to see how they are related. Intuitive learners may use the concept map and pre-requisites view to focus on conceptual interrelationships, while sensing learners may favour the simpler lecture-oriented presentation as a link with the real world. The lectures and related concepts views are more sequentially organised while the concept map and pre-requisites view may more suit the global learner.

3 The Study

A group of students were given the 30-question test and presented with the four views on their open learner model. They completed questionnaires indicating their opinions on the usefulness of the different views, and the experience in general.

3.1 Subjects

Subjects were 23 Electronic, Electrical, and Computer Engineering students studying a module entitled "Educational Technology". Eighteen of these, on a one-year MSc programme, had undertaken the course called "Introduction to Procedural Programming and Software Design". The remainder, finalists on a four-year MEng programme, had previously covered the similar "Introduction to Computing Systems and C Programming". The subjects had yet to be introduced to the idea of open learner modelling or indeed intelligent tutoring systems more generally.

3.2 Materials and Methods

Subjects received the test simultaneously online. On completion, a web page was generated showing alternative views of their learner model. Students then completed a six-item questionnaire, indicating choices on a five-point Likert scale and providing additional comments where necessary. They were asked how useful they found each view of the learner model, how easily the model enabled them to assess their knowledge, how useful they found multiple views, and how accurate they believed their model to be. They were also asked about the usefulness of comparing one's model with that of a peer or the whole group. As the subjects took the test in the same location they could examine each other's models but were never explicitly asked to do so.

Next, subjects compared correct solutions to the test with their own solutions, and completed a second questionnaire concerning how accurate they now believed their model to be and how important it is for a system to give the reasoning behind its representation. Suggestions were sought for additional information that the system should provide as part of its feedback. On a separate occasion, subjects completed the self-scoring Index of Learning Styles (ILS) [18] online. Though used extensively, the ILS has not been validated [19] so in an attempt to assess its usefulness for our purposes, students were asked to rate their agreement with their diagnosed style on a five-point scale (strongly agree, agree, partly agree, disagree, strongly disagree).

3.3 Results

Students spent between 8 and 30 minutes on the test, scoring from 8 to 29 out of 30. All but two students were identified as holding at least one misconception. None had more than four. Seven students discovered that they could send multiple test submissions. The maximum number of submissions from an individual was seven.

Table 1. Preference for individual views

	degree of usefulness						preference	
	<- very useful.............not very useful ->					Avg.	favourite	least
	(5)	(4)	(3)	(2)	(1)	score		favoured
Lecture	6	11	5	1	0	4.0	6	5
Related concepts	3	12	5	3	0	3.7	6	10
Concept map	9	9	2	1	2	4.0	10	5
Pre-requisites	6	7	9	1	0	3.8	4	6

In the first questionnaire, students rated, on a five-point scale, how useful they found each view. The number selecting each option is shown in Table 1. For comparative purposes, assigning a value from 1 to 5 to each option allows averages to be calculated. The penultimate column lists, for each view, the number of people that rate it more highly than the other views. The seven students favouring three or four views equally are excluded from this total, as this does not suggest real preference. Similarly, the final column shows, for each view, the number of people that give it a lower rating than the other views.

With similar average scores, no view is considered better than the others overall. The results show that each view has a number of students that consider it to be the most useful and a number of students who consider it to be the least useful.

Table 2 summarises responses to the other questionnaire items. Students reacted positively to the idea of multiple views, with an average response of 4.2 out of 5 and only one neutral reaction. They were also positive about how easily they could assess the strength of their knowledge on various domain aspects using their model. This received an average response of 4.0, with just two students giving 2 out of 5.

The high scores for perceived accuracy of the model show that there was little disagreement from students about the system's representation of them, either before or after they had seen the correct solutions. Despite agreeing with the system, students were keen for the system to offer some explanation and reasoning for its representation of them. This issue received an average score of 4.2 in the questionnaire. There were comments asking for more detailed feedback, such as "[the system should] give the possible reason why you make these mistakes" and for the system to identify which answers indicate which misconceptions: "I would like to see my misconceptions with examples [of my mistakes added] when the user clicks on red boxes".

Table 2. Summary of questionnaire responses and average scores. A scale from 1 to 5 is used, with 5 representing a postive response, 3 neutral, and 1 a negative response.

	(5)	(4)	(3)	(2)	(1)	Avg
Usefulness of multiple views	5	16	1	0	0	4.2
Ease of understanding strength of knowledge on various aspects	9	8	4	2	0	4.0
Perceived accuracy of model before seeing solutions	7	13	3	0	0	4.2
Perceived accuracy of model after seeing solutions	7	14	1	0	0	4.3
Importance of system giving reasons for its feedback	12	5	4	2	0	4.2
Usefulness of comparing own model with peer's model	4	8	5	3	3	3.3
Usefulness of comparing own model with a group model	5	8	6	3	1	3.6

Responses appear more neutral regarding comparisons with peer or group models. More detailed analysis of the individual responses shows a number of students are very interested in comparing models, but this is offset by a number of students who have very little interest. During the study, many students were seen viewing each other's models for comparison purposes, without any prompting to do so. One student remarked that he would like to see "the distribution of other participant's answers", another said: "Feedback in comparison to other students would be useful".

Nineteen students completed the ILS questionnaire [18]. Table 3 shows the average learning style scores (in each of the four dimensions) for the group as a whole compared to the average scores for the students who favour each view. The similarity between the overall figures and the figures for each view indicates no obvious link between any of the style dimensions and preferences for presentation form. The results also show that in most style categories the distribution is biased towards one end of the scale. In the poll regarding accuracy of the ILS, seventeen students voted that they "agreed" with their results, while two abstained.

Table 3. Average learning style scores for students favouring each view, compared to average learning style scores for the whole group. Scores from 0-11 describe each dimension.

	Active 11 – 0 – Reflective 11	Sensing 11 – 0 – Intuitive 11	Visual 11 – 0 – Verbal 11	Sequential 11 – 0 – Global 11
Overall scores	3.3	3.0	6.7	0.5
Lectures	3.5	5.0	8.0	0.5
Related concepts	2.5	3.5	7.5	3.0
Concept map	2.8	2.6	5.9	0.6
Pre-requisites	3.5	2.5	5.5	3.0

3.4 Discussion

The important question is whether providing multiple views of an open learner model may enhance learning. It is argued that an open learner model may help the learner to become aware of their current understanding and reflect upon what they know, by raising issues that they may not otherwise have considered [20]. A motivation for providing multiple views of the learner model is that this reflection may be enhanced, if the learner may view their model in a form they are most comfortable with. As each representation was found to have several students regarding it the most useful, then if any view were removed, some students would be left using a form they consider less useful, and their quality of reflection may reduce. Providing a representation students find more useful may help to counter problems discussed by Kay [21] or Barnard and Sandberg [22], where few or no students viewed their model.

In addition to having knowledge represented in the most useful form, results show that having multiple representations is considered useful. Students are not confused by the extra information, as indicated by the fact that only two gave a negative response to how easily they could tell the strength of their knowledge from the model.

It is important to remember that the information for the study comes from students' self-reports on an open learner model in isolation. It does not necessarily follow that a multiple-view system helps provide better reflection or increased learning, only that students *believe* it may help. Nor can we assume students know which representation is best for them. Such a system needs evaluating within an intelligent tutoring system. Positive results here suggest this may be a worthwhile next step.

High levels of agreement with the system's representation validate the modelling technique used. However, they raise questions about the possibility of including a negotiation mechanism, the intention of which would be to improve the accuracy of the model and provide more dynamic interaction for active learners. While Bull & Pain [1] conclude that students will negotiate their model with the system in cases of disagreement, this disagreement would appear to be lacking in our case. Nevertheless, in a complete system used in parallel with a course, rather than after students completed the course, there may be more disagreement and scope for negotiation.

The asymmetric distribution of learning styles is expected as "many or most engineering students are visual, sensing and active" [7]. With an unbalanced distribution, and a small number of subjects, it is difficult to draw firm conclusions, although clear differences in preference of view observed between learners of the same style corroborate recent findings [23] of only weak linkages between learning style and learning preference. With no obvious link between preferred view and learning style, it seems unwise to use style to make decisions about which view to present to a user. As students were not confused by being presented with multiple views, it is easiest to let them choose their own view. There may be other uses for learning style, as the idea of how to present the model is just one aspect of an adaptive open learner model system. There are other areas of interaction that may be style dependent: for example, how much negotiation is sought from the learner when arguing over their model, or the degree of interpretation of the model the system provides.

The interest from some students in comparing models show there may be benefit in compiling a group model (such as the OWL [24] skill meters) and in providing a mechanism for students to view each other's individual models (such as in [25]). Which types of learner may benefit from this and how such a comparison is presented could form the subject of a study in its own right.

Students' comments expressing a desire for feedback about why they have chosen an incorrect answer highlight the need in a complete system for a much larger misconception library and better justification on the part of the system.

Incremental increases in proficiency shown by students sending repeated test submissions, indicate that they did so after viewing their model, but before seeing the correct solutions. This shows that some learners like to watch their model update as they answer questions. Thus the process of viewing the model must be heavily integrated with the process of building the model and not carried out as separate tasks.

The "unsure" option on the test was provided to reduce the amount of guessing and avoid misdiagnosis of misconceptions, yet only 8 students used it and 90% of failed questions were answered incorrectly rather than with an "unsure" response. The system's diagnosis may be improved if students guessed fewer answers, but only attempting a question if you are "sure" represents too negative an attitude to be encouraged. A method is required where students can attempt a question, but state that they are unsure about it. The practice of soliciting such confidence measures has been found to be valuable in informing construction of the learner model [1], [26].

As students believe an open learner model with multiple views may be beneficial, investigation in the context of a full intelligent tutoring system seems worthwhile.

4 Summary

This paper has described a study where students were presented with their open learner models and offered a choice of how to view them. The aim was to investigate whether this may be beneficial, and how it might integrate into an intelligent tutoring system where the interaction with the open learner model is individualised.

Results suggest students can use a simple open learner model offering multiple views on their knowledge without difficulty. Students show a range of preferences for presentation so such a system can help them view their knowledge in a form they are comfortable with, possibly increasing quality of reflection. Results show no clear link with learning styles, but students were capable of selecting a view for themselves, so intelligent adaptation of presentation to learning style does not seem beneficial.

A colour-based display of topic proficiency proved effective in conveying knowledge levels, but to improve the quality of the experience, a much greater library of misconceptions must be built with more detailed feedback available in the form of evidence from incorrectly answered questions. Allowing the student to state confidence in answers may be investigated as a means of improving the diagnosis. The student should have the facility to inspect their learner model whenever they choose.

The limitations of self-reports and using a small sample of computer-literate subjects necessitate further studies before drawing stronger conclusions. The educational impact of multiple presentations must be evaluated in an environment where increases in subjects' understanding may be observed over time, and using subjects with less computer aptitude. A learner model with several presentations is only the first part of an intelligent tutoring system where the interaction with the model is personalisable. Further studies may investigate individualising other aspects of the interaction, such as negotiation of the model. Students like the idea of comparing models with others and investigation may show which learners find this most useful.

References

1. Bull, S. and Pain, H.: "Did I Say What I Think I Said, and Do You Agree With Me?": Inspecting and Questioning the Student Model. Proceedings of World Conference on Artificial Intelligence in Education, Charlottesville, VA (1995) 501-508
2. Dimitrova, V.: StyLE-OLM: Interactive Open Learner Modelling. International Journal of Artificial Intelligence in Education, Vol 13 (2002) 35-78
3. Kay, J.: Learner Know Thyself: Student Models to Give Learner Control and Responsibility. Proc. of Intl. Conference on Computers in Education, Kuching, Malaysia (1997) 18-26
4. Zapata-Rivera, J.D., and Greer, J.: Externalising Learner Modelling Representations. Workshop on External Representations of AIED: Muliple Forms and Multiple Roles. International Conference on Artificial Intelligence in Education (2001) 71-76
5. Weber, G. and Specht, M.: User Modeling and Adaptive Navigation Support in WWW-Based Tutoring Systems. Proceedings of User Modeling '97 (1997) 289-300
6. Kolb, D. A.: Experiential Learning: Experience as the Source of Learning and Development. Prentice-Hall, New Jersey (1984)
7. Felder, R. M. and Silverman, L. K.: Learning and Teaching Styles in Engineering Education. Engineering Education, 78(7) (1998) 674-681.

8. Collins, A. and Brown, J. S.: The Computer as a Tool for Learning through Reflection. In H. Mandl and A. Lesgold (eds.) Learning Issues for Intelligent Tutoring Systems. Springer-Verlag, New York (1998) 1-18
9. Bajraktarevic, N., Hall, W., and Fullick, P.: Incorporating Learning Styles in Hypermedia Environment: Empirical Evaluation. Proceedings of the Fourteenth Conference on Hypertext and Hypermedia, Nottingham (2003) 41-52
10. Carver, C. A.: Enhancing Student Learning through Hypermedia Courseware and Incorporation of Learning Styles. IEEE Transactions on Education 42(1) (1999) 33-38
11. Cimolino, L., Kay, J. and Miller, A.: Incremental Student Modelling and Reflection by Verified Concept-Mapping. Proc. of Workshop on Learner Modelling for Reflection, International Conference on Artificial Intelligence in Education, Sydney (2003) 219-227
12. Carnot, M. J., Dunn, B., Cañas, A. J.: Concept Maps vs. Web Pages for Information Searching and Browsing. Available from the Institute for Human and Machine Cognition website: http://www.ihmc.us/users/acanas/Publications/CMapsVSWebPagesExp1/CMapsVSWebPagesExp1.htm, accessed 18/05/2004 (2001)
13. O'Donnell, A. M., Dansereau, D. F. and Hall, R. H.: Knowledge Maps as Scaffolds for Cognitive Processing. Educational Psychology Review, 14 (1) (2002) 71-86
14. Shang, Y., Shi, H. and Chen, S.: An Intelligent Distributed Environment for Active Learning. Journal on Educational Resources in Computing 1(2) (2001) 1-17
15. Riding, R. and Rayner, S.: Cognitive Styles and Learning Strategies. David Fulton Publishers, London (1998)
16. Witkin, H.A., Moore, C.A., Goodenough, D.R. and Cox, P.W.: Field-Dependent and Field-Independent Cognitive Styles and Their Implications. Review of Educational Research 47 (1977) 1-64.
17. Pask, G.: Styles and Strategies of Learning. British Journal of Educational Psychology 46. (1976) 128-148.
18. Felder, R. M. and Soloman, B. A.: Index of Learning Styles. Available: http://www.ncsu.edu/felder-public/ILSpage.html, accessed 24/02/04 (1996)
19. Felder, R.: Author's Preface to Learning and Teaching Styles in Engineering Education. Avail.: http://www.ncsu.edu/felder-public/Papers/LS-1988.pdf, accessed 05/03/04 (2002)
20. Bull, S., McEvoy, A. and Reid, E.: Learner Models to Promote Reflection in Combined Desktop PC/Mobile Intelligent Learning Environments. Proceedings of Workshop on Learner Modelling for Reflection, International Conference on Artificial Intelligence in Education, Sydney (2003) 199-208.
21. Kay, J.: The um Toolkit for Cooperative User Modelling. User Modelling and User Adapted Interaction. 4, Kluwer, Netherlands (1995) 149-196
22. Barnard, Y., and Sandberg, J. Self-explanations, Do We Get them from Our Students? Proc. of European Conf. on Artificial Intelligence in Education. Lisbon (1996) 115-121
23. Loo, R.: Kolb's Learning Styles and Learning Preferences: Is there a Linkage? Educational Psychology, 24 (1) (2004) 98-108
24. Linton, F., Joy, D., Schaefer, P., Charron, A.: OWL: A Recommender System for Organization-Wide Learning. Educational Technology & Society, 3(1) (2000) 62-76
25. Bull, S. and Broady, E.: Spontaneous Peer Tutoring from Sharing Student Models. Proceedings of Artificial Intelligence in Education '97. IOS Press (1997) 143-150
26. Beck, J., Stern, M. and Woolf, B. P.: Cooperative student models. Proceedings of Artifical Intelligence in Education '97. IOS Press (1997) 127-134

Modeling Students' Reasoning About Qualitative Physics: Heuristics for Abductive Proof Search

Maxim Makatchev, Pamela W. Jordan, and Kurt VanLehn

Learning Research and Development Center, University of Pittsburgh
{maxim,pjordan,vanlehn}@pitt.edu

Abstract. We describe a theorem prover that is used in the Why2-Atlas tutoring system for the purposes of evaluating the correctness of a student's essay and for guiding feedback to the student. The weighted abduction framework of the prover is augmented with various heuristics to assist in searching for a proof that maximizes measures of utility and plausibility. We focus on two new heuristics we added to the theorem prover: (a) a specificity-based cost for assuming an atom, and (b) a rule choice preference that is based on the similarity between the graph of cross-references between the propositions in a candidate rule and the graph of cross-references between the set of goals. The two heuristics are relevant to any abduction framework and knowledge representation that allow for a metric of specificity for a proposition and cross-referencing of propositions via shared variables.

1 Introduction

1.1 Why2-Atlas Overview

The Why2-Atlas tutoring system is designed to encourage students to write their answers to qualitative physics problems along with detailed explanations to support their arguments [1]. For the purpose of eliciting more complete explanations the system attempts to provide students with substantive feedback that demonstrates understanding of a student's essay. A sample problem and a student's explanation for it is shown in Figure 1.

The sentence level understanding module in Why2-Atlas parses a student's essay into a first-order predicate representation [2]. The discourse-level understanding module then resolves temporal and nominal anaphora within the representation [3] and uses a theorem prover that attempts to generate a proof, treating propositions in the resolved representation as a set of goals, and the problem statement as a set of given facts. An informal example proof for a fragment of the essay in Figure 1 is shown in Figure 2. The proof is interpreted as a model of the reasoning the student used to arrive at the arguments in the essay, and provides a diagnosis when the arguments are faulty in a fashion similar to [4,5]. For example, the proof in Figure 2 indicates that the student may have

J.C. Lester et al. (Eds.): ITS 2004, LNCS 3220, pp. 699–709, 2004.

Question: Suppose a man is in a free-falling elevator and is holding his keys motionless right in front of his face. He then lets go. What will be the position of the keys relative to the man's face as time passes? Explain.

Explanation: The keys are affected by gravity which pulls them to the elevator floor, because the keys then have a combined velocity of the freefall and the effect of gravity. If the elevator has enough speed the keys along with my head would be pressed against the ceiling of the elevator, because the acceleration of the elevator car along with me and the keys would overwhelm the gravitational pull.

Fig. 1. The statement of the problem and an example explanation.

Step #	Proposition	Justification
1	before the release, the keys have been in contact with the man, and the man has been in contact with the elevator	given
2	at the moment of release, velocity of the keys is equal to velocity of the elevator	bodies in contact over a time interval have same velocities
3	after the release, nothing is touching the keys	given
4	after the release, the keys are in freefall	if there is no any contact then the body is in freefall
5	after the release, the keys' acceleration is not equal to the elevator's acceleration	*elevator is not in freefall
6	after the release, the keys' velocity is not equal to the elevator's velocity	if initial velocity is the same and accelerations are different the final velocities are different
7	the keys touch the ceiling of the elevator	if the keys' velocity is smaller than the elevator's velocity, the keys touch the ceiling

Fig. 2. An informal proof of the excerpt "The keys would be pressed against the ceiling of the elevator" (From the essay in Figure 1). The buggy assumption is preceded by an asterisk.

wrongly assumed that the elevator is not in freefall. A highly plausible wrong assumption in the student's reasoning triggers an appropriate tutoring action [6].

The theorem prover, called Tacitus-lite+, is a derivative of SRI's Tacitus-lite that, among other extensions, incorporates sorts (sorts will be described in Section 2.3) [7, p. 102]. We further adapted Tacitus-lite+ to our application by (a) adding meta-level consistency checking, (b) enforcing a sound order-sorted inference procedure, and (c) expanding the proof search heuristics. In the rest of the paper we will refer to the prover as Tacitus-lite when talking about features present in the original SRI release, and as Tacitus-lite+ when talking about more recent extensions.

The goal of the proof search heuristics is to maximize (a) the measure of plausibility of the proof as a model of a student's reasoning and (b) the measure of utility of the proof for generating tutoring feedback. The measure of plausibility can be evaluated with respect to the misconceptions that were identified as present in the essay by the prover and by a human expert. A more precise plausibility measure may take into account plausibility of the proof as a whole. The measure of utility for the tutoring task can be interpreted in terms of relevance of the tutoring actions (triggered by the proof) to the student's essay, whether the proof was plausible or not.

A previous version of Tacitus-lite+ was evaluated as part of the Why2-Atlas evaluation studies, as well as on its own. The stand-alone evaluation uses manually constructed propositional representation of essays, to measure the performance of the theorem prover (in terms of the recognition of misconceptions in the essay) on 'gold' input [8]. The results of the latter evaluation were encouraging enough for us to continue development of the theorem proving approach for essay analysis.

1.2 Related Work

In our earlier paper [9] we argued that statistical text classification approaches that treat text as an unordered bag of words (e.g. [10,11]) do not provide a sufficiently deep understanding of the logical structure of the student's essay that is essential for our application. Structured models of conceptual knowledge, including those based on semantic networks and expert systems, are described in [12]. Another structured model, Bayesian belief networks, is a popular tool for learning and representing student models [13,14]. By appropriately choosing the costs of propositions in rules, weighted abductive proofs can be interpreted as Bayesian belief networks [15,4]. In general, the costs of propositions in abductive theorem proving do not have to adhere to probabilistic semantics, providing greater flexibility while also eliminating the need to create a proper probability space. On the other hand, the task of choosing a suitable cost semantics in weighted abduction remains a difficult problem and it is out of scope of this paper.

Theorem provers have been used in tutoring systems for various purposes, e.g. for building the solution space of a problem [16] and for question answering [17], to mention a few. Student modeling from the point of view of formal methods is reviewed in [18]. An interactive construction of a learner model that uses a theorem proving component is described in [19].

In this paper we focus on the recent additions to the set of proof search heuristics for Tacitus-lite+: a specificity-sensitive assumption cost and a rule choice preference that is based on the similarity between the graph of cross-references between the propositions in a candidate rule and the graph of cross-references between the set of goals. The paper is organized as follows: Section 2 introduces knowledge representation aspects of the prover; Section 3 defines the order-sorted abductive inference framework and describes the new proof search heuristics; finally, a summary is given in Section 4.

2 Knowledge Representation for Qualitative Mechanics

In addition to the domain knowledge that is normally represented in qualitative physics frameworks (e. g. [20]), a natural language tutoring application requires a representation of possibly erroneous student beliefs that captures the differences between beliefs expressed formally and informally, as allowed by natural language. The process of building a formal representation of the problem can be described in terms of envisionment and idealization.

2.1 Envisionment and Idealization

The internal (mental) representation of the problem plays a key role in problem solving among both novices and experts [21,22]. The notion of an internal representation, described in [22] as "objects, operators, and constraints, as well as initial and final states," overlaps with the notion of *envisionment* [23], i.e. the sequence of events implied by the problem statement. While envisionment can be expressed as a sequence of events in common-sense terms, a further step towards representing the envisionment in formal physics terms (bodies, forces, motion) is referred to as *idealization* [8].

For example, consider the problem in Figure 1. A possible envisionment is: (1) the man is holding the keys (elevator is falling); (2) the man releases the keys; (3) the keys move up with respect to the elevator and hit the elevator ceiling.

The idealization would be:

Bodies: Keys, Man, Elevator, Earth.
Forces: Gravity, Man holding keys
Motion: Keys' downward velocity is smaller than the downward velocity of the elevator.

Because envisionment and idealization are important stages for constructing an internal representation, they fall under the scope of Why2-Atlas' tutoring. However, reasoning about the multitude of possible envisionments would require adding an extensive amount of common-sense knowledge to the system. To bypass this difficulty, we consider problems that would typically have few likely envisionments. Fortunately (for the knowledge engineers), there is a class of interesting qualitative physics problems that falls into this category. We therefore developed a knowledge representation that is capable of representing common correct and erroneous propositions at both the levels of envisionment and idealization.

2.2 Qualitative Mechanics Ontology

The ontology is designed to take advantage of the additional capability provided by an order-sorted language (described in Section 2.3). Namely, constants and variables, corresponding to physical quantities (e. g. force, velocity), physical bodies (man, earth) and agents (air) are associated with a sort symbol. The domains of the predicate symbols are restricted to certain sorts (so that each argument position has a corresponding sort symbol). These associations and constraints constitute an *order-sorted signature* [24].

The ontology consists of the following main concept classes: bodies, physical quantities, states, time, relations, as well as their respective slot-filler concepts. For details of the ontology we refer the reader to [8].

```
((acceleration a1 keys vertical ?d-mag
                 ?d-mag-num nonzero ?mag-num neg ?dir-num ?d-dir ?t1 ?t2)
(Quantity1b Id Regular-body Axial D-mag
                 D-mag-num Mag-zero Mag-num Dir Dir-num D-dir Time Time))
((due-to d1 a1 ph1)  (Due-to Id Id Id))
((phenomenon ph1 gravity)  (Phenomenon Id Field-interaction))
```

Fig. 3. Representation for "The keys have a downward acceleration due to gravity." The atoms are paired with their sorted signatures.

2.3 Order-Sorted First-Order Predicate Language

We adopted first-order predicate logic with sorts [24] as the representation language. Essentially, it is a first-order predicate language that is augmented with an *order-sorted signature* for its terms and predicate argument places. For the sake of computational efficiency and since function-free clauses are the natural output of the sentence-level understanding module (see Section 1), we do not implement functions, instead we use cross-referencing between atoms by means of shared variables. There is a single predicate symbol M_i for each i-place relation. For this reason predicate symbols are omitted in the actual representation. Each atom is indexed with a unique *identifier*, a constant of sort `Id`. The identifiers, as well as variable names, can be used for cross-referencing between atoms. For example, the proposition "The keys have a downward acceleration due to gravity" is represented as shown in Figure 3, where `a1`, `d1`, and `ph1` are atom identifiers. For this example we assume (a) a fixed coordinate system, with a vertical axis pointing up (thus `Dir` value is `neg`); (b) that the existence of an acceleration is equivalent to existence of a nonzero acceleration (thus `Mag-zero` value is `nonzero`).

2.4 Rules

As we mentioned in Section 2.1, it is important to have rules about both envisionment and idealization when modeling students' reasoning. The idealization of the canonical envisionment is represented as a set of givens for the theorem prover, namely rules of the form $\rightarrow a$. A student's reasoning may contain false facts, including an erroneous idealization and envisionment, and erroneous inferences. The former are represented via *buggy givens* and the latter are represented via *buggy rules*. Buggy rules normally have their respective correct counterparts in the rule base. Certain integrity constraints apply when a student model is generated, based on the assumption that the student is unlikely to use correct and buggy versions of a rule (or given) within the same argument.

An example of a correct rule, stating that "if the velocity of a body is zero over a time interval then its initial position is equal to its final position", is shown in Figure 4. Note that the rules are *extended Horn clauses*, namely the head of the rule is an atom or a conjunction of multiple atoms.

```
((velocity v1 ?body ?comp ?d-mag
                  ?d-mag-num zero ?mag-num ?dir ?dir-num ?d-dir ?t1 ?t2)
(Quantity1b Id Body Comp D-mag
                  D-mag-num Mag-zero Mag-num Dir Dir-num D-dir Time Time))
→
((position p1 ?body ?comp ?d-mag1
          ?d-mag-num1 ?mag-zero1 ?mag-num1 ?dir1 ?dir-num1 ?d-dir1 ?t1 ?t1)
(Quantity1b Id Body Comp D-mag
                  D-mag-num Mag-zero Mag-num Dir Dir-num D-dir Time Time))
((position p2 ?body ?comp ?d-mag1
          ?d-mag-num1 ?mag-zero1 ?mag-num1 ?dir1 ?dir-num1 ?d-dir1 ?t2 ?t2)
(Quantity1b Id Body Comp D-mag
                  D-mag-num Mag-zero Mag-num Dir Dir-num D-dir Time Time))
```

Fig. 4. Representation for the rule "If the velocity of a body is zero over a time interval then its initial position is equal to its final position."

3 Abductive Reasoning

3.1 Order-Sorted Abductive Logic Programming

Similar to [25] we define the *abductive logic programming framework* as a triple $\langle T, A, I\rangle$, where T is the set of *givens* and *rules*, A is the set of abducible atoms (potential hypotheses) and I is a set of integrity constraints. Then an *abductive explanation* of a given set of sentences G (observations) consists of (a) subset Δ of abducibles A such that $T \cup \Delta \vdash G$ and $T \cup \Delta$ satisfies I together with (b) the corresponding *proof* of G. Since an abductive explanation is generally not unique, various criteria can be considered for choosing the most suitable explanation (see Section 3.2).

An *order-sorted abductive logic programming framework* $\langle T', A', I'\rangle$ is an abductive logic programming framework with all atoms augmented with the sorts of their argument terms (so that they are sorted atoms) [8]. Assume the following notation: a *sorted atom* is of the form $p(x_1, \ldots, x_n) : (\tau_1, \cdots, \tau_n)$, where the term x_i is of the sort τ_i. Then, in terms of unsorted predicate logic, formula $\exists x\; p(x) : (\tau)$ can be written as $\exists x\; p(x) \wedge \tau(x)$. For our domain we restrict the sort hierarchy to a tree structure that is naturally imposed by set semantics and that has the property $\exists x\; \tau_i(x) \wedge \tau_j(x) \rightarrow (\tau_i \preccurlyeq \tau_j) \vee (\tau_j \preccurlyeq \tau_i)$, where $\tau_i \preccurlyeq \tau_j$ is equivalent to $\forall x\; \tau_i(x) \rightarrow \tau_j(x)$.

Tacitus-lite+ does backward chaining using the order-sorted version of modus ponens:

$$\frac{\begin{array}{l} q(x', z') : (\tau_5, \tau_6) \\ p(x, y) : (\tau_1, \tau_2) \leftarrow q(x, z) : (\tau_3, \tau_4) \\ \tau_5 \preccurlyeq \tau_3,\; \tau_6 \preccurlyeq \tau_4 \end{array}}{p(x', y') : (\min(\tau_5, \tau_1), \tau_2)} \qquad (1)$$

3.2 Proof Search Heuristics

In building a model of the student's reasoning, our goal is to simultaneously increase a function of measures of utility and plausibility. The utility measure is an estimate of the utility of the choice of a particular proof for the tutoring application given a plausibility distribution on a set of alternative proofs. The plausibility measure indicates which explanation is the most likely.

For example, even if a proof does not exactly coincide with the reasoning the student used to arrive at a particular conclusion that she stated in her essay, the proof may be of a high utility value, provided it correctly indicates the presence of certain misconceptions in the student's reasoning. However, generally plausible explanations have a high utility value and we deploy a number of heuristics to increase the plausibility of the proof.

Weighted abduction. One of the characteristic properties of abduction is that atoms can be assumed as hypotheses, without proof. Normally it is required that the set of assumptions is minimal, in the sense that no proper subset of it is sufficient to explain the observation (or, in other words, to prove the goals). While this preference allows us to compare two explanations when one is a subset of another, *weighted abduction* provides a method to grade explanations so we can compare two arbitrary explanations.

Tacitus-lite extends the weighted abductive inference algorithm described in [26] for the case where rules are expressed as Horn clauses to the case where rules are expressed as extended Horn clauses, namely the head of a rule is an atom or a conjunction of atoms. Each conjunct p_i from the body of the rule has a weight w_i associated with it:

$$p_1^{w_1} \wedge \cdots \wedge p_m^{w_m} \rightarrow r_1 \wedge \cdots \wedge r_n$$

The weight is used to calculate the cost of abducing p_i, instead of proving it, via the formula $cost(p_i) = cost(g) \cdot w_i$, where g is the goal atom that has been proved via the rule at a preceding step (by unifying, say, with atom r_j). The costs of the observations are supplied with the observations as input to the prover.

Given a subgoal or observation atom to be proven, Tacitus-lite takes one of three actions; (a) assumes the atom at the cost associated with it; (b) unifies it with an atom that is either a fact or has already been proven or is another goal (in the latter case the cost of the resultant atom is counted once in the total cost of the proof, as the minimum of the two costs); (c) attempts to prove it with a rule. Tacitus-lite calls the action (b) *factoring*.

To account for the fact that in the order-sorted abductive framework a rule can generate new goals of various specificity (depending on the goals that were unified with the head of the rule), we adjust the weight of the assumed atom according to the sorts of its terms: a more general statement is less costly to assume, but a more specific statement is more costly. For example, the rule from Figure 4 can be applied to prove the goal "(Axial, or total) position of ?body3 has magnitude ?mag-num3":

```
((position p3 ?body3 ?comp3 ?d-mag3
        ?d-mag-num3 ?mag-zero3 ?mag-num3 ?dir3 ?dir-num3 ?d-dir3 ?t3 ?t3)
(Quantity1b Id Body Axial D-mag
                D-mag-num Mag-zero Mag-num Dir Dir-num D-dir Time Time)),
```

which generates the subgoal "(Axial or total) velocity of ?body3 is zero":

```
((velocity v2 ?body3 ?comp3 ?d-mag2
        ?d-mag-num2 zero ?mag-num2 ?dir2 ?dir-num2 ?d-dir2 ?t3 ?t4)
(Quantity1b Id Body Axial D-mag
                D-mag-num Mag-zero Mag-num Dir Dir-num D-dir Time Time))
```

The same rule can be applied to prove the more specific goal "Horizontal position of ?body3 has magnitude ?mag-num3":

```
((position p4 ?body3 horizontal ?d-mag3
        ?d-mag-num3 ?mag-zero3 ?mag-num3 ?dir3 ?dir-num3 ?d-dir3 ?t3 ?t3)
(Quantity1b Id Body Axial D-mag
                D-mag-num Mag-zero Mag-num Dir Dir-num D-dir Time Time)),
```

and will generate the more specific subgoal "Horizontal velocity of ?body3 is zero":

```
((velocity v3 ?body3 horizontal ?d-mag2
        ?d-mag-num2 zero ?mag-num2 ?dir2 ?dir-num2 ?d-dir2 ?t3 ?t4)
(Quantity1b Id Body Axial D-mag
                D-mag-num Mag-zero Mag-num Dir Dir-num D-dir Time Time))
```

Since the variables are assumed to be existentially quantified, in accordance with the sort semantics (see Section 3.1), the latter, more specific subgoal implies the former subgoal. Also, according to the ordered version of modus ponens (1), more rules can be used to prove the more general atom, increasing the chances for the atom to be proven, rather than assumed. These considerations suggest that *it should be less costly to assume more general atoms than more specific atoms.* The cost adjustment for the assumptions is implemented by computing a metric of specificity for the sorted signature of each assumed atom.

Rule choice heuristics. Although the rules in Tacitus-lite are applied to prove individual goal atoms, a meaningful proposition usually consists of a few atoms cross-referenced via shared variables (see Section 2.3). When a rule is used to prove a particular goal atom, (a) a unifier is applied to the atoms in the head and the body of the rule; (b) atoms from the head of the rule are added to the list of proven atoms; and (c) atoms from the body of the rule are added to the list of goals. Consequently, suppose there exists a unifier θ that unifies both (a) a goal atom g_1 with an atom r_1 from the head of the rule $R : p_1 \wedge p_2 \rightarrow r_1 \wedge r_2$ so that g_1 can be proved with R via modus ponens, and (b) a goal atom g_2

with an atom r_2 from the head of the rule R so that g_2 can be proved via R. Then, proving goal g_1 via R (and applying θ to g_1 and r_1) adds the atom $r_2\theta$ to the list of provens thus allowing for its potential factoring with goal g_2. In effect, a single application of a rule in which its head atoms match multiple goal atoms can result in proving multiple goal atoms via a number of subsequent factoring steps. This property of the prover is consistent (a) with backchaining using modus ponens (1), and (b) with the intuitive notion of cognitive economy, namely that the shortest (by the total number of rule applications) proofs are usually considered good by domain experts.

Moreover, if an atom $p_1\theta$ in the body of R can be unified with a goal $g_3\theta$, then the application of rule R will probably not result in an increase of the total cost of the goals due to the new goal $p_1\theta$, since it is possible to factor it with $g_3\theta$ and set the cost of the resultant atom as the minimum of the costs of $p_1\theta$ and $g_3\theta$. In other words, applying a rule where multiple atoms in its head and body match multiple goal atoms is likely to result in a faster reduction of the goal list, and therefore a shorter final proof.

The new version of Tacitus-lite+ extends the previous rule choice heuristics described in [9] with rule choice based on the best match between the set of atoms in a candidate rule and the set of goal atoms. To account for the structure of cross-references between the atoms, a labeled graph is constructed offline for every rule, so that the atoms are vertices labeled with respective sorted signatures and the cross-references are edges labeled with pairs of respective argument positions. Similarly a labeled graph is built on-the-fly for the current set of goal atoms. The rule choice procedure involves comparison of the goal graph and graphs of candidate rules so that the rule that maximizes the graph matching metric is preferred.

The match metric between two labeled graphs is based on the size of the largest common subgraph (LCSG). We have implemented the decision-tree-based LCSG algorithm proposed in [27]. The advantage of this algorithm is that the time complexity of its online stage is independent of the size of the rule graph: if n is the number of vertices in the goal graph, then the time complexity of the LCSG is $O(2^n n^3)$.

Since the graph matching includes independent subroutines for matching vertices (atoms with sorted signatures) and matching edges (cross-referenced atom arguments), the precision of both match subroutines can be varied to balance the trade-off between search precision and efficiency of the overall matching procedure. Currently we are evaluating the performance of the theorem prover under various settings.

4 Conclusion

We described an application of theorem proving for analyzing student's essays in the context of an interactive tutoring system. While formal methods have been applied to student modeling, there are a number of challenges to overcome: representing varying levels of formality in student language, the limited scope of the rule base, and limited resources for generating explanations and consistency checking. In our earlier paper [9] we argued that a weighted abduction theorem proving framework augmented with appropriate proof search heuristics provides a necessary deep-level understanding of a student's reasoning. In this paper we describe the recent additions to our proof search heuristics that have the goal of improving the plausibility of the proofs as models of students' reasoning as well as the computational efficiency of the proof search.

Acknowledgments. This work was funded by NSF grant 9720359 and ONR grant N00014-00-1-0600. We thank the entire Natural Language Tutoring group, in particular Michael Ringenberg and Roy Wilson for their work on Tacitus-lite+, and Uma Pappuswamy, Michael Böttner, and Brian 'Moses' Hall for their work on knowledge representation and rules.

References

1. VanLehn, K., Jordan, P., Rosé, C., Bhembe, D., Böttner, M., Gaydos, A., Makatchev, M., Pappuswamy, U., Ringenberg, M., Roque, A., Siler, S., Srivastava, R.: The architecture of Why2-Atlas: A coach for qualitative physics essay writing. In: Proceedings of Intelligent Tutoring Systems Conference. Volume 2363 of LNCS., Springer (2002) 158–167
2. Rosé, C., Roque, A., Bhembe, D., VanLehn, K.: An efficient incremental architecture for robust interpretation. In: Proceedings of Human Language Technology Conference, San Diego, CA. (2002)
3. Jordan, P., VanLehn, K.: Discourse processing for explanatory essays in tutorial applications. In: Proceedings of the 3rd SIGdial Workshop on Discourse and Dialogue. (2002)
4. Poole, D.: Probabilistic Horn abduction and Bayesian networks. Artificial Intelligence **64** (1993) 81–129
5. Young, R.M., O'Shea, T.: Errors in children's subtraction. Cognitive Science **5** (1981) 153–177
6. Jordan, P., Makatchev, M., Pappuswamy, U.: Extended explanations as student models for guiding tutorial dialogue. In: Proceedings of AAAI Spring Symposium on Natural Language Generation in Spoken and Written Dialogue. (2003) 65–70
7. Hobbs, J., Stickel, M., Martin, P., Edwards, D.: Interpretation as abduction. In: Proc. 26th Annual Meeting of the ACL, Association of Computational Linguistics. (1988) 95–103
8. Makatchev, M., Jordan, P.W., VanLehn, K.: Abductive theorem proving for analyzing student explanations to guide feedback in intelligent tutoring systems. To appear in Journal of Automated Reasoning, Special issue on Automated Reasoning and Theorem Proving in Education (2004)
9. Jordan, P., Makatchev, M., VanLehn, K.: Abductive theorem proving for analyzing student explanations. In: Proceedings of International Conference on Artificial Intelligence in Education, Sydney, Australia, IOS Press (2003) 73–80
10. Landauer, T.K., Foltz, P.W., Laham, D.: An introduction to latent semantic analysis. Discourse Processes **25** (1998) 259–284

11. McCallum, A., Nigam, K.: A comparison of event models for naive bayes text classification. In: Proceeding of AAAI/ICML-98 Workshop on Learning for Text Categorization, AAAI Press (1998)
12. Jonassen, D.: Using cognitive tools to represent problems. Journal of Research on Technology in Education **35** (2003) 362–381
13. Conati, C., Gertner, A., VanLehn, K.: Using bayesian networks to manage uncertainty in student modeling. Journal of User Modeling and User-Adapted Interaction **12** (2002) 371–417
14. Zapata-Rivera, J.D., Greer, J.: Student model accuracy using inspectable bayesian student models. In: International Conference of Artificial Intelligence in Education, Sydney, Australia (2003) 65–72
15. Charniak, E., Shimony, S.E.: Probabilistic semantics for cost based abduction. In: Proceedings of AAAI-90. (1990) 106–111
16. Matsuda, N., VanLehn, K.: GRAMY: A geometry theorem prover capable of construction. Journal of Automated Reasoning **32** (2004) 3–33
17. Murray, W.R., Pease, A., Sams, M.: Applying formal methods and representations in a natural language tutor to teach tactical reasoning. In: Proceedings of International Conference on Artificial Intelligence in Education, Sydney, Australia, IOS Press (2003) 349–356
18. Self, J.: Formal approaches to student modelling. In McCalla, G.I., Greer, J., eds.: Student Modelling: the key to individualized knowledge-based instruction. Springer, Berlin (1994) 295–352
19. Dimitrova, V.: STyLE-OLM: Interactive open learner modelling. Artificial Intelligence in Education **13** (2003) 35–78
20. Forbus, K., Carney, K., Harris, R., Sherin, B.: A qualitative modeling environment for middle-school students: A progress report. In: QR-01. (2001)
21. Ploetzner, R., Fehse, E., Kneser, C., Spada, H.: Learning to relate qualitative and quantitative problem representations in a model-based setting for collaborative problem solving. The Journal of the Learning Sciences **8** (1999) 177–214
22. Reimann, P., Chi, M.T.H.: Expertise in complex problem solving. In Gilhooly, K.J., ed.: Human and machine problem solving. Plenum Press, New York (1989) 161–192
23. de Kleer, J.: Multiple representations of knowledge in a mechanics problem-solver. In Weld, D.S., de Kleer, J., eds.: Readings in Qualitative Reasoning about Physical Systems. Morgan Kaufmann, San Mateo, California (1990) 40–45
24. Walther, C.: A many-sorted calculus based on resolution and paramodulation. Morgan Kaufmann, Los Altos, California (1987)
25. Kakas, A., Kowalski, R.A., Toni, F.: The role of abduction in logic programming. In Gabbay, D.M., Hogger, C.J., Robinson, J.A., eds.: Handbook of logic in Artificial Intelligence and Logic Programming. Volume 5. Oxford University Press (1998) 235–324
26. Stickel, M.: A Prolog-like inference system for computing minimum-cost abductive explanations in natural-language interpretation. Technical Report 451, SRI International, 333 Ravenswood Ave., Menlo Park, California (1988)
27. Shearer, K., Bunke, H., Venkatesh, S.: Video indexing and similarity retrieval by largest common subgraph detection using decision trees. Pattern Recognition **34** (2001) 1075–1091

From Errors to Conceptions – An Approach to Student Diagnosis

Carine Webber

Computer Science Department - University of Caxias do Sul
C.P.1352 – Caxias do Sul, RS, Brazil
cgwebber@ucs.br
http://www.dein.ucs.br

Abstract. A particular challenge in the domain of student diagnosis concerns how to 'recognize' and 'remediate' student errors. Machine learning techniques have been successfully applied to identify categories of errors and then to discriminate a new error in order to provide feedback to the student. However, remediation very often requires interpreting student errors in terms of knowledge in the context of a specific learning situation. This work is mainly concerned with this problem area. In this sense, we present here an approach to student diagnosis founded on a cognitive framework, called Conception Model, developed in the domain of educational research. The main issue about the Conception Model is the fact that it allows representing student errors in terms of knowledge applied to a learning context. We describe the main aspects of the student diagnosis system we have implemented, and then we evaluate the diagnosis results by comparing them to human diagnoses.

1 Introduction

An important aspect of learning environments is the ability of taking into account students' knowledge in order to generate new learning situations or to intervene during problem solving activities. A particular challenge for researchers in the domain concerns how to recognize and remediate student errors. One origin of this problem is the large variety of students' possible conceptions, either correct or not. The problem of diagnosing students' conceptions is actually one of the bottlenecks of research on learning environments. Indeed anyone in the field can acknowledge the extraordinary capacity of students to adapt to certain specific circumstances or environments, but contradicting the current knowledge of reference. In fact, students are likely to develop significantly new knowings based on the strategies they develop to face the challenge of adapting to the new context.

Cognitive modeling is a way of taking into account student knowledge. In this paper we start by reviewing classical approaches to model student knowledge (section 2). We define student diagnosis as a process of building a computer-based model from student's behavior on the interface of a learning environment. The purpose of this paper is to present a novel approach to student diagnosis in which beyond simply

J.C. Lester et al. (Eds.): ITS 2004, LNCS 3220, pp. 710–719, 2004.

taking into account student's actions related to a particular task, the system is able to provide explanation on the student's reasoning by recognizing subjacent knowledge. More precisely, we consider that a learning system must be able to represent student's actions in terms of knowledge used in a problem solving activity. In this direction, we will introduce the Conception Model (section 3), which allows the representation of errors in terms of knowledge having a specific domain of validity. Next, we will briefly describe the spatial multiagent diagnosis approach we have implemented (section 4). Finally, experiments we have carried out and the evaluation of the results that have been obtained will be presented (sections 5 and 6).

2 Cognitive Modeling Approaches

In educational technology, the user model has deserved intensive research effort in the last three decades but, so far, the best method has not been found. The very first method employed was the method of overlay. This method assumes that student's knowledge is a subset of the expert's knowledge in one domain. Learning is related to the acquisition of expert's knowledge, which is absent from the incomplete student's model. A learning environment based on this approach will try to create interactions with the student in order to enrich student's model and approximate it to the expert one. Easy to implement, the overlay method was unable to give account of the student's misconceptions in the domain. Once the overlay model represents student's knowledge according to the scope of an expert model, it does not take into account anything beyond that. It means that any knowledge outside expert's knowledge is not recognized and often taken by the system as incorrect knowledge. On these terms, overlay modeling situates student's knowledge as correct or incorrect regarding expert's knowledge. If the student fails, the environment tries to apply different available learning strategies until the student succeeds. West [5] and Guidon [7] are systems based on overlay model.

The first solution to overcome limitations on the overlay model was to construct *bug libraries*, or databases of misconceptions, which have originated the perturbation model. The term *bug*, imported from computer science, was used to represent the errors of systematic type. As static libraries have very quickly proved to be difficult to construct and to maintain, machine learning algorithms have been applied in order to overcome limitations of bug libraries construction and maintenance by inducting bugs from examples of student's behaviors. The perturbation model differs from the overlay model since it does not perceive student's knowledge as a simplification of expert knowledge, but rather like perturbations over the expert knowledge.

Perturbation model is the first considered as a dynamic one, since it could evolve using machine learning techniques. Such techniques were employed for the learning and the discrimination of systematic errors and procedures of resolution. Errors were identified from the analyses of protocols of students, or they were learned by using machine learning algorithms (and in this case a representative set of examples were required). Such algorithms allow as well modeling student's intentions when solving problems by associating actions with plans of resolution, that students could use in the context of a problem. Ideally each systematic error could be associated to an erroneous conception in the domain. Among the systems built on the perturbation model, we quote Buggy [4], and Andes [8]. Buggy is a system developed as an educational game to prepare future teachers. In another field, Andes is a tutoring system in the domain of physics for college students.

The third approach that we discuss here is the model tracing, which comes from ACT theory (Active Control of Thought), proposed by Anderson [1]. Systems based on the model tracing approach work in parallel with the student, simulating his behavior on each step toward the problem solution. This allows the system to interact with him on each step. However, the system must be able to reconstruct each step of a solution in order to simulate and understand student's reasoning about the problem. Each step of the resolution is a production rule; correct and incorrect rules need to be represented. Once an error is detected by the system, an immediate feedback is generated. In fact, this model exerts a control on the solution built by the student, by protecting him from developing his solution in a direction that would not lead it to the correct solution. Knowledge acquisition is attested by the application of correct rules. This approach was implemented by John Anderson and his group in three domains: LISP language with Lisp Tutor, the elementary geometry with Geometry Tutor, and the algebra with Algebra I e II.

3 The Conception Model

Important research has been developed about student's conceptions. A relevant synthesis is presented by Confrey, whose work has concerned the paradigm of "misconceptions" (erroneous conceptions) [9]. According to Confrey, if we attentively look for a sense to a wrong answer given by a student, we may discover that it is reasonable. The problem of dealing with student's mistakes and misconceptions has been as well deeply studied by Balacheff [2]. According to him, when analyzing students' behavior, it must be considered the existence of contradictory and incorrect mental structures from the viewpoint of an observer. Such (contradictory and incorrect) mental structures may however be seen as coherent once applied to a particular context (a class of problems or tasks). Following these important principles, when a student solves a problem, he employs coherent and justifiable knowledge related to the particular learning situation.

Although student's knowledge may be recognized as contradictory or wrong throughout multiple interactions, they can be taken as temporarily stable knowledge structures. One main principle of our work is to consider that any topic of knowledge has a valid domain, which characterizes it as knowledge. The matter of understanding which valid domain was given by a student to one topic of knowledge is a condition for a computer-based system to construct hypothesis about student's behavior. In this sense, the Conception Model, that we introduce here, constitutes a model with cognitive and epistemic basis for representing and formalizing the student's knowledge and its valid domain. The conception model has been developed by researchers in the field of mathematics education and the formalization that we employ was proposed by Balacheff [2]. On the purpose of this work, we consider the conception model as the appropriated theoretical framework for representing student's knowledge; its formal model is presented in the next section.

3.1 Formal Model of a Conception

Usually the word conception is taken in a very general sense for authors in the computers in education's field. Some of them use the word conception concerning something conceived in the mind, like a thought or an idea. In our sense, a conception is a well-defined structure that can be ascribed by an observer to a student according to his behavior. As our work is concerned with problem solving, we consider that a conception has a valid domain; a domain in which the conception applies correctly. Nonetheless describing precisely conceptions is a difficult problem, thus we use a model developed in mathematics education with a cognitive foundation. In this model a conception is characterized by a quadruplet C (P, R, L, Σ) where:

- P represents a set of problems, which describe the conception's domain of validity, it is the seminal context where the conception may appear;
- R represents a set of operators or rules, which are involved in the solutions of problems from P;
- L is a representation system, it allows the representation of problems and operators;
- Σ is a control structure, which guarantees that the solution holds the conception's definition, it allows making choices and decision in the solution process.

We pursue this section by presenting examples of conceptions in the domain of reflection.

3.2 Conceptions in the Domain of Reflection

A common conception that students hold about reflection is the conception of "parallelism" (figure 1). Holding such conception, students believe that two line segments are symmetrical if they are parallel. We can easily observe that for some configurations (figure 1, frame a), two symmetrical line segments are effectively parallels, even though this condition is not always true (figure 1, frame b).

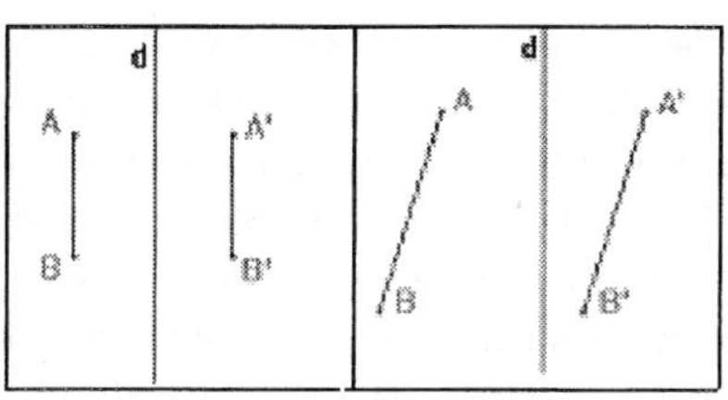

Fig. 1 (frames a and b). Conceptions about reflection

The field of reflection gave matter to several studies on the conceptions carried by students and on their evolution in a learning process [3, 10]. Additional conceptions in the domain of reflection include the conception of "central symmetry", the "oblique symmetry" and the "orthogonal symmetry" (the correct one). Indeed, the research field of conceptions is rather vast, for this reason we recommend to consult [13], where a list of relevant bibliographical references can be found.

4 Multiagent Diagnosis System

From a theoretical perspective, the conception model allows the formalization of students' conceptions. However, the main challenge has been to develop its computer-based counterpart. It is important to remark that the only available information are the problem statement and the solution. Besides, one conception is not an observable element; observable elements are operators used by student, the problem solved, the language used to express them, and theoretical control structures.

In order to develop a computer-based approach to the conception model we have followed a multiagent and emergent approach [12]. We recognize in the theoretical model two distinct levels of knowledge: a micro-level containing the elements characterizing conceptions (as problems and operators), and a macro-level (the conceptions), as shown on figure 2.

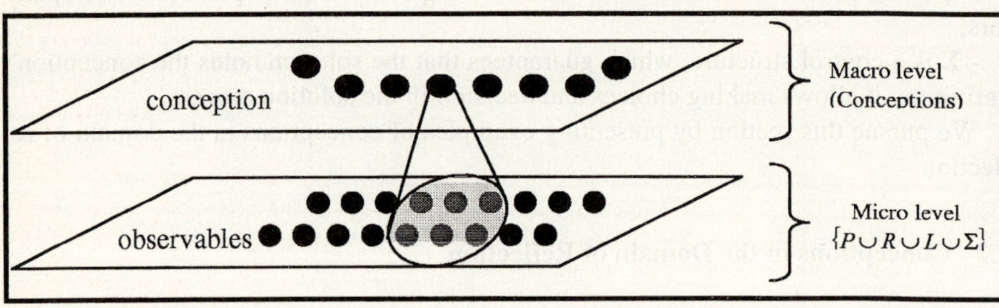

Fig. 2. A macro-level observer interpret micro-level particles in terms of conceptions

We have adopted an emergent approach for diagnosing conceptions since we recognize the necessity of two different ontologies: a first one to describe problems, operators and control structures, and a second one to describe conceptions. The micro-level represents the way any conception may be revealed by students (through sets of operators and problems), whereas macro-level represents conceptions in terms of knowledge. While an observer, placed in the micro-level, is only able to recognize problems, operators, control rules, a second observer placed in the macro-level, must be able to interpret micro-level particles in terms of conceptions. Macro-level corresponds actually to an abstraction (in terms of knowledge) of what is represented in the micro-level.

We pursue this section describing the implementation of micro and macro levels.

4.1 The Micro Level

The purpose of the micro level is to characterize the students' state of knowledge during a problem solving activity, in order to construct an image of students' cognitive abilities. A set of these images will allow observing the behavior of a particular student and attesting changes in problem solving procedures, for instance.

The micro level is modeled by a multiagent system whose agents have sensors to elements from the conception model (problems, operators, and control structures). The multiagent system is composed by 150 different agents. They share an environment where the problem configuration and the proof (representing student solution) are described. Agents react to the presence (of an encapsulated element) in the environment. Interactions between agents and the environment follow the stimulus-response model.

Once an agent perceives its own encapsulated element in the environment, it becomes active. Active agents have a particular behavior towards the spatial organization of the society. Agents' behavior has been formally described at [12]. A spatial multiagent approach has been implemented where agents share a n-dimensional issue space and form coalitions according to their proximity. Agents' behavior is based on group-decision making strategies (a spatial voting mechanism) and coalition formation [11]. Diagnosis is not seen as an exclusive function of an agent, but the result of a collective decision making process. Dynamically agents organize themselves in a spatial configuration according to the affinity of the particles they encapsulate. Agents form coalitions, which positions in the Euclidian space represent conceptions. When the process of coalition formation ends, groups of agents as spatially organized. The winner coalition represents the conception(s) held by the student (as parallelism shown on figure 1, for instance) that the majority considers to be the state of knowledge of the student being observed. Coalitions of agents are observed and finally interpreted by the macro-level in terms of conceptions.

4.2 The Macro Level

Macro level has as a main goal to observe and interpret the final state of micro-level agents in terms of a diagnosis result. The macro level has been modeled as a multi-agent learning environment called Baghera [3]. One or more agents may have the role of observing and interpreting the micro level. In the case of our implementation, we have ascribed this role to a Tutor agent.

The role of tutor agents comprehends as well to decide about the better strategy to apply in order to reach the goal of learning. It may include to propose a new activity to the student in order to reinforce correct conceptions or to confront the student with more complex situations; to show examples or counterexamples; to promote interactions with pairs or teachers.

5 Carrying Out Experiments

In order to carry out the necessary tests and analyze the results obtained from the diagnoses of conceptions, we have created a corpus of solutions of students for five problems. Problems that have been proposed belong to the domain of reflection and involved proving that a line segment has a symmetrical one with respect to an axis. As an example, consider for instance figure 3, where the problem was to prove, using geometrical properties of reflection, that the line segment [NM] has a symmetrical segment with respect to axis (d).

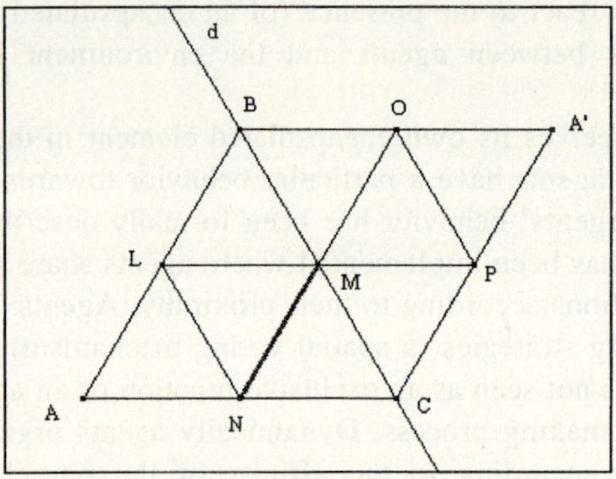

Fig. 3. A problem on the domain of reflection

A strategy that some students have applied to solve the problem above involves the so-called (mis)conception of 'central symmetry'. Holding it, students have proven that [OM] is the symmetrical line segment of [NM]. The conception of central symmetry usually appears on problems where the original segment has one extremity placed on the axis of symmetry. In order to prove which segment is symmetrical to [NM], students apply two main properties (or operators according to the Conception Model): as point M is placed on the axis, it is your own symmetrical point (a correct property); as point O is equidistant of point N with respect to line (d), and they are over the same line segment (NO), they are symmetrical (incorrect property).

Next section analyzes the results obtained through experiments.

6 Evaluating Results

The purpose of this evaluation it to compare results coming from automatic diagnosis to those obtained from human diagnosis. In order to realize this task, it has been created a corpus containing students' solutions given to five problems in the domain of reflection. Around 150 students (11-15 years old) have participated solving problems in a paper-pencil format. From the whole corpus, the work done by 28 students has been chosen to be analyzed. The choice of students was made based on their diversity of solutions presented and on the apparent engagement of students in the activities.

Once these two-steps have been concluded, students' solutions were submitted to the diagnosis of 3 teams of researchers in mathematics education (Did@TIC team from Grenoble (France), Math Education teams from the University of Pisa (Italy) and University of Bristol (UK) [3]). Besides ascribing a diagnosis in terms of four different conceptions to the solution presented by each student, each team of researchers was asked to present arguments in order to justify their diagnosis. In parallel, solutions were submitted as well to the automatic diagnosis system.

Once human and automatic diagnoses concluded, we were able to compare their results. Four situations have been identified among human and automatic diagnoses: total convergence, partial convergence, divergence and finally, situations were a comparison was not possible to be realized.

Situations of total convergence: in 17 cases (out of 28) human and automatic diagnoses have fully converged to the same diagnosis.

Situations of partial convergence: in 4 cases (out of 28) a situation of partial convergence was observed. This situation occurs when at least one human diagnosis converges to the automatic diagnosis. In a few cases, human teams have ascribed a low degree of confidence to the diagnosis to reflect their uncertainty.

Situations of divergence: in 2 cases automatic and human teams have diverged about the diagnosis ascribed to the solution.

Impossible to compare: in 5 cases comparison among the diagnoses could not be carried out because of the great number of divergences between human teams and abstentions.

In the next section, we proceed with an analysis of the divergent situations.

6.1 Divergence Among Diagnoses

Two cases of divergence between human and automatic diagnoses were detected. In both cases, the three human teams have converged towards an identical diagnosis. In order to understand the divergent behavior of the system, it is important to verify the arguments given by human teams used to justify the diagnoses. At this point, differences between human and automatic diagnoses become apparent.

In both cases of divergence, human teams have made a remark that students have not employed clear steps to construct the solutions. Note that all problems have involved the construction of a proof. It happened actually that they have employed rather general properties and operators of Geometry trying to justify a preconceived solution based on the graphical representation of the problem. Because of that, the steps of the proof given by the students were not logically coherent with the given answer. Human teams were able, without any effort, to identify such behavior, whereas automatic diagnosis was not. Thus answers given by students strongly guided human diagnoses. Concerning automatic diagnosis, agents engaged in the diagnosis task were representing rather general notions of reflection. Even though students have chosen a wrong answer to the 2 problems, they were not able to justify them by the means of proving. This explains why the system was not able to exhibit a convergent diagnosis.

6.2 Analyzing the Coherence of Diagnoses

We have attested a strong coherence between automatic and human diagnoses. In clear cases when human diagnoses fully converged with a high degree of confidence (17 cases), automatic diagnoses have as well converged to the formation of one unique coalition.

When handling incomplete or not easily interpretable cases, we have observed that human teams had ascribed a low degree of confidence to the diagnoses (4 cases). Moreover, for certain cases, the diagnosis task could not be carried out by some teams (5 cases), not allowing any comparison between human and automatic diagnoses. In addition, divergent human diagnoses were noticed. Concerning automatic diagnosis for these incomplete cases, diagnosis has as well received a low degree of confidence. Regarding some students' solutions, neither humans nor the system were able to decide between two or three candidate conceptions. In a few cases, the system converged in a more restrictive way with at least one human team.

To conclude this analysis, we have observed that in the majority of the cases, when the three human teams converged towards a diagnosis, the system arrived to this same diagnosis. However, when humans diverged or they expressed a low degree of confidence concerning the diagnosis, system has also exhibited this same behavior. Even tough convergence of all diagnoses was not observed in all the cases, we consider that the spatial multiagent approach to diagnosis is an effective and coherent approach. We consider that any diagnosis system must not only "imitate" human behavior in cases of convergence between them, but also in more difficult cases where there no convergence is observed.

7 Conclusion

In this paper, we have described an approach to student diagnosis founded on a cognitive framework, called Conception Model. The main focus of this paper has been on the representation of student's errors in terms of knowledge, since if an environment intends to provide personalized feedback, then it must be able to interpret student's actions in the interface of a computer in terms of knowledge.

We have implemented a diagnosis multiagent-based system, which has been integrated to the Baghera learning platform. We have followed an emergent and multiagent approach since we consider that, from the computing perspective, a cognitive diagnosis is a complex task. Existing approaches of diagnosis are usually based on complex theoretical frameworks, from which only a partial computer-based model can be built. Besides that, their results are not easily exploitable by the overall learning environment, which has to be built based on the same paradigm. It is as well important to mention that pioneer ideas of cognitive modeling have not been explored further due to the lack of proper computational platform. Recently multiagent architecture has proven to be flexible enough to build learning environment. We believe that multiagent approach is very well suited for the domain of learning environments once it deals well with applications where crucial issues (distance, cooperation among different entities and integration of different components of software) are found.

To conclude, the process of evaluating the automatic diagnosis has involved three teams of researchers on mathematics education. Results obtained from the computer-based diagnosis system have been positively evaluated by the human teams. As the most important perspective so far, we have been working to apply the diagnosis approach to diagnose conceptions in the domain of programming learning.

Acknowledgement. The author would like to thank Did@ctic and Magma Teams, from Leibniz Laboratory (Grenoble, France) where this work was developed when the author was a PhD candidate (1999-2003).

References

1. Anderson, J.: The Architecture of Cognition. Cambridge: Harvard University Press (1983)
2. Balacheff, N.: A modelling challenge: untangling students'knowing. Journées Internationales d'Orsay sur les Sciences Cognitives: L'apprentissage (JIOSC'2000). (http://www-didactique.imag.fr/Balacheff) (2000)
3. BAP: Designing an hybrid and emergent educational society. Research Report, Laboratoire Leibniz, April, number 81. (http://www-leibniz.imag.fr/NEWLEIBNIZ/LesCahiers/) (2003)
4. Brown, J.S., Burton, R.: Diagnostic models for procedural bugs in basic mathematical skill. Cognitive Science, 2, (1978) 155-192
5. Burton, R., Brown, J.S.: An investigation of computer coaching for informal learning activities. In: Sleeman, D., Brown, J. (eds.): Intelligent Tutoring Systems. Academic Press Orlando FL (1982)
6. Carr, B., Goldstein, I.P.: Overlays: a theory of modeling for computer-aided instruction, AI Memo 406, MIT, Cambridge, Mass (1977)
7. Clancey, W.J.: GUIDON. Journal of Computer-Based Instruction, Vol.10,n.1 (1983) 8-14
8. Conati, C., Gertner, A., VanLenh, K.: Using Bayesian Networks to Manage Uncertainty in Student Modeling. J. of User Modeling and User-Adapted Interaction, Vol.12(4) (2002)
9. Confrey, J.: A review of the research on students conceptions in mathematics, science, and programming. In: Courtney C. (ed.): Review of research in education. American Educational Research Association, Vol.16 (1990) 3-56
10. Hart, K.D.: Children's understanding of mathematics: 11-16.Alden Press, London (1981)
11. Sandholm, T.W.: Distributed Rational Decision Making. In: Weiβ, G. (ed.): Multiagent Systems: A Modern Introduction to Distributed A. I. MIT Press (1999) 201-258
12. Webber, C. Pesty, S.: Emergent diagnosis via coalition formation. In: Garijo, F. (ed.): Proceedings of Iberamia Conference. Lecture Notes in Computer Science, Vol.2527. Springer-Verlag, Berlin Heidelberg New York (2002) 755-764
13. WebSite Conception, Knowledge and Concept Discussion Group. http://conception.imag.fr

Discovering Intelligent Agent: A Tool for Helping Students Searching a Library

Kamal Yammine, Mohammed A. Razek, Esma Aïmeur, and Claude Frasson

Département d'informatique et de recherche opérationnelle
Université de Montréal
C.P. 6128, Succ. Centre-ville, Montréal,
Québec Canada H3C 3J7
{yamminek, abdelram, aimeur, frasson}@iro.umontreal.ca

Abstract. Nowadays, the explosive growth of the Internet has brought us such a huge number of books, publications, and documents that hardly any student can consider all of them. Finding the right book at the right time is an exhausting and time-consuming task, especially for new students who have diverse learning styles, needs, and interests. Moreover, the growing number of books in one subject can overwhelm students trying to choose the right book. This paper overcomes this challenge by ranking books using the pyramid collaborative filtering method. Based on this method, we have designed and implemented an agent called Discovering Intelligent Agent (DIA). The agent searches both the University of Montreal's and Amazon's library and then returns a list of books related to students' models and contents of the books.

Keywords: Recommendation Systems, learning style, intelligent agent, pyramid collaborative filtering.

1 Introduction

Currently, the rapid spread of the Internet has become a great resource for students searching for papers, documents, and books. However, the variety of students' learning styles, performances, and needs make finding the right book a complex task. Frequently, students rely on recommendations from their colleagues or professors to get the required books.

There are several methods used to support students. Recommendation systems try to personalize users' needs by building up information about their likes, dislikes and interests [14]. Those systems rely on two techniques: the content-based filtering (CB) and the collaborative filtering (CF) [2].

These approaches are acceptable and relevant; however, none of them considers students' models. To solve this problem, this paper uses a Pyramid Collaborative Filtering Model (PCFA) [18] for filtering and recommending books. PCFA has four levels. Moving from one level to another depends on three filtering techniques: domain model filtering, user model filtering, and credibility model filtering. Based on these techniques, we have designed and implemented an agent called Discovering Intelligent Agent (DIA). This agent searches both the University of Montreal's and Ama-

J.C. Lester et al. (Eds.): ITS 2004, LNCS 3220, pp. 720–729, 2004.

zon's library and then returns a list of books related to students' models and contents of the books.

This paper is organized as follows. Section 1 the above-mentioned introduction. Section 2 briefly describes some related work. In section 3, we present, in detail, the architecture of DIA. Section 4 shows the methodology of DIA. Section 5 discusses the pending problems of implementation. Section 6 presents an online scenario. And finally, section 7 concludes the paper and suggests future projects.

2 Related Work

Recommendation systems have been widely discussed in the past decade and two main approaches have emerged: the *Content-Based filtering* (CB) and the *Collaborative Filtering* (CF) [2], [6], [20]. The first approach recommends items to a user, similar to those he liked in the past by studying the content of the item. Libra [15] for example, proposes books based on the user's ratings and the description of the book. WebWatcher [10] and Letizia [12] use the CB filtering to recommend links and Web pages to users.

The second approach, CF recommends items for which other users, with matching tastes, have liked. In other words, the system determines a set of users similar to the active user, and then recommends the items they have chosen (i.e. items highly rated or already bought). Many CF systems have been implemented in research, with projects such as GroupLens [11] and MovieLens [5]. The first one is a Usenet news recommender; where as the second one is a movie recommender.

Each of these approaches (CB, CF), has its own advantages and disadvantages. Since content-based filtering gets its influence from the information retrieval field, it can be applicable only in text based recommendations. On the other hand, CF is suitable for most recommendable items; however, it suffers from the problem of scalability, sparsity and synonymy [19]. Nevertheless, these two techniques should not be seen as competing with one another, but as complementary to each other. Many developed systems have used both approaches, and thus, took advantage of the benefits of both approaches while eliminating most, if not all, their weaknesses. Fab [1] and METIOREW [3], for example, use this hybrid approach to recommend Websites meeting the users' interests.

In the past years, recommendation systems have witnessed a growing popularity in the commercial field [8], [13], [21] and can be found at many e-commerce sites, such as Amazon[1] [13], CDNow[2] and Netflix[3]. These commercial systems suggest products to consumers based on previous transactions and feedbacks or based on the content of the shopping cart. They are becoming part of a global e-marketing schema that can enhance e-commerce sales by converting browsers to buyers, increasing cross-selling, and building customer loyalty [22].

More recently, recommendation systems have entered the e-learning domain. In [24], the system guides the learners by recommending online activities, based on their profiles, their access history, and their collected navigation patterns. A pedagogy-

---

[1] http://www.amazon.com

[2] http://www.cdnow.com

[3] http://www.netflex.com

oriented paper recommender [23] was developed to recommend papers based on the learners' profile and their expertise.

Book recommenders could be helpful for students. While many book recommendation systems have been implemented [8], [9], [13], to our knowledge none of them are well adapted for e-learning since they exploit the user profile in its general basic form, and not in its academic form. In other words, these systems are not using student models.

In this paper we propose a book recommendation system, adapted to an e-learning environment, taking into consideration the learning style of each student, so it can predict the most pedagogically and academically suitable book for him. To maximize the utility of the system, it should recommend books from the local university library due to its easy access and the lack of any additional cost to the student.

3 The Architecture of DIA

DIA is designed as a specific process for Web-based systems. It aims at recommending the right books for students according to their user modeling. Figure 1 represents the proposed form of the DIA architecture.

The architecture consists of three tiers: user interface, application server, and database. The user interface tier is where the learner establishes contact and interacts with the agent services, such as the login and the prediction of the users' learning style. The application server tier provides the process management services of DIA (such as processing the XML database, processing the dominant meaning XML files, computing recommendations). The third tier provides XML-database management functionality dedicated to XML files, which contain users' profiles, dominant meanings [17] or keywords of books and book data files.

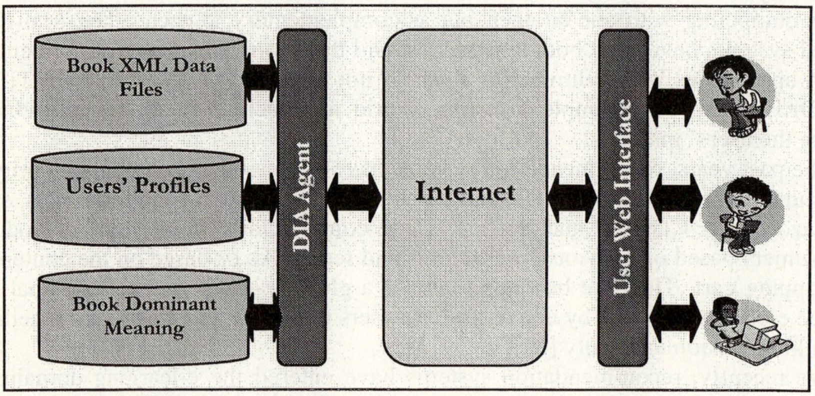

Fig. 1. The architecture of DIA

4 The Methodology

We have applied on Université de Montréal library books the first two levels of the Pyramid Collaborative Filtering Approach (PCFA): domain model filtering and user model filtering.

4.1 Domain Model Filtering

We use the dominant meaning distance between a query and the concept of the book to measure the closeness between them [17]. That is to say, the less distance between them, the more related they are. Suppose that C_h is a concept of a book and $\{w_1,\ldots,w_m\}$ is the set of this concept's dominant meanings. Suppose also that $\{q_1,\ldots,q_s\}$ is the dominant meaning set of a query Q. So, the aim is to evaluate books that have the highest degree of similarity to the query Q. We can calculate the dominant meaning similarity $S(Q, C_h)$ as follows,

$$S(Q, C_h) = \frac{1}{s}\sum_{i=1}^{s}\frac{1}{m}\left[\sum_{j=1}^{m}\Theta(w_i, q_j)\right] \tag{1}$$

$$\text{where} \quad \Theta(w_i, q_j) = \begin{cases} 1 & w_i = q_j \\ 0 & w_i \neq q_j \end{cases}$$

4.2 User Modeling Filtering

Since users' profiles contain many attributes, several of them might have sparse or incomplete data [7]; the task of finding appropriate similarities is usually difficult. To avoid this situation, we classify users according to their learning styles. Following [16], we distinguish several learning styles (*LS*): visual (*V*), auditory (*A*), kinesthetic (*K*), visual & kinesthetic (*VK*), visual & auditory (*VA*), auditory & kinesthetic (*AK*) and visual & auditory & kinesthetic (*VAK*). Therefore, we can calculate the learning style similarity *LSS* between users' as follows,

$$LSS(LS_u, LS_v) = \begin{cases} 1 & LS_u = LS_v \\ 2/3 & LS_u \in \{VK, VA, AK\} \,\&\, LS_v \in \{VAK\} \\ 1/2 & LS_u \in \{V, A\} \,\&\, LS_v \in \{VA\} \\ 1/2 & LS_u \in \{V, K\} \,\&\, LS_v \in \{VK\} \\ 1/2 & LS_u \in \{A, K\} \,\&\, LS_v \in \{AK\} \\ 1/3 & LS_u \in \{V, A, K\} \,\&\, LS_v \in \{VAK\} \\ 0 & else \end{cases} \tag{2}$$

5 System Overview

5.1 System Implementation and Description

This system is mainly implemented with Java (J2SE v1.4.2_04) and XML, on a Windows NT environment. For the Web interface we have used the Java Servlet technology v.2.3 and Tomcat v. 4.1.30. Essentially, the system is divided into 3 stages: the offline or the data collection stage, the profile update stage, and the online stage. In the following section, we will present a brief description of each.

The Offline Stage

The offline stage can be characterized as the data extraction and analysis phase. First, a search in the Université de Montréal library database is performed to obtain a list of books related to a given subject. Since the library uses the Z39.50 standard [4], a client/server-based protocol for searching and retrieving information from remote databases, the JAFER toolkit [4] is used to retrieve the bibliographical information (i.e. ISBN, title, authors, publisher, shelving code, and in some cases the table of contents) of relevant titles and saves them in the "*Book XML Data files*" database.

However, this collected data is not descriptive enough to be used by the domain model filtering. In other words, the system doesn't have a sufficient amount of descriptions about the books so it can filter efficiently the most relevant titles. To remedy the situation, DIA enriches the data it has already gathered from the university library by searching the Internet, predominantly on Amazon's Website, for synopses and book reviews. DIA downloads each pertinent page, and extracts the appropriate data and incorporates it in its database.

Once the information retrieval and extraction are completed, the dominant meaning of each book is computed using the previously seen equation 1. For testing purposes, we decided to cover 4 subjects: *Artificial Intelligence*, with 932 titles, *Java Programming* with 62, *Data Structure* and *Machine learning* with 52 titles found in the local library (Université de Montréal).

Updating the Learner's Profile Stage

The learner's profile contains static and dynamic data. Static data does not change over a longer period of time, like the user's name and login. On the other hand, the user's learning style and the preferred titles are dynamic data; they are in constant change. As we previously explained, DIA bases its predictions on these evolving data. Hence, the system needs to have constantly updated profiles, so it can produce correct recommendations.

After reviewing the suggested books, a learner can select the titles he is interested in. Effectively, DIA updates the learner's profile each time a title is chosen. The system stores the ISBN and the dominant meaning words $W = \{w_1, \ldots, w_n\}$ of the selected book in the learner's profile (see figure 2). Any future recommendation will be based on this updated profile. This step can be repeated a number of times in order to improve the recommendations. From now on, as new selections are provided, the system

---

[4] http://www.loc.gov/z3950/agency/

tracks any changes in the user's preferences and adapts its future recommendations due to the additional data.

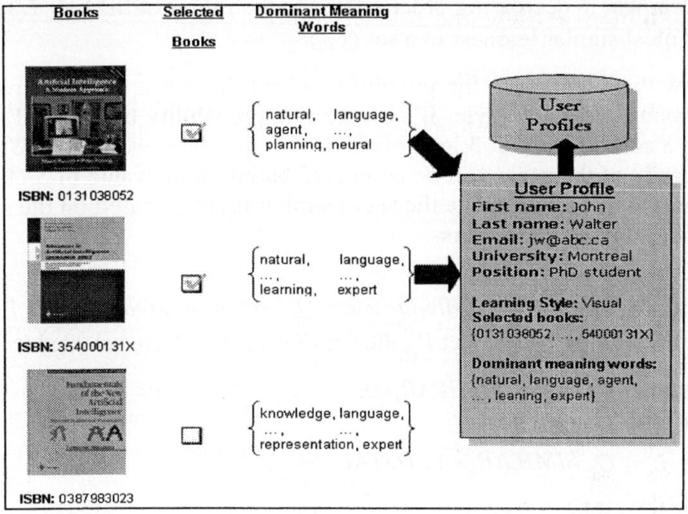

Fig. 2. Profile update example

Online Stage

The online stage represents the interaction between the user and DIA during a Web session. There are 3 key tasks:

User modeling: A first-time user has to register using the registration form. During this process, following [16], the user is asked a series of questions and depending on the answers, DIA classifies the user by his learning style. The system will associate one of the following learning styles to each user: visual, auditory, kinesthetic, visual-auditory, visual-kinesthetic, auditory-kinesthetic, and visual-auditory-kinesthetic style. This learning style is then saved in the learner's profile since it will be used in the computation of the users' similarity.

Search Process: Once the user is registered or logged-in, he has access to the search interface. When the user submits the query Q, the system compares it with the dominant meaning of the previously analyzed subjects during the offline stage. Then, DIA looks for books that match this query. This is achieved by building an ordered set of books $\{B_q\}$, using the value of $S(Q, C_h)$ as seen in equation (1).

Recommendation: Based on the predicted learning style and the users' selected books, DIA computes the most suitable books for the active learner. This task has two main subtasks: the computation of the user similarity and the ranking of the pertinent books. By "*active learner*", we mean the user seeking the recommendation. We compute the user similarity *(SIM)* as the average of the learning style similarity $LSS\ (LS_v, LS_u)$ as seen in equation (2) and the dominant meaning distance between the dominant meaning words W available in the users' profile (see figure 2),

$$SIM\left(L_u, L_v\right) = \frac{LSS\ (LS_u, LS_v) + S(W_u, W_v)}{2} \qquad (3)$$

K most similar Algorithm [Learner L_v]

1. for each learner $L_u \in \{L_u\}_{u=1}^{N}, L_u \neq L_v$ compute *SIM* (L_u, L_v)
2. Sort the learners in decreasing order related to the values of SIM (L_u, L_v)
3. Put the κ most similar learners in a set Q_v

Let's draw the attention to the possibility where the system might have a user L_v, with an unpopular learning style. It's a very rare probability because all learners are classified in a combination of 3 learning styles. In this case, we have *LSS* (L_v, L_u) = *0*. So the similarity of the users will be computed based on the value of *S* (W_v, W_u). That is to say, the system will calculate the set of similar users Q_v based on the similarity of book selections among other users.

Book Ranking Algorithm [set of similar users Q_v, set of ordered books B_q]

1. **for each book** $B_h \in \{B_q\}_{q=1}^{M}$ get P_h, the list of users that have selected it
   a. Instantiate $TOTAL_h$=0, $SIMILAR_h$=0;
   b. **for each user** $L_u \in P_h$
      If user $L_u \in Q_v$ $SIMILAR_h$ ++; $TOTAL_h$ ++
      else $TOTAL_h$ ++;
2. Sort the books in decreasing order related to the values of $SIMILAR_h$. If there are books with equal values, give a higher ranking to the book with the highest value of *TOTAL*.

6 The Online Searching Session Scenario via DIA

Basically, students borrow books from the university library so they could deepen their knowledge in a domain, understand a course, or solve a special problem. By submitting a simple query to the library database, they are faced with a huge number of titles. Obviously, they do not have the time or the resources to choose the right books. Some of them may feel the need to get personalized advice about which book to look for.

Let us take the example of Frederic, a student following the artificial intelligence course at the Université de Montréal. If he looks for books in the library, he will have more then 900 books to choose from. Evaluating all of these books is not an easy task. Since he wants the books most adapted to his learning style, he decides to use DIA to get what he needs.

When Frederic enters the site for the first time, he must register. During this phase, DIA will ask Frederic some questions so it can evaluate his learning style. The system will save the obtained learning style in Frederic's profile, so it can be accessed easily the next time Frederic logs in.

When this process is finished, Frederic is invited to enter his search query. Since he wants books about artificial intelligence, he submits to the system a query composed of the following two keywords: "*artificial*" and "*intelligence*". Consequently, DIA searches the dominant meaning XML files so it can check to which domain this query belongs. If the domain is found, using equation (3), the system looks for Frederic's most similar users (figure 3a) and recommends the books they have liked in the past (figure 3b).

Finally, the list of the recommended books is shown to the user (figure 4).

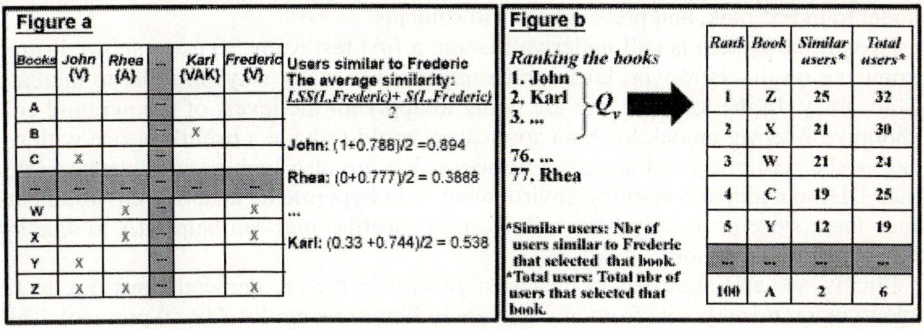

Fig. 3. 3a illustrate the *K* most similar Algorithm. 3b shows the application of the Book Ranking Algorithm

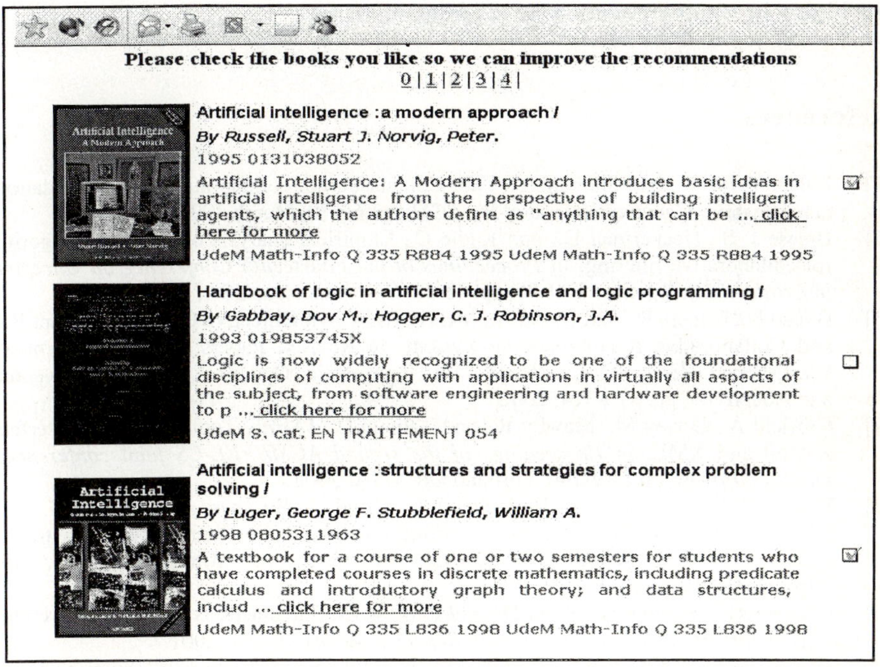

Fig. 4. Titles predicted for a given user

7 Conclusion and Future Work

Frequently, recommender systems use collaborative and content-based filtering for recommending books. Although these approaches are acceptable and relevant, they do not consider student models. In contrast, this paper takes into consideration not only the contents of books but also students' learning styles (visual, auditory, kinesthetic).

We have developed a book recommending agent called Discovering Intelligent Agent: DIA. DIA employs the first two levels of the pyramid collaborative filtering model to index, rank, and present books to students.

Even if the system is still under validation, a first test using 30 users showed some promising results. However, DIA can be improved in many ways in order to increase its accuracy. In the long run, we are going to apply all the levels of the pyramid collaborative filtering model. Such an application could provide a useful service with regard to the credibility and accuracy of books. We are also looking into ways to integrate DIA in a global e-learning environment or in hypermedia adaptive environments since these systems usually have rich learners' profiles that can help DIA to ameliorate its recommendations.

Finally, we are interested in means to generalize the recommendations, i.e. to be able to recommend books from any university library using the Z39.50 protocol. This protocol, which is used by many university libraries like McGill or Concordia University (Canada), enables the client to query the database server without any knowledge of its structure. By implementing this protocol, DIA is able to access and search all the libraries employing this standard, and thus allows the learner to select the university library he wants recommendations from.

References

[1] Balabanovic M., and Shoham Y., Fab: Content-based, collaborative recommendation as classification. *Communications of the ACM*, pp. 66-70, March 1997.

[2] Breese J. S., Heckerman D., and Kadie C., Empirical analysis of predictive algorithms for collaborative filtering. In *Proceedings of the Fourteenth Conference on Uncertainty in Artificial Intelligence, UAI-98*, pp. 43-52, San Francisco, USA, July 1998.

[3] Bueno D., Conejo R., and David A., METIOREW: An Objective Oriented Content Based and Collaborative Recommending System. In Revised Papers from the international Workshops OHS-7, SC-3, and AH-3 on Hypermedia: Openness, Structural Awareness, and Adaptivity, pp. 310-314, 2002.

[4] Corfield A., Dovey M., Mawby R., and Tatham C., JAFER ToolKit project: interfacing Z39.50 and XML. In *Proceedings of the second ACM/IEEE-CS joint conference on Digital libraries*, pp. 289-290, Portland OR, USA, 2002.

[5] Dahlen B. J., Konstan J. A., Herlocker J. L., Good N., Borchers A., and Riedl J., Jump-starting movielens: User benefits of starting a collaborative filtering system with "dead data". *Technical Report TR 98-017*, University of Minnesota, USA, 1998. http://movielens.umn.edu

[6] Goldberg K., Roeder T., Gupta D., and Perkins C., Eigentaste: A constant time collaborative filtering algorithm. *Information Retrieval*, 4(2):133–151, 2001.

[7] Herlocker J. L., Konstan J. A., and Riedl J., Explaining Collaborative Filtering Recommendations. In *Proceedings of the ACM 2000 Conference on Computer Supported Cooperative Work, CSCW'00,* pp. 241-250, Philadelphia PA, USA, 2000.

[8] Hirooka Y., Terano T., Otsuka Y., Recommending books of revealed and latent interests in e-commerce. In *Industrial Electronics Society, the 26th Annual Conference of the IEEE, IECON 2000,* pp. 1632-1637 vol: 3, Nagoya, Japan, October 2000.

[9] Huang Z., Chung W., Ong T., and Chen H., Studying users: A graph-based recommender system for digital library. In *Proceedings of the second ACM/IEEE-CS joint conference on Digital libraries*, pp. 65-73, Portland OR, USA, 2002.
[10] Joachims T., Freitag D., and Mitchell T., WebWatcher: A Tour Guide for the World Wide Web. In *Proceedings of the Fifteenth International Joint Conference on Artificial Intelligence, IJCAI97*, pp. 770-777, Nagoya, Japan, 1997
[11] Konstan J. A., Miller B. N., Maltz D., Herlocker J. L., GordonL. R., and Riedl J., GroupLens: Applying collaborative filtering to Usenet news. *Communications of the ACM* 40 (3), pp. 77-87, 1997.
[12] Lieberman H., Letizia: An Agent That Assists Web Browsing. *International Joint Conference on Artificial Intelligence, IJCAI-95*, pp. 924-929, Montreal, Canada, August 1995.
[13] Linden G., Smith B., and York J., Amazon.com recommendations: item-to-item collaborative filtering. *Internet Computing, IEEE*, 7(1):76-80, 2003
[14] Lynch C. Personalization and Recommender Systems in the Larger Context: New Directions and Research Questions. *Second DELOS Network of Excellence Workshop on Personalization and Recommender Systems in Digital Libraries*, Dublin, Ireland, June 2001.
[15] Mooney R. J., and Roy L., Content-based book recommending using learning for text categorization. In *Proceedings of the Fifth ACM Conference on Digital Libraries, DL'00*, pp. 195–204, San Antonio TX, USA, June 2000. http://www.cs.utexas.edu/users/libra/
[16] Razek M. A., Frasson C., and Kaltenbach M., Using Machine Learning approach To Support Intelligent Collaborative Multi-Agent System. *Technologies de l'Information et de la Communication dans les Enseignements d'ingénieurs et dans l'industrie, TICE2002*, Lyon, France, November 2002.
[17] Razek M. A., Frasson C., and Kaltenbach M., A Context-Based Information Agent for Supporting Intelligent Distance Learning Environments. In *the Twelfth International World Wide Web Conference*, Budapest, Hungary, May 2003.
[18] Razek A. M., Frasson C., and Kaltenbach M., Building an Effective Groupware System. *IEEE/ITCC 2004 International Conference on Information Technology*, Las Vegas NV, USA, April 2004.
[19] Sarwar B. M., Karypis G., Konstan J. A., and Reidl J., Analysis of recommendation algorithms for e-commerce. In *Proceedings of the ACM Conference on Electronic Commerce*, pp. 158-167, New York NY, USA, 2000.
[20] Sarwar B. M., Karypis G., Konstan J. A., and Reidl J., Item-based collaborative filtering recommendation algorithms. In *Proceedings of the 10th International World Wide Web Conference, WWW10*, pp. 285-295, Hong Kong, May 2001.
[21] Schafer J. B., Konstan J. A., and Riedl J., Recommender systems in e-commerce. In *Proceedings of the ACM Conference on Electronic Commerce, EC'99*, pp. 158-166, Denver CO, USA, November 1999.
[22] Schafer J., Konstan J., and Riedl J., E-commerce recommendation applications. *Data Mining and Knowledge Discovery,* pp. 115-153 vol:5, 2001.
[23] Tang T.Y., and McCalla G., Towards Pedagogy-Oriented Paper Recommendation and Adaptive Annotations for a Web-Based Learning System. In the *18th International Joint Conference on Artificial Intelligence, Workshop on Knowledge Representation and Automated Reasoning for E-Learning Systems, IJCAI-03,* pp. 72-80, Acapulco, Mexico, August 2003
[24] Zaïane O. R., Building a Recommender Agent for e-Learning Systems. In *Proceedings of the 7th International Conference on Computers in Education, ICCE 2002*, pp. 55-59, Auckland, New Zealand, December 2002.

Developing Learning by Teaching Environments That Support Self-Regulated Learning

Gautam Biswas[1], Krittaya Leelawong[1], Kadira Belynne[1], Karun Viswanath[1], Daniel Schwartz[2], and Joan Davis[2]

[1] Dept. of EECS & ISIS, Box 1824 Sta B, Vanderbilt University
Nashville, TN 37235. USA.
{gautam.biswas, krittaya.leelawong, kadira.belynne, karun.viswanath}@vanderbilt.edu
http://www.vuse.vanderbilt.edu/~biswas

[2] School of Education, Stanford University
Stanford, CA 94305. USA.
{daniel.schwartz, joan.davis}@stanford.edu

Abstract. Betty's Brain is a teachable agent system in the domain of river ecosystems that combines learning by teaching and self-regulation strategies to promote deep learning and understanding. Scaffolds in the form of hypertext resources, a Mentor agent, and a set of quiz questions help novice students learn and self-assess their own knowledge. The computational architecture is implemented as a multi-agent system to allow flexible and incremental design, and to provide a more realistic social context for interactions between students and the teachable agent. An extensive study that compared three versions of this system: a tutor only version, learning by teaching, and learning by teaching with self-regulation strategies demonstrates the effectiveness of learning by teaching environments, and the impact of self-regulation strategies in improving preparation for learning among novice learners.

1 Introduction

Advances in computer technology have facilitated the development of sophisticated computer-based Intelligent Tutoring Systems (ITS) [1]. The ITS paradigm is problem-based, and has been very successful in developing three core technologies: curriculum sequencing, intelligent analysis of student's solutions, and interactive problem solving support [2]. At the same time, these systems provide localized feedback, and do not emphasize practicing higher-order cognitive skills in complex domains, where problem solving requires active decision-making to set learning goals and to apply strategies for achieving these goals. Our goal has been to introduce effective learning paradigms that advance the state of the art in computer-based learning systems and support students' abilities to learn, even after they leave the computer environment. To achieve this, we have adopted a *learning by teaching* paradigm where students teach computer agents. This paper discusses the design and implementation

J.C. Lester et al. (Eds.): ITS 2004, LNCS 3220, pp. 730–740, 2004.

of a teachable agent system, Betty's Brain, and reports the results of an experiment that manipulated the metacognitive support students received when teaching the agent to determine its effects on the students' abilities to subsequently learn new content several weeks later.

Studies of expertise have shown that knowledge needs to be connected and organized around important concepts, and these structures should support transfer to other contexts. Other studies have established that improved learning happens when the students take control of their own learning, develop metacognitive strategies to assess what they know, and acquire more knowledge when needed. Thus the learning process must help students build new knowledge from existing knowledge (constructivist learning), guide students to discover learning opportunities while problem solving (exploratory learning), and help them to define learning goals and monitor their progress in achieving them (metacognitive strategies).

The cognitive science and education research literature supports the idea that teaching others is a powerful way to learn. Research in reciprocal teaching, peer-assisted tutoring, small-group interaction, and self-explanation hint at the potential of learning by teaching [3,4]. The literature on tutoring has shown that tutors benefit as much from tutoring as their tutees [5]. Biswas et al. [6] report that students preparing to teach made statements about how the responsibility to teach forced them to gain deeper understanding of the materials. Other students focused on the importance of having a clear conceptual organization of the materials.

Teaching is a problem solving activity [7]. Learning-by-teaching is an open-ended and self-directed activity, which shares a number of characteristics with exploratory and constructivist learning. A natural goal for effective teaching is to gain a good understanding of domain knowledge before teaching it to others. Teaching also includes a process for structuring knowledge in communicable form, and reflecting on interactions with students during and after the teaching task [5]. Good learners bring structure to a domain by asking the right questions to develop a systematic flow for their reasoning. Good teachers build on the learners' knowledge to organize information, and in the process, they find new knowledge organizations, and better ways for interpreting and using these organizations in problem solving tasks. From a system design and implementation viewpoint, this brings up an interesting question: "How do we design learning environments based on the learning by teaching paradigm?" This has led us to look more closely at the work on pedagogical and intelligent agents as a mechanism for modeling and analyzing student-teacher interaction.

2 Learning by Teaching: Previous Work

Intelligent agents have been introduced into learning environments to create better and more human-like support for exploratory learning and social interactions between tutor and tutee [8,9]. Pedagogical agents are defined as "animated characters designed to operate in an educational setting for supporting and facilitating learning" [8]. The agent adapts to the dynamic state of the learning environment, and it makes the user aware of learning opportunities as they arise, much as human mentor can. Agents use speech, animation, and gestures to extend the traditional textual mode of interaction, and this may increase students' motivation and engagement. They can gracefully combine individualized and collaborative learning, by allowing multiple students and their agents to interact in a shared environment [10]. However, the locus of control stays with the intelligent agent, which plays the role of the teacher or tutor.

Recently, there have been efforts to implement the learning by teaching paradigm using agents that learn from examples, advice, and explanations provided by the student-teacher [11]. A primary limitation of these systems is that the knowledge structures and reasoning mechanisms used by the agent are not made visible to the student, therefore, they find it difficult to uncover, analyze, and learn from their interactions with the agent. Moreover, some of the systems provide outcome feedback or no feedback at all. It is well known that outcome feedback is less effective in supporting learning and problem solving than *cognitive feedback* [12].

On the positive side, students like interacting with these agents. Some studies showed increased motivation but it was not clear that this approach helped achieve deep understanding of complex domain material. We have adopted a new approach to designing learning by teaching environments that supports constructivist and exploratory activities, and at the same time suggests the use of metacognitive strategies to promote learning that involves deep understanding and transfer.

3 A New Approach: Betty's Brain

Betty's Brain provides important visual structures that are tailored to a specific form of knowledge organization and inference to help shape the thinking of the *learner-as-teacher*. In general, our agents try to embody four principles of design: (i) they teach through visual representations that organize the reasoning structures of the domain; (ii) they build on well-known teaching interactions to organize student activity; (iii) they ensure the agents have independent performances that provide feedback on how well they have been taught, and (iv) they keep the start-up costs of teaching the agent very low (as compared to programming). This occurs by only implementing one modeling structure with its associated reasoning mechanisms.

Betty's Brain makes her qualitative reasoning visible through a dynamic, directed graph called a *concept map* [13]. The fact that the TA environments represent knowledge structures rather than the referent domain is a departure from many simulation-based learning environments. Simulations often show the behavior of a process, for example, how an algal bloom increases the death of fish. On the other hand, TAs simulate the behavior of a person's thoughts about a system. Learning empirical facts is important, but learning to use the expert structure that organizes those facts is equally important. Therefore, we have structured the agents to simulate particular forms of thought that help teacher-students structure their thinking about a domain.

Betty's Brain is designed to teach middle school students about the concepts of interdependence and balance in river ecosystems [6,14]. Fig. 1 illustrates the interface of Betty's Brain. Students explicitly teach Betty, using the *Teach Concept*, *Teach Link* and *Edit* buttons to create and modify their concept maps in the top pane of the window. Once taught, Betty can reason with her knowledge and answer questions. Users can formulate queries using the *Ask* button, and observe the effects of their teaching by analyzing Betty's answers. Betty provides explanations for her answers by depicting the derivation process using multiple modalities: text, animation, and speech. Betty uses qualitative reasoning to derive her answers to questions through a chain of causal inferences. Details of the reasoning and explanation mechanisms in Betty's Brain are presented elsewhere [15].

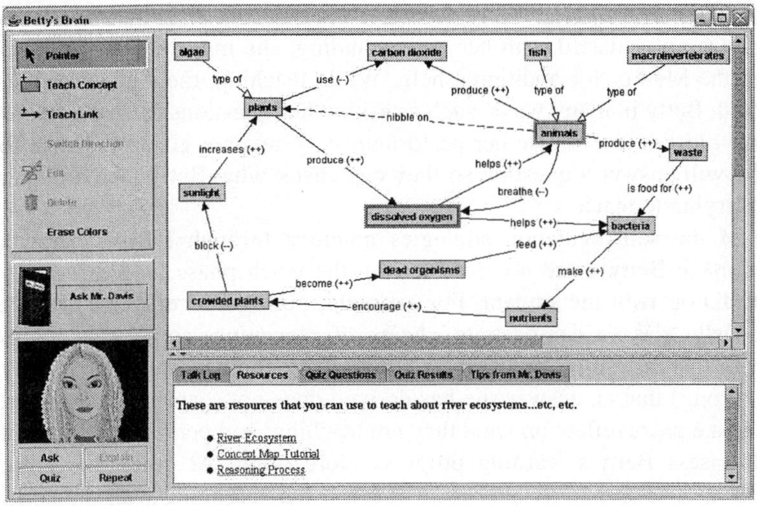

Fig. 1. Betty's Brain

The visual display of the face with animation in the lower left is one way in which the user interface attempts to provide engagement and motivation to users by increasing social interactions with the system. We should clarify that Betty does not use machine learning algorithms to achieve automated learning. Our focus is on the well-defined schemas associated with teaching that support a process of instruction, assessment, and remediation. These schemas help organize student interaction with the computer.

To accommodate students who are novices in the domain knowledge and in teaching, the learning environment provides a number of scaffolds and feedback mechanisms. The scaffolds are in the form of well-organized online resources, structured quiz questions that support users in systematically building their knowledge, and Mentor feedback that is designed to provide hints on domain concepts along with strategies on how to learn and how to teach. We adopted the framework of *self-regulated learning,* described by Zimmerman [16] as situations where students are "*metacognitively, motivationally, and behaviorally participants in their own learning process.*" Self-regulated learning strategies involve actions and processes that can help one to acquire knowledge and develop problem-solving skills [17]. Zimmerman describes a number of self-regulated learning skills that include goal setting and planning, seeking information, organizing and transforming, self-consequating, keeping records and monitoring, and self-evaluation. We redesigned the characteristics of both Betty and the Mentor agent to help users develop these skills as they teach and learn.

This has produced a number of unique characteristics in the learning environment. For example, when a student begins the teach phase by constructing the initial concept map, both the Mentor and Betty make suggestions that the student *set goals* on what to teach, and make efforts to gain the relevant knowledge by studying the river ecosystem resources. The Mentor continues to emphasize the reading and understanding of resources, whenever students have questions on *how to improve their learning*. The user is given the opportunity to *evaluate her knowledge* while studying. If she is not satisfied with her understanding, she may *seek further information* by asking the Mentor for additional help. While teaching, the student as teacher can interact with Betty in many ways, such as asking her questions (*querying*), and getting her to take *quizzes* to evaluate her performance. Users are given a chance to predict how Betty will answer a question so they can check what Betty learned against what they were trying to teach.

Some of the self-regulation strategies manifest through Betty's persona. These strategies make Betty more involved during the teach phase, and drive her interactions and dialog with the student. For example, during concept map creation, Betty spontaneously tries to demonstrate *chains of reasoning*, and the conclusions she draws from this reasoning process. She may query the user, and sometimes remark (right or wrong) that an answer she has derived does not seem to make sense. This is likely to make users reflect on what they are teaching, and perhaps, like good teachers they will assess Betty's learning progress more often. At other times, Betty will prompt the user to *formulate queries* to check if her reasoning with the concept map produces correct results. There are situations when Betty emphatically refuses to take a quiz because she feels that she has *not been taught enough*, or that the student has not given her *sufficient practice by asking queries* before making her take a quiz.

After Betty takes a quiz offered by the Mentor agent, she discusses the results with the user. Betty reports: (i) her view of her performance on the particular quiz, and if her performance has improved or deteriorated from the last time she took the quiz, and (ii) the Mentor's comments on Betty's performance in the quiz, such as: "*Hi, I'm back. I'm feeling bad because I could not answer some questions in the quiz. Mr. Davis said that you could ask him more about river eco-systems.*" The Mentor agent's initial comments are general, but they become more specific (*"You may want to study the role of bacteria in the river"*) if errors persist, or if the student seeks further help. Specific mentor feedback explains *chains of events* to help students better understand Betty's reasoning processes. The online resources are structured to make explicit the concepts of interdependence and balance. A hypertext implementation and an advanced keyword search technique provide easy access to information.

Overall, we believe that the introduction of self-regulation strategies provides the right scaffolds to help students learn about a complex domain, while also developing metacognitive strategies that promote deep understanding, transfer, and life-long learning. All this is achieved in an exploratory environment, with the student primarily retaining the locus of control. Only when the student seems to be hopelessly stuck, does the Mentor intervene with specific help.

4 A Computational Architecture for Betty's Brain

With time, as we refined the system, it became clear that an incremental, modularized design strategy was required to keep to a minimum the changes to be made to the code as and when we felt the need to further refine the system. We turned to multi-agent architectures to achieve this goal. The current multi-agent architecture in Betty's Brain is organized into four agents: the teachable agent, Betty, the mentor agent, Mr. Davis, and two auxiliary agents, the student agent and the environment agent. The last two agents help achieve greater flexibility by making it easier to update the scenarios in which the agents operate without having to recode the communication protocols. The student agent represents the interface of the student teacher into the system. It provides facilities that allow the user to manipulate environmental functions and to teach the teachable agent.

All agents interact through the Environment Agent, which acts as a "Facilitator." This agent maintains information about the other agents and the services they provide. When an agent sends a request to the Environment Agent, it decomposes the request if different parts are to be handled by different agents and sends them to the respective agents, and translates the communicated information to match an agent's vocabulary.

A variation of the FIPA ACL agent communication language [18] is used for agent communication. Each message sent by an agent contains a description of the message, message sender, recipient, recipient class, and the actual content of the message. Communication is implemented using a Listener interface, where each agent listens only for messages from the Environment Agent and the Environment Agent listens for messages from all other agents.

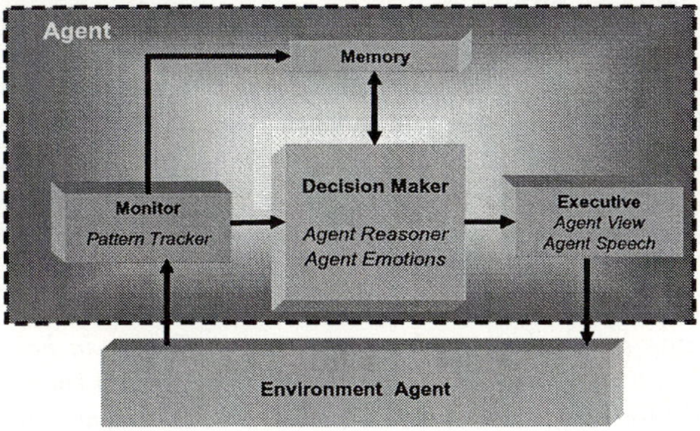

Fig. 2. Agent Components

The system is implemented using a generic agent architecture shown in Fig. 2. Each agent has a Monitor, Decision Maker, Memory, and an Executive. The Monitor listens for events from the environment, and using a pattern tracker, converts them to the appropriate format needed by the agent. The decision maker, the agent's brain, contains two components: the *reasoner* and the *emotion generator*. It performs reasoning tasks (e.g., answering questions) and updates on the state of the agent. The Executive posts multimedia (speech, text, graphics, animation) information from an agent to the environment. This includes the agent's answer to a question, explanation of an answer and other dialog with the user. The Executive is made up of Agent Speech and Agent View, which handle speech and visual communication, respectively.

5 Experiments

An experiment was designed for fifth graders in a Nashville school to compare three different versions of the system. The version 1 baseline system (ITS) did not involve any teaching. Students interacted with the mentor, Mr. Davis, who asked them to construct concept maps to answer three sets of quiz questions. The quiz questions were ordered to meet curricular guidelines. When students submitted their maps for a quiz, Mr. Davis, the pedagogical agent, provided feedback based on errors in the quiz answers, and suggested how the students may correct their concept maps to improve their performance. The students taught Betty in the version 2 and 3 systems. In the version 2 (LBT) system, students could ask Betty to take a quiz after they taught her, and the mentor provided the same feedback as in the ITS system. Here the feedback was given to Betty because she took the quiz. The version 3 (SRL) system had the new, more responsive Betty with self-regulation behavior (section 3), and a more extensive mentor agent, who provided help on how to teach and how to learn in addition to domain knowledge. But this group had to explicitly query Mr. Davis to receive any feedback. Therefore, the SRL condition was set up to develop more active learners by promoting the use of self-regulation strategies. The ITS condition was created to contrast learning by teaching environments from tutoring environments. The two other groups, LBT and SRL, were told to teach Betty and help her pass a test so she could become a member of the school Science club. Both groups had access to the query and quiz features. All three groups had access to identical resources on river ecosystems, the same quiz questions, and the same access to the Mentor agent, Mr. Davis.

The two primary research questions we set out to answer were:

1. Are learning by teaching environments more effective in helping students to learn independently and gain deeper understanding of domain knowledge than pedagogical agents? More specifically, would LBT and SRL students gain a better understanding of interdependence and balance among the entities in river ecosystems than ITS students? Further, would SRL students demonstrate deeper understanding and better ability in transfer, both of which are hallmarks of effective learning?

2. Does self-regulated learning enhance learning in learning by teaching environments? Self-regulated learning should be an effective framework for providing feedback because it promotes the development of higher-order cognitive skills [17] and it is critical to the development of problem solving ability [13]. In addition, cognitive feedback is more effective than outcome feedback for decision-making tasks [10].

Cognitive feedback helps users monitor their learning needs (achievement relative to goals) and guides them in achieving their learning objectives (cognitive engagement by applying tactics and strategies).

Experimental Procedure

The fifth grade classroom in a Nashville Metro school was divided into three equal groups of 15 students each using a stratified sampling method based on standard achievement scores in mathematics and language. The students worked on a pretest with twelve questions before they were separately introduced to their particular versions of the system. The three groups worked for six 45-minute sessions over a period of three weeks to create their concept maps. All groups had access to the online resources while they worked on the system.

At the end of the six sessions, every student took a post-test that was identical to the pretest. Two other delayed posttests were conducted about seven weeks after the initial experiment: (i) a *memory test*, where students were asked to recreate their ecosystem concept maps from memory (there was no help or intervention when performing this task), and (ii) a *preparation for future learning transfer test*, where they were asked to construct a concept map and answer questions about the land-based nitrogen cycle. Students had not been taught about the nitrogen cycle, so they would have to learn from resources during the transfer phase.

In this study, we focus on the results of the two delayed tests, and the conclusions we can draw from these tests on the students' learning processes. As a quick review of the initial learning, students in all conditions improved from pre- to posttest on their knowledge of interdependence (p's<.01, paired T-tests), but not in their understanding of ecosystem balance. There were few differences between conditions in terms of the quality of their maps (the LBT and SRL groups had a better grasp of the role of bacteria in processing waste at posttest). However, there were notable differences in their use of the system during the initial learning phase.

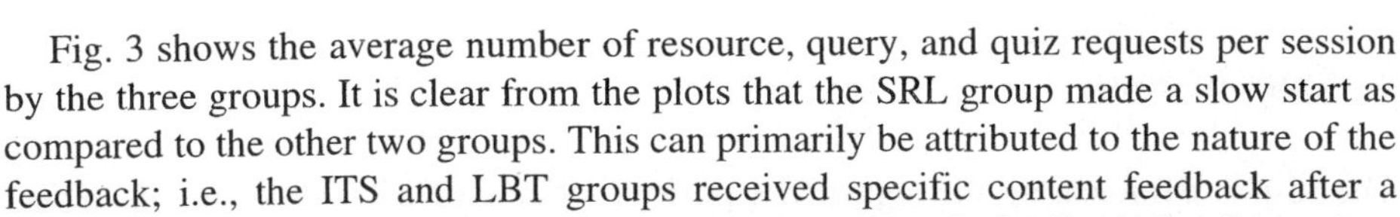

Fig. 3. Resource Requests, Queries Composed, and Quizzes Requested per session

Fig. 3 shows the average number of resource, query, and quiz requests per session by the three groups. It is clear from the plots that the SRL group made a slow start as compared to the other two groups. This can primarily be attributed to the nature of the feedback; i.e., the ITS and LBT groups received specific content feedback after a quiz, whereas the SRL group tended to receive more generic feedback that focused on self-regulation strategies. Moreover, in the SRL condition, Betty would refuse to take a quiz unless she felt the user had taught her enough, and prepared her for the quiz by asking questions. After a couple of sessions the SRL group showed a surge in map creation and map analysis activities, and their final concept maps and quiz performance were comparable to the other groups. It seems the SRL group spent their first few sessions in learning self-regulation strategies, but once they learned them their performance improved significantly. Table 1 presents the mean number of expert concepts and expert causal links in the student maps for the delayed memory test. Results of an ANOVA test on the data, with Tukey's LSD to make pairwise comparisons showed that the SRL group recalled significantly more links that were also in the expert map (which nobody actually saw).

Table 1. Results of the Memory Test

Student Map Included:	SRL Mean (se)	LBT Mean (se)	ITS Mean (se)
Expert Concepts	6.7 (.6)	6.4 (.5)	5.8 (.6)
Expert Causal Links	3.3[a] (.6)	1.7 (.6)	2.0 (.6)

[a] Significantly greater than LBT, $p < .05$;

We thought that the effect of SRL would not be to improve memory, but rather to provide students with more skills for learning subsequently. When one looks at the results of the transfer task in the test on preparation for future learning, the differences between the SRL group and the other two groups are significant. Table 2 summarizes the results of the transfer test, where students read resources and created a concept map for the land-based nitrogen cycle with very little help from the Mentor agent (and which they had not studied previously). The Mentor agent's only feedback was on the correctness of the answers to the quiz questions. All three groups received the same treatment. There are significant differences in the number of expert concepts in the SRL versus ITS group maps, and the SRL group had significantly more expert causal links than the LBT and ITS groups. The effects of teaching self-regulation strategies had an impact on the students' abilities to learn a new domain.

Table 2. Results of the Transfer Study

Student Map Included:	SRL Mean (sd)	LBT Mean (sd)	ITS Mean (sd)
Expert Concepts	6.1[a] (.6)	5.2 (.5)	4.1 (.6)
Expert Causal Links	1.1[ab] (.3)	0.1 (.3)	0.2 (.3)

[a] Significantly greater than ITS, $p < .05$; [b] Significantly greater than LBT, $p < .05$

6 Conclusions

The results demonstrate the significant positive effects of SRL strategies in understanding and transfer in a learning by teaching environment. We believe that the differences between the SRL and the other two groups would have been even more pronounced if the transfer test study had been conducted over a longer period of time. Last, we believe that the concept map and reasoning schemes have to be extended to include temporal reasoning and cycles of behavior to facilitate students' learning about the concept of balance in ecosystems.

Acknowledgements. This work has been supported by a NSF ROLE Award #0231771. The assistance provided by the Teachable Agents group, especially John Bransford and Nancy Vye are gratefully acknowledged.

References

[1] Wenger, E. (1987). Artificial Intelligence and Tutoring Systems. Los Altos, California: Morgan Kaufmann Publishers.
[2] Brusilovsky, P. (1999). Adaptive and Intelligent Technologies for Web-based Education, Special Issue on Intelligent Systems and Teleteaching, C. Rollinger and C. Peylo (eds.), 4: 19-25.
[3] Palinscar, A. S. & Brown, A. L. (1984). Reciprocal teaching of comprehension-fostering and comprehension -monitoring activities. Cognition and instruction, 1: 117-175.
[4] Chi, M. T. H., De Leeuw, N., Mei-Hung, C., & Levancher, C. (1994). Eliciting self explanations. Cognitive Science, 18: 439-477.
[5] Chi, M. T. H., et al. (2001). "Learning from Human Tutoring." Cognitive Science 25(4): 471-533.
[6] Biswas, G., Schwartz, D., Bransford, J., & The Teachable Agents Group at Vanderbilt University. (2001). Technology Support for Complex Problem Solving: From SAD Environments to AI. In Forbus & Feltovich (eds.), Smart Machines in Education, 71-98. Menlo Park, CA: AAAI Press.
[7] Artzt, A. F. and E. Armour-Thomas (1999). "Cognitive Model for Examining Teachers' Instructional Practice in Mathematics: A Guide for Facilitating Teacher Reflection." Educational Studies in Mathematics 40(3): 211-335.
[8] G. Clarebout, J. Elen, W. L. Johnson, and E. Shaw. (2002). "Animated Pedagogical Agents: An Opportunity to be Grasped?" Journal of Educational Multimedia and Hypermedia, 11: 267-286.
[9] Johnson W., Rickel, J.W., and Lester J.C. (2001). "Animated Pedagogical Agents: Face-to-Face Interaction in Interactive Learning Environments", International Journal of Artificial Intelligence in Education11: 47-78
[10] Moreno, R. & Mayer, R. E. (2002). Learning science in virtual reality multimedia environments: Role of methods and media. Journal of Educational Psychology, 94: 598-610.
[11] Nichols, D. M. (1994). Intelligent Student Systems: an application of viewpoints to intelligent learning environments, Ph.D. thesis, Lancaster University, Lancaster, UK.
[12] Butler, D. L. and P. H. Winne (1995). "Feedback and Self-Regulated Learning: A Theoretical Synthesis." Review of Educational Research 65(3): 245-281.
[13] Novak, J.D. (1996). Concept Mapping as a tool for improving science teaching and learning, in Improving Teaching and Learning in Science and Mathematics, D.F. Treagust, R. Duit, and B.J. Fraser, eds. Teachers College Press: London. 32-43.
[14] K. Leelawong, K., et al. (2003), "Teachable Agents: Learning by Teaching Environments for Science Domains," Proc. 15th Innovative Applications of Artificial Intelligence Conf., Acapulco, Mexico, 109-116.
[15] Leelawong, K., Y. Wang, et al. (2001). Qualitative reasoning techniques to support learning by teaching: The Teachable Agents project. 15th International Workshop on Qualitative Reasoning, San Antonio, Texas, AAAI Press, 73-80.

[16] Zimmerman, B. J. (1989). "A Social Cognitive View of Self-Regulated Academic Learning." Journal of Educational Psychology 81(3): 329-339.
[17] Pintrich, P. R. and E. V. DeGroot (1990). "Motivational and self-regulated learning components of classroom academic performance." Journal of Educational Psychology 82: 33-40.
[18] Labrou. Y, T. Finin and Peng, Y. (1999) "Agent Communication Languages: The Current Landscape", IEEE Intelligent Systems, 14(2): 45-52.

Adaptive Interface Methodology for Intelligent Tutoring Systems

Glória Curilem S. [1], Fernando M. de Azevedo[2], and Andréa R. Barbosa[2]

[1] Electrical Engineering Department, La Frontera University,
Casilla 54-D. Temuco, Chile. Phone: 56 +45 325518;
millaray@ufro.cl.

[2] Biomedical Engineering Institute. Electrical Engineering Department. Universidade Federal de Santa Catarina. Campus Trindade. CEP: 88040-900, Florianópolis/ SC, Brasil. Phone: 55 +48 3329594
{azevedo; riccio}@ieb.ufsc.br.

Abstract. In a Teaching–Learning Process (TLP) teachers have to support student's learning using diverse pedagogical resources. One of teachers' task is to create personalized Learning Environments. Intelligent Tutoring Systems (ITS) try to imitate adaptation capacity of a human teacher. The Interface is the Learning Environment and the system stores knowledge that defines how to adapt it to respond to certain student's characteristics. Adaptation is particularly important for TLP oriented to carriers of chronic diseases like Diabetes, which represent very heterogeneous groups of persons. This article presents a Methodology to model a TLP and to build an automatic adaptation (adaptive) mechanism for ITS Interfaces, based in a Neural Network [1]. The diabetes education was used as a case study to apply and validate the proposed methodology. The most important results of this work are presented here.

1 Introduction: Personalization in Pedagogical Software

This work is inserted in a global context characterized by the diversifications of educational needs. Not all the apprentices have the same interests, previous knowledge, or assimilate the information the same way. A pedagogical method can be effective for one student and not for another. Different studies in the area brought a consensus that underline personalization as a strategic goal for education. Educational technology can have a valuable impact supporting this goal. Personalization is particularly relevant for adults' education or for TLP applied to very heterogeneous groups of persons.

Nowadays, Interfaces are considered to have a fundamental role in software [2], but their insertion in pedagogical systems is recent [3] and was due to the increase of interface technologies and to new conceptions of learning processes. Intelligent Learning Environments represent an actual tendency of ITS [4].

In another context, the world is living an increment of degenerative chronic diseases. Preserving health requires an appropriate planning of the daily activities based on reliable and constantly updated knowledge [5]. Diabetes Mellitus Insulin Dependent (DMID) affects people of all ages. Several studies demonstrated that the incidence

J.C. Lester et al. (Eds.): ITS 2004, LNCS 3220, pp. 741–750, 2004.

of diabetes complications decreases if a rigorous treatment is adopted. Educational focus propitiates a more effective participation on the treatment [6].

Due to the heterogeneity of the target group, an adaptive TLP is considered essential to give information in situated and real contexts, making more significant the impact of the educational interventions [7]. DMID educational need was selected as the case study to develop the adaptive methodology. This work was supported by professionals (endocrinologist, nurses, nutritionists, psychologists, etc.) that belong to the Multidisciplinary Group for Diabetes Care (GRUMAD) of the University Hospital of the Santa Catarina Federal University in Florianópolis, Brazil.

2 Modeling a Teaching – Learning Process

2.1 Didactic Ergonomics

The concept of Didactic Ergonomy involves the problematic of making an interface efficient to support learning [8] and was defined specifically for this work to establish how to configure the environment for different kind of users [9]. Didactic Ergonomy establishes that the Interface of pedagogical software should facilitate interactions with the studied object, privileging pedagogical choices over user's commodity [10]. The communication forms available in the interface must be adapted to the cognitive needs and interests of each apprentice.

A great number of cognitive theories provides apprentices' characteristics and suggests compatible learning environments. Didactic Ergonomy is based on the combination of these theories, establishing pedagogical strategies and tactics. Pedagogical strategies define general actions to support learning and were extracted from behaviorism [11] and constructivism [12]. Pedagogical tactics define specific actions that should be executed to carry out a pedagogical strategy. Pedagogical tactics were extracted from theories that define capacities and individual styles in the apprentices, for example, the Learning Styles [13] or the Multiple Intelligences [14] theories. These theories allow the obtaining of apprentice's profiles and suggest supporting technologies. So, if the pedagogical strategy points out that "it is necessary to get the apprentice's attention on the most important matters", the tactics settle down "how to get the attention of each particular apprentice", according to his/her characteristics.

Each specific TLP requires a particular analysis, in order to identify the variables that define the apprentices, the variable that define the elements of the interface and the relationships between both kind of variables. The task of extracting the most representative variables from a specific TLP is called "TLP modeling process" and the resulting model is the base for ITS construction. The advantage of didactic ergonomics is that it suggests how to model a TLP establishing different student's needs and defining how to use technology to support them. So the develpment of the system is no more blind but guided, in all the steps, by pedagogical considerations.

2.2 Variables and Their Relationships

To model a TLP using Didactic Ergonomy it is necessary to know which apprentice characteristic are relevant to the process, how to identify them and which elements must be available in the screen to respond to these characteristics. The theories described before establish these elements. In this work, all the variables regarding the apprentice are contained in the *Characteristics* set, representing the Student's Model and all the variables regarding the interface are contained in the *Attributes* set, representing the content and its presentation form.

It is necessary to underline that the specific needs of a TLP orient which variables are important to be included in the model. That is why it is necessary to work very close to persons with experience in the specific TLP. To Model an educational process in diabetes treatment, some of the considered variables and some of their values were:

Student's Characteristics:

- Intellectual development stages. (Concrete Operational: OpC)
- Diagnosis Phase. (recently diagnosed: Phase1)
- Multiple intelligences. (Kinestesic: CIN, Interpersonal: INTP, Musical: MUS)
- Learning styles. (Visual: VIS, Sequential: SEQ, Active: ACT).

Interface's Attributes:

- Content. (Content 1 to 11).
- Navigation. (Free Navigation: Free, or Predetermined: PRE).
- Interaction. (High: H or Low: L).
- Media. (Text: TXT, Speech: SP, Sound: SND, Music: MUS, Image: IMG, Video: VD, Animation: AN, Animated Character: PER).
- Pedagogical activity. (Pedagogical environments considered are: Tutorials: TUT (behaviorist approach), Exploration Environments: SIM (constructivist approach), Examples: EX, Games: JOG, Question and Answers: PR, Problems' Resolution: RES, Encyclopedia: ENC).

Relationship between variables:

Table 1. Relations between Characteristics (lines) and Attributes (columns)

	CONTENTS											MEDIA								NAV.		INT		ACTIVITIES						
	1	2	3	4	5	6	7	8	9	10	11	Txt	SP	SND	MUS	VD	AN	IMG	PER	Free	Pre	H	L	RES	PR	ENC	EX	JOG	TUT	SIM
OpC	1	1		1	1	1	1	1	1			1	1			1	1		1		1		1				1	1	1	
Phase1		1			1	1	1	1	1												1									
CIN																1	1		1			1							1	1
INTP											1		1						1			1								
MUS													1	1	1			1												
VIS																1	1	1		1								1		
SEQ																					1			1	1				1	
ACT					1	1	1	1	1							1	1		1			1		1		1		1	1	1

Didactic Ergonomy relates *Characteristics* and *Attributes* [15]. For example, for visual students more images or animations, for active students, more exploration environments, etc. Table 1 establishes the relationship between *Attributes* and *Char-*

acteristics. The Tutor Module stores the knowledge of this table, that represents the pedagogical conceptions of the human designer. It is interesting to note that all these conceptions can be changed, as well as the variables, depending on the specific TLP and on pedagogical conceptions of the educators in charge. An adaptation mechanism was created to store and process correctly this knowledge.

3 Adaptive Mechanism (AM)

3.1 Mathematical Formalization of ITS

Theorem: An Intelligent Tutoring System can be defined formally as a finite automata.

Demonstration: An ITS can be represented or defined by a set of six elements:

$$S = \{U, Y, X, xo, \lambda, \eta\}$$

where:

X: Student's Model: is the finite set of system's states. Each state corresponds to a Student's Model formed by the set of detected characteristics. The models are inferred by the systems, during pedagogical activities.

xo: Student's Initial Model: is the initial state of the system. This state corresponds to a default model or to an initial diagnosis of the apprentice and is the starting point for the system's operation.

U: Student's Action: is the finite set of inputs. Each input is a user action on the interface. The set is formed by the commands, selections, questions, etc. requested by the user. The user acts through the interface by means of controls (menus, icons, etc.) or commands.

Y: System's Interface: is the finite set of outputs. Each output is a specific interface. The outputs depend on the selected attributes. To configure the output, the system evaluates the user's actions (inputs) and the Student's Model (state).

λ: UxX → X is the transition state function. Depending on the apprentice's actions (inputs) and on the ITS's pedagogical knowledge a new Student's Model can be reached (new model).

η: UxX → Y is the output function. Given an input and a specific state, the ITS's pedagogical knowledge determines how to configure next screen (new output).

As these elements define an automata [16], it can be concluded that the behavior of an Intelligent Tutoring System can be modeled by means of the automata defined by the sets U, Y and X, by the initial state xo and by the functions λ and η. The theorem is therefore demonstrated.

Didactic Ergonomics defines the six elements that define an automata: the attributes of the interface define the input and outputs of the system; the apprentice's characteristics define the states; the pedagogical conceptions determine the λ and η functions. So, didactic ergonomics can be implemented as an ITS.

3.2 IAC Neural Networks

The IAC (Interactive Activation and Competition) ANN type is an Associative Memory like ANN whose original model was proposed by [17]. In this model, neurons representing specific "properties" or "values" are grouped in categories called pools representing "concepts". These pools, called visible pools, receive excitations from the exterior. Connections among groups are carried out by means of an intermediary pool, also called mirror pool (or hided pool), because it is the copy of the biggest pool of the net. This pool has no connections with the exterior and its function is to spread the activations among groups, contributing with a new competition instance. The connections among neurons are bi-directional and have weights that can take only the values –1 (inhibition), 1 (activation) or 0. Inside a pool, the connections are always inhibitory taking the value -1, so the neurons compete to each other, resulting in a winner (the "competition" of IAC). Among groups, the connections can be excitatory taking the value 1, or null. When two neurons have excitatory connections, if one is excited, the other one will be excited also (the "activation" of IAC). The connection's weights constitute a symmetric matrix *W* of dimension *mXm* where *m* is the number of existent neurons in the network. So, if there is a connection from neuron *i* to neuron *j*, it exists also a connection with the same value from neuron *j* to neuron *i*. As a result, processing becomes interactive since processing in a given pool influences and is influenced by processing in other pools (the "interactive" of IAC). Figure 1 shows the IAC original model.

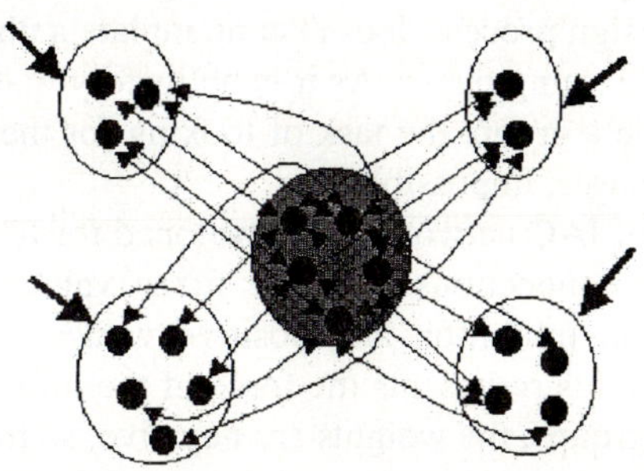

Fig. 1. The IAC original model: intermediary and visible pools

In this model, knowledge is not distributed among the weights of the net, like in most ANN. Here knowledge is represented by the processing neurons, organized in groups and by the connections among them.

The same as in many models, the net input of a neuron *i* is the pondered sum of the influence from the connected neurons to that neuron, and the external input, as shown in (1):

$$net_i = \sum_j w_{ij} y_j + x_i \qquad (1)$$

where w_{ij} represents the weight between neuron i and neuron j; y_j are outputs from other neurons and x_i are external inputs.

The output is given by (2), as follows:

$$y_i = \begin{cases} y_i, \text{ if } net_i > 0 \\ 0, \text{ otherwise} \end{cases} \quad (2)$$

The new activation of the neuron *i* of an IAC network is given by (3).

$$a_i = a_i + \Delta a_i \; . \quad (3)$$

It is observed that the new activation depends on the current activation and on its variation. The variation in the activation is proportional to the net inputs coming from the other neurons, the external inputs and the decay factor, as shown in (4).

$$\begin{aligned} \Delta a_i &= (\max - a_i) net_i - decay\,(a_i - rest) \text{ for } net_i > 0 \\ \Delta a_i &= (a_i - \min)\, net_i - decay\,(a_i - rest) \text{ for } net_i < 0 \end{aligned} \quad (4)$$

The parameters *max*, *min*, *decay* and *rest* of equation (4), define the values *maximum*, *minimum*, the *decay* factor and the *rest* value of the neurons, respectively. The *decay* spreads to recover the *rest* value of the neurons.

The computer model presents other parameters such as α, γ, and *estr* which ponders the influences of the activations, inhibitions and external input that arrive to each neuron. Their influences affect all the neurons at the same time.

In opposition to other paradigms where the main problem is the learning process, in IAC network, the design task consists on defining the best topology that represents a given problem. The design process doesn't contemplate a phase of adjustment of the weights, also known as learning phase. As it is obligatory that a total inhibition exists among the neurons inside a group, the task of looking for the appropriate topology is not trivial and, in many cases, impossible.

The "A" model [18] of IAC network was developed for trying to solve this restriction. In this model, the connections can take fuzzy values, in the interval [-1 1]. Negative values represent inhibition and positive values represent activation. The absolute value of the weights represents the force of the influence that exists between two neurons. Inside the groups, the weights are negative, so the neurons compete with each other. Among the groups, the values of the weights depend on the force of the relationship that exists among the corresponding neurons.

The equations and parameters of the "A" model are similar to the Rumelhart´s. Nevertheless a weights´ adjustment has to be performed by an activity similar to knowledge engineering which is used in the implementation of Expert Systems [18].

As an algorithm of standard learning doesn't exist for this model, the adjustment of the weights is carried out in a manual way. The specialist should determine which are the values and signs of the weights among all the neurons. This task is complex, because from –1 to 1 there exists infinite possible combinations. De Azevedo [18] demonstrated that IAC ANN behaves like automata.

3.3 Computational Model of TLP

To satisfy the requirements of didactic ergonomics, the AM should store the pedagogical knowledge of the ITS. To do so, the AM should fulfill three indispensable properties: parallelism, bi-directionality and uncertainties treatment. The first one guarantees that the apprentice's characteristics are all processed simultaneously by the system. The bi-directionality allows the AM to configure Interface, starting from the apprentice's characteristics (function η), but also to update the Student's Model (function λ) according to the apprentice actions. Uncertainties treatment allows obtaining reasonable output with incomplete or uncertain data as input.

Several aspects led to the suitability of IAC networks for the implementation of the AM. The first one is the automata formalization that relates the two approaches. IAC also fulfill the three requirements exposed. The structure of groups whose concepts or neurons compete internally and activate externally other concepts, offers a natural problem representation, increasing system's selectivity to some students' stereotypes.

To implement the IAC network, the variables of the problem (*Characteristics* and *Attributes*) were represented by neurons and their relationships by weights. The groups of neurons were formed by excluding categories as shown in table 2, where some of the groups are presented.

Table 2. Example of Groups and neurons of the IAC neural network

Groups	# of Neurons
1.- Stage of Development	3
2.- Interest	7
3.- Diagnosis Phase	2
4.- Multiple Intelligences	5
5.- Visual-Verbal Styles	2
6.- Sequential-Global Styles	2
1.- Content	11
2.- Media	8
3.- Activity	7
4.- Navigation	2

The parameters of the net were configured as: $max = 1$; $min = -0.2$; $\alpha = \gamma = 0.1$ and $estr = 0.4$ and 60 cycles. The most difficult task was to determine the weights of the net, which represent the pedagogical concepts, stored in table I.

Two kinds of tests were developed to adjust the weights consequently with the pedagogical conceptions:

C → A Tests: the Characteristics are placed at the net input and the activated Attributes are analyzed at the output (η function).

A → C Tests: the Attributes are placed at the input of the net and the activated Characteristics are analyzed at the output (λ function).

The IAC network performed correctly 94% of the *C → A Tests* and 70% of the *A → C Tests*. For this last case, the reasons of the errors were identified, so corrections can be made in future versions. The main conclusion of simulations is that an IAC network is able to store and process knowledge on pedagogical relationships between student's characteristics and interface configuration. That is to say, an IAC network is able to store Didactic Ergonomy knowledge.

4 ITS Design

The methodology obtained from this work, establishes how to model a TLP and how to design each ITS module. The design method is resumed next.

Student Module stores the Student's Models (States) and is formed by the apprentice's characteristics. The methodology uses two ways to update the Student's Model. First, to obtain the initial State, the ITS presents a diagnostic activity implemented by questionnaires. Once the system identified the apprentice, the initial state is reached, the corresponding environments are configured and the system is ready to work. The second way to update the Student's Model occurs during the TLP. The Tutor Module evaluates the student's actions and updates the model using the η function.

Tutor Module stores pedagogical knowledge (λ and η functions) and is implemented by an "A" model IAC ANN. This module is permanently processing the apprentice's inputs to determine changes at the outputs or states. Once the Initial Student's Model is established, the Tutor Module configures the interface and waits for the student's actions. If the student's actions are consequent with tutor's plan, the outputs are updated and the actual state is maintained. If the student's actions change tutor's plan, by selecting new attributes of the interface (another topic or medias, for example), the state changes: the Tutor Module analyses the new attributes and updates the Student's Model reaching a new state, that will influence future presentations.

Specialist Module stores the contents. To facilitate the design and implementation of this module, contents are structured as a set of topics. Each topic is stored in several files called nodes. Each node contains the topic's information using a specific media and a specific pedagogical activity (Figure 2a). Buttons and other controls are also available as nodes. Links between nodes represent the relationship: "next node to be presented". The establishment of the links is dynamic and depends on the Student's Model and actions (Figure 2b). At the end of the process the system generates a specific graph for each student (Figure 2c). To facilitate the management of the great variety of interface attributes, each node must be stored in an independent file. A database allows the Tutor Module to load in the screen the files corresponding to each attribute activated by the specific Student's Model. The design process is facilitated by the construction of a table that stores all the possible files needed to satisfy a specific TLP.

Interface Module allows inputs and outputs. Once the initial state is reached, the Tutor Module configures a specific interface (output). The interface offers controls (icons, menus, buttons) or commands to make possible student's interactions (input). The Tutor Module processes this input, updates the interface and, eventually, the Student's Model. The interface is updated or reconfigured. As the output depends on the student's input and model (which is continually being updated), the resulting interface is configured at run – time and is highly personalized and dynamical.

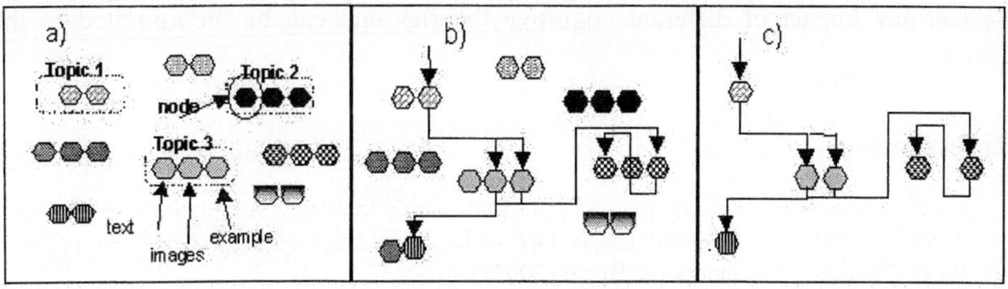

Fig. 2. Content Organization: a) Set of information, b) Student's Path, c) Personalized Graph

5 Final Considerations

The formalization of ITS as an automata was necessary to have a mathematical vocabulary to describe the components of the system and to unify the different approaches involved in its design and implementation.

The proposed system doesn't try to solve all the problems that arise from the development of ITS. Nevertheless this project tries to simplify the Student's Model, designing it as a group of characteristics that offers an approach to select pedagogical activities. On the other hand, the domain is modeled using several strategies what increases the possibilities of interacting in an appropriate way with the student. The interface design is strongly bounded to didactic criteria, and can lead to the construction of more effective and efficient systems. Effective by interacting in an appropriate way with the student. Efficient because technological resources are used strictly when requested by pedagogical criteria on the specific TLP.

The contribution of this system depends in a large part of the relevance of its content, of the correct selection and identification of the users and the capacity of the Tutor Module to suggest pedagogical activities appropriately. The interdisciplinary work is an indispensable condition to achieve the proposed objectives. A great effort in this sense can contribute to increase impact of pedagogical software.

The problem of "who has the control" during the process is a very polemic matter in pedagogical software research. The system here described, allows that as much the system as the student can have the control of the process, depending on the characteristics detected in the student. Some characteristics, like "active" learning style, inhibit the action of the system, leaving it in second plane and suggesting interactive activities like exploration environments. Other characteristics require that the system takes the control, planning the activities like in a tutorial. All this makes that the resulting interface adapts the contents, the presentation form and also the pedagogical strategy to the apprentice.

The case study allowed the design of a specific system. The design used Didactic Ergonomy to model the TLP for diabetic people. The experimental model based on an IAC ANN validated the Adaptive Mechanism. Future works must be developed to implement an ITS prototype to validate Didactic Ergonomy, that is to say, to evaluate the impact on learning of the adaptive Interface. A system designed with the methodology proposed in this work can be evaluated by pedagogical specialists to measure the learning impact of different cognitive theories that can be incorporated to the system.

References

1. Curilem GMJ.: Metodologia para a Implementação de Interfaces Adaptativas em Sistemas Tutores Inteligentes. Doctoral Thesis. Dpt. of Electrical Engineering Federal University of Santa Catarina.), Florianópolis, Brasil (2002)
2. Brusilovsky, P.: Methods and techniques of adaptive hypermedia. In: P. Brusilovsky, A. Kobsa and J. Vassileva (eds.): Adaptive Hypertext and Hypermedia. Kluwer Academic Publishers, Dordrecht (1998) 1-43
3. Wenger E.: Artificial intelligence and Tutoring Systems. Computational and Cognitive Approaches to the Communication of Knowledge, Morgan Kaufmann, San Francisco (1987)
4. Bruillard E.: Les Machines a Enseigner. Editions Hermes, Paris (1997)
5. Briceño L.R.: Siete tesis sobre la educación sanitaria para la participación comunitaria. Cad. Saúde Públ., v. 12, n. 1, Rio de Janeiro (1996) 7-30.
6. Zagury L. Zagury T.: Diabetes sem medo, Ed. Rocco Ltda (1984)
7. Curilem, G.M.J., Brasil, L.M., Sandoval, R.C.B., Coral, M.H.C., De Azevedo F.M., Marques J.L.B.: Considerations for the Design of a Tutoring System Applied to Diabetes. In Proceedings of World Congress on Biomedical Engineering' Chicago, USA 25-27 July (2000)
8. Rouet J.F.: Cognition et Technologies d'Apprentissage. http://perso.wanadoo.fr/arkham/thucydide/rouet.html (Setembro 2001)
9. Curilem, G.M.J., De Azevedo, F.M.: Didactic Ergonomy for the Interface of Intelligent Tutoring Systems in Computers and Education: Toward a Lifelong Learning Society. Kluwer Academic Publishers (2003) 75-88
10. Choplin H., Galisson A., Lemarchand S.: Hipermedias et pedagogie: Comment promouvoir l'activité de l'élève? Congrès Hypermedia et Apprentissage. Poitiers, France (1998)
11. Gagne R.M., Briggs L.J., & Wagner W.W.: Principles of instructional design. Third edition: Holt Rinehart and Winston, New York (1988)
12. Piaget J.: A psicologia da Inteligência. Editora Fundo de Cultura S.A Lisboa (1967).
13. Felder R.M.: Matters of Styles ASEE Prism 6(4), December (1996) 18-23
14. Gardner H.: Multiple Intelligences: The Theory in Practice. NY: Basic Books. (1993).
15. Curilem, G.M.J., De Azevedo, F.M.: Implementação Dinâmica de Atividades num Sistema Tutor Inteligente. In Proceedings of the XII Brazilian Symposium of Informatics in Education, SBIE2001, , Vitória, ES, Brasil 21-23 November (2001).
16. Hopcroft J.E., Ullman J.D.: Introduction to automata theory, Languages and Computation. Addison-Wesley. (1979).
17. Rumelhart, D.E., McClelland, J.L.: Explorations in Distributed Processing. A Handbook of Models, Programs and Exercises. Ed. Bradford Book. Massachusetts Institute of Technology. (1989).
18. De Azevedo, F. M.: Contribution to the Study of Neural Networks in Dynamical Expert System, PhD Thesis – Facultés Universitaires Notre-Dame de la Paix, Namur, Belgium. (1993).

Implementing Analogies in an Electronic Tutoring System

Evelyn Lulis[1], Martha Evens[2], and Joel Michael[3]

[1] CTI, DePaul University
243 S. Wabash Avenue
Chicago, IL 60604 USA
elulis@cti.depaul.edu
[2] Department of Computer Science, Illinois Institute of Technology
10 West 31st Street, Chicago, IL 60616 USA
evens@iit.edu
[3] Department of Molecular Biophysics and Physiology, Rush Medical College
1750 W. Harrison St., Chicago, IL 60612 USA
jmichael@rush.edu

Abstract. We have built an ITS system for cardiovascular physiology that carries on a natural language dialogue with students and simulates our expert tutors' behavior. The tutoring strategies and language are derived from a corpus consisting of eighty-one hour long expert human tutoring sessions with first-year medical students at Rush Medical College. In order to add analogies to the available tutoring repertoire, we analyzed the use of analogies in the human tutoring sessions. Two different types of analogies were discovered: one involves reflection on students' earlier work and the other refers to familiar things outside the physiological domain, like balloons and Ohm's Law. The two types involve different implementation approaches and different language. We are now implementing analogies of the first type in our ITS using the same schemas and rule-based Natural Language Generation techniques as in the rest of the dialogue that CIRCSIM-Tutor generates. We are using the Gentner's model of analogy and Forbus' Structure Mapping Engine to implement the second type.

1 Introduction

Advances in the research on analogies in cognitive science, new work in electronic tutor construction, and progress in discourse planning have provided a solid foundation to build an electronic tutoring system that uses natural language to simulate the human use of analogies in tutoring sessions. We began by analyzing eighty-one human tutoring sessions, identifying the analogies, and studying their use by our experts. Our intelligent tutoring system currently carries on a natural language dialogue with the students. We are now adding analogies to the tutoring strategies available in our system by using natural language generation techniques and by modeling the behavior of our experts.

J.C. Lester et al. (Eds.): ITS 2004, LNCS 3220, pp. 751–761, 2004.

2 CIRCSIM-Tutor

CIRCSIM-Tutor is an electronic tutoring system designed to tutor medical students on the baroreceptor reflex, a physiological negative feedback system. The baroreceptors measure the mean arterial pressure (MAP) in the carotid arteries, which run up both sides of the neck and supply blood to the brain. The reflex uses the central nervous system (CNS) to alter neurally controlled components of the system variables to move MAP back toward its normal value.

The tutor uses natural language discourse derived from studies of human tutoring sessions [1]. Its natural language dialogue is designed to encourage a wide variety of student responses and encourage self-explanation. Pre- and post-tests administered to students before and after one-hour sessions with the tutor have demonstrated it to be effective—students performed significantly better on post-tests than pre-tests ($p<.001$) [1]. Positive responses were received when surveying student attitudes towards the system. Students reported that the tutor "helped them better understand the baroreceptor reflex and helped them learn to predict responses" [1].

3 Analogies Found in the Corpus

Eighty-one hour long human tutoring sessions—seventy-five keyboard-to-keyboard and six face-to-face—with first year medical students solving problems about the baroreceptor reflex were conducted by two professors of physiology, Joel Michael and Allen Rovick, at Rush Medical College. Face-to-face sessions were audio recorded and transcribed, while keyboard-to-keyboard sessions were recorded using the Computer Dialogue System [2]. The human sessions were marked up by hand using an annotation language based on SGML [3]. A representative subset of examples using analogies found in the corpus follows. The identifiers F or K indicate whether the session was face-to-face or keyboard-to-keyboard; the session number follows; who is speaking/typing is indicated by st (student) or tu (tutor); following is the turn number and the sentence number within the turn. Transcripts will be provided on request.

Example 1: Balloons and the Elastic Properties of Tissues Model
Face-to-face session number one (F1) shows the tutor offering a better analogy than the one proposed by the student (as discussed in 4, 5, 6) and demonstrates how a working knowledge of the elastic properties of tissues model [1, 7] increased understanding of pressure change in the right atrium when it distends. Students experience great trouble understanding compliance, the relationship between the pressure in a distensble structure and its volume. In fact, Feltovich et al. [8] have shown this problem to be a source of misconceptions in practicing physicians as well as students. The student proposes comparing the right atrium, as it fills with blood, to a sink. The sink is not a distensible object. The tutor employs the use of the elastic properties of tissues model by suggesting a comparison of the right atrium to a balloon instead.

F1-st-62-1: If I make an analogy of you try to fill a sink with water and you
F1-tu-63-1: Try to fill a balloon with water, since that's what we're dealing with, a distensible object.
F1-st-64-1: OK.
F1-st-64-2: We're filling a balloon with water, and the rate at which the water empties out is slower than before, but you're filling it at the same rate, so it's going to be easier to distend the balloon.
F1-tu-65-1: So the balloon will distend.
F1-st-66-1: So the balloon will distend and we will have -- oh, OK, according to Starling's
F1-tu-67-1: Well, let's stay with the balloon first.
F1-tu-67-2: What's going to happen when the balloon distends?
F1-st-68-1: In terms of the volume or the pressure?
F1-tu-69-1: In terms of the pressure.
F1-st-70-1: Pressure in the balloon will increase.
F1-tu-71-1: OK, good.
F1-tu-71-2: What is this balloon we're talking about?
F1-st-72-1: This balloon is the right atrium.
F1-tu-73-1: So can we say something about happens to right atrial pressure when cardiac pressure goes down?
F1-st-74-1: Right atrial pressure goes up when cardiac output goes down.
F1-tu-75-1: They are inversely related, right?
F1-st-76-1: Right, OK.

The session continues with the correct mapping of the balloon (base) to the right atrium (target) resulting in a correct inference by the student.

Example 2: Ohm's Law and the Pressure/Flow/Resistance Model
Face-to-Face session number five (F5) demonstrates how a working knowledge of the pressure/flow/resistance model [7, 9], using Ohm's Law as a base, facilitated understanding of MAP. The equation MAP = CO * TPR is the cardiovascular version of the pressure/flow/ resistance model, which states that the pressure is the flow times the resistance. This equation is analogous to Ohm's Law (V = IR), which states that the voltage (the electrical pressure) is the current (the flow of electrons) times the electrical resistance.

F5-st-343-5: Like MAP = CO x TPR.
F5-tu-344-1: Of course!
F5-st-345-1: I'll think about that...
F5-st-345-2: I just did five problems on this.
F5-st-345-3: So...
F5-st-345-4: I don't know why this is true though.
F5-tu-346-1: You don't know why that is true.

```
F5-tu-346-2: Do you recognize that that equation is
             identical in principle to Ohm's Law which
             says that electrical potential is equal to
             the current times resistance.
F5-st-347-1: V = IR.
F5-tu-348-1: Or V = IR.
F5-tu-348-2: Right.
F5-tu-348-3: The push equals the flow times the
             resistance.
F5-st-349-1: Well, OK, Yeah, this one makes sense to me
             and I can see that this is the same thing.
```

Example 3: Accelerator and Brake Analogy

Session K44 demonstrates the use of a commonly used analogy in physiology, the "brake and accelerator." The nervous system affects the neural variable called heart rate via the sino-atrial node. The sympathetic and parasympathetic branches of the autonomic nervous system usually have antagonistic effects on the organs or tissues that they innervate. The sino-atrial node determines heart rate, the sympathetic input is the accelerator (it speeds up heart rate), and the parasympathetic input is the brake (it slows heart rate).

```
K44-tu-106-2: What I mean is, what physiological
              signals reach the heart that determine
              the value of hr?
K44-st-107-1: Action potentials from the ans either
              para or sympathetic
K44-tu-108-1: So, if parasymp.
K44-tu-108-2: Signal increases to heart what happens to
              hr?
K44-st-109-1: Decrease
K44-tu-110-1: And if sympath.
K44-tu-110-2: Signal to heart decreases, what happens
              to hr?
K44-st-111-1: Decrease
K44-tu-112-1: Right, think of P and S as the brake and
              accelerator.
```

Example 4: Reflex and the Control Systems Model

K32 demonstrates the use of the control systems model [1, 7] using the reflex—an analogy commonly used in physiology—as a base. In the following example, the tutor uses an analogy to point out that since the baroreceptor reflex is a reflex, and it cannot completely compensate for the change produced by the initial perturbation.

```
K32-tu-236-1: The baroreceptor reflex, like all
              reflexes, partially corrects for any
              disturbance to the regulated variable,
              MAP, in this case.
K32-tu-236-2: Hence, your original prediction of MAP D
              was correct.
```

Example 5: Another Neural Variable Analogy

In session K1 the tutor has already tutored the behavior of TPR in the DR phase and prompts the tutor to make an analogy between it and other neurally controlled variables in this phase (as discussed in 4, 5, 6). The student understands the analogy and correctly infers that all neurally controlled variables will behave in the same manner in this phase.

```
K1-st-29-1: During the DR period it would remain
            unchanged.
K1-tu-30-1: Correct.
K1-tu-30-2: What other variables are neurally
controlled?
K1-st-31-1: CC, HR
K1-tu-32-1: Again correct.
K1-tu-30-1: Correct.
K1-tu-30-2: What other variables are neurally
controlled?
K1-st-31-1: CC, HR
K1-tu-32-1: Again correct.
K1-tu-32-2: Now we know that in this guy HR is under
            the control of the artificial pacemaker.
K1-tu-32-3: But what would happen toCC?
K1-st-33-1: CC 0
K1-tu-34-1: Right on!
```

Example 6: Ohm's Law – Demonstration of Student Misunderstanding

In session K44 there is an example of the student not understanding the Ohm's Law analogy. As a result, the tutor explains the analogy.

```
K44-tu-128-1: Do you know ohm's law for electrical
              circuits?
K44-st-129-1: V=ir
K44-tu-130-1: Well, the circulation is exactly
              analogous.
K44-tu-130-2: That being the case, in the ci rculation,
              what does v represent?
K44-st-131-1: Im embarrased i cant remember what they
              mean
K44-tu-132-1: Well, v is the potential gradienmt
              (electrical) and the equivalent hydrauli
              c parameter is the pressure gradient or
              map.
K44-tu-132-2: Does that help to define map = ...?
K44-st-133-1: Ive got the map =pressure part but if you
              tell me what i and r are ill extr apolate
              to the real situation here
K44-tu-134-1: Well, i = current (flow of electrons) and
              r = resistance to flow.
K44-tu-134-2: Does tha t help?
K44-st-135-1: Isnt it hr and tpr
```

```
K44-tu-136-1: Well, its true that tpr is the total
              peripheral RESISTANCE.
K44-tu-136-2: But, how can h eart rate (beats/min) be a
              flow?
K44-st-137-1: I know it didnt make sense.
K44-st-137-2: Its got to have something to do with the
              fluid o bviously
K44-tu-138-1: What do we call the amount of blood per
              minute that leaves the heart?
K44-st-139-1: Co
K44-tu-140-1: Sure!
K44-tu-140-2: So we have the following relationship:
              map = co x tpr where co is  the cardiac
              output (ml/min) and tpr is the resistance
              to flow posed by the entire cirulcatoy
              system.
K44-tu-140-3: This relationship must always hold in the
              CV system.
```

Example 7. Traffic Cop/Traffic Jam

In session K64 contains an inappropriate analogy proposed by the student (st) between the heart and a traffic cop (as discussed in 4, 5, 6). The tutor suggests a more suitable analogy between the heart and a traffic jam.

```
K64-st-54-1: Would it be a reasonable analogy to look
             at the heart like a traffic cop?
K64-st-54-2: If it slows down the rate of blood flow
             (lets fewer cars through) then there will
             be a backup behind it (a backflow of blood
             prior to the heart, and therefore an
             increase in CVP) and fewer cars coming
             through (less blood coming out of the
             heart and therefore a decrease in MAP)
K64-tu-55-1: The analogy is OK.
K64-tu-55-2: But just as a traffic jam does not occur
             because cars back up, the increase in CVP
             caused by a fall in CO is not the result
             of blood BACKING UP.
K64-tu-55-3: Everything soes in one direction.
K64-st-56-1: well, slowing down would be a better way
             to put it then
K64-tu-57-1: Yes.
K64-tu-57-2: A traffic jam caused by everybody piling
             into the same area at once.
```

Tables 1 and 2 [5, 6] present a synopsis of our analysis of the analogies found in the corpus. The tutors proposed fifty-one analogies in the eighty-one hour long sessions they conducted. Nine of these analogies were used to enhance the student's understanding of the material discussed and did not lead to further development. In another five instances, no inference was requested by the tutor. However, of these five, correct inferences were made by the student four times. In the remaining thirty-seven examples, inferences were requested by the tutor resulting in fifteen successful mappings (correct inferences) and twenty-two failed mappings (incorrect inferences). Out of the twenty-two failed mappings, the tutor successfully repaired/explained the analogy resulting in correct inferences by the student fifteen times. The corpus reflected an 81% success rate—the use of analogy, after an incorrect inference was made by students, resulted in a correct inference made by students in 34 of the 42 times the tutors employed the strategy. The tutor abandoned the analogy in favor of a different teaching plan only seven times.

Table 2 [5, 6] lists the different bases that appeared in the corpus with the number of times they were found. Tutors proposed "another neural variable" twenty-nine times resulting in successful inferences made by the students twenty-four times—83% success rate. More interesting bases—balloons, compliant structures, Ohm's Law, and traffic jam—were used less frequently by tutors and students. However, their use resulted in interesting and successful structural mappings, and was followed by successful inferences by students.

Table 1. Use and results of observed analogies proposed by tutors

Type	Number of times seen
enhancement only	**9**
no inference requested	**5**
successful mapping	4
failed mapping	1
inference requested	**37**
successful inference	15
failed inference	
success after repair	15
failure after repair	7
Total:	**51**

4 Implementation

Joel Michael reviewed the examples of analogies identified and decided that we should implement: "another neural variable," "another procedure," "Ohm's Law" (pressure/flow/resistance model), "balloons/compliant structure" (elastic properties of tissues model), the "reflex and the control systems" model, and the "accelerator/brake" analogy. "Another neural variable," is most often used in tutoring Direct Response phase (although it can be used in the RR and SS phases). It is always invoked when the student gets one or two neural variables correct, but gets the other(s) wrong. It is generally very effective. The work of Kurtz et al. [10] and Katz's series of experiments at Pittsburgh [11, 12, 13] have confirmed the importance of this kind of explicit discussion of meta-knowledge and of reflective tutoring in general. The use of this analogy to test Gentner's mutual alignment theory of analogies [10] is

Table 2. Bases seen in the corpus

Base	Number of times seen in the corpus	Base	Number of times seen in the corpus
Airplane wing	1	Elastic reservoir	1
Another algorithm	2	Flight or fight	1
Another neural variable	29	Gravity	1
Another	3	Last problem	1
Balloon	1	Ohms law	2
Balloon as a compliant	2	Physician	1
Black box	1	Pump	1
Bootstrap	1	Reflex	2
Brake & accelerator	1	Sugar or glucose	1
Compliant structure	3	Summation	1
Dimmer switch	1	Traffic jam	2

being explored. Analogies to other procedures are only evoked after the student has been exposed to a number of different procedures. As a result, there are not many examples of the use of this base in the human tutoring sessions, which typically involve only one or two procedures. However, we expect students to complete 8-10 procedures in hour-long laboratory sessions with the ITS. Joel Michael believes that it would be especially beneficial for students to be asked to recognize parallels between different procedures that move MAP in the same direction.

4.1 Implementing the Another–Neural–Variable Analogy with Schemas

Schemas have been created for the "another neural variable" and "another procedure" analogies, based on the examples found in our human-human tutoring sessions. A successful use of another neural variable analogy was seen in Example 5. The tutor requests an inference and the student infers (that the new variable behaves like the earlier one) correctly. This sequence happens most of the time and the tutor moves to the next
topic. The tutor explains the analogy only when the student fails to understand the analogy or fails to make the inference [5].

> If the tutor decides to explore the analogy further
> the tutor asks the student to map the analogs (or tells the student the mapping)

the tutor asks the student to map the relationships (or tells the student …)
the tutor prompts the student to make an inference to determine understanding

Another neural variable analogy can be used in any phase (DR or RR or SS), whenever the student has made an error in two or three of the neural variables, just after the tutor has finished tutoring the first one. Assume that the tutor has just tutored neural variable (NV1) successfully and that another non-clamped neural variable was incorrectly predicted by the student.

If there is one other neural variable that was not predicted correctly and
if that variable is not clamped
the tutor asks "What other variable is neurally controlled?"

If there are two left and neither is clamped
"What other variables are neurally controlled?"
"Are there other neurally controlled variables that would change at the s ame time?"

If the student answers with the name of a clamped neural variable (which cannot change precisely because it is clamped – this is what happens to HR in our examples), then the tutor asks the student to read the procedure description over again if s/he is doing well, else says:

"In this procedure <the clamped variable> cannot change."

If the student answers with the name of a hemodynamic (nonneural) variable the tutor asks:

"Which variables are directly changed by the reflex?" and a new tutoring goal (teach the neural variables) is placed at the top of the stack.

If the student answers with the name of a neural variable <NV2> that is not clamped, the system asks for an inference:

"What happens to NV2 in this case?"

If the student gives a wrong answer but is otherwise doing well

the tutor will gives a hint "Like <NV1>"
otherwise the tutor teaches NV2 by the method that succeeded with NV1

Note, that in order to make this schema readable, we used actual text examples. In reality, the schemas contain logic forms that are expanded by the Turn Planner [14]. Johanna Moore [15] implemented some language for retrospective tutoring in Sherlock II, and we are using this work as a guide in the language generation process [16].

4.2 Implementing Other Analogies with the Structure Mapping Engine

The explicit analogies that involve bases outside the domain, such as the balloon analogies, are interesting to implement, but more complex. These analogies initiate the biggest revelation, the most effective "aha" experience for the students. They also provide the most opportunities for student misconceptions. It is, therefore, very important for the tutor to forestall these possible misunderstandings by pointing out where the analogy applies and where it does not and to correct any misconceptions that may show up later.

We have chosen the Structure Mapping Engine (SME) [17, 18, 19] to implement this second group of analogies. SME utilizes alignment-first mapping between the target and the base, and then selects the best mapping and all those within 10% of it, as described in Gentner [20]. SME appears to model our expert tutors' behavior as seen in the corpus, especially the example using Ohm's Law as a base. In most of the examples using this analogy, students understood the mapping, resulting in an immediate clarification of the issue. This was not the case in Example 6 above. As a result, we can observe the tutor pushing the student through each step in the mapping process. SME will be used for handling the Ohm's law (pressure/flow/resistance model), balloons/compliant structure (elastic properties of tissues model), reflex and the control systems model, and the accelerator/brake analogies.

5 Conclusion

In order to implement analogies in our ITS, CIRCSIM-Tutor, we analyzed eighty-one human tutoring sessions conducted by experts Michael and Rovick for the use of analogies. Although analogies were not very frequent, they were highly effective when used. The analogies were categorized by the base and the target according to Gentner's [20] structure-mapping model. Analogies and models to implement in CIRCSIM-Tutor have been chosen by Michael, who uses this system in a course he teaches at Rush Medical College. CIRCSIM-Tutor already has a rule-based system set up to utilize the schemas described here to generate tutor initiated "another neural variable" and "another procedure" analogies. The SME model [17, 18, 19] is being used to generate the other analogies—Ohm's law (pressure/flow/resistance model), balloons/compliant structure (elastic properties of tissues model), reflex and the control systems model, and the accelerator/brake analogy. During the human tutoring sessions, students also proposed analogies. Future research will include the mechanisms for recognizing and responding to these proposals using the SME.

Acknowledgments. This work was partially supported by the Cognitive Science Program, Office of Naval Research under Grant 00014-00-1-0660 to Stanford University as well as Grants No. N00014-94-1-0338 and N00014-02-1-0442 to Illinois Institute of Technology. The content does not reflect the position or policy of the government and no official endorsement should be inferred.

References

1. Michael, J., Rovick, A., Glass, M., Zhou, Y., & Evens, M. (2003). Learning from acomputer tutor with natural language capabilities. *Interactive Learning Environments, 11*(3): 233-262.
2. Li, J., Seu, J. H., Evens, M. W., Michael, J. A., & Rovick, A. A. (1992). Computer dialogue system: A system for capturing computer-mediated dialogues. *Behavior Research Methods, Instruments, and Computer (Journal of the Psychonomic Society), 24*(4): 535-540.

3. Kim, J. H., Freedman, R., Glass, M., & Evens, M. W. (2002). Annotation of tutorial goals for natural language generation. Unpublished paper, Department of Computer Science, Illinois Institute of Technology.
4. Lulis, E. & Evens, M. (2003). The use of analogies in human tutoring dialogues. AAAI 7:2003 Spring Symposium Series Natural Language Generation in Spoken and Written Dialogue, 94-96.
5. Lulis, E., Evens, M., & Michael, J. (2003). Representation of analogies found in human tutoring sessions. *Proceedings of the Second IASTED International Conference on Information and Knowledge Sharing,* 88-93. Anaheim, CA:ACTA Press.
6. Lulis, E., Evens, M., & Michael, J. (To appear). Analogies in Human Tutoring Sessions. In *Proceedings of the Twenty-Sixth Conference of the Cognitive Science Society*, 2004.
7. Modell, H. I. (2000). How to help students understand physiology? Emphasize general models. *Advances in Physiology Educ.* 23: 101-107.
8. Feltovich, P.J., Spiro, R., & Coulson, R. (1989). The nature of conceptual understanding in biomedicine: The deep structure of complex ideas and the development of misconceptions. In D. Evans and V. Patel (Eds.), *Cognitive Science in Medicine.* Cambridge, MA: MIT Press.
9. Michael, J. A. & Modell, H. I. (2003). Active learning in the college and secondary science classroom: A model for helping the learner to learn. Mahwah, NJ: Lawrence Erlbaum Associates.
10. Kurtz, K., Miao, C., & Gentner, D. (2001). Learning by analogical bootstrapping. *Journal of the Learning Sciences,* 10(4):417-446.
11. Katz, S., O'Donnell, G., & Kay, H. (2000). An approach to analyzing the role and structure of reflective dialogue. *International Journal of Artificial Intelligence and Education,* 11, 320-343.
12. Katz, S., & Albritton, D. (2002). Going beyond the problem given: How human tutors use post- practice discussions to support transfer. *Proceedings of Intelligent Tutoring Systems 2002,* San Sebastian, Spain, 2002. Berlin: Springer-Verlag. 641-650.
13. Katz, S. (2003). Distributed tutorial strategies. *Proceedings of the Cognitive Science Conference.* Boston, MA.
14. Yang, F.J., Kim, J.H., Glass, M. & Evens, M. (2000). Turn Planning in CIRCSIM-Tutor. In J. Etheredge and B. Manaris (Eds.*), Proceedings of the Florida Artificial Intelligence Research Symposium.* Menlo Park, CA: AAAI Press. 60-64.
15. Moore, J.D. (1995). *Participating in explanatory dialogues.* Cambridge, MA: MIT Press.
16. Moore, J.D., Lemaire, B. & Rosenblum, J. (1996). Discourse generation for instructional applications: Identifying and using prior relevant explanations. *Journal of the Learning Sciences,* 5(1), 49-94.
17. Gentner, D. (1998). Analogy. In W. Bechtel & G. Graham (Eds.), *A companion to cognitive science,* (pp. 107-113). Oxford: Blackwell.
18. Gentner, D., & Markman, A. B. (1997). Structure mapping in analogy and similarity. *American Psychologist, 52*(1): 45-56.
19. Forbus, K. D. Gentner, D., Everett, J. O. & Wu, M. (1997) Towards a computational model of evaluating and using analogical inferences, *Proc. of the 19th Annual Conference of the Cognitive Science Society*, Mahwah, NJ, Lawrence Erlbaum Associates.229-234.
20. Gentner, D. (1983). Structure-mapping: A theoretical framework for analogy. *Cognitive Science 7*(2):155-170.

Towards Adaptive Generation of Faded Examples*

Erica Melis and Giorgi Goguadze

Universität des Saarlandes and
German Research Institute for Artificial Intelligence (DFKI)
Stuhlsatzenhausweg, 66123 Saarbrücken, Germany
phone: +49 681 302 4629, fax: +49 681 302 2235

Abstract. Faded examples have been investigated in pedagogical psychology. The experiments suggest that a learner can benefit from faded examples. For realistic applications, it makes sense to generate several variants of an exercise by fading a worked example and to do it automatically. For the automatic generation, a suitable knowledge representation of examples and exercises is required which we describe in the paper. The structures and metadata in the knowledge representation of the examples are the basis for such an adaptation. In particular, it allows to fade a variety of parts of the example rather than only solution steps.

1 Introduction

Worked-out examples proved to be learning-effective in certain contexts because they are a natural vehicle for practicing self-explanation. *Faded* examples provide another ground for self-explanation that is slightly more difficult for a learner. Here, faded example means a worked-out example from which one or more parts have been removed (faded) deliberately. Those faded examples are exercises in which the learner has to find an equivalent for what has been removed.

Faded examples are of interest because

- the working memory load is not as heavy as for totally faded examples – the typical exercises – so there is a gradual transition to 'full' exercises
- the example context might act as a reminder
- an active analysis of the problem solution is necessary to fill in the faded details – a superficial processing of the example is hardly possible
- there is less stress on performing and more on the actual understanding
- fading can be used to stimulate limited problem solving, reflection, and self-explanation.

* This publication is partly a result of work in the context of the LeActiveMath project, funded under the 6th Framework Programm of the European Community – (Contract IST-2003-507826). The authors are solely responsible for its content. The European Community is not responsible for any use that might be made of information appearing therein

J.C. Lester et al. (Eds.): ITS 2004, LNCS 3220, pp. 762–771, 2004.

So far, faded examples have been produced manually. However, for realistic applications, as opposed to lab experiments, it makes sense to generate several variants of an exercise by fading and to do it *automatically.* For such an automatic generation, a suitable knowledge representation of examples and exercises is needed.

In our mathematics seminars we experienced the value of faded examples for learning. We are now interested in generating adaptively faded examples which can then be used in our learning environment for mathematics, ACTIVEMATH. Several steps are needed before ACTIVEMATH' course generator and suggestion mechanism can present appropriate faded examples to the learner: the knowledge representation has to be extended in a general way, the adaptive generation procedure has to be developed, and finally, the ACTIVEMATH-components have to request the dynamic generation of specially faded examples in response to learners actions. This article concentrates on a knowledge representation of examples and exercises that allows for distinguishing parts to be faded and for characterizing those parts. This is a non-trivial work because worked examples from mathematics can have a pretty complex structure, even more so, if innovative pedagogical ideas are introduced. We discuss general adaptations of the fading procedure we are currently implementing.

2 Example

Example. [1], p. 82, provides a worked-out solution of the problem

$$\textit{The sequence } ((-1)^n) \textit{ is divergent}$$

Solution
Step 1. This sequence $X := ((-1)^n)$ is bounded (take $M := 1$), so we cannot invoke Theorem 3.2.2. ...
Step 2. ... However, assume that $a := limX$ exists. ...
Step 3. ... Let $\epsilon := 1$ ...
Step 4. ... so that there exists a natural number K_1 such that

$$|(-1)^n - a| < 1 \ \ for \ \ all \ \ n \geq K_1 \ ...$$

Step 1 is, formally seen, not necessary for the solution. But it provides a meta-cognitive comment showing why an alternative proof attempt would not work. It would be sensible to fade this step, and request from the learner to indicate valid or invalid alternatives or to fade parts of this step.

In steps 2 and 3 two hypotheses are defined. These hypotheses are dependent. Fading both hypotheses introduces more under-specification than fading only one assumption.

Some good textbook authors omit little subproofs or formula-manipulations and instead ask "Why?" in order to keep the attention of the reader and make her think. For instance, the proof of the example in [1] contains:
... If n is an odd number with $n \geq K_1$, this gives $|(-1)^n - a| < 1$ so that $-2 < a < 0$. (Why?) ...
A response trains *application* skills.

3 Psychological Findings

Some empirical studies investigated faded examples [11,12,10,9]. Merrienboer [12] suggests positive effects of faded examples in programming courses. In a context in which the subjects have little pre-knowledge Stark investigates faded examples and shows a clear positive correlation of learning with faded examples and performance on near and medium transfer problems [10]. He also suggests that in comparison with worked-out examples, faded examples better prevent a passive and superficial processing. His experiments included an immediate feedback in form of a complete problem solving step.

Renkl and others found that *backward fading* of solution steps produces more accurate solutions on far transfer problems [9] – an effect that was inconsistent across experiments in other studies. These studies suggest that mixing faded examples with worked-out examples (with self-explanation) is more effective than self-explanation on worked-out examples only.

4 Preliminaries from ActiveMath

ActiveMath is a user-adaptive, web-based learning environment for mathematics [7]. It dynamically generates learning material for the individual learner according to her learning goals, preferences, and mastery of concepts as well as to the goal level corresponding to Bloom's [2] competencies.

The content to be assembled and presented by ActiveMath is separately stored in a knowledge base. It is represented in the XML language for mathematical documents OMDoc [6]. In OMDoc, mathematical knowledge is represented as learning objects annotated with metadata and relations This knowledge representation allows for better reuse and interoperability of content.

5 Knowledge Representation in ActiveMath

OMDoc has to be enhanced with rich internal structure for generating exercises by fading examples.

A prior extension of OMDoc, described in [5], refined the micro-structure of interactive exercises. The goal of this exercise representation language is to describe a plan of the solution, partial, final results. This is the target format of the faded examples/exercises.

5.1 Anatomy of Mathematical Example

Mathematical examples can possess a complex internal structure depending on the kind of example considered. Their worked solutions may contain a mathematical proof, calculation, exploration, construction of a model etc.

Since in a faded example one introduces under-specifications in a worked-out example, i.e. in its problem statement or its solution, these places have to be marked and annotated with metadata to characterize them. The original information from the example can be used later for diagnosis purposes.

The knowledge representation we suggest is experimental, mostly based on the experience with authors and teachers using ACTIVEMATH.

The first extension in 5.2 targets automatic generation. The extensions in 5.3 target the adaptivity in a generation.

5.2 Different Fadable Parts in the Original Examples

Depending on the content and structure of a worked-out example different parts can be faded. At the top-level, either parts of the problem itself (such as a condition), parts of the problem solution, parts of a meta- cognitive Polya framework [8] of the solution can be faded.

In more detail, faded parts may include (no completeness postulated)

- one or several assumptions of the problem
- a full problem solving step or its textual description
- the reason for applying a step, condition of a step
- a sub-proof or sub-solution
- goal statements
- subgoals
- parameters of a problem solution or a method application
- explanations and auxiliary information
- the reference to a justification (e.g., a theorem, principle)
- references/links to other instructional items such as similar solutions
- anticipatory information
- meta-cognitive structure and heuristics such as headings of Polya-phases and their content

As described in [6] the `proof` element in OMDOC is a directed acyclic graph of steps, connected by cross-references. Each derivation step in the proof can consist of textual content, formal content, it can possess a justification in form of a reference to a derivation rule or method used or a sub-proof. Apart from derivation steps there can occur a number of `hypothesis` elements, containing local hypothesis in the proof. The last step of the proof is called `conclude`.

For meta-cognitive explanatory texts that are not necessarily a logical part of the proof, the element `metacomment` is used.

We generalize the element `proof` to the element `solution` and allow it as a child element within the OMDOC element `example`. A worked `solution` is a hierarchy of steps (including reasoning, calculation, modeling), each of which is potentially fadable completely or partially. We allow authors to annotate parts of steps to be faded with unique identifiers using the container element `with` for marking.

For representing meta-cognitive explanations of different types, we refine the element `metacomment` by introducing the `type` of `metacomment` with possible values *alternative*, *comparison* and *explanation*. Each of the comments may have more then one type.

Finally, we extend the solution format to represent a meta-cognitive framework. We introduce following four meta-steps

1. Understand the problem
2. Devise a plan
3. Carry out the plan
4. Look back at the solution

Understand the Problem. The description of the initial problem includes markup elements `situation-description` and `problem-statement`. The first element describes what is given and what it depends on. Dependencies can be provided in the metadata of `situation-description`. The second element encodes the question (statement) of the problem, i.e. what has to be found, proven, etc. These elements prove to be useful not only for faded examples.

Devise a Plan. We use slightly modified OMDoc markup in order to simulate the plan of the solution. For this, each step of the solution might not directly contain the actual calculation or derivation, but an intermediate step, containing a brief description of one or more steps of the solution. The `derive` element encodes this step and may contain a child element `solution` for a sub-solution or just group a sequence of steps. Note that not only the plan of the solution can be encoded in this way, but more complex solution plans may consist of sequence of sub-solution plans.

Carry out the Plan. The sequence of bottom nodes of the `solution` element is the actual solution. In the encoding of the solution the steps, carrying out the plan, occur inside the corresponding plan steps, in the presentation they can be separated from the plan steps, if wished.

Look Back at the Solution. Here, an element `conclude` is used. This element has the same meaning as in OMDoc and is used not only if the solution is the proof of some fact. For example, if the root of the equation is calculated in the solution, in the `conclude` step the result is verified.

The reference to other problems for which the result of the current problem can be useful, is provided in the metadata record, as discussed below.

Figure 1 shows the internal representation of the previously considered example [1], embedded into the Polya framework. The bold case shows the actual steps of the exercise, italic shows additional steps, introduced for building the Polya framework.

5.3 Adding Metadata

In order to enable adaptive generation of faded examples we need to know what to fade according to capability of the learner and to the learning situation.

[1] Mathematical formulas in OMDoc are represented in OpenMath format, but in this paper we shorten them due to lack of space

```
<example id="div_seq_1" for="def_divergence">
<metadata>...</metadata>
 <situation-description>
  <CMP>Given the sequence ((−1)^n) </CMP>.
 </situation-description>
 <problem-statement>
  <CMP> The given sequence is divergent. </CMP>
 <problem-statement>
<solution>
 <metacomment id="c1" type="alternative">
   <CMP>This sequence X := ((−1)^n) is bounded so we
   can not invoke Theorem 3.2.2.</CMP>
  </metacomment>
 <derive id="plan_step1">
  <CMP>Assume the sequence is convergent</CMP>
  <hypothesis id="hyp1" discharged-in="last_step">
   <CMP> Assume that a := limX exists. </CMP>
  </hypothesis>
 </derive>
 <derive id="plan_step2">
  <CMP>Come to the contradiction.</CMP>
   <hypothesis id="hyp2" discharged-in="step_1">
    <CMP> Let ε := 1 </CMP>
   </hypothesis>
   <derive id="step1">
    <CMP>so that there exists a natural number K_1 such that
    <with id="obj1"> |(−1)^n − a| < 1 </with> for all
    <with id="obj2"> n ≥ K_1 </with> </CMP>
   </derive> ...
   <conclude id="last-step">
    <CMP>Since a cannot satisfy both of these inequalities, the
    hypothesis that X is convergent leads to a contradiction.
    Therefore, the sequence X is divergent. </CMP>
   </conclude>
 </derive>
 <conclude />
 </solution>
 </example>
```

Fig. 1. OMDoc Example enhanced with Polya-structure in the solution

The characterization by a learning-goal level is necessary in order to fade adaptively w.r.t. the learning goal, other properties such as difficulty and abstractness of a step can help to adapt metadata to the skills of the learner.

Metadata also assign dependencies to the `situation-description` element. It also characterizes the `conclude` element with its references to other problems. Metadata records are possible for each structural element of the solution. A metadata record consists of ActiveMath metadata elements, such as `difficulty`, `abstractness`, `competence-level`, `relation` of types *depends_on*, *is_useful_for*, and others.[2]

```
<metadata for="c1">
 <competence-level use="meta_cognition"/>
 <relation type="depends_on"><ref xref="thm_3_2_2"></relation>
</metadata>
<metadata for="hyp1">
 <competence-level use="knowledge"/>
</metadata> ... (the same for "hyp2")
<metadata for="step1">
 <difficulty level="fair"/>
 <competence-level use="application"/>
 <relation type="depends_on"><ref xref="def_limit"></relation>
</metadata>
<metadata for="obj1">
 <difficulty level="easy"/>
 <competence-level use="application"/>
 <relation type="depends_on"> <ref xref="def_limit"></relation>
</metadata> ... (the same for "obj2")
```

Fig. 2. Sample Metadata Record for Solution Steps

The described knowledge representation provides the basis for automatically generating faded examples as a type of exercises and for integrating such exercises into a learning material or into a suggestion.

6 (Adaptive) Generation of Faded Examples

Varying the faded places in examples is more interesting and less schematic for the learner. In addition, adapting the actual fading with a specific purpose in mind adds value to faded examples. The adaptivity has at least two dimensions: the choice of the worked example to be faded (e.g., depending on the interests and ability of the learner) and the choice of the gaps to be introduced.

Choice of Fading. The structure of the worked-out example determines the possibilities of fading. The annotation of fadable parts gives rise to a reasoning about the choices depending on the purpose of the faded example.

To start with, for adaptation we consider the student's mastery of the concept and the learning goal level. This information is available in ActiveMath' user model. The rules we use for fading are still prototypical and not tested with students. The reasoning underlying those fading rules includes

[2] For full reference to all metadata extensions made by ActiveMath, see [3].

- if a concept or rule C is in the current learning focus and if the mastery of C is at least medium, then fade one or several parts which require C as a prerequisite
- if low-ability student, then prefer fading steps backwardly in the solution
- if low-ability student, then prefer fading parts *inside* a problem solving step rather than parts *between* steps
- if the goal level is *knowledge*, then fade parts of problem statement, subgoals, known assumptions or used facts
- if the goal level is *comprehension*, then fade reference, justification for a step, explanations, or auxiliary information
- if the goal level is *application*, then fade a step, a condition of a step, or a sub-solution, (sub)goal statements
- if the goal level is meta-cognition, then fade meta-cognitive structure (headlines), or meta-cognitive steps
- start with smaller gaps and enlarge them gradually towards the end of exercising

This collections of fading 'rules' will be enlarged as soon as we gain more experience with students.

Example. Fading the worked solution of the example "$((-1)^n)$ *is divergent*", represented in Figure 1 with metadata record from Figure 2

The first step of the solution is a meta-comment. It contains reasoning about alternatives and can be faded, if the learning goal is meta-cognition.

By fading $|(-1)^n - a| < 1$ in in 'step1' or the complete step the application of the definition of the limit can be trained. As we see from the metadata records in Figure 2, fading 'step1' completely results in a more difficult exercise than fading only parts 'obj1' or obj2'.

The result of the fading procedure is an exercise. Each of the derive steps becomes an interaction in that exercise. This interaction has all the information, needed for fading: the place to be faded is marked, the type of interactive element to be placed instead is provided and a correct answer to be compared to the input of the learner is obtained from the faded part.

7 Conclusion and Future Work

Because of the length restrictions, more examples could not be presented in this paper. They will be described in the technical report summerizing this work. In order to improve learning within the learning environment ActiveMath we build on the empirical investigations of cognitive psychology about learning with faded examples. Interestingly, a truly user-adaptive presentation of faded examples has not been considered in psychological experiments.

We investigated *what* can be faded. For this, we extended the OMDoc representation for mathematical examples and exercises underlying ActiveMath and refined their internal structure. Moreover, we include the possibility to manually determine what to fade because teachers/authors have a lot of experience on how to 'fade' worked examples and they might want to be in command.

As future work we will improve generation by considering the current tutorial goal and other characteristics of the learner. The domain knowledge and the underlying content model including the dependency of concepts will also influence the fading process.

One of the next steps will evaluate the suitability of the rules theoretically and empirically

- test generated exercises with students (e.g., compared with backward fading)
- confront teacher with a student's characteristics and compare his fading with the automatically generated

Moreover, our knowledge representation has to be compared with results of manual fading by tutors.

Related Work. One obvious alternative to present different faded examples to students is to select handcrafted ones. The heuristics for adaptive choice would be very similar to those informing the generation process. However, this approach would require to predefine and store all faded examples and to characterize each one. Moreover, hand-crafting a variety of elaborate faded examples is a very skillful and laborious work.

The natural-language part of example generation has been addressed by [4]. It generates a natural language example solution and then introduces gaps into that solution according to the user model's predictions about the mastery of a rule. These gaps are restricted to propositions corresponding to communicative act of a particular explanation strategy (e.g., Polya-like structuring elements are not planned) not dependent on preferences or goals of the learner. It may be possible to unify this language- based approach with our's that is based on the structure and annotation of worked example representations.

References

1. R.G. Bartle and D.R. Sherbert. *Introduction to Real Analysis.* John Wiley& Sons, New York, 1982.
2. B.S. Bloom, editor. *Taxonomy of educational objectives: The classification of educational goals: Handbook I, cognitive domain.* Longmans, Green, New York, Toronto, 1956.
3. J. Büdenbender, G. Goguadze, P. Libbrecht, E. Melis, and C. Ullrich. Metadata in activemath. Seki Report SR-02-02, Universität des Saarlandes, FB Informatik, 2002.
4. C. Conati and G. Carenini. Generating tailored examples to support learning via self-explanation. In *Seventeenth International Joint Conference on Artificial Intelligence*, 2001.
5. G. Goguadze, E. Melis, C. Ullrich, and P. Cairns. Problems and solutions for markup for mathematical examples and exercises. In A. Asperti, B. Buchberger, and J.H. Davenport, editors, *International Conference on Mathematical Knowledge Management, MKM03*, LNCS 2594, pages 80–93. Springer-Verlag, 2003.

6. M. Kohlhase. OMDoc: Towards an OPENMATH representation of mathematical documents. Seki Report SR-00-02, Fachbereich Informatik, Universität des Saarlandes, 2000.
7. E. Melis, E. Andrès, J. Büdenbender, A. Frischauf, G. Goguadze, P. Libbrecht, M. Pollet, and C. Ullrich. ActiveMath: A generic and adaptive web-based learning environment. *International Journal of Artificial Intelligence in Education*, 1002(4):385–407, 2001.
8. G. Polya. *How to Solve it.* Princeton University Press, Princeton, 1945.
9. R.K.Atkinson, A. Renkl, and M.M. Merrill. Transitioning from studying examples to solving problems: Effects of self-explanation prompts and fading worked-out steps. *Journal of Educational Psychology*, 2003.
10. R. Stark. *Lernen mit Lösungsbeispielen.* Münchener Universitätsschriften, Psychologie und Pädagogik. Hogrefe, Göttingen, Bern, Toronto, Seattle, 1999.
11. J. Sweller and G.A. Cooper. The use of worked examples as a substitute for problem solving in learning algebra. *Cognition and Instruction*, 2:59–89, 1985.
12. J.J.G. van Merrienboer and M.B.M. DeCrook. Strategies for computer-based programming instruction: Program completion vs. program generation. *Journal of Educational Computing Research*, 1992.

A Multi-dimensional Taxonomy for Automating Hinting

Dimitra Tsovaltzi, Armin Fiedler, and Helmut Horacek

Department of Computer Science, Saarland University
P.O. Box 15 11 50, D-66041 Saarbrücken, Germany
{tsovaltzi,afiedler,horacek}@ags.uni-sb.de

Abstract. Hints are an important ingredient of natural language tutorial dialogues. Existing models of hints, however, are limited in capturing their various underlying functions, since hints are typically treated as a unit directly associated with some problem solving script or discourse situation. Putting emphasis on making cognitive functions of hints explicit and allowing for automatic incorporation in a natural dialogue context, we present a multi-dimensional hint taxonomy where each dimension defines a decision point for the associated function. Hint categories are then conceived as convergent points of the dimensions. So far, we have elaborated four dimensions: (1) domain knowledge, (2) inferential role, (3) elicitation status, (4) problem referential perspective. These fine-grained distinctions support the constructive generation of hint specifications from modular knowledge sources.

1 Introduction

Empirical evidence has shown that natural language dialogue capabilities are a crucial factor to making human explanations effective [16]. Moreover, the use of teaching strategies is an important ingredient for intelligent tutoring systems. Such strategies, normally called dialectic or *socratic*, have been demonstrated to be superior to pure explanations, especially regarding their long-term effects [6,18,1]. Consequently, an increasing though still limited number of state-of-the-art tutoring systems use natural-language interaction and automatic teaching strategies, including some notion of hints.

Ms. Lindquist [9], a tutoring system for high-school algebra, uses some domain specific types of questions in elaborate strategies, such as breaking down a problem into simpler parts and elaborating examples. Thereby, the notion of gradually revealing information by rephrasing the question is prominent, which can be considered some sort of hint. The CIRCSIM-Tutor [10], an intelligent tutoring system for blood circulation, applies a taxonomy of hints, relating them to constellations in a planning procedure that solves the given tutorial task. AutoTutor [17] uses curriculum scripts on which the tutoring of computer literacy is based, where hints are associated with each script. AutoTutor also aims at making the student articulate expected answers and does not distinguish between the cognitive function and the dialogue move realisation of hints. The emphasis is put on self-explanation, in the sense of re-articulation, rather than on trying to help the student to actively produce the content of the answer itself. Matsuda and VanLehn [14] research hinting for helping students with solving geometry proof problems. They orient themselves towards tracking the student's mixed directionality,

J.C. Lester et al. (Eds.): ITS 2004, LNCS 3220, pp. 772–781, 2004.

which is characteristic of novices, rather than assisting the student with specific reference to the directionality of a proof. Melis and Ullrich [15] are looking into Polya scenarios in order to extract possible hints. They aim these hints for a proof presentation approach.

On the whole, these models of hints are somehow limited in capturing their various underlying functions explicitly. Putting emphasis on making cognitive functions of hints explicit, we present a multi-dimensional hint taxonomy where each dimension defines a decision point for the associated function. Such hints are part of a tutoring model which promotes actively producing the content of the answer itself, rather than just phrasing it. We, thus, cater for over-emphasising self-explanation, which can be counter-productive to learning as it directs the student's attention to consciously tractable knowledge. The latter can potentially hinter intractable forms of learing taking place, which is considered superior [12].

The approach to automating hints presented here, is also oriented towards integrating hinting in natural language dialogue systems [23]. In the framework of the DIALOG project [2], we are currently investigating tutoring mathematics in a system where domain knowledge, dialogue capabilities, and tutorial phenomena can be clearly identified and intertwined for the automation of tutoring. More specifically, we aim at modelling a socratic teaching strategy, which allows us to manipulate aspects of learning, such as help the student build a deeper understanding of the domain, eliminate cognitive load, promote schema acquisition, and manipulate motivation levels [25,13,24], within natural language dialogue interaction.

The overall goal of the project is (i) to empirically investigate the use of flexible natural language dialogue in tutoring mathematics, and (ii) to develop an prototype system gradually embodying empirical findings. The prototype system will engage in a dialogue in written natural language to help a student construct mathematical proofs. In contrast to most existing tutorial systems, we envision a modular design, making use of the powerful proof system ΩMEGA [19]. This design enables detailed reasoning about the student's action and bears the potential of elaborate system feedback [21].

The structure of the paper is as follows: Section 2 looks at the pedagogical motivations for our amended taxonomy. Section 3 reports on a preliminary evaluation on which our enhanced taxonomy is based. Section 4 presents the taxonomy itself and briefly talks about its different dimensions and classes.

2 Motivation – The Teaching Model

The tutoring framework that we presuppose for our tutoring phase consists of the phases of reading some lesson material that exposes pieces of domain knowledge and getting acquainted with proving skills. The latter phase is an interactive tutoring session, which aims at teaching primarily the application of declarative domain information and correct argumentation for the final proving skill acquisition. Our pedagogical aims include learning maintenance, transferability and motivation. Our means for achieving those cognitive goals build around promoting the construction of cognitive schemata, reducing cognitive load when possible, and doing so in a motivating way for the student.

In more concrete terms, we propose the simulation of a non-goal-specific instructional teaching model, based on studies in the learning sciences. First, we want to combine the benefits of worked examples [20], which we presuppose as a tutoring framework, and problem solving [26], which is our target. Second, we use non-goal-specific problem solving, which better supports problem solving in the training phase, as it takes care of the extra cognitive load imposed by goal-oriented methods. This is necessary as cognitive load interferes with learning [13]. Third, we advocate the use of instructional problem solving and with it the socratic teaching model, which enables us to further reduce any unnecessary cognitive goal, by providing anchoring points to facilitate schema acquisition, take motivational issues into account, and in general to allow for more fine-grained manipulation of the tutoring session towards our overall tutorial goal [25]. Fourth, since the defining characteristic of the socratic teaching method is hinting, we use a kind of hinting that promotes implicit learning with moderate explicit learning in order to guide the student to intractable forms of learning that have been proven beneficial, which the students cannot deliberate themselves [4,12]. *Hinting* itself is defined as a method that aims at encouraging active learning. It can take the form of eliciting information that the student is unable to access without the aid of prompts, or information which they can access but whose relevance they are unaware of with respect to the problem at hand. A hint can also point to an inference that the student is expected to make based on knowledge available to them [11].

The model presented here strikes a balance between (i) how frivolous one can be with non-goal-specific tutoring, which allows students to build their own knowledge on existing structures and form helpful schemata, and (ii) making use of the tutor's expertise without super-imposing a solution.

3 Experiment Results

In order to test the adequacy of the hint categories and other tutoring components, we have conducted a *WOz* experiment [3] with a simulated system [7], thereby also collecting a corpus of tutorial dialogues in the naive set theory domain. In the course of these experiments, a preliminary version of the hinting taxonomy was used, with very limited meta-reasoning hints, and without the functional problem referential perspective. 24 subjects with varying educational background and prior mathematical knowledge ranging from little to fair participated in the experiment. The experiment consisted of three phases: (1) *preparation and pre-test* on paper, (2) *tutoring session* mediated by a *WOz* tool, and (3) *post-test and evaluation questionnaire*, on paper again. During the session, the subjects had to prove three theorems (K and P stand for set complement and power set respectively): (i) $K((A \cup B) \cap (C \cup D)) = (K(A) \cap K(B)) \cup (K(C) \cap K(D))$; (ii) $A \cap B \in P((A \cup C) \cap (B \cup C))$ and (iii) If $A \subseteq K(B)$, then $B \subseteq K(A)$. The interface enabled the subjects to type text and insert mathematical symbols by clicking on buttons. The subjects were instructed to enter steps of a proof rather than a complete proof at once, in order to encourage guiding a dialogue with the system. The tutor-wizard's task was to respond to the student's utterances following a given algorithm, which selected hints from our preliminary hint taxonomy [8].

In the experiments, our pre- and post-tutoring test comparison supported the didactic method, which explained the solution without hinting, as opposed to the socratic condition and a control group that received only minimal feedback on the correctness of the answer. However, through the analysis of our data, we spotted some experimental confounds, which might have been decisive [3]. For instance, the socratic subjects had a late start due to the nature of the strategy, and it was de-motivating to be stopped because of time constraints just as they had started following the hints. In fact, four out of six subjects in the socratic condition who tried to follow hints did indeed improve during tutoring, as evidenced by their attempts. Nonetheless, their performance did not improve in the post-test. We also found that the didactic condition subjects spent significantly more time on the post-test ($t = .82 < 1.825, a = 0.05$). This can exactly derive from parameters like frustration and low motivation. A side-effect of the above confounds was that the didactic condition subjects were tutored on a larger part of every proof. The same subjects also had a significantly higher level at set-off, as evidenced by the pre-test ($t = 0.865 < 1.825, a = 0.05$). This fact might explain their relative higher improvement as depicted in the post-test.

Moreover, despite the results of the test, the analysis of questionnaires filled in by the subjects after the post-test showed that the socratic condition subjects stated that they learned significantly more about set theory than the didactic condition subjects did ($t = -0.99 < 1.825, a = 0.05$). However, the didactic condition subjects stated significantly more that they had fun with the system ($t = 1.0273 < 1.825, a = 0.05$). That might explain why they were motivated to reach a solution (i.e., spend more time on it) in the post-test, which followed immediately after tutoring, and hence performed better. In addition, all subjects of the didactic condition complained about the feedback in open questions about the system, either for not having been given the opportunity to reach the solution themselves, or for not having received more step-by-step feedback, or for having been given too much feedback for their level. All these complaints can be taken care of by the socratic method. On the contrary, most of the socratic condition subjects chose aspects of the feedback as the best attribute of the system (four out of six). In addition, all but one subjects said that they would use the system in a mathematics seminar at university. The subject who would not use the system had one of the best performances among all conditions, and was taught with the didactic method. This subject also explicitly said that they would like a more eliciting feedback.

Such issues allow us to conclude that although the hinting tutoring strategy undoubtedly needs improvements, it can, contingent upon the specific improvements, become better than the didactic method. Extra support for this claim comes from the psychological grounding of hinting as a teaching method (cf. Section 2). The fact that the didactic condition was nonetheless better, led us to search for improvements in the way this strategy was performed. Our objective is to get the best of both worlds.

The most striking characteristic of the didactic method was the fact that the tutor gave accompanying meta-reasoning information every time along with the proof step information. However, he still avoided to giving long explanations, a characteristic of the didactic method, which renders it easier for us to adapt such feedback. Not only can such meta-reasoning reinforce the anchoring points necessary for the creation of a schema, but it also reduces the cognitive load. This probably means for the socratic condition that among the reasons why we did not manage to achieve the goal of self-sufficiency, necessary for the post-test, was the of lack of meta-reasoning hints. Therefore, our major improvement to hinting was to formalise meta-reasoning, deduced from suggestions by our human tutor, our own observations, the didactic condition feedback, and our new in-detail defined teaching model for psychological motivation.

4 The Philosophy and Structure of the Taxonomy

Our hint taxonomy was derived with regard to the function that can be common for different surface realisations. This function is mainly responsible for the educational effect of hints. To capture all the functions of a hint, which ultimately aim at eliciting the relevant inference step in a given situation, we define four dimensions of hints:

1. The ***domain knowledge*** dimension captures the needs of the domain, distinguishing different anchoring points for skill acquisition in problem solving.
2. The ***inferential role*** dimension captures whether the anchoring points are addressed from the inference per se, or through some control on top of it.
3. The ***elicitation status*** dimension distinguishes between the information being elicited and degrees in which it is provided.
4. The ***problem referential perspective*** dimension distinguishes between views on discovering an inference, including conceptual, functional and pragmatic perspectives.

A hint category is described by the combination of the four dimensions. All combinations are potentially useful, even if it is for different teaching models. We shall first describe the four dimensions in more detail and then give example hint categories.

4.1 The *Domain Knowledge* Dimension

In our domain, we defined the inter-relations between mathematical concepts as well as between concepts and inference rules, which are used in proving [22]. Through those definitions, domain information aspects are derived, which constitute instructional anchoring points aiming at promoting schema acquisition [25]. The following anchoring points have been defined:

1. A *domain relation*, that is, a relation between mathematical concepts. We have defined such relations in a mathematical ontology [22]. Examples are antithesis, duality, hypotaxis, specialisation and generalisation – e.g., $\in$ is in *antithesis* to $\notin$.
2. A *domain object*, that is, a mathematical concept, which is in the focus of the current proof step. Examples are the *relevant concept*, that is, the most relevant concept in the premises or the conclusion of the current proof step; the *hypotactical concept*, that is, a concept used in the definition of the relevant concept; or the *primitive concept*, that is, a concept whose definition is independent of other concepts.
3. The *inference rule* that justifies the current proof step. Examples are theorems and lemmata, but also entire proof methods, such as proof by contradiction.
4. The *substitution* needed to apply the inference, that is, for example, the values to which the variables of a theorem must be assigned during its application.
5. The *proof step* itself, that is, the premises, conclusion and applied inference rule.

Note that the anchoring points are ordered with respect to the amount of information they reveal. This ordering relation, which we call *subordination*, also captures the forward-looking proving technique typically used by experts [5].

4.2 The *Inferential Role* Dimension

This dimension captures, based on the domain, whether the anchoring points are addressed from the perspective of their physical appearance in the formal proof or from some higher perspective, making a distinction between *Performable steps* and *Meta-reasoning*. The latter consists of everything that explains the performable step, but cannot be found in the formal proof, building the motivation for the anchoring points.

The meta-reasoning could be abstracted from performable step hints in the form of schemata built by the student and suiting their cognitive state. If the student is not capable of this abstraction, meta-reasoning hints help him do so by motivating the performable step anchoring points. This way some cognitive load is elevated, the student is further motivated and the anchoring points, which hints point to anyway, are reinforced. Active meta-reasoning hints are, pedagogically speaking, appropriate for students who already have some schema, but get stuck in applying it, as our experiments (see Section 3) have shown. Meta-reasoning subclasses capture the classes' subordination in so far as they motivate the domain hints, which themselves follow it. Furthermore, the passive meta-reasoning hints (see the elicitation status), subsume the corresponding passive performable step information hints, that is, they include their information.

4.3 The *Elicitation Status* Dimension

This dimension distinguishes between the active and passive function of hints. The difference lies in the way the information to which the tutor wants to refer is approached. The *active* function of hints looks forward and seeks to help the student in accessing a further bit of information, by means of *eliciting*, that will bring them closer to the solution. The student has to think of and produce the answer that is hinted at. The *passive* function of hints refers to the small piece of information that is provided each time in order to bring the student closer to some answer. The tutor *gives away* some information, which they might have previously tried to elicit without success. Note, however, that in order to elicit some piece of information, another piece of information has to be given away. Therefore, a passive hint of one class of the proof step information dimension is also an active hint of the subordinate class. For example, a hint that gives away the relevant concept of some proof step also elicits the inference rule used in that step.

4.4 The *Problem Referential Perspective* Dimension

This dimension distinguishes between modes of referring to the anchoring points, according to the context of the tutorial session, differentiating between *conceptual*, *functional* and *pragmatic* hints. Conceptual hints directly refer to domain anchoring points, that is, they make use of mathematical concepts or reasoning.

The *functional* view, which emphasizes the effect imposed on the conclusion of an inference under consideration. In our domain, a conceptual view encompasses axioms which relate a central property of a mathematical concept to some assertion other than a purely taxonomic relation to a more general or more specific concept. Depending on the direction of the implication, that axiom expresses a condition for the property of the mathematical concept under consideration, or a consequence. For the functional view, the applicability of some descriptions is tested by comparing structural properties of the premise and conclusion of an inference rule: the number of operators, the number of parentheses, and the appearance of a variable.

Pragmatic hints refer to pragmatic aspects, as opposed to the reflection of the analytic, deductive way of thinking of the conceptual function and the structural approach of functional hints. Such hints increase the motivation of the student by allowing them to provide as much of the information as they are capable of. They thus take the cognitive state of the student into account. In particular, if the student has an understanding of the conceptual and functional aspect, they only need this kind of pragmatic information to move on. We distinguish between three classes of pragmatic hints:

1. *Speak-to-answer* hints refer to the preceding answer of the student. They, for example, indicate that some elements of a list are missing, narrow down possible choices, or elicit a discrepancy between the student's answer and the expected answer.
2. *Point-to-information* hints refer the student to some information given previously, either during the dialogue or in the lesson material.
3. *Take-for-granted* hints ask the students to accept some information without further explanation, for example, because that would require to delve into another mathematical topic, which would shift the focus of the session to its detriment. This is motivated by *local axiomatics* [26], a prominent notion in teaching mathematics.

4.5 Example Hint Categories

On the whole, the elicitation status dimension is the only one that most other approaches capture explicitly, through designing sets of related hints with increasing degrees of precision in revealing required information. Moreover, the three dimensions domain knowledge, inferential role, and problem referential perspective, are typically combined into a unique whole.

We now determine hint categories in terms of the four dimensions. We elucidate the combinatory operation of the four dimensions by giving example hint categories.

The first example we consider is an active conceptual inference-rule performable-step hint, which elicits the inference rule used in the proof step. This can be done by giving away the relevant concept of the proof step: "You need to make use of P"[1], where P is the relevant concept. The passive counterpart would give away the inference rule: "You need to apply the definition of P.". An equivalent example of an active functional inference-rule performable-step hint would be: "Which variable can you eliminate here?". Its passive counterpart would be: "You have to eliminate P".

As a second example, consider an active conceptual inference-rule meta-reasoning hint, which leads the student through a way of choosing with reference to the concrete anchoring points. Such a hint produced by our human tutor is: "Think of a theorem or lemma which you can apply and involves P and $\subseteq$", where P is the relevant concept and $\subseteq$ the hypotactical concept. If the student already knows the general technique to be applied, e.g. elimination, but they still do not know which specific inference rule can

[1] Realisation examples come from the corpus collected in the WOz experiments, unless otherwise stated.

help them realise this, the latter only needs to be elicited. A constructed example of the active conceptual hint appropriate in this case is: "Can you think of a theorem or lemma that would help you eliminate P?".

The proof-step meta-reasoning hints address the step as a whole. However, because of their overview nature their production makes sense at the beginning of the hinting session to motivate the whole step. This way, these hint capture a hermeneutic process formalised in the actual hinting algorithm. That is, the hinting session for a step starts with a proof-step meta-reasoning hint and finishes with a proof-step performable-step hint. A constructed active conceptual realisation is: "Do you have an idea where you can start attacking this problem?". Or it may recapitulate the meta-reasoning of the step. Other proof-step meta-reasoning hints deal with techniques (methodology) and technique-related concepts (e.g., premise, conclusion) in the domain. To name a constructed example, the passive conceptual hint of this sort could be realised as: "Your aim is to try to manipulate the given expression in order to reach the conclusion."

Let us now turn our attention to some pragmatic hints as well. Consider the situation, where the student has mentioned two out of three properties of the definition that must be applied and the one needed is missing. In this case, different forms of an active speak-to-answer inference-rule proof-step hint can be used, according to the specific needs of the hinting session. If the properties in the definition are ordered, a possible realisation of the hint would be: “You missed the second property.” If the properties are unordered, the hint could be realised simply as: “And?”. When the student gives an almost correct answer, our tutor often elicited the discrepancy to the correct answer by a plain but very helpful “Really?”. Another example for a pragmatic hint is an active point-to-information hint where the student is conferred to the lesson material: “You didn’t use the de Morgen rule correctly. Please check once again your accompanying material.” The pedagogical motivation of this pragmatic aspect is that the student is pointed to consulting the available material better, while being at the same time directed to the piece of information currently needed for the task, which addresses the anchoring points. When it appears that the student cannot be helped by tutoring because they have not read the study material carefully enough, hint would point the student to the lesson in general: “Go back and read the material again.”

So far, we have only seen combinations of the four dimensions which are motivated by our teaching model. However, combinations like active conceptual domain-relation performable-step hint, would serve the specific purpose of explicitely teaching such relations in the form of declarative knowledge, which is not among our tutoring goals. Such hints would elicit the relation between two mathematical objects in the proof step (e.g., the duality between $\subseteq$ and $\supseteq$). The passive counterpart, in contrast, can be used to elicit, for example, the relevant concept. If the student mentioned $\subseteq$ instead of $\supseteq$ a hint could be formulated “Not really $\subseteq$, but something closely related.”

5 Conclusions and Future Work

In this paper, we have motivated and presented a multi-dimensional hinting taxonomy, distinguishing explicitly between various cognitive functions of hints. This taxonomy is used in an adaptive hinting algorithm based on session modelling, which aim at dynamically producing hints that fit the needs of the student with regard to the particular proof and the hinting situation. Hinting situations are defined based on the values of information fields, which are pedagogically relevant and relate to the dialogue context as well as to the more specific tutoring status.

A significant portion of the taxonomy has been tested in a *WOz* experiment, which has inspired us to incorporate improvements in the taxonomy. In terms of evaluating the improved taxonomy and algorithm in our next phase of experiments, particular care will be taken of issues like the sufficient preparation of subjects and of assigning them the right level of tasks. Moreover, we want to evaluate the effectivity over time of our modelled teaching method, taking into account how well declarative and procedural knowledge have improved. This presupposes that the possibility of fatigue is minimised from the experiment design and that the post-test is carefully chosen to test the results of the aimed qualifications.

References

1. Kevin D. Ashley, Ravi Desai, and John M. Levine. Teaching case-based argumentation concpets using dialoectic arguments vs. didactic explanations. In *Proceedings of the 6th International Conference on Intelligent Tutoring Systems*, pages 585–595, 2002.
2. Chris Benzmüller, Armin Fiedler, Malte Gabsdil, Helmut Horacek, Ivana Kruijff-Korbayová, Manfred Pinkal, Jörg Siekmann, Dimitra Tsovaltzi, Bao Quoc Vo, and Magdalena Wolska. Tutorial dialogs on mathematical proofs. In *Proceedings of the IJCAI Workshop on Knowledge Representation and Automated Reasoning for E-Learning Systems*, pages 12–22, Acapulco, 2003.
3. Chris Benzmüller, Armin Fiedler, Malte Gabsdil, Helmut Horacek, Ivana Kruijff-Korbayová, Manfred Pinkal, Jörg Siekmann, Dimitra Tsovaltzi, Bao Quoc Vo, and Magdalena Wolska. A Wizard-of-Oz experiment for tutorial dialogues in mathematics. In *aied03 Supplementary Proceedings, Workshop on Advanced Technologies for Mathematics Education*, pages 471–481, Sidney, Australia, 2003.
4. D. Berry and D. Broadbent. On the relationship between task performance and the associated verbalizable knowledge. *Quarterly Journal of Experimental Psychology*, 36(A):209–231, 1984.
5. M. T. H. Chi, R. Glaser, and E. Rees. Expertise in problem solving. *Advances in the Psychology of Human Intelligence*, pages 7–75, 1982.
6. Michelene T. H. Chi, Nicholas de Leeuw, Mei-Hung Chiu, and Christian Lavancher. Eliciting self-explanation improves understanding. *Cognitive Science*, 18:439–477, 1994.
7. Armin Fiedler, Malte Gabsdil, and Helmut Horacek. A Tool for Supporting Progressive Refinement of Wizard-of-Oz Experiments in Natural Language. In *Intelligent Tutoring Systems — 6th International Conference, ITS 2002*, 2004. In print.
8. Armin Fiedler and Dimitra Tsovaltzi. Automating hinting in mathematical tutorial dialogue. In *Proceedings of the EACL-03 Workshop on Dialogue Systems: Interaction, Adaptation and Styles of Management*, pages 45–52, Budapest, 2003.
9. Neil T. Heffernan and Kenneth R. Koedinger. Building a 3rd generation ITS for symbolization: Adding a tutorial model with multiple tutorial strategies. In *Proceedings of the ITS 2000 Workshop on Algebra Learning*, Montréal, Canada, 2000.
10. Gregory Hume, Joel Michael, Allen Rovick, and Martha Evens. Student responses and follow up tutorial tactics in an ITS. In *Proceedings of the 9th Florida Artificial Intelligence Research Symposium*, pages 168–172, Key West, FL, 1996.

11. Gregory D. Hume, Joel A. Michael, Rovick A. Allen, and Martha W. Evens. Hinting as a tactic in one-on-one tutoring. *Journal of the Learning Sciences*, 5(1):23–47, 1996.
12. Pawel Lewicki, Thomas Hill, and Maria Czyzewska. Nonconscious acquisition of information. *Journal of American Psychologist*, 47:796–801, 1992.
13. Eng Leong Lim and Dennis W. Moore. Problem solving in geometry: Comparing the effects of non-goal specific instruction and conventional worked examples. *Journal of Educational Psychology*, 22(5):591–612, 2002.
14. Noboru Matsuda and Kurt VanLehn. Modelling hinting strategies for geometry theorem proving. In *Proceedings of the 9th International Conference on User Modeling*, Pittsburgh, PA, 2003.
15. Erica Melis and Carsten Ullrich. How to Teach it - Polya-Inspired Scenarios In ActiveMath. In *Proceedings of*, pages 141–147, Biarritz, France, 2003.
16. Johanna Moore. What makes human explanations effective? In *Proceedings of the Fifteenth Annual Meeting of the Cognitive Science Society*, Hillsdale, NJ, 1993.
17. Natalie K. Person, Arthur C. Graesser, Derek Harter, Eric Mathews, and the Tutoring Research Group. Dialog move generation and conversation management in AutoTutor. In Carolyn Penstein Rosé and Reva Freedman, editors, *Building Dialog Systems for Tutorial Applications—Papers from the AAAI Fall Symposium*, pages 45–51, North Falmouth, MA, 2000. AAAI press.
18. Carolyn P. Rosé, Johanna D. Moore, Kurt VanLehn, and David Allbritton. A comparative evaluation of socratic versus didactic tutoring. In Johanna Moore and Keith Stenning, editors, *Proceedings 23rd Annual Conference of the Cognitive Science Society*, University of Edinburgh, Scotland, UK, 2001.
19. Jörg Siekmann, Christoph Benzmüller, Vladimir Brezhnev, Lassaad Cheikhrouhou, Armin Fiedler, Andreas Franke, Helmut Horacek, Michael Kohlhase, Andreas Meier, Erica Melis, Markus Moschner, Immanuel Normann, Martin Pollet, Volker Sorge, Carsten Ullrich, Claus-Peter Wirth, and Jürgen Zimmer. Proof development with ΩMEGA. In Andrei Voronkov, editor, *Automated Deduction — CADE-18*, number 2392 in LNAI, pages 144–149. Springer Verlag, 2002.
20. J. Sweller. Cognitive technology: Some procedures for facilitating learning and problem solving in mahtematics and science. *Journal Educational Psychology*, 81:457–466, 1989.
21. Dimitra Tsovaltzi and Armin Fiedler. An approach to facilitating reflection in a mathematics tutoring system. In *aied03 Supplementary Proceedings, Workshop on Learner Modelling for Reflection*, pages 278–287, Sydney, Australia, 2003.
22. Dimitra Tsovaltzi and Armin Fiedler. Enhancement and use of a mathematical ontology in a tutorial dialogue system. In *Proceedings of the IJCAI Workshop on Knowledge and Reasoning in Practical Dialogue Systems*, pages 19–28, Acapulco, Mexico, 2003.
23. Dimitra Tsovaltzi and Elena Karagjosova. A dialogue move taxonomy for tutorial dialogues. In *Proceedings of 5th SIGdial Workshop on Discourse and Dialogue*, Boston, USA, 2004. In print.
24. B Weiner. *Human Motivation: metaphor, theories, and research.* Sage Publications Inc., 1992.
25. Brent Wilson and Peggy Cole. Cognitive teaching models. In D.H. Jonassen, editor, *Handbook of Research for educational communications and technology*. MacMillan, 1996.
26. H. Wu. What is so difficult about the preparation of mathematics teachers. In National Summit on the Mathematical Education of Teachers: Meeting the Demand for High Quality Mathematics Education in America, November 2001.

Inferring Unobservable Learning Variables from Students' Help Seeking Behavior

Ivon Arroyo[1], Tom Murray[1], Beverly P. Woolf[1], and Carole Beal[2]

[1] Computer Science Department, University of Massachusetts Amherst
{ivon, tmurray, bev}@cs.umass.edu
[2] Information Sciences Institute, University of Southern California
cbeal@isi.edu

Abstract. Results of an evaluation of students' attitudes and their relationship to student behaviors within a tutoring system are presented. Starting from a correlation analysis that integrates survey-collected student attitudes, learning variables, and behaviors while using the tutor, we constructed a Bayesian Network that infers attitudes and perceptions towards help and the tutoring system.

1 Introduction

One of the main components of an interactive learning environment (ILE) is the help provided during problem solving. Some studies have found a link between students' help seeking and learning, suggesting that higher help seeking behaviors result in higher learning (Wood&Wood, 1999; Renkl, 2002). However, there is growing evidence that students may have non-optimal help seeking behaviors, and that they seek and respond to help depending on student characteristics, motivation, attitudes, beliefs, gender (Aleven, 2003; Ryan&Pintrich, 1997; Arroyo, 2001). There are yet many questions to answer in relation to suboptimal use of help in tutoring systems, such as: 1) How do different attitudes towards help and beliefs about the system get expressed in actual help seeking behavior? 2) Can attitudes be diagnosed from students' behavior with the tutoring system? 4) If non-productive attitudes, goals and beliefs can be detected while using the system, what are possible actions that can be taken to encourage positive learning attitudes? This paper begins to explore these questions by showing the results of a quantitative analysis of the presence and strength of these links, and our work towards building a Bayesian Network that diagnoses attitudes from behaviors, with the final goal of building tutoring systems that are responsive and adaptable to students' needs.

2 Methodology

The tutoring system used was Wayang Outpost, a geometry tutor that provides multimedia web-based instruction. If the student requests help, step-by-step guidance is provided. The hints provided in Wayang Outpost therefore resemble what a human teacher might provide when explaining a solution to a student, e.g., by drawing, pointing, highlighting critical parts of geometry figures, and talking. Wayang was used in October 2003 by 150 students (15–18 year olds) from two high schools in Massachusetts. Students were

J.C. Lester et al. (Eds.): ITS 2004, LNCS 3220, pp. 782–784, 2004.

provided headphones, and used the tutor for about 2 hours. After using the tutor, students filled out a survey about their perceptions of the system, and attitudes towards help and the system. Results of a correlation analysis of multiple student variables are shown in figure 1.

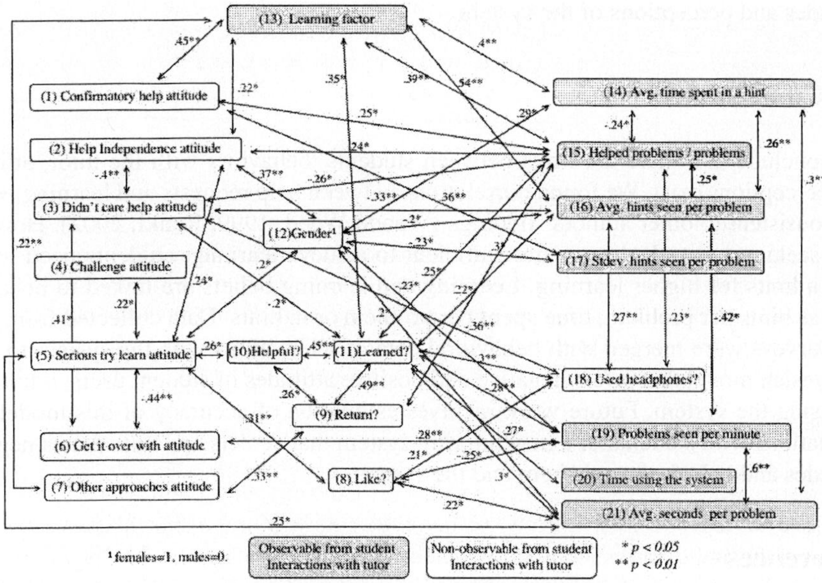

Fig. 1. Correlations among attitudes, perceptions and student behaviors in the tutor

Variables on the left of figure 1 are survey questions about attitudes, those on the right are obtained from log files of students' use of the system. Two learning measures were considered. One of them is students' perception of how much they learned (*Learned?*), collected from surveys. The second one is a *'Learning Factor'* that describes how students decrease their need for help in subsequent problems during the tutoring session. Performance at each problem is defined as the 'expected' number of requested hints for this problem (for all subjects) minus the help requests made by the student at the problem, divided by the expected number of requested hints for the problem by the current student. For instance, if students on average tended to ask for 2 hints in a problem before answering it correctly, and the current student requested 3 hints, performance was 50% worse than expected, and thus performance is -0.5. Ideally, students would perform better as tutoring progresses, so these values should increase with time. The average difference of performance between pairs of subsequent problems ($\text{performance}_t - \text{performance}_{t-1}$) in the whole tutoring session becomes a measure of how students' need for help fades away before choosing a correct answer. This measure of learning is higher when students learn more.

From the correlation graph in figure 3, a directed acyclic graph was created by: 1) eliminating the links among observable variables; 2) giving a single direction to the links from non-observable to observable variables; 3) for links between non-observable variables, unidirectional links were created; 4) eliminating or changing the direction of links that create cycles. The resulting DAG was turned into a Bayesian Network by: 1) discretizing variables; 2) creating conditional probability tables from those new discrete variables. Preliminary analysis suggest that feeding this BBN built from data with different values for the observable variables result in the diagnosis of different attitudes and perceptions of the system.

3 Conclusions

We conclude that there are links between students' behaviors with the tutor, attitudes and perceptions exist. We found correlations between help requests and learning, which are consistent to other authors' findings (Wood&Wood, 1999; Renkl, 2002). However, help seeking by itself does is not sufficient to achieve learning: students need to stay within hints for higher learning. Learning and learning beliefs are linked to behaviors such as hints per problem, time spent per problem or in hints. Data collected from post-test surveys were merged with behavioral data of interactions with the system to build a Bayesian model that infers negative and positive attitudes of student users, while they are using the system. Future work involves estimation of accuracy of this model, and evaluations with students of a new tutoring system that detects and remediates negative attitudes and beliefs towards help and the system.

References

Aleven, V., Stahl, E., Schworm, S., Fischer, F., & Wallace R. (2003) Help Seeking and Help Design in Interactive Learning Environments Review of Educational Research.

Arroyo, I., Beck, J. E., Beal, C. R., Rachel E. Wing, Woolf, B. P. (2001) Analyzing students' response to help provision in an elementary mathematics Intelligent Tutoring System. Help Provision and Help Seeking in Interactive Learning Environments Workshop. Tenth International Conference on Artificial Intelligence in Education.

Renkl, A., & Atkinson, R. K. (2002). Learning from examples: Fostering selfexplanations in computer-based learning environments. Interactive Learning Environments, 10, 105–119.

Ryan, A. & Pintrich,P (1997) Should I ask for help? The role of motivation and attitudes in adolescents' help-seeking in math class. Journal of Educational Psychology, 89, 1–13

Wood, H.; Wood, D. (1999). Help seeking, learning and contingent tutoring. Computers & Education, 33(2-3):153–169.

The Social Role of Technical Personnel in the Deployment of Intelligent Tutoring Systems

Ryan Shaun Baker, Angela Z. Wagner, Albert T. Corbett, and Kenneth R. Koedinger

Human-Computer Interaction Institute, Carnegie Mellon University,
5000 Forbes Avenue, Pittsburgh, PA, 15217, USA
{rsbaker, awagner, corbett, koedinger}@cmu.edu

Abstract. We present a model – developed using Contextual Inquiry – of how prototype intelligent tutors are deployed into classrooms, focusing on how field technical personnel can serve as vital conduits for information and negotiation between ITS researchers and school personnel such as teachers and principals.

1 Introduction

In recent years, Intelligent Tutoring Systems (ITSs) have emerged from the research laboratory and pilot research classrooms into widespread use [2]. Before one of our laboratory's ITSs reaches a point where it is ready for large-scale distribution, it goes through multiple cycles of iterative development in research classrooms. In the first stage of tutor development, this process is supported by a teacher who both teaches the tutor class and participates in its design. In a second stage, the tutoring curriculum is deployed from the teacher-designer's classroom to further research classrooms, and refined based on feedback and data from those classrooms. Finally, a polished tutoring curriculum is disseminated in collaboration with our commercial partner, Carnegie Learning Inc. This process requires considerable collaboration and cooperation across several years from individuals at partner schools, from principals and assistant superintendents, to teachers, to school technical staff.

In this paper, we briefly discuss how the deployment of prototype ITSs to research classrooms is facilitated by the creation of working and social relationships between school personnel and project technical personnel. We discuss the role played by a member of our research laboratory, "Rose" (a pseudonym) , whose job was first conceived as being primarily technical -- including tasks such as writing tutor problems, testing tutoring software, installing tutoring software on school machines (in collaboration with school technical staff), and developing workarounds for bugs. We studied Rose's work practices and collaborative relationships by conducting a set of retrospective contextual inquiries [1], an interview technique based on developing understanding of how a participant understands his or her own process.

J.C. Lester et al. (Eds.): ITS 2004, LNCS 3220, pp. 785–787, 2004.

2 An Important Relationship in Intelligent Tutoring Projects

Rose plays a central role in the collaboration between our laboratory and the schools we work with. In order to discuss this, we introduce a model of (a subset of) the relationships important to Intelligent Tutor projects, building off of earlier models of these roles and relationships [4,5]. Prior models have envisioned project technical staff as liaisons between project programmers, school administrators, and school facilities [5]; Rose, however, primarily acts as a liaison to school teachers. By filling this alternate role, shown in Figure 1, Rose is not only more effective at installing and maintaining our software at the schools, but has also been able to assist our project in many other ways. She has been a key conduit for essential information between the schools and our lab, helping to keep the relationship between the two organizations smooth and mutually beneficial. She has also facilitated negotiations about new studies for many members of research group, and has assisted in scheduling those studies.

Her "primary" role as a technical liaison enables her to fill this role. In particular, she has been able to gain the advantages of proximity to teachers in ways that other members of our research lab cannot, because there are few circumstances when it is normal for other project researchers to be at a school. Rose is frequently at one of our partner schools, and thus has many opportunities to briefly speak with a teacher between (or during) classes – enabling Rose to propose ideas, make requests, and learn about concerns. These conversations of opportunity provide the setting for conducting a considerable amount of important business, in a way that is casual and comfortable for both Rose and the teacher – especially when working with teachers who are not easily reached by phone or email. Such informal contact has been identified by organizational researchers as a crucial element in the coordination between teams [3].

Rose's presence in schools also allows information to informally travel in the opposite direction -- from teachers to programmers and researchers. Teachers often do not feel comfortable telling lab researchers that a tutor lesson is difficult for students to understand or has a number of bugs – but the teachers are comfortable telling Rose about these issues, because she did not write the software or the lesson. Hence, she is

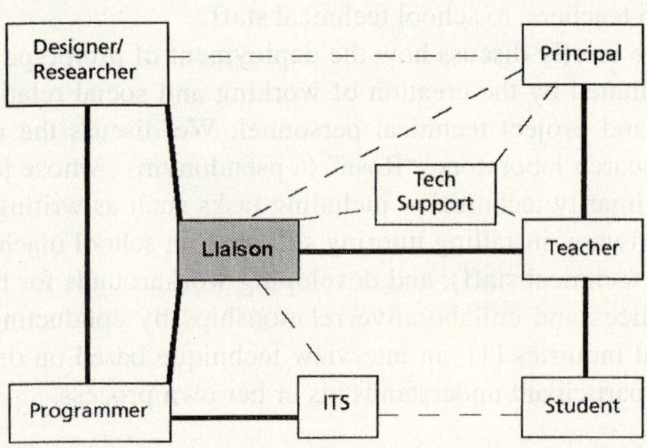

Fig. 1. The primary roles in our project, according to our contextual inquiry

able to commiserate with the teachers about the problem and then bring the information back to the programmer or researcher who can fix the problem.

Rose's relationships with teachers have also aided her in the technical part of her job. Interviews with staff at other intelligent tutoring projects suggest that it is common for project staff to have difficulty obtaining cooperation from school technical staff (the "techs"). Getting the tutor software working is a low priority for the techs -- since the tutor software is supplied and supported by our laboratory, there is simultaneously comparatively little reward for the techs if the tutor software is working properly, and a natural and credible scapegoat (our programmers) if it is working poorly. By contrast, teachers have a strong interest in getting the software to work, since if it fails to work, it is very disruptive to their classes. Hence, Rose enlists teacher assistance in getting cooperation from the techs.

3 Conclusions

Our findings suggest that even in an educational project built around technology, the human relationships supporting that technology are essential to the project's success. Rose's example shows a way to enhance the communication between large-scale educational projects and partner school, by placing an individual in regular and mutually beneficial contact with teachers -- creating an informal conduit for negotiation, communication, and problem-solving. Our wider research (discussed in a CMU technical report available off of the first author's website) suggests that other individuals can also play a similar role – but however it is accomplished, educational technology projects will benefit from having an individual on their team who serves as a bridge to partner schools.

As a final note, we would like to thank Jack Mostow, Laura Dabbish, Shelley Evenson, John Graham, and Kurt vanLehn for helpful suggestions and feedback.

References

1. Beyer, H., Holtzblatt, K. Contextual Design: Defining Customer-Centered Systems. London, UK: Academic Press. (1998)
2. Corbett, A.T., Koedinger, K.R., & Hadley, W. S. Cognitive Tutors: From the research classroom to all classrooms. In P. Goodman (Ed.), Technology enhanced learning: Opportunities for change. Mahwah, NJ : Lawrence Erlbaum Associates (2001) 235-263
3. Kraut, R.E., Fish, R., Root, R., Chalafonte, B. Informal communication in organizations: Form, function, and technology. In S. Okamp & S. Spacapan (Eds.), Human Reactions to technology: Claremont symposium on applied social psychology. Beverly Hills, CA: Sage Publications. (1990) 145-199
4. Schofield, J.W. Computers and Classroom Culture. Cambridge, UK: Cambridge University Press. (1995)
5. Steuck, K., Meyer, T.N., Kretschmer, M. Implementing Intelligent Learning Technologies in Real Settings. Artificial Intelligence in Education Amsterdam, NL: IOS Press. (2001) 598-600.

Intelligent Tools for Cooperative Learning in the Internet

Flávia de Almeida Barros[1], Fábio Paraguaçu[2], André Neves[1], and Cleide Jane Costa[3]

[1]Universidade Federal de Pernambuco
Centro de Informática
fab@cin.ufpe.br, andreneves@projetovirtus.com.br
[2]Universidade Federal de Alagoas
Departamento de Tecnologia da Informação
Maceió – AL-Brazil
fabioparagua2000@yahoo.com.br
[3]SEUNE
Av. Dom. Antonio Brandão, 204-Maceió-Alagoas-Brazil
cleidejane@yahoo.com.br

Abstract. The FIACI project aimed to develop a methodology for the construction of software tools to give support to cooperative learning in the Internet. These tools are based on the Intelligent Agents and objects technology, and they are being applied in the construction of virtual learning environments based on the Web. These environments can be used as a complement to ordinary classes as well as in distance learning. We present here a general description of the project, as well as the main obtained results.

1 Introduction

The growth of the Internet in the past decade, together with the emergence of the social-interactive-constructivism pedagogical approaches [5], has posed a new demand for computational tools capable of supporting cooperation during computer mediated learning processes. Some attempts have been made by the Computer Science community to build such tools. However, in general, the systems available so far are either incomplete regarding pedagogical needs, or they offer domain-dependent solutions. In this sense, the Internet has emerged as a promising media to overcome these problems, offering information regarding the most varied domains (subjects), as well as synchronous and asynchronous communication via the so-called Virtual Learning Environments (VLEs) [1].

In this light, we are developing the FIACI project based on the experience acquired in the construction of tools that follow the cooperative pedagogical approach. These tools are being applied to the construction of virtual learning environments based on the Web. The VLEs can be used as a complement to ordinary classes as well as in distance learning.

We present here a general description of the FIACI project, as well as the main obtained results. Section 2 gives a general description of the project. Section 3 presents the development phases of our research work, as well as results obtained so far. Finally, we have the conclusions in the section 4.

J.C. Lester et al. (Eds.): ITS 2004, LNCS 3220, pp. 788–790, 2004.

2 Project's Overview

The FIACI project falls within the cooperative model, following the social-interactive-constructivism pedagogical approaches [5], which (we believe) are the most appropriated to lead learning (virtual or real) groups. Our central aim was to provide software tools to give support to the construction of *cooperative virtual learning environments* based on the Web. As we have said before, these VLEs can be used as a complement to ordinary classes as well as in distance learning.

This project was developed by a consortium of three groups, and two different kinds of VLEs were investigated in a collaborative fashion. The group SIANALCO concentrated on the development of VLEs to teach children between 6 and 7 years old how to read, which was already their main research interest. Their starting point was the SIANALCO environment (*Sistema de Análise da Alfabetização Colaborativa*) [2], [3]. The group Virtus, on the other hand, focused on VLEs for mature students, having as a starting point the VIRTUS project [1].

Both systems were used in the initial fieldwork phase, reaching some common conclusions. In the following, they were modified to incorporate some features that would help them to provide for cooperative VLEs: (1) *communication* between teachers and students as well as between students; (2) *easiness* of use of the environment for non-expert users in Computer Science; and (3) students' individual *monitoring* within the environment. The main inovation of this FIACI methodology is its empirical nature through the realisation of three phases: intitial design, experimentation, and changes and experimentation. In what follows, we describe the tools development and obtained results.

3 Tool's Development and Obtained Results

This section presents the current level of development of our tool, as well as the results obtained with the initial experiments.

3.1 Communication Agents

The SIANALCO group worked with the intermediate representation to help and communicate with the children in literacy process. The VIRTUS group worked with chaterboot PIXEL to communication in portuguese language with the learner.

3.2 Assistance Agents

The agents in this class are been built by both groups.

- *Editor*:The SIANALCO group invested on the implementation of a tool to construct the VLE's Glossary based on a colaborative multiuser environment to build conceptual graphs [4]. *Chatterbot*: PIXEL can also be used here. The only difference is that it must consult the answer box related to the environment's use.

3.3 Monitoring Agents

The agents in this class are also been built by both groups.

- *Presenter*: so far, this agent has been implemented only for the literacy VLE. It is responsible for showing the interactive stories (course material) to the students. *Librarian*: this agent has been implemented by the group VIRTUS. It searches the Web for pages with bibliography citations and/or tutorials related to the course domain. *Monitor*: two versions of this agent are needed, due to the environments' implementation differences. As it stands, the VIRTUS just keeps the logs of each student's session and creates individual reports. In the SIANALCO environment, this agent also offers some help to the students in the resolution of proposed exercises. *Case-based*: this agent is particular to the literacy VLEs. It presents to the students tasks which are similar to the one he/she has executed wrongly, as well as fragments of stories related to the one being learned.

4 Final Remarks

We presented here the FIACI project, whose main aim is to develop a methodology for the construction of software tools to give support to cooperative learning on the Internet, following the social-interactive-constructivism pedagogical approaches. The Agents technology was used, since it offers the needed functionalities for such kind of VLE.

As a result, teachers will be able to easily build new VLEs or to update existing ones, and students will work within easy-to-use VLEs which facilitate their cooperation and the learning process as a whole.

References

1. Neves, A.M.M. "Ambientes Virtuais de Estudo Cooperativo". Master Dissertation, Universidade Federal de Pernambuco. 1999.
2. Paraguaçu, F. & Jurema, A. "Literacy in a Social Learning Environment (SLE): collaborating with cognitive tools". *X Simpósio Brasileiro de Informática na Educação (SBIE'1999)*. pp. 318-324. Curitiba, PR. Editora SBC. 1999.
3. Paraguaçu, F. & Costa, C. "Em direção a novas tecnologias colaborativas para alfabetizar crianças em idade escolar". *XI Simpósio Brasileiro de Informática na Educação (SBIE'2000)* pp. 148-153. Editora SBC. 2000.
4. Paraguaçu, F., Prata, D. & Reis, A. "A Collaborative Environment for Visual Representation of the Knowledge on the Web – VEDA". *ED-MEDIA Word Conference on Educational Multimedia, Hypermedia & Telecommunications*. Pp. 324-325. Tempere, Finlândia, Editora AACE. 2001.
5. Vygotsky LS. "The Genesis of Higher Mental Functions". In J. V. Wertsch (ed.) *The concept of activity in Soviet Psychology*. Armonk: Sharp. 1981.

A Plug-in Based Adaptive System: SAAW

Leônidas de Oliveira Brandão, Seiji Isotani, and Janine Gomes Moura

Institute of Mathematics and Statistics, University of São Paulo, Postfach 66.281,
05315-970 São Paulo, Brazil
{leo, isotani, janine}@ime.usp.br

Abstract. The expansion of the *World Wide Web* and the use of computers in education have increased the demand for *Web* courses and, consequently, the need for systems that simplify their production and reuse. Such systems must provide means to show the contents in an individualized and dynamic way, which requires they present flexibility and interactivity as main characteristics. Nowadays, *Adaptive Hypermedia Systems* (AHS) have been released to support these characteristics. However, most of them do not allow the extension or modification of their resources. In this work we present the *SAAW*, a prototype of an AHS that allows the insertion/removal of plug-ins, among them the *iGeom*, an application for geometry learning, that makes it more interactive and dynamical.

1 Introduction

Despite the importance of the mathematics and geometry in the engineering and computer sciences, there are a lot of difficulties in developing mathematical and geometric abilities among the university students, as well as among high school students. In this work we present a prototype of such an AHS, *SAAW* (*Adaptive System for Learning on the Web*). We also present a plug-in for geometry, *iGeom - Interactive Geometry for Internet*. The *iGeom* is a complete multi-plataform dynamic geometry software (*DGS*), that we are developing since 2000. *iGeom* can be freely downloaded from *http://www.matematica.br/igeom*. The *SAAW* isn't available since it is in its first test.

2 The Architecture (SAAW)

The SAAW is an AHS whose architecture is component-based and it is divided in two main sections: the web manager system and the learning enviromment (i.e., plug-in). Thus, plug-ins can be added or removed depending on the target subject. Other AHS have a component-based architecture, for example [2], [3] and [4], but ours emphasizes the learning enviromment. The plug-in is related with the subject domain and must increase the interactivity with the user.

The plug-ins reside in the client and they can be used in automatic student evaluation. This results in a reduction of the work load into the server. A detailed vision of this architecture is shown in figure 1.

J.C. Lester et al. (Eds.): ITS 2004, LNCS 3220, pp. 791–793, 2004.

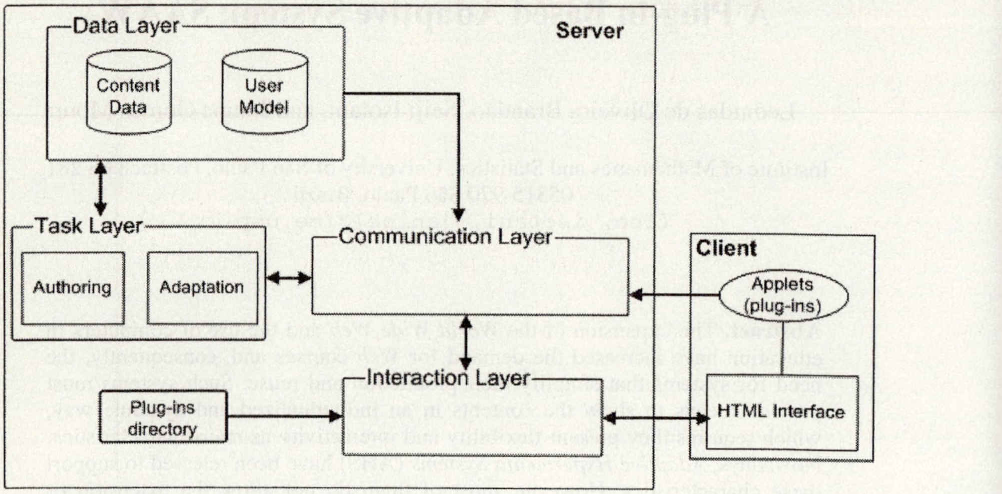

Fig. 1. SAAW. The Adaptive Hypermedia Systems Architecture based in plug-ins

The plug-in is an important part of the SAAW architecture, because they are directly related to the application domain. In addition, they are responsible for the evaluation of the user's interactions and for the largest interactivity with the system.

3 The Prototype and the iGeom

The *iGeom* [1] is a DGS, used to draw any euclidean constructions that are traditionally made with ruler and compass. However, with a DGS the student gets a more precise drawing and can freely move points over the screen. *iGeom* is implemented in Java and can be used as an stand-alone application or as an applet. It has some specific features as "recurrent scripts" and "automatic evaluation of exercises". The use of *iGeom* in *SAAW* allows: the creation/edition of exercises; automatic evaluation; the adaptation of resources, taking into account the exercises evaluation; to communicate to the server results of interactions with the user.

The *SAAW* prototype use the language *PHP*, the database manager *MySQL* and the first plug-in used is the *iGeom*. This prototype dynamically generates *HTML* pages adapted for each course and user, considering the system preferences and the student's model. This prototype (figure 2) is being used by students and teachers in a compulsory discipline offered for an undergraduate course in mathematics in the University of São Paulo (http://www.ime.usp.br/~leo/mac118/04).

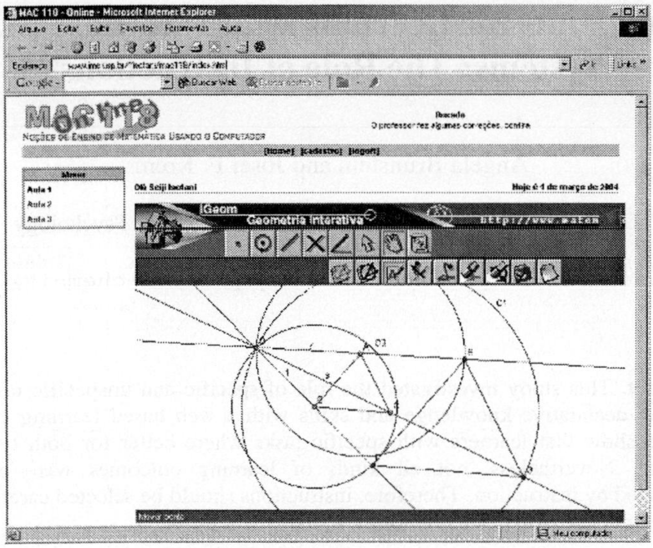

Fig. 2. Resolution of an exercise in the prototype using the plug-in iGeom

4 Conclusion

In this work we present the architecture for an AHS (SAAW), based on plug-ins. The plug-in is responsible for subject related interactivity with user. A prototype (SAAW) of this system is in use with a plug-in to teach/learn geometry (iGeom). The iGeom and SAAW produce an interactive environment allowing: teachers to produce on-line lessons, with automatic evaluation of exercises; students to make geometry constructions directly over the Internet pages; an individualized instruction considering the student navigation style, knowledge level and learning rhythm.

References

1. Brandão, L. O., Isotani, S.: A tool for teaching dynamic geometry on Internet: iGeom. In Proceedings of the Brazilian Computer Society Congress, Campinas, Brazil (2003) 1476-1487
2. Brusilovsky, P. and Nijhawan, H. (2002) A Framework for Adaptive E-Learning Based on Distributed Re-usable Learning Activities. In: M. Driscoll and T. C. Reeves (eds.): Proceedings of World Conference on E-Learning, Montreal, Canada (2002) 154-161
3. Fiala, Z., Hinz, M., Houben, G., Frasincar, F.: Design and implementation of component-based adaptive Web presentations. In Proceedings of ACM Symposium on Applied Computing, Nicosia, Cyprus (2004) 1698-1704
4. Ritter, S., Brusilovsky, P., Medvedeva, O.: Creating more versatile intelligent learning environments with a component-based architecture. In Proceedings of International Conference on Intelligent Tutoring Systems, Texas, USA (1998) 554-563

Helps and Hints for Learning with Web Based Learning Systems: The Role of Instructions*

Angela Brunstein and Josef F. Krems

Chemnitz University of Technology, Department of Psychology
D-09107 Chemnitz, Germany
{Angela.Brunstein,Josef.Krems}@phil.tu-chemnitz.de

Abstract. This study investigated the role of specific and unspecific tasks for learning declarative knowledge and skills with a web based learning system. Results show that learners with specific tasks where better for both types of learning. Nevertheless, not all kinds of learning outcomes were equally influenced by instruction. Therefore, instructions should be selected carefully in correspondence with desired learning goals.

1 Introduction

Web based learning systems have some interesting properties that make them suitable for knowledge acquisition and are expected to support an active, self guided, and lifelong learning.

An advanced design of web based learning systems and an appropriate instruction are both expected to improve E-Learning. So it is often reported that presented instruction is an essential factor for navigating and learning with hypertext [e.g. 1]. Instructions sometimes dominate the influence of hypertext design [e.g. 2]. Or it is at least postulated that different forms of design may be appropriate for different tasks [3].

Two plausible goals for using hypertext systems are either unspecific as *reading* chapters of a learning system or specific as *searching* for details within them or *practicing* specific tasks with help of the system. *Reading* a hypertext requires to decide which information is essential. However, there are only few navigation decisions. *Searching* for details and *practicing* specific tasks within the hypertext require to decide where to go next to find the desired information. However, they do not have to separate central and secondary information already given by their tasks. [cf. 4]

In one of our studies we tested the following hypotheses: We expected that *readers* should acquire unspecific knowledge and *searchers* and *users* should acquire specific knowledge and skills without piggyback details beside their tasks. Therefore *searchers* should demonstrate more declarative knowledge after processing the learning system than *readers* and *users* should demonstrate a higher amount of skill

* This study was supported by German Research Foundation Grant KR 1057.

J.C. Lester et al. (Eds.): ITS 2004, LNCS 3220, pp. 794–796, 2004.

acquisition afterwards than *readers*. In contrast, neither *searchers* should demonstrate advanced skills nor *users* a detailed understanding of declarative knowledge.

2 Methods

56 students of the Chemnitz University of Technology (M = 21 years, SE = 2 years; 16 men and 46 women) took part in the study. All students were native speakers of German. They studied English language for 2 semesters on average (SE = 2) and attended English lessons at school for about 9 years before studying.

One chapter dealing with the present continuous of the Chemnitz Internet Grammar (www.tu-chemnitz.de/phil/InternetGrammar) was chosen for this study. The Internet Grammar is a web based learning system and consists of an explanation section, an exercise section, and a discovery section. The Continuous chapter contains about 75 pages.

Factual knowledge was measured by two questionnaires consisting of 10 multiple choice items and 10 detailed open ended questions each. Skill level was measured by two performance tests each consisting of 21 items. The questionnaires were presented as html pages on the computer screen before and after processing the chapter.

All subjects processed the chapter for 30 minutes and navigated freely within the hypertext. The time seems to be enough to read all cards once, but it doesn't prove to be sufficient to get all details.

The study was conducted in group-sessions of up to twenty subjects at a time. The *reading* group was instructed to process the chapter to learn about the present continuous. The *searching* group was instructed to answer detailed questions corresponding to the text online. The *application* group (*users*) was instructed to use the chapter for performing application tasks. All groups performed a skill test and answered detailed questions before and after processing the chapter. Altogether a session lasted about one hour.

3 Results

Factual Knowledge. As expected, there was a trend that *searchers* answered correctly a higher amount of multiple choice items after processing the chapter than *searchers* and *users*, F (2, 53) = 2.03, p = .06. The former on average answered 4.4 out of 10 questions, while the latter had an average of 4.2 and 3.8 answers.

However, there was no effect of performed task on answering open ended questions after processing the chapter. Here students of all groups answered about 5.5 out of 10 open ended questions.

Skills. All three groups performed better after processing the chapter (64% of the items answered correctly) than before (58% of the items answered correctly), F (1, 53) = 7.14, p = 0.01). Moreover, there was an effect of performed task on skill level improvement, F (2, 53) = 3.31, $p < .05$. Contrary to our expectations, *searchers* performed best after processing the chapter (68%) and improved most by processing the chapter (7.1%). *Users* (3.5%) and *readers* (6.4%) both improved their performance. Nevertheless, their gain in experience was less pronounced than the improvement of *searchers*. Moreover, *users* (M = 65%) and *readers* (M = 59%) performed worse than *searchers* after processing the chapters.

4 Discussion

This study has shown that knowledge and skill acquisition is affected by instructions even with exactly the same hypertext design: *Searchers* answered more multiple choice items on declarative knowledge than *readers* and *users*. Moreover, *searchers* also demonstrated better application skills than *readers* and users. Therefore, only one of two specific learning tasks affected better learning with a web based learning system for advanced learners. One reason for these findings could be that learning to practice a foreign language is a difficult task that can be hardly managed within 30 minutes. In contrast, it is much easier to answer detailed questions *on* application instead. Remarkable is also that not all tasks were affected by instruction in the same manner: open ended questions were answered equally well after processing the chapter for all three groups.

For the design of web based learning tools, the results show the following: First, it can be useful not only to manipulate the appearance of the system but also to guide learners through the material by instruction relevant to their goals.

Second, not all kinds of desired knowledge are susceptive to manipulation of instruction and web design. It seems so that some of them have to be practiced in "real life" instead of been simulated by learning systems.

References

1. Chen, C., Rada, R.: Interacting with Hypertext: A Meta-Analysis of Experimental Studies. Human-Computer-Interaction **11** (1996) 125-156
2. Foltz, P.W.: Comprehension, Coherence, and Strategies in Hypertext and Linear Text. In: Rouet, J.F., Levonen, J.J., Dillon, A.P., Spiro, R.J. (eds.): Hypertext and Cognition. Erlbaum, Hillsdale, NJ (1996) 109-136
3. Dee-Lucas, D.: Instructional Hypertext: Study strategies for different types of learning tasks. Proceedings of the ED-MEDIA 96. AACE, Charlottesville, VA (1996)
4. Dee-Lucas, D., Larkin, J.H.: Hypertext Segmentation and Goal Compatibility: Effects on Study Strategies and Learning. Journal of Educational Multimedia and Hypermedia **9** (1999) 279-313

Intelligent Learning Environment for Film Reading in Screening Mammography

Joao Campos[1], Paul Taylor[1], James Soutter[2], and Rob Procter[2]

[1] Centre for Health Informatics, University College London, UK
[2] School of Informatics, University of Edinburgh, UK

Abstract. We are developing a computer based training system to support breast cancer screening, designed for use in training new staff and also to help experienced readers enhance their skills. We discuss the design architectures used by computer based training systems, intelligent tutoring systems and intelligent learning environments. The basic skills involved in mammogram reading are investigated. Particular attention is given to the understanding of mammogram reading practices and the diversity of ways in which readers acquire their practical reading skills.

1 Introduction

In this paper we describe our work on building a computer based training system to support breast cancer screening. We examine the design constraints required by screening practices and consider the contributions of teaching and learning principles of existing theoretical frameworks. Breast cancer is one of the main forms of cancer. In Britain more than 40,000 cases are diagnosed each year [1]. The scale of the problem has led several countries to implement screening programmes. In the UK, the women aged between 50 and 64 are invited for screening every three years.

2 Screening Practice

Breast screening demands a high level of skill. Readers must identify abnormal features and then decide whether or not to recall the patient. Radiological signs may be very small, faint and are often equivocal. The interpretation of such signs involves setting a threshold for the risk of disease that warrants recall. The threshold should maximise the detection of cancer without recalling too many healthy women. The boundary between recallable and non-recallable will vary. Interpretation, therefore, involves recognising signs of both normal and abnormal appearance and also an understanding of the consequences of decision errors.

3 Mammography Training and Reading Expertise

Trainee film readers learn either by examining cases under supervision or by comparing their analysis against others' assessments. They learn with reference to the *screening decision* rather than final outcome. As a result, film readers may only have a rough picture of their strengths and weaknesses as there is a delay between the decision and the final diagnosis. Studies have shown a correlation between the

J.C. Lester et al. (Eds.): ITS 2004, LNCS 3220, pp. 797–799, 2004.

number of cases read and the sensitivity and specificity of readers [2]. However, the low prevalence of cancer means radiologists must examine a large number of cases to detect even a small number of cancers. The quality of feedback is also a factor [3]. Side-by-side mentoring, third reading, assessment clinics and reviews of missed cancers all provide opportunities for feedback.

4 Designing a Computer Based Training System for Screening

A successful computer-based training system for screening would provide tools that support work practice: for example using simulated screening sets, tutorials illustrating the appearance of lesions, use of standard reporting forms, provide feedback etc. Well-designed systems can be of value [4]. Simple interfaces, engage the user in a problem solving processes presented one step at a time. The system reacts to the success or failure of each step and adjusts the difficulty of the tasks that they present (within limited parameters).

We want to consider what can be added by incorporating artificial intelligence. Intelligent Tutoring Systems (ITS) are based on the cognitive theory of skill acquisition and incorporate instructional principles and methods from this theoretical framework. Such systems follow an *objectivist* view of knowledge: the knowledge to be learned is pre-specified. In contrast, intelligent learning environments (ILEs) follow a *constructivist* view, assuming that knowledge is individually constructed from what the learners do. Akhras and Self [5] highlight the following aspects of the constructivist approach: (i) *Context* - the learner's physical and social environment (ii) *Activity* - learners experience a domain and interpret their experiences; (iii) *Cognitive structures* - previously constructed knowledge influences the way learners interpret new experiences and (iv) *Time-extension* - the construction of knowledge occurs over time as learners connect previously developed experiences to new ones.

Screening interactions reflect the social nature of reading. It is hard to model as the objectivist approach would require. The constructivist approach, however, could allow for exploratory learning in which the user chooses different ways of doing things, reflects on the actions taken and the system, based on observation of the user's actions, suggest alternative pathways. In this way the system will fit the user without being prescriptive about what and how he or she learns.

5 Our Design

Our work is carried out as part of a larger project [6] to demonstrate the advantages of a digital infrastructure for breast screening. The aim is to trial a small high-bandwidth network providing access to a substantial database of digital mammograms and to demonstrate a number of applications including a CBT. The data used in this work have been gathered through interviews, group discussions and observational work.

The aim of the first prototype is to provide readers with additional reading experience from a broad range of cases accompanied by immediate, appropriate and accurate feedback. Training will be provided using high-resolution digital images and a soft copy reading workstation. The Grid infrastructure allows both the cases and work involved in annotating them to be shared between centres.

Our design allows for exploratory and experiential learning. It will permit experiments to evaluate how users explore the available data; to collect data on user performance, skill and expertise; and on individual case difficulty and roller composition. The course of a typical training session would be: start by choosing which set of cases to view, then for each case, identify all the notable features on each mammogram. Next, decide whether the case as a whole is recallable or non-recallable and, after all the cases have been read, complete the session by reviewing the correct solutions and performance statistics. Feedback would be provided on each task and on the overall progress of the user. The difficulty of the tasks may be adjusted. The system would also present suggestions of areas that the user might wish to review again or to concentrate on, and would keep a record of what the user has done. In this way, the training system can induce users to reflect on strategy and plans.

6 Discussion and Future Work

We have shown how the nature of screening work influences the design of a CBT tool. Some aspects of screening are embedded in a context and therefore hard to formalise. Some of the knowledge used in screening is implicit in the process of reading and therefore easily overlooked. Using a pragmatic approach, we are designing a system to allow for exploratory and experiential learning. Learning will be provided in part through measures of overall performance and in part through users' comparison of their own findings with the underlying pathology. Such a design is more likely to succeed because the system will fit the needs of readers without being prescriptive about how and what they should learn. We have looked at the contribution of ITS and ILE frameworks and highlighted the advantages of the ILE approach, as well as the benefits of incorporating both approaches on the design of an ILE for screening. Further work includes adding intelligence to the existing system using elements of the ILE and ITS designs and exploring the Grid-enabled vision of the training application using intelligent agents.

Acknowledgements. The authors wish to thank other members of the eDiaMoND consortium, in particular our clinical collaborators, and acknowledge the support of the DTI, EPSRC and IBM.

References

1. Cancer Research UK: Press Release, (2003) 2 June.
2. L. Esserman, H. Cowley, C. Eberle, et al. Improving the accuracy of mammography: volume and outcome relationships, JNCI (2002) 94 (5), 369-375.
3. M. Trevino and C. Beam: Quality trumps quantity in improving mammography interpretation, Diagnostic Imaging Online, (2003)18 March.
4. B. du Boulay. What does the AI in AIED buy? In Colloquium on Artifficial Intelligence in Educational Software, (1998) .3/1-3/4. IEE Digest No: 98/313.
5. Akhras, F. and Self, J.: System Intelligence in Constructivist Learning. International Journal of Artificial Intelligence in Education,(2000)11(4):344-376.
6. J.M. Brady, D.J. Gavaghan, A.C. Simpson et al. eDiaMoND: A Grid-enabled federated database of annotated mammograms. In Berman, Fox, and Hey, Grid Computing: Making the Global Infrastructure a Reality, (2003) 923-943, Wiley.

Reuse of Collaborative Knowledge in Discussion Forums

Weiqin Chen

Department of Information Science and Media Studies, University of Bergen,
PostBox 7800, N-5020 Bergen, Norway
Weiqin.Chen@infomedia.uib.no
http://www.ifi.uib.no/staff/weiqin/

Abstract. This paper presents an ongoing research on reusing collaborative knowledge in discussion forums as new learning resources. There is a large amount messages posted in a knowledge building process, including problems, hypothesis and scientific material. By adding semantic information into the collaborative knowledge, the reusing mechanism can detect messages and teaching material from the previous knowledge building process which are relevant to current discussion topics and present them to the students. In doing so, a new knowledge building process can be built upon previous accumulated knowledge instead of starting from scratch.

1 Introduction

Discussion forums have been widely used in Web-based education and computer supported collaborative learning (CSCL) to assist learning and collaboration. These discussion forums include questions and answers, examples, articles posted by former students, thus they contain tremendous educational potentials for future students [1]. By reusing these discussion forums as new learning resources, future students can benefit from previous students' knowledge and experiences.

However, it is not a trivial task to extract relevant information from discussion forums given the thread-based structure of them. Some efforts have been made on reusing the discussion forms. Helic and his colleagues [1] described a tool to support conceptual structuring of discussion forums. They attached a separate conceptual schema to a discussion forum and the students manually assigned their messages to the schema. From our experience in fall 2003, this method has two drawbacks. First, some messages could be assigned to more than one concept in the schema. Second, the students were not motivated enough to make extra effort in assigning their messages to concepts.

In our research, we combine an automatic document classification approach with a domain model to find relevant messages (with a certainty factor) from previous knowledge building process and present them to students. The students' feedback is used to improve its performance of the system.

J.C. Lester et al. (Eds.): ITS 2004, LNCS 3220, pp. 800–802, 2004.

2 Reusing the Knowledge Building Material

In this section we present the main elements in reusing the collaborative knowledge, including the conceptual domain model, the message classification method and the integration with a learning environment.

2.1 Conceptual Domain Model

A conceptual domain model is used to describe the domain concepts and the relationships among them, which collectively describe the domain space. A simple conceptual domain model can be represented by a topic map. Topic maps [4] are a new ISO standard for describing knowledge structures and associating them with information resources. It is used to model topics and their relations in different levels. The main components in Topic maps are topics, associations, and occurrences. The topics represent the subjects, i.e. the things, which are in the application domain, and make them machine understandable. A topic association represents a relationship between topics. Occurrences link topics to one or more relevant information resources. Topic maps provide a way to represent semantically the conceptual knowledge in a certain domain.

In our prototype, we use a topic map to represent the domain model of Artificial Intelligence (AI). This domain model includes AI concepts and their relations such as machine learning, agents, knowledge representation, searching algorithm, etc. These concepts are described as topics in the topic map. Relations between the concepts are represented as associations. The occurrence describes the links to the messages where the concept was discussed in the discussion forum. The occurrence is generated by the automatic classification algorithm presented in next subsection.

2.2 Message Classification

Once the conceptual domain model is constructed, messages from previous knowledge building can be classified based on this model [2].

In the prototype we designed a keyword recognizer and an algorithm to determine the relevance of a message to a concept in the domain model. The keyword recognizer identifies the occurrence of the concepts, including their basenames and variants of the basenames in the domain model. Relevance is determined using an algorithm that applies a weight to the keywords in the documents. There are several factors that the algorithm uses to compute the relevance. For example:

- Keyword weight is based on where a concept or its variant is located within a message. A keyword receives the highest rating if it appears in a title.
- Frequency of occurrence is based on the number of times a concept or its variant appears in a message in relation to the size of the message.

The classification results are stored in a MySQL database. The database includes both the messages (title, author, timestamp, thread information) and the concepts they are related to with values of relevance.

2.3 Integration with FLE3

FLE3 is a web-based groupware for computer supported collaborative learning (CSCL).The reusing module is a plug-in to FLE3 environment. It is a domain-independent module. Instructors can build up their own topic maps for their courses or they can use existing topic maps.

The reusing module takes the domain model and the messages as input, and puts the classification of the messages into the database. When a new message comes, the classification module decides its relevant concepts. Then it searches for the relevant messages in the database, computes the certainty factor based on the relevance of the messages, and sends it to the relevant messages interface in FLE3. In the relevant message interface students can browse the relevant messages and comment on them. They can also rank the message according to its relevance and view the whole thread where the messages belong to. The learning module learns from the feedback of the students and adjusts the weights used in the classification algorithm accordingly.

3 Conclusion and Future Plans

This paper presents an ongoing research on reusing collaborative knowledge in discussion forums as new learning resources. A prototype of the reusing mechanism has been developed and is being tested. A formative evaluation of the prototype will be undertaken at the Introductory Artificial Intelligence course in fall, 2004. At this point we focus on the functionality issues. A more thorough evaluation will focus on the performance of the reusing module.

Acknowledgments. The author would like to thank the anonymous reviewers for their constructive comments which helped improve this paper.

References

1. Helic, D., H. Maurer, and N. Scerbakov, Reusing discussion forums as learning resources in WBT systems, in Proc. of the IASTED Int. Conf. on Computers and Advanced Technology in Education. 2003: Rhodes, Greece. p. 223-228.
2. Craven, M., et al. Learning to extract symbolic knowledge from the World Wide Web. in Prof. of the 15th National Conference on AI. 1998: Madison, Wisconsin. p. 509-516
3. Muukkonen, H., K. Hakkarainen, and M. Lakkala. Collaborative technology for facilitating progressive inquiry: future learning environment tools. in Proc. of the Int. Conf. on Computer Supported Collaborative Learning (CSCL'99). 1999. Palo Alto, CA. p. 406-415.
4. Pepper, S. and G. Moore, XML Topic Maps (XTM) 1.0 -TopicMaps.Org Specification. 2001. http://www.topicmaps.org/xtm/1.0/

A Module-Based Software Framework for E-learning over Internet Environment*

Su-Jin Cho[1] and Seongsoo Lee[2]

[1] Department of Korean Language Education, Seoul National University, 151-742, Korea
chosoojin@chollian.net

[2] School of Electronics Engineering, Soongsil University, 156-743, Korea
sslee@ssu.ac.kr

Abstract. This paper presents a novel module-based software framework for multimedia E-learning. Interface of each module is standardized based on IEEE P1484 LTSA so that it easily communicates and combines with other modules. It can be easily reconfigured to various education models with flexibility and adaptability, since it only needs to change connection status between modules. A user can search other users with same educational interests over Internet, and he can easily drag and add various modules of other users to his learning engine, saving a lot of time and money by reusing them.

1 Introduction

E-learning overcomes spatial and temporal limitations of traditional education, promotes interaction between teachers and learners, and enables personalized instruction [1]. However, in many countries, E-learning is not as much popularized yet as we expect, although Internet infrastructure and number of Internet users grow rapidly. This leads to an important idea: most problems of E-learning lie in its contents, software, and human aspect, not in the Internet infrastructure. This paper discusses various problems of E-learning, and proposes a novel software framework to avoid them.

2 Problems of Conventional E-learning

The quality of practical E-learning is often far from satisfactory, while it is theoretically regarded as one of the most effective teaching/learning method. In this paper, the problems of conventional E-learning are classified into three categories.

Teachers: Most teachers utilize computers merely as word processors. It is difficult and time-consuming to develop high-quality multimedia contents. Acceptability of E-learning materials depends on the activeness of individual learner, but learners easily lose their concentration due to indirect interaction with teachers or other learners [2].

Learners: While searching educational material, learners are exposed to almost infinite information, and they easily get lost their sense of direction. They easily fall

* This work was supported by the Soongsil University Research Fund.

J.C. Lester et al. (Eds.): ITS 2004, LNCS 3220, pp. 803–805, 2004.

into cognitive overload, because they have to judge whether it is helpful to their learning whenever they encounter searched or linked materials. They sometimes miss core information, since they have to understand and process it by themselves.

Contents: Internet educational contents often lacks of systematic, well-organized and well-developed materials. Many web sites have duplicated or overlapped contents. Many educational contents on free web sites lack profundity, because in many cases, volunteers prepare them as their hobbies. Teachers hardly discover useful materials from Internet since they are widely spread over Internet without systematic connections, systematic arrangement, and mutual correlation.

3 The Proposed E-learning Software Framework

This paper proposes Modular Learning Engines with Active Search (MOLEAS), an E-learning software framework over Internet environment. It overcomes some problems in Sect. 2 by employing information technologies. It has the following features:

- Standardized architecture based on IEEE P1484 Learning Technology Standard Architecture (LTSA) [3]
- Flexible architecture with module-based learning engine
- Distributed architecture over Internet with P2P and intelligent software agent
- Reconfigurable architecture covering various E-learning models
- Learning inclination analyzer, enabling personalized instruction
- Various communication tools between teachers and learners
- Powerful authoring tools with MPEG-7 [4] multimedia search engine

MOLEAS consists of five basic modules: learning module, teaching module, content module, search module, and control module. Each module has standardized LTSA interface scheme so that any two modules can communicate and combine with each other. Some modules locate in the users' personal computers, some in the web sites, and some in the Internet. By reconfiguring connection status, this module-based approach enables flexible system architecture for various education models. Furthermore, when learners register their own interests and preferences, intelligent software agents automatically finds other learners with common interest by exploiting peer-to-peer. Once they are found, he can access and utilize their modules to compose an effective learning engine. In this case, the learning engine is not stand-alone software on his personal computer, but distributed software over Internet. It has following advantages:

- A user can easily find other learners and teachers with common interest or proper educational materials he really needs.
- It can be easily applied to various education models with flexibility and adaptability, since it only needs to change connection status between modules.
- A user can easily drag and add various modules of other users to his learning engine, meaning that it saves a lot of time and money by reusing them.
- With powerful built-in tools, it can be applied to various fields of E-learning including distance learning, personalized instruction, and collaborative learning.

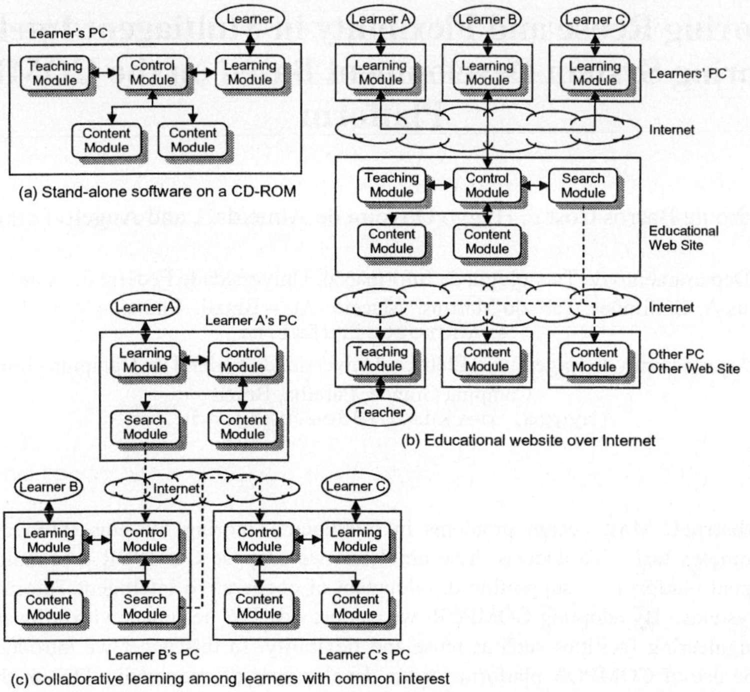

Fig. 1. Reconfiguration of MOLEAS modules to implement various E-learning models

4 Conclusion

In this paper, a novel E-learning software framework in the Internet environment is proposed. It is a module-based learning engine with five modules. By reconfiguring connection status, it can be adopted with flexibility for various educational applications such as distance education and collaborative learning. A user can search other users with same interests over Internet, and he can access and utilize their modules to compose an effective learning engine, saving a lot of time and money by reusing them.

References

1. Moore, M.G., Kearsley, G.: Distance Education, Wadsworth Publishing (1996)
2. Yi, D.B.: The Psychology of Learners in Multimedia Assisted Language Learning, Multimedia-Assisted Language Learning **1** (1998) 163-176
3. IEEE P1484 LTSA Draft 8: Learning technology standard architecture, http://ltsc.ieee.org/doc/wg1/IEEE_1484_01_D08_LTSA.doc4.
4. ISO/IEC JTC1/SC29/WG1 15938: Multimedia Content Description Interface, http://www.cselt.it/mpeg/standards/mpeg-7/mpeg-7.zip

Improving Reuse and Flexibility in Multiagent Intelligent Tutoring System Development Based on the COMPOR Platform

Evandro de Barros Costa[1], Hyggo Oliveira de Almeida[2*], and Angelo Perkusich[2]

[1] Departamento de Tecnologia da Informação, Universidade Federal de Alagoas, Campus A. C. Simões, Tab. do Martins, Maceió -AL – Brazil, Phone: +55 82 214-1401
evandro@tci.ufal.br

[2] Departamento de Engenharia Elétrica, Universidade Federal de Campina Grande
Campina Grande, Paraíba, Brazil
{hyggo, perkusic}@dee.ufcg.edu.br

Abstract. Most design problems in Intelligent Tutoring Systems (ITS) are complex tasks. To address these problems, we propose COMPOR as a multiagent platform for supporting development of cooperative Intelligent Tutoring Systems. By adopting COMPOR, we can provide ITS designers with software engineering facilities such as reuse and flexibility. In this paper we introduce the use of COMPOR platform for the development of cooperative ITS on the Web, based on MATHEMA environment. We focus on how COMPOR supports the reuse of components in multiagent intelligent tutoring systems development.

1 Introduction

Currently, multiagent systems have been widely used as an effective approach for developing different kinds of complex software systems. Indeed, Intelligent Tutoring Systems can be considered as complex systems and have been influenced by this trend. The designer of an ITS must take into account different kinds of complex and dynamic expertise such as the domain knowledge and pedagogical aspects, among others. Thus, the design of an ITS is difficult and a time-consuming task. To build an ITS requires not only knowledge of the tutoring domain and different pedagogical approaches, but also various technical efforts in terms of software engineering.

In this paper we adopt the COMPOR platform [1] as a multiagent development infraestructure to support the development of Cooperative Intelligent Tutoring Systems (ITS) based on the Mathema environment [2], as shown in the next section. By adopting COMPOR, we can provide the ITS designers with software engineering facilities such as reuse and flexibility, saving time on ITS development.

---

* Scholarship CNPQ. Electrical Engineering Doctorate Program COPELE/DEE.

J.C. Lester et al. (Eds.): ITS 2004, LNCS 3220, pp. 806–808, 2004.

2 The Mathema Society of Agents

The general architecture of Mathema was defined around a cooperative multiagent ITS to provide human learners with cooperative a learning environment. The learning process is based on problem solving activities and their consequences leading to the accomplishment of other pedagogical functions, such as, instruction, explanation, hint, among others. In this context, we defined and developed a model of a system that corresponds to a computer-based cooperative interactive learning environment for distance education on the Web that adopts a multiagent approach [3]. From an external point view, the conceptual model of this system consists of five main entities: the *Human Learner*, who is interested in performing learning activities for a given knowledge domain; the *Human Teacher*, responsible for promoting assistance to the learner; a *Society of Artificial Tutoring Agents (SATA)*, responsible for assuring productive interactions with Learner/Teacher. This society represents the multiagent ITS. It implements the idea of distributing the complex expertise among multiple tutoring agents; the *Human Expert Society (HES)*, which makes available a source of knowledge to the *SATA*; and the *Interface Agent*, which mediates the interactions with the Learner, the Teacher, and the *HES*.

In [3], the internal architecture of an agents is detailed. Such architecture is composed by components, named *reasoners*, which implement tutoring functionalities. From the software engineering perspective, we observed that the object-oriented paradigm was not abstract enough to allow the implementation of such functionalities and promote the required reuse and flexibility. This is mainly due to the lack of well defined interfaces among functionalities. Moreover, because of the object explicit references, it is not possible to avoid the high coupling degree among the functionalities (Fig.1). Thus, the reuse of a given functionality imposes the need to reuse other coupling functionalities. Therefore, making very hard, or even impossible, to make changes for agent functionalities without changing others.

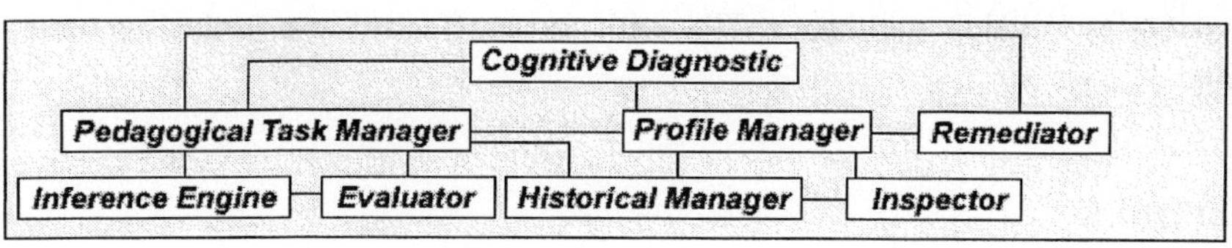

Fig. 1. High coupling among internal agent components

3 Improving Reuse and Flexibility with COMPOR

COMPOR was defined to provide mechanisms to implement the functionalities of agents that belong to a multiagent system architecture. For the COMPOR architecture, an agent is composed by three systems that represent the context of its functionalities: the *intelligent system*, with the functionalities related to the pedagogical task to solve problems on the application domain; the *social system*, with the functionalities related to the agent interaction mechanisms; and the *distribution system*, with the communication functionalities. According to the design of the COMPOR platform the functionalities implemented by each system should be encapsulated in functional components, in order to increase the flexibility and reusability. Such components do not have explicit references to other functional components, there are only references to their parent, called container. Each system (intelligent, social, and distribution) should be represented by a container. Containers are structures composed by functional components, or other containers, but they do not implement any functionality. They only delegate requests to their child components. Thus, if a functional component needs to request a service implemented by other functional component, it requests to its parent. Then, there are no references between the client and server functional components.

Without references among components, it is possible to make runtime changes on the functionalities of agents. Moreover, since functionalities are encapsulated in components, more reuse in multiagent systems development is reached (Fig.2).

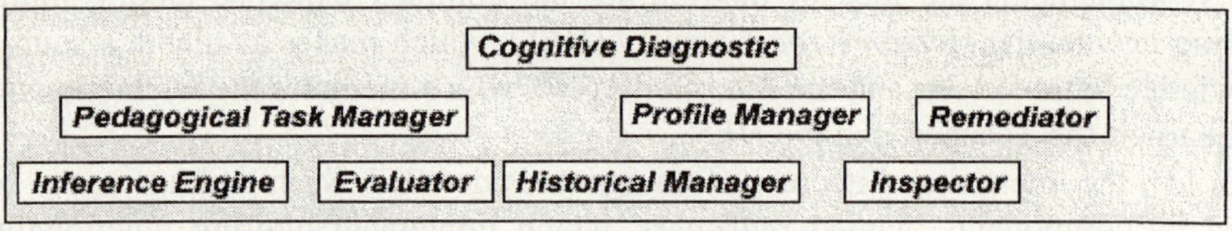

Fig. 2. Low coupling among internal components of an agent

4 Final Remarks

In this paper we have briefly introduced the use of COMPOR as a software engineering platform to improving reuse and flexibility in multiagent intelligent tutoring system development. By means of the encapsulation of the ITS functionalities in functional components and using the COMPOR for assembling these components, it is possible to develop multiagent ITS with more effectiveness, reducing time consuming.

References

1. Costa, E. B., Almeida, H. O., Perkusich, A., Paes, R. B. COMPOR: A component-based framework for building Multi-agent systems. In Proceedings of Software Engineering Large-scale Multi-agent systems - SELMAS'03, Portland – Oregon - USA, (2003) 84-89
2. Costa, E.B.; Perkusich, A.; Ferneda, E. From a Tridimensional view of Domain Knowledge to Multi-agent Tutoring System. In F. M. De Oliveira, editor, Proc. of 14th Brazilian Symposium on Artificial Intelligence, Volume 991, LNAI 1515, Springer-Verlag, Porto Alegre, RS, Brazil, (1998) 61-72
3. Costa, E. B., Almeida, H. O., Lima, E. F., Nunes Filho, R. R. G, Silva, K. S., Assunção, F. M. A Cooperative Intelligent Tutoring System: The case of Musical Harmony domain. Proceedings of 2nd Mexican International Conference on Artificial Intelligence - MICAI'02, Mérida, Yucatán, México, LNAI, Springer Verlag (2002) 367-376.

Towards an Authoring Methodology in Large-Scale E-learning Environments on the Web

Evandro de Barros Costa[1], Robério José R. dos Santos[2], Alejandro C. Frery[1], and Guilherme Bittencourt[3]

[1] Departamento de Tecnologia da Informação, Universidade Federal de Alagoas, Campus A. C. Simões, Tab. do Martins, Maceió -AL – Brazil, Phone: +55 82 214-1401
{Evandro, frery}@tci.ufal.br

[2] Instituto de Tecnologia em Informática e Informação do Estado de Alagoas
Maceió, Alagoas, Brazil
roberio@itec.al.gov.br

[3] Universidade Federal de Santa Catarina
Santa Catarina, Brazil
gb@das.ufsc.br

Abstract. In this position paper, we make a critical evaluation of some assumptions and paradigms adopted by the AI community during the last three decades, mainly examining the gap between perception and description. In particular, we focus on AI-ED research in the context of distributed learning environments speculating about the content annotation process in authoring systems. The problem of authoring educational content for limited and controlled communities has been extensively studied. This paper tackles the broader problem of authoring for large-scale, distributed, fuzzy communities, as those emerging in modern e-Learning systems on the Web. Differently from other approaches in such authoring environments, we consider epistemological aspects regarding the construction of a domain knowledge model. After this, we deal with aspects of knowledge engineering. Then, this paper describes steps towards a new authoring environments along with a methodology for content annotation in large-scale e-Learning environments on the Web. To support such a methodology, a multi-dimensional approach to model domain knowledge is defined aiming to provide its association with a multi-agent society.

1 Problem Statement

We propose a critical evaluation of some assumptions and paradigms adopted by the AI community during the last three decades, mainly examining the gap between perception and description in the process of content annotation. In particular, we focus on that gap in AI-ED research in the context of distributed environments speculating about the content annotation process in authoring systems.

The problem of authoring educational content for limited and controlled communities has been extensively studied. This paper tackles the broader problem of authoring for large-scale, distributed, fuzzy communities, as those emerging in modern e-learning systems on the Web. Differently from other approaches in such

J.C. Lester et al. (Eds.): ITS 2004, LNCS 3220, pp. 809–811, 2004.

authoring environments, we consider epistemological aspects regarding the construction of a domain knowledge model.

In this paper we describe a new methodology, that has already been successfully applied to build AI-ED systems in several knowledge domains, keeping the commitment among knowledge description/representation richness (multidimensional view), development flexibility (frameworks of domains) and intelligent behavior (multi-agent society). From the conceptual point of view, we are extending existing approaches embedding epistemological and ecological elements [4, 6].

In [2,3], an analysis of the state of the art of AI-ED is made and remarks about several drawbacks in current approaches are drawn up. The authors argue that those issues are content annotation related and not just a matter of better formalisms or better inference schemes, therefore, they claim, only content annotated approaches can overcome those serious drawbacks. The authors also advocate that precise ontological engineering assumptions should improve the quality of content annotation in AI-ED systems.

Our proposal deals with the issues presented by Mizoguchi and Bourdeau [2] with a new set of requirements grounded on a new framework based on a multi-dimensional approach, which is a generalization of that proposed in [2]. We also review traditional AI paradigms concerned with the problem involving the perception/description gap.

2 The Proposal and Its Significance

The requirements to maintain an adaptive behavior in the annotation content process can be stated as: i) Content domain should be annotated with ontological guidelines, i.e., descriptions and models about descriptions have to be maintained. ii) Content domain should be annotated with epistemological guidelines, i.e., rules for inspection and review of the content annotation process must be provided. iii) Content domain should be annotated with methodological guidelines, i.e., methods and strategies to deal with ontological objects must be supplied. iv) Content domain should be annotated with ecological guidelines, i.e., shared resources and other facilities to improve the content annotation process quality must be furnished.

The external view of the proposal submits the body of annotated content (viewed as a domain) to a partitioning scheme leading to subdomains in order to link (annotated content in) those subdomains with a more specific body of knowledge about that annotated content. This is ruled only by epistemological assumptions and standard views of that domain, so this process is driven to bind a specialized body of knowledge about annotated content distributed in a three dimensional perspective [5, 6], given by Context, Depth and Laterality.

The Context dimension maps possible points of view about reality. Each one of these points of view can, in turn, lead to a different ontology, based on epistemological assumptions shared by a community about the interpretations of the objects in the real world, from this specific point of view.

The Depth dimension provides room for epistemological refinements in our perceptions of each context, depending on the methodologies used to deal with objects and their relationships inside that context.

The Laterality dimension describes ecological facilities for each context and depth. These facilities allow grasping other related bodies of annotated content, favoring reuse and share of annotated content.

Consider the problem of modeling the classical logic domain for pedagogical purposes. Should it be made with an axiomatic, with a natural deduction or with a semantic approach (three possible contexts for the same domain)? If we choose the semantic approach, to which depth should one go, namely, to the zero order (propositional logic), to the first order (predicate logic) or to higher order logics?

Assume that the axiomatic context with zero order depth have been chosen. Two possible lateralities for this view are set theory and the principle of finite induction.

3 Conclusions

In this work we made a critical review of some assumptions and paradigms adopted by the AI community during the last three decades with special attention in examining the gap between perception and description. A new set of requirements to maintain an adaptive behaviour in the process of content annotation and authoring for large-scale, distributed, fuzzy communities was identified. Such communities emerge, for instance, in modern e-learning systems on the Web. In doing so, we have presented steps towards a formal definition of a new methodology for generating annotated content in the context of AI-ED community.

References

1. Sowa, J.F., Conceptual Structures: Information Processing in Mind and Machine, Addison Wesley Publishing Company, Reading, MA (1984)
2. Mizoguchi, R.; Bourdeau J. - Using Ontological Engineering To Overcome Common AI-ED Problems, IJAIED (2000)
3. Staab, S.; Maedche A - Ontology Engineering Beyond The Modelling of Concepts and Relations In Proceedings of the ECAI'2000 Workshop on Application (2000)
4. Costa, E.B.; Lopes, M.A.; Ferneda, E. "MATHEMA: A Learning Environment Based On Multi-Agent Architecture", Proceedings of the 12th Brazilian Symposium on Artificial Intelligence, Campinas-Brazil, Wainer J.;Carvalho A. (Eds), Volume 991 of Lecture Notes in Artificial Intelligence, SPringer-Verlag (1995) 141-150
5. Costa, E.B.; Perkusich, A. "A Multi-Agent Interactive Learning Environment Model", Proceedings of the 8th World World Conference on Artificial Intelligence in Education / Workshop on Pedagogical Agents, Kobe (Japão), august (1997)
6. Costa, E.B.; Perkusich, A.; Ferneda, E. "From a tridimensional view of domain knowledge to multi-agents tutoring systems", Advances in Artificial Intelligence. 14th Brazilian Symposium on Artificial Intelligence, SBIA´98, Campinas Brazil, Lecture Notes in Artificial Intelligence, Vol. 1010. Springer (1998)

ProPAT: A Programming ITS Based on Pedagogical Patterns

Karina Valdivia Delgado and Leliane Nunes de Barros

Universidade de São Paulo, Instituto de Matemática e Estatística, 05508-090 SP, Brasil
{kvd, leliane}@ime.usp.br

Abstract. Research on cognitive theories about programming learning suggests that experienced programmers solve problems by looking for previous solutions that are related to the new problem and that can be adapted to the current situation. Inspired by these ideas, programming teachers have developed a pattern based programming instruction. In this model, learning can be seen as a process of pattern recognition, which compares experiences from the past with the current situation. In this work, we present a new Eclipse programming environment in which a student can program using a set of *pedagogical patterns*, i.e., elementary programming patterns recommended by a group of teachers.

1 Introduction

Research on programming psychology points out two challenges that a novice programmer has to handle: (i) *learning a new programming language*, requiring learning and and memorizing the syntax and semantics of a programming language; (ii) *learning how to solve problems to be executed by a computer*: where the student has to learn the computer operations.

Although a programming language has a lot of details, the first challenge is not the most difficult part. Evidences show that learning a second language is, in general, easier. A hypothesis is that the student has already acquired abilities to solve problems using the computer which is the common skill for learning different languages.

In relation to the second challenge, research on cognitive theories about programming learning has shown evidences that experienced programmers store and retrieve old experiences on problem solving that can be applied to a new problem and can be adapted to solve it. However, a novice programmer does not have any real experiences but the primitive structures from the programming language he is currently learning [3].

Inspired by these ideas, the *Pedagogical Patterns* community proposes a strategy to teach how to program by presenting small programming pieces (*elementary programming patterns*), instead leaving the student to program from scratch. Supposing that students who learned elementary programming patterns will, in fact, construct programs with them, an Intelligent Tutoring System (ITS) could take a number of advantages from this teaching strategy, such as: (i) the tutor can establish a dialogue with the student in terms of problem solving strategies [3]; (ii) the tutor module for

J.C. Lester et al. (Eds.): ITS 2004, LNCS 3220, pp. 812–814, 2004.

diagnosing the program of the student would be able to reason about the patterns in a hierarchical fashion, i.e., to detect program faults in different levels of abstraction.

In this paper, we present a new Eclipse IDE for programming learning based on the Pedagogical Patterns teaching strategy, extended with a *Model Based Diagnosis* system, to detect errors in the student program in terms of: (1) wrong use of the language sentences and; (2) wrong use and decomposition of Pedagogical Patterns.

2 Pedagogical Programming Patterns and PROPAT Eclipse Plug-In

Programming Patterns [4] can help novice programmers in two ways: (1) to learn general strategies (in a higher abstraction level); (2) to memorize the syntax and use of a programming language, once its documentation include a program, which is an example for that pattern application. Programming patterns can also help a human tutor to: (1) recognize the student's intentions; (2) establish a better communication with the student, since they provide a common vocabulary about general strategies for programming problem solving.

PROPAT is a programming learning environment using pedagogical patterns, built as an Eclipse plugin, that has being devceloped as part of an IME-IBM project. PROPAT provides an IDE for a first Computer Science course. In this environment the student can choose a programming exercise and solve it by selecting patterns. PROPAT also allows a teacher to specify new patterns, exercises and bench tests.

Our proposal is to add a diagnosis module to PROPAT in order to detect errors in the student program. In the next section we show how a classical model based diagnosis technique [1] can be used to programs [2].

3 Diagnosis

The basic idea for diagnosing programs is to derive a *component model* directly from the program and from the programming language semantics. This model must distinguish components, connections, describe their behavior and the program structure. Similar to diagnosis of physical devices, the system description, in this case, is the student program behavior which reflects its errors. The observations are the incorrect outputs in the different points of the original program code. The predictions are not made by the system, but by the student and therefore in this situation it is possible for the student to communicate her programming goals to the tutor. We propose an addition to the diagnosis method described in [2] so that Programming Patterns can also be modeled as new components. Thus, the diagnosis module would be able to reason about patterns in a hierarchical fashion, i.e., to detect program faults in different levels of abstraction.

Figure 1 shows the component model (for a C program) for the problem: *Read numbers, taking their sum until the number 99999 is seen. Report the average. Do not include the final 99999 in the average*. By identifying patterns in the program model, we can construct a new model with a reduced number of components. By doing so, besides getting a model that can improve efficiency on the diagnosis process, the student will be asked to make predictions in terms of high-level strategies and goals.

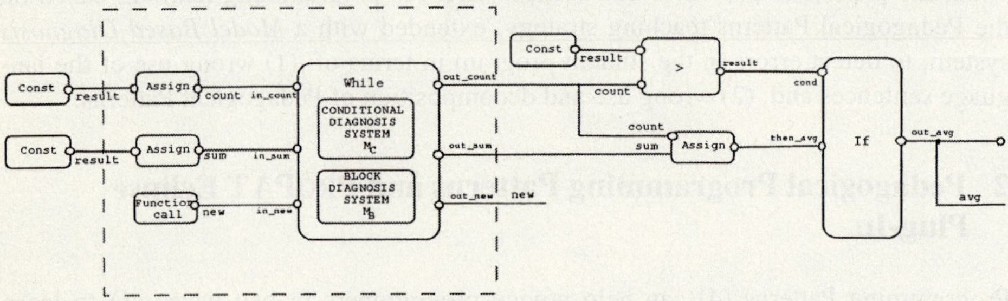

Fig. 1. A structural model of a program solution. The box including four components represents a pattern that can be treated as a regular component of the language for the MBD system.

The identification of the patterns used by the student can be done in two different programming modes in PROPAT: (I) *high control mode*, where the teacher has to specify all the problem subgoals and the student has to select a pattern to solve each one of them; (II) *medium control mode*, where the student can also freely type his own code.

4 Conclusions

PROPAT is a new programming environment, that allows the student to program using *pedagogical patterns*. By using a model based diagnosis approach for detecting the student errors, we add to PROPAT the state of the art on program diagnosis. We also propose the identification of the patterns used by the student to create a program model including these patterns as components. This idea will allow for a better communication between the tutor system and the student. The PROPAT programming interface is already implemented, as an Eclipse plug-in, in two programming modes: *high control* e *medium control*.

References

1. Benjamins, R.: Problem Solving Methods for Diagnosis. PhD thesis, University of Amsterdam (1993)
2. Stumptner, M, Mateis, C., Wotawa, F.: A Value-Based Diagnosis Model for Java Programs. In: Eleventh International Workshop on Principles of Diagnosis (2000)
3. Jonhson, W. L.: Understanding and Debugging Novice Programs. In: Artificial Intelligence, Vol. 42. (1990) 51-97
4. Wallingford, E.: The Elementary Patterns home page, http://www.cs.uni.edu/~wallingf/patterns/elementary (2001)

AMANDA: An ITS for Mediating Asynchronous Group Discussions

Marco A. Eleuterio and Flávio Bortolozzi

Pontifícia Universidade Católica do Paraná – PUCPR
Rua Imaculada Conceição, 1155 –Curitiba, PR –80215-901,
{marcoa, fborto}@ppgia.pucpr.br

Abstract. This paper describes AMANDA, an intelligent system designed to mediate asynchronous group discussions in distance learning environments. The objective of AMANDA is to help on-line tutors achieve better results from group discussions by fostering interaction among distance learners. The overall idea is to organize group discussions in argumentation trees and involve the participants in successive discussion rounds through intelligent mediation. The mediation of the discussion is entirely computational, i.e. no human mediating intervention is required. Mediation is accomplished by a set of mediation algorithms that reason over the argumentation tree and propose new interactions among the participants. Field experiments have shown that AMANDA improves interaction in distance learning situations and can be particularly useful for supporting online tutors in conducting group discussions.

1 Introduction

Collaborative learning is about promoting knowledge transfer among the apprentices through a series of learning interactions. Among these interactions is the *group discussion*, a collective process of articulating knowledge into a series of argumentative statements. Several works, such as [1] and [2] investigate the role of argumentative discussions in learning. In distance learning environments, group discussions are mainly carried out in the so-called *discussion forums*. In practice, however, discussion forums often fail to promote group learning. They either suffer from the lack of participation or grow two much to be efficiently followed up by the tutor [3], [4]. In order to overcome these problems we propose AMANDA, an intelligent system designed to mediate argumentative group discussions. The objective of AMANDA is to relieve tutors from the time consuming task of mediating discussions among a group of distance learners and foster interactivity in asynchronous group discussions. The main features that distinguish AMANDA from a traditional discussion forum are: (i) the use of an argumentation structure to organize the participants' postings; (ii) the capability of reasoning over the discussion structure and (iii) the dynamic generation of customized discussion tasks to the participants. The mediation strategy is based on independent algorithms - called *mediation mechanisms* - that reason over the discussion and propose new interactions among the participants in order to advance the discussion in an intentional manner.

J.C. Lester et al. (Eds.): ITS 2004, LNCS 3220, pp. 815–817, 2004.

2 The Mediation Principle

AMANDA is an autonomous domain-independent intelligent system developed to mediate group discussions among distant learners. For this purpose, it organizes the participants' postings (answers and argumentations) in an 'argumentation tree', where each node represents a posting from a specific participant. By inferring over the topology of the argumentation tree, AMANDA detects potential interactions and redistributes the existing nodes among the participants in successive *discussion rounds*.

At each *discussion round*, the ideas posted by each participant are progressively confronted with the opinions expressed by his peers. AMANDA identifies disagreements, attempts to resolve them collectively, spreads the participants evenly over the discussion tree and attempts to keep a level of participation until a satisfactory degree of discussion is achieved. By triggering successive discussion rounds, AMANDA expands the discussion tree in a purposive way. As new rounds are created, the discussion tree expands either in depth or in breadth in successive configurations. This expansion is due to the aggregation of new nodes and the assignment of such nodes to specific (target) participants, which in practice generates new peer-to-peer interactions. In order to achieve an intentional mediation, AMANDA applies a set of algorithms - called *mediation mechanisms* - that attempt to fulfill their specific objectives, as described below.

Five mediation mechanisms are proposed. The REPLY mechanism detects disagreements (counter-arguments) and relaunches the refuting node to the author of the refuted node, assuring that every participant is given the right-of-response in the case of disagreements. Analogously, other mechanisms are proposed, such as the BUDDY mechanism, that finds peers that have answered the same question, the SPREAD mechanism that spreads the participants evenly throughout the discussion, the VALIDATE mechanism that detects unresolved disagreements which might require human tutoring intervention and the CHECK-ALT mechanism that makes every answer to be checked and validated among the group. In fact, the assignment mechanisms attempt to fulfill their own objectives in order to accomplish a higher mediation task. Details on the assignment mechanisms and their respective formal descriptions can be found in [5].

3 System Implementation

AMANDA was firstly implemented in Lisp, where most of the research on its mediation mechanisms was conducted. When the algorithms were properly tested and tuned, the system was redeveloped in Java. The current version of AMANDA [6] is composed of a Java core on the server side and a web-based interface on the client side. The Java core comprises the mediation algorithms, while the web-based interface provides tutors and learners with a suitable means for interacting with the discussion.

4 Results and Conclusions

AMANDA has been used in several group discussions and the results obtained in the field so far are promising. AMANDA is capable to autonomously mediate collective discussions and motivate the students by finding patterns of interaction among the group, regardless of the type of learners, the subject under discussion and the number of participants. AMANDA has proven to be advantageous over traditional (human-mediated) forum systems by improving group interaction. In AMANDA-mediated discussions, with no human mediating effort, we have observed high participation rates (over 78% in average). Another positive outcome is that AMANDA discussions tend to remain focused on the proposed issues, with little or no deviations of subject, due to the strong argumentative nature of the mediation.

In addition, AMANDA has proven to be an effective tool for online tutors. It is known that in traditional discussion forums, tutors spend considerable effort in articulating the students' ideas, filtering unrelated postings and keeping track of the discussion. In AMANDA discussions, tutors tend to play more cognitive roles, such as resolving specific disagreements, clarifying concepts and providing disturbing ideas to motivate reflection and debate.

Ongoing research on AMANDA involves the design of algorithms that assess the learners according to their contribution for the discussion. This research aims at providing online tutors with a computational assessment method that takes into account the contribution of each participant to the collective learning.

References

1. Quignard M., Baker M. Favouring modellable computer-mediated argumentative dialogue in collaborative problem-solving situations; Proceedings of the 9th Conference on Artificial Intelligence in Education (AI-Ed 99) 1-8, Le Mans. IOS Press, Amsterdam, 1999.
2. Veerman, A. Computer-supported collaborative learning through argumentation; PhD Thesis; University of Utrecht, 2000.
3. Leary D. Using AI in Knowledge Management: Knowledge Bases and Ontologies; IEEE Intelligent Systems, May/June, 1998.
4. Greer, Jim et al. Lessons Learned in Deploying a Multi-Agent Learning Support System: The I-Help Experience. Artificial Intelligence in Education; J.D. Moore et al. (Eds.). IOS Press 410-421, 2001.
5. Eleuterio M. AMANDA – A Computational Method for Mediating Asynchronous Group Discussions. PhD Thesis. Université de Technologie de Compiègne and Pontifícia Universidade Católica do Paraná, 2002.
6. Amanda website, available at www.amanda-system.com.br

An E-learning Environment in Cardiology Domain

Edílson Ferneda[1], Evandro de Barros Costa[2], Hyggo Oliveira de Almeida[3]*, Lourdes Matos Brasil[1], Antonio Pereira Lima Jr[1], and Gloria Millaray Curilem[4]

[1] Universidade Católica de Brasília, Campus Universitário II,
Pró-Reitoria de Pós-Graduação e Pesquisa, SGAN 916, Módulo B – Asa Norte, 70.790-160
Brasília, DF – Brazil
{eferneda,lmb}@pos.ucb.br, pereira@ucb.br

[2] Departamento de Tecnologia da Informação, Universidade Federal de Alagoas
Maceió, Alagoas, Brazil
evandro@tci.ufal.br

[3] Departamento de Engenharia Elétrica, Universidade Federal de Campina Grande
Campina Grande, Paraíba, Brazil
hyggo@dee.ufcg.edu.br

[4] Departamento de Ingenieria Electrica, Universidade de La Frontera
Temuco, Chile
millaray@ufro.cl

Abstract. The research reported in this short paper explores the integration of virtual reality, case-based reasoning, and multiple linked representations in a learning environment concerning medical education. We have focused on cardiology domain by adopting a pedagogical approach based on case-based teaching and cooperative learning. Our aim is to engage apprentices in appropriate problem situations connected with a rich and meaningful virtual medical world. To accomplish this, we have adopted the MATHEMA environment to model knowledge domain and to define an agent society in order to generate productive interactions with the apprentices during problem solving regarding a given case. Also, the agent society may provide apprentices with adequate multimedia content support and simulators to help them in solving a problem.

1 Introduction

Case-based learning has been used in medical schools [2][3]. In this approach, apprentices learn by solving clinical problems, as for instance, engaged in a problem situation where actual patient cases are presented for diagnosis. In so doing, for example, the apprentices have the opportunity to summarize what they know, what their hypotheses are, and what they still need to know. Also, they can plan their next steps; and separately do whatever research is needed to continue solving the problem.

The research reported in this paper is part of an ongoing project which aims to simulate a Web-based virtual medical office. In this paper, we present an e-Learning

* Scholarship CNPQ. Electrical Engineering Doctorate Program COPELE/DEE.

J.C. Lester et al. (Eds.): ITS 2004, LNCS 3220, pp. 818–820, 2004.

environment concerning medical education focused on Cardiology domain. This environment relies on an integration of virtual reality, intelligent agent, case-based reasoning, and multiple linked representations. We have adopted a pedagogical approach based on case-based teaching and cooperative learning. Our aim is to engage apprentices in appropriate problem situations connected with a rich and meaningful virtual medical world. To accomplish this, we have adopted the MATHEMA environment [1] to model knowledge domain and to define an agent society in order to generate productive interactions with the apprentices during problem solving regarding a given case. Also, the agent society may provide apprentices with adequate multimedia content support and simulators to help them in solving a problem. Concerning this content support we have provided the apprentices with theoretical and practical material. Medical education involves an apprentice in complex studies including notions on the life, the body, its behavior, its structure, and therefore, all the complexity of the biological functions of a live being. In order to support this study in a suitable way, it is important to envisage both practical and theoretical materials. In special, our e-learning environment provides apprentices with biological systems functioning in real time, through virtual, three-dimensional models.

2 The Virtual Medical Office Project

We have developed a Web-based virtual environment that is called Virtual Medical Office (VMO). Its main goal is to simulate the process of decision making in a clinical surgical judgment for the definition of a therapeutic conduct for patients with coronariopathy. The VMO will allow: (i) virtual consultations that will provide diagnosis suggestions for the user through his own system or contact with experts from previously defined areas; (ii) a database, constantly renewed with real, updated cases; (iii) discussions involving highly qualified professionals and students from several levels and medical areas; (iv) access to previously registered clinical cases, with the intention of assisting the decision of a medical team, initially in cardiology area, on the definition of a therapeutic conduct for patients, in order to suggest, by the end of processing, a clinical conduct, a surgical conduct or an interventionist treatment for the patient. The major system entities are: student, expert and patient. As mentioned before, the present work is based on MATHEMA learning environment model. The architecture of MATHEMA is defined over a cooperative multiagent ITS to provide human learners with cooperative learning. Learning is mainly based on problem solving activities and their consequences leading to accomplishment of other pedagogical functions: instruction, explanation, hints and so on. In this perspective, we defined a Web-based learning environment which adopts a multiagent approach. This approach was motivated by a particular view of domain knowledge (DK) providing it with multiple linked representations. It means to consider multiple views on *DK* and then providing it with a suitable organization in terms of computational structure. Then, a particular *DK* is viewed as a set of interrelated sub-domains. To obtain these subdomains, we defined three dimensions for *DK*: *context*, *depth*, and *laterality*. The first one, the *context* provides multiple representations of knowledge by leading to different interpretations. The second one, the *depth*, provides different levels of language refinement of DK. The last dimension, the *laterality*, provides dependent knowledge that is, in this work, considered as prerequisites and co-requisites of a particular *DK*. Once established this organization, we define a *DK* decomposition into sub-domains and identify micro worlds and tutoring agents from this decomposition to approach *DK* [1].

3 E-learning Environment

Our e-learning environment is based on Mathema. In so doing, it adopts problem solving and cooperative learning as pedagogical approach. In particular, we have focused on case-based learning where the apprentices are engaged in problem situations connected with appropriate content support. These situations are defined with respect to knowledge domain. We follows Mathema´s proposal by providing cardiology domain D, in terms of contexts and depths, as follow. D = Cardiology, Contexts = C_1: Anatomy, C_2: Physiology e C_3: Pathology. Depth concerned C1 =P11: Pericardium, P12: Heart – General Vision, P13: Size and Position, P14: External Anatomy, P15: Internal anatomy of the Atrium, P16: Internal anatomy of the Ventricles.

4 Conclusion

We present a preliminary proposal concerning the development of an e-Learning environment in the cardiology domain. Our aim is to offer an effective learning environment where the users are able to interact with the system with respect to actual clinical problems, including in this problem solving a suitable support in terms of knowledge.

References

1. E. Costa, Um Modelo de Ambiente Interativo de Aprendizagem Baseado Numa Arquitetura Multi-Agentes, Doctorate Thesis Federal University of Paraíba, Brazil, 1997.
2. J. Kolodner, Case-Based Reasoning, Morgan Kaufmann, San Francisco, California, 1993.
3. I. Bichindaritz and K Sullivan. 'Generating Practice Cases for Medical Training from a Knowledge-Based Decision-Support System', Proc. Workshop on Case-Based Reasoning for Education and Training, 6th ECCBR, Aberdeen, Scotland, 2002.

Mining Data and Providing Explanation to Improve Learning in Geosimulation

Eurico Vasconcelos Filho, Vladia Pinheiro, and Vasco Furtado

University of Fortaleza, Mestrado em Informática Aplicada,
Av. Washington Soares 1521, Edson Queiroz, Fortaleza, CE, Brazil
Jose_eurico@yahoo.com
vladiacelia@zaz.com.br
vasco@unifor.br

Abstract. This poster describes the pedagogical aspects of the ExpertCop tutorial system, a multi-agent geosimulator of the criminality in a region. Assisting the user, a pedagogical agent aims to define interaction strategies between the student and a geosimulator in order to make simulated phenomena better understood.

1 Introduction

This poster refers to an educational geosimulator, the ExpertCop System. Geosimulators are characterized by the association of a Geographical Information Systems (GIS) to a Multi-Agent System (MAS) in the simulation of social or urban environments (Benenson & Torrens 2004). ExpertCop aims to enable police officers to better allocate their police force in an urban area. This system produces, based on a police resource allocation plan, simulations of how the criminality behaves in a certain period of time based on the defined allocation. The goal is to allow a critical analysis by police officers, the system's user/student, making them to understand the cause-and-effect relation of their decisions. Particularly, we describe an intelligent tutor agent, the Pedagogical Agent. This agent uses a machine learning concept formation algorithm for the identification of patterns on simulation data. The patterns are presented to the student by means of questions about the formulated concepts. It also explores the reasoning process of the domain agents for providing explanations, which help the student to understand individually the simulation events.

2 The ExpertCop System

The police force allocation in an urban area to perform a preventive policing is a tactical management activity that is usually decentralized by sub sectors in police departments spread in this area. What is intended from these tactical managers is that they analyze the disposition of crime in their region and that they perform the allocation of the police force based on this analysis.

J.C. Lester et al. (Eds.): ITS 2004, LNCS 3220, pp. 821–823, 2004.

Experiments in this domain cannot be performed without a high risk and high costs once they involve human lives and public patrimony. In this context, simulation systems for teaching and decision support are a primordial tool. The ExpertCop system aims to support education through the induction of reflection on simulated phenomena of crime rates in an urban area. The system receives as input a police resource allocation plan and it makes simulations of how the crime rate would behave in a certain period of time. The goal is to lead the student to understand the consequences of his/her allocation as well as the cause-and-effect relations.

In the ExpertCop system, the simulations occur in a learning environment and along with graphical visualizations that helps the student's learning. The system allows the student to enter parameters dynamically and analyze the results, besides giving support to the educative process by means of an intelligent tutorial agent, the pedagogical agent.

2.1 The Pedagogical Agent in ExpertCop

The pedagogical agent (PA) is responsible for helping the student to understand the implicit and explicit information generated during the simulation process. It is also a PA mission to induct the student to reflect about the causes of the events.

PA, endowed with a set of pedagogical strategies, contemplates the tutorial module of the ExpertCop system. These strategies are the following:

- The computational simulation *per si*, which leads the student to learn by doing and to understand the cause-effect relationship of his/her interaction;
- An interactive system providing usable interface with graphics showing the evolution of the simulation and allowing user/student intervention;
- User-adaptive explanation capabilities, which allow *macro* and *micro* level explanation of the simulation. Adaptation is done in terms of vocabulary and level of detail according to the user's profile.

Micro-level explanation refers to the agent's individual behavior. The criminal behavior in ExpertCop is modeled in terms of Problem Solving Method - PSM (Fensel et al 2000), where the phases of the evaluation reasoning process of committing a crime is represented. ExpertCop explains the simulation events by accessing a log of the evaluation PSM of criminals for all crimes.

Macro-level explanation refers to emergent or global behavior. In ExpertCop the emergent behaviour represents the growth or reduction of the crime and its tendencies. This emergent behavior reflects the effect of the events generated by the agents and their interaction on the environment. To identify this emergent behavior, the pedagogical agent applies a Knowledge Data Discovery – KDD process (Fayyad 1996), searching for patterns, in the database generated by the simulation process (Fig. 1). First it collects the simulation data (events generated from the interaction of the agents as date, motive, crime type, start time, final time and patrol route) and pre-processes them, adding geographic information as escape routes, notable place coordinates, distance between events, agents and notable places and social and

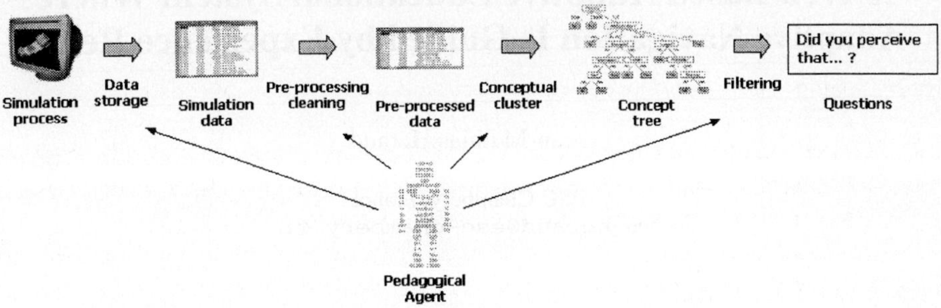

Fig. 1. Pedagogical Agent applying the KDD process.

economical data associated to geographic areas. After pre-processing, PA submits data to the concept formation algorithm FormView (Reboucas 2004). The generated concepts are characterized according to their attribute/value conditional probabilities. That is to say, a conceptual description is made of attribute/values with high probability. Having the probabilistic concept formation tree constructed, the agent identifies and filters the adequate concepts. Finally, PA evaluates the concepts and selects those attributes having values with at least 80% of probability. These filtered concepts are shown to the user by means of questions. An example of question, formulated by the agent applying KDD on the ExpertCop simulation data was: **"Did you realize that *crime*:** theft, ***object*:** vehicle, ***week day*:** saturday, ***period*:** nigth, ***local*:** residential street, ***neighborhood*:** aldeota **frequently ocurr together?".** Having this kind of information, the user/student can make changes in the police alocation, aiming to avoid this situation.

References

1. Benenson, I. and Torrens, P.M. *Geosimulation:object-based modeling of urban phenomena.* Computers, Environment and Urban Systems. Forthcoming (2004).
2. Fayyad, U. M.; Piatetsky, G.; Smyth, P.; Uthurusamy, R. *From Data Mining to Knowledge Discovery: An Overvie.w* In: *Advances in Knowledge Discovery and Data Mining.* California: AAAI Press/The MIT Press (1996)
3. Fensel, D. Benjamins, V.R. Decker, S. Gaspari, M. Groenboom, R. Grosso, W. Musen, M. Plaza, E. Schreiber, G. Studer, R. and Wielinga, B. *The Unified Problem-Solving Method Development Language UPML.* In: IBROW3 ESPRIT Project 27169 (1999)
4. Gibbons, A. S., Lawless, K. A., Anderson, T. A., & Duffin, J. *The web and model-centered instruction.* In B. H. Khan, *Web-based training.* Englewood Cliffs, NJ: Educ. Tech. Publications (2001)
5. Mann, M.D. and S. Batten. *How to accommodate different learningstyles in computer-based instruction.* Slice of Life Abstracts. Toronto (2002)
6. Reboucas R. Furtado, V.: *Formation of Probabilistic Concepts using Discrete and continous attributes.* FLAIRS, Miami (2004)

A Web-Based Adaptive Educational System Where Adaptive Navigation Is Guided by Experience Reuse

Jean-Mathias Heraud

ESC Chambéry, France
jm_heraud@esc-chambery.fr

Abstract. Pixed (Project Integrating eXperience in Distance Learning) is a research project attempting to use past learning episodes to provide contextual help for learners trying to navigate their way through an adaptive learning environment. Case-based reasoning is used to offer contextual help to the learner, providing her/him with an adapted link structure for the course.

1 Introduction

During a learning process, when a learner hesitates when choosing what educational activity to do next, it would be interesting to use similar situations to propose a new way to learn the targeted concept. Therefore we propose an adaptation of a path with alternate educational activities which has been successful in the past in a similar situation. In Pixed, teachers can index educational activities by concepts of the domain knowledge ontology. Next, learners can access these educational activities via three navigation modes according to a chosen concept. These modes are:

- The free path mode: a hyperspace map representing the whole domain knowledge ontology is the only navigation means available. The learner is free to navigate among all the course concepts. Moreover, for each concept s/he can choose among associated educational activities.
- The assisted mode: the learner gets a graphical map representing a conceptual path. This map represents the concepts semantically close to the concepts preceding the goal concept.
- The experience-based mode: the learner gets an experience path. The learner can navigate in this experience path, choose notions, play educational activities that previously have helped other learners to reach the same goal, and consult annotations on these educational activities. This navigation mode is described in the next section.

2 Reusing Concrete Experience in Pixed

When the learner navigates, the system traces learning interactions as *learning episodes*. Using *episode dissimilarity*, the system retrieves similar episodes to this desired situation. From these episodes, the system creates an adapted episode, trying

J.C. Lester et al. (Eds.): ITS 2004, LNCS 3220, pp. 824–826, 2004.

to maximize the *episode potential.* Then an experience path is extracted from this adapted episode.

2.1 Learning Episodes

A learning episode is a high level modeling of the student's learning task composed of the learning context, the actions performed and the episode result.

The different parts of the learning context are the learner identifier, the timestamp, the list of previous educational activities exploited by the learner with optional evaluation results, the domain knowledge ontology, the goal concept in this episode, the current conceptual path and the concepts the learner is supposed to master represented by the learner's domain knowledge model.

Actions performed by the learner to try to reach the targeted concept make up a sequence of elements called trials. A trial is an ordered sequence of logged elements. A trial always begins with a unique concept currently selected by the learner to try to progress towards the targeted concept: the current concept. The following elements are a combination of educational activities, annotations, and quizzes about the mastering level of the current concept. A trial ends with the beginning of a new trial (the choice of a new current concept) or by the last part of an episode.

The different parts of the episode result are quizzes played by the learner concerning the goal concept and the learner's domain knowledge model at the end of the episode.

2.2 Similarity Measures and Adaptability

In order to use the past users' experience to guide future users, it is important that the system has some way of evaluating the quality of those past experiences. However, before selecting good cases, we filter the experience base to the similar experience. We use a set of similarities and dissimilarities according to the specificities of a learning episode's features. We choose a metric for both notions and trial dissimilarities.

Notions dissimilarities : Let $d(N_1, N_2)$ the dissimilarity between N_1 and N_2.

If N_1=N_2 then $d(N_1, N_2) = 0$

Else $d(N_1, N_2) = \dfrac{2 - (sufficiancy\_propagation(N_1, N_2) + (sufficiancy\_propagation(N_2, N_1))}{2 * (1 + precedence\_threshold(N_1, N_2) + precedence\_threshold(N_2, N_1))}$ w

here *sufficiency_propagation*(N_1,N_2) is the value of the mastering level of N_1 propagated to N_2 through *R*, and *precedence_threshold*(N_1,N_2) is the sum of the values of precedence from N_1 to N_2.

Simple trials dissimilarity : Let $d(T_s,T_t)$ the dissimilarity between T_s and T_t, and N_s and N_t the corresponding current Notions.

$$d(T_s, T_t) = d(N_s, N_t) * (1 + abs(NbEA_s, NbEA_t))$$

where NbEAi is the number of Educative Activities exploited during the Trial i.

Beyond the measure of similarity, we try to capture the "adaptability" assessment of the episode on the basis of this source trial. Quiz results are taken into account when computing the "trial sequence potential".

Trial potential: Let $tp(T_s,T_t)$ the trial potential of T_s for T_t.

$$tp(T_s,T_t) = d(T_s,T_t) * (Sqz_s - Sqz_t) * NbEA_{t\_non\_s}$$

where Sqz_i is the score carried off by the learner at the Quiz i, $NbEA_{t\ non\text{-}s}$ is the number of educative activities present in T_t and not present in T_s.

The analysis of simple dependences between how trials work and the result of the episodes allow us to build what we called the "potential" of a source trial, which will be combined with other trial potentials to get the episode potential.

We compose trial dissimilarities and trial potentials in order to respectively build what we call *trials sequence dissimilarities* and *trials sequence potential*. Moreover, we propose to calculate the potential of educational activities for a specific goal, in order to enable a finer adaptation of the episode.

2.3 Adaptation and Experience Path

The adaptation consists of building and proposing a new episode adapted from existing ones. This episode is presented as an adapted path in existing experience. The learner can navigate in this *experience path* through the interface. The adaptation is based on the addition of best potential educational activities within an adapted list of the best potential trials (worst ones are cancelled, new ones are added on their potential value).

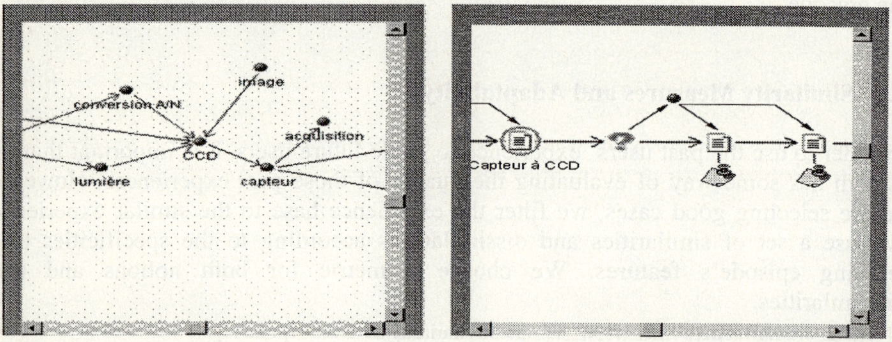

Fig. 1. Left) a conceptual path and Right) an experience path in the Pixed navigation frame

Figure 1 is composed of two screenshots of the system Pixed. The left one illustrates a frame containing a conceptual path and the right one contains an *experience path*. When the learner navigates in the *experience path*, s/he can choose notions (dots), quizzes (question marks) or educational activities (document icons) already played by past users, and annotations written by past users (note icons) concerning these educational activities.

Improving Knowledge Representation, Tutoring, and Authoring in a Component-Based ILE

Charles Hunn[1] and Manolis Mavrikis[2]

School of Informatics & School of Mathematics,
The University of Edinburgh
charles@thr.co.uk, M.Mavrikis@ed.ac.uk

Abstract. With the objective of improving the tutoring and authoring capabilities of an existing ILE we describe how an open architecture and the use of the JavaBean specification helps to integrate JESS, improves its knowledge representation and opens up the system to interoperability and component reuse. In addition, we investigate the feasibility of integrating the suite of Cognitive Tutor Authoring Tools (CTAT) and illustrate issues which concern its use for authoring exploratory activities and representing instructional knowledge.

1 Introduction

Research into reducing the high expense and complexity of ITS development is taking on increased significance as progressively more and more systems are built for use in the classroom. The rationale for such research is clear, it takes approximately 100-200 hours of development time to produce 1 hour of instruction from an ITS [7]. Although a reusable interface and a separate tutoring component can reduce the complexity it does not overcome one of the major challenges; that of enabling domain experts to be directly involved in authoring. This can be achieved by appropriate authoring tools which have the potential to decrease the time, cost and skill threshold as well as support the whole design process and enable rapid prototyping [7]. Additionally, the expense of system development can be reduced by designing with interoperability and component reusability in mind. This approach has been successfully demonstrated in [4].

This paper highlights work in progress to improve the authoring and tutoring capabilities of DANTE; an applied ILE in the field of mathematics (see [5],[6]). We discuss the improvements made in the system's knowledge representation by the employment of the Java Expert System Shell (JESS[3]). In addition, we outline our evaluation of CTAT; a suite of Cognitive Tutor Authoring Tools [3] and present our research into the feasibility of integrating it with the existing framework.

---

[1] Parts of the research reported here have been completed while the first author was studying for an MSc in the School of Informatics and other while he was employed in the School of Mathematics under a University of Edinburgh Moray Endowment Fund.

[2] Corresponing author: M.Mavrikis@ed.ac.uk. School of Mathematics, The University of Edinburgh, Mayfield Road, EH93JZ, Edinburgh, UK. Tel: +44-131-6505086

[3] JESS: http://herzberg.ca.sandia.gov/Jess

J.C. Lester et al. (Eds.): ITS 2004, LNCS 3220, pp. 827–829, 2004.

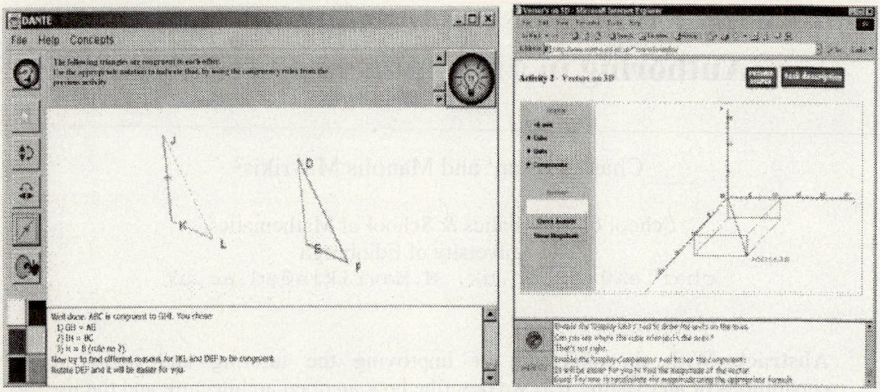

Fig. 1. DANTE applied in different situations with activities for triangles and vectors

2 Employing Jess

Although DANTE's framework was adequate for observations, cognitive task analysis and small activities, it was quite limited particularly with respect to the time taken to author and modify the embedded knowledge. Therefore, we first employed the Java Expert System Shell (JESS). The execution engine of JESS offers a complete programming language from which one can invoke JavaBean code (allowing us to use DANTE's state-aware JavaBean objects). In addition, it gives us the flexibility to have an advanced solution even on the web. JESS has a storage area which can be used to store and fetch Java objects. This allows inputs and results to be passed between JESS and Java. More importantly, facts and rules can be comprised from properties of Java objects as well as fuzzy linguistic terms.

By employing JESS, DANTE's architecture includes the inference engine that JESS provides, a working memory where the current state of the student is kept, and a rule base that provides the generic mechanism that tackles general aspects of user behaviour and goal-subgoal tracking. For each activity a second set of rules represent the domain knowledge. Authoring is now easier both in a conceptual and at a technical level and the rules in Jess are isolated from each other both procedurally and logically and the semantics of the syntax (even for authors with less programming experience) are a lot more intuitive than in a procedural programming language.

3 Cognitive Tutor Authoring Tools

The suite of Cognitive Tutor Authoring Tools (CTAT) [3] facilitates the authoring of cognitive tutors in a number of powerful ways. CTAT is conceptually similar to earlier tools such as 'Demonst8' [1] which enables programming by demonstration. CTAT allows authors to build interfaces from specialised Java components ('Dormin Widgets'). Its central tool is a behaviour recorder which records the interface actions of the author as they demonstrate correct and incorrect paths through the problem space and provides a visualisation of the cognitive model which is particularly useful for debugging the model.

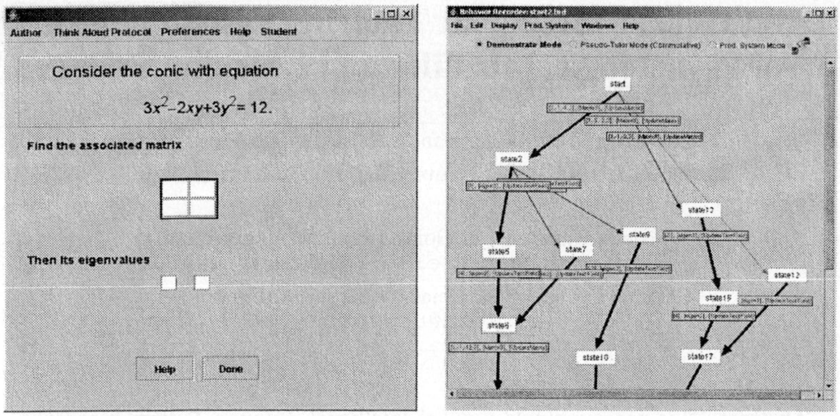

Fig. 2. An exercise as it appears in CTAT and the corresponding solution path

In order to reduce the authoring time for activities, we tried to integrate CTAT with DANTE and highlighted differences between the frameworks. For example, a limitation in representing ranges of values at the state-aware components presents problems in using some of DANTE's components (eg. a slider). In addition, CTAT tutors are based on modeling discrete states, thus the modeling of DANTE's exploratory activities presented a problem. However, we were able to replicate, other purely procedural, activities. We constructed a custom Dormin Widget (a matrix control) for using it with activities which involve matrices. Using this widget we authored a tutor that can teach conversion of quadratic equations to their standard form. Using the behaviour recorder, debugging and validation our rules was substantially faster. Our study indicates favorably that there is a basis for further integration of CTAT with elements of DANTE.

References

1. S. B. Blessing. A Programming by Demonstration Authoring Tool for Model-Tracing Tutors. *International Journal of AIED (1997), 8, 233-261*
2. Hunn, C. Employing JESS for a web-based ITS. Master's thesis, The University of Edinburgh, School of Informatics (2003)
3. Koedinger, K., Aleven, V. & Heffernan, N.T. Toward a Rapid Development Environment for Cognitive Tutors. *12th Annual Conference on Behaviour Representation in Modelling and Simulation*. SISO (2003)
4. Koedinger, K. R., Suthers, D. D., & Forbus, K. D. Component-based construction of a science learning space. *International Journal of AIED, 10* (1999).
5. M. Mavrikis. Towards more intelligent and educational DGEs. Master's thesis, The University of Edinburgh, Division of Informatics; AI, 2001.
6. M. Mavrikis and A. Maciocia. WaLLiS: a web-based ILE for science and engineering students studying mathematics. Workshop of Advanced Technologies for Mathematics in 11th International Conference on AIED, Sydney, 2003.
7. Murray, T. An Overview of ITS Authoring Tools: Updated analysis of the state of the art in *Authoring Tools for Advanced Learning Environments*. Murray, T., Blessing, S. and Ainsworth S. Kluwer Academic Publishers (2003)

A Novel Hybrid Intelligent Tutoring System and Its Use of Psychological Profiles and Learning Styles

Weber Martins[1,2], Francisco Ramos de Melo[1],
Viviane Meireles[1], and Lauro Eugênio Guimarães Nalini[2]

[1] Federal University of Goias, Computer Engineering,
{weber, chicorm, vmeireles}@pireneus.eee.ufg.br

[2] Catholic University of Goias, Department of Psychology,
legn@ucg.br

Abstract. This paper presents a novel Intelligent Tutoring System based on traditional and connectionist Artificial Intelligence. It is adaptive and reactive and has the ability to offer customized and dynamic teaching. Features of apprentice's psychological profile or learning style are employed as basic elements of customization, and they are complemented by (human) expert rules. These rules are represented by probability distributions. The proposed system is implemented on web environment to take advantages such as wide reach and portability. Three types of navigation (on course contents) are compared based on user performances: free (user has full control), random (user is controlled by chance) and intelligent (navigation is controlled by the proposed system: neural network combined with expert rules). Descriptive and inferential analysis of data indicate that the application of proposed techniques is adequate, based on (significant at 5%) results. The main aspects that have been studied are retention ("learning improvement") normalized gain, navigation total user time and number of steps (length of visited content). Both customizations (by psychological profiles and learning styles) have shown good results and no significant difference has been found between them.

1 Introduction

In classical tutorial, users access the content in basic, intermediary and advanced levels progressively. In the tutorial focused in activities, another activity with some information or additional motivations precedes the accomplishment of the goal activity. In the tutorial customized by the apprentice, between the introduction and the summary, there are cycles of pages of options (navigation) and content pages. The page of options presents a list of alternatives for the apprentice or a test in the sense of defining the next step. In the progress by knowledge tutorial, the apprentice can omit contents dominated already, being submitted to tests of progressive difficulty to determine the entrance point in the sequence of contents. In exploratory tutorial, the initial page of exploration has access links to documents, databases or other information sources. In lesson generating tutorial, the result of the test defines the personalized sequence of topics to be exposed the apprentice [1].

J.C. Lester et al. (Eds.): ITS 2004, LNCS 3220, pp. 830–832, 2004.

Recently, connectionist tutoring systems have been proposed [2]-[3]. Despite of the promising results, two problems emerge: the need of retraining neural networks and the occurrence of serious mistakes (incoherencies) during tutoring.

2 Proposed System

The presented work is based on the capacity of artificial neural networks (ANN) [4] to extract useful patterns to content navigation in intelligent tutor systems by selection of better historical examples. This proposal improves the student's performance through the consideration of personal characteristics (and technological ability of interface usage) in the perception of proper navigation patterns [5]-[6]. A navigation pattern establishes global distributions of probabilities of visitations of the five levels in each context in the structure of the connectionist tutoring system. To treat the local situation, expert (human) rules [7] are introduced by means of probability distributions. By integrating the global and local strategies, we have composed a hybrid intelligent tutoring system. In the proposed structure (see Figure 1), there is a single and generic net for the whole tutor. The decision of the proposed ITS is based on the navigation pattern (defined by ANN) and on the apprentice's local acting (current level and the score at the test).

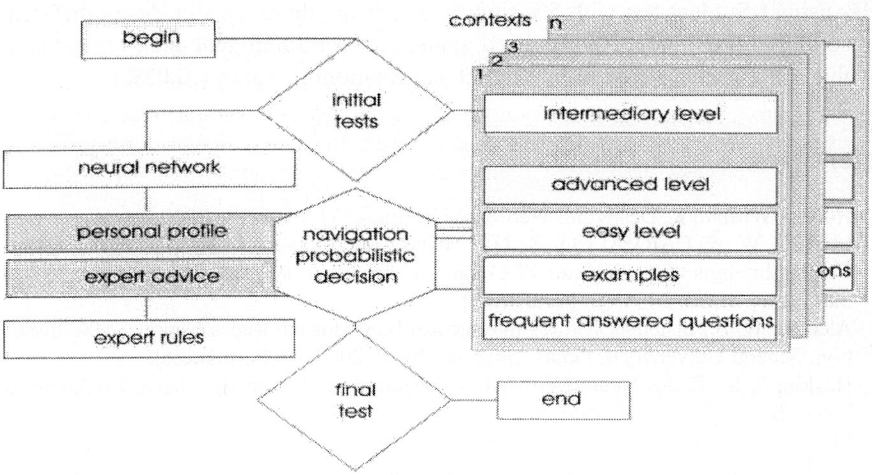

Fig. 1. The proposed system

The use of individual psychological and learning styles characteristics in the tutor's guidance through the course contents allows the system to decide what should be presented based on the student's individual preferences. The dimensions that characterize the psychological characteristics [8] and learning styles [9] are used in the determination of the navigation patterns. Such patterns are extracted for the neural networks starting from individual preferences (dimensions that characterize the type) of the best students.

3 Experiments and Results

The composition of the (neural) training set has lead to the implementation of a tutoring system for the data collection, called Free Tutor, and a guided tutor (without intelligence) denominated Random Tutor for evaluation of the decisions of navigation of the intelligent tutor. The Free Tutor and the Random Tutor possess the same structure of the Intelligent Tutor, but with no advice of the ANN and the set of expert rules. The Intelligent Tutor has employed two individual characterizations: psychological profiles (PP) and learning styles (LE). Descriptive results are shown in Table 1.

Table 1. Comparison among Free, Random and Intelligent navigations

Navigation	Duration (min)	Visited Levels	Incoherencies	Final Mark	Gain (%)
Free	37.88	35.34	0.63	6.87	39.6
Random	35.97	45	1.06	5.93	32.6
Intelligent PP	26.80	26.71	0	7.21	58.0
Intelligent LE	36.99	25.70	0	7.29	57.8

By using t-Student test with 5% significance level, there are significant differences of resulting improvements (normalized gains) between Intelligent and Free navigation (p-value = 0.2%) and between Intelligent and Random (p-value = 0.02%).

References

1. Horton, William K. Designing Web-based Training, Wiley, USA, 2000.
2. Martins, W. & CARVALHO, S. D. "Mapas Auto-Organizáveis Aplicados a Sistemas Tutores Inteligentes". *Anais do VI Congresso Brasileiro de Redes Neurais*, pp. 361-366, São Paulo, Brazil, 2003. [in Portuguese].
3. Alencar, W. S., Sistemas Tutores Inteligentes Baseados em Redes Neurais. MSc dissertation. Federal University of Goias, Goiânia, Brazil, 2000. [in Portuguese].
4. Haykin, S. S.; Redes Neurais Artificiais - Princípio e Prática. 2ª Edição, Bookman, São Paulo, Brazil, 2000 [in Portuguese].
5. Martins, W. Melo, F.R. Nalini, L. E. G. Meireles, V. "Características psicológicas na condução de Sistemas Tutores Inteligentes". *Anais do VI Congresso Brasileiro de Redes Neurais*, pp. 367-372, São Paulo, Brazil, 2003. [in Portuguese].
6. Martins, W. Melo, F.R. Nalini, L. E. G. Meireles, V. "Sistemas Tutores Inteligentes em Ambiente Web Baseados Em Tipos Psicológicos". *X Congresso Internacional de Educação A Distancia – ABED.* Porto Alegre, Brazil. 2003. [in Portuguese].
7. Norvig, P. & Russel, S. Artificial Intelligence: a modern approach. Prentice-Hall, USA, 1997.
8. Keirsey, D. and Bates, M. Please Understand Me – Character & Temperament Types, Intelligence, Prometheus Nemesis Book Company, USA, 1984.
9. Kolb, D. A. Experiential Learning: Experience as The Source of Learning and Development. Prentice-Hall, USA, 1984.

Using the Web-Based Cooperative Music Prototyping Environment CODES in Learning Situations

Evandro M. Miletto, Marcelo S. Pimenta, Leandro Costalonga, and Rosa Vicari

Instituto de Informática - Universidade Federal do Rio Grande do Sul (UFRGS)
PO.Box 15.064 – 91.501-970 – Porto Alegre – RS – Brazil. Phone: +55 (51) 3316-6168
{miletto,mpimenta,llcostalonga,rosa}@inf.ufrgs.br

Abstract. This poster presents CODES - Cooperative Sound Design, a web-based environment for cooperative music prototyping, that aims to provide users (musicians or non-specialists in music) with the possibility of creating musical examples (prototypes) that can be tested, modified and constantly played, both by their initial creator and by their partners, who will cooperate for the refining of the initial musical prototype. CODES main aspects – mainly with respect to interaction and cooperation issues in learning situations are briefly discussed.

1 Music Prototyping: What Is This?

Prototyping is a cyclic process used in industry for the creation of a simplified version of a product in order to understanding its characteristics and the process of conception and construction. This process aims at creating successive product versions incrementally, providing improvements from one version to the next. The final product is that result of several modifications that occurred since the first version. However, in the musical field, some peculiarities make the creation and conception process different from those carried out in other fields. Musical composition is a complex activity with no consensually established systematization: each person has a unique style and way of working. Most composers still do not have a tradition of sharing their musical ideas.

In our point of view, music is an artistic product that can be designed through prototyping. A musical idea (either a note, a set of chords, a rhythm, a structure or a rest) is created by someone (typically for a musical instrument) and afterwards cyclically and successively modified and refined according to her initial intention or to ideas that come up during the prototyping process. Besides musicians, non-specialists (laymen) in music are also probably interested in creating and participating in musical experiments.

CODES - Cooperative Sound Design is a web-based environment for cooperative music prototyping, that aims to provide users (musicians or non-specialists in music) with the possibility of interacting with the environment and each other in order to create musical prototypes. In fact, CODES is related to other works – like FMOL System (F@ust Music On Line) [6] , EduMusical System [3] , TransJam System [1] , PitchWeb [2], CreatingMusic [4] and HyperScore [5] – that enable nonmusicians to

J.C. Lester et al. (Eds.): ITS 2004, LNCS 3220, pp. 833–835, 2004.

compose – collectively or not. CODES associates concepts of Computer Music, Human-Computer Interaction (HCI) and Computer Supported Cooperative Work (CSCW) to allow people to experience the feelings of creating and developing their own artistic and cultural skills through music. This poster summarizes aspects of interaction and cooperation of CODES in learning situations.

2 CODES: Interaction and Cooperation in Learning Situations

CODES considers that the musical prototype is formed by Lines (tracks) of instruments, arrangements, effects, such as bass, arpeggios, and drum lines, etc. Each line belongs to a user who ahs the privilege of editing (selecting other sonic patterns). However, it is allowed the user to create more than one line (see picture 2).

User interaction, therefore, basically includes actions such as "selecting" (by clicking) and playing sonic patterns, combining them with other patterns selected by the "partners" (users) of the same musical prototype. This combination can occur in different ways: overlapping (simultaneous playing), juxtaposition (sequencing), etc .

Many music elements are pre-defined in CODES including concepts such as rhythm, tempo, melody, harmony and timbre. A user does not need to know the conventional music notation (score) to create prototypes: she may select, play and combine such patterns in an interactive way by direct manipulation.

Cooperative music prototyping is here defined as an activity that involves people working together in a musical prototype. Cooperation in CODES is asynchronous, since it is not necessary to manage the complexity of real-time events for development of musical prototypes. Users can access the prototype, doing their experiments and writing comments at different times. CODES, through a group memory mechanism, controls and stores all actions making them available for all partners to aware what was carried out.

In learning situations, CODES usage can provide interesting alternatives for beginners in music. Groups of students can carry out sonic experiments creating a musical prototyping where each student takes over a defined role and an activity to be developed in this prototype. The group, through interactions and advices of a teacher, decides which musical gender will be studied, as well as the number and the kind of instruments and music structures will be put together in the prototype. Then, it is possible to work in music creation collectively, using the metaphor of a musical orchestra: each student has a defined role in the final result. In addition, the teacher can enable many patterns related to the same instrument for different students and all students can compare the different contributions, choosing or mixing alternatives. The teacher can also apply concepts of musical dynamics and expressiveness, indicating different sonic structures in different moments of the prototyped musical discourse. CODES provides a support for students positive interdependency, encouraging collaborative actions, argumentation, discussion and cooperative learning during the development of a cooperative musical prototype.

3 Final Considerations

CODES approach for cooperation among users in order to create collective music prototypes is an example of a very promising educational tool for musicians and laymen because it enables knowledge sharing by means rich interaction and argumentation mechanisms associated to each prototype modification. Consequently, each participant may understand the principles and the rules involved in the complex process of music creation and experimentation.

Our cooperative approach for music prototyping has been applied in private actual case study in order to validate the results obtained , to identify and correct problems and to determine new requirements. An ultimate goal of our work is to make CODES available to public usage to amplify our audience.

References

[1] Burk, P. (2000) Jammin' on the Web - a new Client/Server Architecture for Multi-User Musical Performance – International Computer Music Conference - ICMC2000.

[2] Duckworth, W. Making Music on the Web. Leonardo Music Journal, Vol. 9, pp. 13 – 18, MIT Press, 2000

[3] Ficheman, I. K.(2002) Aprendizagem colaborativa a distância apoiada por meios eletrônicos interativos: um estudo de caso em educação musical. Master Thesis . Escola Politécnica da Universidade de São Paulo. São Paulo, 2002. (in portuguese)

[4] Subotnick, M. Creating Music. Available in the web at http://creatingmusic.com/, accessed in June/2004.

[5] Farbood, M.M.; Pasztor, E.; Jennings, K. Hyperscore: A Graphical Sketchpad for Novice Composers, IEEE Computer Graphics and Applications, Volume: 24, Issue: 1, Year: Jan.-Feb. 2004

[6] Jordà, S. (1999) Faust Music On Line: An approach to real-time collective composition on the Internet. Leonardo Music Journal, Vol 9, 5-12., 1999.

A Multi-agent Approach to Providing Different Forms of Assessment in a Collaborative Learning Environment

Mitra Mirzarezaee[1,3], Kambiz Badie[1], Mehdi Dehghan[2], and Mahmood Kharrat[1]

[1] Iran Telecommunication Research Center (ITRC)
{k_badie, kharrat}@itrc.ac.ir
[2] Dept. of Computer Eng., Amirkabir University of Technology
dehghan@ce.aut.ac.ir
[3] Dept. of Computer Eng., Islamic Azad University-Science and Research Branch
m_rezaee@itrc.ac.ir

Abstract. This paper proposes a multi-agent framework that facilitates provision of different forms of assessment by means of an integrated basis for comparative analysis of different forms of assessment. It is adaptive in the sense that it automatically changes forms of assessment to reach better performance and learning outcomes. The proposed system can be tuned to different contexts and learning materials.

1 Introduction

A collaborative learning environment is an environment that allows participants to collaborate and share access to information, instrumentation, and colleagues [1]. It is recognized that the main goal of professional education is to help students develop into reflective practitioners who are able to reflect critically upon their own professional practice. Assessment is now represented as a tool for learning, and present approaches to it focus at one new dimension of assessment innovation, namely the changing place and function of assessor. Therefore alternatives in assessment have received many attentions in the last decade, and with respect to this, several forms of more authentic assessments such as skills of self-, peer- and co-assessment are introduced [4].

As building assessment systems in different contexts and for different forms of assessment is a very expensive, exhaustive and time-consuming process [2,3], a multi-agent approach to design an Intelligent Assessment System, has been used that provides three advantages for the developers: easier programming and expansion, harmless modification, and distribution of the system within different computers [2].

In the next sections, the proposed multi-agent framework and its components are introduced, and finally arguments of possibility and applicability of the system are presented.

2 The Proposed Multi-agent Framework

The proposed framework, which enables the construction of different forms of assessment within a single integrated skeleton, is a two-layered architecture and its general

J.C. Lester et al. (Eds.): ITS 2004, LNCS 3220, pp. 836–838, 2004.

schema is illustrated in Figure 1.The first layer is called the test layer, which is similar to the general multi-agent architecture of an Intelligent Tutoring System, but also concerns the basic requirements of an assessment process. The second layer is called the assessor layer, and is responsible to set the best form of assessment for the current situation based on the decision made by the test administrator or the critic agent.

2.1 Test Layer

This is the main underlying part of the system, where selected theory of measurement, methods of adaptive testing, activity selection, response processing and scoring exists. The task library is a database of task materials (or references to such materials) along with all the information necessary to select, present, and score the task. The test layer consists of four different agents (tutor, assessor, student model and presentation), each of which has its own responsibilities.

Tutor agent is responsible for managing and administrating the tests. Estimation of item parameters, test calibration, equation and selection of the next task to be represented to the user, are among its main responsibilities.

Assessor agent is responsible for response processing (key matching) and also estimation of students' abilities according to their obtained raw scores. This agent focuses on aspects of the student response and assigns them to categories. The results of assessor agent estimations of learners' abilities are used as the criterion for evaluation of results obtained from other forms of assessment.

Student Model agent is responsible for modeling individual students' knowledge and abilities in that special domain.

Presentation agent is responsible for presenting the task to the examinee and also collecting his/her responses.

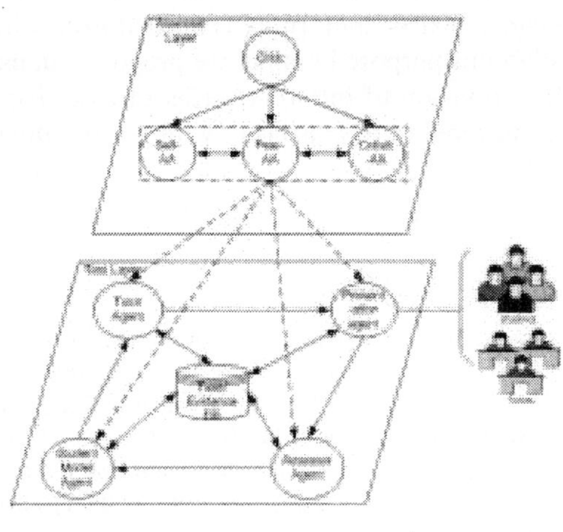

Fig. 1. A multi-agent architecture for implementing different forms of assessment

2.2 Assessor Layer

The assessor layer, comprising of three different assessor agents and one critic, has the duty of identifying and setting the best form of assessment. The minimum required assessor agents are self-, peer- and collaborative assessors. This layer has the ability to perform each of the nine mentioned forms of assessment by activating one or more of the agents simultaneously.

The *critic agent* as its name says, is responsible for deciding on the best possible forms of assessment or a combination of them according to the involving factors.

3 Concluding Remarks

The framework envisioned in this paper is an environment where non-co-located learners can gather and interact with each other to reach goals of assessments. One can construct a class of students from different parts of the world, whom can be assessed according to the modern learner-centered methods of assessment and can benefit from the advances of technology to attend more reliable learning courses and receiving feedbacks of their peers, and tutors. Also, they can evaluate themselves and finally reach a better agreement on their abilities and failures.

The proposed framework has certainly some other advantages: First, it can be seen as a general standard framework of assessment that can be easily added to the former designs with fewer modifications. Secondly, educational researches can benefit from having an integrated basis for comparative analysis of different forms of assessment, which, not only brings them more accuracy and precisions in research outcomes, but also reduces the complexity of their work. And finally, using artificial intelligence techniques, it can be the basis for building an adaptive assessment system that changes its forms of assessment to reach better performance and learning outcomes accordingly.

To sum up, for maintaining different forms of learner assessment, where a variety of possible forms of assessment exists, uniformity is needed from which we can converge in several directions. With this purpose in mind, we proposed an integrated multi-agent framework that enables provision of different forms of assessment. In designing the proposed system, we considered to be consistent with general multi-agent frameworks of Intelligent Tutoring Systems.

References

1. M.c. Dorneich, P.M. Jones, *The Design and Implementation of learning collaboratively,* IEEE International Conference on Systems Man and Cybernetics, (2000).
2. M. Badjonski, M. Ivanovic, Z. Budimac, *Intelligent Tutoring System as Multi-agent System,* IEEE International Conference on Intelligent Processing Systems,(1997).
3. L.M.M. Giraffa, R.M. Viccari, *The use of Agents Techniques on Intelligent Tutoring Systems,* IEEE International Conference on Computer Science,SCCC'98, (1998).
4. D. Sluijsman, F. Docky, G. Moerkerky, *The use of self-,peer- and co-assessment in higher education a review of litreture, Studies in Higher Education*, Vol. 24, No. 3, (1991), p. 331.

The Overlaying Roles of Cognitive and Information Theories in the Design of Information Access Systems

Carlos Nakamura and Susanne Lajoie

McGill University
Education Building, room 513
3700 McTavish Street
Montreal, Quebec H3A 1Y2
cnakam@po-box.mcgill.ca

Abstract. In this paper we discuss how information theories influenced by cognitive theories are shaping the redesign of the online library of BioWorld, a problem-based learning environment. The design of the online library involves four main tasks: (1) the definition of the library's content; (2) the design of the database structure; (3) the definition of how information will be presented; and (4) the design of the user-interface. The outcomes of these four tasks will define the effectiveness of the online library in supporting BioWorld's instructional goals.

1 Introduction

When designing a problem-based learning environment (PBLE), instructional designers should always consider the inclusion of an information access system (IAS) module. Unlike electronic tutorials, PBLE's do not concern the transmission of declarative or propositional knowledge, only the application of that knowledge in a problem-solving context. Because PBLE's focus on knowledge application rather than knowledge accumulation, it is always convenient to couple such learning environments with an IAS that can fill in the gaps in students' knowledge so that they can concentrate on the use of higher level cognitive and metacognitive skills.

While the design of PBLE's is mainly guided by cognitive and instructional theories, the design of IAS's is mainly guided by information theories. However, there is strong evidence that both approaches can benefit from each other. The use of cognitive and instructional approaches coupled with an information science/information architecture approach can greatly improve the design of both PBLE's and the IAS's that support them.

In this paper, we initiate a discussion about the positive implications and applications of such a mixed approach in the specific context of BioWorld, a computer-based learning environment designed to promote scientific reasoning in high school students [1]. Bioworld complements the biology curriculum by providing a hospital simulation where students can apply what they have learned about body systems to problems where they can reason about diseases. Students work

J.C. Lester et al. (Eds.): ITS 2004, LNCS 3220, pp. 839–841, 2004.

collaboratively at collecting evidence to confirm or refute their hypothesis as they attempt to solve BioWorld cases.

Research on the BioWorld project has extend over a decade now. We are currently involved in a new upgrade process which gives us the opportunity to test new features that were derived from two complementary perspectives: a cognitive approach influenced by information theories; and an information-centered approach influenced by cognitive theories. In this paper we will focus the discussion on more recent generations of information theories that were influenced by cognitive theories and how they shape the redesign of BioWorld's online library.

2 Information Access Systems – The BioWorld Online Library

The BioWorld online library and the patient chart are the two sources of additional information that students can use to solve a patient case. From an information science perspective, the patient chart does not represent a great design challenge since it only contains a very limited amount of information that is directly related to the virtual patient's disease. If students work from the hypothesis that the patient is afflicted by diabetes, for example, they can order urine and blood glucose tests to confirm or refute their hypothesis. The online library, on the other hand, contains a much larger body of information that is not directly related to any specific patient case. Therefore, it is a much more prolific ground to test and find new ways of facilitating access to information.

The design of the online library involves four main tasks: (1) the definition of the library's content; (2) the design of the database structure; (3) the definition of how information will be presented; and (4) the design of the user-interface. The outcomes of these four tasks will define the effectiveness of the online library in supporting BioWorld's instructional goals.

3 Helping People Find What They Don't Know

Belkin [2] describes the complexity of an information-seeking task in the following way:

> When people engage in information-seeking behavior, it's usually because they are hoping to resolve some problem, or achieve some goal, for which their current state of knowledge is inadequate. This suggests they don't really know what might be useful for them, and therefore may not be able to specify the salient characteristics of potentially useful information objects.

Consequently, it makes sense to develop IAS's that can help users to find the answers to their questions by helping them to formulate and reformulate queries. An IAS can provide information-seeking guidance to its users in two different ways: direct but decontextualized recommendations, and contextualized but indirect recommendations. Direct but decontextualized recommendations explicitly tell the user what to do but do not apply to the specific search the user is performing.

Contextualized but indirect recommendations relate to the specific search the user is performing but have a less explicit directive character.

4 Implications

We can argue that IAS's provide indirect support to the development of higher order cognitive skills in a PBLE by delivering just-in-time declarative knowledge. However, we are still trying to define to what extent can IAS's provide direct support the development of higher order cognitive skills. Even among the educational research community there is not a full consensus about the interplay between lower and higher order cognitive skills in problem-solving contexts. Back in the seventies, the work of Minsky and Papert on artificial intelligence had already suggested a shift from a power-based to a knowledge-based paradigm. In other words, machine performance-wise, better ways to express, recognize, and use particular forms of knowledge were identified as more important than computational power per se [3]. However, tracing the connection between expert performance and domain-specific problem-solving heuristics does not necessarily mean being able to precisely identify at what point, in a problem-solving context, lower order cognitive skills become insufficient and higher order cognitive skills take over. Even in ill-structured domains, the most trivial problems can be solved by a simple pattern-matching strategy. As the complexity of the problems increase, more robust analogies, more complex reasoning, becomes necessary. Establishing how far one can go with a pattern-matching strategy will define an IAS' limits in providing direct support to problem-solving skills. Hence, the next question becomes: how atypical a patient case must be in order to define a problem that goes beyond the kind of help an IAS can provide. That is one of the questions that the BioWorld research team is currently trying to answer, and that could have only emerged from an interdisciplinary approach that feeds both on cognitive and information theories.

References

1. Lajoie, S., Lavigne, N. C., Guerrera, C., & Munsie, S. D. (2001). Constructing knowledge in the context of BioWorld. Instructional Science 29: 155-186.
2. Belkin, N.J., (2000). Helping People Find What They Don't Know. In Communications of the ACM, vol. 43, no. 8, pp.58-61,
3. Minsky, M. & Papert, S. (1974). Artificial intelligence. Condensed lectures, Oregon State System of Higher Education, Eugene.

A Personalized Information Retrieval Service for an Educational Environment

Lauro Nakayama, Vinicius Nóbile de Almeida, and Rosa Vicari

UFRGS - Federal University of Rio Grande do Sul
Information Institute
Av. Bento Gonçalves, 9500 - Campus do Vale - Bloco IV
Bairro Agronomia - Porto Alegre - RS -Brasil
CEP 91501-970 Caixa Postal: 15064
{naka, nobile, rosa}@inf.ufrgs.br

Abstract. The paper presents the PortEdu Project (an Educational Portal), which consists of a MAS (MultiAgent System) architecture for a leaning environment in the web strongly based on personalized information retrieval. Experiencing search mechanisms it has been detected that the success of distance learning mediated by computer is linked to the contextual search tools quality. Our goal with this project is to aid the student in his learning process and retrieve information pertaining to the context of the problems, which are being studied by the students.

1 Introduction

The experience about distance learning demonstrates that students with difficulties in specifics, during the use of a distance learning environments, going though, in most cases, in web research with the intention to find additional information on the studied topic. However, this search is not always satisfactory. The existing tools make a result classification in a generic way not taking in consideration the specific needs of the user, nor the purpose of the search.

Most of the personalized search tools simply ranking, in a binary way, the obtained results. That is, "interesting" and "non-interesting" according to previous and explicitly elaborated user profile.

Before this problem, it has been idealized a model to toil with these difficulties in the educational context. This model is based on two autonomous agents: User Profile Agent (UP Agent) and Information Retrieving Agent (IR Agent). Such agents will be communicating with each other and among other agents of the learning environment "anchored" in the portal, through the multiagent platform FIPA-OS [1].

In our system, the search refinement is done automatically, based on available info in the users profiles, student's models (information about the student cognitive level) and ontology (learning environment has its own ontology). So, the student makes a high-level information request and receives a distilled reply.

J.C. Lester et al. (Eds.): ITS 2004, LNCS 3220, pp. 842–844, 2004.

2 Software Agents Issues

The term agent is very much diffused and has several definitions. This work is based on the definition made by Russel and Norvig who determines an agent as being all that which may be seen as something that perceives its surroundings by the use of sensors and that may act directly to its causes in this environment. These authors define agent as software used in Artificial Intelligence techniques [5].

In order to bestow intelligence to the consultation, two agents that compose the multiagent society will provide information to the IR Agent: the agent that obtains the user profile making available search terms starting with information on students behavior when he interacts with his classmates and uses the web; and student model agent (from the educational application running in PortEdu, which has information on the knowledge of each student concerning the pedagogical content at issue and specific information on each student's cognitive level.

The UP Agent has the following characteristics: reactivity and continuity. It is reactive because it perceives some changes in the student's behavior as to his deportment once away from the foreseen activities in learning application. That is, it perceives the actions done by the student in the PortEdu. It is continuous due to its constant execution in the portal.

The IR Agent is cognitive and proactive for it elaborates search plans starting with received info by the UP Agent and the students model. Different from the UP Agent, this agent does not have the continuous characteristic. It acts when requested by the student or offers help to the student (a search result, for example) when activated by the students model. Thence, our research is based on additional cognitive information, different from [4], where the extra information used to improve the search is obtained through DNA algorithms.

3 The Agents

The creation of parameters for intelligent search must be taken in account the result to be obtained. In this work, the intention is to aid the student in his learning during the use of the learning systems anchored to the portal.

The aid to the student will be carried out by the obtained contents through the intelligent search mechanism or the indication of a participant in the group that has the knowledge to help him out in the learning of a specific subject. UP Agent is independent from the educational application nowadays.

The Learner Model Agent is who will supply the UP Agent the pertinent info on specific knowledge of the educational system in use. By the attained info as much as from the pedagogical agent as of the interface, summing the inferred info by the student's behavior, a search term will be made to carry out into effect the retrieving desired information.

We may observe that the user profile will be updated at all times. Thus, there is the intention to obtain a closer modeling to that in which represents the user at his last instant in the environment and not only a historical profile.

Nowadays, there are many applications based on intelligent agents, such as Letizia[3], and InfoFinder[2]. However, few agents are capable to obtain knowledge on the profile of an student's interest, to communicate with other agents, to store links in a links repository using integrity classification. As the IR agent will be offering services in an educational environment, it can automatically retrieve information and offer to the student the text content, image, sound, and knowledge.

In PortEdu, there are a navigational monitor that will try to obtain the educational user interests and update a database (UP Agent task).

The sensor receives information from both, the UP Agent and Student Model Agent.

In this context, process of automatic content search (using Google and NetClue), based on user profile and user student's model is the differential in our project. For an effective search it becomes necessary to bring up search terms efficacious.

Once the filter and link classification is done, the IR Agent communicates to the learning environment that there is available URLs with content to complement the info on the topic in which the student is working. The exact moment to present this content to the learner is determined by the set of learning environment agents, as it depends on the pedagogical model.

To increase the level at efficiency in following searches, links are stored in a link repository, considering the impact rate and the comments made by the expert and students.

4 Final Considerations

In this short paper, we have presented the ongoing project PortEdu, a distance learning portal based on a multiagent architecture with the intention to aid the student in the learning process through a personalized search tool.

The main contribution in this work is to make available a personalized search tool considering the specific needs of the educational context and user preference. We believe that a refined and personalized retrieving information in this context contributes to distance learning via Web.

References

1. FIPA – FIPA2000 Specification Part 2, Agent Communication Language. URL: www.fipa.org
2. Krulwich, B. and Burkley, C., (1997) 'The InfoFinder Agent: Learning User Interests through Heuristic Phrase Extraction', IEEE Intelligent Systems, Vol. 12, No. 5, pp. 22-27
3. Lieberman, Henry. (1995). Letizia: An agent that assist web browsing. In Proceeding IJCAI-95. URL: http://lieber.www.media.mit.edu/people/lieber/Lieberary/Letizia/Letizia.html
4. MacMillan, I. C. (2003) 'In Search of Serendipity: Bridging the Gap That Separates Technologies and New Markets', 2 July, http://knowledge.wharton.upenn.edu/index.cfm?fa=viewarticle&id=812
5. Russell, S., Norvig, P., (1995) Artificial Intelligence A Modern Approach, Prentice Hall, Upper Saddle River, NJ, USA.

Optimal Emotional Conditions for Learning with an Intelligent Tutoring System

Magalie Ochs and Claude Frasson*

Département d'informatique et de recherche opérationnelle
Université de Montréal, C.P. 6128, Succ. Centre-ville, Montréal, H3C 3J7, Canada.
{ochsmaga, frasson}@iro.umontreal.ca

Abstract. Intelligent tutoring systems that are also *emotionally* intelligent—i.e., able to manage a learner's emotions—can be much more effective than traditional systems. In this paper, we make a step towards the realization of such systems. First, we show how adding an emotional charge to the learning content can support cognitive processes related to learning such as memorization. Secondly, we determine the optimal emotional conditions for learning.

1 Introduction

People often separate emotions and reason, believing that emotions are an obstacle in rational decision making or reasoning. However, recent research has shown that in every case, the cognitive process, for instance decision making [3], of an individual is strongly dependent on his emotions.

An important special case of a cognitive process, involving a variety of different cognitive abilities, is the learning process. Learning requires to fulfill a variety of tasks such as understanding, memorizing, analyzing, reasoning, or applying. Given the above-mentioned relation between *feeling* and *thinking,* the student's performance in these different learning tasks will depend on his emotions. Systems have been proposed for modeling learners' emotions and their variation during a learning session with an *Intelligent Tutoring System (ITS)*. However, all previous work is based on the hypothesis that only a very restricted class of—mainly positive—emotions can have a positive influence on learning.

The goal of this paper is to improve the effectiveness of emotion-based tutoring systems by determining in much more detail than previously done the impact of different emotions on learning. This analysis allows us to define the optimal emotional conditions of learning. More precisely, we aim at determining the *optimal emotional state* of the learner which leads to the best performance, and how an ITS can directly use the influence of emotions connected to the learning content to improve learner's cognitive abilities.

* Supported by Valorisation Recherche Québec (VRQ).

J.C. Lester et al. (Eds.): ITS 2004, LNCS 3220, pp. 845–847, 2004.

2 Emotionalizing the Learning Content

Teaching and learning are emotional processes: a teacher who communicates the content in an emotional way will be more successful than another who behaves and communicates unemotionally. In fact, situations, objects, or data with emotional charge are better memorized [1]. An ITS should be able, like a successful human teacher, to emotionalize the learning content by giving it an emotional connotation. This connotation can be naturally linked to the learning content: for instance, events in history can naturally generate certain emotions. However, emotions can also be artificially added to a learning content which is a priori unemotional, for example by associating images with emotional charge to random words or numbers.

It has been shown that people in a given emotional state will attribute more attention to stimulus events, objects, or situations that are affectively congruent with their emotional state [1]. An ITS can use this fact for gaining more attention from the learner by *emotionalizing* the learning content. Two approaches can be used: In fact, it can adaptively add an emotional charge to the learning content which is similar or related to the present emotional state of the learner, who will then pay more attention to the material presented to him. On the other hand, an ITS can as well change the emotional state of the learner such as to make it more similar to the emotional charge of the content to be learned.

When a large quantity of data lacking any emotional content has to be memorized and later retrieved, i.e., distinguished, then adding emotional charges with respect to very different emotions—saddening, comforting, disturbing, disgusting, arousing—can help the memorization process. If, during the step of memorization, an ITS associates the learning content with an emotional charge, the learner will be conditioned such as to establish a connection between the subject matter and his specific emotional reaction. Then, so conditioned on having certain emotional reactions to different matters, the learner will be able to recall and distinguish the (non emotional) learning contents as easily as his emotional reactions to them. An ITS therefore pushes the learner to structure and memorize the knowledge in categories of emotion, which is in fact precisely the natural organization of memory [1].

3 Internally and Externally Generated Emotions

During interaction with an ITS, a learner will experience a variety of different emotions. We distinguish between two classes of emotions with respect to their origin: *Internally generated emotions* result directly from the interaction with the ITS, *externally generated emotions* have their origin outside. If a learner is anxious because of some external situation or event—say because his car is parked in a tow-away zone (i.e., the emotion is externally generated)—he will be less able to focus and will, hence, suffer from a weaker learning performance. If, on the other hand, the anxiety stems from the urge to perform well on a test proposed by the ITS, then it can increase the learner's motivation and hence performance. Although it is exactly the same emotion, its effect on the learning performance is opposite in the two cases due to the different origins. Let us analyze the impact of positive and negative emotions on performance, depending on whether they have been externally or internally generated.

Positive emotions: *Internally generated* positive emotions have a strong positive effect on learning for two reasons: First, positive emotions in general allow for a more creative and flexible thinking process. They also increase motivation, such that learners will in general try harder and give up less quickly [4]. The second reason is that the learner wants to keep—and possibly increase—his positive emotional state (which in this case originates from the system) by having good performance. The origin of *externally generated* positive emotions is not directly linked to the learning process; the learner is not necessarily attached to maintain good performance, and has, thus, less motivation. The positive effect of these emotions is hence less strong, and can even turn into a negative one if the emotions are too strong.

Negative emotions: *Internally generated* negative emotions can have a positive effect on the performance. An ITS can generate certain negative emotions, for example anxiety or stress, which reflect the probability of an unpleasant event [6]. These emotions push a person to act in order to avoid this event, which would cause negative emotions, from occurring. In the context of learning, these emotions, therefore, act as a motivating factor for encouraging the learner to work harder and replace them by positive emotions. Similarly, being jealous, envious, or resentful about someone else's performance can have the same positive effect on motivation. However, the other categories of negative emotions (for instance anger, distress, etc.) are disadvantageous for learning [2], [4], [5]. *Externally generated* negative emotions reduce the learner's concentration and turn his focus to different matters.

In general, strong emotions, both positive and negative, can block parts of the brain involved in the thinking process and, therefore, prevent the learner from concentrating, memorizing, retrieving from memory, and reasoning [1].

In conclusion, an ITS can determine the optimal emotional conditions for learning by distinguishing the type, intensity, and origin of the different emotions present in the learner. An *emotionally intelligent tutoring system* is defined by the ability of detecting and managing a learner's emotions with the objective of improving his performance. The strength of such a system comes from the two aspects presented in detail in this paper, and in particular from their combination.

References

1. Bower G. 1992. *How Might emotions affect learning?*. Handbook of emotion and memory, edited by Sven-Ake Christianson.
2. Compton R. 2000. *Ability to disengage attention predicts negative affect.* Cognition and Emotion.
3. Damasio. 1995. Eds. *L'erreur de Descartes: La raison des émotions.* Edition Odile Jacob.
4. Isen A. M. 2000. *Positive Affect and Decision making.* Handbook of emotions, second edition, Guilford Press.
5. Lisetti, Schiano. 2000. *Automatic Facial Expression Interpretation : Where Human-Computer Interaction, Artificial Intelligence and Cognitive Science Intersect.* Pragmatics and Cognition, Vol 8(1): 185-235.
6. Orthony A., Clore G.L, Collins A. 1988. *The cognitive Structure of Emotions.* Cambridge University Press.

FlexiTrainer: A Visual Authoring Framework for Case-Based Intelligent Tutoring Systems

Sowmya Ramachandran, Emilio Remolina, and Daniel Fu

Stottler Henke Associates, Inc., 951 Mariner's Island Blvd. #360, San Mateo, CA, 94404
{sowmya, remolina, fu}@stottlerhenke.com

Abstract. The need for rapid and cost-effective development Intelligent Tutoring Systems with flexible pedagogical approaches has led to a demand for authoring tools. The authoring systems developed to date provide a range of options and flexibility, such as authoring simulations, or authoring tutoring strategies. This paper describes FlexiTrainer, an authoring framework that enables the rapid creation of pedagogically rich and performance-oriented learning environments with custom content and tutoring strategies. FlexiTrainer provides tools for specifying the domain knowledge and derives its power from a visual behavior editor for specifying the dynamic behavior of tutoring agents that interact to deliver instruction. The FlexiTrainer runtime engine is an agent based system where different instructional agents carry out teaching related actions to achieve instructional goals. FlexiTrainer has been used to develop an ITS for training helicopter pilots in flying skills.

1 Introduction

As Intelligent Tutoring Systems gain currency in the world outside academic research, there is an increasing need for re-usable authoring tools that will accelerate creation of such systems. At the same time there exists a desire for flexibility in terms of the communications choices made by the tutor. Several authoring frameworks have been developed that provide varying degrees of control, such as content, student modeling and instructional planning [3]. Some allow the authoring of simulations [2], while some provide a way to write custom tutoring strategies [1, 4]. However, among the latter type, none can create tutors with sophisticated instruction including rich interactions like simulations [3]. Our goal was to develop an authoring tool and engine for domains that embraced simulation-based training. In addition, our users needed facilities for creating and modifying content, performance evaluation, assessment procedures, student model attributes, and tutoring strategies. In response, we developed the FlexiTrainer framework which enables rapid creation of pedagogically rich and performance-oriented learning environments with custom content and tutoring strategies.

2 FlexiTrainer Overview

FlexiTrainer consists of two components: the authoring tool, and the runtime engine. The core components of the FlexiTrainer authoring tool are the Task-skill-principle Editor, the Exercise Editor, the Student Model Editor, and the Tutor Behavior Editor.

J.C. Lester et al. (Eds.): ITS 2004, LNCS 3220, pp. 848–850, 2004.

The *Task-skill-principle Editor* enables the definition of the knowledge of what to teach and includes the following default types of knowledge objects: tasks, skills, and principles. These define the core set of domain knowledge. The *Exercise Editor* facilitates the creation of a library of such exercises for the tutor to draw upon as it trains the students. The *Tutor Behavior Editor* has the author specify two kinds of knowledge: how to assess the student and how to teach the student. Both types of knowledge are captured in the form of behavior scripts that specify tutor behavior under different conditions. These behaviors are visualized in a "drag and drop" style canvas.

Except for the Behavior Editor, all the other editors employ a uniform method for creating knowledge structures. An atomic structure consists of a *type* which is a set of properties common to a number of instances that distinguish them as an identifiable class. For example, the author may want to define "definition" as a separate knowledge type by creating a "definition" type with properties "name", "description", and "review content". An instance would be a definition of "groundspeed" with values filled in, such as "speed relative to the ground" and "ground speed review.html".

Types and instances provide a way for gathering knowledge. Ultimately, there are two ways in which the knowledge will become operational: evaluating and teaching the student. The ways in which the training system fulfills these functions are driven by behavior scripts that dictate how the training system should interact with the student.

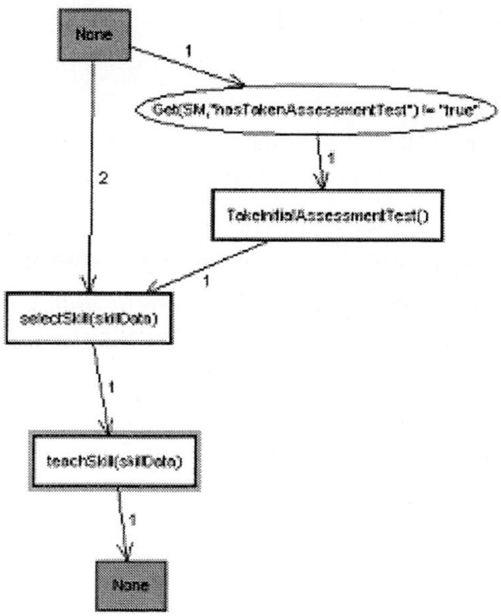

Fig. 1. Example of a dynamic behavior specification

FlexiTrainer's behavior model is a hierarchical finite state machine where the flow of control resides in stacks of hierarchical states. Condition logic is evaluated according to a prescribed ordering, showing very obvious flow of control. FlexiTrainer employs four constructs: *actions*, which define all the different actions FlexiTrainer can perform; *behaviors* that chain actions and conditional logic; *predicates*, which set the conditions under which each action and behavior will happen; and *connectors*, which control the order in which conditions are evaluated, and actions and behaviors take place. These four allow one to create behavior that ranges from simple sequences to complex conditional logic. Figure 1 shows an example "teach for mastery" behavior invoked whenever the student wants to improve his flying skills. It starts in the upper left rectangle. The particular skill to practice is determined by the selectSkill behavior. Once the skill to practice is chosen, the teachSkill behavior is invoked: it will pick an exercise that reinforces the skill (and is appropriate for the student mastery level) and then will call the teachExercise behavior to actually carry out the exercise. If the student has not taken the assessment test yet, he will take the test before any skills are selected.

Instructional agents carry out teaching-related actions to achieve instructional goals. The behaviors specified with the Behavior Editor define how agents satisfy different goals. The engine also incorporates a student modeling strategy using Bayesian inference.

So far the FlexiTrainer framework has been used to develop an ITS to train novice helicopter pilots in flying skills [5]. We plan to add other functionality such as: ability to support development of web-based tutoring systems; support for creating ITSs for team training; a pre-defined library of standard tutoring behaviors reflecting diverse instructional approaches for different types of skills and knowledge.

The work reported here was funded by the Office of the Secretary of Defense under contract number DASW01-01-C-5317.

References

1. Major, N., Ainsworth, S. and Wood, D. (1997) REDEEM: Exploiting symbiosis between psychology and authoring environments. *International Journal of Artificial Intelligence in Education*, 8 (3-4) 317-340.
2. Munro, A., Johnson, M.C., Pizzini, Q.A., Surmon, D.S., Towne, D.M. and Wogulis, J.L. (1997). Authoring simulation-centered tutors with RIDES. *International Journal of Artificial Intelligence in Education*. 8(3-4), 284-316.
3. Murray, T (1999). Authoring Intelligent Tutoring Systems: An analysis of the state of the art. *International Journal of Artificial Intelligence in Education*, 10, 98-129.
4. Murray T. (1998). Authoring knowledge-based tutors: Tools for content, instructional strategy, student model, and interface design. *Journal of the Learning Sciences*, 7(1).
5. Ramachandran, S. (2004). An Intelligent Tutoring System Approach to Adaptive Instructional Systems, Phase II SBIR Final Report, Army Research Institute, Fort Rucker, AL.

Tutorial Dialog in an Equation Solving Intelligent Tutoring System

Leena M. Razzaq and Neil T. Heffernan

100 Institute Road, Computer Science Department, Worcester Polytechnic Institute
Worcester, MA, USA

Abstract. A new intelligent tutoring system is presented for the domain of solving equations. This system is novel, because it is an intelligent equation-solving tutor that combines a cognitive model of the domain with a model of dialog-based tutoring. The tutorial model is based on the observation of an experienced human tutor and captures tutorial strategies specific to the domain of equation-solving. In this context, a tutorial dialog is the equivalent of breaking down problems into simpler steps and asking new questions before proceeding to the next step. The resulting system, named E-tutor, was compared, via a randomized controlled experiment, to a traditional model-tracing tutor that does not engage students in dialog. Preliminary results using a very small sample size showed that E-tutor capabilities performed better than the control. This set of preliminary results, though not statistically significant, shows promising opportunities to improve learning performance by adding tutorial dialog capabilities to ITSs. The system is available at www.wpi.edu/~leenar/E-tutor.

1 Introduction

This research is focused on building a better tutor for the task of solving equations by replacing traditional model-tracing feedback in an ITS with a dialog-based feedback mechanism. This system, named "E-tutor", for Equation Tutor, is novel because it is based on the observation of an experienced human tutor and captures tutorial strategies specific to the domain of equation-solving. In this context, a tutorial dialog is the equivalent of breaking down problems into simpler steps and then asking new questions before proceeding to the next step. This research does not deal with natural language processing (NLP), but rather with dialog planning.

Studies indicate that experienced human tutors provide the most effective form of instruction known [2]. They raise the mean performance about two standard deviations compared to students taught in classrooms. Intelligent tutoring systems can offer excellent instruction, but not as good as human tutors. The best ones raise performance about one standard deviation above classroom instruction [7]. Although Ohlsson [9] observed that teaching strategies and tactics should be one of the guiding principles in the development of ITSs, incorporating such principles in ITSs has remained largely unexplored [8].

2 Our Approach

E-tutor is able to carry on a coherent dialog that consists of breaking down problems into smaller steps and asking new questions about those steps, rather then simply giving hints. Several tutorial dialogs were chosen from the transcripts of human

J.C. Lester et al. (Eds.): ITS 2004, LNCS 3220, pp. 851–853, 2004.

tutoring sessions collected to be incorporated in the ITS. The dialogs were designed to take the place of the hints that are available in the control condition. E-tutor does not have a hint button. When students make errors they are presented with a tutorial dialog if one is available. The student must respond to the dialog to exit it and return to solving the problem in the problem window. Students stay in the loop until they respond correctly or the tutor has run out of dialog. This forces the student to participate actively in the dialog. It is this loop that we hypothesize will do better at teaching equation-solving than hint sequences do. When the tutor has run out of dialog, the last tutorial response presents the student with the correct action and input similar to the last hint in a hint sequence. A close mapping between the human tutor dialog and the ITS' dialog was attempted.

Evaluation. E-tutor was evaluated with a traditional model-tracing tutor as a control. We will refer to this tutor as "The Control." The Control did not engage a student in dialog, but did offer hint and buggy messages to the student. Table 1 shows how the experiment was designed.

Because of the small sample size, statistical significance was not obtainable in most of the analyses done in the following sections. It should be noted that with such small sample sizes, detecting statically significant effects is less likely. A large note of caution is also called for, since using such small sample sizes does make our conclusions more sensitive to a single child, thus possibly skewing our results.

Table 1. Experimental Design

Time	**Control Condition (7 students)**	**Experimental Condition (8 students)**
20 minutes	Paper and pencil pre-test	
5 minutes	Demonstration of both systems	
Control: average 47.8 minutes Experimental: average 55.6 minutes	Used Control Tutor	Used E-tutor
20 minutes	Paper and pencil post-test	

Learning Gains by Condition. To check for learning by condition, a repeated measure ANOVA was performed using experimental or control condition as a factor. The repeated measure of pre-test and post-test was a factor, with prediction of test score as the dependent variable. Due to the small sample size, we found that the experimental group did better on the pre-test by an average of about 1.5 points; the difference was bordering on statistical significance ($F(1,9) = 3.9$, $p = 0.07$). There was marginally statistically significant greater learning in the experimental condition than in the control condition ($F(1,9) = 2.3$, $p = 0.16$). The experimental condition had average pre-test score of 5.67 and post-test score of 6.67, showing a gain score of 1 problem. The control had average pre-test score of 4 problems correct and average post-test score of 4.2 problems correct. The effect size was a reasonable 0.4 standard deviations between the experimental and control conditions, that is, an effect size for E-tutor over the Control.

3 Conclusion

The experiment showed evidence that suggested incorporating dialog in an equation-solving tutor is helpful to students. Although the sample size was very small, there were some results in the analyses that suggest that, when controlling for number of problems, E-tutor performed better than the Control with an effect size of 0.4 standard deviations for overall learning by condition.

There were some limitations in this research that may have affected the results of the experiment. E-tutor presented tutorial dialogs to students when they made certain errors. However, the Control depended on student initiative for the appearance of hints. That is, the students had to press the Hint button if they wanted a hint. Although students in the control group were told that they could request hints whenever they wanted, the results may have been confounded by this dependence on student initiative in the control group. We may also be skeptical about the results because the sample size was very small. Additionally, the experimental group performed better on the pre-test than the control group, so they were already better at solving equations than the control group.

In the future, an experiment could be run with a larger and more balanced sample of students which would eliminate the differences between the groups on the pre-test. The confound with student initiative could be removed for a better evaluation of the two conditions. Another improvement would be to employ more tutorial strategies. Another experiment that controls for time rather than for the number of problems would examine whether E-tutor was worth the extra time.

References

1. Anderson, J. R. & Pelletier, R. (1991). A development system for model-tracing tutors. In *Proceedings of the International Conference of the Learning Sciences*, 1-8. Evanston, IL.
2. Bloom, B. S. (1984). The 2 Sigma Problem: The Search for Methods of Group Instruction as Effective as One-to-one Tutoring. *Educational Researcher*, 13, 4-16.
3. Graesser, A.C., Person, N., Harter, D., & TRG (2001). Teaching tactics and dialog in AutoTutor. *International Journal of Artificial Intelligence in Education.*
4. Heffernan, N. T., (2002-Accepted) Web-Based Evaluation Showing both Motivational and Cognitive Benefits of the Ms. Lindquist Tutor. *SIGdial endorsed Workshop on "Empirical Methods for Tutorial Dialogue Systems" which was part of the International Conference on Intelligent Tutoring System* 2002.
5. Heffernan, N. T (2001) *Intelligent Tutoring Systems have Forgotten the Tutor: Adding a Cognitive Model of Human Tutors.* Dissertation. Computer Science Department, School of Computer Science, Carnegie Mellon University. Technical Report CMU-CS-01-127 <http://reports-archive.adm.cs.cmu.edu/anon/2001/abstracts/01-127.html>
6. Koedinger, K. R., Anderson, J. R., Hadley, W. H. & Mark, M. A. (1995). Intelligent tutoring goes to school in the big city. *In Proceedings of the 7th World Conference on Artificial Intelligence in Education*, pp. 421-428. Charlottesville, VA: Association for the Advancement of Computing in Education.
7. Koedinger, K., Corbett, A., Ritter, S., Shapiro, L. (2000). Carnegie Learning's Cognitive Tutor™: Summary Research Results. http://www.carnegielearning.com/research/research_reports/CMU_research_results.pdf
8. McArthur, D., Stasz, C., & Zmuidzinas, M. (1990) Tutoring techniques in algebra. *Cognition and Instruction*. 7 (pp. 197-244.)
9. Ohlsson, S. (1986) Some principles for intelligent tutoring. *Instructional Science, 17*, 281-307.
10. Razzaq, Leena M. (2003) *Tutorial Dialog in an Equation Solving Intelligent Tutoring System.* Master Thesis. Computer Science Department, Worcester Polytechnic Institute. <http://www.wpi.edu/Pubs/ETD/Available/etd-0107104-155853>

A Metacognitive ACT-R Model of Students' Learning Strategies in Intelligent Tutoring Systems

Ido Roll, Ryan Shaun Baker, Vincent Aleven, and Kenneth R. Koedinger

Human Computer Interaction Institute, Carnegie Mellon University,
5000 Forbes Ave, Pittsburgh, PA 15218
{iroll, rsbaker, aleven}@cs.cmu.edu, koedinger@cmu.edu

Abstract. Research has shown that students' problem-solving actions vary in type and duration. Among other causes, this behavior is a result of strategies that are driven by different goals. We describe a first version of a computational cognitive model that explains the origin of these strategies and identifies the tendencies of students towards different learning goals. Our model takes into account (i) interpersonal differences, (ii) an estimation of the student's knowledge level, and (iii) current feedback from the tutor, in order to predict the next action of the student – a solution, a guess or a help request. Our long-term goal is to use identification of the students' strategies and their efficiency in order to better understand the learning process and to improve the metacognitive learning skills of the students.

1 Introduction

Studies have found some evidence to the connection between students' metacognitive decisions while working with ITS and their learning gains (Aleven et al. in press, Baker et al. 2004, Wood and Wood 1999). We describe here a computational model that explains such relations, by identifying various learning goals and strategies, assigning them to students, and relate them to learning outcomes.
We based our model on log-files of students working with the Geometry Cognitive Tutor, an ITS based on ACT-R theory (Anderson et al, 1995), which is now in extensive use in American public high schools.

2 The Model

The model identifies various goals and associates each goal with a different local-strategy that attempts to accomplish it. It assumes that students' actions, which are determined by the strategies, are driven by (i) their estimated ability to solve the step, (ii) their earlier actions and the system's feedback (e.g., error messages), and (iii) their tendency towards the different goals. The model assumes that every student has some tendency towards all goals. The exact combination of tendencies uniquely identifies the pattern of the individual student.

J.C. Lester et al. (Eds.): ITS 2004, LNCS 3220, pp. 854–856, 2004.

Currently, the model includes the following goals and strategies:

Table 1. The goals and strategies in the model

Goal	Strategy
Learning Oriented (Learn as much as possible)	After thinking about the question, I solve it if I can or ask for a hint.
Performance Oriented (Solve quickly, pretend to be working hard...)	I repeatedly ask for hints until the answer is revealed to me.
Least Effort Oriented (Make progress with minimal thinking effort)	I guess repeatedly until I get it right.
Help Avoider (I want to do it myself)	After thinking about the question, I solve it if I can. Otherwise I guess.

As seen in figure 1, the model has the following stages:

- The student evaluates her ability to solve the question correct immediately (1). If she thinks she can, she does so (2).
- If the student decides that she needs to spend more time thinking 3), she chooses a local strategy (4) and acts upon it (5).

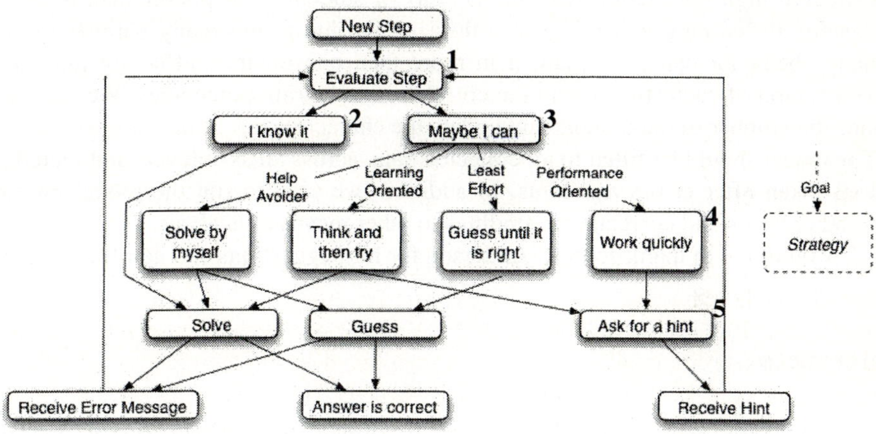

Fig. 1. Student's local goals determine their strategies and actions.

The model is implemented in ACT-R, a theory of mind and a framework for cognitive modeling (Anderson et al., 1998)

2.1 Fitting Data

We used data from Aleven et al. (in press), to identify the students' tendencies according to the model. We included only "new questions" data at this point (and not "after a hint" or "after an error"), for tractability. In addition, only questions to which the Cognitive Tutor evaluates the skill-level of the student as intermediate were included since these actions had the most between-student variance. 1400 actions, performed by 11 students, were analyzed in total.

The correlation between the data to the model's prediction is 1.00 for all students, and the average SD across all students is 0.09 (SD = 0.02). The high correlation is probably an over-fit as a result of too many parameters.

We see a high tendency towards Learning-Orientated and Help-Avoider (0.29 and 0.28 respectively), whereas tendencies towards I-know-it, Performance-Oriented and Least-Effort are 0.15, 0.15 and 0.12 respectively. These values make sense, given that students take their time and rarely use hints on their first actions on a new step.

We calculated the correlation between these tendencies and an independent measure of learning outcomes (as measured by the progress students made from pre- to post-test, divided by their maximum possible improvement). The only significant result is that Help-Avoider is highly correlated with learning gain, $F(1,9)=5.14$, $p<0.05$, $r=0.58$, suggesting that students with higher tendency to avoid help on their first actions did better in the overall learning experience.

3 Conclusions and Future Work

We observe high correlation with the actions of students, but poorer than expected correlation to learning gains. We hypothesize that due to too many parameters, the students' behavior can be explained in more than one manner, affecting the single representation of each student and the correlation to learning outcomes. We currently reduce the number of parameters and update the characteristics of the strategies.

The model should be fitted to all collected data, across all skill levels and including actions taken after errors and hints. In addition, we plan to run the model on data from other tutors and correlate the findings to other means of analysis.

We would like to thank John R. Anderson for his suggestions and helpful advice.

References

1. Aleven, V., McLaren, B., Roll, I., Koedinger, K. Toward Tutoring Help Seeking: Applying Cognitive Modeling to Meta-Cognitive Skills. To appear at Intelligent Tutoring Systems Conference (2004)
2. Anderson, J. R., A. T. Corbett, K. R. Koedinger, and R. Pelletier, (1995). Cognitive tutors: Lessons learned. The Journal of the Learning Sciences, 4, 167-207.
3. Baker, R. S., Corbett, A. T., Wagner, A. Z. & Koedinger, K. R., Off-Task Behavior in the Cognitive Tutor Classroom: When Students "Game the System", Proceedings of the SIGCHI conference on human factors in computing systems (2004), p. 383-390, Vol. 6 no. 1.
4. McNeil, N.M. & Alibali, M.W. (2000), Learning Mathematics from Procedural Instruction: Externally Imposed Goals Influence What Is Learned, Journal of Educational Psychology, 92 #4, 734-744.
5. Wood, H., & Wood, D. (1999). Help seeking, learning and contingent tutoring. Computers and Education, 33, 153-169.

Promoting Effective Help-Seeking Behavior Through Declarative Instruction

Ido Roll, Vincent Aleven, and Kenneth Koedinger

Human Computer Interaction Institute, Carnegie Mellon University,
5000 Forbes Avenue, Pittsburgh, PA 15218, USA
{idoroll, koedinger}@cmu.edu, aleven@cs.cmu.edu

Abstract. Research has shown that students' help-seeking behavior is far from being ideal. In trying to make it more efficient, 27 students using the Geometry Cognitive Tutor regularly received individual online instructions. The instruction to the HELP group, aimed to improve their help-seeking behavior, included a walk-through metacognitive example. The CONTROL group received "placebo instruction" with a similar walk-through but without the help-seeking content. In two subsequent weeks, the HELP group used the system's hints more frequently than the CONTROL group. However, we didn't observe a significant difference in the learning outcomes. These results suggest that appropriate instruction can improve help-seeking behavior in ITS usage. Further evaluation should be performed in order to design better instruction and improve learning.

1 Introduction

Efficient help-seeking behavior in intelligent tutoring systems (ITS) can improve learning outcomes and reduce learning duration (Renkl, 2002; Wood & Wood, 1999). Nevertheless, studies have shown that students use help in suboptimal ways in various ITS (Mandl et al. 2000, Aleven et al. 2000).

The Geometry Cognitive tutor, investigated in this study, is now in extensive use in American public high schools. The tutor has two forms of on-demand help: Context-sensitive hints and decontextualized glossary.

One way to try to improve students' help use is through guiding students to more effective one. White et al. (1998) showed that by developing students' metacognitive knowledge and skills the students learn better. McNeil et al. (2000) showed that students' goals can be modified in lab settings by prompting them appropriately. These studies suggest that appropriate instruction about desired help seeking behavior might be effective in improving that behavior.

2 Experiment

Students from an urban high school were divided into two groups:

The HELP group (including 14 students) received instruction aimed to improve their help-seeking behavior. The CONTROL group (including 13 students) received

J.C. Lester et al. (Eds.): ITS 2004, LNCS 3220, pp. 857–859, 2004.

"placebo-instruction" which focused only on the subject matter without any metacognitive content.

The instructions were given through a website, and students read it at their own pace. Both the HELP and CONTROL instruction led the students through solved examples in the unit the students were working on. The HELP instruction incorporated the desired help-seeking behavior into it, and included the following principles: (i) Ask for a hint when you don't know what to do (ii) read the hint before you ask for an additional one, and (iii) don't guess quickly after committing an error.

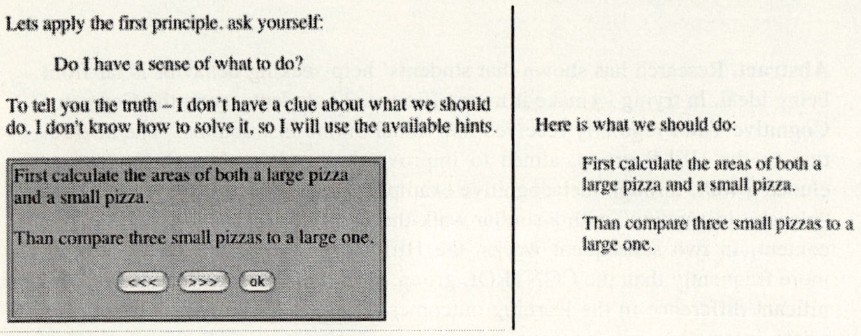

Fig. 1. A snapshot from the instruction. Both the HELP instruction (left hand side) and the CONTROL instruction (right hand side) convey the same cognitive information. In addition, the help-instruction offers a way to obtain that information.

The study was built into the students' existing curriculum, and the students were proficient in working with the Geometry Cognitive Tutor. Students took a pre- and post-test before and after the study, and reported how much attention they paid to the instruction. Since the students were in different lessons of the same unit, each student took a test that matched her progress in the curricula.

On the first day students went individually through the help-seeking instruction, which took about 15 minutes. In the second day, the students went through additional 5 minutes of similar instruction. This time they had to solve a question. In addition to the feedback on the cognitive level, which students in both groups received from the tutor, students in the HELP group received feedback on their help-seeking actions.

In total, students worked on the tutor for approximately 3 hours spread out across 2 weeks. At the end of the two weeks, the students took a post-test.

3 Results

As in Wood & Wood (1999), we calculated the ratio of hints to errors, measured by hints/(hints+errors). This ratio was much higher for the HELP group (0.24) than for the CONTROL group (0.09). The result is marginally significant ($F(1,21)=2.96$, $p=0.10$). However, this does not reveal whether the hint-requests were appropriate.

The students' self-reported attention didn't affect the help-use of the CONTROL group (the hints-to-errors ratio for both low- and high-attention students was 0.09).

However, students which reported paying low attention in the HELP group used significantly more help than those reported paying high attention (0.43 hints-to-errors for low-attention students vs. 0.12 for the high-attention ones, $F(1,11)=8.31$, $p=0.01$). We hypothesize that students who paid low attention to the instruction understood only that they should use help a lot, and thus engaged in an inappropriate hint abuse.

Students showed learning during the experiment (average pre-test score: 1.15 out of 4; average post-test score: 1.67). This improvement was significant, $T(0,26)=2.10$, $p=0.04$. Direct comparison between conditions was difficult, given the design of our study where students were working on different tutor lessons, and thus we did not observe any significant influence of the condition on the learning outcomes.

4 Conclusions and Future Work

Declarative instruction has the potential to influence help-seeking behavior in real classroom environments. More studies should be done to determine the impact of the instruction (e.g., how does it influence learning, for how long the influence persists and whether it extends to other tutor lessons).

The instruction should be combined with other supporting tools such as tracing the students' help seeking behavior in real time and promoting self-assessment.

We would like to thank Matthew Welch and Michele O'Farrell for assisting us in conducting this study, and to Ryan S. Baker for helpful suggestions and comments.

References

1. Aleven, V., & Koedinger, K. R. (2000). Limitations of student control: Do students know when they need help? In C. F. G. Gauthier & K. VanLehn (Eds.), Proceedings of the 5th International Conference on Intelligent Tutoring Systems, ITS 2000 (pp. 292-303).Berlin: Springer Verlag.
2. Anderson, J. R., A. T. Corbett, K. R. Koedinger, and R. Pelletier, (1995). Cognitive tutors: Lessons learned. The Journal of the Learning Sciences, 4, 167-207.
3. Mandl, H., Gräsel, C. & Fischer, F. (2000). Problem-oriented learning: Facilitating the use of domain-specific and control strategies through modeling by an expert. In W. J. Perrig & A. Grob (Eds.), Control of Human Behavior, Mental Processes and Consciousness (pp.165-182). Mahwah: Erlbaum.
4. McNeil, N.M. & Alibali, M.W. (2000), Learning Mathematics from Procedural Instruction: Externally Imposed Goals Influence What Is Learned, Journal of Educational Psychology, 92 #4, 734-744.
5. Renkl, A. (2002). Learning from worked-out examples: Instructional explanations supplement self-explanations. Learning & Instruction, 12, 529-556.
6. White, B.Y. & Federistan, J.R. (1998), Inquiry, Modeling, and Metacognition: Making Science Accessible to All Students. Cognition and Instruction, 16(1), 3-118
7. Wood, H., & Wood, D. (1999). Help seeking, learning and contingent tutoring. Computers and Education, 33, 153-169.

Supporting Spatial Awareness in Training on a Telemanipulator in Space

Jean Roy[1], Roger Nkambou[1], and Froduald Kabanza[2]

Département d'informatique,
[1] Université du Québec à Montréal, Montréal (Québec) H3C 3P8 Canada
[2] Université de Sherbrooke, Sherbrooke (Québec) JIK 2R1 Canada
{roy.jean-a, nkambou.roger}@uqam.ca, kabanza@usherbrooke.ca

Abstract. In this paper, we present an approach for supporting spatial awareness in an intelligent tutoring system, the purpose of which is to train astronauts to operating tasks of a telemanipulator. Our aim is to propose recommendations regarding knowledge structures and cognitive strategies relevant in this context. The spatial awareness is supported through efficient use of animations presenting different tasks.

1 Introduction

The capabilities of spatial representation and reasoning required by the operation of a remote manipulator, such as Canadarm II on the International Space Station (ISS) or other remotely operated devices, are often compared to those required by the operation of a sophisticated crane. In the case of a remote manipulator, however, the manipulator has several joints to control and there can be several operating modes based on distinct frames of reference. Furthermore, and most importantly, the task is remotely executed and controlled on the basis of feedback from video cameras. The operator must not only know how to operate the arm, avoiding singularities and dead ends, but he must also choose and orient the cameras so as to execute its task in the safest and most efficient manner. Computer 3D animation provides an complementary tool for increasing the safety of operations.

The goal of training on operating a telemanipulator like Canadarm II is notably to improve the situation awareness (Currie & Peacock, 2002) and the spatial awareness (Wickens 2002) of astronauts. Distance evaluation, orientation and navigation are basic dimensions of spatial awareness. Two key limits of traditional ITS in this respect are cognitive *tunnelling*, i.e. the fact that observers tend to focus attention on information from specific areas of a display to the exclusion of information presented outside of these highly attended areas, and the difficulty to integrate different camera views. Our challenge is to produce animations (as learning resources) that are efficient in restoring spatial awareness, i.e. in improving the distance estimation, the orientation and the navigation. A training environment based on the use of automatically generated animations offers a natural integration of different camera views that represents a spatial and temporal continuity. Pedagogically, the use of such anima-

J.C. Lester et al. (Eds.): ITS 2004, LNCS 3220, pp. 860–863, 2004.

tions is justified by the fact that astronauts who look alternatively at different displays are compelled to achieve such an integration of different camera views.

To examine the learning of these three tasks, we have developed a 3D environment (figure 1) reproducing different configurations of the International Space Station and Canadarm II. This environment includes a simulator enabling the manipulation of Canadarm II robot manipulator, different viewpoints and camera functionalities, as well as an automated movie production module.

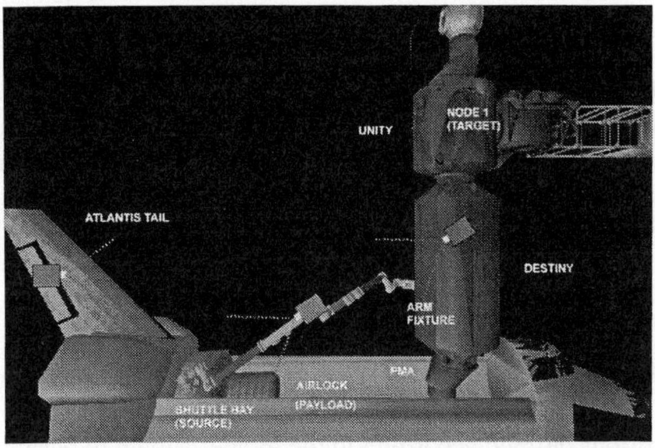

Fig. 1. A screen shot of the working environment.

2 A Model for Automatic Production of Pedagogic Movies

Movies used in our learning environment are pedagogic resources which can be generated automatically depending on formal task specifications. In order to make such an automated generation possible and to reason about the movie structure, cognitive task and navigation constraints, we use a graph-based movie model (Berendt, 1999) called *FILM route graph*. This graph combines properties of a film tree and a basic route graph, using concepts from cognitive modelling and computer graphics.

A film tree is a tree describing a film partitioned into sequences, scenes and frames; the partitioning may be based on the type or theme of activity in each sequence or the episodes in the movie. The basic route graph allows the reproduction of the process of distance inference between two landmarks. Typically, it models the capacity to memorise and process information used in distance evaluation. In the perception of distances covered, it is assumed that subjects have already covered a route and they are therefore requested to memorise the distances between the landmarks. The model is therefore useful inasmuch as the goal is to bring astronauts to learn a certain route.

The integration of the basic route graph into the broader structure of a film tree creates two challenges. First, the basic route graph has been validated in a virtual environment which proposes an egocentric camera viewpoint. It is therefore necessary to verify through experiment, whether the conclusions applicable in such an environment can be transposed into an exocentric shot. Secondly, it is important to clarify which cognitive mechanisms play a part in the interpretation of successive shots according to cinematic heuristics, in particular the integration of egocentric and exocentric viewpoints. This requires an experimental clarification.

3 The Experiment and the Lessons Learned

Our experiment aimed at clarifying the extent to which the integration of viewpoints with cinematic heuristic rules does facilitate the integration of different viewpoints. It must validate the three following hypotheses: 1) cognitive rules can be associated to cinematographic rules; 2) the cognitive model for the evaluation of travelled distances can be adapted to the case of a representation based on several camera shots; 3) the main distortions in the evaluation of travelled distances are caused less by 3D perception problems than by problems linked to the films composition.

3.1 The Main Conclusions of the Experiment

The experiment lasted about one hour. A total number of 16 participants took part in the experiment. They were distributed into three groups corresponding to three experimental conditions defined according to the movies shown to participants.

Three conclusion could be drawn from the results of experiments on the subjective evaluation of distances: 1) the viewpoint of the egocentric camera makes distance evaluation more difficult and even contributes to the distortion in the evaluation of distance travelled; 2) the omission of the presentation on the screen of a stretch of movement is likely to distort the evaluation of distance travelled, even if the subjects have additional information such as maps and pictures enabling them to infer a movement that is not observed; 3) the magnitude of distortions observed in distance evaluation seems to confirm that in the use of movies for learning, cinematographic distortions are more important than effects related to such factors as 3D perception.

3.2 Learner's Model and Cognitive Strategies

The FILM route graph provides a model which is quite appropriate for orienting learning, since it values the analysis of encoding mechanisms which allow a better retrieval of information from the long term memory. Also, the proposed representation does not include any additional assistant device for distances and orientation evaluation. The graph helps in the formulation of display specifications (colours, shapes, etc) used for the identification of natural landmarks as well specifications for camera shots used to achieve a cinematographic representation that allows a better application of the model.

The results analysis of our experiment clearly shows different cognitive strategies used for space navigation. The main cognitive strategy is the evaluation of covered distance according to the size of an object. A second strategy used in the evaluation of distances covered is the distance evaluation according to an assessment of movement speed and duration. A third strategy resides directly on the study of maps.

References

Berendt, B. 1999. *Representation and Processing of Knowledge about Distances in Environmental Space.* Amsterdam: IOS Press.

Currie, N. and B. Peacock 2002. International Space Station Robotic Systems Operations: A Human Factors Perspective. Habitability & Human Factors Office (HHFO). NASA.

Wickens, C. D. 2002. Spatial Awareness Biases, *University of Illinois Institute of Aviation Final Technical Report* (ARL-02-6/NASA-02-4). Savoy, IL: Aviation Research Lab.

Validating DynMap as a Mechanism to Visualize the Student's Evolution Through the Learning Process

U. Rueda, M. Larrañaga, J.A. Elorriaga, and A. Arruarte

University of the Basque Country (UPV/EHU)
649 P.K., E-20080 Donostia
{jibrumou, jiplaolm, elorriaga, arruarte}@si.ehu.es

Abstract. This paper describes a study conducted with the aim of validating *DynMap*, a system based on Concept Maps, as a mechanism to visualize the evolution of the students through the learning process of a particular subject. DynMap has been developed with the aim of providing the educational community with a tool that facilitates the inspection of the student data. It offers the user a graphical representation of the student model and enables learners and teachers to understand the model better.

1 Introduction

Up to now, the research community has considered visualization and inspection of the student model [9]. This component collects the learning characteristics of the student and his/her evolution during the whole learning process. [6] collects some of the reasons that different authors argue for making the learner model available. [1] claims that the use of simple learner models, easy to show in different ways, allows teachers and students to improve the understanding of students' learning of the target domain.

2 DynMap

CM-ED (Concept Map EDitor) [8] is a general purpose tool for editing Concept Maps (CMs) [7]. The aim of the tool is to be useful in different contexts and uses of the educational agenda, concretely inside the computer-based teaching and learning area.

DynMap [8] uses the core of CM-ED and facilitates the inspection of the student data. Taking into account that the student's knowledge changes along the learning process it will be useful if the student module reflects this evolution. Unlike most of the revised student models, DynMap is able to show graphically this evolution. It shows student models based on CMs following the overlay approach [5]. Thus, the knowledge that a student has about a domain is represented as a subset of the whole domain, which is represented in a CM. Considering Bull's classification [2] DynMap would be included in the viewable models. It is designed for student models automatically inferred by a teaching/learning system or manually gathered from the teacher.

J.C. Lester et al. (Eds.): ITS 2004, LNCS 3220, pp. 864–866, 2004.

3 Study: Evaluating DynMap in a Real Use Context

Understandability [3] is the first criteria that an open student model should meet. Focusing on this criteria and, after validating in a preliminary study [8] the set of graphical resources selected to show different circumstances of the student model, a second experiment has been carried out. The main aim of the new study is to evaluate DynMap, as a mechanism for visualising the evolution of the students through the learning sessions of a particular subject.

Context. The study has been conducted in the context of a Computer Security course in the Computer Science Faculty at the University of the Basque Country [4]. In order to carry out continuous assessment, the teachers gather information on the students' performance throughout the term. Due to the complexity and dynamism of the assessment system, the students need to check their marks frequently.

Participants. A group of 32 students from the Computer Security course in 03-04.

Procedure. A questionnaire was constructed to investigate students' opinions about DynMap. It was conducted anonymously during the first part of a normal lab session and they did not receive any help in using the tool. First at all, they were asked to search for some data in the CM that represented the learner model. Next, each student answered a questionnaire composed of 6 open questions and 17 multiple choice questions, where they had to choose a number between 1 and 5.

Results. The first part of the questionnaire was related to the *accessibility* of the information that DynMap offered in carrying out the above mentioned searches. 63,6% of students considered it easy to look for specific data. In the second part the participants were asked about the *organization* of the presented CM. 66,6% of students thought a CM organization is a good approach for representing the student's knowledge. The third part evaluated the suitability of the *information* that DynMap provided. 73,9% of students considered the information provided by the CM was sufficient. In part four, participants were questioned about accessing *individual* and *group data*. 78,9% of students considered students' data private. Even more, 92,8% of students did not have much interest in accessing other students' models. However, 64,03% of students thought that knowing the marks of his/her group was valuable. 46,87% agreed with knowing the marks of other groups learning the same subject. Part five explored *new uses* of CMs in the teaching of a subject. 72,2% of students were in favour of using CMs for management purposes inside the teaching/learning process. CM would be useful for organizing the subject material (68%), for planning the whole course (66,6%) or for managing personal assignments with the teacher (50%). Finally, in part six users had the opportunity to contribute *suggestions*. Most comments suggested improvements in the visualization of the student model such as including the whole information on just a single screen or using some graphical resources for highlighting special circumstances.

Regarding the other partner of the teaching/learning, the teacher of the subject said that the tool could help in assessment decisions and also that it could be useful as a medium to communicate the marks to the students. He added the next issues:

- The graphical view of the student model allows the teacher to analyse the distribution of the students' activities among the units of the subject. This is useful in identifying weaknesses and strengths in the student's knowledge and also to detect learners that are focussing exclusively on some parts.

- It is interesting to observe the evolution of the student through the learning process due to the continuous assessment of the subject.

The teacher was more convinced about the utility of having group models. Again, this feature would be useful in detecting weaknesses and strengths but at group level and also to identify most popular contents.

4 Conclusions

The experiment confirmed that the graphical representation of the student model provided by DynMap is easily understandable. Even more, DynMap offers handy mechanisms for inspecting the student information such as showing the evolution of the learner's knowledge. The study results confirmed that users are able to read, manipulate and communicate with conceptual maps.

The assessment of the subject here presented is carried out continuously along the term and, therefore, it needs an appropriate medium to show the evolution of the marks. Hence, the preparation of the study reported along this paper has got a tool for visualizing graphically student's marks for both teachers and students.

Acknowledgements. This work is funded by the University of the Basque Country (UPV00141.226-T-14816/2002), the Spanish CICYT (TIC2002-03141) and the *Gipuzkoa* Council in an European Union program.

References

1. Bull, S. and Nghiem, T.: Helping Learners to Understand Themselves with a Learner Model Open to Students, Peers and Instructors. In: Brna, P. and Dimitrova, V. (eds.): Proceedings of Workshop on Individual and Group Modelling Methods that Help Learners Understand Themselves, ITS2002 (2002) 5-13.
2. Bull, S., McEvoy, A.T. & Reid, E.: Learner Models to Promote Reflection in Combined Desktop PC/Mobile Intelligent Learning Environments. In: Aleven, V., Hoppe, U., Kay, J., Mizoguchi, R., Pain, H., Verdejo, F., Yacef, K. (eds): AIED2003 Sup. Proc.(2003)199-208.
3. Dimitrova, V.: Interactive cognitive modelling agents – potential and challenges. In: Brna, P. and Dimitrova, V. (eds.): Proceedings of Workshop on Individual and Group Modelling Methods that Help Learners Understand Themselves, ITS2002, (2002) 52-62.
4. Elorriaga, J.A., Gutiérrez, J., Ibáñez, J. And Usandizaga, I.: A Proposal for a Computer Security Course. ACM SIGCSE Bulletin (1998) 42-47.
5. Golstein, I.P.: The Genetic Graph: a representation for the evolution of procedural knowledge. In: Sleeman, D. and Brown, J.S. (eds.): ITSs, Academic Press (1982) 51-77.
6. Kay, J.: Learner Control. User Modelling & User-Adapted Interaction, V.11(2001)111-127.
7. Novak, J.D.: A theory of education. Cornell University, Ithaca, NY (1977)
8. Rueda, U., Larrañaga, M., Ferrero, B., Arruarte, A., Elorriaga, J.A.: Study of graphical issues in a tool for dynamically visualising student models. In: Aleven, V., Hoppe, U., Kay, J., Mizoguchi, R., Pain, H., Verdejo, F., Yacef, K. (eds): AIED (2003) Suppl. Proc. 268-277.
9. Workshop on Open, Interactive, and other Overt Approaches to Learner Modelling. AIED'99, Le Mans, France, July, 1999 (http://cbl.leeds.ac.uk/ijaied/).

Qualitative Reasoning in Education of Deaf Students: Scientific Education and Acquisition of Portuguese as a Second Language*

Heloisa Salles[1], Paulo Salles[2], and Bert Bredeweg[3]

[1] University of Brasília, Department of Linguistics,
Campus Universitário Darcy Ribeiro, Asa Norte,
70.910-900, Brasília, Brasil
hsalles@unb.br
[2] University of Brasília, Institute of Biological Science,
Campus Universitário Darcy Ribeiro, Asa Norte,
70.910-900, Brasília, Brasil
psalles@unb.br
[3] University of Amsterdam, Department of Social Science and Informatic,
Roeterstraat, 15 / 1018WB Amsterdam, The Netherlands,
bert@swi.psy.uva.nl

Abstract. Brazilian educational system is faced with the task of integrating deafs along with non-deafs in the classroom. A requirement of a bilingual education arises, with the Brazilian Sign Language as the native language and Portuguese as the second language. Qualitative Reasoning may provide tools to support Portuguese acquisition while developing scientific concepts. This study describes an experiment with eight deaf students being exposed to three qualitative models. Five students were successful in exploring causal relations and in writing up a composition about an ecological accident. The results encourage us to explore the potential of qualitative models in second language acquisition.

1 Aspects of the Educational Situation of Deaf Students in Brazil

Brazilian deaf students are nowadays integrated in the classroom along with non-deaf students. In spite of all sorts of limitations for implementing bilingual education [6], most educational methods have been oriented by the assumption that the Brazilian Sign Language (henceforth, LIBRAS) is the native language of the deaf community, Portuguese being their second language. In this context, tools to articulate knowledge and mediate second language acquisition are required. Qualitative Reasoning (QR) may support the education of deaf students, as they are articulate knowledgeable models with explicit representations of causality. Our objective here is to verify the understanding and use of the causal relations by deaf students, assuming that (i) the causal relations represented in the models should be understood, due to their ability to

* An extended version of this paper can be found in the Proceedings of the 18th International Workshop on Qualitative Reasoning, held in Evanston, Illinois, August 2004.

J.C. Lester et al. (Eds.): ITS 2004, LNCS 3220, pp. 867–869, 2004.

work out logical deductions; (ii) the understanding of the causal relations and the articulation of old and new vocabulary can be read off the linguistic description of processes and the textual connectivity in their written composition in Portuguese; (iii) while conceptual connectivity (*coherence*) is a function of the understanding of the causal relations, grammatical connectivity (*cohesion*) is a function of the level of proficiency in each language, LIBRAS and Portuguese [3].

2 Models, Simulations, and Evaluation of the Experiment

We adopt the Qualitative Process Theory [2], an ontology that has been the basis for a number of studies in cognitive science (for example, [4]), and implemented the models in the qualitative simulator GARP [1]. Causal relations are modelled by using two primitives: direct *influences* that represent processes (I+ and I–), and qualitative *proportionalities* (P+ and P–) to represent how changes caused by processes propagate through the system (see Figure 1).

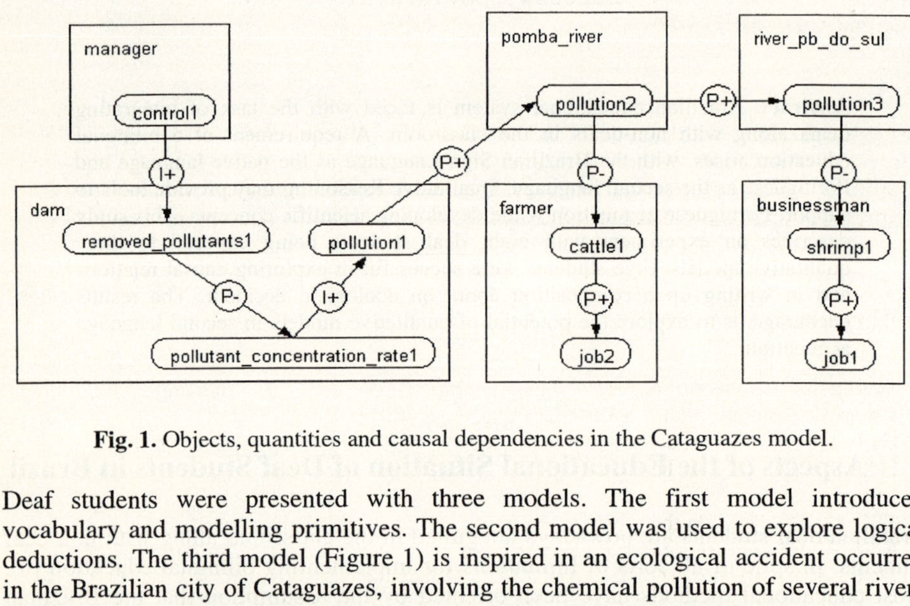

Fig. 1. Objects, quantities and causal dependencies in the Cataguazes model.

Deaf students were presented with three models. The first model introduced vocabulary and modelling primitives. The second model was used to explore logical deductions. The third model (Figure 1) is inspired in an ecological accident occurred in the Brazilian city of Cataguazes, involving the chemical pollution of several rivers in a densely populated area in the Paraíba do Sul river water basin [5].

The study was run in a secondary state school in Brasília, with deaf students from the 2nd year, their teachers and interpreters of LIBRAS-Portuguese in the classroom. Questionnaires and diagrams were used as evaluation tools, and explored the formulation of predictions and explanations about changes in quantities, by means of exploring the causal model. The final question was a written composition about the third model. The performance of five out of eight students allows for interesting observations. They were successful in recognizing objects, quantities and changes of quantity values during the simulations and building up causal chains based on the given models. They were partially successful in building up causal chains given initial values for some quantities, and identifying processes. Finally, they were successful in reporting the consequences of the ecological accident in a (written) composition. The results of the remaining three students are not conclusive at present.

3 Discussion

This paper describes exploratory studies on the use of qualitative models to mediate the second language acquisiton by deaf students in the context of science education. The consistence in the results allows for a correlation between the writing skills of the students and their understanding of the causal model. In particular, conceptual connectivity in the text seems to be a function of the ability to recognize objects and processes, to build up causal chains and to apply them to a given situation, assessing derivative values of quantities and making predictions about the consequences of their changes. The results reported here constitute a first approach in a research program concerned with the acquisition of Portuguese as second language by deaf students (see below). Ongoing work includes a similar experiment with a qualitative model developed for the understanding of electrochemistry in secondary schools [7].

Acknowledgements. We thank the deaf students that took part in the experiment, as well as their teachers and educational coordinators and the APADA for their support. H. and P. Salles are grateful to CAPES/MEC/ PROESP for the financial support to the project Portuguese as a second language in the scientific education of deaf.

References

1. Bredeweg, B. (1992) *Expertise in Qualitative Prediction of Behaviour*. Ph.D. thesis, University of Amsterdam, Amsterdam, The Netherlands, 1992.
2. Forbus, K.D. (1984) Qualitative process theory. Artificial Intelligence, 24:85–168.
3. Halliday, M. A. K. & R. Hasan (1976) *Cohesion in Spoken and Written English*. London: Longman.
4. Kuhene, S. (2003) On the representation of physical quantities in natural language. In Salles, P. & Bredeweg, B. (eds.) *Proceedings of the Seventeenth International Workshop on Qualitative Reasoning (QR'03)*, pages 131-138 Brasília, Brasil, August 20-22, 2003.
5. Martins, J. (2003) Uma onda de irresponsabilidades. *Ciência Hoje*, 33(195): 52-54.
6. Quadros, R. (1997) *Educação de Surdos: a Aquisição da Linguagem*. Porto Alegre: Artes Médicas.
7. Salles, P.; Gauche, R. & Virmond, P. (2004) A qualitative model of the Daniell cell for chemical education. This volume.

A Qualitative Model of Daniell Cell for Chemical Education

Paulo Salles[1], Ricardo Gauche[2], and Patrícia Virmond[2]

[1] University of Brasília, Institute of Biological Sciences,
Brasília, Brasil
psalles@unb.br
http://www.unb.br/ib-n/index.htm
[2] University of Brasília, Institute of Chemistry,
Brasília, Brasil
gauche@unb.br, patriciavirmond@bol.com.br
http://www.unb.br/iq-n/index.htm

Abstract. Understanding how students learn chemical concepts has been a great concern for researchers of chemical education, who want to identify the most important misunderstandings and develop strategies to overcome conceptual problems. Qualitative Reasoning has great potential for building conceptual models that can be useful for chemical education. This paper describes a qualitative model for supporting understanding the interaction between chemical reactions and electric current in the Daniell cell. We discuss the potential of the model for science education of deaf students.

1 Introduction

Why does the colour of copper sulphate changes when the Daniell cell is functioning? Any Brazilian student in a secondary school should be able to answer this question, given that the Daniell cell is largely used to build up concepts on the relation between chemical reactions and electric current. However, the students can hardly give a causal account of the Daniell cell typical behaviour. Textbooks are widely used in Brazilian schools, but they fail in developing fundamental concepts [3]. The laboratory is not an option in this case, because experiments in general do not work very well. Computer models and simulations are interesting alternatives. However, are they actually being used by the teachers? Ribeiro [5] reviewed papers published in 15 leading international journals of chemical education during a period of 10 years (up to 2002) and showed that the use of software is far less than expected. Qualitative Reasoning (QR) has great potential for supporting science education. This potential was explored by Mustapha [4], who describe a system for simulating a chemistry laboratory. Here we describe a qualitative model for understanding the structure and behaviour of the Daniell cell.

J.C. Lester et al. (Eds.): ITS 2004, LNCS 3220, pp. 870–872, 2004.

2 The Daniell Cell and the Modelling Process

The Daniell cell consists of a zinc rod dipping in a solution of zinc sulphate, connected by a wire to a copper rod dipping in a copper sulphate (II) solution. Spontaneous oxidation and reduction reactions generate electric current, with electrons passing from the zinc rod (the anode) to the wire and from it to the copper rod (the cathode). While the battery works, the zinc rod goes under corrosion and its mass decreases, while concentration of ions Zn^{2+} increases in the half cell. The copper rod receives a deposit of metal and its mass increase, so that concentration of ions Cu^{2+} in the solution decreases. A bulb that goes on and off and the colour of the solution in the cathode cell are external signs of the battery functioning. Copper sulphate produces a blue coloured solution. As the concetration of this substance decreases, the liquid becomes colourless. The process centred approach [2] was chosen as an ontology for representing the cell and the models were implemented in GARP [1]. Causality is represented by direct *influences* and qualitative *proportionalities*. The former represents processes, the primary cause of change. Proportionalities propagate to other quantities changes caused by processes. In this case, the causal link is established via the derivatives (see Figure 1):

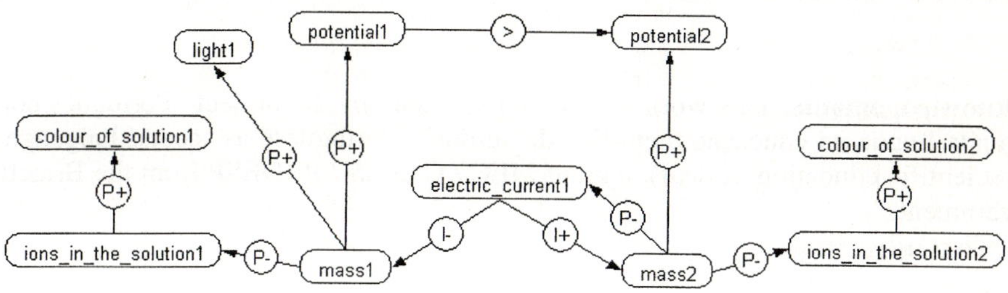

Fig. 1. Dependencies between quantities in state 1 of a simulation.

3 Simulation and Results

Simulation with this model generates only two states: the initial and the final states, respectively states 1 and 2. In state 1, the potential in the anode is greater than the potential in the cathode. This situation creates a flow of electrons that leave the rod with greater potential and move to the rod with lower potential, setting the value *on* to the bulb connected to the wire. This flow of electrons increases the mass at the cathode and decreases the amount of ions copper in the solution, while decreases the mass of the anode and increases the amount of ions zinc in the solution. Variations in the mass of the metals also affect the potential of the electrodes. This situation leads to a state transition. In state 2, the process stops because there is no longer difference potentials between the electrodes (the chemical equilibrium), and the battery does not work. The bulb is off and the copper sulphate solution becomes colourless.

4 Discussion and Final Remarks

This work describes a qualitative model of the Daniell cell. Textbooks do not describe how chemical energy transforms into electric energy. A QR approach has an added value because it focus on the causal relations that determine the behaviour of the cell. A description of the mechanism of change, the electric current generation process, indicates the origin of the dynamic phenomenon, which is then propagated to and observed in the rest of the system. This way, inspecting only the causal model of the battery the student can explain why the mass of rods change, and why the bulb goes off while the colour of the solution at the cathode disappears. The work described here is part of an umbrella project that aims at the development of Portuguese as a second language for deaf students (see below). The use of qualitative models to support second language acquisition by deaf students is already being investigated and the results obtained so far are encouraging. Ongoing work includes exploring the qualitative model of the Daniell cell with a group of deaf students in an experiment similar to the one described in Salles [6], improved by the lessons learned.

Acknowledgements. This work was partially funded by the project "Português como segunda língua na educação científica de surdos" (Portuguese as second language in the scientific education of deaf), a grant MEC / CAPES / PROESP from the Brazilian government.

References

1. Bredeweg, B. (1992) Expertise in Qualitative Prediction of Behaviour. Ph.D. thesis, University of Amsterdam, Amsterdam, The Netherlands, 1992.
2. Forbus, K.D. (1984) Qualitative process theory. *Artificial Intelligence*, 24:85–168.
3. Lopes, A. R. C. (1992) Livros didáticos: obstáculo ao aprendizado da ciência Química. *Química Nova*, 15(3): 254-261.
4. Mustapha, S.M.F.D.; Jen-Sen, P. & Zaim, S.M. (2002) Application of Qualitative Process Theory to qualitative simulation and analysis of inorganic chemical reaction. In: N. Angell & J. A. Ortega (Eds.) *Proceedings of the International workshop on Qualitative Reasoning, (QR'02)*, pages 177-184, Sitges - Barcelona, Spain, June 10-12, 2002.
5. Ribeiro, A.A. & Greca, I.M. (2003) Simulações computacionais e ferramentas de modelização em educação química: uma revisão de literatura publicada. *Química Nova*, 26(4): 542-549.
6. Salles, H.; Salles, P. & Bredeweg, B. (2004) Qualitative reasoning in education of deaf students: scientific education and acquisition of Portuguese as a second language. This volume.

Student Representation Assisting Cognitive Analysis

Antoaneta Serguieva and Tariq M. Khan

Brunel Business School, Brunel University, Uxbridge UB8 3PH, UK
{Antoaneta.Serguieva, Tariq.Khan}@brunel.ac.uk

Abstract. A central concern when developing intelligent tutoring systems is student representation. This paper introduces work-in-progress on producing a scheme that describes various imprecision in student knowledge. The scheme is based on domain representation through multiple generalized constraints. The adopted approach to domain and student representation will facilitate cognitive analysis performed as propagation of generalized constraints. Qualitative reasoning provides the basis for the approach and Zadeh's computational theory of perception complements the technique with the ability to process perception-based information.

1 Introduction

The development of intelligent educational systems faces the challenging problem of cognitive diagnosis. This necessitates approaches to analyzing student performance and inferring cognitive states. The end aim of our work is to develop techniques that evaluate the current state of a student's understanding of domain concepts and their interrelations by identifying those domain models or constraints thought to be held by the student. On the one hand, learning progresses cyclically with knowledge being revisited, and it is difficult to claim one model that represents a student's understanding absolutely. On the other hand, there is a degree of uncertainty regarding any student's understanding, and ways to represent that uncertainty or imprecision are being researched. A solution to both these tendencies is provided by first employing multiple-model student representation, and then incorporating imprecise knowledge by transforming the models into generalized constraints. Generalized constraints – introduced by Zadeh [11],[12] – are a generalization of the notion of model and describe knowledge involving various imprecision. Both quantitative and qualitative models form important, though special classes of generalized constraints. A student's perception of domain information is characterized with imprecision and reflects her bounded ability to resolve detail and unbounded capability for information compression. We recommend imprecision as one of the perspectives [8],[9] in the multi-dimensional knowledge framework [4],[5]. The contribution of the computational theory of perception [12] to the capability of qualitative diagnostic methods [1],[2],[3] to process and reason with perception-based information will allow the reformulation of performance analysis. Thus, it will be possible to associate observed student performance with a subset of generalized constraints.

J.C. Lester et al. (Eds.): ITS 2004, LNCS 3220, pp. 873–876, 2004.

2 Student Framework

Let us describe domain knowledge through four-dimensional generalized constraints:

$$X\ isr_{resolution} r_{scope} r_{generality} r_{imprecision}\ R \tag{1}$$

$$r_{resolution} \in \{compositional\ levels\}$$

$$r_{scope} \in \{taxonomy\ classes\}$$

$$r_{generality} \in \{temporal, cooccurrence, correlational, enablement, teleological, causal\}$$

$$r_{imprecision} \in \{equal, possibilistic, veristic, probabilistic, probability\ value, usuality, random\ set, random\ fuzzy\ set, fuzzy\ graph\},$$

where X is a constrained variable, R is a modeled constraining relation, and $r_{resolution}$, r_{scope}, $r_{generality}$, $r_{imprecision}$ are indexing variables standing for the relational types. The adopted relational types along the dimension of imprecision correspond to the types defined in [11],[12]. Overall, represented domain information may be singular, crisp granulated or fuzzy granulated. Then, student description is introduced by exploiting the wealth of domain constraints while following three guiding principles – the description is model-choice dependent, experience related and perception based.

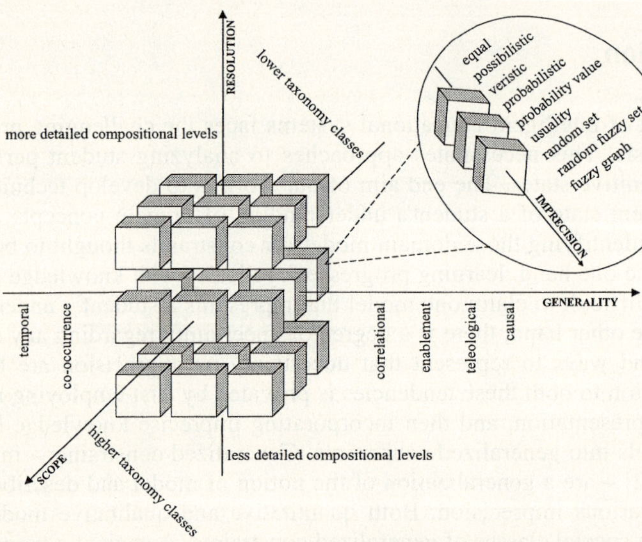

Fig. 1. Multiple-constraint multi-perspective student representation.

Solving a domain problem usually employs a set of generalized constraints, and there may exist several sets providing solutions with different characteristics. The student's choice of a constraint set will reflect her understanding of the problem and related domain concepts. The choice may include an incorrect set or one of the correct sets. Gaining experience in a target domain, a student will progress from a novice to an expert, and her choice will rather focus on the most appropriate among the correct sets. For example, providing a satisfactory solution that concerns the lowest necessary level of relational strength along the generality dimension, or recommending the sufficient level of precision for an efficient solution along the imprecision dimension.

Next, the student's perception of a target domain will reflect the bounded human ability to resolve detail and unbounded capability for information compression [10]. Human cognition is by definition fuzzy granular, as a consequence of the fuzziness of concepts like indistinguishability, proximity and functionality. Student perceptions will be extracted as propositions in natural language. It is demonstrated in [11],[12] how propositions in natural language translate into generalized constraints. Conveniently, the framework in Fig. 2 is already described through generalized constraints. Therefore, we can introduce a unified approach to student representation based on both their performance and perceptions.

3 Further Research

Further work involves developing a diagnostic strategy able to determine cognitive states in terms of subsets of generalized constraints. According to the complexity of the task, the strategy will employ propagation of generalized constraints or evolutionary computation [6]. A demonstration application will illustrate how the overall approach works in a real setting. This involves instantiating the domain framework within the area of risk analysis, particularly assets and derivatives valuation and risk analysis [6],[7],[8].

Acknowledgements. This work is supported by the EPSRC Grant GR/R51346/01 on cognitive diagnosis in intelligent training (CODIT), and developed within the European Network of Excellence in model based systems and qualitative reasoning (MONET).

References

1. de Koning, K., Bredeweg, B., Breuker, J., Wielinga, B.: Model-Based Reasoning About Learner Behaviour. Artificial Intelligence 117 (2000) 173-229
2. Forbus, K.: Using Qualitative Physics to Create Articulate Educational Software. IEEE Expert 12 (1997) 32-41
3. Forbus, K., Whalley, P., Everett, J., Ureel, L., Brokowski, M., Baher, J., Kuehne, S.: Cyclepad: An Articulate Virtual Laboratory for Engineering Thermodynamics. Art. Intell. 114 (1999) 297-347
4. Khan, T., Brown, K., Leitch, R.: Managing Organisational Memory with a Methodology Based on Multiple Domain Models. Proceedings of the Second International Conference on Practical Application of Knowledge Management (1999) 57-76
5. Leitch, R., et al.: Modeling choices in intelligent systems. Artificial Intelligence and the Simulation of Behavior Quarterly 93 (1995) 54-60
6. Serguieva, A., Kalganova, T.: A Neuro-fuzzy-evolutionary classifier of low-risk investments. Proceedings of the IEEE Int. Conf. on Fuzzy Systems (2002) 997-1002 IEEE Press
7. Serguieva, A., Hunter, J.: Fuzzy interval methods in investment risk appraisal. Fuzzy Sets and Systems 142 (2004) 443-466
8. Serguieva, A., Khan, T.: Modelling techniques for cognitive diagnosis. EPSRC Deliverable Report on Cognitive Diagnosis in Training. Brunel University (2003)

9. Serguieva, A., Khan, T.: Domain Representation Assisting Cognitive Analysis. In Proceedings of the Sixteenth European Conference on Artificial Intelligence. IOS Press (2004) to be published
10. Zadeh, L.: Toward a theory of fuzzy information granulation and its centrality in human reasoning and fuzzy logic. Fuzzy Sets and Systems 90 (1997) 111-127
11. Zadeh, L.: Outline of Computational Theory of Perceptions Based on Computing with Words. In: Soft Computing and Intelligent Systems, Academic Press (2000) 3-22
12. Zadeh, L.: A new direction in AI: Toward a computational theory of perceptions. Artificial Intelligence Magazine 22 (2001) 73-84

An Ontology-Based Planning Navigation in Problem-Solving Oriented Learning Processes

Kazuhisa Seta[1], Kei Tachibana[1], Motohide Umano[1], and Mitsuru Ikeda[2]

[1] Department of Mathematics and Information Sciences, Osaka Prefecture University, Japan, 1-1, Gakuen-cho, Sakai, Osaka 599-8531, Japan
{seta, umano}@mi.cias.osakafu-u.ac.jp,
http://ks.cias.osakafu-u.ac.jp

[2] School of Knowledge Science, JAIST, 1-1, Asahidai, Tatsunokuchi, Nomi, Ishikawa 923-1292, Japan
ikeda@jaist.ac.jp
http://www.jaist.ac.jp/ks/labs/ikeda/

Abstract. Our research aims are to propose a support model for problem-solving oriented learning and implement a human-centric system that supports learners and thereby develops their ability. The characteristic of our research is that our system understands the principle knowledge (ontology) to support users through human-computer interactions.

1 Introduction

Our research aims are to propose an ontology-based navigation framework for Problem-Solving Oriented Learning (PSOL) [1], and implement a human-centric system based on the ontology to support learners and thereby develop their ability. By ontology-based, we mean that we do not develop the ad hoc system but the theory-aware system based on the principle knowledge.

We define problem-solving oriented learning as learning whereby a learner must not only accumulate sufficient understanding for planning and performing problem-solving processes but also acquire capacity for making efficient problem-solving processes according to a sophisticated strategy. Therefore, in PSOL it is important for learner not only to execute problem-solving processes or learning processes (Object activity) but also to encourage meta-cognition (Meta activity) that monitors/controls her internal mental image.

2 Problem-Solving Oriented Learning Task Ontology

Rasmussen's cognitive model [2] is adopted as a reference model in the construction of the ontology for supporting PSOL. Rasmussen's cognitive model simulates the process of human cognition in problem-solving based on cognitive psychology. Cognitive activity in PSOL is related to this model, based on which PSOL task ontology is constructed. This provides with useful information for effective performance of cognitive activity at each state, according to Rasmussen's theoretical framework [2]

J.C. Lester et al. (Eds.): ITS 2004, LNCS 3220, pp. 877–879, 2004.

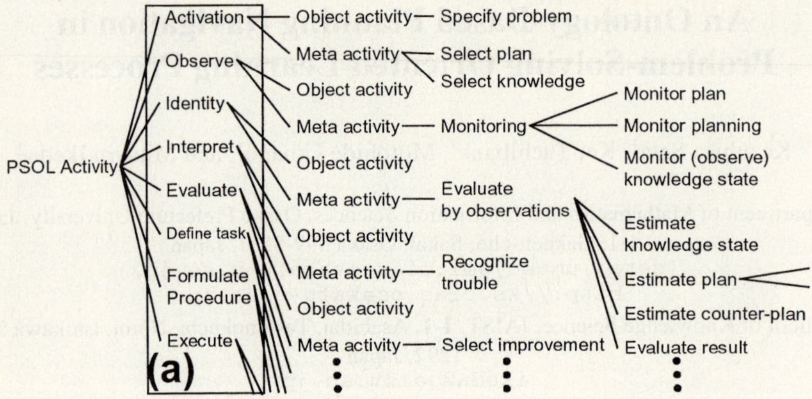

Fig.1. A hierarchy of problem-solving oriented learning task ontology

Figure 1 presents an outline of the Problem-Solving Oriented Learning Task Ontology constructed in this study. Ovals in the figure express a cognitive activity performed by a learner in which a link represents an "is-a" relationship. The PSOL task ontology defines eight cognitive activities modeled in Rasmussen's cognitive model ((a) in the figure). They are refined through an is-a hierarchy to cognitive activities on the meta-level (Meta activity), and cognitive activities on the object level (Object activity). Moreover, they are further refined in detail as their lower concepts: a cognitive activity in connection with learning activities and a cognitive activity in connection with problem-solving activities. For example, typical meta-cognitive activities that a learner performs in PSOL, such as "Monitor knowledge state" and "Monitor learning plan", are systematized as lower concepts of meta-cognition activities.

3 Planning Navigation in Kassist

The screen image of our system (Kassist), a system based on the PSOL task ontology, is shown in Fig. 2. Kassist is an interactive open learner-modeling environment [1]. A learner describes a problem-solving plan, own knowledge state about the object domain, and a learning process in each panels of (a), (b), and (c), respectively. It then encourages her spontaneous meta-cognition activities. The upper panel in (d) represents the flow of cognitive processes according to the Rasmussen's cognitive model. Cognitive activities performed by the learner is recorded in (d) corresponded to the cognitive processes.

Moreover, we can implement a more positive navigation function that encourages a learner's meta-cognition activity in the subsequent cognitive process by making ontology into the basis of a system. Such navigation allows a learner to comprehend knowledge required to carry out problem-solving, but missing herself, and to understand at what occasion in a problem solving process such knowledge is required and on what processes it gives influence.

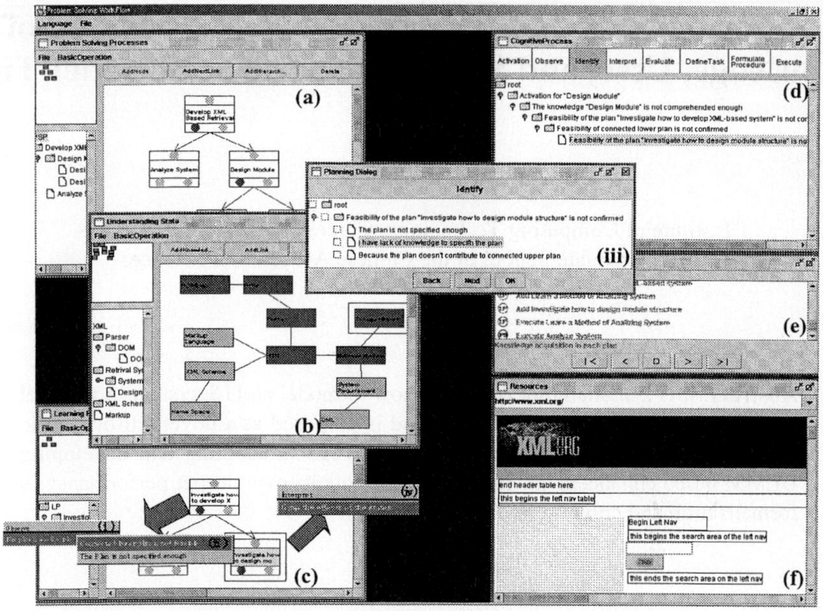

Fig.2. Planning Navigation based on PSOL task ontology

Figure 2 shows that the system provides appropriate information for a learner when she reaches an impasse because the feasibility of learning process is not confirmed. Here by suggesting the causes of the impasses as well as showing the influence on problem-solving, the system encourages the learner to observe and control her internal mental image (meta-cognition), which contributes to effective PSOL.

4 Concluding Remarks

This paper systemized PSOL task ontology and then proposed a human-computer interactive navigation framework based on the ontology.

References

1. Kazuhisa Seta, Kei Tachibana, Ikuyo Fujisawa and Motohide Umano: "An ontological approach to interactive navigation for problem-solving oriented learning processes," International Journal of Interactive Technology and Smart Education, (2004, to appear)
2. Rasmussen, J.: "A Framework for Cognitive Task Analysis", Information Processing and Human-Machine Interaction: An Approach to Cognitive Engineering, North-Holland, New York, (1986) pp.5–8.

A Formal and Computerized Modeling Method of Knowledge, User, and Strategy Models in PIModel-Tutor

Jinxin Si[1,2]

[1] Institute of Computing Technology, Chinese Academy of Sciences
[2] The Graduate School of the Chinese Academy of Sciences
jxsi@ict.ac.cn

Abstract. It is a challenging issue that how to model an ITS system in a global way. In this background, ULMM method is proposed as a novel uniform logic modeling method. Our new project PIModel-ITS is adopting and developing ULMM based enhancements in order to promote its own deeper performance in formalization and computerization.

1 Introduction

Some researchers proposed that an ITS can be regarded as a framework of multi-agent multi-user environment, each component of which can use a common communication language to negotiate and regulate [4]. According to two viewpoints of knowledge design (KD) and instructional design (ID), there are many interwove and contextual clews among knowledge, users and strategies in ITS systems [5]. Furthermore, it becomes more and more important that how to avoid deploying the "isolationism" opinion to study three issues which consist of knowledge domain model (ab. DM), user model (ab. UM) and pedagogical strategy model (ab. PM). In an ITS, DM emphasizes on what the "right" knowledge is, UM concentrates on why the delivery knowledge is valid and PM addresses how the knowledge will be recognized and constructed effectively by students. The paper mainly centers on the possible difficulties around ITS modeling which should be consolidated in our further works.

2 ULMM Overview

ULMM is a uniform logic modeling method in ITSs which should be a correlative and hierarchical environment. Therefore, ITS researchers and designers can depict knowledge and user characters, teaching and learning strategies [2, 3]. ULMM can provide three layers of modeling languages in order to represent an ITS, which consists of the knowledge layer, the user layer and the strategy layer.

J.C. Lester et al. (Eds.): ITS 2004, LNCS 3220, pp. 880–882, 2004.

2.1 Knowledge Layer

Knowledge logic model is the fine-grained knowledge base about concepts and relations for pedagogical process. We define a knowledge logic model to be a 4-tuple KLM := $\{C, R_s, R_p, A\}$, where C is the concept set, R_s is the set of semantic relations, R_p is the set of pedagogical relations, A is the set of axioms among concepts and their relations.

In many cases, the designation of pedagogical relations de facto can be combined intimately with semantic relations. Some literatures proposed that the whole is more than the sum of its parts and the "glue" is specified to tie together the pieces of knowledge. So, we give two examples about the translation rule involved some semantic relations (i.e. "part-of", "has-instance" and prerequisite) depicted as bellow.

$$\text{part-of}(c_1, c_2, c_3; C) \wedge \text{glue}(c_2; c_1, c_3) \rightarrow \text{prerequisite}(c_1 \wedge c_3, c_2)$$
$$\text{has-instance}(C, i_1, i_2, i_3) \wedge \text{glue}(i_2; i_1, i_3) \rightarrow \text{prerequisite}(i_1 \wedge i_3, i_2)$$

2.2 User Layer

User logic model can help ITSs to determine static characters and dynamic requirements for a given user in an interactive manner. Inspired by performance and expectation of leaning event, student states can be depicted by the tuple $\langle S_s, S_t \rangle$ anytime, where symbol S_s indicates practical student states from student perspectives and symbol S_t indicates planned student states from tutor perspectives. Both unit exercises and class quizzes need to be considered during the pedagogical evaluation.

Error identification and analysis is a central task in user logic model as other UM methods including bug library, model-tracing, constraint-based method etc. However, concrete errors are thought to be dependent strongly on domain, pedagogical, even psychological theory. To some extent the error abstraction decreases the complexity of state computation, and increases the facility of state expression. For example, some detailed explanations for misclassification and misattribution, which are two classical error types in concept leaning, can be formalized with first-order logic as follows, where the suffix-w denotes wrongness of atomic predicate:

$$\text{class1.slot} \in_w \text{class2.slotset} \rightarrow \text{misclassification(class1,class2)}$$
$$\text{is-a(instance2, class)} \wedge \text{Resemble (instance1, instance2)} \rightarrow \text{misclassification(instance1, class)}$$
$$\text{subclass.slot} \in_w \text{class.slotset} \rightarrow \text{Misattribution(subclass.slot, class)}$$
$$\text{slot} \in \text{instance1.slotset} \wedge \text{Resemble(instance1, instance2)} \rightarrow \text{Misattribution(slot, instance2)}$$

2.3 Strategy Layer

Strategy logic model should be regarded as a runnable decision-making system, through which ITS can provide individualized content and navigation to students, and can decide and modify student states in offline and online ways. In principle, tutoring strategies are the sequence of interactive actions and events initiated by tutor and student [1]. Obviously, the pedagogical strategy is connected closely with pedagogical actions and goals. However, constraint-base method proposed that the diagnosis of student state does not reside in sequence of actions the student executed, but in the situation the student created. In fact some empirical research proposed that it is uncertain for the effects on student state which results from imposed action. As a result, it is a vital task for ITS designer to build large testing, feedback and remedial strategies in order to obtain and evaluate student states. At the same time, strategy layer should be able to provide an open authoring portal to formalize versatile sound-psychological learning strategies.

3 Conclusions and Further Work

The novelty of ULMM lies in that it can give a formal representation schema in global modeling of an ITS architecture rather than local modeling of every components. We think that it is not considerate that the modeling strategy in ITS research domain should be regarded as "divide and rule". Until now the ULMM method has not been subject to an overall evaluation in our PIModel-Tutor system. In our future works, we need to evaluate some issues to promote validness and soundness in concrete implementation of PIModel-Tutor. During the process of ITS authoring, how can ULMM provide the mechanism about conflict detection and resolution to facilitate system construction? As a central element, how can the effective and automated instructional remedy be generated as to adapt to student requirements in psychological and pedagogical aspects? How should ULMM ease the difficulty of computation about student states through a flexible interface?

References

1. Kay, J. 2001. Learner control, User Modeling and User-Adapted Interaction, Tenth Anniversary Special Issue, 11(1-2), Kluwer, 111-127.
2. Si J. ; Yue X.; Cao C.; Sui Y. 2004. PIModel: A Pragmatic ITS Model Based on Instructional Automata Theory, To appear in the proceedings of The 17th International FLAIRS Conference, Miami Beach, Florida, May 2004. AAAI Press.
3. Si J.; Cao C.; Sui Y.; Yue X.; Xie N. 2004. ULMM: A Uniform Logic Modeling Method in Intelligent Tutoring Systems, To appear in the proceedings of The 8th International Conference on Knowledge-based Intelligent Information & Engineering Systems, Springer.
4. Vassileva, J.; McCalla, G.; and Greer, J. 2003. Multi-Agent Multi-User Modelling in I-Help, User Modelling and User Adapted Interaction, 2003, 13(1) 179-210.
5. Yue X.; and Cao C. 2003. Knowledge Design. In Proceedings of International Workshop on Research Directions and Challenge Problems in Advanced Information Systems Engineering, Japan, Sept.

SmartChat – An Intelligent Environment for Collaborative Discussions

Sandra de Albuquerque Siebra[1,2], Cibele da Rosa Christ[1], Ana Emília M. Queiroz[1], Patrícia Azevedo Tedesco[1], and Flávia de Almeida Barros[1]

[1] Centro de Informática – Universidade Federal de Pernambuco (UFPE)
Caixa Postal 7851 – Cidade Universitária – 50732-970 – Recife – PE – Brasil
{sas,crc2,aemq,pcart,fab}@cin.ufpe.br
[2] Faculdade Integrada do Recife (FIR)
R. Abdias de Carvalho, 1678 – Madalena – Recife – PE – Brasil

1 Introduction

Using Computer Supported Collaborative Learning Environments (CSCLE) two or more participants can build their knowledge together, through reflection, collaborative problem resolution, information exchange, and decision-making. The majority of these environments provide tools for communication (e-mails, chats, and forums). However, there are no mechanisms for the evaluation of the interaction contents. The lack of a mechanism to evaluate the interactions could prevent the users from discussing about a specific theme or collaborating among themselves.

Among the communication tools available in CSCLEs, the chat is one of the most effective. Since it is synchronous, it is the one that mostly resembles the conventional classroom. In this context, we developed SmartChat, an intelligent chat environment. The SmartChat has two main components: the chat interface, and the reasoning mechanism. This mechanism consists of an agent society that monitors the users' discussion, and intervenes in the chat trying to make the collaboration more productive. Preliminary tests with its prototype yielded promising results.

2 Chat Environments

We have analyzed three environments: jXChat [1], Comet [2] and BetterBlether [3], according to the following criteria: (1) record of the interaction log; (2) technique employed in the interaction analysis; (3) goal of the interaction analysis; (4) way of intervening in the conversation; (5) provision of feedback for the teacher or the student; (6) use of an argumentation model; (7) interface usability. We have observed that when a chat offers more resources to support teachers and/or students during the discussion, its interface becomes a hindrance to the users. We have also observed that these systems only provide feedback to the teacher. Furthermore, even the systems that provide feedback, do so through reports or statistics generated from the interaction log, and only at the end of the discussion. And none of the systems make use of the argumentation model to structure the conversation.

J.C. Lester et al. (Eds.): ITS 2004, LNCS 3220, pp. 883–885, 2004.

3 SmartChat

SmartChat's prototype was implemented using RMI (Remote Method Invocation). Its reasoning mechanism uses an agent society composed by two intelligent agents: The Monitor Agent that is responsible for getting all the perceptions necessary for deciding whether to interfere or not in conversation. And the Modeller Agent centralizes the main activities in the chat, models the profile of the users logged-in. This agent communicates with the rule database generated by JEOPS [4], which is used to classify the user as one of the stereotypes [5] stored in the user model. The Modeller interferes in the discussion to perform one of three actions: (1) send support messages to the users according to their stereotype; (2) suggest references related to the subject being discussed; and (3) name another user that may collaborate with the user having difficulties. Fig.1 shows the SmartChat architecture.

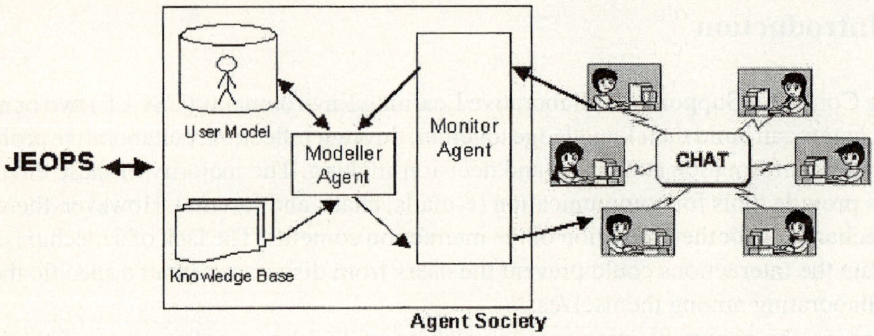

Fig. 1. SmartChat's Architecture

SmartChat uses a simplified argumentation model, based on the IBIS model [6], to structure the information contained in the interactions and to categorize the messages exchanged between students. The user that wishes to interact with the environment should select an abstraction from a predefined set (for example, Argument, Question, etc.), in order to provide explicit information about the intention of her/his messages. The use of an argumentation model favours the resolution of conflicts and the understanding of problems, helping the participants to structure their ideas more clearly. Fig. 2 shows the argumentation model used by SmartChat.

4 Conclusions and Further Work

In CSCLE, the interaction is fundamental to understand the process of building knowledge and the role of each student in the process. In this article, we presented SmartChat, a chat environment that monitors online discussions, and interacts with the users to motivate them, to point references or to suggest the collaboration between two peers. The initial tests performed with SmartChat indicated good interface usability, good acceptance of the interventions performed by the SmartChat Agents, and the correctness of

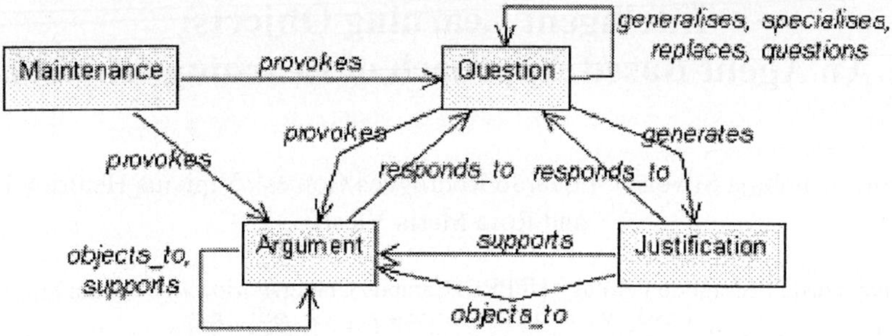

Fig. 2. Argumentation Model used in SmartChat

the classification of the users using the environment. In the near future, we intend to extend the domain ontology, implement an on-line feedback area to inform the students about their performance, and to enrich the student and teacher reports with more relevant information.

References

1. Martins, F. J.; Ferrari, D. N.; Geyer, C. F. R. jXChat - Um Sistema de Comunicação Eletrônica Inteligente para apoio a Educação a Distância. *Anais do XIV Simpósio de Informática na Educação* - SBIE - NCE/UFRJ. (2003).
2. Soller, A.; Wiebe, J. ; Lesgold, A. A Machine Learning Approach to Assessing Knowledge Sharing During Collaborative Learning Activities. In: *Proceedings of Computer Support for Collaborative Learning 2002*. Boulder, CO, (2002). 128-137.
3. Robertson, J.; Good, J.; Pain, H. BetterBlether: The Design and Evaluation of a Discussion Tool for Education. In: *International Journal of Artificial Intelligence in Education*, N.9 (1998), 219-236.
4. Figueira Filho, C.; Ramalho G. JEOPS - Java Embedded Object Production System. Monard, M. C; Sichman, J. S (Eds). IBERAMIA-SBIA 2000, Proceedings. Lecture Notes in Computer Science 1952. Springer (2000), 53-62.
5. Rich, E. Stereotypes and user modeling. A. Kobsa & W. Wahlster (Eds.), User Models in Dialog Systems. Berlin, Heidelberg: Springer, (1989). 35-51.
6. Conklin, J.; Begeman, M. L. gIBIS: A Hypertext Tool for Exploratory Policy Discussion. In: *ACM Transactions on Office Information Systems.* V. 16, N.4, (1998).

Intelligent Learning Objects: An Agent Based Approach of Learning Objects

Ricardo Azambuja Silveira[1], Eduardo Rodrugues Gomes[2], Vinicius Heidrich Pinto[1], and Rosa Maria Vicari[2]

[1] Universidade Federal de Pelotas - UFPEL, Campus Universitário, s/nº - Caixa Postal 354
{rsilv, vheidrich}@ufpel.edu.br

[2] Universidade Federal do Rio Grande do Sul – UFRGS
Av. Bento Gonçalves, 9500 - Campus do Vale - Bloco IV Porto Alegre - RS -Brasil
{ergomes,rosa}@inf.ufrgs.br

Abstract. Many researchers on Intelligent Learning Environments have proposed the use of Artificial Intelligence through architectures based on agents' societies. Teaching systems based on Multi-Agent architectures make possible to support the development of more interactive and adaptable systems. At the same time many people have been working to produce metadata specification towards a construction of Learning Objects in order to improve efficiency efficacy and reusability of learning content based on Object Oriented design paradigm. This paper proposes an agent based approach to produce more intelligent learning objects according to FIPA agent architecture reference model and LOM/IEEE 1484 learning object specification learning objects

1 Introduction

Many people have been working hard to produce metadata specification towards a construction of Learning Objects in order to improve efficiency, efficacy and reusability of learning content based on Object Oriented design paradigm. According to Sosteric and Hesemeier [7], learning objects have been on the educational agenda now. Organizations such as the IMS Global Learning Consortium [4] and the IEEE [3] have contributed significantly by helping to define indexing (metadata) standards for object search and retrieval. There has also been some commercial and educational work accomplished.

Learning resources are objects in an object-oriented model. They have methods and properties. Typically methods include rendering and assessment methods. Typical properties include content and relationships to other resources [5]. Downes [2] points out that a lot of work has to be done to use a learning object. You must first build an educational environment in which they can function, you need, somehow, to locate these objects, arrange them in their proper order, according to their design and function. And you must arrange for the installation and configuration of appropriate viewing software. Although it seems to be easier to do all this with learning objects, we need smarter learning objects.

J.C. Lester et al. (Eds.): ITS 2004, LNCS 3220, pp. 886–888, 2004.

2 Pedagogical Agents: The Intelligent Learning Objects

The idea of **Pedagogical Agents** in the context of this project was conceptualized in the same spirit as the learning objects in the sense of efficiency, efficacy and reusability of learning content. In addiction, the **Intelligent Learning Objects** (or Pedagogical Agents) improve adaptability and interactivity of complex learning environments built with this kind of components by the interaction among the learning objects and between learning objects and other agents in a more robust conception of communication than a single method invocation as the object oriented paradigm use to be. **Intelligent Learning Objects** (ILO) must be designed according to the Wooldridge, Jennings and Kinny conceptions of agents [8] considering an agent as coarse-grained computational systems, each making use of significant computational resources that maximizes some global quality measure, but which may be sub-optimal from the point of view of the system components.

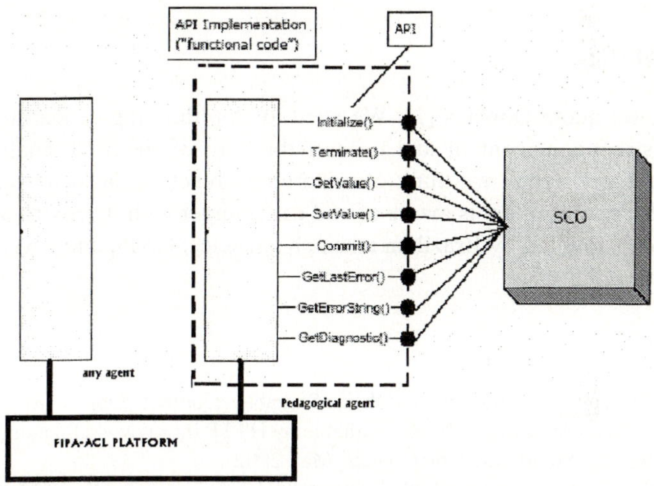

Fig. 1. The Intelligent Learning Object designed as a Pedagogical FIPA agent implements the same API specification, performs messages sending and receiving, and performs agents' specific task, according to its knowledge base. As the agent receives a new FIPA-ACL message it processes the API function according to its content, performing the adequate behavior and act on SCO. According to the agent behavior model, the message-receiving event can trigger some message sending, mental model updating and some particular specific agent action on the SCO

ILOs must be heterogeneous, in that different agents may be implemented using different programming languages and techniques and make no assumptions about the delivery platform The ILOs are created according to the course design in order to perform specific tasks to create some significant learning experience by interacting with the student. But the object must do it in a smaller sense as possible in order to promote reusability and efficiency, and permit a large amount of different combination with other objects. In addition, an most important, the ILOs must be designed by the course specialist The smaller and most simple is the pedagogical task performed by the ILO, the most adaptable flexible and interactive is the learning experience provided by it.The FIPA-ACL protocol performed by a FIPA agent communication manager platform ensures an excellent support for cooperation. Fig 1 shows the proposed architecture of the set of pedagogical agents.

The Sharable Content Object Reference Model (SCORM®) [1] is maybe the best reference to start a thinking of how to build learning objects based on a agent architecture. The SCORM defines a Web-based learning "Content Aggregation Model" and "Run-time Environment" for learning objects. At its simplest, it is a model that references a set of interrelated technical specifications and guidelines designed to meet the requirements for object learning. Learning content in its most basic form is composed of Assets that are electronic representations of media, text, images, sound, web pages, assessment objects or other pieces of data that can be delivered to a Web client.

3 Conclusions

At this point, we quote Downes [2]: We need to stop thinking of learning objects as chunks of instructional content and to start thinking of them as small, self-reliant computer programs. When we think of a learning object we need to think of it as a small computer program that is aware of and can interact with its environment.

This project is granted by Brazilian research agencies: CNPq and FAPERGS.

References

1. Advanced Distributed Learning (ADL)a. Sharable Content Object Reference Model (SCORM ®) 2004 Overview. 2004. Available by HTTP in: <www.adlnet.org>.
2. Downes , Stephen Smart Learning Objects, May 2002
3. IEEE Learning Technology Standards Committee (1998) Learning Object Metadata (LOM): Draft Document v2.1
4. IMS Global Learning Consortium. IMS Learning Resource Meta-data Best Practices and Implementation Guide v1.1. 2000.
5. Robson, Robby (1999) Object-oriented Instructional Design and Web-based Authoring. [Online] Available by HTTP in: <www.eduworks.com/robby/papers/objectoriented.pdf>
6. Shoham, Y Agent-oriented programming. Artificial Intelligence, Amsterdam, n.60, v.1, p.51 - 92, Feb. 1993.
7. Sosteric, Mike, Hesemeier Susan When is a Learning Object not an Object: A first step towards .a theory of learning objects International Review of Research in Open and Distance Learning (October - 2002) ISSN: 1492-3831
8. Wooldridge, M.; Jennings, N. R.; Kinny, D. A methodology for agent-oriented analysis and design. In: International Conference on Autonomous Agents, 3. 1999. Proceedings

Using Simulated Students for Machine Learning

Regina Stathacopoulou[1], Maria Grigoriadou[1], Maria Samarakou[2], and George D. Magoulas[3]

[1] Department of Informatics and Telecommunications, University of Athens, Panepistimiopolis, GR-15784 Athens, Greece
{sreg, gregor}@di.uoa.gr

[2] Department of Energy Technology, Technological Education Institute of Athens, Ag. Spyridonos Str. GR 12210, Egaleo, Athens, Greece
marsam@teiath.gr

[3] School of Computer Science and Information Systems, Birkbeck College, University of London , Malet Street, London WC1E 7HX, United Kingdom
gmagoulas@dcs.bbk.ac.uk

Abstract. In this paper we present how simulated students have been generated in order to obtain a large amount of labeled data for training and testing a neural network-based fuzzy model of the student in an Intelligent Learning Environment (ILE). The simulated students have been generated by modifying real students' records and classified by a group of expert teachers regarding their learning style category. Experimental results were encouraging, similar to experts' classifications.

1 Introduction

One of the critical issues that are currently limiting the real world application of machine learning techniques for user modeling is the need for large data sets of explicitly labeled examples [7]. Simulated students, originally proposed as a modeling approach 6, have been used in ITS studies [1] [6]. This paper presents how simulated students have been generated in order to train a neural network-based fuzzy model that updates the student model on student's learning style in a Intelligent Learning Environment (ILE). The ILE consists of the educational software *"Vectors in Physics and Mathematics"* [4], and the neural network-based fuzzy model [5].

The educational software *"Vectors in Physics and Mathematics"* [4], is a discovery learning environment that allows students carrying out selected activities which refer to real-life situations, e.g. they experiment with forces acting on objects and run simulations.

The neural network-based fuzzy model makes use of neuro-fuzzy synergism is order to evaluate, taking into consideration teacher's personal opinion/judgment, an aspect of the surface/deep approach [3] of student's learning style, in order to be used to sequencing the educational material. Deep learners often prefer self-regulated learning; conversely, surface learners often prefer externally regulated learning [2]. *"Student's tendency to learn by discovery in a deep or surface way"* is described with

J.C. Lester et al. (Eds.): ITS 2004, LNCS 3220, pp. 889–891, 2004.

the term set {*Deep, Rather Deep, Average, Rather Shallow, Shallow*}. This process involves dealing with uncertainty, and eliciting and expressing teacher's qualitative knowledge in a convenient and interpretable way. Neural networks are used to equip the fuzzy model with learning and generalization abilities, which are eminently useful when teacher's reasoning process cannot be defined explicitly.

2 Generating Simulated Students

In order to construct simulated students' patterns of interaction with the learning environment that are "close" to real students' behaviour patterns, we modified the patterns of a small set of pre-classified real students' patterns. The real students' interaction patterns (two from each of the five learning style categories) have been provided during an experiment which was carried out with the assistance of a group of five experts in teaching the subject content. All the available information on what a student is doing, together with a time stamp is stored on a log file.

Student's observable behavior recorded in the log files, is fuzzified and described with three linguistic variables B_1, B_2, B_3. Fuzzification is performed by associating the universe of discourses U_k (k=1,2,3) for each numeric input x_1, x_2, x_3 representing the measured values of B_1, B_2, B_3, respectively with the linguistic values of each linguistic variable B_k. The numeric values x_1, x_2, x_3 are calculated by pre-processing the log files. For example, the time needed to find the correct solution was compared against the time the group of experts defined as "average estimation" × 2. Thus, in Fig. 1, the linguistic variable B_3="*problem solving speed*" is described with the term set $T(B_3)$={*slow, medium fast*} defined in U_3 (percentage of time in [0, 100]).

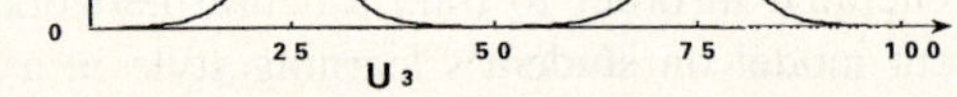

Fig. 1. Membership functions for the linguistic variable "*problem solving speed*".

In order to construct the simulated students' records, student's actions until s/he quits an activity are decomposed in terms of episodes of actions. Each episode includes a series of actions which begins or ends when the student clears the screen in order to start a new attempt on the same activity, or a new equilibrium activity. Within each episode the student conducts, successfully or unsuccessfully, an experiment. The simulated students' records have been produced by modifying the number of episodes or elements of patterns within each episode or between episodes, i.e. inserting, deleting or changing actions that are used to calculate the values x_1, x_2, x_3 which represents the measured values of B_1, B_2, B_3. Thus, starting with 10 real students' records we can generate simulated students, altering the values of x_1, x_2, x_3 in the students' patterns by giving appropriate values within their universes of discourse U_1, U_2, U_3.

For example, reducing the number of episodes will cause a decrease to the value of x_3, which gives the measured value of B_3 Thus, a particular student performing an unsuccessful experiment, needs 5 episodes and 18 minutes overall to produce a correct solution in this activity. For the particular activity that the student is performing, the group of experts estimated the average time is 10 minutes. Thus, calculating the percentage that corresponds to 10 minutes multiplied by 2 (i.e. 20 minutes) for this student $x_3 = 90\%$ which corresponds to the linguistic value "*Slow*" with membership degree very close to 1 (see Fig. 1). Reducing the number of episodes of this activity to 4, the total time of the episodes needed to find the correct solution is 15 minutes; this corresponds to a value of $x_3 = 75\%$, and the linguistic value for problem solving speed is now "*slow*" with a degree of 0.5 and "*Medium*" with a degree of 0.5 (see Fig. 1).

3 Results and Future Work

The performance of neuro-fuzzy model has been tested with three test sets created and labelled from a group of experts. The first set contains patterns with clear-cut descriptions of students' observable behaviour and the results of the model were 100% similar to the group of experts classifications. The second set involves a lot of uncertainty; there are no clear-cut cases due to lack of well-defined boundaries in describing students' observable behaviour. The results of the model were 96% similar to experts' classifications. The third set consists of special marginal cases that could cause conflicting judgment from rule-based classifiers. The results of the model were 86% similar to experts' classification. We are currently conduct experiments with real students to fully explore the benefits and limitations of this approach.

References

1. Beck J. E. (2002). Directing Development Effort with Simulated Students. In Proc. of ITS 2002, Biarritz, France and San Sebastian, Spain, June 2-7, pp. 851-860, LNCS, Spr.-Verl.
2. Beshuizen J. J., Stoutjesdijk E. T., Study strategies in a computer assisted study environment, Learning and Instruction 9 (1999) 281-301.
3. Biggs J., Student approaches to learning and studying, Australian Council for Educational Research, Hawthorn Victoria, 1987.
4. Grigoriadou M., Mitropoulos D., Samarakou M., Solomonidou C., Stavridou E. (1999). Methodology for the Design of Educational Software in Mathematics and Physics for Secondary Education. Computer Based Learning in Science, Conf. Proc. 1999 pB3.
5. Stathacopoulou R, Magoulas GD, Grigoriadou M., Samarakou M. (2004). Neuro-Fuzzy Knowledge Processing in Intelligent Learning Environments for Improved Student Diagnosis. Information Sciences, in press, DOI information 10.1016/j.ins.2004.02.026
6. Vanlehn K., Niu Z. (2001). Bayesian student modeling, user interfaces and feedback: A sensitivity analysis. Inter. Journal of Artificial Intelligence in Education 12 154-184.
7. Webb G. I., Pazzani M. J., Billsus D.(2001) Machine Learning for User Modeling User Modeling and User-Adapted Interaction 11, 19-29.

Towards an Analysis of How Shared Representations Are Manipulated to Mediate Online Synchronous Collaboration

Daniel D. Suthers

Dept. of Information and Computer Sciences, University of Hawaii, 1680 East West Road
POST 317, Honolulu, HI 96822, USA
suthers@hawaii.edu
http://lilt.ics.hawaii.edu/

Abstract. This work is concerned with an analysis of how shared representations – notations that are manipulated by more than one person during a collaborative task – are used as resources to support that collaboration. The analysis is built on the concept of "informational uptake": how information moves and is transformed between individuals via a graphical representation as well as a verbal "chat" tool. By examining patterns of such uptake, one can see ways in which the activity of two individuals is coupled and joined into a larger cognitive (and sometimes knowledge-building) activity distributed across the persons and representations they are manipulating.

1 Introduction

The author is studying how software tools that support learners' construction of knowledge representations (e.g., concept maps, evidence maps) are used by collaborating learners, and consequently how to design such tools to more effectively support collaboration. A previous study [6] found that online collaborators treated a graphical evidence map as a medium through which collaboration took place, proposing new ideas by entering them directly in the graph before engaging in (usually brief) confirmation dialogues in a textual chat tool. In general, actions in the graph appeared to be an important part of participants' conversations with each other, and in fact was at times the sole means of interaction. These observations led to the questions of whether and in what sense we can say that participants are having a conversation through the graph, and whether knowledge building taking place. To answer these questions, the author identified interactions from the previous study that appeared to constitute collaboration through the nonverbal as well as verbal media, and is engaged in a qualitative analysis of these examples. The purpose of this analysis is to understand how participants made use of the structured graph representation to mediate meaning making activity, by examining how participants use actions on the representations to build on each others' ideas. The larger goal is to identify affordances of shared representations for face-to-face and online collaboration and their implications for the design of representational support for collaborative knowledge building.

J.C. Lester et al. (Eds.): ITS 2004, LNCS 3220, pp. 892–894, 2004.

2 The Study

The participants' task was to propose and evaluate hypotheses concerning the cause of ALS-PD, a neurological disease with an unusually high occurrence on Guam that has been studied by the medical community for over 50 years. The experimental software provided a graphical tool for constructing representations of the data, hypotheses, and evidential relations that participants gleaned from information pages. An information window enabled participants to advance through a series of textual pages presenting information on ALS-PD. The sequence was designed such that later pages sometimes affected upon the interpretation of information seen several pages earlier, making the use of an external memory important. In the study on which this analysis derives its data [6], the software was modified for synchronous online collaboration with the addition of a chat tool. Transcripts were automatically logged in the online sessions.

3 The Analysis

In order to "see" how participants were interacting with each other, the author and his student (Ravikiran Vatrapu) began by identifying "information uptake" relations between actions. Information uptake is said to hold between action A1 and action A2 if A2 builds on the information in A1. Examples include editing or linking to prior information, or cross-modal references such as a chat comment about an item in the graph. This uptake must be plausibly based on the informational content or attitude towards that information of the uptaken act or representation. There must be evidence that the uptaker is responding to one of these. For example, merely moving things around to make the graph pretty is not counted.)

The analysis then proceeds in a bottom-up manner, working from the referential level to the intentional level, similar to [5]. After having identified ways in which information "flows" between participants, as evidenced by their references to information in the graph, interpretations of the intentions behind these references are then made.

The analysis seeks evidence of *knowledge building*, using a working definition of knowledge building as the *accretion of interpretations on an information base that is simultaneously expanded by information seeking*. Collaborative knowledge building takes place when multiple participants contribute to this accretion of interpretations by building, commenting on, transforming and integrating an information base. In defining what counts as evidence for knowledge building, the analysis draws upon several theoretical perspectives. Interaction via a graphical representation can be understood as similar to interaction via language in terms of Clark's model of grounding [4] if grounding is restated in terms of actions on a representation: a participant expresses an idea in the representation; another participant acts on that representation in a manner that provides evidence of understanding the first participant's intent in a certain way; the first participant can choose to accept this action as evidence of sufficient understanding, or, if the evidence is insufficient, initiate repair. Under the grounding perspective, one would look for sequences of actions in which one participant's action on a representation is taken up by another participant in a manner that indicates understanding of its meaning, and the first participant signals acceptance (usually implicitly). Yet other theoretical perspectives are needed to identify how interpretations are collaboratively constructed. Under the socio-cognitive conflict perspective [2], the analyst would identify situations in which the externalization of ideas led to identification of differences of interpretation that were subsequently taken up by at least one of the individuals involved. A distributed cognition perspective [3] suggests that cognitive activities such as knowledge building are distributed across individuals and information artifacts through and with which they interact. Then, the analyst would look for transformations of representations across individuals, especially if those transformations can be interpreted as an intersubjective cognitive process. Although the activity theoretic perspective [1] offers many ideas, this work draws primarily on the concept of mediation. The analyst looks for ways in which the representation mediates (makes possible and guides) interactions between participants by virtue of its form. This viewpoint is consistent with the distributed cognition perspective. In addition to the foregoing, the work draws on ideas in [7] about how representations support collaborative activity: the constructive actions afforded by a representation initiate negotiations about those actions, and the representations resulting from such constructive actions serve as proxies for the meanings so negotiated, supporting further conversation through deictic reference.

References

1. Bertelsen, Olav W. and Bødker, Susanne (2003). Activity Theory. In J. M. Carroll (Ed.), HCI Models, Theories and Frameworks: Towards a Multidisiplinary Science. San Francisco, Mogan Kaufmann: 290-315.
2. Doise, W., and Mugny, G. (1984) The Social Development of the Intellect, International Series in Experimental Social Psychology, vol. 10, Pergamon Press
3. Hollan, J., E. Hutchins, & Kirsh, D. (2002). Distributed Cognition: Toward a New Foundation for Human-Computer Interaction Research. Human-Computer Interaction in the New Millennium. J. M. Carroll. New York, ACM Press Addison Wesley: 75-94.
4. Monk, A. (2003). Common Ground in Electronically Mediated Communication: Clark's Theory of Language use. In J. M. Carroll (Ed.), HCI Models, Theories and Frameworks: Towards a Multidisiplinary Science. San Francisco, Mogan Kaufmann: 265-289.
5. Mühlenbrock, M., & Hoppe, U. (1999). Computer Supported Interaction Analysis of Group Problem Solving. In Proceedings of the Computer Support for Collaborative Learning (CSCL) 1999 Conference, C. Hoadley & J. Roschelle (Eds.) Dec. 12-15, Stanford University, Palo Alto, California. Mahwah, NJ: Lawrence Erlbaum Associates.
6. Suthers, D., Girardeau, L. and Hundhausen, C. (2003). Deictic Roles of External Representations in Face-to-face and Online Collaboration. Designing for Change in Networked Learning Environments, Proceedings of the International Conference on Computer Support for Collaborative Learning 2003, B. Wasson, S. Ludvigsen & U. Hoppe (Eds), Dordrecht: Kluwer Academic Publishers, pp. 173-182.
7. Suthers, D., and Hundhausen, C. (2003). An Empirical Study of the Effects of Representational Guidance on Collaborative Learning. Journal of the Learning Sciences, 12(2), 183-219

A Methodology for the Construction of Learning Companions

Paula Torreão, Marcus Aquino, Patrícia Tedesco, Juliana Sá, and Anderson Correia

Centro de Informática – Universidade Federal de Pernambuco (UFPE)
Caixa Postal 7851 – 50732-970 – Recife – PE – Brasil – Phone 55-81-2126-8430
{pgbc, msa, pcart, jcs}@cin.ufpe.br; anderson3d@yahoo.com.br

One of the essential factors for the success of any software is the use of a methodology. This increases the probability of the final system being complete, functional and accessible. Furthermore, such practice reduces risks, time and cost. However, there is no clear description of a methodology for the construction of LCs.

This paper presents a proposal for a methodology for the construction of a LC used to build a collaborator/simulated peer LC [1], VICTOR[1], applied to a web-based virtual learning environment, PMK Learning Environment[2] (or PMK), which teaches Project Management (PM). The PMK has the content of PMBOK®[3], which provides a basic knowledge reference and practices for PM, thus being a worldwide standard. The construction of an intelligent virtual environment using a LC to teach PM is a pioneer proposal. The application of the methodology described in this paper permitted a better identification of the problem and the learning bottlenecks. Furthermore, it also helped us to decide on a proper choice of domain concepts to be represented, as well as clarifying the necessary requirements for the design of a more effective LC.

Several authors describe methodologies for the construction of Expert Systems (ES) (e.g. [2]). A Learning Companion is a type of ES, used for instruction that diagnoses the student's behavior and cooperates with him/her learning [3,4]. The methodology here presented is based on Levine et al. [4] and has the following six stages: (1) identifying the problem; (2) eliciting relevant domain concepts; (3) conceptualizing the pedagogical tasks; (4) building the LC's architecture; (5) implementing the LC; and (6) evaluating and refining the LC.

Identifying the Problem: At this stage, a preliminary investigation of the main domain characteristics should be considered for the formalization of the knowledge. Following, one should identify in which subjects there are learning problems and of what type they are. This facilitates the conception of adequate pedagogical strategies and tactics that the LC should use for the student's learning. At the end of this stage, two artifacts should be produced: (1) a document relating the most relevant domain characteristics; and (2) a document enumerating the main learning problems found.

Eliciting Relevant Domain Concepts: After defining the task at hand (what are the domain characteristics? Which type of LC is needed?), one should choose which are the most important concepts to represent in the domain. Firstly, one should define the

---

[1] Virtual Intelligent Companion for TutOring and Reflection

[2] http://www.cin.ufpe.br/~pmk - Oficial Project Site

[3] Project Management Body of Knowledge – http://www.pmi.org

J.C. Lester et al. (Eds.): ITS 2004, LNCS 3220, pp. 895–897, 2004.

domain ontology and choose how to represent domain knowledge. At the end of this stage, two artifacts should be produced: (1) a model of the domain ontology and; (2) a document containing the ontology constraints.

Conceptualizing the Pedagogical Task: After modeling the domain ontology, it is necessary to define the LC's goals, pedagogical tactics and strategies. In order to define the LC's behaviour three questions should be answered: What to do? When? And How? The understanding of the learning process and of any factors (e.g. reflection, aims) relevant to the success of this process facilitates this specification. There are various ways of selecting a pedagogical strategy and tactics, one of them being the choice of the teaching strategy according to the domain and the learning goal [5]. For instance, agent LUCY [1] uses the explanation-based teaching strategy to teach students physical phenomena about satellites. Choosing an adequate teaching strategy depends on the following criteria: size and type of the domain, learning goals, and safety and economical questions (e.g. training firefighters would qualify as a non-safe domain). At the end of this stage, two artifacts should be produced: (1) a document specifying the LC's goal, pedagogical strategies and tactics; and (2) a document specifying the LC's actions and behaviors.

Building the LC's Architecture: At this stage, the documents previously constructed are used as a basis for the detailed project of the LC's architecture. This project should include the Behavior Model of LC and Knowledge Base (KB). The LC's behavior should be modeled according to tactics, strategies, and goals defined previously. This behavior determines how, when and what the LC perceives and in what way it responds to the student's actions. The KB stores the contents defined during the elicitation of domain concepts. It should contain all domain concepts, terms and relationships among them. The representation technique chosen for the KB will also determine which Inference Engine will be used by the LC. The LC's Architecture contains four main components: the student's model, the pedagogical module, the domain knowledge and the communication modules [6]. The student´s model stores the individual information about each student and provides information to the pedagogical module. The pedagogical module provides a model of the learning process and contains the model of Behavior of LC. The domain knowledge module contains information about what the tutor should teach. The communication module mediates the LC's interaction with the environment. It captures the student's actions in the interface and sends the actions suggested by the pedagogical module to the interface. At the end of this stage, a document containing the detailed project of the architecture should be produced.

Implementing the LC: At this stage, all the components of the architecture of LC should be implemented, as well as the character's animation, if any, according to the emotional states defined in the behavior of the LC. A good implementation practice is to construct first a prototype of the LC with the minimum set of functionalities necessary for the system to run. This prototype is then used to validate the designed LC's behavior. At the end of this stage, the artifact produced is the prototype itself.

Evaluating and Refining the LC: The tests will validate the architecture of LC and point out any necessary adjustments. At the end of this stage, two artifacts should be produced: (1) a test and evaluation report, with any changes performed; (2) the final version of the LC.

This paper proposes a novel methodology for the construction of LCs. The methodology allowed a better organization, structuring, shaping of the system and the common understanding of the development team about fundamental details for the construction of VICTOR. The benefits of using the methodology could be observed mainly at the stage of implementation, where all the requisites were clearly elicited, modeled at previous stages and the nuances were perceived. Some risks could be eliminated or mitigated in the beginning of this work, allowing us to cut costs and save time. The definition of a methodology before starting the construction of VICTOR facilitated greatly the achievement of the purposes of this work.

Integrating VICTOR to the PMK environment has enabled us to gather evidence of the greater efficiency of an intelligent learning environment and of the various behaviors of LC in different situations. This type of system helps the overcome the main difficulties of the Distance Learning systems: discouragement and dropouts. The LC here proposed aims at meeting the student's needs in a motivational, dynamic and intelligent way. VICTOR's integration with the PMK resulted in an Open Source Software research project[4].

In the future, VICTOR will also be able to use the Case-based Teaching Strategy as a pedagogical strategy, presenting PM real-world project scenarios. Another researcher in our group is working on improving VICTOR's interaction through the use of natural language. In the near future, we intend to carry out more comprehensive tests with users aspiring to PMP certificates, by comparing the performance of those who used LC with those who did not.

References

1. Goodman, B., Soller, A., Linton, F., Gaimari, R.: Encouraging Student Reflection and Articulation Using a Learning Companion. International Journal of Artificial Intelligence in Education, Vol. 9 (1998) 237-255
2. Schreiber, A., Akkermans, J., Anjewierden, A., Hoog, R., Shadbolt, N., Velde, W., Wielinga, B.: Knowledge Engineering and Management: The CommonKADS Methodology. MIT Press (2000)
3. Chou, Chih-Yueh., Chan Tak-Wai., Liin Chi-Jen.: Redefining the Learning Companion: The Past, Present, and Future of Educational Agents Source. Computers & Education. Elsevier Science Ltd., Vol. 40, Issue 3, Oxford UK (2003) 255-269
4. Levine, R., Drang, D., Edelson, B.: Inteligência Artificial e Sistemas Especialistas. McGraw-Hill, São Paulo Brazil (1988)
5. Giraffa, L. M. M.: Uma Arquitetura de Tutor Utilizando Estados Mentais. Doctorate Thesis in Computer Science. Instituto de Informática/UFRGS, Porto Alegre, Brazil (1999)
6. Self, J.: The Defining Characteristics of Intelligent Tutoring Systems Research: ITSs Care, Precisely. International Journal of Artificial Intelligence in Education, Vol 10 (1999) 350-364

[4] Project PMBOK-CVA approved by CNPq in November/2003, in the call for the Program of Research and Technological Development in Open Source Software.

Intelligent Learning Environment for Software Engineering Processes

Roland Yatchou[1], Roger Nkambou[1], and Claude Tangha[2]

[1] Département d'Informatique
Université du Québec à Montréal, Montréal, H3C 3P8, Canada
ryatchou@yahoo.fr, nkambou.roger@uqam.ca

[2] Département de Génie Informatique
École Polytechnique de Yaoundé, BP 8392 Yaoundé, Cameroun
ctangha@yahoo.fr

Abstract. The great number of software engineering processes and their deep granularity constitute important obstacles for these to be taught properly. Teachers generally train on what they master best and focus on the respect of high-level representation formalisms. Consequently, it is up to the learner to go in depth. An alternative for this situation is to build tools for learner to be quickly qualified. Existing tools are generally "monoprocesses" and are developers oriented. In this article, we propose a "multiprocesses" intelligent learning environment that is opened to several software engineering processes. This environment is facilitates the learning of processes compliant to SPEM (Software Process Metamodel Engineering).

1 Introduction

The mastery of software engineering processes is more and more important for the success of computer science projects. However, using a software development process is not an obvious task. At least two levels of complexity are identifiable. The first one is related to the problem to be solved, and the second one is related to the method itself which presents large panel of solutions. With the numerous technological orientations, these processes vary, merge or simply disappear with corresponding tools.

Another concern is the number of design approaches. Their great number has pointed out the need for standardization. Based on this, a recommendation of the Object Management Group (OMG) has defined a common description language that resulted in the SPEM metamodel [1]. The mastery of their production strategy requires a lot of knowledge and experience that learner's memory cannot recall without practice.

This work presents an approach of learning by doing or training through practice. We suggest an open tool facilitating the knowledge acquisition on several processes. To this effect, we have developed a set of intelligent agents that guide the learner through the life cycle of a project and particularly during the production of artifacts. We focus on the stability and the consistency of productions by an approach of verification linked to the constraints of the process in use. This research is conducted within the framework of the ICAD-IS [2] project.

J.C. Lester et al. (Eds.): ITS 2004, LNCS 3220, pp. 898–900, 2004.

2 System Modeling

Building training tools is not a novelty. The literature review shows that efforts were also oriented toward automated solutions aiming to help developers. It should be noticed that the existing tools are as numerous as processes. Every editor comes with his approach and a tool that teaches it. Therefore, to master many processes, one should acquire each of the corresponding tools. These limits led to numerous initiatives for independence of software engineering teaching environments.

Jocelyn Armeno proposes an online training system that allows students to exercise and evaluate their experience in the acquirement of a given domain knowledge [3]. The SETLAS (Software Engineering Teaching and Learning System) and Webworlds environments are as much experience that permitted to improve performances and motivation of learners [4]. However, there are no generic tools to teach knowledge on several existing processes and teaching.

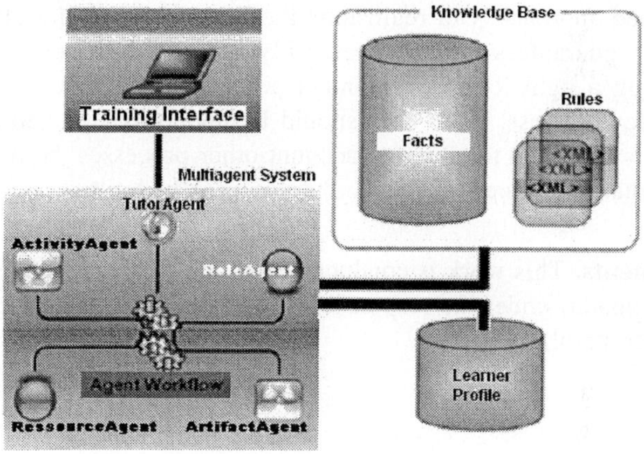

Fig.1. System architecture

Our system model has been built with consideration to the ontology of the process and the rules on artifacts. The figure 1 shows the system architecture. Our ontologies are centered on the SPEM concepts and artifacts of the used process. As state by the model that we have built, processes specify realization guides of different activities and artifacts. They will also identify the check points for verifications on artifacts. Depending on the process, the validity of artifacts should respect this implemented rules.

The architecture of our environment is built on four components: the multiagent system (SMA), the training interface (TI), the learner profile (LP), the knowledge and rule base (KRB). The multiagent system is made of six agents interacting through a blackboard. They use data from the knowledge base to assess the rules to be applied to a project. The training interface interacts with the agents of the system. All activities concerning the learner are sent to or capture from this interface that unify all the element of the system. The learner profile records the learning activities of the student. It contains all management elements of concerning the learner and is used by the Tutor-Agent. The knowledge base includes: ontologies of tasks (tasks and links between tasks), Ontologies of the domain (concepts and links between concepts) of the process. It constitutes the knowledge of agent associate to Workflow, Activity and Role.

3 Conclusion and Prospects

In this study, we have proposed a learning environment that is opened to several software engineering processes. In our approach, we showed that the multiplicity and the deep granularity of processes constitute a barrier to software engineering processes teaching. Therefore it was important for teachers to have tools on which they can rely in for their activities and particularly for student practices. We noticed that tools were generally "one process" based. This led us to suggest an opened "multi-processus" based approach. Our realization has been based on the SPEM meta-model and XMI. This guarantees the interoperability with other system. The environment was tested using a light RUP development process. The results obtained so far are satisfactory. Nevertheless, more tests should be undertaken to validate some of the results. Work is going on to take into account other processes, be it in computer science or any industrial process for which ontology can be built.

Acknowledgments. This work is conducted with the financial support of Le Groupe Infotel Inc. (Canada) under the responsibility of laboratory GDAC of the Université de Québec à Montreal.

References

1. OMG, Software Process Engineering Metamodel Specification, Spécification de l'Object Management Group (OMG), (2002)
2. Bevo, V., Nkambou, R., Donfack, H.,: Toward A Tool for Software Development Knowledge Capitalization. In Proceedings of the 2nd international conference on information and knowledge sharing. ACTA press, Anaheim, (2002) pp. 69-74
3. Ratcliffe, M., Thomas, L., Woodbury, J.: A Learning Environment for First Year Software Engineers. p. 268-275, 14th Conference on Software Engineering Education and Training, February 19 - 21, 2001, Charlotte, North Carolina
4. Armarego, J., Fowler, L., Geoffrey, G.,: Constructing Software Engineering Knowledge: Development of an Online Learning Environment. P 258-267, 14th Conference on Software Engineering Education and Training, February 19 - 21, 2001, Charlotte, North Carolina

Opportunities for Model-Based Learning Systems in the Human Exploration of Space

Bill Clancey

Computational Sciences Division, NASA, USA
william.j.clancey@nasa.gov

The international space program is at a crossroads: Advanced technology in automation and robotics is motivating moving beyond low Earth orbit for extended lunar stays and multiple-year missions to Mars. This presentation relates the various themes of ITS to new plans for the human-robot exploration of space. Opportunities include: adapting student modeling to the problem of instructing robotic systems in cooperative assembly and maintenance tasks, providing astronauts with refresher training and tutorials for new engineering procedures, web-based systems for representing and sharing scientific discoveries, multiagent systems using natural language for life support and surface exploration, and virtual reality for design and training of human-robotic systems. I will illustrate these ideas with current projects carried out by NASA and the Mars Society. Throughout I emphasize how the scientific understanding of the differences between present technology and people is essential for both exploiting and improving computational methods.

J.C. Lester et al. (Eds.): ITS 2004, LNCS 3220, p. 901, 2004.

Toward Comprehensive Student Models: Modeling Meta-cognitive Skills and Affective States in ITS

Cristina Conati

University of British Columbia, Canada
conati@cs.ubc.ca

Student modeling has played a key role in the success of ITS by allowing computer-based tutors to dynamically adapt to a student's knowledge and problem solving behaviour. In this talk, I will discuss how the scope and effectiveness of ITS can be further increased by extending the range of features captured in a student model to include domain independent, meta-cognitive skills and affective states. In particular, I will illustrate how we are applying this research to improve the effectiveness of exploratory learning environments and educational games designed to support open ended, student-led pedagogical interactions.

J.C. Lester et al. (Eds.): ITS 2004, LNCS 3220, p. 902, 2004.

Having a Genuine Impact on Teaching and Learning – Today and Tomorrow

Elliot Soloway[1] and Cathleen Norris[2]

[1] University of Michigan, USA
soloway@umich.edu
[2] University of North Texas, USA
norris@tac.coe.unt.edu

Education – especially for those in the primary and secondary grades – is in desperate need of an upgrade. Children are bored in class; teachers still use 19th century materials. And, as for the content, well, we still teach children about Mendel's darn peas. We are failing to prepare our children to be productive and effective in the 21st century.

There is an opportunity, however, to make a change: we need to use the digital resources inside of school that today's digital children find so compelling and engaging outside of school. Research is most assuredly needed in order to produce effective materials. Yes, next-generation work needs to be carried out, but more near-term work needs to be done – and inform those next-generation efforts. In our presentation, we will describe our efforts in today's classrooms, and on the basis of that work, suggest three next-generation problems that cry out for exploration.

J.C. Lester et al. (Eds.): ITS 2004, LNCS 3220, p. 903, 2004.

Interactively Building a Knowledge Base for a Virtual Tutor

Liane Tarouco

Federal University of Rio Grande do Sul, Brazil
liane@penta.ufrgs.br

The area of knowledge acquisition research concerned with the development of knowledge acquisition tool is always looking for new approaches for building knowledge acquisition. This paper will describe our experimental methodology to create and add knowledge to a FAQ Robot. It will describe the evolutionary process based on reading the dialogues, analyzing the responses, and creating new replies for the patterns detected.

And will report the lessons learned from several experiments that we have performed on the process of build the knowledge base for a virtual tutor to help remote students and network operators to learn on networking and network management area. It will describe how contextualization trough access to cases, animations and network management tools is implemented allowing the tutor to become more than a FAQ robot that uses only static data to answer.

J.C. Lester et al. (Eds.): ITS 2004, LNCS 3220, p. 904, 2004.

Ontological Engineering and ITS Research

Riichiro Mizoguchi

Osaka University, Japan
miz@ei.sanken.osaka-u.ac.jp

Ontology has attracted much attention recently. Semantic Web (SW) is accelerating it futher. As far as the author is concerned, however, ontology as well as ontological engineering is not well-understood by people. There exist two types of ontology: One is computer-understandable vocabulary for SW and the other is something related to deep conceptual structure closer to philosophical ontology. In this talk, I would like to explain the essentials of ontological engineering laying much stress on the latter type ontology.

The talk will be composed of two parts. The first part is rather introductory and includes: (1) how ontological engineering is different from knowledge engineering, (2) what is ontology and what is not, (3) what benefits it brings to ITS research, (4) state of the art of ontology development, etc. The second part is an advanced course and includes (1) what is an ontology-aware system, (2) knowledge systematization by ontological engineering, (3) a successful deployment of ontological framework of functional knowledge of artifacts, etc. To conclude the talk, I will envision the future of ontological engineering in ITS research.

J.C. Lester et al. (Eds.): ITS 2004, LNCS 3220, p. 905, 2004.

Agents Serving Human Learning

Stefano A. Cerri

University of Montpellier II, France
cerri@lirmm.fr

The nature of the Intelligent Tutoring System research has evolved during the years to become one of the major conceptual as well as practical source of innovation for the wider area of Human Learning support by advancements in Informatics. In the invited paper we present our view on the synergic support of Informatics research and the Human Learning context – in the tradition started by Alan Kay with Smalltalk and the Dynabook more that 30 years ago – down to the most concrete plans and results around Agents, the GRID and Human learning as a result of Human and Artificial Agent's conversations. The paper will be organised around three questions: what?, why?, how?.

What: Current research priorities in the domain: the historical shift from a product oriented view of the Web to a service oriented view of the Semantic Grid, with its potential implications for Agent's research and Intelligent Tutoring, and its consequent methodological proposal for a different life cycle in service research embodied in the concept of Scenarios for Service Elicitation, Exploitation and Evaluation (SEES).

Why: Current motivation for research on service oriented models, experiments, tools, applications and finally theories: the emergent impressive growth of the demand in technologies supporting Human Learning as well as human ubiquitous bidirectional access to Information and collaboration among Virtual Communities, with examples ranging from empowerment of human Communities for their durable development (the Virtual Institute for Alphabetisation for Development), to communities of top scientists remotely collaborating for an Encyclopedia of Organic Chemistry, to Continuing Education and dynamic qualification of learning services as well as their concrete effects on human learners - the three being ongoing subprojects of ELEGI, a long term EU project recently started - finally to the necessary integration scenario of digital Information and biological Information supporting human collaboration and Learning in the two most promising areas of competence for the years to come.

How: Our research approach and results for the integration of the above describes themes, consisting of a model – STROBE – , a set of prototypical experiments, an emerging architecture for the integration of components of the solution and the expected results both within ELEGI and independently from it.

J.C. Lester et al. (Eds.): ITS 2004, LNCS 3220, p. 906, 2004.

Panels

Affect and Motivation

W. Lewis Johnson (Moderator), USC/ISI
Panelists: Cristina Conati, Ben du Boulay, Claude Frasson, Helen Pain, Kaska Porayska-Pomsta

This panel brings together researchers who are addressing the topic of affect and motivation in intelligent tutoring systems. The panelists will address the following questions: Which affective and motivational states are most important for an intelligent tutoring system to assess and influence? For example, should an ITS infer learner emotional state, infer states and attitudes that lead to emotional states, or both? What techniques are effective for assessing and influencing these states? How do these concerns influence the learner's perception of the tutoring system, e.g., as appearing caring, empathetic, or socially intelligent?

Inquiry Learning Environments: Where is the field and what needs to be done next?

Ben MacLaren (Moderator), Carnegie Mellon University
Panelists: Lewis Johnson, Ken Koedinger, Tom Murray, Elliot Soloway

Inquiry learning systems allow students to learn in a more authentic manner than traditional tutoring systems. They offer the potential for students to acquire more general problem solving and metacognitive skills that may transfer more broadly than domain specific knowledge. The goal of this panel is to bring together researchers in the field to take inventory of what has been learned, and to ask what important questions remain to make inquiry learning environment more effective in real world educational settings.

Towards Encouraging a Learning Orientation Above a Performance Orientation

Carolyn P. Rose (Moderator), Carnegie Mellon University
Panelists: Lisa Anthony, Ryan Baker, Al Corbett, Helen Pain, Kaska Porayska-Pomsta, Beverly Woolf

It is well known that student engagement is important for learning. Nevertheless, a major problem hindering the effectiveness of intelligent tutoring systems is that students do not necessarily have a proper learning orientation when they interact with these systems. The theme of this panel is to discuss evidence for relationships between student orientation, student behavior, and student learning with a view towards detecting and improving poor student orientations, and enhancing students' interactions with intelligent tutoring systems.

J.C. Lester et al. (Eds.): ITS 2004, LNCS 3220, p. 907, 2004.

Workshop on Modeling Human Teaching Tactics and Strategies

Fabio Akhras (Co-chair), Renato Archer Research Center
Ben du Boulay (Co-chair), University of Sussex
Art Graesser, University of Memphis
Susanne Lajoie, McGill University
Rose Luckin, University of Sussex
Natalie Person, University of Memphis

The purpose of this workshop is to explore the issues concerned with capturing human teaching tactics and strategies as well as attempts to model and evaluate those and other tactics and strategies in Intelligent Tutoring Systems (ITSs) and Intelligent Learning Environments (ILEs). The former topic covers studies both of expert as well as "ordinary" teachers. The latter includes issues of modeling motivation, timing, conversation, learning as well as simply knowledge traversal.

One of the promises of ITSs and ILEs is that they will teach and assist learning in an intelligent manner. While ITSs have historically concentrated on issues of representing the domain knowledge and skills to be learned and modeling the student´s knowledge in order to guide instructional actions, addressing a more teacher-centred view of AI in Education, ILEs have explored a more learner-centered perspective in which the system plays a facilitatory role providing appropriate situations and conditions that can lead the learners to experience their own knowledge construction processes. One of the aims of this workshop is to explore the implications of this change in perspective to the issue of modeling human teaching tactics and strategies.

The issue of teaching expertise has been central to AI in Education since the start. What the system should say or do, when to say or do it, how best to present its action or express its comment have always been questions at the heart of the enterprise. Note that this is intended to be a broad notion of teaching that includes issues of help provision, choice of activity, provision of support and feedback, introduction and fading of scaffolding, taking charge or relinquishing control to the learner(s) and so on.

The workshop's theme is modeling teaching tactics and strategies addressing the following issues:

- Empirical studies of human teaching
- Modeling human teaching expertise
- Development of machine-based teaching tactics and strategies
- Evaluations of human and/or machine teaching tactics and strategies
- Comparisons of human and machine teaching

J.C. Lester et al. (Eds.): ITS 2004, LNCS 3220, p. 908, 2004.

Workshop on Analyzing Student-Tutor Interaction Logs to Improve Educational Outcomes

Joseph Beck (Chair), Carnegie Mellon University
Ryan Baker, Carnegie Mellon University
Albert Corbett, Carnegie Mellon University
Judy Kay, University of Sydney
Diane Litman, University of Pittsburgh
Tanja Mitrovic, University of Canterbury
Steve Ritter, Carnegie Learning

The goal of this workshop is to better understand how and what we can learn from data recorded when students interact with educational software. Several researchers have been working in these areas, largely independent of what others are doing. The time is ripe to exchange information about what we've learned.

There are five major objectives for this workshop:

1. Learn about existing techniques and tools for storing and analyzing data. Although there are many efforts in the ITS community to record and analyze tutorial logs, there is little agreement on good approaches for storing and analyzing such data. Our goal is to create a list of "best practices" that others in the community can use, and to create a list of existing software that is helpful for analyzing such data.

2. Discover new possibilities in what we can learn from log files. Currently, researchers are frequently faced with a large quantity of data but are uncertain about what they can learn. Looking at the data in the proper way can uncover a variety of information ranging from student motivation to the efficacy of tutorial actions.

3. Share analysis techniques. As data become more numerous, the analysis techniques change, and a straightforward pre- to post-test approach is not likely to be applicable.

4. Create sharable resources. Currently the only way to test a theory about how students interact with educational software, or a theory about how to model such data, is to construct the software, gather a large number of students, and collect their interaction data.

5. Create higher-level, visual, representations. There are multiple possible consumers for data collected by educational software, including teachers, administrators, and researchers. What are good abstractions of low-level information for each of these groups? How should the information be presented?

J.C. Lester et al. (Eds.): ITS 2004, LNCS 3220, p. 909, 2004.

Workshop on Grid Learning Services

Guy Gouardères (Co-chair), Université de Pau & des Pays de l'Adour
Roger Nkambou (Co-chair), Université du Québec à Montréal
Colin Allison, University of St Andrews
Jeff Bradshaw, University of South Florida
Rajkumar Buyya, University of Melbourne
Stefano A. Cerri, LIRMM: CNRS & Université Montpellier II
Marc Eisenstadt, Open University
Guy Gouardères, IUT de Bayonne, Université de Pau & des Pays de l'Adour
Michel Liquière, LIRMM: CNRS & Université Montpellier II
Roger Nkambou, Université de Québec à Montréal
Liana Razmerita, University of Toulouse III
Pierluigi Ritrovato, CRMPA, Salerno
David de Roure, University of Southampton
Roland Yatchou, Université de Québec à Montréal

The historical domain of ITS is currently confronted with a double challenge. On the one side the availability of Internet worldwide and the globalisation have tremendously amplified the demand for distance learning (tutoring, training, bidirectional access to Information, ubiquitous and lifelong education, learning as a side effect of interaction). On the other, technologies evolve with an unprecedented speed as well as their corresponding computational theories, models, tools, applications. One of the most important current evolution in networking is represented by GRID computing. Not only the concept promises the availability of important computing resources to be significantly enhanced by GRID services, but identifies an even more crucial roadmap for fundamental research in Computing around the notion of Semantic GRID services, as opposed/complementary to the traditional one of Web accessible products and, more recently, Web services. We do not discuss here the two alternative viewpoints; just anticipate their co-existence, the scientific debate about them and the choice in this workshop of the approach Grid Service.

Assuming a service view for e-Learning, the adaptation to the service user – be it a human, a community of humans or a set of artificial Agents operating on the GRID – entails the dynamic construction of models of the service user by the service provider. Services need to be adapted to users, thus they have to compose their configuration according to their understanding of the user. When the user is a learner – as it is the case in e-Learning – the corresponding formal model has to learn during its life cycle. Machine learning meets necessarily human learning in the sense that it becomes a necessary precondition for composing adaptive services for human needs.

The workshop addresses the issues of integrating human and machine learning into models, systems, applications and abstracting them into theories for advanced Human learning, based on the dynamic generation of GRID services.

J.C. Lester et al. (Eds.): ITS 2004, LNCS 3220, p. 910, 2004.

Workshop on Distance Learning Environments for Digital Graphic Representation

Ricardo Azambuja Silveira (Co-chair), Universidade Federal de Pelotas
Adriane Borda Almeida da Silva (Co-chair), Universidade Federal de Pelotas
Demetrio Arturo Ovalle Carranza, U. Nacional de Colombia
Antônio Carlos Rocha Costa, UCPEL
Heloísa Rocha, UNICAMP
Marcelo Payssé, Universidad de la Republica
Mary Lou Maher, University of Sydney
Monica Fernandez, Universidad de Belgrano
Neusa Felix, UFPEL
Rosa Vicari, Federal U. of Rio Grande do Sul

Graphic Representation is a considerable activity for architects during the development of design, and Architectural Design has been, for centuries, concerned with the design of physical objects and physical space to accommodate various human needs and activities, creating new environments in the physical world.

New technologies opens up new directions in architecture and related areas, not only in terms of the kinds of objects that they produce, but in redefining the role of architects and designers in society. Recently, cyberspace, or the virtual world, a global networked environment supported by Information and Communication Technologies (TIC) has become a field of study and work for Architects and Designers as an excellent approach to build virtual environments and to use it for educational purposes.

The relationship among Architecture and Intelligent Learning Environments is a two directions way: Architecture supports virtual world design for educational purposes and Learning Environments supports the apprenticeship of design and related areas.

The 1st LEDGRAPH workshop (Distance Learning Environments for Digital Graphic Design Representation) intends to create a space to discuss the problems involved in the construction and use of learning environments for distance education in Digital Graphic Representation of Architectural Design and related areas, and intends to create a researcher community composed by different areas involved in educational, technological and architectural issues of this field.

J.C. Lester et al. (Eds.): ITS 2004, LNCS 3220, p. 911, 2004.

Workshop on Applications of Semantic Web Technologies for E-learning

Lora Aroyo (Co-chair), Eindhoven University of Technology
Darina Dicheva (Co-chair), Winston-Salem State University
Peter Brusilovsky, University of Pittsburgh
Paloma Diaz, Universidad Carlos III de Madrid
Vanja Dimitrova, Univeristy of Leeds
Erik Duval, Katholieke Universiteit Leuven
Jim Greer, University of Saskatchewan
Tsukasa Hirashima, Hiroshima Univeristy
Ulrich Hoppe, University of Duisburg
Geert-Jan Houben, Technische Universiteit Eindhoven
Mitsuru Ikeda, JAIST
Judy Kay, University of Sydney
Kinshuk, Massey Univeristy
Erica Melis, Universität des Saarlandes, DFKI
Tanja Mitrovic, University of Canterbury
Ambjörn Naeve, Royal Institute of Technology)
Ossi Nykänen, Tampere University of Technology
Gilbert Paquette, LICEF
Simos Retalis, University of Cyprus
Demetrios Sampson, Center for Research and Technology - Hellas (CERTH)
Katherine Sinitsa, Kiev University
Amy Soller, ITC-IRST
Steffen Staab, AIFB, University of Karlsruhe
Julita Vassileva, University of Saskatchewan
Felisa Verdejo, Ciudad Universitaria
Gerd Wagner, Eindhoven University

SW-EL'04 will focus on issues related to using concepts, ontologies and semantic web technologies to build e-learning applications. It follows the successful workshop on Concepts and Ontologies in Web-based Educational Systems, held in conjunctions with ICCE'2002 in Auckland, New Zealand. Due to the great interest, the 2004 edition of the workshop will be organized in three sessions held at three different conferences. The aim is to discuss the current problems in e-learning from different perspectives, including those of web-based intelligent tutoring systems and adaptive hypermedia courseware, and the implications of applying semantic web standards and technologies for solving them.

J.C. Lester et al. (Eds.): ITS 2004, LNCS 3220, p. 912, 2004.

Workshop on Social and Emotional Intelligence in Learning Environments

Claude Frasson (Co-chair), University of Montreal
Kaska Porayska-Pomsta (Co-chair), University of Edinburgh
Cristina Conati (Organizing Committee), University of British Columbia
Guy Gouarderes (Organizing Committee), University of Pau
Lewis Johnson (Organizing Committee), USC, Information Sciences Institute
Helen Pain, (Organizing Committee), University of Edinburgh
Elisabeth Andre, University of Augsburg, Germany
Tim Bickmore, Boston School of Medicine
Paul Brna, University of Northumbria
Isabel Fernandez de Castro, University of Basque Country
Stephano Cerri, University of Montpellier
Cleide Jane Costa, UFAL
James Lester, North Carolina State University
Christine Lisetti, EURECOM
Stacy Marsella, USC, Information Sciences Institute
Jack Mostow, CMU
Roger Nkambou, UQAM
Magalie Ochs, University of Montreal
Ana Paiva, INESC-ID
Fabio Paraguacu, UFAL
Natalie Person, Rhodes College
Rosalind Picard, MIT
Candice Sidner, MERL Cambridge Research
Angel de Vicente, University of La Laguna, Tenerife

It has been long recognised in education that teaching and learning is a highly social and emotional activity. Students' cognitive progress depends on their psychological predispositions such as their interest, confidence, sense of progress and achievement as well as on social interactions with their teachers and peers who provide them (or not) with both cognitive and emotional support. Until recently the ability to recognise students' socio-affective needs constituted exclusively the realm of human tutors' social competence. However, in recent years and with the development of more sophisticated computer-aided learning environments, the need for those environments to take into account the student's affective states and traits and to place them within the context of the social activity of learning has become an important issue in the domain of building intelligent and effective learning environments. More recently, the notion of emotional intelligence has attracted increasing attention as one of tutors' pre-requisites for improving students' learning.

J.C. Lester et al. (Eds.): ITS 2004, LNCS 3220, p. 913, 2004.

Workshop on Dialog-Based Intelligent Tutoring Systems: State of the Art and New Research Directions

Neil Heffernan (Co-chair), Worcester Polytechnic University
Peter Wiemer-Hastings (Co-chair), DePaul University
Greg Aist, University of Rochester
Vincent Aleven, Carnegie Mellon University
Ivon Arroyo, University of Massachusetts at Amherst
Paul Brna, University of Northumbria at Newcastle
Mark Core, University of Edinburgh
Martha Evens, Illinois Institute of Technology
Reva Freedman, Northern Illinois University
Michael Glass, Valparaiso University
Art Graesser, University of Memphis
Kenneth Koedinger, Carnegie Mellon University
Pamela Jordon, University of Pittsburgh
Diane Litman, University of Pittsburgh
Evelyn Lulils, DePaul University
Helen Pain, University of Edinburgh
Carolyn Rose, Carnegie Mellon University
Beverly Woolf, University of Massachusetts at Amherst
Claus Zinn, University of Edinburgh

Within the past decade, advances in computer technology and language-processing techniques have allowed us to develop intelligent tutoring systems that feature more natural communication with students. As these dialog-based tutoring systems are maturing, there is increasing agreement on the fundamental methods that make them effective in producing learning gains. This workshop will have two goals. First, we will discuss current research the techniques that make these systems effective. Second, especially for the benefit of researchers just starting tutorial dialog projects, we will include a how-to track where experienced system-builders describe the tools and techniques that form the cores of successful systems.

J.C. Lester et al. (Eds.): ITS 2004, LNCS 3220, p. 914, 2004.

Workshop on Designing Computational Models of Collaborative Learning Interaction

Amy Soller (Co-chair), ITC-IRST
Patrick Jermann (Co-chair), EPFL
Martin Muehlenbrock (Co-chair), DFKI
Alejandra Martínez Monés (Co-chair), University of Valladolid
Angeles Constantino González, ITESM Campus Laguna
Alain Derycke, Université des Sciences et Technologies de Lille
Pierre Dillenbourg, EPFL
Brad Goodman, MITRE
Katrin Gassner, Fraunhofer ISST
Elena Gaudioso, UNED
Peter Reimann, University of Sydney
Marta Rosatelli, Universidade Católica de Santos
Ron Stevens, University of California
Julita Vassileva, University of Saskatchewan

During collaborative learning activities, factors such as students' prior knowledge, motivation,roles, language, behavior and interaction dynamics interact with each other in unpredictable ways, making it very difficult to predict and measure learning effects. This may be one reason why the focus of collaborative learning research shifted in the nineties from studying group characteristics and products to studying group process. With an interest in having an impact on the group process in modern distance learning environments, the focus has recently shifted again – this time from studying group processes to identifying computational strategies that positively influence group learning. This shift toward mediating and supporting collaborative learners is fundamentally grounded in our understanding of the interaction described by our models of collaborative learning interaction. In this workshop, we will explore the advantages, implications, and support possibilities afforded by the various types of computational models of collaborative learning processes.

Computational models of collaborative learning interaction provide functional computer-based representations that help us understand, explain, and predict patterns of group behavior. Some help the system automatically identify group members' roles, while others help scientists understand the cognitive processes that underlie collaborative learning activities such as knowledge sharing or cognitive conflict. Some computational models focus specifically on social factors, and may be applied to many different domains, while others are designed to facilitate aspects of task oriented interaction and may be bound to a particular domain. In this workshop, we will discuss the requirements for modeling different aspects of interaction.

J.C. Lester et al. (Eds.): ITS 2004, LNCS 3220, p. 915, 2004.

Author Index

Lecture Notes in Computer Science

For information about Vols. 1–3075

please contact your bookseller or Springer

Vol. 3220: J.C. Lester, R.M. Vicari, F. Paraguaçu (Eds.), Intelligent Tutoring Systems. XXI, 920 pages. 2004.

Vol. 3207: L.T. Jang, M. Guo, G.R. Gao, N.K. Jha, Embedded and Ubiquitous Computing. XX, 1116 pages. 2004.

Vol. 3205: N. Davies, E. Mynatt, I. Siio (Eds.), UbiComp 2004: Ubiquitous Computing. XVI, 452 pages. 2004.

Vol. 3198: G.-J. de Vreede, L.A. Guerrero, G. Marín Raventós (Eds.), Groupware: Design, Implementation and Use. XI, 378 pages. 2004.

Vol. 3194: R. Camacho, R. King, A. Srinivasan (Eds.), Inductive Logic Programming. XI, 361 pages. 2004. (Subseries LNAI).

Vol. 3186: Z. Bellahsène, T. Milo, M. Rys, D. Suciu, R. Unland (Eds.), Database and XML Technologies. X, 235 pages. 2004.

Vol. 3184: S. Katsikas, J. Lopez, G. Pernul (Eds.), Trust and Privacy in Digital Business. XI, 299 pages. 2004.

Vol. 3183: R. Traunmüller (Ed.), Electronic Government. XIX, 583 pages. 2004.

Vol. 3182: K. Bauknecht, M. Bichler, B. Pröll (Eds.), E-Commerce and Web Technologies. XI, 370 pages. 2004.

Vol. 3178: W. Jonker, M. Petkovic (Eds.), Secure Data Management. VIII, 219 pages. 2004.

Vol. 3177: Z.R. Yang, H. Yin, R. Everson (Eds.), Intelligent Data Engineering and Automated Learning – IDEAL 2004. XVIII, 852 pages. 2004.

Vol. 3174: F. Yin, J. Wang, C. Guo (Eds.), Advances in Neural Networks - ISNN 2004. XXXV, 1021 pages. 2004.

Vol. 3172: M. Dorigo, M. Birattari, C. Blum, L. M.Gambardella, F. Mondada, T. Stützle (Eds.), Ant Colony, Optimization and Swarm Intelligence. XII, 434 pages. 2004.

Vol. 3166: M. Rauterberg (Ed.), Entertainment Computing – ICEC 2004. XXIII, 617 pages. 2004.

Vol. 3158: I. Nikolaidis, M. Barbeau, E. Kranakis (Eds.), Ad-Hoc, Mobile, and Wireless Networks. IX, 344 pages. 2004.

Vol. 3157: C. Zhang, H. W. Guesgen, W.K. Yeap (Eds.), PRICAI 2004: Trends in Artificial Intelligence. XX, 1023 pages. 2004. (Subseries LNAI).

Vol. 3156: M. Joye, J.-J. Quisquater (Eds.), Cryptographic Hardware and Embedded Systems - CHES 2004. XIII, 455 pages. 2004.

Vol. 3155: P. Funk, P.A. González Calero (Eds.), Advances in Case-Based Reasoning. XIII, 822 pages. 2004. (Subseries LNAI).

Vol. 3154: R.L. Nord (Ed.), Software Product Lines. XIV, 334 pages. 2004.

Vol. 3153: J. Fiala, V. Koubek, J. Kratochvíl (Eds.), Mathematical Foundations of Computer Science 2004. XIV, 902 pages. 2004.

Vol. 3152: M. Franklin (Ed.), Advances in Cryptology – CRYPTO 2004. XI, 579 pages. 2004.

Vol. 3150: G.-Z. Yang, T. Jiang (Eds.), Medical Imaging and Augmented Reality. XII, 378 pages. 2004.

Vol. 3149: M. Danelutto, M. Vanneschi, D. Laforenza (Eds.), Euro-Par 2004 Parallel Processing. XXXIV, 1081 pages. 2004.

Vol. 3148: R. Giacobazzi (Ed.), Static Analysis. XI, 393 pages. 2004.

Vol. 3146: P. Érdi, A. Esposito, M. Marinaro, S. Scarpetta (Eds.), Computational Neuroscience: Cortical Dynamics. XI, 161 pages. 2004.

Vol. 3144: M. Papatriantafilou, P. Hunel (Eds.), Principles of Distributed Systems. XI, 246 pages. 2004.

Vol. 3143: W. Liu, Y. Shi, Q. Li (Eds.), Advances in Web-Based Learning – ICWL 2004. XIV, 459 pages. 2004.

Vol. 3142: J. Diaz, J. Karhumäki, A. Lepistö, D. Sannella (Eds.), Automata, Languages and Programming. XIX, 1253 pages. 2004.

Vol. 3140: N. Koch, P. Fraternali, M. Wirsing (Eds.), Web Engineering. XXI, 623 pages. 2004.

Vol. 3139: F. Iida, R. Pfeifer, L. Steels, Y. Kuniyoshi (Eds.), Embodied Artificial Intelligence. IX, 331 pages. 2004. (Subseries LNAI).

Vol. 3138: A. Fred, T. Caelli, R.P.W. Duin, A. Campilho, D.d. Ridder (Eds.), Structural, Syntactic, and Statistical Pattern Recognition. XXII, 1168 pages. 2004.

Vol. 3137: P. De Bra, W. Nejdl (Eds.), Adaptive Hypermedia and Adaptive Web-Based Systems. XIV, 442 pages. 2004.

Vol. 3136: F. Meziane, E. Métais (Eds.), Natural Language Processing and Information Systems. XII, 436 pages. 2004.

Vol. 3134: C. Zannier, H. Erdogmus, L. Lindstrom (Eds.), Extreme Programming and Agile Methods - XP/Agile Universe 2004. XIV, 233 pages. 2004.

Vol. 3133: A.D. Pimentel, S. Vassiliadis (Eds.), Computer Systems: Architectures, Modeling, and Simulation. XIII, 562 pages. 2004.

Vol. 3132: B. Demoen, V. Lifschitz (Eds.), Logic Programming. XII, 480 pages. 2004.

Vol. 3131: V. Torra, Y. Narukawa (Eds.), Modeling Decisions for Artificial Intelligence. XI, 327 pages. 2004. (Subseries LNAI).

Vol. 3130: A. Syropoulos, K. Berry, Y. Haralambous, B. Hughes, S. Peter, J. Plaice (Eds.), TeX, XML, and Digital Typography. VIII, 265 pages. 2004.

Vol. 3129: Q. Li, G. Wang, L. Feng (Eds.), Advances in Web-Age Information Management. XVII, 753 pages. 2004.

Vol. 3128: D. Asonov (Ed.), Querying Databases Privately. IX, 115 pages. 2004.

Vol. 3127: K.E. Wolff, H.D. Pfeiffer, H.S. Delugach (Eds.), Conceptual Structures at Work. XI, 403 pages. 2004. (Subseries LNAI).

Vol. 3126: P. Dini, P. Lorenz, J.N.d. Souza (Eds.), Service Assurance with Partial and Intermittent Resources. XI, 312 pages. 2004.

Vol. 3125: D. Kozen (Ed.), Mathematics of Program Construction. X, 401 pages. 2004.

Vol. 3124: J.N. de Souza, P. Dini, P. Lorenz (Eds.), Telecommunications and Networking - ICT 2004. XXVI, 1390 pages. 2004.

Vol. 3123: A. Belz, R. Evans, P. Piwek (Eds.), Natural Language Generation. X, 219 pages. 2004. (Subseries LNAI).

Vol. 3122: K. Jansen, S. Khanna, J.D.P. Rolim, D. Ron (Eds.), Approximation, Randomization, and Combinatorial Optimization. IX, 428 pages. 2004.

Vol. 3121: S. Nikoletseas, J.D.P. Rolim (Eds.), Algorithmic Aspects of Wireless Sensor Networks. X, 201 pages. 2004.

Vol. 3120: J. Shawe-Taylor, Y. Singer (Eds.), Learning Theory. X, 648 pages. 2004. (Subseries LNAI).

Vol. 3118: K. Miesenberger, J. Klaus, W. Zagler, D. Burger (Eds.), Computer Helping People with Special Needs. XXIII, 1191 pages. 2004.

Vol. 3116: C. Rattray, S. Maharaj, C. Shankland (Eds.), Algebraic Methodology and Software Technology. XI, 569 pages. 2004.

Vol. 3114: R. Alur, D.A. Peled (Eds.), Computer Aided Verification. XII, 536 pages. 2004.

Vol. 3113: J. Karhumäki, H. Maurer, G. Paun, G. Rozenberg (Eds.), Theory Is Forever. X, 283 pages. 2004.

Vol. 3112: H. Williams, L. MacKinnon (Eds.), Key Technologies for Data Management. XII, 265 pages. 2004.

Vol. 3111: T. Hagerup, J. Katajainen (Eds.), Algorithm Theory - SWAT 2004. XI, 506 pages. 2004.

Vol. 3110: A. Juels (Ed.), Financial Cryptography. XI, 281 pages. 2004.

Vol. 3109: S.C. Sahinalp, S. Muthukrishnan, U. Dogrusoz (Eds.), Combinatorial Pattern Matching. XII, 486 pages. 2004.

Vol. 3108: H. Wang, J. Pieprzyk, V. Varadharajan (Eds.), Information Security and Privacy. XII, 494 pages. 2004.

Vol. 3107: J. Bosch, C. Krueger (Eds.), Software Reuse: Methods, Techniques and Tools. XI, 339 pages. 2004.

Vol. 3106: K.-Y. Chwa, J.I. Munro (Eds.), Computing and Combinatorics. XIII, 474 pages. 2004.

Vol. 3105: S. Göbel, U. Spierling, A. Hoffmann, I. Iurgel, O. Schneider, J. Dechau, A. Feix (Eds.), Technologies for Interactive Digital Storytelling and Entertainment. XVI, 304 pages. 2004.

Vol. 3104: R. Kralovic, O. Sykora (Eds.), Structural Information and Communication Complexity. X, 303 pages. 2004.

Vol. 3103: K. Deb, e. al. (Eds.), Genetic and Evolutionary Computation – GECCO 2004. XLIX, 1439 pages. 2004.

Vol. 3102: K. Deb, e. al. (Eds.), Genetic and Evolutionary Computation – GECCO 2004. L, 1445 pages. 2004.

Vol. 3101: M. Masoodian, S. Jones, B. Rogers (Eds.), Computer Human Interaction. XIV, 694 pages. 2004.

Vol. 3100: J.F. Peters, A. Skowron, J.W. Grzymała-Busse, B. Kostek, R.W. Świniarski, M.S. Szczuka (Eds.), Transactions on Rough Sets I. X, 405 pages. 2004.

Vol. 3099: J. Cortadella, W. Reisig (Eds.), Applications and Theory of Petri Nets 2004. XI, 505 pages. 2004.

Vol. 3098: J. Desel, W. Reisig, G. Rozenberg (Eds.), Lectures on Concurrency and Petri Nets. VIII, 849 pages. 2004.

Vol. 3097: D. Basin, M. Rusinowitch (Eds.), Automated Reasoning. XII, 493 pages. 2004. (Subseries LNAI).

Vol. 3096: G. Melnik, H. Holz (Eds.), Advances in Learning Software Organizations. X, 173 pages. 2004.

Vol. 3095: C. Bussler, D. Fensel, M.E. Orlowska, J. Yang (Eds.), Web Services, E-Business, and the Semantic Web. X, 147 pages. 2004.

Vol. 3094: A. Nürnberger, M. Detyniecki (Eds.), Adaptive Multimedia Retrieval. VIII, 229 pages. 2004.

Vol. 3093: S. Katsikas, S. Gritzalis, J. Lopez (Eds.), Public Key Infrastructure. XIII, 380 pages. 2004.

Vol. 3092: J. Eckstein, H. Baumeister (Eds.), Extreme Programming and Agile Processes in Software Engineering. XVI, 358 pages. 2004.

Vol. 3091: V. van Oostrom (Ed.), Rewriting Techniques and Applications. X, 313 pages. 2004.

Vol. 3089: M. Jakobsson, M. Yung, J. Zhou (Eds.), Applied Cryptography and Network Security. XIV, 510 pages. 2004.

Vol. 3087: D. Maltoni, A.K. Jain (Eds.), Biometric Authentication. XIII, 343 pages. 2004.

Vol. 3086: M. Odersky (Ed.), ECOOP 2004 – Object-Oriented Programming. XIII, 611 pages. 2004.

Vol. 3085: S. Berardi, M. Coppo, F. Damiani (Eds.), Types for Proofs and Programs. X, 409 pages. 2004.

Vol. 3084: A. Persson, J. Stirna (Eds.), Advanced Information Systems Engineering. XIV, 596 pages. 2004.

Vol. 3083: W. Emmerich, A.L. Wolf (Eds.), Component Deployment. X, 249 pages. 2004.

Vol. 3080: J. Desel, B. Pernici, M. Weske (Eds.), Business Process Management. X, 307 pages. 2004.

Vol. 3079: Z. Mammeri, P. Lorenz (Eds.), High Speed Networks and Multimedia Communications. XVIII, 1103 pages. 2004.

Vol. 3078: S. Cotin, D.N. Metaxas (Eds.), Medical Simulation. XVI, 296 pages. 2004.

Vol. 3077: F. Roli, J. Kittler, T. Windeatt (Eds.), Multiple Classifier Systems. XII, 386 pages. 2004.

Vol. 3076: D. Buell (Ed.), Algorithmic Number Theory. XI, 451 pages. 2004.